To My Friend, Rifka

Because you and Harry are very dear to me, I sincerely hope you both will find this token of my deep friendship a source of real pleasure, You, the Chef De Cuisine, and, Harry, always the gourmet.

Happy Birthday to

Bon Appetite

Bill Adams

GREAT ITALIAN COOKING

La Grande Cucina Internazionale

LA GRANDE CUCINA

Edited by *MICHAEL SONINO*

LUIGI CARNACINA'S

GREAT ITALIAN COOKING

INTERNAZIONALE

ABRADALE PRESS *PUBLISHERS* NEW YORK

Library of Congress Catalog Card Number: 68—28378

Printed and bound in Italy

CONTENTS

EDITOR'S FOREWORD

This book endeavors to present as wide a range as possible of recipes falling within the limitations defined by "Italian" and "international." Of all the Continental European countries, Italy is perhaps the least chauvinistic in its gastronomic outlook. Restaurants in France, for instance, are pretty much limited to French cuisine, but in the larger Italian cities many restaurateurs serve delicacies drawn with happy impartiality from the best of various Continental cuisines, albeit with a slightly Italian "accent."

After examining many of the strictly Italian recipes in this book the reader may be surprised to discover that Italian cookery is quite refined, subtle, and delicate; some will detect the fact that it is equal to many of the great preparations that are the ornament of French *haute cuisine*. Actually, French cooking owes more to Italy than most people realize. Until the sixteenth century, cooking in France was not much different from that of the rest of northern Europe: highly spiced meats, overseasoned or undercooked and generally rather "high" (which accounted for the overspicing). Vegetables were chiefly turnips or other roots (potatoes and tomatoes had not yet been brought from the New World), and salads were not terribly popular. Sweets consisted of "sugarplums" and lumps of crystallized honey. Wine was either almost as strong as brandy or a weak, watery drink; and beer (the most favored beverage of all classes) was a thin, mildly alcoholic gruel.

This state of affairs was changed, practically overnight, by the arrival of Catherine de' Medici, who had come to France to marry King Henry II. Catherine's entourage included a full complement of Italian cooks, and these kitchen artists succeeded in instituting sweeping reforms in French culinary practices; through them French cooking began to gain ascendancy.

According to contemporaneous accounts, the Italian cuisine of the sixteenth century was quite elegant. This is not too surprising when one recalls that the first extant cookbook, Apicius', was compiled in the heyday of the Roman Empire. Because of Italy's geographic location and wide-ranging mercantile interests, Renaissance Italians were familiar with such Saracenic favorites as sugar, oranges, coffee, and spices so rare in the north of Europe that their price was greater than gold. (Whether or not Marco Polo brought back spaghetti from Cathay in the fourteenth century has yet to be established—it may have made its appearance before then.)

The food of Italy covers a wide spectrum: in the north it is a subtle blend of French and Austrian, with a uniquely Italian flavor. In Tuscany, beef and game-birds are favored. The Bolognese cuisine relies heavily on butter in almost everything. Genoa features the incomparable Pesto, a subtle blend of basil and cheese. Lombardy glories in the white truffle. As one goes south, tomato sauces and the heavier forms of pasta appear. And as one enters Sicily, the food takes on a curiously exotic touch, reminiscent of North Africa and the Levant.

Many of the well-known pasta preparations (chiefly macaroni and spaghetti) are far more popular in the South. The Northerners favor risottos and polentas. The latter (a cornmeal dish) takes the place of pastas in the majority of homes around Venice and in Friuli, while the risottos (rice-based dishes) occupy a favored place on Lombardian and Piedmontese tables. The favored pastas of the regions above Rome are home-made egg noodles (fettuccine or tagliatelle) and filled noodle doughs (ravioli or cappelletti); the lasagna dishes are prepared with squares of noodle dough rather than the wide strips of spaghetti dough favored

7

in Naples and farther south, and well-known as "typical Italian lasagna" in America.

Many recipes in this volume suggest that one use a homemade pasta or stock as their base. In case this does not prove practical, we have given substitute stocks, and suggestions for using commercial pastas. However, one must realize that even though the Italian cook may not turn out homemade pastas, there are shops where one may purchase the freshly made product, still soft and moist, and made for cooking the same day. The texture and flavor of freshly made pasta is a sublime delight, and if you have any culinary ambitions at all, we heartily endorse the purchase of a pasta-making machine, and the involvement in this truly Italian art.

National cookery is, to a certain extent, governed by a state of mind, and the success with which you will be able to present a typically "Italian" (or "French" or "Chinese") meal rests not so much on your skill in the kitchen as on an instinctive feeling for the underlying taste (both aesthetic and gastronomic) of the country. Therefore, one can in theory prepare a Chinese dinner that is basically Italian in concept, and vice-versa. Taking this into consideration, do not expect that this volume will be a means to transform you magically into an "Italian" cook. But if you wish to approximate the ideas inherent in Italian cuisine, turn to the menus offered at the end of this book, and follow them to the letter. You will then see that you have approximated an authentic Italian meal.

The majority of the recipes in this book reflect the food that the tourist is apt to sample in the better hotels and restaurants throughout Italy. The regional dishes here reflect what is best in the many delicious specialties developed up and down the boot of Italy. To simplify the task of those who may be searching for special old favorites, we have included an Italian index of recipes. Many readers will doubtless rediscover some favored preparation in these pages. Others will be delighted to find a recipe for a long-remembered dish described with nostalgia by their parents. Still others will embark upon an entirely new field of gastronomical adventures.

Do not, however, expect that a dish you may have enjoyed in a restaurant or *trattoria* in Italy can be duplicated exactly in your own kitchen. There are many factors which make this an impossibility. First of all, even the simplest basic ingredients found in America will differ subtly from their Italian counterparts. Also, your mood will not be the same. There is a vast difference between sitting down to a meal after spending a stimulating day exploring the Roman Forum, enjoying the pictures in the Uffizi Gallery, or attending a brilliant performance at La Scala, and sitting down to a meal in your own dining room after having spent a number of hours over the stove. Your memory, too, plays tricks, and in retrospect the wonderful pasta dish you relished in Italy a few months or years ago becomes even more delectable with the passing of time, the flavors heightened by the sauce of happy reminiscence. This is best demonstrated by the following: when the famous Russian impresario, Serge Diaghilev, contemplated a revival of one of his first sensational successes, the ballet *Scheherazade*, he instructed the scene painters to make the colors far brighter than they were originally, for he knew that the audience would remember the first performances as being more brilliant than they actually were. The same holds true for those wonderful taste memories we all cherish.

It is hoped that this book will do much to dispel the popular American notion that Italian cooking is based on tomato sauces overflavored with oregano and garlic; that pasta is soggy spaghetti swimming in watery tomatoes and studded with overcooked, anonymous meatballs; that meat is "Veal Parmigian"—a concoction of veal "cutlets" thickly coated with breadcrumbs, fried to leathery toughness in oil, bathed in the omnipresent tomato sauce, and overcooked until the sauce and meat achieve the same texture; that antipasto consists of a platter graced with a slice of greasy salami, a tired sardine, a too-salty anchovy fillet, red peppers preserved in too much vinegar, wrinkled black olives, and a stalk of celery; that Italian wine is "red ink"; and that dessert is either Biscuit Tortoni or "rum" cakes. These gastronomic horrors, served in all too many "Italian" restaurants throughout the United States are, unfortunately, the popular American conception of typical Italian foods. Italians do not subsist on these dishes, nor upon pizzas or over-garlicked, vinegary salads, and their soups are not "pasta fazool" or "minestrone." (These two soups are, however, abundantly represented in these pages—the former in at least five variations, though not under the name of "Pasta e Fagioli," and the latter in a special subsection in the Soup chapter.)

It would be, of course, impossible to list *all* the Italian regional specialties in a book of less than five volumes. Additionally, many of these are so local, and within their localities vary so from cook to cook, from *trattoria* to *trattoria*, that definitive recipes do not exist. It might also be stated that certain regional specialties vary according to the mood of the individual cook, and to the range of produce available in the market on the day the dish is being prepared, so that a dish (although basically the same in its concept) can run the gamut of subtle taste variations each time it is made. However, the recipes included in this book cover a wide range: from luscious Italian regional specialties to sophisticated preparations that are the proud adornment of the great hotels and restaurants in Venice, Milan, Turin, Florence, Bologna, Rome, and other centers. Also included are Signor Carnacina's own creations, which are here printed for the first time.

This volume has been adapted to present-day American cooking methods. In no way, however, has it been transformed into an "Italo-American" cookbook. In a few instances, where ingredients are simply not available in American markets, substitutions have been made. In most cases, however, the ingredients called for in the recipes can be found at any grocery store carrying Italian products. In this connection it may be mentioned that a group of recipes calling for "songbirds" has been omitted. These are considered a great delicacy in Italy, but in the United States they are not only unpurchasable—but illegal to hunt.

There is one section of cookery not covered in this book: breadmaking. Few urban Italians bake bread, and the purchased product is just as fine as any home-baked loaf (in fact, sometimes better). Even if bread recipes had been included in the Italian edition, it would have been almost impossible to duplicate them in the United States. Flour is milled differently here, and it has become increasingly difficult to purchase "bread" flour these days (an unbleached type with a high gluten content). Water is also an important factor, and most of our water is too highly chlorinated to react properly with flour and yeast to give the bread its proper Italian flavor and crumb. Yeast, too, differs considerably, and the Italian strain is a far wilder strain than our own. Finally, a home gas or electric oven is not able to produce real Italian-type bread.

Many of the recipes here may seem especially elaborate and time-consuming to speed-conscious Americans. One must realize that the Italian householder spends a good deal of time on the preparation of food and does not usually attempt to pursue a career at the same time. For Europeans in general, and Italians and Frenchmen in particular, cooking is a serious art; the final result amply justifies the means (all day in the kitchen, if necessary). However, the American cook should not be frightened off by seemingly complicated dishes:

many may be prepared ahead of time and reheated before serving, and the majority of the recipes are not overly involved or lengthy in their preparation.

When using this book, it might be useful to keep in mind the difference between Italian and American marketing methods. The supermarket is a recent development on the Italian scene and only in the past decade has this type of shop made its appearance in the larger Italian cities.

Most Italians market every day, stopping at different shops for dairy products, baked goods, fish, meat, wine, pastas, fruits, and vegetables. Since refrigeration is still a recent "luxury" in many homes, perishable items are acquired in quantities sufficient for the day on which they are purchased. In the Italian edition of this book most of the recipes call for the "freshest" butter, cream, milk, fish, etc. This prerequisite was, with very few exceptions, not carried over into this edition, since it was taken for granted that we do not employ perishable items whose freshness is suspect.

Despite the inconvenience of daily shopping in small amounts, the Italian consumer rejoices in a wide selection of the freshest possible fruits and vegetables. The reason is simple: the produce is fresh because it has been gathered on farms not more than a few hours' journey from the markets. Fruit has not languished in railway cars for days (and was not for that reason picked "green" so that it would survive the trip) and vegetables have not been subjected to a few weeks' cold storage: therefore these items have not been robbed of their flavor and texture. True, this means that strawberries and asparagus, for instance, are not available in midwinter as they are here, but as seasonal and freshly picked items are always the best, the Italians do not consider themselves underprivileged.

The size of produce is not of paramount interest to the Italians. In fact, what Americans would call "baby" fruits and vegetables are the most highly prized, and jumbo sized items (much sought-after here) are not always regarded as superior. The Italians feel that the smaller and more perfect a fruit or vegetable the better the flavor: it is fresh, newly picked; and in growing, chemical processes have not been lavished on making it big, they have been channeled into its flavor.

On page 13 there is a selected gastronomic dictionary that may prove helpful to many. It defines a number of terms, and clarifies the type of many ingredients called for in the recipes. Also, on page 794 there are a number of menus which will no doubt prove to be useful if you wish to prepare a typically Italian meal.

You will note that they are seasonal, and therefore take advantage of the freshest possible foods available during the course of the year.

About this book:

When this volume was published in Italy it was perhaps the first cookbook issued there to include Continental as well as Italian recipes. It was also noteworthy because it endeavored to give the cook more directions than is usual in an Italian cooking manual. Earlier, even in such outstanding works as Artusi's magnificent cookbook, which was (and still is for many) the standard kitchen guide for the Italian home cook, recipes were set forth in the sketchiest manner possible. Amounts, cooking time, and temperatures were hardly ever stated, and although the recipes themselves are a delight to read, they are quite impossible for all but the most experienced cook to follow.

Luigi Carnacina, the author of *Great Italian Cooking,* was a protege of the almost-legendary Auguste Escoffier. This great French gastronome and chef selected Signor Carnacina to be the chef at his hotel in Ostende, Belgium. Subsequently, he became the "official" chef at the Italian pavilions at international world's fairs, notably Paris in 1937, New York in 1939 (a restaurant still spoken of with wistful longing by New York gourmets), and Brussels in 1958. Many of the dishes created for these restaurants may be found in these pages, and they are identified as such by their titles.

It might also be of interest to note that all recipes with the name "Germana" in their title are Signor Carnacina's tribute to his wife, Germana. All those subtitled "Villa Sassi" are named in honor of Signor Carnacina's house. And, finally, "Luigi Veronelli" in a recipe title refers to a noted Italian food expert and wine connoisseur, who was the editor of the Italian edition of this volume and a close friend and collaborator of the author's. It was Signor Veronelli who wrote the section on wine at the end of this volume.

The majority of the various sections and sub-sections are prefaced by introductory remarks. We strongly advise that these remarks be read with care, as they contain a great deal of useful information on the ingredients discussed and also the basic preparation.

If you wish to make substitutions in any of the ingredients and/or components of a recipe, this is of course up to you and your skill. If you are an experienced cook and are familiar with all the various subtleties of taste, texture, and procedure, then you have instinctive knowledge as to what is "right." If, however, you are a tyro cook, we advise that you keep to the recipe as closely as possible.

Remember, adding or subtracting ingredients is a dangerous practice, and using 5 eggs where 3 are called for does not necessarily guarantee the improvement of a recipe.

All recipes are identified by both their English and Italian names. For convenience, we have cross-referenced all recipes within a recipe by number and in this way the reader may locate them with a minimum of effort.

M.S.

AUTHOR'S INTRODUCTION

The Preparation of Food

The preparation of any elaborate and successful dish is within the ability of almost anyone who will keep in mind that such a dish is merely the crowning point of a series of basic operations, most of them simple enough. It is very important to be familiar with the fundamental procedures and, at the risk of repeating information well known to many, we will list them here.

While most meats today are purchased in ready-to-cook condition, they should be given a thorough inspection and be trimmed of skin, membranes, veins (or "tubes"), and any other parts that interfere with palatability or digestion.

Vegetables should be washed in plenty of running water and leaf vegetables should be inspected, trimmed, and washed leaf by leaf. In Europe, the tough outer surface is often peeled away from many vegetables, such as asparagus, broccoli, mushrooms, fennel, and oyster plant.

The scales, fins, gills, and intestines of fish should be removed, and, since many people are prejudiced against fish because of the bones, they may be filleted before cooking.

Some foods have a better flavor if marinated before cooking. This is especially true of all game, but a good cook's repertoire should include the marinating of regular meats, poultry, and fish as a change of pace from direct cooking. Some vegetables that are almost always cooked are just as delicious raw. Try raw spinach in salads and raw cauliflower flowerets dipped in cocktail sauces.

The freezing of foods has become so highly perfected, and their distribution so widespread, that their use is accepted everywhere. Directions for the proper defrosting of foods, so that texture and flavor are not impaired, will be given wherever necessary throughout this book.

After the food is cleaned and ready, the moment of cooking arrives. To cook means basically to bake, fry, roast, or boil the food with fats, spices, and other seasoning in order to make it flavorful, tender, and digestible. Temperature and timing are the two most important factors in the cooking process and must be uppermost in the cook's mind.

While lengthy cooking makes certain vegetables and farinaceous products more digestible, this does not always hold true for meats cooked at higher temperatures, so care must be taken to keep the heat process from overcooking meat and reversing the effect desired. Fish, especially, needs little cooking—just enough to coagulate the protein—and more or longer heat results in loss of the moist, flaky quality which makes a properly prepared fish dish such a particular delight.

FOOD CAN BE:

1. *Roasted, Baked,* or *Broiled:* that is, exposed directly to the heat of charcoal, wood, a gas flame, or electric coils. This is the oldest process known to man. Today, most roasting and baking is done in the oven. One method is to expose the food to an initial high temperature (to seal in the juices), then to turn down the heat, and cook for the specified time at a lower heat. More recently there have been many advocates of a steady, medium heat.

2. *Boiled:* here, too, the matter of temperature is important. Meat cooked this way should be put into cold water and gradually brought to a boil, especially if it is to be used to obtain broth, when it should be put in cold water with aromatic vegetables and herbs. Fish requires special attention. The ancient Greeks divided fish into hard and soft varieties and only boiled the soft, with aromatic herbs and vinegar or lemon, placing the fish in a snug container with just enough water to cover. Today, steaming is a popular and effective way

of cooking fish, especially since it eliminates shrinkage, and for this purpose special steamers are used. Similar utensils for vegetables are becoming more and more widely used, because of their tenderizing effect.

3. *Stewed* or *Braised*: that is, placed in a saucepan or casserole over heat with water, broth, or fat. This is a slower method of cooking, and the food never reaches the high temperatures of roasting.

4. *Fried*: either in a skillet or pan, or in a deep-fat kettle with metal basket. Butter, fats, olive and cooking oils are the principal materials for shallow frying, while melted shortening or oil at 375° for uncooked foods (unless the recipe calls for another temperature) is recommended for deep-fat frying, especially vegetable oil and the canned shortenings, which do not smoke unduly at high temperatures.

5. *"Over hot water"*: in the home kitchen almost always refers to double-boiler cookery, but any large container, placed over heat and filled with simmering water in which smaller utensils are set functions as a *bain-marie*. Especially useful for sauces, soufflés, puddings, and for reheating foods, including leftovers.

These are the principal methods of cooking food. Variations and more details are given in the different sections.

In conclusion: in cookery, as everywhere else in life, moderation, good temper, and good timing are fundamental qualities. The secret of being a good cook is in controlling temperatures—yours as well as that of the food—from start to finish.

L.C.

GASTRONOMIC DICTIONARY

Dizionario gastronomico

The following is a selected dictionary of technical cooking terms, ingredients, and utensils, including some professional words and phrases which appear in this book and may not be familiar to all readers. Many of the methods described, and much of the nomenclature, are used by kitchen staffs in homes, clubs, hotels, and restaurants all over Europe, and, consequently, have been imported to similar institutions in the United States and England. In most definitions, the term is followed by its Italian equivalent.

ACIDULATED WATER—Water to which lemon juice or vinegar has been added; the usual proportions are 1 tablespoon of lemon juice or vinegar to 1 quart of water.

AL DENTE—Used to describe foods, especially pasta, cooked until just barely done and their texture still resilient and chewy. In other words: not overcooked.

ARROWROOT—A starch used to thicken sauces and soups; finer textured than flour, it gives gloss and a translucent quality to sauces. About 1 teaspoon of arrowroot will lightly thicken 1 cup of liquid.

AU GRATIN *(gratinare)*—To obtain a golden, crisp crust on a dish by browning under a broiler flame, usually done with dishes dressed with sauces, grated cheese, crumbs, or melted butter.

BAIN MARIE *(placca per bagno-maria)*—Professional version of the double boiler; a large container intended to hold hot water which is placed in the oven and in which smaller cooking utensils are partially immersed. The hot water acts as insulation from the direct heat of the oven and thus provides very slow, uniform heat for such dishes as molded soufflés, custards, etc.

BAKING SHEET *(placca per pasticceria)*—Large rectangular metal pan with or without very low sides. *See* Cooky Sheet.

BARD—To cover meat, poultry, or game with thin sheets of fat (usually fresh pork fat or salt pork) before cooking.

BASTE—To spoon fat or liquid over a food as it cooks, in order to keep it from drying out or to glaze or crisp its surface.

BATTER *(apparecchio)*—1) The blended ingredients for pancakes, custards, etc. 2) The mixture of eggs, flour, butter, milk, sugar, and flavorings for cakes. 3) Combinations of flour and liquid used to coat foods before frying in deep fat.

BLANCH—To partially cook foods in boiling water for a short time. Some vegetables are frequently blanched in order to remove outer skins; some meats, such as sweetbreads or brains, are blanched in order to firm them up prior to their being sautéed. *See* Parboil.

BLEND *(amalgamare)*—To combine materials until they are smoothly and evenly mixed.

BONE *(scalcare)*—To remove the bones of poultry, meat, etc., either before or after cooking. Directions for boning poultry will be found on page 436

BOUQUET GARNI *(mazzetto guarnito)*—A bunch of aromatic herbs used to flavor cooking. If fresh sprigs of herbs are available, they need only be tied with a string to facilitate their later removal; if dried herbs are used, they should be tied in a muslin or cheesecloth bag. The most commonly used Bouquet Garni is a combination of parsley, thyme, and bay leaf.

13

BRAISE *(far sudare)*—To tenderize food by long, slow cooking with a small amount of liquid in a covered pot or casserole over direct heat or, more frequently, in the oven.

BREADCRUMBS—Classically, breadcrumbs are the center portion of a loaf of bread with all trace of crust removed. Fresh breadcrumbs are most easily made by blending fresh slices of bread, cubed, in the electric blender at low speed for a few seconds, or slightly stale bread may be grated. More finely grained crumbs are made by drying slices of bread very slowly in the oven and then crushing them on a board.

BREADING *(panare)*—To dip food to be fried (especially croquettes or cutlets) in beaten egg and then to roll them in breadcrumbs.

BUTTER *(burro)*—The flavor of sweet butter is incomparably superior to that of salted butter, and it is recommended that only sweet butter be used for all of the recipes in this book.

CARAMEL *(caramello)*—Sugar that has been cooked with a very small amount of water over low heat until it has melted and turned brown. It is used to color various dishes and in the preparation of desserts and candies. *See* recipe No. 2293.

CASSEROLE—A heavy earthenware or enameled cooking pot with a lid.

CAYENNE PEPPER *(pepe di caienna)*—Condiment obtained by crushing the seeds and pods of small, fiery chili peppers of the *capsicum* family.

CLARIFY—To clear a liquid and remove all impurities. Stocks and soups are clarified by cooking them briefly with slightly beaten egg whites and then straining them through several thicknesses of cheesecloth. Specific directions for clarifying soups and stocks will be given with the recipes.

CLARIFIED BUTTER—*See* recipe No. 102.

COCOTTE—A fire-resistant pottery or glass cooking utensil, similar to a casserole.

CORAL *(corallo)*—The roe or eggs found in female lobsters which becomes red after cooking and is used for coloring foods, especially hot and cold sauces served with boiled fish.

CORRECT *(correggere)*—To modify a flavor and obtain a desired result by the addition of another spice or ingredient.

CROÛTONS *(crostini e crostoncini)*—Small cubes of bread either fried in fat or browned in the oven. They are most often served as a garnish with soups, vegetables, or scrambled eggs. *See* recipe No. 332.

CUBE—To cut into square shapes, larger than dice.

DE-GLAZE *(deglassare)*—To blend liquid with meat drippings in a pan by scraping the bottom and sides with a wooden spoon until the drippings are dissolved in the liquid. This operation is the usual basic step in preparing a sauce for fried and sautéed meats.

DE-GREASE—*See* Skim.

DICE *(dadolata)*—Bread, vegetables, or any food cut into tiny squares.

DRAIN *(sgocciolare)*—To dry food by letting it drip through a sieve, strainer, or colander; to dry food fried in deep fat briefly on absorbent paper to remove excess grease.

DRAINER *(scolafritti)*—Special Italian utensil, with grid, on which fried food is placed to drain off excess fat.

DRESS *(parare)*—To shape a portion of meat, cutting out nerves, tendons, fat, and bones with a sharp knife; to dress a salad is to mix in salad dressing; to dress vegetables with butter means to coat them with softened or melted butter just before serving.

DRIPPINGS *(fondo di cottura)*—Meat juices which have coagulated in the bottom of a pan after roasting or sautéeing.

DRIPPING PAN *(leccarda)*—Rectangular metal utensil put under meat roasting on a spit to gather the drippings.

ENTRÉE—Fourth course served at a formal Italian dinner, coming after soup, fish, and *relevé*. It can be a boiled, fried, or even a cold dish, such as timbales, meat or vegetable pies, variety meats, various croquettes, vol-au-vents, etc. *See* Relevé.

ENTREMETS—French term used to indicate two types of dishes: the first, prepared by the so-called *entremetier*, consists of soups, farinaceous dishes, and vegetables; the second, under the direction of a confectioner, includes all pastries and cakes.

ESSENCES *(essenze)*—Reduced concentrates of stocks prepared from meats, fish, vegetables, etc.; also flavorings, extracts, and syrups made from the zest or peel of citrus fruits.

EXTRACT *(estratto)*—Condensation of meat, vegetable, or other food juice, reduced by evaporation to a syrup or paste.

FINES HERBES *(erbe fini)*—A finely chopped mixture of any desired fresh herbs, such as parsley, tarragon, basil, marjoram, chervil, etc.

FLAMBÉE—To pour heated brandy or other liquor over a dish, ignite, and burn off the alcohol.

FOOD MILL—A round, sieve-like utensil through which foods may be puréed.

FORTIFY *(dar corpa)*—To give body, increase consistency, or sharpen the flavor of sauces or gravies by adding meat extract or other strongly flavored seasonings.

FROST *(glassare)*—To coat cakes with icing after baking.

FUMET—A fish or game stock.

GLAZE *(glassare)*—To make a thin, golden surface on any sauced food by subjecting it to high heat in the oven or under a broiler flame; to cover food with a thin coating of a shiny sauce; to brush the top of bread dough or pastry with beaten egg to achieve a golden color during the baking.

LARD *(lardellare)*—To introduce strips of seasoned fat into lean meat before cooking, using a special larding needle; *(picchettare)*—to introduce fats, aromatic herbs, or other ingredients by making incisions in meat, fish, or vegetables before cooking to improve flavor.

MASK *(velare)*—To cover with a thin, even layer of sauce.

MELON BALL CUTTER *(scavino)*—Kitchen tool used to cut small round balls of potato, apple, melon, or other vegetables and fruits.

MINCE *(tritare)*—To chop very finely meat, vegetables, or other foodstuffs.

MIREPOIX—Finely diced carrots, onions, and celery (with or without ham) cooked in butter; used as foundation to season prepared meat and fish dishes. *See* recipe No. 141.

MORTAR AND PESTLE *(mortaio e pestello)*—Marble, stone, or wooden bowl and hard pestle, used to grind and reduce foods to paste. Very small wooden mortars are used to prepare oil mixtures.

MUSTARD *(mostarda)*—Dry mustard is made by milling mustard seed; prepared mustard is the moist, spreading type. Wherever prepared mustard is required throughout this book, it is recommended that the more strongly flavored Dijon-type be used.

OIL *(olio)*—Whenever oil is required in any of the recipes throughout this book, it is recommended that only pure, virgin olive oil be used.

EN PAPILLOTE—Used to describe small cuts of sauced meat, poultry, or fish which are placed on one half of heavy sheets of white paper cut in the shape of hearts; the other half of the paper heart is folded over, the edges crimped to form a very tight seal, and the packets are then baked in the oven until the paper is browned and puffed. These are usually served by allowing each guest to open his own packet.

PARBOIL—To partially cook foods in boiling water; the operation is very similar to blanching, although it is generally understood that parboiling means a longer period of cooking than blanching. *See* Blanch.

PASTA MACHINE *(passatello)*—Metal utensil, rather like a laundry mangle, used for rolling out and cutting pasta dough.

PASTRY BAG *(tasca o cornetto)*—Cone-shaped funnel of cloth at the small end of which a metal tip or tube may be attached; the tips come in a large variety of sizes and decorative shapes.

PASTRY CLOTH—A large cloth on which to roll out pastry, frequently made of heavy linen whose coarse weave holds the flour and thereby helps keep pastry from sticking and enables it to be rolled to any desired thinness.

PASTRY WHEEL *(tagliapasta)*—Tool with a serrated wheel, used to cut egg pasta, biscuits, pastry, etc.

PEPPER *(pepe)*—Fruit of an East Indian shrub, also found in tropical Asia and equatorial America. Pepper comes in two forms, black and white. The black has a hull which is black and green striped; white pepper is simply black, without the covering, and is both less bitter and less aromatic. Since ground pepper loses strength rapidly, it is advisable to buy whole peppercorns and grind them, either in a pepper mill or in a mortar, as they are to be used.

POACH *(affogare)*—To cook foods in a barely simmering liquid.

PURÉE—To reduce cooked foods to a finely grained, paste-like consistency by mashing and pressing them through a sieve, food mill, ricer, or by blending them in the electric blender.

REDUCE *(ridurre)*—To cook a sauce or other liquid over heat until it has evaporated to the desired consistency and flavor; to change the consistency of foods.

RELEVÉ—In the lexicon of professional cookery, the main meat dish, served after the soup and fish courses.

15

SAUTÉ *(saltare)*—To cook meat, fish, or vegetables until brown and tender in an uncovered frying pan, using only a small amount of butter, oil, or other fat and agitating the pan to keep the food from sticking.

SCALD *(sbollentare)*—Usually directed for heating milk until small bubbles appear around the edge of the pan.

SEAR *(scottare)*—To brown the outside of food, sealing in juices and flavor, by roasting quickly in a hot oven or frying in very hot fat.

SIEVE *(cinese o passino fine)*—Cone-shaped or hemispherical strainer with tiny holes, used to strain sauces, clear soups, and other liquids; *(calza)*—cheesecloth or hair cloth strainer used to strain fruit juices and filter foods; *(stamigna)*—cloth strainer for sauces, etc. with wooden spatula to press material through cloth; *(colapasta o colatoio)*—colander or large metal bowl with holes for draining pasta and other foods.

SIMMER *(sobbollire)*—To cook in a liquid just below the boiling point.

SKIM *(schiumare)*—To remove with a spoon the scum and other impurities from the surface of sauces, stocks, and soups after simmering; *(sgrassare)*—to remove fats from surface of boiling or cold liquids.

SLIVER *(affilare)*—To cut almonds, pistachio nuts, string beans, etc. into thin lengthwise slices, using a very sharp knife.

SPICE BAG *(quattro spezie o spezie composte)*—Mixture of spices, tied in cheesecloth bag for easy removal, classically consisting of 4 ounces white pepper, 1 ounce nutmeg, 1 ounce juniper berries, 10 cloves.

SPRING FORM—A round mold or pan whose sides may be detached from the bottom by loosening a metal clasp.

STONER *(snocciolatore)*—Tool used to take stones, pits, and kernels out of fruits, especially cherries.

STRAIN *(passare)*—To pass food or liquid through a filtering surface, such as a sieve, in order to make it finer in consistency or to remove undesired elements.

STUFF *(farcire o riempire)*—To introduce stuffing into any other foodstuff, such as meat, poultry, fish, or vegetables.

STUFFING *(farce)*—Different ground and chopped foods, mixed with spices and crumbs, usually bound together with egg.

SUGAR *(zucchero)*—Ordinary granulated sugar should be used throughout the recipes in this book, unless another type is specified. Care should be taken not to confuse superfine sugar with confectioners' (the latter being flour-fine and containing cornstarch).

SUPRÊME—Originally the fillet or breast of poultry, now the word includes the best part of any meat, fish, or other favored food.

SWIRL—To agitate a pan in a circular motion in order to incorporate an ingredient into a sauce without stirring. Softened butter is frequently swirled into a thin sauce off the heat just before serving to thicken it very slightly.

TOMALLEY—The liver of male and female lobsters, a soft paste-like substance which becomes green after cooking. *See* Coral.

TRIM—To cut off or remove undesired elements from any food.

TRUSS *(accosciare)*—To tie meat or poultry with string so that it will retain its shape while cooking.

VEGETABLE SLICERS *(mandolini)*—Plane-like utensils, usually grooved, to cut potatoes and other vegetables; especially useful to prepare julienne vegetables and potato chips.

VENT—A cone of heavy paper or a pastry tube with a round opening inserted in the top of pastry-wrapped meats or pâtés to allow steam to escape and to keep the pastry casing from bursting during the cooking.

WELL *(fontana)*—In making pastry or dough, flour is usually piled in a mound on a board or hard surface and a "well" hollowed out in the center to facilitate incorporating other ingredients into the flour.

WHIP *(montare)*—To blend fresh butter into a sauce by whipping it in; to beat cream until it doubles in size and stiffens; to beat egg whites until they are stiff; *(mantecare)*—to work a food to make it softer and more tender, generally with a whisk; to paddle ice cream.

WHISK *(frusta)*—Kitchen tool of looped wires held together by a handle, used to whip eggs, cream, white of egg, sauces, etc. In Italy, *vimini,* a special type of broom straw, is considered the best whip for cream.

16

KITCHEN STOCKS, SAUCES, AND BASIC PREPARATIONS

KITCHEN STOCKS
Fondi di cucina

Stocks are the basic elements for many sauces and they are used to strengthen and enrich many others. They should be prepared in advance and kept under refrigeration or frozen.

It is often faster and more convenient to substitute canned beef bouillon, canned chicken consommé, or bottled clam juice for these stocks. Although they may be used just as they come, it is relatively easy to disguise their "canned" taste. Recipes for doing so are given in this section: No. 1a, No. 2a, and No. 4a. Bouillon cubes or dehydrated stocks may also be substituted, but they are less successful and should be used only if necessary. While all of these substitutes can be satisfactory, we should add that for a special occasion or a special dish, nothing can equal the indefinable perfection of a well-prepared, homemade stock.

1. WHITE STOCK
Fondo bianco

By definition, this is light-colored and should always be very clear. See No. 1a *for a substitute.*

½ pound lean veal
¾ pound veal shin (bone and meat), cracked
2 pounds chicken necks, backs, or wings
8 cups cold water

1 teaspoon salt
2 large onions, sliced
1 large carrot, sliced
3 stalks celery with leaves, sliced
1 bay leaf
4 sprigs parsley
2 sprigs fresh thyme (or ½ teaspoon dried)
2 egg whites
2 egg shells, crushed

Place the meat, shin, and chicken in a large soup pot, add the water and salt, bring slowly to a boil, and reduce the heat. Stir meat occasionally. As scum rises to the surface, skim frequently until the liquid is clear. Add the remaining ingredients, except the egg whites and shells, and again skim until clear. Simmer gently for 3 hours, remove from fire, and strain through a fine sieve or cheesecloth-lined colander. For extra clarity, return stock to the pot and add the egg shells and egg whites, beaten until soft peaks form. Bring to boil, stirring constantly, then strain again through clean cheesecloth. Before using the stock, fat should be carefully removed from top. If it has been kept in refrigerator, the fat will have solidified and is easy to remove. Stock keeps better if crust of fat is not broken. *Makes about 1 quart.*

NOTE: Carcasses of roast or fried (but not boiled) chicken may be substituted for the chicken parts, along with gizzards.

1a. SUBSTITUTE WHITE STOCK

4 cups canned chicken consommé
1 onion, sliced
1 carrot, sliced
2 stalks celery, sliced
Bouquet Garni:
    2 sprigs parsley
    1 bay leaf
    1/2 teaspoon dried thyme

Place all ingredients in a heavy saucepan, bring to a boil, reduce heat, and simmer for 30 minutes. Strain through a fine sieve. *Makes about 3 cups.*

2. FISH STOCK or FUMET
Fondo bianco di pesce

Fish stock will not keep quite as well under refrigeration as other stocks, and thus it is wise to make it fresh for each use. The heads and bones of filleted fish may be used, or it may be necessary to buy pieces of less expensive fish, such as whiting, flounder, or cod. Do not use oily fish, such as mackerel. See No. 2a for a substitute.

2 pounds raw fish: lean meat, heads, bones, and
    trimmings
2 cups dry white wine
6 cups water
1 onion, peeled and sliced
3 sprigs parsley
1 bay leaf
1 teaspoon lemon juice
Optional: 1/2 cup mushroom stems
1/2 teaspoon salt
2 egg whites, lightly beaten
2 egg shells

Place all the ingredients, except the egg whites and shells, in a large pot and bring slowly to a boil. Simmer gently for 2 hours, strain, clarify with the egg whites and shells [*see* No. 1], chill, and skim any fat from top. *Makes about 1 quart.*

2a. SUBSTITUTE FISH STOCK or FUMET

2 cups bottled clam juice
1 cup water
1 cup dry white wine
1 onion, sliced
1 carrot, sliced
2 stalks celery, sliced

Bouquet Garni:
    2 sprigs parsley
    1 bay leaf
    1/2 teaspoon dried thyme
Optional: 1/2 cup mushroom stems, sliced

Place all ingredients in a heavy saucepan, bring to a boil, turn down heat, and simmer for 30 minutes. Strain through a fine sieve. *Makes 3 cups.*

3. CHICKEN STOCK
Fondo bianco di pollame

Prepare a White Stock [No. 1], using 1 additional pound of chicken meat, bones, or giblets.

4. BROWN STOCK
Fondo bruno o sugo di carne

See No. 4a for a substitute.

1/2 pound cracked soup bones
1 pound veal shin (bone and meat)
1 pound lean soup beef (shank or shin), in 2-inch
    cubes
1 tablespoon butter or rendered beef fat
8 ounces lean raw ham, diced
2 ounces pork rind, in one piece
1 medium carrot, diced
1 large onion, diced
1 stalk celery with leaves, chopped
1 clove
1 bay leaf
1 clove garlic
4 sprigs parsley
4 sprigs thyme (or 1/2 teaspoon dried)
1 teaspoon salt
8 cups water

Brown the bones, veal shin, and beef cubes for 15 minutes in a hot (450°) oven. Melt the butter in a large, heavy pot over medium heat and add the ham, pork rind, carrot, celery, and onion. Arrange the meat and bones on top, add 1/2 cup of the water, and cook until the water has evaporated. Remove the rind. Add remainder of water, salt, clove, bay leaf, garlic, parsley, and thyme. Bring to a rapid boil, reduce heat, and simmer 4 to 5 hours, skimming scum from top and replenishing water if needed. Remove from flame and strain immediately through hair sieve or cheesecloth-lined colander. Chill, and remove fat before using. *Makes about 1½ quarts.*

NOTE: For meat glaze, reduce Brown Stock further by boiling until it becomes syrupy. Meat glaze may be used, a spoonful at a time, for flavoring sauces or reinforcing weak gravies or soups. [*see also* No. 10]

4a. SUBSTITUTE BROWN STOCK

Make exactly as Substitute White Stock [No. 1a], but use canned beef bouillon.

5. BROWN VEAL STOCK
Fondo bruno di vitello

1 pound boned shoulder of veal, tied in a roll
1 tablespoon butter or rendered beef fat, melted
1 medium carrot, finely sliced
1 medium onion, finely sliced
½ pound veal bones, cracked
1½ pounds chopped veal shin (bone and meat)
3 sprigs parsley
2 sprigs thyme (or ½ teaspoon dried)
1 bay leaf
6 cups (or more, as needed) White Stock [No. 1]

Brush the veal shoulder with the melted butter or fat. Brown it in a hot (450°) oven for 15 to 20 minutes. Place the carrot and onion in a large, heavy pot. Add the cracked bones, the veal shin, the herbs, ¼ cup white stock, and the oven-browned shoulder. Cover the pot and cook over a medium flame for about 15 minutes. Add another ¼ cup of the stock, and cook uncovered until the stock has almost evaporated. Add the remaining stock and bring rapidly to a boil, skimming carefully. Reduce heat and simmer for about 5 hours. Be careful that liquid does not boil away; add another cup of white stock or water from time to time, as needed. Strain through a fine sieve or cheesecloth-lined colander and chill. Remove the fat before use. It may be clarified as in No. 1, if you wish. *Makes about 1 quart.*

NOTE: The veal shoulder meat should be saved for other uses.

6. THICKENED BROWN VEAL STOCK
Fondo legato di vitello o fondo bruno legato

Boil 1 quart of Brown Veal Stock [No. 5] over high heat until it is reduced to 3 cups. Blend in 2 tablespoons of arrowroot or cornstarch mixed with ¼ cup cold stock or cold water, stirring constantly until it thickens.

7. GAME STOCK
Fondo di cacciagione o fondo di selvaggina

⅔ pound shoulder or breast of venison
½ pound hare or wild rabbit
½ pound pheasant or partridge
3 tablespoons butter or rendered beef fat
¼ pound fresh pork rind, parboiled in water for
    10 minutes
1 teaspoon salt
1 tablespoon diced carrot
4 tablespoons minced onion
1 cup white wine
3 cups White Stock [No. 1], or water seasoned with
    ½ teaspoon salt
2 juniper berries, bruised
1 clove
1 sprig fresh sage (or ¼ teaspoon dried)
3 sprigs parsley
2 sprigs fresh thyme (or ½ teaspoon dried)
1 bay leaf

Trim the game meats, spread with butter, season with salt, and sauté in a frying pan over high heat for about 5 minutes or until nicely browned. Place the carrot, onion, and pork rind in the bottom of a heavy pot. Arrange the game meats on top, and add the wine and 2 tablespoons of white stock. Cook over medium heat until the liquid is reduced to ⅓. Add the remaining stock, bring to a boil, skim, and add the juniper, clove, sage, parsley, thyme, and bay leaf. Reduce the heat and simmer for about 3 hours. Strain through several thicknesses of cheesecloth and chill. Remove fat from the surface before using. *Makes about 1 pint.*

8. CHICKEN FUMET
Fumetto di pollame

Follow the directions for Game Stock [No. 7] but use trimmings, carcasses, and bones of chicken and/or turkey instead of the game meat and omit the juniper berries, clove, and sage.

9. GAME FUMET
Fumetto di cacciagione o di selvaggina

Follow the same directions as for Game Stock [No. 7] but use trimmings, carcasses, and bones of game and/or wild birds instead of the meat.

10. MEAT ESSENCE
Essenza di carne

This essence, also called meat glaze, is made by reducing Brown Stock [No. 4] or White Stock [No. 1]. While making it, strain through a fine sieve several times. As the essence gets thicker, gradually reduce the heat. When it is thick enough to make a shiny coating on a wooden spoon, it is done. Pour it in a small, sterilized bottle and keep in refrigerator. A teaspoon added to a simple sauce will greatly enhance its flavor.

A commercial meat or beef extract, such as Bovril, may be used as a substitute.

11. FISH ESSENCE
Essenza di pesce

Prepare in the same manner as Meat Essence [No. 10] but use Fish Fumet [No. 2].

12. CHICKEN or GAME ESSENCE
Essenza di pollame o cacciagione o selvaggina

Prepare in the same manner as Meat Essence [No. 10] but use Chicken Stock [No. 3] or Game Stock [No. 7].

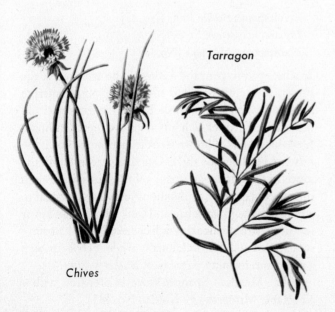

Tarragon

Chives

SAUCES
Salse

A sauce is to a dish as a piano accompaniment is to a singer: it isn't the same as the voice part, but it enriches the main theme, underlines its beauty, and fills in the rest with a flavor of its own. The one thing it should *never* do is overpower the dish it accompanies, or clash with it. Beef, mutton, and game can take a rather "loud" sauce, but sauces for veal, chicken, and delicate fish should be much more lightly seasoned. It is easier to add more flavoring at the end than attempt to take seasonings out once they are in.

In the section on stocks, a minimum amount of salt has been specified. This is so that the finished sauces will not be too salty after the other ingredients have been added.

In this book, almost all of the sauces have been divided into four groups and, after learning the four primary sauces, any cook should be able to face all the different sauce recipes calmly and confidently. In addition to the many important sauces which are part of the Italian gastronomic repertory, a number of other classic sauces, especially French, have been included.

A sauce thickened with flour, and/or egg yolks, should be stirred constantly while at cooking heat and should have the cook's undivided attention.

To make a good sauce, it is essential that the ingredients be of the best quality, especially the oil and butter. As egg yolks have such an important function in thickening and enriching many sauces, always use the freshest obtainable.

After cooking a sauce, skim all the fat remaining from the surface. If fat is needed for preserving, use a film of fresh butter.

When a sauce is too thin, thicken by adding an

21

appropriate amount of Kneaded Butter [No. 107], blending it in with a wire whisk over a low flame until it reaches the right consistency. Sauces may also be thickened by the addition of cornstarch or arrowroot mixed with a little water.

While they may be stored in the refrigerator or frozen, most sauces are best when made fresh, just before they are to be used.

ROUX
Roux

A roux is a cooked mixture of flour and butter used to thicken basic sauces. Although it is simple to prepare, a certain amount of care is required to achieve a smooth sauce, free of lumps.

There are two methods of making a flour-thickened sauce. The first, which is favored by most professional chefs, is to heat the specified liquid to the boiling point and then add it *all at once* to the cooking butter and flour; the liquid will thicken almost immediately. The alternative method is to add cold liquid very gradually to the cooking butter and flour. In both methods the sauce must be stirred constantly until the boiling point is reached and the heat lowered. The thickened sauce then should simmer for 5 to 10 minutes to rid it of its floury flavor. A wire whisk is an invaluable tool in achieving a smooth sauce.

13. WHITE ROUX
Roux bianco

Melt 3 tablespoons butter in a pan over medium heat, stir in 3 tablespoons flour, and simmer for 3 or 4 minutes, but do not let it brown. A cup of liquid added to this mixture, by either method outlined above, will become very thick. *Makes 3 tablespoonsful.*

14. BLOND ROUX
Roux biondo

Prepare in the same manner as No. 13 but let butter and flour cook to a dark golden hue before adding liquid. *Makes 3 tablespoonsful.*

15. BROWN ROUX
Roux bruno

Use 3 tablespoons Clarified Butter [No. 102] and 3 tablespoons flour and cook as in No. 13 but let flour become well browned before adding liquid. Care must be taken that the flour does not actually burn, as this will not only impair its flavor, but will also lessen its thickening power. *Makes 3 tablespoonsful.*

PRIMARY SAUCES
Salse madri

Traditionally, only Spanish sauce is considered the basic or primary sauce. However, we are including in this primary category Velouté, Béchamel, and tomato sauces, since Velouté and Béchamel form the bases of a great many other compounded sauces, and tomato sauce is used so frequently to season and enrich a wide variety of dishes.

16. SPANISH SAUCE
Salsa spagnola

3 tablespoons Brown Roux [No. 15]
2 quarts hot Brown Stock [No. 4]
2 tablespoons Mirepoix [No. 141]

In a heavy saucepan, add 3 cups hot brown stock to the brown roux and bring to the boiling point, stirring constantly with a wire whisk. Lower the flame and add the mirepoix. Cook 2 hours over low heat, adding a few tablespoons of brown stock from time to time if the mixture becomes too thick. Using fine sieve, strain the sauce into another saucepan, gently pressing through the mirepoix. Add an amount of brown stock equal to strained sauce in saucepan and cook 3 hours more over low heat. Strain sauce through cheesecloth or hair sieve into a bowl and stir occasionally while it cools to keep a skin from forming on surface. *Makes 1 pint.*

NOTE: Meatless Spanish sauce is prepared with a Vegetable Mirepoix [*see* Note to No. 141].

22

17. VELOUTÉ SAUCE
Salsa vellutata o salsa bianca

3 tablespoons butter
3 tablespoons sifted flour
2 cups White Stock [No. 1]
3 sprigs parsley
Pinch white pepper
$\frac{1}{2}$ teaspoon salt
Pinch nutmeg
1 tablespoon butter, melted

Melt butter in a saucepan over a medium flame, stir in the flour, and, as soon as the mixture begins to color, add stock little by little. Slowly bring to boil. Add parsley, pepper, and nutmeg. Cook over moderate heat for 15 minutes. Add salt, remove from stove, and strain the sauce through a fine sieve into a bowl. Float the melted butter on the surface to avoid the formation of skin on the top and cool. *Makes 1 pint.*

17a. VELOUTÉ SAUCE FOR FISH

This is prepared exactly like Velouté Sauce [No. 17], except that Fish Fumet [No. 2] replaces the white stock.

17b. VELOUTÉ SAUCE FOR CHICKEN

This is prepared exactly like Velouté Sauce [No. 17], except that Chicken Stock [No. 3] is substituted for the white stock.

18. BÉCHAMEL SAUCE
Salsa besciamella

4 tablespoons butter
Optional: $\frac{1}{2}$ tablespoon finely chopped onion
3 tablespoons sifted flour
2 cups hot milk
$\frac{1}{2}$ teaspoon salt
Pinch pepper
Pinch nutmeg
Bouquet Garni:
   2 sprigs parsley
   1 sprig thyme (or $\frac{1}{4}$ teaspoon dried)
   1 bay leaf

Melt the butter in a heavy saucepan over medium heat. (Cook the optional onion in the butter until transparent but not brown.) Add flour, and stir for 1 minute. Gradually add the milk, stirring constantly, and season with salt, pepper, and nutmeg. Add Bouquet Garni, bring

to boil, lower the flame, and cook over low heat for 15 minutes, stirring occasionally. Strain sauce through a fine sieve into a bowl, stirring now and then as it cools to keep skin from forming on surface. *Makes 1 pint.*

19. TOMATO SAUCE
Salsa al pomodoro

2 tablespoons oil
$\frac{1}{2}$ onion, finely chopped
4 tablespoons ham (or fresh pork), fat and lean, chopped
1 tablespoon flour mixed with 1 teaspoon oil
2 pounds fresh tomatoes, peeled, seeded, drained, and
    chopped (or 1 No. $2\frac{1}{2}$ can Italian-style plum
    tomatoes, drained)
1 sprig thyme (or $\frac{1}{4}$ teaspoon dried)
1 bay leaf
1 teaspoon salt
$\frac{1}{2}$ teaspoon sugar (more, if tomatoes are tart)
$\frac{1}{4}$ teaspoon pepper

Heat the oil in a heavy saucepan, add the chopped onion and ham, and brown them over fairly high heat for 5 to 6 minutes. Add the flour and mix well. Turn the heat down to moderate and add tomato pulp (or the canned tomatoes, drained). Season with the salt, pepper, and sugar; and add the thyme and bay leaf. Cook for about 45 minutes, stirring from time to time. The sauce may be strained through a fine sieve, if desired. *Makes 1$\frac{1}{2}$ pints.*

SECONDARY SAUCES
Salse di base

Although the three following sauces are derived from Spanish or Velouté sauces, each is the starting point for so many other sauces that they deserve their own category.

20. DEMI-GLAZE SAUCE
Salsa demi-glace

This is the name for a Spanish Sauce [No. 16] which is simmered until it is reduced by half. This concentrate is further strengthened by the addition of Meat Glaze [No. 10]. Taste as you add the latter as it is very salty and too much will ruin the sauce. When the mixture has cooled, add wine at the rate of $\frac{1}{3}$ cup per quart of sauce. Choose a wine (Port, Marsala, Madeira, sherry, Burgundy, etc.) appropriate to the dish the sauce will be served with.

21. SAUCE PARISIENNE
Salsa parigina

¼ pound mushrooms
1 cup water
3 egg yolks
3 tablespoons White Stock [No. 1]
½ cup light cream
½ teaspoon salt
Pinch pepper
Pinch nutmeg
1 teaspoon lemon juice
2 cups Velouté Sauce [No. 17]
3 tablespoons butter

Cook the mushrooms and water in a saucepan over moderate heat for 25 minutes or until the liquid is reduced to ⅓ cup. Strain this liquid into a bowl (the mushrooms may be reserved for other uses) and allow to cool for a few minutes. Add the stock and mix well. Add the egg yolks and cream and beat the mixture thoroughly. Bring the Velouté to a simmer in a heavy saucepan. Remove from the fire and gradually add it to the egg-yolk mixture, stirring constantly with wire whisk. When well incorporated, pour the mixture back into the saucepan, add the salt and pepper and lemon juice, and cook over low heat for 10 minutes, stirring constantly, until slightly thickened. Do not allow to boil. Off the heat beat in the butter, bit by bit, and then strain the sauce through a very fine sieve. The sauce may be kept warm in the top of a double boiler over warm, *not hot*, water, with another tablespoon of melted butter floated over the top to keep a skin from forming. *Makes 2½ cups.*

22. SAUCE SUPRÊME
Salsa suprema

1 pint Chicken Stock [No. 3]
¼ cup mushroom liquid [*see* No. 21]
1 cup Velouté Sauce for Chicken [No. 17b]
½ cup heavy cream
4 tablespoons butter
Optional: 1 tablespoon chopped black truffle
    [or No. 1819a] and 2 teaspoons lemon juice
Salt and freshly ground white pepper

Cook the chicken stock and mushroom liquid in a saucepan over high heat until reduced to ⅔. Add the Velouté and cook over medium heat for 1 hour or until mixture reaches a slightly thickened consistency, adding the cream little by little during cooking. Remove from the heat, strain through cheesecloth or a

fine sieve, and beat in the butter bit by bit. Season with salt and white pepper to taste. Optional: add 1 tablespoon chopped black truffle and 2 teaspoons lemon juice. If sauce is not used immediately, melt a little butter and float it over the surface to prevent a crust from forming. *Makes 1 pint.*

COMPOUND
BROWN SAUCES
Salse brune composte

Compound brown sauces are:
1. Those derived from Spanish Sauce [No. 16]
2. Those derived from Demi-Glaze Sauce [No. 20]
3. Those derived from Brown Veal Stock [No. 5]; from red wine; or from Italian Meat Sauce [No. 45]

23. GENEVA SAUCE
Salsa génevoise

For fish

½ cup butter
2 tablespoons Vegetable Mirepoix [*see* Note to No. 141]
1 pound raw fish pieces: bones, heads, fins, etc.
2 cups dry red wine
1 cup Fish Stock [No. 2]
4 tablespoons chopped mushrooms
1 cup Meatless Spanish Sauce [*see* Note to No. 16]
½ teaspoon anchovy paste

Melt 1 tablespoon of the butter in a saucepan over moderate heat, add the mirepoix and the pieces of fish, cover, and let steam 15 minutes. Drain off resulting liquid into a saucepan and to it add the wine, the fish stock, and the mushrooms. Cook over a brisk flame until the liquid is reduced by ½. Add the Spanish sauce, reduce the heat, and simmer for 1½ hours, adding a spoonful of fish stock now and then if it becomes too thick. Strain through cheesecloth or a fine sieve and reheat, but do not boil again. Add the anchovy paste and the remaining butter, bit by bit, beating briskly. Serve immediately. *Makes about 1 pint.*

24. AU GRATIN SAUCE
Salsa al gratino

For fish

1 cup dry white wine
1 cup Fish Stock [No. 2]
1 tablespoon finely chopped scallion
1 cup Duxelles Sauce [No. 31]
1⅔ cups Spanish Sauce [No. 16]
1 tablespoon chopped parsley

Cook the wine, fish stock, and the scallion in a saucepan over fairly high heat until reduced to ½ its quantity. Add the Duxelles and Spanish sauces and simmer for 5 minutes longer. Taste for seasoning and sprinkle with the parsley. *Makes 3½ cups.*

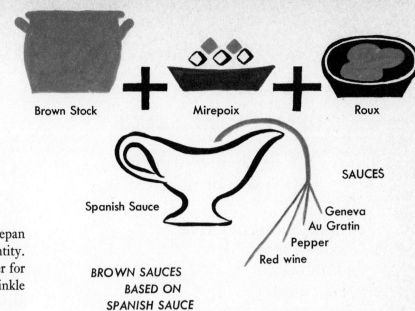

Brown Stock + Mirepoix + Roux

Spanish Sauce

SAUCES

Geneva
Au Gratin
Pepper
Red wine

**BROWN SAUCES
BASED ON
SPANISH SAUCE**

25. PEPPER SAUCE
Salsa peperata

For red meats

2 tablespoons butter
2 tablespoons Vegetable Mirepoix [*see* Note to No. 141]
⅓ cup white wine vinegar
⅓ cup dry white wine
⅔ cup Spanish Sauce [No. 16]
⅓ cup (slightly more, if needed) White Stock [No. 1]
¼ teaspoon freshly ground pepper

Melt 1 tablespoon butter in a saucepan over moderate heat, add the mirepoix, and simmer for 5 minutes. Add the vinegar and white wine and cook until liquid is reduced by half. Add the Spanish sauce and stock and continue cooking over a moderate flame for 1 hour, adding more stock if sauce boils away too quickly. Strain through a fine sieve, pressing the juices out of the residue. Just before serving, reheat and season with pepper. Remove from stove and beat in the other tablespoonful of butter. If the meat with which the sauce is being served has been marinated, you may add a spoonful of marinade. *Makes about 1 cup.*

26. RED WINE SAUCE
Salsa al vino rosso

For red meats and chicken casseroles

4 tablespoons butter
2 tablespoons finely chopped onion
1⅔ cup dry red wine
1 bay leaf
2 tablespoons mushroom stems or 1 tablespoon dried mushrooms, soaked for 1 hour, squeezed dry, and coarsely chopped
4 sprigs parsley
4 sprigs thyme (or ½ teaspoon dried)
1 cup Spanish Sauce [No. 16]
Salt to taste

Cook the minced onion in 1 tablespoon of the butter in a saucepan over medium heat until golden. Add wine, mushrooms, herbs, and a pinch of salt. Cook over a brisk flame until only ⅓ of the liquid remains. Add the Spanish sauce and cook again until ½ has evaporated. Strain through a fine sieve, taste, add salt if necessary, and keep warm until ready to use. Just before serving, beat in the remaining 3 tablespoons of the butter, bit by bit. *Makes 1 scant cup.*

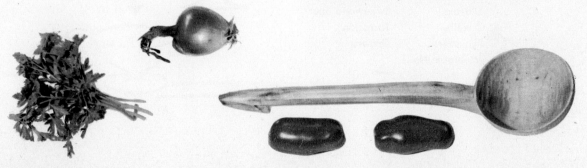

COMPOUND BROWN SAUCES DERIVED FROM DEMI-GLAZE SAUCE

Salse brune di derivazione dalla salsa demi-glace

27. SAUCE BORDELAISE
Salsa bordolese

For broiled meats

¾ cup red wine
1 tablespoon finely chopped scallion
1 tablespoon chopped fresh thyme (or ½ teaspoon dried)
1 bay leaf, crumbled
¾ cup Demi-Glaze Sauce [No. 20]
1 tablespoon butter
1 tablespoon beef marrow, finely diced and parboiled
1 teaspoon minced parsley

Simmer wine with scallion, thyme, and bay leaf until ⅔ evaporated. Add the Demi-Glaze and simmer again until ⅓ has evaporated. Remove from flame, and beat in the butter. Strain through a fine sieve. Just before serving add marrow and parsley. *Makes 1 cup.*

28. CACCIATORA SAUCE
Salsa alla cacciatora

For broiled meat or chicken

¼ pound mushrooms, sliced
4 tablespoons butter
Salt and pepper
1 tablespoon finely chopped onion
½ cup dry white wine
2 tablespoons flour
2 cups Demi-Glaze Sauce [No. 20]
⅓ cup Tomato Sauce [No. 19], or canned tomatoes, drained
1 tablespoon parsley and tarragon, chopped together

Sauté the mushrooms for 5 minutes in 2 tablespoons of the butter in a saucepan over moderate heat and season them lightly with salt and pepper. Add onion and continue cooking for another 10 minutes or until the mushrooms are very tender. Remove mushrooms, leaving their juices in the saucepan. To the juice add wine and boil until only 4 tablespoons of liquid remain. Cool, and blend in the flour, making a smooth paste. Return to a low flame and stir until mixture starts to thicken. Add the Demi-Glaze and Tomato sauces, bring to a boil, and simmer for 5 minutes. Add cooked mushrooms, remaining butter, chopped parsley and tarragon; and stir well. *Makes 2½ cups.*

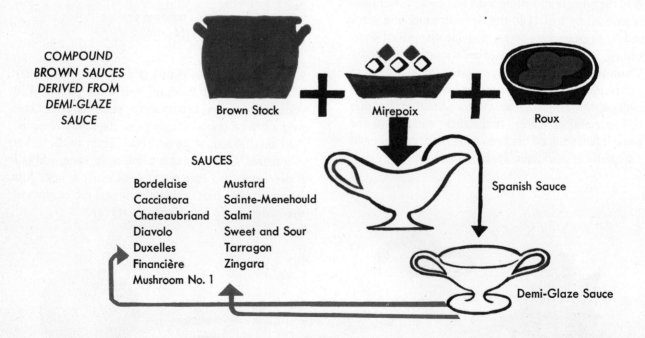

COMPOUND BROWN SAUCES DERIVED FROM DEMI-GLAZE SAUCE

Brown Stock + Mirepoix + Roux

Spanish Sauce

Demi-Glaze Sauce

SAUCES

Bordelaise
Cacciatora
Chateaubriand
Diavolo
Duxelles
Financière
Mushroom No. 1

Mustard
Sainte-Menehould
Salmi
Sweet and Sour
Tarragon
Zingara

29. CHATEAUBRIAND SAUCE
Salsa chateaubriand

For steaks

⅔ cup white wine
1 tablespoon finely chopped scallion
⅔ cup Demi-Glaze Sauce [No. 20]
½ cup butter, softened
1 tablespoon finely chopped tarragon (or 1 teaspoon dried)
Pinch Cayenne pepper (or 1 drop Tabasco sauce)
1 teaspoon lemon juice

Cook scallion and wine in a saucepan over medium heat until only ⅓ of the liquid remains. Add Demi-Glaze sauce and boil until liquid is reduced by half. Strain through fine sieve into another saucepan. Just before using, reheat; then remove from flame and add butter, bit by bit, stirring vigorously. Add Cayenne pepper and lemon juice and serve immediately, before butter can separate. *Makes about 1 cup.*

30. DIAVOLO SAUCE
Salsa alla diavola

For roast chicken, Cornish hens, squab, etc.

½ cup dry white wine
1 tablespoon wine, or cider, vinegar
1 tablespoon finely chopped onion
1 teaspoon chopped thyme (or ½ teaspoon dried)
½ small bay leaf
¼ teaspoon coarsely ground black pepper
¾ cup Demi-Glaze Sauce [No. 20]
Pinch Cayenne pepper (or 1 drop Tabasco sauce)
1 tablespoon minced parsley
2 tablespoons butter, softened

Put wine, vinegar, onion, thyme, bay leaf, and pepper into a heavy saucepan. Boil rapidly over high heat until liquid is reduced by ⅔. Add Demi-Glaze sauce and simmer for 5 minutes. Strain through a fine sieve, add Cayenne (or Tabasco) and parsley, and beat in the butter. *Makes 1 scant cup.*

31. DUXELLES SAUCE
Salsa Duxelles

For eggs, fish, poultry, broiled or sautéed meat

⅔ cup juice drained from cooked mushrooms
⅔ cup dry white wine
2 tablespoons grated onion
2 cups Demi-Glaze Sauce [No. 20]
2 tomatoes, peeled, seeded, drained, and puréed through a food mill
4 tablespoons Duxelles [No. 138]
1 teaspoon minced parsley

In heavy saucepan or skillet put mushroom juice, wine, and onion. Cook over brisk fire until ⅔ of liquid has boiled away. Add the Demi-Glaze, puréed tomatoes, and Duxelles and cook for another 5 minutes, stirring gently. Just before serving, add the parsley. *Makes about 2 cups.*

32. SAUCE FINANCIÈRE
Salsa finanziera

This sauce is usually used to bind the ingredients for the filling of Vol-au-Vent Financière [No. 648] and also for timbales and chicken dishes.

2 cups Demi-Glaze Sauce [No. 20]
¾ cup Marsala wine
½ cup liquid from canned truffles [or No. 1819a]
12 thin slices canned truffles [or No. 1819a]
½ pound cooked veal sweetbreads, in small slices [see introduction to No. 1434]
6 mushroom caps, sautéed in 1 tablespoon butter for 10 minutes
6 tablespoons veal purée (cooked veal puréed in electric blender)

Mix the Demi-Glaze and Marsala with the truffle juice in a saucepan. Place the pan over high heat and reduce the liquid to ½ its quantity. Strain through a fine sieve, blend in the veal purée, and stir in the sweetbreads, truffles, and mushroom caps. Return to a medium flame and heat only until the whole mixture is thoroughly hot. *Makes about 3 cups.*

33. MUSHROOM SAUCE NO. 1
Salsa con funghi

1½ tablespoons butter
¼ pound sliced, or tiny whole mushrooms
¾ cup Demi-Glaze Sauce [No. 20]
1 tablespoon dry Marsala or Madeira wine
Salt and freshly ground pepper

Melt the butter in a frying pan over moderate heat, add the mushrooms, and sauté gently for about 8 minutes, stirring often and seasoning the mushrooms lightly with salt and pepper as they cook. Add the Demi-Glaze sauce and the wine, bring to a boil, and simmer for 2 minutes. *Makes 1 scant cup.*

34. MUSTARD SAUCE
Salsa mostarda

For broiled meat, especially pork

5 tablespoons butter
1 small onion, finely chopped
¼ teaspoon salt
Pinch black pepper
Pinch powdered thyme
Pinch powdered bay leaf
½ cup dry white wine
¾ cup Demi-Glaze Sauce [No. 20]
2 tablespoons prepared mustard (Dijon-type preferred)
Juice of ½ lemon

Brown the onion lightly in 2 tablespoons of the butter in a saucepan over medium heat and season with salt, pepper, thyme, and bay leaf. Add the Demi-Glaze sauce and reduce to ⅔ its quantity. Just before serving, finish sauce by briskly stirring in the mustard, the rest of the butter, bit by bit, and the lemon juice. *Makes 1 scant cup.*

35. SAUCE SAINTE-MENEHOULD
Salsa Sainte-Menehould

For broiled pork and pig's feet

1 tablespoon butter
2 tablespoons finely chopped onion
¼ teaspoon salt
Pinch powdered thyme
Pinch powdered bay leaf
2 pinches Cayenne pepper
⅓ cup dry white wine
1 tablespoon vinegar
⅔ cup Demi-Glaze Sauce [No. 20]
1 tablespoon finely chopped sour pickles
1 tablespoon finely chopped parsley

28

Cook the onion in the butter in a saucepan over medium heat for 3 minutes; season with salt, thyme, bay leaf, and Cayenne. Add the wine and vinegar and boil until the liquid has almost evaporated. Add Demi-Glaze sauce and bring to rolling boil. Remove from flame almost immediately and mix in pickles and parsley. *Makes ¾ cup.*

36. SALMI SAUCE
Salsa salmi

This sauce is for game and utilizes the trimmings and bones of the bird or animal.

3 tablespoons Vegetable Mirepoix [*see* Note to No. 141]
Game trimmings, roasted and cut into small pieces
⅓ cup dry white wine
⅔ cup Demi-Glaze Sauce [No. 20]
7 tablespoons White Stock [No. 1]

Heat mirepoix and remnants of game in a heavy frying pan over medium heat. Add wine and let this boil away almost completely. Add Demi-Glaze sauce and 5 tablespoons of the stock. Simmer for 15 minutes and then strain through a sieve, pressing firmly to extract all the juices. Return the strained sauce to the fire, add remaining 2 tablespoons of stock, and simmer for 20 minutes. The sauce should be fairly thick. *Makes ¾ cup.*

37. SWEET-AND-SOUR SAUCE
Salsa agrodolce

For ham, beef tongue, etc.

3 lumps sugar, quickly dipped in vinegar and removed at once
¾ cup dry white wine
1 tablespoon finely chopped onion or scallion
¾ cup Demi-Glaze Sauce [No. 20]
1 tablespoon capers
2 tablespoons seedless grapes, or plumped raisins

Melt the sugar lumps in a small, heavy frying pan over moderate heat until they begin to caramelize. When the sugar becomes light brown and bubbly, quickly add wine and chopped onion. Bring to rapid boil and let liquid reduce almost entirely. Add Demi-Glaze sauce, heat through, and then strain through a fine sieve. A few minutes before serving, add the capers and grapes. *Makes 1 scant cup.*

38. TARRAGON SAUCE
Salsa al dragoncello

For eggs, poultry, or veal

2/3 cup dry white wine
4 sprigs fresh tarragon (or 1 teaspoon dried)
1 cup Demi-Glaze Sauce [No. 20] or Thickened Brown
    Veal Stock [No. 6]
1 teaspoon chopped tarragon leaves

Bring wine to a boil in a saucepan over high heat and remove from fire. Steep tarragon in the wine (use more tarragon for stronger flavor) for 10 minutes, keeping the saucepan covered. Add the Demi-Glaze sauce and return to fire. Cook until 1/3 of liquid has evaporated. Strain through fine sieve and add the chopped tarragon (or substitute 1 teaspoon of chopped parsley). *Makes 1 cup.*

39. ZINGARA SAUCE
Salsa zingara

For tender roasts, especially lamb or veal

2/3 cup Demi-Glaze Sauce [No. 20]
3 tablespoons Tomato Sauce [No. 19]
3 tablespoons mushroom liquid [*see* No. 21]
1 tablespoon diced, cooked lean ham
1 tablespoon diced, cooked tongue
1 tablespoon chopped mushrooms
1 teaspoon finely chopped truffle [or No. 1819a]
Pinch paprika

Mix Demi-Glaze, tomato sauce, and mushroom liquid in a saucepan; bring to a boil over medium heat. Add ham, tongue, mushrooms, truffle, and paprika. Heat thoroughly, but do not boil again. *Makes 1 cup.*

VARIOUS COMPOUND
BROWN SAUCES
Salse brune di derivazione da
fondi bruni

Most of these sauces are based on Brown Veal Stock [No. 5] or red wine. Also included in this category is a basic Italian meat sauce which may successfully be substituted for many of the sauces based on brown stocks.

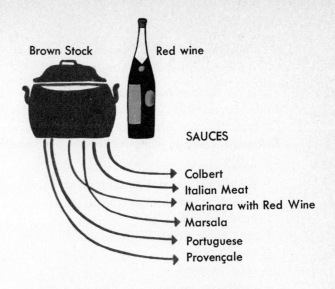

Brown Stock   Red wine

SAUCES

Colbert
Italian Meat
Marinara with Red Wine
Marsala
Portuguese
Provençale

**COMPOUND BROWN SAUCES BASED
ON BROWN VEAL STOCK AND/OR WINE**

40. SAUCE COLBERT
Salsa Colbert

For grilled meats

1 tablespoon Meat Essence [No. 10]
1 tablespoon Brown Veal Stock [No. 5] or water
1 tablespoon Madeira wine
1/4 teaspoon nutmeg
Pinch Cayenne pepper
1/2 cup butter, softened
Juice of 1/2 lemon
1 tablespoon finely chopped parsley

Bring to a boil the meat glaze, stock, and Madeira in a saucepan over medium heat. Mix nutmeg and Cayenne with the butter and, off the heat, beat into the sauce, bit by bit. Add lemon juice and parsley. *Makes 2/3 cup.*

29

41. ITALIAN MEAT SAUCE
Sugo di carne all'italiana

This is the sauce mentioned earlier, which may be substituted for many of the sauces based on brown stocks. The quantities given here will yield about 4 cups of sauce. The sauce may also be frozen and kept for 2 or 3 months.

⅛ pound ham fat, chopped or ground
⅛ pound fresh pork rind (or salt pork, cut in
    strips, and parboiled and cooled)
1 pound beef shank
1 carrot, cut in slivers
½ teaspoon salt
⅛ teaspoon pepper
4 strips bacon, parboiled
½ pound veal shank
1 veal knuckle (or ½ calf's foot), split
⅛ pound mushrooms, sliced (or 1½ tablespoons dried
    mushrooms, soaked for 1 hour, squeezed dry, and
    coarsely chopped)
1 medium carrot, sliced
2 onions, sliced
1 stalk celery with leaves, sliced
1 clove
Bouquet Garni:
    1 bay leaf
    ¼ teaspoon dried thyme
    ¼ teaspoon dried marjoram
1 clove garlic, crushed in the garlic-press
¼ cup red wine (or Marsala wine)
2 teaspoons flour, mixed with 2 teaspoons oil
1 medium tomato, peeled, seeded, drained, and chopped
1 teaspoon sugar
8 cups boiling water (or more if necessary)
Additional salt and pepper to taste

Line bottom of a large, heavy pot with ham fat and pork rind (or parboiled salt pork). Insert the slivers of carrot in the beef shank, season with the salt and pepper, cover with strips of parboiled bacon, and place it on top of fat in the pot. Add veal shank, veal knuckle, mushrooms, carrot, onion, celery, and clove. Place in a 450° oven for 15 to 20 minutes, stirring occasionally. When meat begins to brown, remove from oven, add Bouquet Garni, garlic, and wine; cook uncovered over medium heat on top of the stove until liquid has nearly boiled away. Remove from heat for a moment while adding flour, then return to the stove and stir contents thoroughly for a few minutes. Add the tomato and sugar. Now add sufficient boiling water to cover the meat; add salt to taste (about 1 teaspoon) and mix well. Bring to a boil again, cover, and return to a 300°

oven for 4 hours. Remove meat and veal knuckle and reserve for another use. Strain liquid into another pot through a fine sieve and continue to cook on top of stove over medium heat until the desired thickness has been achieved, skimming fat from surface from time to time. Pour into a container and store in refrigerator until needed. This sauce keeps well. *Makes approximately 1 quart.*

NOTE: The beef and veal knuckle (boned) may be served reheated in a little of the sauce. The veal may be ground and used for meatballs.

42. MARINARA SAUCE WITH RED WINE
Salsa alla marinara al vino rosso

For eels and fresh-water fish

2 cups red wine
2 tablespoons Vegetable Mirepoix [*see* Note to No. 141]
1 clove garlic, crushed in the garlic-press
1 tablespoon mushroom peelings
1 tablespoon Kneaded Butter [No. 107]
2 tablespoons butter
½ teaspoon anchovy paste
Pinch Cayenne Pepper
Salt and freshly ground white pepper

Put the red wine, mirepoix, garlic, and mushroom peelings in a heavy saucepan, bring to a boil over medium heat, and simmer for 15 minutes. Raise the heat and reduce quickly to ⅓ its original quantity. Strain through a fine sieve into another saucepan over medium heat, blend in the kneaded butter with a wire whisk, and simmer for 10 minutes. Remove from the heat, stir in the anchovy paste and the Cayenne, and swirl in the butter, bit by bit. Taste, and adjust seasoning. *Makes 1 scant cup.*

NOTE: The flavor of this sauce will be greatly enhanced if the fish with which it is to be served is simmered in the wine with the mirepoix, garlic, and mushrooms (see the section on Fish for exact directions and cooking time); the cooked fish should be kept warm on a hot platter while the sauce is being completed.

43. MARSALA SAUCE
Salsa al marsala

Marsala is a delicious Sicilian wine, either sweet or dry, which resembles Madeira. The two can nearly always be used interchangeably. Dry Marsala is best for meat sauces, while the sweet variety lends itself naturally to desserts. The following sauce is excellent for dressing up leftover meat or any small pieces of meat.

2 cups Italian Meat Sauce [No. 41]
⅓ cup dry Marsala wine
1 tablespoon butter

Bring the meat sauce to a brisk boil in a saucepan over high heat and let it reduce a little. Strain, and reduce again until only 1 cup remains. Remove from the flame, add the Marsala, then add the butter, bit by bit. If the sauce is to be kept warm, do not boil again, but keep hot in double boiler over warm water. *Makes 1¼ cups.*

44. ORANGE SAUCE
Salsa all'arancia

For duck or duckling

4 lumps sugar dipped in vinegar
⅔ cup Brown Veal Stock [No. 5]
Juice of 1 orange
1 teaspoon lemon juice
2 tablespoons orange peel (no white part) cut into fine strips and parboiled
1½ tablespoons Curaçao or other orange liqueur

Caramelize the sugar in a heavy saucepan over medium heat until light gold in color and then add the veal stock. Bring to rolling boil, cook for 5 minutes, and add the orange and lemon juice. Stir occasionally to dissolve the caramelized sugar. Strain through a fine sieve, and add orange peel and Curaçao. *Makes ¾ cup.*

NOTE: If a thicker sauce is desired, blend in 1 tablespoon Kneaded Butter [No. 107] with a wire whisk when the stock comes to a boil.

45. PORTUGUESE SAUCE
Salsa portoghese

For eggs, fish, meat, or poultry

1 tablespoon oil
2 tablespoons finely chopped onion
2 medium tomatoes, peeled, seeded, drained, and cut into strips
1 clove garlic, crushed in the garlic-press
½ teaspoon salt
⅛ teaspoon pepper
½ cup Thickened Brown Veal Stock [No. 6]
1 tablespoon finely chopped parsley

In a small, heavy saucepan, cook the chopped onion in the oil over medium heat until golden; add tomato, garlic, and the salt and pepper. Bring to boil, turn flame down, and simmer, covered, for about 15 minutes, stirring occasionally. Add veal stock, mix thoroughly, and bring to a boil again. Serve at once, topped with the parsley and a grating of black pepper. *Makes about ¾ cup.*

46. SAUCE PROVENÇALE
Salsa alla provenzale

For eggs, fish, and small pieces of meat

1 tablespoon oil
3 tablespoons finely chopped onion
½ cup dry white wine
1 medium tomato, peeled, seeded, drained, and chopped
1 clove garlic, bruised
Salt and freshly ground pepper
1 cup Thickened Brown Veal Stock [No. 6]
½ teaspoon chopped parsley

Cook the onion in the oil in a saucepan over medium heat until golden. Add the wine and reduce over high heat until only one or two tablespoons of liquid remain. Add the tomato and garlic, season with salt and pepper to taste, and simmer 5 minutes. Add veal stock and simmer for 15 minutes longer. Remove garlic clove and add parsley. *Makes 1 cup.*

COMPOUND
WHITE SAUCES

Salse bianche composte

Compound white sauces are:

1. Those derived from Velouté Sauce
2. Those derived from Béchamel Sauce
3. Those derived from Sauce Parisienne
4. Those derived from Sauce Suprême

47. ANDALUSIAN SAUCE
Salsa andalusa

For eggs, poultry, and fish

½ green pepper, roasted, scraped, seeded, and diced
    [*see* No. 145]
2 tablespoons butter
⅔ cup Velouté Sauce [No. 17]
2 tablespoons Tomato Sauce [No. 19]
2 teaspoons finely chopped parsley
1 clove garlic, crushed in the garlic-press
Salt and freshly ground pepper

Gently sauté the diced pepper in the butter in a sauce-pan over medium heat for 3 minutes. Add the 2 sauces, garlic, and parsley. Cook only until thoroughly hot and season to taste with salt and pepper. *Makes ¾ cup.*

NOTE: Omit the garlic if the sauce is to be served with fish.

48. AURORA SAUCE
Salsa aurora

For eggs, sweetbreads, poultry

Heat ¾ cup of Velouté Sauce [No. 17] with ¼ cup of very concentrated Tomato Sauce [No. 19] in a saucepan over medium heat until very hot. Strain through a fine sieve and beat in, bit by bit, 2 tablespoons of softened butter. *Makes 1 cup.*

If the sauce is to be served with fish, use Velouté Sauce for Fish [No. 17a] or White Wine Sauce [No. 76] in place of plain Velouté sauce.

49. SAUCE BERCY
Salsa Bercy

For fish

3 tablespoons butter
1 tablespoon finely chopped onion
⅓ cup dry white wine
⅓ cup Fish Essence [No. 11]
⅔ cup Velouté Sauce for Fish [No. 17a]
1 tablespoon finely chopped parsley

Cook the onion in a teaspoon of the butter in a saucepan over moderate heat until it is transparent, but not brown. Add the wine and fish essence and boil rapidly for half a minute. Add the Velouté sauce, simmer for 3 minutes; remove from the flame, and add the rest of the butter, beaten in bit by bit, and the parsley. *Makes 1⅓ cups.*

NOTE: This sauce may also be made with red wine to accompany a robustly flavored fish.

50. SAUCE BRETONNE
Salsa bretonne

For fish

3 cups Velouté Sauce for Fish [No. 17a]
3 tablespoons butter
2 tablespoons finely chopped leek
2 tablespoons finely chopped celery
2 tablespoons finely chopped white onion
4 tablespoons sliced mushrooms
3 tablespoons heavy cream

Reduce the Velouté sauce slightly by cooking in a saucepan over moderate heat for about 15 minutes. Melt half of the butter in another saucepan over moderate heat; add the leek, celery, onion, and mushrooms; and cook for about 5 minutes, or until the vegetables are soft. Add the Velouté sauce, bring slowly to a boil, and simmer for 5 minutes longer. Remove from the heat, add the cream, and swirl in the remaining butter, bit by bit. *Makes 3 generous cups.*

NOTE: To accompany sweetbreads or poultry, the same sauce may be made with Velouté Sauce for Chicken [No. 17b].

51. IVORY SAUCE
Salsa avorio

For boiled chicken

⅔ cup Velouté Sauce [No. 17]
⅓ cup heavy cream
1 teaspoon Meat or Chicken Essence [No. 10 or 12]
1 tablespoon butter

Bring the Velouté sauce to a boil in a saucepan over medium heat and add the cream, a spoonful at a time. Cook until only ⅔ cup remains. Remove from the fire, blend in the essence, and beat in the butter, bit by bit. *Makes ⅔ cup.*

52. SAUCE NORMANDE
Salsa normanda

For fish

⅔ cup Velouté Sauce for Fish [No. 17a]
⅓ cup Fish Essence [No. 11]
⅓ cup mushroom juice (made by cooking ¼ cup finely grated mushrooms in ¼ cup water for 15 minutes then pressing through a fine sieve)
5 tablespoons heavy cream
2 egg yolks
2 tablespoons butter

Mix the Velouté sauce, fish essence, and mushroom juice in a heavy saucepan. Bring to boil over medium heat and cook until ⅓ has evaporated. Off the fire blend in the egg yolks which have been mixed with half the cream. Return to the stove and cook very slowly until thickened, stirring constantly. Do not boil. Remove from the fire, beat in the butter, bit by bit, and add the rest of cream. *Makes 1 cup.*

Alternate method
Cook 4 tablespoons of chopped mushrooms in ⅓ cup of water and ⅓ cup of fish essence in a saucepan over medium heat until the liquid is reduced by ½. Add ⅔ cup of Velouté sauce and ⅓ cup of heavy cream. Bring slowly to a boil and continue cooking until the liquid is again reduced by ½. Remove from the fire, stir in ⅓ cup of heavy cream, and beat in 1½ tablespoons of butter, bit by bit.

53. PAPRIKA SAUCE
Salsa ungherese o alla paprika

½ cup butter, softened
1 medium onion, minced
2 cups Velouté Sauce [No. 17]
2 tablespoons paprika

Gently sauté the onion in 2 tablespoons of the butter in a saucepan over medium heat until transparent but not brown. Add the paprika and the Velouté sauce, and simmer 15 minutes. Remove from the heat and beat in the rest of the butter, bit by bit. *Makes 2 cups.*

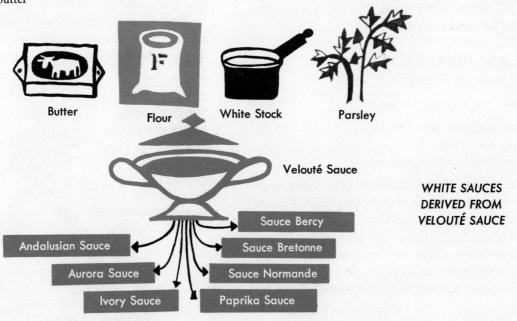

Butter   Flour   White Stock   Parsley

Velouté Sauce

Sauce Bercy
Andalusian Sauce
Sauce Bretonne
Aurora Sauce
Sauce Normande
Ivory Sauce
Paprika Sauce

WHITE SAUCES DERIVED FROM VELOUTÉ SAUCE

54. ANCHOVY SAUCE
Salsa d'acciughe

Bring 1 cup of Béchamel Sauce [No. 18] to a boil in a saucepan over medium heat. Remove from the heat and blend in 3 tablespoons of Anchovy Butter [No. 108] with a wire whisk. *Makes 1 cup.*

NOTE: White Wine Sauce [No. 76], Bastard Sauce [No. 66], or Sauce Normande [No. 52] may be substituted for the Béchamel.

55. CREAM SAUCE
Salsa alla crema

For eggs, fish, vegetables, or poultry

⅔ cup Béchamel Sauce [No. 18]
½ cup heavy cream
1½ tablespoons butter, softened

Put the Béchamel sauce and half of the cream into a heavy saucepan and heat to the boiling point. Remove from the flame and add the butter and the rest of the cream alternately, stirring well after each addition. If it is not for immediate use, float a thin film of melted butter over the top to prevent a skin from forming. This is stirred in when sauce is reheated. *Makes 1¼ cups.*

56. SAUCE MORNAY
Salsa Mornay

For au gratin dishes : eggs, vegetables, or fish

⅔ cup Béchamel Sauce [No. 18]
⅓ cup heavy cream
3 tablespoons grated Parmesan cheese
1½ tablespoons butter

Put the Béchamel sauce and the cream in a heavy saucepan, bring to a boil over medium heat, and reduce to ⅔ its quantity. Add the cheese and stir until the cheese is melted and well blended with the sauce. Remove from the heat and beat in the butter, bit by bit. *Makes ⅔ cup.*

NOTE: For a slightly stronger flavor, substitute Chicken Stock [No. 3] for the cream. For fish dishes, add 2 tablespoons Fish Essence [No. 11] while the sauce is reducing.

57. SAUCE NANTUA
Salsa Nantua

For eggs, fish, and seafood

⅔ cup Béchamel Sauce [No. 18]
⅔ cup Fish Fumet [No. 2]
⅔ cup heavy cream
½ cup shrimp butter [*see* Note]
1 teaspoon brandy
Small pinch Cayenne pepper

Put the first 3 ingredients into a heavy saucepan; bring to rolling boil and reduce by ½. Remove from heat and beat in the shrimp butter, a little at a time; add the brandy and season with the Cayenne. *Makes 1½ cups.*

NOTE: To make shrimp butter take ½ cup shelled and de-veined shrimp and cook them in ¼ cup butter over a medium flame for 5 minutes. Add a grating of

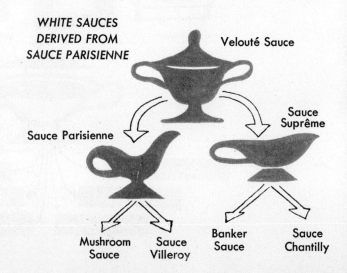

freshly ground white pepper and a dash of salt to taste and cook over high heat for 2 more minutes. Pour shrimp and butter into container of electric blender or put through a food mill (using fine cutter). *Makes ½ cup.*

58. MUSHROOM SAUCE NO. 2
Salsa ai funghi

For poultry

1 cup mushroom juice [*see* No. 52]
3 cups Sauce Parisienne [No. 21]
¼ pound button mushroom caps, cooked for 7 minutes in 2 tablespoons butter

Reduce the mushroom juice in a saucepan over a brisk flame until only ⅓ cup is left. Add the Parisienne sauce and simmer again for 5 minutes. Add the mushroom caps just before serving. *Makes 3⅓ cups.*

NOTE: If this sauce is to be used for fish, use Velouté Sauce for Fish [No. 17a] instead of Parisienne sauce.

59. SAUCE VILLEROY
Salsa Villeroy

For coating Spiedini, fried foods, etc.

To 2 cups of Sauce Parisienne [No. 21] add 2 tablespoons bottled truffle essence. Reduce this over brisk flame, stirring constantly, until slightly thickened. *Makes 2 scant cups.*

NOTE: If bottled truffle essence is unavailable, put the contents of a 1-ounce can of black or white truffles (the white have a more pronounced flavor and perfume), with their juice, in electric blender and blend for 10 seconds on high speed, or put through a food mill. The resulting purée will serve just as well as the bottled essence [*see also* No. 1819a].

WHITE SAUCES DERIVED
FROM SAUCE SUPRÊME
Salse bianche di derivazione
dalla salsa suprema

60. BANKER SAUCE
Salsa banchiera

For eggs, croquettes, poultry, variety meats
Mix ⅔ cup Sauce Suprême [No. 22] with 2 tablespoons

Madeira wine. Heat only until thoroughly hot and add 2 tablespoons finely chopped truffles or Mock Truffles [No. 1819a]. *Makes ⅔ cup.*

61. SAUCE CHANTILLY
Salsa chantilly

For poultry, vegetables

Just before serving, mix ⅔ cup of very thick, hot Sauce Suprême [No. 22] with the same amount of unsweetened whipped cream. *Makes 1½ cups.*

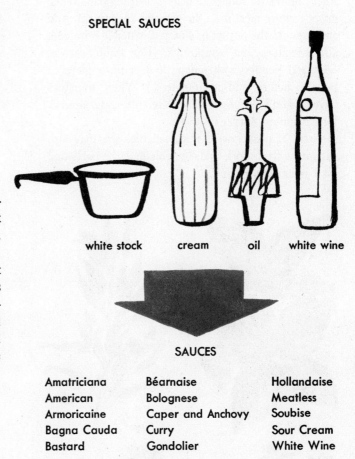

SPECIAL SAUCES

white stock   cream   oil   white wine

SAUCES

Amatriciana	Béarnaise	Hollandaise
American	Bolognese	Meatless
Armoricaine	Caper and Anchovy	Soubise
Bagna Cauda	Curry	Sour Cream
Bastard	Gondolier	White Wine

SPECIAL SAUCES
Salse per elezione

We are placing in this special category a diverse group of sauces which are not chiefly based on any of the basic stocks or the primary sauces.

62. SAUCE AMATRICIANA
Salsa amatriciana

For noodles, spaghetti, etc.

½ pound lean pork jowl
2 tablespoons oil
1 small onion, chopped
4 tomatoes, peeled, seeded, drained, and chopped
    (or 1 large can Italian-style plum tomatoes, drained)
Small piece hot red pepper (or pinch Cayenne pepper)
Salt and pepper to taste
¼ teaspoon sugar

Cut pork jowl into ½-inch cubes and cook in the oil for ½ hour over moderate heat in a frying pan. When crisp, remove meat from the pan and keep warm. Add the onion to the hot fat in pan and, when it is golden, add tomatoes and seasonings. (For milder sauce, cook red pepper with onions and remove piece of pepper before adding tomatoes.) When tomatoes have cooked 8 minutes, add browned meat, and simmer for 3 minutes. *Makes 1½ cups.*

NOTE: If pork jowl is not available, one may also substitute fresh pork rind, but this must be parboiled for 1 hour before using.

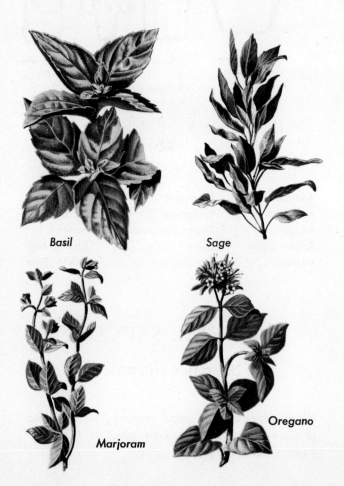

Basil

Sage

Marjoram

Oregano

63. AMERICAN SAUCE
Salsa all'americana

No research has yet shown that this is a sauce of American origin. The name is believed to come from Armoricaine [see No. 64], Armorica being the ancient name for Brittany. The sauces are similar and are the classic accompaniment for lobster in that French coastal province, where they are served over the lobster, shell and all. This sauce is a welcome change when used for seafood in patty shells, or for sole and similar bland fish. It is wasted on highly flavored fish, such as mackerel, and too highly seasoned for any delicate fish that is relished for its own flavor.

⅓ cup oil
¼ cup butter
½ pound (more or less) shrimp, crayfish, or lobster
    tails, with shells (shrimp or crayfish should be
    halved; lobster tails cut in 1-inch chunks)
½ teaspoon salt
⅛ teaspoon pepper
¼ cup brandy
1 tablespoon finely chopped onion
⅔ cup dry white wine
3 large tomatoes, peeled, seeded, drained, and chopped
Pinch Cayenne pepper
3 tablespoons heavy cream
1 tablespoon chopped tarragon leaves

Put oil and 1 tablespoon of the butter in a saucepan and heat over a brisk flame until bubbling. Add shellfish, season with the salt and pepper, and stir for 4 minutes. Spoon off as much of the fat as possible, add brandy, and heat a few seconds until the brandy is quite hot. Ignite by tipping the pan, so that gas flame reaches brandy, or light with a match. Shake the pan until the flames die out. Add onion, wine, tomatoes, and Cayenne. Cook over medium flame about 20 minutes until only 1 cup of sauce remains (estimating amount after shellfish is removed). Remove from the heat. Remove the shellfish pieces and reserve them for another use. Stir in remainder of butter, a little at a time; then add the cream and tarragon (if fresh tarragon is not available, substitute ½ teaspoon of dried tarragon, but add it to the sauce earlier, with the wine). Correct the seasoning and keep warm in the top part of a double boiler over warm water until used. *Makes 1 cup.*

NOTE: If you wish, the shellfish may be shelled, finely chopped, and added to the sauce. Also, some of the butter and oil may be put back in to make a more unctuous sauce.

64. SAUCE ARMORICAINE
Salsa all'armoricaine

For shellfish, fish, and seafood

Prepare an American Sauce [No. 63] but at the end, after removing shellfish pieces, blend in off heat ½ teaspoon mild curry powder and 2 egg yolks mixed with 4 tablespoons heavy cream. Cook over low heat, stirring constantly, until thickened. Do not boil. Remove from stove and stir in the remaining butter. *Makes 1⅓ cups.*

65. BAGNA CAUDA
Bagna cauda

This is a famous specialty of the Piedmont region, a hot dip for hearts and stalks of celery, raw cardoons (a relative of the artichoke), etc. One of the ingredients is a large quantity of chopped white truffles, which are not easy to obtain in America. Half a pound of chopped mushrooms, mixed with bottled truffle essence, anchovy paste, and garlic juice, or No. 1819a may be substituted. The dip is a traditional delicacy for Christmas Eve.

    5 tablespoons butter
    5 tablespoons oil
    3 cloves garlic, crushed in the garlic-press
    4 anchovy fillets, washed free of salt [*see* No. 220] and mashed
    1 cup chopped white truffles [or No. 1819a]

Put butter and oil into a heavy saucepan with garlic and anchovies. Cook gently over medium heat until garlic begins to turn yellow. Add the truffles. Heat through and serve very hot in a chafing dish. *Makes 1½ cups.*

66. BASTARD SAUCE
Salsa al burro o salsa bastarda

For boiled fish or asparagus.
This is essentially a Béchamel sauce with some additions that make it resemble Hollandaise. Because of its mixed attributes it has been given its unusual name.

    ½ cup butter, softened
    1 tablespoon flour
    1 cup milk
    2 egg yolks beaten with 1 tablespoon cold milk
    1 teaspoon lemon juice

Melt 2 tablespoons of the butter in a saucepan over medium heat and add flour, mixing well. Add milk gradually and heat until the mixture thickens, stirring to keep flour from becoming lumpy. Simmer 5 minutes and beat in the egg yolks and milk. Continue stirring briskly. The moment the sauce shows signs of thickening, remove from fire and stir in the rest of the butter, bit by bit. Add lemon juice last. Do not boil again. *Makes 1½ cups.*

67. SAUCE BÉARNAISE
Salsa béarnaise

For fish and broiled meats

    5 tablespoons dry white wine
    5 tablespoons tarragon wine vinegar
    1 tablespoon finely chopped onion or chives (or 1 teaspoon chopped shallots)
    4 sprigs fresh tarragon (or 1 teaspoon dried)
    2 crushed peppercorns
    3 egg yolks
    ¾ cup butter
    1 tablespoon chopped chervil
    1 tablespoon chopped fresh tarragon (or substitute parsley)
    ½ teaspoon salt

Put wine, vinegar, onion, sprigs of tarragon, and pepper into a small saucepan and boil briskly until only 2 or 3 tablespoons of liquid remain. Remove from stove, and let stand for 5 minutes so herbs can infuse liquid. Strain through a fine sieve into the top section of a double boiler, pressing well with a spoon to get all the juice out of the herbs. Add egg yolks, beaten with 1 tablespoon water. Place over barely simmering water. The water should not come up to the bottom of top pot or the sauce may curdle. Add the butter, a tablespoon at a time, beating continually with a wire whisk or rotary hand beater and scraping the sides of the pot from time to time with rubber spatula. When the sauce has reached the consistency of fluffy custard, remove the top pan quickly from the heat and add the salt, fresh chervil, and tarragon. The sauce is usually served lukewarm. Do not overcook or eggs will curdle and separate from butter. *Makes ¾ cup.*

NOTE: This sauce may also be made in the electric blender. Strain the herb vinegar infusion into blender container. Add the egg yolks (having previously warmed the unbroken eggs by running hot water over them for 2 minutes, then separating them). Melt the butter until it bubbles, pour over the egg vinegar mixture in a steady stream, running the blender at high speed. Pour into serving bowl and mix in the chopped herbs. Do *not* add the herbs while the sauce is in blender, or they will be mashed and give the sauce a greenish look.

68. BOLOGNESE SAUCE
Salsa bolognese

For noodles and spaghetti

3 tablespoons oil
¼ pound chopped smoked ham (preferably prosciutto)
    or smoked pork jowl
1 onion, chopped
1 stalk celery, finely chopped
1 small carrot, finely chopped
1 small clove garlic, finely chopped, or crushed in the
    garlic-press
½ pound lean beef, coarsely ground
1 ounce dried imported mushrooms, softened in warm
    water for 30 minutes, and chopped (or substitute
    ⅛ pound fresh mushrooms)
⅓ cup dry red (or dry Marsala) wine
1 teaspoon chopped parsley
1 teaspoon chopped marjoram (or ¼ teaspoon dried)
Pinch nutmeg
1 teaspoon salt
⅛ teaspoon pepper
1 teaspoon sugar
Optional: 2 teaspoons flour mashed with 2 teaspoons
    of butter
½ pound tomatoes, peeled, seeded, drained, and
    chopped (or 1½ cups canned Italian-style plum
    tomatoes, drained)

Fry the ham lightly in 2 tablespoons of the oil in a heavy pot. When it begins to get golden in color, add onion, celery, carrot, and garlic; continue cooking gently for 10 to 15 minutes, or until the vegetables are soft. Meanwhile, in a frying pan, brown the chopped meat in 1 tablespoon oil, separating it into bits with a wooden spoon. When well seared, add mushrooms and cook for 5 minutes. Add wine, and cook 5 minutes more, scraping the bottom of the pan. Add parsley, marjoram, nutmeg, salt, pepper, and sugar; and cook until wine has completely evaporated. Remove briefly from the flame and mix in the optional butter and flour, the tomatoes, the previously sautéed ham, and vegetables. Bring all to a boil once more, then simmer uncovered for 1 to 1½ hours, adding a little water, if necessary, and stirring from time to time. If the optional flour was not used, cook slightly longer until the sauce is of the desired consistency. *Makes 2½ cups.*

69. CAPER AND ANCHOVY SAUCE
Salsa con capperi e acciughe ·

For broiled steaks

2 tablespoons drained capers
6 anchovy fillets, washed free of salt [*see* No. 220]
½ cup butter

Chop capers and the anchovy fillets together until very fine. Melt butter in a saucepan over medium heat until bubbling and add the chopped mixture. *Makes ½ cup.*

70. CURRY SAUCE
Salsa al curry o salsa all'indiana

For lamb, mutton, poultry, eggs

1 tablespoon butter
½ cup finely chopped onion
1 tablespoon chopped parsley
1 stalk celery, finely chopped
Pinch dried thyme
Pinch nutmeg
Pinch mace
½ bay leaf
1 tablespoon flour
1 tablespoon curry powder (or more, to taste)
1½ cups White Stock [No. 1] or any good broth
⅓ cup heavy cream
¼ teaspoon lemon juice
Salt and freshly ground pepper

Cook the onion in the butter in a saucepan over medium heat until it turns golden; add parsley, celery, thyme, nutmeg, mace, and bay leaf. Sprinkle with flour and curry powder and mix well, cooking until mixture is well colored with the curry. Slowly add the stock or broth and stir until it comes to boil. Reduce heat and simmer 40 minutes. Strain, carefully pressing out juices. Reheat in the saucepan and add the cream. Remove from fire, correct the seasoning, and add lemon juice. *Makes 1⅓ cups.*

71. GONDOLIER SAUCE
Salsa canottiera

For fish

Reduce to ⅔ its quantity a Court Bouillon [Nos. 763 or 765] in which a fish has been cooked. Thicken with Kneaded Butter [No. 107] using 1½ tablespoons for each cup of reduced liquid. Cook again for 10 minutes over moderate heat, remove from the fire, and beat in, a little at a time, 2 tablespoons of butter for each cup of sauce. Strain if necessary. Taste for seasoning and add a pinch of Cayenne pepper and dash of lemon juice.

72. SAUCE HOLLANDAISE
Salsa olandese

For fish and certain vegetables

2 tablespoons lemon juice
5 egg yolks
1 cup butter, softened
Salt and freshly ground white pepper

Put lemon juice (or vinegar) in the top pan of a double boiler. Add egg yolks and 1 tablespoon of the butter. Put the pan over simmering water but do not allow the water to touch the bottom of the top pan. Beat mixture with wire whisk, or with an electric hand beater at low speed, until the butter melts. Immediately begin adding the rest of the butter, a small piece at a time, speeding up beating. Each piece of butter must be absorbed before adding the next. When all the butter has been incorporated, and the sauce is the consistency of fluffy custard, remove immediately from over water and beat for 30 seconds. Add salt and pepper to taste, and more lemon juice, if it is too bland. To keep warm for any length of time, add cold water to bottom of double boiler so that it no longer steams and replace the top pot and cover. *Makes 1¾ cups.* (*See* Blender Recipes, f, for another version.)

73. MEATLESS SAUCE
Sugo finto

For noodles, spaghetti, croquettes, rice dishes, tripe

1 tablespoon oil
¼ cup ham fat, diced (or ¼ cup butter)
1 onion, sliced
1 small carrot, sliced
1 celery stalk, with leaves, sliced
1 tablespoon chopped parsley and marjoram (or ¼ teaspoon each, dried)
1 clove garlic, bruised
1 whole clove
1 ounce imported dried mushrooms, soaked for 30 minutes in warm water and chopped (or ⅛ pound fresh mushrooms, chopped)

½ cup dry white wine
2 pounds tomatoes, peeled, seeded, drained, and chopped (or 1 No. 2½ can Italian-style plum tomatoes, drained)
½ teaspoon sugar
1 teaspoon salt
¼ teaspoon freshly ground pepper

Heat oil and ham fat together over medium heat in a heavy saucepan. When ham fat is transparent, add onion, carrot, celery, parsley, marjoram, garlic, clove, mushrooms, and sugar. Simmer, stirring from time to time, for 10 minutes or until vegetables begin to color. Add wine and cook until almost all of it has boiled away. Add tomatoes and season with the salt and pepper. Cover and simmer gently for 1 hour, adding a little water from time to time, if necessary. It will only be necessary if fresh small Italian plum tomatoes, which are rather dry, are used. Purée through a food mill before serving. If too thin, cook uncovered until sauce has reduced further. *Makes 2 cups.*

74. SAUCE SOUBISE or ONION PURÉE SAUCE
Salsa soubise o purea di cipolle

For fish and meats

1 pound onions, finely chopped
4 slices salt pork, parboiled for 20 minutes
½ cup uncooked rice
1½ cups White Stock [No. 1] or Chicken Stock [No. 3]
Pinch sugar
3 tablespoons butter
⅓ cup heavy cream
Salt and freshly ground pepper

Parboil the chopped onions 5 minutes in lightly salted water to cover. Meanwhile, line top pot of a double boiler with salt pork slices. Drain onions and put them and the rice on top of salt pork. Add stock and sugar. Set the pot over the bottom pan of the double boiler containing enough boiling water to come well up the sides. Cover, and cook over a low flame for 1½ to 2 hours, depending on variety of rice used. (For this purpose soft, starchy short-grain rice is best.) Discard the strips of pork and force the mixture through a fine sieve or food mill, or put in blender at low speed for 10 seconds. Return to the fire, bring to a boil, and add butter and cream. Taste, and adjust seasoning. Can be kept, covered, in refrigerator, until needed. *Makes about 1½ cups.*

74a. Second Method

The same quantity of chopped onions is used in this version as in the above recipe, but instead of the rice and broth, the sauce is made with Béchamel Sauce [No. 18].

1 pound onions, finely chopped
7 tablespoons butter
$\frac{1}{2}$ teaspoon salt
$\frac{1}{8}$ teaspoon freshly ground pepper
Pinch sugar
$1\frac{1}{2}$ cups thick Béchamel Sauce [No. 18]
3 tablespoons cream

Begin by parboiling onions [*see* No. 74]; melt 5 tablespoons of the butter in a heavy saucepan; add the onions, salt and pepper, and pinch of sugar; cook slowly, covered, for 10 minutes. Add the Béchamel sauce and continue cooking, covered, over low heat for another half hour. Pass through a fine sieve, pressing through well (or put into blender for 10 seconds at low speed), and add remaining butter and the cream. *Makes about $1\frac{1}{2}$ cups.*

75. SOUR CREAM SAUCE
Salsa smitana

For stewed or pan-broiled game

2 tablespoons butter
2 medium onions, finely chopped
$\frac{3}{4}$ cup dry white wine
2 tablespoons flour
2 cups sour cream at room temperature
$\frac{1}{2}$ teaspoon salt

Melt the butter in a saucepan over medium heat and add onions, letting them cook gently until they are soft but have not begun to brown. Add the wine and let it cook almost completely away over brisk fire (watch carefully so that the onions do not burn). Immediately blend in flour; gradually add sour cream and simmer 5 minutes. Pass through a fine sieve (or put in blender at low speed for 10 seconds). Reheat, and add salt. *Makes 2 cups.*

76. WHITE WINE SAUCE
Salsa al vino bianco

For fish.

There are two methods of making this sauce, and two steps in each method. In both cases they make use of fish trimmings (from the fish to be sauced) made into a broth.

Skin, bones, and other trimmings from fish
1 cup dry white wine
1 tablespoon finely chopped onion
1 teaspoon minced parsley
3 peppercorns

Make a broth from the above ingredients, and cook it down until $\frac{2}{3}$ of the liquid remains. Strain through a fine sieve.

$\frac{2}{3}$ cup fish broth (*see* above)
1 cup Fish Fumet [No. 2], reduced to $\frac{1}{4}$ cup
$1\frac{1}{2}$ tablespoons Kneaded Butter [No. 107]
6 tablespoons butter, at room temperature
Freshly ground white pepper
1 teaspoon lemon juice

Put the fish broth into a saucepan over medium flame. Add kneaded butter, bit by bit, stirring until smooth. Bring to a boil and remove from heat. Add butter, little by little, stirring constantly. Then add a grating of white pepper, lemon juice, and the concentrated fish Fumet. Serve at once. *Makes about $1\frac{1}{2}$ cups.*

76a. Second Method

$\frac{2}{3}$ cup fish broth (*see* above)
1 cup Fish Fumet [No. 2] reduced to $\frac{1}{4}$ cup
3 tablespoons mushroom stems and peelings
1 tablespoon Kneaded Butter [No. 107]
$\frac{1}{3}$ cup light cream
2 egg yolks, beaten
1 tablespoon whipped cream
6 tablespoons butter, at room temperature
Juice of $\frac{1}{4}$ lemon
Pinch paprika

Cook the mushroom scraps in the fish broth over a brisk flame until the liquid is reduced by $\frac{1}{2}$. Add the Fumet and thicken with the kneaded butter, added bit by bit. Simmer for 2 minutes, add the light cream, and cook down to reduce sauce slightly. Strain into another saucepan and add the beaten egg yolks in which the whipped cream has been folded. Reheat over a moderate flame, stirring constantly until the sauce begins to thicken. Remove from fire and complete the sauce with the butter, added bit by bit, the lemon juice, and a pinch of paprika. *Makes about $1\frac{1}{2}$ cups.*

Pike

COLD SAUCES
Salse fredde

Included in this section are all the sauces that are served cold. Many of them are derivations of mayonnaise, which we therefore put at the head of the section.

77. MAYONNAISE
Salsa maionese

Commercial mayonnaise almost always contains too much sugar, going well with vegetable salads, but rather poorly with meat or fish. A homemade version can be varied to suit the dish that it is to accompany. For meat and fish, part mild olive oil, part vegetable oil makes a tasty mayonnaise; however, if for vegetable salads, one of the blander salad or cooking oils may be preferred. Lemon juice makes a lighter colored sauce than vinegar, but the taste is tarter.

3 egg yolks
$\frac{1}{2}$ teaspoon salt
Pinch white pepper
2 cups oil
1 tablespoon vinegar or lemon juice

It is important to have all ingredients at room temperature. But if "room temperature" means 100° in summer, first put ingredients in refrigerator for $\frac{1}{2}$ hour. Warm ingredients make it difficult to tell whether the mayonnaise is thickening as it should; if too cold, eggs and oil will not form an emulsion.

Lightly break egg yolks with a fork in a bowl, add salt, pepper, and a few drops of vinegar. Begin to beat, either with wire whisk or electric mixer at medium speed. Pour in the oil *very* slowly, by droplets, beating constantly. Stop adding oil whenever traces float to top; do not add more until previously added oil has been absorbed. After the first few spoons of oil have been incorporated, the mayonnaise will suddenly become quite thick. From then on add oil more freely, as it is no longer so likely to separate from the eggs. Continue beating and adding oil, alternating it with the rest of vinegar or lemon juice, until all has been

used up. If weather is hot and mayonnaise seems thin, it will stiffen in refrigerator.

In the event that the mayonnaise separates, in spite of care taken, it is simple to rescue. Begin again with 1 egg yolk and instead of plain oil, add the "spoiled" mayonnaise to it very slowly, beating constantly. (*See* Blender Recipes, c, for another version.)

78. MAYONNAISE CHANTILLY
Maionese Chantilly

For cold asparagus, salads, etc.

1 cup Mayonnaise [No. 77], made with vegetable oil
1 cup heavy cream
Pinch salt

Whip cream with a pinch of salt until stiff and fold it into the mayonnaise. *Makes $2\frac{1}{2}$ cups.*

79. ESCOFFIER MAYONNAISE
Maionese Escoffier

1 cup Mayonnaise [No. 77]
$\frac{1}{4}$ cup finely chopped radishes
1 teaspoon finely chopped chervil
1 tablespoon finely chopped parsley

Mix all ingredients together. *Makes $1\frac{1}{4}$ cups.*

80. GARLIC MAYONNAISE
Salsa all'aglio

For cold fish, salads, etc.

To 1 cup Mayonnaise [No. 77] add 1 clove garlic, crushed in the garlic-press. More garlic may be added if desired, but it should be used sparingly, to give a lift to the sauce but not to overpower it. It is a simple matter to add more to taste, but not to subtract it once it has been added. *Makes 1 cup.*

81. MAYONNAISE INDIENNE
Salsa indiana

For cold meats

1 cup Mayonnaise [No. 77]
1 teaspoon curry powder
1 teaspoon grated raw onion

Mix all ingredients together. More curry powder may be added to taste. *Makes 1 cup.*

41

82. ANDALUSIAN SAUCE
Salsa andalusa

For cold boiled beef or fish

1 cup Mayonnaise [No. 77]
¼ cup Tomato Sauce [No. 19] or 2 tablespoons canned
    tomato purée
1 small green pepper, roasted, scraped, seeded, and cut
    into fine strips [*see* No. 145]

Mix the tomato sauce thoroughly with the mayonnaise and pepper strips. Canned pimento may be substituted for the pepper. *Makes 1½ cups.*

83. ANCHOVY SAUCE
Salsa di acciughe

For salads and canapés

2 hard-boiled egg yolks
6 anchovy fillets, washed free of salt [*see* No. 220]
½ cup oil
1 teaspoon wine vinegar
Pinch pepper

Pound egg yolks with anchovies in a mortar until they become a smooth paste. Stirring steadily, add, little by little, oil, vinegar, and pepper. *Makes ⅔ cup.*

84. CASALINGA SAUCE
Salsa casalinga

For boiled fish.
This is a sauce that can be prepared either in the electric blender or by hand chopping. In Italy the latter is often done with a "half moon"—a rocker chopper or curved blade with handle on each end, used with a wooden board. This method has the effect of bruising the aromatic herbs, releasing the aroma, instead of liquefying them or turning them into mush, as a blender is likely to do.

½ small bunch parsley
3 sprigs fresh chervil
3 sprigs fresh tarragon leaves
2 tablespoons celery leaves
1 small onion
2 anchovy fillets
4 slices dill pickle
1½ teaspoons capers
½ teaspoon grated orange peel
½ teaspoon grated lemon peel
1 cup oil (or more, as desired)
1 teaspoon lemon juice

Chop all ingredients except oil and lemon juice together until very fine. Or blend in electric blender. Gradually stir in enough oil in a thin trickle to get consistency of thin mayonnaise and add the lemon juice. *Makes 1½ cups.*

85. SAUCE CITRONNETTE
Salsa citronnette

For salads

Mix ⅔ cup oil and ⅓ cup lemon juice and season to taste with salt and a little pepper. Proportions can vary according to taste. *Makes 1 cup.*

86. FANTASIA SAUCE
Salsa fantasia

For cold fish

½ cup olive oil
2 hard-boiled egg yolks
1 tablespoon prepared mustard (Dijon-type preferred)
1 tablespoon lemon juice
1 tablespoon fresh basil
1 scallion, with the green ends
2 hard-boiled egg whites
1 teaspoon Worcestershire sauce

Mash the egg yolks to a paste with the mustard. Slowly add the oil in a fine, steady stream, then add the lemon juice. Chop the basil and the scallion together and add to sauce. Cut the hard-boiled egg whites into thin slivers, add to the sauce, and finally add the Worcestershire sauce. *Makes about ¾ cup.*

87. GENOESE SAUCE
Salsa genovese

For cold fish

2 tablespoons shelled, skinned pistachio nuts
1 tablespoon pine nuts
1 tablespoon Béchamel Sauce [No. 18]
3 egg yolks
2 cups oil
Juice of 1 small lemon
½ teaspoon salt
⅛ teaspoon pepper
⅓ cup mixed fresh herb purée

Pound nuts, moistened with Béchamel sauce, in a mortar to make a smooth paste. Press through a fine sieve into a bowl. Add egg yolks, beat well, and add oil alternately with lemon juice in the same manner as for Mayonnaise [No. 77]. Season with salt and pepper.

Finish by adding the herb purée, made by parboiling a mixture of fresh herbs (tarragon, basil, parsley, chervil), which may include spinach, for 2 minutes; pressing dry in a cloth; and then forcing through a sieve or putting in blender until puréed. *Makes about 2½ cups.*

NOTE: This sauce may be made in the blender. Put egg yolks, pine nuts, pistachio nuts (omit Béchamel) in blender container. Mix at high speed for 10 seconds. Add the parboiled herbs, unchopped, and mix for 2 seconds, then pour in the oil in a thin, steady stream, then add lemon, salt, and pepper. Turn off blender as soon as all ingredients have been blended.

88. GREEN SAUCE
Salsa verde

This is an herb vinaigrette sauce that is used everywhere in Italy. It can be served with cold or hot (usually boiled) meats.

1 cup parsley, without stems
3 anchovy fillets, washed free of salt [*see* No. 220]
1 small boiled potato, cold
1 small dill pickle
1 clove garlic
1 small onion
1 cup oil
2 tablespoons white wine vinegar
1 teaspoon salt
⅛ teaspoon pepper

Chop parsley, anchovy, potato, pickle, garlic, and onion very fine. Put in a bowl, season with the salt and pepper, and beat in oil, little by little, and the vinegar.

Many variations are possible, depending on herbs at hand. Only parsley, onion, and anchovy are always used. Capers may be substituted for the pickle and lemon juice for the vinegar; fresh basil leaves and tarragon can also be used. By omitting the oil, this makes a very low-calorie dressing for reducing diets. *Makes 1¾ cups.*

89. HORSERADISH SAUCE
Salsa al rafano

This is the Italian version of the usual dressing for boiled beef made by mixing grated horseradish with whipped or sour cream.

4 tablespoons horseradish
1 cup fresh white breadcrumbs (crusts removed)
½ cup milk
½ teaspoon salt
½ teaspoon superfine sugar
½ cup whipped cream (or sour cream)
1 teaspoon vinegar

Mix grated horseradish with breadcrumbs that have been soaked in the milk and squeezed dry. Season with salt and sugar, add the cream (whipped or sour) and, when ready to serve, complete with the vinegar. *Makes 1½ cups.*

90. MALTESE SAUCE
Salsa maltese fredda

For cold asparagus

1 cup Mayonnaise [No. 77]
Juice of ½ orange, strained
2 tablespoons orange peel (no white part)

Gradually add orange juice to the mayonnaise, stirring constantly to make a smooth, rather thin, sauce. Cut orange peel into very fine strips, parboil for 5 minutes, and drain on paper towel. Mix peel into the sauce. *Makes 1¼ cups.*

91. MINT SAUCE
Salsa di menta

For hot or cold roast lamb

4 tablespoons finely chopped mint leaves
2 tablespoons sugar
1 cup hot vinegar
Pinch each of salt and pepper
4 tablespoons water

Mix together all ingredients, pour into a bottle, and keep in a cool place until needed. *Makes 1¼ cups.*

92. ORIENTAL SAUCE
Salsa orientale

For cold antipasti

¾ cup Mayonnaise [No. 77]
¼ cup thick Tomato Sauce [No. 19] (or commercial catsup)
⅛ teaspoon powdered saffron
½ small can pimento

Mix the mayonnaise with the tomato sauce or catsup. Add powdered saffron (make sure the saffron is powdered, not shredded). Chop the pimento and fold into sauce. *Makes slightly more than 1 cup.*

Basil

93. PESTO GENOVESE
Pesto alla genovese

For pasta, soups, or boiled fish
This is one of the most famous of all the Italian pasta sauces.

1 cup fresh basil leaves, washed and thoroughly dried
4 spinach leaves, washed and dried
6 sprigs parsley
3 sprigs marjoram
½ cup pine nuts
3 cloves garlic, crushed in the garlic-press
⅓ cup grated Parmesan cheese
⅓ cup Pecorino (or Romano) cheese
3 tablespoons oil
2 tablespoons butter, softened
¼ teaspoon salt

Pound all of the ingredients in a mortar or blend very briefly in blender. *Makes 1 cup.*

NOTE: By omitting the cheeses and increasing the amount of pine nuts to ¾ cup, this is delicious over a hot boiled fish, such as cod or halibut. One may also add a spoonful to hot consommé (using the regular recipe for the sauce given above).

94. PIQUANT SAUCE
Salsa piccante

For cold hard-boiled or poached eggs

3 tablespoons pine nuts
3 egg yolks
2 anchovy fillets, washed free of salt [*see* No. 220]
2 cloves garlic
1 teaspoon capers
1 tablespoon soft breadcrumbs, soaked in vinegar and squeezed dry
12 green olives, pitted
1⅓ cups oil
2 tablespoons vinegar
Pinch salt

Put pine nuts, egg yolks, anchovy fillets, garlic, capers, bread crumbs, and olives into the blender and blend at low speed until it forms smooth paste, or pound the ingredients in a mortar. Add oil, alternating with vinegar, as in Mayonnaise [No. 77]. Season to taste. *Makes 2 cups.*

95. SAUCE PROVENÇALE
Salsa provenzale

For hard-boiled eggs, or mixed boiled meats

2 tablespoons vinegar
¼ cup oil
1 teaspoon salt
⅛ teaspoon pepper
4 tomatoes, peeled, seeded, drained, and chopped
1 hard-boiled egg, chopped
1 teaspoon capers, chopped
2 teaspoons chopped parsley
½ clove garlic, crushed in the garlic-press

Make a French dressing of the vinegar, oil, salt, and pepper. Add chopped tomato and chopped mixture of garlic, egg, capers, and parsley. *Makes 1½ cups.*

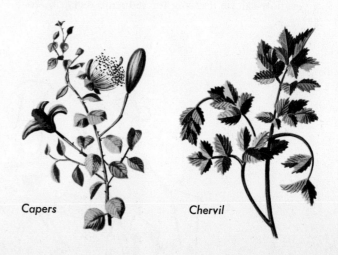

Capers   Chervil

44

96. SAUCE RAVIGOTE
Salsa ravigotta

For various cold dishes

1 cup oil
½ cup white wine vinegar
1½ tablespoons capers
2 teaspoons each parsley, chervil, scallions, and
    tarragon, chopped together
1½ tablespoons grated raw onion
½ teaspoon salt
⅛ teaspoon pepper

Mix all ingredients together very thoroughly. *Makes*
1½ cups.

Salmon

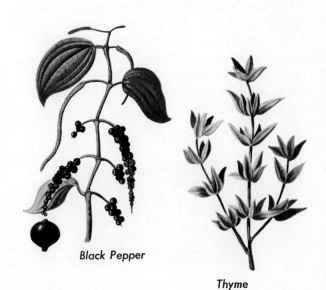

Black Pepper

Thyme

97. SAUCE REMOULADE
Salsa remolata

For cold fish, cold meat, and hard-boiled eggs

1⅓ cups Mayonnaise [No. 77]
1 teaspoon prepared mustard
½ teaspoon anchovy paste
1 teaspoon finely chopped capers
3 small sour pickles, drained and finely chopped
1 tablespoon finely chopped fresh herbs (tarragon,
    parsley, chervil, basil, etc.)

Mix all ingredients well. *Makes about 1½ cups.*

98. TARTAR SAUCE
Salsa tartara

There are many versions of Tartar sauce, but this is the
classic recipe.

4 hard-boiled egg yolks
1 tablespoon prepared mustard (Dijon-type preferred)
2 cups oil
1 tablespoon minced scallion
1 tablespoon vinegar
1 teaspoon salt
¼ teaspoon freshly ground pepper
Optional: ½ cup Mayonnaise [No. 77]

Mash the egg yolks with the mustard into smooth
paste; add oil, little by little, beating constantly as for
Mayonnaise [No. 77]. Finish with the scallion, vinegar,
salt and pepper, and the optional mayonnaise. *Makes*
2¼ cups.

99. SAUCE VINAIGRETTE
Salsa vinaigrette

For salads.
This is the traditional oil-and-vinegar "French" dressing,
and many variations may be made by adding or substitut-
ing various ingredients. Olive oil, nut oil, or vegetable
oil may be used, depending upon personal taste.

The classic proportions of a Vinaigrette are 1 part
vinegar to 3 parts oil, with salt and pepper to taste,
dissolved in the vinegar. The oil and vinegar can be
mixed together and poured over salad greens or
applied separately. In the latter case, for an aromatic
wilted salad of greens with their own flavor, first pour
vinegar and seasonings over the leaves, thus wilting
them slightly and bringing out their flavor. For a
crisp salad, put oil on first, insulating leaves from
vinegar and salt. A pre-mixed dressing has almost the
same effect.

  Grated cheese, egg yolk mixed with the vinegar,
dry or prepared mustard, herbs, or hard-boiled eggs
are some of the variations suggested.

45

HOW TO CHOOSE
THE RIGHT SAUCE FOR
THE RIGHT DISH

EGGS

Andalusian Sauce [No. 47] Aurora Sauce [No. 48]
Banker Sauce [No. 60] Béchamel Sauce [No. 18]
Cream Sauce [No. 55] Curry Sauce [No. 70] Mayonnaise [No. 77] Sauce Mornay [No. 56] Sauce Nantua
[No. 57] Paprika Sauce [No. 53] Piquant Sauce [No.
94] Sauce Provençale [No. 95] Tarragon Sauce [No.
38] Tomato Sauce [No. 19]

FISH

Anchovy Sauce [No. 83] American Sauce [No. 63]
Andalusian Sauce [No. 47] Sauce Béarnaise [No. 67]
Sauce Bercy [No. 49] Sauce Bretonne [No. 50] Sauce
Colbert [No. 40] Cream Sauce [No. 55] Geneva Sauce
[No. 23] Gondolier Sauce [No. 71] Au Gratin Sauce
[No. 24] Sauce Hollandaise [No. 72] Mayonnaise
[No. 77] Marinara Sauce with Red Wine [No. 42]
Sauce Nantua [No. 57] Paprika Sauce [No. 53] Pesto
Genovese [No. 93] Sauce Normande [No. 52] Sauce
Provençale [No. 95] Sweet and Sour Sauce [No. 37]

LAMB

Curry Sauce [No. 70] Mint Sauce [No. 91] Paprika
Sauce [No. 53] Sauce Villeroy [No. 59] Zingara Sauce
[No. 39]

BEEF AND VEAL

Banker Sauce [No. 60] Sauce Béarnaise [No. 67] Sauce
Bordelaise [No. 27] Cacciatora Sauce [No. 28] Caper
and Anchovy Sauce [No. 69] Chateaubriand Sauce
[No. 29] Sauce Colbert [No. 40] Sauce Financière
[No. 32] Green Sauce [No. 88] Horseradish Sauce
[No. 89] Marsala Sauce [No. 43] Meatless Sauce
[No. 73] Pepper Sauce [No. 25] Sauce Provençale [No.
46] Red Wine Sauce [No. 26] Tarragon Sauce [No. 38]
Tartar Sauce [No. 98] Zingara Sauce [No. 39]

POULTRY

Andalusian Sauce [No. 47] Aurora Sauce [No. 48]
Banker Sauce [No. 60] Sauce Bretonne [No. 50]
Cacciatora Sauce [No. 28] Sauce Chantilly [No. 61]
Cream Sauce [No. 55] Curry Sauce [No. 70] Diavolo
Sauce [No. 30] Sauce Financière [No. 32] Ivory Sauce
[No. 51] Mushroom Sauce [No. 33 or No. 58] Orange
Sauce [No. 44] Tarragon Sauce [No. 38]

PORK

Mustard Sauce [No. 34] Sauce Saint-Menehould
[No. 35]

GAME

Marsala Sauce [No. 43] Pepper Sauce [No. 25] Salmi
Sauce [No. 36]

VEGETABLES

Bagna Cauda [No. 65] Bastard Sauce [No. 66] Sauce
Chantilly [No. 61] Sauce Citronnette [No. 85] Cream
Sauce [No. 55] Maltese Sauce [No. 90] Sauce Hollandaise [No. 72] Sauce Mornay [No. 56] Vinaigrette
Sauce [No. 99]

BUTTER: HOT, COLD, AND COMPOUNDED

Burri: freddi, caldi, semplici, composti

In addition to simple hot butter sauces, the classic culinary repertoire includes a number of cold butters compounded, or creamed, with a variety of flavoring ingredients. These compound butters are used for canapés, as flavoring agents in sauces, or for decorating cold meats, vegetables, or fish. Formerly only restaurants or houses with large staffs would bother with compound butters, as pounding them in a mortar was a laborious and time-consuming process. Now, however, the electric blender has simplified the process to a few seconds' labor. Some of these compound butters, such as Garlic Butter or Anchovy Butter, may be easily made, even without the blender. The freshest sweet butter is preferable in all of these preparations.

HOT BUTTERS

Burri caldi

100. BLACK BUTTER

Burro nero

For eggs, fish, boiled beans and peas, and brains

½ cup butter
1 tablespoon white wine vinegar
1 tablespoon coarsely chopped parsley
1 tablespoon capers

Cook the butter in a heavy saucepan over medium heat to a dark brown color and pour into a bowl. Add the vinegar to the hot pan and let it fizz. Add this to the butter, mix in the capers and parsley, and stir well. *Makes ½ cup.*

101. CAPER BUTTER

Burro di cappero

For fish or vegetables

¾ cup butter
¼ cup capers
Juice of ½ lemon
Salt and freshly ground pepper

Melt the butter over low heat, skim off the foam, add the capers and lemon juice, and season lightly with salt and generously with pepper. *Makes ¾ cup.*

102. CLARIFIED BUTTER

Burro chiarificato o epurato

Clarified butter is butter reduced to pure fat, purified of all milky particles and sediment. It is frequently used for sautéing foods, since the pure fat will not burn as quickly as butter that contains milk solids. It is also used in many delicate cakes and pastries and for greasing cake pans where the milk content of ordinary butter might make dough or batter stick.

Melt any given quantity of sweet butter in a heavy saucepan over very low heat (or in a low—200°—oven) until white foam rises to the top. Skim off the foam and continue cooking until no more foam rises and all particles in the butter sink to the bottom of the pan. Be very careful not to allow the butter to color too much, especially when using for cakes or pastries, as it will acquire a nutty flavor. Pour off the clear, purified butter from the top into a container or remove it with a bulb-baster. The residue may be used as a final enrichment for sauces and soups. Both may be stored for as long as a week in the refrigerator or kept frozen for several weeks.

Clarified butter may be used as is, or with the addition of lemon juice, salt, and pepper, as a simple sauce for a wide variety of vegetables.

103. HAZELNUT BUTTER

Burro nocciola

For vegetables, meats, and rice dishes

Melt any given quantity of butter in a heavy saucepan over medium heat until it is dark gold. Remove immediately from the fire and pour from the saucepan. The cooking process may be brought to an instant halt by the addition of a few drops of cold water.

104. MELTED BUTTER
Burro fuso

For fish, vegetables, and other uses

Melt any given quantity of butter in a double boiler. Season with salt, pepper, and dash of lemon juice.

105. MEUNIÈRE BUTTER
Burro meunière

For sautéed fish

Meunière butter is Hazelnut Butter [No. 103] to which a dash of lemon juice is added at the last minute.

Perch

106. MILLER'S WIFE BUTTER
Burro alla mugnaia

For sautéed fish

Melt any given quantity of butter in a heavy saucepan over medium heat until brown. Immediately add a dash of lemon juice, chopped parsley, and salt and pepper.

107. KNEADED BUTTER
Burro maneggiato

Kneaded butter is not a sauce or a butter spread, but a simple mixture of flour and butter used as a thickening agent for sauces or, occasionally, soups. It is, in effect, an uncooked roux [see Nos. 13, 14, and 15]. Sauces may be thickened with flour mixed with water, but it is nearly impossible to avoid small lumps forming by this method, and this necessitates straining the sauce. Flour mixed with butter, on the other hand, will blend evenly into a hot sauce as the butter melts. Constant stirring is necessary until it is well blended into the sauce, and the sauce should then be simmered for a minimum of 5 minutes to eliminate any floury taste.

Cream slightly softened butter with an equal amount of flour, or, to facilitate its even blending into a sauce, use slightly more butter. Use 1 tablespoon of flour to 1 cup of liquid for a thin sauce, 1 1/2 tablespoons of flour for a medium sauce, and 2 tablespoons of flour for a thick sauce.

COMPOUND BUTTERS
Burri composti

108. ANCHOVY BUTTER
Burro d'acciuga

Anchovy butter is used very often as a flavoring agent for sauces, as a spread for canapés, or for decorating cold dishes.

Cream 1 cup of sweet butter with 3 tablespoons of mashed anchovy fillets. If Italian-style salted anchovies are used, wash them free of salt before chopping [*see* No. 220].

109. GARLIC BUTTER
Burro d'aglio

For canapés and flavoring sauces

Cream 1/2 cup of butter with two cloves of garlic which have been crushed in the garlic-press.

110. GREEN BUTTER
Burro verde

For decorating hot or cold fish

8 tablespoons assorted chopped green herbs or leafy green vegetables (spinach leaves, parsley, tarragon, chervil, basil, etc.)
1/2 cup butter, creamed

Parboil the greens for 5 minutes in just enough water to cover. Drain, pat dry in a paper towel, rub through a fine sieve, cool, and blend with the butter.

111. MAÎTRE D'HÔTEL BUTTER
Burro maître d'hôtel

For broiled meats and fish

1 cup butter
1 tablespoon chopped parsley
1/2 teaspoon salt
1/4 teaspoon freshly ground white pepper
1 teaspoon lemon juice

Cream the butter with the other ingredients.

112. MUSTARD BUTTER
Burro di mostarda

For canapés

Blend 1/2 cup softened butter with 1 tablespoon (or more, to taste) of prepared mustard (Dijon-type preferred), or 1/2 teaspoon dry mustard.

48

SEE
REVERSE
FOR
CAPTION

Suggested presentation of canapés. Among the varieties shown are Canapés of San Daniele Prosciutto (No. 231), Caviar (No. 221), Italiana (No. 228), Shrimp (No. 233), and Shrimp Canapés Gourmet (No. 234). Precision and neatness are the watchwords when making canapés. One need not strive to achieve the effects shown (the canapés pictured have been glazed with a brushing of aspic). The flowers decorating this tray might be duplicated by cutting thin strips from yellow and white turnips in a continuous spiral, using a rotary peeler. The strips are then twisted about the index finger to form a rose.

113. TUNA BUTTER
Burro di tonno

For canapés and cold antipasti

Pound 4 tablespoons Italian-style tuna, canned in oil, in a mortar, blend in ½ cup butter, and press through a fine sieve (or whirl all ingredients in the blender at high speed for 10 seconds).

114. WHITE BUTTER
Burro bianco

For broiled fish

½ cup vinegar
2 teaspoons chopped chives
½ cup butter, softened
½ teaspoon salt
⅛ teaspoon pepper

Boil the vinegar with the chopped chives in a small, heavy saucepan until liquid has almost evaporated. Remove from fire, allow to cool, stir in, bit by bit, the softened butter, and season with the salt and pepper.

GELATIN AND ASPICS
Gelatine

Gelatin is a nutritive substance, abundantly present in the bones and connective tissues of most young animals and in all kinds of fish and fowl. A liquid blended with a required amount of gelatin will become firmly jellied when chilled. In culinary terms, this jelly is called aspic and is used as a flavorful and decorative coating or garnish for cold meats, chicken, fish, eggs, or vegetables.

Aspics may be made naturally by preparing an appropriate stock with, in addition to its normal ingredients, a quantity of bones. By long simmering, the bones will render a sufficient amount of gelatin to jell the stock when it is chilled. A much simpler method,

however, especially if there is an appropriate stock on hand, is simply to use a small amount of commercial gelatin, softened in a little water. To simplify the process even further, canned beef bouillon, chicken consommé, or bottled clam juice may be substituted for homemade stocks.

To achieve a sparkling clear aspic, only two simple rules need be followed. First, the stock must be absolutely free of fat; even a particle of fat is apt to make the aspic cloudy, once it is chilled. The simplest method, although it is time-consuming, is to chill the stock in the refrigerator until thoroughly cold and then scrape every trace of fat from the surface. Second, the stock must be clarified by the addition of a few beaten egg whites and crushed egg shells; it is then brought slowly to a boil, stirred constantly, allowed to stand for 5 minutes, and strained through several thicknesses of cheesecloth.

The flavor of aspics may be further heightened by the addition of wine or herbs—tarragon and chervil are particularly flavorsome in aspics. Fortified wines, such as sherry, Port, or Madeira, are better than unfortified wines, since the flavor of the latter tends to disappear once the aspic is chilled. It is also wise to allow hot stock to cool slightly before adding a wine flavoring and then add it more "to smell" than to taste; too much wine will turn the aspic into a wine jelly.

Each envelope of commercial gelatin contains slightly in excess of 1 tablespoon and is sufficient to firmly jell 2 cups of liquid. It is important to gauge the amount of gelatin accurately. If too little gelatin is used, the aspic will melt quickly at room temperature; if too much is used, it will have a distasteful, rubbery consistency.

To coat a dish or food with aspic, the aspic should be lukewarm and then stirred in a bowl placed over a bowl containing cracked ice until it becomes thick and syrupy. The coating process should then be begun immediately, and, if the aspic becomes too stiff, remove it from the ice, stir vigorously, or place it for a moment over a bowl of warm water. It is extremely important that any food which is to be coated with aspic be very cold; if it is warm, the aspic will simply melt and run off. Metal molds are frequently lined with aspic, filled with a variety of ingredients, chilled, and then unmolded. These molds should first be chilled in the freezer to allow the aspic to adhere to their sides.

Highly decorative garnishes for cold dishes may be made from thin sheets of aspic, chilled in the refrigerator, turned out onto a board, and then cut into fancy shapes or chopped.

gelatin base

egg white and shell

bring to a boil

meat and bones and aromatic herbs and vegetables

filter

STANDARD PROCEDURE FOR GELATIN BASES

115. REGULAR GELATIN BASE
Fondo per gelatina ordinaria

1/2 pound leg of veal
1/3 pound chopped veal bones
1/3 pound beef round
1 calf's foot, blanched for 10 minutes
2 tablespoons diced salt pork rind, blanched for 10 minutes
1 carrot, sliced
1 onion, sliced
1 leek (white part only), sliced
1 stalk celery, sliced
Bouquet Garni:
  2 sprigs parsley
  1/4 teaspoon dried thyme
  1 bay leaf
2 quarts water

Roast veal, bones, calf's foot, and beef in a hot (450°) oven until brown, about 10 to 15 minutes. Proceed as described under Brown Stock [No. 4], cooking very slowly for 6 hours. Strain. *Makes 1 quart.*

116. FISH GELATIN BASE
Fondo per gelatina di pesce

5 cups Fish Fumet [No. 2]
1/2 pound inexpensive raw fish, such as cod
1/3 pound of fish bones, tails, or heads
1 small onion, chopped
6 fresh mushrooms, chopped
2 sprigs parsley

50

Simmer all ingredients for 1 hour and strain.

NOTE: Do *not* use flesh and bones of oily, strongly flavored fish, such as mackerel or bluefish.

117. CHICKEN GELATIN BASE
Fondo per gelatina di pollame

1/2 pound chopped leg of veal
1/3 pound chopped beef bones
1 pound raw chicken carcasses, chicken parts, or giblets
1/2 pound chicken feet
1 small calf's foot, split and blanched for 10 minutes
1 carrot, sliced
1 onion, sliced
1 leek (white part only), sliced
1 stalk celery, sliced
Bouquet Garni:
  2 sprigs parsley
  1/4 teaspoon dried thyme
  1 bay leaf
2 quarts water

Proceed as for Brown Stock [No. 4], cooking for 4 hours. Strain. *Makes 1 quart.*

118. REGULAR ASPIC
Gelatina ordinaria

1 quart Regular Gelatine Base [No. 115], free of fat
2 sprigs chervil, chopped
2 sprigs tarragon, chopped
1 egg white, lightly beaten
1 egg shell, crushed

Check the stiffness of the gelatin base by chilling a small amount in the refrigerator; if it is too thin, add a small amount of commercial gelatin, softened in a little water. Place all ingredients in a heavy saucepan over medium heat, bring to a boil, stirring constantly to mix the egg whites with the stock, and simmer for 5 minutes. Remove from the heat, allow to stand for 5 minutes, and then strain through several thicknesses of cheesecloth. *Makes 1 scant quart.*

118a. SUBSTITUTE REGULAR ASPIC

1 quart Substitute Brown Stock [No. 4a]
2 envelopes commercial gelatin, softened in ¼ cup
    water
2 sprigs chervil, chopped
2 sprigs tarragon, chopped
1 egg white, lightly beaten
1 egg shell, crushed

Place all ingredients in a heavy saucepan over medium heat, bring to a boil, stirring constantly, and simmer for 5 minutes. Remove from the heat, allow to stand for 5 minutes, and then strain through several thicknesses of cheesecloth. *Makes 1 quart.*

119. FISH ASPIC WITH WHITE WINE
Gelatina di pesce al vino bianco

1 quart Fish Gelatin Base [No. 116], free of fat
2 ounces minced, fatless white fish (cod, halibut, etc.)
1 egg white, lightly beaten
1 egg shell, crushed
¼ cup dry white wine

Prepare exactly as Regular Aspic [No. 118], except that the wine is added immediately after the hot aspic is removed from the heat.

119a. SUBSTITUTE FISH ASPIC WITH WHITE WINE

1 quart Substitute Fish Stock [No. 2a]
2 envelopes commercial gelatin, softened in ¼ cup
    water
1 egg white, lightly beaten
1 egg shell, crushed
¼ cup dry white wine

Prepare exactly as Substitute Regular Aspic [No. 118a], adding the wine immediately after the hot aspic is removed from the heat.

120. CHICKEN ASPIC
Gelatina di pollame

1 quart Chicken Gelatin Base [No. 117], free of fat
2 sprigs chervil, chopped
2 sprigs tarragon, chopped
1 egg white, lightly beaten
1 egg shell, crushed

Prepare exactly as Regular Aspic [No. 118].

120a. SUBSTITUTE CHICKEN ASPIC

1 quart Substitute White Stock [No. 1a]
2 envelopes commercial gelatin, softened in ¼ cup
    water
2 sprigs chervil, chopped
2 sprigs tarragon, chopped
2 egg whites, lightly beaten
1 egg shell, crushed

Prepare exactly as Substitute Regular Aspic [No. 118a].

MARINADES AND PICKLING BRINES
Marinate e salamoie

Marinades are liquids seasoned with various condiments, herbs, and vegetables, which are used to soak meats, fish, or game in order to give them added flavor, as well as to tenderize them and preserve them for a time. The length of time that they stay in the marinade varies according to the type of meat, the size of the piece, and the temperature. In the refrigerator, or in a cold storeroom, marinated meats will keep for a week or more. In summer, without refrigeration, they will not keep more than a day or two.

Cooked marinades will keep well in the refrigerator, especially if a pinch of boric acid is added to each quart while it is boiling. In a warm place they may be preserved by removing the marinating item, bringing them to a boil every other day, and adding more wine and vinegar.

Pickling brines are a solution of non-iodized salt in water, often with the addition of sugar and spices, in which meats may be preserved.

51

Never use metal pots or bowls when preparing marinades and brines or for soaking food in them. The acids in the preparations will act upon the metal chemically and produce an unpleasant (and sometimes harmful) taste.

121. WHITE WINE MARINADE FOR FISH

Marinata cotta per pesce al vino bianco

This marinade is used for small whole fish and shrimp before frying in batter. The marinade should be poured hot over the fish and they should be marinated for 2 hours, turning them occasionally. This recipe is sufficient for 3 pounds of fish.

½ cup oil
2 scallions, chopped
1 stalk celery, chopped
1 carrot, chopped
1 onion, chopped
2 small cloves garlic, crushed in the garlic-press
¼ teaspoon powdered thyme
½ bay leaf
Few sprigs of parsley
1 whole clove
Pinch of pepper
2 quarts dry white wine such as a Rhine or Moselle
   (do not use a sweet wine like Sauternes)
1 cup white wine vinegar or cider vinegar

Pour the oil into a large, heavy saucepan and sauté the vegetables and spices in it over medium heat until they begin to turn yellow. Add the wine and vinegar and let the mixture simmer for about 35 minutes.

Tuna

122. RED WINE MARINADE FOR FISH

Marinata cotta per pesce al vino rosso

Prepare exactly as the preceding recipe, using the same quantity of dry red wine instead of white.

123. COOKED MARINADE FOR MEAT OR GAME

Marinata cotta per pezzi di carne da macello e selvaggina

For every 2 pounds of meat use the following:

¼ pound chopped onions and/or scallions
1 tablespoon chopped parsley
1 bay leaf, crumbled
½ teaspoon thyme
1 clove garlic, crushed in the garlic-press
½ cup oil
1 teaspoon salt
Enough dry white wine and vinegar to cover the meat
   (The quantity will depend on how tightly the meat fits into the bowl in which it is soaked. The proportions should be 1 part vinegar to 4 parts wine; for example, ½ cup vinegar to 2 cups wine.)

Lightly sauté, but do not brown, the onion and all of the seasonings in the oil in a saucepan over medium heat. If the marinade is to be used for game, other seasonings such as 1 teaspoon rosemary, 1 teaspoon bruised juniper berries, or 1 teaspoon coriander seeds may be added. Add the wine and vinegar and let all boil together for about 30 minutes. Cool completely and pour over the meat. Keep in a cold place for several days.

124. COOKED RED WINE MARINADE FOR MEAT

Marinata cotta per pezzi di carne da macello al vino rosso

Prepare exactly as described for No. 123, above, substituting red wine for white wine.

125. UNCOOKED MARINADE FOR MEAT AND GAME

Marinata cruda per pezzi di carne da macello e selvaggina

For every 2 pounds of meat use:

2½ cups dry white wine
1 cup oil
1 medium onion, chopped
1 tablespoon chopped scallion
1 tablespoon chopped celery leaves
1 clove garlic, crushed in the garlic-press
4 sprigs of parsley, coarsely chopped
1 bay leaf

½ teaspoon dried thyme
1 whole clove
8 peppercorns
1 tablespoon salt
¼ teaspoon ground pepper

Spread half the vegetables and seasonings (except salt and pepper) in the bottom of the bowl in which the meat is to be marinated. Place the meat on top, season with the salt and pepper, and spread the rest of the vegetables and seasonings over the meat. Gently pour in the liquids. Keep in a cool place for several days, turning the meat every day, so that it absorbs the liquid.

If used for game, coriander, juniper berries, or rosemary may be added.

Second Method

Omit the oil from the above ingredients and add ¼ cup brandy. Marinate the meat or game for only 6 hours, turning it occasionally. The marinade may be used in the cooking process, if desired.

126. UNCOOKED MARINADE FOR SMALL PIECES OF MEAT, CHICKEN, OR FISH

Marinata cruda per pezzi piccoli di carne da macello, pollame, pesci

1 onion, finely chopped
3 sprigs parsley, chopped
3 scallions, chopped
¼ teaspoon powdered bay leaf
¼ teaspoon dried oregano
1 clove garlic, crushed in the garlic-press
Juice of 1 lemon
¾ cup oil
1 teaspoon salt
¼ teaspoon freshly ground pepper

Mix all the ingredients together thoroughly. Pour the mixture over the meat, chicken, or fish to be marinated and allow to steep for 2 hours, turning occasionally.

127. PICKLING BRINE FOR TONGUE OR CORNED BEEF

Salamoia liquida per lingue salmistrate e pressed beef

Enough for 5 to 6 pounds of meat

5 quarts cold water
4 pounds non-iodized salt (Kosher salt is excellent)
¾ cup saltpeter
¾ pounds brown sugar
15 peppercorns, lightly crushed
15 juniper berries, bruised
Pinch thyme
1 bay leaf, crumbled

Put all ingredients in a large pot except for the saltpeter and 2 cups of the salt. Boil briskly for ½ hour and then cool until cold. Puncture the meat to be treated all over with a small skewer or the tines of a large fork. Rub it with the remaining salt and saltpeter and place it in a large bowl or crock (do *not* use a metal container). Cover it completely with the cold brine. Place a piece of wood over it (the same size, or a bit smaller, as the opening of the crock) and weight this down with a stone or brick so that the meat cannot rise to the top and become exposed to the air. Keep in a cool place.

The meat will be pickled in the course of 8 days in winter (6 in summer) and will keep longer if not exposed to too high temperatures.

128. "DRY" BRINE FOR MEATS

Salamoia secca per pezzi di carni da macello diverse

Puncture a piece of meat deeply all over with a skewer. Rub on all sides with a generous amount of saltpeter and non-iodized (or Kosher) salt. Place in a crock and sprinkle with more salt (using 1 rounded tablespoon of salt per pound of meat). Crumbled bay leaf and thyme may be added to the salt, if desired. Cover with a wooden board and weight it with a large stone or brick. The pickling time will vary with the size of the piece of meat. For 5–6 pounds the time will be about 8 days in winter, or 6 in summer.

53

FORCEMEAT AND STUFFINGS
Farce

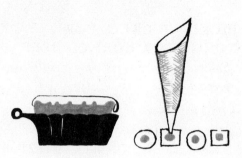

All of these may be used as the bases for pâtés [*see* Nos. 1566–71]. However, many of these preparations provide exquisite quenelles or dumplings. To prepare these, butter a large enamel skillet, take the forcemeat mixture up in a moistened tablespoon, round off the top with another moistened spoon, and carefully place in the skillet. Leave enough space between each of the quenelles for expansion. Carefully pour in enough simmering broth or salted water to barely cover the quenelles, place skillet over low heat, cover, and simmer for about 15 minutes. Remove quenelles carefully with a slotted spoon and place on a warm platter. Mask with any preferred sauce, preferably a delicate one such as Mornay or Nantua.

Very tiny quenelles for garnishes may be prepared by placing the mixture into a pastry bag fitted with a large plain tip (or the nozzle of the bag) and squeezing small amounts of the mixture into barely simmering broth or water. Cook covered over very low heat for 5 minutes and remove with a slotted spoon.

129. FORCEMEAT
Farcia di carne di vitello o di pollame o di cacciagione

This is a basic forcemeat which may be made of veal, pork, poultry, or game. It is used for dumplings, quenelles, mousses, or mousselines.

2 pounds of lean meat: veal, pork, poultry, or game, cut into small pieces with all the fat, tendons, nerves, and larger blood vessels removed

4 cups heavy cream
4 egg whites
2 teaspoons salt
1/4 teaspoon white pepper

Place the meat 1/2 pound at a time in the blender along with 1 egg white and 1/4 cup cream and blend for 1/2 minute at medium speed and 1/2 minute at high. Repeat until all has been processed. Put into a bowl placed over a bowl of ice for a couple of hours. Then, still on ice, work in the remaining cream, a little at a time, with a wooden spoon. Season, and set aside in the refrigerator until needed. *Makes about 2 quarts.*

130. FORCEMEAT AU GRATIN
Farcia al gratino

This forcemeat is used in hot hors d'oeuvres, such as meat tartlets.

6 tablespoons butter
1/4 pound fat pork, diced
1/4 pound trimmed lean veal, diced
1/4 pound calf's liver, diced
1 teaspoon sliced truffle [or No. 1819a]
2 scallions, chopped
1/4 teaspoon powdered bay leaf
Pinch powdered thyme
1 teaspoon salt
1/4 teaspoon pepper
Pinch allspice
1/4 cup dry Madeira wine
3 egg yolks
1/4 cup Spanish Sauce [No. 16]

Sauté the fat pork dice in 1 tablespoon of the butter in a frying pan over medium heat for 2 or 3 minutes. When it begins to color, remove with a slotted spoon and set aside. Add the veal dice to the pan, cook for about 3 minutes, remove with a slotted spoon, and set aside with the pork dice. Add the liver to the pan, cook for 1 minute, return the pork and veal dice to the pan, and add the truffle, scallions, herbs, and seasoning. Raise the heat and cook for 2 minutes. Pour the contents of the pan into the blender container and deglaze the pan with the Madeira, scraping the bottom well. Add this juice to the blender, together with the egg yolks, Spanish sauce, and the remaining butter. Blend at high speed for 1 minute, or until the mixture is smooth. Store in a covered bowl until needed. *Makes about 2 1/2 cups.*

131. CHICKEN FORCEMEAT FOR PÂTÉS
Farcia di pollame per pâtés e terrine

1 pound raw chicken meat, skinned and boned
$\frac{1}{4}$ pound lean veal
$\frac{3}{4}$ pound fat pork (or beef or pork kidney fat)
1 tablespoon salt
2 eggs
$\frac{1}{2}$ cup brandy

Place half of all ingredients in the blender container and blend for 30 seconds at high speed. Put in a bowl, blend the remaining ingredients, mix the 2 batches well, cover with wax paper or foil, and place in refrigerator until needed. *Makes about 4 cups.*

132. MOUSSELINE FISH FORCEMEAT
Farcia mousseline per pesci

This is a light forcemeat used for mousses and quenelles.

$1\frac{1}{2}$ pounds skinned, boned, raw fish or shellfish
3 egg whites
2 cups heavy cream
1 teaspoon salt
Pinch nutmeg
Pinch white pepper

Pat fish dry with a paper towel. Cut in small pieces and put in blender container. Add the egg whites, 1 at a time, blending 10 seconds after each addition. Chill thoroughly. Place the mixture in a bowl placed over another bowl with ice and gradually add the cream, mixing and stirring continuously with a wooden spoon until well blended. Season and chill until needed. *Makes about 6 cups.*

133. FANCY PORK FORCEMEAT
Farcia fine di maiale

Blend equal parts of lean and fat pork pieces chopped very fine, adding $\frac{1}{2}$ tablespoon salt for each pound of the meat. Keep in refrigerator until needed.

134. VEAL FORCEMEAT FOR PÂTÉS
Farcia di vitello per galantine, pâtés, terrine

$\frac{1}{2}$ pound lean veal, free of white tissue, nerves, and fat
1 pound pork fat (or beef or pork kidney fat)

$1\frac{1}{2}$ tablespoons salt
2 eggs
$\frac{1}{2}$ cup brandy

Place all ingredients in the blender container, $\frac{1}{3}$ at a time, blending each batch for 30 seconds at high speed. Put in a bowl, mix well, cover with wax paper or foil, and place in refrigerator until needed. *Makes about 4 cups.*

135. SIMPLE FISH STUFFING
Farcia di pesce ordinaria

$1\frac{1}{4}$ pounds fillet of fresh cod (or other white fish)
1 teaspoon salt
$\frac{1}{4}$ teaspoon pepper
Pinch nutmeg
$1\frac{1}{2}$ cups cold Panade [No. 137]
$\frac{1}{2}$ pound butter
2 whole eggs or 4 egg yolks

Put $\frac{1}{2}$ of the fish and the seasonings into the blender container and blend for 30 seconds at high speed. Add $\frac{1}{2}$ of the cold panade and blend for 20 seconds; add $\frac{1}{2}$ of the butter, a piece at a time, and blend until all of it is incorporated. Then, one at a time, add the eggs or egg yolks, blending briefly after each. If necessary, blend a few seconds longer to make a smooth mixture. Pour the mixture into a bowl. Repeat the process with the remaining ingredients. Combine the 2 mixtures, cover with wax paper or foil, and put in refrigerator until needed. *Makes about 4 cups.*

136. STUFFING FOR BRAISED FISH
Farcia per pesce da brasare

1 tablespoon butter
4 tablespoons chopped onion
2 tablespoons chopped scallion
Optional: ½ pound fish milt
4 medium whiting or other white fish, skinned,
    boned, and chopped
¼ pound breadcrumbs soaked in milk and squeezed dry
2 eggs
1 tablespoon chopped parsley
1 clove garlic, crushed in the garlic-press
1 teaspoon salt
⅛ teaspoon pepper
Pinch nutmeg

Cook onion and scallion in the butter in a frying pan over medium heat for 3 minutes, or until soft. Cool. Put all ingredients in a bowl, mix thoroughly, cover with wax paper or foil, and keep in the refrigerator until used.

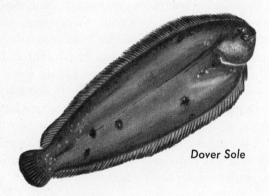

Dover Sole

137. PANADE
Panata per farce

This is used to extend the simpler kinds of forcemeat, using half as much panade as forcemeat.

To any desired quantity of soft, crumbled, fresh white bread (no crust) gradually add enough scalded milk so that the bread will be soaked but not swimming. All the milk should be absorbed. Put in a heavy saucepan over a brisk flame and mix vigorously with a wooden spoon, scraping the sides and bottom frequently. When the paste begins to stick to the spoon, remove from fire and pour onto a buttered platter. Cover it with buttered paper so that no skin can form, and cool.

If desired, the panade may be enriched by the addition of 1 egg yolk and 1 tablespoon of melted butter for each cup of breadcrumbs. These are added before cooking.

MISCELLANEOUS PREPARATIONS
Preparazione ausiliare

138. DUXELLES
Purea di funghi duxelles

1 pound mushrooms, finely chopped
1½ teaspoons salt
2 tablespoons finely chopped onion
1 tablespoon butter
1 tablespoon oil
1 teaspoon finely minced parsley
⅛ teaspoon pepper

Place the mushrooms in a bowl, sprinkle with the salt, and allow them to stand for 30 minutes. Gather them up in a strong cloth, twist to form a bag, and squeeze out as much of their juice as possible. Cook the onion in the oil and butter in a saucepan over moderate heat for 3 minutes, add the mushrooms, and cook very slowly until all moisture has evaporated. Add the pepper and parsley, cool, and store in the refrigerator, covered, until needed. *Makes 1 cup.*

139. DUXELLES CASALINGA
Purea di funghi Duxelles casalinga

Add 1 cup pre-cooked sausage meat to 1 cup Duxelles [No. 138].

140. MATIGNON
Matignon

1 tablespoon butter
1 onion, finely chopped
2 stalks celery, finely chopped
1 carrot, finely chopped
¼ pound ham or parboiled salt pork (part fat, part
    lean), chopped
⅛ teaspoon powdered thyme
½ teaspoon powdered bay leaf
¼ teaspoon salt (omit if using salt pork)
Pinch sugar
⅓ cup dry white wine

Melt the butter in a small saucepan over low heat. Add the onion, celery, carrots, ham, thyme, bay leaf, salt, and sugar. Cook for 30 minutes, or until the vegetables are reduced to mush, but *not* browned. Add the wine and continue cooking until it has evaporated. *Makes about 1 cup.*

NOTE: This may also be prepared without meat, in which case it is called Vegetable Matignon.

141. MIREPOIX
Mirepoix

1 tablespoon butter
1 carrot, finely diced
1 onion, finely diced
2 stalks celery, finely diced
¼ pound ham (both fat and lean) or parboiled lean
    salt pork, chopped
½ teaspoon salt
Pinch powdered thyme
Pinch powdered bay leaf

Melt the butter in a saucepan over medium heat and add all the other ingredients. Stir until the onions begin to turn light yellow. Reduce heat, cover pan, and continue cooking until vegetables are soft but not mushy. *Makes about 1 cup.*

NOTE: This may also be prepared without meat, in which case it is called Vegetable Mirepoix.

142. SALPICON
Dadolata

A Salpicon is any diced, cooked meat, usually employed as a garnish. The dice should not be larger than ¼ inch. Ham, tongue, goose or chicken livers, sweetbreads, chicken, etc., may be used.

143. MIXED SALPICON
Dadolata composta

A mixed Salpicon uses 2 or more different meats, such as tongue and chicken. Diced mushrooms or truffles may be added, if desired.

144. TOMATO PASTE
Essenza—o salsina—di pomodoro

Although canned tomato paste is satisfactory and convenient, freshly made paste is simple to prepare. Peel, seed, and drain any quantity of dead-ripe tomatoes, purée them in the blender or through a food mill, and then simmer them very gently in a heavy enamel saucepan over moderate heat until thickened to the desired consistency.

Chervil

Savory

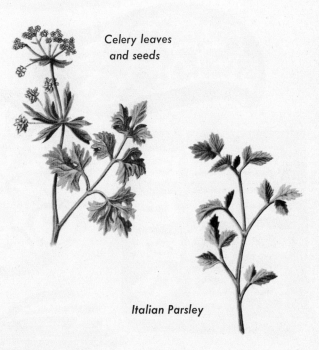

Celery leaves and seeds

Italian Parsley

57

ANTIPASTI

ANTIPASTI

Antipasti (literally, "before the pasta") are the splendid Italian version of hors d'oeuvres (literally, "apart from the main works"). They may be hot or cold, and in Italy they are most often served at table as the first course for lunch or dinner, although the only cold antipasti considered suitable for a formal dinner are caviar, pâté de foie gras, smoked salmon, oysters, or shellfish cocktails.

They may also be served as an accompaniment to aperitifs or cocktails. In Italy this was originally a carry-over of the old Imperial Russian tradition of *zakousky,* when etiquette demanded that appetizers and delicacies be served in a room adjoining the dining room, accompanied by a generous flow of vodka and wines.

Antipasti should not be so copious or overpowering that they will ruin the appetite for the meal to follow. However, a judicious selection may serve as a pleasant summer buffet or as a late supper after the theater.

While some antipasti can be fairly elaborate, many of them are quite simple to prepare and are economical, since leftovers may often be used in both the hot and cold varieties.

Antipasti requiring forks and knives are best served at table, and those which can be held in the fingers are more suitable when served before dinner, with drinks.

COLD ANTIPASTI

Antipasti freddi

Cold antipasti are cheerful, colorful, and appetizing. Their most commonly used ingredients are: fresh sweet butter, crisp salad greens, cold cuts, stuffed hard-boiled eggs, olives, tuna, anchovies, sardines, caviar, smoked or marinated herring fillets, marinated mushrooms or artichokes, pickled vegetables, shellfish, and bivalves. Most of these are readily available in local markets, and some of the more special ingredients are easily found in Italian food markets and delicatessens. When butter is called for in a recipe, only sweet butter should be used—and sweet butter with the highest butterfat content available. Fresh tub-butter is ideal if available. Make sure that your raw vegetables are the freshest and best, that your oil is the finest virgin olive oil, and that your preparations are as delightful to the eye as they should be to the palate.

145. ANTIPASTO CASALINGA
Antipasto alla casalinga

Sweet (or mild) peppers, red, green, or yellow
  (or Italian-style peppers packed in jars)
Ripe tomatoes
Onions, sliced
Olive oil
Vinegar
Salt and pepper to taste
Sardines or canned Italian-style tuna in olive oil

Choose the quantity of ingredients in proportion to the number of persons you wish to serve. Roast the peppers. This is most easily accomplished by placing them directly over the gas flame until they become black, turning them to char all surfaces, and peeling them under cold running water. Do not let them stay over the flame too long after they are charred or they will become too soft. Each section to be charred should be black within 1 or 2 minutes. Once the peppers are peeled, discard the seeds and whitish membranes. Cut them into strips and arrange them on a platter. Surround with a border of sliced, peeled, and seeded tomatoes, alternating with onion rings that have been soaked in water (or wine) for 40 minutes to remove some of their sharpness. Sprinkle all with olive oil and 1/3 as much vinegar and season with salt and freshly ground black pepper. Serve with an accompanying dish of sardines or tuna in olive oil.

146. ANTIPASTO ITALIANA
Salumi misti all'italiana

Mixed cold cuts might well be considered the Italian national antipasto. On a large platter serve a variety of the following: prosciutto from San Daniele, Parma, or Modena; salami from Milan, Cremona, or Felino (or with garlic, from Genoa); sopressata (picnic bologna) from Verona; mortadella from Bologna; bondiola (a Po Valley salami made with wine); culatello (ham butt) from Parma; bresaola (rolled beef) from Colico; pork shoulder from San Secondo; or zampone (stuffed pig's foot) from Modena.

147. ANCHOVIES CARABINIERA
Acciughe alla carabiniera

24 anchovy fillets, washed free of salt [*see* No. 220]
2 cups potato salad
1 medium onion, peeled and thinly sliced
½ cup olives, stuffed with anchovy fillets
Freshly ground pepper

Prepare a potato salad by boiling 1 pound of "new" potatoes in lightly salted water for about 20 minutes, or until tender; peel and slice the potatoes while still hot; and toss them lightly in a bowl with ½ cup Sauce Vinaigrette [No. 99]. The salad may be chilled, if desired, but the flavor will be stronger if it is served at room temperature. Garnish the salad with the anchovy fillets, olives, and the onion slices, broken up into rings, and grate the pepper over all. *Serves* 4.

148. ANCHOVIES CONTADINA
Acciughe alla contadina

24 anchovy fillets, washed free of salt [*see* No. 220]
  and sprinkled lightly with oil
1 tablespoon finely chopped parsley
1 teaspoon capers
1 small onion, sliced and broken into rings
½ cup pitted ripe olives, stuffed with Anchovy Butter
  [*see* No. 108]

Arrange anchovy fillets close together on a plate. Cover with the finely chopped parsley, capers, and small onion rings. Garnish the platter with the olives. *Serves* 4.

149. ANCHOVY AND EGG SALAD
Acciughe in insalata con uova sode

6 hard-boiled eggs
24 anchovy fillets washed free of salt [*see* No. 220]
½ cup Sauce Vinaigrette [No. 99] or Mayonnaise
  [No. 77]
3 tablespoons chopped parsley

Chop the eggs and the anchovy fillets rather coarsely. Sprinkle with the Vinaigrette sauce or mix with the mayonnaise, and garnish with the parsley. *Serves* 4.

150. ANCHOVIES WITH YELLOW PEPPERS
Acciughe con peperoni gialli

24 anchovy fillets washed free of salt [*see* No. 220]
1 yellow pepper, roasted, peeled, and cut into strips
  [*see* No. 145]
1 teaspoon capers
2 hard-boiled eggs
4 tablespoons oil
4 teaspoons vinegar
1 tablespoon chopped parsley

Place crisscross rows of the anchovy fillets and the strips of yellow pepper on a platter. Decorate with the capers and hard-boiled eggs, chopped separately. Sprinkle with oil, vinegar, and finely chopped parsley. *Serves* 4.

151. MARINATED FRESH ANCHOVIES
Acciughe fresche marinate

2 pounds fresh anchovies, filleted
7 tablespoons olive oil
6 small white onions, sliced
1 cup dry white wine
Juice of 1 lemon
1 clove garlic, crushed in the garlic-press
Bouquet Garni:
  2 tablespoons chopped fennel
  3 sprigs parsley
  ¼ teaspoon dried thyme
  1 bay leaf
1 teaspoon salt
⅛ teaspoon pepper
1 teaspoon coriander

Anchovy and Egg Salad (No. 149)

60

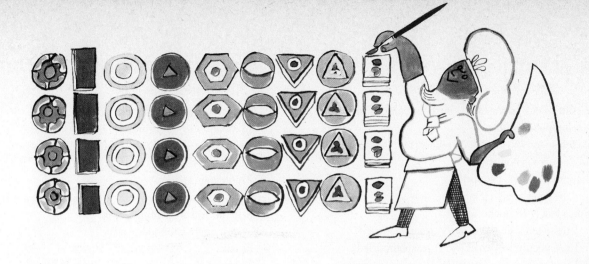

Brown the onions in a saucepan over medium heat with 3 tablespoons of the oil; add the wine, lemon juice, crushed garlic, and Bouquet Garni. Season with ½ teaspoon of the salt and the pepper and coriander. Simmer briskly for 10 minutes, remove from flame, and cool off completely. Place anchovies in 1 layer in a baking dish, season with ½ teaspoon salt, sprinkle with remaining 4 tablespoons oil, and bake in hot (400°) oven until golden, about 12 minutes. Cool, place in a bowl, and cover with the cooked marinade. Keep in cool place for about 2 days before serving. *Serves* 4.

152. CAVIAR
Caviale

This name is given to several kinds of fish roe. Sturgeon roe is the best and most expensive and comes from Russia, but the Iranian variety is very highly prized. If it is shipped fresh (unsalted) on ice, the cost is astronomical. However, the salted kind that comes in vacuum-packed jars is also very good. There are persons who eschew any but the fresh roe; however, certain great chefs and gourmets prefer the salted, pressed, caviar. Except for red salmon caviar, which is of good consistency though it is quite salty and lacks the delicate flavor of the sturgeon roe, the cheaper kinds (such as lumpfish) are best avoided. They are hard and grainy, with no particular flavor, and the charcoal with which they are colored to make them resemble real sturgeon roe has a disagreeable way of oozing onto the canapés and making them gray all over.

Russian or Persian caviar should be handled as little as possible so as not to crush the delicate eggs. Just open the container and imbed it in crushed ice. Serve chilled, with buttered toast points and lemon slices. Let each guest spoon out his own. Use a wooden spoon if possible, since caviar will discolor silver.

153. EELS BURGUNDY
Anguilla fresca alla borgognona

2 pounds eels, skinned [*see* introduction to Fish section]
3 tablespoons oil
1 clove garlic, crushed in the garlic-press
2 tablespoons chopped scallion
3 tablespoons brandy
1 cup dry red wine
Bouquet Garni:
   2 sprigs thyme (or ¼ teaspoon dried)
   1 bay leaf
   2 sprigs parsley
1 teaspoon salt
⅛ teaspoon pepper
2 tablespoons Anchovy Butter [No. 108]

Skin and clean eels, chop into 2-inch pieces, and brown in a skillet over high heat with the oil, garlic, and scallions. Add the brandy and cook until the liquid has almost completely evaporated. Add the wine and Bouquet Garni, season with salt and pepper, cover the pan, and simmer 15 minutes. Remove eels with a slotted spoon to a serving dish. Reduce the cooking liquid over high heat to ½ its quantity, remove from heat, discard the Bouquet Garni, and add, bit by bit, the anchovy butter. Pour the sauce over the eels and cool to room temperature, or serve hot, if desired. *Serves* 4.

Eel

61

154. FLEMISH EELS
Anguilla fresca alla fiamminga

2 pounds eels, skinned [*see* introduction to Fish section]
4 tablespoons butter
2 tablespoons Vegetable Mirepoix [*see* Note to No. 141]
1 cup sorrel, chopped
1 cup watercress, chopped
1 tablespoon finely chopped parsley
Spice bag (tied in cheesecloth):
   1 teaspoon sage leaves (or ¼ teaspoon dried)
   1 teaspoon mint leaves (or ¼ teaspoon dried)
   1 teaspoon savory leaves (or ¼ teaspoon dried)
¾ teaspoon salt
⅛ teaspoon pepper
2 cups dry white wine
4 egg yolks
½ cup cream

Clean and skin the eels and then cut them into 2-inch pieces. Melt the butter in a frying pan over fairly high heat and add the eels, mirepoix, sorrel, watercress, parsley, spice bag, wine, and salt and pepper. Cook for 15 to 20 minutes, or until the eel pieces are tender. Remove from the heat and discard the spice bag. Beat the egg yolks with the cream and pour the mixture slowly into the pan, stirring constantly. Return the pan to a low flame and stir for about 5 minutes until the sauce has thickened slightly. Do not boil. Remove from the heat and allow to cool completely, stirring occasionally. This dish may also be served hot, if desired. *Serves* 4.

155. EELS WITH ONIONS AND MUSHROOMS
Anguilla fresca con cipolline e funghi

Prepare exactly as Eels Burgundy [No. 153], adding 1 cup each Braised White Onions [No. 1721], sautéed mushrooms, and a little oil before serving. *Serves* 4.

156. ANTIPASTO FANTASIA
Antipasto fantasia

18 oysters on the half shell
18 medium raw shrimp
1 cup Mayonnaise [No. 77]
2 tablespoons heavy cream
2 tablepoons sherry
1 tablespoon prepared mustard (Dijon-type preferred)
Salt and freshly ground pepper
½ cup finely chopped parsley
Paprika
18 lemon slices

Remove oysters from their shells and place in a saucepan over medium heat with their own juices. The moment the liquid comes to a boil, remove from fire, drain and dry the oysters, and trim off their "beards." Scrub and dry their bottom shells and put aside.

Boil the shrimp in salted water for 8 minutes. Cool, peel off shells, and de-vein.

Mix together the mayonnaise, cream, sherry, and mustard. Add salt and freshly ground pepper to taste and enough paprika to color the sauce a pale pink.

Put an oyster on its shell, top with a shrimp, and carefully cover both with the sauce so that they are well masked, but do not allow the sauce to run over the shells. Dust with finely chopped parsley. Arrange on a platter decorated with thin lemon slices. Serve with a side dish of celery, cut in fine strips.

NOTE: If served as a first course, allow 5 oysters per person; if served in combination with other antipasti, let your judgment be your guide as to the proper helping.

157. FRUTTI DI MARE
Frutti di mare

Serve any combination of bivalves, such as oysters, mussels, clams, etc., on the halfshell. They should be kept on ice, opened just before serving, decorated with sections of lemon, and accompanied by slices of buttered rye bread. It is vitally important that they be absolutely fresh.

158. SALT HERRING
Aringhe salate alla semplice

Briefly pass salt herrings over a gas flame, skin, fillet them, and soak fillets in milk for 4 hours to eliminate some of the salt. Dry the fillets with a cloth, arrange on a dish, cover with 1 onion sliced into thin rings, and sprinkle with 4 tablespoons olive oil.

159. SALT HERRING GOURMET
Aringhe salate del ghiottone

12 small salt herring fillets (or 6 medium)
1½ cups milk
2 tablespoons finely chopped onion
2 tablespoons finely chopped scallions
3 tablespoons finely chopped parsley
1 tablespoon finely chopped fresh basil
1 tablespoon finely chopped celery
1 cup Mayonnaise [No. 77]

Soak the herring fillets in milk for 4 hours. Drain, dry, and remove bones. Blend the mayonnaise with all of the vegetables and herbs and cover the herring, arranged on a platter, with this mixture. *Serves* 4.

NOTE: If herring has milt, strain the milt, mix with a little vinegar, and add to the chopped vegetables and mayonnaise.

160. MARINATED SALT HERRING
Aringhe salate marinate

6 salt herring with milt and eggs
1 carrot, sliced
2 medium onions, sliced
2 cloves garlic, crushed in the garlic-press
3 sprigs parsley
½ bay leaf, crushed
Pinch Cayenne pepper
2 cups dry white wine
½ cup white wine vinegar
⅓ cup oil

Singe herring rapidly over a gas flame, remove eggs and milt, skin and cut into fillets; place the fillets in a skillet with their milt and eggs. Put carrot, onions, garlic, parsley, bay leaf, Cayenne, wine, and vinegar in an enamel saucepan over a moderate flame. Bring to a boil, lower flame and simmer 20 minutes or until the carrot is tender. Pour this hot marinade over the herring fillets, cover skillet with oiled white paper (or aluminum foil) and its lid. Cook 15 minutes over moderate flame. Cool to room temperature. Arrange fillets, with eggs and milt, in a deep dish, pour marinade over them, cover with oil, and keep in a cool place for 2 or 3 days. *Serves* 4.

161. SCANDINAVIAN SALT HERRING (ROLLMOPS)
Aringhe alla scandinava

12 salt herrings, with milt (if possible)
3 cups milk

½ cup prepared mustard (Dijon-type preferred)
  mixed with ½ cup finely chopped onion
24 slices dill or garlic pickle
1 quart vinegar (cider vinegar preferred)
1 onion, minced
Bouquet Garni:
  ¼ teaspoon dried thyme
  3 sprigs parsley
  1 bay leaf
8 peppercorns
2 cloves
½ cup oil

Pass herrings over gas flame, skin and clean (reserving milt). Soak in milk 4 hours, changing the milk after 2 hours. Drain, dry with 2 cloths, and cut into fillets on a kitchen board. Spread mustard/onion mixture on the top of each fillet, place 2 pieces of pickle on each, roll up, tie with white thread, and place rolls upright, close together, in a crock.

Pour the vinegar into an enamel saucepan, add minced onion, Bouquet Garni, peppercorns, and cloves; bring to boil over medium heat. After 5 minutes remove from flame, strain through a fine sieve, and cool. Force any milt and eggs removed from the herring through a sieve, place in a bowl, and slowly add the oil. Blend oil/milt mixture with the cold marinade and cover herring rolls with this combination. Store in a cool place for 2 to 3 days. *Serves* 6.

162. SMOKED HERRING SALAD
Aringhe affumicate in insalata

12 smoked herrings
1 tart apple, peeled, cored, and cut into dice
1 tablespoon chopped parsley
1 tablespoon chopped basil
1 teaspoon fennel seeds
6 tablespoons oil
2 tablespoons vinegar
Pinch Cayenne pepper

Choose meaty smoked herrings. Singe them for a few minutes under the broiler or over a gas flame, skin, and remove bones. Cut fish meat into dice. Add the diced apples and mix. Add mixture of chopped parsley, chopped basil, and fennel seeds. Sprinkle with a dressing made of the oil, vinegar, and the pinch of Cayenne pepper. *Serves* 6.

NOTE: Kippered herrings may be used instead of herring. Remove kippers from can, drain, remove skin and bones, and cut into dice. Proceed as above.

163. LENTEN ANTIPASTO
Antipasto quaresimale

6 slices cold, boiled carp
3 hard-boiled eggs, chilled
¾ cup Mayonnaise [No. 77]
1 small jar mushrooms (Italian-style, preserved in oil)
1 small jar artichokes (Italian-style, preserved in oil)
1 cup Sicilian (or Greek) olives

Halve the hard-boiled eggs and cover each half with a tablespoon of mayonnaise. Arrange all of the ingredients decoratively on a platter. *Serves* 6.

164. LOBSTER COCKTAIL
Cocktail di aragosta

6 perfect lettuce leaves (Boston lettuce or romaine)
1 pound cooked lobster meat, diced
12 pickle slices
12 small capers

Place 1 lettuce leaf in each of 6 crystal coupes or small glass bowls. Divide lobster meat among the coupes and cover with Lobster Cocktail Sauce [No. 164a]. Decorate each with 2 pickle slices and 2 capers. Place each cup in a small silver bowl filled with chopped ice. *Serves* 6.

164a. LOBSTER COCKTAIL SAUCE

2 egg yolks
2 tablespoons oil
½ teaspoon lemon juice
½ teaspoon salt
⅛ teaspoon pepper
Pinch paprika
6 tablespoons tomato catsup
Dash Worcestershire sauce
3 tablespoons brandy
2 tablespoons heavy cream

Mix egg yolks with oil and lemon juice, season with salt, pepper, and paprika; beat well to obtain a smooth mixture. Still beating, add tomato catsup, Worcestershire sauce, brandy, and cream; mix well.

165. MULLET WITH SAFFRON
Trigliette allo zafferano

12 ½-pound mullet, cleaned
3 tablespoons oil
Pinch salt
1 clove garlic, crushed in the garlic-press
Bouquet Garni:
   2 sprigs thyme (or ¼ teaspoon dried)
   1 bay leaf
   3 sprigs parsley

Mullet with Saffron (No. 165)

64

SEE
REVERSE
FOR
APTION

1, 3–6. Suggested elaborate presentation of canapés (see Nos. 220–49)

2. Cheese Tartlets (No. 316)

7. Suggested presentation of Tartlets Italiana (No. 317), further garnished with pieces of sweet red pepper, roasted, scraped, and seeded (see No. 145), and small pieces of ham.

1 teaspoon fennel seeds
4 peppercorns, coarsely ground
Pinch saffron
3 tomatoes, peeled, seeded, drained, and chopped
2 cups dry white wine
12 lemon slices, peel removed

Place the fish in a heavy enameled pan which has a tight lid, sprinkle with oil, add salt, garlic, Bouquet Garni, fennel seeds, pepper, saffron, and tomatoes. Cover with the white wine. Slowly bring to boil over moderate heat. Seal pan with oiled white paper (or aluminum foil), then fit lid on. Simmer 15 minutes. Cool in same pan and chill in refrigerator. When ready to serve, arrange fish on oval platter, cover with the sauce, removing Bouquet Garni. Decorate each mullet with a peeled slice of lemon. *Serves* 6.

Mussels in Aspic with Sardine Butter (No. 168)

166. MUSSELS CAPRICCIOSE
Cozze capricciose

2 pounds mussels
1 cup dry white wine
1 cup Mayonnaise [No. 77]
1 tablespoon prepared mustard (Dijon-type preferred)
2 medium cold boiled potatoes, peeled and sliced
2 tablespoons chopped parsley

Scrub the mussels under running water and remove their "beards." Place them in a heavy pot with the wine, cover tightly, and shake the pot over a high flame for 5 minutes, or until the shells open. Pour the contents of the pot into a colander placed over a bowl. Remove the mussels from their shells, allowing any liquid in the shells to drain into the bowl. Strain the mussel liquid through several thicknesses of cheesecloth into a saucepan and boil over high heat until it is reduced to ¼ cup. Cool this reduced liquid and the mussels in the refrigerator. Blend the cooled liquid with the mayonnaise and the mustard, add the mussels, and mix thoroughly. Mound the mussels on a platter, surround with the potato slices, and sprinkle with parsley. *Serves* 4.

167. MUSSELS WITH LEMON
Cozze crude al limone

In Naples at noontime, a variety of succulent mollusks are habitually served, freshly gathered and resting in large, flat baskets on beds of glistening green seaweed. Among the most popular is the mussel, whose flesh, eaten raw, has a delicate and spicy flavor.

2 dozen small, or 1 dozen large, mussels per person, well scrubbed and "beards" removed
Lemon quarters
Parsley sprigs

Open the mussels, or have them opened at the fishmarket. Serve them on the halfshell, resting on beds of chopped ice and garnished with sprigs of parsley; decorate each serving with 2 or 3 lemon quarters. Serve at once. *Serves* 4.

NOTE: Only the *freshest* mussels may be eaten raw. If you have gathered them yourself, make sure that their bed was located in an unpopulated area, or one washed by the cleanest waters. If you purchase them from a fishmarket, be sure to stipulate that you will be eating them raw, so that you will be sold mussels of impeccable reputation.

168. MUSSELS IN ASPIC WITH SARDINE BUTTER
Cozze con purea di sardine alla gelatina

4 pounds mussels, well scrubbed and "beards" removed
1 cup dry white wine
½ envelope commercial gelatin
¼ cup cold water
1 6-ounce can skinless, boneless sardines in olive oil, drained
6 tablespoons butter, softened
Parsley sprigs

Steam the mussels in the wine as directed in No. 166, but reduce the liquid to only ¾ cup. While the liquid is still hot, add to it the gelatin which has been dissolved

65

in the cold water. Stir thoroughly to blend. Chill the mixture in the refrigerator, stirring occasionally, until it becomes syrupy (if it stiffens completely, soften it over hot water). While awaiting the gelatin, mash the sardines with the butter until a smooth blend is obtained. Take half the mussel shells (the better-looking ones) and spoon a little of the sardine butter in each. Place a cold mussel on top, and dribble some of the half-set gelatin over them to mask them completely. Chill until set, and serve garnished with sprigs of parsley. *Serves 6 as a first course, and quite a number of people as a cocktail appetizer.*

169. MUSSELS RAVIGOTE
Cozze alla ravigotta

3 pounds mussels
1 cup dry white wine
2 tablespoons finely chopped onion
½ bay leaf
¼ teaspoon dried thyme
¼ teaspoon coarsely ground (or crushed) black pepper

Clean the mussels as in No. 166. Cook them the same way, but add the above-listed herbs and spices to the wine. After the mussels are cooked, strain the liquid and reduce it to ½ cup. Shuck the mussels and let them cool in the strained liquid. Meanwhile, prepare the following dressing:

½ cup oil
2 tablespoon white wine vinegar
1 tablespoon chopped parsley
1 tablespoon capers
½ small onion, finely chopped
1 teaspoon dried tarragon (or 1 tablespoon fresh, finely chopped)
½ teaspoon salt
⅛ teaspoon pepper
½ cup chopped parsley

Mix all the ingredients together, drain the mussel liquid into it, blend thoroughly, pour over the mussels, and marinate for a few hours in a cool place. *Serves 4.*

170. MUSSELS IN SAFFRON SAUCE
Cozze allo zafferano

2 pounds of cooked shelled mussels [*see* No. 166], reserving the cooking liquid for another use
3 tablespoons oil
2 leeks (white part only), finely chopped
¼ onion, chopped

⅔ cup dry white wine
1 tomato, peeled, seeded, drained, and chopped
½ teaspoon Spanish saffron
Pinch powdered bay leaf
Pinch powdered thyme
¼ teaspoon salt
2 tablespoons chopped parsley

Put the chopped leek and onion with the oil in a saucepan over medium heat. Sauté until they turn yellow, about 2 minutes. Add the wine, tomato pulp, and all the seasoning and herbs except the chopped parsley. Simmer until the liquid is reduced to ½ its quantity. Pour over the cooked mussels in a serving dish and mix. Chill for at least 2 hours. Before serving sprinkle with chopped parsley. *Serves 4.*

171. OYSTERS
Ostriche

Raw oysters on the halfshell are often served alone or as part of more elaborate cold antipasti. Oyster Fritters [No. 1027] or Curried Oysters [No. 1026] may be used as hot antipasti. A full discussion of oysters is given in the section preceding those recipes.

172. NORWEGIAN OR SCOTTISH SMOKED SALMON
Salmone affumicato di Norvegia o di Scozia

Cut smoked salmon in thin slices, place on a platter, overlapping or rolled [*see* page 68], and decorate with sprigs of parsley and lemon quarters or peeled lemon slices. Serve with butter curls and triangles of toast.

NOTE: Nova Scotia smoked salmon may be used, but the Scottish is the best.

173. MARINATED SARDINES
Sardine fresche in escabecio

2 pounds fresh sardines
Flour
1 cup oil
1 small onion, sliced
1 carrot, sliced
5 whole cloves garlic
¾ cup white wine vinegar
2 tablespoons water
1 teaspoon salt
¼ teaspoon pepper

1 bay leaf
Pinch dried thyme
$\frac{1}{4}$ cup chopped parsley

Clean the fish, dip in flour, and fry in hot oil in a frying pan over high heat, a few at a time. Set them aside in a glass or china dish. To the hot oil, add the onion, carrot, and garlic. Stir for half a minute, and then add the vinegar and water. Add the seasonings and herbs and boil for 20 minutes. Pour over the fish, and chill in the refrigerator for at least 2 days before serving to give the vinegar a chance to dissolve the fish bones. The fish should be completely covered with the marinade. *Serves* 6.

NOTE: Almost any small fish may be prepared in this manner.

174. SARDINES IN OIL
Sardine sott'olio

3 tins sardines packed in olive oil
3 hard-boiled eggs, whites and yolks chopped
    separately
1 lemon, cut in 6 sections
2 tablespoons finely chopped parsley
1 sweet pepper, roasted, scraped, and seeded
    [*see* No. 145]

Drain the sardines and remove the skin and bones (or purchase skinless, boneless sardines). Arrange the filleted sardines fanwise on a round platter, alternating with little mounds of egg yolk and egg white. Decorate with the parsley, the pepper, cut in fine strips, and the lemon sections. *Serves* 6.

NOTE: The entire dish may be sprinkled with olive oil and a grating of freshly ground black pepper before serving.

175. SARDINES VENETA
Sardine sott'olio alla veneta

3 tins sardines packed in olive oil
3 tomatoes, peeled, seeded, drained, and chopped
1 clove garlic, crushed in the garlic-press
4 sage leaves (or $\frac{1}{4}$ teaspoon powdered sage)
3 tablespoons butter
Pinch sugar
$\frac{1}{2}$ teaspoon salt
$\frac{1}{8}$ teaspoon pepper
3 hard-boiled eggs, whites and yolks chopped
    separately
1 sweet pepper, roasted, scraped, seeded, and cut into
    strips [*see* No. 145]

Drain the sardines and remove skin and bones (or else purchase skinless, boneless sardines). Arrange fanwise on a platter and put in refrigerator while you make the following sauce: melt the butter in a small saucepan, add the garlic, sauté for 3 minutes, and add the tomato pulp, sage, salt, pepper, and sugar. Cook over a medium flame for $\frac{1}{2}$ hour, stirring frequently to prevent scorching. If too much moisture evaporates, add a very little water. Cool the sauce and pour over the sardines. Decorate with mounds of egg yolk, egg white, and strips of the pepper. *Serves* 6.

176. SHRIMP COCKTAIL
Cocktail di gamberetti o di scampi

1 pound cooked, de-veined shrimp (or scampi)
Lettuce leaves

Proceed as in No. 164, but omit the capers and pickles. Cover the shrimp or scampi with the following sauce:

176a. SHRIMP COCKTAIL SAUCE

1 hard-boiled egg yolk
1 teaspoon prepared mustard (Dijon-type preferred)
3 tablespoons oil
Juice of $\frac{1}{4}$ lemon
Pinch paprika
6 tablespoons tomato catsup
3 dashes Worcestershire sauce
2 tablespoons dry sherry (or 1 tablespoon brandy)
2 tablespoons heavy cream
$\frac{1}{2}$ teaspoon salt
Freshly ground black pepper to taste

Mash the egg yolk with the mustard and add the oil, drop by drop, as for Mayonnaise [No. 77]. Alternate the oil with the lemon juice. When all has been added, mix in the rest of the ingredients. Chill well. *Serves* 6.

Norwegian or Scottish Smoked
Salmon (No. 172): see page 66

177. TUNA SALAD BORGHESE
Tonno sott'olio alla borghese

1 cup Italian-style canned tuna in olive oil
1 cup cold boiled "new" potatoes, diced small
¾ cup Mayonnaise [No. 77]
¼ cup cold mashed potatoes
1 tablespoon finely chopped parsley
1 tablespoon finely chopped uncooked spinach
1 tablespoon finely chopped tarragon (or ½ teaspoon dried)
3 medium tomatoes, cut into wedges
2 hard-boiled eggs, cut in quarters
6 anchovy fillets, washed free of salt [*see* No. 220]
1 pimento (sweet red pepper), roasted, scraped, seeded, and cut into strips [*see* No. 145]
½ cup pitted ripe olives

Mash tuna in its oil, gently fold in diced potatoes, and bind with a sauce made from the mayonnaise mixed with the mashed potatoes and herbs, which have previously been parboiled for 1 minute and drained. Mix all together and mound onto a platter. Garnish with an ornamental arrangement of the tomato sections, hard-boiled eggs, anchovy fillets, slivers of pimento, and olives. Chill thoroughly. *Serves* 4.

178. TUNA-STUFFED ONIONS
Cipolle farcite con purea di tonno

6 medium onions, peeled
1 cup dry white wine

1 cup white wine vinegar
Bouquet Garni:
　¼ teaspoon dried thyme
　1 bay leaf
　3 sprigs parsley
1 clove garlic, crushed in the garlic-press
3 tablespoons oil
1 cup Italian-style canned tuna in olive oil, mashed in its oil

Put the onions in an enameled saucepan with the wine, vinegar, Bouquet Garni, garlic, and oil. Bring to a boil over medium heat, and simmer for about 18 minutes, or until just barely tender. Do not overcook. Allow the onions to cool in the liquid, remove them with a slotted spoon, and chill in the refrigerator. Reduce the cooking liquid over high heat to ½ its quantity; remove from the heat and chill. Remove the core of the onions, fill with the mashed tuna, arrange them on a platter, and chill again. Just before serving, pour the reduced cooking liquid over them. *Serves* 6.

179. TUNA WITH ONIONS
Tonno sott'olio con cipollina fresca

1 cup Italian-style canned tuna in olive oil
1 teaspoon capers
1 small Bermuda onion, peeled and cut in rings
Freshly ground black pepper

Pull tuna into chunks and arrange on a small round platter. Sprinkle with the tuna oil, capers, and black pepper. Arrange onion rings in a linked pattern over the top and serve chilled.

NOTE: Onion rings may be marinated in white wine for ¾ hour. This takes away some of their pungency (the wine may be reserved for future use in salad dressings or sauces).

180. ARTICHOKES VINAIGRETTE
Carciofi alla vinaigrette

12 small young artichokes
Juice of 2 lemons
3 cups White Foundation for Vegetables [No. 1576]
1 cup Sauce Vinaigrette [No. 99]

Remove the tough outer leaves of the artichokes, peel the stem and cut off the end. Cut off the tips of the leaves with scissors and cut out the inner choke by scraping it out with a grapefruit spoon or paring knife. Cut longitudinally into quarters, sixths, or eighths (depending on the size of the artichoke; the sections should be thin). As soon as each artichoke has been prepared, plunge sections immediately into a pan of water containing the juice of 2 lemons. This keeps the vegetable from turning black.

Bring the white foundation for vegetables to a boil in a large saucepan or enamel pot (do not use aluminum or iron), add artichokes and cook for 15 minutes or until done (the outer leaves will come off easily). Drain, rinse with cold water, shake off all excess moisture, chill, and serve with Vinaigrette sauce. *Serves* 4.

NOTE: The artichokes should be quite small, about $3\frac{1}{2}$ to 4 inches long (including stem).

181. ARTICHOKE HEARTS BORGHESE
Fondi di carciofi alla borghese

6 artichoke hearts [*see* introduction to No. 1578]
2 cups White Foundation for Vegetables [No. 1576]
$\frac{1}{2}$ cup oil
$\frac{1}{2}$ cup white wine vinegar (or $\frac{1}{4}$ cup lemon juice)
$\frac{1}{2}$ teaspoon salt
$\frac{1}{8}$ teaspoon white (or black) pepper

Cook the fresh artichoke hearts about 30 minutes in the white foundation for vegetables. When tender, drain and pat dry. While still warm, cover with a marinade made of the oil, vinegar (or lemon juice), and salt and pepper. Leave for 1 hour, and then place in refrigerator until well chilled. When ready to serve, drain, arrange on a small platter, and pour a spoonful of marinade over each heart (remainder of marinade may be reserved for use in salad dressings, etc.). *Serves* 6.

NOTE: Use an enamel or stainless steel pan to cook the artichokes. Aluminum or iron will turn them gray.

182. ARTICHOKE HEARTS, GREEK STYLE
Carciofi alla greca

12 medium artichoke hearts [*see* introduction to No. 1578]
6 tablespoons oil
3 cups water
1 tablespoon fennel seeds
Bouquet Garni:
   1 sprig thyme (or $\frac{1}{4}$ teaspoon dried)
   1 bay leaf
   1 tablespoon celery leaves
$\frac{1}{2}$ teaspoon freshly ground pepper
1 teaspoon salt
4 lemons

As soon as each artichoke heart is prepared, place it in a bowl of water containing the juice of 2 lemons. This prevents them from discoloring. When all the hearts have been prepared, place them in a pot (not iron or aluminum) of boiling, salted water. When the water comes to a boil again, cook them for 8 minutes. Drain, plunge into cold water, and drain again.

While the artichokes are cooking, pour 3 cups of water into a medium-sized saucepan (again, not iron or aluminum), add the Bouquet Garni, the oil, fennel seeds, juice of two lemons (or the juice of 1 lemon and the other thinly sliced and seeded), salt, and pepper. Bring to a boil over moderate heat and boil for 6 minutes. Add the artichoke hearts and cook slowly for 15 minutes. Remove artichoke hearts, reduce liquid over high heat to $1\frac{1}{2}$ cups, put artichokes into a crock or bowl, cover with reduced liquid, let cool, and place in refrigerator overnight. *Serves* 6.

NOTE: Also see Hearts of Fennel, Greek Style [No. 195], and Leeks, Greek Style [No. 197].

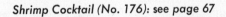

Shrimp Cocktail (No. 176): see page 67

183. ARTICHOKE HEARTS WITH TUNA MAYONNAISE
Fondi di carciofi con purea di tonno

6 artichoke hearts [*see* introduction to No. 1578]
2 cups White Foundation for Vegetables [No. 1576]
½ cup (3½-ounce can) Italian-style tuna in olive oil
½ cup Mayonnaise [No. 77]
1 tablespoon capers

Cook the fresh artichoke hearts in white foundation for vegetables for 30 minutes, or until tender. Drain, rinse with cold water, and pat dry. Mash tuna with its own oil until it is a smooth paste, and mix with the mayonnaise. Spoon the mixture in mounds on the artichoke hearts, smoothing it with the back of the spoon. Decorate with capers and chill for 1 hour. *Serves* 6.

184. MARINATED BEETS
Barbabietole aromatizzate con aceto

Use unpeeled, tender beets of good color. Place on a baking pan or sheet in a medium (375°) oven and bake until done, 25 to 45 minutes, depending on size and age of beets. Cool, peel, and slice. Place in a jar or bowl, cover with an herb vinegar of your choice, and leave in a cold place for 3 or 4 days.

185. MARINATED BEETS, RUSSIAN STYLE
Barbabietole marinate alla russa

Cook beets as in preceding recipe [No. 184]. Peel and slice them, and place in a jar, alternating with thin layers of freshly grated horseradish. Add boiling vinegar (cider or white wine) to cover and marinate 24 hours or more.

186. CANTALOUPE
Melone cantaloup

Cantaloupes should be purchased when exactly ripe, and then kept in the refrigerator until needed. When chilled, they are cut in two, the seeds removed, and the halves garnished with lemon quarters or slices.

In buying cantaloupes, be guided by the aroma indicating ripeness, and the feel of yielding firmness.

187. CARDOONS AND BEETS ITALIANA
Cardi e barbabietole all'italiana

2 pounds cardoons
1 pound beets
4 cups White Foundation for Vegetables [No. 1576]
¾ cup oil
¼ cup lemon juice
1 teaspoon salt
¼ teaspoon pepper

Remove the tough outer stalks from the cardoons, and trim the tops of the stalks. Cut them into 3-inch sections. Cook them in the white foundation for vegetables until tender, about 1½ to 2 hours (they need a great deal of time to cook). If too much liquid evaporates, add more boiling water to keep them covered. Meanwhile, cook beets as described in No. 184. Peel beets when done, slice, and put aside in a bowl. When cardoons are cooked, drain, run cold water over them, and add to beets. Cover the vegetables with a marinade made from the olive oil, lemon juice, and the salt and pepper. Put in refrigerator, and allow to marinate for 24 hours. Serve in the marinade or drain slightly and arrange on a platter. *Serves* 6.

NOTE: Cardoons are a stalky vegetable, looking like an enlarged and coarsened cross between celery and fennel. They are related to the artichoke/thistle family. Cardoons are an indispensable part of the famous *Bagna Cauda* [No. 65] where the inner stalks are eaten raw. The flavor is somewhat bitter, but pleasant, and cardoons are usually found in Italian vegetable markets. They may be grown in the garden. Celery may be substituted if cardoons are not available, but the flavor and texture of this dish will be totally different.

188. MARINATED CARROTS
Carote marinate

1 pound tender young carrots
¾ cup dry white wine
¾ cup white wine vinegar
4 cups water
6 tablespoons oil
2 cloves garlic
Small bunch parsley
1 teaspoon sugar
1 teaspoon salt
Pinch Cayenne pepper
1 teaspoon finely chopped basil (or ½ teaspoon dried)
1 teaspoon prepared mustard (Dijon-type preferred)

Wash and scrape the carrots and cut in medium julienne strips. Put the wine, wine vinegar, water, oil, garlic cloves (uncrushed), parsley, sugar, salt, and Cayenne in an enamel saucepan or small pot. Bring to a boil over moderate heat and cook until the carrots are done (about 10 to 15 minutes; they should still be somewhat crisp). Let them cool in this marinade. When cool, remove them and cook the marinade until it is reduced to about 2 cups. Mix in the mustard, pour over the carrots, sprinkle with the basil, and chill. *Serves* 4.

189. CAULIFLOWER IN VINEGAR
Cavolfiore all' aceto

1 firm, medium head cauliflower (or 1 medium bunch broccoli)
1 small bunch basil (or 1 tablespoon dried)
2 cups white wine vinegar
1 small clove garlic, crushed in the garlic-press
4 tablespoons oil
1 teaspoon finely chopped parsley
1 teaspoon finely chopped chives
Salt and freshly ground pepper to taste

Separate the cauliflower (or broccoli) into small flowerets. Cook in boiling, salted water for 5 minutes. Drain, and place in a fireproof casserole or small enamel pot (do *not* use metal), in which you have placed the basil. Bring the vinegar and garlic to a boil in an enamel or Pyrex saucepan (again, do *not* use metal). Pour over the cauliflower, place the casserole over medium heat, and bring to a boil. Remove at once, cover with a plate, allow to cool, and place in refrigerator overnight. When ready to serve, remove vegetable, shake or pat dry of excessive marinade, sprinkle with oil, herbs, and pepper (salt if necessary). *Serves* 6.

190. CELERY
Sedani alla semplice

Remove outer stalks from celery, trim in even lengths, cut hearts in quarters, prick with fork, and serve them in a tall glass almost filled with ice water.

191. CELERY, GREEK STYLE
Sedani alla greca

2 bunches celery (Pascal or white)
Ingredients for Archichoke Hearts, Greek Style [No. 182], omitting 2 of the lemons

Discard tough outer stalks of celery. Trim off tops, small branches, and leaves, and cut the trimmed stalks into 3½-inch sections. Cook and serve as described in No. 182. Celery may require slightly longer cooking. *Serves* 6.

192. CELERY ROOT (CELERIAC) SALAD
Sedano-rapa alla semplice

1 large celery root
½ cup Escoffier Mayonnaise [No. 79] or Sauce Vinaigrette [No. 99], mixed with 1 tablespoon prepared mustard (Dijon-type preferred)

Peel, wash, and cut the celery root into paper-thin slices about 1½ inches wide. Blanch in slightly salted water for about 5 minutes to remove the bittersweet flavor of the raw root. Drain, let cool, dry between 2 cloths or double thicknesses of paper towels. Cover with the Escoffier mayonnaise or the Vinaigrette sauce mixed with prepared mustard. Serve well chilled. Serves 4 to 6 depending upon the size of the celery root.

193. PICKLED CUCUMBERS
Cetriolini al sale

3 quarts young cucumbers, about 3 inches long
2 quarts water
1 cup salt
¼ pound sugar
Spice Bag:
   1 teaspoon peppercorns
   ¼ teaspoon whole cloves
   1 bay leaf
   ½ teaspoon dried tarragon
   1 clove garlic, crushed in the garlic-press
   ½ teaspoon shredded horseradish

Carefully wash and dry cucumbers; pack in sterilized quart jars. Place remaining ingredients in a saucepan and simmer over moderate heat for 30 minutes. Cool, then pour over cucumbers; seal jars and keep in refrigerator. *Makes 3 quarts.*

71

Eggplant Oriental (No. 194)

194. EGGPLANT ORIENTAL
Melanzane all'orientale

1 cup oil (or more as needed) for frying
2 medium globe eggplants
1 small eggplant
1 clove garlic, crushed in the garlic-press
6 tomatoes, peeled, seeded, drained, and chopped
    (or 2 cups canned Italian-style plum tomatoes,
    drained)
Pinch sugar
1 teaspoon salt
¼ teaspoon pepper
1 tablespoon breadcrumbs
1 teaspoon chopped parsley
Lemon quarters
Stuffed olives

Use the more rounded eggplant, if available, rather than the elongated variety. Peel the two larger eggplants and slice each one lengthwise into 6 equally thick slices. Sprinkle the slices rather heavily with salt and allow them to rest on paper towels for an hour or so. This permits a good deal of their juice to drain off. The process may be speeded up by placing a weight, such as a large platter, or a wax paper-covered cooky sheet, over the slices. Wash off the salt thoroughly and pat slices dry with a paper towel. Quickly fry slices in about ⅓ inch of olive oil until golden brown on each side. As the slices are done, place them on a platter to cool. Meanwhile coarsely chop, but do not peel, the smaller eggplant, salt, and allow to drain, wash and dry it well, and sauté it in a saucepan over medium heat in 3 tablespoons of oil for about 10 or 12 minutes. Remove it to a bowl with a slotted spoon and to the oil

remaining in the pan add the crushed garlic (there should be about 2 tablespoons of oil left; if not, add enough oil to make this amount). Sauté the garlic over rather high heat for 1 minute, add tomatoes and the sautéed chopped eggplant. Season with salt and freshly ground black pepper, add a pinch sugar, the breadcrumbs, and parsley. Simmer, stirring occasionally, for about 15 minutes, or until quite thick. Put aside and cool.

When everything has cooled, assemble as follows: pair eggplant slices so that they are matched in size; spread one slice with the tomato mixture, and cover it with the other slice. Bake the "sandwiches" in a moderate, 350°, oven for 30 minutes, and then cool again. Allow to chill slightly before serving. Garnish with lemon wedges and side dishes of stuffed olives [*see* photograph]. *Serves 4 to 6.*

195. HEARTS OF FENNEL, GREEK STYLE
Cuori di finocchi alla greca

3 bunches fresh fennel
Ingredients for Artichokes, Greek Style [No. 182],
    omitting fennel seeds and 2 of the lemons

Trim the tough outer stalks and feathery tops from the fennel. Cut the hearts into 4 parts each, and proceed as described in Artichokes, Greek Style [No. 182]. (The soaking in acidulated water is not necessary, as the fennel will not discolor when exposed to air.) *Serves 6.*

NOTE: Fresh fennel (which looks somewhat like celery) is available at Italian markets and grocery stores. It may be grown in the home garden.

72

196. GRATED HORSERADISH
Ramolaccio grattugiato

Peel a horseradish root and grate across the grain. This is used to decorate various types of antipasti and as a condiment with bland foods.

NOTE: Freshly grated horseradish is *very* powerful and must be employed with care.

197. LEEKS, GREEK STYLE
Porri alla greca

12 large leeks
Ingredients for Artichokes, Greek Style [No. 182],
   omitting 2 of the lemons

Carefully wash the leeks—as they contain a good deal of sand and gritty soil, great care must be taken to wash it out of the layers that lie near the top of the trimmed stalk. Trim each stalk, leaving about 1 inch of the pale-green top (the tightly layered part, not the looser leaves). Pour the liquid ingredients and seasonings called for in Artichokes, Greek Style into an enamel saucepan and boil them for 6 minutes, add the leeks, bring to a boil, and cook for 8 minutes longer. Remove leeks, reduce liquid as indicated in No. 182, and proceed as in that recipe. *Serves 6.*

198. MACEDOINE OF VEGETABLES
Macedonia di legumi

¾ cup cooked carrots, cut into small cubes
¾ cup cooked peas (petits pois, or small spring peas,
   if available; frozen petits pois may also be used)
¾ cup cooked string beans, cut in ¼-inch pieces
¾ cup cooked celery, cut in small pieces
¾ cup cooked baby lima beans
¾ cup Sauce Vinaigrette [No. 99]
2 tablespoons Worcestershire sauce
3 tablespoons prepared mustard (Dijon-type preferred)
Salt and freshly ground pepper to taste

Mix all the ingredients together and place in refrigerator for 3 hours or more. Serve in a shallow bowl, well chilled. *Serves 6 to 8.*

NOTE: 4 cups of frozen mixed vegetables, cooked according to directions, may be substituted for the vegetables listed above. Also, many combinations of leftover cooked vegetables may be used; i.e. mushrooms, sweet peppers, corn, beets, cucumbers (blanched), broccoli, cauliflower, etc. Leafy vegetables are to be avoided, as they will wilt.

199. MELON CUP
Cocktail di melone

1 large melon (or enough for 6 people) in season
½ cup superfine sugar, or more to taste
¼ cup kirsch, brandy, maraschino, or Port
1 teaspoon lemon juice

Scoop out the melon with a ball cutter, or cut it into neat 1-inch squares. Sprinkle over sugar to taste and the lemon juice. Chill for about 1 hour. Just before serving, drench with the liquor and mix gently but thoroughly. Divide among six glass bowls or coupes and serve at once. *Serves 6.*

200. MUSHROOMS ITALIANA
Funghi di serra marinati all'italiana

1 pound large, perfect mushrooms
¼ cup dried, imported mushrooms
¼ cup oil
3 cloves of garlic, crushed in the garlic-press
1 bay leaf
2 cloves
4 peppercorns
1 sprig rosemary (or 1 teaspoon dried)
Salt to taste
2 jiggers (ounces) of brandy
Juice of ½ lemon

Soak the dried mushrooms in hot water for ½ hour, drain, sauté them in 1 tablespoon of the oil for 10 minutes, and reserve. Wipe the fresh mushrooms with a damp cloth, trim stems, and cut into thick slices. Heat the rest of the oil in an enameled saucepan over

Boletus scaber

Imperial Agaric

Boletus badlus

moderate heat and add both kinds of mushrooms, the garlic, bay leaf, cloves, peppercorns, rosemary, and salt to taste. Simmer gently for about 8 minutes. Add the brandy, allow it to become very hot, ignite, and shake the pan until the flames subside. Add the lemon juice, cover the pan, and simmer for 5 minutes longer. Cool and store in the refrigerator until needed. *Serves* 6.

201. MARINATED MUSHROOMS
Funghi di serra alla semplice

1 pound mushrooms, sliced
3 tablespoons oil
3 cloves garlic, crushed in the garlic-press
1 bay leaf
2 cloves
4 peppercorns
½ cup white wine
Juice of 1 lemon
1 teaspoon salt
⅛ teaspoon pepper

Heat the oil in an enameled saucepan over moderate heat, add garlic, and cook until golden. Add mushrooms, bay leaf, cloves, and peppercorns. Sauté for 3 minutes, mixing well. Add wine and lemon juice, season with salt, cover, and cook over moderate heat 10 minutes, stirring occasionally. Remove to a bowl, season with freshly ground pepper, and keep in refrigerator until needed. *Serves* 6.

202. MARINATED DRIED MUSHROOMS
Funghi porcini marinati

Prepare exactly as Marinated Mushrooms [No. 201], using 4 ounces of dried, imported mushrooms which have first been soaked in warm water for ½ hour and squeezed dry. Cut the mushrooms in small pieces before cooking, if desired. *Serves* 4.

203. OLIVES STUFFED WITH ANCHOVY BUTTER
Olive farcite

Fill large, pitted green olives with Anchovy Butter [No. 108], and chill. Serve mixed with ripe black or green olives.

204. STUFFED OLIVES SICILIANA
Olive farcite alla siciliana

½ teaspoon (¼ envelope) commercial gelatin
½ cup Tomato Paste [No. 144] (or canned tomato paste)
½ cup roast sweet pepper purée (*see* Note below)
1 pound pitted ripe olives, drained

In top of double boiler moisten gelatin with 2 tablespoons of tomato paste and beat over boiling water until dissolved; put to one side. Put the remaining tomato paste and the pepper purée in a small saucepan over moderate heat and cook till thick. Cool, mix with gelatin mixture, place in pastry tube fitted with a small round tube, and fill olives. Serve well chilled. *Serves* 4.

NOTE: The pepper purée is made by first roasting, scraping, seeding, and cutting into strips 4 sweet peppers [*see* No. 145]; sauté the strips gently in a little oil for 15 minutes; and then purée in the blender or through a food mill.

205. BLACK GAETA OLIVES
Olive nere di Gaeta

These olives are available in certain specialty stores. Pile the olives on a round platter; sprinkle them with a little olive oil and a few drops of lemon juice.

NOTE: Gaeta is a resort about 45 miles northwest of Naples. Its olives are famous for their flavor. Greek or Sicilian olives are similar, but the small Gaeta variety are incomparable.

206. NEAPOLITAN BLACK OLIVES
Olive nere alla napoletana

Remove pits from black Gaeta olives. Place in a marinade, to cover, of oil, a little lemon juice, and a pinch each of marjoram and oregano. Marinate in a cool place (not refrigerator) from 1 hour to overnight. Serve on small platter.

74

207. BAKED ONIONS ITALIANA
Cipolle al forno all'italiana

12 medium or 6 large onions, unpeeled
¾ cup oil
¼ cup lemon juice or ½ cup wine vinegar
1 teaspoon dried mustard
1 teaspoon salt
¼ teaspoon pepper
1 sweet pepper, roasted, scraped, seeded, and cut into
  strips [see No. 145]

Trim tops and bottoms of onions, place in a roasting pan, and roast in a moderate oven until they are easily pierced with a fork, about 25 minutes. Cool somewhat, and peel them. Place in a flat bowl and cover with a dressing made from the oil, vinegar, mustard, and salt and pepper. Chill for at least 6 hours in refrigerator, and serve decorated with the strips of pepper (or use canned pimento). *Serves* 6.

208. ONIONS IN VINEGAR
Cipolline all'aceto

24 white onions
6 small hot peppers (fresh, or canned in jars),
  coarsely chopped
1 tablespoon dried tarragon (or 1 small bunch fresh
  tarragon, chopped)
6 cups boiling white wine vinegar

Select small, even-sized onions. Peel and place in an earthenware jar or crock, sprinkling bits of pepper and tarragon throughout. Cover with the boiling vinegar and marinate in a cool place for 8 days. Drain off vinegar and cover again with fresh, boiling vinegar. Cover and store in a cool place. *Serves* 6.

209. MARINATED ONIONS
Cipolline marinate

1 pound small white onions
Marinade for Marinated Carrots [No. 188]

Peel onions and cook as described in No. 188. *Serves* 4.

210. ALGERIAN SWEET PEPPER SALAD
Peperoni dolci all'algerina

8 sweet peppers (green, red, or yellow)
⅓ cup oil
2 tablespoons vinegar
½ teaspoon salt
⅛ teaspoon pepper

Char and peel the peppers as described in No. 145. Remove the stems, seeds, and white membranes. Cut into strips and marinate for at least 1 hour in the oil, vinegar, salt, and pepper. *Serves* 4.

NOTE: Canned Italian-style peppers (packed in water, not brine or vinegar) may be used instead; do *not* use canned pimentos as they are too soft and tasteless.

211. SWEET PEPPER SALAD ITALIANA
Peperoni dolci all'olio e prezzemolo

8 sweet peppers (green, red, or yellow)
⅓ cup oil
3 tablespoons chopped parsley
¼ clove garlic, crushed in the garlic-press
½ teaspoon salt
⅛ teaspoon pepper

Proceed as in the preceding recipe. Do not marinate, but serve at once. *Serves* 4.

212. PROSCIUTTO AND FIGS
Prosciutto di San Daniele con fichi

If prosciutto is not available, use cold Westphalian, Virginia, or country ham. It should be saltier and tangier than ordinary boiled ham. Arrange paper-thin slices on a chilled platter and serve with an appropriate quantity of fresh ripe figs in a bowl over crushed ice. The figs may be peeled, if desired.

NOTE: *See* No. 231 for further information on prosciutto.

213. PROSCIUTTO AND MELON
Prosciutto di Parma e melone

If Italian prosciutto is not available, use cold Westphalian, Virginia, or country ham. It should be saltier and tangier than ordinary boiled ham. Roll in paper-thin slices and serve several to each person with a slice of ripe melon (any kind except watermelon). The only seasoning used is coarsely ground fresh black pepper.

The melon may be detached from the rind and cut into wedges, if desired.

This may also be served as a cocktail snack by skewering a melon ball and a small roll of ham on a toothpick.

NOTE: *See* No. 231 for further information on prosciutto.

214. RED OR WHITE RADISHES
Ravanelli rosa o grigi

Trim the radishes by cutting off the rootlets and most of the leafy tops, leaving a small green stem to facilitate handling and to lend an appetizing color to their appearance. Scrub clean, slash them to make "roses," if desired, but do not peel, as it is the peel that lends the radish its "bite" and savor. Soak in ice water for about 1 hour. Serve ice-cold, or resting on a bed of crushed ice, accompanied by curls of sweet butter and salt.

NOTE: The combination of salt, radish, and sweet butter is typically Continental and extremely delicious.

215. GREEN TOMATO SALAD ITALIANA
Pomodori all'italiana

18 plum tomatoes, slightly underripe and greenish
1 small clove garlic, crushed in the garlic-press
⅓ cup oil
2 tablespoons coarsely chopped basil leaves
1 teaspoon salt
¼ teaspoon pepper

Cut plum tomatoes in half (do not try and substitute regular tomatoes for this, as plum tomatoes are sweeter and, even when underripe, do not have such a high acidity). Mix with oil, garlic, basil, and salt and pepper. *Serves* 6.

NOTE: Because tomatoes are greenish and tart, vinegar should not be used.

216. TOMATOES STUFFED WITH CUCUMBERS
Pomodori con cetrioli

2 large cucumbers
4 medium tomatoes
1½ tablespoons salt
1 tablespoon finely chopped parsley or dill

Peel cucumbers and chop them into small dice. Salt them well and let them stand for ½ to 1 hour. Peel the tomatoes and cut off their tops. Scoop out the seeds and pulp, sprinkle the cavities with a bit of salt and let them stand for ½ hour. Wash the cucumbers by putting them in a sieve and running cold water over them until all the salt has been washed out. Press out all excess moisture, sprinkle with parsley or dill, and fill the tomatoes with the mixture. Sprinkle with additional parsley and serve ice-cold. *Serves* 4.

217. CHILLED GRATINÉE OF TOMATOES AND ZUCCHINI
Zucchine e pomodori gratinati e raffreddati

6 medium tomatoes, slightly underripe
6 small zucchini, unpeeled but thinly sliced
1 tablespoon coarsely chopped basil (or 1 teaspoon dried)
6 tablespoons oil
2 tablespoons breadcrumbs
Pinch sugar
Salt and freshly ground pepper to taste

Cut the tomatoes into halves, horizontally. Remove the stem ends, and gently squeeze the tomato halves to extract as much moisture and as many seeds as possible. Put 2 tablespoons of the oil in a frying pan over medium heat, add the tomatoes, season with salt and pepper and add a pinch sugar, and fry them flat side down for about 5 minutes. Remove them from the frying pan, put in the zucchini and the basil, add 2 more tablespoons of oil, and fry at rather high heat for 5 or 6 minutes until the zucchini are beginning to brown, turning them gently every so often with a wooden spoon to ensure even cooking. Add salt and pepper to taste (*after* frying).

Put 6 of the tomato halves in a straight-sided baking dish, which should be large enough to hold the tomatoes snugly. Cover them with half the zucchini (including the oil they have cooked in), repeat with a layer of the remaining tomato halves, and top with the rest of the zucchini. Sprinkle with the breadcrumbs and the remaining 2 tablespoons of oil, and bake in a 375° oven until the crumbs are slightly browned. Remove, cool, and serve cold, but *not* chilled. *Serves* 6.

218. FRESH TOMATO JUICE COCKTAIL

Cocktail di pomodoro

6 pounds dead-ripe tomatoes
1/4 cup Worcestershire sauce
1/3 cup superfine sugar
2 tablespoons boiling water
1 teaspoon salt
Few grains Cayenne pepper

Use only the reddest and ripest tomatoes. Peel them—either by plunging them in boiling water for 30 seconds or by spearing them with a fork and turning them over a gas flame until their skins split. Pass the tomatoes through a food mill, or press them through a fine strainer into a bowl (putting them in a blender is *not* advisable as the seeds must be eliminated, and the action of the blender will produce a pink foam instead of a rich, red juice). After all the liquid has been extracted, mix in the Worcestershire, salt, Cayenne, and the sugar which has been dissolved in the boiling water. Allow the juice to chill thoroughly, stir it up before serving, and pour into glasses. Serve with lemon quarters, and allow the guests to adjust the seasoning to their own taste with additional salt, freshly ground pepper, and Worcestershire sauce. *Makes about 1 1/2 quarts.*

NOTE: If you have never tried fresh tomato juice before, this is quite a treat. The result is quite unlike the commercially prepared variety and more like a liquid salad. The peak of the tomato season is the best time to try this recipe. The juice may also be frozen for later use, although the freezing takes away much of the freshness.

219. VEGETABLE ANTIPASTO

Antipasto di ortaggi

White truffles, cut in julienne strips
Fresh mushroom caps (or small, whole button mushrooms)
Artichoke hearts
Fennel, sliced
Pickles (a variety to your taste)
Sweet peppers, roasted, scraped, seeded, and cut into strips [*see* No. 145]
White celery, trimmed and cut in even sized stalks
Sauce Vinaigrette [No. 99]

Choose the quantity of ingredients in proportion to the number of persons you wish to serve. On a large platter, arrange neat little mounds of the vegetables.

Cover with a simple Vinaigrette sauce (or with a sprinkling of olive oil, half as much white wine vinegar, salt, and freshly ground pepper).

NOTE: Most of the vegetables may be those found in cans or jars in Italian stores. The only vegetables that should be raw are the fennel, celery, and, if desired, the mushrooms (using only the freshest, whitest, and cleanest ones available).

CANAPÉS

Canapés

Canapés consist of a small piece of bread, toast, or a cracker which is topped by a savory preparation—actually a tiny open-face sandwich. The word *canapé* is French and means "couch" or "sofa." Translated into culinary terms, the base of bread, toast, or cracker acts as a "couch" on which the topping "sits." The ancestor of the canapé was probably the open-face sandwich that is one of the main features of the Scandinavian *smörgåsbord* (*smörgås* is the Swedish name for an open-face sandwich) or Russian *zakousky*.

The bread or toast to be used should be thinly sliced and the crusts removed. The shape of the canapé is limited only to the imagination of the cook—rounds, squares, triangles, diamonds, hearts, etc.; *see* illustration on page 80—and fancy cutters may be purchased for this purpose. As canapés are usually served before dinner, as an accompaniment to cocktails or aperitifs, they should be bite size (no larger than about 1 1/2 inches square), as they ideally are meant to be consumed in one bite.

Meats, fish, poultry, etc. should be thinly sliced or finely chopped. If shrimp are used, they should be very tiny (the Scandinavian variety that come packed in jars are ideal). In other words, all the ingredients should be cut into small pieces no larger than the base, and the edges of the topping should not extend over the

77

base. The beauty of a plate of canapés adds much to its gustatory enjoyment.

To prevent the base from getting soggy, the canapé should be generously spread with butter, at times a flavored butter, before adding the desired topping. The butter acts as a moisture-proofing agent (besides enhancing the flavor of the canapé), but it should be remembered that canapés with toast or cracker bases should not be made more than 1 hour in advance as they tend to become soggy faster than those made with bread bases. Commercially prepared crackers or melba toast are too dry and will become sodden rapidly, and there is nothing so unpalatable as a limp cracker. Besides the fact that their dryness causes them to become sponges, commercial crackers and toasts are far too crisp and their overly crunchy texture does not blend with the smoother preparations used to cover them. Also, crackers are mostly too salty or too individually flavored and tend to overpower the butters and toppings. In all, freshly made toast or fresh bread is preferable, both for its taste and because it will take to longer periods of storage (a slightly soggy piece of toast is much less objectionable than a limp cracker). Bread-based canapés have a slightly higher tolerance, and may be stored for 2 hours or more, unless their topping is very moist (such as fresh tomato or cucumber). When making canapés in advance, remember to cover them with wax paper, aluminum foil, or clear plastic food wrap. Many of the toppings discolor with exposure to air, and some dry out, so a covering is vital.

After a little experience, imaginative cooks may experiment with their own combinations, keeping in mind that certain flavors blend more successfully than others (anchovies and pineapple are *not* recommended, for example). Another point to remember is that ideally the butter should complement the topping—i.e. Anchovy Butter [No. 108] for anchovy canapés, etc.

Note: In most cases actual amounts are not given, only proportions. This is because it will be up to the individual to decide how many canapés are needed. Do remember, however, not to feed your guests too many canapés so that their appetites will be dulled for dinner. On the other hand, if one is giving a cocktail party, a wide variety and plenteous assortment of canapés is a definite asset.

220. ANCHOVY CANAPÉS
Canapés di acciughe

Lightly butter canapé squares with Anchovy Butter [No. 108]. Cover with anchovy fillets arranged in overlapping parallel rows, and garnish with chopped hard-boiled eggs mixed with $\frac{1}{2}$ their amount of finely chopped parsley.

NOTE: Salted whole anchovies should be used in place of the usual canned-in-oil variety. Available in certain Italian specialty stores, one must first wash off the excess salt, then soak them in two changes of water, each soaking lasting about $\frac{1}{2}$ hour. After the excess salt has been washed and soaked away (you can judge their salinity by tasting—they should be less salty than the canned variety), fillet them, wash again, pat them dry on paper towels, place them in a jar, cover them with olive oil (and a few slivered garlic cloves, if desired), and keep them in the refrigerator until needed. If jar is tightly covered and the fillets are immersed in oil at all times, they will last for at least a month.

Anchovy fillets prepared in this manner are much firmer in texture than the canned variety, and also far less salty. Their flavor is incomparably superior.

221. CAVIAR CANAPÉS
Canapés di caviale

White bread, toasted or plain
Sweet butter, softened
Fresh Russian or Iranian caviar
Hard-boiled eggs, the whites and yolks chopped
    separately
Finely chopped scallions or white onions
Lemons

Choose a quantity of ingredients in proportion to the number of persons you wish to serve. Cut thin slices of white bread or toast diagonally, and remove crusts. Spread with softened sweet butter. Cover with caviar, and edge with 2 borders of finely chopped hard-boiled eggs (yolks and whites, mixed together or chopped separately). Serve with side dishes of chopped hard-boiled egg whites, finely chopped scallions or white onions, and thin lemon slices. All should be ice-cold.

NOTE: Do *not* serve caviar in a silver container or with a silver spoon.

222. CONNOISSEUR'S CANAPÉS
Canapés del conoscitore

4 slices white bread, crusts removed and quartered
2 tablespoons butter
$\frac{1}{2}$ cup Piedmontese Fondue [No. 274]
4 slices bacon, sautéed or broiled crisp
Optional: 16 very small slices white truffles
    [or No. 1819a]

Sauté the squares of bread in the butter until golden. When ready to serve, top with a teaspoonful of Piedmontese fondue, crown with a square of crisp bacon, and a slice of white truffle. Serve immediately. *Makes* 16.

NOTE: The bacon may be blanched for 5 minutes to remove excess salinity. Drain and dry before sautéing.

223. DANISH CANAPÉS
Canapés alla danese

4 slices pumpernickel, crusts removed, and quartered
$\frac{1}{2}$ cup Mustard Butter [No. 112]
4 slices smoked salmon, each cut into 4 small pieces
4 slices smoked herring, each cut into 4 small pieces
$1\frac{1}{2}$ tablespoons caviar

Butter the squares of pumpernickel with mustard butter and cover with alternate slices of smoked salmon, herring, and a little caviar. Pipe on a border of mustard butter if you wish. *Makes* 16.

224. EGG CANAPÉS
Canapés di uova sode

4 slices white bread, crusts removed
2 tablespoons butter
2 tablespoons Mayonnaise [No. 77]
3 hard-boiled eggs
3 tablespoons finely chopped tarragon, basil, or parsley

Spread bread first with butter, then with mayonnaise, and then quarter the slices. Center the squares with a slice of hard-boiled egg yolk and surround with finely chopped egg whites. Dust with any combination of the finely chopped fresh herbs. *Makes* 16.

225. EMMENTHAL CANAPÉS
Canapés di emmenthal

Spread bread with Mustard Butter [No. 112] and place a slice of Emmenthal (or Swiss) cheese to fit on top. Trim edges neatly, and cut to desired sizes.

226. FANTASY CANAPÉS
Canapés "Fantasia"

4 slices white toast, quartered
2 tablespoons sweet butter
$\frac{1}{2}$ cup flaked, cooked fish or crabmeat
$\frac{1}{2}$ cup Mayonnaise [No. 77]
1 tablespoon capers

Spread the quarters of white toast with sweet butter. Place a heaping teaspoon of flaked, cooked fish or crabmeat on top of each quarter, cover with mayonnaise, and decorate with a few capers. *Makes* 16.

227. GAME CANAPÉS
Canapés di cacciagione

Spread sweet butter on canapé bases and decorate with thin slices of any type of leftover game, such as venison, hare, pheasant, etc.

228. CANAPÉS ITALIANA
Canapés all'italiana

Butter canapé bases of your choice with sweet butter, over this place a thin slice of Genoa (or any other variety of Italian) salami, trimmed to fit the canapé, and garnish with a border of chopped, hard-boiled egg.

229. CANAPÉS NICE
Canapés alla nizzarda

Spread Anchovy Butter [No. 108] on canapés; cover with sliced, stuffed, black olives, arranged in a decorative pattern, and sprinkle finely chopped fresh onion on top.

230. POKER CANAPÉS
Canapés "Poker d'assi"

These are made exactly as Connoisseur's Canapés [No. 222] except the white truffle slices are eliminated and Mustard Butter [No. 112] is piped around the border of the canapés before serving.

231. CANAPÉS OF SAN DANIELE PROSCIUTTO
Canapés di prosciutto di San Daniele

Spread bread (not toast or cracker) bases with Mustard Butter [No. 112]. Cover with paper-thin slices of prosciutto, trimmed to fit the bases.

Suggested presentation of canapés, from left to right on large trivet: Cheese and Salami Canapés (No. 238); Shrimp Canapés (No. 233); Connoisseur's Canapés (No. 222); and Caviar Canapés (No. 221)

NOTE: Prosciutto is a "raw" ham, that has been cured and prepared in a special manner; it does not need to be (nor, indeed, should it be) cooked. Prosciutto should be sliced paper-thin, and should be eaten as soon as sliced, otherwise it will dry out—the slices being literally as thin as paper. The best prosciutto comes from either San Daniele di Friuli or from Parma. Imported prosciutto is available at most specialty shops in the United States, and the San Daniele variety is available in cans (this variety is excellent, and the fact that it is canned in no way compromises its quality, which in most cases is superior to many "fresh-cut" varieties).

Certain large meat packers in the United States have tried their hand at domestic prosciutto with signal success. As the imported variety is quite expensive, the domestic kind may be recommended as a substitute.

Always buy your prosciutto sliced, as this can be best accomplished by a commercial slicing machine (the canned variety, and certain of the domestic kinds that come pre-packed, are already sliced).

An excellent substitute may be found in Westphalian ham, which is cured by almost the same process. Regular boiled ham makes a very poor substitute as the flavor and texture are totally different.

232. SARDINE CANAPÉS
Crostini di sardella

Using bread or toast squares on which Mustard Butter [No. 112] has been spread, either place skinless, boneless sardines on each, or mash sardines in their oil and spread this mixture on the canapés.

233. SHRIMP CANAPÉS
Canapés di scampi

Spread canapés with Mustard Butter [No. 112]; cover with a whole shrimp (or tiny canned shrimp); and decorate edges with chopped hard-boiled egg.

234. SHRIMP CANAPÉS GOURMET
Canapés di gamberetti

16 medium-sized rounds white bread
2 tablespoons butter
16 large, cooked, peeled, and de-veined shrimp (or about 50 tiny canned shrimp)
½ cup Mayonnaise [No. 77]
2 tablespoons capers

Butter the rounds of bread (butter may be colored pink, if desired, with paprika or a drop of red vegetable coloring). On each round place one large, cooked, peeled shrimp, or several tiny canned ones. Garnish with a border of mayonnaise piped around the edges and a few capers in the center. *Makes* 16.

235. TONGUE CANAPÉS
Canapés di lingua salmistrata

¼ cup Mustard Butter [No. 112]
16 small squares white bread (or pumpernickel)
4 slices cooked smoked tongue, cut into thin strips
4 slices boiled ham, cut into thin strips
2 tablespoons horseradish (commercially prepared)

Butter bread squares with mustard butter. Cover with alternate strips of the smoked tongue and boiled ham. Garnish with horseradish to taste. *Makes 16.*

236. TUNA-CHEESE CANAPÉS
Canapés con formaggio di tonno

1 6-ounce can tuna (Italian-style in oil)
¾ cup provolone cheese, grated
1 tablespoon finely chopped onion
1 tablespoon (or more) heavy cream

Mash the tuna in its own oil until smooth. Add the cheese and onion. Mix well. If the mixture seems too dry, thin with heavy cream. Use as a spread for canapés or sandwiches.

HOT CANAPÉS
Crostini caldi

The bases for these canapés consist of day-old sliced white bread, trimmed of crust and cut into pieces about 2½ by 1½ inches. These are then fried in a mixture of half butter and half oil until they are light brown on each side. The canapés should be served as soon as prepared to avoid their becoming soggy.

HOT ANTIPASTI
Antipasti caldi

These may be served alone, or mixed with the preceding cold appetizers in any combination. They may also be served as a first course, or in place of a fish or egg course at an elaborate dinner. Increase the quantity if they are to be used for a main course.

237. CHEESE CANAPÉS
Crostini al formaggio

2 tablespoons butter
2 tablespoons flour
½ teaspoon salt
Pinch white pepper
Pinch nutmeg
1 cup heavy cream
¾ cup grated Emmenthal (or Swiss) cheese
2 eggs, separated
6 slices bread, prepared for canapés (*see* above)

Melt butter in a saucepan over medium heat and add flour and seasonings. Stirring constantly, add the cream, little by little. When all the cream has been added, cook over a low flame for 5 minutes, stirring occasionally to prevent scorching. Add cheese, and stir until it has melted. Remove from fire and add 2 egg yolks, beating well until they are incorporated into the cheese mixture. Beat the 2 egg whites in a bowl with a pinch of salt. Carefully fold them into the cheese/egg mixture. Spread on bread bases, and place in a hot (400°) oven until well puffed and glazed. Serve at once. *Serves 6.*

238. CHEESE AND SALAMI CANAPÉS
Crostini "moda del fattore"

6 ⅛-inch-thick slices of Swiss cheese
24 thin slices of Genoa salami
6 slices white bread, prepared for canapés (*see* above)

Cover fried bread bases with a slice of Swiss cheese and cover this with salami. Cut each bread base in half, diagonally, and put in a hot (375°) oven for 10 minutes. Serve immediately. *Serves* 6.

239. EGG AND TRUFFLE CANAPÉS
Crostini con uova rimestate e tartufi

6 slices white bread
6 eggs
½ teaspoon salt
⅛ teaspoon freshly ground pepper
1-ounce can of white (Alba) truffles [or No. 1819a]
3 tablespoons butter
½ cup grated Parmesan cheese

Remove the crusts from 6 slices white bread, toast them, butter them, and keep them warm. With a large fork beat the eggs and add the salt and a bit of pepper. Open the can of truffles and drain the liquid into the eggs. Beat well with the fork. Melt the butter in a frying pan, add the eggs, and scramble lightly until they are creamy but *not* overcooked or dry. Slice the truffles thin, arrange the eggs on the toast slices, put one or two slices of truffle on each, sprinkle with Parmesan cheese, and place under a hot broiler for a few seconds to glaze. *Serves 6 as a first course or late snack, or makes 24 canapés if cut in quarters.*

240. CANAPÉS FINANCIÈRE
Crostini con finanziera

⅓ cup Demi-Glaze Sauce [No. 20]
or
A mixture of:
  3 tablespoons Bovril
  3 tablespoons dry Marsala wine
  4 tablespoons brown meat gravy
½ recipe Sauce Financière [No. 32], cooled
2 tablespoons fine breadcrumbs
2 tablespoons butter, melted
6 slices bread, prepared for canapés (*see* above)

Combine the Bovril, Marsala, and gravy in a small saucepan. Cook over a high flame until reduced by 1/3 (or use Demi-Glaze sauce). Combine with the cold Financière sauce. Spread on canapé bases, sprin-kle with breadcrumbs and melted butter, and put in a hot (400°) oven for 2 minutes, or until well glazed. *Serves* 6.

241. GORGONZOLA CANAPÉS
Crostini con gorgonzola

½ cup crumbled gorgonzola cheese, at room temperature
½ cup sweet butter, softened
2 tablespoons brandy
⅛ teaspoon paprika
6 slices bread prepared for canapés (*see* above)

Cream the butter and gorgonzola together until they are totally blended. Add the brandy and paprika, mix in well, and spread on canapé bases or buttered toast bits. Serve at once. *Serves* 6.

242. HAM AND CAPER CANAPÉS
Crostini con capperi e prosciutto in agro-dolce

3 tablespoons superfine sugar
3 tablespoons white wine vinegar
½ teaspoon cornstarch dissolved in 1 tablespoon water
4 tablespoons capers
¼ cup smoked ham, with fat, cut julienne
2 tablespoons small raisins (or dried currants)
1 tablespoon candied fruit, chopped very finely
2 tablespoons pine nuts, cut in half
6 slices white bread, prepared for canapés (*see* above)

Put the sugar in a small enamel saucepan (do not use aluminum), add the vinegar and cornstarch/water mixture. Place over a medium flame and bring to a boil. Cook and stir until mixture becomes transparent. Add the remaining topping ingredients and cook over a low flame for 5 minutes. Taste, and, if too sweet, add a little more vinegar which has previously been reduced in a small saucepan; if too tart, add more sugar. Spoon mixture over canapés and serve at once. *Serves* 6.

243. MIDNIGHT CANAPÉS
Crostini "ghiottoneria di mezzanotte"

6 eggs
¼ teaspoon salt
Grating of black pepper
4 tablespoons butter
6 anchovy fillets
1 tablespoon capers
12 ripe or black olives, pitted and sliced lengthwise
6 slices bread, prepared for canapés (*see* above)

Beat the eggs in a bowl and season with salt and pepper. Melt the butter in a heavy frying pan over moderate heat, add eggs, and scramble until creamy (they should not be dry). Spoon over the slices of bread, prepared as described above for canapé bases. Garnish each slice with an anchovy fillet, some capers and olives, and serve immediately. *Serves 6.*

244. FONDUE CANAPÉS PIEDMONTESE
Crostini con fonduta piemontese

½ recipe Piedmontese Fondue [No. 274]
Optional: 1 small can (1 ounce) white (Alba) truffles
    [or substitute No. 1819a]
6 slices bread prepared for canapés (*see* above)

Allow fondue to cool a little. When thick enough to spread, cover bread bases with the mixture, garnish with chopped white truffles, and glaze in a hot (400°) oven for 3 or 4 minutes. Serve at once. *Serves 6.*

245. SARDINE CANAPÉS SCANDINAVIAN
Crostini "moda del nord"

24 canned, boneless sardines, drained
5 tablespoons Mustard Butter [No. 112]
6 slices white bread, prepared for canapés (*see* above)

Spread fried bread bases with mustard butter. Cover each slice with four sardines, cut diagonally in half, and put in a hot (375°) oven for 10 minutes. Serve immediately. *Serves 6.*

NOTE: A little mustard may be spread over the sardines before they are placed in the oven, if desired.

246. SEAFOOD CANAPÉS
Crostini con frutti di mare

2 tablespoons butter
1 small can tiny shrimp (or ¼ cup small, fresh, shelled), chopped
1 small can mussels (or ¼ cup fresh, shelled), chopped
1 small can chopped clams (or ¼ cup, fresh, shelled, and chopped)
¾ cup very thick Sauce Mornay [No. 56]
Salt and freshly ground pepper to taste
4 tablespoons breadcrumbs browned in 1 tablespoon butter
6 slices bread, prepared for canapés (*see* above)

Melt the butter in a small saucepan, and briefly sauté the shellfish (if they are raw, cook them for 5 minutes at high heat). Incorporate the Mornay sauce and then add salt and pepper to taste. Spread the seafood mixture on hot canapés and sprinkle them with breadcrumbs. Place them in a 450° oven for 5 minutes or until nicely browned and glazed. Serve at once. *Makes 2 dozen small canapés.*

247. TOMATO AND ANCHOVY CANAPÉS
Crostini con alici e pomodoro

8 anchovy fillets
2 cloves garlic, crushed in the garlic-press
3 tablespoons oil
1 tablespoon finely chopped onion
3 unripe green tomatoes, peeled, seeded, drained, and cut into strips
Freshly ground pepper to taste
6 slices bread, prepared for canapés (*see* above)

Mash 5 of the anchovy fillets with the garlic. Sauté the chopped onion in the oil in a frying pan over medium heat until it becomes golden; then add the mashed anchovies and garlic. Add the tomatoes and sauté briskly for about 5 minutes, being careful that the tomatoes do not become mushy. If moisture in pan has not reduced sufficiently (the mixture should be on the dry side), raise flame and cook for a minute or two more. Grate some pepper on the mixture and spread it on the canapés. Garnish with the remaining anchovy fillets, coarsely chopped. Serve at once. *Serves 6 as an appetizer.*

248. LUIGI VERONELLI CANAPÉS
Crostini alla Luigi Veronelli

½ recipe Piedmontese Fondue [No. 274]
12 slices bacon
6 tablespoons sweet butter
12 slices white bread, each cut in 4 triangles and prepared for canapés (*see* above)

Prepare the fondue and let it cool somewhat. Grill bacon in the oven, drain on absorbent paper, and cut each slice into 4 sections. Spread fondue on canapé bases, previously buttered with a little softened sweet butter. Cover fondue topping with a piece of bacon. Put in a hot (375°) oven for 2 or 3 minutes. Serve at once accompanied by some Dijon- or German-type mustard and mustard pickles. *Serves 6.*

83

249. WINE MERCHANTS' CANAPÉS
Crostini "Mercante di vini"

5 or 6 sweet Italian sausages, cooked and skinned
¾ cup Red Wine Sauce [No. 26]
6 slices of white bread, prepared for canapés (see above)

Cut the fried bread bases in half, diagonally. Slice sausages and arrange on bread, cover with red wine sauce, and place in a hot (375°) oven for 8 to 10 minutes. Serve immediately. *Serves 6.*

CROQUETTES
Crocchette

Croquettes usually consist of finely chopped cooked meats and/or vegetables that have been combined with a thick sauce that binds them together. For each 2 cups of basic ingredients, about ¾ cup of sauce is the standard mixing proportion. Both are mixed together while the sauce is still warm and the mixture is then left to cool or chill. In this way the croquette mixture becomes easier to shape. The size of the croquettes varies according to whether they are to be served at the table or passed around with cocktails or aperitifs and thereby meant to be eaten with the fingers. However, it is a good idea to remember not to make them too large or unwieldy as they have a tendency to split open during the cooking process if they have been made outsized. The largest should be about the size of a large egg.

Cooking croquettes: When you have shaped the croquettes into the desired forms—cones, cylinders, balls—they must be first dipped into beaten egg and then carefully rolled in fine breadcrumbs. After this has been accomplished, they may be allowed to rest for an hour or so in a cool place before they are to be cooked. Just before serving, place a few at a time in a frying basket, leaving about 1 inch between each croquette, for if they touch they may burst open during the frying process. Immerse the frying basket into deep fat or oil which has been pre-heated to 375°. Cook them until they are golden brown, drain them, and place on absorbent paper for further draining. Keep in a warm place until all are cooked and serve accompanied by the indicated sauce. They should be served as soon after cooking as possible, as long standing or reheating tends to dull their flavor and make them soggy.

250. ARTICHOKE CROQUETTES
Crocchette con fondi di carciofi

8 tablespoons butter
2 large onions, thinly sliced
3 tablespoons flour
3 cups Chicken Bouillon [No. 326], or Substitute White Stock [No. 1a]
1 medium bunch parsley, tied with a string
Pinch nutmeg
1 cup mushrooms
½ cup water or Chicken Bouillon [No. 326]
5 cooked artichoke hearts [see introduction to No. 1578]
Optional: 2 tablespoons chopped truffles or Mock Truffles [No. 1819a]
2 egg yolks
Salt and freshly ground pepper to taste
1 egg, beaten with 1 tablespoon water
Flour
Breadcrumbs
Fat for deep frying
2 cups Cream Sauce [No. 55] or Tomato Sauce [No. 19]

Melt butter in a saucepan. Measure out 1½ tablespoons and put aside. Add sliced onions to remaining butter and cook over medium heat, covered, until the onions are translucent but not browned. Sprinkle with the 3 tablespoons flour, stirring to obtain a smooth mixture. Slowly add the chicken bouillon, stirring to prevent lumps. Add the parsley bunch and nutmeg. Cook over medium heat, uncovered, for 15 minutes. Meanwhile, take the 1½ tablespoons of reserved butter and place in a small saucepan together with the mushrooms and ½ cup water (or broth, for added flavor). Add a grating of pepper, and cook for 10 minutes, covered, over a medium flame. Drain, reserving cooking liquid, chop mushrooms, and put them aside.

Remove parsley bunch from the simmering sauce, and then pass sauce through a fine sieve to obtain a purée (or put in blender at high speed for 10 seconds). Return purée to the stove, add ½ of the liquid the mushrooms cooked in and a grating of pepper, and simmer over medium flame until the mixture has been reduced by ½. To avoid scorching, it is best to temper the flame by placing the saucepan on an asbestos pad and to stir from time to time. Taste and adjust seasoning.

Chop artichoke hearts and truffles, and mix with chopped mushrooms. Beat the egg yolks with remaining mushroom liquid and, off the heat, add to the purée mixture, stirring constantly to prevent curdling. Return to low heat and cook for 2 minutes; then remove from fire again and add chopped ingredients. Pour onto a buttered platter and let cool for at least 2 hours. When cool and solidified, turn out by tablespoonful onto a lightly floured board and shape into the form of miniature artichoke bottoms (or shape into little rounds). Dip in beaten egg and then roll gently in breadcrumbs. Cook according to directions above for Cooking Croquettes (page 84). Serve at once accompanied by a bowl of Cream Sauce [No. 55] or Tomato Sauce [No. 19]. *Serves* 4.

251. CHICKEN CROQUETTES
Crocchette di pollo

2 cups cooked chicken, very finely diced
3 cups Béchamel Sauce [No. 18]
$\frac{1}{4}$ pound mushrooms, sliced
3 egg yolks
2 tablespoons butter
Salt and pepper to taste
1 egg beaten with 1 tablespoon water
Flour
Breadcrumbs
Fat for deep frying
2 cups Tomato Sauce [No. 19]

Make certain the chicken contains no skin or bits of bone before dicing. Put the Béchamel into an earthenware casserole or heavy enamel saucepan, place over medium heat on an asbestos pad, and simmer until reduced to about 1 generous cup. Stir from time to time to prevent scorching. In another pan, cook the mushrooms, covered, in 1 tablespoon of butter for 8 minutes. Drain, chop, and reserve the liquid they cooked in. When cool, pour this liquid into the egg yolks, beat well, and slowly add this mixture, off the heat, to the reduced Béchamel. Cook, stirring constantly, over low heat for 2 minutes; then remove from stove. Add the remaining butter, the diced chicken, and the chopped mushrooms; taste and adjust seasoning. Pour onto a buttered platter and cool for at least 2 hours. When sufficiently cool and solidified, form into little croquettes with moistened hands, dredge lightly with flour, dip into beaten egg, and roll gently in breadcrumbs. Cook according to directions above for Cooking Croquettes (page 84). Serve accompanied by a bowl of tomato sauce or any other desired sauce. *Serves* 4 *to* 6.

252. CODFISH CROQUETTES ITALIANA
Crocchette di baccalà all'italiana

1 pound dried salt cod
$\frac{1}{2}$ pound mushrooms
6 tablespoons butter
$\frac{1}{4}$ cup prosciutto [*see* Note to No. 231], cut in small strips
3 cups thick mashed potatoes (cold)
2 egg yolks
1 whole egg, beaten
Breadcrumbs
Flour
Fat for deep frying
Parsley
Optional: 1 truffle (white or black), sliced
$1\frac{1}{2}$ cups Tomato Sauce [No. 19]

Soak the salt codfish in a large enamel, pottery, or glass bowl for 12 hours, changing the water at least 3 times during the process. Put fish in an enamel saucepan with fresh water to cover, bring to a boil, and cook for 20 minutes over a low flame. Drain and cool. Flake the cooled fish, discarding bones and skin (if any). Cook the mushrooms in $1\frac{1}{2}$ tablespoons of the butter for 8 minutes, covered; drain; chop coarsely; and add to flaked fish. Melt the rest of the butter in a saucepan over medium heat, add the fish, mushrooms, optional truffle, and the prosciutto. Remove from flame after 1 minute, let cool for a minute or two, and beat in the mashed potatoes alternately with the egg yolks. Let mixture stand until completely cool. Taste and add salt only if necessary. Form into little pear-shaped croquettes, dredge them lightly in flour, dip gently in the beaten egg, and then roll in breadcrumbs. They may rest at this point in a cool place. When all are made, fry them, a few at a time, in deep fat at 375°. Place on absorbent paper and keep warm until all are cooked. Garnish with parsley and serve accompanied by the tomato sauce. *Serves* 6.

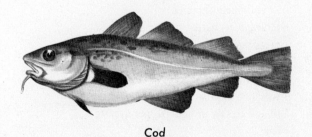

Cod

253. GAME CROQUETTES
Crocchette di selvaggina

2 cups cooked leftover game (venison, rabbit, etc.)
1 cup mushrooms, finely chopped
4 tablespoons butter
1 tablespoon chopped truffle or prosciutto
3 cups Demi-Glaze Sauce [No. 20], reduced to 1 cup
3 tablespoons dry Marsala wine
Flour
1 egg, beaten with 1 tablespoon water
Fine breadcrumbs
Freshly ground black pepper
Fat for deep frying

Cook the chopped mushrooms in 3 tablespoons of butter in a frying pan over medium heat for 10 minutes. Dice the game meat finely and add to the mushrooms, along with the truffle or prosciutto, the reduced Demi-Glaze, the Marsala, and a grating of pepper. Heat through, remove from fire, and pour onto a buttered platter, brushing the top of the mixture with the remaining tablespoon of butter (this keeps a crust from forming). Cool for at least 2 hours. When cool and solidified, take a tablespoonful at a time and, with moistened hands, roll into balls, dredge lightly in flour, dip in beaten egg, and roll lightly in breadcrumbs. Cook according to directions above for Cooking Croquettes (page 84). *Serves 4 to 6.*

NOTE: These may be served with an accompanying bowl of Marsala Sauce [No. 43].

254. GAMEBIRD CROQUETTES
Crocchette alla cacciagione

Make exactly as Game Croquettes [No. 253], substituting leftover cooked gamebird meat (pheasant, mallard, quail, partridge, etc.) for the game meat.

255. SEAFOOD CROQUETTES DIEPPE
Crocchette alla dieppoise

1 cup cooked, shelled mussels [*see* introduction to No. 1019] finely chopped
1 cup peeled shrimp, cooked [*see* No. 256], de-veined, and finely chopped
6 tablespoons butter, melted
1 tablespoon oil
1 cup mushrooms, sliced
3 cups Béchamel Sauce [No. 18]
1 teaspoon paprika
Salt and freshly ground pepper to taste
Flour

Breadcrumbs
1 egg beaten with 1 tablespoon water
Fat for deep frying
Parsley
1 cup White Wine Sauce [No. 76]

Put the oil and 1 tablespoon of the butter into a saucepan, and cook the mushrooms, covered, over medium heat for 8 minutes. Drain, chop them finely, and combine with the shrimp and mussels. In an earthenware casserole or a heavy enamel saucepan, reduce the Béchamel to 2 scant cups. This is best accomplished by placing an asbestos pad between the heat and the utensil, stirring frequently to prevent scorching. When reduced, add the paprika, the seafood/mushroom mixture, and the remaining butter. Mix well, season to taste, and remove from heat. Pour onto a buttered platter and let cool for at least 2 hours. When cool and solidified, take a tablespoonful at a time and with moistened hands roll into little balls, dredge lightly with flour, dip in beaten egg, and roll lightly in breadcrumbs. Cook according to directions above for Cooking Croquettes (page 84). Garnish with parsley and serve with an accompanying bowl of white wine sauce. *Serves 4 to 6.*

256. SHRIMP CROQUETTES
Crocchette di scampi

1 pound shrimp, peeled
4 tablespoons butter
1 cup mushrooms
3 cups Béchamel Sauce [No. 18]
2 egg yolks
Salt and pepper to taste
Flour
1 egg beaten with 1 tablespoon water
Breadcrumbs
Fat for deep frying
1½ cups Marsala Sauce [No. 43] or Cream Sauce [No. 55]

Cook shrimps in butter over high heat until they are pink and have lost their transparent look (this should take no more than 5 minutes, as overcooking will toughen them). Remove shrimp with a slotted spoon, cool, de-vein, and chop. Add mushrooms to butter in pan and cook, covered, for 8 minutes over moderate heat; when cooked, remove them, reserving cooking liquids, and chop them finely. In an earthenware casserole or a heavy enamel saucepan, simmer the Béchamel on an asbestos pad over medium heat until reduced by $\frac{1}{2}$. Stir occasionally to prevent scorching. When sufficiently reduced, take off the heat, add the egg yolks which have been beaten with the cooking liquid from the mushrooms, return to low heat, stir constantly for 2 minutes, and remove from the stove. Add the shrimp and mushrooms and mix well. Pour onto a buttered platter and cool for at least 2 hours. When cool and solidified, form into balls with moistened hands, dredge lightly with flour, dip into beaten egg, and roll gently in breadcrumbs. Cook according to directions above for Cooking Croquettes (page 84). Serve accompanied by a bowl of Marsala sauce or cream sauce. *Serves 4 to 6.*

SMALL CROQUETTES

Fondanti

Small croquettes constitute one of the best ways to utilize leftover game, chicken, meat, fish, shellfish, and vegetables. The usual proportions for this type of croquette are 3 parts leftovers, finely chopped or puréed, to 1 part of very thick reduced sauce.

257. ASPARAGUS CREAM CROQUETTES

Fondanti di crema di asparagi

1 pound fresh asparagus, peeled and trimmed (or 2 packages frozen)
$\frac{3}{4}$ cup very thick Béchamel Sauce [No. 18], or undiluted, condensed canned cream of asparagus soup
Salt and pepper to taste
1 egg yolk
Flour
1 beaten egg
Breadcrumbs
Fat for deep frying
Parsley sprigs

Cook the asparagus until they are barely tender, drain, and cool. Chop or purée only those parts which are not woody or tough (or use frozen asparagus—do *not* use canned, as they are too mushy). You should have slightly more than 2 cups. Mix with the Béchamel or canned cream of asparagus soup, salt and pepper to taste, and egg yolk. Chill until quite cold to facilitate handling. Take a large teaspoonful of the mixture and form it into whatever shape is desired (round, pear-shaped—using a sliver of truffle as a stem—etc.).

Dredge lightly with flour, dip in beaten egg, and roll lightly in fine breadcrumbs (extreme deftness should be employed, as these little croquettes should be delicate in texture, and heavy handling will cause them to fall apart). Allow them to rest for 1 hour, or longer, in a cool place and then fry in deep hot (375°) fat until they are golden brown. Drain well on absorbent paper and then arrange them in a pyramid shape on a platter covered with a paper doily, garnished with sprigs of parsley. *Makes about 24 small croquettes.*

258. CARROT CROQUETTES

Fondanti di carote

$\frac{1}{2}$ pound cooked carrots
$\frac{3}{4}$ cup very thick Béchamel Sauce [No. 18]
Salt and pepper to taste
1 egg yolk
Flour
1 egg, beaten
Breadcrumbs
Fat for deep frying

Purée the cooked carrots by passing them through a fine sieve or whirling them in the blender for a few seconds. Mix in the thick Béchamel, which should be cool, salt and pepper to taste, and the egg yolk. Proceed in the same manner as described in Asparagus Cream Croquettes [No. 257]. *Makes about 24 small croquettes.*

259. GAME CROQUETTES

Fondanti di cacciagione

$2\frac{1}{4}$ cups finely chopped or ground leftover game (pheasant, partridge, rabbit, etc.)
$\frac{3}{4}$ cup puréed chestnuts (canned or freshly made)
$\frac{1}{2}$ cup finely chopped truffles, or substitute Mock Truffles [No. 1819a]
Salt and freshly ground pepper to taste
1 egg yolk
Flour
1 egg, beaten
Breadcrumbs
Fat for deep frying
2 cups Pepper Sauce [No. 25]

Mix game, chestnut purée, truffles, and egg yolk until well blended. Proceed in the same manner as described in Asparagus Cream Croquettes [No. 257]. Serve accompanied by the pepper sauce. *Makes about 24 small croquettes.*

260. HAM CROQUETTES
Fondanti di prosciutto

2¼ cups finely ground lean cooked ham
¾ cup very thick Béchamel Sauce [No. 18], made
    without salt
Pepper to taste
1 egg yolk
Flour
1 egg, beaten
Breadcrumbs
Fat for deep frying

Mix ground ham, cooled Béchamel, pepper, and egg yolk until well blended. (If ham is very salty—such as prosciutto, or Virginia—blanch in simmering water for 5 minutes and cool before chopping.) Proceed in the same manner as described in Asparagus Cream Croquettes [No. 257]. *Makes about 24 small croquettes.*

261. CROQUETTES LUCULLUS
Fondanti "Lucullo"

1½ cups pâté de foie gras (or any good liver pâté)
¾ cup finely ground cooked chicken
¾ cup very thick Sauce Parisienne [No. 21], cooled
    (or undiluted condensed canned cream of chicken
    soup enriched with an egg yolk)
Salt and pepper to taste
Flour
1 beaten egg
Breadcrumbs
Fat for deep frying

Mix together the pâté, ground chicken, and cooled Parisienne sauce. (If using condensed cream of chicken soup, after adding an egg yolk to it cook it in a double boiler over hot, not boiling, water, stirring constantly until it coats a spoon. Allow it to cool before adding to the pâté and chicken.) Add salt and pepper to taste. Proceed in the same manner as described in Asparagus Cream Croquettes [No. 257]. *Makes about 24 small croquettes.*

262. PARMESAN CREAM CROQUETTES
Fondanti di crema al parmigiano

¾ cup plus 1 tablespoon sifted flour
1 cup grated Parmesan cheese
½ teaspoon salt
⅛ teaspoon freshly ground white pepper
2 whole eggs and 6 egg yolks
2 cups rich milk
4 tablespoons butter
Flour
1 egg, beaten
Fine breadcrumbs
Fat for deep frying

Mix the sifted flour, Parmesan, salt, and pepper in a saucepan. Blend in the whole eggs and yolks, adding them one at a time and beating well after each addition. Put the milk into a small saucepan, bring it just to a boil, and pour it into the cheese/flour/egg mixture, stirring constantly. As soon as all the milk has been added, place the mixture over a medium flame and slowly bring to a boil, stirring constantly. Cook for 1 minute, then remove from the stove, and beat in 3 tablespoons of the butter. Pour the mixture into a buttered, shallow baking dish and spread the top with the remaining butter to prevent a crust from forming. Allow the mixture to cool thoroughly. Just before serving, take heaping teaspoonsful of the mixture, roll lightly with floured hands, brush with beaten egg, and toss lightly in fine breadcrumbs. Fry in deep hot (375°) fat, and serve in the same manner as described in Asparagus Cream Croquettes [No. 257]. *Makes about 24 small croquettes.*

263. SOLE CROQUETTES
Fondanti di sogliola

1½ cups finely ground cooked sole (or flounder) fillets
¾ cup finely ground cooked, shelled, and de-veined
    shrimp
¾ cup very thick Béchamel Sauce [No. 18]
½ teaspoon paprika
Salt and pepper to taste
1 egg yolk
Flour
1 egg, beaten
Breadcrumbs
Fat for deep frying

Mix ground sole (or flounder) fillets, shrimp, cooled Béchamel, paprika, salt and pepper, and egg yolk until well blended. Proceed in the same manner as described in Asparagus Cream Croquettes [No. 257]. *Makes about 24 small croquettes.*

264. SWEETBREAD CROQUETTES
Fondanti di animella

2 cups leftover sweetbreads (broiled or boiled)

1 cup Sauce Parisienne [No. 21], reduced and quite thick

½ cup chopped white truffles, or substitute Mock Truffles [No. 1819a]

1 egg, beaten

Salt and pepper to taste

Flour

Breadcrumbs

Fat for deep frying

Parsley sprigs, fried in deep fat [*see* Note to No. 276]

Lemon wedges

Chop the sweetbreads and the truffles finely, or put them through the meat grinder, using the finest blade. Mix them with the Parisienne sauce, which should be quite cold and thick. Taste, and adjust seasoning. Proceed in the same manner as described in Asparagus Cream Croquettes [No. 257]. *Makes about 24 small croquettes.*

Finished Croustades (see Nos. 265-73)

CROUSTADES
(BREAD TARTLETS)

Croste

Croustades are little filled tartlets whose crusts are made from squares of crustless white bread, hollowed out, deep fried until golden brown, and filled. Instead of frying them, the Croustades may be brushed with melted butter and baked in a 300° oven for about 30 minutes or until crisp and nicely browned. They may also be baked or fried in large sizes and used as crusts for pies. Croustades are made as follows:

Take a loaf of unsliced white bread that is about a day old. Carefully remove the crusts so that the bread has straight sides (*see* photograph). Cut the loaf into thick slices, at least 1½ inches thick, and cut each of these slices into 4 cubes or squares. With the tip of a small, sharp knife cut half way down, about ¼ inch inside the edge (see picture). A grapefruit knife is useful for this purpose as it is curved and this makes the square easier to remove later on. Fry the bread squares until brown in deep fat or oil, heated to about 375°, or brush with melted butter and bake in the oven. When cooked (if fried, they must be well drained on absorbent paper) and cool enough to handle, carefully remove the pre-cut center with the tines of a small fork. Pick out the soft bread from the inside and from the bottom of the little lid, fill as desired, replace the lid, and serve as shown in the photograph above.

Preparing the bread cases for Croustades: see text above

265. CROUSTADES OF BEEF MARROW WITH RED WINE
Croste con midollo di bue al vino rosso

1½ cups beef marrow
½ cup Red Wine Sauce [No. 26]
2 truffles (white or black), sliced, or substitute Mock Truffles [No. 1819a]
Salt and freshly ground pepper to taste
12 Croustades with their lids (see above)
12 thin lemon wedges
Sprigs of parsley

Gently poach the marrow in barely simmering lightly salted water for 4 minutes. Drain and cut into coarse dice. Gently fold in red wine sauce, taste and adjust seasoning, and pour into warm Croustades. Top with a slice of truffle and cover with lids. Serve garnished with lemon wedges and sprinkle with finely chopped parsley. *Serves 6 as an appetizer.*

266. CROUSTADES OF LAMB'S OR CALF'S BRAINS
Croste con cervella d'agnello

3 tablespoons butter
3 tablespoons finely chopped scallions (including some of the green part)
1 pound calf's or lamb's brains, blanched [see Preparation of Brains: introduction to No. 1385]
½ teaspoon salt
Freshly ground pepper to taste
12 Croustades with their lids (see above)
6 lemon wedges
6 sprigs parsley

Melt 2 tablespoons of the butter in a frying pan over medium heat and cook the scallions until translucent but not brown. Add the brains, the salt, and pepper to taste. Sauté gently for 5 minutes. Remove the brains and the scallions with a slotted spoon. Chop the brains coarsely and mix well with the scallions. To the remaining butter in the frying pan add an additional tablespoon and turn up the flame to allow the butter to become browned (be careful not to burn it, though). Add the brains and scallions and turn off the flame. Mix well, season to taste, and spoon into the little Croustades. Place in a hot (400°) oven for 5 minutes and serve at once garnished with parsley and lemon quarters. *Serves 6 as an appetizer.*

90

267. CHEESE CROUSTADES
Croste al formaggio

These are a cross between French toast and a grilled cheese sandwich. In classic French cuisine they are known as Croques Madame *or* Croques Monsieur *and are made in the same way, except the bread is not soaked in an egg/milk mixture. This type of Croustade differs from the other types in this section in that one need not prepare a separate bread base.*

12 slices of day-old sandwich bread (or thinly cut French or Italian bread), crusts removed
¾ pound Swiss, Gruyère, or mozzarella cheese, thinly sliced
1 cup scalded milk
2 whole eggs
1 egg yolk
½ teaspoon salt
Pinch white pepper
6 tablespoons butter
Freshly ground pepper

Beat the eggs in a wide, shallow bowl. Add the scalded milk, beating well, and the salt and pepper. Dip each slice of bread in the mixture, and when all have been immersed, leave them in the bowl for ½ to 1 hour. Melt some of the butter in a large skillet (an electric frying pan is useful here) and, when it sizzles, place as many slices of bread in the pan as will fit without crowding. Cover each slice with cheese, taking care that the cheese does not overlap the edge of the bread. Grate a small amount of pepper on the cheese. Cover with another slice of the soaked bread and fry over low heat until the bottom is brown. Carefully turn with a spatula and fry until the second side is brown. When first batch is done, transfer to an oven-proof platter and keep in a warm oven until all the sandwiches have been cooked. *Makes 6 sandwiches.*

NOTE: These sandwiches may be made more festive by adding a slice of prosciutto (or smoked ham) on top of the cheese and serving the cooked sandwiches with an unctuous Béchamel Sauce [No. 18] made with heavy cream and seasoned with a little grated Parmesan or Gruyère cheese.

268. GAME CROUSTADES
Croste di cacciagione

1 cup leftover cooked game (venison, hare, pheasant, mallard, etc.), chopped
½ cup Demi-Glaze Sauce [No. 20]

1 tablespoon Game Essence [No. 12] or bottled meat
  extract
3 tablespoons soft breadcrumbs (utilizing bread removed
  from the center of the Croustades), fried in 1
  tablespoon butter
12 Croustades with their lids (*see* above)
6 lemon wedges
6 sprigs parsley

Mix the first three ingredients in a small enamel sauce-pan over medium heat until heated through (do *not* cook for any length of time). Fill the Croustades, cover with their lids, and sprinkle with the fried breadcrumbs. Serve plain, or garnished with lemon quarters and sprigs of parsley. *Serves 6 as an appetizer.*

269. CROUSTADES OF VEAL KIDNEYS MARSALA

Croste con rognoncino al marsala

1½ cups cooked Veal Kidneys Trifolato [No. 1428]
¼ cup Marsala wine
12 Croustades with their lids (*see* above)
Parsley sprigs

Prepare Veal Kidneys Trifolato as described in No. 1428, substituting the Marsala for the lemon juice. Fill warm Croustades and cover with their lids. Serve at once, garnished with sprigs of parsley. *Serves 6 as an appetizer.*

270. LIVER CROUSTADES

Croste con fegatelli di maiale

Although the original Italian recipe calls for pork liver, calf's or lamb's liver may be used. Do not use beef liver, as it is too strong.

½ pound pork, calf's, or lamb's liver
3 tablespoons butter
1 bay leaf
½ teaspoon salt
¼ teaspoon freshly ground black pepper
½ cup Tomato Sauce [No. 19]
12 Croustades with their lids (*see* above)

Cut the liver into ½-inch-thick slices, and then cut these slices into diamond-shaped pieces with sides ½ inch long. Trim off any membranes or tubes. Melt the butter in a frying pan over medium heat, add the bay leaf and the liver, and season with the salt and pepper. Turn up the flame and sauté rapidly, turning the pieces so that they will brown evenly. Sauté 2 or 3 minutes, depending on the size of the pieces of liver.

Do not overcook or they will be tough. Add the tomato sauce and heat through. Remove the bay leaf and spoon into warm Croustades. Cover with their lids and serve at once. *Serves 6 as an appetizer.*

NOTE: The livers from a suckling pig should be used if pork liver is employed.

271. CHICKEN LIVER AND SAGE CROUSTADES

Croste con fegatini di pollo all'erba salvia

½ pound chicken livers
3 tablespoons butter
½ teaspoon dried sage
½ teaspoon salt
⅛ teaspoon freshly ground pepper
½ cup White Wine Sauce [No. 76]
12 Croustades with their lids (*see* above)

Wash chicken livers and cut them into small pieces. Dry well and sauté them in the butter over a high flame for 5 minutes, seasoning them with the sage and salt and pepper. When they are well browned, add the white wine sauce and cook over very high heat for 5 minutes more. Pour into the Croustades and serve at once. *Serves 6 as an appetizer.*

272. MUSHROOM AND CREAM CROUSTADES

Croste con funghi alla crema

1 pound mushrooms, sliced
¼ cup imported, dried mushrooms
4 tablespoons butter
½ teaspoon salt
½ teaspoon freshly ground pepper
1½ cups heavy cream
12 Croustades with their lids (*see* above)
2 lemons, thinly sliced
6 sprigs parsley

Soak the dried mushrooms in hot water for 1 hour. Drain, chop, and cook them in a little water for about ½ hour (very little water should remain in pan, about 1 or 2 tablespoons). Melt the butter in a large enamel saucepan or frying pan, add the cooked dried mushrooms and their remaining liquid. Sauté gently for about 5 minutes. Add the sliced mushrooms and cook for about 5 minutes, turning often to ensure even cooking, over moderate heat. Add the salt, pepper, and cream and cook at high heat for 5 minutes, stirring to prevent sticking. Lower heat and continue cooking until liquid has reduced by 2/3. Taste and adjust seasoning. Add 2 or 3 tablespoons additional cream if the sauce seems too thick, and spoon into warm Croustades, cover with their lids, and serve garnished by slices of lemon and sprigs of parsley. *Serves 6 as an appetizer.*

273. CROUSTADES REGINA
Croste alla reine

1½ cups cooked chicken (all white meat, if possible)
½ cup heavy cream (or sour cream)
½ teaspoon salt
¼ teaspoon white pepper
¼ teaspoon paprika
4 tablespoons butter, softened
2 tablespoons breadcrumbs
12 Croustades with their lids (*see* above)
6 lemon wedges
2 tablespoons chopped parsley

Grind chicken in meat grinder twice, using the finest blade. Place in a bowl and slowly add the cream, working it in with a wooden spoon. Add seasonings and 2 tablespoons of softened butter. Beat well for a minute or two. Melt remaining butter in a small pan, add breadcrumbs and brown them lightly. Spoon the filling into the Croustades, cover with a sprinkling of the butter-browned breadcrumbs, and place in a 375° oven for 5 to 10 minutes to glaze the tops. Cover with their lids, and serve garnished with lemon wedges and finely chopped parsley. *Serves 6 as an appetizer.*

FONDUE

Fonduta

In Italy, fondue is a Piedmontese specialty. It may be served as an especially delicious hot antipasto or as a light supper or luncheon dish.

274. PIEDMONTESE FONDUE
Fonduta piemontese

2 cups fontina cheese, cut in tiny cubes
½ cup rich milk, or light cream, scalded
2 egg yolks beaten with 2 tablespoons hot milk
2 tablespoons butter, melted
½ teaspoon salt
1-ounce can white (Alba) truffles, or substitute Mock Truffles [No. 1819a]
4 slices toast, crusts removed, each cut in 4 triangles

Put the cubed fontina in the top of a double boiler, add scalded milk or cream. Place over simmering (not boiling) water and stir vigorously until smooth and creamy. Do not overcook beyond this point as the mixture will become stringy. Add the egg yolks mixed with the 2 tablespoons hot milk, the melted butter, and salt. Stir constantly until thick and shiny. Arrange toast triangles in 4 previously heated ramekins or small casseroles and pour the fondue over these. Garnish with the white truffles, which have been sliced paper thin. Serve at once. *Serves 4.*

NOTE: Do not attempt to make this ahead of time and reheat it in the oven before serving. This will only coagulate the mixture and give it a "skin" over the top.

The truffles, though not obligatory, give the dish its characteristic flavor and should not be omitted. The accompanying photographs show an alternative method of preparing the dish that does not call for the use of a double boiler. If using this latter method, make sure the water bath is not boiling or simmering, merely scalding hot.

If fontina cheese is not available, sweet (non-aged) Munster cheese might be substituted, although the result will not be as creamily unctuous.

The preparation of Piedmontese Fondue (No. 274): see text above

FRITTERS
Bignè

Fritters as appetizers are usually savory bits that have been dipped into a batter and deep fried. They may also be made from cream-puff dough which has been specially seasoned and augmented, usually with cheese, or with mashed potatoes enriched with egg yolks and specially seasoned. Remember to make these fritters bite size. A mild vegetable oil is best for frying, and should be heated to about 375°. Never fry too many of these small fritters at the same time and always be sure to drain them well on absorbent paper.

275. FRITTER BATTER
Pastella per bignè

¼ cup sifted flour
3 whole eggs
¼ teaspoon salt
Few grains Cayenne pepper
½ to ⅔ cup light cream

Mix flour with eggs, salt, and Cayenne until a smooth mixture is obtained. Stirring briskly, add the cream in a slow stream until the batter is the consistency of very heavy cream. Another method is to put all ingredients into the blender and mix for 10 seconds at high speed. After batter is mixed, it should be placed in the refrigerator for at least 2 hours, and beaten lightly before using. *Makes about 1 ¼ cups.*

276. ANCHOVY FRITTERS
Bignè di acciughe salate

½ pound salted anchovies, boned and washed free of
    salt [*see* No. 220]
Fritter Batter [No. 275]
Fat for deep frying
Parsley
Lemon quarters

Canned anchovy fillets, packed in oil, are not recommended for this dish as they will be too flimsy in texture and probably too salty. Dip the fillets individually into the fritter batter and fry them in deep fat pre-heated to 375° until they are well puffed and golden-brown. Drain well and keep them in a warm place on absorbent paper until all are cooked. Do not pile them one on top of another as this will make them soggy. Serve at once, accompanied by lemon quarters and fried or fresh parsley.

NOTE: Fried parsley is an unusually tasty garnish and may be prepared as follows—select luxuriant sprigs of fresh parsley, dredge in a *little* flour, fry in deep, hot (375°) fat for about 2 or 3 minutes, drain well, and keep until needed in a warm place on absorbent paper.

277. FISH FRITTERS
Bignè di pesce

1 cup salt herring
1 cup leftover cooked fish, boned and mashed
1 cup Cream Puff Dough [No. 1990], omitting sugar
Fat for deep frying
2 lemons, cut in quarters
6 parsley sprigs, deep fried [*see* Note to No. 276]

Scald herring, then skin it. Remove bones and cut into small pieces. Mix herring and mashed fish into cream puff dough. Drop a few teaspoonsful at a time into fat which has been pre-heated to 375°, and fry until they are brown on both sides. Remove with slotted spoon and drain on absorbent paper. Serve hot, on a folded napkin, decorated with lemon quarters and fried parsley sprigs. *Serves 6.*

278. FRITTERS ITALIANA
Bignè all'italiana

2 cups cooked white meat of chicken, finely diced
1 cup lean cooked ham, finely diced
1 cup cooked lamb's brains, prepared as indicated in
    the introduction to No. 1385 and finely diced
1⅓ cups freshly grated Parmesan cheese
3 egg yolks
⅛ teaspoon pepper
Fritter Batter [No. 275]
Fat for deep frying
2 cups Tomato Sauce [No. 19]

Place the first 6 ingredients in a bowl and mix well. With moistened hands, shape the mixture into walnut-sized balls, place on a platter, and chill for about 2 hours. Just before serving, dip them into the fritter batter and fry a few at a time in the fat, pre-heated to 375°, until browned. Drain well on absorbent paper and serve hot, accompanied by the tomato sauce. *Serves 6.*

Anchovy

279. PARMESAN FRITTERS
Bignè al parmigiano

1½ cups Cream Puff Dough [No. 1990], omitting sugar
⅓ pound freshly grated Parmesan cheese
Pinch paprika
6 sprigs parsley, deep fried [*see* Note to No. 276]
Fat for deep frying

When making the cream puff dough, add the grated cheese and paprika at the same time as the flour. When prepared, drop by teaspoonful, a few at a time, into the fat, pre-heated to 375°. Let brown nicely, being sure they turn over once while cooking. Remove with slotted spoon and drain well on absorbent paper. Serve on a folded napkin garnished with fried parsley sprigs. *Serves 6.*

280. WHITEBAIT FRITTERS
Bignè di bianchetti

1 pound whitebait
1 cup sifted flour
2 tablespoons oil or melted butter
1 cup tepid water
1 teaspoon salt
2 egg whites, beaten
Fat for deep frying
3 lemons, quartered
6 sprigs parsley, deep fried [*see* Note to No. 276]

Make a smooth batter from the flour, butter (or oil), water, and salt. Carefully fold in the beaten egg whites and the whitebait. Drop by spoonsful into deep hot (375°) fat. Remove with a slotted spoon when crisp and brown and drain on absorbent paper. Sprinkle with a little salt. Garnish with lemon quarters and the parsley deep fried in fat for two seconds. *Serves 4 to 6.*

PASTIES OR TURNOVERS
Pâtés

In Italy, these are preparations of cooked meat, poultry, fish, shellfish, or game, enclosed in a crust: ordinary pie crust dough, Puff Paste [No. 1960], or Rich Pastry [No. 1955].

Basic preparation:
These pasties are usually served as an antipasto or a light luncheon entrée. Roll out the dough to ⅛-inch thickness. With a cookie cutter or pastry cutter, cut into 3-inch rounds or rectangles 3 by 3½ inches. Place a rounded tablespoon of the stuffing on half the pieces, moisten the edges with water (to effect a perfect seal), and cover with the remaining pieces of dough, whose edges have also been moistened. Press the edges together well with your finger or with the floured tines of a fork to seal in the stuffing. Prick the tops once with a fork, brush with beaten egg, and arrange on a baking sheet slightly moistened with water. Bake in a hot (375° or 400°) oven for 15 minutes, or until nicely browned. If you want to serve the pasties with cocktails or aperitifs, make them smaller in size.

281. HAM PASTIES
Pâtés piccoli con prosciutto

1½ cups Forcemeat [No. 129] made with cooked lean ham
½ recipe Puff Paste [No. 1960], or any other flaky pie crust desired
1 egg, beaten

Proceed as described above. *Makes 12 pasties.*

282. ONION PASTIES
Pâtés piccoli con cipollina fresca

1½ cups Forcemeat [No. 129], made with veal
2 tablespoons finely chopped scallions
½ recipe Puff Paste [No. 1960], or any other flaky pie crust desired
1 egg, beaten

On a lightly floured board or pastry cloth, roll out the puff paste ⅛ inch thick. Cut into 24 round or rectangular pieces with a cooky or pastry cutter. Arrange 12 of these on a lightly floured surface. Mix the chopped scallions with the forcemeat. Divide the mixture evenly among the 12 pieces of pastry, leaving a margin of about ¼ to ½ inch around the edge. Brush the edges of these with a little water and do the same for the remaining 12 pieces. Cover with the remaining 12, pressing the edges together well with a floured fork or fingers to effect a perfect seal. Prick the tops once or twice with the tines of a fork, brush the pasties with the beaten egg, and place on an unbuttered cooky sheet. Bake in a 400° oven for about 15 minutes, or until well puffed and golden brown. Serve at once on a warm platter which has been covered with a napkin or paper doily. *Makes 12 pasties.*

283. SHRIMP PASTIES

Pâtés piccoli con code di scampi

1½ cups Forcemeat [No. 129], made with cooked
    shrimp (or scampi)
1 tablespoon butter
Pinch salt
½ recipe Puff Paste [No. 1960], or any other flaky pie
    crust desired
1 egg, beaten

Add the butter and salt to taste to the shrimp forcemeat, and proceed as described above. *Makes* 12
pasties.

284. SMOKED TONGUE PASTIES

Pâtés piccoli con lingua salmistrata

1½ cups Forcemeat [No. 129], made with cooked
    smoked tongue
1 tablespoon finely chopped scallions
½ recipe Puff Paste [No. 1960], or any other flaky pie
    crust desired
1 egg, beaten

Add the chopped scallions to forcemeat made with
tongue, and proceed as described above. *Makes* 12
pasties.

PIES AND TARTS

Crostate

Pies served as a first course may be made with the
following crusts: Flaky Pastry [No. 1954], Rich Pastry
[No. 1955], and the finest, Puff Paste [No. 1960].
Of course, any non-sweet crust of your choice may be
used, the only reservation being that one should keep
in mind the filling to be used; if the filling to be baked
in an uncooked crust is very moist, a less rich pastry
will have less chance of becoming soggy. If the crust
is to be pre-baked, then richness does not matter.
In fact, the richer the better, just so long as it is not so
fragile that the pie cannot be served without the support of its baking pan. Other crusts may be Egg Pasta
Dough [No. 482], or the almost strudel-type dough
called for in the Easter Pie Genovese [No. 288].

None of the crusts for these first-course pies should
contain sugar. The choice of fillings is almost limitless,
and the imaginative cook will find this diversity of
choice both delightful to the palate and helpful to the
budget, as leftovers may be served up in as grand a
style as one could desire. The fillings may consist of
creamed vegetables, enriched with plenty of butter;
chopped chicken or meat; shellfish or fish; rich stews
or ragouts; or cheese or vegetable custards.

If served as a first course, the portions should be
small, so as not to glut the diners. However, these pies
make perfect supper or luncheon dishes when served
as the main course, and accompanied by a salad and
a light dessert.

Two standard methods of baking crusts for first-
course pies are listed below; however, if one's pastry
hand is "heavy," or if a pleasant change is desired, a
hollowed-out loaf of unsliced white bread, with its top
sliced off, its crust removed, liberally buttered on the
inside, and browned in a hot oven, makes a delicious
pre-baked crust. The top may be employed as a cover,
or the bread tart may be served uncovered. It is important to remember that for this bread-crust, the
filling must be added at the last moment before serving,
otherwise the crust will be soggy and the retaining walls
of crisp bread may give way—thus causing an unsightly
dish. This is also advisable for pre-baked pastry crusts
that are to be served after they have been removed from
the pie tin or tart ring in which they have been baked.
(*See* Croustades, page 89.)

If the filling to be baked in an uncooked crust is
very moist, select a crust that is not too rich. (Puff paste
should always be pre-baked, as a filling will impede its
rising and the bottom will be unpleasant: heavy and
very soggy.) Bake the filled crust in a 375° oven for
40 to 50 minutes for an uncooked filling, and in a 400°
oven 15 to 20 minutes for fillings whose ingredients
are pre-cooked (considerably less time is necessary if
both pre-cooked crust and filling are hot).

Pre-baked crusts may be baked by the following
classic methods:

First method

Butter a pie tin, straight-sided spring form, or
bottomless tart ring set on a baking sheet. These should
be about 8 inches in diameter, and about 1 to 1½ inches
deep. Line with desired crust which should be pre-
chilled for at least 2 hours and rolled out about ⅛ inch
thick, except for noodle-like pastry, which should be
almost paper thin, or puff paste, which should be
slightly more than ¼ inch thick. Prick the crust all
over with the tines of a fork (this prevents air bubbles
from blistering the crust during baking), line the inside
with white parchment paper or aluminum foil, and fill
this with dried beans, peas, or rice. This keeps the
crust from slipping down the sides of the tin—which
it tends to do if rich—and also keeps the bottom from

95

rising in bumps and bubbles. If using a puff-paste dough, *do not line the crust in this manner,* but proceed as follows: cut a circle of puff paste the exact size desired, and place on a baking sheet, then cut a long strip about ⅜ of an inch wide, moisten the perimeter of the bottom crust with water or milk, gently lay the strip around the edge to form a little "fence" and lay another strip on top of this, moistening the first strip. The moistening helps the "fence" to adhere to the bottom crust, and the method of making this "fence" of pastry allows the puff paste to rise in its full glory.

Bake the crust in a hot oven, about 400°, for 15 to 20 minutes. If the lining has been employed, remove the paper and the peas, beans, or rice after about 15 minutes of baking when the pastry is "set." This allows the crust to brown more easily. Continue baking for another 5 minutes, or until brown. The dried peas, beans, or rice are not wasted; one merely cools them off, puts them in an airtight container, and uses them over and over again for this purpose. This method is by far the best for producing an evenly shaped crust and cannot be recommended too highly for both first-course or dessert pies and tarts.

Second method

This is recommended for a less rich crust and for puff paste, which, as noted above, should be baked without a lining. Line your buttered tin with the desired crust and prick the bottom all over with the tines of a fork. Bake at 400° until well browned. To lessen the danger of the crust sliding away from the side, do not butter the tin, but moisten the sides slightly.

NOTE: *Never fill an unbaked crust with a hot filling—the heat of the filling will destroy the unbaked pastry by melting the shortening.*

Most professional chefs and experienced cooks prefer to use bottomless tart or "flan" rings, since the baked pie can easily be slid off the baking sheet onto a serving dish by pushing the ring, and then the ring is removed by simply lifting straight up. The result is an attractive, free-standing pastry. (*See* also Flans, page 213.)

285. BURGUNDIAN PIE
Crostata salata alla moda di Borgogna

This is the Italian version of the classic French Quiche Lorraine.

½ pound lean bacon or parboiled, sliced lean salt pork
Optional: ½ pound Swiss or Gruyère cheese

4 eggs
2 cups heavy cream
¼ cup melted butter
Rich Pastry [No. 1955] for a one-crust, 8-inch pie

Grill bacon lightly until it is slightly brown but not crisp. If using salt pork, boil in 2 changes of water for a total of 30 minutes, drain, and grill the same as the bacon. Drain bacon or salt pork on absorbent paper, cut into bite-sized pieces, and cool slightly. Line an 8-inch spring form or pie pan with the pastry, rolled out to ⅛-inch thickness. Put pieces of bacon on bottom of crust (an equal amount of Swiss or Gruyère cheese may also be added, if desired). Add the butter to the eggs, beat lightly, add the cream, and pour the resulting mixture over the crust. Bake in a 350° oven for 35 minutes, or until the top is well-browned and glazed. Serve at once, or serve slightly warm. *Serves 4 to 6.*

NOTE: If a crisper undercrust is desired, pre-bake pie crust for 10 to 15 minutes, and then add filling.

286. CAPRICE TART
Crostata salata capricciosa

3 tablespoons butter
1 cup boiled ham, cut in strips
1 pound Gruyère or Swiss cheese, cut in strips
4 eggs
2 cups heavy cream (or 1 cup milk and 1 cup heavy cream)
1 teaspoon salt
½ teaspoon freshly grated white pepper
Pinch nutmeg
2 tablespoons freshly grated Parmesan cheese
1 unbaked 8-inch pie shell, made with Rich Pastry [No. 1955]

Melt 1 tablespoon of the butter in a small frying pan. Add the ham, which has been cut in fine julienne strips no more than 2 inches long, and frizzle over a medium flame until the ham begins to brown. Classically, the unbaked pie shell should now be filled, but, since this has a custard filling, the best way to avoid a soggy undercrust is as follows: line the pie tin with the pastry (it would be best to use a straight-sided spring form or tart ring on a baking sheet) and fill it with beans, rice, or peas as previously described. Bake in a 400° oven 10 minutes, or until the crust has set but not browned. The upper edges may brown a bit, but this may be avoided by folding the paper or foil lining over them to protect them. While the crust is baking, cut the cheese into julienne strips about 2 inches long and ⅛-inch square. Lightly beat the eggs; add the salt, pepper, and nutmeg; and gradually beat or stir in the cream. When the crust has been in the oven for 10 minutes, remove it, carefully pour off the peas, beans, or rice, with equal care lift out the paper or foil liner, and add the ham and cheese, distributing them in an even layer over the bottom. Gently pour over the egg/cream mixture, dust the top with Parmesan, dot with the remaining butter, and place in a 375° oven for 30 minutes, or until a knife blade thrust into the center of the filling comes out clean. Let the tart rest for about 10 minutes after removal from the oven. This allows the custard to set. Serve then, or serve when barely lukewarm (do *not* serve chilled, as cold ruins the texture and makes the filling tough). *Serves 5 as a main course or 8 as a first course.*

287. FONTINA PIE ITALIANA
Crostata salata italiana di fontina

1½ cups sifted all-purpose flour
½ cup butter, softened
¼ cup dry white wine and White Stock [No. 1], mixed
  (⅛ cup of each)
½ teaspoon salt

On a pastry board, or smooth-surfaced table, arrange the flour in a well. In the center of the well put the butter, salt, and wine and stock mixture. Incorporate all these ingredients with the tips of your fingers until a light dough has been formed. If it is too moist, add a bit more flour. Take care not to overmix or dough will be tough. When mixed, wrap lightly in a floured cloth and place in a cool place for ½ to ¾ of an hour. Meanwhile, prepare a filling of the following ingredients:

½ pound fontina cheese, cubed in small pieces
2 eggs, beaten
½ cup dry white wine
2 tablespoons freshly grated Parmesan cheese
½ teaspoon salt
Pinch nutmeg

Beat the eggs and wine together, using a fork. Add the Parmesan, salt, and nutmeg. Roll out the pastry on a lightly floured pastry cloth or board and line an 8-inch spring form with it, trim, and fold edges neatly all around. Distribute the fontina evenly over the bottom of the crust, pour the wine/egg mixture over this, and bake in a 350° oven for 35 minutes, or until the top is nicely browned and well puffed Serve at once. *Serves 4 to 6.*

NOTE: Fontina is a mild Italian cheese, rather like Munster in texture, but slightly nuttier than the latter. Half Swiss and half Munster may be substituted in this recipe, but the flavor and texture of the pie will not be the same.

288. EASTER PIE GENOVESE
Crostata salata alla genovese—Torta pasqualina

This is a traditional regional specialty. It is rather difficult to make, but, as it is delicious and very festive in appearance, it is well worth the effort by the venturesome or the experienced cook.

2 pounds all-purpose flour (unbleached)
1½ cups water, more or less
3 tablespoons oil
2 teaspoons salt

Place the flour on a smooth surface and make a well in the center; add the water, salt, and oil to make a firm but moist dough, rather like the consistency of a noodle dough [*see* No. 482]. Knead this for about 15 minutes, or until it is smooth to the touch and no longer sticks to the hands. The kneading process is important as it releases the gluten in the flour and makes the dough elastic and workable. The amount of water varies with the quality of the flour; more may be added if necessary. After the dough has been kneaded, place it in a warm bowl, cover it with a clean cloth, and let it rest for about ½ hour. After this time has elapsed, remove the dough, divide it into 20 equal pieces (reserving a few trimmings), place on a lightly floured cloth, and cover with a *slightly* dampened (*not* wet) cloth. Let it rest while you prepare the following filling:

2 pounds beet greens (very small artichokes are a traditional substitute, or spinach—not traditional, but good)
2 tablespoons butter
¾ cup oil, or more as needed
2 tablespoons chopped fresh marjoram or parsley
¾ cup freshly grated Parmesan cheese
1¼ pounds ricotta cheese (if absolutely necessary, small-curd creamed cottage cheese may be substituted)
½ cup heavy cream
⅓ cup melted butter
12 eggs
2 tablespoons flour
Salt and freshly ground pepper to taste
1 egg beaten with 1 tablespoon oil

Wash the beet tops or spinach in several changes of water to rid them of sand. Pat dry, and chop finely with a kitchen knife (do *not* use a chopper or blender as they will liquefy the vegetables). Put the 2 tablespoons of the butter in a large enamel or stainless steel saucepan, add the beet greens or spinach, sprinkle with 1 teaspoon of salt, and cook for 5 minutes, covered. Remove cover, raise heat, and cook for another 5 minutes, stirring the chopped leaves so that all are evenly cooked. There should be very little liquid in the pan, but if the mixture seems soggily damp, remove the leaves with a slotted spoon, pressing out the moisture against the side of the pan, and allow the resulting liquid to reduce to about 2 tablespoons. If artichokes are to be used, cook only the hearts, peeled stems, and tenderest inner leaves of the fresh kind. Either frozen or fresh, there should be about 2½ cups of artichokes, cooked until *almost* done [*see* introduction to No. 1578] drained, and chopped coarsely. When the vegetables have been cooked and drained, place them on a plate, sprinkle them with about 2 tablespoons of oil, 1 tablespoon of marjoram, and ½ cup of the Parmesan.

Mix the ricotta with the cream in a large bowl and add the 2 tablespoons of flour and 1 teaspoon of salt. Beat well to obtain a smooth mixture.

By this time the pieces of dough will be ready to roll out. Take one at a time, and roll it out very thinly on a lightly floured pastry cloth. It should form a large circle about 14 inches in diameter, and be as thin as noodle dough. Place the first layer of dough into a 12 inch, deep spring form which has been lightly oiled. Press it in gently, being careful not to tear the dough. When snugly in place, roll out the second piece of dough until it is the same size and thickness as the first, and with a pastry brush, paint the first layer with a generous coating of oil, place the second layer over this, and repeat the process until 10 layers have been used up. Do *not* oil the top of the last layer. Now spoon in the beet greens, forming an even layer, sprinkle with a tablespoon of oil, and cover them with a layer of the ricotta (or mix both together with 3 tablespoons of oil). With a spoon make 12 evenly spaced hollows around the edge of the filling big enough to receive an egg. Carefully break 1 egg into each of these hollows, endeavoring to keep it to itself as much as possible (it should not spread out, but almost act as though it were egg-shaped, with the filling serving as its retaining shell). Sprinkle each egg with a grating of fresh pepper, a few grains of salt, the remaining marjoram, and Parmesan; sprinkle the melted butter over the top of the filling. Roll out the other 10 pieces of dough,

one by one, and cover the pie as follows: toss on the first layer lightly, trapping as much air as possible between it and the filling, press lightly around the edges to keep the air in, brush lightly with oil, and repeat this until all 10 layers are used. As much air should be trapped between the layers as possible (the original recipe calls for one to "blow air between each layer," which is not only difficult, but perhaps indelicate to the Anglo-Saxon mind). Before placing the last layer of dough, prick the other nine with the tines of a fork (or an ice pick) to allow some of the steam to escape during baking (this causes a domed effect on the top crust). Cover with the tenth layer, trim the edges evenly, folding to seal them; make a long braided rope with the trimmings. This goes around the edge, serving both as decoration and sealer. Moisten this slightly with water before pressing down. Brush the top of the pie with the beaten-egg/oil mixture, put in a 350° oven, and bake for about 1½ hours. Serve at once. *Serves* 12.

NOTE: Photograph facing page 144 shows a pie that was baked with the cheese and vegetable layers mixed together, and eggs that were soft boiled and shelled before setting into the pie. Ideally, the crust should rise as depicted, but even if it doesn't this is a delicious dish. It may also be served lukewarm or cold.

289. CREAMED MUSHROOM TART
Crostata salata di funghi alla crema

¾ pound white mushrooms
6 tablespoons butter
½ small onion, finely chopped
¼ clove garlic, crushed in the garlic-press
½ cup imported, dried mushrooms, soaked in hot water
     for ½ hour, drained, and cooked for ½ hour in
     1 tablespoon butter
2 tablespoons dry Marsala wine
1 cup heavy cream
1 cup thick Béchamel Sauce [No. 18]
½ cup freshly grated Parmesan cheese
Salt and freshly ground pepper to taste
1 baked 8-inch pie shell, made with Rich Pastry [No.
     1955]

Pre-cook the pie crust as directed in the First Method on page 95. Cut the white mushrooms into thick slices, sauté over a medium flame in 4 tablespoons of the butter, adding the chopped onion, garlic, a generous grating of pepper, and the cooked dried mushrooms.

When they have begun to brown slightly, add the Marsala and turn up the flame. Scrape the pan with a wooden spoon to loosen any of the crusty particles that might have adhered. Cook briskly until only a tablespoon of liquid (exclusive of melted butter) remains. Add the cream and simmer over a medium flame for 5 minutes, stirring from time to time. Add the Béchamel, salt to taste, and bring to a boil. Pour into the baked pie shell, sprinkle the top with Parmesan, dot with remaining butter, and place in a hot (400°) oven for 5 minutes. Serve at once. *Serves* 6.

NOTE: This is equally delicious when served in a puff paste shell. *See* introduction above.

290. REGENCY TART
Crostata salata "Régence"

$\frac{1}{2}$ recipe Puff Paste [No. 1960]
1 cup mushrooms
4 tablespoons butter
$\frac{1}{4}$ pound chicken livers
$\frac{1}{2}$ cup milk
3 tablespoons imported, dried mushrooms, soaked in
    hot water for $\frac{1}{2}$ hour, drained, and cooked for
    $\frac{1}{2}$ hour in 1 tablespoon butter
2 tablespoons dry Madeira wine
$1\frac{1}{2}$ cups Sauce Suprême [No. 22]
12 Chicken Quenelles [*see* No. 339]
Salt and freshly ground pepper

Bake an 8-inch puff-paste crust as described in the directions for making pies, Second Method, page 96. If mushrooms are large, slice them; if small, trim stems and leave whole. Cook them in the butter in a large frying pan over a hot flame, covered, for about 5 minutes, stirring so that they all cook evenly. At this point uncover and add the chicken livers, which have been soaked in the milk for about $\frac{1}{2}$ hour, drained, patted dry, and cut into small pieces. Cook them at high heat, turning them often to distribute the heat evenly, for about 3 or 4 minutes. Add the pre-soaked and pre-cooked dried mushrooms and the Madeira, tipping the pan in all directions and scraping with a wooden spoon to allow the wine to loosen any crusty bits adhering to the bottom and sides. Let liquid cook away almost completely, add the Sauce Suprême, heat thoroughly, taste for seasoning, and remove from heat. Fold in the quenelles gently, so as not to break them; pour into the baked puff paste; and put into a 400° oven for 5 minutes, or until the top is well glazed and browned. Serve at once. *Serves 4 to 6.*

291. SHRIMP TART
Crostata di code di scampi

1 8-inch pie shell, made with Rich Pastry [No. 1955]
2 cups mushrooms, sliced
3 tablespoons butter
1 pound uncooked large shrimp, peeled and de-veined
    (or frozen, thawed, imported scampi, if available)
$1\frac{1}{4}$ cups Béchamel Sauce [No. 18]
3 tablespoons Tomato Sauce [No. 19]
Optional: 12 Chicken Quenelles [*see* No. 339]
Salt and freshly ground white pepper to taste

Line a spring form or straight-sided tart ring with pastry, line with paper, and weight with dried beans, etc., as described in the First Method above. Bake for about 15 minutes in a 400° oven, then carefully remove lining paper and dried beans, and return to the oven for another 7 to 10 minutes to brown.

Meanwhile, sauté the mushrooms in the butter over a high flame, covered, for about 5 minutes; uncover, and add the shrimp or scampi and continue cooking for another 5 minutes, stirring from time to time so that all the shrimp are cooked evenly (do not overcook, as they will toughen). Add the Béchamel and tomato sauces, a generous grating of pepper, and salt to taste. Heat through over a moderate flame. When tart crust is nicely browned, remove from oven, arrange the quenelles over the bottom, and pour in the shrimp mixture. Return to the oven for about 5 minutes to glaze the top slightly (*see* photograph facing page 144). Serve at once. *Serves* 6.

NOTE: If the quenelles are omitted, increase the shrimp to $1\frac{1}{2}$ pounds. The quenelles may be cooked the day before and allowed to stand in the refrigerator (not the freezer) until needed. In this case they should be warmed through before placing in the tart.

SAVOURIES

Savouries

Savouries are British in origin, and are usually served at the end of an elaborate meal, after the dessert and before the Port and nuts, although they may be served after the soup course, or as a midnight snack. Savouries are usually highly seasoned, especially with hot spices such as Cayenne pepper. Being highly flavored, they are thirst inducing. Many gourmets frown upon their all-too-vigorous assault on the tastebuds. However, because of their over-assertive flavor, they may be successfully served as an accompaniment to cocktails or aperitifs.

292. ALGERIAN TONGUES
Lingue algerine

1 large eggplant (about 1 pound)
1 tablespoon salt
Flour
¼ cup oil
1 cup heavy cream
4 egg yolks
¼ teaspoon pepper
1½ cups freshly grated Parmesan cheese
Fritter Batter [No. 275]
Fat for deep frying

Peel eggplant and cut into ¼-inch crosswise slices. Sprinkle liberally with salt and allow them to drain on absorbent paper for about 1 hour. Wash slices free of all traces of salt and press dry between paper towels. Cut them into equal-sized pieces, about 2 inches long by 1 inch wide, dust in flour, and fry on both sides in hot oil (as eggplant soaks up oil, more than indicated

may be needed). Drain slices well, and place in refrigerator to chill.

Beat cream with egg yolks and pepper. Add Parmesan, and pour into a small, heavy saucepan. Cook over low heat, stirring constantly with a wire whisk until thick and creamy. Do not boil, or the eggs will curdle. Pour into a bowl and place in refrigerator until thoroughly chilled and very thick.

Prepare fritter batter as indicated in No. 275.

When all the components are well chilled, proceed as follows: cover half the eggplant pieces with the cream/Parmesan mixture and cover these with the remaining eggplant. Press together firmly but lightly so that the "sandwiches" will not come apart. Dip into fritter batter and fry a few at a time in the deep hot (375°) fat. Drain on absorbent paper and keep in a warm place until all the fritters have been fried. Serve at once. *Serves* 6.

293. "AMERICAN" DELICACIES
Delizie all'americana

8 slices white bread
1 cup Bastard Sauce [No. 66], hot
2 tablespoons anchovy paste
2 tablespoons capers

Remove crusts from bread. Cut each slice into 3 equal-sized strips. Toast strips until golden brown. Arrange them on warm platter and pour over the hot Bastard sauce which has been mixed with the anchovy paste. Garnish with capers and serve at once. *Serves* 6.

NOTE: This may be divided among six oven-proof ramekins and placed in a hot (375°) oven to glaze for a few minutes.

294. CAMEMBERT FRITTERS
Bignè di Camembert

1 pound Camembert cheese
2 eggs, beaten with ⅛ teaspoon Cayenne pepper
Breadcrumbs
Fat for deep frying
Parsley sprigs

Choose a Camembert that is not too ripe; if it is runny, it will be impossible to handle. Chill it well. When cold, carefully pare off the rind. Cut cheese into small strips, like miniature French fried potatoes. Dip into beaten egg/Cayenne mixture and roll in breadcrumbs, and then repeat this process. When dipped twice, these strips may be returned to the refrigerator for a few hours until just before serving time. Heat fat to 375°.

Place some of the fritters in the bottom of a frying basket but do not overcrowd so that they touch each other. Carefully lower basket into fat and fry until golden brown. Remove and drain on absorbent paper in a warm place. Repeat until all fritters have been fried. Serve at once, garnished with parsley. *Serves 6 as an appetizer.*

295. CAVIAR TOAST
Toasts di caviale

1 cup red (salmon) caviar
2 tablespoons grated onion
1 teaspoon lemon juice
3 tablespoons oil
12 slices toast, crusts removed and diagonally cut in
   half
4 tablespoons butter, softened
Lemon quarters

Taking great care, place the caviar in a fine sieve. Place this under the *gentlest possible* stream of lukewarm water from the sink tap. This must all be performed with great delicacy, as one does not wish to bruise the eggs, but merely to wash away the excess salt. When salt, water, and packing liquid has drained away, carefully place caviar in a small bowl and add onion, lemon juice, and oil. Carefully mix with a wooden spoon or rubber spatula (1 or 2 turns should suffice, as the eggs must not burst). Cover and place in re-frigerator overnight.

Before serving, liberally butter toast triangles with the butter. Spread with marinated caviar, and place in a hot (400°) oven for 5 minutes. Serve at once, garnished with lemon quarters.

NOTE: The original Italian recipe calls for fresh sturgeon caviar. We feel that this is too cavalier a treatment for this imperial roe, and have therefore substituted red caviar. The washing and marinating of the latter do much to reduce its saltiness and enhance its flavor. However, to repeat, the process must be carried out with the utmost gentleness, as a heavy stream of water, or mixing too strenuously, will result in a red fish mush.

296. CHEESE CUSTARD CROQUETTES
Crema fritta al formaggio

3/4 cup sifted flour
1/4 cup plus 1 heaping tablespoon rice flour
1 teaspoon salt

Pinch nutmeg
Pinch Cayenne pepper
3 whole eggs
5 egg yolks
4 cups milk
1 1/2 cups grated Emmenthal or Swiss cheese
2 eggs, beaten with 1 tablespoon melted butter
Breadcrumbs
Fat for deep frying

Mix sifted flour, rice flour, salt, nutmeg, and Cayenne. Sift them into a heavy enamel saucepan. Lightly beat the whole eggs and the yolks, add milk, mix well, and slowly pour onto flour mixture, beating constantly with a wire whisk to avoid lumps. When the mixture is smooth, place over moderate flame and bring to a boil, beating constantly with the whisk. When boiling, reduce flame, add grated cheese, and cook for 5 minutes, stirring occasionally. Remove from stove and pour onto a buttered platter or dish which is large enough so that the mixture is 1/2-inch deep. Place in refrigerator and chill for at least 6 hours, or overnight.

Before serving, dip the bottom of the platter into hot water for a moment to loosen mixture. With a wet knife, cut into 2-inch squares or diamonds, or into rectangles 2 1/2 by 1 inches. Carefully dip into the beaten eggs, and then roll in breadcrumbs until thoroughly coated. (At this point you may refrigerate the breaded squares for a few hours.)

Heat fat to 375°, carefully place a few breaded squares in the bottom of a frying basket, making sure they do not touch each other. Lower basket into fat, fry until golden brown, drain, and place on absorbent paper or paper towels. Keep in a warm place until all the squares have been fried. Serve at once. *Serves 6.*

297. CHESHIRE CAKE
Chester cake

1¼ cups sifted flour
7 tablespoons sweet butter
1¼ cups grated Cheshire cheese (*see* Note below)
½ teaspoon salt
2 pinches Cayenne pepper
3 egg yolks
1 egg, beaten
¾ cup very thick Béchamel Sauce [No. 18]

Sift the flour into a bowl. Add 5 tablespoons of the butter, half the grated cheese, salt, and 1 pinch Cayenne. Mix with the tips of the fingers or with a pastry blender until the mixture resembles cornmeal. Add 2 of the egg yolks, and mix with a fork until the dough leaves the sides of the bowl and forms a ball. If dough is too dry, add a little ice water (the dough should be the same consistency as pie crust). When mixed, gently pat into a solid ball, cover with foil or wax paper, and place in refrigerator (*not* the freezer) for 1 hour. Prepare the Béchamel sauce while the dough is resting. On a floured board or pastry cloth, roll out dough until ⅛-inch thick. Cut into 1¼-inch rounds with a cooky cutter or glass. Place on a slightly dampened baking sheet, brush with the beaten egg, and bake in a 375–400° oven for 15 minutes, or until golden brown. Just before the rounds are completely baked, beat the remaining butter, cheese, egg yolk, and 1 pinch of Cayenne into the hot Béchamel. Remove rounds from oven, place 1 teaspoon of the mixture onto ½ of the rounds and top them with the remaining half. Serve at once. *Serves 6 as an appetizer.*

NOTE: If Cheshire cheese is unavailable, a reasonable substitute might be ½ grated Parmesan cheese and ½ grated well-aged, hard Cheddar cheese. In Italy, Cheshire cheese is called "Chester."

298. CURRIED EGGS ON TOAST
Toasts con uova all'indiana

6 eggs, poached or soft boiled and shelled
¾ cup Curry Sauce [No. 70], hot
6 thick slices toast, crusts removed

It is best to use unsliced bread for this. Slice each piece about ¾ inch thick and remove crust. If desired, one may hollow out the center of each slice, about ¼ inch deep, before toasting. Poach or soft boil the eggs (shell carefully after cooking in the latter case). Toast bread on both sides. Spoon curry sauce over each slice, reserving some for later use. Place an egg over this (resting in the hollow) and cover with remaining sauce. Do not mask too heavily with sauce, as it should not run over the sides. Place toasts in a baking pan in a 400° oven for 2 or 3 minutes to glaze. Do not leave in longer as the eggs should not overcook. Serve at once. *Serves 6.*

299. FONTINA CROQUETTES
Crocchette di fontina

½ cup plus 2 tablespoons butter
⅓ cup plus 1 tablespoon flour
⅓ cup plus 1 tablespoon rice (or potato) flour
1 cup milk
4 egg yolks
2 whole eggs
Pinch nutmeg
Pinch Cayenne pepper
1 pound fontina cheese (or Munster), rind removed and coarsely grated
1 teaspoon oil
2 eggs, beaten
Breadcrumbs
Fat for deep frying

Melt the butter in a heavy saucepan. Add both flours and mix well. Add the milk, stirring well, and cook over moderate heat until a very heavy mixture is formed. Beat the 4 yolks and 2 whole eggs together. Remove flour/milk mixture from the stove, and beat in the eggs with a wire whisk until mixture is smooth. Add nutmeg and Cayenne. Place over medium heat, with an asbestos pad between saucepan and flame. Gradually add the grated cheese, and stir constantly until cheese has melted and mixture is very thick and smooth (about 5 minutes). Remove from stove and pour into a buttered, deep-sided dish. Brush top with a bit of oil or melted butter to keep a crust from forming, and chill for at least 3 hours.

Before serving, take spoonsful of the cheese mixture, and with moistened hands roll into croquettes about the size of a walnut. Carefully dip in beaten egg and roll in breadcrumbs until well coated. Repeat this process once again. Fry in deep hot (375°) fat until golden. Drain well and place on absorbent paper in a warm place until all the croquettes have been fried. Serve at once. *Makes about 36 small croquettes.*

300. GOURMET TOAST
Toasts del ghiottone

6 medium tomatoes of equal size
5 tablespoons butter
6 slices bread
6 eggs
½ teaspoon salt
¼ teaspoon pepper
Pinch sugar

Cut tops off the tomatoes and scoop out the pulp, taking care not to pierce the skin. Wash out the hollowed tomatoes to rid them of all adhering seeds and pulp. Dry thoroughly. Melt 2½ tablespoons of the butter and brush this on the tomatoes, inside and out. Season with ½ the salt and pepper and the pinch sugar. Place in a baking pan and bake in a 375° oven for about 15 minutes, or until tender. Do not, however, overcook so that they lose their shape and become pulpy. Meanwhile cut the bread into circles slightly larger than the circumference of the tomatoes and toast lightly on both sides. Melt the remaining butter in a frying pan and carefully fry the eggs. Do not use too large a pan as the eggs should not spread out too much. Season with the remaining salt and pepper. Cook until whites are set and yolks are still runny. Remove tomatoes from oven when done. Place them on the toast circles and cover them with the juices and butter remaining in pan. Carefully fill each tomato with a fried egg, and drizzle over the remaining butter from egg pan. Serve at once. Garnish with chopped parsley, if desired. *Serves* 6.

NOTE: Instead of being fried, the eggs may be poached, well drained, and patted dry before filling the tomatoes. In this case reduce the butter to 3 tablespoons, and use this to coat the tomatoes before baking.

301. HAM AND MOZZARELLA TOAST
Toasts di mozzarella con prosciutto

6 thin slices cooked smoked ham (Virginia or Smithfield, if possible)
6 slices toast, crusts removed
1 cup mozzarella cheese, thinly sliced
3 tablespoons butter, melted
2 tablespoons freshly grated Parmesan cheese
Grating of freshly ground black pepper

Place a slice of ham on each piece of toast, folding the edges over so that they do not hang over the sides of the toast. Carefully cover this with the mozzarella. Drizzle melted butter over the top and sprinkle with

grated Parmesan and pepper. Place in a 375° oven for about 7 minutes until heated through. Serve at once. *Serves* 6.

302. OYSTERS ON HORSEBACK
Oysters on horseback

2 dozen oysters, shucked and drained
12 strips bacon, cut in half, crosswise
6 wooden skewers
¼ cup fine breadcrumbs
¼ cup Hazelnut Butter [No. 103]
Salt and pepper to taste
6 pieces toast, crusts removed, lightly buttered
Pinch Cayenne pepper
Lemon quarters

Lightly season each oyster with salt and pepper. Wrap each oyster in ½ slice of bacon, and thread them on the skewers, 4 bacon-wrapped oysters to a skewer. Place in a baking pan and broil under a very high flame for 6 or 7 minutes, turning each skewer once. Mix breadcrumbs with hazelnut butter and heat through over moderate heat. When oysters are cooked, unskewer each set on a buttered slice of toast, sprinkle with the buttered crumbs, and *lightly* dust each portion with a grain or two of Cayenne. Serve at once, garnished with lemon quarters. *Serves* 6.

303. PARMESAN MARCHESAS
Marchesa al parmigiano

6 unbaked tart shells, or 12 tartlets [*see* No. 1959]
2 cups thick Béchamel Sauce [No. 18]
2 cups freshly grated Parmesan cheese
Pinch Cayenne pepper
½ recipe Cream Puff Dough [No. 1990], omitting sugar

Line tart or tartlet tins with dough. Prick well with a fork. Mix warm Béchamel with 1½ cups of the Parmesan and Cayenne, stir well until smooth, and let cool. Fill tart shells ⅔ full of this mixture. Top each tart with a layer of cream puff dough, being careful that the filling is completely covered by this. Sprinkle the rest of the Parmesan over the tops, and bake in a 350° oven for about 40 minutes, or until the tarts are puffed and golden brown. Serve at once. *Serves* 6.

304. DEVILED SARDINES ON TOAST
Toasts di sardine sott'olio alla diavola

⅓ cup Mustard Butter [No. 112]
Pinch Cayenne pepper
6 slices toast, crusts removed
2 tins boneless, skinless sardines, packed in olive oil

Season mustard butter with Cayenne. Spread ⅓ of this on the toast while the latter is still warm. Drain sardines and arrange neatly on top. Cover with remaining mustard butter. Place in a 375° oven for 4 minutes. Serve at once. *Serves* 6.

305. SIGHS
Sospiri

2 cups light cream
2 whole eggs
3 egg yolks
Pinch nutmeg
Pinch Cayenne pepper
½ teaspoon salt
12 slices Brioche [*see* No. 1890] or purchased egg bread (Challah), sliced ½-inch thick
2 tablespoons butter, softened
2 tablespoons freshly grated Parmesan cheese
2 tablespoons freshly grated Swiss or Emmenthal cheese

Heat the cream to scalding. Lightly beat the whole eggs with the yolks and add the scalded cream, beating well. Add salt, Cayenne, and nutmeg. Lightly butter 12 small molds, tartlet tins, or very small custard cups.

Chicken in Scallop Shells (No. 306)

Pour in the custard. Place molds in a pan containing 1 or 2 inches of hot water. Bake in a 300° oven for 30 minutes, or until a knife blade inserted in the custard comes out clean. Cut slices of brioche or egg bread the same diameter as the molds and arrange them on a serving dish (they may be lightly toasted and buttered, if desired). When custards are cooked, carefully unmold each one on the brioche bases. Sprinkle carefully with the grated cheeses, and place in a 375° oven for 5 minutes to glaze. Serve at once. *Serves* 6.

SCALLOP SHELLS
Conchiglie

A number of hot hors d'oeuvres are most attractive when served in fluted scallop shells. These can be bought in housewares stores if there is no seashore handy. Large clam shells serve as well, though they are not quite as attractive. Failing shells, the contents will taste as good baked in ovenware.

Many of the recipes can be stuffed into small cream puff shells, as finger food. They may be put together an hour in advance and heated before serving, but don't try to prepare them earlier or the cream puffs will be soggy.

NOTE: When heating the filled scallop or clam shells, keep them from tipping and spilling by imbedding them in a panful of rock salt or small pebbles instead of simply setting them on baking sheets.

306. CHICKEN IN SCALLOP SHELLS
Conchiglie di pollo all'italiana

25 button mushroom caps, or 12 medium mushrooms, sliced
3 tablespoons butter
3 cups cooked chicken meat, finely diced
1 scant tablespoon water or bouillon
1½ cups Sauce Parisienne [No. 21]
1 cup Duchesse Potatoes, prepared with 2 additional tablespoons of butter [No. 1771]
Optional: 24 slices truffle (*see* Note below)
Salt and freshly ground pepper to taste
6 large (or 12 small) scallop shells

Clean mushroom caps, but do not peel them. Melt the butter in a small saucepan; add the mushroom caps, 1 scant tablespoon water (or bouillon for added flavor), a pinch of salt, and a grating of pepper. Cook, covered, over medium heat for about 8 minutes. When mushrooms are cooked, remove them and heat the diced chicken in the mushroom liquid, stirring constantly. Do not allow the chicken to fry, but make sure it is heated through; then remove from the heat. Place a few spoonsful of chicken in the bottom of the shells, cover with some of the Parisienne sauce, then add another layer of chicken and top with the remaining sauce. Pipe a border of Duchesse potatoes around the scallop shells, using a pastry bag with a medium star tube. Place mushroom caps and truffles decoratively on top of the sauce [*see* photograph] and place in a 400° oven until the sauce becomes glazed, but not too brown. Serve at once. *Serves* 6.

NOTE: In place of truffles, the following may be used: take the best mushroom stems, slice them crosswise, and sauté them gently in 1 tablespoon butter, with a grating of fresh pepper. When they start to brown, add ¼ clove of garlic, crushed in the garlic-press, remove from stove and cover the saucepan for 10 minutes [*see also* No. 1819a].

307. SHRIMP IN SCALLOP SHELLS LUCULLUS
Conchiglie di scampi "Lucullo"

2 tablespoons butter
¼ pound mushrooms, sliced
¾ pound peeled, de-veined raw shrimp (if they are large, cut them in pieces)
2 tablespoons dry Madeira wine
1½ cups Sauce Mornay [No. 56]
Optional: 24 slices truffle [*see* Note to No. 306]
3 tablespoons grated Parmesan cheese
Salt and freshly ground pepper to taste
6 large or 12 small scallop shells

Melt the butter in a frying pan and cook the mushrooms and shrimps over medium heat until the shrimp turn pink and lose their transparent look. Season lightly with salt and pepper and remove the pieces from the pan. Add the wine to the remaining pan juices and cook, scraping the pan well with a wooden spoon, until only a spoonful of liquid is left. Combine this with the Mornay sauce. To half of the sauce, add the shrimp and mushrooms and mix gently until they are well coated. Divide this among the shells, and arrange truffle slices on top. Then top with a thin coating of the remaining sauce and sprinkle with Parmesan. Put in a 400° oven until glazed but not brown. *Serves* 6.

NOTE: Scallops may be substituted for the shrimp,

but they should be simmered in dry white wine to cover for 8 minutes, drained, and cut in small pieces if very large, before adding them to half of the Mornay sauce as above. You may also use a combination of equal amounts of scallops and shrimp.

SPIEDINI
Spiedini

This Italian specialty is almost impossible to translate. "Skewered" does not adequately describe these superbly luxurious preparations, and "en brochette" merely means skewered in French. The skewers employed may be of wood, silver, or metal (such as aluminum or stainless steel) and should be about 6 inches long. Wooden skewers are perhaps the best choice, although the metal variety are excellent heat conductors and ensure that the spiedini will be heated through.

The spiedini may be deep fried in hot fat, cooked under the broiler, or fried in about ½ inch of butter. Deep frying is recommended for most of these recipes, however, as they are rather delicate in their construction, and a minimum of handling is recommended.

Chicken Liver Spiedini (No. 309)

308. SPIEDINI CASALINGA
Spiedini alla casalinga

4 cups Chicken Stock [No. 3], or Substitute White
    Stock [No. 1a]
1 cup semolina (or farina)
1/2 teaspoon salt
1/4 teaspoon white pepper
Pinch nutmeg
1 1/4 cup grated Parmesan cheese
3/4 cup butter
6 skewers
18 pieces Swiss cheese, cut in 1 1/2-inch cubes
2 eggs, beaten with 1 tablespoon oil
Breadcrumbs
Fat for deep frying
Parsley sprigs, thoroughly dried and deep fried
    [see Note to No. 276]

Bring stock to a rolling boil, then slowly add the semolina, stirring constantly. When all semolina has
been added, reduce flame and cook for about 1/2 hour,
stirring occasionally to prevent scorching (or cook for
3/4 hour in a double boiler). When mixture is cooked
(it will be *very* thick), add salt, pepper, nutmeg,
Parmesan cheese, and all but 2 tablespoons of the
butter. Beat well and set aside. With 1 tablespoon of
the remaining butter, grease an 8- by 8-inch square
baking pan. Pour in the hot semolina mixture and
spread the remaining butter over the top to prevent
a skin from forming. Let cool to room temperature,
then place in refrigerator for at least 3 hours. When
semolina mixture is cold, dip the bottom of the pan
briefly in warm water and carefully turn out the solidified mixture onto a large platter. With a knife dipped
in cold water, cut it into 24 squares. Starting with a
square of molded semolina, alternate with a square of
Swiss cheese, impaling them on wooden skewers
(metal skewers are too fine, and there is a danger of
their splitting these delicate squares). The last piece
to be impaled should be a square of semolina mixture.
Carefully dip each skewer into beaten egg and roll in
breadcrumbs. This must be done with great care so
as not to break the fragile squares. Place in refrigerator
for an hour and then fry in deep hot (375°) fat until
golden brown. Since the squares are so fragile, a
frying basket should be used and only a few of the
spiedini should be cooked at a time in order that they
do not touch each other during the frying. Remove
them to a warm place to drain on absorbent paper
while the remainder are being fried. When all are
cooked, serve as quickly as possible on a hot platter
garnished with the fried parsley. *Serves* 6.

309. CHICKEN LIVER SPIEDINI
Spiedini di fegatini di pollo

1/2 pound chicken livers
1 pound salt pork
18 medium mushroom caps
3/4 cup butter
12 slices, 1/2-inch thick, Italian-style bread, trimmed
    to 2-inch squares
Optional: 18 slices white truffle [or No. 1819a]
12 fresh sage leaves
6 skewers
Salt and freshly ground pepper
Breadcrumbs
6 thick slices buttered toast

Wash chicken livers and soak in acidulated water for
1/2 hour. Meanwhile, slice salt pork 1/2 inch thick and
cut into 2-inch squares. Blanch these in a large pan of
boiling (unsalted) water for 20 minutes, drain, broil
in a 375° oven until crisp, and put aside on paper towels.
Cook mushroom caps in a small, covered saucepan
with 3 tablespoons of the butter and a little salt and
pepper for 5 minutes over medium heat. Drain, and
reserve pan juices. Melt 6 tablespoons of the butter in a
large frying pan. Drain chicken livers, separate them,
pat dry, and sauté them over a high flame for 5 minutes.
Remove the livers, add the mushroom liquid and
remaining 3 tablespoons butter to the pan, tilt and
scrape with a wooden spoon to de-glaze, and remove
pan from fire. Quickly dip the 12 slices of bread (cut
into 2-inch squares) in this gravy.

Alternately thread livers, sage leaves, broiled salt
pork, mushrooms, bread, and optional truffles on 6
skewers. Dust lightly with breadcrumbs, salt, and
pepper. Place in a baking dish. Pour over the remaining pan juices (or brush with a little melted butter),
and broil under a medium flame until well browned.
Place each of the skewers on a slice of buttered toast,
spoon over any pan juices, and serve at once. (*See*
photograph on page 105 for serving suggestion and
preparation.) *Serves* 6.

NOTE: If only dried, or powdered, sage is available,
1/2 teaspoon may be sprinkled over the livers before
sautéing.

310. SPIEDINI GOURMET
Spiedini del ghiottone

18 pieces mild cheese (Munster, fontina, mozzarella,
    etc.), cut into 1 1/2-inch squares
24 slices Italian-style bread, trimmed into 2-inch
    squares

¾ cup butter
1 small can anchovy fillets, drained
6 skewers

Thread the bread and cheese on skewers, beginning and ending with squares of bread. Melt 4 tablespoons of the butter, arrange spiedini in a baking dish, cover them with melted butter, and toast them under the broiler, turning them so that they brown evenly. Baste with additional melted butter if necessary.

Put the drained anchovy fillets in a sieve, run hot water over them for a minute or two, chop them finely, and put in a saucepan with the remaining butter. Melt butter over low heat. Cook for about 3 minutes.

Remove spiedini from broiler when evenly toasted. Place on a hot platter, and pour a spoonful of anchovy butter over each and serve at once. Serve remaining anchovy butter separately. *Serves* 6.

311. LAMB SPIEDINI
Spiedini di filetti di agnello

½ to ¾ pound shoulder or leg meat of lamb, without fat
Same ingredients as indicated in Chicken Liver Spiedini [No. 309]

Proceed exactly as indicated in No. 309, except: cut lamb into small pieces, about 1½ to 2 inches square; do not soak in acidulated water; sauté them for 5 minutes; omit the sage and sprinkle ½ teaspoon dried rosemary over lamb before sautéing. *Serves* 6.

312. SPIEDINI LUCULLUS
Spiedini luculliani

½ pound chicken livers
18 pieces cooked smoked tongue, cut in 1½-inch cubes
18 pieces Swiss cheese, cut in 1½-inch cubes
6 skewers
2 cups very thick Béchamel Sauce [No. 18]
2 eggs, beaten with 1 tablespoon oil
Salt and pepper to taste
Flour
Breadcrumbs
Parsley sprigs
Fat for deep frying

Wash chicken livers and soak for ½ hour in acidulated water. Drain and plunge into boiling, salted water. Lower flame, simmer for 5 minutes, drain, and cool. Separate livers, cut into 18 equal pieces, and season

lightly with salt and pepper. Alternately thread on skewers the cheese, tongue, and chicken livers. Place skewers on a large, lightly buttered platter. Mask them completely with warm Béchamel, smoothing it evenly with a moistened spatula and making sure the ends are well covered. Chill for 1 hour, then dredge lightly with flour, dip in beaten egg, and roll in bread-crumbs, being careful that they are completely coated with the breadcrumbs. Chill for another hour or until ready to serve.

Heat fat to 375°. Place 2 or 3 of the spiedini in a frying basket, taking care that they do not touch, and fry until golden brown. Remove them to a warm place to drain on absorbent paper while the remainder are being fried. Serve as quickly as possible on a hot platter garnished with the parsley. *Serves* 6.

313. OYSTER SPIEDINI VILLEROY
Spiedini di ostriche alla Villeroy

24 shucked oysters
3 tablespoons butter
24 medium-to-large mushroom caps, cooked (should be same size as oysters)
½ teaspoon salt
¼ teaspoon pepper
6 skewers
2 cups very thick Sauce Villeroy [No. 59], warmed
2 eggs, beaten with 1 tablespoon oil
Flour
Breadcrumbs
Parsley sprigs
Lemon quarters
Fat for deep frying
2 cups Tomato Sauce [No. 19]

Poach fresh, shucked oysters in their own liquid for 2 or 3 minutes, or until their edges curl; drain, trim, and place on paper towels. Reduce oyster liquid to about 2 scant tablespoons, add butter, raise flame, add mushrooms, and sauté rapidly for 8 minutes. Remove from fire and drain. Alternately thread mushrooms and oysters on skewers, salt and pepper them lightly, place them on a lightly buttered platter, and mask them with the still warm, thick Villeroy sauce. Proceed exactly as indicated in No. 312. Serve accompanied by the tomato sauce. *Serves* 6.

314. SWEETBREAD SPIEDINI
Spiedini di animella di vitello

¾ pound veal sweetbreads, cleaned, parboiled for 20
   minutes, cut in 1½-inch cubes, and fried lightly in
   butter for 5 minutes

18 medium mushroom caps, cooked 5 minutes in butter

Optional: 18 slices truffle [or No. 1819a]

6 skewers

3 cups Sauce Parisienne [No. 21], reduced until very
   thick

2 eggs, beaten with 1 tablespoon oil

Salt and freshly ground black pepper to taste

Breadcrumbs

Flour

Fat for deep frying

Parsley sprigs

Lemon quarters

Alternate sweetbreads, mushrooms, and optional
truffle slices on skewers. Season lightly with salt and
pepper. Place skewers on a large, lightly buttered
platter. Mask them completely with warm, very thick
Parisienne sauce. Proceed exactly as described in
No. 312. *Serves* 6.

315. VEAL KIDNEY SPIEDINI
Spiedini di rognoni di vitello

½ to ¾ pound veal kidneys

Same ingredients as indicated in No. 314, omitting the
   truffles and sweetbreads

Slice veal kidneys, remove hard fatty core. Soak in
acidulated water for ½ hour. Drain, pat dry, cut into
pieces about 2 inches square, and sauté in butter over
a high flame for 6 minutes. Proceed exactly as indicated
in No. 314. *Serves* 6.

Spiedini Gourmet (No. 310): see page 106

TARTLETS AND BARQUETTES
Barchette e tartelette

These may be prepared from the standard crust indicated in No. 1959, or any favorite recipe you prefer.
They may be made in many sizes, although for appetizers they should either be 3 inches in diameter for
individual servings, or 1 to 1½ inches in diameter
(or smaller) for serving as a finger food. Little puff-
paste patty shells may also be used with equal success.
The pastry cases may also be formed into barquettes
("little boats") of any size desired. The larger tarts
and barquettes should be served at table as a first course
before the soup course. The smaller, bite-sized varieties are suitable for passing around at cocktails.

All of the following recipes may be converted into
delicious main courses for luncheons or late suppers
by tripling the ingredients for the fillings, and placing
the filling into a 10-inch pre-baked tart crust or puff-
paste shell. Served in this manner and followed by a
salad and dessert, they make superb light meals.

The fillings may be made ahead of time, and the
crusts may also be baked in advance. However, do not
fill the crusts until just before you place them in the
oven or they will become soggy. If you have made the
filling ahead of time and allowed it to cool, double the
time it is to remain in the oven. If you are making the
larger size for a main course, allow at least 20 to 25
minutes in the oven for a warm, freshly made filling,
and about 20 minutes longer for a pre-cooked and
chilled filling.

316. CHEESE TARTLETS
Tartelette con mozzarella e emmenthal

1 1/2 cups Béchamel Sauce [No. 18]
2 whole eggs, beaten
Pinch nutmeg
1/2 pound mozzarella cheese, diced small
1/4 pound Swiss cheese, grated
Salt and freshly grated white pepper to taste
6 baked tartlet shells [see No. 1959]

Heat the Béchamel sauce to the boiling point and remove from stove; quickly beat in the eggs, seasonings, and both cheeses. Fill the tartlet shells to 1/2 inch from the top. Bake in 400° oven on the second rack from the bottom until tops are well glazed, about 10 minutes. Serve at once. *Serves 6.*

317. TARTLETS ITALIANA
Tartelette all'italiana

1/4 cup pastina
1 cup Tomato Sauce [No. 19]
3 tablespoons dry Marsala wine
1/2 cup boiled ham, diced small
1/2 cup smoked tongue, diced small
1 cup cooked mushrooms, diced small
1/4 cup butter, melted
3/4 cup freshly grated Parmesan cheese
6 baked tartlet shells [see No. 1959]

Cook the pastina in salted, boiling water until barely done (about 11 minutes, or according to directions on the manufacturer's package). Drain. Add Marsala to the tomato sauce, bring to a boil, and simmer for 5 minutes. Add the ham, tongue, cooked mushrooms, and pastina to sauce, mix well, and remove from fire. Stir in 2 tablespoons of melted butter and 1/2 cup of Parmesan. Place this mixture in baked tart shells, sprinkle with remaining cheese, and drizzle over with the rest of the butter. Glaze in a 400° oven for 5 minutes. Serve at once. *Serves 6.*

318. TARTLETS MARION DELORME
Tartelette Marion Delorme

1 cup cooked chicken meat
1 cup mushrooms (caps and stems)
2 tablespoons butter
1 cup Béchamel Sauce [No. 18]
Salt and freshly ground white pepper
Pinch nutmeg
3 egg yolks, beaten with 2 tablespoons cream
6 baked tartlet shells [see No. 1959]
1/4 cup chopped parsley
1/2 teaspoon lemon juice

Grind chicken meat twice, using finest blade of meat grinder (or mix with the Béchamel and whirl in blender at high speed for 10 seconds). Grind mushrooms and pass them through a fine sieve (or put them in blender with 1 tablespoon cream and mix at high speed for 5 seconds). Melt the butter in a saucepan and cook the mushroom purée over medium heat for about 10 minutes, adding a few drops of lemon juice to keep it from turning brown. When cooked, add the puréed chicken and the Béchamel. Season to taste with salt, pepper, and pinch nutmeg. Stir constantly over medium heat until mixture comes to a boil. Remove from heat, cool for a few seconds, and beat in the egg yolks mixed with the cream. Fill tartlet shells with the mixture and place in a 375° oven for 10 minutes, or until the filling is well glazed. Serve at once garnished with fresh parsley. *Serves 6.*

319. MUSHROOM TARTLETS MORNAY
Barchette di funghi Mornay

1/4 cup dried, imported mushrooms (soaked for 1/2 hour in hot water and drained)
3 tablespoons butter
2 tablespoons water (or broth)
1 pound fresh mushrooms
1 1/2 cups thick Sauce Mornay [No. 56]
Salt and freshly ground pepper
1/3 cup freshly grated Parmesan cheese
6 baked tartlet shells [see No. 1959]
Paprika

Melt the butter in a saucepan over medium heat and add the pre-soaked, drained, dried mushrooms. Cover, and cook for 1/2 hour. After the first five minutes add 2 tablespoons water (or broth). Chop the fresh mushroom stems. If caps are very fresh and white, do not peel; only rinse lightly in a colander. Add chopped stems and caps to dried mushrooms and season lightly with salt and pepper. Cook, covered, over high heat for 10 minutes, stirring occasionally. Add the Mornay sauce, mix well and season to taste with salt and pepper, pour into tartlet shells, sprinkle tops with Parmesan and a dusting of paprika. Put into a 375° oven for 10 minutes, or until tops are lightly browned. *Serves* 6.

320. ROMAN TARTLETS
Barchette alla romana

1½ cups Marsala Sauce [No. 43]
1 cup diced, cooked chicken
½ cup small mushroom caps, cooked in 1 tablespoon
   butter, covered, for 10 minutes
Optional: 1 or 2 truffles (white or black), finely chopped
   [or No. 1819a]
⅓ cup freshly grated Parmesan cheese
2 tablespoons butter, melted
6 baked tartlet shells [*see* No. 1959]

Cook the Marsala sauce down until it is reduced by one half. Mix in the diced chicken, mushroom caps (if small mushrooms are not available, cut larger caps into quarters), and the optional truffles. Taste and adjust seasoning if necessary. Fill baked tartlet shells, sprinkle with Parmesan, and drizzle with melted butter. Place in a 375° oven for 10 minutes, or until well browned. *Serves* 6.

321. SHRIMP TARTLETS
Barchette di gamberetti

1 pound fresh shrimp, peeled and de-veined
3 tablespoons butter
3 egg yolks
⅓ cup heavy cream
1½ cup hot Béchamel Sauce [No. 18]

¼ cup sherry
Salt and freshly ground white pepper
¼ cup grated Swiss or Gruyère cheese
6 baked tartlet shells [*see* No. 1959]

Melt the butter in a heavy frying pan and cook the shrimp over a high flame for 5 minutes. Beat the yolks with the cream and add to the hot Béchamel, stirring constantly. Add the shrimp. De-glaze the frying pan in which the shrimp cooked with the sherry, tipping the pan in all directions to dissolve any shrimp and butter particles that might have remained; cook over high heat for a minute or two and add to the Béchamel/shrimp mixture. Season to taste with salt and pepper and pour into tartlet shells. Sprinkle cheese over the top and bake in a 375° oven for 10 minutes, or until the tops are well browned. *Serves* 6.

322. SWEETBREAD TARTLETS
Barchette di animella di agnello ò di vitello

2 cups parboiled, diced sweetbreads
1½ cups thick Béchamel Sauce [No. 18]
3 tablespoons sherry wine
⅓ cup fine breadcrumbs
2 tablespoons butter, melted
Salt and freshly ground pepper
6 baked tartlet shells [*see* No. 1959]

Prepare sweetbreads as indicated in introduction to No. 1434. Prepare tartlet shells. (Both these tasks may be accomplished the day before.) Mix diced sweetbreads with the Béchamel and sherry, and season to taste. Divide among the tartlet shells. Top with the breadcrumbs which have been lightly browned in the melted butter. Put into a 375° oven for 10 or 15 minutes. *Serves* 6.

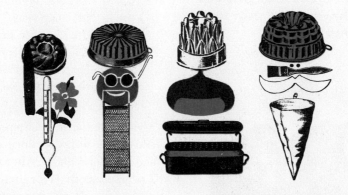

SOUPS

SOUPS
Minestre

Because of the immense variety of soups, their classification has been a problem for almost a century.

The problem is further compounded by the changing character of some soups and by the different interpretation of the same term from country to country and, within countries, from cookbook to cookbook. Thus, what is "basic stock" in one may be "broth" or "bouillon" in another, and "consommé" in a third. For some characteristically national dishes, there may be no equivalent English term. Thus, the Italian *Zuppa*, defined below, if translated literally as "soup," would give no hint of the fact that a *Zuppa* invariably includes vegetables.

We shall try to establish a classification which, while simple enough to be a dependable guide, will also be logical and, above all, adhere to the fundamental principles of fine cooking.

Soups may be divided into clear soups, thick soups based on purées and/or white sauces, and vegetable soups.

CLEAR SOUPS: BOUILLONS and CONSOMMÉS

Bouillons should be served boiling hot in hot soup plates. They may be garnished with rice, pasta, or croûtons; or with slivers or cubes of vegetables, meat, or other substances. The outstanding example of clear soups is the *Brodo Classico,* or Classic Bouillon.

Bouillon is the basis of various concentrated consommés, each with its own characteristic spices and flavorings. The preparation of these is a fine but not difficult art, dependent on following a few simple basic instructions.

Consommés are served in cups, usually without grated cheese. They are often accompanied by a delicate garnish appropriate to the base of the consommé and served either in the soup or on the side.

Very concentrated bouillons, called double consommés, are usually reserved for ceremonial dinners and more formal or elaborate supper parties. They are rarely served with a garnish, or, when they are, the garnish is served on the side. Such consommés are flavored and made fragrant by the addition of fortified wines (sherry, Madeira, Marsala, etc.) or essences of truffles or vegetables (tomatoes, celery, etc.). Double consommés may also be served cold in well-chilled cups.

PURÉES, CREAM SOUPS, and VELOUTÉ SOUPS

Thick soups may be divided into three major groups: purées or potages, cream soups, and Velouté soups. (The French "Velouté" is retained since it appears as commonly on American and English menus as on Italian and French. Its literal English translation, "velvet," describes the characteristic texture.)

The purée, traditionally known as a *potage,* is so called from its base which may be a single purée or a combination of purées. Purées are served with garnishes appropriate to their basic ingredients. Such garnishes may be rice, fried bread, a starchy vegetable (potatoes, lentils, chickpeas), etc.

Cream soups based on purées of meat, poultry, vegetables, fish, or shellfish are flavored with butter, usually thickened with Béchamel sauce or a white roux, and finished off with heavy cream. They are served with garnishes appropriate to the basic ingredients of the soup: rice, pasta, or tiny dumplings; slivers of poultry, meat, truffles, or mushrooms; custard royales; croûtons browned in butter; or a sprinkling of fresh herbs.

Velouté soups are generally composed of purée, bouillon, flour, butter, cream, and eggs. Their essential ingredient is a Velouté sauce, and they are invariably thickened at the end with butter and the yolks of eggs. They receive the same garnishes as creamed soups.

BISQUES and COULIS

The old terms for thick soups based on purées of fish —especially shellfish—and of poultry and game are included in the larger categories of cream or Velouté soups.

VEGETABLE SOUPS

Known in Italy as *Zuppe*, these soups are distinguished by their content of vegetables and, usually, pasta or bread. Vegetables normally form the larger part of the soup and, before being added, they are often pre-cooked in butter. *Zuppe* also include soups, such as the famous Zuppa Pavese, which contain no vegetables, but their richly flavored broth contains bread or pasta. *Minestroni* are a rather special class of Italian soups. These are so heavily laden with vegetables and pasta that a large bowl might almost serve as a meal in itself.

BOUILLONS
Brodi

The two bouillons [No. 323, No. 324] which begin this section may be served directly from the pot. Very frequently, however, they are used as a base for a more elaborate soup. While the hurried cook may substitute commercially available canned, powdered, or cubed concentrates, these will never provide the characteristically Italian body and flavor that distinguishes the homemade product.

A savory and delicious bouillon depends on knowing how to choose the ingredients, how to put them together, and how to superintend their cooking. The first essential in the preparation of bouillon or any other soup that begins with meat, poultry, game, or fish covered with cold water is to bring the cold water to a boil *very slowly* over *moderate heat*. Half an hour is by no means too long for this opening step. This long, slow, preliminary heating helps to extract the juices from the meat and make the soup flavorsome. If the water is rapidly brought to a boil, the albumen congeals and the essential nutrients and flavors of the meat are sealed in, rather than released. Thus, the novice, who has used the best ingredients and apparently carefully followed every other direction, may wonder why, after 2 or 3 hours of correct simmering, a tasteless, cloudy bouillon with tough, stringy meat is the result. The answer is often that a high heat has been initially employed to bring the water rapidly to the boiling point. Turning down the heat to a proper simmer after this initial error will not repair the damage.

It is by following this and a few other simple rules, embodied in the following recipes, that the preparation of a savory bouillon becomes a fine art.

323. WHITE BOUILLON
Brodo bianco

4 quarts cold water
Basic nutritive elements:
  2 pounds lean veal shank
  2 pounds raw, cracked veal bones
Basic aromatic elements:
  2 onions, peeled and each stuck with 1 clove
  3 carrots, thinly sliced
  3 leeks (white part only), finely sliced
  2 stalks celery with leaves, sliced or chopped
Bouquet Garni:
  Few sprigs of parsley
  Optional: 1 clove garlic, crushed in the garlic-press
  Few sprigs of thyme (or ¼ teaspoon dried)
  1 bay leaf
2 teaspoons salt
¼ teaspoon ground pepper

Put the meat and bones into a large kettle (preferably earthenware, but enamel or tinned copper may be used), cover with cold water, and bring *very slowly* to a boil over *moderate heat*. Simmer for a few minutes, drain, wash the meat and bones with cold water, and rinse out the kettle thoroughly. Return the meat and bones to the kettle, cover with 4 quarts of cold water, bring *very slowly* to a boil again, reduce heat so that the liquid barely simmers, and skim off any scum that rises to the

113

surface. The scum is merely coagulated albumen, but for a clear bouillon it must be carefully skimmed off several times at this early stage of the cooking. If a tablespoon of cold water is thrown into the pot from time to time, more of the scum will rise and can be removed. As soon as all of the scum is removed and no more is rising to the surface, add the aromatics, the Bouquet Garni, and the salt and pepper. Simmer for 3 to 4 hours (never more than 5). The time will depend upon the flavor, which the cook will recognize as just right or whether it is in need of further reducing. Remove from the fire. Skim off fat and strain soup through a colander lined with cheesecloth into another container. The cheesecloth should first be dipped in warm water and well wrung out to prevent its absorbing too much of the soup. Keep until ready to serve or to use as a base for other soups. *Makes about 2 quarts or serves 6.*

NOTE: The preliminary step of first blanching the veal and bones is highly recommended, since veal gives off more albumen than other meats, and the simplest means of getting rid of it is this blanching process.

324. CLASSIC BOUILLON
Brodo classico

Classic bouillon is more often used as a base for a wide variety of soups than the preceding white bouillon. Using both beef and chicken as its nutritive elements, it is both more strongly flavored and more subtle. The best cuts of beef for a classic bouillon are parts of the leg, shoulder, or the ribs nearer the shoulder. These cuts are sold in the United States under various names, depending upon the section of the country. Shank or shin is excellent, as it is very flavorsome; bottom round makes a fine bouillon, but tends to become rather dry after being simmered; or chuck is very satisfactory. Sirloin makes a succulent soup, especially when reinforced with veal bones, and this cut is particularly delicious eaten separately with a bit of the broth.

4 quarts cold water
Basic nutritive elements:
  2 pounds beef (*see above*)
  1 pound raw chicken giblets, necks, etc. (or other chicken parts)
  1 or 2 carcasses of chicken (if available), from a roasted (not boiled) chicken
  1 to 2 pounds marrow bones, cracked
  1 veal knuckle, cracked

Basic aromatic elements:
  2 onions, each stuck with 1 clove
  Optional: 1 clove garlic
  3 carrots, sliced
  3 leeks (white part only), finely sliced
  2 stalks celery with leaves, sliced or chopped
Bouquet Garni:
  3 sprigs parsley
  2 sprigs thyme (or ½ teaspoon dried)
  1 bay leaf
2 teaspoons salt
¼ teaspoon pepper (or 2 whole, bruised peppercorns)

Place the meats and bones in a roasting pan and roast in a 450° oven for 10 to 15 minutes until brown. Turn them occasionally to ensure even browning. Remove the chicken parts or bones sooner than the beef or other bones, as soon as they brown. As soon as all are brown, transfer to a 6- to 10-quart earthenware (or enamel or tinned copper) kettle and cover with the 4 quarts cold water. Bring *slowly* to a boil over *moderate heat;* turn down heat to a simmer; skim off scum with care and do so twice more by adding a tablespoon of cold water to the simmering soup to raise further scum. As soon as no more scum is rising, add all of the other ingredients. Simmer very gently for 3½ hours. Take the pot from the fire and skim off fat. Remove meat (if it is a good cut which you intend to serve separately, keep warm with a little of the broth) and correct for salt (being very careful not to oversalt). Strain into another receptacle through cheesecloth dipped in warm water and well wrung out. *Serves 6.*

325. FISH BOUILLON
Brodo di pesce

1¼ quarts dry white wine
1¼ quarts water
Nutritive elements:
  1½ to 2 pounds of fish (solid weight, without bones, skin, etc.), such as halibut, flounder, etc. (avoid oily fish, such as mackerel)
  1 pound fish heads, bones, and other available parts
Aromatic elements:
  1 cup chopped onion
  2 tablespoons chopped leeks (white part only)
  3 tablespoons chopped celery
Bouquet Garni:
  2 sprigs thyme (or ½ teaspoon dried)
  3 sprigs parsley
  1 bay leaf
1 tablespoon coarse salt

Proceed as in Classic Bouillon [No. 324], but omit the browning process and simmer gently for only 45 minutes over a moderate flame. Strain the bouillon through cheesecloth dipped in warm water and well wrung out. *Makes 2 quarts or serves 8.*

326. CHICKEN BOUILLON
Brodo di pollo

3 quarts cold water
Nutritive elements:
   1 4- to 5-pound stewing hen (the hen may be cut into
      pieces)
   3 sets of raw giblets, chopped
Aromatic elements:
   1 carrot, chopped
   1 leek (white part only), finely sliced
Bouquet Garni:
   1 bay leaf
   3 sprigs parsley
   2 sprigs thyme (or $1/2$ teaspoon dried)
2 teaspoons salt
$1/4$ teaspoon freshly ground pepper

Brown the hen and giblets in a 450° oven for about 15 to 20 minutes. Remove and put in a large earthenware (or enamel) pot with the water. Proceed as for Classic Bouillon [No. 324] but simmer for only $1 1/2$ to 2 hours (or more, if the hen is not sufficiently tender by that time). Taste and adjust seasoning. Remove from fire and skim off fat. Strain through cheesecloth dipped in warm water and well wrung out. *Makes 2 quarts or serves 6.*

327. VEGETABLE BOUILLON
Brodo vegetale o brodo di magro

$2 1/2$ quarts cold water
$1 1/2$ pounds potatoes, thinly sliced
2 onions, chopped
1 small bunch celery (or 6 stalks) with leaves, chopped
2 carrots, chopped
3 tomatoes, peeled, seeded, and thinly sliced
1 teaspoon salt
$1/4$ teaspoon freshly ground pepper
Bouquet Garni:
   1 clove
   3 sprigs parsley
   2 sprigs thyme (or $1/2$ teaspoon dried)
   1 bay leaf

Put all ingredients together in a large earthenware (or enamel) pot and bring slowly to a boil over *moderate*

heat. After it has reached a boil, reduce heat so that bouillon just simmers for $1 1/2$ hours. Remove the vegetables, which may be used as a garnish (unless they are too pulverized), and put the bouillon through a fine strainer. A small lump of butter added to each serving improves the flavor of the bouillon. *Makes 2 quarts or serves 8.*

GARNISHES FOR SOUPS
Guarnizioni per minestre

Garnishes for soups may be quite simple or very elaborate. Some are cooked in the soup, others are cooked separately and added to the soup at the moment it is served. Only rarely are they served on the side. We are including in this section a representative range of garnishes most widely used with both clear and thick soups.

Various garnishes for soups (see Nos. 328-42)

328. BRUNOISE
Brunoise

The ingredients of a Brunoise vary according to the character of the soup for which it is intended. It may be made up of single type of vegetable (carrots, celery, leeks, turnips, or artichokes) or of a mixture of vegetables. A general rule is to estimate 2 to 3 tablespoons of Brunoise for each quart of soup or bouillon. For particular soups, other ingredients are included in the Brunoise, such as chicken, game, smoked tongue, fish, etc.

General directions: Cut the vegetables into small dice, add a pinch of salt, cook them gently in butter (2 tablespoons per cup of vegetables) covered (do not brown), for 15 to 20 minutes; add bouillon, and continue cooking until they are tender.

329. CHEESE STRAWS
Pagliette al parmigiano

1 recipe Puff Paste [No. 1960] or an equal amount of
    leftover pieces from this or any similar dough
1 cup plus 3 tablespoons grated Parmesan cheese
1/8 teaspoon Cayenne pepper or 1 teaspoon paprika
1 egg, beaten

Turn [*see* No. 1960] the dough once or twice, incorporating the cheese and pepper at each turn. (If leftover dough is used, a scant tablespoon of cold water may be needed to bind it.) Roll out into a sheet 1/8 inch thick. Cut into 4- by 4-inch squares, and from these cut "sticks" or "straws" about 1/4 inch wide. Butter a pan lightly, spread the straws on it and, using a pastry brush, brush them lightly with beaten egg. Sprinkle lightly with the remaining grated Parmesan cheese and brown them in a 375° oven, about 10 minutes.

As a full recipe of puff paste makes a large quantity: the straws may be stored in an airtight container and crisped in the oven before using.

330. CRÊPES CÉLESTINE
Crespelle Célestine

3/4 cup flour, sifted
1/2 teaspoon salt
2 eggs, slightly beaten
1 tablespoon parsley, finely chopped
2 cups scalded milk (or boiling bouillon)
2 tablespoons butter, melted
Butter for frying

Mix the flour, salt, eggs, and parsley in a bowl. Slowly blend in the boiling liquid until the batter is smooth. Add the melted butter, mix thoroughly, and chill in the refrigerator for at least 2 hours. Heat a small frying pan, 7 inches in diameter (or use two or more if you

wish to speed the operation), add 1/4 teaspoon of butter, and when this is bubbling hot (not brown), pour in 2 tablespoons of the batter. Tilt the frying pan in all directions so that the mixture spreads evenly over its whole surface. As soon as the crêpe is lightly browned underneath, turn it and finish cooking the other side. Continue, using more butter, as needed, until the batter has been used up. Roll, and cut into fine strips before adding to soup. [For additional crêpe-making hints and instructions, *see* introduction to No. 2017]

NOTE: Crêpes may be made well in advance, even a day ahead, and stored, well wrapped, in the refrigerator.

331. SALTED CRÊPES
Crespelle salate

Use the same ingredients and method as in the preceding recipe, but increase the salt to 1 tablespoon.

332. CROÛTONS
Crostoncini

Remove the crusts from 4 slices of bread (use proportionately more if you are using French or Italian bread) and cut into 1/2-inch cubes. Sauté the cubes in 2 tablespoons of butter (use more as necessary) in a large skillet until golden brown. Toss them well during the cooking to ensure that they brown evenly on all sides.

The bread cubes may also be browned in a 375° oven, either brushed with melted butter or toasted dry. For some soups, as later recipes indicate, the bread is first lightly browned in the oven and then fried in butter.

This will make about 1 1/2 cups of croûtons, or enough for 2 quarts of soup.

333. DIAVOLINI
Diavolini

4 slices white bread, 1/4 inch thick
3/4 cup Béchamel Sauce [No. 18], reduced to 1/2 cup
1/4 cup grated Parmesan cheese
Pinch of Cayenne pepper

Cut 3/4-inch rounds from the slices of bread. Spread them with the reduced Béchamel sauce, sprinkle with the cheese and Cayenne, and brown in a 375° oven. *Makes 30 to 40 Diavolini, sufficient for 1 quart of soup.*

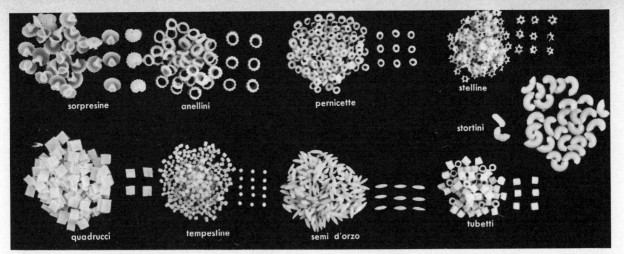

sorpresine   anellini   pernicette   stelline

stortini

quadrucci   tempesline   semi d'orzo   tubetti

Commercially available tiny pastas for soup garnishes, shown actual size. As their English-language names vary throughout various sections of the United States while their Italian names are standard, the names are untranslated.

334. JULIENNE VEGETABLES
Giuliana di legumi

Julienne vegetables are only used as garnishes for clear soups. Carrots, celery, onions, white part of leeks, turnips, tender white celery, or any other firm vegetable may be used, in any amount desired, first cut into little sticks about an inch long. The following model recipe provides enough for 2 quarts of soup, or sufficient to serve 8 :

2 small carrots
1 small turnip (about same amount as carrot)
2 leeks, white part only (about half the amount as
    turnip)
½ medium onion
2 stalks white celery (no leaves; no tough outer stalks)
½ teaspoon salt
3 tablespoons butter
4 cups Classic Bouillon [No. 324]
5 cups bouillon or consommé

Cut the vegetables as indicated above and cook, covered, in the butter and salt in a saucepan over very low fire, for about 15 minutes. Add the bouillon and simmer gently for 20 minutes. When ready to serve, add the vegetables and liquid to 5 cups of bouillon or consommé of your choice, bring to a simmer, and keep at a simmer for a few minutes to blend the flavors. If necessary, skim. *Serves 8.*

335. PARMESAN GÉNOISE
Génoise al parmigiano

2 eggs, separated
¼ cup all-purpose flour, sifted
½ cup grated Parmesan cheese
¼ teaspoon nutmeg

Beat the egg whites until stiff peaks form. In a larger bowl, beat the yolks slightly and blend in the flour, nutmeg, and cheese. Gently fold in the egg whites. Spread the mixture about 1 inch thick in a buttered 8-inch square baking pan and bake in a slow oven (250° to 300°) for 20 to 25 minutes. Cook, and slice or cut into desired shapes. This is one of the best garnishes for consommés. *Makes enough for* 1 *quart.*

336. PASTINE
Pastine

The very tiny pastas are best adapted to soups. Commercially available, these include *anellini* (tiny rings), *quadrucci* (tiny squares), *capelli d'angelo* (the finest of noodles), *tubetti* (tiny tubes), and other tiny shapes *(sorpresine, permicette, stelline*—tiny stars—*tempestine, semi d'orzo*—beads of pasta the size of barley—etc.). About ½ cup, uncooked, should be added for each quart of soup.

337. PRIMAVERILE
Primaverile

This is the classic garnish for Consommé Printanier.

2 quarts consommé of your choice
2 carrots, cut in julienne
1 turnip, peeled and cut in julienne
½ cup tender young peas
½ cup green beans, shredded French-style
Optional: ½ cup asparagus tips (the very tender ends
    only)

Blanch the carrots and turnips for 5 minutes in boiling, salted water. Drain and cook them in the 2 quarts of boiling consommé for 10 to 15 minutes until just tender. Cook the peas, beans, and optional asparagus, each separately, in lightly salted water until just tender and add them to the consommé just before serving. *Serves* 8.

338. PROFITEROLES
Profiteroles

Prepare ½ a recipe of Cream Puff Dough [No. 1990]—omitting sugar—and put in a pastry bag. Using a small round nozzle, squeeze out tiny balls, about the size of a large bean, onto a baking sheet slightly dampened with water and bake for 10 to 12 minutes in a 425° oven. These are one of the best garnishes for a good consommé. *Makes a sufficient amount for 2 quarts of consommé.*

339. QUENELLES
Morbidelle o chenelline

These are tiny dumplings, not much larger than a lima bean, either round or slightly oblong. They are made from various forcemeats of meat, chicken, game, or fish [Nos. 129-34]. A pastry bag (or a paper cornucopia) is filled with the mixture which is then forced through the nozzle in tiny balls onto a large, buttered frying pan. About ten minutes before serving, pour boiling salted water very slowly and gently over them and place in a hot (400°) oven for 8 to 10 minutes. Estimate about 30 of these tiny dumplings (about 1 cup of forcemeat) for a quart of consommé if no other garnish is used. If a second garnish is included, 20 of these for each quart are sufficient.

340. RAVIOLINI
Raviolini mignons

These are one of the most delicious garnishes for a good bouillon or consommé. Follow the directions given for preparation of Ravioli [Nos. 505-10], and make tiny ravioli of your choice ¾ inch square. Cook them in a little bouillon, drain, and add to the clear boiling soup just at the moment of serving. Serve with grated Parmesan cheese on the side.

341. ROYALES
Reale

Royales are an excellent garnish for clear soups (only rarely are they served with thickened soups). They vary in name according to the purée on which they are based, as: royale of carrots, celery, asparagus tips, peas, tomatoes, chicken, or game.

2 eggs
1 cup Consommé [No. 360]

2 tablespoons any purée of cooked vegetable or very finely ground cooked meat (*see* above)
1 tablespoon heavy cream

Beat the eggs until very light and gradually add the consommé. Blend in the purée and cream, fill royale molds *(darioles)*, and bake in a *bain marie* (hot water bath) in a moderate oven for 20 to 25 minutes. Remove from the oven, cool, chill, and, when completely cold, remove from the molds. Cut into fancy shapes. *Makes sufficient for 2 quarts of consommé.*

NOTE: If royale molds are not available, the mixture may be poured into a buttered baking dish large enough so that the custard will be ½ inch deep. Bake for 20 minutes or until it is set in the middle. Cool, turn out, and cut into squares or small fancy shapes.

342. STRACCIATA
Stracciata

These are usually leaves of lettuce or of fresh savory, very finely shredded and cooked until transparent in butter. They are used as a supplementary garnish for several soups.

GARNISHED BOUILLONS
Minestre chiare all'italiana

Italian cooks over the years have adapted basic bouillons and imbued them with distinctive regional flavors, ingredients, garnishes, and styles. We include in this section a characteristic selection of these delicious soups.

343. BOUILLON BOLOGNESE
Brodo alla bolognese

2 quarts White or Classic Bouillon [No. 323 or No. 324]
3 eggs, separated
6 tablespoons breadcrumbs
6 tablespoons grated Parmesan cheese
¼ teaspoon salt
Pinch freshly ground pepper
Pinch nutmeg

Beat the egg whites until stiff. Lightly fold into them the well-beaten egg yolks, breadcrumbs, grated Parmesan cheese, salt, pepper, and nutmeg. Do *not* overmix. The mixture should be very light.

Bring the bouillon to a boil, turn down flame, and keep it at a simmer. Drop the egg/cheese mixture into the simmering bouillon, a teaspoonful at a time. Simmer uncovered for about 8 minutes. Additional grated Parmesan cheese may be served on the side. *Serves* 6.

344. BOUILLON WITH BREADCRUMBS
Brodo con pangrattato

2 quarts White or Classic Bouillon [No. 323 or 324]
8 slices day-old bread
3 eggs
1 cup grated Parmesan cheese

Toast the slices of bread in a slow (275°) oven until lightly golden and crush to provide about 8 tablespoons of crumbs (or whirl in electric blender). Beat the eggs until frothy and add 5 tablespoons of the cheese. Bring the bouillon to a boil and drop the breadcrumbs in all at once. Keep the bouillon at a boil for 2 or 3 minutes so that it thickens slightly. Pour the egg/cheese mixture into a warm tureen and, little by little, pour the slightly thickened boiling broth over it gently, beating the mixture continuously with a wire whisk. Serve with the remaining grated Parmesan cheese on the side. *Serves* 6.

345. BOUILLON WITH CAPPELLETTI ROMANA
Brodo con cappelletti alla romana

2 quarts White or Classic Bouillon [No. 323 or 324]
Dough for cappelletti:
  3 cups sifted flour
  1 teaspoon salt
  4 eggs
  2 tablespoons water (if needed)
Filling for cappelletti:
  ¼ pound raw pork
  1 thick slice Bologna sausage (or sweet Italian sausage)
  1 thick slice prosciutto
  ¼ pound white meat of either chicken or turkey
  2 ounces lamb brains (or substitute sweetbreads or chicken liver)
  2 tablespoons grated Parmesan cheese
  Pinch nutmeg
  1 teaspoon salt
  ¼ teaspoon freshly ground pepper
  1 egg, beaten
  ¼ cup Marsala wine

Prepare a noodle-type dough [*see* No. 482], which should not be too stiff, and let it rest while preparing the filling.

Put all the filling ingredients (except the egg and wine) through the food chopper, using the finest blade. Work the beaten egg and Marsala into the mixture until it is smooth. Keep in a cool place. The filling is improved by a little "ripening" and can be prepared earlier in the day, or even the day before. It should be left covered in a cold place. If kept in refrigerator, bring to room temperature before use.

Roll out the dough into a thin sheet and cut out rounds of dough with a cooky cutter (or round glass) about 3 inches in diameter. Fill each round with a scant teaspoon of filling, fold over dough to form a half moon. Seal the edges well by moistening with a little water and pressing together firmly. Then bring the two ends of the half moon together to form the cappelletti or "little hats." Remove to a clean cloth. Gather remaining pieces of dough, roll out, cut and fill, and repeat until all the dough and filling have been used up. (If the last pieces of dough fail to roll easily, add a *very* little water to bind them.) The filled cappelletti may rest, covered, in a cool place for 24 hours before cooking.

Drop the cappelletti into the boiling bouillon and cook about 10 to 15 minutes. Serve with grated Parmesan cheese on the side. *Serves* 6.

NOTE: Roman cappelletti are larger in size and use uncooked filling, in contrast to the smaller-sized tortellini which are of the same shape but employ cooked fillings. Bouillon with tortellini is more often found in the Romagna, the region north of Florence.

Bouillon with Spinach Gnocchi
(No. 350): see page 121

119

346. BOUILLON WITH EGG RIBBONS
Brodo con uova filate

2 quarts White or Classic Bouillon [No. 323 or 324]
2 cups sifted flour (or slightly more)
3 eggs
1 tablespoon grated Parmesan cheese
½ teaspoon salt
Pinch nutmeg
Pinch freshly ground pepper

Bring the bouillon to a boil and turn heat down to a simmer. Mix the remaining ingredients to make a soft dough. Use a little more flour if the dough is too wet, but it should be quite soft. Fill a pastry bag with the dough. Using a very small round tube, press slowly but steadily on the bag so that a thin, continuous ribbon of dough emerges. The ribbon should be about the size of vermicelli. Use a circular motion as it falls into the lightly bubbling bouillon, taking care that it does not double over on itself into a solid mass. When all the dough has been squeezed into the broth, stir it very gently with a wooden spoon and keep it simmering for a few minutes. Serve very hot. *Serves 6.*

347. BOUILLON WITH MEAT GNOCCHI
Brodo con gnocchetti di carne

These tiny gnocchi or dumplings are made by combining a rich, soft dough with finely ground meat or poultry.

2 cups milk
1 teaspoon salt
Pinch nutmeg
½ cup butter
2½ cups flour
6 eggs

¾ pound raw lean beef (or raw chicken meat), very finely ground
3 quarts Bouillon [Nos. 323 or 324, or No. 326 if chicken is used]
½ cup grated Parmesan cheese

Put the milk, salt, nutmeg, and butter in a saucepan; bring to a boil over high heat; and remove from the fire. Stir in the flour and mix thoroughly. Return the pan to the heat and cook for 1 or 2 minutes until the mixture comes away from the sides of the pan. Remove from the heat and, one by one, add the eggs, beating well after each addition.

Mix the finely ground meat thoroughly into the soft dough. Let it rest for 1 hour in a cool place and then shape into tiny balls the size of a hazelnut. Bring the bouillon to a boil and drop in gnocchi, one by one. As they float to the surface, remove with a slotted spoon and drop into a tureen, warmed with a little of the hot bouillon in the bottom. When all the dumplings have been removed, bring remaining bouillon to a rapid boil and gently pour through a fine sieve over dumplings in tureen. Serve with grated Parmesan cheese on the side. *Serves 8.*

348. BOUILLON WITH POTATO GNOCCHI
Brodo con gnocchetti di patate

2 quarts White or Classic Bouillon [No. 323 or 324]
1 pound "old" potatoes
3 tablespoons butter, softened
1 cup grated Parmesan cheese
3 egg yolks, well beaten
¼ teaspoon salt
Pinch nutmeg
Flour

Cook the potatoes in their jackets in boiling water until tender, peel, and, while still hot, mash them in a warm bowl. Add the butter and ⅓ of the Parmesan cheese. Season with salt and nutmeg. Make a smooth dough by incorporating the beaten egg yolks thoroughly. With slightly floured hands, shape the mixture on a floured board into a thin roll 1 inch in diameter and let it rest for ½ hour. Bring the bouillon to a boil, slice off pieces of the dough the size of an olive, and drop them into the boiling bouillon. As soon as the bouillon returns to a boil remove the pan from the fire. Serve at once with grated Parmesan cheese on the side. *Serves 6.*

349. BOUILLON WITH SEMOLINA GNOCCHI
Brodo con morbidelle piccole di semolino

2 quarts White or Classic Bouillon [No. 323 or 324]
1 cup semolina (or farina)
2 eggs
3 tablespoons butter, melted
Pinch nutmeg
$\frac{1}{2}$ teaspoon salt
$\frac{1}{8}$ teaspoon freshly ground pepper
2 quarts boiling water

Put the eggs and melted butter into a bowl and beat vigorously with a wire whisk until they become frothy. Add seasonings, and pour in semolina gently but steadily, beating continuously all the while with a wooden spoon so that a smooth paste, without lumps, results. Bring 2 quarts of water to a boil in a large saucepan. Using an after-dinner coffee spoon (the dumplings must be very tiny), scoop up a little of the semolina mixture. Using a second spoon of the same size, first dipped into the boiling water, push the mixture off into the boiling water. Continue until all of the semolina mixture is used up. Cover the pot and, without boiling but at a fairly high temperature, cook the dumplings until firm—about 10 minutes. Drain, distribute in soup plates, and cover them with boiling bouillon. Grated Parmesan cheese may be served on the side. *Serves* 6.

350. BOUILLON WITH SPINACH GNOCCHI
Brodo con gnocchetti malfatti

2 quarts White or Classic Bouillon [No. 323 or 324]
$\frac{1}{4}$ pound raw spinach
1 cup grated Parmesan cheese
2 tablespoons breadcrumbs
2 tablespoons flour
$\frac{1}{2}$ teaspoon salt
$\frac{1}{8}$ teaspoon freshly ground pepper
Pinch nutmeg
2 egg yolks
1 tablespoon heavy cream (plus $\frac{1}{2}$ tablespoon more if necessary)

Wash the spinach thoroughly, drain well, and cook for 5 minutes, covered, in only the water that clings to the leaves. Cool, squeeze thoroughly between hands to remove excess water, and pass it through a food mill (or chop it and blend in electric blender on high speed

very briefly being careful not to liquefy). Add $\frac{1}{3}$ cup of the cheese, the breadcrumbs, flour, salt, pepper, and nutmeg. Beat the egg yolks thoroughly with the cream and incorporate with the spinach. Scoop out small teaspoonsful of the mixture and drop into boiling bouillon. As soon as the bouillon returns to a boil, remove the pot from the fire and serve at once with the remaining grated Parmesan cheese on the side. *Serves* 6.

351. BOUILLON WITH CHOPPED LETTUCE
Brodo con lattughe

Boiling water
1 head of lettuce (preferably Boston lettuce, *never* iceberg)
$2\frac{1}{2}$ quarts Bouillon [No. 323 or 324]

Pour boiling water over a head of tender lettuce and let it stand for 5 minutes. Drain, cool, squeeze well between the hands to remove excess water, and chop very fine. Bring $\frac{1}{3}$ of the bouillon to a boil and cook the lettuce in it at a moderate heat. When the bouillon has been reduced by $\frac{1}{2}$, add the rest of the bouillon, raise the heat and cook for about 10 minutes more. Serve very hot with toast and grated Parmesan cheese on the side. *Serves* 6.

352. BOUILLON WITH PASSATELLI MARCHIGIANA
Brodo con passatelli alla marchigiana

2 quarts White or Classic Bouillon [No. 323 or 324]
6 tablespoons fine breadcrumbs
2 eggs
2 tablespoons grated Parmesan cheese
2 tablespoons beef marrow
$\frac{1}{2}$ teaspoon salt
$\frac{1}{8}$ teaspoon freshly ground pepper

Bring the bouillon to a boil. Mix together all the other ingredients very thoroughly and force the mixture through a colander or a ricer. With a sharp knife or

121

scissors, cut the emerging cylinders of the dough free at about ½-inch lengths and let them drop directly into the boiling bouillon. When all of the mixture has been dropped into the bouillon, reduce the heat to the lowest possible point and cook 5 minutes. Grated Parmesan cheese may be served on the side. *Serves 6.*

NOTE: Passatelli, in the Marches, are made with a special utensil, *ferro per passatelli* or passatelli iron, a circular, convex, iron utensil with holes through which the paste is pushed with wooden sticks. When cut free they resemble fine vermicelli.

353. BOUILLON WITH GRATED PASTA
Brodo con pasta grattugiata

2 quarts White or Classic Bouillon [No. 323 or 324]
1¼ cups sifted flour
¼ cup semolina
3 eggs, beaten
Pinch nutmeg
½ teaspoon salt
1 cup grated Parmesan cheese

Make a rather dry, stiff noodle-type dough [*see* No.482] of the flour, semolina, beaten eggs, salt, and nutmeg. Let it rest, covered, for 1 hour. Grate the dough using the coarse side of the grater, and let the pieces dry thoroughly for 3 or 4 hours on a lightly floured board. Bring the bouillon to a boil; drop in the grated dough, and cook at a moderate simmer for 10 to 15 minutes. Serve with the grated Parmesan cheese on the side. *Serves 6.*

354. BOUILLON WITH PASTINA
Brodo con pastina

1¼ cups pastina [*see* No. 336]
2 quarts White or Classic Bouillon [No. 323 or 324]
1 cup grated Parmesan cheese

Drop the pastina into boiling bouillon. When it returns to a boil, lower the flame and continue cooking for 10 minutes. Serve with grated Parmesan cheese on the side. *Serves 6.*

355. BOUILLON WITH SEMOLINA
Brodo con semolino

3 quarts Classic Bouillon [No. 324]
⅔ cup semolina (or farina)
1 cup grated Parmesan cheese

Bring the bouillon to a boil and, very slowly but steadily, pour in the semolina, stirring constantly to prevent lumps, until it has all been added. Cook gently for about ½ hour. Serve with grated Parmesan cheese on the side. *Serves 8.*

356. BOUILLON WITH HOMEMADE TAGLIARINI
Brodo con tagliarini

4 cups flour, sifted
4 eggs
½ teaspoon salt
3 quarts White or Classic Bouillon [No. 323 or 324]
1 cup grated Parmesan cheese

Prepare a noodle dough with the flour, salt, and eggs [*see* No. 482], and let it rest, covered, for ½ hour. Break off some of the dough and roll out paper-thin on a lightly floured board. Cut off any thick edges and roll up, jelly-roll fashion, making a loose, flattish roll about 4 or 5 inches wide. Using a sharp knife with a wide blade, cut the roll into narrow strips about ¼ inch wide. Repeat this process until all of the dough has been used. Spread the noodles out on a lightly floured cloth (or in a large colander) so that they may dry slightly.

Bring the bouillon to a boil, drop in the noodles, and let them boil over moderate heat for about 10 minutes. Serve with grated Parmesan cheese on the side. *Serves 8.*

357. BOUILLON WITH TORTELLINI BOLOGNESE
Brodo con tortellini alla bolognese

3 quarts White or Classic Bouillon [No. 323 or 324]
Tortellini dough [*see* No. 518]
Tortellini filling:
  ¼ pound cooked smoked ham (both fat and lean)
  ¼ pound beef marrow
  ¾ pound ground pork loin, cooked for 10 minutes in 2 tablespoons butter
  1 thick slice Bologna sausage
  1 egg yolk
  ¼ cup grated Parmesan cheese
  Pinch nutmeg

Prepare the tortellini dough and let it rest as directed in No. 518. Using the fine blade, put the meats and the beef marrow through the food chopper. Then work in the egg yolk, cheese, and nutmeg; mix very thoroughly. Prepare the tortellini, making them as small as possible (about 1 inch square), and fill them with the filling, as described in No. 518. Allow them to rest, covered, in a cool place for 24 hours. Just before serving, bring the soup to a boil in a large saucepan, drop in the tortellini, and cook for about 15 minutes. Grated Parmesan cheese may be served on the side. *Serves 8.*

358. BOUILLON WITH TORTELLINI MODENESE
Brodo con tortellini alla modenese

It is a comment on the intensely individualistic character of food in each region of Italy that although Modena is only a scant hour's train ride from Bologna, the filling for these tortellini differs considerably from that of the preceding Bologna recipe.

3 quarts White or Classic Bouillon [No. 323 or 324]
Tortellini dough [*see* No. 518]
Tortellini filling:
   $\frac{1}{2}$ the breast of either a roasted turkey or capon, with the skin removed
   $\frac{1}{2}$ pound ricotta cheese
1 heaping cup grated Parmesan cheese
2 egg yolks
Pinch white pepper
Pinch nutmeg
$\frac{1}{4}$ teaspoon salt
$\frac{1}{2}$ teaspoon grated lemon rind

Follow the procedure for preparing, filling, and cooking the tortellini as in the preceding recipe, No. 357. Grated Parmesan cheese may be served on the side. *Serves 8.*

359. STRACCIATELLA
Stracciatella

2 quarts White or Classic Bouillon [No. 323 or 324]
4 eggs
4 tablespoons semolina (or farina)
4 tablespoons grated Parmesan cheese
Pinch nutmeg
$\frac{1}{2}$ teaspoon salt

Reserve 1 cup of cold bouillon; put the rest over medium heat in a heavy pot and bring to a boil. Put the eggs, semolina, cheese, and seasonings into a bowl and slowly add the 1 cup of cold broth, beating continuously with a wire whisk to avoid lumps. Pour all at once into the boiling bouillon and reduce heat to a simmer. Stir vigorously for 3 or 4 minutes. This will give you a slightly flaky stracciatella. Grated Parmesan cheese may be served on the side. *Serves 6.*

CONSOMMÉS
Brodi ristretti

Consommés are prepared by reducing a bouillon made from beef, poultry, or fish. Consommés should not be served with grated cheese, as the heightened flavor of a consommé should be savored alone. Often, the consommé is thickened with tapioca which gives it a certain delicacy and an especially pleasant flavor and consistency. Before serving, the consommé should be strained through a cheesecloth which has been dipped in warm water and wrung out well. Consommés may be served hot or very cold, jellied.

360. CONSOMMÉ
Brodo ristretto—consommé

For 2 quarts:
   $2\frac{1}{2}$ quarts Classic Bouillon [No. 324]
   $\frac{3}{4}$ pound very lean beef (trimmed of gristle and sinews), chopped
   1 carrot, sliced
   1 leek (white part only), finely sliced
   1 egg white
   1 egg shell, crushed

Put the beef, vegetables, egg shell, and egg white into a large earthenware (or enamel or tinned copper) pot. Add the bouillon all at once if cold, but a little at a time if it is hot, stirring constantly, in order to avoid instantaneous cooking of the egg white, which would interfere with its clarifying function. The egg white may be lightly beaten before it is added, but constant stirring is still necessary. Put the pot over a very low flame, and without stopping the beating, bring it gently to a simmer: discontinue beating, cover, and let it barely simmer for 1 hour. During this time, the meat will release its juices, the vegetables their fragrance, and the egg white and shell will clarify the consommé. Pour into a bowl, straining consommé through a triple thickness of cheesecloth, dipped in warm water and wrung out well. *Makes 2 quarts or serves 6.*

123

361. CHICKEN CONSOMMÉ
Brodo di pollo ristretto—consommé

2½ quarts Chicken Bouillon [No. 326]
¾ pound chicken meat (trimmed of all sinews, skin, and gristle), chopped
1 egg white
1 egg shell, crushed

Prepare exactly as in the preceding recipe.

362. FISH CONSOMMÉ
Brodo di pesce ristretto

2½ quarts Fish Bouillon [No. 325]
1½ pounds fish (solid weight, after skin, bones have been removed), chopped or cut in small pieces
2 tablespoons coarsely chopped parsley
2 egg whites
2 egg shells, crushed

Prepare exactly as Consommé [No. 360].

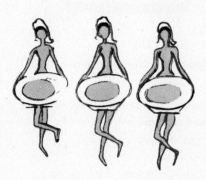

GARNISHED CONSOMMÉS
Consommés con guarnizioni

363. CONSOMMÉ AURORA
Consommé Aurora

2 quarts Chicken Consommé [No. 361]
6 tablespoons canned tomato purée (*not* paste)
Pinch sugar
½ cup cooked chicken, cut into slivers

Bring the consommé to a boil. Add the tomato purée and sugar, bring to a boil again, and garnish with the slivers of chicken. *Serves 6.*

364. CONSOMMÉ WITH BARLEY
Consommé con orzo perlato

1 quart Consommé [No. 360]
1 quart White Bouillon [No. 323]
¾ cup pearl barley
1 stalk celery, finely sliced

Wash the barley in warm water and then parboil it in 2 quarts boiling, salted water for 20 minutes; drain, rinse under cold water, and put it into a pot. Cover it with the bouillon, add the sliced celery, and bring it to a boil. Reduce the heat to moderate and continue cooking for 45 minutes. When ready to serve, bring the consommé to a boil. Drain the barley and celery, add them to the consommé, and then turn into a tureen. *Serves 6.*

NOTE: Although the bouillon is discarded, it may be saved and used in the preparation of sauces, other soups, etc.

365. CONSOMMÉ WITH BEEF MARROW
Consommé con midollo di bue

2½ quarts Consommé [No. 360]
6 beef marrow bones, cut into sections 3 inches long
1 recipe Diavolini [No. 333]

Poach the marrow bones for 6 minutes in 2 cups of the consommé. Scoop out the marrow from the bones and cut into thin slices. Bring the remaining consommé to a boil, reduce heat, add the slices of marrow, and simmer for 2 minutes. Serve the diavolini on the side. *Serves 6.*

366. CONSOMMÉ CASALINGA
Consommé all'italiana a mio modo

2 quarts Consommé [No. 360]
½ cup tomato paste
½ recipe Risotto Milanese [No. 578]
2 white truffles, thinly sliced [or No. 1819a]
1 cup grated Parmesan cheese

Beat the tomato paste into the consommé, which has been heated to the boiling point. Simmer for 15 minutes. Serve it garnished with Risotto Milanese mixed with the sliced white truffles, and sprinkle the grated Parmesan cheese on top. *Serves 6.*

367. CONSOMMÉ CÉLESTINE
Consommé Célestine

2 quarts Chicken Consommé [No. 361], or Consommé
   [No. 360]
4 tablespoons quick-cooking tapioca
½ cup dry sherry, dry Madeira, or dry Port wine
1 recipe Crêpes Célestine [No. 330]

Bring the consommé slowly to a boil with the tapioca, stirring constantly. Just before serving, add the wine and the Crêpes Célestine cut into fine strips. *Serves* 6.

368. CONSOMMÉ CHASSEUR
Consommé chasseur

2 quarts Chicken Consommé [No. 361]
4 tablespoons quick-cooking tapioca
½ cup Port wine
2 truffles, thinly sliced
1 recipe Profiteroles [No. 338]

Bring the consommé slowly to a boil with the tapioca, stirring constantly. Add the wine and garnish with sliced truffles. Serve the profiteroles on the side. *Serves* 6.

369. CONSOMMÉ WITH CHICKEN WINGS
Consommé con alette di pollo

2 quarts Chicken Consommé [No. 361]
8 chicken wings
1 cup Chicken Bouillon [No. 326]
2 tablespoons butter
Salt and freshly ground pepper
½ cup white rice, cooked just *al dente* in bouillon
   [*see* No. 592]

Put the chicken wings, chicken bouillon, and butter in a small casserole, season lightly with salt and pepper, cover the casserole tightly, and place it in a moderate (350°) oven for 25 minutes. Remove from the oven and bone the wings. Bring the consommé to a boil and garnish with the meat from the wings and rice. *Serves* 6.

370. CONSOMMÉ DIANA
Consommé Diana

3½ quarts Game Stock [No. 7]
¾ cup pearl barley
Quenelles [No. 339] made with 1 cup Game Forcemeat
   [No. 129]
3 tablespoons diced celery, cooked for 10 minutes in
   1 tablespoon butter

Parboil the barley in 1 quart water for 20 minutes; drain, rinse well, and cook the barley in 4 cups of the stock until tender (about 1 hour) and then drain it. Bring the remaining stock to a boil and reduce to 2 quarts, or until it has a good strong flavor. Garnish with the barley, celery, and quenelles. *Serves* 6.

371. CONSOMMÉ WITH DIAVOLINI
Consommé con diavolini

2 quarts of Chicken Consommé [No. 361]
4 tablespoons quick-cooking tapioca
1 recipe Diavolini [No. 333]

Bring the consommé slowly to a boil with the tapioca, stirring constantly. Then garnish with the Diavolini. *Serves* 6.

372. CONSOMMÉ DORIA
Consommé Doria

2 quarts Chicken Consommé [No. 361]
1 recipe Quenelles [No. 339] made with 1 cup chicken
   Forcemeat [No. 129] and ¼ cup finely chopped
   gherkins
1 cup Cream Puff Dough [No. 1990]—made without
   sugar—mixed with ½ cup grated Parmesan cheese
Fat for deep frying

Cook the quenelles made with chicken forcemeat and the chopped gherkins as indicated in No. 339. Fry tiny bits of the cream puff dough mixed with the grated Parmesan cheese in deep hot (375°) fat. Bring the consommé to a boil and garnish with the quenelles and the tiny fried puffs. *Serves* 6.

373. ENGLISH CONSOMMÉ
Consommé Albione

2 quarts Fish Consommé [No. 362]
Quenelles [No. 339] made from 1½ cups Mousseline
  Fish Forcemeat [No. 132]
4 tablespoons quick-cooking tapioca
2 white truffles, very thinly sliced

Cook the quenelles as indicated in No. 339, and reserve. Add the tapioca to the consommé and bring it slowly to a boil, stirring constantly. Garnish with the quenelles and the truffle slices. *Serves* 6.

374. CONSOMMÉ ITALIANA
Consommé all'italiana

2 quarts Chicken Consommé [No. 361]
1 recipe Raviolini [No. 340]
A sauce made of:
  2 cups Brown Veal Stock [No. 5], reduced to 1 cup
  ½ cup Tomato Sauce [No. 19]
  3 tablespoons fresh sage, chopped (or 1 teaspoon
    dried)
  1 cup grated Parmesan cheese

Serve the consommé very hot in heated cups. Serve with it plates of tiny ravioli sprinkled with fresh sage and with a sauce made of the reduced veal stock mixed with the tomato sauce. If fresh sage is not available, simmer the dried sage for 10 minutes in the tomato sauce. Sprinkle the whole lightly with the Parmesan cheese. *Serves* 6.

375. CONSOMMÉ WITH JULIENNE VEGETABLES
Consommé con nastrini di ortaggi

2½ quarts Consommé [No. 360]
¼ medium cabbage
¼ head lettuce (*not* iceberg)
1 onion
2 small carrots
1 small turnip
1 leek (white part only)
2 stalks celery
3 tablespoons butter
Pinch sugar
¼ teaspoon salt
4 tablespoons cooked peas

Shred the cabbage into fine strips, pour boiling water over it, and let it stand for ten minutes. Shred the lettuce finely. Cut the onion, carrots, turnip, leek, and celery into very thin strips; season with the salt and sugar; and sauté them gently in the butter, covered, for 5 minutes. Pour 2 cups of the consommé over the vegetables and bring to a boil. Reduce heat, add the parboiled cabbage, and simmer until the vegetables are tender (but not mushy), about 10 minutes. When ready to serve, bring the remaining 2 quarts of consommé to a boil, add the cooked peas, the shredded lettuce, and the other vegetables with their liquid. Pour into a warm soup tureen and serve at once. *Serves* 6.

376. CONSOMMÉ MADRILENA
Consommé alla madrilena

2½ quarts Chicken Consommé [No. 361]
6 stalks celery with leaves, sliced
6 small Italian plum tomatoes, peeled, seeded, and
  thinly sliced
1 sweet yellow pepper roasted, skinned, and cut into
  fine strips [*see* No. 145]

Simmer the consommé with the celery for 40 minutes, strain, discard celery, and reheat to the boiling point. Serve the consommé garnished with small slices of raw tomato and the strips of roasted pepper. *Serves* 6.

377. CONSOMMÉ MESSALINA
Consommé Messalina

2 quarts Chicken Consommé [No. 361]
1 cup canned tomato purée (*not* paste)
12 chicken hearts, boiled for 5 minutes in 1 cup
  Classic Bouillon [No. 324], and chopped
1 yellow pepper, roasted, skinned, and cut into fine
  strips [*see* No. 145]
½ cup rice, cooked in 1½ cups Classic Bouillon [No.
  324] until just *al dente*

Mix the tomato purée thoroughly with the consommé, which has been heated to the boiling point. Garnish with the chopped boiled chicken hearts, the strips of roasted peppers, and the rice. *Serves* 6.

378. CONSOMMÉ POLAIRE
Consommé polaire

2 quarts Chicken Consommé [No. 361]
4 tablespoons quick-cooking tapioca
6 raw egg yolks

Bring the consommé to a boil with the tapioca, stirring constantly. Simmer for 5 minutes. Serve the consommé in heated cups and carefully drop 1 raw egg yolk in each cup. *Serves* 6.

379. CONSOMMÉ À LA REINE
Consommé à la reine

2 quarts Chicken Consommé [No. 361]
4 tablespoons quick-cooking tapioca
1 recipe Royales [No. 341], made with 2 tablespoons
    cooked, finely ground chicken
¾ cup cooked chicken (all white meat), cut into slivers

Bring the consommé to a boil with the tapioca, stirring constantly. Simmer for 5 minutes. When ready to serve, garnish with the royales, diced or cut into fancy shapes, and the slivers of chicken. *Serves 6.*

380. CONSOMMÉ ROSSINI
Consommé Rossini

2 quarts Chicken Consommé [No. 361]
4 tablespoons quick-cooking tapioca
½ cup pâté de foie gras
½ cup truffles [or No. 1819a]
1 recipe Profiteroles [No. 338], baked about the size of
    a hazelnut

Bring the consommé to a boil with the tapioca, stirring constantly. Simmer 5 minutes. Purée truffles in electric blender. Thoroughly blend the pâté de foie gras and truffle purée, put the mixture into a pastry bag fitted with a very small round tip, and fill the tiny profiteroles. Garnish the soup with these profiteroles. *Serves 6.*

381. CONSOMMÉ TREVISO
Consommé Treviso—ai tre filetti

2 quarts Chicken Consommé [No. 361]
4 tablespoons quick-cooking tapioca
½ cup slivered white meat of cooked chicken
½ cup slivered tongue (pickled or smoked)
¼ cup slivered truffles [or No. 1819a], sprinkled with
    1 tablespoon dry Marsala wine

Bring the consommé to a boil with the tapioca, stirring constantly. Simmer 5 minutes. Garnish with the chicken, tongue, and truffles. *Serves 6.*

CONSOMMÉS WITH SPECIAL ESSENCES
Consommés con fumetti

These consommés are heightened by the addition of just a single strong flavor or essence. No additional garnish is served with them, as this would detract from the enjoyable taste of the one heightened flavor.

382. CONSOMMÉ WITH CELERY ESSENCE
Consommé all'essenza di sedano

2 quarts Consommé [No. 360]
1 cup finely chopped celery (inner stalks only), leaves
    removed

Bring consommé to a boil, add the chopped celery, and simmer for 10 minutes. *Serves 6.*

383. CONSOMMÉ WITH MUSHROOM ESSENCE
Consommé all'essenza di fungo

2 quarts Consommé [No. 360]
1 cup mushrooms, finely minced (Morel mushrooms are
    best. In parts of the United States they are available in the early spring.)
¼ cup *Boletus edulis* mushrooms [*see* **introduction to No. 1701**], finely minced

Bring consommé to a boil, add the mushrooms, and simmer for 15 minutes. *Serves 6.*

384. CONSOMMÉ WITH TOMATO ESSENCE
Consommé all'essenza di pomodoro

2 quarts Consommé [No. 360]
4 large (or 6 small) very ripe tomatoes, peeled, seeded,
    chopped, and puréed through a sieve or a food mill (do not press so hard as to crush any remaining seeds; this will make the consommé bitter)

Bring the consommé to a boil, add the puréed tomatoes, and simmer for 10 minutes. *Serves 6.*

385. CONSOMMÉ WITH TRUFFLE ESSENCE
Consommé all'essenza di tartufo

2 quarts Consommé [No. 360]
6 fresh truffles (only fresh may be used), very finely chopped

Bring the consommé to a boil, add the finely chopped truffles (including the peelings), and simmer for 10 minutes. *Serves 6.*

386. CONSOMMÉ WITH WINE
Consommé con vini liquorosi

2 quarts Chicken Consommé [No. 361]
1 cup of any of the following wines: Marsala, Madeira, Malvasia, dry sherry, Cyprus, Samos, or other not-too-dry fortified wine

Bring the consommé to a boil, add the wine, and serve immediately. *Serves 6.*

THICK SOUPS: PURÉES AND POTAGES

Purées o potages

(*See* page 112 for introductory remarks)

387. PURÉE OF CELERY SOUP
Potage di sedani

2 quarts White or Classic Bouillon [No. 323 or 324]
2 bunches white celery, leaves removed (about 1½ pounds)
½ cup butter
½ pound potatoes, thinly sliced

½ teaspoon salt
¼ teaspoon pepper
Optional: 1 cup milk, scalded (use only if the soup is too thick)
1 cup Croûtons [No. 332]

Slice the celery very thinly and parboil it for 5 minutes in boiling water; drain thoroughly. Melt 2 tablespoons of the butter in a large, heavy (preferably earthenware) pot; add the celery, potatoes, bouillon, and salt and pepper. Cook very slowly over low heat, covered, for 40 to 50 minutes, or until potatoes and celery are soft. Purée the mixture through a food mill or through a fine sieve (or whirl in electric blender for 10 seconds on high speed). Taste, and add more salt if needed. Return to the pot and bring back to a boil. If a thinner consistency is desired, add the scalded milk. Just before serving, swirl in the remaining butter, off the heat. Serve the croûtons on the side. *Serves 6.*

388. POTAGE PARMENTIER
Potage Parmentier

1½ quarts White or Classic Bouillon [No. 323 or 324]
1½ pounds potatoes, finely sliced
½ cup butter
3 leeks (white part only), finely sliced
2 cups milk, scalded
1 teaspoon salt (or less if the bouillon is well seasoned)
¼ teaspoon white pepper
1 cup Croûtons [No. 332], fried in butter
1 tablespoon fresh chervil leaves (or substitute chopped parsley)

Melt 2 tablespoons of the butter in a large, heavy (preferably earthenware) pot; add the leeks and cook for 5 minutes, or until they are golden. Add the potatoes, bouillon, salt, and pepper; and cook, covered, over very low heat until the potatoes are very soft, about 40 to 50 minutes. Purée the mixture through a food mill or through a sieve (or whirl in electric blender on high speed for 10 seconds). Return the purée to the pot and blend in scalded milk. Correct seasoning. Just before serving, swirl in the rest of the butter off the heat. Sprinkle with the chervil leaves and serve with croûtons on the side. *Serves 6.*

SEE
VERSE
FOR
PTION

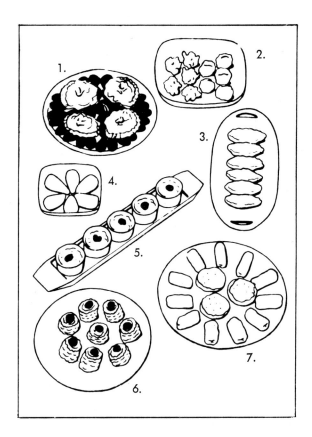

1. Parisian Mussels (No. 1024) prepared as an antipasto. They are served in scallop shells (*see* introduction to No. 306), and the platter is garnished with mussel shells.

2. Whitebait Fritters (No. 280) and Parmesan Fritters (No. 279)

3. Mushroom Tartlets Mornay (No. 319) baked in barquette shells (*see* introduction to No. 316)

4. Sweetbread Croquettes (No. 264)

5. Small individual casseroles filled with the filling for Creamed Mushroom Tart (No. 289) make an excellent antipasto. Here, they have been garnished with slices of truffle. Any of the fillings called for in the pies, tarts, and tartlet recipes in the Hot Antipasto section may be treated in this manner.

6. Little puff paste patty shells (*see* No. 1960 and introduction to No. 316)

7. Chicken Croquettes (No. 251) and Tartlets Marion Delorme (No. 318)

389. PURÉE OF DRIED PEA SOUP
Potage di piselli

2 cups dried peas (soaked overnight in cold water, unless the ready-to-use type is available, in which case soaking is unnecessary)
4 cups cold water
Mirepoix [No. 141] composed of:
   1 small carrot
   $\frac{1}{2}$ medium onion
   1 stalk celery
   $\frac{1}{8}$ pound raw pork
2 leeks (*green* part only), thoroughly washed and chopped
Bouquet Garni:
   $\frac{1}{4}$ teaspoon dried thyme
   1 bay leaf
   3 sprigs parsley
1 tablespoon fresh chervil leaves (or substitute chopped parsley)
1 cup Croûtons [No. 332]
1 teaspoon salt
$\frac{1}{4}$ teaspoon pepper
1 quart hot White or Classic Bouillon [No. 323 or 324] (or substitute scalded milk)
4 tablespoons butter

Drain the soaked peas or, if the ready-to-use type are available, wash and drain them well. Put them into a large, heavy (preferably earthenware) pot. Add the cold water, the mirepoix, leeks, Bouquet Garni, and salt and pepper. Cook over moderate heat for $1\frac{1}{2}$ to 2 hours, or until peas are tender. Remove Bouquet Garni and purée the mixture through a food mill or through a fine sieve (or in blender container on high speed for 10 seconds). Return the purée to the pot, pour in the boiling bouillon (or scalded milk), and mix thoroughly. Bring it back to a boil and, just before serving, swirl in the butter off the heat. Garnish with the chervil leaves and serve the croûtons on the side. *Serves 6.*

390. PURÉE OF PUMPKIN SOUP BORGHESE
Potage di zucca alla borghese

3 cups pumpkin, peeled and seeded
$\frac{1}{2}$ cup butter
1 quart White or Classic Bouillon [No. 323 or 324]
1 tablespoon sugar
1 teaspoon salt
$\frac{1}{4}$ teaspoon pepper

2 cups milk (or more, if soup is very thick)
$\frac{1}{4}$ pound very thin, narrow noodles, broken up (capelli d'angelo type)

Cut the pumpkin into slices; put it in a pot with 2 tablespoons of the butter, bouillon, sugar, and salt and pepper. Cook over moderate heat, covered, for 30 to 40 minutes, or until very soft. Purée through a food mill or through a fine sieve (or in electric blender container on high speed for 10 seconds). Return the purée to the pot and thin to desired consistency with milk. Correct the seasoning. Bring to a boil and drop in the pieces of capelli d'angelo. Cook for about 5 minutes or until just *al dente*. Just before serving, swirl in the remaining butter, off the heat. *Serves 6.*

391. PURÉE OF TOMATO SOUP
Potage di pomodoro

$1\frac{1}{2}$ pounds fresh tomatoes, peeled, seeded, drained, and chopped (there should be 2 generous cups)
1 onion, finely chopped
$\frac{1}{2}$ cup butter
2 quarts White or Classic Bouillon [No. 323 or 324]
Bouquet Garni:
   $\frac{1}{4}$ teaspoon dried thyme
   3 sprigs parsley
   1 bay leaf
4 tablespoons uncooked rice, well washed
$\frac{1}{2}$ teaspoon salt
1 teaspoon sugar
Pinch white pepper

Melt 2 tablespoons of the butter in a large, heavy (preferably earthenware) pot, add the finely chopped onion, and cook until soft but not brown, about 5 minutes. Add the tomato pulp and the rest of the ingredients. Bring to a boil, reduce heat to moderate, and continue cooking for 40 minutes. Remove Bouquet Garni and purée the soup through a food mill or through a fine strainer (or whirl in electric blender on high speed for 10 seconds). Return the purée to the pot. If it seems too thick, dilute to desired consistency with a little more bouillon. Correct the seasoning. Bring it back to a boil, and, just before serving, swirl in the remaining butter, off the heat. *Serves 6.*

129

CREAM SOUPS

Creme

Cream soups are based on purées of meat, poultry, vegetables, or fish, flavored with a little butter, thickened with Béchamel sauce, and finished off with a little heavy cream. They are garnished with rice, pasta, or many of the traditional garnishes outlined in the section on garnishes.

In the preparation of the basic purée (whether meat, vegetable, or fish), the electric blender can save much time and effort.

392. CREAM OF ARTICHOKE SOUP
Crema di carciofi

8 large artichoke hearts [see introduction to No. 1578]
4 tablespoons butter
4 cups Béchamel Sauce [No. 18]
1½ cups White or Classic Bouillon [No. 323 or 324]
½ teaspoon salt
4 tablespoons heavy cream, heated
1 tablespoon fresh chervil leaves (no stems), or substitute chopped parsley

Slice the artichoke hearts; cook in acidulated water for 20 to 30 minutes or until tender; drain well. Sauté the slices gently in the butter for a few minutes. Add the Béchamel sauce, mix thoroughly, and simmer for 15 minutes. Purée the mixture through a food mill or through a fine sieve (or whirl in electric blender very briefly on high speed). Return to the pot, add the bouillon, bring gently to a boil, and remove from the fire. Add the salt and the hot cream; taste, and adjust seasoning; and sprinkle the chervil leaves or parsley over the top. *Serves* 6.

393. CREAM OF WHITE ASPARAGUS SOUP
Crema di asparagi bianchi

5 cups White or Classic Bouillon [No. 323 or 324]
1 pound white asparagus (if available; if not, use all green, well peeled—see Note below)
1 cup butter
¼ cup flour
¼ cup heavy cream, boiling
½ teaspoon salt
Pinch freshly ground pepper
½ pound green asparagus tips

Scrub the asparagus stalks and, if not tender, peel them. Cut them off at the point where they toughen and discard the tough ends. Make a roux with 4 tablespoons of the butter and the ¼ cup of flour in a large, heavy (preferably earthenware) pot. Cook over moderate heat for 3 minutes, add the bouillon slowly, stirring constantly; bring to a boil and lower the flame so that the bouillon simmers. Add the white asparagus and the salt and pepper. Continue cooking over moderate heat for about 30 minutes, or until the asparagus is very soft. Purée the mixture through a food mill or through a fine sieve, or whirl in electric blender on high speed for 10 seconds.

While the white asparagus is cooking, cook the green asparagus in very slightly salted boiling water, using only the very tender tips. Cook only for 12 to 15 minutes, or until just done *(al dente)*; drain and keep warm.

Return the white asparagus purée to the pot, bring it to a boil, and remove it from the fire. Add the rest of the butter, the boiling cream, and the garnish of green asparagus tips. *Serves* 6.

NOTE: Although highly prized in Italy and in Europe generally, white asparagus is rarely found in American markets. There is a canned white asparagus commercially available, but its texture is mushy and its flavor bears little resemblance to the fresh vegetable. Nevertheless, we have included this recipe since white asparagus makes a particularly fine soup. As you will see from the following recipe, this soup can, of course, be made with green asparagus.

394. CREAM OF GREEN ASPARAGUS SOUP
Crema di asparagi verdi

This reverses the preceding soup, making the purée base of green asparagus and the garnish of tips of white asparagus. Prepare it exactly in the same way, except reversing the quantities of green and white asparagus.

395. CREAM OF BARLEY SOUP
Crema d'orzo

½ cup pearl barley, well washed and drained
2 quarts White or Classic Bouillon [No. 323 or 324],
    or substitute either milk or ½ milk and ½ bouillon
Bouquet Garni:
    1 stalk celery
    3 sprigs parsley
    ¼ teaspoon dried thyme
    1 bay leaf
½ teaspoon salt
⅛ teaspoon freshly ground pepper
1 cup barley meal (see Note below)
1 cup heavy cream, boiling
4 tablespoons butter

Put the bouillon and the pearl barley into a large heavy (preferably earthenware) pot, add the Bouquet Garni and seasonings, and simmer for ½ hour. Pour in the barley meal in a continuous stream and cook for another 30 minutes. Discard the Bouquet Garni. Remove the pot from the fire, correct the seasoning, and add the butter and boiling cream. *Serves 6.*

NOTE: If barley meal is unavailable, take 1 cup raw pearl barley and place in electric blender ½ cup at a time to whirl on high speed for 10–20 seconds.

396. CREAM OF CHICORY SOUP
Crema di cicoria

This is prepared in exactly the same way as Cream of Artichoke Soup [No. 392], except that a head of tender white chicory, boiled for 5 minutes, drained, and thoroughly squeezed until dry, is substituted for the artichoke hearts. Garnish with Croûtons [No. 332]. *Serves 6.*

Chicory

397. CREAM OF CHESTNUT SOUP BRUNOISE
Crema di marroni à la brunoise

4 tablespoons vegetable Brunoise [No. 328] using:
    2 parts diced carrots
    1 part diced celery
    1 part finely chopped onion
36 chestnuts
3 cups rich milk (or more if needed)
Bouquet Garni:
    1 stalk celery
    3 sprigs parsley
    ¼ teaspoon dried thyme
    1 bay leaf
3 tablespoons heavy cream
3 tablespoons butter
Salt and freshly ground pepper to taste

Prepare the Brunoise and set aside. Cut a small cross on each of the chestnut shells (or "stab" them with a sharp knife); boil them for 10 minutes in water to cover; drain; and peel off the shells and the inner skin. Put them in a pot with the milk and the Bouquet Garni. Cook over moderate heat until quite tender, about 45 to 60 minutes; remove Bouquet Garni. Purée the chestnut/milk mixture through a food mill or through a fine sieve (or whirl in electric blender on high speed for 10 seconds). Return the purée to the pot, thin it with more milk, if it seems too thick, and bring to a boil. Add the Brunoise and the cream to the purée and cook over moderate heat for 10 minutes. Add salt and pepper to taste. Remove from fire and swirl in the butter. *Serves 6.*

398. CREAM OF MUSHROOM SOUP
Crema di funghi di serra

Only the freshest, whitest cultivated mushrooms will do for this soup. Proceed as for Cream of Artichoke Soup [No. 392], substituting 1 pound of unpeeled mushrooms for the artichoke hearts. The mushroom liquid may be reduced and added to the soup. Garnish with Croûtons [No. 332]. *Serves 6.*

purée (2 cups)

cream and bouillon
(2 cups altogether)

butter
(4 tbs.)

flour
(4 tbs.)

VELOUTÉ
BASE

stock
(1 quart)

eggs

butter

=VELOUTÉ SOUP FOR 6 PEOPLE

BASIC PREPARATION OF VELOUTÉ SOUPS

VELOUTÉ SOUPS

Vellutate

Velouté soups require very careful preparation and, hence, are usually reserved for more elaborate meals.

399. VELOUTÉ BASE
Base vellutata

Prepare a White Roux [No. 13] and mix it with stock made from beef, poultry, game, or fish [Nos. 1, 2, 3, 4, or 5], according to the requirements of the particular recipe. For every quart of stock, the roux will require 4 tablespoons each of butter and flour.

Half the finished velouté soup will be composed of the Velouté base; the other half will be divided equally between a purée (of poultry, game, fish, shellfish, or vegetables according to the specific character of the particular soup) and bouillon mixed with heavy cream.

Thus, to prepare a velouté soup for 6 to 8 people, you will need about 2 quarts in the following proportions:

1 quart Velouté base (*see* above)
2 cups purée

1 cup bouillon
1 cup heavy cream

These are not rigid proportions and may be changed according to varying needs and taste.

Every velouté soup is finished off with the yolk of egg and butter, which thicken the soup and give it the characteristic "velvety" texture which gives it its name.

400. ARTICHOKE VELOUTÉ SOUP
Vellutata di carciofi

1 quart Velouté Base [No. 399], made with White Stock [No. 1]
$2\frac{1}{2}$ cups artichoke purée (*see* Note below)
$1\frac{1}{2}$ cups Classic Bouillon [No. 324]
4 egg yolks
1 cup heavy cream
$\frac{1}{2}$ cup sweet butter, softened
1 artichoke heart cooked in white stock until just *al dente,* diced

Blend the Velouté base, the artichoke purée, and the bouillon all together. Press it through a fine sieve, or whirl for a few seconds in the electric blender on high speed. Put the mixture in a large, heavy (preferably earthenware) pot, bring to a boil, and remove from the heat. Beat the eggs with the heavy cream and pour

132

them very slowly into the hot soup, stirring vigorously. Return to the fire and heat very gently for 5 to 10 minutes, stirring constantly. Do not boil. When slightly thickened, remove from the fire, correct for salt if needed, and add the softened butter piece by piece, stirring each piece in well. Garnish with the cubed, cooked artichoke heart. *Serves* 6.

NOTE: To make artichoke purée, take 2 boxes of frozen artichoke hearts, cook for 10 minutes, drain, put in electric blender, and whirl for 15 seconds at high speed (or, lacking a blender, pass through a food mill or fine sieve). One may also use fresh artichoke hearts; 8 large ones will make 2½ cups purée [*see* No. 638].

401. ASPARAGUS VELOUTÉ SOUP
Vellutata di asparagi

This is prepared in exactly the same way as Artichoke Velouté Soup [No. 400], substituting 1½ pounds of asparagus tips, cooked, drained, and puréed, in place of the artichoke purée. Garnish the soup with a few asparagus tips cooked *al dente* in a little bouillon. Either green or white asparagus may be used for this soup.

402. CELERY VELOUTÉ SOUP
Vellutata di sedano

1 quart Velouté Base [No. 399], made with White
    Stock [No. 1]
1 medium bunch celery, finely sliced (without leaves)
½ cup butter, softened
1½ cups Classic Bouillon [No. 324]
1 cup heavy cream
4 egg yolks
1 heart of celery, diced (about ½ cup), cooked *al dente*
    in a little bouillon
Salt and pepper to taste

Cook the celery for 25 minutes in lightly salted boiling water and drain. Melt 2 tablespoons of the butter in a heavy saucepan, add the celery, and cook over low heat for 15 minutes, covered, or until the celery is very soft. Purée it through a food mill or a fine sieve, or whirl in electric blender at high speed for 10 seconds.

Mix the Velouté base with the celery purée and the bouillon in a heavy pot, bring this mixture to a boil, and remove from the heat. Beat the egg yolks with the cream and pour them gradually into the hot soup, stirring constantly. Return the pot to the fire and stir over very gentle heat until slightly thickened. Do not boil. Correct the seasoning, remove from fire, and add

the remaining butter, bit by bit. Garnish with the diced heart of celery. *Serves* 6.

403. LETTUCE VELOUTÉ SOUP
Vellutata di lattuga

This is prepared in exactly the same way as Artichoke Velouté Soup [No. 400], substituting puréed Boston lettuce for the artichoke purée.

For the puréed lettuce, wash 4 heads of Boston lettuce thoroughly, shred it, and cook in salted boiling water for 3 minutes. Drain, cool, and press out excess water with the hands. Melt 3 tablespoons of butter in a heavy pot and cook the lettuce gently for 5 minutes, and purée.

NOTE: Bibb or oak-leaf lettuce may also be used. Do *not*, however, employ iceberg lettuce.

404. RED PEPPER VELOUTÉ SOUP
Vellutata Carmen

1½ quarts Velouté Base [No. 399], made with White
    Stock [No. 1]
½ pound sweet red peppers, roasted and peeled
    [*see* No. 145]
¾ cup butter
4 egg yolks
1½ cups Chicken Bouillon [No. 326]
1 cup heavy cream
¼ cup rice cooked *al dente* in Chicken Bouillon
    [No. 326]

Cook the roasted and peeled peppers, covered, for 15 minutes in ¼ cup of the butter until very soft. Purée them through a food mill or through a fine sieve (or whirl in electric blender on high speed for 10 seconds). Mix together the pepper purée, the Velouté base, and the bouillon. Bring the mixture slowly to a boil in a large, heavy (preferably earthenware) pot. Remove from the fire. Beat the egg yolks with the cream and add them, very slowly, to the hot soup, stirring vigorously. Return the soup to the fire and cook gently, stirring constantly, for 5 to 10 minutes. Do not boil. As soon as it is slightly thickened, remove from the fire and add the remaining butter, bit by bit. Garnish with the cooked rice. *Serves* 6.

405. SHELLFISH VELOUTÉ SOUP
Vellutata di gamberetti

1 quart Velouté Base [No. 399], made with White Stock
    [No. 1]
1½ cups Fish Stock [No. 2]
1 pound shelled lobster (or substitute shelled shrimp
    or crab)
½ cup butter.
1 small carrot, chopped
½ medium onion, chopped
1 celery stalk, chopped
4 egg yolks
1 cup heavy cream
5 drops red vegetable coloring
Freshly grated white pepper

Set aside ¼ of the lobster leaving a few choice bits for a garnish. Melt 2 tablespoons of the butter in a heavy pot, add the chopped vegetables, and cook over moderate heat, covered, for 10 minutes. Add about ¾ of the shellfish (exclusive of the reserved pieces), and cook for 5 minutes more. Mix with the Velouté base and purée through a food mill or a fine sieve, or whirl in electric blender on high speed for 10 seconds.

While the fish and vegetables are cooking, prepare a lobster butter as follows: take the remaining ¼ of the lobster meat (exclusive of the reserved pieces) and all of the shells and pound them to a paste in the mortar (or place them in the electric blender with ½ cup of the stock and whirl at high speed for 10–15 seconds). Cream this mixture with the remaining butter and place in a small saucepan with 1 cup of the stock (½ cup if you have used the blender method). Melt this over high heat and allow to boil vigorously for 2 minutes, then pour through a strainer lined with a triple thickness of cheesecloth, previously dipped in cold water and well wrung out.

Put the lobster/vegetable mixture and the rest of the fish stock in a heavy pot, bring to a boil, and remove from fire. Beat the egg yolks with the cream and a few gratings of white pepper and add very slowly to the soup, stirring constantly with a wire whisk. Return pot to fire, lower flame to a minimum, and cook soup very gently, stirring continuously. Do *not* boil. When soup is slightly thickened, remove pot from fire, and, bit by bit, add the lobster butter. Taste, and add salt if necessary. Mix in the vegetable coloring, pour into a pre-heated tureen, and garnish with the reserved lobster meat cut into neat, small pieces. *Serves* 6.

406. SPINACH VELOUTÉ SOUP
Vellutata di spinaci

This is prepared in the same way as Artichoke Velouté Soup [No. 400], substituting a spinach purée for the artichoke purée.

For the spinach purée, wash 1 pound of spinach thoroughly and cook, covered, in an enamel or stainless steel saucepan, with only the water that clings to the leaves, for 6 minutes. Drain it, squeeze thoroughly between the hands to remove excess water, and cook it again with ½ teaspoon salt and 3 tablespoons of butter, covered, for 20 minutes or until very soft. Purée it through a food mill or a fine sieve, or whirl in the electric blender at high speed for 10 seconds.

ZUPPE

(*See* page 112 for introductory remarks)

407. BEAN SOUP BORGHESE
Zuppa di fagioli alla borghese

1 pound cannellini beans (or white navy beans),
    soaked 12 hours and drained
½ pound lean raw pork
½ pound prosciutto in one piece, without fat
    (or substitute smoked ham)
3 quarts cold water
2 ounces ham fat, finely chopped
Diced vegetables:
    3 small turnips
    3 small carrots
    1 small celery heart
1 medium onion stuck with 1 clove
3 sprigs rosemary tied together (or ½ teaspoon dried
    tied in a cloth bag)
2 cloves garlic, split
1 pound beets, well scrubbed, peeled, and sliced
2 teaspoons salt

¼ teaspoon freshly ground pepper
1 cup grated Parmesan cheese
30 small, thin slices of French bread, crusts removed,
    lightly browned in oil

Put the soaked beans, pork, and prosciutto into a large earthenware pot, cover with the cold water, and bring to a boil over moderate heat. Skim off any scum that rises to the surface. Add the ham fat, the diced vegetables, onion, rosemary, garlic, and the beets. Season with the salt and pepper. Cook over moderate heat for 2 hours. When ready to serve, discard the rosemary and onion. Remove the pork and ham, dice the meat, and return it to the pot. Place the bread that has been browned in oil in soup plates, cover with the hot soup, and serve the grated Parmesan cheese on the side. *Serves* 6.

408. BEAN SOUP CIOCIARA
Zuppa di fagioli alla ciociara

3 quarts cold water
1 pound dried white beans, soaked 12 hours and drained
½ cup oil
1 stalk celery, finely sliced
1 clove garlic, split
3 sprigs parsley, chopped
½ small yellow pepper, roasted, peeled, and cut into
    strips [*see* No. 145]
2 teaspoons salt
1½ cups Croûtons [No. 332], fried in oil

Put all of the ingredients except the croûtons into a large earthenware (or enamel) pot and bring to a boil. Reduce the heat to moderate and simmer until the beans are tender, about 1½ hours. Scatter the croûtons in the soup plates and pour the hot soup over them. *Serves* 6.

409. BEAN SOUP NAPOLETANA
Zuppa di fagioli alla napoletana

2 cloves garlic, crushed in the garlic-press
1 yellow or sweet red pepper, roasted, peeled, and cut
    into fine strips [*see* No. 145]
½ cup oil
2 pounds tomatoes, peeled, seeded, and chopped
    (retain as much of the liquid as possible)
1 pound fresh string beans, trimmed and cut in 1-inch
    pieces
2 teaspoons salt

1 tablespoon minced fresh basil
30 small thin slices of French bread, crusts removed,
    lightly browned in the oven

Put the oil, garlic, and pepper into a large, heavy pot over moderate heat for 6 minutes. Add the tomato pulp and cook for 15 minutes. Add the beans and a few tablespoons of water, if necessary, to cover the beans, but add the least amount of water possible. Season with the salt and continue cooking over moderate heat, covered, stirring from time to time, for 25 to 30 minutes. When ready to serve, add the basil, divide the toast in the soup plates, and cover with the hot soup. *Serves* 6.

410. CABBAGE SOUP
Zuppa di cavolo nero

¾ cup oil
1 bunch kale, shredded
1 small head Savoy cabbage, shredded
1 pound broccoli di rape (broccoli-rave), shredded
3 cloves garlic, split
1 carrot, diced
2 leeks (white part only), chopped
1 stalk celery, chopped
2 quarts cold water
1 teaspoon salt
¼ teaspoon freshly ground pepper
30 small thin slices dark bread, crusts removed,
    toasted
1 cup grated Parmesan cheese

Pour ½ cup of the oil into a large earthenware (or enamel) pot and heat well. Add all of the shredded and chopped vegetables, the garlic, salt, pepper, and the water. Bring to a boil, lower the heat, and continue cooking for 1 hour, or until the vegetables are tender. Near the end of the cooking, toast the bread in the oven and lightly brush with the rest of the oil while still warm. When ready to serve, put the toast in the bottom of the tureen and pour the soup over it. Serve the grated Parmesan on the side. *Serves* 6.

NOTE: The Italian version calls for *cavolo nero* ("black cabbage"), a kale-and-broccoli-like leafy vegetable unavailable here. The above substitute will approximate the flavor. Broccoli di rape [sometimes called broccoli-rave; *see* Nos. 1625-27] is found in Italian vegetable markets and in supermarkets in Italian neighborhoods.

135

411. GNOCCHI SOUP
Zuppa di gnocchetti

For the gnocchi:
    2 eggs (1 separated, 1 whole)
    $\frac{1}{3}$ cup flour, sifted
    4 tablespoons grated white breadcrumbs
    4 tablespoons butter, softened
    $\frac{1}{2}$ teaspoon salt
    Pinch white pepper
    Pinch nutmeg
For the soup:
    8 tablespoons flour
    8 tablespoons butter
    2 quarts White or Classic Bouillon [No. 323 or 324], heated to the boiling point
    Bouquet Garni:
        $\frac{1}{4}$ teaspoon dried thyme
        1 bay leaf
        3 sprigs parsley
    $\frac{1}{2}$ teaspoon salt
    $\frac{1}{8}$ teaspoon freshly ground pepper
    Pinch nutmeg
3 egg yolks mixed with 2 tablespoons heavy cream
1 cup grated Parmesan cheese

Gnocchi:

Beat the 1 separated egg white until stiff. Mix in a bowl the flour, breadcrumbs, butter, and the 1 whole egg plus the 1 egg yolk. Season with salt, pepper, nutmeg, and, as gently as possible, fold in the beaten egg white. Bring 2 quarts of salted water to a boil in a pot. Using a very tiny spoon, scoop up the mixture in amounts the size of a lima bean and, little by little, drop them into the boiling water. Keep the water just below boiling and cook the gnocchi for 10 to 12 minutes. Remove them carefully with a slotted spoon and keep warm in a little bouillon.

Soup:

Melt the butter in a large earthenware (or enamel) pot over moderate heat and add the flour. As soon as the mixture turns barely golden, gradually add the hot bouillon, beating the mixture well with a wire whisk. Add the Bouquet Garni and season with salt, pepper, and nutmeg. Keep at a gentle simmer for about 20 minutes, stirring from time to time. Remove from the fire and discard the Bouquet Garni. Beat the egg yolks with the cream. Add them very gradually to the hot soup, stirring vigorously. Return the soup to the fire and cook gently for another 5 minutes, stirring constantly. Do not boil or the eggs will curdle. Add the gnocchi, remove from fire, and serve immediately. Serve grated Parmesan on the side. *Serves* 6.

412. LEEK AND POTATO SOUP
Zuppa di porri Germaine

2 heads tender lettuce (Boston or Bibb, *not* iceberg), shredded
2 tablespoons chopped sorrel
4 tablespoons chopped chervil (or 2 teaspoons dried)
1 tablespoon chopped basil (or $\frac{1}{2}$ teaspoon dried)
6 medium leeks (white part only), finely sliced
6 medium potatoes, thinly sliced
2 teaspoons salt
$\frac{1}{3}$ cup butter
4 quarts cold water
2 vegetable bouillon cubes
1 cup Croûtons [No. 332]

Put all of the ingredients, except the croûtons, in a large earthenware (or enamel) pot. Mix thoroughly, cover the pot, bring to a boil over moderate heat, and keep barely simmering for 2 hours. When ready to serve, mash the potatoes down with a potato masher (they will be well cooked down, in any case), and correct the seasoning. Serve with the croûtons which have been browned in butter at the very last moment before bringing the soup to the table. *Serves* 6.

413. LENTIL SOUP
Zuppa di lenticchie alla paesana

2 cups dried lentils
2 quarts water
4 tablespoons oil
$4\frac{1}{2}$ tablespoons butter
4 stalks celery
2 cloves garlic
4 dried sage leaves
12 salted anchovy fillets, washed free of salt [*see* No. 220]
$\frac{1}{2}$ pound tomatoes, peeled, seeded, drained, and chopped (or two cups canned Italian tomatoes, well drained)
18 thin slices Italian or French bread, toasted
1 cup freshly grated Parmesan cheese
Salt and freshly grated pepper

Soak the lentils in a few quarts cold water for an hour. In a large earthenware (or enamel) pot bring the 2 quarts of water to a boil. Add 1 teaspoon salt and the lentils, drained, and cook until they are tender, about 1 hour. Melt the oil and the butter in a large, heavy saucepan over medium heat and sauté the chopped celery, garlic, and sage until they turn golden. Mash the anchovies to a fine paste and add to the vegetables. Add the well-drained tomatoes and cook over medium heat for 15 minutes, stirring every so often to prevent scorching. Drain the cooked lentils, reserving their cooking liquid, and add them to the mixture. Stirring them gently, let them cook for 5 minutes, then add their cooking liquid. Taste for salt, add more if necessary, and grate in a little black pepper. Bring to a boil again, and lower heat to a simmer. Toast the bread slices in a 375° oven until they are golden brown and dry, distribute them among six soup plates, sprinkle with half the grated Parmesan, and ladle the soup over them. Serve the remaining Parmesan on the side. *Serves* 6.

414. PORK AND BEAN SOUP ROMANA
Zuppa di ventresca alla romana

½ pound lean salt pork in 1 piece
1½ cups dried white beans, soaked for 12 hours and
    drained
2 quarts water
Bouquet Garni:
    1 leek
    1 celery stalk
    3 sprigs parsley
4 medium onions, very finely chopped
3 tablespoons oil
1 large celery heart, cooked whole in boiling water
    until tender and finely chopped
1 teaspoon salt
¼ teaspoon freshly ground pepper
30 thin slices bread, crusts removed, browned in
    the oven
1 cup grated Parmesan cheese

Parboil the salt pork for 20 minutes in plenty of boiling water; and put the beans in a large earthenware (or enamel) pot with the 2 quarts of water, the salt pork, and the Bouquet Garni. Bring slowly to a boil and skim off any scum that rises to the surface. Simmer for 1½ hours or until the pork and beans are just tender. While the beans are cooking, sauté the onions with the oil in a frying pan over moderate heat until golden. Add the celery and blend both thoroughly. When the beans and pork are tender, remove the Bouquet Garni and discard. Remove the salt pork and cut it into small cubes. Return it to the soup with the onion/celery mixture and correct the seasoning. Distribute the toasted bread in soup plates, pour the hot soup over them, and serve with the grated Parmesan cheese on the side. *Serves* 6.

415. PUMPKIN SOUP CASALINGA
Zuppa di zucca alla casalinga

3 leeks (white part only) chopped
6 tablespoons butter
½ very small pumpkin (¾ to 1 pound), peeled, seeded,
    and coarsely chopped
3 large potatoes, sliced
Bouquet Garni:
    3 sprigs parsley
    1 bay leaf
    2 sprigs thyme (or ½ teaspoon dried)
1 quart White or Classic Bouillon [No. 323 or 324]
1 teaspoon salt
½ teaspoon freshly ground pepper
Pinch nutmeg
½ teaspoon sugar
3 cups scalded milk
¼ cup uncooked rice
½ pound spinach, thoroughly washed
1 cup grated Parmesan cheese

Cook the leeks until golden in 2 tablespoons of butter in a large, heavy pot over medium heat. Add the pumpkin, potatoes, Bouquet Garni, and the bouillon. Season with the salt, pepper, sugar, and nutmeg; bring to a boil. Turn the heat down to moderate and continue cooking, covered, for 1 hour. Discard the Bouquet Garni. Pound the vegetables to a pulp (or purée them in a food mill) and return them to the pot. Add the hot milk and bring back to a boil. Add the rice and cook until just *al dente*, about 20 minutes. While the rice is cooking, cook the washed spinach for 8 minutes in a covered enamel or stainless steel saucepan, using only the water that clings to the leaves, turning occasionally with a fork to ensure even cooking. Drain it, press out all of the moisture, chop finely, and then sauté it gently for 5 minutes in 2 tablespoons of butter. When the rice is done, add the spinach, correct the seasoning, and, if the soup is too thick, add a little more bouillon. Remove from the fire and swirl in the remaining 2 tablespoons of butter. Serve very hot with grated Parmesan cheese on the side. *Serves* 6.

416. SPINACH SOUP
Zuppa di spinaci

2 pounds spinach
6 cups White or Classic Bouillon [No. 323 or 324]
2 egg yolks
2 cups heavy cream
Salt and pepper to taste
Pinch nutmeg
$\frac{1}{2}$ cup grated Parmesan cheese
30 thin slices French bread, crusts removed, lightly
    buttered and browned in the oven

Wash the spinach thoroughly, sprinkle it with $\frac{1}{2}$ teaspoon salt, and cook it in a covered enamel or stainless steel saucepan for 8 minutes, using only the water that clings to the leaves. Drain it, squeeze moisture out thoroughly with the hands, and chop it coarsely. Bring the bouillon to a boil, add the chopped spinach, and turn down to a simmer. Beat the egg yolks slightly, mix them well with the cream, and add the nutmeg. Gradually add this mixture to the soup, stirring rapidly. Stir it constantly over a very low fire for 5 minutes. Do not allow to boil or the eggs will curdle. Taste, and adjust seasoning. Sprinkle the cheese over the soup and serve the toast on the side. *Serves 6.*

417. STUFFED BREAD SOUP
Zuppa di pane farcito

1 $2\frac{1}{2}$-pound cooked chicken (either boiled or roasted),
      boned, with sinews and skin removed
6 thin slices (2 ounces) prosciutto
4 tablespoons beef marrow
1 egg
$\frac{1}{2}$ teaspoon salt
$\frac{1}{8}$ teaspoon freshly ground pepper
$\frac{1}{2}$ cup grated Parmesan cheese
1 loaf very fresh bread, unsliced
6 tablespoons butter
2 quarts boiling White or Classic Bouillon
    [No. 323 or 324]

Chop and mix thoroughly (or put through the food chopper with the medium blade) the chicken, prosciutto, and marrow; make a smooth mixture by adding the egg, slightly beaten, salt, pepper, and 1 tablespoon of the cheese. Remove the crust from the bread with a sharp knife and cut into slices $\frac{1}{8}$ inch thick; cut out rounds with a cooky cutter $1\frac{1}{2}$ inches in diameter. Spread half of these rounds with the chicken mixture and cover with the remaining rounds, pinching the edges together firmly to make sure they will hold

138

together. Melt 2 tablespoons of the butter in a frying pan and fry the pieces on both sides to a golden brown, adding more butter as necessary. Distribute these in deep soup plates when ready to serve and pour over them the hot bouillon. Pass the remaining grated cheese on the side. *Serves* 6.

418. TOMATO SOUP WITH TARRAGON
Zuppa di pomodoro con erba serpentaria

$\frac{2}{3}$ cup butter
2 large onions, finely chopped
$\frac{1}{4}$ cup flour
2 pounds tomatoes, peeled, seeded, drained, and finely
    chopped
2 tablespoons finely chopped tarragon (or 1 teaspoon
    dried)
$\frac{1}{2}$ teaspoon sugar
1 teaspoon salt
7 cups White or Classic Bouillon [No. 323 or 324]
4 tablespoons grated Parmesan cheese
10 thin slices French or Italian bread, crusts removed
$\frac{1}{4}$ teaspoon freshly grated white pepper

Melt 4 tablespoons of the butter in a heavy pot. Stir in the onions, cover, and cook over moderate heat until the onions are soft and transparent but not brown. Stir in the flour thoroughly and cook long enough to blend smoothly. Add the tomato pulp and $\frac{1}{2}$ of the fresh tarragon (if dried tarragon is used, add it *all* at this point). Add the salt and sugar and continue cooking over low heat for 15 minutes, stirring occasionally. Gradually pour in the bouillon and continue cooking for another $\frac{1}{2}$ hour. Mix 4 tablespoons of the butter with the cheese, spread on the slices of bread, and toast in a hot oven for 10 minutes, or until delicately brown. When ready to serve the soup, correct the seasoning, add the rest of the fresh tarragon, and swirl in the remaining butter. Serve the toasted bread on the side. *Serves* 6.

419. TOMATO SOUP WITH VEAL MEATBALLS

Zuppa di pomodoro con polpettine di vitello

2 quarts White or Classic Bouillon [No. 323 or 324]

3 ounces ham fat, preferably prosciutto

1 small carrot

1 medium onion

1 clove garlic

1 stalk celery

3 sprigs parsley

2 pounds potatoes, thinly sliced

2 pounds tomatoes, peeled, seeded, drained, and finely chopped

1 teaspoon salt

$\frac{1}{8}$ teaspoon pepper, freshly ground

For the meatballs:

    1 very small onion, very finely chopped

    1 tablespoon butter

    $\frac{1}{3}$ pound lean veal, very finely ground

    $\frac{1}{2}$ cup cubed stale bread, moistened with $\frac{1}{2}$ cup milk and then thoroughly squeezed out with the hands

    2 egg yolks

    $\frac{1}{2}$ teaspoon salt

    $\frac{1}{8}$ teaspoon pepper

    Pinch nutmeg

    $\frac{1}{2}$ cup flour

Chop together, very finely, the ham fat, carrot, onion, garlic, celery, and parsley. Place this mixture in a large, heavy pot (preferably earthenware); add the potatoes, tomato pulp, salt and pepper, and $\frac{1}{2}$ cup of the bouillon. Bring to a boil, reduce heat to low, cover, and cook for $1\frac{1}{2}$ hours. Stir occasionally to make sure the potatoes do not scorch. While this is cooking, prepare the meatballs: cook the finely chopped onion in a frying pan over moderate heat with the butter for 10 minutes or until it is tender but not brown. In a bowl mix the cooked onion, the veal, the soaked bread, egg yolks, nutmeg, and salt and pepper. Beat this mixture smooth with a fork and then form it into tiny balls about the size of a grape. Bring the bouillon to boil in a pot, roll the veal balls lightly in the flour, drop them very gently into the bouillon, one by one, and let them poach at a barely perceptible simmer for 15 minutes. Remove them with a slotted spoon and set them aside for the moment. When the potato/tomato mixture is done, purée it through a food mill and return it to the pot. Pour the remaining bouillon into the purée, stir thoroughly, and correct the seasoning. Bring to a boil, drop the meatballs into the soup, and serve very hot. *Serves* 6.

420. FARMER'S VEGETABLE SOUP

Zuppa del coltivatore

2 cups cooked lean pork

1 medium potato

1 carrot

1 turnip

1 medium onion

1 leek (white part only)

1 cup shelled peas

2 quarts White or Classic Bouillon [No. 323 or 324]

4 tablespoons butter

$\frac{1}{2}$ teaspoon salt

$\frac{1}{8}$ teaspoon freshly ground pepper

Cut the meat and vegetables into dice as small as the peas. Heat the butter in an earthenware (or enamel) pot, add all of the ingredients except the peas, potatoes, and the pork; cook, covered, for 10 minutes over low heat. Pour in the bouillon, cover, and bring slowly to a boil over moderate heat. Simmer gently for 30 minutes, add the diced pork, peas, and potatoes, and cook for another 20 minutes or until the potatoes are tender and all the flavors are mingled. *Serves* 6.

421. GRANDMOTHER'S VEGETABLE SOUP

Zuppa della nonna

5 tablespoons butter

1 heart of celery, finely sliced

3 leeks (white part only), finely sliced

1 medium onion, finely sliced

1 teaspoon salt

3 cups warm water

3 large potatoes, finely sliced

1 heart of Boston lettuce, coarsely shredded

4 tablespoon grated carrot

$\frac{1}{2}$ teaspoon sugar

2 cups rich milk, scalded

30 thin slices of French or Italian bread, crusts removed, spread with a mixture of 4 tablespoons softened butter and 4 tablespoons of grated Parmesan cheese

Melt 3 tablespoons of the butter in a large, heavy earthenware (or enamel) pot. Add the celery, leeks, and onion. Season with the salt, cover, and cook over moderate heat for 15 minutes. Do not allow the vegetables to brown. Add the water, the potatoes, and the lettuce. Continue cooking, covered, over moderate heat for 30 minutes, or until the vegetables are tender and their flavors well blended. Melt the remaining 2 tablespoons of butter in a smaller pot and add the grated carrot, sugar, and a pinch of salt. Cook gently for 5 minutes, or until barely tender. Add the carrots and scalded milk to the soup. Keep very hot, but do not allow to boil. Bake the slices of bread spread with the butter and cheese mixture in a hot oven for 10 minutes or until delicately brown. Correct the seasoning of the soup and pour into deep soup plates. Serve the toast on the side. *Serves* 4.

422. PEASANT'S VEGETABLE SOUP
Zuppa alla campagnola

2 quarts cold water
½ pound very lean bacon, cooked for 10 minutes in boiling water
1 ½-pound ham bone (with a little meat clinging to it)
Coarsely chopped vegetables:
   3 onions
   2 carrots
   3 small turnips
1 cup dried split peas, soaked overnight in cold water (unless the ready-to-use kind are available, in which case wash and drain them well)
Bouquet Garni:
   3 sprigs parsley
   1 bay leaf
1 teaspoon salt
¼ teaspoon freshly ground pepper
1 cup grated Parmesan cheese
30 thin slices of French bread, crusts removed, lightly browned in the oven

Put the bacon and ham bone into a large earthenware (or enamel) pot and add the chopped vegetables, pre-soaked and drained peas, Bouquet Garni, and the salt and pepper. Cover with the cold water and cook, covered, at a gentle simmer for about 1½ hours. Toward the end of the cooking, remove the Bouquet Garni and the ham bone. Remove and cut up the bacon into fine strips; and return it to the pot. Serve the toast and grated cheese on the side. *Serves* 6.

423. ZUCCHINI SOUP
Zuppa di zucchine alla moda del fattore

3 tablespoons butter
1 tablespoon finely minced onion
1 pound small zucchini, unpeeled and cut into ½-inch slices
Bouquet Garni:
   1 bay leaf
   3 sprigs parsley
   ½ teaspoon dried thyme

2 quarts Vegetable Bouillon [No. 327]
Pinch nutmeg
2 teaspoons salt
⅛ teaspoon freshly ground pepper
2 eggs
10 slices bread, crusts removed, quartered, and browned in oven
1 cup grated Parmesan cheese

Brown the onion slightly in 1 tablespoon of the butter in a large, heavy earthenware (or enamel) pot over medium heat; add the zucchini, Bouquet Garni, bouillon, nutmeg, salt, and pepper. Bring to a boil, reduce heat to moderate, and continue cooking, covered, for 10 minutes, or until the zucchini are tender. Remove the Bouquet Garni. Beat the eggs slightly, dilute with a little of the soup liquid, and slowly add to the soup, stirring briskly. Remove from the fire at once, swirl in the remaining butter, and stir in half the grated cheese with a wooden spoon. Serve immediately with the rest of the grated Parmesan and the toast on the side. *Serves* 6.

NOTE: Take great care when adding eggs; stir briskly to prevent curdling.

424. ZUPPA BUONA DONNA
Zuppa buona donna

This is the well-known French Potage bonne-femme.

4 leeks (white part only), finely sliced
½ cup butter
1½ quarts Classic Bouillon [No. 324]
½ pound potatoes, very finely sliced
1 tablespoon finely chopped parsley
½ cup heavy cream
Salt to taste
30 small slices bread, crusts removed, lightly browned in the oven

Cook the leeks in a large covered pot over moderate heat with 2 tablespoons of the butter for 6 minutes, or until soft (do not let them brown). Add the bouillon and bring to a boil. Add potatoes and continue cooking over moderate heat for 20 minutes, or until the potatoes are just tender. Remove from fire and add the remaining butter, the cream, and the parsley. Correct for salt. Serve the toasted bread on the side. *Serves* 4.

425. ZUPPA PAVESE
Zuppa pavese

We give here a variant of the classic Zuppa pavese. *This delicious soup, so popular throughout Italy, is so easily and quickly made that we give here the recipe for one person.*

2 tablespoons butter, softened
3 tablespoons grated Parmesan cheese
4 slices French or Italian bread, crusts removed
1 cup hot White or Classic Bouillon [No. 323 or 324]
1 egg
Pinch freshly ground white pepper

Mix the softened butter with 2 tablespoons of the cheese and spread on the slices of bread. Toast the bread in a hot (400°) oven for 10 minutes or until delicately brown. Set aside. Turn the oven down to moderate. Break the egg into a saucer. Pour the hot bouillon into an oven-proof dish and slide the egg into it, being careful not to break the yolk, and grate the pepper over it. Place in the oven for 5 minutes or just long enough for the yolk to set. Serve at once with the toast and sprinkle the remaining tablespoon of cheese over the soup. *Serves 1.*

REGIONAL ITALIAN SOUPS
Minestre all'italiana

All of the following soups are uniquely Italian, many of them traditional specialties of a particular region.

426. BEAN SOUP CASALINGA
Minestra di fagioli alla casalinga

3 quarts water
2 cups dried white beans, soaked overnight in water and drained
2 ripe tomatoes, peeled, seeded, drained, and chopped
A chopped mixture:
  $\frac{1}{4}$ pound ham fat
  3 sprigs parsley
  3 sprigs basil (or $\frac{1}{2}$ teaspoon dried)
  1 stalk celery
  1 small onion
  1 clove garlic
1 tablespoon oil
$\frac{1}{4}$ teaspoon freshly ground pepper
2 teaspoons salt
$\frac{1}{2}$ pound spaghetti, broken into pieces

Put all of the ingredients except the spaghetti in a large earthenware (or enamel) pot. Bring slowly to a boil and simmer for $1\frac{1}{2}$ hours, or until the beans are barely tender. Raise the flame and add the broken spaghetti. Reduce the flame as soon as the soup returns to a boil and cook until the pasta is just *al dente*, 10 to 12 minutes. *Serves 6.*

427. BEAN SOUP WITH PASTA
Minestra di fagioli con la pasta

$\frac{3}{4}$ pound dried white beans, soaked 12 hours and drained
$1\frac{1}{2}$-pound ham bone with a little of the meat clinging to it
$\frac{1}{4}$ pound pork rind
3 quarts cold water
$\frac{1}{4}$ teaspoon freshly ground pepper
1 teaspoon salt
A chopped mixture:
  $\frac{1}{4}$ pound ham fat
  $\frac{1}{2}$ onion
  1 clove garlic
  2 stalks celery
  3 sprigs parsley
3 tomatoes, peeled, seeded, drained, and chopped
$\frac{1}{2}$ pound elbow macaroni (or fine spaghetti, broken into pieces)

Parboil the ham bone and pork rind for 10 minutes. Drain and cut the rind into slivers. Wash the beans under running water and put into an earthenware (or enamel) pot with the ham bone and pork rind. Cover with the cold water, and season with the salt and pepper. Bring to a boil, reduce heat to moderate, and cook, covered, for $1\frac{1}{2}$ hours or until the beans are tender. In a separate saucepan brown the chopped mixture over medium heat, add the chopped tomatoes, blend well, and cook gently for about 10 minutes. When the beans are tender, remove the ham bone, cut off the meat from it, cut it into slivers, and add it to the soup along with the tomato mixture. Bring the soup back to a boil, drop in the pasta (whichever has been chosen), and cook until the pasta is just *al dente,* 10 to 12 minutes. Correct the seasoning, let it rest a few minutes, and, if desired, serve with grated Parmesan cheese on the side. *Serves 6.*

428. BEAN SOUP VENETA
Minestra di fagioli con pasta veneta

1 pound dried cranberry beans (borlotti beans), soaked
    12 hours and drained
1 $\frac{1}{2}$-pound ham bone with some of the meat clinging
    to it
$\frac{1}{2}$ pound fresh pork rind
A finely chopped mixture:
    $\frac{1}{2}$ pound ham fat
    1 medium onion
3 tablespoons oil
1 teaspoon salt
$\frac{1}{8}$ teaspoon cinnamon
9 cups cold water
$\frac{1}{2}$ pound flat egg noodles, broken into pieces about
    2 inches long
$\frac{1}{2}$ teaspoon freshly ground pepper

Parboil the ham bone and pork rind in boiling water
for about 10 minutes. Remove the meat from the bone
and cut the meat and rind into small slivers. Wash the
soaked beans under running water and put them into
a large, heavy earthenware (or enamel) pot with the
pork rind and ham slivers, the ham bone, the chopped
mixture, and the oil. Season with salt and cinnamon.
Add the water, cover, bring *slowly* to a boil, and simmer
until the beans are tender, about 1$\frac{1}{2}$ hours. Remove
the ham bone and bring the soup to a fast boil. Add the
pasta and cook for 8 to 10 minutes or until the pasta
is just *al dente*. Taste and adjust seasoning and add the
freshly ground pepper just before serving. *Serves 6.*

429. BROCCOLI SOUP ROMANA
Minestra di pasta e broccoli alla romana

$\frac{1}{2}$ pound pork rind
2 quarts water
1$\frac{1}{2}$ tablespoons oil
1 onion, finely chopped
2 cloves garlic, crushed in the garlic-press
$\frac{1}{2}$ pound smoked ham (lean and fat), chopped
2 teaspoons salt
$\frac{1}{4}$ teaspoon freshly ground pepper
1 medium bunch broccoli
$\frac{1}{3}$ pound spaghetti, broken into 2-inch pieces
1 cup grated Pecorino (or Parmesan) cheese

Boil the pork rind in the water for about 1$\frac{1}{2}$ hours,
drain, reserving cooking water, and cut rind into slivers.
Add more water to the cooking liquid to bring it up to
2 quarts again. Heat the oil in an earthenware (or
enamel) pot over medium heat, add the onion and

garlic, and cook until golden. Add the ham, pork rind
slivers, the cooking liquid, salt, and pepper. Bring to a
boil, reduce heat, and simmer for 30 minutes. Trim
the stems of the broccoli and cook it in slightly salted
boiling water to cover for 12 to 15 minutes, or until
just tender; drain, chop it coarsely, and keep it warm.
Bring the soup to a fast boil, drop in the broken
spaghetti, and cook until just *al dente*, about 10 to 12
minutes. About 5 minutes before the spaghetti is
done, add the cooked broccoli and correct the seasoning. Serve the grated Pecorino or Parmesan on the
side. *Serves 6.*

430. BRODETTO ALLA ROMANA
Brodetto alla romana

This is the traditional soup for Roman families at Easter.

2 pounds beef (boneless rump or bottom round)
2 pounds breast of lamb (boneless)
6 quarts cold water
1 onion stuck with 2 cloves
Bouquet Garni:
    3 sprigs parsley
    1 stalk celery
    1 small carrot
1 tablespoon coarse salt
6 egg yolks
1 cup grated Parmesan cheese
1 teaspoon lemon juice
$\frac{1}{2}$ teaspoon freshly ground white pepper
1 teaspoon salt (if necessary)
1 tablespoon chopped marjoram (or 1 teaspoon dried)
24 thin slices French or Italian bread, browned in
    the oven

Put the two meats into a large earthenware (or enamel)
pot with 6 quarts of cold water, cover, and bring it
slowly to a boil. Skim any scum from the top. Add the
onion, Bouquet Garni, coarse salt, and reduce flame to
keep at a barely perceptible simmer. After 1$\frac{1}{2}$ hours,
remove the lamb and keep in another pot covered with
a little of the cooking liquid. After another 1$\frac{1}{2}$ hours
(or as soon as the beef is tender), remove the beef to the
same pot containing the lamb. Strain the cooking
liquid into another pot and reduce it over a high flame
to about 2 quarts. Beat the egg yolks in a bowl with
2 tablespoons of the grated Parmesan cheese and the
lemon juice. Add 1 cup of the broth, mix well, and, off
the heat, pour this mixture slowly into the soup,
stirring vigorously. Return the pot to the lowest possible fire and, stirring with a wooden spoon, cook for
5 minutes or until the soup has thickened slightly.

Do not boil. Add the white pepper, additional salt if needed, and marjoram. Pour the soup into bowls in which the toast first has been distributed. Serve the rest of the grated Parmesan on the side. The meat may be served as a separate main course. *Serves 6.*

431. CABBAGE SOUP MILANESE
Verzata alla milanese

2 very solid heads of Savoy cabbage
¼ pound fresh pork rind
½ pound sweet Italian sausage
2 tablespoons butter
A chopped mixture:
  ½ medium onion
  ½ small carrot
  1 stalk celery
2 quarts White or Classic Bouillon [No. 323 or 324]
A second chopped mixture:
  4 slices bacon, parboiled for 5 minutes
  2 sprigs parsley
  6 leaves fresh sage (or ⅛ teaspoon dried)
Salt and freshly ground pepper
24 slices French bread, crusts removed, lightly
  browned in oven
1½ cups grated Parmesan cheese

Remove the leaves from the cabbage, wash, trim off tough parts, shred it coarsely, and cook in slightly salted boiling water for 8 minutes. Drain, cool thoroughly, squeeze with hands to remove excess water, and set aside. Cook the pork rind in boiling water for 1½ hours, drain it, and cut into slivers. Boil the sausage in water for 10 minutes, drain, skin it, and cut it into ½-inch pieces.

Put the first chopped vegetable mixture and the butter in a large, heavy pot and sauté over medium heat until golden. Add the bouillon, bring it to a simmer, and add the second chopped mixture, the cabbage, cooked pork rind, and cooked sausage. Correct seasoning and continue cooking for 10 minutes. When ready to serve, distribute the toasted bread in deep soup bowls and pour the soup over. Serve the grated Parmesan cheese on the side. *Serves 6.*

432. CHICKPEA SOUP CONTADINA
Minestra di ceci alla contadina

2 cups dried chickpeas, soaked overnight in water and
  drained
A chopped mixture:
  ¼ pound ham (fat and lean), preferably prosciutto
  ½ onion
  1 clove garlic
  3 sprigs parsley
  3 sprigs fresh marjoram (or ½ teaspoon dried)
1 heart very white escarole, well washed and shredded
½ pound fresh ham, cut into thin strips 2 inches long
2 ripe tomatoes, peeled, seeded, drained, and chopped
2 teaspoons salt
3 quarts cold water
¼ teaspoon pepper, freshly ground
24 thin slices bread, crusts removed, browned in
  oven
1 cup grated Parmesan cheese

Put the chickpeas in a large earthenware (or enamel) pot with the chopped mixture, escarole, fresh ham, tomatoes, salt, and the water (the chickpeas should be covered generously; add a little more water, if necessary). Bring slowly to a boil and simmer for 1½ hours, or until the chickpeas are tender. Season with a liberal amount of freshly ground pepper and add more salt if necessary. Divide the toasted bread among individual soup bowls and pour the soup over them. Serve the grated Parmesan on the side. *Serves 6.*

433. CHICKPEA SOUP ROMANA
Minestra di ceci alla romana

2 cups dried chickpeas, soaked overnight in water and
  drained
3 quarts cold water
Bouquet Garni:
  3 sprigs rosemary (or ½ teaspoon dried)
  1 clove garlic
2 teaspoons salt
½ cup oil
A small bunch rosemary, tied with string (or ½
  teaspoon dried)
2 cloves garlic, crushed in the garlic-press
3 anchovy fillets, washed free of salt [*see* No. 220]
¼ teaspoon freshly ground pepper
½ pound elbow macaroni

Put the dried chickpeas into an earthenware (or enamel) pot with the 3 quarts of cold water, the Bouquet Garni, and the salt. Bring slowly to a boil, and continue cooking, covered, over moderate heat for about 1½ hours, or until the chickpeas are tender. Meanwhile, put the oil in a saucepan with the second bunch of rosemary and the garlic; season with several turns of the pepper mill, and cook over medium heat until the garlic is golden. Remove the pan from the fire, discard the rosemary (unless dried has been used), add the anchovies, and crush to a pulp with a pestle or spoon. When the chickpeas are tender, add the anchovy/garlic mixture to the soup, and mix well. Bring the soup to a boil, add the elbow macaroni, and cook until the pasta is just *al dente,* about 10 to 12 minutes. Remove the Bouquet Garni and correct seasoning. *Serves* 8.

434. CHICKPEA SOUP TOSCANA
Minestra di ceci alla toscana

2 cups dried chickpeas, soaked overnight and drained
2 teaspoons salt
1 small bunch rosemary, tied with a string (or 1 teaspoon dried)
3 quarts cold water
2 cloves garlic, crushed in the garlic-press
½ cup oil
½ cup tomato paste
3 anchovy fillets, washed free of salt [*see* No. 220]
½ teaspoon freshly ground pepper
½ pound shell-shaped pasta

Put the soaked chickpeas, salt, and the rosemary into an earthenware (or enamel) pot and cover with the 3 quarts of cold water. Bring to a boil and cook over moderate heat for 2 hours, or until the chickpeas are very tender. Remove the rosemary and purée the peas through a food mill together with their liquid. Wash and dry the pot and in it put the garlic and oil. Cook until brown over medium heat, add the tomato paste, and cook gently for a few minutes to blend well. Add the anchovy fillets, which have been thoroughly crushed with a pestle in the mortar. Add the chickpea purée and, if the whole is too thick, add enough water or bouillon to bring to the desired consistency. Bring to a boil, drop in the pasta, and cook until just *al dente,* 10 to 12 minutes. Correct seasoning and pour into soup plates. This is a rather thick soup. *Serves* 6.

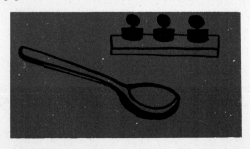

435. FANTASY SOUP GOURMET
Minestra fantasia del ghiottone

2½ quarts Chicken or Vegetable Bouillon [No. 326 or 327]
4 sets chicken parts (about 1½ pounds): giblets, necks, wings, and feet
Aromatic seasoning:
  1 carrot, sliced
  1 onion stuck with 1 clove
  2 leeks (white part only), sliced
  1 stalk celery, sliced
Bouquet Garni:
  3 sprigs thyme (or ¼ teaspoon dried)
  1 bay leaf
  3 sprigs parsley
2 teaspoons salt
⅛ teaspoon freshly ground white pepper
3 tablespoons butter
3 tablespoons flour
2 tablespoons chopped parsley
Pinch Cayenne pepper
½ cup dry Marsala wine, reduced to ¼ cup

Cut up the chicken parts in the following fashion: cut the necks and wings in half, the gizzards (from which the heavy lining has first been removed) into quarters, the feet (which have first been scalded in boiling water) in half, and the hearts and livers (from which tough parts or tendons have been removed) in half. Put all of these, except the hearts and livers, into a large earthenware (or enamel) pot, add the aromatic seasoning, the Bouquet Garni, and the salt and pepper. Cover with the bouillon, bring *slowly* to a boil, and simmer for about 1½ hours. About 6 minutes before removing the soup from the fire, add the hearts and livers. Strain through cheesecloth dipped in warm water and well wrung out. Transfer all of the strained material in the cheesecloth, except the feet and the Bouquet Garni, to a bowl and keep warm with some of the hot soup. In a separate pot, melt the butter, add the flour, cook over gentle heat, stirring continuously, until it is golden, and then gradually blend all of the soup into it. Bring it to boil, stirring occasionally, lower the flame, and cook at the barest simmer for 25 minutes. Pour the soup into a hot tureen and add the chicken parts and the chopped parsley (parboiled for a moment and well drained). Add the Cayenne, correct the seasoning, and add the reduced Marsala. *Serves* 6.

SEE
VERSE
FOR
PTION

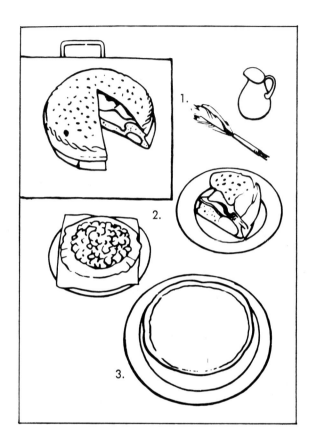

1. Easter Pie Genovese (No. 288)
2. Shrimp Tart (No. 291)
3. Caprice Tart (No. 286)

Chickpea Soup Romana (No. 433):
see page 143

436. FARRICELLO SOUP ROMANA
Minestra di farricello con cotiche alla romana

$\frac{1}{4}$ pound pork rind
3 quarts hot water, slightly salted
A chopped mixture:
   $\frac{1}{8}$ pound ham fat
   1 clove garlic
   3 sprigs fresh marjoram (or $\frac{1}{4}$ teaspoon dried)
   1 onion
1$\frac{1}{2}$ pounds tomatoes, peeled, seeded, drained, and chopped
1 tablespoon each parsley and fresh basil, chopped together
1 pound farricello or any similar pasta
1 cup grated cheese (Parmesan or Pecorino)

Blanch the pork rind for 30 minutes in boiling water and drain. Cut it into small slivers. Put it into a large earthenware (or enamel) pot with the 3 quarts slightly salted water. Bring to a boil, turn heat down to moderate, and simmer for 1 hour. In another pan, brown the chopped mixture over medium heat, add the tomatoes and the chopped herbs, cook gently for about 10 minutes to blend, and then add to the soup pot containing the pieces of pork rind and water. Bring to a boil and drop in, little by little, the farricello, carefully washed with cold water and picked over (as one does rice). Stir several times to prevent the farricello from sticking to the pot and cook until just *al dente*, about 15 minutes. Remove from the fire and add the grated cheese. Serve very hot. *Serves* 6.

437. GENOESE SOUP WITH LINGUINE
Minestra di bavette alla genovese

This is a well-known Genoese specialty that is generally prepared with the broth made from the famous Cima [No. 1545]. *When* Cima *is being prepared for a family dinner, this soup is also often served.*

8 cups broth from Cima Genovese [No. 1545]
1$\frac{1}{2}$ cups linguine (or comparable pasta), broken into $\frac{1}{2}$-inch pieces
1 tablespoon fresh chopped marjoram (or $\frac{1}{2}$ teaspoon dried)
4 eggs, beaten
1$\frac{1}{2}$ cups grated Parmesan cheese
Salt and freshly ground pepper

Bring the broth to a boil and drop in the linguine and the chopped marjoram. Cook only until the pasta is just *al dente*, 10 to 12 minutes. Meanwhile, mix the beaten eggs with $\frac{1}{2}$ cup of the grated Parmesan cheese and dilute it with 1 cup of the broth. As soon as the pasta is cooked, remove pot from the fire, add the beaten eggs slowly, stirring briskly to prevent curdling. Return soup to the lowest possible heat and cook for 5 minutes, stirring constantly. Correct the seasoning. Serve with the remaining grated Parmesan on the side. *Serves* 6.

Lima Bean Soup Romana (No. 438):
see page 146

145

438. LIMA BEAN SOUP ROMANA
Minestra di fave fresche alla romana

1 pound large Fordhook lima beans (weight after shelling)
A finely chopped mixture:
   $\frac{1}{4}$ pound hog jowl
   1 stalk celery
   1 onion
   1 clove garlic
   3 sprigs parsley
2 tablespoons oil
2 tomatoes, peeled, seeded, drained, and chopped
2 quarts Chicken or Vegetable Bouillon [No. 326 or 327]
$\frac{1}{2}$ pound elbow macaroni
Salt and freshly ground pepper
$\frac{2}{3}$ cup grated Pecorino cheese

Brown the chopped mixture in the oil in a large pot over medium heat, add the tomatoes, and season with a little salt and freshly ground pepper. Add the beans and cook very gently, covered, for 10 minutes. Add the bouillon, check for seasoning, and bring to a boil. Add the macaroni, cook until just *al dente,* pour into a tureen, and add the grated cheese. Let the soup rest for a few minutes before bringing it to the table. *Serves* 6.

439. MID-CENTURY SOUP
Minestra demi-siècle

$2\frac{1}{2}$ quarts water
2 pounds large fresh peas (weight after shelling)
2 tender heads of Boston lettuce, well washed and finely shredded
1 large onion, finely chopped
Bouquet Garni:
   3 sprigs parsley
   $\frac{1}{2}$ teaspoon dried thyme
   1 bay leaf
1 teaspoon sugar
$\frac{1}{2}$ teaspoon freshly ground white pepper
$2\frac{1}{2}$ teaspoons salt
1 2-pound chicken
Aromatic vegetables used in cooking the chicken:
   2 stalks celery, sliced
   1 onion, sliced
   1 small carrot, sliced
$\frac{1}{3}$ pound very tiny fresh peas—petits pois (weight after shelling)
4 egg yolks

2 tablespoons heavy cream
3 tablespoons butter, softened

Put 1 cup of the water into a large earthenware (or enamel) pot with the large peas, lettuce, chopped onion, Bouquet Garni, sugar, pepper, and $\frac{1}{2}$ teaspoon of the salt. Bring barely to a boil and cook, covered, over low heat for about 45 minutes, or until vegetables are cooked down to a pulp. At the same time, cook the chicken in another pot, covered with the remaining water. Add the remaining salt and the aromatic vegetables, bring to a boil, then turn heat down to moderate, and simmer for 45 minutes, or until the chicken is tender. Remove the chicken and let it cool for a few minutes. Turn the flame high under the chicken broth, allowing it to reduce to a good flavor. When the chicken is cool enough to handle, cut the breast free, skin it, cut it into slivers, and keep it hot, covered with $\frac{1}{2}$ cup of its broth in a covered bowl. Chop the dark meat finely, dilute it with a few tablespoons of the hot broth, and force it through a fine sieve or blend for 20 seconds in the electric blender on high speed. Remove the Bouquet Garni from the pulped vegetables and purée the latter in a food mill or blender. Mix the two purées thoroughly in a large pot. Degrease and strain the reduced chicken broth and pour it into the combined purées. Cook the tiny peas in salted water for 8 minutes or until tender, add them to the puréed soup, and correct the seasoning. Stirring steadily, bring the whole to a boil, remove from the fire, and slowly add the slightly beaten egg yolks which have been well mixed with the cream and $\frac{1}{2}$ cup of the soup. Return to the fire, stirring constantly, and at the first sign of boiling pour the soup into a hot tureen and add the slivers of white meat and softened butter. *Serves* 6 *to* 8.

440. MUSHROOM SOUP
Minestra di funghi

Markets in Italy provide a wide range of mushrooms of varying sizes and colors, few of which are available in this country. For this soup the preferred mushrooms are very small, very firm, and lightish yellow, known as galinette. *Button mushrooms found in American markets may be substituted* [*see* introduction to No. 1761].

2 quarts White or Classic Bouillon [No. 323 or 324]
2 pounds button mushrooms, unpeeled
3 tablespoons butter
1 tablespoon finely chopped onion
2 cloves garlic, finely sliced

1 tomato, peeled, seeded, drained, chopped, and cooked
    for 10 minutes to a paste
1 tablespoon finely chopped parsley
2 egg yolks
2 eggs
$\frac{1}{2}$ cup grated Parmesan cheese
Pinch nutmeg
$\frac{1}{2}$ teaspoon salt
$\frac{1}{8}$ teaspoon freshly ground pepper
1 cup Croûtons [No. 332]

Wash, trim, and slice the mushrooms. Melt the butter in a large pot over medium heat, add the chopped onion and garlic, cook till golden, add the mushrooms, blend well for a few moments, add the tomato and chopped parsley, and season with the salt and pepper. Pour the bouillon over, bring to a boil, turn the heat down to moderate, and continue cooking for 1 hour. When ready to serve, beat the 2 eggs and 2 yolks in a bowl with a wire whisk, mix in the grated cheese and the pinch of nutmeg, salt, and pepper, and dilute with $\frac{1}{2}$ cup of the soup. Remove the soup from the fire, pour in the beaten egg mixture slowly, stirring vigorously. Return the soup to the fire and, stirring continuously, heat very slowly for 5 minutes until slightly thickened. Do not boil. Correct the seasoning and serve in a tureen with the croûtons which should be browned in butter just before serving. *Serves* 6.

441. NEAPOLITAN SOUP
Minestra di erbe maritata

This is a traditional Neapolitan specialty.

3 quarts water
1 2-pound chicken
$1\frac{1}{4}$ pound beef (rump or bottom round)
1 tablespoon coarse salt
Aromatics for the bouillon in which the chicken is
    cooked:
    1 onion stuck with 1 clove
    1 clove garlic
    1 small carrot
    1 celery stalk
1 small green cabbage
1 head chicory
1 head escarole
$\frac{1}{4}$ pound ham fat, finely chopped, with 2 cloves garlic
$\frac{1}{4}$ pound Genoa salami, skinned, in one piece
$\frac{1}{4}$ pound prosciutto, in one piece
$\frac{1}{4}$ pound very lean hog jowl, in one piece

$\frac{1}{4}$ pound fresh pork rind, in one piece, pre-cooked
    for $\frac{1}{2}$ hour in boiling water, drained, and cubed

Put the chicken and the beef in a large earthenware (or enamel) pot, cover with 3 quarts of water, season with the coarse salt, cover, and bring slowly to a boil. Skim off any scum that rises to the surface. When no more scum rises, add the aromatic vegetables. Simmer for 1 hour or until the chicken and meat are just tender (the beef may take slightly longer). Remove them to a covered bowl and keep them warm with a little of the liquid in which they have been cooking. Strain the rest of the liquid through cheesecloth dipped in warm water and well wrung out. Cut out the hard core of the cabbage with a sharp knife and quarter the head. Wash the chicory and the escarole thoroughly and quarter them. Drop all three vegetables into 3 quarts of lightly salted boiling water and boil for 5 minutes. Drain, cool, and wring them out well by hand. Put them into good-sized pot together with the chopped ham fat/garlic mixture, salami, hog jowl, and cubed pork rind; cover the whole with the bouillon from the chicken, bring to a boil, reduce to a gentle simmer, and continue cooking, covered, for 2 hours or until the meats are tender. Remove the salami, hog jowl, and prosciutto; cut them into fairly large pieces and return them to the soup. Let it cook for a few minutes to blend, correct seasoning, and serve. The chicken and beef may be served on the side with appropriate seasonal vegetables amply dressed in butter and oil. *Serves 6 to 8.*

442. PEA AND PASTA SOUP
Minestra di quadrucci e piselli

2 quarts Chicken or Vegetable Bouillon [No. 326 or 327]
A chopped mixture:
    $\frac{1}{4}$ pound pork jowl
    1 small onion
    1 clove garlic
2 tablespoons oil
$\frac{1}{2}$ pound small, tender peas (weight after shelling)
$\frac{1}{2}$ teaspoon salt
$\frac{1}{4}$ teaspoon freshly ground white pepper
$\frac{1}{2}$ pound thin egg noodles
1 cup grated Parmesan cheese

Lightly brown the chopped mixture in the oil in a large earthenware pot over medium heat. Add the peas, season with the salt and pepper, add 3 tablespoons of the bouillon, and cook over moderate heat for 3 minutes, covered. Add the rest of the bouillon, bring to a boil, drop in the noodles, and cook just to the *al dente* stage, about 8 to 12 minutes. Correct the seasoning and serve at once with the grated cheese on the side. *Serves 6.*

443. RICE SOUP WITH CHICKEN LIVERS
Minestra di riso con fegatini di pollo

$\frac{1}{3}$ pound chicken livers
2 quarts Chicken Bouillon [No. 326]
1 cup rice, washed and drained
2 tablespoons chopped parsley
Salt and freshly ground pepper
1 cup grated Parmesan cheese

Wash and dry the chicken livers. Chop them into small pieces, and scald them for 2 minutes in 4 tablespoons of the bouillon. Bring the remaining bouillon to a boil in a large, heavy pot, drop the rice in gradually, and cook for 17 to 20 minutes, or until just *al dente*. Add the chicken liver pieces with their bouillon. Add the chopped parsley; taste, and correct the seasoning. Serve the grated cheese on the side. *Serves 6.*

444. RICE AND PARSLEY SOUP CASALINGA
Minestra di riso e prezzemolo alla casalinga

3 tablespoons oil
1 small onion, finely chopped
4 medium potatoes, grated through the round holes of the grater
4 tablespoons chopped parsley
2 quarts cold water
4 vegetable bouillon cubes
$\frac{3}{4}$ cup uncooked rice
3 tablespoons butter, softened
$\frac{1}{2}$ cup grated Parmesan cheese
Salt and freshly ground pepper

Heat the oil in a large earthenware (or enamel) pot over medium heat and add the chopped onion. As soon as the onion is golden add the grated potatoes, 2 tablespoons of the chopped parsley, the 2 quarts of water, $\frac{1}{2}$ teaspoon salt and $\frac{1}{4}$ teaspoon pepper, and the vegetable bouillon cubes. Bring slowly to a boil, add the rice, reduce heat, cover, and cook until rice is *al dente*, about 17 to 20 minutes. Correct the seasoning, remove from the fire, and add the butter, grated Parmesan cheese, and the remaining chopped parsley. *Serves 6.*

Neapolitan Soup (No. 441): see page 147

148

445. RICE AND PEA SOUP
Minestra di "risi e bisi"

Risi e bisi *soup is a specialty of the Veneto, the north-eastern part of Italy west of and above Venice. The success of this soup, which is a combination of rice and peas, depends on the quality of the peas, which must be the freshest and tenderest procurable.*

3 tablespoons butter
2 tablespoons oil
1/8 pound very lean salt pork, diced and parboiled for 10 minutes
1 small onion, chopped
2 quarts Chicken Bouillon [No. 326]
1 cup uncooked rice, well washed and drained
1 pound (weight when shelled) small tender peas (or 2 packages frozen petits pois)
2 tablespoons chopped parsley
Salt and freshly ground pepper
1 cup grated Parmesan cheese

Put the butter, oil, diced salt pork, and onion into a large earthenware pot over moderate heat, and, as soon as the onions are transparent, add the rice. Cook very gently for 5 minutes. Add the bouillon, bring to a boil, add the peas, and cook until the rice is just *al dente*, about 17 to 20 minutes. Remove from the fire, correct the seasoning, add 2 tablespoons of the cheese and parsley, and serve with the remaining cheese on the side. *Serves 6.*

NOTE: If frozen peas are used, add during the last 7 minutes of cooking.

446. RICE AND POTATO SOUP
Minestra di riso e patate

2 quarts White or Classic Bouillon [No. 323 or 324]
3 tablespoons oil
A chopped mixture:
1/4 pound ham fat
1 small onion
1 stalk celery
1 1/2 pounds medium potatoes (2 of them whole and the remainder cut into small pieces)
1/4 pound smoked ham, cut into slivers
1 cup rice, cooked *al dente* in bouillon
2 tablespoons minced parsley
Salt and freshly ground pepper

Put the oil and the chopped mixture into a large, heavy pot over medium heat. When the onion is golden, add all of the potatoes and the ham. Mix well, add the bouillon, bring to a boil, and cook, covered, over

Rice and Sausage Soup Veneta (No. 447)

moderate heat for about 20 minutes, or until the potatoes are just tender. Remove the whole potatoes, mash them to a purée (or put them through a ricer), and return to the soup. Add the chopped parsley and the cooked rice, correct the seasoning, and remove from the fire. Serve with grated Parmesan cheese on the side. *Serves 6.*

447. RICE AND SAUSAGE SOUP VENETA
Minestra di "risi e luganeghe" alla veneta

1 pound sweet Italian sausage
1 turnip, diced
1/4 pound ham fat, put through the fine blade of the food chopper with 1 small onion
2 quarts White or Classic Bouillon [No. 323 or 324]
1 cup rice
1 tablespoon chopped parsley
3 tablespoons butter, softened
1 1/2 cups freshly grated Parmesan cheese

Cook the sausage for 10 minutes in boiling water, drain, cut into 1-inch slices, and reserve. Cook the turnip in boiling water for 15 to 20 minutes, or until just tender, and drain. Put the ham fat in a large earthenware (or enamel) pot over medium heat and cook until golden. Add the sausage, turnip, and the bouillon. Bring it to a boil and drop in the rice. After it has cooked for 20 minutes or until just *al dente,* add the chopped parsley, butter, and 1/2 cup of the grated cheese. Correct the seasoning and serve with the remaining cheese on the side. *Serves 6.*

448. RICE AND SPINACH SOUP
Minestra di riso e spinaci

2 quarts White or Classic Bouillon [No. 323 or 324]
1 pound spinach
1 tablespoon oil
A finely chopped mixture:
    1/4 pound ham fat
    1 onion
    1 stalk celery
1 cup rice
1/4 pound prosciutto, cut into slivers
2 tablespoons chopped parsley
Salt and freshly ground pepper
1 cup grated Parmesan cheese

Wash the spinach thoroughly, drain it, and cook it in only the water clinging to its leaves in a covered enamel or stainless steel saucepan over medium heat for about 5 minutes. Stir it once or twice and add a pinch of salt during the cooking. Drain it, press out excess water with the hands when it is cool enough to handle, chop it coarsely, and reserve. Heat the oil in a large earthenware (or enamel) pot over medium heat; add the chopped mixture. When the onion is golden, add the rice, stir for a minute so that every grain of rice is covered with the fat in the pot, and pour in the bouillon. Correct the seasoning, bring to a boil, and cook for 17 to 20 minutes, or until the rice is just *al dente*. Add the spinach, prosciutto, and the parsley 5 minutes before the rice is done. Serve the grated cheese on the side. *Serves* 6.

449. RICE AND VEGETABLE SOUP
Minestra di riso e verdure

2 1/2 quarts Chicken Bouillon [No. 326]
1 1/2 cups rice, cooked until just *al dente* in the bouillon
4 tablespoons butter
3 large potatoes, diced
1/2 pound tiny peas (weight when shelled)
3 zucchini, diced
1 tablespoon chopped parsley
1 small head green cabbage
Salt and freshly ground pepper
1 cup grated Parmesan cheese

Cook rice, and strain, reserving bouillon. Keep rice in a bowl until needed. Melt the butter in a large, heavy pot, add the potatoes, and sauté gently over moderate heat for 10 minutes, stirring occasionally. Add the bouillon, bring to a boil, and cook for 10 minutes.

Add the peas, zucchini, and parsley and continue simmering, covered, for another 10 minutes, or until the peas are just tender. Meanwhile, wash the cabbage, discard the tough white core, and shred it. Cook it for 10 minutes in lightly salted water and drain. Add the cabbage and the rice to the soup and correct the seasoning. Simmer for 1 or 2 minutes longer. Serve the grated cheese on the side. *Serves* 6.

450. RICE AND ZUCCHINI SOUP
Minestra di riso e zucchini

This is prepared the same way as Rice and Spinach Soup [No. 448], except that 1 pound of finely sliced zucchini is substituted for the spinach. The zucchini should be cooked for 6 to 8 minutes in bouillon or lightly salted water, drained, and added to the soup a few minutes before serving.

451. ROMAN SOUP
Minestra col battuto alla romana

This is a traditional Roman specialty.

1/3 cup ham fat, preferably prosciutto
2 medium onions
2 cloves of garlic
1 tablespoon oil
Optional: 1 fresh tomato, peeled, seeded, and sliced
2 quarts cold water
2 teaspoons salt
1/4 teaspoon freshly ground pepper
1/2 pound spaghetti, broken into pieces 1 1/2 inches long
1 cup grated Pecorino cheese (or substitute Parmesan)

Put the ham fat, onions, and garlic cloves through the food chopper. Put them in a large, heavy pot over moderate heat and sauté mixture gently in the oil until onions are transparent. Add, if you wish, several slices of tomato and, immediately thereafter, the cold water and salt and pepper. Bring to a boil, drop in the broken spaghetti, and cook until just *al dente,* about 10 to 12 minutes. Serve with the grated Pecorino on the side. *Serves* 6.

452. TRIPE SOUP MILANESE
Minestra di trippe alla milanese

4 pounds honeycomb tripe
For cooking the tripe:
    5 quarts White or Classic Bouillon [No. 323 or 324]
    1 onion, stuck with 2 cloves
    2 stalks celery

For the soup:

    1 cup dried white beans, soaked overnight and drained

    1 medium cabbage, well washed, trimmed, and the leaves separated

    3 tablespoons butter

    ½ pound sliced bacon, cut into 1-inch pieces and parboiled for 5 minutes

    1 medium onion, thinly sliced

    3 leeks (white part only), thinly sliced

    1 celery heart, thinly sliced

    4 small carrots, thinly sliced

    2 tomatoes, peeled, seeded, drained, and chopped

    3 medium potatoes, cubed

    Salt and freshly ground pepper

    A chopped mixture:

        4 tablespoons ham fat

        1 clove garlic

    2 cups grated Parmesan cheese

    2 cups Croûtons [No. 332]

Clean the tripe, wash it thoroughly, cut it into 4-inch squares, and put it into a large earthenware (or enamel) pot. Add the 5 quarts of bouillon (or substitute lightly salted water, if you wish, although the soup will not be so flavorsome), the onion, and the celery stalks. Bring it to a boil, reduce heat to moderate, and cook, covered, for about 4½ hours. Drain the tripe, slice it into thin strips, and put aside. Strain the broth through a very fine strainer and reserve.

Meanwhile, in another pot cook the beans in lightly salted water for 1½ hours or until tender. Cook the cabbage in boiling water for 10 minutes, drain, and cut into fine shreds. Melt the butter in a large, heavy pot over medium heat, add the bacon, the onion, and leeks. As soon as they are lightly golden, add the celery, carrots, tomatoes, and blend well. Cook gently, stirring occasionally, for 10 minutes. Add the sliced tripe, pour in 4 quarts of the tripe/bouillon liquid, add salt and pepper if necessary, return to a boil, and reduce heat. Add the potatoes and simmer, covered, over moderate heat for 20 minutes. Then add the cooked beans and cabbage and simmer for about another 5 minutes. When ready to serve, sauté the chopped mixture in a frying pan for 5 minutes and add to the soup. Pour into soup bowls and serve with the grated Parmesan cheese and the croûtons on the side. *Serves 10 to 12.*

453. PURÉE OF VEGETABLE SOUP ITALIANA
Minestra di legume passati all'italiana

1 medium cabbage

1 pound spinach, thoroughly washed

4 turnips

4 carrots

4 medium potatoes

3 tablespoons butter

2 quarts water

2 teaspoons salt

¼ teaspoon freshly ground pepper

2 eggs

½ cup rich milk

1 cup Croûtons, browned in butter [No. 332]

Separate the cabbage leaves. Wash, trim, and slice very finely the cabbage and spinach. Wash, peel, and slice very finely the turnips, carrots, and potatoes. Melt the butter in a large earthenware (or enamel) pot over moderate heat. Add all the vegetables and cook gently, covered, for 10 minutes, stirring occasionally. Add 2 quarts of water, season with the salt and pepper, and continue cooking over moderate heat for 1 hour or until the vegetables are very soft. Purée them through a food mill and correct the seasoning. In a deep tureen beat the eggs with the milk and pour the hot vegetable purée over them, stirring to blend well. Serve in deep soup plates with the croûtons which have been browned in butter just before serving. *Serves 6.*

MINESTRONE
Minestroni

"Minestrone" is a flexible term, the interpretation of which varies not only from region to region in Italy (as the recipes below illustrate), but often from restaurant to restaurant, or from cook to cook. It invariably implies vegetables in the soup and, usually, a starchy supplement—small pastine, cubed potatoes, dried beans, or rice. However, the contents of a particular minestrone may depend upon the prevailing regional produce, what the cook has available, and the cook's expertise and taste. In any case, minestroni are never thin, watery soups, but soups so amply laden with vegetables or pasta that they may be described more accurately as eaten rather than drunk.

454. MINESTRONE BORGHESE
Minestrone alla borghese

1/4 pound prosciutto (or smoked ham), fat and lean, sliced

3 tablespoons butter

2 tablespoons finely chopped onion

1 clove garlic, crushed in the garlic-press

2 tomatoes, peeled, seeded, drained, and chopped

1 small celery heart, finely sliced

2 teaspoons salt

1/4 teaspoon freshly ground pepper

2 quarts water

4 vegetable bouillon cubes

4 medium "old" potatoes, cubed

1 1/2 cups elbow macaroni

4 medium zucchini, finely sliced

2 sweet yellow peppers, roasted, peeled, and cut into fine strips [*see* No. 145]

10 fresh basil leaves (or 1 teaspoon dried)

1 cup grated Parmesan cheese

Cut the prosciutto into fine slivers and brown it in the butter in a large, heavy pot over medium heat. Add the chopped onion and garlic and, when these are transparent, add the tomatoes. Cook, covered, over low heat for about 10 minutes, add the celery, and season with the salt and pepper. Add the 2 quarts of water in which the vegetable bouillon cubes have been dissolved, cover the pot, and simmer for 1/2 hour. Correct seasoning, add the potatoes, and cook 10 minutes longer. Then add the macaroni (it may be necessary to add a little water at this point to provide sufficient liquid to cook the macaroni) and cook 10 minutes more. Finally, add the zucchini, the strips of peppers, and the basil and cook for 6 to 8 minutes longer. Taste, and adjust seasoning. Serve the grated cheese on the side. *Serves 6.*

NOTE: If dried basil is used, add with the tomatoes.

455. CABBAGE MINESTRONE
Minestrone di cavoli

1 1/2 cups dried white beans, soaked overnight and drained

1 medium head cabbage

1/2 head Savoy cabbage

Aromatic mixture:
   1 medium onion
   1 leek (white part only)
   1 medium carrot
   1 stalk celery
   3 sprigs parsley

6 medium potatoes, thinly sliced

2 turnips, thinly sliced

1/4 pound bacon, cut into 1-inch pieces and parboiled for 5 minutes

2 teaspoons salt

1/4 teaspoon freshly ground pepper

2 quarts White or Classic Bouillon [No. 323 or 324]

3/4 cup pastine (rice or broken-up spaghetti may be substituted)

4 tablespoons butter, softened

1 cup grated Parmesan cheese

Cook the beans in salted water to cover for 1 1/2 hours, or until tender, drain, and reserve. Separate the leaves from the cabbages, trim off the tough parts at the base of the leaves, wash, shred coarsely, cook in lightly salted boiling water to cover for 5 minutes. Drain, cool, and squeeze out excess water with the hands. Put the cabbage, aromatic mixture, potatoes, turnips, and bacon into a large earthenware (or enamel) pot. Season with the salt and pepper, add the 2 quarts of bouillon, and bring *slowly* to a boil. Cover the pot and continue simmering for 1/2 hour. The heat should be low enough so that the vegetables are tender and firm, but not mushy. Bring the soup to a rolling boil, add the pastine, and cook for 10 to 12 minutes longer. About 5 minutes before the pastine are done, add the beans. When ready to serve, taste, and adjust the seasoning, add the butter, a grating or two of pepper, and the grated cheese. *Serves 6.*

152

Minestrone Borghese (No. 454)

456. MINESTRONE GENOVESE
Minestrone alla genovese

This characteristically Genoese minestrone contains a Genoese specialty, the Pesto (literally "pounded"), an aromatic mixture of pounded ingredients, colored green by the use of various vegetable leaves and delicately redolent of garlic. It is famous throughout Italy as the Genoese accompaniment for spaghetti and other pastas. Its fresh green color distinguishes it from the red tomato sauces of the rest of Italy.

For the Pesto:

   1 cup fresh basil leaves, loosely packed

   1 cup fresh spinach leaves, trimmed of stems, loosely packed

   4 tablespoons Pecorino cheese (or substitute Parmesan)

   3 cloves garlic, crushed in the garlic-press

   2 tablespoons chopped parsley

   6 tablespoons oil

   3 tablespoons butter, softened

3 tablespoons oil

¼ pound spinach, washed and chopped

¼ pound beet greens, washed and chopped

¼ pound (weight when shelled) lima beans

½ Savoy cabbage, trimmed, washed, shredded, and parboiled in salted water for 5 minutes

2 potatoes, cubed

2 tablespoons finely chopped onion

1 leek (white part only), finely sliced

2 teaspoons salt

½ teaspoon freshly ground pepper

2 quarts water

½ pound trenette (or linguine or similar pasta), broken into 1-inch pieces

Pound all of the Pesto ingredients in a mortar with a pestle until a smooth paste is obtained and set aside. (Or whirl in blender at high speed for 30 seconds.)

  Heat the oil in a large earthenware (or enamel) pot over medium heat. Add the spinach, beet greens, lima beans, cabbage, potatoes, chopped onion, leek, and salt and pepper. Cover with the 2 quarts of water and simmer very gently for 1½ hours. Raise heat, bring to a rolling boil, add the pasta, and cook until it is just *al dente* (the time will depend on the type of pasta employed). Taste, and adjust seasoning; then blend in the Pesto with a wire whisk, and cook for a minute or so to blend all the flavors. *Serves 6.*

Minestrone Genovese (No. 456)

457. MINESTRONE ITALIANA
Minestrone all'italiana

1 pound beet greens

4 tablespoons oil

⅓ pound fresh pork rind, parboiled for 10 minutes and cut into slivers

1 onion, finely chopped

2 tablespoons chopped parsley

¼ pound prosciutto (fat and lean), cut into slivers

¾ pound white beans (either cannellini or borlotti), soaked overnight and drained

2 quarts water

1 teaspoon salt

¼ teaspoon freshly grated pepper

½ pound very fine spaghetti (or similar pasta, such as cannolicchietti), broken into 1-inch pieces

⅓ pound young zucchini, cut into small cubes

1 cup grated Parmesan cheese

Wash the beet greens and chop coarsely. Heat the oil in a large earthenware (or enamel) pot over medium heat. Add strips of pork rind, chopped onion, and parsley; as soon as the onion begins to turn golden, add the prosciutto, beans, and the water; season with the salt and freshly ground pepper. Bring to a boil, cover pot, and simmer over moderate heat for 1½ hours, or until the beans are barely tender. Raise the heat toward the end and, when the soup is boiling, add the beet greens. When the soup comes back to a boil, add the spaghetti (or whatever pasta has been chosen) and cook until just *al dente*. About 8 minutes before the pasta is done, add the cubed zucchini. The finished soup must not be watery but rather thick with vegetables and pasta. Serve with the grated Parmesan cheese on the side. *Serves 6.*

153

458. MINESTRONE MILANESE
Minestrone alla milanese

2 quarts White or Classic Bouillon [No. 323 or 324]

$\frac{1}{4}$ pound lean salt pork

$\frac{1}{2}$ cup butter

1 small onion, chopped

1 leek (white part only), chopped

Bouquet Garni:

   3 sprigs parsley

   1 sprig rosemary (or $\frac{1}{4}$ teaspoon dried)

   1 bay leaf

$\frac{1}{2}$ pound tomatoes, peeled, seeded, drained, and coarsely chopped

2 medium potatoes, diced

2 carrots, scraped and diced

$\frac{1}{4}$ pound asparagus, cut into $\frac{1}{2}$-inch pieces

$\frac{1}{4}$ pound zucchini, diced

$\frac{1}{4}$ pound fresh lima beans (or, lacking these, dried beans soaked overnight and cooked until tender)

$\frac{1}{4}$ pound fresh string beans

$\frac{1}{4}$ pound fresh peas

1 tiny heart of celery, finely chopped

1 cup rice

A mixture of fresh herbs, chopped together:

   $\frac{1}{4}$ cup basil leaves

   1 clove garlic

   4 sprigs parsley

Salt and freshly ground pepper

1 cup grated Parmesan cheese

Parboil the salt pork in boiling water for ten minutes and dice it. Melt 2 tablespoons of the butter in a large earthenware (or enamel) pot; add the onion, leek, and salt pork. Cook gently over moderate heat until the onion is transparent. Add the tomatoes, the Bouquet Garni, and season with salt and freshly ground pepper. Melt the remaining butter in another saucepan; add all of the vegetables and sauté gently for about 4 minutes, stirring and mixing them as they cook; then add them to the onion/tomato mixture. Cook for a few minutes to blend; add the bouillon and bring to a boil. Drop in the rice and cook until just *al dente,* about 17 to 20 minutes. It may be necessary to add a little more bouillon to keep the rice and vegetables well covered. A few minutes before taking the soup from the stove, blend in the basil/garlic/parsley mixture thoroughly. Discard the Bouquet Garni. Taste the various vegetables to make certain they are tender and, if not, cook a little longer. They should not be mushy. Serve the grated Parmesan cheese on the side. *Serves* 6.

459. COLD MINESTRONE MILANESE
Minestrone alla milanese freddo

The Milanese are connoisseurs of good minestrone. In summer they generally prefer it served cold.

Prepare cold minestrone as the preceding hot one [No. 458], except for the following changes: do not dice the salt pork, but cut it into small thin slices. Season the minestrone as soon as the rice is cooked *al dente* with a good, freshly grated Parmesan cheese. Pour it into deep soup bowls and garnish with a few slices of the salt pork. Keep in a cool place (not the refrigerator, if possible) until ready to serve. *Serves* 6.

460. MINESTRONE MONTEFREDINE
Minestrone alla montefredine

$2\frac{1}{2}$ quarts cold water

4 pig's feet

4 pig's ears

$\frac{3}{4}$ pound dried vegetables (such as beans, chickpeas, lentils, fave beans, etc.), soaked overnight and drained

1 slice prosciutto (or smoked ham), $\frac{1}{4}$ inch thick

4 tablespoons butter

3 medium onions, sliced

A finely chopped mixture:

   2 ounces ham fat

   $\frac{1}{2}$ carrot

   $\frac{1}{2}$ onion

   $\frac{1}{4}$ pound each of fresh vegetables in season—use at least 4 or 5 varieties (such as potatoes, leeks, carrots, peas, green beans, zucchini, yellow squash, asparagus, lima beans, tomatoes, etc.) all washed, trimmed, and cut into dice

Bouquet Garni:

   3 sprigs parsley

   2 sprigs marjoram (or $\frac{1}{2}$ teaspoon dried)

   1 bay leaf

Greens:

   1 small heart celery, finely chopped

   $\frac{1}{2}$ cup fennel, diced small

   $\frac{1}{4}$ pound spinach, washed and coarsely chopped

   $\frac{1}{4}$ pound beet greens, washed and coarsely chopped

2 teaspoons salt

$\frac{1}{2}$ teaspoon freshly ground pepper

$\frac{1}{2}$ pound pasta (such as spaghetti, linguine, macaroni, etc.), broken into $\frac{1}{2}$- to 1-inch pieces

1 cup grated Parmesan cheese

Cover the pig's feet and ears with the cold water in a large earthenware (or enamel) pot. Bring slowly to a boil, turn heat down, and simmer for 1½ hours. Skim off any scum that rises to the surface. Add the dried vegetables and the prosciutto and continue cooking for another 1½ hours, or until the beans are tender.

Meanwhile, melt the butter in another large saucepan; add the onion and the chopped ham fat/carrot/onion mixture; and sauté over medium heat until the onion is transparent. Add all of the other fresh vegetables and the Bouquet Garni. Cook very gently for 10 minutes, stirring and mixing the vegetables as they cook. Remove from the stove and set aside.

About 20 minutes before the beans are done add the greens to the soup pot, season with the salt and pepper, and bring the mixture slowly to a boil. Add whatever pasta you have chosen and cook until just *al dente*. It may be necessary to add a little more water to keep the pasta and vegetables well covered. Test the various vegetables to make certain they are tender, and, if not, cook a little longer. The vegetables must not be mushy. Remove the prosciutto and the pig's feet and ears; discard the Bouquet Garni. Pick the meat off the feet, discarding the bones; cut the ears in very small pieces; cut the prosciutto into dice; and return all of the meats to the pot. Taste, and adjust seasoning. Serve the grated Parmesan cheese on the side. *Serves* 8.

461. MINESTRONE TOSCANA
Minestrone alla toscana

1½ cups dried white beans, soaked overnight
    and drained
2½ quarts cold water
Bouquet Garni:
    1 sprig rosemary (or ¼ teaspoon dried)
    1 bay leaf
1 tablespoon salt
½ cup oil
A chopped mixture:
    1 small onion
    3 sprigs parsley
    1 stalk celery
1 pound escarole (weight after trimming), well washed
    and coarsely chopped
3 medium tomatoes, peeled, seeded, drained, and
    chopped
½ teaspoon freshly ground pepper
½ pound pasta (spaghetti, linguine, or any preferred
    variety), broken into 1-inch pieces
1 cup grated Parmesan cheese

Put the pre-soaked beans in a large, heavy pot. Add the water, Bouquet Garni, and salt and cook over

moderate heat for 1¾ hours, or until the beans are almost mushy. Discard the Bouquet Garni and purée the beans and their liquid by passing through a fine strainer or a food mill. Return the purée to the pot. In the meanwhile, heat the oil in another saucepan with the chopped onion mixture. As soon as it begins to take on color, add the escarole and the tomato pulp. Cook for about 10 minutes, and then turn the mixture into the pot with the bean purée. Season with the freshly ground pepper and additional salt, if necessary. Mix all the ingredients thoroughly and bring slowly to a boil. Drop in the pasta and cook until just *al dente*. Serve the grated Parmesan cheese on the side. *Serves* 6.

SPECIAL SOUPS AND ONE-DISH MEALS OF MANY LANDS
Minestre Tipiche di Vari Paesi

ALGERIA

462. COUSCOUS or THA'AM
Cus cus—tha'am

Rich and poor, all North Africans delight in this traditional specialty.

½ pound large-grained semolina
½ cup slightly salted water
4 tablespoons butter

Put the semolina in a wooden bowl (North Africans use one especially designed for it, called a "djefna"), add ½ cup of slightly salted water, work it with both hands to make a smooth paste, and then knead it with the right hand, fingers spread apart, until, little by little, it separates into tiny balls the size of peppercorns. Put these into a strainer and shake it so as to remove any loose grains of the semolina that have not been worked into pellets. Put the pellets on a clean cloth and let them dry out in the sun or in a 200° oven. When ready to cook, put them into a colander (North Africans use a special pan called a "keskès") over boiling water (the water should not touch the colander) and cook for ½ hour. Then pour the semolina into a bowl, add the butter, and mix with a fork. Replace any water that may have boiled away in the lower pan, put back the "keskès" with the semolina, and cook it for another half hour as before. Sugar, honey, raisins, and hard-boiled eggs may be served with it. *Serves 6.*

BELGIUM

463. WATERZOI (BELGIAN NATIONAL SOUP)
Waterzoi—zuppa nazionale belga

1 4-pound stewing chicken, or hen
3 tablespoons butter
1 large onion, finely sliced
3 hearts of celery, finely sliced
3 leeks (white part only), finely sliced
2 quarts White Stock [No. 1]
3 peppercorns tied in a cheesecloth bag
3 egg yolks
½ cup finely grated parsley root
1½ cups Croûtons [No. 332]
1 teaspoon salt
¼ teaspoon finely ground pepper

Cut up the chicken as for frying: separate the drumsticks, thighs, wings, and the 2 breast halves; cut the back in half. Season the pieces with the salt and pepper. Melt the butter in a large earthenware pot, add the sliced vegetables, and sauté them gently for 10 minutes. Arrange the pieces of chicken on top of the vegetables, add the bouillon and the bag of peppercorns, bring slowly to a boil over moderate heat, and simmer for about 1½ to 2 hours, or until the chicken pieces are just tender. When they are done, remove the pot from the fire and discard the bag of peppercorns. Remove the pieces of chicken and put them in a warmed soup tureen. Beat the egg yolks with the grated parsley root and 4 tablespoons of the broth. Pour this mixture gradually into the soup, stirring constantly. Return the pot to the fire and cook very gently, stirring continuously, until the soup is slightly thickened. Do not boil. Correct the seasoning. Pour the soup over the chicken pieces and serve the croûtons on the side. *Serves 6.*

BRAZIL

464. CAMARO (CHICKEN AND RICE SOUP)
Camaro brasilero—minestra di gallina e riso

1 2½-pound stewing chicken, or hen
2½ quarts water
1 onion stuck with 1 clove
Bouquet Garni:
  3 peppercorns
  1 sprig chervil
  1 sprig parsley
⅔ cup rice
2 teaspoons salt
¼ teaspoon freshly ground pepper

Put the chicken in a large earthenware (or enamel) pot with the 2½ quarts water. Bring slowly to a boil; skim; and add the onion, Bouquet Garni, and pepper and salt. Lower the heat and cook at a gentle simmer for 1½ to 2 hours, or until the chicken is tender. Remove it from the soup, disjoint it into serving pieces, and keep warm with a little of the bouillon in a tureen. Strain the rest of the soup through cheesecloth, return the strained soup to the pot, and bring it to a boil. Drop in the rice and cook until it is just barely tender, 17 to 20 minutes. Taste, and correct seasoning and pour over the chicken and serve. *Serves 6.*

CHINA

465. BIRD'S NEST SOUP
Brodo ristretto al nido di rondini

Gourmets in China and epicures in Europe serve these "nests" in a very concentrated consommé. The nests are built by a genus of swallow called salangani. *Built one upon the other, they hang from the ceilings of enormous caves in Annam, Java, and in several of the Malayan islands. Secured with great difficulty and danger, it is only the high price they command that explains why anyone would risk the hazards involved in gathering them. The nests must be subjected to long processing to eliminate every trace of feathers and down, and then are carefully boxed.*

Soak 6 nests in cold water for a couple of hours; as soon as they begin to swell and take on a transparent, gelatinous appearance, check to see that they contain no foreign substances that have to be removed. Blanch them in boiling water for about 10 minutes, then put them into 2 quarts of a reduced, boiling consommé [No. 324 or 325], and cook them for about 30 to 40 minutes. Serve in well-heated cups. *Serves* 6.

ENGLAND

466. CHICKEN BROTH
Zuppa di pollo

1 3-pound stewing chicken
2 quarts White Bouillon [No. 323]
1 onion stuck with 1 clove
Bouquet Garni:
   1 sprig thyme (or $\frac{1}{4}$ teaspoon dried)
   1 bay leaf
   2 sprigs parsley
1 stalk celery
$\frac{1}{2}$ cup rice
Salt to taste
3 tablespoons Brunoise [No. 328], cooked until
   tender in $\frac{1}{2}$ cup bouillon

Put the chicken in a large earthenware (or enamel) pot, pour in the bouillon, and bring to a boil over moderate heat. Skim carefully. Add the onion, Bouquet Garni, celery, rice, and a dash of salt (unless the bouillon is already well seasoned). Continue cooking over moderate heat for 1 to $1\frac{1}{2}$ hours, or until the chicken is tender. Remove and drain the chicken when it is done, skin it, bone it, and cut it into small pieces, and return it to the soup. Remove the Bouquet Garni, onion, and celery. Add the Brunoise and correct the seasoning. *Serves* 6.

467. CLEAR OXTAIL SOUP
Minestra di coda di bue chiara

$2\frac{1}{2}$ pounds oxtail
$\frac{1}{2}$ pound veal knuckle, cracked
$\frac{1}{2}$ pound beef shin bones, cracked
3 quarts water
1 tablespoon salt
1 onion stuck with 2 cloves
2 carrots
Bouquet Garni:
   3 leeks (white part only), sliced
   2 stalks celery, sliced
   1 sprig fresh thyme (or $\frac{1}{4}$ teaspoon dried)
   1 bay leaf
3 tablespoons butter
1 turnip, peeled and diced
2 carrots, scraped and diced
2 stalks celery, sliced
2 leeks (white part only), sliced
1 cup Classic Bouillon [No. 324]
To clarify the soup:
   $1\frac{1}{2}$ pounds lean beef, chopped
   White and shell of 1 egg
$\frac{1}{2}$ cup dry Madeira wine

Cut up the oxtail at the joints and wash thoroughly under running water. Use not only the solid chunks, but all the odd bits and pieces. Tie these bits into a muslin bag (they will be used to strengthen the soup). Put the oxtail chunks in a large earthenware (or enamel) pot with the bag of odd pieces and the veal knuckle and the bones; season with the salt; and add 3 quarts of cold water. Bring it slowly to a boil over moderate heat and skim off any scum that rises to the

Bird's Nest Soup
(No. 465)

surface. Add the clove-stuck onion, two carrots, and the Bouquet Garni. Continue cooking at a bare simmer for 4 hours. Remove the pot from the stove and take out the oxtail pieces; keep them in a covered bowl with a little of the soup. Discard the muslin bag containing the odd pieces of oxtail and pour the soup through a fine strainer. Thoroughly rinse out the pot and return the soup to it. Skim off excess fat from the surface. Allow to cool.

While cooling, melt the butter in a heavy saucepan; add the carrot and turnip dice and the slices of celery and leeks; and cook very gently for 10 minutes. Add the cup of bouillon and continue cooking for 20 minutes, or until the vegetables are just barely tender. Mix the chopped beef and the white and shell of egg thoroughly together. Pour this into the cooled oxtail soup, and, stirring continuously, bring it to a boil over medium heat. Lower the flame and simmer the soup at a hardly perceptible boil for 1 hour. Strain the clarified soup through cheesecloth dipped in warm water and well wrung out. Return the soup to the pot, add the chunks of oxtail and the cooked vegetables, and heat well. Add the Madeira a moment before it goes to the table. *Serves 6 to 8.*

468. GREEN TURTLE SOUP
Zuppa di tartaruga verde chiaro

1 2-pound can of green turtle meat
1 4-pound stewing chicken or hen
½ pound veal knuckle
2½ quarts White or Classic Bouillon [No. 323 or 324]
1 onion, stuck with 1 clove
Bouquet Garni:
 3 sprigs parsley
 ·1 stalk celery
 1 sprig thyme (or ¼ teaspoon dried)
 1 bay leaf
 3 sprigs basil (or ¼ teaspoon dried)
 2 sprigs marjoram (or ¼ teaspoon dried)
2 tablespoons arrowroot or potato starch
Pinch Cayenne pepper
Salt to taste
Few drops Worcestershire sauce
½ cup dry sherry wine

Brown the chicken in a hot (400°) oven for 20 minutes (do not smear it with any fat), until it is just lightly colored. Put it in an earthenware (or enamel) pot and add the veal knuckle, the onion, and the Bouquet Garni. Pour in the bouillon and bring it slowly to a boil; simmer for 2 hours. Remove the bones and the

chicken. Reserve the chicken for other uses. Strain the soup through cheesecloth dipped in warm water and wrung out well, and then return it to the pot. Mix the potato starch or arrowroot with a little cold water and blend it into the soup with a wire whisk. Season with salt, bring it to a boil over moderate heat, and cook for 15 minutes, skimming carefully. During this time heat the can containing the turtle meat in a *bain-marie* (pan of hot water), open it, drain the pieces, cut them into 1-inch cubes, add them to the soup, and heat them through. Just before serving, add the dash of Cayenne, a few drops of Worcestershire sauce, and the sherry. *Serves 6.*

469. MOCK-TURTLE SOUP
Zuppa di finta tartaruga

It is not known whether the origin of this soup is English or American. In any case, it has been baptized "mock-turtle" by the English, since a calf's head is substituted for the turtle. Prepared with care, it merits its international fame.

1 calf's head (boned by the butcher), soaked
 2 hours in water
3 quarts White Bouillon [No. 323]
A chopped mixture:
 1 carrot
 1 onion
 1 stalk celery
Bouquet Garni:
 2 sprigs thyme (or ¼ teaspoon dried)
 1 bay leaf
 2 sprigs parsley
White Roux [No. 13], made of 4 tablespoons each
 butter and flour
¼ pound ham, coarsely chopped
1 quart White Stock [No. 1]
Salt and freshly ground pepper to taste
Aromatic infusion made by soaking the following
 herbs in ¼ cup dry Madeira wine:
 1 teaspoon chopped marjoram
 1 teaspoon chopped thyme
 1 bay leaf, crumbled
Optional: 40 Quenelles [No. 339] made with a veal
 Forcemeat [No. 129] which has been mixed with
 the chopped yolks of 2 hard-boiled eggs

Put the soaked calf's head in a large earthenware (or enamel) pot. Cover it with the bouillon and add the chopped vegetable mixture and Bouquet Garni. Bring to a boil, turn down heat, skim off all scum, and simmer for about 2 hours. When the meat is tender, remove

158

the head, drain, and slice the meat in pieces $\frac{1}{4}$ inch thick. Put these slices between two plates with a weight on the top plate. Allow to cool; cut the meat into small square or round pieces; and reserve.

While the calf's head is cooking, prepare the white roux in another large, heavy pot. Heat the stock until boiling and add it to the roux, stirring constantly. Bring to a boil, turn heat down to a slow boil, and add the ham. Continue cooking for about $1\frac{1}{2}$ hours, or until the stock is reduced by $\frac{1}{2}$ and is very thick. Stir often to prevent scorching. Add the bouillon in which the calf's head cooked, turn heat down, and simmer for 2 hours. While this is cooking, prepare the aromatic infusion by soaking the various crushed herbs in the wine. (Prepare the—optional—tiny quenelles.) When ready to serve, strain the soup through a cheesecloth into a fresh pot, reheat it, and pour in the aromatic-wine infusion through a fine strainer. Taste for seasoning. Garnish with the (optional) quenelles and/or the pieces of meat from the calf's head. *Serves* 8.

FRANCE

470. CRAYFISH BISQUE or CULLIS
Bisque o coulis d'écrevisses—bisque di gamberi d'acqua dolce

$2\frac{1}{2}$ pounds crayfish (or substitute lobster), thoroughly washed and cleaned
2 quarts Fish Bouillon [No. 325]
$\frac{1}{2}$ cup rice, well washed
$\frac{1}{2}$ cup butter
1 small onion, finely chopped
1 small carrot, finely chopped
3 tablespoons brandy
1 cup dry white wine
Bouquet Garni:
   1 sprig thyme (or $\frac{1}{4}$ teaspoon dried)
   1 bay leaf
   2 sprigs parsley
40 tiny Quenelles [No. 339], made from Mousseline Fish Forcemeat [No. 132]
1 cup heavy cream
1 teaspoon salt
$\frac{1}{4}$ teaspoon white pepper

Bring the rice and 1 quart of the bouillon to a boil in a large earthenware (or enamel) pot, cover, and cook over moderate heat for 40 minutes, or until the rice is very soft. Melt 3 tablespoons of the butter in a large

saucepan. Add the onion and carrot and cook for 10 minutes, or until the onion is transparent. Add the crayfish, cover pot, and continue cooking until the crayfish turn a bright rose color, about 15 minutes. Add the brandy and, as soon as it is well heated, ignite. Shake the pan vigorously until all the flames have died out. Add the wine and the Bouquet Garni and continue cooking until the liquid has almost disappeared. Add 2 cups of the bouillon and cook for another 15 minutes. Discard the Bouquet Garni. Shell the crayfish. Crush the shells with 1 cup of the cooking liquid in blender (or pound them in a mortar with a pestle). Strain the crayfish-shell purée through several thicknesses of cheesecloth to remove any tiny particles of shell. Purée both the rice with its liquid and the crayfish with their remaining liquid in the electric blender for 20 seconds on high speed. This will require several operations, since the blender container will not hold enough to do it all at once. Combine all purées in a large earthenware (or enamel) pot, add the remaining bouillon and the cream, and bring just to the boiling point. Add the quenelles, salt, and pepper, lower the heat, and simmer for 5 minutes. Remove the bisque from the heat and swirl in the remaining butter, bit by bit. *Serves* 6.

471. CREAM OF CHICKEN SOUP
Crème de volaille à la reine

In the complex repertory of French soups, cream of chicken soup occupies a pre-eminent place. Its smoothness, delicacy, and subtle flavors make it a true masterpiece.

1 $2\frac{1}{2}$- to 3-pound stewing hen, cut up
2 quarts Chicken Bouillon [No. 326]
$\frac{3}{4}$ cup butter
4 tablespoons flour
2 large leeks (white part only), sliced
1 stalk celery, sliced
1 carrot, finely sliced
1 cup heavy cream
1 teaspoon salt
$\frac{1}{4}$ teaspoon white pepper

Heat the bouillon to the boiling point in a saucepan. Melt 4 tablespoons of the butter in a large earthenware (or enamel) pot, add the flour, and cook gently for 3 or 4 minutes, being careful not to allow it to brown. Add the boiling bouillon, stirring vigorously with a wire whisk. Still stirring, bring it to a boil and cook for 5 minutes. Remove from the fire and allow to cool until tepid. Put the chicken in the pot (there should be sufficient thickened bouillon to cover it) and add the leeks, celery, and carrot. Season with the salt and simmer over moderate heat for $1\frac{1}{2}$ to 2 hours, or until the chicken is just barely tender. Then remove the chicken; bone, and skin it. Cut the white meat of the breast into slivers and reserve. Cut up the rest of the chicken meat and pound it to a pulp in the mortar, incorporating with it 4 tablespoons of butter and $\frac{1}{2}$ cup of the cream (or this may be done more simply by puréeing in the electric blender for 20 seconds on high speed). Strain the soup through cheesecloth into another pot. Return it to the fire and add the chicken purée and the slivers of white meat. Bring it back to a boil and remove from the fire. Blend in the remaining butter (which should be softened, but not melted) and the rest of the cream. Check for salt and season with the pepper. Pour into a hot soup tureen. *Serves* 6.

472. PETITE MARMITE HENRI IV
or CHICKEN IN THE POT
Petite marmite Henri IV—poule au pot

$1\frac{1}{2}$ pounds rump of beef (or top round)
1 $3\frac{1}{2}$- to 4-pound hen
1 set chicken giblets
$\frac{1}{2}$ pound beef marrow bones
$2\frac{1}{2}$ quarts White or Classic Bouillon [No. 323 or 324], or more as needed
Vegetables tied in a cloth bag:
  2 leeks (white part only) sliced
  3 stalks celery, sliced
Bouquet Garni:
  3 sprigs parsley
  1 bay leaf
  1 sprig fresh thyme (or $\frac{1}{4}$ teaspoon dried)
6 carrots, scraped and cut into small ovals the size of an olive
$\frac{1}{2}$ pound small white onions, peeled
2 turnips, peeled and cut into small ovals the size of an olive
1 small cabbage, tough white core removed, cut into 6 pieces
12 thin slices bread cut into large rounds and browned in the oven
Salt and pepper to taste

This French specialty is traditionally served in an earthenware stewing pot. Put the meats, giblets, marrow bones, and the bouillon in a large earthenware (or enamel) pot. Bring very slowly to a boil and skim off carefully any scum that rises to the surface. Add the vegetables tied in a cloth bag and the Bouquet Garni. Return to a boil, lower the heat, and simmer *very*

slowly for about 3 hours (adding more bouillon if necessary). Add the carrots, turnips, and onions during the last $\frac{1}{2}$ hour of the cooking. After the first hour test the chicken and remove it as soon as it is tender. Keep it warm in a covered bowl. Meanwhile, boil the cabbage in lightly salted water for 12 minutes, or until it is just tender; drain it; and keep it hot in another bowl with a few tablespoons of the broth. Remove the beef rump (or round) as soon as it is tender and cut into small pieces. Skin and bone the chicken and pull or cut the meat into bite-size pieces. Remove the vegetables in a bag, the Bouquet Garni, and the giblets and discard. Remove the marrow bones. Skim off excess fat from the surface of the soup; taste for seasoning and add salt and pepper, if necessary. Add the chicken and beef pieces to the soup and heat for a few more minutes. Scoop the marrow from the bones and spread it onto the freshly browned bread rounds. Pour the soup into heated soup plates, portioning the meat and vegetables out evenly. Serve the cabbage and the bread rounds on the side. *Serves* 6.

473. POT-AU-FEU
Pot-au-feu

Pot-au-feu is a kind of everyday Petite Marmite, a family-type soup prepared in an earthenware casserole. Beef is generally the only meat used in it (although it may be enriched with veal, turkey, mutton, or chicken). Pot-au-feu provides two courses. The first is the soup, which is delicious, and which may contain rice, pastine, tiny ravioli, tortellini, cappelletti, or any of the other garnishes already described as appropriate for clear soups. The second course is provided by the meat, which is served separately and garnished with appropriate seasonal vegetables. A number of condiments and sauces are appropriate with boiled beef, such as coarse salt, grated horseradish with vinegar, horseradish sauce, various kinds of mustard, sweet pickles, and, if one prefers, a good and fragrant tomato sauce. Follow recipe No. 472, Petite Marmite, omitting the chicken, if desired.

474. ONION SOUP
Soupe à l'oignon—zuppa di cipolle alla francese

2 pounds yellow onions, thinly sliced
6 tablespoons butter
2 tablespoons oil
2 tablespoons flour
2 quarts Classic Bouillon [No. 324]

160

Paella Valenciana (No. 481). Here are assembled all the components for this elaborate and truly festive preparation.

18 thin slices French or Italian bread, crusts removed,
   browned in butter
1 cup grated Parmesan cheese
Salt and freshly grated pepper to taste

In the pot (preferably earthenware) in which the soup is to be cooked, melt 3 tablespoons of the butter with the oil. Add the onions and season with salt and pepper. Stew the onions over moderate heat, covered, until they are very soft but not brown. Add the flour, stirring in well, and, when the mixture is a pale gold, remove half the onions. Purée them through a strainer or food mill (or whirl in blender on high speed for 10 seconds) and return them to the pot. Stir thoroughly so that the flour does not stick to the bottom. Pour in the bouillon, correct the seasoning, and continue simmering for about 20 minutes over moderate heat. When ready to serve, pour the soup into six individual oven-proof earthenware bowls or casseroles. On top of each put 3 slices of bread spread with a mixture of grated cheese and the remaining butter. Put the casseroles into a hot (450°) oven for 6 to 8 minutes and serve as soon as the cheese has turned golden. *Serves* 6.

GERMANY

475. BEER SOUP
Bier suppe—zuppa di birra

4 tablespoons butter
4 tablespoons flour

1½ quarts light German beer
1 teaspoon sugar
1 teaspoon salt
¼ teaspoon pepper
⅛ teaspoon cinnamon
⅔ cup heavy cream
12 slices of bread, crusts removed, browned
   in the oven

Melt the butter in a heavy pot, stir in the flour to make a roux, and cook over medium heat until it is barely golden. Add the beer, sugar, and seasonings. Keep at a boil for a few minutes, then blend in the cream. Heat for a few moments more, but do not boil. Distribute the pieces of toast in 6 soup bowls, pour the boiling soup over it. *Serves* 6.

476. CHERRY SOUP
Kirschen suppe—zuppa di ciliege

1 pound Bing cherries, stoned (reserve ½ the pits)
1 stick cinnamon
1 strip lemon rind (no white part)
1 cup hot water
2¼ cups dry red wine
1 scant tablespoon sugar
½ tablespoon cornstarch
8 rusks, coarsely crumbled

Put the stoned cherries, stick cinnamon, and lemon rind into a large earthenware pot, and pour the hot water over them. Cook over a high flame for about 10 minutes and then purée through a fine sieve or food mill (or whirl in blender on high speed for a few sec-

Olla Podrida
(No. 479):
see page 162

onds). Put the purée back into the pot and pour the wine over it. Pound the reserved cherry stones in a mortar, add to the soup, and bring it to a boil. Keep at a boil for 4 minutes, and then strain the purée through a triple thickness of cheesecloth dipped in water and well wrung out. Return the purée to the pot, bring it back to a boil, and add the sugar and the cornstarch which has been first mixed to a paste with a little cold water. Continue boiling for 5 minutes. Pour into a hot tureen, add the crumbled rusks, and serve. *Serves* 4.

477. SOUR CREAM SOUP
Zuppa di crema acida

3 cups Velouté Base [No. 399]
3 cups White Bouillon [No. 323]
1 small onion stuck with 1 whole clove
Bouquet Garni:
   1 sprig thyme (or ¼ teaspoon dried)
   1 bay leaf
   3 sprigs parsley
Pinch cumin
Pinch nutmeg
Salt to taste
2 cups sour cream, at room temperature
18 thin slices bread, crusts removed, browned in butter

Pour the Velouté base and bouillon into an earthenware pot; add the clove-stuck onion, Bouquet Garni, cumin, nutmeg, and salt to taste. Bring to a gentle simmer and cook for about 20 minutes. Strain the soup through a fine sieve, return it to the pot, and gradually beat in the sour cream. Bring it to a simmer (do *not* boil) and cook for a few seconds longer. Serve with the browned slices of bread on the side. *Serves* 6.

NOTE: If this soup is brought to a boil, or cooks too long after the addition of the sour cream, the cream will curdle.

478. BORSCH (BEET AND BEEF SOUP)
Bortsch-koop—zuppa di bue e barbatietole

3 tablespoons butter
1 pound brisket of beef, cut into small dice
4 chicken necks, skinned and cut into pieces
1¾ quarts Classic Bouillon [No. 324]
The following vegetables, all sliced:
   3 leeks (white part only)
   2 carrots
   1 medium onion
   2 stalks celery
¼ pound beets, parboiled, peeled, and thinly sliced
Juice of one grated beet
Bouquet Garni:
   1 tablespoon chopped fennel
   2 sprigs marjoram (or ¼ teaspoon dried)
1½ cups sour cream
Salt and freshly ground pepper

Melt the butter in a large, heavy pot over medium heat; add all of the sliced vegetables except the beets, cook gently for a few minutes, and pour in the bouillon. Add the diced beef, chicken necks, and the Bouquet Garni. Season with salt and a pinch of pepper, and cook over moderate heat for 1 hour. When the meat is tender, strain the soup through a fine sieve and return it to the pot. Pick out the pieces of beef and chicken and keep them warm in a covered bowl. Add the sliced beets and beet juice to the broth, bring to a boil, reduce heat to moderate, and cook for 15 minutes. Correct the seasoning and garnish with the diced meat and chicken necks. Serve sour cream on the side. *Serves* 6.

SPAIN

479. OLLA PODRIDA
Olla podrida

½ pound pig's ears
1 pound pig's feet
1 small pig's tail
5 quarts water
1 pound brisket of beef (in a single piece)
1 pound breast of lamb or mutton (in a single piece)
1 small partridge (or squab), cleaned
1 2½-pound stewing hen, cleaned
¾ pound raw ham (in single piece)

½ pound lean salt pork, parboiled for 10 minutes
½ pound carrots, cut in pieces
4 leeks (white part only), sliced
1 onion, sliced
1 cabbage heart, cooked 10 minutes in boiling water
    and shredded
3 large potatoes, sliced
1½ cups chickpeas, soaked overnight and drained
2 small Spanish sausages (chorizos)
3 cloves garlic
1 small head of lettuce, shredded
1½ tablespoons salt
50 thin slices bread, crusts removed, browned in
    the oven

Parboil the pig's ears, feet, and tail in boiling water for 10 minutes. Put all the meats and vegetables in a very large earthenware (or enamel) pot. Cover with about 5 quarts of cold water and bring slowly to a boil over moderate heat. Skim carefully several times. Season with the salt. Continue cooking over moderate heat for 2½ hours (or longer if any one of the meats is not tender at the end of that time). Remove the meats and the vegetables from time to time, as each becomes tender, and keep warm with a little broth. When all are cooked, pour the soup into a hot tureen, arrange the meat and vegetables on a platter, and serve at the same time. Serve the browned slices of bread on the side. *Serves* 12.

480. PUCHERO
Puchero

Puchero *is a regional variation of* Olla Podrida [No. 479]. *It is more austere than the latter and contains less meat, but the dried chickpeas and the sharp, hot sausage* (chorizos) *are increased.*

To make the Puchero, follow the directions for Olla Podrida exactly, except decrease the amount of the various meats by ¼ and double the amount of dried chickpeas and sausage.

481. PAELLA VALENCIANA
Paella alla valenzana

This famous Spanish dish, containing various meats, fish, shellfish, frogs' legs, snails, rice, and vegetables, provides a complete and plentiful meal in itself. Since the variety of its ingredients makes it impossible to assign it to a more exact category, we include it here with the soups. The expense of the ingredients and the work involved make this a dish best reserved for times when a number of guests are invited.

½ cup oil, or more as needed
1 3-pound chicken, cut up into 10 pieces, as for frying
1 4-pound duckling, cut in pieces
1½ pounds loin of pork, cut into large dice
2 onions, chopped
4 cloves garlic, crushed in the garlic-press
6 sweet red peppers, roasted, peeled, and cut in strips
    [*see* No. 145]
4 sausage links (sweet Italian or *chorizos*), sliced
1 pound eel, head removed, skinned, and cut into
    1-inch pieces
1 pound dried codfish, soaked in 3 changes of water for
    24 hours, boned, and cut into small pieces
8 tomatoes, peeled, seeded, drained, and chopped
4 artichoke hearts, blanched with a little vinegar in
    boiling water and cut into julienne strips
    (or use frozen)
½ pound peas (weight after shelling)
½ cauliflower (flowerets only)
½ pound fresh lima beans
1 pound dried peas, soaked overnight and cooked
    separately for 1 hour, or until about ½ done
1½ pounds rice, washed and drained
1 teaspoon saffron, soaked in ¼ cup water
3 quarts White Bouillon [No. 323]
1½ pounds lobster tail, cut into 2-inch pieces
36 small frogs' legs
36 crayfish (or substitute medium shrimp)
36 snails, canned—or fresh, cooked and removed from
    shells [*see* introduction to No. 1038]
½ teaspoon paprika
Salt and freshly ground pepper
½ cup chopped parsley

Heat 4 tablespoons of the olive oil in a heavy frying pan. Lightly salt the pieces of chicken, add them, a few at a time, to the hot oil, and sauté until golden. As the pieces are done, remove them to a platter. Sauté the duck pieces and the pork dice in the same manner and remove them to the same platter. Using the same oil, adding to it if necessary, cook the chopped onion and

163

garlic until golden; add the strips of pepper; cook for 5 minutes longer; and remove from the fire.

Heat 3 tablespoons of the olive oil in a very large earthenware (or enamel) pot and remove from the fire. Now add, in any order that is convenient, all of the following: the browned meats, the sautéed onion/pepper mixture, the sausage, eel, codfish, tomatoes, artichokes, peas, cauliflower, lima beans, the half-cooked dried peas, rice, saffron and its water, salt, and a good grating of pepper (the amount of salt will depend on how seasoned the bouillon is; 1 tablespoon will be about right if the bouillon is only lightly seasoned). Using a wooden spoon or a rubber spatula, gently jumble all the ingredients until they are thoroughly mixed. Add the bouillon and heat over a fairly high flame just until the boiling point is reached. Remove from the flame and put the pot in a moderate (350°) oven for 40 minutes, tightly covered. As the Paella cooks, check occasionally to see whether more bouillon

is needed. All of the liquid should be absorbed by the rice and beans by the end of the cooking period, but the Paella must not be dry.

After 20 minutes, remove the pot from the oven for a moment. Distribute the lobster tail pieces, frogs' legs, crayfish (or shrimp), snails, and paprika over the top of the paella. Cover tightly and return to the oven for 20 minutes. Just before serving sprinkle the chopped parsley over the top. *Serves* 12.

NOTE: In the event a pot large enough to comfortably contain all of the ingredients is not available, use 2 or more pots, portioning out the various ingredients and bouillon accordingly. Traditionally in Spain a paella may be served in 6 different serving dishes. Each dish has a layer of rice, peas, and beans. The first is topped with the eel and codfish; the second with lobster and crayfish; the third with snails and frogs' legs; the fourth with vegetables; the fifth with pork and sausages; and the sixth with duck and chicken.

PASTAS AND OTHER FARINACEOUS DISHÈS

PASTAS
Paste alimentari

In addition to the traditional pastas—the fresh ones, commonly prepared with eggs at home, and the dried ones, commercially available—this chapter will include all the starchy specialties which either resemble pastas or are used in the same way, such as Neapolitan pizzas, polentas, rice dishes, flans, soufflés, gnocchi, and timbales.

Cooking pasta in boiling water or broth is very simple, but is does require attention to a few basic rules. The pot or pan in which it is cooked must be large enough to contain sufficient water; each 4 ounces of pasta requires a minimum of 1 quart of boiling water, but an even greater proportion of water is desirable both because it will keep the cooked pasta from becoming sticky and because a larger quantity of water will return more quickly to the proper boiling temperature after the pasta is dropped in. The water should be generously salted; estimate $1\frac{1}{2}$ teaspoons of salt for each quart of water. It must be brought to a vigorous, rolling boil, and the pasta should not be dropped in all at once, but added little by little, so the water remains as close to a boil as possible. It must be stirred often to prevent the pasta from sticking together. Bring the water back to a vigorous boil when all has been dropped in, and continue cooking, covered, stirring it once in a while.

It is not possible to give a fixed time for the cooking since this depends in part upon the quality and type of pasta, its thickness, and the taste of those who are to eat it. Most Italians prefer it *al dente;* that is, they cook it just long enough so that it retains some chewiness and resilience (literally, "to the tooth," but resistance to the teeth is implied by the phrase). When it is ready, remove it from the heat (a little cold water may be added to stop the cooking) and drain it as quickly as possible in a colander. Do not *ever* rinse it with water after draining.

If the pasta is to be dressed with butter and grated Parmesan cheese, keep a few tablespoons of the cooking water to add in case any of the pasta sticks together before it is served.

A wide range of (mostly) Italian-named pastas is commercially available in American markets. The following is a partial list:

Bows	Manicotti	Rotelloni (spiral macaroni)
Capellini	Mezzani	Rotini
Cavatelli	Mezze ziti	Shells (in various sizes)
Ditalini (macaroni cut into ¼-inch pieces)	Mostaccioli	Spinach (or green) noodles
Egg flakes (quadrucci)	Mostaccioli rigati (with lines)	Spaghetti
Egg rings (also egg flakes ¼-inch square)	Maruzzeli (shells)	Spaghettini
Farfalle	Noodles (in a wide range of widths)	Spedini
Fuselli ("slip-proof spaghetti")	Perciatelli	Tubellini (tiny narrow tubes, ¼-inch long)
Lasagne	Pastina (also spinach or carrot pastina)	
Linguine (ribbons of flat spaghetti)	Rigatoni	Vermicelli
Macaroni	Rigatti	Ziti (or Zite)
Macaroncelli	Rigoletti	Ziti rigati

166

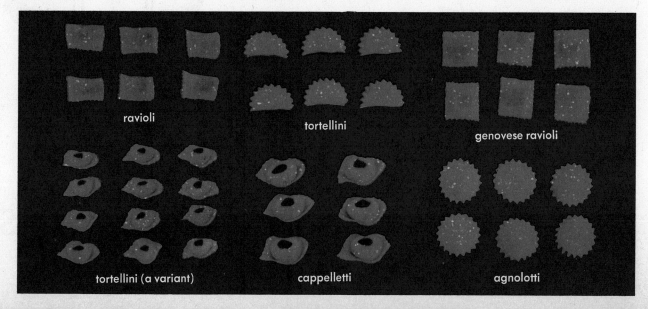

ravioli · tortellini · genovese ravioli

tortellini (a variant) · cappelletti · agnolotti

EGG PASTAS

Paste all'uovo

VARIOUS TYPES OF EGG PASTA
I diversi tipi

Egg pasta, rolled out into sheets of varying thickness, is the basic preparation of an immense range of pasta types, each characterized by its own shape and cut. Here are some of the most common that you will find cited in the various recipes that follow:

Tortellini, agnolotti, cappelletti, ravioli, cannelloni, tortelli, tortellini, etc. all have a filling. The dough is usually the one described above, or a slight variation of it.

The only difference between cappelletti and tortellini is their size and shape. The dough for both should be smooth and glossy. After a brief rest, it should be rolled out into sheets and, with a cooky cutter, cut into circles a scant 1½ inches in diameter.

The sheets of dough for tortelli and for tortellini are rolled more thinly, and are left to rest for a scant hour, after which they are cut into rounds of 2 to 3 inches in diameter. These will be filled and folded over in the middle so that when sealed they form half moons.

In Genoa, dough for ravioli, generally prepared according to the directions given above, usually re-quires only 3 eggs for each 4 cups flour, a pinch of salt, and enough water to blend. The sheets of dough are rolled out exceedingly thin, little pellets of stuffing are set out on one sheet, the covering sheet of dough laid on the top, and the ravioli are then cut out with a little pastry wheel *(rotella dentellata)* into small squares (or other shapes) with fluted edges, each one about 1½ inches wide.

Agnolotti are prepared and stuffed like ravioli but are larger and round rather than square in shape.

The dough for cannelloni is generally the same as that described above. It is then divided and rolled out into oblongs 4 inches long by 3 inches wide, cooked in a liberal amount of slightly salted water, drained, and lined up on a clean cloth which has been dipped in warm water and well wrung out. Cannelloni must be cooled before they are filled and rolled.

Tagliatelle (also called fettuccine), lasagne, taglierini, and noodles of similar types are also cut from sheets of dough but have no filling. They are also prepared commercially. All of these types vary in shape and size, but rarely in the dough from which they are made. The precise variations appear in the different recipes. Fettuccine or tagliatelle are rather narrow; lasagne range from the medium sized, about 1 inch wide, to the large sized, 3 inches wide. The large sized are generally used in recipes for *lasagne pasticciata,* that is, lasagne baked in layers, with a filling between each layer, and then cut into individual portions.

Various types of homemade egg pastas.
Below left: Pasta shapes with stuffings. Below: Simple rolled varieties.
Many of both types may be purchased commercially
(the stuffed varieties are available frozen in many communities).

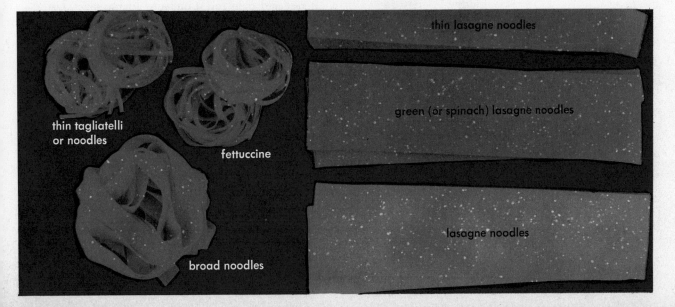

thin lasagne noodles

green (or spinach) lasagne noodles

lasagne noodles

thin tagliatelli
or noodles

fettuccine

broad noodles

482. EGG PASTA DOUGH
Preparazione della pasta all'uovo

3½ cups sifted flour
5 eggs
1 tablespoon oil
1 teaspoon salt

Make a little mound of the sifted flour on a pastry board and scoop out the center to form a well. Break the eggs into a deep bowl, beat them with the tablespoon of olive oil and the salt, and pour them into the center of the flour well. Working with the fingers, mix the flour into the eggs a little at a time until it is all thoroughly combined; then knead it with both hands until it is quite firm and very smooth to the touch. Dip a clean white cloth in warm water, wring it out *well*, wrap the ball of dough in it to keep it from drying out, and set it aside to rest for a half hour. Roll the dough into sheets with a rolling pin to a thickness suitable for the particular kind of pasta you intend to make. There are available inexpensive pasta-rolling machines that are great time and effort savers.

For certain dishes for which a more "porous" dough is desirable, more flour may be added to the above recipe and the dough rolled out rather thick.

NOTE: Commercial egg pasta may be employed in any of the following recipes (except, of course, the filled varieties and the lasagne). Use 1 pound of the best quality egg noodles in place of the above recipe. However, the taste and texture of the homemade variety is incomparable.

483. AGNOLOTTI WITH SAUCE
Agnolotti con sugo d'umido

Dough:
  3½ cups sifted flour
  3 eggs
  1 tablespoon oil
  1 teaspoon salt
  1 egg beaten with ½ teaspoon water
Filling:
  ½ pound raw veal or chicken meat (all fat, skin, and tendons removed), finely ground
  4 tablespoons prosciutto (meat and fat), finely ground
  1 onion, chopped
  3 tablespoons butter
  ½ cup dry white wine
  ½ teaspoon salt
  ⅛ teaspoon freshly ground pepper
  Pinch nutmeg
  ¼ cup grated Parmesan cheese
Alternative filling:
  ¾ cup fresh ricotta cheese
  ½ cup spinach purée, lightly salted [*see* No. 622]
  ¼ pound calves' brains, parboiled, cooled, and finely chopped
  ¼ cup soft breadcrumbs, soaked in milk and squeezed out
  2 egg yolks
  2 tablespoons grated Parmesan cheese
  ½ teaspoon salt
  ⅛ teaspoon freshly ground pepper
  Pinch nutmeg
Sauce:
  2 cups Italian Meat Sauce [No. 41]
  ½ cup butter, melted
  1 cup grated Parmesan cheese

Prepare the dough as described above [No. 482]. Let it rest and then roll it out into a large sheet. Using a pastry brush, paint the surface with an egg that has been beaten with a few drops of water. Put whichever of the two fillings you prefer into a pastry bag fitted with a medium-sized round tip (or use a stiff piece of paper rolled into a cornucopia, snip off the end, and press the filling through the tip) and press small pellets of filling out onto ½ the sheet of dough, spacing them about 2½ inches apart. Cover this ½ sheet with the other ½ and press down hard with the finger on all the unfilled spaces to seal the dough around each filling. Then cut the agnolotti apart by running a pastry wheel between the filled parts, or cut them out with a round cooky cutter a scant 2½ inches in diameter. As you cut out the agnolotti, line them up on a clean cloth that has been very lightly sprinkled with flour, separating each from the next.

Fillings:

1. Put the chopped onion and ham into a frying pan with the butter and cook gently until just light brown; add the chopped veal (or chicken), stir well, and let it cook a moment to blend. Add the wine and cook until it has completely evaporated. To prevent the filling's sticking to the bottom of the pan, add a few tablespoons of the meat sauce. Season with salt, pepper, and the nutmeg. Continue cooking until the filling thickens. Put it into a bowl, mix in the grated Parmesan cheese, and allow it to cool.

2. Put all of the ingredients of the alternative filling into a heavy saucepan and cook over moderate heat for 15 minutes, stirring often. Remove from the heat and cool.

When ready to serve, cook the filled agnolotti in plenty of boiling salted water, drain, and spread them in layers on a warm platter. Brush each layer with melted butter and spoon over some of the meat sauce. Serve the grated Parmesan cheese on the side. *Serves* 6.

484. CANNELLONI HOTEL EXCELSIOR
Cannelloni "Excelsior di Napoli"

Crêpe batter:
  1½ cups sifted flour
  4 eggs
  3 cups milk, boiled until reduced to 2½ cups
    (or 2½ cups heavy cream)
  ½ teaspoon salt
Filling:
  1 pound mozzarella cheese, diced
  2½ cups thick Béchamel Sauce [No. 18]
  ¼ pound prosciutto (including a little fat), coarsely
    chopped
  5 egg yolks
  1½ cups Italian Meat Sauce [No. 41]
  ¼ pound mushrooms, sliced
  2 tablespoons butter
  1½ cups grated Parmesan cheese

Mix together all the ingredients of the crêpe batter until they are thoroughly blended and smooth; let batter stand for at least 2 hours. Make crêpes from this batter [*see* No. 330], but fry on one side only. Place all of the filling ingredients in a heavy saucepan and cook over very low heat, stirring constantly, for 10 minutes. Remove from the heat and spread a little of the filling

in the center of the browned side of each crêpe, rolling each up as it is filled. Line up the filled crêpes in 2 shallow, well-buttered baking dishes. Cook the mushrooms, covered, over moderate heat for 10 minutes in the butter. Spoon these and the meat sauce over the crêpes. Place the baking dishes in a 375° oven for 15 minutes, or until the crêpes are thoroughly heated. Just before serving, sprinkle the top with a little grated cheese and serve the remaining cheese on the side. *Serves* 6.

485. CANNELLONI ITALIANA
Cannelloni all'italiana

Dough:
  2½ cups sifted flour
  4 eggs
  1 tablespoon oil
  1 teaspoon salt
Filling:
  3 tablespoons butter
  A chopped aromatic mixture:
    1 small carrot
    1 onion
    1 stalk celery
    3 sprigs parsley
  ½ pound lean beef (all fat and tendons removed),
    ground
  A second chopped mixture:
    2 ounces prosciutto (both fat and meat)
    1 tablespoon chopped truffles
      [or substitute No. 1819a]
    1 ounce dried mushrooms, soaked for 1 hour and
      then parboiled until they are soft
  ½ cup dry white wine
  4 tomatoes, peeled, seeded, drained, and chopped
  1 tablespoon flour
  1 teaspoon salt
  ¼ teaspoon freshly ground pepper
  Pinch nutmeg
Sauce:
  1½ cups Italian Meat Sauce [No. 41]
  2 cups grated Parmesan cheese
  6 tablespoons butter

Prepare the dough as described in No. 482, let it rest, and roll it out. Cut it into oblongs 3 by 4 inches, cook these in plenty of salted, boiling water, drain them, and line them up on a clean cloth dipped in warm water and thoroughly wrung out. Let them cool while you prepare the filling.

Put the butter into a large frying pan with the

chopped aromatic vegetables. Cook over moderate heat until the mixture turns a pale gold, add the ground beef, stir it well, and cook a few minutes to blend thoroughly. Add the second chopped mixture, season with salt, pepper, and pinch of nutmeg. Mix thoroughly, add the wine, and let it cook away completely. Scatter over the tablespoon of flour, stir it in well, add the tomatoes, 2 tablespoons of the meat sauce, and continue cooking over moderate heat until it has slightly thickened. Remove to a bowl and cool. Spread a little of the filling along the long edge of each cannelloni, rolling each up as it is filled. Line the filled cannelloni up in a single layer in a buttered, shallow baking dish. Cover them with the meat sauce and a little of the grated Parmesan cheese and dot with tiny pieces of butter. Heat thoroughly in a 375° oven for about 15 minutes. Sprinkle more cheese over them, and serve very hot, with the remaining cheese served on the side. *Serves 6.*

486. CANNELLONI PARTENOPE
Cannelloni alla partenopea

The Via Partenope is the wide avenue running along the magnificent Bay of Naples. Here are found the finest of Naples' fashionable hotels, among them the Excelsior Hotel, which contributed the cannelloni recipe No. 484.

Dough:
  2½ cups flour
  4 eggs
  ½ tablespoon oil
  1 teaspoon salt
Filling:
  ¾ cup ricotta cheese
  ½ pound mozzarella cheese, finely diced
  2 ounces slightly fat prosciutto, cut into thin strips
  2 eggs
  ½ teaspoon salt
  A grating of freshly ground pepper
Sauce:
  6 tablespoons butter
  4 tomatoes, peeled, seeded, drained, and chopped
  1 tablespoon chopped basil (or 1 teaspoon dried)
  ½ teaspoon salt
  ¼ teaspoon freshly ground pepper
  1½ cups grated Parmesan cheese

Prepare the dough, let it rest, and roll it out as described above [No. 482]. Cut into oblongs 3 by 4 inches and cook them in plenty of salted, boiling water. Drain them, and set them out to cool on a clean cloth

dipped in warm water and wrung out well. Press the ricotta through a very fine sieve (Italians would use a hair sieve) into a bowl (or whirl it in the blender for 10 seconds); add the mozzarella, the strips of prosciutto, salt, pepper, and eggs; and work the whole with a fork until it is a smooth paste. Spread a little of the filling along the long edge of each cannelloni, rolling each up as it is filled. Line them up in a single layer in a buttered, shallow baking dish.

To make sauce, melt 3 tablespoons of the butter in a heavy saucepan; add the tomato, salt, pepper, and basil; and cook for 15 minutes over medium heat. Spoon the sauce over the cannelloni, sprinkle with a little grated Parmesan cheese, and dot with remaining butter. Heat for 15 minutes in a 375° oven, sprinkle a little more grated cheese over the top, and serve the rest of the cheese on the side. *Serves 6.*

487. CAPPELLETTI WITH PISTACHIOS
Cappelletti con pistacchi

Dough:
  3½ cups sifted flour
  5 eggs
  1 tablespoon oil
  2 tablespoons water
  Pinch of salt
Filling:
  ¼ pound prosciutto (without fat), chopped or ground
  ½ pound beef marrow, parboiled and diced
  1 lamb's brain, parboiled and finely chopped
  1½ tablespoons butter
  2 tablespoons grated Parmesan cheese
  Pinch of nutmeg
  ½ teaspoon salt
  ⅛ teaspoon freshly ground pepper
  2 eggs
Sauce:
  ¾ cup Hazelnut Butter [No. 103], prepared just before serving
  1½ cups grated Parmesan cheese
  ½ cup blanched pistachio nuts, finely ground

Filling: Place all of the filling ingredients, except the eggs, in a bowl and mix thoroughly. Add the eggs and work the mixture until it is a smooth paste.
Dough: Prepare the dough as directed above [No. 482], let it rest, and roll it out into very thin sheets. Cut into 2-inch squares or rounds 2 inches in diameter. Line them up on a bread board or lightly floured clean cloth,

and in the center of each put a little filling (about the size of a lima bean); fold over the dough to form a half moon (if you are using rounds of dough) or a triangle (if you have cut the dough into squares) and join the two ends of the half moon or triangle, pressing them firmly together with the fingers, thus forming the cappelletti or "little hats." Gather up the dough left on the board, roll out again, cut, and continue making the cappelletti with the filling, until all the dough has been used.

Cook the filled cappelletti in plenty of salted, vigorously boiling water *al dente*; drain; put on a heated platter; sprinkle them with a little of the grated Parmesan cheese and all of the chopped pistachio nuts, and pour the Hazelnut butter over them. Serve at once with the remaining grated Parmesan cheese on the side. *Serves* 6.

488. CAPPELLETTI ROMANA WITH MEAT SAUCE
Cappelletti al sugo di carne alla romana

Dough:
    3½ cups sifted flour
    5 eggs
    1 tablespoon oil
    2 tablespoons water
    1 teaspoon salt
Filling:
    ⅓ pound raw turkey meat (sausage may be substituted
        for a more zestful, but less subtle, flavor), ground
    2 ounces prosciutto (or substitute Bologna sausage),
        chopped

2 tablespoons ricotta cheese
1 small lamb's brain, parboiled for 10 minutes and
    finely chopped
2 tablespoons Marsala wine
Pinch of nutmeg
½ teaspoon salt
⅛ teaspoon freshly ground pepper
3 tablespoons grated Parmesan cheese
2 egg yolks
Sauce:
    2 cups Italian Meat Sauce [No. 41]
    5 tablespoons butter
    1 cup grated Parmesan cheese

To prepare the filling, put all of the ingredients into a bowl, adding the egg yolks last. Work with a fork until the mixture is a smooth paste. Set aside.

Prepare the dough as directed in No. 482, let it rest, and roll it out into very thin sheets. Cut it into rounds 2 inches in diameter or into 2-inch squares. Align these on a lightly floured board or clean cloth, on each put a mound of filling the size of a lima bean, fold in half (making a half moon if you are using circular cappelletti, or triangles if you are using square), join the two ends, and press them firmly together with the fingers, forming the "little hats" or cappelletti. Gather up any remaining pieces of dough on the board, roll them out, cut, fill, form the cappelletti, and repeat until all the dough or filling has been used up.

Cook the cappelletti in vigorously boiling, salted water until *al dente*; drain and put on warm serving platter. Spoon over the meat sauce, dot with tiny pieces of butter, and sprinkle with a few tablespoons of grated cheese. Serve very hot with the remaining Parmesan on the side. *Serves* 6.

Preparation of cappelletti.
Left: Small amounts of filling are spaced out on the dough,
which has already been cut into squares.
Right: The squares are folded over the filling and
then pinched and twisted into the characteristic shape.

489. FETTUCCINE (TAGLIATELLE) WITH BUTTER AND ANCHOVIES
Fettuccine—tagliatelle—con burro e alici

Dough:
    3½ cups sifted flour
    5 eggs
    1 tablespoon oil
    1 teaspoon salt
Sauce:
    ⅔ cup butter
    ¼ cup anchovy fillets, washed free of salt
        [*see* No. 220], and very finely chopped
    1 cup grated Parmesan cheese
    Freshly ground white pepper

Prepare the dough as directed above [No. 482], let it rest, and then roll it out rather thin. Fold it over on itself several times, and cut it into noodles about ⅛ inch wide. Spread these well apart on a clean cloth that has been lightly floured, and leave them to dry a little.

While they are drying, heat the butter in a saucepan over low heat; as soon as it melts, add the chopped anchovies. Remove at once from the stove.

Cook the fettuccine (noodles) in salted, boiling water for about 8 minutes, or until *al dente,* drain them, place them on a hot platter, sprinkle over a little of the grated Parmesan cheese which has been mixed with a liberal dash of white pepper. Pour the butter/anchovy sauce over them. Serve with the remaining grated Parmesan cheese on the side. *Serves* 6.

490. FETTUCCINE (TAGLIATELLE) WITH TRIPLE BUTTER
Fettuccine—tagliatelle—al triplo burro

Dough:
    3 cups sifted flour
    ½ cup semolina
    6 eggs
    1 tablespoon oil
    1 teaspoon salt
Sauce:
    ½ pound best butter, softened
    1½ cups grated Parmesan cheese (use the very
        center of a large wheel of cheese and grate
        just before serving)

Prepare the dough as described above [No. 482], allow it to rest, roll it out, and cut into noodles ¼ inch wide. Cook the noodles in plenty of salted, boiling water and, when they have just reached the *al dente* stage,

drain them. Put them into a hot porcelain bowl. Quickly sprinkle the grated Parmesan cheese over them and dot with pieces of the softened butter. Mix well but very lightly and serve as hot as possible. *Serves* 6.

491. FETTUCCINE (TAGLIATELLE) CIOCIARA
Fettuccine—tagliatelle—alla ciociara

The peasant women of the Roman countryside (the ciociare*) are famous for their preparation of egg noodles.*

Dough:
    3½ cups sifted flour
    5 eggs
    1 tablespoon oil
    1 teaspoon salt
Sauce:
    ½ cup butter, melted
    1 cup Italian Meat Sauce [No. 41]
    1½ cups grated Parmesan cheese

Prepare the dough as described in No. 482, and cut it as directed in the preceding recipe [No. 490], rolling out the dough extremely thin and cutting it into noodles about ¼ to ½ inch wide. Cook them in plenty of boiling, salted water, then lift them, when ready, a few at a time, out of the water with two forks. Put them into a deep bowl and let them thoroughly absorb the dressing of fresh, sweet butter, grated Parmesan cheese, and meat sauce. *Serves* 6.

492. FETTUCCINE (TAGLIATELLE) GERMANA
Fettuccine—tagliatelle—Germana

Dough:
    3½ cups flour
    5 eggs
    1 tablespoon oil
    1 teaspoon salt
Dressing:
    1 2½-pound broiling chicken
    ⅔ cup butter
    2 tablespoons brandy
    ½ cup heavy cream, heated
    1 white truffle, finely chopped [or No. 1819a]
    1½ cups grated Parmesan cheese
    1 teaspoon salt

Prepare the dough, let it rest, and roll it out as described above [No. 482]. Cut it into noodles ¼ inch wide and keep then from drying out too much by covering with a barely damp cloth.

Brown the chicken in 3 tablespoons of butter, in a heavy frying pan over medium heat, adding a little salt as it begins to cook. Turn the heat down, add the brandy, cover tightly, and continue cooking for about ½ hour. From time to time baste it with the butter and juices in the bottom of the pan. When it is just barely tender, remove from the pan, let it cool, discard the skin and bones, and cut the meat into julienne strips. Keep them until needed in the butter and juices in which the chicken was cooked.

Cook the noodles in plenty of vigorously boiling, salted water. When they are *al dente,* drain them, put them on a rather large oval platter, and cover them with ½ the grated cheese and with the remaining butter, which has been slightly softened and cut into small pieces. Mix the whole very lightly. Add the heavy cream which has been heated (but not allowed to boil), and the chicken meat with its juices; mix a second time very lightly. Divide into serving portions, scatter each with a few shreds of the chopped truffle, and serve with the rest of the Parmesan on the side. *Serves 6.*

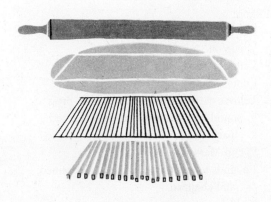

493. FETTUCCINE GUITAR
Fettuccine o maccheroni alla chitarra

This is a regional specialty of the Abruzzi that takes its name from the guitar-string-like shape of the form through which the noodles are pressed. The Abruzzi "guitar" is a rectangular loom of wood across the length of which steel wires are stretched at narrow intervals. These "guitars" are usually about 20 inches long and 10 inches wide.

Prepare a dough as directed in No. 482 and roll it out into rather thick sheets the size of the loom. Lay the sheets, one at a time, across the metal strings and run the rolling pin over the dough. Long, rectangular, heavy ribbons of dough will fall out beneath. Spread these on a lightly floured cloth and let dry slightly.

Noodles or fettuccine "guitar" are cooked in the same way as other pastas. They are served with various home-style sauces, but the real Abruzzi *alla chitarra* sauce is actually two sauces: equal amounts of Bolognese Sauce [No. 68] and Sauce Amatriciana [No. 62], mixed together and enriched with a few pieces of butter and plenty of grated Parmesan cheese.

494. FETTUCINE (TAGLIATELLE) PIEMONTESE
Fettuccine—tagliatelle—alla piemontese

Dough:
  3 cups flour
  5 eggs
  1 tablespoon oil
  2½ tablespoons grated Parmesan cheese
Sauce:
  2 cups Italian Meat Sauce [No. 41]
  8 tablespoons butter, softened
  1 cup grated Parmesan cheese
  1 white truffle, sliced [or No. 1819a]
  Freshly ground white pepper
  Pinch nutmeg

Prepare the dough, let it rest, and roll it out as described above [No. 482]. Cut it into noodles about ¼ inch wide. Cook the noodles in plenty of vigorously boiling, salted water; drain them; and put them on a large, very hot, oval platter. Dot them with the butter which has been cut into small pieces. Sprinkle over half the Parmesan cheese which has been mixed with the nutmeg and a very little white pepper (1 or 2 turns of the pepper mill) and top with the sliced truffle. Serve the rest of the grated Parmesan cheese and the meat sauce on the side. *Serves 6.*

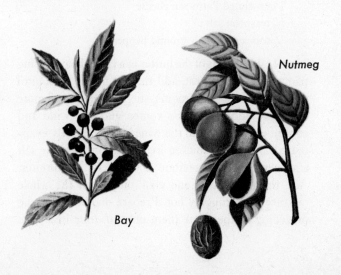

Nutmeg

Bay

495. FETTUCCINE (TAGLIATELLE) ROMANA
Fettuccine—tagliatelle—alla romana

Dough:
    3½ cups sifted flour
    5 eggs
    1 tablespoon oil
    1 teaspoon salt
Dressing:
    2 cups Italian Meat Sauce [No. 41]
    ½ cup butter
    1 cup grated Parmesan cheese
    Freshly grated white pepper

Prepare the dough as directed above [No. 482] and let it rest for ½ hour; roll it out into slightly thick sheets, fold it over several times on itself, and cut it into noodles ¼ inch wide. Cook these in a liberal amount of salted, boiling water and drain when they are *al dente*. Dress them with the butter, a little grated Parmesan cheese, and a little white pepper. Spoon over the meat sauce and serve the remaining cheese on the side. *Serves 6.*

496. GOURMET FETTUCCINE (TAGLIATELLE) ROMANA
Fettuccine—tagliatelle—alla romana del ghiottone

Dough:
    Use the preceding recipe [No. 495]
Sauce:
    1 onion, finely chopped
    8 tablespoons butter
    ¼ pound cock's combs (*see* Note below)
    ¼ pound fresh mushrooms, sliced
    ¼ pound chicken livers, coarsely chopped
    1 cup Italian Meat Sauce [No. 41]
    ½ cup dry white wine
    1 cup grated Parmesan cheese
    ½ teaspoon salt
    ⅛ teaspoon freshly ground pepper

Melt 4 tablespoons of the butter in a large, heavy frying pan over medium heat, add the onion, and cook until golden. Add the mushrooms, stir, and cook for 5 more minutes. Add the cock's combs and the wine and continue cooking until the wine has completely evaporated. Stir in the chicken livers, season with the salt and pepper, and continue cooking for 3 minutes. Add the meat sauce and cook only until the whole mixture is thoroughly hot. Prepare noodles as in the preceding recipe, cook them until *al dente* in a large

quantity of salted, boiling water; drain them, and place them on a large, hot serving platter. Pour the sauce over, sprinkle over half the grated Parmesan cheese, and dot with the remaining butter. Mix it at the table, and serve with the rest of the Parmesan cheese on the side. *Serves 6.*

NOTE: Cock's combs are prepared as follows: place combs in a small saucepan filled with water and bring them slowly to a simmer over medium heat. The moment the water begins to simmer, plunge the combs into cold water, drain, and rub each one with a fine cloth which has been sprinkled with a little salt. Rub gently until the skin is detached. Ready-to-serve cock's combs are also available in cans at certain specialty shops.

497. LASAGNA CACCIATORA
Lasagna alla cacciatora

Dough:
    3½ cups sifted flour
    5 eggs
    1 tablespoon oil
    1 teaspoon salt
Filling:
    1 2½- to 3-pound chicken, cut in half
    ½ cup oil
    3 tablespoons butter
    1 onion, chopped
    2 cloves garlic, crushed in the garlic-press
    ¼ pound lean salt pork, cut into dice and parboiled for 10 minutes
    ½ cup Marsala wine
    2 pounds tomatoes, peeled, seeded, drained, and chopped
    1 tablespoon chopped parsley
    1 tablespoon chopped basil (or 1 teaspoon dried)
    1 teaspoon salt
    ¼ teaspoon freshly ground pepper
    1 cup grated Parmesan cheese

Prepare the dough, let it rest, and roll it out into sheets, as described above [No. 482]. Cut it into 3-inch squares and let these dry slightly by spreading them out on a cloth that has been lightly dusted with flour.

Put the butter, oil, chopped onion, and garlic into a heavy saucepan large enough to hold the chicken. Cook gently over moderate heat until the onion is transparent (do not allow it to brown). Add the parboiled salt pork and chicken halves; season with salt and pepper; raise the flame; pour in the Marsala; and, stirring occasionally, cook until the wine has com-

174

pletely evaporated. Add the tomatoes, cover saucepan, and continue cooking for 25 minutes, stirring from time to time. Remove the chicken halves, allow to cool slightly, pull the meat apart into large bite-size pieces, and discard the skin and bones. Return the pieces to the sauce and add the chopped basil and parsley.

Cook the lasagna squares in plenty of vigorously boiling, salted water and, when they are *al dente*, drain. Line the bottom of a large, lightly greased, shallow baking dish with the squares of the pasta, cover them with a layer of the sauce and chicken pieces, and continue layering, ending with the sauce. Put the dish in a moderate (350°) oven for 25 to 30 minutes. Serve the grated Parmesan on the side. *Serves* 6.

498. LASAGNA WITH HAM AND MUSHROOMS

Lasagna pasticciata con prosciutto e funghi

Dough:
    3½ cups sifted flour
    5 eggs
    1 tablespoon oil
    1 teaspoon salt
Filling:
    ½ cup butter
    A chopped mixture:
        1 onion
        1 carrot
        1 stalk celery
        3 sprigs parsley
    ¼ pound ham, including both the fat and meat,
        cut into thin strips
    ¾ pound fresh mushrooms, diced (or 5 ounces dried
        mushrooms, soaked for ½ hour and squeezed
        out well)
    ½ pound lean beef or veal, finely chopped
    3 tablespoons tomato paste
    ½ teaspoon sugar
    1 teaspoon salt
    ¼ teaspoon freshly ground pepper
    ½ cup water in which the pasta has cooked
    1 cup grated Parmesan cheese
    3 tablespoons butter, melted

Prepare the dough, let it rest, and roll it out, rather thin, as described above [No. 482]. Cut it into 3-inch squares. Cook 6 to 8 squares of the pasta at a time in plenty of salted, boiling water. As soon as the pieces become *al dente,* remove them with a slotted spoon, and set them out on a clean cloth which has been dipped

in warm water and well wrung out. Continue until all the pasta squares are cooked.

Put 1½ tablespoons of the butter into a large, heavy saucepan, add the chopped vegetables, and cook over moderate heat until they are golden; add the chopped beef and ham; stir thoroughly; add the mushrooms; mix again; add the tomato paste; season with the sugar, salt, and pepper; dilute with the water; reduce the flame; and continue cooking for 25 minutes.

Butter a shallow baking dish and arrange in alternate layers the lasagna noodles and the filling. Begin and end with a layer of the noodles and dot each filling layer with bits of the remaining butter and a few strips of ham. Spread the melted butter and a little of the grated Parmesan cheese over the top layer of noodles. Put the dish in a moderate (350°) oven for 30 to 40 minutes, or until the top is well browned. Serve with the rest of the Parmesan cheese on the side. *Serves* 6.

499. LASAGNA ITALIANA

Lasagna pasticciata all'italiana

Dough:
    3½ cups sifted flour
    5 eggs
    1 tablespoon oil
    1 teaspoon salt
Filling:
    2 cups Bolognese Sauce [No. 68]
    3 ounces dried mushrooms, soaked for ½ hour,
        parboiled till soft, squeezed out thoroughly,
        chopped, and moistened with 1 tablespoon butter
    1¾ pounds mozzarella cheese, sliced
    1½ cups grated Parmesan cheese
    3 tablespoons melted butter
    Grated fresh breadcrumbs

Prepare the dough, let it rest, and roll it out (slightly thicker than for fettucine) as described above [No. 482]. Cut it into 3-inch squares. Cook them a few at a time in plenty of salted, boiling water, remove with a slotted spoon when they have reached the *al dente* stage, and let them cool on a clean cloth that has been dipped in hot water and well wrung out.

Add the mushrooms to the Bolognese sauce. Butter a large, shallow baking dish and line the bottom with a single layer of the pasta squares. Cover these with a few tablespoons of the sauce, a few slices of mozzarella, and 1 tablespoon of grated Parmesan cheese. Continue layering and filling until all the pasta and filling have been used, ending with a top layer of pasta. Top with

175

a little grated Parmesan cheese, the rest of the melted butter, and the breadcrumbs. Heat in a moderate (350°) oven for 20 to 30 minutes and serve with the rest of the grated Parmesan cheese on the side. *Serves 6.*

500. LASAGNA NAPOLETANA
Lasagna alla napoletana

This is a traditional dish in Naples during the pre-Lenten carnival season, especially on Shrove Tuesday.

Dough:
    Use the ingredients specified in the preceding recipe
        [No. 499]
Filling:
    2 cups ricotta cheese
    ½ Fresh Ham Braised in Marsala [No. 1233], or a
        4-pound pork loin braised in the same manner
    1½ cups grated Parmesan cheese

Time the preparation of the braised ham so that it is ready and hot by the time the lasagna noodles are cooked.

Prepare the dough, let it rest, and roll it out into sheets as described above [No. 482]. Cut these into 3-inch squares and cook them a few at a time in plenty of boiling, salted water. Remove them with a slotted spoon when they are *al dente* and place them on a large oval platter that has been thoroughly heated and lightly buttered.

While the lasagna noodles are cooking, beat the ricotta cheese until it is smooth and free from lumps, add 3 tablespoons (or more) of the lasagna cooking water and stir until the ricotta becomes as smooth as thick sour cream. Stir the ricotta into the drained lasagna noodles on the platter, sprinkle with half the grated Parmesan cheese, and mix in half the sauce from the braised ham. Serve very hot with the rest of the sauce and the remaining grated Parmesan cheese, in separate dishes, on the side. *Serves 6.*

NOTE: The braised ham or pork is served as the second course, with a leafy vegetable (spinach or whatever is in season), cooked with garlic and oil.

501. LASAGNA PARTENOPE
Lasagna imbottita—pasticciata—alla partenopea

Dough:
    3½ cups sifted flour
    5 eggs
    1 tablespoon oil
    1 teaspoon salt
Sauce:
    2½ cups Italian Meat Sauce [No. 41]
    ½ pound sweet Italian sausage, cut into tiny pieces,
        parboiled for 5 minutes (or sautéed for 5 minutes),
        and crumbled
    2 cups ricotta cheese, creamed
    1 pound mozzarella cheese, sliced
    6 hard-boiled eggs
    1 cup grated Parmesan cheese
    5 tablespoons butter, softened

Prepare the dough, let it rest, and roll it out as described above [No. 482]. The rolled out dough should be slightly thicker than for fettucine. Cut it into 3-inch squares. Drop 6 or 8 of these into a very large quantity of vigorously boiling, salted water and remove them with a slotted spoon as soon as they are *al dente*, or rise to the surface. Spread them out on a cloth that has been dipped in warm water and well wrung out. Continue cooking, a few at a time, until all have been spread out on the cloth. Butter a large, shallow baking dish and line the bottom with a single layer of the pasta squares. Spoon several tablespoons of meat sauce over these and dot with several teaspoons of ricotta, several slices of mozzarella, a few slices of hard-boiled egg, pieces of sausage, and a little of the grated Parmesan cheese. Cover with another layer of the pasta, repeat the same filling as just described, and continue to make layers in this fashion until the dish is full, ending with a layer of the pasta. Spread the top with the softened butter and a sprinkling of grated Parmesan cheese. Put the pan into a moderate (350°) oven and heat for about 40 minutes, or until the cheese bubbles. Serve very hot with the rest of the grated cheese on the side. *Serves 6.*

Preparation of Lasagna Partenope (No. 501). Left: The pieces of rolled-out dough are being poached, and those that have already been poached are resting on a cloth. Right: The various components of the recipe are being put together.

EE
ERSE
OR
TION

1. Lasagna Piemontese (No. 502)
2. Cannelloni Hotel Excelsior (No. 484)
3. Ricotta Ravioli (No. 509)

502. LASAGNA PIEMONTESE
Lasagna alla piemontese

Dough:
  3½ cups sifted flour
  3 eggs
  3 egg yolks
  1 or 2 tablespoons water
  1 tablespoon oil
  3 tablespoons grated Parmesan cheese
  1 teaspoon salt
Sauce:
  6 tablespoons butter, softened
  Freshly ground pepper
  Pinch nutmeg
  2 cups Italian Meat Sauce [No. 41]
  1 truffle, sliced [or No. 1819a]
  1 cup grated Parmesan cheese

Prepare the dough with all the ingredients listed above, as described in No. 482, and let it rest 30 minutes. Roll it into rather thin sheets and cut out oblong lasagne about 2 by 3 inches. Drop, a few at a time, into vigorously boiling, salted water; remove them with a slotted spoon when they are *al dente ;* and put them on a rather large, hot platter. Toss lightly with the butter, and season with a few turns of the pepper mill, and the nutmeg. Cover with the meat sauce. Stir it up at the table and scatter the sliced truffle over the top. Serve the grated Parmesan cheese separately. *Serves* 6.

503. LASAGNA VERDE MARCHIGIANA
Lasagna verde incassettata alla marchigiana

Dough:
  3½ cups sifted flour
  2 eggs
  ½ pound well-drained cooked spinach (or 1 box
      frozen chopped spinach, cooked) puréed in the
      electric blender or through a food mill
  1 tablespoon oil

  1 teaspoon salt
Filling:
  2½ cups Bolognese Sauce [No. 68]
  ½ pound chicken livers, cooked for 5 minutes in
      4 tablespoons butter, and diced
  1 small truffle, sliced [or No. 1819a]
  1 cup grated Parmesan cheese
  4 tablespoons butter, melted
  Salt and freshly ground pepper

Prepare the dough, incorporating the spinach; let it rest; and roll it out as described above [No. 482]. Cut into 3-inch squares. Cook the squares, 6 to 8 at a time, in a large pot containing plenty of salted, boiling water; when *al dente* remove them with a slotted spoon and let them cool on a clean cloth that has been dipped in warm water and well wrung out.

Butter a shallow baking dish and line the bottom with a single layer of the pasta squares. Cover these with a layer of the filling: several tablespoons of Bolognese sauce mixed with the cooked livers, a sprinkling of grated Parmesan cheese, and a few slices of truffle. Continue to form the layers of pasta and filling until the dish is full, ending with a top layer of pasta. Sprinkle ½ cup of the grated Parmesan cheese and the melted butter on top. Bake in a moderate (350°) oven for 30 to 40 minutes and serve with the rest of the Parmesan cheese on the side. *Serves* 6.

NOTE: After the spinach is cooked, be very careful to press out as much of the water as possible before puréeing; otherwise the dough will become sticky.

504. LASAGNA VERDE
Lasagna verde pasticciata

This is a variation of the preceding baked Green Lasagna Marchigiana. It is made in exactly the same way except that the chicken livers and truffle slices are omitted, and 1½ cups Béchamel Sauce [No. 18] is also portioned out between the layers.

177

Lasagna Verde
(No. 504),
or green lasagna

505. RAVIOLI GENOVESE
Ravioli alla genovese

Dough:
>   3½ cups sifted flour
>   5 eggs
>   1 tablespoon oil
>   1 teaspoon salt
> 1 egg beaten with a little water

Filling:
>   ½ pound beet greens (weight when cleaned, trimmed, and ready to cook)
>   ¼ pound spinach, thoroughly washed
>   ¼ pound cooked, skinned chicken meat
>   2 ounces sweet Italian sausage (or cooked ham)
>   1 ounce ham fat
>   2 tablespoons fresh breadcrumbs, soaked in milk and thoroughly squeezed out
>   1 teaspoon salt
>   ¼ teaspoon freshly ground pepper
>   Pinch nutmeg
>   2 eggs, beaten
>   Flour

Sauce and seasoning:
>   2 cups Italian Meat Sauce [No. 41]
>   3 tablespoons butter
>   1 cup grated Parmesan cheese

Cook the spinach and beet greens in the water clinging to their leaves, covered, for 8 minutes. Drain, press out all excess water, and purée in the electric blender or through a food mill. Using the fine blade, put the chicken, sausage (or ham), ham fat, and breadcrumbs through the meat grinder. Put the mixture into a deep bowl; add the puréed greens and 2 tablespoons of the grated Parmesan cheese; season with the salt, freshly ground pepper, and nutmeg. Work the 2 beaten eggs into the mixture until it is a smooth paste. Put a little flour on a plate and taking up small bits of the filling, dip them lightly into the flour and roll them in the palm of the hand to form small balls about the size of a small grape. Set them aside until needed.

Prepare the dough, let it rest, and roll it out into very thin sheets as described above [No. 482]. Brush the sheets lightly with the egg/water mixture. Arrange the small balls of filling on the lower half of one sheet of dough, about 2 inches apart; cover with the other half sheet of dough and with the fingers press firmly all the space around the balls of filling. Using a pastry cutter, cut out ravioli about 2 inches square; line them up on a tray, covered with a lightly floured cloth.

Cook the ravioli, a few at a time, in plenty of vigorously boiling, salted water. As they float to the top, cook 5 more minutes, and remove with a slotted spoon to a colander. When all have been cooked and drained, put them in layers in a large, oval oven-proof dish, seasoning each layer with meat sauce, a few dots of butter, and half the grated Parmesan cheese. Heat for a few minutes in a medium (350°) oven and serve very hot, with the rest of the Parmesan on the side. *Serves* 6.

506. LENTEN RAVIOLI
Ravioli di magro stretto

Dough:
>   4 cups sifted flour
>   2 tablespoons oil
>   5 to 8 tablespoons water (or just enough to form a stiff dough)
>   ¾ teaspoon salt

Filling:
>   1 pound filleted fish (sole, flounder, or halibut)
>   2 tablespoons oil
>   2 tablespoons chopped parsley
>   Juice of ½ lemon
>   ½ teaspoon salt
>   ⅛ teaspoon freshly ground pepper
>   1 tablespoon potato flour

Seasonings:
>   ½ cup oil
>   1 tablespoon chopped onion
>   2 cloves garlic, crushed in the garlic-press
>   2 ounces dried mushrooms, soaked for ½ hour and well squeezed out
>   1 pound uncooked shelled lobster tail, cut into small pieces

178

Preparation of Ravioli (see text above). Left: *The top sheet of dough has been placed over the evenly spaced portions of filling, and the dough is being pressed together.* Right: *The squares are being cut with a serrated pastry wheel.*

1 pound uncooked shelled clams
6 anchovy fillets, washed free of salt [*see* No. 220],
    and crushed to a pulp in a mortar
1 tablespoon chopped parsley
1½ pounds tomatoes, peeled, seeded, drained, and
    chopped
1 teaspoon salt
¼ teaspoon freshly ground pepper

Cut the filleted fish into very small pieces. Put the pieces in a saucepan with the oil, 2 tablespoons of water, the chopped parsley, salt, pepper, and lemon juice. Cook over moderate heat for 10 minutes; drain well (reserving the liquid); and mash fish thoroughly. Blend 1 tablespoon of water into the potato flour, mixing it to a smooth paste; add to the fish liquid; and cook over low heat until thick. Add to the chopped fish, stirring it in thoroughly, and set aside to cool.

Prepare the (eggless) dough as described in No. 482, let it rest, and roll it out as thin as possible in two sheets. With a pastry brush dipped in cold water, dampen the surface of each sheet slightly. Using an afterdinner coffee spoon, drop spoonsful of the fish mixture on one sheet of dough at regular intervals about 1½ inches apart. Cover with the other sheet and, with the fingers, press the two sheets firmly together in all spaces around the fillings. Cut out the squares of ravioli with a pastry wheel and line them up on a cloth which has been lightly dusted with flour.

Sauté the chopped onion and garlic in a saucepan with the oil. When they are barely colored, add the mushrooms, the lobster tail, and clams, mixing thoroughly. After a few minutes add the chopped parsley, the crushed anchovies, and the tomato pulp. Season with the salt and pepper, and continue cooking over moderate heat for 10 minutes.

Drop the ravioli into plenty of boiling, salted water. Cook until just *al dente* and drain. Put them in layers on a hot serving dish and cover each layer with the sauce. *Serves* 6.

507. LITHUANIAN RAVIOLI
Ravioli alla lituana

Dough:
    3½ cups sifted flour
    5 eggs
    2 tablespoons water
    1 tablespoon oil
    1 teaspoon salt

Filling:
    ½ pound raw fillet of beef, ground
    ½ pound beef kidney fat, ground
    1 onion, finely chopped
    3 tablespoons sweet butter
    ½ cup very thick Béchamel Sauce [No. 18]
    1 teaspoon salt
    ¼ teaspoon freshly ground pepper
¾ cup Hazelnut Butter [No. 103]

Prepare the dough as directed in No. 482, let it rest, and roll it out into the thinnest possible sheets.

Cook the chopped onion in the butter in a frying pan over medium heat and, when it is barely colored, add the ground beef and kidney fat; season with the salt and pepper; and cook, stirring occasionally, over moderate heat for 15 minutes. Put the mixture into a bowl, add the Béchamel sauce, mix thoroughly, and let it cool. Roll bits of the mixture on a floured board into pellets the size of a hazelnut.

Put a half sheet of dough, thoroughly stretched out, onto a lightly floured board or cloth. At regular intervals, rather farther apart than usual, line up the small bits of filling. Cover with the other half sheet of dough and press the spaces around the fillings firmly with the finger. Using a pastry cutter, cut the ravioli a little larger than usual. Drop them, a few at a time, into vigorously boiling, salted water; remove them with a slotted spoon when they are *al dente*. When all are cooked and drained, arrange them on a hot platter; cover liberally with the Hazelnut butter and serve. *Serves* 6.

508. RAVIOLI NIÇOISE
Ravioli alla nizzarda

Dough:
    Use ingredients of No. 482
Filling:
    1 pound braised beef [*see* No. 1080]
    ¾ pound beet greens (weight when washed and
        trimmed)
    1 egg
    2 tablespoons finely chopped onion, cooked for
        6 minutes in 1 tablespoon of butter
    1 heaping tablespoon grated Gruyère or Parmesan
        cheese
Sauce:
    Gravy from the braised beef
    Freshly ground pepper to taste
    1 cup grated Parmesan cheese

Prepare the dough, following directions given in No. 482, and proceed, after rolling out, to fill and make into ravioli, as in preceding recipes.

For the filling: braise the beef, pass the sauce through a fine strainer and reserve until needed. Put the beet greens into a very small amount of salted, boiling water and cook for 10 minutes. When tender, drain well, press out excess water with the hands, and cool. Chop very finely, or grind the beef and beet greens in the meat grinder. Put them into a deep bowl and add the egg, the sautéed onion, and the grated cheese (either Gruyère or Parmesan). Mix thoroughly until smooth. Roll into small balls and distribute over the dough. Finish making the ravioli as described in preceding recipes. Drop them into vigorously boiling, salted water, and drain. Dress with the beef gravy, which has been reheated, a few gratings of pepper, and with the grated Parmesan cheese. *Serves* 6.

509. RICOTTA RAVIOLI
Ravioli con la ricotta

Dough:
  3½ cups sifted flour
  3 eggs
  3 tablespoons oil
  1 teaspoon salt
1 egg, beaten with a little cold water
Filling:
  2 cups ricotta cheese, the freshest available
  4 egg yolks
  3 tablespoons grated Parmesan cheese
  Pinch nutmeg
  1 teaspoon salt
  ¼ teaspoon freshly ground pepper
⅔ cup Hazelnut Butter [No. 103], cooked with a few
    fresh (or dried) sage leaves
1½ cups grated Parmesan cheese

Press the ricotta through a fine strainer into a deep bowl. Add the grated Parmesan, eggs, and the nutmeg, salt, and pepper. Mix thoroughly.

Prepare the dough as described above [No. 482], let it rest, and roll it out into two large, very thin sheets. Brush the surface of one leaf with a pastry brush dipped into the beaten egg and water and, using a pastry bag (or a piece of stiff paper wound into a cornucopia), force out small bits of filling the size of a large grape onto the dough at regular intervals 2 inches apart. Brush the other sheet of dough with the egg and water and cover the first sheet with it. Press down firmly with the fingers all the spaces around the fillings. Cut

out the ravioli with a pastry wheel in 2-inch squares, lining them up as they are finished on a lightly floured cloth.

Cook them, a few at a time, in plenty of vigorously boiling, salted water. As they float to the surface, in about 5 minutes, remove them with a slotted spoon and drain in a colander. When all have been cooked and drained, put them into a well-heated oval dish in layers, dressing each layer with the hazelnut/sage butter. Sprinkle with the grated Parmesan cheese. *Serves* 6.

510. SPINACH AND CHEESE RAVIOLI
Ravioli vegetariani

Dough:
  3½ cups sifted flour
  5 eggs
  1 tablespoon water
  1 tablespoon oil
  1 teaspoon salt
Filling:
  2 pounds spinach, thoroughly washed
  1½ cups ricotta cheese, pressed through a sieve
  1 tablespoon butter, softened
  3 egg yolks
  ½ cup grated Parmesan cheese
  1 teaspoon salt
  ¼ teaspoon freshly grated pepper
1 cup heavy cream, brought to a boil
½ cup butter, softened
1 cup grated Parmesan cheese

Cook the spinach in just the water that clings to the leaves for 10 minutes over medium heat, covered; drain it thoroughly (squeezing between the hands is best); chop it; and purée in the electric blender or through a food mill. Add a tablespoon of butter and put it into a bowl to cool. Add the sieved ricotta, the egg yolks, and ½ cup of the grated Parmesan cheese. Season with the salt and pepper and blend into a smooth paste.

Prepare the dough, let it rest, and roll it out into two large, very thin sheets as described in No. 482. Put one sheet on a lightly floured board. Line up small bits of filling the size of a large grape on it at regular intervals, about 2 inches apart. Cover with the second sheet of dough and press the dough together firmly with the fingertips in the empty spaces between the fillings, sealing the two sheets of dough together. Cut out 2-inch squares with a pastry wheel. As they are cut out, line them up on a lightly floured cloth. Cook the ravioli, a few at a time, in plenty of boiling, salted water; remove and drain them as soon as they float to the surface. When all have been cooked, put them into a well-heated oval serving dish. Season them with bits of the remaining softened butter, the hot cream, and the rest of the grated Parmesan cheese. Toss lightly and serve at once. *Serves* 6.

511. TAGLIARINI WITH HAM AND PEAS
Tagliarini con prosciutto e pisellini

Dough:
    3½ cups sifted flour
    5 eggs
    1 tablespoon oil
    ½ teaspoon salt
Sauce:
    ¼ pound prosciutto or smoked ham (including lean meat and fat), cut into thin strips
    ½ pound tiny peas (weight after shelling), or 1 box frozen petits pois
    1 onion, finely chopped
    ¾ cup butter, softened
    1 cup grated Parmesan cheese
    ½ teaspoon salt
    ⅛ teaspoon freshly ground white pepper

Prepare the dough as described above [No. 482], let it rest, roll it out into two rather thin sheets, flour them lightly, fold each sheet over on itself several times, and slice into thin noodles about ⅛ inch wide. Spread the noodles well apart on a lightly floured tray and let them dry a bit.

Melt 6 tablespoons of butter in a saucepan, add the chopped onion, and cook over moderate heat until the onion is limp (but not colored). Add the peas and season with the salt and freshly ground white pepper. Stir (add 2 tablespoons water if not using frozen peas), raise the flame, and cook for 5 or 6 minutes, or until the peas are tender. Add the prosciutto strips, cook for a moment longer, and reserve.

Drop the noodles into vigorously boiling, salted water. Cook for just 4 minutes after the water has returned to a boil. Drain them and put them into a well-heated oval serving dish. Cover with the peas and ham, the remaining softened butter, and half the grated Parmesan cheese. At the table, stir the whole carefully and pass the rest of the grated Parmesan cheese on the side. *Serves* 6.

NOTE: This dish should be planned so that the peas are ready at the moment that the noodles are drained.

512. TAGLIARINI ITALIANA
Tagliarini pasticciati all' italiana

Dough:
    3½ cups sifted flour
    5 eggs
    1 tablespoon oil
    ½ teaspoon salt
Sauce:
    2½ cups Italian Meat Sauce [No. 41], heated
    ⅔ cup butter, melted
    ½ pound chicken livers
    ½ cup Marsala wine
    1 truffle, sliced [or No. 1819a]
    1 cup grated Parmesan cheese
    Salt and freshly ground pepper to taste

Prepare the dough as directed in No. 482, let it rest, and roll it out into two very thin sheets, and flour them very lightly. Fold the dough over on itself several times, cut into thin noodles about ⅛ inch wide, and spread them out well to dry on a lightly floured cloth.

Put 2 tablespoons of butter into a frying pan and sauté the chicken livers in it for 5 minutes. Add the Marsala, mixing it in well, and cook until it has evaporated. Remove from the heat and add the livers to the meat sauce. Season with salt and pepper, if necessary.

Drop the noodles in plenty of salted, boiling water and drain them in exactly 4 minutes after the water has returned to a boil. Put them in a large, shallow baking dish and add the remaining butter and the meat sauce. Mix thoroughly and then top with a few tablespoons of the grated cheese and slices of truffle. Heat in a hot (400°) oven for 15 to 20 minutes, or until the cheese is well browned, and serve with the remaining grated Parmesan cheese on the side. *Serves* 6.

513. COLD SUMMER TAGLIARINI
Tagliarini freddi estivi

This is an excellent dish to serve at a late supper after the theater. The noodles—spaghetti may be substituted—must be cooked al dente.

Dough:
  3½ cups flour
  5 eggs
  1 tablespoon oil
  1 teaspoon salt
Sauce and seasoning:
  2 cloves garlic, crushed in the garlic-press
  1 tablespoon chopped parsley
  A few leaves of fresh basil
  ½ cup oil
  2½ cups Tomato Sauce [No. 19], cooled

Prepare the dough, let it rest, and roll it out as described above [No. 482]. Fold it over on itself several times and cut into fine noodles, ⅛ to ¼ inch wide. Cook these in plenty of boiling, salted water and drain when they are just *al dente*. Put them into a porcelain dish, and while they are still very hot season with the garlic, parsley, basil, oil, and mix thoroughly. Set aside to cool. When ready to serve, add the cold tomato sauce and toss lightly. *Serves* 6.

NOTE: It is recommended that this dish be kept in a cool place, but *not* the refrigerator. It should be served cool, *not* cold.

514. TAGLIATELLE BOLOGNESE
Tagliatelle—fettuccine—alla bolognese

Dough:
  3½ cups sifted flour
  5 eggs
  1 tablespoon oil
  1 teaspoon salt
Sauce:
  2½ cups Bolognese Sauce [No. 68], heated
  8 tablespoons butter, softened
  1 cup grated Parmesan cheese

Prepare the dough as previously described [No. 482], let it rest, roll it out into 2 large sheets, flour lightly, fold each sheet over on itself several times, and cut into noodles about ¼ inch wide. Spread them out at once, well separated, on a lightly floured cloth. Leave them to dry for 30 minutes. When dry, drop them into plenty of vigorously boiling, salted water and drain them when they are just *al dente*. Put them on a well-heated serving platter; scatter tiny pieces of the softened butter and half the grated Parmesan cheese over them, and pour over half the hot sauce. Mix thoroughly at table and pass the rest of the sauce and the grated Parmesan cheese, separately, on the side. *Serves* 6.

515. TAGLIATELLE WITH PESTO GENOVESE
Tagliatelle—fettuccine—col pesto alla genovese

Dough:
  3½ cups sifted flour
  5 eggs
  1 tablespoon oil
  1 teaspoon salt
  4 medium potatoes, thinly sliced
  ½ cup grated Parmesan cheese (or grated Pecorino)
  2 cups Pesto Genovese [No. 93]

Prepare the dough as previously described [No. 482], let it rest, and roll out into 2 very thin sheets. Lightly flour the sheets and fold them over upon themselves several times. Slice them into noodles about ¼ inch wide and spread them well apart on a lightly floured cloth.

Put the sliced potatoes in a large pot with plenty of slightly salted, cold water and bring to a boil. After ten minutes, or when the potatoes are about three-fourths cooked, drop in the noodles and cook until just *al dente*. Drain the noodles and the potatoes, reserving a little of the cooking water. Put the noodles and potatoes into a hot, shallow, oval serving dish. Season at once with the grated cheese and 3 or 4 tablespoons of the hot water in which the noodles were cooked. Mix carefully once, cover with the Pesto, carry to the table, and mix again. Serve at once. *Serves* 6.

516. TAGLIATELLE VERDI WITH MUSHROOMS
Tagliatelle—fettuccine—verdi al funghetto

Dough:
  3½ cups sifted flour
  3 eggs
  ½ pound spinach (or 1 box frozen spinach)
  1 tablespoon oil
  ½ teaspoon salt

182

Sauce:

½ cup butter, softened

1 pound mushrooms, diced

1 onion, chopped

Optional: 1 clove garlic, crushed in the garlic-press

1 tablespoon oil

2 pounds tomatoes, peeled, seeded, drained, and chopped

½ cup dry white wine

Pinch nutmeg

½ teaspoon sugar

1 teaspoon salt

¼ teaspoon freshly ground pepper

1 cup grated Parmesan cheese

Wash, trim, and drain the spinach. Cook it in only the water clinging to the leaves, covered, for 10 minutes. Drain it thoroughly, squeezing it dry with the hands, chop it, and purée in the electric blender or through a food mill.

Heap the sifted flour into a mound on the rolling board and then hollow out a well in the center. Drop the egg, oil, strained spinach, and salt into the well. Mix with the fingers, working a little flour at a time into the center, and, if necessary, adding a little water from time to time, until it is a solid, rather hard dough. Knead until smooth, cover, and let it rest ½ hour; then roll it out into thin sheets, folding each one over on itself several times. Slice into noodles ¼ inch wide.

Heat 3 tablespoons of the butter and the tablespoon of oil in a saucepan. Add the chopped onion and the optional garlic and, as soon as the onion takes on a little color, add the diced mushrooms. Season with the salt and freshly ground pepper, stir, pour in the wine, and let it cook until the wine has evaporated. Add the tomato pulp and season with a pinch of nutmeg and the sugar. Stir, and continue to cook over moderate heat for 15 minutes.

Drop the noodles into plenty of boiling, salted water, and cook until just *al dente*. Drain, and put them on a well-heated serving platter. Scatter pieces of the remaining softened butter over them, sprinkle with half the grated Parmesan cheese, and pour over half the sauce. Mix at table, and serve the rest of the cheese and the sauce separately. *Serves* 6.

517. TORTELLI LOMBARDA
Tortelli alla lombarda

Dough:

3½ cups sifted flour

2 eggs

1 tablespoon oil

1 teaspoon salt

⅓ cup cold water (more or less as needed to form a stiff dough)

Filling:

2 cups pumpkin, cubed, peeled, and seeded

¼ pound almond macaroons, coarsely chopped

3 tablespoons Verona mustard (or substitute Bahamian mustard)

1 tablespoon candied citron, chopped as finely as possible

1 tablespoon grated Parmesan cheese

Pinch nutmeg

2 eggs

Freshly ground pepper to taste

Sauce:

⅔ cup butter

1 cup grated Parmesan cheese

Several fresh sage leaves

Prepare the dough as directed in No. 482, let it rest, roll it out into thin sheets, and cut rounds 2½ inches in diameter out of the sheets. Cook the cubed pumpkin for 25 minutes in boiling, salted water, drain, and mash it. Put the cooked pumpkin, 1 tablespoon of the grated Parmesan cheese, the chopped macaroons, mustard, and citron in a bowl. Season with salt, pepper, and nutmeg. Add the eggs, working the whole into a smooth paste.

Put a teaspoon of the filling in the center of one of the rounds of dough and fold it over to form a half-moon, moistening the edges slightly with water to seal them more securely. Repeat until all of the rounds and filling are used. Cook the tortelli, a few at a time, in plenty of salted, boiling water until just *al dente*. Drain them and, when all are cooked, put them on a large, hot serving platter. Cook the butter with the sage leaves over medium heat until it is a nut brown; pour it over the tortelli; cover with grated Parmesan cheese; and serve at once. *Serves* 6.

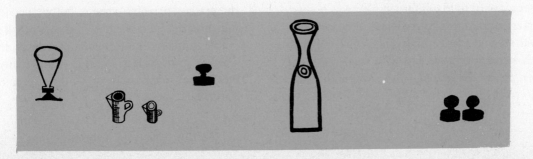

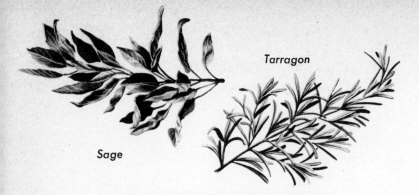

Tarragon

Sage

518. TORTELLINI BOLOGNESE
Tortellini alla bolognese

Dough:

4 cups sifted flour

6 eggs

1 tablespoon oil

1 teaspoon salt

Filling:

½ pound ham, including fat and meat

2 ounces mortadella (Bologna sausage)

¼ pound beef marrow, poached for 5 minutes in simmering water

¼ pound calf's brains, poached for 15 minutes in boiling water

4 tablespoons grated Parmesan cheese

½ teaspoon salt

¼ teaspoon freshly ground pepper

Pinch nutmeg

2 eggs

Sauce:

2 cups Bolognese Sauce [No. 68], heated

½ cup butter, softened

1 cup grated Parmesan cheese

Prepare the dough as directed above [No. 482]. It should be fairly soft. Let it rest 30 minutes; roll it out into thin sheets; and cut rounds 1½ inches in diameter out of the sheets.

Put all of the filling ingredients, except the eggs, through the meat grinder, using a fine blade. Work the eggs into the mixture until it is a smooth paste. Put a small ball of filling in the center of one of the rounds of dough and fold the round in half to form a half-moon, dampening the edges and pressing them down well to seal the filling in firmly. As the tortellini are filled, set them out, carefully keeping them from touching each other, on a lightly floured cloth. Cook them, a few at a time, for 10 to 15 minutes in plenty of boiling, salted water; drain them; place them on a very hot, large, oval serving platter in layers, seasoning each layer with Bolognese sauce and with small pieces of the butter. Serve the grated Parmesan on the side. *Serves* 6.

184

519. TORTELLINI EMILIANA
Tortellini all'emiliana

Dough:

The same ingredients as in Tortellini Bolognese [No. 518]

Filling:

½ pound cooked chicken (skin, bones, and tendons removed)

½ pound cooked ham (with fat)

1 truffle [or No. 1819a]

2 tablespoons grated Parmesan cheese

Freshly ground pepper to taste

2 egg yolks

Sauce:

¾ cup Hazelnut Butter [No. 103] cooked with a few fresh (if possible) sage leaves

1 cup grated Parmesan cheese

Prepare in the manner described in the preceding recipe.

520. TORTELLONI ROMAGNOLA
Tortelloni alla moda di Romagna

Dough:

3½ cups sifted flour

3 eggs

1 tablespoon oil

Pinch salt

Cold water (only as much as needed to form a stiff dough)

Filling:

¾ pound very fresh ricotta cheese

1½ cups grated Parmesan cheese

¾ cup butter

Few leaves of fresh sage, finely chopped

1 tablespoon chopped parsley

2 eggs

Pinch nutmeg

1 teaspoon salt

¼ teaspoon freshly ground pepper

Prepare the dough as directed in No. 482 and let it rest 1 hour. Roll it into thin sheets and cut rounds of dough 3 inches in diameter from these.

Press the ricotta through a strainer into a bowl. Add the grated Parmesan cheese, butter, parsley, seasonings, and the eggs. Blend to make a smooth paste.

Fill and cook the tortelloni exactly as described in Tortelli Lombarda [No. 517]. Choose any butter or meat sauce, such as those in the preceding recipes. *Serves* 6.

521. TORTELLINI WITH SQUAB FILLING

Tortellini con carne di piccione

Dough:
  The same ingredients as in No. 518
Filling:
  1 plump pigeon or squab
  2 tablespoons softened butter
  3 ounces ham (with fat)
  1 lamb's brain, parboiled for 20 minutes in boiling
    water
  2 tablespoons grated Parmesan cheese
  Salt and freshly ground pepper to taste
  Pinch nutmeg
  2 egg yolks, well beaten
Sauce:
  1 recipe Italian Meat Sauce [No. 41]
  ¼ pound chicken giblets, sautéed for 6 minutes in
    2 tablespoons butter and coarsely chopped
  1 cup grated Parmesan cheese

Prepare the dough as in No. 518.

Spread the butter on the pigeon and roast it in a hot (400°) oven for 30 minutes. Remove the skin, bones, and tendons and discard them. Put the pigeon meat and all of the remaining filling ingredients, except the egg yolks, through the meat grinder using fine blade. Put the mixture in a bowl and work in the beaten egg yolks until it is a smooth paste. Fill the tortellini rounds and cook them as in the preceding recipe. Pour over the Italian meat sauce and top with chicken giblets and grated cheese. *Serves 6.*

DRIED PASTAS
Paste secche

This section deals with commercially available dried pastas. They are of infinite variety, shape, and name, some of the names being known only in particular regions. Among them are spaghetti, macaroni, macaroncelli, bucatini or perciatelli, ziti (large macaroni), mezze ziti, linguine (trenette, or lingue di passero, all variations of linguine), maltagliati or penne (literally "pens"), rigatoni (large-sized macaroni with a slightly thicker dough), vermicelli, capelli d'angelo ("angel's hair," a very thin pasta), cannolicchietti or avemarie, etc.

Commercially available dried pastas: see next page for full comment

522. BUCATINI GOURMET

Bucatini del buongustaio

1 pound bucatini, broken into 4-inch pieces
2 cloves garlic, crushed in the garlic-press
Few leaves basil
Few leaves sage
Oil as needed
1½ pounds tomatoes, peeled, seeded, drained, and
  chopped
½ teaspoon sugar
2 eggplant, peeled, thinly sliced, sprinkled with
  1½ teaspoons salt, and pressed under a weight for
  1 hour
½ pound mushrooms, diced
1 cup grated Parmesan cheese
4 tablespoons butter, softened
Salt and freshly ground pepper

Brown the 2 garlic cloves with the basil and sage leaves in 2 tablespoons of oil in a saucepan over medium heat; add the tomato pulp; season with sugar, salt, and pepper; and cook gently for about 20 minutes. While the tomatoes are cooking, parboil the eggplant slices for 10 minutes, drain them, and pat dry with a cloth. Sauté them in a frying pan over medium heat in 2 tablespoons of oil for about 10 minutes until light gold. In a separate saucepan over a high flame, quickly cook the diced mushrooms in 2 tablespoons of oil until a light gold, about 10 minutes.

Cook the bucatini in vigorously boiling, salted water until just *al dente*. Drain and put them into a large shallow bowl. Scatter a little grated Parmesan over them and small pieces of the butter. Cover with the eggplant, the mushrooms, and with the hot tomato sauce. Mix carefully at the table and serve the rest of the grated Parmesan cheese on the side. *Serves 6.*

capellini
vermicellini
vermicelli
spaghetti
bucatini
macaroni
zite
linguine
bavette
trenette

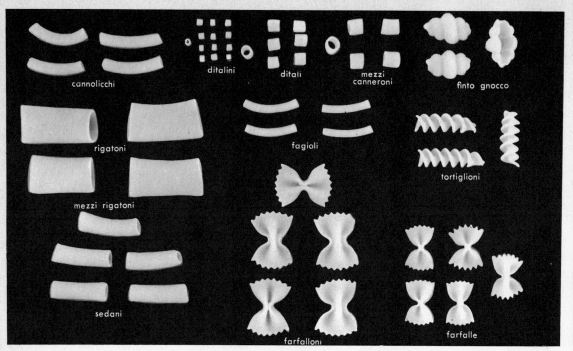

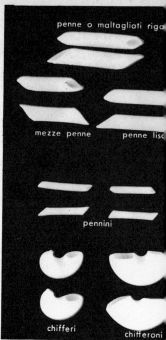

Commercially available dried pastas. As the names of these pastas vary from manufacturer to manufacturer, and also in different parts of the United States, the Italian names of these shapes are left untranslated. The problems of nomenclature may be demonstrated by the type of pasta called sedani (which means "celery") in the picture to the left. Certain pasta companies call these ribbed tubes "mezzani rigati." The penne shown in the picture at right are also called "mostaccioli."

523. BUCATINI DOMENICANA
Bucatini alla domenicana

1 pound bucatini, broken into 4-inch pieces
½ cup oil
4 ounces dried mushrooms, soaked in warm water
   for ½ hour, parboiled for 20 minutes, squeezed
   dry, and chopped finely
2 cloves garlic, crushed in the garlic-press
12 anchovy fillets, washed free of salt [*see* No. 220] and
   pounded to a pulp in the mortar
1 tablespoon chopped parsley
6 tablespoons fresh breadcrumbs browned for a few
   seconds in 2 tablespoons hot oil
Salt and freshly ground pepper to taste

Cook the chopped mushrooms with 1 tablespoon of oil and 2 tablespoons of water in a saucepan over moderate heat for 15 minutes, or until very soft. Purée in the electric blender or through a food mill. Sauté the garlic in a frying pan in the remaining oil until it is golden. Add the mushrooms, remove the pan from the fire, and add the pounded anchovies. Season with salt (if needed) and pepper to taste and keep warm.

Cook the bucatini in plenty of vigorously boiling, salted water until just *al dente*. Drain them and put into a shallow baking dish. Pour the sauce over them,

add the chopped parsley, mix well, and scatter the browned breadcrumbs over the top. Heat in a hot (400°) oven for 10 minutes. Serve at once. *Serves 6.*

524. BUCATINI CASALINGA
Bucatini alla Freda

1 pound bucatini, broken into 4-inch pieces
12 sweet Italian sausages (or 6 sweet and 6 hot sausages)
2 pounds tomatoes, peeled, seeded, drained, and chopped
1 cup grated Parmesan cheese

Prick each sausage 10 times with a fork. Put the tomato pulp in an earthenware (or enamel) pot and arrange the sausages in the pot so that they do not touch each other. (No salt, pepper, or fat are added because the sausages will give all the seasoning necessary to the sauce.) Put the pot over a high flame, bring it to a boil, reduce heat to moderate, and simmer for ¾ hour. Remove the sausages and reserve. Cook the bucatini in plenty of boiling, salted water. Drain them when they are just *al dente*. Put them on a well-heated serving platter, cover with the grated Parmesan cheese, and pour the sauce over them. Mix at the table. Serve the sausages as a second course with cooked turnip greens seasoned with olive oil and very lightly salted.

525. LINGUINE WITH GARLIC AND OIL

Linguine o trenette con aglio e olio

1 pound linguine (or trenette)
½ cup oil
2 cloves garlic, crushed in the garlic-press
Several gratings of pepper
3 tablespoons chopped parsley

Cook the pasta in plenty of rapidly boiling, salted water; drain it when it has reached the *al dente* stage and put it on a large, hot serving platter. A few minutes before draining the pasta, heat the oil in a frying pan and add the garlic and pepper; just as soon as the garlic takes on a little color, pour over the spaghetti, add the parsley, and mix quickly. *Serves* 6.

526. LINGUINE LUIGI VERONELLI

Linguine alla Luigi Veronelli

1 pound linguine
1 pound clams
1 pound mussels
½ pound shrimp
½ pound cuttlefish or squid
½ cup dry white wine
1 tablespoon chopped onion
½ cup oil
2 cloves garlic, crushed in the garlic-press
Bouquet Garni:
  2 sage leaves (or ¼ teaspoon dried)
  1 sprig rosemary (or ¼ teaspoon dried)
1½ pounds tomatoes, peeled, seeded, drained, and chopped
3 ounces Italian-style tuna canned in oil, broken into pieces
2½ tablespoons Anchovy Butter [No. 108]
3 tablespoons chopped parsley
Salt and freshly ground pepper to taste

Scrub the clams, mussels, and wash shrimp and put them all into a heavy pot (preferably earthenware) with the wine and the onion. Cook over high heat, covered, for 12 minutes. Remove the shrimp and then the clams and mussels as soon as their shells have opened. Strain the liquid through a cheesecloth-lined sieve into a bowl. Shell the clams and mussels and shell and de-vein the shrimp. Reduce the strained liquid over lively heat to about 3 tablespoons. Clean the cuttlefish (or squid) and cut it into small ribbon-like strips. Put the oil, garlic, and Bouquet Garni in a large, heavy saucepan. Cook over moderate heat until the garlic takes on color. Add the cuttlefish. Cook for a few moments, stirring to blend, and add the tomato pulp. Season with a pinch of salt and pepper. Cook over moderate heat for about 10 minutes, then add the tuna, mussels, clams, shrimps, and the 3 tablespoons of reduced fish broth. Remove the Bouquet Garni. Cook the linguine in plenty of vigorously boiling, salted water until just *al dente*. Drain and put into a large, hot, shallow serving bowl. Pour the sauce over, top with little pieces of the anchovy butter, and sprinkle lightly with the chopped parsley. Mix lightly at the table. *Serves* 6.

527. MACARONCELLI WITH HAM AU GRATIN

Maccheroncelli al prosciutto gratinati

1 pound macaroncelli, broken into 4-inch pieces
3 cups hot Béchamel Sauce [No. 18]
1½ cups grated Parmesan cheese
¼ pound smoked ham, cut into thin strips
½ cup soft fresh breadcrumbs
3 tablespoons butter

Cook the macaroncelli in plenty of salted, boiling water; drain them when they have reached the *al dente* stage; and put them in a large bowl. Add ¾ of the Béchamel sauce, the ham, a couple of tablespoons of the grated Parmesan cheese, and mix gently. Put the macaroncelli in a buttered, shallow baking dish, pour the rest of the Béchamel over it, cover with the breadcrumbs mixed with ½ cup of grated Parmesan cheese, dot with small bits of the butter, and put the dish into a very hot (450°) oven for about 10 minutes. Serve as soon as the top is well browned and pass the rest of the Parmesan cheese on the side. *Serves* 6.

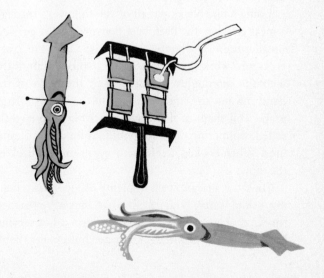

528. MACARONCELLI WITH MEAT BALLS
Maccheroncelli con polpettine di carne

1½ pounds macaroncelli, broken into pieces
1 tablespoon oil
A chopped mixture:
    4 tablespoons ham (fat and meat)
    1 small onion
1 pound rump of beef
½ cup dry white wine
2 pounds tomatoes, peeled, seeded, drained, and passed
    through a food mill or strainer
½ teaspoon sugar
2 ounces uncooked beef marrow
2 cloves garlic
3 sprigs parsley
¼ cup cubed bread (no crusts), soaked in a little milk
    and squeezed dry
¼ teaspoon grated lemon rind (no white part)
2 egg yolks
Flour
4 tablespoons butter, softened
1 cup grated Parmesan cheese
1 teaspoon salt
¼ teaspoon freshly ground pepper

Heat the oil in a large heavy pot over a medium flame and add the chopped mixture and the beef. As soon as the onion and beef begin to take on a little color, pour in the wine and cook until it has completely evaporated. Add the tomato purée and pour in enough water so that the meat is just covered; season with the sugar, salt, and pepper. Cover the pot, bring to a boil, reduce the heat to moderate, and continue cooking for about two hours. When the meat is tender remove it and let it cool. Put the sauce through a fine sieve and return it to the pot.

Using a fine blade, put all of the following through a meat grinder: the beef, beef marrow, garlic, parsley, breadcrumbs, and grated lemon peel. Beat the 2 egg yolks and work them into the meat mixture until the whole is thoroughly blended. With the palm of the hand roll out tiny meat balls about the size of a large grape, roll them in flour, and poach them in slightly salted, simmering water (or bouillon) for about 5 minutes. When cooked, keep them warm on the back of the stove.

Cook the macaroncelli in plenty of vigorously boiling, salted water. Drain them when they have reached the *al dente* stage and pour them into a hot serving bowl. Scatter little pieces of softened butter over them, a little grated Parmesan cheese, and half of the sauce from the stewed meat. Distribute the meat balls on top. Carry to the table, mix with care, and serve the rest of the sauce and grated Parmesan cheese on the side. *Serves 6 to 8.*

529. MACARONI AU GRATIN
Maccheroni gratinati

1 pound macaroni broken into pieces 2½ inches long
½ cup butter
3 tablespoons flour
3 cups scalding medium cream
Dash of salt
Pinch nutmeg
½ cup soft breadcrumbs
1 cup grated Parmesan cheese

Make a roux in a saucepan over medium heat with the flour and 3 tablespoons of the butter. Stirring constantly, add the cream, salt, and nutmeg. Cook over moderate heat for 15 minutes, stirring occasionally.

Cook the macaroni in plenty of vigorously boiling, salted water; drain it when it has reached the *al dente* stage. Put it into a bowl; add 3 tablespoons of butter, ¾ of the hot cream sauce, and 3 tablespoons of grated Parmesan cheese; mix well. Turn the macaroni into a shallow, buttered baking dish, cover it with the rest of the sauce, scatter the breadcrumbs which have been mixed with an equal amount of grated Parmesan cheese over the top, and dot with the rest of the butter. Put the dish into a very hot oven (450°) for 10 minutes. Serve as soon as the top turns a deep gold. Pass the rest of the Parmesan cheese on the side. *Serves 6.*

530. MACARONI SAN GIOVANNIELLO
Maccheroni alla San Giovanniello

1½ pounds macaroni, broken into 2-inch pieces
3 tablespoons butter
3 tablespoons lard
3 cloves garlic, crushed in the garlic-press
⅓ pound prosciutto or smoked ham (fat and meat),
    chopped
3 pounds tomatoes, peeled, seeded, drained, and sliced
1 cup Pecorino cheese, grated
½ cup fresh basil leaves, coarsely chopped
1 teaspoon salt
¼ teaspoon freshly ground pepper

Melt the butter and lard over moderate heat in a very large earthenware (or enamel) pot. Add the crushed garlic and chopped ham and cook until the garlic is golden. Add the tomatoes, season with salt and pepper, and cook gently for 30 minutes. About 15 minutes before the sauce is done, cook the macaroni in plenty of boiling, salted water; drain it when it has reached the *al dente* stage; and put it into the pot with the tomato sauce. Mix carefully. Remove from the fire, pour the macaroni into a well-heated platter, sprinkle with the grated cheese and the basil, and serve. *Serves 6 to 8.*

NOTE: Do not attempt this with dried basil.

531. MACARONI WITH SARDINES SICILIANA
Maccheroni con le sarde alla siciliana

2 pounds macaroni, broken into pieces
1 pound fresh sardines, washed, trimmed, and sliced
Oil as needed
⅔ pound wild fennel (or substitute leaves and stalks of the cultivated kind), parboiled for 15 minutes and coarsely chopped
The water in which the fennel was cooked
3 cloves garlic, crushed in the garlic-press
¼ onion, chopped
⅓ cup anchovy fillets, washed free of salt [*see* No. 220] and pounded to a pulp in the mortar
2 ounces raisins, thoroughly washed
2 ounces pine nuts
2 sprigs parsley, finely chopped
Pinch saffron
1 teaspoon salt
¼ teaspoon freshly ground pepper

Heat 2 tablespoons of oil in a heavy saucepan over moderate heat. Add the garlic, 3 tablespoons of fennel water, the pinch of saffron, and the salt and pepper. When the liquid has evaporated and the garlic has turned golden, add the sardines and cook for 10 minutes longer.

Heat 2 tablespoons of oil in another saucepan. Add the chopped onion, cooked fennel, raisins, pine nuts, anchovies, and the parsley. Cook over moderate heat for 5 minutes until blended.

Bring a large pot of salted water to a boil and add the water in which the fennel was cooked. Bring back to a boil, drop in the macaroni, and cook until it reaches the *al dente* stage. Drain and put the macaroni in an oven-proof dish, alternating it with layers of sauce and of sardines, ending with a top layer of sauce. Put into a moderate (350°) oven for about 20 minutes. *Serves 12.*

532. PENNE OR MALTAGLIATI WITH RICOTTA
Penne o maltagliati con la ricotta

1 pound penne (or maltagliati)
2 cups ricotta cheese
½ teaspoon sugar
1 teaspoon cinnamon

Cook the penne (or maltagliati) in a generous amount of salted, boiling water until just *al dente*. While the penne are cooking, place the ricotta in a large serving bowl, season with the sugar and cinnamon, add a few tablespoons of the water in which the penne are cooking, and mix until smooth. When the penne are done, add to the ricotta and mix very gently. *Serves 6.*

533. RIGATONI RAGOUT WITH EGGPLANT
Rigatoni al ragù e melanzane

1½ pounds rigatoni
3 tablespoons prosciutto (fat and meat), chopped
1 small onion, chopped
2 tablespoons oil
1 pound rump of beef
½ cup dry white wine
2 pounds tomatoes, peeled, seeded, drained, and passed through a food mill or strainer
1 teaspoon sugar
¼ pound chicken livers, sliced, and sautéed in 2 tablespoons of butter for 3 minutes
¼ pound mushrooms, chopped, and sautéed in 2 tablespoons butter for 8 minutes
2 medium eggplant, peeled, thinly sliced, sprinkled with 1 teaspoon salt, weighted down under a plate to drain for 1 hour, well washed, thoroughly patted dry, and sautéed in 4 tablespoons oil until brown
4 tablespoons butter, softened
1 cup grated Parmesan cheese
1 teaspoon salt
¼ teaspoon freshly ground pepper

Cook the chopped prosciutto and onion in a large, heavy saucepan with the oil over high heat. Add the beef and brown the meat and onion, turning them often. Add the wine and cook until it has completely evaporated. Add the tomato pulp and as much water as is needed to cover the meat. Season with the sugar, salt, and pepper, bring to a boil, cover the pan, reduce the heat to moderate, and continue cooking for about 2 hours, or until the meat is tender. Remove it and cut it into

189

dice. Strain the sauce into another pot and add the diced meat, chicken livers, and mushrooms. Bring to a boil and then reduce heat to the barest simmer.

Meanwhile, cook the rigatoni in plenty of vigorously boiling, salted water until just *al dente*. Drain and turn them into a large, shallow serving bowl, dot with pieces of softened butter and a little of the grated Parmesan cheese, add half the meat sauce, mix very gently, and cover the top with the slices of eggplant. Serve the rest of the sauce and the Parmesan cheese on the side. *Serves 6 to 8.*

534. SPAGHETTI AMATRICIANA
Spaghetti all'amatriciana

1 pound spaghetti
½ pound lean hog jowl, cut into 2-inch squares
2 tablespoons oil
Optional: ¼ onion, chopped
1 sweet red pepper, roasted, scraped, seeded, and cut into strips [*see* No. 145]
1 pound tomatoes, peeled, seeded, drained, and chopped
1 cup grated Pecorino cheese
1 teaspoon salt

Cook the hog jowl with the oil in a large, heavy saucepan over a brisk flame until brown and crisp; remove the pieces and reserve, keeping them warm. In the same pan, sauté the onion and red pepper over medium heat; as soon as the onion takes on the slightest color, add the tomatoes and season with the salt. Mix thoroughly, bring to a boil, cook 10 minutes. While the sauce is cooking, drop the spaghetti into plenty of rapidly boiling, salted water; drain at the *al dente* stage and put into a rather large, shallow serving bowl. Add the pork cracklings to the sauce, pour over the spaghetti, and sprinkle with the grated Pecorino cheese. Mix and serve. *Serves 6.*

535. SPAGHETTI WITH ANCHOVIES
Spaghetti o trenette con le acciughe

Trenette, sometimes called linguine or lingue di passero, may be substituted in this dish for the spaghetti.

1 pound spaghetti
½ cup oil
¼ cup anchovy fillets, washed free of all salt [*see* No. 220] and pounded to a paste in the mortar
2 cloves garlic, crushed in the garlic-press
1 pound tomatoes, peeled, seeded, drained, and finely chopped or puréed

2 sweet red or yellow peppers, roasted, scraped, seeded, and cut into strips [*see* No. 145]
½ teaspoon sugar
Salt to taste
¼ teaspoon freshly ground pepper
1 tablespoon chopped parsley

Cook the spaghetti in rapidly boiling, slightly salted water, drain when just *al dente*, and put into a well-heated, shallow serving bowl. While the spaghetti is cooking, quickly prepare the sauce. Sauté the garlic and sweet peppers in the oil; as soon as the garlic takes on a little color, add the mashed anchovies and the tomato pulp. Season with the sugar and pepper, taste for salt, and mix thoroughly. Bring to a boil and cook 10 minutes from the time the sauce begins to boil. Pour the sauce over the spaghetti, scatter the parsley over it, and mix quickly. *Serves 4.*

536. SPAGHETTI BOSCAIOLA
Spaghetti alla boscaiola

1 pound spaghetti
4 ounces canned Italian-style tuna in oil, crumbled
½ pound mushrooms, chopped
½ cup oil
1 clove garlic, crushed in the garlic-press
1 teaspoon salt
¼ teaspoon pepper

Sauté the garlic in the oil in a heavy saucepan for a few minutes until it begins to color; add the mushrooms and salt and pepper. Cook, covered, over medium heat for 10 minutes. Add the crumbled tuna and cook only until the sauce is blended and very hot. Cook the spaghetti as described in the preceding recipes, drain, put on a serving platter, and pour the sauce over it. *Serves 6.*

537. SPAGHETTI WITH BROCCOLI
Spaghetti "chi vruoccoli arriminata"

This dish is a Calabrian specialty.

1 pound spaghetti
1 large head of broccoli
1 tablespoon oil
3 cloves garlic, crushed in the garlic-press
1½ pounds tomatoes, peeled, seeded, drained,
    and chopped
4 tablespoons seeded raisins
4 tablespoons pine nuts
1 tablespoon chopped parsley
1 teaspoon salt
¼ teaspoon freshly ground pepper
1 cup grated Parmesan cheese

Wash the broccoli thoroughly, trim off the tough end of the stalk, and cook it in boiling salted water for 12 to 15 minutes; drain it, remove the flower heads from the stalks, cut the stalks into bite-size pieces, and keep both warm in a covered bowl. Put the oil and garlic into a pot; cook over medium heat until the garlic is lightly browned. Add the tomatoes and salt and pepper and cook over moderate heat for 20 minutes. Stir in the raisins and the pine nuts. Cook the spaghetti in rapidly boiling, salted water and drain when it reaches the *al dente* stage; pour it into a hot, shallow serving bowl; pour the sauce over it; and top with the pieces of broccoli and the chopped parsley. Mix with care and serve the grated cheese on the side. *Serves 6 to 8.*

538. SPAGHETTI BUCANIERA
Spaghetti alla bucaniera

1 pound spaghetti
½ cup oil
2 cloves garlic, crushed in the garlic-press
1 pound tomatoes, peeled, seeded, drained, and chopped
¼ pound baby octopus (or squid), cleaned and diced
1 small lobster tail (or substitute 1 small lobster),
    cleaned, shelled, and cut into pieces
1 pound clams, steamed open, washed free of sand,
    and shelled
3 tablespoons chopped parsley
Several gratings of pepper
1 teaspoon salt

Put half the oil into a large, heavy saucepan over medium heat and brown the garlic in it. Add the tomatoes, season with salt and pepper, and continue cooking for about 15 minutes. Heat the rest of the oil in another saucepan over medium heat, add the

pieces of octopus, reduce heat to moderate, and cook for 20 minutes. Add the lobster tail (or lobster) and cook for 10 minutes longer. Add the clams, remove from the heat, and combine all of the fish with the tomato sauce. Cook the spaghetti in rapidly boiling, salted water; drain at the *al dente* stage, and pour into a large, shallow, hot serving bowl. Add the sauce, sprinkle with parsley, mix, and serve. *Serves 6.*

539. SPAGHETTI CARBONARA
Spaghetti alla carbonara

1 pound spaghetti
¼ pound hog jowl, cut in 1-inch pieces
1 tablespoon oil
4 eggs
¾ cup grated Parmesan cheese
¼ cup heavy cream
4 tablespoons butter
½ teaspoon salt
ı teaspoon freshly ground pepper

Cook the spaghetti in plenty of rapidly boiling, salted water, and drain at the *al dente* stage. While this is cooking, fry the hog jowl with the oil in a frying pan over high heat until crisp and brown. Beat the eggs in a bowl with the cheese, salt, pepper, and the cream. Melt the butter in a heavy saucepan over medium heat and as soon as it turns a dark gold (almost nut colored), gradually beat in the egg mixture. Stir quickly and when it has just begun to thicken, add the spaghetti and the fried hog jowl. Mix very quickly and serve at once. It is important to have the spaghetti cooked and drained when the eggs just begin to thicken. They must not be allowed to overcook and should be moist. *Serves 6.*

NOTE: Parboiled salt pork or bacon, fried crisp, as above, may be substituted for the hog jowl.

191

540. SPAGHETTI CARRATTIERA
Spaghetti alla carrattiera

1 pound spaghetti
4 ounces canned Italian-style tuna in oil, broken into
    pieces or chopped
2 cloves garlic, crushed in the garlic-press
3 tablespoons oil
½ pound mushrooms, diced
¼ pound hog jowl, cut into thin slices
2 cups Italian Meat Sauce [No. 41], heated
1 cup grated Parmesan cheese
Salt and freshly grated pepper to taste

Cook the oil and garlic in a heavy saucepan over medium heat. As soon as the garlic begins to color, add the diced mushrooms and the slices of hog jowl. Season with a pinch of salt and a grating of pepper. Cook for 30 minutes, covered, and then add the pieces of tuna. Cook for a few more minutes to heat through and remove the pan from the fire. Cook the spaghetti in plenty of rapidly boiling, salted water and drain at the *al dente* stage. Put it into a large, shallow serving bowl, cover it with the tuna/mushroom mixture, and pour the meat sauce over it. Mix at the table and serve the grated Parmesan cheese on the side. *Serves* 6.

541. SPAGHETTI WITH CHEESE AND PEPPER ROMANA
Spaghetti con cacio e pepe alla romana

1 pound spaghetti
1 cup grated Pecorino cheese
1 teaspoon whole peppercorns pounded in the mortar
3 tablespoons of the water in which the spaghetti was
    cooked

Cook the spaghetti in plenty of rapidly boiling, salted water and drain at the *al dente* stage. Put it on a hot serving plate, scatter the grated cheese and pepper over the top, and pour over a few tablespoons of the water in which the spaghetti has been cooked. Mix carefully and serve. *Serves* 4.

542. SPAGHETTI WITH CLAMS
Spaghetti con vongole

1 pound spaghetti (or vermicelli or linguine)
¼ cup water
2 pounds clams (preferably steamers)
½ cup oil
3 cloves garlic, crushed in the garlic-press

1½ pounds tomatoes, peeled, seeded, drained, and
    chopped
1 tablespoon chopped parsley
1 teaspoon salt
¼ teaspoon freshly ground pepper

Wash the clams and steam them in a covered pot over a brisk flame with ¼ cup water; as soon as their shells have opened, drain them in a cheesecloth-lined colander placed over a bowl to catch the juices. Shell the clams, wash out any sand, and reserve in a covered bowl. Brown the garlic in another pot in 2 tablespoons of oil over medium heat, add the clam juice, cook until it is reduced to 2 or 3 tablespoons, add the tomato pulp, season with the salt and pepper, and cook over a brisk flame for about 20 minutes. Cook the pasta in a liberal amount of salted, rapidly boiling water, drain it when it reaches the *al dente* stage, and pour it into a well-heated shallow serving bowl. Add the clams to the hot sauce and pour it over the spaghetti. Sprinkle with the chopped parsley and mix carefully. *Serves* 4.

543. SPAGHETTI WITH CUTTLEFISH
Spaghetti con le seppie

1 pound spaghetti
1 pound cuttlefish (or squid), cleaned and tentacles
    removed
A chopped mixture:
    3 sprigs parsley
    1 clove garlic
    The cuttlefish tentacles
1 tablespoon chopped onion
½ cup oil
1 pound tomatoes, peeled, seeded, drained, and
    chopped
1 tablespoon chopped parsley
1 teaspoon salt
¼ teaspoon freshly ground pepper

Clean the cuttlefish; discard the bone, eyes, and ink sac; rinse it thoroughly and cut it into strips. Put the chopped mixture and onion into a heavy saucepan with the oil and cook over medium heat until the onion turns a light gold. Add the cuttlefish strips and tomato pulp, season with the salt and freshly ground pepper, and continue cooking over moderate heat for 20 minutes, or until the cuttlefish is tender. If sauce is too thick, add a few tablespoons of warm water. Cook the spaghetti in plenty of rapidly boiling, salted water and drain when it reaches the *al dente* stage. Pour it

SEE
VERSE
FOR
PTION

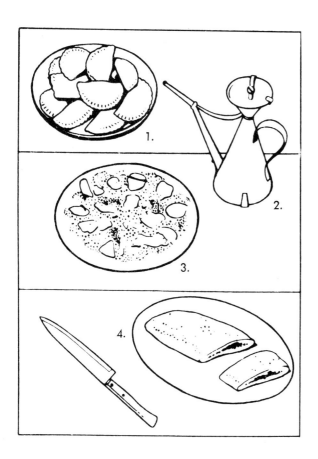

1. Neapolitan Pizza Casalinga (No. 557)
2. Traditional copper oil can used in Italy for sprinkling pizzas with oil
3. Neapolitan Pizza (No. 555)
4. Stuffed Calzone (No. 561)

into a large, heated, shallow serving bowl, cover it with the sauce and cuttlefish, and sprinkle with the chopped parsley. *Serves* 4.

544. SPAGHETTI GOURMET
Spaghetti alla ghiotta

1 pound spaghetti
1 onion, finely chopped
6 tablespoons butter
⅓ cup cooked chicken meat, diced
⅓ cup prosciutto, diced
1 tablespoon brandy
4 tomatoes, peeled, seeded, drained, and chopped
½ teaspoon sugar
1½ cups Bolognese Sauce [No. 68]
1 cup grated Parmesan cheese
¼ pound mozzarella cheese, thinly sliced
½ pound eggplant, peeled, cut in julienne strips, and fried until brown in 3 tablespoons oil
½ teaspoon salt
¼ teaspoon freshly ground pepper

Cook the chopped onion in a large, heavy pot over medium heat in 3 tablespoons of butter; as soon as the onion begins to color, add the diced chicken and prosciutto. Pour in the brandy and let it cook away completely. Add the tomatoes, sugar, salt, and pepper. Stir carefully and continue cooking for 8 minutes. Combine with the Bolognese sauce and keep warm. Drop the spaghetti into plenty of rapidly boiling, salted water, drain it when it reaches the *al dente* stage, and pour it into a large, shallow, hot serving bowl. Dot with pieces of the remaining butter, sprinkle with 2 tablespoons of grated Parmesan cheese, and put the slices of mozzarella over the top. Pour the sauce over it and top with the strips of cooked eggplant. Pass the rest of the grated Parmesan cheese on the side. *Serves* 6 *to* 8.

545. SPAGHETTI MARCHIGIANA
Spaghetti alla marchigiana

1 pound spaghetti
1 pound hog jowl, cut into small pieces
4 tablespoons oil
2 tablespoons lard
1 onion, chopped
A small piece of hot red pepper
1 clove garlic, crushed in the garlic-press
1 cup grated Pecorino cheese

Sauté the hog jowl in the oil and lard in a frying pan over medium heat; as soon as the pork begins to become crisp and golden, add the onion, red pepper, and garlic. Stir, brown the mixture lightly, and remove from the fire. Cook the spaghetti in plenty of salted, rapidly boiling water, drain it at the *al dente* stage, turn it into a heated serving dish, sprinkle the Pecorino cheese over the top, and pour over the browned mixture. This dish is most successful when the browned mixture is ready at precisely the same moment as the spaghetti is being drained. *Serves* 4.

546. SPAGHETTI NAPOLETANA
Spaghetti alla napoletana

Neapolitans prefer a fine spaghetti known as vermicelli.

1 pound fine spaghetti (vermicelli)
6 tablespoons butter
¼ cup chopped ham fat
1 tablespoon chopped onion
1½ pounds tomatoes, peeled, seeded, drained, and chopped
1 tablespoon chopped basil
1 cup grated Parmesan cheese
½ teaspoon salt
¼ teaspoon freshly ground pepper

Put 2 tablespoons of the butter, the chopped ham fat, and the onion in a heavy saucepan and cook over medium heat until the onion turns golden. Add the tomato pulp, season with salt and pepper, and continue cooking over moderate heat for 15 minutes. Cook the spaghetti in a liberal amount of rapidly boiling, salted water. Drain it at the *al dente* stage and pour it into a well-heated, shallow serving bowl. Dot it with small pieces of the remaining butter, sprinkle the basil and 2 tablespoons of grated Parmesan cheese on top, and pour the sauce over it. Mix it carefully and serve the rest of the Parmesan cheese on the side. *Serves* 4.

547. SPAGHETTI WITH SEAFOOD
Spaghetti "tutto mare"

1 pound spaghetti (or trenette)

Oil as needed

A small piece hot red pepper

½ pound squid, cleaned (see page 310) and cut into pieces

½ cup dry white wine

½ pound tomatoes, peeled, seeded, drained, and chopped

½ cup sliced mushrooms

A chopped mixture:
   1 carrot
   1 onion

½ cup raw lobster meat, cut in small pieces

1 teaspoon sage leaves

¼ cup brandy

1 pound mussels, shells scrubbed, steamed open, and shelled

1 pound clams, shells scrubbed, steamed open, and shelled

2 tablespoons chopped parsley

1 teaspoon salt

¼ teaspoon freshly ground pepper

Heat 3 tablespoons of oil in a pot; add the red pepper, sage, and the squid. Cook over a brisk flame for 5 minutes, stir well, pour over half the wine, and cook until it has completely evaporated. Add the tomato pulp and the salt and pepper, cover the pot, reduce flame to moderate, and continue cooking for 20 minutes. In another pan, sauté the sliced mushrooms in 1 tablespoon of oil for 8 minutes, then combine them with the tomatoes and squid. Heat 3 tablespoons of oil in the same pan in which the mushrooms have been cooked; add the chopped carrot/onion and cook over moderate heat until lightly browned. Add the lobster, stir, add the sage, the rest of the wine, and the brandy, and continue cooking for 5 minutes over a brisk flame. Combine the lobster meat mixture with the mussels and clams, mix thoroughly, and keep hot. Cook the spaghetti in plenty of briskly boiling water that has been lightly salted, drain when it has reached the *al dente* stage, and put it into a well-heated, shallow serving bowl. Cover it with half the seafood sauce, sprinkle the chopped parsley over it, mix, and serve. Serve the rest of the sauce on the side. *Serves* 4.

548. SPAGHETTI WITH TUNA
Spaghetti col tonno

1 pound spaghetti (or trenette)

½ cup oil

1 pound tomatoes, peeled, seeded, drained, and chopped

1 4-ounce can Italian-style tuna in oil, broken into pieces

3 tablespoons Anchovy Butter [No. 108]

1 tablespoon chopped parsley

1 teaspoon salt

¼ teaspoon freshly ground pepper

Heat 6 tablespoons of the oil in a heavy saucepan over moderate heat, add the tomatoes, season with the salt and freshly ground pepper, and cook for 15 minutes. Keep warm until needed. Heat the rest of the oil in another saucepan and, as soon as it is hot, add the pieces of tuna. Brown them quickly, remove from the fire, and keep warm. Cook the spaghetti in plenty of rapidly boiling, salted water, drain at the *al dente* stage, and pour into a well-heated, shallow serving bowl. Add the anchovy butter and the tuna to the sauce and pour it over the spaghetti. Sprinkle with the chopped parsley and mix carefully. *Serves* 4.

549. SPAGHETTI TURIDDU
Spaghetti alla Turiddu

1 pound spaghetti (or trenette)

½ cup oil

2 cloves garlic, crushed in the garlic-press

6 anchovy fillets, washed free of salt [see No. 220] and pounded to a paste in the mortar

1 tablespoon capers

⅓ cup Gaeta (or Greek-style) olives, pitted and chopped

1½ pounds tomatoes, peeled, seeded, drained, and chopped

1 tablespoon chopped oregano (or 1 teaspoon dried)

1 tablespoon chopped parsley

1 tablespoon chopped basil (or 1 teaspoon dried)

½ teaspoon salt

¼ teaspoon freshly ground pepper

Put the oil and garlic into a heavy saucepan and heat over a medium flame until the garlic turns a light gold. Add the mashed anchovies, capers, olives, and tomatoes. Season with the salt and pepper, bring to a boil, and continue cooking over moderate heat for 15 minutes. Cook the spaghetti in plenty of rapidly boiling, salted water, drain it at the *al dente* stage, and pour it into a well-heated shallow bowl. Cover it with the hot sauce, and sprinkle over it the oregano, parsley, and basil. Stir it up at the table. *Serves* 4.

NOTE: If dried oregano and/or basil is used, add to the sauce with the tomatoes.

550. SPAGHETTI UMBRIANA
Spaghetti alla moda dell' Umbria

1 pound spaghetti
½ cup oil
3 cloves garlic, crushed in the garlic-press
6 anchovy fillets, washed free of salt [*see* No. 220]
    and pounded to a paste in the mortar
1 pound tomatoes, peeled, seeded, drained, and chopped
1 small can black truffles, finely chopped
    [or No. 1819a]
1 tablespoon chopped parsley
¼ teaspoon salt
¼ teaspoon freshly ground pepper

Put the oil and garlic in a heavy saucepan and cook over medium heat until the garlic is slightly brown. Add the mashed anchovies and the chopped tomatoes. Season with the salt and pepper, mix thoroughly, and continue cooking for 15 minutes. Cook the spaghetti in plenty of rapidly boiling, salted water and drain at the *al dente* stage. Pour it at once into a hot, shallow serving bowl; cover with the chopped truffles, pour the sauce over, and sprinkle the chopped parsley over the top. Mix carefully at the table. *Serves* 4.

551. ZITE NAPOLETANA
Zite alla napoletana

1 pound zite
1½ pounds rump of beef
⅛ pound prosciutto (meat and fat), sliced ⅛ inch
    thick and cut into long strips
A chopped mixture:
  2 ounces ham fat
  2 cloves garlic
  ½ small onion
1 tablespoon oil
½ cup dry white wine
2 pounds tomatoes, peeled, seeded, drained, and
    chopped
4 tablespoons butter, softened
¼ cup Malaga grapes, pitted
2 ounces pine nuts, slightly crushed
1 cup grated cheese (Pecorino or Parmesan)
1 teaspoon sugar

1 teaspoon salt
¼ teaspoon freshly ground pepper

Lard the beef with the strips of prosciutto. Sauté the chopped mixture in the oil in a large heavy pot over medium heat until the onion is limp. Add the larded beef, raise the flame, and brown the meat and onion. Add the wine and cook until the wine has almost entirely evaporated. Add the tomato pulp and sufficient water to cover the meat. Season with the sugar, salt, and pepper and continue cooking over moderate heat for 2 hours, or until the meat is tender. Remove the beef and reserve. Pass the sauce through a strainer or through a food mill. Return it to the pot, add the grapes and pine nuts, and keep hot. Bring a liberal amount of salted water to a brisk boil and drop in the zite, broken into pieces 4 inches long; drain them at the *al dente* stage and put them on a large, hot serving platter. Dot them with pieces of the softened butter, sprinkle over 2 tablespoons of the grated cheese, and pour the sauce over them. Mix with care and serve the remaining cheese on the side. The meat may follow as a second course, accompanied by fresh vegetables. *Serves 4 to 6.*

552. MEZZE ZITE WITH "FOUR" CHEESES
Mezze zite ai "quattro formaggi"

1 pound mezze zite
¼ pound mozzarella, cut in tiny strips
¼ pound Parmesan cheese, cut in tiny strips
¼ pound Holland cheese (Gouda), cut in tiny strips
1 cup Parmesan cheese, grated
¾ cup melted butter, kept warm in the double boiler

Cook the mezze zite in plenty of rapidly boiling, salted water and drain them when they are *al dente*. Pour them into a large, shallow baking dish and add the strips of cheese, half the melted butter, and half the grated Parmesan cheese. Mix very quickly and put into a very hot (450°) oven for 5 minutes. Remove from the oven, cover with the rest of the grated Parmesan cheese and the melted butter. It is important to do all this very quickly and to serve it very hot to avoid giving the top layer of Parmesan time to melt. The butter should be very hot but should never be allowed to brown or frizzle. *Serves* 4.

553. MEZZE ZITE RICCA
Mezze zite alla ricca

1 pound mezze zite
¼ pound ham fat, chopped
1 onion, chopped
2 ounces prosciutto, chopped
½ pound chicken livers, coarsely chopped
¼ pound mushrooms, chopped
1½ pounds tomatoes, peeled, seeded, drained, and
    chopped
1 cup red wine, reduced to ¼ cup
½ cup butter, softened
2 tablespoons chopped basil
Salt and freshly ground pepper
1 cup grated Parmesan cheese

Put the onion and the ham fat in a saucepan and cook over moderate heat until the onion is transparent. Add the prosciutto and chicken livers, stir for 1 minute, add the mushrooms, stir again for 1 minute, add the tomatoes and the reduced wine, season with salt and pepper, and then cook for about 15 minutes. Cook the mezze zite in a large quantity of rapidly boiling salted water and drain when they have reached the *al dente* stage. Spread them out on a hot serving platter, dot with the softened butter, sprinkle with the basil, and pour the sauce over. Serve the grated cheese on the side. *Serves* 6.

NEAPOLITAN SPECIALTIES

Specialità napoletane

554. NEAPOLITAN PIZZA MARINARA
Pizza alla napoletana marinara

This is the traditional Neapolitan homemade pizza.

3½ cups sifted flour
1 envelope dried yeast
1 teaspoon salt
¾ cup lukewarm water
Oil or lard, as needed
1 pound tomatoes, peeled, seeded, drained, and cut
    into strips
2 cloves garlic, sliced
1 tablespoon chopped oregano (or ¼ teaspoon dried)
Salt and freshly ground pepper

Sift the flour onto the board in a little mound and hollow out the center. Dissolve the yeast in the lukewarm water with the salt, let it stand for 10 minutes, until it foams, and pour it into the hollowed center of the flour. Little by little work the flour into the yeast mixture with the fingers. If necessary, add a tablespoon or more of warm water to make a smooth and rather soft dough. Roll it into a ball, put it into a lightly floured bowl, cover, and set in a warm place to rise until doubled in bulk. Lightly flour a board or a marble surface and knead the dough for a few minutes. Divide it into 6 equal portions and roll (or pat) each portion out into a circle about ⅛ inch thick and 6 inches in diameter. The edges should be slightly thicker, to form a rim. Brush each circle with a little lard or oil, put small heaps of tomato strips spaced well apart on each, garnish with the garlic slices and pinches of oregano, sprinkle some more oil over the tops, and season with a dash of salt and pepper. Grease a baking sheet with oil, put the pizzas on it, and put into a very hot (450°) oven for 10 to 15 minutes. Serve as hot as possible. *Serves* 6.

Anchovy

555. NEAPOLITAN PIZZA
Pizza alla napoletana—commerciale

This is the pizza that is served in the pizzerias of Naples.

Prepare this pizza exactly as Neapolitan Pizza Marinara [No. 554], adding pieces of salted anchovy fillets [*see* No. 220] on top of the tomatoes and a few thin slices of mozzarella cheese on each of the rounds of dough before baking.

566. NEAPOLITAN PIZZA WITH FRESH ANCHOVIES
Pizza alla napoletana con alici fresche

This pizza is prepared and baked exactly as in No. 554, except that fresh anchovies are substituted for the tomatoes and the oregano is omitted.

557. NEAPOLITAN PIZZA CASALINGA
Pizzelle casalinghe napoletane

Pizza dough:
  2 cups sifted flour
  2 tablespoons lard
  ½ envelope dried yeast, dissolved in ¼ cup warm
      water
  ½ teaspoon salt
  Warm water as needed
Fat for deep frying
Filling:
  2 bunches escarole
  Oil as needed
  1 clove garlic, peeled
  12 anchovy fillets, washed free of salt [*see* No. 220]
      and cut into pieces
  1 tablespoon capers
  12 black Sicilian (or Greek) olives, pitted and chopped
  2 tablespoons sultana raisins
  1 egg yolk
  ½ teaspoon salt

Make a dough of the flour, lard, yeast, salt, and a few tablespoons of warm water, as described in Neapolitan Pizza Marinara [No. 554], and set it aside to rise. Wash the escarole thoroughly and cook it in boiling, salted water for 10 minutes; drain it thoroughly, squeezing out all the water; chop it fine; and sauté it in a frying pan with 2 tablespoons oil, the garlic, and the salt. When it is tender, remove the garlic and let the escarole cool; then add the anchovy fillets, capers, olives, raisins, and blend in the egg yolk. Sprinkle a pastry board or marble slab with a little flour, knead the dough on it for a few minutes, and divide it into pieces about the size of an egg. Pat these between well-floured hands, pulling them out until you have circles 4 inches in diameter. Line up the circles on a board, put a tablespoon of filling in the center of each, dampen the edges slightly, fold each over on itself, and press the edges together firmly so that the filling will not escape. Fry the pizza pies in hot (375°) fat, drain them well when they are crisp and golden, and serve them at once. *Serves* 6.

558. NEAPOLITAN PIZZA FANTASIA
Pizza alla napoletana "fantasia"

1 pound potatoes, boiled and mashed free of any lumps
2¼ cups flour
½ cup grated Parmesan cheese
Pinch sugar
2 eggs, beaten
4 egg yolks
Oil as needed
4 tomatoes, peeled, seeded, drained, chopped, and
    cooked in 1 tablespoon of oil for 5 minutes
18 anchovy fillets, washed free of salt [*see* No. 220]
2 tablespoons chopped basil
Salt and freshly ground pepper to taste
Fat for deep frying

Blend the mashed potatoes while still warm with the flour, 3 tablespoons of the grated Parmesan cheese, the eggs and egg yolks, a little salt, pinch of pepper, and a pinch of sugar. With this dough prepare small pizzas 5 inches in diameter; fry them in hot (375°) oil and, when they are golden, drain them well. Garnish each with scattered heaps of tomato, pieces of anchovy, the chopped basil, and scatter the rest of the grated Parmesan over the tops. Sprinkle with oil, season lightly with salt and pepper, line them up on a lightly greased baking sheet, and bake them in a hot (375°) oven for about 10 minutes. *Serves* 6.

559. NEAPOLITAN PIZZA HOTEL EXCELSIOR
Pizza alla napoletana "Excelsior di Napoli"

3½ cups sifted flour
7 tablespoons butter, melted
1½ envelopes dried yeast, dissolved in ½ cup lukewarm
    water, and allowed to stand for 10 minutes
1 teaspoon salt
1 egg, lightly beaten
A little warm milk
Fat for deep frying
Garnish:
  4 tomatoes, peeled, seeded, drained, chopped, and
      then sautéed for 5 minutes in 1 tablespoon of oil
  ½ pound fresh mozzarella, thinly sliced
  18 small anchovy fillets, washed free of salt
      [*see* No. 220]
  2 tablespoons chopped basil leaves
  Oil as needed
  ½ cup grated Parmesan cheese

Sift the flour into a little hill on the board; hollow out

the center; and pour in the melted butter, dissolved yeast, egg, and a pinch of salt. Work the flour into the liquid, little by little, with the fingers, adding a tablespoon of warm milk from time to time, as needed, until you have a well-blended, elastic, and rather soft dough; put it aside in a bowl dusted with flour to rise in a warm place until doubled in bulk. From this dough roll out 6 circles $\frac{1}{8}$ inch thick and 6 inches in diameter. Fry them in smoking hot (375°) fat and drain them as soon as they are crisp and lightly browned. Line them up on a lightly oiled baking sheet or cooky tin, and garnish them with small bits of the tomato, slices of mozzarella, pieces of the anchovy fillets, chopped basil, and a sprinkling of grated Parmesan cheese; then sprinkle with oil. Bake them in a 375° oven for 10 minutes. *Serves* 6.

560. NEAPOLITAN PIZZETTE
Pizzette alla napoletana

These are made exactly as Neapolitan Pizza Marinara [No. 554], except they are made smaller, about 4 inches in diameter. Garnish and season them to taste and bake in the oven as described in No. 554.

561. STUFFED CALZONE
Calzone imbottito

4 cups sifted flour
1 envelope dried yeast, dissolved in $\frac{1}{2}$ cup warm water and allowed to stand for 10 minutes
1 teaspoon salt
Warm water as needed
Lard as needed
$\frac{1}{3}$ pound salami or prosciutto, diced
$\frac{2}{3}$ pound mozzarella cheese, sliced
1 egg beaten with a little water

Sift the flour onto a pastry board in a little mound; hollow out the center and pour in the dissolved yeast and salt. Work the flour into the liquid in the center with the fingers, bit by bit, adding a few tablespoons of warm water as needed, until you have a smooth, rather soft dough. Roll it into a ball, put it in a floured bowl, and set it in a warm place to rise until doubled in bulk. When it has risen, knead it for a few minutes on a lightly floured board or marble surface and divide into 6 portions. Roll these into circles a scant $\frac{1}{8}$ inch thick and from 8 to 10 inches in diameter. Brush them with melted lard and in the center of each put a slice of mozzarella and some of the diced salami (or prosciutto). Moisten the edges of each circle with the beaten egg, fold each over on itself, and press the edges

together firmly so that the filling will not escape during the cooking. Brush the outside of each with melted lard, line them up on a baking sheet, and cover with a towel and leave in a warm place for 1 hour; then bake them in a hot (375°) oven for about 30 minutes. Serve at once. *Serves* 6.

562. CHEESE AND HAM PANZAROTTI
Panzarotti di mozzarella e prosciutto

Dough:
   $1\frac{2}{3}$ cups sifted flour
   1 teaspoon salt
   6 tablespoons butter, melted
   1 egg yolk
   A little milk, as needed
Filling:
   $\frac{1}{2}$ pound mozzarella cheese, chopped
   2 ounces prosciutto, cut in slivers
   $\frac{1}{2}$ cup grated Parmesan cheese
   2 eggs, beaten
   1 tablespoon chopped parsley
   Pinch nutmeg
   $\frac{1}{2}$ teaspoon salt
   $\frac{1}{4}$ teaspoon freshly ground pepper
3 eggs, beaten with a little water
Fat for deep frying (half oil and half lard)

Sift the flour with the salt onto a board in a mound, hollow out the center, and pour in the butter and egg yolk. Work the flour into the liquid with the fingers, adding a little milk from time to time, as needed, to make a smooth, well-blended, firm dough. Wrap it up in a clean cloth and let it rest for a half hour. Then put the dough on a lightly floured board, roll it out, and fold it over on itself twice. Wrap it in the cloth again and let it rest while you prepare the filling. Put the chopped mozzarella, prosciutto, grated Parmesan cheese, and parsley in a bowl; season with the salt, freshly ground pepper, and nutmeg. Add the eggs, and blend thoroughly. Divide the dough in half and roll out two sheets, each $\frac{1}{8}$ inch thick. Brush one sheet with beaten egg and space small heaps of the filling on it $1\frac{1}{2}$ inches apart. Brush the second sheet with beaten egg and lay it over the first sheet. Press the fingers on the dough all around the spots of filling. Then, with a pastry wheel, cut out squares, each containing a knob of filling. Press the edges of each square down again to make sure that none of the filling escapes during the cooking. As you finish the panzarotti, line them up on a lightly floured cloth, taking care that they do not touch each other. Dip them in the beaten egg and drop them at once into the hot (375°) fat (traditionally ½ lard, ½ oil). Remove them with a slotted spoon after about 6 minutes. They should be crisp and golden. Drain on absorbent paper. Sprinkle them lightly with salt and serve at once. *Serves* 6.

TIMBALES
Timballi

Timbales are thick-crusted pies, served hot. They may be filled with various pasta, meats, game, fish, poultry, or vegetables. The cases, or crust, should be about ¼ to ½ inch thick. They are sometimes pre-baked and then filled just before serving, or timbale forms may be lined with unbaked pastry, filled, covered with a pastry top, and then baked in a moderate oven for about ¾ of an hour.

563. TIMBALES
Croste per timballi

This recipe makes enough pastry for 2 timbale cases.

    4 cups sifted flour
    1 cup butter, softened
    2 eggs, beaten
    2 teaspoons salt
    ¼ cup cold water

Sift the flour onto a board or marble surface to form a mound. Hollow out the peak and put the butter, eggs, and salt into this hollow. Work the flour quickly into the butter/egg mixture with the fingers, adding the water little by little. Handle the pastry as little as possible and add more water only if necessary. The result will be a rather granular dough. Wrap the dough in a cloth and set it in a cool place for 1 hour. This rest will cause it to lose most of its elasticity. Then place the dough on a lightly floured board and roll it out into sheets about ¼ inch thick. Line the bottom and sides of 2 timbale molds or 2 8-inch spring form pans with some of the dough. Cut 2 8½-inch circles from the remaining dough and place them on a baking sheet (these are the lids for the timbales). Line the 2 molds with aluminum foil and then fill them with dried peas. Put the molds and the baking sheet into a hot (375°) oven for 12 minutes. Carefully remove the dried peas and foil, reduce heat to moderate, and bake 5 to 10 minutes longer. Cool the timbale cases in the molds, and then remove carefully.

564. BUCATINI TIMBALES WITH EGGPLANT
Timballo di bucatini con melanzane

    2 baked Timbales [No. 563]
    1 pound bucatini, or elbow macaroni
    4 large eggplant, peeled, sliced, salted, and
        allowed to stand for 1 hour
    Oil as needed
    2 cloves garlic, crushed in the garlic-press
    1 pound tomatoes, peeled, seeded, drained, and
        chopped
    5 tablespoons butter, softened
    2 tablespoons chopped basil
    1 cup grated Parmesan cheese
    Salt as needed

Wash the eggplant well, and pat dry, then cut them into julienne strips, and sauté several strips at a time in a frying pan over medium heat in several tablespoons of oil; repeat until all are sautéed; sprinkle lightly with salt and keep them hot until needed. Brown the garlic in a saucepan over medium heat in 3 tablespoons of oil, add the tomato pulp, season with 1 teaspoon salt, and cook over a brisk flame for 20 minutes. Cook the bucatini, broken into 2-inch pieces, in plenty of briskly boiling, lightly salted water; drain them at the *al dente* stage; put them into a bowl with the tomatoes, 3 tablespoons of the butter, the basil, and half of the grated Parmesan cheese; mix thoroughly. Spread the inside of the timbale molds with the remaining butter, return the cases to their molds, and fill them with layers of the bucatini and eggplant, ending with a top layer of bucatini. Put the pastry covers on top; bake in a moderate (350°) oven for 15 minutes, or until they are thoroughly hot; remove them from the oven and let rest for 3 minutes. Unmold on a large platter and serve with the grated Parmesan on the side. *Serves* 8 *to* 10.

*Macaroncelli Timbale
à la Ricca (No. 565)*

565. MACARONCELLI TIMBALES À LA RICCA
Timballo di maccheroncelli alla ricca

2 baked Timbales [No.563]
1 pound macaroncelli
1 tablespoon oil
A chopped mixture:
   1 small carrot
   1 small onion
   1 stalk celery
4 tablespoons chopped ham fat
1 3-pound chicken, with its liver
½ cup dry white wine
¼ cup dried mushrooms, soaked in warm water for 1
   hour, drained, squeezed dry, and coarsely chopped
3 tablespoons butter, softened
2½ cups Béchamel Sauce [No. 18]
1 cup grated Parmesan cheese
2 tablespoons lean ham, cut in thin slivers
1 teaspoon salt
½ teaspoon freshly ground pepper

Put the oil, chopped mixture, ham fat, chicken, and chicken liver in a large heavy pot with the salt and pepper. Cook over a brisk flame for 10 minutes, or until the chopped vegetables are golden and the chicken takes on some color; remove the liver and reserve; pour the wine over all; and cook until it has almost completely evaporated. Add 2 tablespoons of water and put the pot, tightly covered, into a moderate (350°) oven for 1 hour, basting from time to time with its own juices from the bottom of the pot. When the chicken is tender, remove from the oven and allow to cool. Remove the skin and

bones and cut the meat into thin slices. Slice the liver and put aside with the chicken slices. Strain the juices from the pot into a bowl and reserve. Soak the dried mushrooms until soft, rinse them, squeeze them out thoroughly, cut them into rather large pieces, and cook them in 1 tablespoon of butter for 10 minutes. Cook the macaroncelli, broken into pieces, in plenty of briskly boiling, lightly salted water; drain them when they have reached the *al dente* stage; put them into a large bowl. Add the Béchamel, the chicken meat and liver slices, the reserved pan juices, grated Parmesan, mushrooms, and ham. Mix thoroughly. Spread the inside of the timbale molds with the remaining butter, return the cases to their molds, fill with the chicken/macaroncelli mixture, and put the pastry covers on top. Bake in a moderate (350°) oven for 15 minutes, or until they are thoroughly hot. Remove from oven and let rest for 3 minutes. Unmold on a large platter and serve the remaining sauce separately. *Serves 8 to 10.*

566. ITALIAN MACARONI TIMBALES
Timballo di maccheroni all'italiana

2 Timbales [No. 563]
1 pound macaroni (or macaroncelli may be substituted)
2½ cups Marsala Sauce [No. 43]
2 cups Sauce Financière [No. 32]
5 tablespoons butter, softened
½ cup each grated Gruyère and Parmesan cheese

Break the macaroni into pieces 2 inches long and cook in plenty of rapidly boiling, lightly salted water; drain them when they have reached the *al dente* stage and put into a bowl. Add half the Marsala sauce, half the Financière sauce, 3 tablespoons of the butter, and ¼ cup each of the cheeses. Spread the insides of timbale molds with the remaining butter, return cases to their molds, fill them with sauced macaroni, and put the pastry covers on top. Bake in a moderate (350°) oven for 15 minutes, or until they are thoroughly hot. Remove from oven and let rest for 3 minutes. Unmold on a large platter, and serve the remaining cheese and the rest of the sauces separately. *Serves* 8 *to* 10.

567. MEZZE ZITE TIMBALES WITH OCTOPUS
Timballo di mezze zite con polpetti

2 baked Timbales [No. 563]
1 pound mezze zite
Olive oil
2 cloves garlic, crushed in the garlic-press
1 tablespoon chopped parsley
1 pound tomatoes, peeled, seeded, drained, and chopped
6 anchovy fillets, washed free of salt [*see* No. 220] and chopped
1 pound young octopus, well cleaned, cut into small pieces, and cooked in 2 tablespoons oil and a pinch of salt for 20 minutes, or until tender
¼ cup dried mushrooms, soaked in warm water for 1 hour, drained, squeezed dry, coarsely chopped, and cooked in 1 tablespoon oil for 15 minutes
½ cup black olives, pitted and chopped
1 tablespoon capers
1 teaspoon salt
¼ teaspoon freshly ground pepper

Cook the mezze zite in plenty of rapidly boiling, salted water. At the same time put into a heavy pot ½ cup of oil and the crushed garlic. Cook over medium heat until the garlic browns, add the chopped parsley and tomatoes. Continue cooking over a brisk flame for 3 or 4 minutes, or until they become pulpy. Season with the salt and pepper. Drain the mezze zite when they are *al dente* and put them into a heated bowl. Pour over them the chopped anchovies, the cooked octopus meat, tomatoes, mushrooms, olives, and capers; mix well. Butter the insides of the timbale molds with a little softened butter, return the cases to their molds, fill them with the mezze zite mixture, and put the pastry covers on top. Bake them in a moderate (350°) oven for 15 minutes, or until they are thoroughly hot. Remove from oven and let rest for 3 minutes. Unmold on a large platter, and serve at once. *Serves* 8 *to* 10.

568. RAVIOLI TIMBALES WITH MEAT SAUCE
Timballo di raviolini al ragù

2 Timbales [No. 563]
1 recipe Ravioli Genovese [No. 505]
5 tablespoons butter
1 teaspoon sage leaves
2½ cups Italian Meat Sauce [No. 41], adding ¼ pound of the beef which cooked in the sauce, chopped
¼ pound lamb's sweetbreads, blanched, sliced, and cooked for 10 minutes in 2 tablespoons of butter
¼ cup dried mushrooms, soaked in warm water for 1 hour, drained, thoroughly squeezed out, and cooked for 10 minutes in 1 tablespoon butter
1 cup grated Parmesan cheese

Cook the ravioli in plenty of rapidly boiling, salted water, and drain them at the *al dente* stage into a bowl. Just before the ravioli are done, heat the butter with the sage leaves until butter is nut brown in color. Pour over the ravioli and mix thoroughly. Add half the meat sauce, the sweetbreads, mushrooms, and half the grated Parmesan cheese; mix well again. Butter the timbale molds, return the cases to them, fill these with the sauced ravioli, and cover with their respective crusts. Put them in a moderate (350°) oven for 15 minutes; remove them; let them rest briefly; and unmold on a serving platter. Pass the rest of the sauce and the grated Parmesan cheese on the side. *Serves* 8.

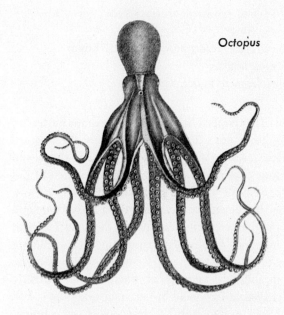

Octopus

201

569. RICE TIMBALES NAPOLETANA
Timballo—sartù—di riso alla napoletana

Neapolitans are veritable gluttons for this specialty, which they call Sartù.

2 cups rice (Italian short-grain rice if possible)

A chopped mixture:

    4 tablespoons ham fat

    1 onion

2 tablespoons butter

2 pounds tomatoes, peeled, seeded, drained, and chopped

Pinch sugar

4 cups White Bouillon [No. 323]

2 eggs

2 cups grated Parmesan cheese

1 teaspoon salt

$\frac{1}{4}$ teaspoon freshly ground pepper

Filling:

    $\frac{1}{3}$ pound lean beef, chopped

    2 cups soft breadcrumbs, soaked in milk and squeezed dry

    $\frac{1}{2}$ teaspoon salt

    $\frac{1}{4}$ teaspoon freshly ground pepper

    Pinch nutmeg

    6 tablespoons lard

    Flour

    1 tablespoon butter

    $\frac{1}{2}$ pound chicken livers, chopped

    $\frac{1}{2}$ pound sweet Italian sausage, cut in small pieces

    $\frac{1}{4}$ cup dried mushrooms, soaked $\frac{1}{2}$ hour in warm water, rinsed, squeezed dry, and cut into pieces

    $\frac{1}{2}$ pound mozzarella cheese, sliced

For the crust:

    3 cups soft breadcrumbs (from fresh bread)

    2 eggs, beaten

    4 tablespoons butter, melted

Brown the chopped ham fat and onion in the butter in a large, heavy pot over medium heat; add the chopped tomatoes; season with the salt, pepper, and sugar; and continue cooking for 30 minutes, or until the sauce is thick. Remove $\frac{1}{3}$ of the sauce and reserve in a bowl. Bring the remainder to a boil over a brisk flame and add the rice; blend it for a minute, then add 3 cups of the bouillon. Continue cooking, uncovered, adding more bouillon as necessary. Remove the rice from the fire in about 17 minutes, or when it is still slightly under-cooked (it should be very moist, not dry). Add the 2 eggs beaten with 2 tablespoons of the bouillon, fold in 1 cup of the grated Parmesan cheese, check the seasoning, pour the mixture out on a very large platter (or on a thoroughly clean marble surface), and let it cool.

Put the chopped beef, moistened bread, and 1 tablespoon of lard into a deep bowl; season with the salt, pepper, and pinch of nutmeg; blend thoroughly and shape into small balls the size of a large grape. Roll them lightly in flour and sauté them in lard over a brisk flame for 5 or 6 minutes, or until browned.

Melt a tablespoon of butter in a small saucepan, add the mushrooms, cook for 10 minutes over medium heat, stir in the sausage and chicken livers, and remove from the fire after 10 minutes.

Put the reserved tomato sauce into another large saucepan, bring it to a boil over moderate heat, and gently stir in the mushroom/sausage/liver mixture and the little meatballs. Cook all together for several minutes and then turn them into a bowl. Keep hot.

Generously butter a 2-quart spring mold; cover it liberally with fresh breadcrumbs and carefully brush the breadcrumbs with beaten egg so that the crumbs are well soaked. Repeat the operation a second, then a third time, until there is a crust about $\frac{1}{4}$ inch thick. Gently pack the bottom and sides of the mold with the rice, leaving the center hollow. Pour the meat filling into this hollow space and add the sliced mozzarella. Cover with a thick layer of rice, smooth it down, and then add a liberal layer of fresh breadcrumbs. Sprinkle well with melted butter. Put it into a moderate (350°) oven for about 25 minutes, or until the surface is beautifully golden. Let it rest for about 20 minutes in order to make the crust firmer, and carefully unmold it directly onto a round serving platter. Serve with the remaining Parmesan cheese on the side. *Serves* 8.

570. SPAGHETTI AND SHELLFISH TIMBALES
Timballo di spaghetti alla marinara

2 baked Timbales [No. 563]

$1\frac{1}{2}$ pounds spaghetti, broken into pieces

Oil as needed

3 cloves garlic, crushed in the garlic-press

2 pounds tomatoes, peeled, seeded, drained, and chopped

1 tablespoon chopped basil

1 tablespoon chopped parsley

3 pounds mussels

3 pounds clams

$\frac{1}{2}$ cup dry white wine

2 tablespoons butter

¼ pound shelled crayfish tails (or substitute lobster), cut in pieces

2 tablespoons butter, softened

1 teaspoon salt

¼ teaspoon freshly ground pepper

Put ½ cup oil into a heavy pot and add the crushed garlic. Cook over a brisk flame until the garlic turns gold; add the tomatoes, basil, parsley, and salt and pepper. Bring to a boil, lower the heat, and continue cooking for ½ hour. While the tomatoes are cooking, put the mussels and clams, first thoroughly rinsed, into a large pot with 1 tablespoon of oil; cook them for a few minutes, tightly covered, over a lively flame until all the shells have opened. Strain them into a colander over a bowl to catch the liquid. As soon as they are cool enough to handle, remove them from their shells. Strain the liquid through cheesecloth into a saucepan, add the wine, and cook down until only 3 tablespoons remain. Heat 2 tablespoons of butter in a pan, add the shelled crayfish tails (or lobster), and after 8 minutes remove from the fire. Combine all of the shellfish and the reduced liquid with the tomato sauce. Cook the spaghetti in plenty of rapidly boiling, salted water, drain at the *al dente* stage, return it to the pot, pour over it half the sauce, and mix. Butter the timbale molds, return the two cases to them, fill the cases with the sauced spaghetti, and cover with their lids. Put them into a moderate (350°) oven for 15 minutes to heat through. Remove them, let them rest a few minutes, and unmold. Serve the rest of the sauce on the side. *Serves* 8.

571. TORTELLINI TIMBALES WITH MEAT SAUCE
Timballo di tortellini al ragù

This is prepared in exactly the same way as Ravioli Timbales with Meat Sauce [No. 568], except that Tortellini Bolognese [No. 518] are substituted for the ravioli.

RICE
Riso

Italian rice is larger grained than the familiar short- or long-grained Carolina rice. Italians nearly always cook rice in broth or stock and, like pasta, it is cooked until just *al dente*. Because of its larger size, it takes slightly longer to cook than American rice. It is generally served very moist, almost wet, with grated cheese on the side. Properly prepared, it should never be gummy; each grain should be separate. The closest American substitute is brown rice, but the Italian variety is well worth trying, if you are not familiar with it. It is readily available in the Italian neighborhoods of larger cities or in specialty stores.

Long-grained white rice or brown rice may be substituted for the Italian rice specified in the following recipes. If brown rice is used, it must be cooked for a longer time and it will be necessary to adjust the recipes accordingly to avoid overcooking other ingredients in a risotto, such as green vegetables, etc.

It is recommended that caution be exercised in seasoning with salt any of the risottos in this section. The amount of salt needed will depend entirely on the seasoning in the stock in which it is cooked. Since the stock reduces as the risotto cooks, its salinity is naturally much increased by the end of the cooking.

572. RISOTTO WITH BUTTER AND PARMESAN CHEESE
Risotto con burro e parmigiano

2 cups Italian rice

½ cup butter

2 ounces beef marrow, diced

1 small onion, chopped

½ cup dry white wine

5 cups White Bouillon [No. 323]

1 cup grated Parmesan cheese

Salt and freshly ground pepper

Melt 5 tablespoons of the butter in a heavy pot over medium heat and add the beef marrow, onion, and a little grated pepper. Cook until the onion is transparent, add the wine, and cook until it has evaporated. Add the rice and stir for a few moments until every grain is coated with the butter. Add 3 cups of the bouillon and about 1 teaspoon of salt (depending on the seasoning of the bouillon), bring to a boil, reduce heat slightly, and cook for about 20 minutes, stirring frequently

203

and adding more bouillon as necessary. Remove from the heat when it has reached the *al dente* stage. Add the remaining butter and a few tablespoons of Parmesan cheese. Turn it out onto a hot serving platter and serve the remaining cheese on the side. *Serves* 6.

573. RISOTTO CAMPO ANTICO
Risotto al campo antico

2 cups Italian rice
⅔ cup butter
1 small onion, chopped
⅓ pound fresh mushrooms, chopped
½ cup dry white wine
5 cups White Bouillon [No. 323], or more as needed
½ teaspoon saffron, soaked in ¼ cup water
3 ripe tomatoes, peeled, seeded, drained, and chopped
1¼ cups freshly grated Parmesan cheese
1 white truffle, sliced [or No. 1819a]
Salt and freshly grated pepper

Melt 3 tablespoons of butter in a large, heavy pot over a medium flame and add the onion and mushrooms; cook for 2 minutes and add the rice. Season with salt and pepper, stir until every grain of rice is coated with butter, and add the wine. As soon as the rice shows a tendency to stick to the bottom of the pan, add 3 cups of the bouillon, and continue cooking over brisk heat for about 10 minutes, adding additional bouillon from time to time as needed. Add the saffron and the tomatoes, bring back to a boil, and cook for about 10 more minutes, or until just *al dente*. Off the heat, add the remaining butter and a few tablespoons of grated cheese. Turn it out onto a hot serving platter, sprinkle the truffle slices over the top, and serve the remaining cheese on the side. *Serves* 6.

574. CARTHUSIAN RISOTTO
Risotto alla certosina

2 cups Italian rice
1 pound shrimp (or lobster), boiled, shelled, de-veined, and cut in pieces
The shellfish cooking liquid
½ cup butter
2 tablespoons oil
A chopped mixture:
    1 onion
    1 small carrot
    few sprigs parsley
2 cloves garlic, bruised
5 cups Fish Bouillon [No. 325], or more as needed
Salt and freshly ground pepper

Using the pestle and mortar, pound the shells of the shrimp and then simmer them in the shrimp cooking liquid for about 15 minutes, or until the liquid is reduced to 1 cup. Strain through cheesecloth and reserve. Brown the chopped vegetables and garlic in 3 tablespoons of butter and the oil in a heavy pot over medium heat, add the strained shellfish liquid, season with salt and pepper; cook over brisk heat for 15 minutes, and then remove the garlic. Add the rice and bring to a boil. Now start adding the bouillon, a little at a time as it is needed, keeping the rice very moist. Cook for about 20 minutes, or until the rice is *al dente*. A few minutes before the rice is done, add the pieces of shrimp. Off the heat, add the remaining butter, turn it onto a hot serving platter, and serve at once. *Serves* 6.

575. RISOTTO WITH CHICKEN GIBLETS
Risotto con rigaglie di pollo

2 cups Italian rice
5 cups White Bouillon [No. 323], or more as needed
¼ pound chicken giblets, cleaned and chopped
¼ pound veal (all fat removed), chopped or finely ground
A chopped mixture:
    ½ onion
    ½ carrot
    ½ stalk celery
½ cup butter
½ cup dry white wine
2 ounces beef marrow, diced
3 tomatoes, peeled, seeded, drained, and chopped
1 cup grated Parmesan cheese
Salt and freshly ground pepper

Put the uncooked marrow and the chopped vegetables into a large, heavy pot with 3 tablespoons of butter and cook over medium heat until they are lightly browned. Add the giblets and veal and cook for 5 minutes, crumbling the veal with a fork. Add the wine, cook until it has evaporated, and then add the tomato pulp. Season with salt and pepper, bring to a boil, reduce heat, add a few tablespoons of bouillon, and continue cooking for 30 minutes. Add the rice, stir, and then add 3 cups of bouillon. Return the rice to a boil and continue cooking for about 20 minutes, adding a little bouillon from time to time as the rice seems to need it. When the rice has reached the *al dente* stage, remove it from the fire; add the rest of the butter in small pieces and several tablespoons of grated Parmesan. Let it rest for a good minute on a corner of the stove and then turn it out onto a hot serving platter. Serve the rest of the grated Parmesan cheese on the side. *Serves 6 to 8.*

576. RISOTTO WITH FROG'S LEGS
Risotto con ranocchi

2 cups Italian rice
24 whole frogs, skinned and the legs separated from the carcasses
A chopped mixture:
   ½ onion
   ½ carrot
   1 clove garlic
   1 tablespoon basil leaves
   2 sprigs parsley
3 tablespoons oil
½ cup dry white wine
2 tomatoes, peeled, seeded, drained, and chopped
3 tablespoons butter
5 cups boiling water, or more as needed
1 cup grated Parmesan cheese
Salt and freshly ground pepper

Put the chopped mixture with the oil in a large heavy skillet and cook over medium heat until it has turned a light gold. Add the frogs' carcasses (reserving the legs), season lightly with salt and pepper, add the wine, cook until it has almost entirely evaporated, and then add the tomato pulp. Mix thoroughly and continue cooking over moderate heat for about 30 minutes, or until the carcasses are reduced to a paste and the sauce has thickened. Pick out any bones and press the remainder through a fine sieve, pushing it through with a pestle, or purée through a food mill. Put this sauce into a heavy saucepan, bring it to a boil, add the frog's legs, cover, cook for 5 to 6 minutes, and remove the legs. Remove the bones from these, return the meat to the sauce, and reserve. Melt the butter in a large, heavy pot over medium heat, add the rice (well picked over, but not washed), season with salt, stir, and cook until the rice is well coated with the butter. Add 3 cups of boiling water, stir it again, and continue cooking, uncovered, over a brisk flame for about 20 minutes. As the rice dries out during the cooking, add the sauce, little by little. (If the rice absorbs too much liquid, add more water.) Remove it from the heat when it is just *al dente* to a corner of the stove and let it rest for

Risotto Paesana (No. 582):
see page 207

a couple of minutes. Add the grated Parmesan cheese, turn it onto a well-heated serving platter, mix again, and serve. *Serves 6.*

NOTE: Usually only cleaned, skinned frog's legs are available in American markets. In this event, omit cooking the carcasses with the tomatoes as described above.

577. RISOTTO GENOVESE
Risotto arrosto alla genovese

2 cups Italian rice
½ cup Italian Meat Sauce [No. 41]
5 cups White Bouillon [No. 323], or more as needed
½ cup butter
1 small onion, chopped
½ pound sausage meat
½ cup dry white wine
1½ cups shelled fresh peas (petits pois if available)
2 uncooked artichoke hearts [*see* introduction to No. 1578], sliced
¼ pound fresh mushrooms, sliced
1 cup grated Parmesan cheese
Salt and freshly ground white pepper

Brown the onion in 3 tablespoons of butter in a large, heavy pot over a medium flame, add the sausage meat, season with a little salt and a pinch of white pepper, cook for 5 minutes, breaking up the meat with a fork. Add the wine and cook until the wine has completely evaporated. Add the peas, artichoke hearts, mushrooms, and the rice; season again with salt and pepper and continue cooking over moderate heat for about

5 minutes, stirring well, until every grain of rice and all of the vegetables are well coated with butter. Add the meat sauce and 3 cups of the bouillon, bring to a boil, and cook for about 20 minutes, adding a little more bouillon from time to time as needed. The rice should absorb most of the bouillon by the end of the cooking time, but it must be moist. Remove it from the fire when it has reached the *al dente* stage. Check the seasoning. Add the remaining butter, in pieces, and a few tablespoons of grated Parmesan cheese. Turn into an oven-proof dish and put into a very hot (450°) oven for about 5 minutes. As soon as a golden crust has formed on the top, serve it with the remaining grated Parmesan cheese on the side. *Serves 6 to 8.*

578. RISOTTO MILANESE
Risotto alla milanese

2 cups Italian rice
1 cup butter
2 ounces beef marrow, diced
1 small onion, chopped
½ cup dry white wine
½ teaspoon saffron, soaked in 2 tablespoons water
5 cups White Bouillon [No. 323], or more as needed
1 cup grated Parmesan cheese
Salt and freshly ground pepper

Melt 5 tablespoons of the butter in a large, heavy pot over moderate heat and add the beef marrow, onion, and a pinch of pepper. As soon as the onion becomes limp (do not allow it to brown), add the wine and cook over a brisk flame until it has evaporated. Add the rice, season with salt, stir it for a few minutes until every grain is coated with the butter, and add the saffron with 3 cups of bouillon. Bring quickly to a boil and as the rice thickens and dries, add more bouillon from time to time. Continue cooking for about 20 minutes over a brisk fire, stirring it frequently. When it has reached the *al dente* stage, remove it from the fire, add the rest of the butter and several tablespoons of grated Parmesan cheese. Let it rest a minute on the corner of the stove, turn it out onto a serving platter, and serve the rest of the grated Parmesan cheese on the side. *Serves 6.*

579. RISOTTO WITH MUSHROOMS
Risotto con funghi

This is prepared with the same ingredients and in the same way as Risotto with Butter and Parmesan Cheese [No. 572], except that to the onion that has been cooked in the butter, you add ¾ pound fresh mushrooms, sliced, or, if these are out of season, 4 ounces of the dried, imported mushrooms, soaked, drained, well wrung out, and cut into rather large pieces.

580. RISOTTO WITH MUSSELS VENETA
Risotto con peoci alla veneta

2 cups Italian rice
2 pounds mussels
4 tablespoons oil
4 cloves garlic, bruised
6 tablespoons butter
1 small onion, chopped
4 cups Fish Bouillon [No. 325], or more as needed
Salt and freshly ground pepper

Wash the mussels in several waters, scrub well, trim off their "beards," put them in a large pot in which 2 garlic cloves have already been browned in 2 tablespoons of oil. Cook tightly covered over brisk heat until the shells open. Drain the mussels in a colander over a bowl to catch the liquid, extract the mussels from their shells, and strain their liquid through a cheesecloth-lined sieve. Heat the remaining 2 tablespoons of oil and 2 tablespoons of the butter with the other 2 cloves of garlic and the chopped onion in a large heavy pot over a medium flame. As soon as the mixture begins to turn golden, remove the garlic, add the rice, season very lightly with salt and pepper, and stir for 2 minutes until the rice is coated with butter. Add the hot mussel liquid, stir, and continue cooking for about 20 minutes over a brisk flame, adding, from time to time, the fish bouillon as the rice requires it. Just before the *al dente* stage is reached, fold in the mussels and complete the cooking. Remove the pot from the fire and add the rest of the butter, divided into small pieces. Let the risotto rest a few minutes on a corner of the stove and turn it onto a well-heated serving platter. *Serves 6.*

581. RISOTTO NAPOLETANA
Risotto alla napoletana

This has the same ingredients and is prepared in the same way as Risotto with Butter and Parmesan Cheese [No. 572] except for the addition of the following sauce:

½ pound lean salt pork, diced and parboiled for 10 minutes
2 tablespoons oil
A chopped mixture:
  1 onion
  1 stalk celery
  1 clove garlic
  A few basil leaves
1½ pounds tomatoes, peeled, seeded, drained, and chopped
Salt and freshly ground pepper

Brown the parboiled, diced pork in the oil in a frying pan over medium heat until it is crisp and brown, remove it with a slotted spoon, and keep it hot. Add the chopped mixture to the oil in the pan and, as soon as it begins to brown, add the tomato pulp. Season with salt and pepper and cook for 15 minutes. Add the diced pork, mix well, pour into sauce bowl, and serve on the side with the rice. *Serves* 6.

582. RISOTTO PAESANA
Risotto alla paesana

2 cups Italian rice
2 tablespoons oil
1 onion, chopped
¼ pound asparagus tips
½ pound zucchini (or other summer squash), sliced
¼ pound shelled peas
¼ pound lima beans
5 cups White Bouillon [No. 323], or more as needed
1 pound tomatoes, peeled, seeded, drained, and chopped
1 cup grated Parmesan cheese
4 tablespoons butter
1 teaspoon salt
¼ teaspoon freshly ground pepper

Lightly brown the onion in the oil in a large, heavy pot over medium heat. Add the peas, asparagus tips, zucchini, and beans. Cook a moment to blend the flavors well, add the tomatoes, and season with salt and pepper. Bring to a boil, add the rice, stir, and, little by little, add enough bouillon to keep the rice moist. Cook for about 20 minutes, or until the rice is just *al dente*. Season with the butter and several tablespoons of grated Parmesan cheese, let it rest a

good minute at the corner of the stove, turn it out onto a well-heated serving platter, and pass the rest of the grated Parmesan on the side. *Serves 6 to 8.*

583. RISOTTO WITH PEAS AND HAM
Risotto con pisellini freschi e prosciutto

Prepare 1 recipe Risotto with Butter and Parmesan Cheese [No. 572]. Just before serving, add to it the following, cooked as noted below:

3 ounces ham fat, chopped
2 tablespoons oil
1 onion, chopped
½ pound shelled tiny peas (or 1 box frozen, thawed petits pois)
Salt and freshly ground white pepper
Pinch sugar
¼ pound ham (fat and meat included), cut in strips

Cook the onion in the ham fat and oil in a heavy skillet over medium heat and, as soon as it begins to turn golden, add the peas; season lightly with salt, a pinch of pepper, and a pinch of sugar. Add a few tablespoons of water, cover, and cook gently for about 10 minutes, or until the peas are just tender. A few minutes before removing the pan from the stove, stir in the ham strips. *Serves* 6.

584. RISOTTO WITH SAUSAGE AND MUSHROOMS
Risotto con salsiccia e funghi

2 cups Italian rice
6 tablespoons butter
1 small onion, chopped
½ pound sweet Italian sausage, removed from its casing
12 little whole sausages
½ pound mushrooms, sliced (or substitute 3 ounces dried, imported mushrooms soaked for ½ hour in water, squeezed dry, and cut into fairly large pieces)
½ cup dry white wine
5 cups White Bouillon [No. 323], or more as needed
1 cup grated Parmesan cheese
Salt and freshly ground pepper

Lightly brown the chopped onion with 3 tablespoons of butter in a large, heavy pot over medium heat. As soon as it turns golden, stir in the sausage meat and mushrooms, season lightly with salt and pepper, and cook for a few moment crumbling the sausage with a fork. Add the wine and cook until it has completely evaporated. Add the rice, stir, and cook until the rice is well coated with butter. Add 3 cups of bouillon and the whole sausages. Continue cooking over a brisk flame, uncovered, for about 20 minutes, adding a little bouillon from time to time as it is needed. When the rice has reached the *al dente* stage, remove it from the fire and add the remaining butter in small pieces with several tablespoons of the grated cheese. Let it rest for a minute on the corner of the stove, turn it out onto a hot serving platter, and serve the remaining cheese on the side. *Serves 6 to 8.*

585. RISOTTO SBIRRAGLIA
Risotto alla sbirraglia

2 quarts water
½ pound lean veal
¼ pound lean raw ham, chopped
1½ pounds raw chicken meat (reserving the skin, bones and giblets for use as described below), diced
Aromatic vegetables:
   1 carrot, sliced
   1 onion, sliced
   2 stalks celery with leaves, sliced
Bouquet Garni:
   1 bay leaf
   2 sprigs parsley
   ½ teaspoon dried thyme
A chopped mixture:
   ¼ pound lean raw ham
   1 small onion

1 small carrot
1 stalk celery
6 tablespoons butter
½ cup dry white wine
3 tomatoes, peeled, seeded, drained, and chopped
2 cups Italian rice
1 cup grated Parmesan cheese
Salt and freshly ground pepper

Prepare a well-flavored bouillon in a large heavy pot with the following: 1½ quarts water, the veal, ham, chicken giblets, skin, bones, aromatic vegetables, Bouquet Garni, and a pinch of salt; cook for 2½ hours over moderate heat. Strain and add a little water, if necessary, to make 5 cups. Reserve the veal for another use. In another large pot, brown the chopped mixture in 2 tablespoons of butter over medium heat and, as soon as it turns a light brown, add the diced chicken, season with salt and pepper, mix well, and cook for 5 minutes. Add the wine and cook until it has completely evaporated. Add the tomatoes and continue cooking for 8 minutes. Add the rice and 3 cups of the bouillon, bring to a boil, and cook, uncovered, for about 20 minutes, or until the rice is *al dente*, adding a little more bouillon from time to time as the rice requires it. Remove it from the fire, add the rest of the butter, in small pieces, and a little grated Parmesan cheese. Let it rest for a good minute on the corner of the stove, turn it out onto a well-heated serving platter, and serve it with the rest of the cheese on the side. *Serves 6.*

Risotto with Shrimp (No. 586): see page 209

Risotto Siciliana (No. 587):
see *page 209*

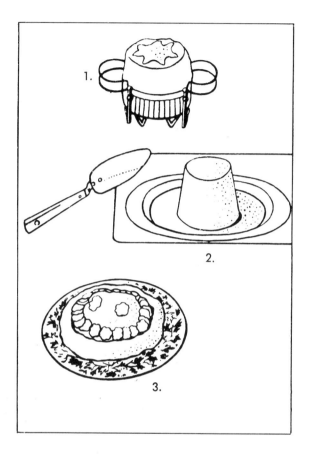

1. Cheese Soufflé (No. 630). The decoration on top of the soufflé in this presentation may be achieved by placing ¼ cup Béchamel (*see* No. 18), 1 tablespoon chopped parsley, and 2 tablespoons grated Parmesan cheese in the blender container and whirling for a few seconds. The resulting mixture may be spooned over the top of the soufflé (using a very light touch) 5 minutes before the soufflé is to be served. Do *not* remove the soufflé from the oven shelf when topping with the mixture, just slide it out of the oven part way. If you remove it completely from the oven, it may fall.

2. Spinach and Ham Soufflé (No. 637). In this presentation, the molded soufflé has been surrounded with Demi-Glaze Sauce (*see* No. 20)

3. Carrot Flan (No. 606)

586. RISOTTO WITH SHRIMP
Risotto con gli scampi

2 cups Italian rice
1 pound shelled, de-veined shrimp (or scampi if available)
4 cups Fish Bouillon [No. 325], or more as needed
½ cup butter
1 tablespoon oil
A chopped mixture:
  ¼ onion
  ½ small carrot
  ½ stalk celery
2 cups dry white wine
¼ cup brandy
Pinch thyme
Salt and freshly ground pepper

Put the chopped vegetables with 3 tablespoons of butter and the oil in a large, heavy skillet and cook over medium heat until they are lightly browned. Add the wine, brandy, and thyme; and cook until the liquid is reduced by half. Add the shrimp (or scampi) and continue cooking for 10 minutes over moderate heat. Keep this sauce hot while you prepare the rice. Bring the 4 cups of bouillon to a boil in an oven-proof casserole; add the rice, season with a little salt, and let it return to a boil. Put the casserole into a moderate (350°) oven, covered, for about 25 minutes. Toss the rice well with a fork, season with the rest of the butter, and turn it out onto a well-heated serving platter. Cover it with the hot shrimp and sauce and serve at once. *Serves* 6.

587. RISOTTO SICILIANA
Risotto "chi cacuoccioli" alla siciliana

2 cups Italian rice
⅓ pound shelled Fordhook lima beans, or fresh fave beans
⅓ pound shelled peas
3 uncooked young artichokes hearts, trimmed and cut in quarters [see introduction to No. 1578]
½ cup oil
1 onion, chopped
1 teaspoon lemon juice
6 tablespoons butter
1 cup grated Parmesan cheese
Salt and freshly ground pepper

Lightly brown the onion in the oil in a heavy saucepan over moderate heat; add the beans, peas, and artichokes; season with salt and pepper; add a few tablespoons of water, and cook, covered, over moderate heat until the vegetables are tender, about 15 to 20 minutes. Melt 3 tablespoons of butter in a heavy saucepan which has a tight-fitting lid. Add the rice and stir over medium heat for 5 minutes until every grain of rice is coated with the butter. Add 4 cups of water, 2 teaspoons of salt, and the lemon juice. Bring to a boil, stir once, reduce heat to the lowest possible flame, cover tightly, and cook for 18 minutes without stirring. Turn the rice out onto a well-heated serving platter, season with the remaining butter divided into tiny pieces and with the grated cheese. Arrange the vegetables around the border and in the center of the plate. *Serves* 6.

588. RISOTTO WITH SQUID
Risotto con le seppie

2 cups Italian rice
1½ pounds squid
4 cups hot Fish Bouillon [No. 325], or more as needed
½ pound fresh mushrooms
½ cup oil
A chopped mixture:
  2 cloves garlic
  1 small onion
½ cup dry white wine
¼ cup butter
Salt and freshly ground pepper

Clean the squid, cut out the yellowish deposit under the head and ink sac (reserving the latter until needed), remove the bone, wash well, and cut into strips. Clean, peel, and chop the mushrooms, including the stems. Put the oil, a little pepper, and the chopped garlic and onion in a large, heavy pot. Cook over medium heat until these are golden, add the strips of squid, season with salt, cook a moment to blend, add the wine, and cook over moderate heat, covered, for about 15 minutes, stirring from time to time. Add the chopped mushrooms and continue cooking, over very moderate heat, for another 10 minutes. A half hour before serving, bring sauce to a boil and add rice. Mix thoroughly and, as soon as the rice swells and tends to stick to the bottom of the pot, add the boiling bouillon and the contents of the ink sac (if desired). Continue cooking for about 20 minutes, adding a few tablespoons of boiling water from time to time, if necessary. When the rice has reached the *al dente* stage, remove the pot to a corner of the stove, let it rest a good moment, add the butter in small pieces, turn it onto a hot serving platter, and serve. *Serves* 6.

589. RISOTTO WITH SWEETBREADS
Risotto con animelle d'agnello

2 cups Italian rice
½ pound lamb's sweetbreads, soaked, trimmed, and
    blanched [see introduction to No. 1434]
2 tablespoons flour
¾ cup butter
A chopped mixture:
    1 onion
    The peel of 1 lemon (no white part)
2 ounces prosciutto, cut in slivers
½ cup dry white wine
5 cups White Bouillon [No. 323], or more as needed
1 cup grated Parmesan cheese
Salt and freshly ground pepper

Dice the sweetbreads and coat them lightly with the flour. Brown them gently in 2 tablespoons of the butter in a heavy skillet for 10 minutes. Remove from stove and keep hot until needed. Heat 3 more tablespoons of the butter in a large, heavy pot over medium heat, add the chopped mixture and, as soon as the onion turns golden, add the slivered prosciutto; stir, add the wine, and cook until it is entirely evaporated. Add the rice, mix thoroughly, and cook for a few minutes, stirring occasionally, until every grain of rice is coated with butter. Add 3 cups of the bouillon, bring to a boil, reduce heat to moderate, and cook for about 20 minutes; add a little more bouillon, little by little, as it is needed. The rice should have absorbed most of the bouillon by the end of the cooking period, but it should not be dry. When it is just *al dente,* remove it from the stove, add the sweetbreads, the rest of the butter divided into little pieces, and a few tablespoons of the grated Parmesan cheese. Taste for seasoning and mix the sweetbreads and rice lightly. Turn out onto a heated serving platter and serve with the remaining Parmesan cheese on the side. *Serves* 6.

590. RISOTTO VERDE
Risotto verde

2 cups Italian rice
½ cup butter
2 tablespoons oil
1 pound spinach, thoroughly washed and chopped
2 stalks celery, chopped
1 carrot, chopped
1 onion, chopped
4 cups White Bouillon [No. 323], or more as needed
½ cup Italian Meat Sauce [No. 41]
Salt and freshly ground pepper
1 cup grated Parmesan cheese

Heat 3 tablespoons of butter and the oil in a heavy saucepan over moderate heat. Add the spinach, celery, carrot, onion, and 2 tablespoons of water; season lightly with salt and pepper; and cook, covered, over moderate heat for 20 minutes. Purée the mixture through a food mill or in the blender. Return the purée to the pot; add the rice and 3 cups of the bouillon; and continue cooking over a brisk flame for about 20 minutes, adding more bouillon, as necessary. A few minutes before the rice has reached the *al dente* stage, add the meat sauce. Remove the pot to a corner of the stove, add the rest of the butter, and a few tablespoons of grated Parmesan cheese. Let it rest a good minute, turn it onto a hot serving platter, and serve with the rest of the Parmesan cheese on the side. *Serves* 6.

591. "AMERICAN" RICE
Riso alla creola

Wash 2 cups of white rice very thoroughly in several changes of water. Cook it in 6 to 8 quarts of rapidly boiling, lightly salted water for 18 minutes. Drain it into a sieve and set the sieve over simmering water to dry (or place the sieve in a moderate oven) for about 10 minutes. Add 2 tablespoons of butter before serving and fluff with a fork. *Serves* 6.

Alternate method: Lightly sauté 2 cups of white rice in 3 tablespoons of butter in a heavy saucepan over medium heat until every grain is coated. Do not brown. Add 3 cups cold water, 2 teaspoons of salt, and 2 teaspoons of lemon juice. Bring to a boil over a brisk flame. Lower the flame to the least possible heat and cover very tightly. Cook for 18 minutes. Do not stir. The water will have been completely absorbed by the rice. Fluff with a fork before serving.

592. RICE CAGNONE
Riso in cagnone

2 cups Italian rice
6 quarts boiling water
¾ cup butter
3 cloves garlic, bruised
2 tablespoons fresh sage leaves
1 cup grated Parmesan cheese
Salt

Cook the rice in a large pot containing 6 quarts of rapidly boiling, salted water for about 20 minutes and then allow it to dry as described in No. 591. A few minutes before serving, prepare the sauce. Melt the butter in a saucepan over medium heat with the bruised cloves of garlic and the sage leaves; cook until the butter has turned nut brown; remove at once from the stove; and discard the garlic. Turn the rice out onto a hot serving platter. Pour the sauce over it and mix well. Serve the grated cheese on the side. *Serves 6.*

593. FRIED RICE
Riso al salto

This is a characteristically Lombard dish.

1 recipe Risotto Milanese [No. 578]
½ cup butter
1 cup grated Parmesan cheese

Melt a teaspoon of butter in each of 6 small frying pans, each the size of a serving portion. Put a ½-inch layer of cold Risotto Milanese in each pan. Smooth out the surface of each with a wooden spoon. Cook over moderate heat until a golden crust has formed on the bottom; turn out bottom side up very carefully on service platter; heat more butter in the frying pans, slip the little "pies" back and fry them on the other side until they are golden. Serve very hot with grated Parmesan cheese on the side. *Serves 6.*

NOTE: One may also make individual patties and fry them in a large frying pan.

594. INDIAN RICE
Riso all'indiana

This dish is generally served with shellfish, or else with cooked fish accompanied by some appropriate sauce.

Cook 1 cup of white rice in 2 quarts of rapidly boiling, salted water; while it is cooking, stir it from time to time with a wooden spoon. After 15 minutes, drain it into a sieve. Wash it thoroughly under running cold water and drain it again. Spread it out in a thin layer on a large flat pan or baking sheet and dry it out in a moderate oven. Serve in a vegetable dish. *Serves 3.*

595. PILAF
Riso pilaff

2 cups Italian rice, well washed
½ cup butter
1 large onion, chopped very fine
3¼ cups White Bouillon [No. 323]
Salt

Lightly sauté the onion in 3 tablespoons of the butter over moderate heat in an oven-proof pot until it be-

comes limp but not brown. Add the rice, season with a pinch of salt (the quantity will depend on the seasoning of the bouillon), and cook it, stirring occasionally, for 5 minutes over a high flame so that the rice becomes thoroughly covered with the butter. Add the bouillon, bring it to a boil, cover the pot, and put it into a moderate (350°) oven for 20 minutes. Remove it from the oven, turn it lightly into a vegetable dish, add the rest of the butter in pieces, and separate the grains carefully with a fork. The outstanding characteristic of a good pilaf is that each grain of rice is completely separate from every other. *Serves 6.*

596. PILAF WITH CHICKEN LIVERS AND GIBLETS
Riso pilaff di fegatini e rigaglie di pollo

1 recipe Pilaf [No. 595]
½ pound chicken livers, sliced
¼ pound chicken gizzards and hearts trimmed of tough parts, sliced, and parboiled for 20 minutes
6 tablespoons butter
½ cup dry white wine (or Marsala)
2 cups Italian Meat Sauce [No. 41]
Salt and freshly ground pepper

Prepare the pilaf as directed in No. 595. While the rice is cooking, melt half the butter in a pot over medium heat and add the giblets. Cook 5 minutes. Stir in the chicken livers, season with salt and pepper, and cook 5 minutes more, stirring frequently. Remove the chicken livers and giblets with a slotted spoon and keep warm. Add the wine to the juices remaining in the pan and cook until it is reduced by ⅔; then add 1 cup of the meat sauce.

Grease a 10-inch spring mold with the remaining butter, and when the pilaf is done, half fill it with rice. Cover the rice with the chicken livers and giblets and top with the rest of the rice. Put it into a hot (400°) oven briefly to heat through. Remove from the oven, let it rest for a few minutes at the back of the stove, and unmold onto a hot serving dish. Serve with the remaining meat sauce on the side. *Serves 6.*

597. CHICKEN PILAF ITALIANA
Riso pilaff di pollo all'italiana

2 cups Italian rice
1 3-pound chicken
½ cup butter
1 onion, chopped
3 tomatoes, peeled, seeded, drained, and chopped
1 bay leaf
Pinch thyme
4 cups White Bouillon [No. 323]
Salt and freshly ground white pepper

Cut the chicken into the following pieces: 2 thighs, 2 legs, 2 wings (without tip ends), 2 halves of breast, and 2 halves of the back. Brown these lightly in a large pot in 3 tablespoons of butter over high heat; season with salt and black pepper; add the chopped onion; and, when it has lightly browned, add the rice. Cook and stir a few minutes, so that the rice is well coated with the butter. Add the tomatoes, a little pepper, the bay leaf, thyme, and the bouillon. Bring to a boil, cover, and put into a fairly hot (375°) oven for ½ hour. Remove from the oven when the rice has completely absorbed all the liquid and the chicken is tender. The grains of rice should be separate. Add the rest of the butter, put the pieces of chicken in the center of a well-heated serving platter, arrange the rice around them, and serve the whole very hot. *Serves* 6.

598. GREEK PILAF
Riso pilaff alla greca

1 recipe Pilaf [No. 595]
½ pound sweet Italian sausage, cut in ½-inch pieces
½ cup butter
1 small onion, chopped
1 tablespoon oil
2 heads Boston lettuce, trimmed, shredded, parboiled for 3 minutes in lightly salted boiling water, and pressed dry
2 sweet red peppers, roasted, peeled, scraped, and cut into strips [*see* No. 145]
¼ pound shelled fresh little peas (petits pois if available)
Salt and freshly ground pepper

Prepare the pilaf as directed in No. 595. While the rice is cooking, sauté the pieces of sausage in the oil in a small frying pan over medium heat for 5 minutes and reserve. Melt the butter in a heavy saucepan over a moderate fire and lightly brown the onion; add the cooked lettuce, the peas, and the pepper strips; season lightly with salt and a little pepper; and cook gently together for about 10 minutes over moderate heat until the vegetables are tender. When the pilaf is done, add the vegetables and sausage to the rice; turn into a vegetable dish, and serve at once. *Serves* 6.

599. LOBSTER PILAF
Riso pilaff di aragosta

1 recipe Pilaf [No. 595]
6 tablespoons butter
2 cups lobster meat (shelled and trimmed), sliced
2 cups American Sauce [No. 63]
Salt and freshly ground pepper

Prepare the pilaf as described in No. 595. While the rice is cooking, melt 3 tablespoons of butter in a pot over medium heat and add the sliced lobster; season with a pinch of salt and pepper and cook over moderate heat for about 10 minutes. Grease a 10-inch spring mold with the rest of the butter and, when the pilaf is done, fill it with the rice and sliced lobster, in alternate layers, beginning and ending with the rice. Put it into a hot (400°) oven for a few minutes and, as soon as it is thoroughly heated through, remove it to a corner of the stove. Let it rest there for a few moments and unmold onto a round serving platter. Serve the sauce on the side. *Serves* 6.

600. PILAF WITH MUSHROOMS
Riso pilaff con funghi

This is prepared in exactly the same way as Pilaf with Chicken Livers and Giblets [No. 596] except that ¾ pound of mushrooms replaces the chicken parts and they are sautéed in the same manner as the giblets.

601. PILAF WITH SHRIMP OR CRABMEAT
Riso pilaff con granzevola o scampi

This is prepared in the same way as Lobster Pilaf [No. 599] except for two changes: substitute the same quantity of shelled crabmeat, shrimp, or scampi for the lobster and substitute White Wine Sauce [No. 76] for the American sauce.

NOTE: The sauce may be finished off with a few tablespoons of shellfish butter (using crab, shrimp, or scampi) for added flavor. Shellfish butter is prepared by pounding equal amounts of butter and the shells (of the shellfish being used) in a mortar until shells are reduced to a paste; the mixture is then pressed through a hair sieve or, more simply, heated to a boiling point in $\frac{1}{2}$ cup water, strained through a fine sieve, chilled in the refrigerator, and the hardened butter removed from the surface.

602. PILAF WITH SWEETBREADS
Riso pilaff con animelle

1 recipe Pilaf [No. 595]
$\frac{1}{2}$ cup butter
$\frac{1}{4}$ pound mushrooms, chopped
$\frac{1}{2}$ pound sweetbreads, blanched, drained, and sliced
    [see introduction to No. 1434]
$\frac{1}{2}$ cup dry white wine (or Marsala)
2 cups Italian Meat Sauce [No. 41]
Salt and freshly ground pepper

Prepare the pilaf as described in No. 595. While the rice is cooking, melt half the butter in a heavy saucepan over medium heat and add the mushrooms. Cook 3 to 4 minutes, stir in the sliced sweetbreads, season lightly with salt and pepper, and braise for another 3 to 4 minutes. Remove the mushrooms and sweetbreads with a slotted spoon and keep them hot. Pour the wine into the pan and cook until it is reduced by $\frac{2}{3}$. Add $\frac{1}{3}$ of the meat sauce, return the sweetbreads and mushrooms to the pot, cook for a few moments to blend, and remove from the fire. When the pilaf is done, butter a 10-inch spring form mold with the remaining butter, fill it half full with the pilaf, over this put the sweetbread/mushroom mixture, fill the mold with the rest of the rice, and put the whole into a hot (400°) oven for 10 minutes, or until the rice is thoroughly hot. Remove the mold from the oven, let it rest on a corner of the stove for a few minutes, and unmold onto a large, round, serving platter. Serve the remaining meat sauce on the side. Serves 6.

NOTE: This may also be served with the rice pressed into a ring mold, turned out on a platter, and the sweetbreads and the mushrooms placed in the center.

603. TURKISH PILAF
Riso pilaff alla turca

This is prepared in the same way and with the same ingredients as Greek Pilaf [No. 598] except for the addition of 4 tomatoes which are peeled, seeded, drained, chopped, and sautéed (separately from the other ingredients) in 1 tablespoon of butter for 15 minutes. They are added to the rice at the last minute with the other vegetables. Serves 6.

NOTE: $\frac{1}{2}$ teaspoon powdered saffron, soaked for one hour in $\frac{1}{4}$ cup water, may be added to the rice before cooking.

604. PILAF WITH VEAL KIDNEYS
Riso pilaff con rognoni di vitello

This is prepared in the same way as Pilaf with Sweetbreads [No. 602], except that the same quantity of veal kidneys are substituted for the sweetbreads. The kidneys, however, should not be blanched, but trimmed, sliced, and cooked in the same way as the sweetbreads. Serves 6.

FLANS
Flans

Flans, in classic cooking, are open tarts or pies with a sweet filling. They may, however, also be used as light entrées, naturally without sugar and filled with savory ingredients. The flan crust or case may be baked separately and filled at the last moment, just before the flan is to be carried to the table, thus avoiding any chance of a soggy crust; or, like timbales (the molds for which are deeper than those for flans), the crust may be filled before baking. A flan ring is a simple circle of aluminum or steel with 1-inch sides and no bottom. It is placed on a baking sheet and then fitted with pastry. When ready to serve, the flan ring is slid off the baking sheet onto a serving dish and the ring lifted off, leaving an attractive, free-standing pie.

605. FLAN CRUST
Crosta per flan

Prepare 1 recipe of Rich Pastry [No. 1955], omitting the sugar, and roll it out $\frac{1}{8}$ inch thick into a circle about 2 inches larger than your flan ring (flan rings come in varying sizes, but throughout this chapter we are recommending the use of an 8-inch ring). Place the ring on a baking sheet and place the dough over the ring. Lightly press the dough into the bottom of the ring and then, working with your fingers, work the dough to form sides about $\frac{3}{8}$ inch thick. Excess dough may be snipped off with scissors or by simply rolling the rolling pin across the top of the ring. The sides of the ring should be sturdier than the bottom to avoid their breaking when the flan is filled. Press the dough sides so that they are slightly higher than the ring and then, with your fingers and thumb or with the dull edge of a knife, press a decorative border around the top rim of the pastry. Prick holes in the bottom with a fork. For the best results the pastry should now be

213

thoroughly chilled for 2 hours in the refrigerator or it may be frozen (once the pastry is frozen it may be carefully lifted off the baking sheet, well wrapped, and kept for weeks in the freezer); this step may be omitted, but the pastry will "set" during the baking before the sides have a chance to fall if it is first well chilled.

Bake the chilled or frozen pastry in a 400° oven for 15 to 20 minutes. After 7 minutes of baking, prick the bottom again several times; do this very quickly to avoid the loss of too much heat. When the pastry is golden brown, remove from the oven and keep in the flan ring until filled, reheated, and slid off the baking sheet onto a serving dish.

NOTE: If the pastry is not chilled, it may be lined with foil or parchment paper and filled to the top with dried peas or beans. It is then baked for 10 minutes, removed from the oven, the paper and beans carefully lifted out (reserving the beans for future use), the bottom pricked once more with a fork several times, and returned to the oven for another 8 to 10 minutes to brown lightly.

606. CARROT FLAN
Flan di carote

1 baked 8-inch Flan Crust [No. 605], prepared with
    Rich Pastry [No. 1955], omitting the sugar, or with
    Puff Paste [No. 1960]
2 cups hot carrot purée (made with 2 bunches carrots),
    sweetened with 1 teaspoon sugar
4 tablespoons melted butter
1/4 pound tiny, young carrots, boiled for about 15
    minutes or until they are 3/4 cooked, sliced, and
    glazed for 5 minutes in 3 tablespoons butter
1/4 cup grated Parmesan cheese
1 tablespoon chopped parsley

Cook 2 bunches carrots in boiling salted water until tender; drain, scrape carrots if necessary, and purée them in a blender or food mill with 2 tablespoons of the butter and the sugar. Fill the flan crust with this purée; cover the top with sliced carrots; sprinkle with grated Parmesan cheese and melted butter. Heat for 15 minutes in a hot (400°) oven. Sprinkle with parsley just before serving. *Serves* 6.

607. CRABMEAT FLAN
Flan di granzevola

1 baked Flan Crust [No. 605], prepared with Rich
    Pastry [No. 1955] omitting the sugar
3/4 pound crabmeat, flaked

1/4 pound mushrooms, sliced
1 1/2 cups Sauce Normande [No. 52]
3 tablespoons fresh breadcrumbs, finely grated
5 tablespoons butter
Salt and freshly ground pepper

Cook 5 tablespoons of the butter until it is nut brown, add the flaked crabmeat and the sliced mushrooms, season lightly with salt and pepper, and cook over a brisk flame for 8 minutes. Add the Sauce Normande. Fill the pastry case with this mixture, sprinkle the surface with fresh breadcrumbs and the melted butter, and bake in a hot (400°) oven briefly until the top is golden. *Serves* 6.

608. FLAN FINANCIÈRE
Flan alla financiera

1 baked Flan Crust [No. 605], prepared with Rich
    Pastry [No. 1955], omitting the sugar
1 recipe Sauce Financière [No. 32]
1 cup Demi-Glaze Sauce [No. 20]
2 tablespoons breadcrumbs, freshly browned

Combine the Financière and Demi-Glaze sauces and fill the pastry case with this mixture. Scatter the browned breadcrumbs over the top, and bake in a 400° oven until the top is golden. *Serves* 6.

609. FLAN ITALIANA
Flan all'italiana

1 baked Flan Crust [No. 605], prepared with Rich
    Pastry [No. 1955], omitting the sugar
1/2 cup butter
3/4 pound chicken livers, sliced
1/4 pound mushrooms, sliced
1 cup dry Marsala wine
1 1/2 cups Béchamel Sauce [No. 18]
1 cup heavy cream
4 eggs, beaten
1/2 cup grated Parmesan cheese
Salt and freshly grated pepper

Melt 3 tablespoons of the butter in a skillet and sauté the chicken livers for 5 minutes over a very high flame. Season lightly with salt and pepper, remove the livers with a slotted spoon, and keep them warm. In the same butter, sauté the mushrooms for 8 or 10 minutes with a pinch of salt, remove them with a slotted spoon, and add them to the livers. Pour the Marsala into the juices left in the pan and cook until reduced to 1/4 cup. Add the Béchamel and the cream, cook over brisk heat, stirring constantly, until reduced by 1/3, add the livers and mushrooms, remove from the fire, and keep hot. Heat 3 tablespoons of the butter in another skillet over a brisk flame and, when it has turned a rich nut brown, add the beaten eggs. Season with a pinch of salt and scramble them only until creamy and still moist. Add half of the grated Parmesan cheese and mix well. Pour the sauced livers and mushrooms into the crust, cover smoothly with the scrambled eggs, scatter the rest of the grated Parmesan cheese and bits of the remaining butter over the top, and bake in a 400° oven until golden. *Serves* 6.

610. LEEK FLAN
Flan di porri

1 baked Flan Crust [No. 605], prepared with Rich Pastry [No. 1955], omitting the sugar
10 leeks (white part only), sliced
2 cups Béchamel Sauce [No. 18] mixed with ½ cup heavy cream
6 tablespoons butter
3 tablespoons grated Parmesan cheese
Salt and freshly ground pepper

Cook the Béchamel and the cream in a heavy saucepan over medium heat until reduced by ⅓. Melt 3 tablespoons of the butter in a skillet, add the sliced leeks, season with salt and pepper, and cook over moderate heat until they are limp but not brown. Stir in the reduced Béchamel and mix well. Fill the crust with the mixture, sprinkle the top with grated Parmesan cheese and the remaining butter, melted, and brown in a hot (400°) oven for about 10 minutes. *Serves* 6.

Flan Italiana (No. 609)

611. PARMESAN CHEESE FLAN
Flan al parmigiano

1 baked Flan Crust [No. 605], prepared with Rich Pastry [No. 1955], omitting the sugar
2 cups heavy cream
4 tablespoons butter
¾ cup sifted flour
4 eggs, separated
1¼ cups grated Parmesan cheese
Pinch nutmeg
Salt and freshly grated white pepper

Bring the cream and the butter to a boil in a heavy saucepan; season with a pinch of salt, white pepper, and nutmeg; add the flour in a steady stream; and mix to a smooth, creamy, and very thick consistency. Remove it from the fire and add the egg yolks, beaten, and the grated Parmesan cheese, stirring constantly. Beat the egg whites until stiff peaks form and gently fold these into the filling. Pour the mixture into the crust, smooth the surface, and bake for about 20 minutes, or until golden in a hot (400°) oven. *Serves* 6.

612. SHRIMP FLAN
Flan di scampi

This is prepared in the same way and with the same ingredients as Crabmeat Flan [No. 607], except that slices of shelled and de-veined shrimp (or scampi) are substituted for the crabmeat.

613. SHELLFISH FLAN
Flan con frutti di mare

1 baked Flan Crust [No. 605], prepared with Rich Pastry [No. 1955], omitting the sugar
2 cups raw shellfish (shelled), such as clams, shrimp, crayfish tails, or lobster, cut into bite-size pieces
6 tablespoons butter
2 cups thick Sauce Mornay [No. 56]
Fresh breadcrumbs
Salt and freshly ground white pepper

Cook 2 tablespoons of the butter in a heavy saucepan over medium heat until it is nut colored; add the shellfish; season lightly with salt and freshly ground white pepper; and cook over high heat until just tender (the time will vary slightly according to the fish). Add the Mornay sauce. Fill the case with this mixture, cover the top with grated fresh breadcrumbs and the remaining butter, melted, and brown quickly in a 400° oven. *Serves* 6.

215

GNOCCHI
Gnocchi

Gnocchi are delicious poached dumpling-like preparations. They are typically North Italian, although Roman gnocchi (made with potatoes) are a regional specialty rarely found in Northern home kitchens. A light hand is the watchword for these delicacies, otherwise they will be soggy and leaden.

614. GNOCCHI AU GRATIN
Gnocchi delicati gratináti

3/4 cup sifted flour
3/4 cup butter
2 cups milk
1 cup grated Parmesan cheese
1/2 cup Gruyère (or Swiss) cheese, cut in thin strips
5 tablespoons butter, melted
3 eggs
1 teaspoon salt

Put the unmelted butter with the salt and milk in a saucepan over a moderate fire and bring to a boil. When the butter has melted add the flour all at once and cream it in with a wooden spoon. Continue cooking for 1 minute, pressing the mixture against the sides of the pan until it no longer sticks against the pan. Remove it from the fire and add the Gruyère strips and 1/2 cup of the grated Parmesan cheese. Add the eggs, one at a time, beating well after each addition. Moisten a shallow baking dish with water, turn the paste into it, smooth it down into an even layer about 3/4 inch thick, and let it get completely cold. Turn the cold paste out on a lightly floured board and cut into any desired shapes, such as 3-inch oblongs. Butter an oven-proof dish and line up the gnocchi in it; sprinkle them with melted butter and a little Parmesan; and brown them

*Preparation of Parisian Gnocchi (No. 618).
Here, the dough has been placed in the pastry bag and is being squeezed out into the simmering water. Note the knife being held at the nozzle of the bag, cutting off cylinders of dough as they emerge.*

216

in a hot (400°) oven for 15 to 20 minutes. Serve them very hot with the rest of the grated Parmesan cheese on the side. *Serves 6.*

615. OLD-FASHIONED GNOCCHI AU GRATIN
Gnocchi gratinati all'antica

1 cup sifted flour
2 cups grated Gruyère (or Swiss) cheese
1 1/4 cups milk
1/2 cup butter
3 eggs
3 slices fresh bread, dried in a 200° oven, and grated into crumbs
Pinch nutmeg
3 tablespoons butter, melted
Salt

Put the milk, 1/2 cup butter, nutmeg, and 1/2 teaspoon of salt into a saucepan over a moderate flame. As it approaches a boil and the butter is melted, remove it from the fire. Add the flour all at once, stirring rapidly with a wooden spoon. Return the pot to the fire and stir over a brisk flame until the mixture comes away from the bottom and sides of the pan and forms a ball. Remove from the fire and add the 3 eggs, one by one, beating thoroughly after each addition. Add 1 cup of the grated Gruyère cheese. Bring a liberal amount of salted water to a boil in a large pot, and lower flame to a simmer. Using 2 afterdinner coffee spoons, push small bits of the dough into the simmering water. Since the gnocchi will almost double in size, do not cook too many at one time; simmer them for about 10 minutes. Remove them with a slotted spoon as they are cooked and drain on a damp cloth. When all are cooked and drained, butter a rather deep oven-proof dish and sprinkle the bottom with a little grated Gruyère cheese; arrange the gnocchi in it in layers, sprinkling each layer with more of the grated Gruyère mixed with fresh breadcrumbs; pour the melted butter over the top and brown in a hot (400°) oven for about 15 minutes. *Serves 6.*

616. CREAM GNOCCHI
Gnocchi teneri alla crema

1 cup sifted flour
2 tablespoons potato flour
6 egg yolks
1 tablespoon cornstarch
1 tablespoon superfine sugar
Salt

Pinch cinnamon
Pinch nutmeg
$1\frac{1}{4}$ cups heavy cream
1 cup butter
$\frac{1}{2}$ cup butter, melted
1 cup grated Parmesan cheese

Put the flour, potato flour, egg yolks, cornstarch, sugar, cinnamon, a pinch of salt, and nutmeg in a bowl. Blend them thoroughly, then mix in the cream and pass the mixture through a fine strainer into a heavy saucepan. Add the unmelted butter and place the pot over moderate heat. Beat with a wire whisk as it cooks to prevent lumps from forming. Bring it to a boil and cook it exactly 5 minutes, stirring constantly. By that time you should have a rather heavy, but smooth and creamy, mixture. Moisten a marble or enameled surface with cold water, turn the mixture out onto it, and, with the flat part of a knife frequently dipped in boiling water, smooth it out until it is $\frac{1}{2}$ inch thick. Let it cool. When solidified, cut into $\frac{1}{2}$-inch squares. Grease an oven-proof dish with a little of the melted butter, arrange the tiny gnocchi in layers, sprinkling each layer with a little grated Parmesan cheese and melted butter. Put the dish into a hot (400°) oven and, when the surface has turned golden, serve with the rest of the grated Parmesan cheese on the side. *Serves* 6.

617. GNOCCHI GENOVESE
Gnocchi alla genovese

These are prepared in the same way as Potato Gnocchi Romana [No. 620] except that Pesto Genovese [No. 93], slightly diluted with a little water in which the gnocchi have been cooked, is substituted for the Italian meat sauce. *Serves* 6.

618. PARISIAN GNOCCHI
Gnocchi alla parigina

$2\frac{1}{2}$ cups milk
$\frac{1}{2}$ cup butter
2 cups sifted flour
6 eggs
1 cup grated Parmesan cheese
2 cups Sauce Mornay [No. 56]
4 tablespoons butter, melted
Pinch nutmeg
Salt

Heat the milk in a saucepan over a moderate flame with $\frac{1}{2}$ cup of butter, $\frac{1}{2}$ teaspoon of salt, and the nutmeg. When it boils, add the flour all at once, working it energetically with a wooden spoon. When the mixture comes away from the sides and bottom of the pan and forms a ball, remove from the fire, let it cool a bit, and add the eggs, one at a time, beating well after each addition. Blend in $\frac{3}{4}$ cup of the grated Parmesan cheese. Put the mixture into a pastry bag fitted with a round tube about $\frac{3}{4}$ inch in diameter. Press out small cylinders of the gnocchi dough about 1 inch long, cutting them off with a knife or scissors into a large pot of simmering, salted water. Cook for about 10 minutes; do not cook too many at one time. Continue until all the paste in the pastry bag has been used. Remove them with a slotted spoon as they are cooked and drain on a cloth. Cover an oven-proof dish with several tablespoons of the Mornay sauce and arrange the cooked gnocchi on top; cover them with the rest of the sauce; sprinkle with the remaining grated Parmesan cheese and the melted butter; and put them into a hot (400°) oven for about 15 minutes, or until the surface is golden. *Serves* 6.

619. GNOCCHI PIEMONTESE
Gnocchi filanti alla piemontese

1 recipe Potato Gnocchi Romana [No. 620]
Flour
$\frac{1}{4}$ pound fontina cheese (or substitute Munster), sliced
$\frac{1}{2}$ cup butter
Optional: 2 truffles, sliced [or No. 1819a]
2 cups Tomato Sauce [No. 19]
1 cup freshly grated Parmesan cheese

Prepare a dough as directed in Potato Gnocchi Romana [No. 620]. Lightly flour your hands, then take small pieces of dough between the palms, and roll them into cylinders or rods $\frac{1}{2}$ inch in diameter. Cut off pieces from the roll about 1 inch long and slightly flatten them in the center by pressing them between the index finger and the thumb. As you form them, set them out on a lightly floured cloth, being careful that they do not touch each other. Drop them into a large pot of simmering, lightly salted water; cook 5 to 7 minutes; and remove them with a slotted spoon to a very large, oven-proof platter. Heat for 5 minutes in a hot (400°) oven. Cover them with very thin slices of fontina cheese and the optional sliced truffles and sprinkle them with the butter that has been cooked over medium heat until it is nut brown. Serve the tomato sauce and grated Parmesan cheese on the side. *Serves* 6.

620. POTATO GNOCCHI ROMANA
Gnocchi di patate alla romana

This typical Roman dish is not to be confused with the semolina gnocchi that are served in restaurants. Neapolitans prepare this dish in the same way and then sprinkle rather coarsely chopped basil leaves over the cooked gnocchi. They call it, in the local dialect, Stranogolaprievete.

4 pounds large, "old" potatoes, peeled, and cut into pieces
3 cups sifted flour
1/2 cup butter, melted
1 cup grated Parmesan cheese
2 1/2 cups Italian Sauce [No. 41]
Salt

It is best to prepare the dough for the gnocchi just before cooking, since it becomes damp and gluey if allowed to sit. Put the potatoes into a large saucepan with sufficient cold water to cover and 2 teaspoons of salt. Bring them to a boil over medium heat and cook for about 18 to 20 minutes. Drain them while they are tender but still firm, and put them through a ricer or food mill onto a lightly floured board or marble surface. Taste, and salt them lightly, if necessary. While they are still warm, work the flour into them until they become a firm, but delicate and soft, dough. Divide the dough into pieces and roll these between well-floured hands to form long cylinders about 1/2 inch in diameter. Cut these into pieces about 1 inch long and pinch the center of each lightly between the index finger and thumb. Line them up on a lightly floured cloth taking care that they do not touch each other. Drop the gnocchi in a large pot of rapidly boiling, salted water and remove them with a slotted spoon as soon as they float to the surface of the water. Drain them on a cloth. When they are all cooked and drained, put them into a large ovenproof dish, sprinkle with butter, several tablespoons of grated Parmesan cheese, and with half the meat sauce. Heat for 5 to 10 minutes in a hot (400°) oven and serve. Serve the rest of the meat sauce and the Parmesan cheese separately. *Serves 6.*

621. SEMOLINA GNOCCHI ROMANA
Gnocchi di semolino alla romana

1 cup semolina
1 quart milk
1/4 cup butter, melted
1 cup grated Parmesan cheese
3 egg yolks, beaten with 1 tablespoon milk
1/2 cup butter, softened
Pinch nutmeg
Salt and freshly ground pepper

Bring the milk to a boil in a saucepan over medium heat and add the semolina in a steady stream, stirring constantly. Add the 1/4 cup of butter, 1 teaspoon of salt, a grating of pepper, and the pinch of nutmeg. Stir vigorously from time to time, scraping the sides and bottom of the pan. Remove from the heat after 20 minutes and add 2 tablespoons of the grated cheese and the egg yolks. Dampen a large, shallow baking dish with water, pour in the semolina, and smooth it out evenly with the flat side of a knife. Chill it for 1 hour, or until it solidifies. Turn it out onto a floured cloth or pastry board and cut out rounds 1 1/2 inches in diameter with a drinking glass or a cooky cutter. Grease a large, shallow baking dish with some of the softened butter and arrange the gnocchi rounds in it in 3 or 4 layers, sprinkling each layer with a little of the grated cheese and dots of softened butter. Put the pan into a hot (400°) oven for about 15 minutes, or until the gnocchi are golden. Serve at once. *Serves 6.*

Preparation of Potato Gnocchi Romana (No. 620). Here, the long cylinders of dough have already been cut into sections, and the final touch is being added by pinching each piece.

622. GNOCCHI VERDI ITALIANA
Gnocchi verdi all'italiana

2 pounds spinach
3/4 cup butter, softened
1/3 cup sifted flour
1/2 cup very dry mashed potatoes
1 cup very fine fresh breadcrumbs
3 eggs, beaten
Milk, if needed
Flour
1 teaspoon fresh sage leaves
1 cup grated Parmesan cheese

Salt and freshly ground pepper
2½ cups Tomato Sauce [No. 19]

Wash and trim the spinach and cook in a heavy saucepan over medium heat, covered, in just the water that clings to its leaves, for 8 minutes; drain it; squeeze it out well with the hands; chop it fine; cook it gently in a skillet with 3 tablespoons of the butter and a dash of salt for 5 minutes and then purée it through a sieve, food mill, or blender. Put the purée in a bowl with the flour, ¼ cup softened butter, mashed potatoes, breadcrumbs, and the beaten eggs. Season with salt and pepper and mix thoroughly. If the resulting dough is too stiff, add a very little milk. Divide the dough into pieces and roll each between well-floured hands into a long cylinder about ¾ inch in diameter. Cut these into 1-inch lengths and hollow each out slightly in the middle by pressing lightly between the index finger and the thumb. As they are formed, line the gnocchi up on a lightly floured cloth so that they do not touch each other. Drop them, a few at a time, into plenty of rapidly boiling, lightly salted water; remove them with a slotted spoon after 6 to 8 minutes; and drain on a cloth. When all are cooked and drained, place them on a large, oven-proof platter and heat in a hot (400°) oven for 10 minutes. Melt the rest of the butter with the sage leaves, heat thoroughly for a few moments, and pour it over the gnocchi. Sprinkle with a little of the grated Parmesan cheese and serve the tomato sauce and the rest of the grated Parmesan on the side. *Serves 6.*

Gnocchi Verdi Italiana (No. 622)

POLENTA
Polenta

623. POLENTA
Polenta

Polenta is best cooked in a copper pan. Italian cooks use a "paiolo," which is a kind of caldron with a rounded bottom and, unlike most copper pots, it is not lined with tin. Polenta meal is usually maize flour (comparable to the American cornmeal) but it may also be made of chestnuts. The following is the traditional Italian method of preparing polenta:

4 cups polenta
2½ teaspoons salt
3 quarts boiling water (or more, as needed)

Bring 2 quarts of water to a boil with the salt in a large copper pot. Bring another quart of water to a boil in a saucepan; this will be needed as the cooking proceeds. As soon as the water boils, add 2½ cups of polenta, stirring constantly with a wooden spoon. Traditionally, the stirring is clockwise only. Reduce the heat. As the polenta thickens, add a little more boiling water. After 15 minutes, add the remaining polenta and continue stirring and cooking, adding boiling water when it becomes too thick. The polenta should cook for about 1 hour; it will be more digestible and lose any underlying bitterish taste if the cooking can be extended that long. However, it is cooked when it comes easily away from the sides of the pan. The polenta may then be enjoyed soft and very hot, accompanied by any one of a number of sauces and garnishes; or it may be allowed to cool and harden, cut into various shapes, sprinkled with fresh butter and grated Parmesan cheese, arranged in layers with various fillings between, and baked, etc. The sliced, hardened polenta may be substituted for bread, especially when it is accompanied by a good gravy or a dish of braised meat.

Alternate method:
If Italian polenta is not available, bring 4 cups of water

to a rapid boil with 2 teaspoons of salt in the top half of a double boiler directly over a brisk flame. When the water is at a rolling boil, slowly pour in 1 cup of water-ground cornmeal (white or yellow), stirring constantly. Cook until it thickens slightly. Then place it into the bottom half of the double boiler containing boiling water. Simmer for 45 minutes, stirring occasionally.

624. POLENTA CASALINGA
Polenta col sugo alla casalinga

This is an excellent winter dish that handsomely complements roast pork or hot sausage.

Prepare 1 recipe hot Polenta [No. 623]. Turn it out into a deep, heated serving dish, sprinkle a little grated Parmesan cheese over it, and pour over it about 1 cup of Meatless Sauce [No. 73]. Serve another cup of the sauce on the side and a generous amount of grated Parmesan. *Serves 6.*

NOTE: The pan gravy from a pork roast may be substituted for the meatless sauce.

625. POLENTA CIOCIARA
Polenta pasticciata alla ciociara

Ciociare, *it will be recalled from other recipes, are the peasant women of the Roman countryside.*

4 cups hot Polenta [No. 623]
1 recipe Tomato Sauce [No. 19]
½ pound rump of beef, ground
⅓ cup butter
3 ounces dried, imported mushrooms, soaked ½ hour in warm water, squeezed dry, and cut into rather large pieces
½ pound sweet Italian sausage meat
½ pound mozzarella cheese, thinly sliced
1 cup grated Parmesan cheese
Salt and freshly ground pepper

Prepare the tomato sauce, adding ½ pound of ground beef to the other required ingredients. Turn the hot polenta out on a marble or enameled surface that has been dampened with water and smooth it out ¼ inch thick with the flat part of a broad knife, dipped frequently into boiling water. Let it cool and then cut into 2- by 4-inch pieces. Melt 3 tablespoons of butter in a large, heavy pot, add the mushrooms, cook for a few seconds over medium heat, add the sausage meat, season with a pinch of salt and pepper, cook for 5 minutes, and then add the tomato sauce. Butter a large baking dish; arrange 3 or 4 layers of the sliced polenta in it, placing them lengthwise in the first

layer and crosswise in the next; and cover each layer with several tablespoons of the sauce, a few slices of mozzarella, and a little of the grated Parmesan cheese. Cover the top layer with a little of the sauce and a few bits of butter. Put the dish into a hot (400°) oven for 15 minutes and serve very hot. Serve the rest of the Parmesan cheese on the side. *Serves 8.*

626. POLENTA FRITTERS LODIGIANA
Frittelle di polenta alla lodigiana

3 cups hot Polenta [No. 623]
2 eggs, beaten
Breadcrumbs
Fat for deep frying
2 cups Tomato Sauce [No. 19]

Pour the polenta out on a smooth surface as described in the preceding recipe to a thickness of ½ inch. Let it cool and cut out small circles with a cooky cutter or a drinking glass. Dip each of these into beaten egg, sprinkle with fresh breadcrumbs, and fry in deep hot (375°) fat. Drain them when they are a deep gold, put them on a serving platter, and serve them with the tomato sauce. *Serves 4.*

627. POLENTA LOMBARDA
Polenta con gli uccelli

This is a North Italian specialty, served often in Lombardy.

1 recipe Polenta [No. 623]
¼ cup butter
1 onion, chopped
1 teaspoon fresh sage leaves (or ¼ teaspoon dried)
2 ounces salt pork, diced and parboiled for 10 minutes
3 ounces dried, imported mushrooms, soaked ½ hour in warm water and squeezed dry
6 very small squab or woodcock
½ cup dry white wine
Salt and pepper
Fat for deep frying

Prepare slices of cold polenta about 4 inches square and ½ inch thick, as described above [No. 625]. Brown the chopped onion in the butter with a few sage leaves in a large, heavy skillet. Add the salt pork dice and the mushrooms and cook for 5 minutes. Add the small birds and wine, season with salt and pepper, and cook over a brisk flame until the wine has completely evaporated. Cover the pan and cook for another 15 minutes over very low heat. Plunge several of the polenta slices into deep hot (375°) fat and remove them when they are a golden brown; repeat until all are browned. Put them on a serving platter and cover them with the birds, pouring over them the pan juices, pork dice, and mushrooms. *Serves 6.*

NOTE: In Italy, songbirds such as thrushes or larks are the proper ingredients for this dish.

628. POLENTA ROMAGNOLA
Polenta pasticciata alla romagnola

This is prepared in the same way as the preceding Polenta Ciociara [No. 625], except that Bolognese Sauce [No. 68] is substituted for the tomato sauce and a few tablespoons of Béchamel Sauce [No. 18] are spooned between each layer of polenta. *Serves 8.*

629. POLENTA WITH VEAL
Polenta con oseleti scampai

This is a specialty of Venetian cooking.

6 large, ¾-inch-thick slices of cold Polenta [No. 623]
½ pound very lean salt pork, cut into 24 large cubes, ¾ inch thick
24 thick mushroom slices
12 chicken livers
24 slices of fillet of veal, ¼ inch thick and 2 inches square
12 thick slices of veal sweetbreads, soaked and blanched [*see* introduction to No. 1434]
¾ cup butter
1 teaspoon fresh sage leaves (or ¼ teaspoon dried)
Salt and freshly ground pepper

Cut each of the livers in half, season them with salt and pepper, and brown them lightly for 3 minutes in a skillet in 1 tablespoon of butter. Parboil the salt pork cubes for 15 minutes. Cut each of the 6 slices of sweetbreads in half (they should be the same size as the pieces of veal). Using 6 small metal skewers, alternate the pieces of the salt pork, liver, mushroom, veal, and sweetbread, inserting an occasional sage leaf at intervals. Season with salt and pepper and brush with melted butter. Broil them for about 5 minutes on each side under a high flame, basting often with more melted

butter. While these are cooking, sauté the slices of cold polenta in butter until golden brown, put them on a hot serving plate, and arrange 1 skewer over each slice. Remove the meats from the skewers at the table. *Serves 6.*

ENTRÉE SOUFFLÉS
Soufflés

A soufflé, briefly, is a very thick Béchamel sauce combined with egg yolks and a flavoring agent or purée (fish, meat, vegetables, or cheese), into which stiffly beaten whites of eggs are folded. The mixture is turned into a mold or baking dish and then baked in the oven until more than doubled in size and the top browned.

A beautifully puffed and browned soufflé is one of the glories of any cook's repertoire, and its successful preparation is not difficult, if one adheres to a few simple rules.

Since egg whites are the only leavening agent in a soufflé, special care must be taken in beating and folding them into the mixture. The bowl in which they are beaten must be absolutely dry and clean. If you are fortunate enough to have an *unlined* copper bowl, this makes the best container, but a stainless steel or porcelain bowl will give satisfactory results. An electric mixer or hand beater is satisfactory, but the whites will rise even higher if they are beaten with a large wire whisk. The egg whites must not contain even a particle of yolk or they will not rise sufficiently. They should be at room temperature, not taken directly from the refrigerator. They should be beaten just until they stand in soft peaks or until they will remain in the bowl when it is turned upside down; they should not be beaten until they are dry. The sauce into which the whites are folded must be thick, but not so heavy and gummy as to cause the whites to break down when they are folded in. The temperature of the sauce should be warm; if it is cold, it will have become too thick. Best results will be achieved if a small amount of the beaten whites, about $^1/_5$, is first folded, or even stirred, into the sauce before gently folding in the remainder.

Traditionally, a soufflé dish is of white porcelain and the outside is fluted. However, Pyrex, earthenware, or even metal molds can be satisfactory. The soufflé batter, when poured into the baking dish, should come to within about an inch of the top, or, for a spectacular effect, fill the dish to the top and tie a collar of a double thickness of wax or brown paper around the bowl so that it extends 4 or 5 inches above the top edge of the dish; the soufflé will thus be guaranteed to rise straight up out of the dish and give the appearance of a "hat." The dish (and collar, if used) should be generously buttered and sprinkled with breadcrumbs or grated cheese, before pouring in the batter; roll or shake the dish so that it is evenly coated; and then knock out excess crumbs or cheese by inverting the dish and tapping it lightly.

The cooking time and temperature may be varied as experience and the temperament of your oven dictate, but excellent results will be obtained by baking it in an oven preheated to 400° and reducing the heat to 375° when the soufflé goes in. Bake at this temperature for 30 to 35 minutes. The dish should always be placed in the middle level of the oven. Test the soufflé for doneness by inserting a sharp knife into the center; if the knife comes out clean, the souffle is done.

A baked soufflé will collapse very quickly, once it is removed from the oven. Hence, never keep a soufflé waiting for your guests, but keep them waiting for it. Waiting in happy anticipation for a soufflé is rarely a chore for any diner.

222

630. CHEESE SOUFFLÉ
Soufflé al formaggio

4½ tablespoons flour
3½ tablespoons butter
1½ cups hot milk
6 egg yolks
1 cup grated Parmesan cheese
7 egg whites
Pinch nutmeg
½ teaspoon salt
¼ teaspoon freshly grated white pepper
1 8-cup soufflé dish, buttered and sprinkled with grated Parmesan cheese

Prepare a thick Béchamel sauce by making a roux with the flour and butter in a heavy saucepan over medium heat, add the hot milk all at once, and stir vigorously with a wire whisk. Add the salt, pepper, and nutmeg and cook for about 5 minutes. Remove from the fire and stir in the egg yolks and all but 2 tablespoons of the grated cheese. Beat the egg whites with a pinch of salt until stiff peaks form. Fold 1/5 of them into the cheese mixture until thoroughly incorporated, and then delicately fold in the remainder. Turn the mixture into a well-buttered 8-cup soufflé dish that has been sprinkled with 1 tablespoon grated cheese. Sprinkle the remaining tablespoon of cheese over the top. Place in a preheated 400° oven, turn the heat down to 375°, and bake for 30 minutes. Test for doneness and bake 5 minutes longer, if necessary. Serve at once. *Serves 6.*

631. GRUYÈRE CHEESE SOUFFLÉ
Soufflé al formaggio a modo mio

Prepare exactly as Cheese Soufflé [No. 630], substituting Gruyère cheese for the Parmesan.

632. CHICKEN SOUFFLÉ
Soufflé di pollo

1½ cups cooked chicken meat, finely diced
4½ tablespoons flour
3½ tablespoons butter
¾ cup hot milk
¾ cup hot Chicken Stock [No. 3]
6 egg yolks
7 egg whites
Pinch nutmeg

Polenta with Veal (No. 629):
see *page 221*

½ teaspoon salt
¼ teaspoon freshly ground pepper
2 tablespoons breadcrumbs
1 8-cup soufflé dish, buttered and sprinkled with the
breadcrumbs

Prepare a thick Béchamel, as in the Cheese Soufflé [No. 630], with the flour, butter, milk, chicken stock, and seasonings. Remove from the fire and add the egg yolks and diced chicken. Follow recipe No. 630 for beating and folding in the egg whites, sprinkle buttered dish with the breadcrumbs, and bake as indicated in No. 630. Bake for 30 minutes, test for doneness, and bake 5 minutes longer, if necessary. Serve at once. *Serves* 6.

633. CHICKEN SOUFFLÉ WITH TRUFFLES
Soufflé di pollo con tartufi

This has the same ingredients and is prepared in the same way as the preceding recipe (Chicken Soufflé, No. 632), except that ½ cup sliced white (or black) truffles are added to the mixture before baking.

634. FISH SOUFFLÉ
Soufflé di pesce alla casalinga

1½ cups cooked, flaked fish (such as salmon, flounder, or halibut)
4½ tablespoons flour
3½ tablespoons butter
¾ cup hot milk
¾ cup hot Fish Fumet [No. 2]
6 egg yolks
7 egg whites
1½ cups Croûtons [No. 332]
Pinch Cayenne
1 teaspoon salt
¼ teaspoon freshly ground white pepper
2 tablespoons fresh breadcrumbs, dried in the oven
1 8-cup soufflé dish, buttered and sprinkled with the
breadcrumbs

Prepare a thick Béchamel, as in Cheese Soufflé [No. 630], with the butter, flour, milk, Fumet, and seasonings. Remove from the fire and add the egg yolks. Gently fold in the flaked fish and croûtons. Follow recipe No. 630 for beating and folding in the egg whites, sprinkle buttered dish with breadcrumbs, and bake in a 375° oven, preheated to 400°. Bake for 30 minutes, test for doneness, and bake 5 minutes longer, if necessary. Serve at once. *Serves* 6.

*Molded Harlequin Soufflé
(No. 645): see page 226*

635. INDIVIDUAL MOZZARELLA SOUFFLÉS
Soufflé in tazzette con mozzarella

Prepare exactly as Cheese Soufflé [No. 630], adding ½ cup finely diced mozzarella cheese to the mixture and baking in 6 individual soufflé dishes that have been generously buttered and sprinkled with grated Parmesan cheese. *Serves* 6.

636. SHRIMP OR SCAMPI SOUFFLÉ ITALIANA
Soufflé di scampi all'italiana

This has the same ingredients as Fish Soufflé [No. 634], except that cooked, diced shrimp or scampi are substituted for the flaked fish and 2 thinly sliced white truffles or Mock Truffles [No. 1819a] are added to the mixture before baking. *Serves* 6.

NOTE: The preparation may be varied by placing alternate layers of the fish, truffles, and soufflé mixture in the dish before baking.

223

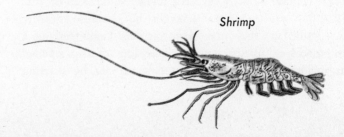

Shrimp

637. SPINACH AND HAM SOUFFLÉ
Soufflé con spinaci e prosciutto

1 cup cooked, puréed spinach (*see* No. 622)
½ cup finely diced boiled ham (or prosciutto)
4½ tablespoons flour
3½ tablespoons butter
1½ cups hot White Bouillon [No. 323]
7 egg whites
6 egg yolks
¼ cup grated Parmesan cheese
Pinch nutmeg
½ teaspoon salt
¼ teaspoon freshly grated white pepper
1 8-cup soufflé dish, buttered and sprinkled with grated cheese

Prepare a thick Béchamel, as in Cheese Soufflé [No. 630], with the butter, flour, hot bouillon, and seasonings. Remove from the fire and add the egg yolks, spinach, ham, and all but 1 tablespoon of the grated cheese. Follow the directions for beating and folding in the egg whites given in No. 630. Sprinkle buttered dish with the remaining cheese and bake in a 375° oven, preheated to 400°, for 30 minutes. Test for doneness and bake 5 minutes longer, if necessary. Serve at once. *Serves 6.*

MOLDED ENTRÉE
SOUFFLÉS
Sformati

Molded entrée soufflés generally follow the same principles and methods of preparation as regular soufflés, but they are cooked more slowly in a metal mold set in a pan of hot water in the oven. Usually they do not contain as many eggs as a regular soufflé and they do not rise to as great a height, but, because they are sturdier, they may be attractively unmolded on a serving platter without collapsing. Test a molded soufflé for doneness in the same manner, by inserting a knife through the top; if it comes out clean, the soufflé is done.

638. MOLDED ARTICHOKE SOUFFLÉ
Sformato di carciofi

2 cups artichoke purée (*see* Note below)
Lemons
1 cup thick Béchamel Sauce [No. 18]
2 tablespoons grated Parmesan cheese
6 eggs, separated
2 tablespoons butter
Flour
1 teaspoon salt
¼ teaspoon freshly ground pepper

Break or cut off the stems of a sufficient number of artichokes to provide 2 cups of purée. Remove all of the outer leaves by bending them back until they snap. Pull or slice off the rest of the leaves just over the heart. With a teaspoon, scoop out the choke. Throughout all of these operations, rub any exposed parts of the bottoms immediately with lemon juice, and, as soon as the bottoms are completely trimmed, drop them in acidulated water; this prevents the bottoms from turning an unattractive gray color. Boil the artichokes in the acidulated water for about 30 minutes, or until they are very tender. Drain and purée the bottoms through a food mill or in the blender. Mix thoroughly together the purée, Béchamel sauce, grated cheese, and the egg yolks. Season with the salt and pepper. Beat the 6 egg whites until they form stiff peaks and gently fold them into the mixture. Butter and lightly flour a 2-quart mold and pour in the mixture. Put it in a pan of very hot water in a moderate (350°) oven for 40 minutes, or until a knife blade inserted in the center comes out clean. Remove the mold from the oven, let it rest for a moment, and unmold on a round platter. Serve at once. *Serves 6.*

NOTE: Frozen artichoke hearts may be substituted for the fresh. Purée these as described in the Note for No. 400.

639. MOLDED BEEF AND POTATO SOUFFLÉ
Sformato di patate con ragù

This dish is actually not a soufflé but it is included in this category since its preparation is similar.

¾ pound top round of beef, braised [*see* No. 1080] and diced
1 pound potatoes

SALE

1. Frittata Savoiarda (No. 711)
2. Shirred Eggs Gourmet (No. 679)
3. Creamed Eggs and Onions (No. 686)
4. Poached Eggs with Red Peppers (No. 656)
5. Omelet Chasseur (No. 718)

¾ cup butter
4 egg yolks and 1 whole egg
4 egg whites
½ cup grated Parmesan cheese
½ teaspoon salt
¼ teaspoon freshly ground pepper
Pinch nutmeg
Flour

Peel the potatoes, cut them in pieces, and cook them in lightly salted water for about 20 minutes. Drain them when they are tender but still firm. Pass them through a ricer or food mill, put them into a heavy saucepan, and place the pan over very low heat for a few minutes, stirring constantly, to dry them thoroughly. Add ½ cup of the butter and the three seasonings and mix thoroughly until the butter is melted and absorbed. Remove from the fire; beat in the egg yolks, the whole egg, and the grated Parmesan cheese. Beat the egg whites until stiff and gently fold into the potato mixture. Butter and lightly flour a 2-quart mold and pour in some of the potato mixture, smoothing it against the sides (reserving a little of the mixture to use as a cover). Fill the center with the braised diced meat, mixed with its gravy, and then cover with a layer of the potato mixture. Put it into a moderate (350°) oven for 20 minutes, or as soon as the surface is well browned. Let it rest for a few minutes and unmold it on a round serving platter. Serve at once. *Serves* 6.

640. MOLDED CHICKEN SOUFFLÉ
Sformato di pollo

⅔ pound cooked chicken meat (weight when trimmed
    and boned)
5 tablespoons butter
1 tablespoon chopped onion
2 ounces boiled ham
1 cup thick Béchamel Sauce [No. 18]
2 tablespoons grated Gruyère cheese
4 eggs, separated
Pinch nutmeg
1 teaspoon salt
Flour

Cook the onion over moderate heat in a small saucepan in 3 tablespoons of butter until it is limp, but not brown, and let it cool. Put the chicken, ham, and onion into the mortar and pound them until they form a paste or blend for a few seconds in the blender; press through a sieve into a bowl. Add the Béchamel, the Gruyère, and the egg yolks; and season with salt and nutmeg. Stir well until blended, then fold in the egg whites

which have been beaten stiff. Butter and lightly flour a 1½-quart mold, pour the chicken/ham mixture into it, and put the mold into a pan of hot water in a moderate (350°) oven for 40 minutes, or till a knife inserted in the center comes out clean. Remove it from the oven, let it rest for a few minutes, unmold it on a round serving platter, and serve at once. *Serves* 6.

641. MOLDED EGGPLANT SOUFFLÉ
Sformato di melanzane

This is prepared in the same way as Molded Artichoke Soufflé [No. 638], substituting a purée of cooked eggplant for the artichoke purée. The eggplant is prepared as follows: Slice 1 large eggplant into ¼-inch-thick slices, and sprinkle each slice with salt. Let the slices drain for 1 hour, then wash off all the salt thoroughly and pat the slices dry with a towel. Dip each slice in a little flour and fry them in 4 tablespoons olive oil until well browned. When all slices are cooked, press them through a food mill or blend in the electric blender for a few seconds. *Serves* 6.

642. MOLDED GAME SOUFFLÉ
Sformato di cacciagione

⅔ pound cooked game meat (weight after boning and
    trimming)
6 tablespoons butter
1 tablespoon chopped onion
3 ounces boiled ham
1 cup thick Béchamel Sauce [No. 18]
4 eggs, separated
Flour
Salt and freshly ground pepper

Cook the onion in 3 tablespoons of butter in a small skillet over medium heat until it is limp, but not brown, and let it cool. Chop the game meat with the ham, place it in a mortar, add the onion, and pound with a pestle until it is a paste (or purée for a few seconds in the blender). Press this paste through a fine sieve into a bowl. Add the Béchamel and the egg yolks, season lightly with salt and pepper, and then fold in the egg whites which have been beaten until they stand in firm peaks. Butter and lightly flour a 1½-quart mold, pour the mixture into the mold, and set it in a pan of hot water in a moderate (350°) oven. Bake for 1 hour or until a knife inserted in the center comes out clean. Remove the mold from the oven, let it rest for a few minutes, and unmold it on a round serving platter. Serve at once. *Serves* 6.

643. MOLDED GOOSE LIVER SOUFFLÉ
Sformato di fegato d'oca

¼ pound canned goose liver (or pâté de foie gras)

¼ pound raw chicken meat (weight after removing skin, tendons, and bones)

3 ounces truffles, or substitute Mock Truffles [No. 1819a]

½ cup heavy cream

3 egg whites

Coarsely chopped ice

Pinch nutmeg

1 teaspoon salt

¼ teaspoon freshly ground pepper

3 tablespoons butter

Flour

1½ cups Marsala Sauce [No. 43]

Put the chicken, truffles, and goose liver through the meat grinder, using a fine blade. Turn this mixture into a mortar and pound with a pestle until it is a finely grained paste. Add the white of 1 egg, slowly, bit by bit, working it in well. Press the mixture through a fine sieve into a bowl. Season with the salt and pepper. Place the bowl in a larger one filled with chopped ice and work the cream into the paste with a wooden spoon a very little at a time. When completely blended, beat the remaining 2 egg whites until they stand in stiff peaks and fold them into the goose-liver mixture. Butter a 1½-quart metal mold with a tight-fitting lid, flour it lightly, pour in the mixture, cover it, and place it in a pan of hot water in a moderate (350°) oven for 1¼ hours. Remove it, uncover, let it rest, unmold it on a round serving platter, and serve at once with the Marsala sauce on the side. *Serves* 6.

644. MOLDED GRUYÈRE CHEESE SOUFFLÉ
Sformato di groviera

½ pound Gruyère cheese, finely diced

5 tablespoons butter

5 tablespoons sifted flour

1½ cups milk, scalded

6 eggs, separated

1 teaspoon salt

¼ teaspoon freshly ground pepper

Pinch nutmeg

1 cup Croûtons [No. 332]

Melt the butter in a heavy saucepan over moderate heat and add the flour. Cook for a few moments, stirring continuously, and then add the hot milk all at once. Cook for 5 minutes, stirring constantly over moderate heat. Remove from the stove and cool slightly. Add the egg yolks, beating vigorously with a wire whisk. Add the seasonings and the Gruyère cheese and mix well. Beat the egg whites until they form stiff peaks, and very carefully fold them into the mixture. Butter and lightly flour a 2-quart metal mold with a lid, pour in the cheese mixture, cover, and put into a pan of hot water in a moderate (350°) oven for 1 hour. Remove it from the oven, let it rest a few moments, and unmold. Garnish with the croûtons. *Serves* 6 to 8.

645. MOLDED HARLEQUIN SOUFFLÉ
Sformato di legumi Arlecchino

⅔ cup each of 5 vegetable purées (carrots, celery, spinach, peas, Belgian endive, etc.)

7 tablespoons butter

1⅔ cups Béchamel Sauce [No. 18]

5 eggs, separated

3 tablespoons grated Parmesan cheese

Flour

Salt and freshly ground pepper

2 cups Spanish Sauce [No. 16], blended with ¼ pound chicken livers, chopped, and sautéed for 5 minutes in 3 tablespoons butter

Each of the vegetables must be puréed separately. This is done by first cooking each in lightly salted water until tender: the spinach and peas will be tender in about 10 minutes, the celery and endive in about 30 minutes, and the carrots in about 35 minutes. Drain, and sauté each with 1 tablespoon of butter in a saucepan over moderate heat for 5 minutes and then purée each by pressing through a food mill or blending in the electric blender for a few seconds.

Add separately to each purée ⅓ cup Béchamel sauce, the yolk of 1 egg, and a little grated Parmesan cheese; season each with salt and pepper; and fold into each 1 egg white, beaten stiff. Butter and flour a 3-quart metal mold and carefully fill it with layers of each vegetable mixture. Arrange the layers so that there is a pleasant contrast of colors. Cover the mold, put it into a pan of hot water in a moderate (350°) oven for 1 hour. Remove from the oven, let it rest a few minutes, and unmold it on a round serving platter. Cover it with some of the sauce and pass the remainder on the side. *Serves* 6.

646. MOLDED MUSHROOM SOUFFLÉ
Sformato di funghi

1 pound fresh mushrooms, sliced

5 tablespoons butter
1 tablespoon chopped onion
$\frac{1}{2}$ cup Italian Meat Sauce [No. 41]
1 cup thick Béchamel Sauce [No. 18]
3 ounces grated Parmesan cheese
2 eggs, beaten
Pinch nutmeg
Flour
$\frac{1}{2}$ teaspoon salt
$\frac{1}{4}$ teaspoon freshly ground pepper

Melt 3 tablespoons of the butter in a heavy saucepan, add the chopped onion, and brown lightly over medium heat; add the mushrooms, stir, and cook over moderate heat for about 7 or 8 minutes. Add the meat sauce and continue cooking 5 minutes more. Turn the mixture into a bowl, let it cool slightly, and then add the Béchamel sauce, cheese, and the eggs. Season with salt, pepper, and nutmeg and mix thoroughly. Butter a 1$\frac{1}{2}$-quart mold and flour it very lightly. Turn the mixture into it, and place in a pan of hot water in a moderate (350°) oven for 45 minutes. Remove it, let it rest for a moment, unmold it on a round serving platter, and serve at once. *Serves* 6.

647. MOLDED PEA SOUFFLÉ
Sformato di piselli freschi

This is prepared and cooked in the same way as Molded Artichoke Soufflé [No. 638], substituting a purée of fresh peas [*see* No. 645] for the artichoke purée.

VOL-AU-VENT
Vol-au-vent

A vol-au-vent is a shell, or case, of baked puff paste that is filled with any one of a variety of sauced ingredients. It makes a very elegant dish, and because of the lightness of the pastry the filling is traditionally of a delicate nature—chicken, sweetbreads, mushrooms, etc. If desired, small cases, or patty shells, may be filled and served individually, although these are not quite as impressive as a large vol-au-vent.

Prepare a full recipe of Puff Paste [No. 1960] and roll the dough out into a rectangle $\frac{1}{4}$ inch thick. Using an 8-inch round baking tin (or an 8-inch round of paper) as a guide, cut out 2 8-inch rounds from the dough with a very sharp knife. Place one of the rounds on a baking sheet moistened with cold water. From the other round cut out an inner circle 5 inches in diameter, leaving a rim 1$\frac{1}{2}$ inches wide. Carefully place this rim on top of the round of dough on the baking sheet so that their outside edges line up perfectly. Cut diagonal gashes about $\frac{1}{8}$ inch deep and spaced 1 inch apart all around the sides of the 2 layers with a very sharp knife. Place the remaining 5-inch round of dough on the baking sheet (this will serve as a lid for the filled vol-au-vent). Brush both rounds with beaten egg, but do not allow the egg to drip over the sides. Put the baking sheet in a hot (450°) oven for 5 minutes, reduce the heat to 375°, and bake for 25 to 30 minutes longer. Both the case and the lid will puff up 5 or 6 times their unbaked height. Remove from the oven, fill at once with any desired filling, and place the lid on top.

If desired, the lid may be baked in position on top of the bottom round and inside the outer rim. This will have the effect of leaving the dough inside the vol-au-vent somewhat undercooked. The lid should be removed after baking and the uncooked dough removed with a fork. If baked in this manner, the quantity of the filling may be increased slightly, as there is more space in the interior of the vol-au-vent. It should be noted that this method of baking will provide a great deal less of the delicious layers of flaky pastry that is the characteristic of puff paste.

As a slightly more elegant variation, the bottom round of dough may be cut from a round fluted form. The top rim of pastry should be slightly smaller and should not extend over the outside edges of the flutes, so that they may be fully visible after baking.

648. VOL-AU-VENT À LA FINANCIÈRE
Vol-au-vent alla finanziera

Prepare and bake an 8-inch vol-au-vent as described above, fill it with 2 cups of hot Sauce Financière [No. 32], cover with its lid, and serve immediately. *Serves* 4.

Vol-au-Vent à la Financière (No. 648)

EGGS

EGGS

Uova

Eggs have a very important place in cooking, not only as the prime ingredient of many egg dishes, but also as a leavening, thickening, or binding agent for which nothing else may be substituted.

Freshness of eggs is of the utmost importance, and a very dependable grocer will probably offer you the best chance of obtaining them. However, the following practical tests may prove useful in establishing the freshness of your eggs.

1.) Plunge the egg into fresh water. If it is absolutely fresh, it will lie horizontal at the bottom of your bowl. If it is a week old, it will turn up at an angle of 45 degrees from the bottom. If it is older still, it will stand vertically on end.

2.) Plunge the eggs into a solution of heavily salted water. If the egg has been laid that very day, it will sink at once to the bottom. Depending on its age, it will float at various levels in the liquid, from the bottom to the top.

3.) If you need a test to use when buying eggs, shake an egg close at your ear. If it is fresh you will hear no sound at all since the egg is full and compact, as a fresh egg should be. If it is old you will hear a characteristic rippling sound.

The average weight of a good egg is 2 ounces.

Throughout most of the egg recipes that follow, you will achieve better results if the *eggs are at room temperature* and not used ice-cold, directly from the refrigerator. The shells of cold eggs will crack more easily on contact with boiling water than eggs at room temperature. If the eggs are chilled, run hot tap water over them for 2 minutes.

649. RAW EGG or PRAIRIE OYSTER
Uovo all'ostrica

This is particularly recommended for convalescents or persons in delicate health. The pleasant flavor is surprising.

Separate an egg, reserving the white for another use. Slip the yolk from its shell into a tablespoon without breaking it, season it with a few drops of lemon juice and a pinch of salt. Eat or serve at once. *Serves 1.*

HOT EGG DISHES

Preparazioni calde

POACHED EGGS

Uova affogate o in camicia

650. BASIC RECIPE
Preparazione di base

Freshness of eggs is particularly important in poaching. The whites of stale, older eggs will not cling to the yolks once they are dropped in simmering water, but will separate, spread, and trail off in wispy threads.

Fill a skillet or shallow saucepan, appropriately sized for the number of eggs to be poached, with water and add some lemon juice or vinegar (about 1 tablespoon for each quart of water), which will facilitate the coagulation of the egg albumen and thus keep it from spreading. Bring the water to a boil and then reduce heat to the barest simmer. Break the eggs and drop them into the water one at a time; or break the eggs one at a time into a teacup and slip them gently into the water. Simmer them for 4 minutes. If the whites do not cover the yolks, very gently push some of the whites over the yolks with a wooden spoon. Remove them one at a time with a skimmer or slotted spoon to a clean cloth and trim off any uneven edges with the point of a sharp knife. The whites should be firm and set, the yolks still soft. It is best to prepare the eggs just before serving them. If this is not possible and they are to be kept for any time, immerse them in slightly salted water until they are needed. They may be reheated by immersing them for 1/2 minute in simmering water.

651. POACHED EGGS WITH ANCHOVIES
Uova affogate con acciughe

6 poached eggs [No. 650]
6 slices toasted bread, cut to the size of the eggs
3 tablespoons Anchovy Butter [No. 108]
12 anchovy fillets, washed free of salt [see No. 220]

Arrange the toast on a hot serving plate, place a poached egg on each piece, and cover each with a teaspoon of anchovy butter and with 2 anchovy fillets in the form of a cross. *Serves 6.*

652. POACHED EGGS CASALINGA
Uova affogate alla casalinga

6 poached eggs [No. 650]
3 tablespoons chopped onion
2 tablespoons oil
1 tablespoon chopped fresh basil (or ½ teaspoon dried)
¼ pound sweet Italian sausage
6 tomatoes, peeled, seeded, drained, and chopped
3 tablespoons butter, melted
3 tablespoons grated Parmesan cheese
1 teaspoon salt
¼ teaspoon freshly ground pepper

Put the onion, oil, and basil into a skillet over medium heat and, as soon as the onion is lightly browned, add the sausage meat (withdrawn from its casing just before using). Crumble the sausage with a fork, cook for 3 minutes, add the chopped tomatoes, season with salt and pepper, and continue cooking for about 10 minutes. Poach the eggs as described in No. 650, but for only 3 minutes. Keep them until needed in lightly salted, warm water. Butter an oven-proof dish and cover the bottom with the sausage and tomato sauce. Put the eggs (thoroughly drained) on the sauce, sprinkle with the grated Parmesan cheese and the melted butter, and put in a very hot (450°) oven for about 2 minutes, or until golden. *Serves* 6.

653. POACHED EGGS GENTILUOMO
Uova affogate alla "gentiluomo"

6 poached eggs [No. 650]
6 tablespoons butter (or more, as needed)
¼ pound mushrooms, sliced
6 tomatoes, peeled, seeded, drained, and chopped
2 tablespoons chopped fresh basil (or 1½ teaspoons dried)
6 slices boiled ham, cut ⅛ inch thick and trimmed to the size of the eggs
6 slices toast, cut to the size of the eggs
1 teaspoon salt
¼ teaspoon freshly ground pepper

Melt 1 tablespoon of butter in a frying pan and add the sliced mushrooms. Cook over moderate heat, covered, for about 8 minutes. Season to taste, and set aside until needed. Cook the tomatoes with 1 tablespoon of butter, the chopped basil, salt, and pepper over medium heat in another saucepan for about 10 minutes. Poach the eggs [see No. 650] and keep them in slightly salted warm water. Sauté the ham very

lightly for 2 or 3 minutes in a frying pan in 1 tablespoon of butter. Brown the toast for 1 minute in bubbling butter in a frying pan over medium heat, place the pieces on a serving platter, put a slice of the grilled ham on each, and top each with a poached egg, well drained. Garnish one side of the platter with small heaps of the mushrooms and the other side with the tomatoes. Serve at once. *Serves* 6.

654. POACHED EGGS ITALIANA
Uova affogate all'italiana

6 poached eggs [No. 650]
4 tablespoons butter
¼ pound veal (or lamb's) kidneys, chopped
Optional: ¼ cup cock's combs [*see* Note to No. 496]
¼ pound mushrooms, sliced
1 cup Italian Meat Sauce [No. 41]
6 slices of truffle, or substitute Mock Truffles [No. 1819a]
6 slices toast, cut slightly larger than the eggs
Salt and freshly ground pepper

Melt 2 tablespoons of butter in a frying pan, add the kidneys and optional cock's combs, season lightly with salt and pepper, and sauté over medium heat for 10 minutes (if lamb's kidneys are used, sauté for only 5 or 6 minutes). Remove the kidneys and cock's combs with a slotted spoon. Add the mushrooms to the pan and cook, covered, for about 8 minutes. Slice the kidneys. Add them, the cock's combs, and the mushrooms to the Italian meat sauce, stir it well, and heat in a saucepan only until it is hot. Poach the eggs as directed in No. 650 and keep them warm in lightly salted warm water until needed. Melt the rest of the butter in a frying pan over medium heat until it bubbles and fry the pieces of toast until golden. Place them on a serving platter, put a well-drained poached egg on each, and cover each with a liberal spoonful of the sauce and top with a slice of truffle. Serve very hot. *Serves* 6.

655. POACHED EGGS MARINARA
Uova affogate alla marinara

6 poached eggs [No. 650]
24 mussels
1 onion, very finely chopped
Bouquet Garni:
   3 sprigs parsley
   $\frac{1}{4}$ teaspoon dried thyme
   1 bay leaf
1 cup dry white wine
1 clove garlic, bruised
2 tablespoons Kneaded Butter [No. 107]
2 egg yolks
$\frac{1}{2}$ cup heavy cream
2 tablespoons chopped parsley
Freshly ground white pepper

Poach the eggs as described in No. 650 and keep in slightly salted warm water. Scrub the mussels under running water, trim off their "beards," put them into a large pot, add the onion, Bouquet Garni, a pinch of pepper, and $\frac{1}{2}$ cup of the wine. Cover, bring to a boil over a brisk flame, and shake the pot from time to time until the mussels are fully open. Turn them into a colander over a bowl to catch all the liquid. Extract the mussels from their shells and strain the liquid in the bowl through several thicknesses of cheesecloth that has been dipped in cold water and thoroughly wrung out. Put the bruised clove of garlic and the rest of the wine into a saucepan and cook over high heat until the wine has been reduced by $\frac{1}{3}$; add the mussel liquid and blend in the kneaded butter. There should be about $1\frac{1}{2}$ cups. Cook over moderate heat for about 10 minutes, but do not allow the sauce to become too thick; it should be about the consistency of very heavy cream. Remove from the fire and add the egg yolks that have been beaten with the cream, stirring continuously. Return to a moderate flame and, stirring constantly, cook only until slightly thickened, about 5 minutes. Do not boil. Remove the garlic and add the mussels during the last minute of cooking. Reheat the eggs for $\frac{1}{2}$ minute in simmering water. Drain them well and place on a serving platter. Pour the sauce over them and sprinkle with chopped parsley. Serve very hot. *Serves* 6.

656. POACHED EGGS WITH RED PEPPERS
Uova affogate con pancetta di lardo e peperoni

6 poached eggs [No. 650]
3 sweet red peppers
2 tablespoons oil
12 slices of very lean salt pork, $\frac{1}{2}$ inch thick
4 tablespoons butter, melted
$\frac{1}{3}$ cup grated Parmesan cheese
Salt and freshly ground pepper

Roast the peppers over the flame on the top of the stove, scrape, seed, and slice them into 1-inch strips [*see*

231

No. 145]. Cook them gently in the oil over moderate heat in a frying pan for 5 minutes. Parboil the salt pork in 2 changes of water for 20 minutes, drain it, and broil it until crisp. Poach the eggs as described in No. 650, and keep them hot in slightly salted warm water. Grease an oven-proof dish with half the melted butter, arrange the slices of broiled salt pork on it, and cover each slice with a well-drained poached egg. Season lightly, garnish with the slices of red pepper, and sprinkle with the grated Parmesan cheese and the rest of the melted butter. Put the dish into a hot (400°) oven for 2 minutes and serve very hot. *Serves* 3.

SOFT-BOILED EGGS

Uova barzotte

657. SOFT-BOILED EGGS
Uova barzotte o semidure

Put the required number of eggs into a saucepan and cover with cold water. Bring to a boil and cook for exactly 4 minutes from the time the boiling begins. Remove the pot from the fire and plunge the eggs into cold water. Shell them quickly and carefully and keep in a bowl of warm water until needed.

658. SOFT-BOILED EGGS ALSACIENNE
Uova barzotte all'alsaziana

6 soft-boiled eggs [No. 657]
1½ cups hot braised sauerkraut [*see* No. 1261]
6 tablespoons Demi-Glaze Sauce [No. 20]
6 slices boiled ham

Prepare the braised sauerkraut and the Demi-Glaze sauce and heat the slices of ham. The soft-boiled eggs should be cooked at the last moment. Spread the sauerkraut on a hot serving platter; arrange the ham slices on top; and place an egg on each slice. Spoon a tablespoon of Demi Glaze sauce over each and serve at once. *Serves* 6.

659. SOFT-BOILED EGGS WITH ANCHOVIES
Uova barzotte all'acciuga

6 soft-boiled eggs [No. 657]
2 tablespoons oil (or butter)
6 slices toast, each cut into 3-inch rounds
3 tablespoons Anchovy Butter [No. 108]
12 anchovy fillets, washed free of salt [*see* No. 220], rolled

Cook the soft-boiled eggs as indicated in No. 657. Prepare the slices of toast and brown them in oil. Arrange the slices on a serving platter and put an egg on each slice; cover each with a teaspoon of hot anchovy butter and decorate each with two rolled anchovies. *Serves* 6.

660. ASPARAGUS TARTS WITH SOFT-BOILED EGGS
Uova barzotte con punte di asparagi

6 tart shells, 5 inches in diameter, made of Rich Pastry [No. 1955], without sugar
24 asparagus tips
2 tablespoons butter
6 soft-boiled eggs [No. 657]
Salt
¾ cup hot Tomato Sauce [No. 19]

Cook the asparagus, using only 3 inches of the tender tips, in lightly salted water for about 10 minutes, or just until they are tender. Drain and then sauté them for 1 minute in the butter in a frying pan over moderate heat. Reserve and keep hot. Prepare the soft-boiled eggs as described in No. 657. Arrange the tart shells, on a platter, put 4 of the asparagus tips in each tart, top with a soft-boiled egg, and cover each with 2 tablespoons of the tomato sauce. *Serves* 6.

661. SOFT-BOILED EGGS WITH EGGPLANT
Uova barzotte con melanzane

6 soft-boiled eggs [No. 657]
3 very tiny globe eggplants (about the size of a large lemon)
Salt
Oil as needed
1½ to 2 cups Sauce Mornay [No. 56]
6 tablespoons butter, melted

Cut the eggplants in half. Make deep incisions in the cut side of each half with a sharp knife, about 1 inch apart and going to within ¼ inch of the skin. Sprinkle a generous amount of salt on each half and allow them to drain upside down on paper towels for 1 hour. Wash off thoroughly, pat dry, and sprinkle with a little oil; place them in a roasting pan containing ½ inch of water; broil them for about 15 minutes under a moderate flame until their flesh is tender. Scoop out as much of the flesh as possible with a spoon, going to within about ⅛ inch of the skin. Be very careful not to break through the skin. It may be necessary to return them to the broiler a second time to tenderize the flesh. Reserve the skins and put the flesh with 2 tablespoons oil in a frying pan over moderate heat for 5 minutes, mashing the pulp as it cooks. Add about twice as much Mornay sauce as there is pulp and cook until thoroughly hot. Prepare 6 soft-boiled eggs as described in No. 657, except boil them for only 3 minutes. Place some of the eggplant mixture in each of the skins, put an egg in each, and cover with the remaining mixture. Sprinkle a little melted butter over each and place in a lightly buttered baking dish. Bake in a hot (400°) oven for about 10 minutes, or until the tops are golden brown. *Serves 6.*

662. SOFT-BOILED EGGS WITH CHOPPED MEAT

Uova barzotte con trito di carne

12 soft-boiled eggs [No. 657]
1 pound chopped beef, lamb, or veal
1 onion, chopped
2 tablespoons butter
1 cup Italian Meat Sauce [No. 41]
1 tablespoon chopped parsley
Salt and freshly ground pepper

Lightly brown the onion in the butter over a medium flame in a frying pan; add the chopped meat and cook for 5 minutes; then add the meat sauce and cook for 10 minutes longer. Correct the seasoning. Soft boil the eggs as described in No. 657. Pour the sauce into a hot, shallow serving bowl, arrange the soft-boiled eggs on top, sprinkle parsley lightly over the whole, and serve at once. *Serves 6.*

FRIED EGGS

Uova fritte

663. FRIED EGGS

It is equally important for fried eggs, as for poached, that the eggs be absolutely fresh. The whites of even slightly older eggs will not adhere to the yolks in a coagulated mass, as they should, but will spread out over the pan in an unsightly manner. A perfectly fried egg should be tender, its white firm, its yolk soft and still slightly runny, and its surface a pale gold, a result best achieved by frying only one or two eggs at a time. They may be fried in butter or oil. Butter is perhaps preferable, since the heat can be regulated by its color; the butter should be hot, bubbling, and golden before the egg is dropped into it, and the heat throughout the cooking should be as high as possible without actually burning the butter or letting it brown.

Heat 2 tablespoons (or 4 tablespoons, if you are cooking 2 eggs) of butter in a medium-sized, heavy skillet over a medium flame. Tin-lined copper is the best type of pan, since it ensures even heat. Break the egg into a saucer or teacup and, when the butter is bubbling and golden, carefully slide the egg into it without breaking the yolk. Quickly push a little of the white over the yolk with a spoon so that it is well covered. Allow the white to firm up for a moment so that it will not run or spread out when the pan is tilted. Now tilt the pan slightly so that the butter is in a small pool on one side of the pan. Quickly begin basting the surface of the egg with the golden butter, being careful to regulate the heat so the butter does not burn. After basting for 1 or 2 minutes, begin testing for doneness by shaking the pan slightly; when the white ceases to quiver like jelly, it has firmed up sufficiently and the egg is done. Remove it carefully from the pan with a broad spatula and transfer to a hot plate or serving dish.

664. FRIED EGGS AMERICANA

Uova fritte all'americana

6 round slices of eggplant, ¼ inch thick
Salt
4 tablespoons oil
6 slices of ham, ⅛-inch thick and trimmed to the size of the eggplant slices, broiled
6 fried eggs [No. 663]
1 cup Tomato Sauce [No. 19]

Sprinkle the eggplant slices liberally with salt and allow them to drain off their moisture on paper towels for 1 hour. Wash the slices thoroughly under running water, pat dry, and then sauté them in the oil for about 5 minutes. Prepare the tomato sauce, broil the ham, and keep both hot. Fry the eggs as described in No. 663. Arrange the eggplant slices on a hot serving platter, place a slice of ham over each, and top with a fried egg. Serve the tomato sauce on the side. *Serves 6.*

Fried Eggs Italiana (No. 665)

Cook the spaghetti in a large pot of salted, boiling water until just *al dente*. Drain, turn onto a large serving dish, pour 1/2 cup of the melted butter over it, sprinkle with the basil and the grated cheese, and mix thoroughly. Keep warm. Sauté the tomato slices very quickly in the oil in a skillet over a brisk flame, being careful not to overcook them. When just tender, arrange them on top of the spaghetti. Fry the eggs as described in No. 663 and keep warm. Dip the slices of mozzarella in beaten egg and then in flour; fry until golden in the remaining butter over a brisk flame. Arrange these also on top of the spaghetti and place a fried egg on top of each slice. *Serves 6.*

665. FRIED EGGS ITALIANA
Uova fritte all'italiana

6 fried eggs [No. 663]
6 slices of ham, cut 1/8 inch thick
1/2 pound mushrooms, sliced
Oil as needed
1 clove garlic, crushed in the garlic-press
Pinch salt
6 slices toast, cut in rounds the size of the fried eggs

Lightly fry the slices of ham in a little oil in a heavy skillet over medium heat; remove the slices and keep hot. Cook the sliced mushrooms in the same oil for 8 minutes with the crushed garlic and salt. Fry the eggs as described in No. 663 and brown the toast in oil until it is golden. Arrange the toast in a circle on a hot, round serving platter; place a slice of the fried ham between each round of toast; place a fried egg on each piece of toast; and garnish the center with the mushrooms. *Serves 6.*

666. FRIED EGGS NAPOLETANA
Uova fritte alla napoletana

3/4 pound spaghetti
12 thick tomato slices
2 tablespoons chopped basil
2 tablespoons oil
3/4 cup butter, melted
1/2 cup grated Parmesan cheese
6 fried eggs [No. 663]
6 1/4-inch-thick slices mozzarella cheese, about the size of a fried egg
1 egg, beaten
Flour
Salt

667. FRIED EGGS WITH PEAS AND HAM
Uova fritte con pisellini al prosciutto

1 1/2 cups young peas, shelled (or 1 package frozen petits pois)
3 tablespoons butter
2 tablespoons chopped onion
2 ounces prosciutto, cut into fine slivers
6 fried eggs [No. 663]
Salt and freshly ground pepper

Cook the onion in the butter over moderate heat in a heavy saucepan until it is soft and transparent, but not brown. Add the peas and 2 tablespoons of water, season lightly, cover, and cook for about 10 minutes, or until the peas are tender. A few minutes before taking the peas off the stove, add the slivers of prosciutto. While the peas are cooking, fry the eggs as described in No. 663. Put the peas in the center of a hot serving platter, and surround them with the fried eggs. *Serves 6.*

668. FRIED EGGS PIEMONTESE
Uova fritte alla piemontese

1/2 recipe Risotto with Butter and Parmesan Cheese [No. 572]
2 tablespoons butter
6 ripe tomatoes
6 fried eggs [No. 663]
1 truffle, thinly sliced [or No. 1819a]
Salt and freshly ground pepper

Prepare the risotto and keep warm. Slice off the tops of the tomatoes and press out as many of the seeds and as much of the juice as possible without crushing them. Place them in a baking dish, dot the top of each with a little butter, season with salt and pepper, and bake

234

them for 15 minutes in a moderate (350°) oven. Fry the eggs as described in No. 663 and keep warm. Turn the rice out onto a hot serving dish. Arrange the tomatoes on the rice in a circle around the edge of the dish and place a fried egg on each tomato. Garnish with the truffle slices in the center. *Serves* 6.

669. FRIED EGGS WITH SAUSAGE
Uova fritte con luganega

1½ cups Tomato Sauce [No. 19]
6 sweet Italian sausages
6 fried eggs [No. 663]
6 slices toast, cut into rounds the size of a fried egg
Butter as needed

Prepare the tomato sauce and let it reduce until quite thick. Broil the sausages under a hot flame and cut them into 1-inch pieces. Fry the eggs in butter as described in No. 663. Keep them warm while you fry the toast in butter until it is golden. Put the pieces of toast on a serving platter, place the fried eggs and grilled sausages over them, and put a thin border of the thick tomato sauce all around them. *Serves* 6.

670. FRIED EGGS ROMANA
Uova fritte alla romana

2 pounds spinach, well washed
4 tablespoons butter
1 clove garlic, crushed in the garlic-press
6 anchovy fillets, washed free of salt and cut into small pieces [*see* No. 220]
3 tablespoons oil
6 fried eggs [No. 663]
Salt

Cook the spinach, in only the water that clings to its leaves after washing, in large saucepan, tightly covered, over medium heat for 8 minutes. When it is tender, drain it well, let it cool, press out excess water with your hands, then sauté it very gently in a frying pan with the butter and a pinch of salt for 5 to 10 minutes. Fry the eggs as described in No. 663. Sauté the garlic and anchovy pieces in the oil for 1 minute. Place the spinach in the center of a hot, round serving platter. Pour anchovies and garlic over the spinach and surround it with a circle of fried eggs. *Serves* 6.

EGGS IN THE SHELL
Uova al guscio

671. EGGS IN THE SHELL
Uova al guscio o alla coque

The best way to cook eggs in their shells without breaking the shell when it touches simmering water is to make the tiniest possible hole in the pointed end of the shell with a fine pin. The eggs must also be at room temperature. Then lower the eggs one at a time into the water with a tablespoon. Adjust the heat so that the water just simmers. The cooking time may vary according to personal taste, but 4 minutes in simmering water should produce an egg whose white is firm and yolk soft.

672. EGGS SURPRISE
Uova al guscio in sorpresa

6 extra-large eggs
¼ cup Italian Meat Sauce [No. 41]
¼ cup heavy cream
2 tablespoons dry Marsala wine
1 teaspoon salt
¼ teaspoon pepper
Pinch nutmeg
Flour
6 slices buttered toast

Prick the pointed ends of the eggs in a V-shape with a rather large needle (a larding or knitting needle will serve). Then make a small hole at the opposite, round end of the shell with a pin. Blow into the small hole making the contents of the egg run out of the larger hole at the other end. Drain the contents of 4 of the eggs into a bowl. Drain the contents of the remaining 2 eggs into another bowl and reserve for another use. Purée the meat sauce through a food mill or in the electric blender. Add the cream, meat sauce, Marsala, salt, pepper, and nutmeg to the bowl with the 4 eggs and beat the mixture with a fork. Pour the mixture into a pastry bag fitted with a very fine round tube and fill the empty shells of all 6 eggs with the mixture. Seal the holes of each egg with a stiff flour-and-water dough. Cook the eggs in lightly salted, boiling water for 4 minutes and serve in eggcups with buttered toast on the side. *Serves* 6.

SHIRRED EGGS
Uova al piatto

673. SHIRRED EGGS
Uova al piatto o al tegamino

Most recipes for shirred eggs specify that the eggs should be baked in the oven, but, since the enveloping heat of the oven tends to toughen eggs, a better method is to partially cook them on top of the stove and then broil them for a minute or two under a hot flame. Shirred eggs should be cooked in shallow fireproof dishes or ramekins about 4 inches in diameter. Either 1 or 2 eggs may be placed in each ramekin.

Melt a tablespoon of butter in a ramekin over medium heat on top of the stove. Break 1 or 2 eggs into the dish and cook for about $\frac{1}{2}$ minute until a layer of white has filmed the bottom of the dish. Remove from the heat and baste with a little of the butter. Season the white lightly with salt. If you are preparing several ramekins, they may all be prepared in this way up to this point and set aside in a warm place until just before serving. When ready to serve, place the ramekins under a very hot broiler flame. After 10 seconds, baste each with the butter in the dishes. Baste again in 30 seconds. The eggs will be done in less than 2 minutes of cooking if your broiler is hot enough, so watch them carefully to avoid overcooking.

674. SHIRRED EGGS ALI BABA
Uova al piatto "Alì Babà"

Prepare shirred eggs as described in the preceding recipe with Anchovy Butter [No. 108] instead of with plain butter. Slip them carefully out of the ramekins onto pieces of hot toast that have been spread with pâté de foie gras. Garnish the top of each yolk with half an anchovy fillet and serve at once. *Serves 6.*

675. SHIRRED EGGS WITH ANCHOVIES
Uova al piatto con acciuga

Prepare shirred eggs as described in No. 673 with Anchovy Butter [No. 108] instead of plain butter. Garnish the yolk of each egg with half of an anchovy fillet after they are broiled. *Serves 6.*

676. SHIRRED EGGS CONTADINA
Uova al piatto alla contadina

1 onion, chopped
1 clove garlic, crushed in the garlic-press
2 tablespoons chopped parsley
$\frac{3}{4}$ cup butter
12 eggs
6 slices of eggplant, salted liberally, allowed to drain for 1 hour, thoroughly washed, and patted dry with a towel
Flour
Salt

Cook the onion, garlic, and parsley in 3 tablespoons of the butter in a frying pan over medium heat until the onion and garlic are golden. Portion this mixture out into 6 ramekin dishes and prepare shirred eggs, placing 2 eggs in each ramekin, as described in No. 673, up to the point when they are ready to go into the broiler. Cut the slices of eggplant into any desired small shapes, dust them lightly with flour, and brown them in the remaining butter in a frying pan over medium heat. Finish cooking the eggs under the broiler and serve them garnished with the pieces of eggplant. *Serves 6.*

677. SHIRRED EGGS DIAVOLA
Uova al piatto alla diavola

Reduce 6 tablespoons of a good, red wine vinegar to $\frac{1}{2}$ its original volume in a saucepan over medium heat. Prepare 6 ramekins of shirred eggs as described in No. 673 and, 5 seconds before removing them from the broiler, spoon a generous teaspoon of the vinegar into each dish and top each with a generous grating of pepper. *Serves 6.*

678. SHIRRED EGGS FATTORE
Uova al piatto del fattore

Sauté 6 sweet Italian sausages in a little butter in a frying pan over medium heat until they are fully cooked and brown. Cut each sausage into small pieces and keep warm. Prepare 6 ramekins of shirred eggs as described in No. 673, using the butter and sausage fat from the sausages. Just before serving, garnish each with the sausages and 2 tablespoons of Tomato Sauce [No. 19] piped around the edge. *Serves* 6.

679. SHIRRED EGGS GOURMET
Uova al piatto del ghiottone

Precook 6 slices of hog jowl, about 4 inches square, for 1½ to 2 hours in boiling water until tender. Drain and then broil until brown and crisp. Line 6 ramekin dishes with the pork, cover with a thin slice of mozzarella, and then prepare shirred eggs in the ramekins as described in No. 673. Just before serving, each ramekin may be garnished with 2 tablespoons of Tomato Sauce [No. 19], carefully spooned around the edge. *Serves* 6.

680. SHIRRED EGGS WITH LEAN SALT PORK AND CHEESE
Uova al piatto con lardo di petto magro e groviera

These are prepared exactly as Shirred Eggs Gourmet [No. 679] except that slices of lean salt pork replace the hog jowl and slices of Gruyère (or Swiss) cheese replace the mozzarella. The salt pork need be parboiled only 20 minutes in two changes of water. *Serves* 6.

681. SHIRRED EGGS NAPOLETANA
Uova al piatto alla napoletana

1 clove garlic, crushed in the garlic-press
1 tablespoon oil
4 tomatoes, peeled, seeded, drained, and chopped
Pinch oregano
1 teaspoon salt
Pinch sugar
12 eggs

Prepare a light tomato sauce by cooking the garlic in the oil over medium heat in a saucepan until it is golden. Add the tomatoes, oregano, salt, and sugar. Cook for only about 10 minutes, or until the tomatoes are soft, but still retain their shape. Prepare 6 ramekins of shirred eggs as described in No. 673 and garnish with the tomato sauce. *Serves* 6.

682. SHIRRED EGGS WITH PEPPERS
Uova al piatto con peperoni

4 sweet red or yellow peppers, roasted, peeled, seeded, and cut into strips [*see* No. 145]

1 clove garlic, crushed in the garlic-press
3 tablespoons oil
2 tomatoes, peeled, seeded, drained, and chopped
12 eggs
Salt and freshly ground pepper

Brown the garlic very lightly in the oil in a frying pan over medium heat. Add the strips of pepper and cook for about 5 minutes. Add the tomatoes and cook for only 4 to 5 minutes longer. Season with salt and pepper. Portion this mixture out into 6 ramekins and prepare shirred eggs in them as described in No. 673. *Serves* 6.

HARD-BOILED EGG DISHES
Uova sode

683. HARD-BOILED EGGS
Uova sode

Make a tiny hole with the point of a fine pin at one end of an egg which has been brought to room temperature and lower it carefully with a spoon into boiling water. After the water returns to a boil, cook the egg 8 to 10 minutes for medium and 12 to 15 minutes for hard-boiled. Plunge the egg immediately into cold water, crack the shell by rolling it on a hard surface, and peel it off.

684. HARD-BOILED EGGS WITH CREAMED CHICORY
Uova sode con cicoria alla crema

3 heads of chicory
4 tablespoons butter
½ cup heavy cream
Salt and freshly ground pepper
6 hard-boiled eggs, quartered or sliced

Wash the chicory thoroughly and trim off the hard core so that the leaves are separate; boil it in a large quantity of lightly salted water for 4 minutes; and drain it thoroughly, pressing out excess water with the hands. Sauté it very gently in a saucepan with the butter and heavy cream for 10 minutes. Season it lightly with salt and pepper. Turn it out into a vegetable dish and garnish with the hard-boiled eggs. *Serves* 6.

685. HARD-BOILED EGGS OVER CHICORY WITH MEAT SAUCE
Uova sode con cicoria al sugo di carne

This is prepared in the same way as the preceding recipe, Hard-Boiled Eggs with Creamed Chicory [No. 684], substituting 1 cup of Italian Meat Sauce [No. 41] for the cream.

686. CREAMED EGGS AND ONIONS
Uova sode in trippe

12 hard-boiled eggs, sliced
12 white onions
Bouquet Garni:
   1 bay leaf
   2 sprigs parsley
   $\frac{1}{2}$ teaspoon dried thyme
$5\frac{1}{2}$ tablespoons butter
$3\frac{1}{2}$ tablespoons flour
3 cups boiling milk
$1\frac{1}{2}$ teaspoons salt
$\frac{1}{4}$ teaspoon freshly ground white pepper
Pinch nutmeg
2 tablespoons chopped parsley

Peel the onions (a simple and tearless way of doing this is to plunge them, a few at a time, into boiling water for 5 seconds and then plunge them into cold water; trim off a bit of the hard core on the bottom and the outside skin will slip off easily). Cut a cross in the bottom core of each onion about $\frac{1}{8}$ inch deep with a very sharp knife to keep them from bursting during the cooking. Put them in a heavy frying pan, large enough to accommodate them in one layer, with 2 tablespoons of the butter, 2 tablespoons of water, and the Bouquet Garni. Season lightly with salt and pepper, cover very tightly, and cook over the lowest possible flame for 25 to 35 minutes (the exact time will depend on the size of the onions). They should be barely tender.

While the onions are cooking, prepare a Béchamel by making a roux with the remaining butter and the flour; add the boiling milk, salt, pepper, and nutmeg, stirring vigorously with a whisk; and cook over moderate heat for about 20 minutes. Add the onions and their cooking juices to the sauce and cook for another 5 minutes. Add the hard-boiled egg slices, mix gently, correct the seasoning, and turn it carefully into a serving dish. Sprinkle the chopped parsley over the top, and serve at once. *Serves* 6.

NOTE: Light cream may be substituted for the milk to make a more unctuous sauce.

687. EGG CROQUETTES MARSALA
Crocchette di uova sode con salsa al marsala

6 hard-boiled eggs, finely chopped
2 cups Béchamel Sauce [No. 18]
2 tablespoons chopped onion
2 tablespoons butter
3 ounces dried mushrooms, soaked $\frac{1}{2}$ hour in warm water, squeezed dry, and chopped
1 egg, beaten
2 tablespoons grated Parmesan cheese
Flour
Fresh breadcrumbs
Salt and freshly ground pepper
Pinch nutmeg
Fat for deep frying
$1\frac{1}{2}$ cups Marsala Sauce [No. 43]

Reduce the Béchamel to $\frac{1}{2}$ its original volume over very moderate heat. Cool and chill thoroughly. Cook the onion in a frying pan with the butter over moderate heat and, as soon as it begins to turn golden, add the mushrooms. Cook gently for 20 minutes. Remove from the heat and cool. When the Béchamel is quite cold, combine it with the mushroom/onion mixture, grated cheese, and the finely chopped eggs. Add the seasoning and mix thoroughly. Shape the mixture into little croquettes of any desired shape, roll them in flour, dip them in the beaten egg and then in the breadcrumbs. Arrange the croquettes in a wire basket so they do not touch one another, lower them into hot oil preheated to 375°, and drain them when they are golden. Arrange them on a serving platter and serve the Marsala sauce on the side. *Serves* 6.

NOTE: These croquettes are very delicate, so they should be made no larger than 2 inches in diameter.

238

SCRAMBLED EGGS

Uova strapazzate

688. SCRAMBLED EGGS
Uova strapazzate o rimestate

The freshness of eggs is equally important for scrambled eggs as for other egg dishes. Both flavor and consistency will be greatly impaired if older eggs are used. Scrambled eggs must be cooked slowly over moderate heat. You may cook them over a brisk fire, if you wish, but their taste will be quite different and they will lose their creaminess. There are basically two methods for scrambling eggs. We are outlining both below, although the first is preferred and more classic.

Season the required number of eggs lightly with salt and pepper (about ¼ teaspoon of salt for 6 eggs) and beat them with a fork only until the whites are mixed with the yolks. They must not be beaten until they become thin and watery, but must still be partly coagulated. Using a proportion of 1 tablespoon of butter for every 2 eggs, melt the butter in a heavy frying pan of an appropriate size (the eggs should never be more than 1 inch deep when poured into the pan) over a fairly low flame. As soon as the butter is completely melted and before it turns golden-brown, pour in the eggs. Stir them continuously with a wooden spoon or rubber spatula. If the heat is as low as it should be, they will not begin to coagulate for several minutes. When they do begin to thicken, stir more rapidly and continue cooking until they are of the desired consistency. (Italians, generally, prefer scrambled eggs very moist.) Remove them immediately from the fire and quickly stir in a small amount of butter to help stop their cooking. Turn them quickly into a serving dish.

Alternate method:
Follow the directions above for beating the eggs and pouring them into the pan. Instead of stirring them continuously, allow a layer of egg to thicken on the bottom of the pan; lift this layer up gently and allow uncooked egg to run underneath; continue this process and, as more layers are cooked, pile them loosely in the center of the pan, being careful to break the layers as little as possible; lift the center up several times during the cooking to allow air in and thus prevent their overcooking and becoming dry. When cooked to the desired consistency, shake the pan back and forth a few times. The eggs should separate easily from the pan in one mass. Slide them out onto a serving dish in one piece. Eggs scrambled in this manner have a com-

pletely different flavor from those cooked by the first method. They are not as creamy, but they can provide a pleasant change.

689. SCRAMBLED EGGS WITH CHICKEN LIVERS
Uova strapazzate con fegatini di pollo

12 fresh eggs
½ pound chicken livers
½ cup butter
¼ cup Marsala wine
Salt and freshly ground pepper

Clean, trim, and slice the chicken livers. Sauté them for 3 minutes in 2 tablespoons of the butter in a frying pan over fairly brisk heat. Remove them with a slotted spoon and keep warm. Pour the Marsala into the pan, scrape the bottom of the pan with a wooden spoon, and let it cook down to half its original volume. Remove from the heat, return the livers to the pan, and keep warm. Scramble the eggs in 6 tablespoons of the butter as described in No. 688. Turn them into a vegetable dish and garnish with the livers. *Serves 6.*

690. SCRAMBLED EGGS FORESTIERA
Uova strapazzate alla forestiera

12 fresh eggs
¼ pound salt pork, diced and parboiled 10 minutes
¾ cup butter
2 tablespoons chopped onion
¼ pound mushrooms, sliced
1½ cups Italian Meat Sauce [No. 41]
2 tablespoons chopped parsley

Sauté the parboiled salt pork dice in 2 tablespoons of butter over a brisk flame until golden. Remove with a slotted spoon and reserve. Add 2 more tablespoons of butter to the pan and cook the onion until it is golden. Add the mushrooms and continue cooking over moderate heat for 8 minutes. Heat the Italian meat sauce and keep warm. Season the eggs lightly and beat them with a fork. Add the browned salt pork dice to the eggs and scramble them in 6 tablespoons of the butter as described in No. 688. Add the remaining butter to them, turn them into a warm vegetable dish, garnish with the mushrooms, decorate with a thick ribbon of sauce around the dish, and sprinkle the chopped parsley over the top. *Serves 6.*

691. SCRAMBLED EGGS WITH HAM AND CROÛTONS
Uova strapazzate con prosciutto e crostoncini

12 fresh eggs
1 pound cooked ham (in 1 slice, about ½ inch thick)
½ cup butter
¼ cup dry Marsala wine
1½ cups Croûtons [No. 332]

Cook the slice of ham in a frying pan with 2 tablespoons of butter and the Marsala over a brisk fire. Turn the ham once or twice during the cooking. When the Marsala has entirely evaporated, dice the ham and keep the cubes hot until needed. Prepare the croûtons as directed in No. 332. Scramble the eggs in the remaining butter as described in No. 688. Turn the eggs into a serving dish, garnish the center with the cooked ham, and make a circle of croûtons around the edge. *Serves* 6.

692. SCRAMBLED EGGS WITH SAUSAGE
Uova strapazzate con luganega

12 fresh eggs
6 sweet Italian sausages
1 tablespoon oil
6 tablespoons butter
1 cup Tomato Sauce [No. 19]

Slice the sausages and brown them in hot oil in a skillet over a brisk flame. Prepare the scrambled eggs in the butter as directed in No. 688 and turn them out into a serving dish. Garnish the center with the cooked sausage and decorate with a ribbon of the hot tomato sauce around the edge. *Serves* 6.

240

693. SCRAMBLED EGGS WITH SHRIMP
Uova strapazzate con gamberetti

12 fresh eggs
½ pound small shrimp
¾ cup butter
½ cup brandy
Salt

Cook shrimp in a small saucepan over moderate heat in boiling water for 3 minutes after the water comes back to a boil. Shell and de-vein them. Melt 3 tablespoons of butter in frying pan, add the shrimp, and cook for 2 minutes over a brisk flame. Add the brandy and, as soon as it is warm, ignite. Shake the pan until flames disappear and continue cooking until the brandy has evaporated. Beat the eggs lightly in a bowl, season them, and scramble in butter as directed in No. 688. Pour the cooked eggs into a vegetable dish, add the remaining 2 tablespoons of butter, garnish with the shrimp, and serve at once. *Serves* 6.

694. SCRAMBLED EGGS WITH ZUCCHINI AND TOMATOES
Uova strapazzate con zucchine e pomodori

12 fresh eggs
8 tablespoons butter
1 tablespoon oil
1 clove garlic, crushed in the garlic-press
3 tomatoes, peeled, seeded, drained, and sliced
4 zucchini, sliced
1 teaspoon salt
¼ teaspoon freshly ground pepper
2 tablespoons chopped basil

Melt 2 tablespoons of the butter in a frying pan with 1 tablespoon of oil over medium heat. Add the garlic, sauté for a minute, and then add the tomatoes. Cook for 5 minutes, add the zucchini slices, season with salt and pepper, mix gently, and continue cooking for another 5 minutes, or until the zucchini are just tender. Remove from the heat and keep warm. Scramble the eggs in remaining butter as described in No. 688 and turn them into a hot serving dish. Garnish the center with the cooked zucchini and tomatoes (if they have released too much liquid, put them over high heat for a minute to reduce it), and sprinkle the chopped basil over the top. *Serves* 6.

1. Mosaic of Eggs in Aspic (No. 728)

2. Eggs Mayonnaise (No. 727). In this presentation the garnish consists of 4 sweet green and red peppers, roasted, scraped, seeded, and cut into strips (see No. 145). Each egg is topped by a small sour gherkin, partially sliced lengthwise, and spread out fanwise.

3. Prosciutto-Stuffed Eggs Glacée (No. 747)

4. Stuffed Eggs (No. 739) garnished with caviar and rolled slices of smoked salmon served on a bed of crushed ice.

5. Hard-Boiled Eggs Napoletana (No. 735)

CODDLED EGGS
Uova nelle tazzine

695. CODDLED EGGS
Uova nelle tazzine

Eggs are coddled in a cocotte, a small circular fireproof dish, usually of porcelain or earthenware, about 3 to 4 inches in diameter, with low, straight sides. A small ramekin serves the same purpose, although individual soufflé dishes are better.

6 eggs
4 tablespoons butter, softened
6 tablespoons heavy cream (or substitute Meat Sauce, No. 41)
Boiling water
Salt

Heat the cocottes well in the oven, grease each with 1 teaspoon of the butter, put 1 tablespoon of the cream (or meat sauce) in each, break 1 egg into each, season with a little salt, and dot the top of each egg with another teaspoon of butter. Place the cocottes in a shallow roasting pan and pour in enough boiling water to come up to $\frac{1}{2}$ the height of the cocottes. Cook in a moderate (350°) oven for about 10 minutes. Test the eggs for doneness after 8 minutes and cook a little longer if necessary. Wipe the cocottes dry and set them on a round serving platter. *Serves 6.*

696. ALSATIAN CODDLED EGGS
Uova nelle tazzine all'alsaziana

These are prepared exactly as Coddled Eggs [No. 695], except that 1 tablespoon of pâté de foie gras is put in the bottom of each cocotte in place of the cream or meat sauce. Press the foie gras down well in the cocotte, so that it forms a thin layer over the whole bottom.

697. CODDLED EGGS WITH CREAM
Uova nelle tazzine alla crema

These are prepared in the same way as Coddled Eggs [No. 695], except the heavy cream is not added to the cocotte until *after* the eggs are cooked. Heat the cream well before spooning a tablespoon over each egg.

698. CODDLED EGGS WITH MEAT SAUCE
Uova nelle tazzine al sugo di carne

These are prepared in the same way as Coddled Eggs [No. 695], except that the cream is omitted and 1 tablespoon Italian Meat Sauce [No. 41] is spooned over each egg *after* it is cooked.

699. CODDLED EGGS NAPOLETANA
Uova nelle tazzine alla napoletana

This is prepared in the same way as Coddled Eggs [No. 695], except that a tablespoon of a light tomato sauce is substituted for the cream. Prepare the sauce by peeling, seeding, draining, and chopping 2 small, very ripe tomatoes; cook them for only about 5 minutes over medium heat in a small saucepan with 1 tablespoon of butter and a pinch of sugar, salt, pepper, and basil.

OMELETS AND FRITTATE
Frittate e omelette

In Italy, a distinction is made between omelets and frittate. Briefly described, a frittata is beaten eggs cooked and stirred over very high heat and then, when they thicken but are still very moist, they are turned in one mass and cooked on the other side; the resulting shape is round when it is turned onto a serving dish. An omelet is prepared by cooking and stirring beaten eggs over very high heat; as they thicken, the sides are folded toward the center; and then inverted on a serving dish; the resulting shape is oval. Generally, omelets are more moist and creamy than frittate.

The one essential requirement for the successful preparation of frittate or omelets is a good pan. Steel, aluminum, or enameled iron can be successful, but the best is seasoned iron ⅛ inch thick with sloping sides. An omelet pan should not be used for any other purpose, since it will begin to stick if liquids are boiled in it, or if other foods are allowed to stick to its bottom. An omelet pan should never be washed, but merely wiped dry with a paper towel after each use. If it becomes soiled, wipe it clean with a little salt and a paper towel. A new omelet pan must be seasoned. This is best done by first scrubbing it with fine steel wool and salt, filling it with oil, and heating over a very low flame for several hours. Drain off the oil, wipe it dry with a paper towel, and it is ready for its first use.

An omelet or frittata may contain up to 12 eggs, but large ones are difficult to handle. The recommended size for an omelet is 3 eggs, and, if you are serving a number of guests, it is wiser to make several small omelets, rather than one large one. The recommended size for a frittata is 6 eggs, since they are somewhat easier to handle. The eggs in the pan should not be more than ½ inch deep, or they will not cook quickly enough. A pan whose bottom diameter is 7 inches is the perfect size for a 3-egg omelet and a 9-inch bottom is correct for a 6-egg size.

700. PLAIN FRITTATA
Preparazione della frittata

Season 6 eggs lightly with salt and freshly ground pepper. Beat them with a fork only long enough to combine the whites and yolks; they should still be partially coagulated, not thin and watery. Heat 3 tablespoons of butter in a 9-inch omelet pan over high heat. Roll it around in the pan so that the sides are well covered and it cooks evenly. When the butter stops bubbling and is just past the golden stage, becoming a light brown, pour in the eggs. Immediately stir the eggs very rapidly with a circular motion 3 or 4 times with a fork. Then, using a fork or rubber spatula, begin lifting the cooked bottom of the egg mass up lightly from the sides to allow uncooked egg to run underneath. Do not attempt to stir the whole mass so that the butter becomes completely incorporated with the eggs, or you will risk their sticking to the bottom.

Continue this for a few seconds until the eggs look ⅔ cooked. Bang the pan very sharply on the stove and jerk it back and forth once or twice to make certain the frittata is not sticking to the bottom. If it is sticking, quickly slide a broad spatula underneath the eggs to free them. Now, toss the whole frittata lightly up in the air out of the pan, letting it turn over in the air and its uncooked side fall back to the bottom of the pan. This is a good deal easier than it sounds; you can practice the motion with a large, round slice of bread, if you feel uncertain. A less dramatic method is, of course, to turn the frittata with a broad spatula. Cook the underside for only a few more seconds, as the eggs will congeal very rapidly over a high flame. Your taste will have to guide you here for the exact time, but the frittata should not be dry. Bang and jerk the pan several times to make sure the frittata is not sticking to the bottom, and, if it is, slide a spatula underneath to free it. Slide it out of the pan onto a warm serving dish, or invert it onto a dish, if you prefer. *Serves 2 to 3.*

NOTE: Frittate generally contain a variety of ingredients, such as meat, vegetables, or fish. These flavoring ingredients may be sautéed or cooked directly in the omelet pan and then the eggs poured over them, but this method risks the eggs sticking to the pan. We have preferred to cook the flavoring ingredients sepa-

Preparation of a frittata (see No. 700 and Nos. 702-14).
Left: The beaten eggs are poured into the pan.   Center: The pan is being agitated.
Right: The frittata is being flipped over.

Preparation of Plain Omelet (No. 701).
Left: The beaten eggs are poured into the pan. Center: The omelet is turned out
onto a serving plate. Right: The omelet is poked into its "ideal" shape.

rately and then either add them to the eggs just before cooking or add them to the hot butter in the omelet pan just before pouring in the eggs.

Frittate are also good when served cold.

701. PLAIN OMELET
Preparazione dell'omelette

Over the years cooks have devised a variety of ways to prepare a perfect omelet. We are listing below two methods, both of which will give excellent results. The first is more difficult and requires a certain amount of courage from an inexperienced cook, but it is the method preferred by professional chefs. It is also more fun.

Season 3 eggs lightly with salt and freshly ground pepper. Beat them with a fork only long enough to combine the whites with the yolks; they should still be partially coagulated, not foamy on top and watery on the bottom. Heat 2 tablespoons of butter in a 7-inch omelet pan over high heat. Roll it around in the pan so that the sides are well covered and it cooks evenly. When the butter stops bubbling and is just past the golden stage, becoming a light brown, pour in the eggs. Leave them untouched for a moment so that a thin layer of cooked egg forms on the bottom. Take the handle of the pan in both hands (more or less the way a golf club is held with the thumbs on top); tilt the pan very slightly away from you, raising the side closer to you about 1 inch; and begin jerking the pan very sharply toward you. The jerks must be very quick, almost rough; this will cause the cooked layer of egg on the bottom to slide up the far side of the pan and, as you jerk, it will begin to slide over the un-cooked egg on top. Pause for a few seconds between each jerk to allow more egg to cook on the bottom. When the cooked layer slides about halfway over the top of the uncooked egg, tilt the pan more sharply away from you, causing the eggs to become a more compact mass in the far side of the pan. *(If you are putting a filling in the omelet, it should go in just before you tilt the pan more sharply away from you. Be very careful that none of the filling touches the bottom of the pan, since it can cause the omelet to stick.)* Continue jerking at the higher angle and the omelet will fold over on itself several times, becoming oval in shape, and the creamy egg mass in the center will be completely encased in the tender, buttery crust. Turn the heat down slightly and allow the omelet to become golden on one side. Tilt the pan very sharply over a hot serving dish and invert the pan, so that the golden side of the omelet is on top. *Serves 1.*

Alternate method: As described above, season and beat the eggs, and heat the butter in the pan until light brown. Pour in the eggs and immediately stir with a fork in a circular motion 3 or 4 times. Then, just as in preparing a frittata, using a fork or a rubber spatula, begin lifting the cooked bottom of the egg mass up lightly from the sides, to allow uncooked egg to run underneath. As you lift, gently pile the cooked egg in the center. *(A filling should be added at this point.)* Continue this for a few seconds until the eggs thicken and look $2/3$ cooked. Then quickly fold $1/3$ of the omelet over on itself toward the center with a spatula. Turn the heat down slightly and allow the underside to become golden. Do not overcook; the top side of the omelet should be very moist, even partially runny. Holding a warm serving dish in your left hand, slide $1/3$ of the omelet, the side that has *not* been folded over on itself, out of the pan onto the dish. Then very quickly invert the pan so that the omelet folds over on itself. The resulting shape should be oval and puffed in the center.

243

702. FRITTATA AMATRICIANA
Frittata all'amatriciana

12 fresh eggs
2 tablespoons oil
1 onion, finely chopped
1/4 pound lean hog jowl, parboiled for 1/2 hour and diced
2 boiled potatoes, finely sliced
6 tablespoons butter
Salt and freshly ground pepper

Heat the oil in a heavy skillet over medium heat. Add the onion and cook until golden. Add the diced hog jowl and the potatoes and sauté gently for 5 minutes. Break the eggs into a bowl, season them lightly with salt and pepper, and beat them with a fork. Add the pork/potato mixture to the eggs, stir lightly, divide the mixture in two portions, and then prepare 2 frittate from it as described in No. 700. *Serves* 6.

703. FRITTATA AUVERGNE
Frittata alla moda di Auvergne

8 egg yolks
1 pound salted fish (dried cod or haddock)
9 tablespoons oil
1 clove garlic, crushed in the garlic-press
3 tablespoons chopped parsley
1/4 teaspoon freshly ground pepper
1 cup heavy cream

Soak the salted fish for 12 hours, changing the water 3 times. Clean the fish, discard the bones and any tough parts, slice fine, and cook over very low heat with 3 tablespoons of oil in a heavy frying pan for 1 hour, or until it is soft enough to mash into a purée. Place the purée in a bowl and allow to cool. Add the egg yolks, the chopped parsley, pepper, and garlic, and, very slowly, a little at a time, the heavy cream. Divide the mixture in two portions and prepare a frittata with each half, using 3 tablespoons of oil for each, as described in No. 700. *Serves* 6.

704. FRITTATA BASQUE OR PIPÉRADE
Frittata alla basca—pipérade basquaise

12 fresh eggs
2 tablespoons oil
4 tomatoes, peeled, seeded, drained, and chopped
2 red or yellow sweet peppers, roasted, scraped, and
    cut into strips [*see* No. 145]
6 tablespoons butter
Salt and freshly ground pepper

Frittata Basque or Pipérade (No. 704)

Heat the oil in a heavy saucepan over medium heat. Add the tomatoes, season lightly with salt and pepper, and cook for 10 minutes. Add the peppers, lower the heat, and cook for another 10 minutes. Break the eggs into a bowl, season them with a little salt and pepper, and beat them with a fork. Add the peppers and tomatoes to the eggs, stir lightly, divide the mixture in two portions, and prepare 2 frittate in the butter as described in No. 700. *Serves* 6.

705. CHEESE FRITTATA
Frittata al formaggio

12 fresh eggs
1/3 cup Gruyère (or Swiss) cheese, cut into small, thin slices
1/2 cup grated Parmesan cheese
6 tablespoons butter
Salt and freshly ground pepper

Break the eggs into a bowl, add both cheeses, season lightly with salt and pepper, and beat with a fork. Divide the mixture in two portions and proceed to make 2 frittate in the butter as described in No. 700. *Serves* 6.

706. FRITTATA CONTADINA
Frittata alla contadina

12 fresh eggs
8 tablespoons butter
2 tablespoons chopped onion

1 clove garlic, bruised
3 ounces ham (meat and fat), boiled or baked, cut in slivers
3 tomatoes, peeled, seeded, drained, and chopped
1 teaspoon chopped parsley
Salt and freshly ground pepper

Melt 2 tablespoons of the butter in a frying pan over medium heat and add the onion and garlic clove. Cook until the onion is golden, add the slivers of ham, and cook for 5 minutes. Add the tomatoes, season lightly with salt and pepper, and cook for 10 minutes or until they are soft. Remove from the heat and discard the garlic. Break the eggs into a bowl, season lightly with salt and pepper, beat with fork, add the tomato/ham mixture and parsley. Divide the mixture in two portions and proceed to prepare 2 frittate with the remaining butter as described in No. 700. *Serves* 6.

707. FRITTATA GOURMET
Frittata alla ghiotta

12 fresh eggs
8 tablespoons butter
2 tablespoons chopped onion
¼ pound sweet Italian sausage
3 ounces fontina (or Munster) cheese, cut into small, thin slices
Salt and freshly ground pepper

Melt 2 tablespoons of the butter in a frying pan over medium heat and add the chopped onion and the sausages. Sauté for about 10 minutes, or until the sausages are well cooked and the onion golden. Remove from the heat, take the sausage meat out of its casing, and crumble the meat. Break the eggs into a bowl, season lightly with salt and pepper, and beat with a fork. Add the sausage, onion, and cheese; stir once or twice to mix well; and pour ½ the mixture into another bowl. Proceed to make 2 frittate in the remaining butter as described in No. 700. *Serves* 6.

Baked Artichoke Omelet Toscana
(No. 717): see page 247

708. FRITTATA LINA CAVALIERI
Frittata "Lina Cavalieri"

12 fresh eggs
¼ pound salt pork, diced and parboiled for 10 minutes
1 tablespoon chopped onion
7 tablespoons butter
¼ cup finely diced mozzarella cheese
1 tablespoon heavy cream
Salt and freshly ground pepper

Sauté the salt pork dice and the onion in 1 tablespoon of the butter over high heat in a frying pan until both turn golden. Break the eggs into a bowl, season lightly with salt and pepper, and beat with a fork. Add the salt pork, onion, cheese, and heavy cream; stir once or twice to mix well; and pour ½ the mixture into another bowl. Proceed to make 2 frittate in the remaining butter as described in No. 700. *Serves* 6.

NOTE: Lina Cavalieri was a breathtakingly beautiful opera star of the 1900s.

709. FRITTATA MARINARA
Frittata alla marinara

12 fresh eggs
5 tablespoons oil
1 clove garlic, crushed in the garlic-press
3 tomatoes, peeled, seeded, drained, and chopped
6 anchovy fillets, washed free of salt [*see* No. 220] and pounded to a paste in the mortar with 3 sprigs of parsley
Salt and freshly ground pepper

Cook the garlic in 1 tablespoon of the oil in a frying pan over medium heat until the garlic becomes golden. Add the tomatoes and the anchovy/parsley paste, season lightly with salt and pepper, and cook for about 10 minutes, or until the tomatoes are just soft. Remove from the heat and cool slightly. Break the eggs into a bowl, season lightly with salt and pepper, beat with a fork, add the other mixture, stir once to mix well, and pour $\frac{1}{2}$ the mixture into another bowl. Proceed to prepare 2 frittate, using 2 tablespoons of oil for each, as described in No. 700. *Serves* 6.

710. FRITTATA WITH ONIONS
Frittata con le cipolle

12 fresh eggs
8 tablespoons butter
1 tablespoon oil
1 large Bermuda onion, coarsely chopped
Salt and freshly ground pepper

Heat the oil and 2 tablespoons of the butter in a frying pan over medium heat. Add the onion, reduce heat to moderate, and cook until the onion becomes soft and yellow, but not brown. Break the eggs into a bowl, season lightly with salt and pepper, beat with a fork, and pour half of them into another bowl. Heat 3 tablespoons of the butter in a 9-inch omelet pan over high heat until golden, add half of the onions, and cook for 1 minute, stirring constantly to prevent their sticking to the pan. Add 6 of the eggs, and proceed to make a frittata as described in No. 700. Turn it out onto a warm serving dish and keep warm while you prepare the second frittata. *Serves* 6.

711. FRITTATA SAVOIARDA
Frittata alla savoiarda

12 fresh eggs
$\frac{1}{4}$ pound salt pork, diced and parboiled for 10 minutes
10 tablespoons butter
1 tablespoon oil
3 potatoes, diced
3 leeks (white part only), finely sliced
3 ounces Gruyère (or Swiss) cheese, diced
2 tablespoons chopped parsley
Salt and freshly ground pepper

Sauté the salt pork dice in 1 tablespoon of the butter and the oil in a frying pan over high heat until golden. Remove the dice with a slotted spoon and reserve. Sauté the diced potatoes in the same pan, adding more

butter if necessary, for about 10 minutes, or until the potatoes are nicely browned. Cook the leeks in another saucepan over very gentle heat in 1 tablespoon of the butter for about 10 minutes, or until they are tender. Break the eggs into a bowl, season lightly with salt and pepper, and beat with fork. Add the salt pork, potatoes, leeks, cheese, and parsley; stir once or twice to mix well; and pour $\frac{1}{2}$ of the mixture into another bowl. Prepare 2 frittate from the mixture, using 3 tablespoons of butter for each, as described in No. 700. *Serves* 6.

712. SPINACH FRITTATA
Frittata con spinaci

12 fresh eggs
1 pound spinach, well washed
8 tablespoons butter
Salt and freshly ground pepper
Pinch nutmeg

Cook the spinach in a covered saucepan over high heat for 5 or 6 minutes in just the water that clings to the leaves after washing. Drain it well, pressing out excess water with the hands; chop it coarsely; season it with salt, pepper, and nutmeg; and sauté it very gently for another 5 minutes in a saucepan with 2 tablespoons of the butter. Break the eggs into a bowl, season lightly with salt and pepper, beat with a fork, add the spinach, stir once to mix well, and pour $\frac{1}{2}$ of the mixture into another bowl. Prepare 2 frittate from the mixture, using 3 tablespoons of the remaining butter for each, as described in No. 700. *Serves* 6.

713. FRITTATA WITH TRUFFLES
Frittata con tartufi d'Alba

12 fresh eggs
6 ounces white Alba truffles (or substitute Mock Truffles, No. 1819a), finely chopped
6 tablespoons butter
Salt and freshly ground pepper

Break the eggs into a bowl, season lightly with salt and pepper, add the chopped truffles, beat with a fork, and pour $\frac{1}{2}$ the mixture into another bowl. Prepare 2 frittate from the mixture, as described in No. 700, using 3 tablespoons of the butter for each. *Serves* 6.

714. WHITEBAIT FRITTATA
Frittata coi bianchetti

12 fresh eggs
$\frac{1}{2}$ pound whitebait

2 tablespoons oil
1 onion, chopped
1 teaspoon fresh oregano
2 tablespoons grated Parmesan cheese
6 tablespoons butter
Salt and freshly ground pepper

Heat the oil in a frying pan over medium heat and add the onion. Cook until it turns golden, add the whitebait, and cook for 5 minutes. Remove from the heat and reserve. Break the eggs into a bowl; season lightly with the fresh oregano, salt and pepper, and the grated cheese; beat with a fork; divide the mixture in two portions. Heat 3 tablespoons of the butter in a 9-inch omelet pan over high heat until golden, add ½ of the whitebait and onion, and cook for 1 minute, stirring carefully to prevent the whitebait from sticking to the pan. Add ½ the egg mixture and proceed to make a frittata as described in No. 700. Turn it out onto a warm serving dish and prepare the second frittata in the same manner. *Serves* 6.

715. OMELET ARCHDUKE
Omelette all'arciduca

12 fresh eggs
1 small onion, chopped
9 tablespoons butter
1 teaspoon paprika (or more, to taste)
1½ cups Paprika Sauce [No. 53]
2 truffles, thinly sliced [or No. 1819a]
Salt and freshly ground pepper

Cook the onion in 1 tablespoon of the butter in a heavy pan over medium heat until it is soft and transparent. Break the eggs into a bowl, season lightly with salt and pepper, add the onion and paprika, and beat with a fork. Prepare 4 omelets from the mixture as described in No. 701, using 2 tablespoons of butter and a generous ½ cup of egg for each. As each omelet is finished, turn it out onto an individual hot plate or a large, hot serving platter. Garnish with a thick ribbon of paprika sauce spooned across the middle of each omelet and sprinkle a few truffle slices over each. *Serves* 4.

716. ARTICHOKE OMELET
Omelette con carciofi

12 fresh eggs
4 small, young artichokes
1 lemon
2 tablespoons oil
8 tablespoons butter
2 tablespoons chopped parsley
Salt and freshly ground pepper

Remove the tough outer leaves from the artichokes and cut off the sharp tips of all the leaves; cut the artichokes in half and remove the choke with a sharp knife; cut the halves into fine slices; and place them in acidulated water for ½ hour. Drain the slices and dry them on a towel. Heat the oil in a frying pan over moderate heat and add the slices. Season lightly with salt and pepper and cook for 10 to 15 minutes, or until they are tender. Break the eggs into a bowl, season lightly with salt and pepper, and beat with a fork. Prepare 4 omelets as described in No. 701, using 2 tablespoons of butter and a generous ½ cup of egg for each. Spoon ¼ of the artichokes into each at the point where the filling should be added, as indicated in No. 701. Turn the omelets out onto individual hot plates or onto a hot serving platter and garnish with the parsley. *Serves* 4.

717. BAKED ARTICHOKE OMELET TOSCANA
Tortino di carciofi alla toscana

12 fresh eggs
12 small, young artichokes
Flour
Fat for deep frying
4 tablespoons butter, softened
Salt and freshly ground pepper

It is important to use only very young, small artichokes for this dish; older artichokes will be too tough. Remove the tougher outer leaves, trim off the tips of the remaining leaves with scissors, cut the artichokes into quarters, and remove the choke from each quarter. Sprinkle them lightly with flour, fry in deep fat (preheated to 375°) until they are golden, drain, and season lightly with salt and pepper. Break the eggs into a bowl, season lightly with salt and pepper, and beat with a fork. Smear a round baking dish with the softened butter, arrange the artichoke quarters in it, heat for 1 minute over a medium flame on top of the stove, pour in the eggs all at once, place immediately

247

into a hot (400°) oven, and cook for 6 to 8 minutes, or until the eggs are still moist but not runny. Remove the dish from the oven and brown the top for a few seconds under a hot broiler flame. *Serves* 4.

718. OMELET CHASSEUR
Omelette chasseur

12 fresh eggs
³/₄ cup butter
¹/₂ pound chicken livers, coarsely chopped
¹/₂ pound mushrooms, sliced
1¹/₂ cups Cacciatora Sauce [No. 28]
Salt and freshly ground pepper

Sauté the chicken livers in 3 tablespoons of the butter for 5 minutes in a frying pan over medium heat. Remove from the heat and reserve. Cook the mushrooms with 2 tablespoons of the butter in a saucepan, covered, for 5 to 6 minutes over moderate heat: remove the cover during the last minute of cooking and raise the heat to reduce any accumulated juices. Remove from the heat, combine with the chicken livers, and season lightly. Break the eggs into a bowl, season lightly with salt and pepper, and beat with a fork. Prepare 4 omelets with the eggs (approximately a generous ¹/₂ cup of egg and 2 tablespoons of butter for each), as described in No. 701. Spoon ¹/₄ of the liver/mushroom mixture into each omelet at the point indicated in No. 701 when the filling should be added. Turn the omelets out onto individual hot plates or onto a serving platter and garnish each with a thick ribbon of Cacciatora sauce spooned over the center of each. *Serves* 4.

719. OMELET FINES HERBES
Omelette con erbe fini

12 eggs
4 to 6 tablespoons of mixed, chopped, fresh herbs:
    Parsley
    Chervil
    Basil
    Tarragon
    Chives
    Scallions
8 tablespoons butter
Salt and freshly ground pepper

Break the eggs into a bowl, add the chopped herbs (use any combination of available fresh herbs to your taste), season lightly with salt and pepper, and beat with a fork. Prepare 4 omelets from the mixture, as

described in No. 701, using 2 tablespoons of butter and a generous ¹/₂ cup of egg for each. Turn the omelets out onto individual hot plates or onto a hot serving platter. *Serves* 4.

720. SHRIMP OMELET
Omelette con gamberetti

12 fresh eggs
1¹/₂ pounds very small shrimp, peeled and de-veined (or use larger shrimp, cut into pieces after peeling and de-veining)
2 cups Sauce Normande [No. 52]
8 tablespoons butter
Salt and freshly ground pepper

Prepare a Normande sauce as directed in No. 52, adding the shrimp to the other ingredients at the beginning of the preparation. Allow them to cook for only 5 to 8 minutes in the sauce, remove them, finish preparing the sauce, and then return the shrimp to it. Break the eggs into a bowl, season lightly with salt and pepper, and beat with a fork. Prepare 4 omelets as indicated in No. 701, using 2 tablespoons of butter and a generous ¹/₂ cup of egg for each. Spoon ¹/₄ of the shrimp and 2 tablespoons of the sauce into each omelet at the point where the filling should be added, as indicated in No. 701. Turn the omelets out onto individual hot plates or onto a hot serving platter. Garnish with a thick ribbon of the sauce spooned across the center of each. *Serves* 4.

721. OMELET WITH VEAL KIDNEYS
Omelette con rognoni di vitello

12 fresh eggs
³/₄ cup butter
2 veal kidneys, trimmed
¹/₂ cup dry Marsala wine
1 tablespoon Dijon-type mustard
Salt and freshly ground pepper

Melt 4 tablespoons of the butter in a frying pan over medium heat until it becomes golden. Add the trimmed kidneys, roll them around in the pan, and cook for about 10 minutes, turning them often, until they are firm. Remove them from the pan, add the Marsala, and cook until it is reduced to about 3 tablespoons. Slice the kidneys, return them to the pan, season lightly with salt and pepper, reduce heat to moderate, and cook for about 1 minute. Remove the pan from the fire and swirl in the mustard. Keep the kidneys warm while preparing 4 omelets. Break the eggs into a bowl, season lightly with salt and pepper, and beat with a fork. Cook the omelets, using 2 tablespoons of butter and a generous ½ cup of egg for each and adding ¼ of the kidneys as a filling at the point indicated in No. 701. Turn the omelets out on individual hot plates or onto a large serving platter. You may, if you wish, reserve a little of the kidneys and their sauce to spoon over the top of the cooked omelets. *Serves* 4.

COLD EGG DISHES
Uova fredde

722. EGGS ALEXANDRA
Uova affogate Alexandra

6 poached eggs [No. 650], chilled
1½ cups Regular Aspic [No. 118] or Substitute Regular Aspic [No. 118a]
1 cup Mayonnaise [No. 77]
6 slices black truffle, cut into fancy shapes with a truffle cutter
6 baked tart shells, about 3 inches in diameter, made from Rich Pastry [No. 1955], made without sugar, chilled

Trim the poached eggs so that they will fit neatly into the tart shells. If the aspic is jellied, warm it slightly until it is room temperature and liquid. Mix ½ cup of the aspic with the mayonnaise in a bowl, place the bowl over cracked ice, and stir for about 10 minutes, or until the mixture becomes very thick and will adhere to the chilled eggs. Spoon a little of the mixture into each of the tart shells, carefully slide an egg over it, and cover with more of the mixture. Garnish the top of each with a piece of truffle. Stir another ½ cup of liquid aspic over cracked ice until it is thick and syrupy and coat each of the tarts with a thin layer. Place the tarts in the refrigerator to chill thoroughly. Pour the remaining aspic into a shallow dish and chill in the refrigerator until it is firmly jellied. Turn it out onto a board and chop it finely. Serve the tarts on a chilled platter garnished with the chopped aspic. *Serves* 6.

723. EGGS ANDALUSIA
Uova affogate all'andalusa

2 tomatoes, peeled, seeded, drained, and chopped
Salt and freshly ground pepper
½ cup Sauce Soubise [No. 74]

1½ cups Regular Aspic [No. 118] or Substitute Regular Aspic [No. 118a]
6 poached eggs [No. 650], chilled
6 baked tart shells, about 3 inches in diameter, made from Rich Pastry [No. 1955], made without sugar, chilled

Simmer the tomatoes over medium heat in a saucepan for about 15 minutes until they are reduced and fairly thick. Season them lightly during the cooking with salt and pepper. Purée them through a food mill or for a few seconds in the blender. Mix them with the Soubise sauce and 1 cup of the liquid aspic. Place this mixture in a bowl over cracked ice and stir until thick and syrupy. Trim the eggs to fit inside the tart shells. Place a little of the mixture in the bottom of each shell, carefully slide one egg into each, and cover with the remaining mixture. Arrange them in a circle on a serving platter and chill thoroughly. Chop the remaining aspic, as in the preceding recipe, and garnish the center of the platter with it. *Serves* 6.

724. EGGS IN ASPIC WITH ASPARAGUS
Uova affogate con asparagi

6 poached eggs [No. 650], chilled
24 green asparagus tips, cooked
24 white asparagus tips, cooked
2 cups Mayonnaise [No. 77]
2 cups Regular Aspic [No. 118] or Substitute Regular Aspic [No. 118a]

Mix the white asparagus tips gently with 1 cup of the mayonnaise and arrange them in a pattern on the bottom of a shallow, round crystal serving dish. Chill until cold. Place the eggs in a circle on top of the asparagus and cover each egg with a mayonnaise/aspic mixture as described in Eggs Alexandra [No. 722], using the remaining mayonnaise and ½ cup of the aspic. Garnish each egg with 4 green asparagus tips, and spoon a little aspic, which has been stirred over cracked ice until syrupy, over each. Chill and chop the remaining aspic and make a mound of it in the center. *Serves* 6.

NOTE: White asparagus are not generally available in this country except in tins or packed in jars.

249

725. EGGS CASTILLE
Uova affogate alla castellana

2 cups chestnut purée (*see* Note)
1 cup Mayonnaise [No. 77]
1½ cups Regular Aspic [No. 118] or Substitute Regular
    Aspic [No. 118a]
6 poached eggs [No. 650], chilled
6 small circular slices of smoked tongue
6 slices truffle, cut into fancy shapes

Make a layer of chestnut purée in the bottom of 6 individual crystal serving bowls. Chill these in the refrigerator until very cold. Prepare a mayonnaise/aspic mixture, using ½ cup of the aspic and 1 cup of mayonnaise, as in Eggs Alexandra [No. 722]. Place a chilled egg on top of the chestnut purée in each bowl, cover with a coating of the mayonnaise/aspic, garnish with the tongue and truffle, and chill. Place the remaining liquid aspic in a bowl over cracked ice and stir until thick and syrupy. Spoon a generous layer of aspic over the top of each coated egg and chill until very firm. *Serves* 6.

NOTE: Prepare the chestnut purée as indicated in No. 397, except cook the chestnuts in broth instead of milk and use only ½ cup of the cooking broth in the purée.

726. EGGS WITH LOBSTER BON VIVANT
Uova semidure dei viveurs

6 soft-boiled eggs [No. 657] (cooked for 5 minutes,
    instead of 4), chilled
3 cups potato salad [*see* No. 147]
1 cup cubed pickled beets
½ cup Fish Aspic with White Wine [No. 119] or Sub-
    stitute Fish Aspic with White Wine [No. 119a]
1 cup American Sauce [No. 63], made with lobster, and
    cooled

Arrange the potato salad in a shallow crystal serving bowl, piled into a peak in the center and smoothed out flat around the edge of the bowl. Arrange a border of pickled beets around the outside edge. Cut a small slice from one end of each egg so they will stand upright. Arrange these around the center mound of potatoes. Blend the American sauce with the liquid aspic and stir over cracked ice until very thick. Coat the eggs with the mixture and garnish the top of each egg with 1 or 2 slices of the lobster that cooked in the sauce. Chill thoroughly. *Serves* 6.

727. EGGS MAYONNAISE
Copertura delle uova maionese

6 hard-boiled eggs, chilled
½ cup Regular Aspic [No. 118] or Substitute Regular
    Aspic [No. 118a]
1 cup Mayonnaise [No. 77]
Optional: vegetable coloring, red, yellow, or green

Place the eggs on a wire rack. If the aspic is jellied, warm it slightly until it is room temperature and liquid. Mix it with the mayonnaise in a bowl, place the bowl over cracked ice, and stir for about 10 minutes, or until the mixture becomes very thick and will adhere to the cold eggs. Cover all of the eggs with a rather thick coating and chill in the refrigerator. Before placing the aspic/mayonnaise over ice, it may be tinted with a few drops of vegetable coloring for a heightened visual effect. *Serves* 6.

728. MOSAIC OF EGGS IN ASPIC
Uova affogate mosaico

1 quart Regular Aspic [No. 118] or Substitute Regular
    Aspic [No. 118a]
6 poached eggs [No. 650] chilled
¼ cup small slices smoked tongue, cut into diamond
    shapes about ½ inch across
¼ cup small pieces cooked green beans, cut into diamond
    shapes about ½ inch across
¼ cup sliced black truffles, cut into diamond shapes
    about ½ inch across
1½ cups Russian Salad [No. 1879]
Few drops red vegetable coloring

Line with aspic the bottoms and sides of 12 oval or round metal molds which are just large enough to contain easily a trimmed, poached egg. The simplest way of doing this is first to chill the molds in the freezer until very cold. Remove them, one at a time, and pour a little liquid aspic into each, rolling the aspic around until the sides, as well as the bottom, are coated with a thin layer. It may be necessary to repeat this process once or twice with each mold. Return all of the molds to the refrigerator (not the freezer this time) to chill thoroughly. Trim the eggs neatly so that they will fit into the molds. Press a harlequin pattern of the beans, truffles, and tongue into the stiff aspic in the bottom of each mold; carefully dribble a teaspoonful of syrupy aspic over each; and then very carefully invert 1 egg into each of 6 of the molds, so that its more attractive side faces the bottom of the mold. Partially fill the remaining 6 molds with Russian Salad and then fill all of the molds to the brim with liquid aspic. Place all 12 in the refrigerator and chill until firm. Tint the remaining liquid aspic with a few drops of red vegetable coloring, pour into a serving platter, and chill in the refrigerator until firm. When ready to serve, unmold the eggs and salad in an attractive design on top of the chilled sheet of aspic. *Serves* 6.

729. PARISIAN EGGS
Uova semidure ghiacciate alla parigina

6 soft-boiled eggs [No. 657], chilled
½ cup Regular Aspic [No. 118] or Substitute Regular
    Aspic [No. 118a]
2 cups Mayonnaise [No. 77]
2 cups Macedoine of Vegetables [No. 198], substituting
    1 cup of the mayonnaise for the Vinaigrette sauce

Place the macedoine of vegetables mixed with the mayonnaise in a shallow crystal serving bowl, arrange the eggs over the top of the vegetables, and glaze each egg with aspic/mayonnaise as described in Eggs Alexandra [No. 722]. *Serves* 6.

730. EGGS PRINTANIÈRE
Uova affogate alla primaverile

6 poached eggs [No. 650], chilled
3 cups Macedoine of Vegetables [No. 198], substituting
    Mayonnaise [No. 77] for the Vinaigrette sauce
24 fresh tarragon leaves
12 cooked green asparagus tips
1½ cups Regular Aspic [No. 118] or Substitute Regular
    Aspic [No. 118a]

Place the macedoine of vegetables, generously mixed with mayonnaise, in a low, shallow crystal bowl and chill. Place the bunch of asparagus tips, standing up, in the center of the vegetables, arrange the eggs around them, garnish each egg with a spray of 4 tarragon leaves, and cover the whole with a layer of aspic which has been stirred over cracked ice until syrupy. Chill until firm in the refrigerator. *Serves* 6.

731. EGGS PROVENÇALE
Uova affogate ghiacciate alla provenzale

6 poached eggs [No. 650], chilled
6 large tomatoes, peeled
½ eggplant, peeled and cut into small cubes
3 tablespoons oil
2 medium potatoes, boiled, peeled, and cubed
Salt and freshly ground pepper
2 cups Mayonnaise [No. 77]
2 cups Regular Aspic [No. 118] or Substitute Regular
    Aspic [No. 118a]
Few drops red vegetable coloring
24 tarragon leaves

Slice off the top third of each tomato, squeeze them gently to remove seeds and juice, and scoop out most of the pulp with a spoon or sharp knife. Season the interior of each with salt and pepper. Sprinkle the eggplant cubes with a little flour and sauté them in the oil over medium heat in a frying pan until barely tender and golden. Remove from the fire, cool, combine gently with the potato dice and 1 cup of the mayonnaise,

Basic preparation of eggs
in aspic (see Nos. 728, etc.).
Top, left to right: The egg being
trimmed before being placed
in the mold (which has a layer
of solidified aspic on its bottom
holding the desired decorations in place);
the egg being positioned in the mold.
Bottom, left to right: The aspic is
poured over the egg; the now-set
aspic-covered eggs are unmolded
on a serving plate.

and season with salt and pepper, if necessary. Fill the tomatoes with this mixture and chill. Trim the poached eggs to fit over each tomato, place one egg over each, and cover with a layer of aspic/mayonnaise as in Eggs Alexandra [No. 722], using the remaining mayonnaise, a few drops of red vegetable coloring, and ½ cup of the aspic. Garnish with a spray of 4 tarragon leaves on top of each, and cover with a layer of clear aspic which has been stirred over cracked ice until syrupy. Chill in the refrigerator. *Serves 6.*

732. EGGS RAVIGOTE
Uova semidure alla ravigotta

6 soft-boiled eggs [No. 657], chilled
1½ cups Sauce Ravigote [No. 96]
18 fresh leaves of basil or tarragon, blanched in hot water

Cut a tiny slice from one side or end of each egg so they will not roll around. Arrange them on a round serving dish, pour the Ravigote sauce over them, and garnish the top of each egg with 3 basil or tarragon leaves. *Serves 6.*

733. EGGS AND SHRIMP IN ASPIC
Uova semidure con gamberetti

2½ cups Regular Aspic [No. 118] or Substitute Regular Aspic [No. 118a]
36 tiny shrimp, cooked, shelled, de-veined, and chilled
6 soft-boiled eggs [No. 657], chilled
6 slices bread, cut into rounds, toasted, and buttered

Line the bottom and sides of 6 small metal molds with aspic in the manner described in No. 728. The molds should each be large and deep enough to easily contain a whole egg. Press 6 of the tiny shrimp into the aspic in each mold and cover with a teaspoonful of aspic. Chill, and carefully slide a soft-boiled egg into each mold (the egg should not extend over the top of the mold), and fill the mold with aspic. Chill until jellied and, when ready to serve, unmold the eggs onto the rounds of freshly made toast. *Serves 6.*

734. GERMAN HARD-BOILED EGGS
Uova sode alla tedesca

1 8-ounce can of herring in wine sauce
½ cup finely diced apple
½ cup thinly sliced gherkins
6 hard-boiled eggs, chopped
½ cup Sauce Vinaigrette [No. 99]
4 radishes, grated

Drain the herring and cut them into small pieces. Mix them in a serving dish with the diced apple, gherkins, and chopped eggs. Pour the Vinaigrette sauce over and sprinkle the grated radishes over the top. Serve chilled. *Serves 4 to 6.*

735. HARD-BOILED EGGS NAPOLETANA
Uova sode alla napoletana

6 hard-boiled eggs, sliced
6 ripe tomatoes, sliced
1 small Bermuda onion, peeled and sliced
1 cup Sauce Vinaigrette [No. 99]
2 tablespoons chopped fresh basil
1 teaspoon chopped fresh oregano

On a large serving platter, alternate the egg and tomato slices. Arrange the onion slices around the side and pour the Vinaigrette over all. Sprinkle the basil and oregano over the tomatoes and eggs and serve at once. *Serves 6.*

736. PORTUGUESE HARD-BOILED EGGS
Uova sode alla portoghese

6 hard-boiled eggs, quartered and chilled
3 tomatoes, peeled, seeded, drained, and chopped
1 clove garlic, crushed in the garlic-press
1 tablespoon oil
18 small shrimp, peeled and de-veined
2 sweet red or yellow Italian peppers, roasted, peeled, and cut into strips [*see* No. 145]
Salt and freshly ground pepper
½ cup Sauce Vinaigrette [No. 99]
2 tablespoons chopped parsley

Heat the oil in a frying pan over medium heat and add the tomatoes and garlic. Season lightly with salt and pepper and cook for 5 minutes. Add the shrimp and peppers and cook for another 5 to 10 minutes. The tomatoes should be soft but not disintegrated and mushy and there should be very little liquid left in the pan. Remove from the heat and chill. When cold, mix the Vinaigrette sauce with the mixture. Arrange the egg quarters on a serving dish and pour the sauce over. Sprinkle with the parsley and serve at once. *Serves 4 to 6.*

737. SPANISH HARD-BOILED EGGS
Uova sode alla spagnola

4 onions, sliced
2 tablespoons butter, melted
6 hard-boiled eggs, sliced
18 rings of raw green pepper
¾ cup Sauce Vinaigrette [No. 99]

Arrange the onion slices in a round glass baking dish. Brush them with the butter and cook for 15 minutes in a moderate (350°) oven. Remove and chill. When cold, make a circle of sliced eggs around the edge, arrange the pepper rings in the center, and pour the Vinaigrette sauce over all. *Serves 4 to 6.*

738. UKRAINIAN HARD-BOILED EGGS
Uova sode alla ucraina.

3 cups Russian Salad [No. 1879]
6 hard-boiled eggs
1½ cups Mayonnaise [No. 77]
1 tablespoon chopped tongue
1 tablespoon chopped truffles
1 tablespoon chopped ham

Spread the Russian salad in a shallow serving bowl, arrange the eggs on top, spread a coat of mayonnaise over each egg, and sprinkle a little chopped tongue, truffles, and ham over each. Serve cold. *Serves 6.*

STUFFED EGGS
Uova farcite

739. STUFFED EGGS
Uova farcite

Eggs that are to be stuffed should be plunged into cold water immediately after hard-boiling them. They may be allowed to cool in the cold water or peeled immediately by rolling on a hard surface, pressing slightly with the palm of the hand, to crack the shells well; the shells are then easily removed. To enable stuffed egg halves to stand upright on a serving platter, a small slice is cut from each end of the egg. Frequently, however, eggs are cut in half, the yolks removed and mashed with a filling, the white halves are stuffed, and then the eggs are reassembled to give the appearance of whole eggs. Stuffed eggs are usually garnished with either mayonnaise or aspic.

740. ARTICHOKE-STUFFED EGGS
Farcia di carciofi

8 hard-boiled eggs
¾ cup artichoke purée [*see* No. 400 and No. 638]
1 stalk celery, finely chopped
1 apple, finely chopped
¼ cup finely chopped gherkins
1 cup Mayonnaise [No. 77], seasoned with Worcestershire sauce and a pinch of sugar.

Cut a small slice off the bottom of each egg, cut the eggs in half widthwise, and remove the yolks. Mash the yolks and then mix them very thoroughly with all the remaining ingredients. Stuff the white halves with the mixture and then reassemble them to give the appearance of whole eggs. Chill and use as a garnish.

741. STUFFED EGGS CACCIATORA
Farcia alla cacciatora

8 hard-boiled eggs
½ small onion, sliced
2 ounces mushrooms, cooked
2 ounces prosciutto, sliced
2 ounces any cooked game meat (wild fowl, venison, etc.)
¼ cup pickled gherkins
1 teaspoon chopped chervil
1 teaspoon chopped tarragon
1 cup Mayonnaise [No. 77], seasoned with ½ teaspoon dry mustard

Cut a small slice off the bottom of each egg, cut the eggs in half widthwise, and remove the yolks. Chop all the remaining ingredients, except the mayonnaise, very finely together. Mash the yolks into the mixture and combine with the mayonnaise. Stuff the white halves and reassemble them to give the appearance of whole eggs. Chill and use as a garnish.

742. CHICKEN-STUFFED EGGS
Farcia di pollo

8 hard-boiled eggs
½ cup cooked, chopped chicken meat
¼ cup chopped tongue
2 ounces mushrooms, cooked and chopped
¼ cup chopped gherkins
½ tomato, peeled, seeded, thoroughly drained, and chopped
1 cup Mayonnaise [No. 77]

Prepare with the above ingredients in the same manner as described in Stuffed Eggs Cacciatora [No. 741].

743. CHICKEN-STUFFED EGGS GLACÉS
Mezze uova sode con pollo

12 small ripe tomatoes, peeled
6 hard-boiled eggs
1½ cups Mayonnaise [No. 77]
1 cup cooked, chopped white meat of chicken
¼ cup Sauce Vinaigrette [No. 99]
12 thin slices red radish
2 cups cooked tiny peas (petits pois), chilled
2 cups Chicken Aspic [No. 120] or Substitute Chicken
    Aspic [No. 120a]

Cut off the top third of the tomatoes, squeeze gently, and shake out the seeds and juice. Scoop half of the pulp out with a spoon and put a little mayonnaise in each cavity. Cut the eggs in half lengthwise, and remove the yolks. Mash the yolks with the chopped chicken and Vinaigrette sauce to form a paste. Fill the egg halves with this mixture and garnish the top of each with a slice of radish. Press the egg halves down gently into each tomato until a small border of mayonnaise shows around each egg. Chill in the refrigerator until cold. Arrange a border of the peas around the edge of a large serving platter and arrange the filled tomatoes in the center. Stir the liquid aspic over cracked ice until syrupy and coat the filled tomatoes and the peas with it. Chill again until very cold. *Serves* 6.

744. HERRING-STUFFED EGGS GLACÉS
Mezze uova sode con aringhe

12 small, ripe tomatoes, peeled
6 hard-boiled eggs
1½ cups Mayonnaise [No. 77]
½ cup salt herring fillets, washed free of salt and chopped
¼ cup Sauce Vinaigrette [No. 99]
12 thin slices truffle
2 cups Regular Aspic [No. 118] or Substitute Regular
    Aspic [No. 118a]
1 cup Anchovy Butter [No. 108]

Cut off the top third of the tomatoes, squeeze gently, and shake out the seeds and juice. Scoop half of the pulp out with a spoon and put a little mayonnaise in each cavity. Cut the eggs in half and remove the yolks. Mash the yolks with the chopped herring and the Vinaigrette sauce to form a smooth paste. Fill the egg white halves with this mixture and garnish the top of each with a slice of truffle. Press the egg halves down

gently into each tomato until a small border of mayonnaise shows around each egg. Chill in the refrigerator until cold. Stir 1 cup of the liquid aspic over cracked ice until syrupy and spoon a little aspic over each egg and tomato. Arrange them in the center of a serving platter, pipe a border of anchovy butter around the edge, and make another inner border of the remaining aspic, chopped. Chill again until very cold. *Serves* 6.

745. STUFFED EGGS PARTENOPEA
Farcia alla Partenopea

8 hard-boiled eggs
1 tomato, peeled, seeded, drained, and chopped
½ cup pitted green olives, chopped
8 anchovy fillets, washed free of salt [*see* No. 220], and
    cut into tiny pieces
1 cup Mayonnaise [No. 77], seasoned with a little dry
    mustard

Prepare in the same manner as described in Stuffed Eggs Cacciatora [No. 741].

746. PROSCIUTTO-STUFFED EGGS
Farcia di prosciutto

8 hard-boiled eggs
½ cup chopped prosciutto
¼ cup chopped gherkins
½ green pepper, seeded and chopped
½ cup Mayonnaise [No. 77], seasoned with a little dry
    mustard

Prepare with the above ingredients in the same manner as described in Stuffed Eggs Cacciatora [No. 741].

747. PROSCIUTTO-STUFFED EGGS GLACÉS
Mezze uova sode con prosciutto

12 small, ripe tomatoes, peeled
6 hard-boiled eggs
½ cup Mayonnaise [No. 77]
½ cup chopped prosciutto
¼ cup Sauce Vinaigrette [No. 99]
2 cups Regular Aspic [No. 118] or Substitute Regular
    Aspic [No. 118a]
12 thin slices truffle
12 thick slices dill pickle

Proceed generally as in Chicken-Stuffed Eggs Glacés [No. 743], filling the tomatoes with a little mayonnaise, mashing the egg yolks with prosciutto (instead of chicken) and Vinaigrette, filling the eggs, garnishing with slices of truffle, and arranging the filled tomatoes on a serving platter alternately with the slices of pickle. Glaze the whole dish with aspic and chill until cold. *Serves* 6.

748. SALMON-STUFFED EGGS
Farcia di salmone affumicato

8 hard-boiled eggs
1 cup smoked salmon, chopped
1 cup Mayonnaise [No. 77], seasoned with a little dry mustard
¼ cup chopped gherkins
1 tomato, peeled, seeded, thoroughly drained, and chopped

Prepare with the above ingredients in the same manner as described in Stuffed Eggs Cacciatora [No. 741].

749. SHRIMP-STUFFED EGGS
Farcia di gamberetti

8 hard-boiled eggs
12 medium shrimp, cooked, peeled, de-veined, and chopped
1 cup Mayonnaise [No. 77], seasoned with a little dry mustard
¼ cup chopped gherkins
1 tomato, peeled, seeded, drained very thoroughly, and chopped

Prepare with the above ingredients in the same manner as described in Stuffed Eggs Cacciatora [No. 741]

750. SHRIMP-STUFFED EGGS GLACÉS
Mezze uova sode con scampi

6 small, ripe, tomatoes
9 hard-boiled eggs, chilled
1½ cups Mayonnaise [No. 77]
¼ pound shrimp, cooked, shelled, de-veined, and chopped
¼ cup Sauce Vinaigrette [No. 99]
12 small slices of smoked salmon
6 thin slices of truffle
2 cups Fish Aspic [No. 119] or Substitute Fish Aspic [No. 119a]

Proceed generally as in Chicken-Stuffed Eggs Glacés [No. 743]. Drain and seed the tomatoes, scoop out most of the pulp, and place a little mayonnaise in each. Cut a tiny slice from both ends of all the eggs to enable them to stand upright. Cut all of the eggs in half

lengthwise; remove the yolks from 6 of them and mash them to a paste with the chopped shrimp and the Vinaigrette; fill the 12 egg white halves with the mixture; garnish the top of each with a piece of salmon; and arrange them in a circle around the outside edge of a large serving platter. Place the remaining egg halves in the tomatoes, press them down slightly until a border of mayonnaise shows around each, and garnish the top of each with a slice of truffle. Arrange the filled tomatoes in the center of the serving platter. Chill until very cold. Stir the liquid aspic over cracked ice until syrupy and then glaze the eggs and stuffed tomatoes with it. Chill again until the aspic is set. *Serves* 6.

751. TONGUE-STUFFED EGGS
Farcia di lingua salmistrata

8 hard-boiled eggs
¼ cup chopped, boiled (or smoked) tongue
¼ cup chopped celeriac, parboiled for 2 minutes
¼ cup chopped gherkins
1 cup Mayonnaise [No. 77], seasoned with a little dry mustard

Prepare with the above ingredients in the same manner as described in Stuffed Eggs Cacciatora [No. 741].

MISCELLANEOUS EGG SALADS OR GARNISHES
Guarnizioni diverse per uova

752. ARTICHOKES AND EGGS VINAIGRETTE
Guarnizione di carciofi

6 hard-boiled eggs
6 cooked artichoke hearts [*see* introduction to No. 1578], sliced
3 "new" potatoes, cooked, peeled, and sliced
2 ounces mushrooms, sliced and cooked
1 teaspoon chopped tarragon
1 teaspoon chopped parsley
¾ cup Sauce Vinaigrette [No. 99]

Pour the Vinaigrette sauce over the other ingredients in a bowl and toss very lightly. *Serves* 4.

753. ASPARAGUS AND EGGS VINAIGRETTE
Guarnizione di punte d'asparagi

1½ pounds asparagus tips, trimmed, cooked until just
    tender in salted water, and chilled
1 cup Sauce Vinaigrette [No. 99]
6 hard-boiled eggs
2 tablespoons parsley

Pour the Vinaigrette sauce over the asparagus in a bowl
and toss very lightly. Arrange it on a serving platter
and either surround with quarters of the hard-boiled
eggs, or chop the eggs and sprinkle them and the parsley
over the top. *Serves* 4.

754. CELERY AND EGGS VINAIGRETTE
Guarnizione di sedani

6 hard-boiled eggs, sliced
1 bunch white celery, leaves removed, and washed
¾ cup Sauce Vinaigrette [No. 99]

Cut the celery into very fine slices. Put into a bowl, pour
in the Vinaigrette, and toss lightly. Arrange the sliced
eggs on a serving platter and spoon the celery over.
Chill until very cold. *Serves* 4.

755. EGG GARNISH FOR GAME
Guarnizione di cacciagione

6 hard-boiled eggs, sliced
½ cup Sauce Vinaigrette [No. 99]
6 scallions, sliced
1 tablespoon chopped fresh chervil
1 tablespoon chopped fresh tarragon

Pour the Vinaigrette sauce over the other ingredients
in a bowl and toss very lightly.

756. GREEN BEANS AND EGGS VINAIGRETTE
Guarnizione di fagiolini verdi

1½ pounds green beans, cooked in salted water until
    just tender, well drained, and chilled
1 cup Sauce Vinaigrette [No. 99]
6 hard-boiled eggs, chopped

Pour the Vinaigrette sauce over the beans in a bowl
and toss lightly. Arrange the sauced beans either very
neatly in bundles or piled in a mound on a serving
platter. Surround with a border of the chopped eggs.
Serves 4.

757. EGGS ITALIANA
Guarnizione all'italiana

A mixture of cooked, diced vegetables, chilled:
    3 new potatoes
    3 carrots
    2 stalks celery
    ¼ pound green beans
6 hard-boiled eggs, sliced
2 tomatoes, peeled, seeded, drained, and coarsely chopped
½ cup green olives, coarsely chopped
6 anchovy fillets, washed free of salt [*see* No. 220]
    and coarsely chopped
2 cups Mayonnaise [No. 77]

Mix ingredients lightly and chill. *Serves* 4 *to* 6.

758. EGGS WITH POTATO SALAD
Guarnizione di patate

Arrange 3 cups of potato salad [*see* No. 147] in the
center of a serving platter and surround with a circle of
6 sliced hard-boiled eggs. *Serves* 4 *to* 6.

759. PEPPERS AND EGGS VINAIGRETTE
Guarnizione di peperoni

6 hard-boiled eggs, quartered
½ cup Sauce Vinaigrette [No. 99]
4 sweet red or yellow peppers, roasted, scraped,
    seeded, and cut into strips [*see* No. 145]
1 small Bermuda onion, thinly sliced
2 tablespoons chopped parsley

Pour Vinaigrette sauce over the peppers, onions, and
parsley and toss lightly. Arrange in a shallow serving
bowl and place the egg quarters on top. *Serves* 4.

760. SHRIMP AND EGG SALAD
Guarnizione di scampi

18 shrimp, cooked, shelled, and de-veined
2 ounces very fresh white mushrooms, thinly sliced
2 stalks celery, finely sliced
3 new potatoes, cooked, peeled, and diced
3 cooked artichoke hearts [*see* introduction to No. 1578],
    sliced
1½ cups Mayonnaise [No. 77]
6 hard-boiled eggs, quartered
12 asparagus tips, cooked until tender

Combine all ingredients, except eggs and asparagus
tips, with the mayonnaise and mix lightly. Chill mixture, and arrange it in a shallow bowl. Arrange egg
quarters and asparagus tips on the top. *Serves* 4.

FISH

FISH
Pesci

The careful preparation and proper presentation of fish is one of the glories and delights of classic European cuisine. It is more than natural that Italians, particularly, consume large quantities of a variety of seafood, since no point in the long Italian peninsula is very far from a seacoast. Perhaps because of the abundance of fish in the Mediterranean, Italian cooks have devised a variety of delicious seasonings and sauces for fish.

Freshness of fish is absolutely essential. Spoiled fish, especially shellfish, can have disastrous effects on the digestive system. Generally, one can determine the freshness of fish by the freshness of its odor, the brightness of its eyes, the pink color of its gills, and the firmness of its flesh. It is usually wise to cook fish on the same day it is purchased. If it must be bought a day or two ahead, do not store it tightly covered in the refrigerator, since this hastens deterioration; lay it directly on a bed of ice in the refrigerator without any covering and wash it frequently in cold water.

NOTE: Many of the fish called for in the Italian edition are Mediterranean specimens unavailable in the United States. In these cases we have substituted readily available varieties whose taste and texture most closely resemble the originally called-for fish. However, for those people who may be using this book in Italy we have retained the original name of the fish in the Italian title of the recipes.

PRELIMINARY PREPARATION
OF FISH
Preparazione del pesce prima
della cottura

Fish must be scaled and the entrails removed before cooking. This is usually done by a fish dealer, but the occasion may arise when it is necessary for the cook to do it himself.

A fish is scaled by placing it on a board, grasping the tail firmly with the left hand, and, using a fish scaler or very sharp knife, scraping toward the head. If you work very quickly the scales will come off easily. Turn the fish over and scale the other side. Cut off the flaps over the gills and cut off the fins close to the body of the fish. Make a sharp incision lengthwise along the abdomen, spread the slit open, and pull out the entrails. Wash the fish very thoroughly, inside and out, in cold water.

Fish that have a thick, tough skin, like eels, must be skinned. This is done by first making an incision, skin deep, around the circumference of the head; then, with the left hand holding the head wrapped in a cloth to prevent its slipping, turn back the edge of the skin at the incision; and pull the skin firmly toward the tail with the right hand in one quick, long motion. The skin will come off whole. Cut off the head, and it is ready for cooking.

Large, thickly fleshed fish often have slits cut into one or both sides to allow the heat to penetrate and facilitate even cooking.

METHODS OF COOKING
FISH
Modi di cottura

ROASTING
Arrosto

Large, firmly fleshed fish, such as carp or pike, are frequently roasted whole in a hot oven without any liquid in the pan. After being cleaned, their cavity is seasoned with salt and other seasonings and the whole fish is spread with a generous amount of butter before being placed in the oven. During the cooking it is basted frequently with the butter and juices in the pan.

BRAISING

Brasatura

An enameled pan or a Pyrex dish with a lid is best for braising a fish in the oven. The pan is first generously buttered and then may be lined with a layer of sliced carrots and onions. The fish is laid on top; the pan is covered and placed in a hot oven; and it is then allowed to braise for 10 to 15 minutes, as the vegetables become soft and the fish releases some of its juices. It is then removed from the oven and hot liquid, usually wine or fish stock, is poured in to half the depth of the fish. A Bouquet Garni is added, the pan is covered again, and returned to the oven to complete cooking. Generally, the fish is basted from time to time during the cooking. After the fish is cooked, the liquid in the pan is frequently reduced to form the base of an accompanying sauce.

FRYING

Frittura

Smaller fish or fillets are frequently fried quickly in very hot olive oil in a frying pan on top of the stove. Olive oil is preferable to butter as a rule, because it has a higher burning point, although clarified butter is used in some instances. The oil may be reused for frying other fish, but, since the fish will flavor it, it should not be used for frying other foods. The oil must be very hot before placing the fish in the pan, but not actually smoking, as this will not only impair the flavor but result in an unattractive dark brown color. The amount of oil used depends naturally on the size of the pan and the fish, but the quantity should always be generous and more hot oil should be added during the cooking if the coating on the fish absorbs too much of the oil.

After being cleaned, the fish is dipped in liquid, usually milk or beaten egg; it is then dipped or rolled in flour or meal, and the excess is shaken off before frying. Care must be taken in removing larger pieces of fried fish from the pan, since cooked fish is very delicate and can easily break; two slotted spatulas are useful for this.

Fried fish are often served with Tartar sauce, Remoulade sauce, or mayonnaise and are garnished with parsley and lemon quarters.

BROILING

Alla griglia

Most medium-sized, firmly fleshed fish may be broiled. After being cleaned, the fish is seasoned with salt and brushed with oil or generously coated with butter. The broiler should always be preheated. The size of the broiler flame should be in inverse proportion to the size of the fish: very high heat for small fish and moderate heat for larger fish to permit penetration into the thicker flesh. The fish is turned halfway through the cooking and it is basted often with melted butter or oil.

POACHING

Lessatura

Almost all fish may be cooked in a simmering Court Bouillon whose ingredients vary for different types of fish. Listed below are 6 different court bouillons.

761. COURT BOUILLON FOR BASS, COD, MULLET, ETC.

For each quart of water, add 2 teaspoons salt

762. COURT BOUILLON FOR TURBOT

For each quart of water, add:
1 cup milk
2 teaspoons salt
1 slice lemon

763. COURT BOUILLON FOR SALMON AND TROUT

For each 4 quarts water, add:
$\frac{1}{2}$ cup vinegar
1 onion, sliced
1 sprig parsley
1 bay leaf
1 sprig thyme (or $\frac{1}{2}$ teaspoon dried)
4 peppercorns, bruised
4 teaspoons salt

Bring all of the ingredients to a boil over medium heat and cook for 1 hour. Strain before using.

259

764. COURT BOUILLON FOR LOBSTER AND EELS

For each quart water, add:
 1 quart dry white wine
 1 carrot, sliced
 1 onion, sliced
 1 stalk celery, sliced
Bouquet Garni:
 1 bay leaf
 2 sprigs parsley
 1 sprig thyme (or ½ teaspoon dried)
 3 peppercorns

Bring all of the ingredients to a boil over medium heat and cook for 20 minutes.

765. COURT BOUILLON FOR SHRIMP

For each quart water, add the same ingredients as
 No. 764, omitting the wine

Bring all ingredients to a boil over medium heat and cook for 20 minutes. Strain before using.

766. COURT BOUILLON FOR FISH COOKED AU BLEU

For each quart water, add:
 2 teaspoons salt
 2 tablespoons vinegar

A fish may, of course, be poached in any appropriately sized pan, but fish boilers are particularly useful utensils. These are elongated pans, usually enameled or of stainless steel, and are equipped with lids and a rack whose handles extend nearly to the top of the pan for easy submersion and removal of the fish. Removing a large, whole cooked fish, without breaking it into pieces, from a pan of boiling liquid which is not equipped with a rack can be a trying and difficult task. A fish boiler reduces the problem to a satisfying science. They come in a variety of sizes and are readily available at restaurant supply houses.

The fish is usually placed in cold or tepid Court Bouillon, brought rapidly to a boil, and then the fire is reduced to simmering heat. This may be done on top of the stove or in the oven. When cooking large, whole fish in a long fish boiler, it is generally simpler to bring the Court Bouillon to a boil on top of the stove in the boiler placed over 2 burners and then place it in a moderate oven to complete the cooking.

The fish should be completely submerged in the Court Bouillon. Larger fish weighing 4 pounds or more, such as salmon or salmon trout, will require 6 or more quarts of Court Bouillon; a small fish weighing less than a pound will require less than a quart in an appropriatley smaller pan.

Cooking time will naturally vary with different types of fish, but it may be roughly estimated at 15 minutes after the Court Bouillon comes to a boil for a 2-pound fish, 25 minutes for a 4-pound fish, 40 minutes for a 6-pound fish, and 50 minutes for a 6- to 10-pound fish. Thin fillets take about 5 minutes.

Never allow the liquid to boil uncontrollably. This will cause the fish to fall apart.

AU BLEU
Al blu

Small fresh-water fish, such as brook trout, carp, pike, perch, etc., are often cooked in boiling Court Bouillon as soon as possible after they are killed and cleaned. This method causes them to curl slightly and take on a bluish tinge. If the fish is rubbed with a little vinegar before submerging in the Court Bouillon, it will accentuate the bluish color.

Strike the head of the live fish a quick, sharp blow to kill it. Working very quickly, scale and clean it. Rub it with a little vinegar and plunge immediately into boiling Court Bouillon. Turn the heat down, and simmer for about 10 minutes. Serve it with melted butter, lemon quarters, and boiled "new" potatoes.

À LA MEUNIÈRE
Alla mugnaia

This method is well adapted to small, whole fish or to fillets. Season the fish, dip it in milk, dust it with flour, and fry it in very hot oil or clarified butter until it is golden on both sides. Remove from the pan and keep warm. Pour off the butter or oil in the pan, add fresh sweet butter to the pan, and cook over medium heat until nut colored. Pour over the fish and garnish with lemon quarters and chopped parsley.

BROWNING
Doratura

Fish that are completely masked with a sauce are frequently placed in a very hot oven or under the broiler for a few minutes to give the surface an attractive golden or light-brown color. Frequently a little grated cheese is sprinkled over the sauce, or a small amount of the sauce mixed with whipped cream is spread in a thin layer over the surface; this will hasten the browning process. Normally browning must be done very quickly to avoid overcooking the fish and to prevent curdling a sauce containing egg yolks.

AU GRATIN
Gratinatura

Gratin is literally a "covering," usually of breadcrumbs or cheese, and any dish whose preparation is completed in this fashion is said to be cooked "au gratin."

Light gratin:
Remove a boiled fish from its Court Bouillon a few minutes before it is done, drain it for a moment, and then place it on an oven-proof platter or baking dish. Brown a generous amount of fresh, finely grated breadcrumbs in butter for 2 seconds and spread them over the fish. Dot with a few pieces of softened butter and place in a very hot oven until the fish has a crisp, golden crust.

Warmed leftover fish may also be treated this way, either placed in shells or as a garnishing border for another dish.

Full gratin:
Remove the fish from its Court Bouillon, drain, and place on an oven-proof dish. Spoon a Mornay [No. 56] or white wine sauce over it, sprinkle it lightly with grated cheese (breadcrumbs may be mixed with the cheese) and melted butter, and place in a very hot oven until covered with a golden crust.

Anchovy

FRESH- AND SALT-WATER FISH
Pesci di mare e d'acqua dolce

ANCHOVIES
Acciuga

Anchovies are salt-water fish with a unique flavor. They are prepared in many of the same ways as sardines, which will be dealt with later, and are usually served with the heads removed. Commercial anchovy preparations—in salt brine or in oil—are delicious and make one of the best antipasto ingredients.

767. BAKED ANCHOVIES
Acciughe in teglia

2 pounds fresh anchovies, heads removed
2 tablespoons oil
$\frac{1}{4}$ cup wine vinegar
2 tablespoons chopped parsley
2 cloves garlic, crushed in the garlic-press
1 cup fresh breadcrumbs
$\frac{1}{2}$ cup butter, melted
Salt and freshly grated pepper

Clean, wash, and dry the anchovies. Grease with oil a

baking dish large enough to hold the anchovies in one layer and arrange them in it. Season them lightly with salt and pepper and sprinkle the vinegar over them. Sauté the parsley, garlic, and the breadcrumbs in the butter in a frying pan over high heat and spread them over the anchovies. Heat the dish for 1 minute on top of the stove over medium heat and then place it in a very hot (450°) oven for 10 to 12 minutes. The fish should be golden and the breadcrumbs crisp. *Serves* 6.

768. FRIED ANCHOVIES WITH LEMON
Acciughe fritte al limone

2 pounds fresh anchovies, heads removed
Milk
Flour
¾ cup oil
Salt
Parsley sprigs
3 lemons, quartered

Clean the anchovies, wash them, dry them, dip them in milk, then in flour, and drop them into a frying pan in which oil has been heated until smoking hot. Cook them for only a few minutes over medium high heat until they are crisply golden on both sides. Drain them on paper towels and sprinkle them lightly with salt. Heap them on a serving platter spread with a paper doily or a napkin and garnish them with clusters of fried [*see* No. 276] or fresh parsley and the lemon quarters. Serve at once. *Serves* 6.

BASS
Dentice, branzino, detto anche
spigola

Several varieties of bass are available in American markets. The black sea bass of the Atlantic coast and the white sea bass of the Pacific coast are particularly abundant and are similar to the Italian *dentice*. These are generally marketed in sizes of less than 4 pounds. Also usually available is striped sea bass which may weigh as much as 20 pounds. Two varieties of fresh-water bass are taken in great numbers in the Great Lakes region and in the Mississippi Valley. Bass is a rather lean fish, but its flesh is very tender and juicy and it has a delicious flavor. It is cleaned and prepared for cooking as described in the introduction.

769. BASS WITH ANCHOVY BUTTER
Dentice al burro d'acciuga

2 3-pound bass, cleaned
1½ pounds small "new" potatoes
Flour
½ cup butter
6 sprigs parsley
Dash Worcestershire sauce
Salt and freshly ground pepper
¾ cup Anchovy Butter [No. 108]

Peel the potatoes and cook them in lightly salted boiling water for about 20 minutes, or until they are tender. About 10 minutes before they are done, cut each fish into 4 transverse slices, season them lightly with salt and pepper, and dust them with flour. Melt the butter in a large frying pan until almost nut colored, add the pieces of fish, and brown them quickly on both sides. Reduce heat slightly and cook them for about 8 minutes longer on each side. Transfer them to a hot serving platter and garnish with the boiled potatoes and the parsley. Add the Worcestershire sauce to the butter in which the fish cooked, boil for a few seconds, and then pour over the fish. Serve the anchovy butter on the side. *Serves* 6.

770. FILLETS OF BASS AU GRATIN
Filetti di dentice al gratino

6 ½-pound fillets of bass
½ cup butter, softened
1 tablespoon chopped shallots
1 cup dry white wine
1½ cups fresh breadcrumbs
Salt and freshly ground white pepper
Juice of 1 lemon
1 tablespoon chopped parsley

Butter a large baking dish with 3 tablespoons of the butter, sprinkle the shallots in the bottom, arrange the fillets in it, season lightly with salt and pepper, add the wine, cover the dish with a lid or aluminum foil, and put in a moderate (350°) oven for 10 minutes. Remove from the oven and transfer the fillets temporarily to a warm platter. Boil down the cooking liquid over a high flame to ⅓ its volume and, as it reduces, add any juices that have drained from the fish. Return the fillets to the baking dish, sprinkle them with the breadcrumbs, and dot with the remaining butter. Return to a hot (450°) oven for about 4 minutes, or until the surface of the fillets is golden. Squeeze the lemon juice over the fillets, sprinkle with the chopped parsley, and serve in the baking dish. *Serves* 6.

771. BASS CASALINGA
Branzinetti alla casalinga

6 ¾- to 1-pound bass
½ cup butter
1 onion, chopped
½ cup dry white wine
1 tablespoon chopped parsley
1½ tablespoons Kneaded Butter [No. 107]
5 anchovy fillets, washed free of salt [*see* No. 220] and
    pounded to a paste in a mortar
Juice of ½ lemon
Salt and freshly ground pepper

Clean and wash the bass thoroughly. Season the cavity with salt and pepper. Melt 4 tablespoons of the butter in a very large, heavy skillet over medium heat, add the onion, and cook until golden. Add the wine, parsley, and the bass (if the skillet is not large enough to hold all the bass, use 2 pans and slightly more butter); bring to a boil; reduce heat; cover tightly; and cook for about 12 minutes. Remove the bass from the pan, put them on a hot serving platter, and keep warm. The bass will have rendered a good deal of juice during their cooking; you should have about 1 cup. Strain this liquid into a bowl, return it to the pan, blend in the kneaded butter and the anchovy paste, and cook over medium heat, stirring constantly, for 5 to 8 minutes. Taste for seasoning, swirl in the remaining butter off the heat, and add the lemon juice. Pour the sauce over the fish. *Serves* 6.

772. BASS GOURMET
Branzino alla ghiottona

2 3-pound bass
1 quart Fish Fumet [No. 2]
2 cups dry white wine
2 cups red wine
4 carrots, sliced
1 onion, sliced
2 cloves garlic, crushed in the garlic-press
Bouquet Garni:
    2 sprigs thyme (or ¼ teaspoon dried)
    2 sprigs parsley
    1 bay leaf
2 cloves
4 tablespoons Kneaded Butter [No. 107]
1 pound tomatoes, peeled, seeded, drained, and chopped
10 anchovy fillets, washed free of salt [*see* No. 220]
    and chopped
Salt and freshly ground pepper

Clean and wash the bass thoroughly. Place the fish on a rack in a fish boiler and add the fish Fumet, red and white wine, carrots, onion, garlic, Bouquet Garni, and cloves. Season lightly with salt and pepper, bring to a boil over medium heat, reduce the flame, and simmer for 25 to 30 minutes. When the fish are done, place them on a hot serving platter, keep warm, and carefully scrape off the skin from the head to the tail of their top side. Strain the fish liquid through several thicknesses of cheesecloth into bowl, pour 1 quart of it into a saucepan, bring it quickly to a boil, blend in the kneaded butter, add the tomato pulp and the chopped anchovies, and simmer for 5 minutes. Taste for seasoning and pour half of it over the fish. The edge of the platter may be garnished with slices of the cooked carrot. Serve the remaining sauce on the side. *Serves* 6.

773. BASS WITH HOLLANDAISE SAUCE
Dentice lessato con salsa olandese

2 3-pound bass, cleaned
1½ pounds small "new" potatoes
Salt
6 sprigs parsley
2 cups Sauce Hollandaise [No. 72]

Peel and cook the potatoes in lightly salted boiling water for about 20 minutes. Place the fish on a rack in a fish boiler, cover with cold water, add 2 teaspoons of salt, bring to a boil over high heat, cover tightly, reduce the heat, and simmer for about 15 minutes. Transfer the fish to a hot serving platter, surround it with the boiled potatoes, and garnish with the parsley. Serve the Hollandaise sauce on the side. *Serves* 6.

774. BASS ITALIANA
Dentice freddo all'italiana

2 3-pound bass, cleaned
2 lemons, quartered
6 sprigs parsley
3 hard-boiled eggs, quartered
6 small hearts of Boston lettuce
Salt
2 cups Mayonnaise [No. 77]

Place the fish on a rack in a fish boiler, cover with cold water, add 2 teaspoons of salt, bring to a boil over high heat, cover tightly, reduce the heat, and simmer for about 15 minutes. Remove from the fire, add 2 cups of cold water to stop the cooking process, and allow the fish to cool in the liquid. When it is cold, carefully transfer it to a serving platter, remove the skin, and garnish with lemons, parsley, eggs, and lettuce. Serve the mayonnaise on the side. *Serves* 6.

775. BASS MEUNIÈRE WITH PEPPERS
Branzinetti alla mugnaia con peperoni

6 1-pound bass
Flour
½ cup butter
3 sweet peppers, roasted, scraped, seeded, and cut into
    strips [*see* No. 145]
2 tablespoons oil
1 tablespoon chopped parsley
Juice of ½ lemon
Salt

Clean, wash, and dry the bass; season the cavities with salt and pepper; and dust the fish with flour. Melt the butter in a large, heavy skillet (or use 2 skillets) over a medium-high flame until it is golden, add the bass, reduce the heat slightly, and cook them for about 6 minutes on each side. While the bass are cooking, sauté the peppers in the oil in a frying pan over moderate heat for about 10 minutes. When the bass are done, arrange them on a serving platter, season them lightly with salt, and sprinkle them with the parsley and lemon juice. Place a few strips of pepper over each fish and pour the butter in which they cooked over all. *Serves* 6.

776. BASS NIÇOISE
Branzinetti alla nizzarda

6 1-pound bass
⅔ cup pitted black olives
½ cup oil
2 tablespoons chopped onion
½ pound tomatoes, peeled, seeded, drained, and
    chopped
1 tablespoon chopped tarragon
1 tablespoon chopped parsley
12 anchovy fillets, washed free of salt [*see* No. 220]
Salt and freshly ground pepper

Simmer the olives in water for 10 minutes, drain, and keep warm. Clean, wash, and dry the bass. Season the cavities with salt and brush the fish with oil. Broil them under a medium high flame for about 6 minutes on each side, basting with more oil during the cooking. Meanwhile, brown the onion very quickly in 2 tablespoons of oil in a frying pan over high heat, add the

tomatoes, season lightly with salt and pepper, and cook for about 8 minutes. Add the chopped tarragon and parsley and cook for 1 minute more. Spread this sauce on the bottom of a serving platter, arrange the bass over it, decorate each bass with 2 of the anchovy fillets, and garnish the platter with a ring of the warm olives. *Serves* 6.

777. BASS NORMANDE
Branzino lessato con salsa normanda

2 3-pound bass
Salt
Parsley sprigs
2 cups Sauce Normande [No. 52]

Clean and wash bass thoroughly. Place them on the rack in a fish boiler, cover with cold water, add a tablespoon of salt, bring to a boil, reduce the flame, and simmer for 15 minutes. When cooked, place the fish carefully on a serving platter and garnish with the springs of parsley. Serve the Normande sauce on the side. *Serves* 6.

NOTE: Plain, hot, boiled "new" potatoes make an excellent accompaniment for boiled bass.

778. COLD BASS WITH OIL AND LEMON
Branzino freddo con olio e limone

2 3-pound bass
Salt
Parsley sprigs
2 lemons, quartered
1 cup Sauce Vinaigrette [No. 99], mixed with
    1 tablespoon chopped parsley (or substitute 1½
    cups Mayonnaise—No. 77)

Clean and wash the bass thoroughly. Bring it to a boil in lightly salted water and cook for 15 to 20 minutes. Add 2 cups of cold water to stop the cooking process and allow the bass to cool completely in the liquid. Drain and carefully remove skin, and place on a serving platter garnished with the parsley and lemon quarters. Serve the Vinaigrette or the mayonnaise on the side. *Serves* 6.

779. ROAST BASS
Branzino arrosto

2 3-pound bass, cleaned
4 tablespoons butter, softened
1½ cups Sauce Bercy [No. 49]
½ cup oil

2 large onions, sliced and dusted with flour
2 lemons, sliced
Salt and freshly ground pepper

Season the cavity of the fish with salt and pepper, spread the softened butter all over them, place in an oblong baking dish, and bake in a hot (400°) oven for about 20 minutes. Test after 15 minutes and, if it flakes easily, it is done. While the bass is cooking, prepare the Bercy sauce and sauté the onions in smoking hot oil in a frying pan until golden. Arrange the onions in a bed on a serving platter, place the bass on top, and garnish with the sliced lemons. Pass the sauce on the side. *Serves* 6.

CARP

Carpio

Carp is a delicious fresh-water fish which can grow to a considerable size, but the type most commonly found in American markets is from 2 to 7 pounds. Occasionally very small carp are available. The best carp have brown scales on their back, golden yellow sides, and greenish-white stomachs. It is best to avoid carp of a very dark color; these were probably bred in stagnant waters and will have a slightly muddy taste. Carp is at its best when taken from very cold water; therefore, the best season is from October to March. They are scaled and cleaned as described in the introduction. Ideally, carp should be cooked immediately after killing, and it is possible to accomplish this if one is able to purchase the fish live at a Chinese fish market. Certain Italian fish markets also carry live carp.

780. CARP CAPPUCCINA
Carpio alla cappuccina

6 1-pound carp, cleaned
½ cup oil
Salt and freshly ground pepper
1 tablespoon chopped oregano (or ½ teaspoon dried)
1 cup fresh breadcrumbs
2 lemons, sliced

Split the fish in half and remove the central bone, but leave the outside skin intact. Arrange the fillets in an oiled baking dish, skin side down. Season them with salt and pepper, sprinkle with the oregano and breadcrumbs, arrange the lemon slices on top, and pour the oil into the dish. Place them in a hot (400°) oven for about 15 minutes, basting occasionally with the juices in the pan. *Serves* 6.

781. COLD CARP
Carpio fritto in carpione

6 1-pound carp, cleaned and filleted
Milk
Flour
1 cup oil
1 large onion, sliced
3 cloves garlic, crushed in the garlic-press
2 yellow peppers, roasted, scraped, seeded, and cut into strips [*see* No. 145]
1½ cups mild white wine vinegar
12 fresh sage leaves
Pinch sugar
Salt and freshly ground pepper

Dip the fish in milk and then roll them in flour. Heat ¾ cup of the oil in a large frying pan over high heat until smoking hot, add the fish, and brown fairly quickly. Drain them when they are crisp and golden and arrange them in a shallow serving bowl. Heat the remaining oil in a saucepan, add the onion and garlic, cook until they are soft, add the pepper strips, sauté for another 2 minutes, and add the vinegar, sage, sugar, and a generous amount of salt and pepper. Bring just to a boil, pour over the fish, cover the dish, put in a cool place, and allow the fish to steep in the liquid for 24 hours, or longer, if desired. *Serves* 6.

782. COLD CARP ISRAELITA
Carpio freddo all'israelita

1 6-pound carp, cleaned and cut into 2-inch steaks
1 quart dry white wine
1 quart Fish Fumet [No. 2]
3 cups oil
1 onion, chopped
2 shallots, chopped
5 tablespoons flour
2 cloves garlic, bruised
Bouquet Garni:
    2 sprigs thyme (or 1/4 teaspoon dried)
    1 bay leaf
Pinch Cayenne pepper
Salt
Optional: juice of 1 lemon
3 tablespoons chopped parsley

Combine the wine and fish Fumet in a saucepan and heat to the boiling point. Heat 1 cup of the oil in a large, heavy pot over medium heat, add the onion and shallots, and cook until golden. Add the flour, stir for a few seconds, and then add the boiling wine and Fumet, stirring constantly with a whisk. Add the garlic and Bouquet Garni, season very lightly with salt and the Cayenne (be careful of overseasoning, since the sauce will be reduced later on), and bring to a boil. Add the carp slices, including the head; reduce the heat to moderate; and simmer for about 20 minutes. Remove the fish slices to a platter, allow to cool, and then arrange the slices to re-create the form of the original fish. Meanwhile, remove the Bouquet Garni and the garlic and discard; and continue cooking the sauce slowly until it is reduced to 1/3 of its original quantity. Stir occasionally to prevent its sticking to the bottom of the pot. Remove from the fire and cool. Now add the remaining oil, drop by drop, in the same manner as though making mayonnaise. When all the oil has been added, it should have the consistency of a thin mayonnaise. Taste for seasoning, add the optional lemon juice, and pour it over the fish. Sprinkle the parsley over and serve the fish cool, but not chilled. *Serves* 6.

266

783. FRIED CARP
Carpio fritto

3 2-pound carp, cleaned (reserving the milt)
Salt and freshly ground pepper
Flour
3/4 cup oil

Parsley sprigs
2 lemons, quartered

Split the carp lengthwise down their backs, cutting only to the long center bone. Season the inside of this cavity with salt and pepper; dredge the fish lightly with flour. Heat the oil in a very large frying pan (or use 2 pans) over high heat until it is smoking hot, add the fish, and cook them for about 7 minutes on each side. Reduce the heat slightly during the cooking if they brown too quickly. Remove the fish to a hot serving platter and garnish with the parsley and lemon quarters. *Serves* 6.

NOTE: If the carp contain milt, this may be fried with the fish for the last 5 minutes of cooking and served on the same platter.

784. ROAST CARP
Carpio arrosto

6 1-pound carp, cleaned
A marinade of:
    1 cup oil
    1/4 cup lemon juice
    1 teaspoon salt
    1/4 teaspoon freshly ground pepper
2 lemons, quartered

Marinate the carp in the marinade for 1 hour, turning them occasionally. Transfer the fish to a large baking dish, stir the marinade vigorously, pour it over the fish, and bake them for about 15 minutes in a hot (400°) oven, basting them occasionally with the juices in the pan. Place the fish on a hot serving platter, spoon a little of the cooking juices over them, and garnish with the lemon quarters. *Serves* 6.

CUTTLEFISH
Seppia

Cuttlefish are a salt-water mollusk, closely related to squid. They are usually marketed in sizes less than a foot long. Like squid, the eyes, long central bone, sac of ink, and yellowish deposit under the head must be removed. Squid may be substituted in any of the following recipes.

785. CUTTLEFISH WITH ARTICHOKES
Seppie con carciofi

3 pounds cuttlefish, cleaned and cut into pieces, reserving the yellowish deposit

6 small, young artichokes, quartered and soaked in acidulated water for 1 hour

2 tablespoons oil

2 cloves garlic, crushed in the garlic-press

½ cup dry white wine

6 anchovy fillets, washed free of salt [*see* No. 220] and pounded to a paste in the mortar

1 tablespoon chopped parsley

2 lemons, quartered

Salt and freshly ground pepper

Remove the tough, outer leaves from the artichokes, cut off the sharp tips of all the leaves, and remove the chokes with a sharp knife. Heat the oil in a large saucepan over medium heat, add the garlic, and cook until golden. Add the cuttlefish pieces, season lightly with salt and pepper, and stir for 1 minute. Add the wine, blend in the anchovy paste, and cook until the wine has almost evaporated. Reduce the heat, add sufficient water to barely cover the fish, and cook for about 40 minutes, or until the fish is tender. About 20 minutes before the fish is done, add the artichokes. When both are tender, remove them with a slotted spoon to a hot serving dish and keep warm. Add the yellowish deposit to the liquid in the pan and then reduce it over high heat for a few minutes to give it a concentrated flavor. Pour over the fish and artichokes, sprinkle the parsley on top, and garnish with the lemon quarters. *Serves* 6.

786. BROILED CUTTLEFISH
Seppie in gratella

2½ pounds cuttlefish, cleaned, tentacles removed, and cut into long pieces

½ cup oil

Salt and freshly ground pepper

2 lemons, quartered

Place the pieces of fish in a bowl, season them lightly with salt and pepper, add the oil, and marinate for 1 hour, stirring occasionally. Broil the pieces 5 inches below a medium broiler flame for about 12 minutes on each side, basting occasionally with the oil. Remove them to a hot serving platter and garnish with the lemon quarters. *Serves* 6.

787. CUTTLEFISH PAESANA
Seppie alla paesana

2½ pounds cuttlefish, cleaned, tentacles removed, and cut into large pieces

½ cup oil

3 cloves garlic, crushed in the garlic-press

½ cup dry white wine

2 tablespoons chopped parsley

2 lemons quartered

Salt and freshly ground pepper

Marinate (using ¼ cup of the oil) and broil the pieces of fish as in the preceding recipe. While the fish is cooking, heat the remaining ¼ cup of the oil in a frying pan over medium heat, add the garlic, and cook until golden. Add the wine and cook until almost evaporated. Pour over the pieces of fish arranged on a hot serving dish, sprinkle the parsley over the top, and garnish with the lemon quarters.

788. CUTTLEFISH WITH PEAS
Seppie con pisellini dolci

3 pounds cuttlefish, cleaned and cut into pieces, reserving the yellowish deposit

½ cup oil

2 cloves garlic, crushed in the garlic-press

½ cup dry white wine

6 anchovy fillets, washed free of salt [*see* No. 220] and pounded to a paste in the mortar

4 tomatoes, peeled, seeded, drained, and puréed through a food mill or strainer

1 pound small, tender peas (or 1 box frozen petits pois)

1 tablespoon chopped parsley

Salt and freshly ground pepper

Heat the oil in a large, heavy saucepan over medium heat, add the garlic, and cook until golden. Add the pieces of fish, stir for 1 minute, season lightly with salt and pepper, add the wine, blend in the anchovy paste, and cook until the wine has almost entirely evaporated. Reduce the heat, add the tomato purée and sufficient water to barely cover the fish, cover the pan tightly, and cook for about 40 minutes, or until the fish is tender. About 10 minutes before the fish is done, add the peas. When they are tender, drain the peas and fish into a sieve placed over a bowl, invert the sieve onto a hot serving platter, and keep warm. Return the liquid in the bowl to the saucepan, add the yellowish deposit, and reduce over a high flame for about 5 minutes. Check the seasoning, pour over the fish, and sprinkle the top with parsley. *Serves* 6.

789. STUFFED YOUNG CUTTLEFISH
Seppioline alla Cetrullo

12 ½-pound cuttlefish
2 cups fresh breadcrumbs
2 cloves garlic, crushed in the garlic-press
2 tablespoons chopped parsley
½ cup dry white wine
A paste pounded in the mortar:
    2 ounces anchovy fillets, washed free of salt [*see* No. 220]
    1 ounce capers
½ cup oil
½ cup water
Salt and freshly ground pepper

Clean the cuttlefish, but leave the bone intact; discard the eyes, cut off the heads and tentacles, and put these latter through the meat grinder, using the finest blade. Place the ground fish in a bowl and add the breadcrumbs, garlic, parsley, wine, and anchovy/caper paste. Season lightly with salt and generously with pepper. Mix very thoroughly and stuff each of the cuttlefish bodies with a little of the mixture. Tie the openings with string, arrange the fish in a large casserole, add the oil and water, cover tightly, bring to a boil on top of the stove, and then place the casserole in a moderate (350°) oven for 1 hour. They may be served either hot or cold. *Serves* 6.

Preparation of Stuffed Young Cuttlefish (No. 789)

790. DRIED COD BARCAROLA
Baccalà alla barcarola

2 pounds dried cod, soaked for 12 hours in several changes of water
3 large onions, very finely chopped
1 tablespoon chopped parsley
2 cups dry white wine (or more, if needed)
4 tablespoons oil

Trim and dry the soaked cod (the skin may be removed, if desired), cut it into slices 2 inches wide, and put them in a pot with the onions, parsley, white wine, and the oil. Cover the pot, bring to a boil over medium heat, reduce the flame, and cook for 15 minutes. Remove the pieces of cod and arrange them on a hot serving platter. Reduce the liquid to ½ its quantity over high heat and pour it over the fish. Serve very hot. *Serves* 6.

791. DRIED COD BOLOGNESE
Baccalà alla bolognese

2 pounds dried cod, soaked for 12 hours in several changes of water
3 tablespoons oil
1 onion, chopped
1 clove garlic, crushed in the garlic-press
2 tablespoons chopped parsley
3 tablespoons butter
Freshly ground pepper
Juice from 1 lemon

Trim, skin, and dry the soaked cod; cut it into slices 2 inches wide. Heat the oil in a frying pan over medium heat, add the fish pieces, and scatter the chopped onion, garlic, and parsley over them. Dot with the butter, season with 3 turns of the pepper mill, and sauté the pieces of fish for 8 minutes on each side, turning them with great care to prevent their breaking up. Arrange them on a serving platter, pour the sauce left in the pan over them, and squeeze the lemon juice over them. *Serves* 6.

DRIED COD

Baccalà

Cod (dried, and called baccalà in Italy), comes from the Atlantic, particularly along the Newfoundland banks, the coast of Nova Scotia, and the coast of New England. (In the United States, a species of cod is also found in the Pacific.) The cod is cleaned, salted, and then dried. Cod is also packed in brine, but the dried variety is more common. It must be soaked for a minimum of 12 hours—if possible, under a trickle of running water—or the water must be changed very often. The soaking process not only softens the fish, but is necessary to wash away much of the salt taste. The best cod has very white meat and should flake easily.

After soaking and cooking cod, it is wise to taste it for saltiness and be guided in seasoning the accompanying sauce. Do *not* soak dried cod in a metal container, *always* use enamel or earthenware.

SOME POPULAR FRESH- AND SALT-WATER FISH

(not shown to scale)

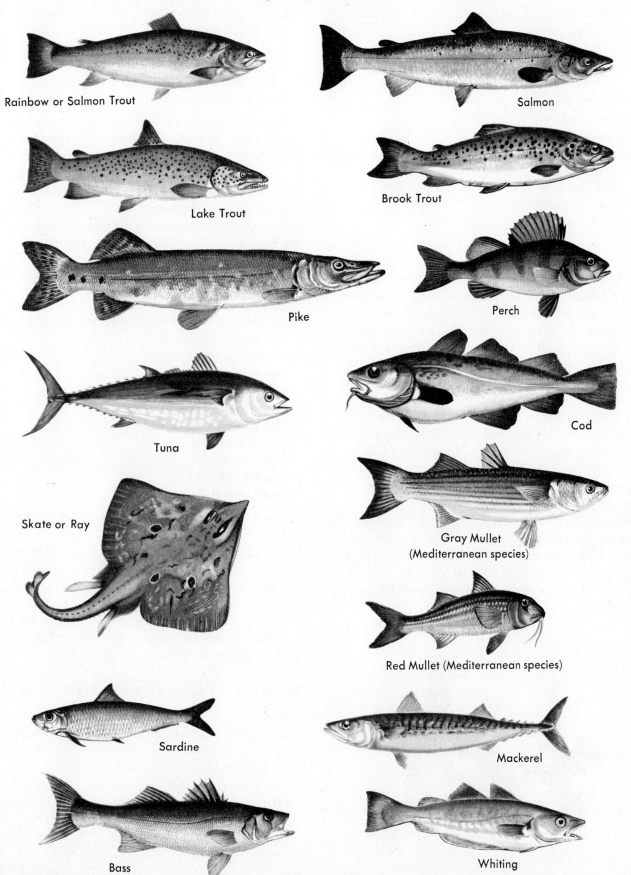

Rainbow or Salmon Trout

Salmon

Lake Trout

Brook Trout

Pike

Perch

Tuna

Cod

Skate or Ray

Gray Mullet
(Mediterranean species)

Red Mullet (Mediterranean species)

Sardine

Mackerel

Bass

Whiting

269

792. DRIED COD CAPPUCCINA
Baccalà alla cappuccina

2 pounds dried cod, soaked for 12 hours in several
    changes of water
2 cups hot Duchesse Potatoes [No. 1771]
3 large onions, sliced
½ cup butter
2 tablespoons flour
1½ cups boiling milk
1 tablespoon chopped parsley
¼ cup grated Parmesan cheese
¼ cup fresh breadcrumbs
Pinch nutmeg
Freshly ground pepper
Salt (if needed)

Trim and dry the cod and cut it into 2-inch pieces.
Put them in a saucepan, cover with cold water, bring
to a boil over medium heat, reduce heat, and simmer
for 5 minutes. Drain the pieces in a colander, remove
all skin and bones, and flake the fish. Parboil the onions
for 8 minutes, drain, and dry them on a paper towel.
Melt 4 tablespoons of the butter in a frying pan over
moderate heat, add the onions, and cook until limp
but do not brown. Add the flour, mix well, and pour
in the boiling milk all at once, stirring constantly.
Season with pepper and nutmeg, add the chopped
parsley, and bring to a boil. Add the codfish flakes,
reduce the heat, and cook for 20 minutes. Taste for
salt and then turn the mixture onto an oven-proof
platter. Sprinkle the grated cheese mixed with the
breadcrumbs over the top, dot with the remaining
butter, and pipe a border of the Duchesse potatoes
around the edge of the platter, using a pastry bag
fitted with a medium star tip. Put the platter in a
very hot (450°) oven and bake for about 10 minutes,
or until the edges of the potatoes are golden brown.
Serves 6.

793. DRIED COD FIORENTINA
Baccalà alla fiorentina

2 pounds dried cod, soaked for 12 hours in several
    changes of water
Flour
¼ cup oil
3 cloves garlic, crushed in the garlic-press
2 cups Tomato Sauce [No. 19]

Trim, skin, and dry the cod and cut it into 2-inch
pieces. Dust the pieces with flour. Heat the oil in a
frying pan over medium heat, add the garlic, cook for
1 minute, and then add the cod pieces. Cook them for
5 or 6 minutes on each side, season them lightly with
pepper, and add the tomato sauce. Bring to a boil,
reduce the heat, simmer for 10 minutes, and turn
the mixture out onto a serving dish. *Serves* 6.

794. COD FRITTERS
Baccalà fritto dorato

2 pounds dried cod, soaked for 12 hours in several
    changes of water
4 tablespoons oil
Juice of 1 lemon
1 tablespoon chopped parsley
2 cups Fritter Batter [No. 275]
1 egg white, beaten stiff
Fat for deep frying
Parsley sprigs
2 lemons, quartered
Freshly ground pepper

Skin and bone the soaked cod and cut the fish into bite-
size pieces. Marinate the pieces for 1 hour in the oil,
lemon juice, and chopped parsley. Fold the beaten
egg white into the fritter batter, dry the pieces of cod,
dip them in the batter, and fry in deep hot (375°) fat
until they are golden. Remove from the fat, drain for
a moment on absorbent paper, and then arrange them
on a platter. Sprinkle lightly with pepper and garnish
with the lemon quarters and parsley. *Serves* 6.

795. FRIED FILLETS OF DRIED COD
Filetti di baccalà in bignè

2 pounds of dried cod, soaked for 12 hours in several
    changes of water
Fritter Batter [No. 275]
1 egg white, beaten stiff
Fat for deep frying
2 lemons, quartered
Parsley sprigs
Freshly ground pepper

Prepare and serve exactly as Cod Fritters [No. 794], except the cod is cut into larger pieces and is not marinated. *Serves* 6.

796. DRIED COD NAPOLETANA
Baccalà alla napoletana

2 pounds dried cod, soaked for 12 hours in several
    changes of water
Flour
$\frac{1}{2}$ cup oil
1 clove garlic, crushed in the garlic-press
2 pounds tomatoes, peeled, seeded, drained, and
    chopped
$1\frac{1}{2}$ cups black olives, pitted
1 tablespoon capers
1 tablespoon chopped oregano (or $\frac{1}{2}$ teaspoon dried)
Salt and freshly ground pepper

Skin and bone the cod, cut it into 2-inch slices, and dust the slices with flour. Heat the oil in a frying pan over medium heat until smoking hot, add the pieces of cod, and cook for 6 or 7 minutes on each side. Drain the pieces and keep hot. Cook the garlic in the oil remaining in the pan over medium heat until golden, add the tomatoes, season lightly with salt and pepper, and cook for 10 minutes. Add the olives, capers, and oregano and cook for 2 minutes longer. Arrange the cod pieces on a hot serving platter and pour the sauce over them. *Serves* 6.

NOTE: If fresh oregano is not available, add the dried oregano to the sauce with the tomatoes.

797. DRIED COD WITH OLIVES
Baccalà con olive verdi

2 pounds dried cod, soaked for 12 hours in several
    changes of water
Flour
$\frac{1}{2}$ cup oil
1 onion, sliced
1 pound tomatoes, peeled, seeded, drained, and chopped
2 tablespoons gherkins, sliced
$1\frac{1}{2}$ cups green ripe olives, pitted
1 tablespoon capers
2 tablespoons chopped parsley
Salt and freshly ground pepper

Skin and bone the soaked cod, cut it into 2-inch slices, and dust the slices with flour. Heat the oil in a frying pan over medium heat until smoking, add the pieces of cod, and brown on both sides. Drain the pieces and keep them hot. Cook the onion in the oil remaining

in the pan over medium heat until golden, add the tomatoes, season lightly with salt and pepper, and cook for 10 minutes. Add the gherkins, olives, capers, and parsley and cook for 5 minutes longer. Arrange the pieces of fish on a serving platter and pour the sauce over them. *Serves* 6.

798. DRIED COD WITH ONIONS AND POTATOES
Baccalà con cipolle e patate

2 pounds dried cod, soaked for 12 hours in several
    changes of water
4 tablespoons oil
3 onions, sliced
2 tablespoons butter
3 potatoes, sliced
3 tablespoons chopped parsley
Salt and freshly ground pepper

Trim and dry the cod and cut it into 2-inch pieces. Put them in a saucepan, cover with cold water, bring to a boil over medium heat, reduce heat, and simmer for 15 minutes. Drain the pieces in a colander, remove all skin and bones, and flake the fish. Cook the onions in a frying pan with 3 tablespoons of oil over medium heat until golden; remove them with a slotted spoon and keep warm. Add the butter and remaining oil to the pan and brown the sliced potatoes over high heat, seasoning them with a little salt and pepper as they cook. As soon as the potatoes are brown and tender, add the onions and flaked fish to the pan, reduce the heat, toss the mixture very lightly, and cook for 1 or 2 minutes to heat it thoroughly. Turn it out onto a warm serving dish and sprinkle the parsley over the top. *Serves* 6.

799. DRIED COD WITH PEPPERS ROMANA
Baccalà con peperoni alla romana

2 pounds dried cod, soaked for 12 hours in several
    changes of water
Flour
$\frac{1}{2}$ cup oil
6 yellow peppers, roasted, scraped, seeded, and
    cut into strips [*see* No. 145]
2 onions, chopped
$1\frac{1}{2}$ pounds tomatoes, peeled, seeded, drained, and
    chopped
Salt and freshly ground pepper

Bone the soaked cod, cut it into 2-inch slices, and dust the slices with flour. Heat the oil in a frying pan over medium heat until smoking, add the pieces of cod, and brown on each side for 6 or 7 minutes. Remove the pieces and keep hot. Cook the peppers for about 5 minutes, or until they are tender, in the oil remaining in the pan over medium heat. Remove them with a slotted spoon and keep warm. In the same oil (adding a little more, if necessary), cook the onions until they are transparent, add the tomatoes, season lightly with salt (if necessary) and pepper, and cook for 15 minutes. Arrange the pieces of cod on a serving platter, pour the tomato sauce over them, and top with the peppers. *Serves* 6.

800. DRIED COD PIZZAIOLA
Baccalà alla pizzaiola

2 pounds dried cod, soaked for 12 hours in several
    changes of water
¼ cup oil
2 tomatoes, peeled, seeded, drained, and sliced
A chopped mixture of:
    1 clove garlic
    2 sprigs basil (or ½ teaspoon dried)
    2 sprigs parsley
    2 sprigs oregano (or ½ teaspoon dried)
Freshly ground white pepper

Trim the soaked cod and cut it into 2-inch slices. Place the slices in a saucepan, cover with cold water, bring to a boil, reduce the heat, and simmer for 5 minutes. Drain the pieces, skin and bone them, and place them in an oiled baking dish. Arrange the tomatoes and chopped mixture over them, season very generously with pepper, sprinkle the oil over the top, and bake in a moderate (350°) oven for 25 minutes. *Serves* 6.

801. DRIED COD ROMANA
Baccalà in guazzetto alla romana

2 pounds dried cod, soaked for 12 hours in several
    changes of water
Flour
½ cup oil
3 cloves garlic, crushed in the garlic-press
2 pounds tomatoes, peeled, seeded, drained, and
    chopped
1 tablespoon chopped parsley
1 tablespoon yellow raisins

1 tablespoon pine nuts
Salt and freshly ground pepper

Trim and bone the soaked cod, cut it into 2-inch slices, and dust the slices with flour. Heat the oil in a frying pan over medium heat until smoking, add the pieces of cod, and cook for 6 minutes on each side. Drain the pieces and keep hot. Cook the garlic in the oil remaining in the pan over medium heat until golden, add the tomatoes, season lightly with salt (if needed) and pepper, and cook for 10 minutes. Add the parsley, pine nuts, and the raisins and cook for 3 minutes longer. Arrange the pieces of hot fish on a serving platter and pour the sauce over them. *Serves* 6.

802. SUNRAY DRIED COD
Baccalà al raggio di sole

2 pounds dried cod, soaked for 12 hours in several
    changes of water
Flour
½ cup oil
1 pound onions, sliced
1 clove garlic, crushed in the garlic-press
3 anchovy fillets, washed free of salt [*see* No. 220],
    and pounded to a paste in a mortar
1 tablespoon capers
1 tablespoon pine nuts
1 tablespoon yellow raisins
2 tablespoons chopped parsley
Juice of ½ lemon
Salt and freshly ground white pepper

Trim and bone the cod, cut it into 2-inch slices, and dust the slices with flour. Heat the oil in a frying pan over medium heat until smoking, add the pieces of cod, brown them on each side for about 6 minutes, remove them with a slotted spoon, and keep hot. Cook the garlic and sliced onions until golden in the oil remaining in the pan; add the anchovy paste, capers, pine nuts, and raisins; and season very lightly with salt (if needed) and generously with pepper. Spread the mixture out on an oven-proof platter, arrange the pieces of cod over it, and place the platter in a hot (400°) oven for 5 minutes. Remove from the oven, squeeze the lemon juice over the fish, and sprinkle the parsley over the top. *Serves* 6.

NOTE: Plain, hot, boiled potatoes are an excellent accompaniment for this dish.

1. Mullet en Papillotes with Anchovy Butter
   (No. 834), shown unwrapped at left
2. Porgy Marina Piccola (No. 864)

STOCKFISH

Stoccafisso

Stockfish is cod that is dried without salt. It is split and hung in fresh air until completely dry. In the United States haddock is sometimes treated and sold in this manner.

Like dried salt cod, stockfish must be soaked in several changes of water for a minimum of 12 hours, or, if possible, under a trickle of running water.

803. STOCKFISH NIÇOISE
Stoccafisso alla nizzarda

2 pounds stockfish, soaked, skinned, boned, and cubed
1 cup oil
2 cloves garlic, crushed in the garlic-press
2 onions, finely sliced
2 leeks (white part only), finely sliced
2 pounds tomatoes, peeled, seeded, drained, and chopped
4 potatoes, quartered
1½ cups pitted black olives
8 anchovy fillets, washed free of salt [see No. 220], pounded to a paste in the mortar, and mixed with
1 tablespoon chopped parsley and ¼ cup brandy
Salt and freshly ground pepper

Lightly brown the onions, leeks, and garlic in the oil in a large earthenware casserole over medium heat. Add the stockfish cubes, tomatoes, and sufficient water to barely cover the fish. Season with salt and pepper, cover tightly, and place in a moderate (350°) oven for 1 hour. Uncover the casserole, add the potatoes and olives, and continue cooking for another 25 minutes, or until the potatoes are tender. A few minutes before removing from the oven, add the anchovy paste mixture. Correct the seasoning and serve very hot in the casserole. *Serves* 6.

804. STOCKFISH SICILIANA
Stoccafisso alla siciliana

2 pounds stockfish, soaked, skinned, boned, and cubed
1 cup oil
1 onion, chopped
2 cloves garlic, crushed in the garlic-press
½ cup dry white wine
2 pounds tomatoes, peeled, seeded, drained, and chopped
4 potatoes, quartered
2 cups pitted black olives
2 tablespoons capers
2 tablespoons pine nuts
2 tablespoons yellow raisins
Salt and freshly ground pepper

Lightly brown the onion and garlic in the oil in a large earthenware casserole over medium heat. Add the stockfish cubes and the wine and cook until the wine has almost evaporated. Add the tomatoes and sufficient water to barely cover the fish, season lightly with salt and pepper, cover tightly, and place in a moderate (350°) oven for 1 hour. Uncover and add the potatoes, olives, capers, pine nuts, and yellow raisins. Continue cooking for another 25 minutes, or until the potatoes are tender. Correct the seasoning and serve in the casserole. *Serves* 6.

805. STOCKFISH VICENTINA NO. 1
Stoccafisso alla vicentina

2 pounds stockfish, soaked, skinned, boned, and cut into serving-size pieces
Pinch cinnamon
Flour
½ cup grated Parmesan cheese
1 onion, chopped
1 clove garlic, crushed in the garlic-press
½ cup oil
8 anchovy fillets, washed free of salt [see No. 220], and pounded to a paste in the mortar
1 tablespoon chopped parsley
½ cup dry white wine
2 cups milk, scalded
2 tablespoons butter, softened
3 cups Polenta [No. 623], chilled, sliced, and fried crisp in oil
Salt and freshly ground pepper

Season the stockfish with salt, pepper, and cinnamon; dust the pieces lightly with flour; and put them in an earthenware casserole large enough to accommodate them in one layer. Sprinkle the grated Parmesan over them. Brown the onion and garlic in oil in a frying pan over medium heat; add the anchovy paste, parsley, and the wine. Cook over a brisk flame until almost evaporated and add the hot milk and the butter. Stir well and pour over the fish. Bring to a boil over high heat and place the casserole in a moderate (350°) oven for 1½ hours. Serve in the casserole with the slices of hot, fried polenta on the side. *Serves* 6.

806. STOCKFISH VICENTINA NO. 2
Stoccafisso alla vicentina a modo mio

2 pounds stockfish, soaked, skinned, boned, and
    cut into serving-size pieces
½ cup oil
1 onion, finely sliced
3 cloves garlic, crushed in the garlic-press
½ cup dry white wine
12 anchovy fillets, washed free of salt [*see* No. 220]
    and finely sliced
1 quart hot milk
1 tablespoon chopped parsley
1 bay leaf
3 cups hot Polenta [No. 623]
Salt and freshly ground white pepper

Lightly brown the onion and garlic in the oil in a large earthenware pot over medium heat. Add the wine and anchovy paste and cook until the wine has almost evaporated. Add the pieces of stockfish, milk, parsley, bay leaf, a pinch of salt, and a generous grating of pepper. Bring to a boil over high heat, cover the pot, and place it in a moderate oven for 2 hours. Transfer the fish and sauce to a large, shallow serving bowl and serve the hot polenta on the side. *Serves* 6.

807. STOCKFISH PURÉE VICENTINA
Stoccafisso mantecato alla vicentina

2 pounds stockfish, soaked, skinned, boned, and
    cut into small pieces
3 cloves garlic, peeled
2 cups milk, or more as necessary
1 cup oil
Pinch cinnamon
Salt and pinch freshly ground pepper
3 cups Polenta [No. 623], chilled, sliced, and
    fried crisp in oil

Rub a large earthenware (or enamel) pot with the garlic, add the fish and milk, bring to a boil, reduce the heat, and cook for 15 minutes. Begin pounding the fish with a wooden pestle or a potato masher until it starts to combine with the milk. Add the oil, bit by bit, and add a little more milk as it becomes necessary. Continue cooking and mashing for about 20 minutes longer, or until the mixture is the consistency of fluffy mashed potatoes. Season with cinnamon, salt, and pepper and pour it into a shallow serving bowl. Serve the slices of fried polenta on the side. *Serves* 6.

Cod

EEL
Anguilla

Like all fish, eels should be very fresh. Many fish dealers keep them in water tanks and sell them live. The best eels are caught in fresh water and this type can be recognized by their striped back, the brown shading to green on their sides, and their silvery undersides. Do not buy eels with all black backs and yellowish undersides; this coloring generally indicates that they have been living in stagnant, muddy waters.

808. EELS AZZALI
Anguilla alla Azzali

2 pounds eels
¼ cup oil
¼ cup butter
½ pound slightly green tomatoes, peeled and sliced
2 cloves garlic, crushed in the garlic-press
½ cup fresh breadcrumbs, browned in butter for
    2 minutes
2 tablespoons chopped parsley
1 tablespoon chopped fresh basil
Salt and freshly ground pepper

Skin and clean the eels as described in the introduction (page 258), season them lightly with salt and pepper, and cut them into pieces 2 to 3 inches long. Heat the butter and oil in a frying pan over high heat until very hot and put the eel pieces in the pan. Do not crowd the pieces; if necessary use 2 frying pans with more butter and oil. Cook between 8 and 12 minutes, depending on the size of the eels. Remove them from the pan and place them on an oven-proof platter. Sauté the tomato slices in the same butter and oil for about 3 minutes on each side over high heat. Remove and arrange them around the eel pieces on the platter. Sprinkle the garlic and breadcrumbs over the eel pieces and place under a hot broiler flame for 2 minutes. Remove and sprinkle with the basil and parsley. *Serves* 6.

809. EELS FATTORE

Anguilla alla moda del fattore

2 pounds eels
1 carrot, sliced
1 onion, sliced
2 cloves garlic, crushed in the garlic-press
1 teaspoon chopped fresh thyme (or ¼ teaspoon dried)
1 bay leaf
2 cups dry white wine
4 hard-boiled egg yolks
2 tablespoons prepared mustard (Dijon-type preferred)
1 cup oil
1 teaspoon vinegar
6 scallions, chopped
1 egg, beaten
1 cup fresh breadcrumbs
Parsley sprigs
1 cup gherkins
Salt and freshly ground pepper

Skin and clean the eels as described in the introduction (page 258), and cut them into 3-inch pieces. Put them in a heavy saucepan with the onion, carrot, garlic, thyme, bay leaf, white wine, and a pinch of salt and pepper. Bring to a boil over medium heat and cook for 8 minutes after the wine comes to a boil.

While the eels are cooking, prepare the sauce: mash the hard-boiled egg yolks in a bowl, mix them with the mustard, beat in ½ cup of oil, add the vinegar, season lightly with salt and pepper, and mix in the chopped scallions; pour the mixture into a sauceboat.

Remove the eels from their cooking liquid and drain them. Dip them in beaten egg, then in breadcrumbs. Heat the remaining oil in a frying pan over high heat until it is smoking hot and fry the eel pieces very quickly until they are crisp and golden. They should not cook for more than 2 minutes. Arrange them on a serving platter, season lightly with salt, garnish with the gherkins and parsley, and serve the sauce on the side. *Serves* 6.

810. EELS WITH PEPPERS AND ONIONS

Anguilla in guazzetto con peperoni e cipolline

2 pounds eels
¼ pound small white onions, parboiled for 5 minutes
½ cup oil
2 yellow peppers, roasted, scraped, seeded, and cut into strips [*see* No. 145]

2 cups dry white wine
1 bay leaf
1 teaspoon chopped fresh thyme (or ¼ teaspoon dried)
2 tablespoons Kneaded Butter [No. 107]
⅓ cup heavy cream
Salt and freshly ground pepper
2 tablespoons chopped parsley

Skin and clean the eels as described in the introduction (page 258) and cut them into 3-inch pieces. Drain the parboiled onions thoroughly, squeezing out any excess water. Heat the oil in a frying pan over high heat until smoking hot. Sauté the eel pieces very quickly until they are golden brown. Reduce the heat to medium and add the onions and the pepper strips. Season lightly with salt and pepper and cook for 5 minutes. Add the wine, bay leaf, and thyme; bring to a boil; blend in the kneaded butter; and cook over moderate heat for 8 minutes. Add the cream and cook only long enough for the sauce to be thoroughly hot. Remove bay leaf. Turn the mixture out on a serving platter and sprinkle with the parsley. *Serves* 6.

811. EELS PROVENÇALE

Anguilla alla provenzale

2 pounds eels
Flour
½ cup butter
A chopped mixture:
   3 sprigs parsley
   1 onion
   1 clove garlic
1 cup fresh breadcrumbs
Salt and freshly ground pepper

Skin and clean the eels as described in the introduction (page 258) and cut them into pieces 2 inches long. Season them lightly with salt and pepper and dust them with flour. Heat the butter until it is golden in a frying pan over medium high heat and add the pieces of eel. Cook them for about 10 minutes, or until they are golden. Spoon them out of the pan and arrange them on a hot serving platter. Add the chopped mixture to the butter and drippings in the frying pan and cook until the onion is golden. Add the breadcrumbs, season lightly with salt, and cook for about 30 seconds longer. Remove from the fire and spoon this mixture over the fish. *Serves* 6.

Mackerel

812. EELS WITH TARTAR SAUCE
Anguilla alla tartara

2 pounds eels
2 cups Court Bouillon [No. 764]
Flour
1 egg, beaten
1 cup fresh breadcrumbs
1/2 cup butter
1/2 cup gherkins, sliced
Salt and freshly ground pepper
1 cup Tartar Sauce [No. 98]

Skin and clean the eels as described in the introduction (page 258) and cut them into 3-inch pieces. Put them in a heavy saucepan with the Court Bouillon over high heat and bring to a boil. Reduce heat and cook for 8 minutes. Drain the eel pieces, dust lightly with flour, dip them in beaten egg, and then in breadcrumbs. Melt the butter in a frying pan over medium high heat until it is golden, add the eel pieces and cook until they are well browned. Sprinkle them lightly with salt and pepper, arrange them on a serving platter, and garnish with the gherkins. Serve the tartar sauce on the side. *Serves* 6.

813. EELS IN WINE
Anguilla al vino rosso

2 pounds eels
18 Glazed Onions [No. 1723]
2 tablespoons oil
2 tablespoons butter
1 large onion, chopped
Pinch nutmeg
2 1/2 cups red wine, mixed with 1/4 cup water
1 bay leaf
12 thin slices French or Italian bread, fried in butter until golden
3 tablespoons Anchovy Butter [No. 108]
Juice of 1/2 lemon
2 tablespoons chopped parsley
Salt and freshly ground pepper

Skin and clean the eels as described in the introduction (page 258), and cut them into 3-inch pieces. Prepare the glazed onions and keep them warm. Heat the butter and oil in a large, heavy saucepan over medium heat. Add the chopped onion and sauté gently until golden. Add eel pieces; season very lightly with salt, pepper, and the nutmeg; turn the eel pieces in the butter after 3 minutes; add the wine/water mixture and the bay leaf. Bring to a boil, reduce heat, and simmer for 8

minutes. Remove eel pieces and keep hot. Reduce the liquid to 1/2 its original quantity over high heat. While it is reducing, brown the slices of bread in butter. Remove the boiling sauce from the fire, discard bay leaf, and swirl in the anchovy butter and the lemon juice. Taste, and correct seasoning. Arrange the eel pieces in the center of the platter, pour the sauce over them, and garnish the edge of the platter with the glazed onions and the bread slices. Sprinkle the parsley over the top. *Serves* 6.

MACKEREL
Sgombro

There are many varieties of mackerel native both to the Atlantic and Pacific. One of the most popular and delicious is the Spanish mackerel. It is a deep, steel-blue color, its flesh is very oily, and it has a strong flavor. Mackerel are usually marketed in about 2-pound sizes, and their best season is from April to November.

814. FILLETS OF MACKEREL AMERICANA
Filetti di sgombro all'americana

3 2-pound mackerel, cleaned
6 thick slices lean salt pork, parboiled for 20 minutes
Flour
1/2 cup oil
3 tablespoons butter
4 tomatoes, seeded and sliced
Salt and freshly ground pepper

Broil the salt pork under a medium flame until crisp, and keep warm. Season the fillets lightly with salt and pepper and dust them with flour. Heat the oil over fairly high heat in a large frying pan until almost smoking and sauté the fillets for about 2 minutes on each side. Melt the butter in another frying pan over high heat until golden, add the tomato slices, season lightly with salt and pepper, and sauté for 2 minutes on each side. Arrange the tomato slices in the center of a hot platter, surround with a circle of the fillets, and garnish with the salt pork slices. *Serves* 6.

276

815. MACKEREL BÉARNAISE
Sgombro farcito alla béarnaise

3 2-pound mackerel, cleaned
1½ cups Simple Fish Stuffing [No. 135], seasoned with
    1 tablespoon each chopped parsley, tarragon, and
    basil
¼ cup butter, softened
2½ cups dry white wine
2 cups Sauce Béarnaise [No. 67]

Remove the heads of the mackerel and split them down their backs with a very sharp knife, but do not separate the 2 halves of the fish. Remove the backbones and spread the fish open on the table. Spread ½ cup of the stuffing on one half of each fish, put the halves back together, and wrap each fish rather tightly in two thicknesses of cheesecloth. Spread the softened butter in a large baking dish, arrange the fish in it, and add the wine. Bake the fish for 25 minutes in a medium (370°) oven, basting them frequently. Transfer them to a hot serving platter, remove the cheesecloth carefully, and serve the Béarnaise sauce on the side. *Serves 6.*

816. MACKEREL FLAMANDE
Sgombro alla fiamminga

3 2-pound mackerel, cleaned
Stuffing:
    ½ cup butter, softened
    3 shallots, finely chopped
    1 large onion, finely chopped
    2 tablespoons chopped parsley
    4 tablespoons fresh breadcrumbs (made from crustless
        bread)
    Juice of ½ lemon
½ cup butter, softened
Lightly oiled brown paper
½ cup oil
3 lemons, quartered
Salt and freshly ground pepper

Split and bone the mackerel as described in the preceding recipe. Spread the halves out on the table and season lightly with salt and pepper. Mix the stuffing ingredients thoroughly in a bowl and spread a little on one half of each of the fish. Put the fish halves back together, spread a little of the softened butter on each fish, and wrap each tightly in oiled brown paper. Butter a baking dish with the remaining butter, arrange the wrapped fish in it, add the oil, and bake in a moderate (350°) oven for 25 minutes. Place the packets on a hot serving dish garnished with the lemon quarters. Allow each guest to unwrap his own fish, since the aroma that escapes from the packets is one of the pleasures of this dish. *Serves 6.*

817. FILLETS OF MACKEREL ITALIANA
Filetti di sgombro all'italiana

3 2-pound mackerel, filleted
1 pound potatoes, sliced
½ cup oil
½ cup Anchovy Butter [No. 108]
2 tablespoons chopped parsley
Juice of ½ lemon
12 slices French or Italian bread, lightly toasted
1½ cups Tomato Sauce [No. 19]
Salt and freshly ground pepper

Sauté the potatoes in 3 tablespoons of the oil over fairly high heat in a large frying pan for about 20 minutes, or until they are tender and golden, seasoning them with a little salt and pepper as they cook. Meanwhile, season the fillets lightly with salt and pepper and brush them with oil. Broil them under a high flame for about 3 minutes on each side, basting with a little more oil as they cook. Blend the anchovy butter with the parsley and lemon juice and spread a little on each slice of toast. Arrange the potatoes in a mound in the center of a hot serving platter, place the slices of toast in a circle around the potatoes, and put one half of a fillet on each slice. Serve the tomato sauce on the side. *Serves 6.*

818. FILLETS OF MACKEREL NORMANDE
Filetti di sgombro alla normanda

3 2-pound mackerel, filleted (reserving the bones and
    heads)
2 tablespoons butter
1 tablespoon chopped chervil
1 tablespoon chopped shallots
1 tablespoon chopped parsley
2 cups Fish Fumet [No. 2], prepared with the mackerel
    bones and heads in addition to the usual ingredients
Salt and freshly ground pepper
2 cups hot Sauce Normande [No. 52]

Butter a large baking dish, arrange the fillets in it, season them lightly with salt and pepper, and sprinkle with the chervil, parsley, and shallots. Add the Fumet, cover the dish with a lid or aluminum foil, and bake in a moderate (350°) oven for 20 minutes. Transfer them carefully to a hot serving platter, allow them to sit for 3 minutes in a warm place, and then remove any juices they have released with a bulb baster. Pour the Normande sauce over them. *Serves* 6.

819. FILLETS OF MACKEREL EN PAPILLOTES CAPRICCIO
Filetti di sgombro al cartoccio "Capriccio"

3 2-pound mackerel, filleted
$\frac{1}{2}$ pound mushrooms, sliced
$\frac{1}{4}$ cup butter, softened
$\frac{1}{4}$ cup oil
2 tablespoons chopped parsley
12 sheets parchment paper, cut in the shape of large hearts
6 sprigs parsley
Salt and freshly ground pepper

Sauté the mushrooms in 2 tablespoons of the butter in a covered frying pan over moderate heat for 8 minutes; remove from the heat and keep warm. Season the fillets lightly with salt and pepper, brush them with oil, and broil under a high flame for about 2 minutes on each side, basting them with a little more oil as they cook. Mix the remaining butter with the chopped parsley in a bowl; grease the paper hearts with oil. Cut each broiled fillet in half. Spread a little of the parsley butter on one half of the paper hearts, top with half of a fillet and a few mushrooms slices, fold the other half of the heart over, and crimp the edges well to form a very tight seal. Arrange the packets in a large, oiled baking dish and place in a hot (450°) oven for 5 minutes, or until they are puffed and turn golden. Transfer packets to a hot serving platter and garnish with the parsley. *Serves* 6.

820. FILLETS OF MACKEREL IN WHITE WINE
Filetti di sgombro al vino bianco

3 2-pound mackerel, filleted
$1\frac{1}{2}$ pounds "new" potatoes
Flour
$\frac{1}{2}$ cup butter, softened
$1\frac{1}{2}$ cups White Wine Sauce [No. 76]
1 tablespoon chopped parsley
Salt and freshly ground pepper

Cook the potatoes in boiling, salted water in a saucepan over medium heat for about 20 minutes, or until tender. A few minutes before the potatoes are done, season the fillets lightly with salt and pepper and dust them with flour. Melt $\frac{1}{4}$ cup of the butter in a large frying

pan over fairly high heat until it is almost nut colored and sauté the fillets in the pan for about 3 minutes on each side. Arrange the fillets in the center of a hot serving platter, pour the wine sauce over them, and garnish with the potatoes which have been rolled in the remaining butter and sprinkled with the parsley. *Serves* 6.

MULLET
Triglia, cefalo

There is both a salt-water and a fresh-water type of mullet native to American waters. The salt-water mullet, sometimes called striped mullet, is found on both the Atlantic and Pacific coasts. The average market weight is about 2 pounds, although sizes of $\frac{1}{2}$ pound or less are occasionally available, and these are especially delicious. Fresh-water mullet, sometimes called white sucker, is slightly less strongly flavored than the salt-water variety. It is particularly abundant in the Mississippi River and in the Great Lakes. Both species are fairly oily. The salt-water variety native to European waters, of which there are two distinct types, is the red and the gray mullet.

Mullet are scaled and cleaned as described in the introduction (page 258).

821. MULLET AU GRATIN
Triglie gratinate

6 $\frac{1}{2}$-pound mullet, cleaned
$\frac{1}{2}$ pound mushrooms, sliced
1 cup dry white wine
2 cups Duxelles Sauce [No. 31]
1 cup fresh breadcrumbs
$\frac{1}{2}$ cup butter, melted
Juice of 1 lemon
2 tablespoons chopped parsley
Salt and freshly ground white pepper

Season the mullet with salt and pepper and arrange them in a generously buttered oven-proof dish. Arrange the mushrooms around them, add the wine, spread the Duxelles sauce over the fish, and sprinkle with the breadcrumbs and melted butter. Place the dish in a moderate (350°) oven for about 15 minutes. Remove from the oven, squeeze the lemon juice over the fish, sprinkle with the parsley, and serve in the baking dish. *Serves* 6.

822. BAKED MULLET
Triglie in teglia

6 ½-pound mullet, cleaned
¼ cup oil
Juice of 1 lemon
2 tablespoons chopped parsley
Salt and freshly ground pepper

Season the cavities of the fish with salt and pepper. Arrange them in a baking dish, pour the oil over them so that each fish is well coated, season again very lightly, and bake in a medium (315°) oven for 15 minutes. Serve them in the baking dish, squeeze the lemon juice over them, and sprinkle with parsley. *Serves 6.*

823. MULLET BORDELAISE
Triglie alla bordolese

6 ½-pound mullet, cleaned
½ cup butter
2 shallots, finely chopped
1 cup dry white wine
1½ cups Velouté Sauce [No. 17]
1 cup Tomato Sauce [No. 19], strained through a fine
　　sieve
1 tablespoon chopped tarragon (or 1 teaspoon dried)
Salt and freshly ground pepper

Season the mullet, inside and out, with salt and pepper. Melt 4 tablespoons of the butter in a baking dish over medium heat, line the fish up in the dish, sprinkle with the shallots, add the wine, cover the dish, bring to a boil, and then place the dish in a moderate (350°) oven for 12 minutes. Transfer the fish to a hot serving dish and keep warm. Combine the cooking liquid with the Velouté and tomato sauces in a saucepan and reduce over fairly high heat to about 2 cups. Strain the sauce through a fine sieve, return it to the saucepan, add the tarragon, correct the seasoning, bring just to a boil, and remove from the heat. Swirl in the remaining butter, bit by bit, and pour over the fish. *Serves 6.*

824. COFFERED MULLET WITH MUSHROOMS
Triglie in cassetta con funghi

6 ½-pound mullet, cleaned
A marinade:
　1 cup oil
　¼ cup lemon juice
　1 onion, sliced

　2 tablespoons chopped parsley
　1 teaspoon fennel seeds, crushed
　1 teaspoon salt
　¼ teaspoon freshly ground pepper
4 tablespoons oil
1 clove garlic, crushed in the garlic-press
½ pound mushrooms, sliced
6 oblong boxes, open on the top, made of parchment
　　paper, each large enough to contain 1 mullet
¾ cup Anchovy Butter [No. 108]
Fresh breadcrumbs
Juice of 2 lemons
12 small sprigs parsley
Salt and freshly ground pepper

Marinate the fish in the marinade for 3 hours, turning them occasionally. Heat 2 tablespoons of the oil in a frying pan over medium heat, add the garlic, cook until golden, add the mushrooms, cover the pan, reduce the heat, and cook for 8 minutes, shaking the pan occasionally. Grease the paper boxes, inside and out, with oil, arrange them in an oiled baking dish, spread 1 tablespoon of the anchovy butter in the bottom of each, place the mullet on top, spread them with another tablespoon of the anchovy butter, add a spoonful of mushrooms, and sprinkle with a generous tablespoon of the marinade. Place the dish in a moderate (350°) oven for 10 minutes. Remove, sprinkle the tops with breadcrumbs and a little oil, raise the oven heat to 400°, and return the dish to the oven for about 5 minutes, or until the tops are brown. Transfer the boxes to individual hot plates, squeeze a little lemon juice into each, and garnish with sprigs of parsley. *Serves 6.*

NOTE: The boxes may be made of heavy-duty aluminum foil, but the effect is garish.

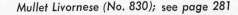

Mullet Livornese (No. 830); see page 281

825. COLD MULLET WITH SAFFRON
Trigliette fredde allo zafferano

6 ½-pound mullet, cleaned
3 tablespoons oil
2 cloves garlic, crushed in the garlic-press
3 cups dry white wine
4 tomatoes, peeled, seeded, drained, and chopped
½ teaspoon saffron, soaked in ¼ cup warm water
1 teaspoon chopped thyme (or ½ teaspoon dried)
1 bay leaf, crumbled
6 sprigs parsley
12 lemon slices, edges scalloped
Salt and freshly ground pepper

Heat the oil in a large earthenware (or enamel) pot over medium heat, add the garlic, cook until golden, and then add the mullet, wine, tomatoes, saffron, thyme, bay leaf, and parsley. Season lightly with salt and pepper, cover, bring to a boil, lower the heat, and simmer for 12 minutes. Transfer the fish to a shallow serving bowl and allow to cool. Reduce the cooking liquid over high heat to ¼ its quantity, discard the parsley, and allow to cool. Pour the sauce over the fish, garnish with the lemon slices, and serve cold. *Serves* 6.

826. MULLET FANTASIA
Triglie alla graticola "Fantasia"

6 ½-pound mullet, cleaned
¼ cup oil
6 tablespoons butter, softened
1 onion, chopped
¼ pound mushrooms, chopped
1 tablespoon chopped chervil
1 tablespoon chopped parsley
1 tablespoon chopped basil
1 tablespoon chopped tarragon
1 cup dry white wine
1 tablespoon Kneaded Butter [No. 107]
Salt and freshly ground pepper

Brush the fish with oil and season them, inside and out, with salt and pepper. Broil them for about 5 minutes on each side under a high broiler flame, basting occasionally with more oil. While the fish is cooking, melt 2 tablespoons of the butter in a frying pan over medium heat, add the onion, cook until transparent, add the mushrooms, stir for 1 minute, and add the chopped herbs and the wine. Bring to a boil, season with salt and pepper, blend in the kneaded butter with a whisk, lower the heat, and

simmer for 10 minutes. Remove the sauce from the fire and swirl in the remaining butter, bit by bit. Arrange the fish on a hot serving platter and serve the sauce separately. *Serves* 6.

827. FRIED MULLET
Frittura di triglie

6 ½-pound mullet, cleaned
Milk
Flour
1 cup oil
Salt and freshly ground pepper
2 lemons, quartered
12 sprigs parsley, fried in deep fat [*see* No. 276]

Season the fish with salt and pepper, dip them in milk, dust them with flour, and sauté them in smoking hot oil in a large frying pan over high heat for about 5 minutes on each side. Transfer them to a hot serving platter, and garnish with the fried parsley and lemon quarters. *Serves* 6.

828. MULLET GOURMET
Triglie alla buongustaia

6 ½-pound mullet, cleaned
¼ cup oil
Salt and freshly ground pepper
1 cup Mustard Butter [No. 112], melted

Brush the fish with oil and season them lightly, inside and out, with salt and pepper. Broil them under a hot broiler flame for about 5 minutes on each side, basting occasionally with more oil. Transfer them to a hot serving platter and pour the mustard butter over them. *Serves* 6.

829. MULLET ITALIANA
Triglie all'italiana

6 ½-pound mullet, cleaned
½ cup butter
6 tomatoes, peeled, seeded, drained, and chopped
2½ cups hot Duxelles Sauce [No. 31]
2 tablespoons chopped parsley
Salt and freshly ground white pepper

Melt 4 tablespoons of the butter in a saucepan over medium heat, add the tomatoes, season with salt and pepper, and cook for about 15 minutes. Season the fish with salt and pepper, spread the remaining butter in a large baking dish, arrange the fish in the dish, and bake them in a medium (375°) oven for about 15 minutes, basting them occasionally with the juices in the dish. Transfer them to a hot serving platter, pour the Duxelles sauce over them, surround them with small heaps of the tomatoes, and sprinkle with the chopped parsley. *Serves* 6.

830. MULLET LIVORNESE
Triglie alla livornese

6 ½-pound mullet, cleaned
3 tablespoons butter
1 tablespoon chopped onion
1 clove garlic, crushed in the garlic-press
8 tomatoes, peeled, seeded, drained, and chopped
1 teaspoon chopped thyme (or ¼ teaspoon dried)
1 bay leaf, crumbled
Flour
½ cup oil
2 tablespoons chopped parsley
Salt and freshly ground pepper

Melt the butter in a saucepan over medium heat, add the onion and garlic, and cook until golden. Add the tomatoes, thyme, and bay leaf; season with salt and pepper; and cook for 15 minutes. Season the fish with salt and pepper, dust them with flour, and sauté them in smoking hot oil in a large frying pan over high heat for about 5 minutes on each side. Transfer them to a hot serving platter, pour the tomato sauce over them, and sprinkle with the chopped parsley. *Serves* 6.

831. MULLET MADRILÈNE
Triglie alla madrilena

1 3- to 4-pound mullet, cleaned and cut into 2-inch slices
2 stalks celery, sliced
1 large onion, finely chopped
4 tomatoes, peeled, seeded, drained, and sliced
4 tablespoons oil
2 cups muscatel wine
3 yellow peppers, roasted, scraped, seeded, and cut into strips [see No. 145]
Salt and freshly ground pepper

Oil a large oven-proof dish and arrange the celery and onion in the bottom. Place the tomato slices on top and season lightly with salt and pepper. Place the fish slices on top of the tomatoes and season lightly again. Sprinkle 2 tablespoons of the oil over all and pour in the muscatel. The wine should come only halfway up the sides of the fish pieces. Place the dish in a moderate (350°) oven for 25 to 30 minutes, basting frequently

with the liquid in the dish. While the fish is cooking, sauté the pepper strips in the remaining oil in a frying pan over moderate heat for about 10 minutes. When the fish is done, serve it in the baking dish and garnish with the strips of pepper. *Serves* 6.

NOTE: If desired, the sauce may be thickened by the addition of 1 tablespoon Kneaded Butter [No. 107].

832. MULLET MARSEILLAISE
Triglie alla marsigliese

6 ½-pound mullet, cleaned
½ cup oil
1 onion, chopped
1 clove garlic, pounded to a paste in the mortar
6 tomatoes, peeled, seeded, drained, and chopped
1 teaspoon saffron, soaked in ¼ cup water
3 cups Fish Fumet [No. 2]
Salt and freshly ground pepper
6 slices bread, crusts removed, toasted, and rubbed with garlic

Season the fish with salt and pepper. Heat the oil in a large enamel skillet over medium heat, add the onion and garlic, cook until transparent, arrange the fish on top, and add the tomatoes, saffron, and Fumet. Season lightly with salt and pepper, cover the dish, bring to a boil, and simmer for 12 minutes. Transfer the fish to a hot serving platter and keep warm. Reduce the cooking liquid to ⅔ its quantity, place the slices of freshly made garlic toast under each fish, and cover with the sauce. *Serves* 6.

833. MULLET NAPOLETANA
Triglie in gratella alla napoletana

6 ½-pound mullet, cleaned
A marinade:
  1 cup oil
  Juice of 1 lemon
  Salt and freshly ground pepper
2 cloves garlic, crushed in the garlic-press
1 tablespoon chopped oregano (or ½ teaspoon dried)
1 tablespoon chopped parsley
3 tablespoons white wine vinegar
½ cup oil
2 lemons, quartered
Salt and freshly ground pepper

Cut a few diagonal slits in the side of each of the fish and marinate them for 2 hours in the marinade liquid. Place them on the rack of the broiler about 5 inches from a hot flame and broil 5 minutes on each side.

While the fish are cooking, prepare the sauce quickly by mixing the garlic, oregano, parsley, vinegar, and oil; season to taste with salt and pepper. Place the fish on a hot serving platter and garnish with the lemon quarters. Serve the (cold) sauce on the side. *Serves* 6.

834. MULLET EN PAPILLOTES WITH ANCHOVY BUTTER
Triglie al cartoccio con burro d'acciuga

6 ½-pound mullet, cleaned
A marinade:
   ¾ cup oil
   ¼ cup lemon juice
   1 onion, chopped
   1 tablespoon chopped tarragon (or ½ teaspoon dried)
   1 tablespoon chopped parsley
   1 teaspoon salt
   ¼ teaspoon freshly ground pepper
¼ cup oil
6 large sheets parchment paper
¾ cup Anchovy Butter [No. 108]

Marinate the fish in the marinade for 2 hours, turning them occasionally. Remove them and carefully wipe off any of the marinade ingredients. Brush fish lightly with oil and broil them quite close to a high broiler flame for 2 minutes on each side. Cut the parchment paper into the shape of hearts, large enough so that each half-heart is somewhat larger than any of the fish. Brush the hearts with oil, spread half of each with a tablespoon of the anchovy butter, place the fish on top, spread with another tablespoon of anchovy butter, and sprinkle with a tablespoon of the marinade liquid. Fold the other half of the hearts over the fish and crimp the edges well so that the fish is tightly enclosed. Grease a large baking dish with oil, arrange the papillotes in it, and bake in a moderate (350°) oven for 20 minutes. Transfer them to individual hot plates and allow each guest to open his own. *Serves* 6.

835. MULLET EN PAPILLOTES WITH FENNEL
Triglie alla graticola con finocchio

6 ½-pound mullet, cleaned
A marinade:
   ½ cup oil
   ¼ cup lemon juice
   1 tablespoon fennel seeds, bruised
   1 teaspoon salt
   ¼ teaspoon freshly ground pepper

¼ cup oil
6 large sheets parchment paper
¼ pound lean salt pork, diced and parboiled for 15 minutes
1 tablespoon chopped parsley

Marinate the fish in the marinade for 2 hours, turning them occasionally. Brush the parchment paper on both sides with oil, place 1 fish on half of each sheet, and sprinkle each with a generous tablespoon of the marinade, a little salt pork, and a little parsley. Fold the other half of the paper over the fish and crimp the edges tightly together. Place the packets in a well oiled baking dish and place the dish in a moderate (350°) oven for 20 minutes. Transfer the packets to individual hot plates and allow each guest to open his own. *Serves* 6.

836. MULLET WITH ZUCCHINI
Triglie con zucchine

1 3- to 4-pound mullet, cleaned
3 tablespoons softened butter
1½ pounds zucchini, sliced
½ cup butter, melted
1 tablespoon chopped parsley
Salt and freshly ground pepper

Season the cavity of the mullet with salt and pepper, cut diagonal slits on each side, and place in a baking dish smeared with the softened butter. Arrange the zucchini slices around the fish, season both with salt and pepper, and sprinkle the melted butter over both. Bake in a moderate (350°) oven for 25 to 30 minutes, basting often with the butter and juices in the dish. Sprinkle the parsley over the top and serve in the baking dish. *Serves* 6.

OCTOPUS
Polpo

Octopuses have short, cylindrical bodies, rounded at the base. Their mouths are surrounded by eight tentacles which are equipped with long, double rows of suckers. While they can grow to enormous size in deep waters, the variety sold in fish markets is about 2 pounds. Occasionally very tiny octopuses are available (in Liguria these are called *moscardini*) and these are particularly tender and delicious. Before cooking, octopuses must be skinned and the insides, eyes, and mouth, or beak, removed; this is usually done by a fish dealer.

Neapolitans are connoisseurs of octopus, and they often eat it simply boiled and seasoned with oil, lemon, and pepper.

837. BOILED OCTOPUS
Polpi di scoglio lessati alla luciana

3 1-pound octopuses
Boiling water
12 peppercorns pounded in the mortar
3 lemons, quartered
1 cup oil
Salt

Place the octopuses in a large earthenware (or enamel) pot, cover with boiling water, add 2 teaspoons of salt for each quart of water, place the pot over a very low flame, cover tightly, and simmer for about 2 hours, or until the octopuses are tender. Drain them and arrange on a serving platter. Cut them into serving pieces at the table and serve the pepper, lemons, and oil separately. *Serves* 6.

838. OCTOPUS GENOVESE
Moscardini alla genovese

6 ½-pound octopuses
½ cup oil
1 onion, chopped
A chopped mixture of:
    2 cloves garlic
    3 sprigs rosemary
    3 sprigs parsley
2 ounces dried, imported mushrooms, soaked ½ hour
    in warm water, squeezed dry, and cut into pieces
2 tomatoes, peeled, seeded, drained, and puréed
    through a food mill
1 cup cold water
1½ cups Croûtons [No. 332]
Salt and freshly ground pepper

Cut the octopuses into strips. Heat the oil in a large earthenware (or enamel) pot over medium heat, add the octopus strips and the onion, and cook until the onion begins to color. Add the chopped mixture, mushrooms, tomato purée, and 1 cup of water. Season with salt and pepper, cover the pot tightly, reduce the heat, and cook for 1½ hours, or until the octopus strips are tender. Turn out onto a serving platter and garnish with the croûtons. *Serves* 6.

839. OCTOPUS À LA GRECQUE
Polpi di scoglio alla greca

3 1-pound octopuses
2 cups water
½ cup oil
½ cup vinegar
2 onions, finely sliced
2 cloves garlic, crushed in the garlic-press
1 clove
1 teaspoon salt
¼ teaspoon freshly ground pepper
½ cup of flour-and-water paste

Cut the octopuses into large pieces and put them in a large earthenware (or enamel) casserole with all of the other ingredients except the flour-and-water paste. Spread the paste around the rim of the pot and press the cover lightly on top of it to make an airtight seal. Place the casserole in a 300° oven for 3 hours. Remove, and unseal the casserole at the table. *Serves* 6.

840. OCTOPUS LUCIANA
Polpi di scoglio affogati alla luciana

3 1-pound octopuses
4 tomatoes, peeled, seeded, drained, and chopped
½ cup oil
2 teaspoons chopped parsley
1 hot red pepper, whole
Pinch sugar
1 teaspoon salt
2 lemons, quartered

Place all of the ingredients except the lemons in a large, heavy earthenware (or enamel) pot, mix them well, place over medium heat, and cook until the tomatoes begin to bubble. Reduce the heat to a very low flame, cover the pot tightly, and simmer for 1½ to 2 hours, or until the octopus is tender. Remove the pepper and discard. Transfer the octopus to a carving board and cut into small pieces. Return the pieces to the pot, allow them to reheat for a moment, and then serve in the pot. Serve the lemon quarters on the side. *Serves* 6.

841. OCTOPUS MARCHIGIANA
Moscardini alla marchigiana

6 ½-pound octopuses
½ cup oil
2 cloves garlic, crushed in the garlic-press
2 anchovy fillets, washed free of salt [*see* No. 220],
    and pounded to a paste in the mortar

½ cup dry white wine
1 cup Fish Fumet [No. 2]
½ hot red pepper
Salt
1 tablespoon chopped parsley
1½ cups Croûtons [No. 332]

Cut the octopuses into strips. Heat the oil in a large earthenware (or enamel) pot over medium heat, add the garlic, and cook until golden. Add the octopus strips and stir for 2 minutes. Season lightly with salt and pepper, blend in the anchovy paste, add the wine, and cook until the wine has almost evaporated. Add the fish Fumet and the red pepper, reduce the heat to a very low flame, cover tightly, and cook for 1 hour. Remove the pepper and discard. Taste, and add salt if necessary. Turn the octopus strips and the sauce out onto a hot serving platter, sprinkle the parsley over the top, and garnish with the croûtons. *Serves* 6.

842. SAVORY OCTOPUS
Moscardini piccanti "à la minute"

6 ½-pound octopuses
½ cup oil
2 cloves garlic, bruised
1 hot red pepper, whole
1 teaspoon chopped parsley
¼ cup fresh breadcrumbs, browned for a few seconds in
    2 tablespoons butter
2 lemons, quartered
Salt

Parboil the octopuses for 20 minutes in lightly salted boiling water. Drain them and cut into strips. Heat the oil in a large frying pan over medium heat, add the garlic, and cook until golden. Add the octopus strips and the pepper, raise the heat slightly, and sauté for 15 minutes. Add the parsley and the breadcrumbs, reduce the heat, and cook for 10 minutes longer. Remove the pepper and discard. Turn out onto a hot serving platter and garnish with the lemon quarters. *Serves* 6.

843. STEWED OCTOPUS WITH TOMATOES
Polpi di scoglio affogati in umido

3 1-pound octopuses
3 tablespoons oil
3 cloves garlic, crushed in the garlic-press
6 tomatoes, peeled, seeded, drained, and puréed
    through a food mill

Salt
6 peppercorns crushed in the mortar
2 tablespoons chopped parsley

Cut octopuses into large pieces, drop them in boiling water for 15 minutes, and drain in a colander. Heat the oil in a large earthenware (or enamel) pot over medium heat, add the garlic, and cook until golden. Add the pieces of octopus, season with salt and pepper, and cook for 5 minutes, stirring occasionally. Add the tomato purée and enough water to barely cover the octopus. Cover tightly and cook for about 1½ hours over a very low flame. Remove the cover during the last ½ hour to allow the sauce to reduce and thicken. Turn the pieces of octopus and the sauce out onto a large serving platter and sprinkle the parsley over the top. *Serves* 6.

844. OCTOPUS IN WHITE WINE
Polpi di scoglio al vino bianco

3 1-pound octopuses
3 tablespoons oil
2 cups dry white wine
2 tablespoons chopped parsley
½ cup flour-and-water paste
Salt and freshly ground pepper

Place the octopuses in a large earthenware (or enamel) casserole and add the oil, wine, and parsley. Season lightly with salt and generously with pepper. Spread the flour-and-water paste around the rim of the casserole and press the cover lightly on top of it to make an airtight seal. Bake in a 300° oven for 2½ hours. Remove from the oven, uncover, cut the octopuses in large pieces, place them on a serving platter, and keep warm. Reduce the sauce in the pot over high heat to ½ its quantity and pour over the octopus pieces. *Serves* 6.

PERCH
Pesce persico

Perch are small fresh-water fish which are more generally known in the United States as yellow perch or yellow pike-perch. Their sides are almost golden in color and their flesh is very white and of a particularly sweet flavor. They are scaled and cleaned as described in the introduction (page 258).

845. FILLETS OF PERCH WITH ANCHOVY BUTTER

Filetti di pesce persico con burro d'acciuga

6 ½-pound perch, filleted
A marinade:
    1 cup oil
    Juice of 1 lemon
    4 scallions, finely chopped
    3 sprigs parsley, finely chopped
    1 teaspoon salt
    ¼ teaspoon freshly ground pepper
1½ cups Croûtons [No. 332]
1 cup Anchovy Butter [No. 108]

Marinate the fillets in the marinade for 1 hour, turning them occasionally. Drain them and broil under a very high broiler flame for about 5 minutes on each side, basting occasionally with the marinade liquid. Transfer the fish to a hot serving platter, garnish with the croûtons, and serve the anchovy butter on the side. *Serves* 6.

846. BOILED PERCH

Pesce persico con burro fuso al prezzemolo

6 perch (½ to ¾ pound each), cleaned
1 tablespoon vinegar
Bouquet Garni:
    2 sprigs thyme (or ½ teaspoon dried)
    1 bay leaf
    2 sprigs parsley
1 cup butter, melted
2 tablespoons chopped parsley
Juice of ½ lemon
Salt and freshly ground pepper

Place the fish on a rack in a fish boiler; cover with cold water; and add the vinegar, 2 teaspoons salt, and the Bouquet Garni. Bring to a boil over high heat, reduce the heat, and simmer for 12 to 15 minutes. Transfer the fish to a hot serving platter. Season the melted butter lightly with salt and pepper, add the parsley and lemon juice to it, and serve on the side in a sauceboat. *Serves* 6.

847. PERCH GRAND HÔTEL

Pesce persico "Grand Hôtel"

6 perch (½ to ¾ pound each), cleaned
6 tablespoons butter, softened
2 carrots, sliced
2 stalks celery, sliced
2 cups dry white wine
2 cups water

3 tablespoons Kneaded Butter [No. 107]
2 tablespoons chopped parsley
Salt and freshly ground white pepper

Melt 3 tablespoons of the butter in a saucepan over medium heat, add the carrots and celery, cook for 5 minutes, add the 2 cups of wine and water, bring to a boil, and cook for ½ hour. Place the fish on a rack in a fish boiler; strain the boiling liquid over them, reserving the carrots and celery; cover the pan; bring to a boil; reduce the heat; and simmer for 12 to 15 minutes. Transfer the fish to a hot serving platter and keep warm. Reduce the liquid over high heat to about 2½ cups, blend in the kneaded butter, and cook for 5 minutes. Correct the seasoning, remove the pan from the fire, swirl in the remaining butter, add the carrots and celery, and pour the sauce over the fish. Sprinkle the top with the parsley. *Serves* 6.

848. PERCH ITALIANA

Pesce persico all'italiana

6 ½- to ¾-pound perch, cleaned
Bouquet Garni:
    2 sprigs thyme (or ½ teaspoon dried)
    1 bay leaf
    2 sprigs parsley
1 tablespoon vinegar
Salt
2 hard-boiled eggs, finely chopped with 3 sprigs parsley
2 cups Bastard Sauce [No. 66]

Cook the fish in the same way as Boiled Perch [No. 846]. When they are done, arrange them on a hot serving platter, sprinkle the chopped eggs and parsley over them, and serve the sauce on the side. *Serves* 6.

849. PERCH MILANESE

Filetti di pesce persico alla milanese

6 small perch, filleted
A marinade:
    ½ cup oil
    Juice of 1 lemon
    4 scallions, chopped
    1 teaspoon salt
    ¼ teaspoon freshly ground pepper
Flour
2 eggs, beaten with a little salt
Fresh breadcrumbs
6 tablespoons butter
3 lemons, quartered

Marinate the fillets for 2 hours in the marinade. Drain,

dust them with flour, dip them in beaten egg, and then dip them in breadcrumbs. Heat the butter until almost nut colored in a large, heavy frying pan over high heat, add the fillets, and cook until golden on both sides. Transfer the fillets to a hot serving platter, pour the butter in the pan over the fish, and garnish with the lemon quarters. *Serves* 6.

850. FILLETS OF PERCH WITH SAGE
Filetti di pesce persico all'erba salvia

6 small perch, filleted
A marinade:
   ½ cup oil
   Juice of 1 lemon
   4 scallions, chopped
   1 teaspoon salt
   ¼ teaspoon freshly ground pepper
Flour
2 eggs, beaten with a little salt
Fresh breadcrumbs
6 tablespoons butter
2 tablespoons fresh sage leaves (do *not* use dried sage)
3 lemons, quartered

Marinate the fillets for 2 hours in the marinade. Drain, dust them with flour, dip them in beaten egg, and then dip them in breadcrumbs. Heat the butter until almost nut colored in a large, heavy frying pan over high heat, add the fillets, and cook until golden on both sides. Transfer the fillets to a hot serving platter, reduce the heat under the frying pan, add the sage leaves, and cook for 2 minutes. Pour the sage-butter over the fish, and garnish with the lemon quarters. *Serves* 6.

NOTE: Dried sage is a little too strong for this. An attempt might be made by plumping 1 teaspoon dried sage in 2 tablespoons heated white wine for 10 minutes, draining, and patting dry on paper towels.

851. FILLETS OF PERCH STRESA
Filetti di pesce persico "Nuova moda di Stresa"

6 ¾-pound perch, filleted
A marinade:
   1 cup oil
   Juice of 1 lemon
   1 teaspoon salt
   ¼ teaspoon freshly ground pepper
6 large slices of eggplant, peeled and sliced ½ inch thick
Flour

2 eggs beaten with a little salt
½ cup butter
Salt
1 cup Garlic Butter [No. 109]

Marinate the fillets in the marinade for 1 hour. At the same time, liberally salt the eggplant slices and let them drain on paper towels for 1 hour; then wash off salt thoroughly, pat dry, and dust the eggplant slices with flour and dip them in beaten egg. Melt the butter in a large frying pan over medium heat until it is almost nut colored, add the eggplant slices, and sauté until golden on both sides. Transfer them to a hot serving platter and keep warm. Broil the fillets under a high broiler flame for about 3 minutes on each side, basting occasionally with the marinade liquid. Place 2 of the fillets on each eggplant slice and serve the garlic butter on the side. *Serves* 6.

852. PERCH SWEDISH STYLE
Pesce persico alla svedese

6 perch (½ to ¾ pound each), cleaned
3 cups Fish Fumet [No. 2]
4 tablespoons Kneaded Butter [No. 107]
Juice of 1 lemon
Salt and freshly ground pepper
2 tablespoons chopped parsley

Place the fish on a rack in a fish boiler, pour in the Fumet, bring to a boil over high heat, reduce the flame, and simmer for 6 to 8 minutes. Transfer the fish to a hot serving platter and keep warm. Bring the liquid to a boil, blend in the kneaded butter, and cook for 5 to 6 minutes. Correct the seasoning, add the lemon juice, pour the sauce over the fish, and sprinkle the top with parsley. *Serves* 6.

PIKE

Luccio

Pike abound in the Great Lakes and are found in fresh waters extending up to the Arctic Circle. They can grow to a considerable size, but the size usually found in fish markets is 3 to 4 pounds. Their flesh is very lean, almost dry, but it has a sweet flavor. Because of the dryness of the flesh, pike is usually served with a sauce. It is one of the best fish for a fish forcemeat or fish stuffing. It is scaled and cleaned as described in the introduction (page 258).

853. BAKED PIKE LUIGI VERONELLI
Luccio arrostito alla Luigi Veronelli

1 4-pound pike, cleaned
2 ounces salt pork, cut into small strips and
    parboiled for 10 minutes
4 tablespoons butter, softened
¾ cups Soave wine (or substitute any good dry white
    wine)
½ pound mushrooms, sliced
3 tablespoons butter
1 tablespoon oil
½ pound "new" potatoes, cut into the shape of olives
    and boiled for 12 minutes
1 tablespoon Kneaded Butter [No. 107]
2 tablespoons chopped parsley
   Salt and freshly ground pepper

Lard the pike with the salt pork strips. Do this either
with a larding needle or cut tiny slits into the sides of
the fish and stuff them with small pieces of the pork.
Season the cavity with salt and pepper, spread the fish
with 2 tablespoons of the softened butter, pour the
wine over it, and place it into a moderate (350°) oven
for 35 minutes, basting often with the juices in the dish.
Cook the mushrooms in the remaining butter and the
oil in a covered saucepan over very low heat for 10
minutes, shaking the pan often to ensure even cooking.
Remove them from the fire and keep warm. Time the
cooking of the potatoes so that they will be ready just
when the pike is done. Remove the pike to a hot serving
platter, blend the kneaded butter into the juices in
the baking dish, and cook it for 4 minutes on top of
the stove over medium heat, stirring constantly. Pour
the sauce over the fish, garnish the platter with the
mushrooms and the potatoes, and sprinkle the parsley
over all. *Serves 6.*

854. PIKE RAVIGOTE
Luccio arrostito con salsa ravigotta

1 4-pound pike, cleaned
8 anchovy fillets, washed free of salt [*see* No. 220]
¼ cup oil
   Oiled brown paper
   Salt and freshly ground pepper
2 cups Sauce Ravigote [No. 96]

Cut small slits into the sides of the fish and insert
small pieces of anchovies into the flesh. Sprinkle the
fish with a little oil and season it all over with salt
(lightly) and pepper. Wrap it well in oiled brown paper
or aluminum foil, place it in a baking dish, and bake

in a moderate (350°) oven for 35 minutes. Carefully
turn the fish out onto a hot serving platter and remove
the paper or foil. Serve the Ravigote sauce on the side.
Serves 6.

855. COLD PIKE RICCA
Maionese di pesce alla ricca

2 3-pound pike, filleted
3 tablespoons butter
3 cups Fish Fumet [No. 2]
2 cups Sauce Vinaigrette [No. 99]
¼ cup diced cooked zucchini, chilled
¼ cup diced cooked artichoke hearts [*see* introduction
    to No. 1578], chilled
¼ cup cooked green beans, cut into ½-inch pieces
    and chilled
¼ cup diced cooked potatoes, chilled
¼ cup coarsely chopped cooked cauliflower, chilled
2 cups Mayonnaise [No. 77]
4 hard-boiled eggs, quartered
12 pitted olives
3 stuffed olives, sliced
4 gherkins, sliced
2 cooked sliced beets, chilled
12 rolled anchovies
6 tiny leaves Boston lettuce

Arrange the fish fillets in a buttered baking dish, add
the fish Fumet, cover the dish with a lid or aluminum
foil, and bake in a moderate (350°) oven for 12 minutes,
or until the fillets are barely done. Do not overcook.
Remove the fillets and allow them to cool in a shallow
glass dish until completely cold. Reserve the fish stock

Cold Pike Ricca (No. 855)

for another use. When the fillets are cold, drain off any liquid they have released, pour 1 cup of the Vinaigrette sauce over them, and marinate for 2 hours. At the same time marinate the cold vegetables in the remaining cup of Vinaigrette. Cut the fillets in half and arrange them around the outside edge of a large platter. Heap all of the marinated vegetables in a large, neat mound in the center. Cover both fish and vegetables with a smooth coating of mayonnaise and garnish the outside edge of the dish with a border of the eggs, olives, gherkins, beets, anchovies, and lettuce leaves. *Serves* 6.

856. PIKE FILLETS IN VIN ROSÉ
Filetti di luccio al vino rosé

2 3-pound pike, filleted
2 truffles, cut in half and sliced
2 ounces salt pork, cut into tiny slivers and parboiled
    for 10 minutes
1 tablespoon butter
1 cup Duxelles [No. 138]
3 cups rosé wine
4 tablespoons Kneaded Butter [No. 107]
3 egg yolks
1/2 cup heavy cream
2 tablespoons chopped parsley
Salt and freshly ground white pepper

Insert the slivers of truffle and salt pork into the fillets with the point of a very sharp knife. Butter a large baking dish, spread the bottom with the Duxelles, arrange the fillets over it, add the rosé, cover the dish with a lid or aluminum foil, and bake in a moderate (350°) oven for about 15 minutes, or until the fish flakes easily. Remove the fillets to a hot serving platter and keep warm. Pour the liquid in which the fish cooked into a saucepan, season lightly with salt and pepper, bring to a boil over medium heat, blend in the kneaded butter with a whisk, and cook for 5 minutes. Mix the egg yolks with the cream, remove the sauce from the fire, and slowly add the egg/cream mixture, stirring constantly with a whisk. Return the pan to the fire, cook very slowly, stirring constantly, until slightly thickened (do not boil), remove from the fire, and pour over the fish. Sprinkle the chopped parsley over the top and serve at once. *Serves* 6.

NOTE: A delicious garnish for this dish is pre-baked rosettes of puff paste [*see* No. 1960].

857. PIKE WITH WHITE BUTTER
Luccio al burro bianco

1 4-pound pike, cleaned
A double recipe of White Butter [No. 114]
2 lemons, scalloped and sliced
Parsley sprigs
Salt to taste

Place the pike on the rack in a fish boiler and cover with cold water. Season the water lightly with salt, bring to a boil over high heat, reduce heat, and simmer for 20 minutes. About 5 minutes before the fish is done, prepare the butter sauce; it should not be prepared in advance. Carefully turn the fish onto a serving platter, garnish with the parsley and slices of lemon, and serve the sauce on the side. *Serves* 6.

PORGY

Orata

Porgies are native to the North Atlantic and they are marketed in sizes of about 2 to 3 pounds. They are brownish in color, tinged with pink, and their flesh is very tender. Porgies are cleaned and prepared for cooking as described in the introduction (page 258).

858. BAKED PORGY
Orata al piatto

2 3-pound porgies, cleaned
1 1/2 pounds very small, "new" potatoes, peeled
Flour
1/2 cup butter, softened
4 tablespoons chopped shallots
2 cups dry white wine
Juice of 1 lemon
Salt and freshly ground pepper

Cook the potatoes in lightly salted boiling water for about 20 minutes, or until they are tender. Season the fish with salt and pepper and dust them with flour. Brown them very quickly in 4 tablespoons of the butter over high heat in a frying pan. Spread a baking dish with the remaining butter, sprinkle the bottom with the shallots, place the fish on top, add the wine and the lemon juice, bring to a boil on top of the stove, and then place, uncovered, in a hot (450°) oven for about 8 minutes, basting often with the wine in the dish. Transfer the fish to a hot serving platter and surround with the cooked potatoes. Reduce the cook-

SEE
VERSE
FOR
PTION

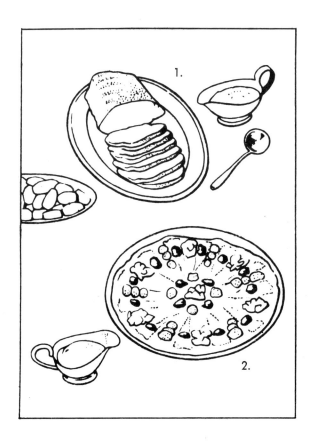

1. Sturgeon Borghese (No. 929)
2. Fillets of Sole Gran Successo No. 1 (No. 905)

ing liquid slightly over high heat, correct the seasoning, and pour over the fish. *Serves* 6.

859. PORGY CASALINGA
Orate piccole alla casalinga

6 ¾-pound porgies, cleaned
Flour
½ cup butter
2 onions, sliced
2 tablespoons chopped parsley
2 teaspoons chopped sage
6 anchovy fillets, washed free of salt [*see* No. 220] and pounded to a paste in the mortar
1 clove garlic, crushed in the garlic-press
½ cup Fish Fumet [No. 2]
1 cup dry white wine
Salt and freshly ground white pepper
Juice of 1 lemon

Season the porgies lightly with salt and pepper and dust them with flour. Melt 4 tablespoons of the butter in a frying pan over high heat until it is nut colored, and brown the fish very quickly on both sides. Remove from the heat. Melt the remaining butter in an enameled baking dish over medium heat, add the onions, cook until golden, add the chopped herbs, anchovy paste, and garlic. Arrange the browned fish on top, add the Fumet and the wine, bring to a boil, reduce the heat, and simmer for 10 minutes, basting occasionally with the liquid in the dish. Transfer the fish to a hot serving platter, reduce the cooking liquid slightly, add the lemon juice, correct the seasoning, and pour over the fish. *Serves* 6.

860. PORGY CONTADINA
Orata in casseruola alla contadina

2 2-pound porgies, cleaned
½ cup butter
½ cup dry white wine
Bouquet Garni:
   2 sprigs thyme (or ¼ teaspoon dried)
   1 bay leaf
   2 sprigs parsley
½ cup water (or bouillon)
1 onion, chopped
1 pound tomatoes, peeled, seeded, drained, and puréed through a food mill
Salt and freshly ground pepper

Melt 4 tablespoons of the butter over fairly high heat in a pan large enough to easily accommodate the fish.

When it is almost nut colored, add the fish and brown very quickly on both sides. Season lightly with salt and pepper; add the wine, the Bouquet Garni, and ½ cup of water; cover the pot; and bring to a boil. Reduce the heat and simmer for 10 to 12 minutes. While the fish are cooking, melt the remaining butter in a saucepan over medium heat, add the onion, cook until golden, add the tomatoes, season with salt and pepper, and cook over high heat for 15 minutes. When the fish are cooked, transfer them to a hot serving platter and keep warm. Discard the Bouquet Garni, reduce the fish cooking liquid to about 3 tablespoons, add it to the tomatoes, and cook for 2 minutes longer. Pour the sauce over the fish and serve at once. *Serves* 6.

861. PORGY FANTASIA
Orata picchettata "Fantasia"

1 3-pound porgy, cleaned
6 anchovy fillets, washed free of salt [*see* No. 220], and cut in half
12 narrow strips salt pork, parboiled for 15 minutes
½ cup butter, softened
Oiled brown paper
½ cup dry white wine
Salt and freshly ground pepper

Lard the porgy all over with the anchovies and the strips of salt pork; this may be done either with a larding needle or by making slits with a sharply pointed knife. Season the fish with pepper and spread it with 4 tablespoons of the butter. Wrap it in oiled brown paper or aluminum foil, place it in a lightly oiled baking pan, and put the pan in a moderate (350°) oven for 25 minutes. Transfer the fish to a hot serving platter, carefully unwrap it, and drain off any liquid which it has rendered into a saucepan. Add the wine, bring to a boil over high heat, boil for 2 minutes, correct the seasoning, and remove from the heat. Swirl in the remaining butter, bit by bit, and pour over the fish. *Serves* 6.

862. PORGY FLAMBÉ
Orata farcita e infiammata al brandy

1 4-pound porgy, cleaned
1½ cups simple Fish Stuffing [No. 135]
¾ cup butter, softened
3 cups Fish Fumet [No. 2]
1 tablespoon chopped parsley
Juice of 1 lemon
Salt and freshly ground pepper
¼ cup brandy

289

Slit the porgy down the back from the head to the tail and remove the backbone; this is most easily done by cutting off the bone near the head and close to the tail with poultry shears and then carefully separating the bone from the flesh with a very sharp knife. Season the cavity lightly with salt and pepper and stuff the fish. Sew the opening with string (or wrap the fish in cheesecloth), spread it with ¼ cup of the butter, place it on the rack in a fish boiler, add the Fumet, bring to a boil over high heat, reduce the heat, cover tightly, and simmer for 20 minutes. Transfer it to a hot baking dish, remove the string (or unwrap the cheese-cloth), and keep warm. Reduce the cooking liquid over very high heat to 1 cup, remove from the heat, allow it to cool for a few minutes, add the lemon juice and the parsley, beat in the remaining butter, bit by bit, and place it in the freezing compartment for about 5 minutes. Drain off any liquid which has drained from fish, pour the brandy over fish, heat the dish over a medium flame until the brandy is very hot, ignite, and shake the dish for 2 or 3 minutes until the flames subside. Serve at once with the cooled sauce on the side. *Serves 6.*

NOTE: The sauce may be cooled more rapidly, if desired, by reducing it to ¾ cup and then beating in 3 ice cubes after the butter has been added.

863. PORGY ITALIANA
Orata all'italiana

1 4-pound porgy, cleaned
½ cup butter, softened
1½ cups dry white vermouth
1 cup Fish Fumet [No. 2], reduced to ¼ cup
2 tablespoons flour
¼ pound mushrooms, chopped
Juice of 1 lemon
½ cup heavy cream
Pinch nutmeg

Porgy Contadina (No. 860): see page 289

3 tablespoons fresh breadcrumbs
¼ cup grated Parmesan cheese
2 tablespoons chopped parsley
Salt and freshly ground pepper

Remove the head and the tail of the fish and discard. Cut it into 6 thick, crosswise slices. Spread 3 table-spoons of the butter in the bottom of a pot large enough to accommodate the fish easily, add the fish slices, season very lightly with salt and pepper, and add the vermouth and sufficient water barely to cover the fish. Bring to a boil over high heat, reduce heat, cover tightly, and simmer for 12 minutes. Remove the fish to a warm oven-proof platter, allow it to cool slightly, carefully remove the bones, and keep warm. Reduce the cooking liquid over high heat to about 1 cup and add the reduced Fumet to it. Prepare a roux in sauce-pan with 2 tablespoons of the butter and the flour, add the boiling liquid all at once, and stir vigorously with a whisk until it returns to a boil. Reduce the heat and simmer for 5 minutes. Add the mushrooms, lemon juice, cream, and nutmeg. Simmer for 5 minutes longer and correct the seasoning. Remove any liquid which has drained from the fish and add it to the sauce. Pour the sauce over the fish, sprinkle with the bread-crumbs mixed with the cheese, and dot with small bits of the remaining butter. Place in a hot (450°) oven for 5 minutes. Remove from the oven and sprinkle the parsley over the top. *Serves 6.*

The Mediterranean dorado ("orata") which is equivalent to the porgy of Atlantic waters

864. PORGY MARINA PICCOLA
Orata Marina piccola

1 4-pound porgy, cleaned
12 oysters
24 mussels, scrubbed, with "beards" removed
1½ cups red wine
6 tablespoons butter
2 onions, sliced
Bouquet Garni:
  2 sprigs thyme (or ¼ teaspoon dried)
  1 bay leaf
  2 sprigs parsley
2 tablespoons Kneaded Butter [No. 107]
Salt and freshly ground pepper
Pinch Cayenne pepper

Place the oysters and mussels with $\frac{1}{4}$ cup of the wine in a tightly covered pot over high heat and steam for a few minutes until all the shells open. Pour them into a colander placed over a bowl, remove them from their shells, allowing any liquid to drain into the bowl. Keep them barely warm in another bowl, covered. Strain the liquid through several thicknesses of cheesecloth. Cook the onions in a frying pan over medium heat in 3 tablespoons of the butter until soft and transparent. Spread them out in the bottom of a large baking dish, place the fish on top, season lightly with salt and pepper, and add the remaining wine, the shellfish liquid, and the Bouquet Garni. Cover the dish with a lid or with aluminum foil and bake in a moderate (350°) oven for about 20 minutes. Transfer the fish to a hot serving platter and keep warm. Reduce the cooking liquid in a saucepan over high heat to about $1\frac{1}{2}$ cups and discard the Bouquet Garni. Blend in the kneaded butter with a whisk, reduce the heat, and simmer for 8 minutes. Add the Cayenne and correct the seasoning. Remove from the heat and swirl in the remaining butter, bit by bit. Arrange the mussels and oysters around the fish, pour the sauce over all, and place in a very hot (450°) oven for 2 or 3 minutes. Serve at once. *Serves* 6.

SALMON
Salmone

In the United States there are two distinct types of salmon, the Atlantic, sometimes called the Kennebec, and the Pacific, of which there are several different varieties. While there is some argument that the Pacific salmon is superior to the Atlantic, both are delicious fish with very tender, moist flesh. The average market weight of most Atlantic salmon is between 10 and 20 pounds, although they can grow considerably larger. Small salmon weighing 5 pounds or less are more frequently found on the Pacific coast than the Atlantic. The larger salmon are marketed in transverse slices, or steaks.

865. BROILED SALMON STEAKS
Fette di salmone alla graticola

6 $\frac{1}{2}$-pound salmon steaks
A marinade:
  1 cup olive oil
  $\frac{1}{4}$ cup lemon juice
  3 sprigs parsley, coarsely chopped
  1 teaspoon salt
  $\frac{1}{4}$ teaspoon freshly ground white pepper
$\frac{1}{2}$ cup Anchovy Butter [No. 108]
6 sprigs parsley

Marinate the salmon steaks in the marinade for 2 hours. Remove them but leave well covered with oil. Broil them under a hot broiler flame for 2 minutes on each side, reduce the heat, and broil for another 4 minutes on each side, basting occasionally with the marinade liquid. Spread the anchovy butter over the bottom of a hot serving platter, place the salmon steaks on top, and garnish with the parsley. *Serves* 6.

866. SALMON CHAMBORD
Darne di salmone Chambord

6 $\frac{1}{2}$-pound salmon steaks
3 tablespoons butter, softened
1 carrot, finely sliced
1 onion, finely sliced
$1\frac{1}{2}$ cups red wine
$\frac{3}{4}$ cup Fish Fumet [No. 2]
Bouquet Garni:
  2 sprigs thyme (or $\frac{1}{4}$ teaspoon dried)
  1 bay leaf
  3 sprigs parsley
Garnishes:
  1 recipe Mousseline Fish Forcemeat [No. 132]
  1 truffle, chopped [or No. 1819a]
  $\frac{1}{2}$ pound large mushroom caps, fluted (*see* Note below) and cooked for 8 minutes in 3 tablespoons of butter
  12 shrimp, cooked in Court Bouillon [No. 765] for 6 minutes, peeled, and de-veined
  6 slices bread, cut into triangles and sautéed until golden in butter just before serving
$1\frac{1}{2}$ cups Geneva Sauce [No. 23]
Salt and freshly ground white pepper

Grease a large baking dish with the softened butter, spread the slices of carrot and onion in the bottom, arrange the fish steaks on top, season lightly with salt and pepper, and add the wine, Fumet, and Bouquet Garni. Cover the dish with a lid or aluminum foil and place it in a moderate (350°) oven for 20 minutes, basting occasionally with the liquid in the pan. While the fish is cooking, add the chopped truffle to the forcemeat; from this mixture form 12 tiny quenelles, or dumplings, and 6 large ones, the shape of an egg; poach the large quenelles for about 10 minutes in barely simmering water and add the tiny ones for the last 5 minutes of simmering; drain on a cloth and keep warm. When the fish is cooked, transfer the steaks to a hot platter and keep warm. Strain the cooking liquid into a saucepan and reduce over high heat to $\frac{1}{2}$ cup. Add the Geneva sauce, cook only until very hot, correct the seasoning, and pour over the fish. Garnish the top of the fish with the tiny quenelles, shrimp, and mushrooms, and arrange the large quenelles and sautéed triangles of bread around the edge of the platter. *Serves* 6.

NOTE: Fluting mushrooms requires practice to execute perfectly, but they make a uniquely attractive garnish and are worth the effort. The mushrooms must be very white and fresh, and the only tool required is a very sharp paring knife. Dip a mushroom cap in water, hold it, cap up, in the fingers of the left hand, hold the knife in the right hand with the blade just touching the center of the cap, and rotate the cap toward you with the left hand while holding the knife rigid. Continue in this manner, cutting shallow crescent-shaped "flutes" from the center to the bottom of the sides, until the whole cap is fluted. The cuts will be more even if you work as quickly as possible.

867. COULIBIAC OF SALMON
Coulibiac di salmone

Dough ingredients:
   1 package dry yeast
   $\frac{1}{2}$ cup warm (85°) water
   $3\frac{1}{2}$ cups sifted all-purpose flour
   4 eggs
   $\frac{3}{4}$ cup butter, softened
   1 teaspoon salt
2 pounds cooked salmon, boned and cut into large
   chunks
2 onions, chopped
4 tablespoons butter
$\frac{1}{2}$ pound mushrooms, sliced
6 cups Rice Pilaf [No. 595]
3 hard-boiled eggs, chopped
Optional: 6 ounces dried salmon marrow soaked in
   water for 6 hours (*see* Note below)
$\frac{1}{2}$ cup butter, melted
$\frac{1}{3}$ cup fresh breadcrumbs
Salt and freshly ground pepper

Sprinkle the yeast on the water, let it stand until it foams up, and then mix with 1 cup of the flour; set in a warm place until it has doubled in bulk. While it is rising, combine the remaining flour with the eggs, butter, and salt; knead until it is an elastic dough; and

let it rest. Combine the 2 doughs and knead until thoroughly blended. Cover, and set the dough in a warm place until it is doubled in bulk. This should take about 2 hours (it is important that the dough does not rise too fast or be more than doubled).

Sauté the onions very lightly in 3 tablespoons of butter in a frying pan over moderate heat until they are transparent, add the mushrooms, season lightly, and cover the pan, and cook for 8 minutes longer, stirring occasionally. Remove from the heat and reserve.

When the dough has just doubled, punch it down, place $\frac{2}{3}$ of it on a floured board, and roll it out into a 12-inch square. Spread 2 cups of the rice in a 7-inch square layer in the center; spread $\frac{1}{2}$ of the salmon, a little salt and pepper, mushroom/onion mixture, hard-boiled eggs, and the optional salmon marrow in a layer on top; add another layer of rice; add another layer of the mixed ingredients; and top with the remaining rice. Roll out the remaining dough into a 9-inch square, place it on top of the rice, brush the edge of the bottom dough with water, pull it up to form sides, and press the edges of the 2 doughs firmly together to form a tight seal. Set the pie in a warm place to rise for $1\frac{1}{2}$ hours. Sprinkle the top with 2 tablespoons of melted butter and the breadcrumbs, cut a slit in the center of the top, insert a small funnel, place the pie on a baking sheet, and bake in a moderate (350°) oven for 50 to 60 minutes. Remove from the oven and pour the remaining melted butter into the funnel. Remove the funnel and serve at once. *Serves* 6.

NOTE: $\frac{1}{4}$ pound beef marrow, poached for 5 minutes, could be substituted for the salmon marrow. However, the marrow can be omitted with very little loss to the flavor of this exceptionally delicious dish.

868. SALMON KEDGEREE
Cadgery di salmone

$1\frac{1}{2}$ pounds cooked salmon, boned and flaked
2 teaspoons curry powder
$2\frac{1}{2}$ cups White Wine Sauce [No. 76]
3 cups rice Pilaf [No. 595]
4 tablespoons butter
5 hard-boiled eggs, quartered

Blend the curry powder with the wine sauce in a saucepan and cook for 5 minutes over medium heat. Add the flaked fish and heat for 2 minutes. Place a layer of the rice in a hot, shallow serving bowl, cover with a layer of the sauced fish, and continue making layers of each, ending with a layer of rice. Heat the butter in a frying pan until nut colored, pour over the top and garnish with the hard-boiled eggs. *Serves* 6.

869. SALMON WITH MOUSSELINE SAUCE
Salmone lessato con salsa mousseline

1 whole 5-pound salmon, cleaned

3 quarts Court Bouillon [No. 763]

2 lemons, quartered

6 sprigs parsley

2 cups Sauce Hollandaise [No. 72]

½ cup heavy cream, beaten stiff

Place the fish on a rack in a fish boiler, add the Court Bouillon, cover the pan, bring to a boil over high heat, reduce the heat, and simmer for 35 minutes. Transfer the fish to hot serving platter, carefully remove skin, and garnish with the lemon quarters and the parsley. Fold the whipped cream into the Hollandaise and serve separately. *Serves* 6.

870. COLD SALMON MUSCOVITE
Darne di salmone fredde alla moscovita

3 1-pound salmon steaks (or 6 ½-pound steaks)

2 quarts Court Bouillon [No. 763]

6 very large dill pickles (the Scandanavian *senf* gherkins, if possible)

1½ cups Russian Salad [No. 1879]

18 tiny shrimp, boiled for 5 minutes in salted water, peeled, and de-veined

6 tartlet shells, made from Rich Pastry [No. 1955]

3 hard-boiled eggs

4 ounces caviar

1 quart Fish Aspic [No. 119] or Substitute Fish Aspic [No. 119a]

2 cups Mayonnaise [No. 77]

Arrange the fish slices on the rack in a fish boiler, add the Court Bouillon, cover tightly, bring to a boil over high heat, reduce the heat, and simmer for 20 minutes (if using the smaller steaks, poach for 10 minutes). Add a little cold water to the pan and allow the fish to cool in the liquid. Transfer the slices to a serving platter, skin, and carefully remove the center bone with a sharp knife; chill salmon in the refrigerator. Slice the pickles in half lengthwise, scoop out most of the pulp from each half, fill each with Russian salad, and chill. Arrange 3 shrimp in each of the tart shells and chill. Cut the hard-boiled eggs in half lengthwise, remove the yolks, fill the white halves with a little caviar, and chill. When all the ingredients are cold, stir the liquid aspic over ice until it becomes thick and syrupy. Decoratively arrange the 3 garnishes around the fish and glaze them and the salmon with aspic; chill again in the refrigerator. Pour the remaining aspic in a large shallow dish, chill in the refrigerator until firm, turn this sheet of aspic out onto a board, chop it finely, and arrange small heaps of it around the platter. Serve the mayonnaise on the side. *Serves* 6.

NOTE: If desired, the hard-boiled egg yolks may be pressed through a sieve and used as an additonal garnish.

871. NORWEGIAN SALMON
Salmone rosso alla norvegese

2 pounds dried, salted salmon, soaked in several changes of cold water for 48 hours

2 carrots, chopped

2 onions, chopped

1 tablespoon vinegar

2 pounds spinach, thoroughly washed

4 tablespoons butter

1 cup butter, melted

Cut the soaked salmon into serving pieces, place them in a large saucepan with the carrots and onions, add the vinegar and sufficient water to cover, bring to a boil over high heat, reduce the heat, and simmer for 15 minutes. While the fish is cooking, cook the spinach in just the water that clings to the leaves in a covered saucepan for 8 minutes over medium heat. Drain, cool, press out excess water with the hands, chop it coarsely, and sauté it for a few minutes in 4 tablespoons of butter in a saucepan over very low heat. Spread the spinach out on a serving platter, arrange the fish on top, and serve the melted butter separately. *Serves* 6.

872. COLD PARISIAN SALMON
Salmone freddo alla francese

1 whole 5-pound salmon, cleaned
3 quarts Court Bouillon [No. 763]
2 cups ice cubes
Sauce:
    2 tablespoons chervil leaves
    2 tablespoons chopped parsley
    2 tablespoons tarragon leaves
    1 small onion, chopped
    6 spinach leaves, coarsely chopped
    3 anchovy fillets, soaked free of salt [*see* No. 220]
    3 pickles, chopped
    2 tablespoon capers
    5 hard-boiled egg yolks
    1 cup butter, softened
    1 tablespoon tarragon vinegar
    1 cup oil
    Cayenne pepper
    Salt and freshly ground pepper
Garnish:
    5 hard-boiled egg whites, cut into fancy shapes
    1 truffle, sliced and cut into fancy shapes
    12 tarragon leaves
    3 hard-boiled eggs, sliced
    6 anchovy fillets, soaked free of salt [*see* No. 220]
    12 large Italian-style capers
    12 pickle slices

Place the fish on the rack in a fish boiler, add sufficient Court Bouillon to cover the fish, bring to a boil over high heat, cover the pan tightly, reduce the heat, and simmer for 35 minutes. Add 2 cups ice cubes to pan, and allow the fish to cool completely in the cooking liquid; then carefully transfer it to a serving platter, remove all of the skin from the head to the tail, and chill in the refrigerator until very cold. Parboil the chervil, parsley, tarragon, onion, and spinach in a small amount of boiling water for 3 minutes. Drain, and squeeze out as much of the water as possible. Place the mixture in a mortar and pound to a paste; add the anchovy fillets, pickles, and capers; pound to a paste again; add, alternately, the egg yolks, one at a time, and the butter, a little at a time, pounding vigorously. Transfer the mixture to a bowl, add the vinegar, mix thoroughly, and add the oil, a drop at a time, beating constantly with a whisk (it should be the consistency of mayonnaise). Press the sauce through a fine strainer and season to taste with salt, pepper, and Cayenne. Remove the fish from the refrigerator and spread a little of the sauce over the exposed flesh.

Decorate the top with the garnish ingredients in decorative patterns. *Serves 6.*

NOTE: The whole preparation of the sauce may be accomplished in the electric blender.

873. SALMON SUPRÊME PHOENICIA
Suprême di salmone phoenicia

6 ⅓-pound salmon steaks
¾ cup butter, softened
12 large leaves of Boston lettuce, parboiled
    for ½ minute and patted dry
1 tablespoon chopped shallots
½ cup dry white wine
½ cup Fish Fumet [No. 2]
½ cup Brown Veal Stock [No. 5], reduced
    to 3 tablespoons
1 clove garlic, crushed in the garlic-press
½ pound mushrooms, sliced
4 tablespoons heavy cream
4 tablespoons chopped parsley
Salt and freshly ground white pepper

Season the fish slices lightly with salt and pepper, spread ½ tablespoon of butter on each, and wrap each in 2 of the lettuce leaves. Grease a large baking dish with 2 tablespoons of the butter, arrange the wrapped fish slices in it, and add the shallots, wine, Fumet, and reduced stock. Cover the dish with a lid or aluminum foil and place it in a moderate (350°) oven for about 20 minutes. While the fish is cooking, melt 3 tablespoons of the butter in a frying pan over medium heat, add the garlic, cook until golden, add the mushrooms, cover the pan, reduce the heat, and cook for 8 minutes, stirring occasionally. Spread the mushrooms and garlic in the bottom of a hot serving platter. When the fish is cooked, carefully transfer the wrapped slices to the platter on top of the mushrooms and keep warm. Strain the cooking liquid into a saucepan and reduce to 1 cup over high heat. Add the cream, cook for 1 minute, correct the seasoning, remove from the heat, and swirl in the remaining butter, bit by bit. Pour the sauce over the fish and sprinkle with the parsley. *Serves 6.*

874. SALMON IN RED WINE
Salmone brasato al barolo

1 whole 4-pound salmon, cleaned
3 quarts Court Bouillon [No. 763]
24 mushrooms
3 tablespoons butter

Bouquet Garni:

    2 sprigs thyme (or ¼ teaspoon dried)

    2 sprigs parsley

    1 bay leaf

3 cups red wine (preferably Barolo)

1 clove garlic, crushed in the garlic-press

1 cup vegetable Mirepoix [*ese* Note to No. 141]

5 tablespoons Kneaded Butter [No. 107]

Salt and freshly ground pepper

Place the fish on the rack in a fish boiler, add enough of the Court Bouillon to just cover the fish, cover the pan tightly, bring to a boil over high heat, reduce the heat, and simmer for about 30 minutes. While the fish is cooking, sauté the mushroom caps (reserving the stems) in the butter in a covered frying pan over moderate heat for 8 minutes. Transfer the fish to a hot serving platter and keep warm. Reduce 1 quart of the cooking liquid to 1½ cups as rapidly as possible in a saucepan over high heat. When it is reduced, add the Bouquet Garni, wine, mushroom stems, garlic, and the vegetable mirepoix. Simmer for 20 minutes, strain into another saucepan, blend in the kneaded butter with a whisk, simmer for 5 minutes longer, correct the seasoning, and pour over the fish. Garnish with the mushroom caps. *Serves* 6.

SARDINES

Sarda e sardina

Sardines are a salt-water fish of the herring family and are especially popular in Italy. Italian cooks prepare fresh sardines in a wide variety of ways, and sardines preserved in oil or brine are nearly always included in a good antipasto. In the United States, sardines come from the north and eastern Atlantic where they are very abundant. Fresh sardines in American markets are usually 3 to 4 inches long, the larger ones being commercially preserved and packed. Usually their heads are removed before cooking, and they are cleaned in the manner described in the introduction (page 258).

875. SARDINES WITH ARTICHOKES
Sarde con carciofi

24 fresh sardines, cleaned

6 very young, tender artichokes

½ cup oil

2 tablespoons chopped parsley

Juice of 1 lemon

½ cup fresh breadcrumbs

Salt and freshly ground pepper

Remove any tough outer leaves from the artichokes, cut off all of the hard tips of the leaves, split them in half, remove the choke with a sharp knife, and then slice them thinly lengthwise. Grease a round oven-proof dish liberally with oil and line the bottom with half of the artichoke slices; season them lightly with salt. Arrange the sardines on top with the tails in the center and the heads at the rim. Sprinkle them lightly with salt, a little oil, a tablespoon of chopped parsley, and a few drops of lemon juice. Over this place a second layer of the sliced artichokes, season them with salt, pepper, chopped parsley, oil, and lemon juice. Cover the top with breadcrumbs, sprinkle with oil, put the dish into a moderate (350°) oven for about 40 minutes. Serve very hot in the baking dish. *Serves* 6.

876. BAKED SARDINES
Sarde in tortiera

24 fresh sardines, cleaned

4 tablespoons fresh breadcrumbs

1 tablespoon chopped parsley

2 cloves garlic, crushed in the garlic-press

½ cup oil

3 tablespoons vinegar

Salt and freshly ground pepper

Mix the breadcrumbs, parsley, garlic, a pinch of salt, and pepper, and 2 tablespoons of oil in a bowl until it is a smooth, thick paste. Grease a baking dish liberally with oil, arrange half the sardines in it, spread them with half the paste, cover with the rest of the sardines, spread these with the remaining paste, sprinkle the top with the vinegar and remaining oil. Place in a hot (400°) oven for 20 minutes. Serve in the baking dish. *Serves* 6.

877. BROILED SARDINES
Sarde arrosto

24 fresh sardines, cleaned
Juice of 1 lemon
¼ cup oil
3 lemons, quartered
Salt and freshly ground pepper

Place the sardines in a bowl, season them lightly with salt and pepper, add the lemon juice and oil, and mix lightly so that each sardine is well coated. Arrange them on the rack of the broiler and broil under a high flame for 2 to 3 minutes on each side. Arrange them on a hot serving platter and garnish with the lemon quarters. *Serves* 6.

878. SARDINES CONTADINA
Sarde alla contadina

24 fresh sardines, cleaned
Flour
5 tomatoes, peeled, seeded, drained, and chopped
1 clove garlic, crushed in the garlic-press
2 tablespoons oil
2 tablespoons chopped parsley
2 tablespoons chopped basil (or 1½ teaspoons dried)
Fat for deep frying
Salt

Split the sardines down the back with a very sharp knife and carefully remove the backbone, cutting it off at the head and close to the tail; be careful to remove as little of the flesh as possible. Season lightly with salt and toss in flour until lightly coated. Let stand while you prepare the sauce: mix the tomatoes, garlic, and oil (and if you are using dried basil add this also) in an oven-proof platter. Season lightly with salt and pepper, and place the platter in a hot (400°) oven while the sardines are being cooked. Heat the fat to 375°, and fry the sardines a few at a time in a frying basket until they are golden brown. Drain on absorbent paper, and when all are fried place them on top of the tomato mixture in the platter, sprinkle with the fresh herbs and a little salt, and serve at once. *Serves* 6.

879. SARDINES WITH FENNEL
Sarde al finocchio

24 fresh sardines, cleaned
½ cup oil
1 large onion, chopped
½ cup dry white wine
3 tomatoes, peeled, seeded, drained, and chopped
½ cup fresh breadcrumbs
1 tablespoon fennel seed, pounded to a powder in the mortar
Salt and freshly ground pepper

Heat ¼ cup of the oil in an earthenware (or enamel) casserole over medium heat, add the onion, and cook until golden. Add the wine, cook until it is reduced by ⅔, and add the tomato pulp. Cook for 8 minutes and remove from the stove. Add the sardines, season with salt and pepper, mix lightly, and cover with the fresh breadcrumbs which have been mixed with the powdered fennel seeds. Sprinkle with the remaining oil and put the casserole into a moderate (350°) oven for 20 minutes. Serve in the casserole. *Serves* 6.

880. SARDINE FRITTERS
Bignè di sardine

2 pounds fresh sardines, cleaned and filleted
A batter composed of:
   ¾ cup flour
   2 tablespoons oil
   1 cup warm water
   ½ teaspoon salt
2 egg whites, beaten stiff
Fat for deep frying
6 sprigs parsley, fried in deep fat [*see* No. 276]
2 lemons, quartered
Salt
Optional: 2 cups Tomato Sauce [No. 19]

Fold the egg whites into the batter; dip the fillets in the mixture, one by one, and drop immediately in deep, hot (375°) fat. Drain them when they are golden, arrange on a hot serving platter, sprinkle with salt, and garnish with the fried parsley and the lemon quarters. A tomato sauce may be served on the side. *Serves* 6.

881. SARDINES WITH GARLIC BUTTER
Sardine sulla graticola con burro d'aglio

2 pounds fresh sardines, cleaned
Juice of 1 lemon

¼ cup oil

6 sprigs parsley, fried in deep fat [*see* No. 276]

3 lemons, quartered

1½ cups Garlic Butter [No. 109]

Salt and freshly ground pepper

Broil the sardines as in No. 877. Arrange them on a hot serving platter and garnish with the lemon quarters and the fried parsley. Serve the garlic butter on the side. *Serves* 6.

882. SARDINES GENOVESE
Sardine fritte alla genovese

2 pounds fresh sardines, cleaned

A stuffing composed of:

  1 cup fresh bread, cubed, soaked in milk, and squeezed dry

  2 eggs

  2 tablespoons grated Parmesan cheese

  1 tablespoon chopped parsley

  1 tablespoon chopped basil (or ½ teaspoon dried)

  1 teaspoon chopped oregano (or ¼ teaspoon dried)

  ½ teaspoon salt

  ¼ teaspoon freshly ground pepper

Flour

2 eggs, beaten

Breadcrumbs

Fat for deep frying

2 lemons, quartered

Salt

Mix all the ingredients for the stuffing together thoroughly (if dried herbs have been used, let the mixture stand for 20 minutes to moisten the herbs). Split the sardines and remove the backbone as in Sardines Contadina [No. 878]. Spread a little of the stuffing mixture inside each sardine, press the two halves together, dust the stuffed fish with flour, dip them in beaten egg, roll in the breadcrumbs, and fry a few at a time in deep, hot (375°) fat until golden. Drain on absorbent paper and keep warm until all are fried. Arrange them on a serving platter, sprinkle with salt, and garnish with the lemon quarters. *Serves* 6.

883. SARDINES GOURMET
Sardine del gourmet

2 pounds fresh sardines, cleaned

1 cup very thick Tomato Sauce [No. 19]

¼ cup Duxelles [No. 138]

¼ cup oil

1½ cups hot Sauce Bercy [No. 49]

3 sweet red peppers, roasted, scraped, seeded, and cut into strips [*see* No. 145]

12 anchovy fillets, washed free of salt [*see* No. 220]

Salt and freshly ground pepper

Split the sardines and remove the backbone as in Sardines Contadina [No. 878]. Combine the tomato sauce and the Duxelles and place a little of the mixture inside each sardine. Oil a baking dish generously, arrange the sardines in it in 1 layer, sprinkle with a little oil, season lightly with salt and pepper, and bake in a hot (400°) oven for 20 minutes. While the sardines are baking, sauté the pepper strips very gently in a frying pan with 2 tablespoons of oil for about 10 minutes. When the sardines are cooked, arrange them on a serving platter, pour the Bercy sauce over them, and decorate with the pepper strips and anchovy fillets. *Serves* 6.

Stuffing sardines for
Sardines Gourmet (No. 883)

884. SARDINES WITH MUSSELS
Sardine con le cozze

2 pounds fresh sardines, cleaned

1½ pounds mussels, scrubbed and "beards" removed

½ cup dry white wine

3 tablespoons oil

1 tablespoon chopped parsley

Juice of 1 lemon

Salt and freshly ground pepper

Split the sardines and remove the backbone as in Sardines Contadina [No. 878]. Place the mussels and wine in a heavy pot, put it over high heat, cover tightly, and steam just until the mussel shells open. Pour the mussels and the liquid into a colander placed over a bowl; remove the mussels from their shells, allowing any juice to drain into the bowl; and keep the mussels warm. Strain the liquid in the bowl into a saucepan through several thicknesses of cheesecloth. Add sardines, season lightly with salt and pepper, bring to a boil over high heat, reduce the heat, and simmer for 10 minutes. Remove the sardines with a slotted spoon and transfer them to a hot serving platter. Arrange the mussels on top. Add the oil, parsley, and lemon juice to the liquid; boil for 2 minutes over a brisk flame; correct seasoning; and pour over the fish. *Serves* 6.

885. SARDINES PALERMO
Sarde ripiene alla palermitana

24 fresh sardines, cleaned
½ cup oil (or more as needed)
1½ cups fine breadcrumbs
⅓ cup yellow raisins
⅓ cup pine nuts
Pinch sugar
1 tablespoon chopped parsley
12 anchovy fillets, washed free of salt [*see* No. 220], and chopped
Pinch nutmeg
Freshly ground pepper
12 bay leaves, halved
Juice of 1 lemon

Split the sardines and remove the backbone as in Sardines Contadina [No. 878]. Heat 4 tablespoons of the oil in a frying pan over medium heat, add half of the breadcrumbs, sauté for 20 seconds, and remove from the fire. Add the raisins, pine nuts, sugar, parsley, anchovies, and nutmeg. Season lightly with pepper and mix thoroughly. Put a little of this mixture into each sardine and close them firmly by pressing the halves together. Grease a baking dish with oil, arrange the sardines in it in 1 layer in even rows, place a halved bay leaf between each, cover with the remaining breadcrumbs, sprinkle with a little more oil, and place the dish in a moderate (350°) oven for 30 minutes. Sprinkle the lemon juice over the top and serve in the baking dish. *Serves* 6.

886. SARDINES ROMANA
Sarde ripiene alla romana

24 fresh sardines, cleaned
1 pound spinach, thoroughly washed
3 tablespoons butter
¼ cup heavy cream
2 eggs beaten

Breadcrumbs
Fat for deep frying
2 lemons, quartered
6 sprigs parsley
Salt and freshly ground pepper

Split the sardines and remove the backbone as in Sardines Contadina [No. 878]. Cook the spinach in a saucepan over medium heat for 8 minutes in just the water that clings to the leaves after washing. Drain it, allow it to cool slightly, press out excess water with the hands, and chop it. Return it to the saucepan, season it lightly with salt and pepper, add the butter and heavy cream, and cook over moderate heat for 5 minutes .The mixture should be moist, but not wet. Spread the sardines open flat, flesh side up, and put a little of the spinach on each of the sardines, roll them up lengthwise, and skewer each with a toothpick to keep their rolled shape. Dip them in beaten egg and then in breadcrumbs. Fry them a few at a time in deep, hot (375°) fat until they are golden, drain, remove the toothpicks, and heap them in a mound on a hot serving platter. Garnish with the parsley and lemon quarters. *Serves* 6.

887. SARDINES IN TOMATO SAUCE
Sarde ripiene alla salsa di pomodoro

24 fresh sardines, cleaned
¼ cup fresh breadcrumbs, soaked in milk and squeezed dry
6 anchovy fillets, washed free of salt [*see* No. 220] and pounded to a paste in the mortar with 1 crushed clove of garlic
Pinch oregano
2 eggs, separated
¼ cup grated Parmesan cheese
Breadcrumbs
Fat for deep frying
6 sprigs parsley, fried in deep fat [*see* No. 276]
1½ cups Tomato Sauce [No. 19]
Salt

Split the sardines and remove the backbone, as in Sardines Contadina [No. 878]. Mix the breadcrumbs with the anchovy/garlic paste, oregano, 2 egg yolks, and the cheese; if the mixture is too dry to hold together, add a very little oil. Place a little of this mixture in each sardine and close the opening with a toothpick. Beat the 2 egg whites until stiff, dip the sardines in the beaten whites, roll them very lightly in breadcrumbs, and fry a few at a time in deep hot (375°) fat until golden. Drain, remove toothpicks, and heap them in a mound on a hot serving platter, sprinkle with a little salt, and garnish with the fried parsley. Serve the tomato sauce on the side. *Serves* 6.

888. SAVORY SARDINES
Sardine fritte piccanti

2 pounds fresh sardines, cleaned
A mixture pounded to paste in the mortar:
   16 anchovy fillets, washed free of salt [*see* No. 220]
   1/2 teaspoon dry mustard
   1/4 teaspoon dried oregano
   6 white peppercorns
   1 tablespoon chopped parsley
Flour
3 eggs, beaten
Fat for deep frying
3 lemons, quartered
Salt

Split the sardines and remove the backbone as in Sardines Contadina [No. 878]. Spread a little of the paste inside each, fold the halves together, dust them with flour, dip in the beaten egg, and fry a few at a time in deep hot (375°) fat until they are golden. Drain and heap them in a mound on a hot serving platter. Sprinkle lightly with salt and garnish with the lemon quarters. *Serves* 6.

SHARK
Palombo

Several varieties of shark are found in American fish markets. Among them, the sand shark is the most common. Usually very thick transverse slices are cut by the fish dealer into thin slices or small fillets. Sharks have a very firm flesh and are somewhat similar to swordfish in flavor. The latter may be substituted in any of the following recipes.

889. SHARK FILLETS WITH MUSHROOMS
Palombo coi funghi

6 shark fillets, 1/2 inch thick
1 1/2 cups oil
Juice of 1 lemon
2 tablespoons butter
1 onion, chopped
1 carrot, chopped
2 cloves garlic, bruised
2 anchovy fillets, washed free of salt [*see* No. 220] and
   pounded to a paste in the mortar
1/2 cup dry white wine
2 tablespoons chopped parsley
1 teaspoon chopped thyme (or 1/4 teaspoon dried)
1 bay leaf, crumbled
2 tablespoons Meat Essence [No. 10] diluted with
   1/4 cup water
4 ounces dried, imported mushrooms, soaked in water
   for 1/2 hour, squeezed dry, and cut into small pieces
Flour
1 cup Croûtons [No. 332]
Salt and freshly ground pepper

Season the fillets lightly with salt and marinate them for 2 hours in the lemon juice and 1 cup of the oil. Heat the butter and 1 tablespoon of the oil in a heavy saucepan over medium heat; add the onion, carrot, and garlic; and cook until golden. Blend in the anchovy paste and then add the wine, parsley, thyme, and bay leaf. Cook until the wine has evaporated and add the diluted meat essence. Reduce the heat and cook for 5 minutes. Meanwhile sauté the mushrooms very gently in 1 tablespoon of oil in a frying pan over moderate heat, season them lightly with salt and pepper, and after 10 minutes transfer them to the other mixture. Remove the fillets from their marinade, dust them with flour, and sauté them in a large frying pan in the remaining oil over high heat for about 3 minutes on each side, or until they are brown. Arrange them on a hot serving platter, pour the sauce over them, and garnish with the croûtons. *Serves* 6.

Shark Fillets with Mushrooms (No. 889)

890. SHARK FILLETS WITH PEAS
Palombo in umido con piselli

6 small shark fillets, ½ inch thick
3 tablespoons oil
1 large onion, chopped
1 pound shelled peas
3 tomatoes, peeled, seeded, drained, and pureéd through
    a food mill
1 tablespoon chopped parsley
Salt and freshly ground pepper

Heat the oil in a large, heavy saucepan over medium heat, add the onion, and cook until golden. Add the peas, reduce the heat, and cook for 2 minutes. Add the tomato purée, the fish fillets, the parsley, and sufficient water barely to cover. Bring to a boil, reduce the heat, and simmer for 10 to 12 minutes. Remove the fillets to a hot serving platter and keep warm. Drain off the liquid in the pan through a sieve into another saucepan and reduce to ⅓ its quantity over high heat. Add the contents of the sieve, and spoon the mixture over the fillets. *Serves* 6.

891. SHARK ROMANA
Palombo alla romana

6 small shark fillets, ½ inch thick
2 eggs, beaten
3 cloves garlic, crushed in the garlic-press
2 tablespoons chopped parsley
3 tablespoons fresh breadcrumbs
3 tablespoons grated Parmesan cheese
½ cup oil
2 lemons, quartered
Salt and freshly ground pepper

Season the eggs lightly with salt and soak the fillets in them for ½ hour. Mix together in a bowl the garlic, parsley, breadcrumbs, and cheese. Season lightly with salt and pepper and mash the mixture to a paste. Spread a little of this on both sides of the fillets and fry them in smoking hot oil for about 3 minutes on each side, or until they are golden. Drain them, arrange them on a serving platter, and garnish with the lemon quarters. *Serves* 6.

300

892. SHARK VIVANDIERA
Palombo alla vivandiera

6 small shark fillets, ¼ inch thick
½ cup oil
4 shallots, finely chopped

1 clove garlic, crushed in the garlic-press
4 anchovy fillets, washed free of salt [*see* No. 220] and
    pounded to a paste in the mortar
½ cup dry white wine
2 tablespoons chopped parsley
Flour
Salt and freshly ground pepper

Heat 2 tablespoons of the oil in a frying pan over medium heat, add the shallots and garlic, and cook until golden. Blend in the anchovy paste, add the wine and parsley, and cook until the wine has almost evaporated. Season the fillets lightly with salt and pepper, dredge them with flour, and sauté them in smoking hot oil in a large frying pan over high heat for about 2 minutes on each side, or until they are golden. Arrange them on a hot serving platter, and spoon the sauce over them. *Serves* 6.

SKATE

Razza

Skate (or ray) is a large salt-water fish that is fairly common in Europe, but not very popular in the United States. The large "wings" that extend from either side of its body are, except for its liver, the only edible parts of a skate. Its flesh is very solid and, unlike other fish, is better if it is "seasoned" for 2 or 3 days before cooking.

Skate are usually cut into convenient-sized serving pieces and have a preliminary cooking in Court Bouillon [No. 763] for 15 to 20 minutes, depending on their thickness. They may be removed at once from the Court Bouillon and skinned or they may be cooled in the Court Bouillon before skinning. The gall sac must be removed from the liver before cooking and the skate is then either poached for 5 minutes in a little Court Bouillon or sautéed gently in a little butter.

893. SKATE IN BLACK BUTTER
Razza al burro nero

3 pounds skate, cut into serving pieces
3 cups Court Bouillon [No. 763]
¼ pound skate liver
1½ pounds "new" potatoes, peeled
½ cup butter
2 tablespoons capers

Salt and freshly ground pepper
Juice of 1 lemon

Put the skate and the Court Bouillon in a saucepan and bring to a boil over high heat; reduce the heat and simmer for 15 to 20 minutes, adding the liver for the last 5 minutes of the cooking. While the skate is cooking, boil the potatoes in salted water for about 20 minutes, or until they are just tender. Drain, skin the skate pieces, and slice the liver. Arrange them on a hot serving platter and keep warm. Melt the butter in a frying pan over high heat until it is nut colored, pour over the fish, season lightly, sprinkle with the capers, and squeeze the lemon juice over. Surround with the boiled potatoes and serve at once. *Serves* 6.

894. SKATE FRITTERS WITH TOMATO SAUCE
Fagottini di razza con salsa di pomodoro

2 pounds skate, cut into serving pieces
3 cups Court Bouillon [No. 763]
Juice of 4 lemons
2 cups sifted flour
3 tablespoons butter, melted
1 egg yolk
$\frac{1}{2}$ teaspoon salt
Fat for deep frying
$1\frac{1}{2}$ cups Tomato Sauce [No. 19]

Place the skate and the Court Bouillon in a saucepan and bring to a boil over high heat; reduce the heat and cook for 15 to 20 minutes. Remove from the heat, add a little cold water to stop the cooking process, and allow the skate to cool in the liquid. Drain the pieces, skin them, dry them well, and marinate them in the lemon juice for 1 hour. While they are marinating, prepare a dough with the flour, butter, egg yolk, salt, and the smallest amount of water possible to make a rather stiff noodle-type dough. Allow it to rest for $\frac{1}{2}$ hour, then roll it out as thinly as possible, and cut into 3-inch squares. Remove the pieces of skate from the lemon juice, dry them well, cut them into bite-size pieces, and wrap each piece in a square of dough, pinching the edges firmly together. Drop these into deep hot (375°) fat and drain when they are golden. Heap them up on a serving platter and serve the tomato sauce on the side. *Serves* 6.

895. SKATE GASTRONOME
Razza alla gastronoma

3 pounds skate, cut into serving pieces
$\frac{1}{4}$ pound skate liver
3 cups Court Bouillon [No. 763]
1 onion, chopped
2 tablespoons Kneaded Butter [No. 107]
4 tablespoons Anchovy Butter [No. 108]
2 tablespoons capers
2 tablespoons gherkins, sliced
1 tablespoon chopped parsley
Juice of 1 lemon
Salt and freshly ground white pepper

Place the skate and the Court Bouillon in a saucepan over high heat and bring to a boil; reduce the heat and simmer for 15 to 20 minutes, adding the liver for the last 5 minutes of the cooking. Remove the skate and the liver with a slotted spoon, skin the skate, slice the liver, place the pieces on a hot serving platter, and keep warm. Add the onion to the cooking liquid and reduce it over high heat to 2 cups, blend in the kneaded butter, reduce the heat, and simmer for 10 minutes. Remove from the heat, swirl in the anchovy butter, and add the capers, gherkins, parsley, and lemon juice. Correct the seasoning and pour over the fish. *Serves* 6.

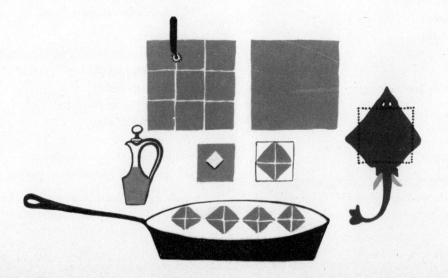

896. GOLDEN SKATE
Razza dorata

3 pounds skate, cut into serving pieces
3 cups Court Bouillon [No. 763]
A marinade:
  1 onion, sliced
  1/4 cup vinegar
  1/2 cup oil
  1 bay leaf, crushed
  1/4 teaspoon dried thyme
  1 teaspoon salt
  1/4 teaspoon freshly ground pepper
Flour
2 eggs, beaten
3/4 cup butter
6 sprigs parsley, fried in deep fat [*see* No. 276]
3 lemons, quartered

Put the skate and the Court Bouillon in a saucepan over high heat and bring to a boil; reduce the heat and simmer for 10 minutes. Remove from the fire, add a little cold water, and allow the skate to cool in the liquid. Drain the pieces, skin them, dry them thoroughly, and marinate them in the marinade for 2 hours. Dry the pieces, dust lightly with flour, dip in beaten egg, then in flour again, and sauté them in foaming hot butter in a large frying pan over high heat until golden on both sides. Transfer the pieces to a hot serving platter and garnish with the lemon quarters and the fried parsley. *Serves* 6.

897. SKATE WITH TARTAR SAUCE
Razza fritta con salsa tartara

3 pounds skate, cut into serving pieces
3 cups Court Bouillon [No. 763]
A marinade:
  2 onions, sliced
  1 tablespoon chopped parsley
  1/2 teaspoon dried thyme
  1 bay leaf, crumbled
  4 tablespoons vinegar
  1/2 cup oil
  1 teaspoon salt
  1/4 teaspoon freshly ground pepper
2 eggs, beaten
Flour
Fat for deep frying
1 1/2 cups Tartar Sauce [No. 98]

Prepare in the same manner as in the preceding recipe, except frying the skate in deep hot (375°) fat, instead of butter. Serve the tartar sauce on the side. *Serves* 6.

SOLE
Sogliola

The true Dover sole

The best sole in the world is taken in the English Channel and adjacent waters. Often called Dover sole, its flesh is rather firm, with a delicate and uniquely distinctive flavor. True Dover sole is imported and sold in better fish markets in the larger American cities; it is naturally expensive, but well worth the cost. Most of the salt-water fish labeled "sole" in American markets is any one of several varieties of flounder. The best of these is the so-called gray sole which is fairly abundant in the North Atlantic. Also distinctive in flavor is lemon sole. Ordinary flounder has a rather soft flesh and is bland in flavor.

Sole and flounder are nearly always filleted before cooking. While this is normally done by a fish dealer, it is not a difficult operation. The skin is removed from both sides of the fish by loosening a little of it near the tail with a very sharp knife and then, holding the tail firmly with a cloth to prevent slipping, it is pulled off in one quick motion. Using the same sharp knife, the fillets are then carefully removed from the backbone.

898. FILLETS OF SOLE AMERICANA
Sogliola all'americana

6 sole fillets
3 cups American Sauce [No. 63], prepared with
  3/4 pound lobster and 3/4 pound shrimp
6 tablespoons butter
1 cup Fish Fumet [No. 2]
1 cup dry white wine
12 mushroom caps
2 tablespoons chopped parsley
Salt and freshly ground white pepper

Prepare the American sauce and keep warm. Shell the lobster and shrimp with which the sauce was prepared and keep warm in a separate bowl. Butter a large baking dish with 3 tablespoons of the butter, arrange the fillets in it, season lightly with salt and pepper, and pour in the Fumet and wine. Cover the dish with a lid or aluminum foil and bake in a moderate (350°) oven for 8 to 10 minutes, being very careful not to overcook. While the fish is cooking, sauté the mushroom caps in the remaining butter over very gentle heat in a covered frying pan for about 8 minutes, remove from the heat, and keep warm. Remove the fish to a hot serving platter and keep warm while reducing its cooking liquid in a saucepan over high heat to $\frac{1}{4}$ its original quantity. Add the reduced stock to the American sauce. Remove any liquid which has drained from the fish with a bulb baster. Arrange the pieces of shellfish and the mushroom caps on top of the fillets, pour the sauce over them, and sprinkle with the chopped parsley. *Serves* 6.

899. FILLETS OF SOLE BONNE FEMME

Sogliola bonne femme

6 sole fillets
6 tablespoons butter, softened
$\frac{1}{2}$ pound mushrooms, sliced
1 tablespoon chopped parsley
2 cups dry white wine
3 tablespoons Kneaded Butter [No. 107]
Juice of 1 lemon
Salt and freshly ground white pepper

Butter a large baking dish with 2 tablespoons of the butter, spread the mushrooms and parsley in the bottom, arrange the fillets over them, season lightly with salt and pepper, and add the wine. Cover the dish with a lid or aluminum foil and bake in a moderate (350°) oven for 8 to 10 minutes, being very careful not to overcook. Transfer the fillets to a hot serving platter and keep warm. Strain the cooking liquid through a sieve into a saucepan, and keep the mushrooms and parsley in the sieve warm. Bring the liquid in the saucepan to a boil over fairly high heat, blend in the kneaded butter, add the lemon juice, and cook for about 5 minutes. Correct the seasoning, remove from the heat, and swirl in the remaining butter, bit by bit. Spoon the mushrooms and the parsley over the fillets, remove any liquid which the fish has released with a bulb baster, and pour the sauce over. *Serves* 6.

900. FILLETS OF SOLE CASALINGA

Filetti di sogliola casa nostra

6 sole fillets
$\frac{1}{2}$ cup butter
2 tablespoons oil
1 onion, chopped
3 tomatoes, peeled, seeded, drained, and chopped
2 sprigs rosemary, tied with string
1 tablespoon chopped basil
1 pound small zucchini, sliced
Flour
Juice of 1 lemon
3 tablespoons butter, melted
1 cup fresh breadcrumbs
Salt and freshly ground pepper

Heat 2 tablespoons of the butter and the oil in a heavy saucepan over medium heat, add the onion, and cook until golden. Add the tomatoes, basil, and rosemary; season with salt and pepper; and cook for 5 minutes. Add the zucchini, mix well, and cook for 8 minutes longer. Remove from the heat, discard the rosemary, and keep warm. Season the fillets lightly with salt and pepper and dust them with flour. Heat the remaining butter in a large frying pan over fairly high heat until almost nut colored and sauté the fillets in it on both sides until golden. Transfer them to an ovenproof platter, squeeze the lemon juice over them, spoon a little of the zucchini/tomato mixture over each fillet, and sprinkle first with breadcrumbs and then with the melted butter. Place the platter under a high flame in the broiler for 1 minute, or until the top is golden. *Serves* 6.

901. FILLETS OF SOLE COLBERT
Sogliola alla Colbert

6 sole fillets
Milk
Flour
2 eggs, beaten
Fresh breadcrumbs
¾ cup oil (or more, if necessary)
¾ cup Maître d'Hôtel Butter [No. 111]
Salt and freshly ground pepper
3 lemons, their edges scalloped, thinly sliced

If the fillets are too large to be turned easily in a frying pan, cut them in half. Season them lightly with salt and pepper, dip them in milk, dust them with flour, dip them in beaten egg, and then cover them completely with breadcrumbs. Heat ½ cup of the oil in a large frying pan (or use 2 frying pans) until smoking, add the fish, and sauté on both sides until golden, adding more oil as necessary. Transfer the fillets to a hot serving platter, put 2 tablespoons of the Maître d'Hôtel butter on each fillet, and garnish with the sliced lemon. *Serves 6.*

902. FILLETS OF SOLE FANTASIA DI BRIDA
Filetti di sogliola "Fantasia di Brida"

6 sole fillets
6 scampi (or substitute large shrimp), shelled
A marinade:
　1 cup oil
　⅓ cup lemon juice
　1 teaspoon salt
　¼ teaspoon freshly ground white pepper
1 cup dry white vermouth
1 tablespoon chopped shallots
½ cup Tomato Sauce [No. 19]
½ cup heavy cream
¼ cup butter, softened
12 small, cooked artichoke hearts [*see* introduction to
　No. 1578]
Salt and freshly ground pepper

Marinate the fillets and the scampi (or shrimp) in the marinade for 1 hour, turning them occasionally. Place both fish in a heavy, shallow pot (or, if the pot is deep, cut the fillets in half to facilitate their easy removal) with ¼ cup of the marinade, the vermouth, shallots, tomato sauce, and ¼ cup of the heavy cream. Season very lightly with salt and pepper, bring to a boil over high heat, reduce the heat, cover tightly, and simmer

for 8 minutes. Transfer the fillets to a hot serving platter, arrange 1 scampi or shrimp on top of each fillet, and keep warm. Reduce the sauce, uncovered, over high heat until it is rather thick, add the remaining cream, reduce again for 5 minutes, and correct the seasoning. Off the heat, swirl in the butter, bit by bit. Place 2 of the artichoke hearts on top of each fillet and pour the sauce over. *Serves 6.*

903. FILLETS OF SOLE FANTASIA MARINA
Filetti di sogliola "Fantasia Marina"

6 sole fillets
36 mussels, scrubbed and "beards" removed
½ cup dry white wine
36 medium shrimp, peeled and de-veined
12 slices of truffle [or No. 1819a]
¾ cup butter, softened
½ cup Scotch whiskey
Salt and freshly ground white pepper

Steam the mussels in the wine over high heat in a tightly covered saucepan for 3 to 5 minutes, or just until their shells open. Pour them into a colander placed over a bowl and remove the mussels from their shells, allowing any liquid in the shells to drain into the bowl. Keep the mussels warm in another covered bowl. Strain the mussel liquid through several thicknesses of cheesecloth and reserve. Sauté the shrimp and truffle slices in ¼ cup of the butter in a frying pan over moderate heat for 6 to 8 minutes, or until the shrimp are tender. Remove from the heat and keep warm. Season the sole fillets lightly with salt and pepper. Heat ¼ cup of the butter in a large frying pan over high heat until almost nut colored and sauté the fillets for about 3 minutes on each side; remove them to a hot serving platter and keep warm. Add the whiskey and the mussel liquid to the pan in which the fillets were cooked and reduce over high heat to ½ its quantity. Remove from the fire and swirl in the remaining butter, bit by bit. Place a few of the shrimp, mussels, and truffles over each fillet and pour the sauce over. *Serves 6.*

904. FILLETS OF SOLE FIORENTINA
Filetti di sogliola alla fiorentina

6 sole fillets
1 pound spinach, thoroughly washed
½ cup butter
1 cup dry white wine
½ cup Fish Fumet [No. 2]
2 cups Sauce Mornay [No. 56]
2 tablespoons melted butter
2 tablespoons grated Parmesan cheese
Salt and freshly ground white pepper

Cook the spinach in just the water that clings to the leaves in a tightly covered saucepan over medium heat for 8 minutes, stirring occasionally. Drain it well, press out excess water with the hands, chop it coarsely, place it in a saucepan, season lightly with salt and pepper, and cook it in 4 tablespoons of the butter for 5 minutes over moderate heat. Remove it from the fire and keep warm. Spread a baking dish with the remaining butter, arrange the fillets in it, season lightly with salt and pepper, add the wine and Fumet, cover with a lid or aluminum foil, and bake in a moderate (350°) oven for 10 to 12 minutes. Remove the fish to a large dish and keep warm. Pour the cooking liquid into a saucepan and reduce it over high heat to ¼ cup. Add the Mornay sauce and cook for another 5 minutes. Spread the spinach on an oven-proof platter, arrange the fillets on top, cover with the sauce, and sprinkle with the grated cheese and melted butter. Place the the platter under a high flame in the broiler for 1 minute, or until the top is golden. *Serves* 6.

905. FILLETS OF SOLE GRAN SUCCESSO NO. 1
Filetti di sogliola "Gran Successo" No. 1

6 sole fillets
4 tomatoes, peeled, seeded, drained, and chopped
6 tablespoons butter, softened
1 cup dry white wine
12 scampi (or substitute shrimp), shelled and diced
Flour
¼ cup oil
1½ cups White Wine Sauce [No. 76]
12 slices of truffle [or No. 1819a]
Salt and freshly ground white pepper

Cook the tomatoes with 3 tablespoons of the butter in a saucepan over medium heat for 10 minutes, seasoning them with a little salt and pepper as they cook.

Remove from the heat and keep warm. Spread the remaining butter in a large baking dish, arrange the fillets in it, season lightly with salt and pepper, add the wine, cover with a lid or aluminum foil, and bake in a moderate (350°) oven for 12 to 15 minutes. Arrange the fillets on a hot round platter, the tail ends in the center, and keep warm. Pour the cooking liquid into a saucepan and reduce over high heat to ¼ cup. While it is reducing, dust the diced scampi (or shrimp) with flour, and sauté them in smoking hot oil in a frying pan over high heat for about 4 minutes, or until they are golden. Add the white wine sauce to the reduced cooking liquid and cook just until thoroughly hot. Remove any liquid which has drained from the fish with a bulb baster and add this to the sauce. Spoon a little of the sauce over half of each fillet lengthwise (*see* illustration) and top these alternately with a little of the tomatoes and diced scampi. Place a truffle slice on each of the unsauced halves of the fillets and arrange the remaining truffles in the center with the rest of the tomatoes. Serve the remaining sauce on the side. *Serves* 6.

906. FILLETS OF SOLE GRAN SUCCESSO NO. 2
Filetti di sogliola "Gran Successo" No. 2

6 sole fillets
4 tomatoes, peeled, seeded, drained, and chopped
6 tablespoons butter, softened
1 cup dry white wine
1½ cups hot Sauce Béarnaise [No. 67]
24 fresh tarragon leaves, parboiled for 1½ minutes
Salt and freshly ground pepper

Cook the tomatoes in 3 tablespoons of the butter in a saucepan over medium heat for 15 minutes, seasoning them with salt and pepper as they cook. Remove from the heat and keep warm. Spread the remaining butter in a large skillet, arrange the six fillets in it, season them lightly with salt and pepper, add the wine, cover tightly, bring to a boil over high heat, reduce the heat, and simmer for 12 minutes. Remove the fillets to a hot serving platter and keep warm. Reduce the cooking liquid over high heat to 3 tablespoons. Add any juices that drain from the fillets and reduce again. Mix this concentrated liquid into the Béarnaise sauce and spoon it over the fillets. Garnish the top of each fillet with 4 tarragon leaves and arrange small heaps of the tomatoes around the platter. *Serves* 6.

907. FILLETS OF SOLE GRAN SUCCESSO NO. 3
Filetti di sogliola "Gran Successo" No. 3

6 sole fillets
1 pound mushrooms, sliced
6 tablespoons butter, softened
Pinch paprika
¾ cup sherry wine
3 egg yolks
¼ cup heavy cream
Juice of 1 lemon
Salt and freshly ground pepper

Sauté the mushrooms very gently in a covered saucepan in 3 tablespoons of the butter for about 8 minutes. Remove from the heat and keep warm. Spread the remaining butter in a large baking dish; arrange the fillets in it; season them lightly with salt, pepper, and paprika; add the sherry; cover the dish with a lid or aluminum foil; and place in a moderate (350°) oven for 12 to 15 minutes, basting occasionally with the liquid in the pan. Remove the fillets to a hot serving platter and keep warm. Pour the cooking liquid into a saucepan, add the liquid which the mushrooms have rendered, and bring to a boil over high heat. Mix the egg yolks with the cream and, off the heat, slowly pour into the sauce, stirring with a wire whisk. Return the pan to a very low fire and, stirring constantly, cook for about 5 minutes, or until it thickens. Remove from the heat, add the lemon juice, and correct the seasoning. Remove any liquid which the fillets have released with a bulb baster, spoon the mushrooms over the fillets, and pour the sauce over them. *Serves 6.*

908. FILLETS OF SOLE GRAN SUCCESSO NO. 4
Filetti di sogliola "Gran Successo" No. 4

6 sole fillets
2 sweet red peppers, roasted, scraped, seeded, and
    cut into strips [*see* No. 145]
1 cup butter
½ pound small zucchini, sliced
4 tomatoes, peeled, seeded, drained, and chopped
Flour
1 tablespoon chopped parsley
Salt and freshly ground pepper

Sauté the pepper strips gently in a saucepan in 2 tablespoons of butter for about 10 minutes; remove from the heat and keep warm. Melt 3 tablespoons of the butter in another saucepan, add the zucchini, season lightly with salt and pepper, and cook over

Fillets of Sole Gran Successo No. 4 (No. 908)

moderate heat, covered, for about 10 minutes, or until the zucchini are tender; remove from the heat and keep warm. Melt 3 tablespoons of the butter in another saucepan, add the tomatoes, season lightly with salt and pepper, and cook for about 10 minutes. Season the fillets lightly with salt and pepper and dust them with flour. Melt the remaining butter in a large frying pan over fairly high heat until it is almost nut colored and sauté the fillets for about 3 minutes on each side. Mix the 3 hot vegetables, spread them out on a hot serving platter, arrange the fillets over them, and sprinkle with the chopped parsley. *Serves 6.*

909. FILLETS OF SOLE INDIENNE
Sogliola al curry con riso pilaff all'indiana

6 sole fillets
½ cup butter, softened
1 onion, chopped
3 tomatoes, peeled, seeded, drained, and chopped
1 tablespoon curry powder (or more to taste)
½ cup Fish Fumet [No. 2]
1 cup Béchamel Sauce [No. 18]
½ cup heavy cream
Juice of 1 lemon
4 cups Indian Rice [No. 594]
Salt and freshly ground white pepper

Melt 2 tablespoons of the butter in a frying pan over medium heat, add the onion, and cook until golden.

306

Add the tomatoes; season with the curry powder, salt, and pepper; and cook for 10 minutes. Spread this mixture on the bottom of a large baking dish, arrange the fillets on top, season them lightly with salt and pepper, and add the Fumet. Cover the dish with a lid or aluminum foil and bake in a moderate (350°) oven for 10 to 12 minutes. Transfer the fillets to the center of a hot serving dish and keep warm. Pour the contents of the baking dish into a saucepan, add the Béchamel sauce and the cream, and cook for 10 minutes over medium heat. Remove from the fire, correct the seasoning, swirl in the remaining butter, bit by bit, and add the lemon juice. Encircle the fillets with a ring of the hot rice, and pour the sauce over the fillets. *Serves* 6.

910. FILLETS OF SOLE INGLESA
Sogliola all'inglese

6 sole fillets
1½ pounds very small, "new" potatoes, peeled
1½ cups butter, melted
4 tablespoons oil
6 sprigs parsley
2 lemons, quartered
Salt and freshly ground pepper

Cook the potatoes in salted boiling water in a saucepan over medium heat for about 20 minutes, or until tender. About 10 minutes before the potatoes are cooked, mix 4 tablespoons of the melted butter with the oil and brush both sides of each fillet. Season the fillets lightly with salt and pepper and broil them under a high flame for about 3 minutes on each side, basting them with a little more melted butter as they cook. Arrange the fillets on a hot serving platter and garnish with the parsley and lemon quarters. Drain the potatoes, turn them into a vegetable dish, add 4 tablespoons of the melted butter, and mix them lightly. Serve the remaining butter separately in a sauceboat. *Serves* 6.

911. FILLETS OF SOLE LOUISIANA
Sogliola alla louisiana

6 sole fillets
3 yellow peppers, roasted, scraped, seeded, and
    cut into strips [*see* No. 145]
1 cup butter
Flour
3 bananas, sliced
1 tablespoon each parsley, chervil, and tarragon,
    chopped
Salt and freshly ground white pepper

Sauté the pepper strips very gently in 3 tablespoons of the butter in a frying pan for 10 minutes. Remove them to a bowl with a slotted spoon and keep warm. Season the fillets lightly with salt and pepper and dust them with flour. Melt 6 tablespoons of the butter in a large frying pan over fairly high heat until it is almost nut colored, add the fillets, and cook on both sides until golden. Arrange the fillets on a hot serving platter and keep warm. In the same pan in which the peppers were cooked, sauté the bananas for about 2 minutes over medium heat, adding a little more butter if necessary. Spoon a little of the bananas and pepper strips over each fillet, add the remaining butter to the pan in which the bananas cooked, heat over a high flame until nut colored, and pour over the fish. Sprinkle with the chopped herbs. *Serves* 6.

912. FILLETS OF SOLE LUIGI VERONELLI
Sogliola alla Luigi Veronelli

6 sole fillets
¼ cup butter, softened
2 shallots, chopped
¼ pound mushrooms, finely sliced
2 tablespoons chopped parsley
½ cup dry white wine
½ cup Fish Fumet [No. 2]
½ cup fresh breadcrumbs
¼ cup butter, melted
12 scampi (or substitute large shrimp), shelled
½ cup heavy cream
1 tablespoon Meat Essence [No. 10], diluted with
    2 tablespoons water
12 slices stale bread, crusts removed, and cut into
    heart shapes
Salt and freshly ground white pepper
Juice of 1 lemon

Spread 2 tablespoons of the softened butter in a large baking dish; sprinkle the chopped shallots, mushrooms, and parsley in the bottom; add the wine and Fumet; arrange the fillets on top; season them lightly with salt and pepper; sprinkle them with the breadcrumbs, lemon juice, and melted butter; and place the dish in a moderate (350°) oven for 5 minutes. Surround the sole with the shelled scampi (or shrimp), add the cream and the meat essence, and return to the oven for another 10 minutes. A few minutes before the fish is cooked, sauté the slices of bread in the remaining butter in a frying pan over high heat until golden on both sides. Arrange these around the fish and serve in the baking dish. *Serves* 6.

913. FILLETS OF SOLE MARIA THERESA
Filetti di sogliola "Maria Teresa"

6 sole fillets
3 tablespoons butter, softened
½ pound mushrooms, sliced
3 shallots, chopped
Bouquet Garni:
   1 sprig thyme (or ¼ teaspoon dried)
   1 bay leaf
   2 sprigs parsley
2 cups dry white wine
½ cup water
4 egg yolks
½ cup heavy cream
Juice of ½ lemon
Salt and freshly ground pepper

Butter a baking dish with the softened butter, spread the mushrooms and shallots in the bottom, arrange the fillets over them, add the Bouquet Garni, season lightly with salt and pepper, add the wine and water, cover the dish with a lid or aluminum foil, and place in a moderate (350°) oven for 8 to 10 minutes. Remove the fillets to a hot serving platter, remove the mushrooms with a slotted spoon, arrange them over the fillets, and keep warm. Pour the cooking liquid into a saucepan and reduce over high heat to 1½ cups. Discard the Bouquet Garni, beat the egg yolks with the cream and, off the heat, pour slowly into the sauce, stirring with a whisk. Return the pan to a very low flame and cook for about 5 minutes, stirring constantly, until the sauce thickens slightly. Do not boil. Remove from the heat, add the lemon juice, correct the seasoning, and pour over the fillets. *Serves 6.*

914. FILLETS OF SOLE MEUNIÈRE WITH EGGPLANT
Sogliola alla mugnaia con melanzane

6 sole fillets
2 eggplant, peeled, cut in half, and cut into thick slices
Flour
6 tablespoons oil
½ cup butter
1 tablespoon chopped parsley
Juice of 1 lemon
Salt and freshly ground white pepper

Liberally salt the eggplant slices and let them drain on paper towels for 1 hour. Season the fillets lightly with salt and pepper and dust them with flour. Thoroughly wash the eggplant slices, pat dry, and dust them with flour. Melt the butter in a large, heavy frying pan until almost nut colored and, at the same time, heat the oil in another large frying pan until smoking. Sauté the fillets in the butter and the eggplant in the oil on both sides until golden; the eggplant will take slightly longer than the fish. Arrange the fillets in the center of a hot serving platter, squeeze the lemon juice over them, sprinkle with the chopped parsley, and surround with the eggplant slices. *Serves 6.*

915. FILLETS OF SOLE ORLY
Filetti di sogliola all'Orly

6 sole fillets
2 cups Fritter Batter [No. 275]
Fat for deep frying
6 sprigs parsley fried in deep fat [*see* No. 276]
2 lemons, quartered
2 cups Tomato Sauce [No. 19]
Salt and freshly ground pepper

Season the fillets with salt and a little pepper, dip them in the batter, and fry them in deep hot (375°) fat. Drain them when they are golden on absorbent paper and sprinkle with a little salt. Heap them in a mound on a serving platter covered with a paper doily or a napkin, garnish them with the fried sprigs of parsley and lemon quarters, and serve the tomato sauce on the side. *Serves 6.*

916. FILLETS OF SOLE SAINT GERMAIN
Filetti di sogliola Saint Germain

6 sole fillets
½ cup butter, melted
1½ cups fine fresh breadcrumbs
1½ cups Sauce Béarnaise [No. 67]
Salt and freshly ground white pepper

Season the fillets with salt and pepper, brush them lightly with butter, and dip them in breadcrumbs. Broil them under a medium flame in the broiler for about 5 minutes on each side, basting often with the remaining butter. Transfer them to a hot serving

platter and decorate with a ribbon of Béarnaise sauce on each fillet. Serve the remaining Béarnaise on the side. *Serves* 6.

917. FILLETS OF SOLE WITH TARTAR SAUCE
Sogliola fritta con salsa tartara

6 sole fillets
Flour
3/4 cup oil
6 sprigs parsley
3 lemons, quartered
2 cups Tartar Sauce [No. 98]
Salt and freshly ground pepper

Season the fillets lightly with salt and pepper and dust them with flour. Heat 1/2 cup of the oil in a large frying pan over fairly high heat until smoking, add the fillets, and cook on both sides until golden, adding more oil as necessary. Arrange the fish on a hot serving platter, garnish with the parsley and lemon quarters, and serve the tartar sauce separately. *Serves* 6.

918. FILLETS OF SOLE IN RED WINE
Filetti di sogliola al vino rosso

6 sole fillets
1/2 cup butter, softened
1 onion, finely sliced
1/2 pound mushrooms, sliced
1 3/4 cups red wine
2 tablespoons Kneaded Butter [No. 107]
2 tablespoons chopped parsley
Salt and freshly ground white pepper

Sauté the onion in 2 tablespoons of the butter in a frying pan over medium heat until it is transparent. Butter a large baking dish with 3 tablespoons of the butter, spread the onions and mushrooms in the bottom, arrange the fillets on top, season them lightly with salt and pepper, add the wine, cover with a lid or aluminum foil, and place the dish in a moderate (350°) oven for 12 to 15 minutes. Transfer the fillets to a hot serving platter, remove the mushrooms and onions with a slotted spoon, arrange them over the fillets, and keep warm. Reduce the cooking liquid in a saucepan over high heat to about 1 1/4 cups. Add any liquid which has drained from the fish and reduce again. Blend in the kneaded butter with a wire whisk and cook for 4 minutes. Correct the seasoning, remove from the heat, and swirl in the remaining butter, bit by bit. Pour over the fish and sprinkle with the parsley. *Serves* 6.

919. FILLETS OF SOLE IN WHITE CHIANTI
Sogliola al chianti bianco

6 sole fillets
3/4 cup butter, softened
3 cups white Chianti
3 tablespoons Kneaded Butter [No. 107]
Juice of 1 lemon
Flour
4 sprigs parsley
Salt and freshly ground white pepper

Cut off about 1/3 of each fillet at the tail end and reserve these pieces. Spread 3 tablespoons of the butter in a large baking dish, arrange the larger pieces of the fillets in it, season lightly with salt and pepper, add the wine, cover the dish with a lid or aluminum foil, and bake in a moderate (350°) oven for 10 to 12 minutes, being careful not to overcook. Remove the fillets to a hot serving platter and keep warm. Pour the cooking liquid into a saucepan and reduce over high heat to 1 1/2 cups, adding any juice which has drained from the cooked fish. Blend in the kneaded butter and cook for 5 minutes longer. Add the lemon juice and correct the seasoning. Remove from the heat and swirl in 4 tablespoons of the butter, bit by bit. While the sauce is reducing, dust the smaller pieces of the fillets with flour, heat the 5 tablespoons of the butter in a frying pan over high heat until almost nut colored, and sauté the fish on both sides until golden. Pour the sauce over the larger fillets, arrange 3 of the smaller fillets on each end of the platter, and garnish with the parsley. *Serves* 6.

920. FILLETS OF SOLE IN WHITE WINE
Sogliola al vino bianco

6 sole fillets
6 tablespoons butter, softened
2 cups Fish Fumet [No. 2], reduced over high heat to 1/4 cup
2 cups dry white wine
2 1/2 tablespoons Kneaded Butter [No. 107]
Juice of 1 lemon
Salt and freshly ground white pepper

Butter a large baking dish with 2 tablespoons of the butter, arrange fillets in it, season them with pepper, add the wine and reduced Fumet, cover with a lid or aluminum foil, and bake in a moderate (350°) oven for 10 to 12 minutes. Transfer the fillets to a hot serving platter and keep warm. Pour the cooking liquid into a saucepan and bring to a boil over high heat. Blend in the kneaded butter, reduce the heat slightly, and cook for 8 minutes. Remove from the fire, correct the seasoning, add the lemon juice, and swirl in the remaining butter, bit by bit. Pour the sauce over the fish and serve. *Serves* 6.

921. FILLETS OF SOLE WITH WHITE WINE SAUCE
Filetti di sogliola al vino bianco

6 sole fillets
3 tablespoons butter, softened
$\frac{1}{2}$ cup dry white wine
$\frac{1}{2}$ cup Fish Fumet [No. 2]
$1\frac{1}{4}$ cups White Wine Sauce [No. 76]
Salt and freshly ground white pepper
Juice of 1 lemon

Butter a large baking dish with the softened butter, arrange the fillets in it, season lightly with salt and pepper, add the wine and Fumet, cover with a lid or aluminum foil, and place in a moderate (350°) oven for 12 to 15 minutes. Transfer the fillets to a hot serving platter and keep warm. Pour the cooking liquid into a saucepan and reduce over high heat to about 3 tablespoons. Add any liquid which has drained from the fish and reduce again. Add the white wine sauce and lemon juice, cook only until thoroughly hot, and pour over the fish. *Serves* 6.

SQUID
Calamaro

Squid, like octopus and cuttlefish, are salt-water mollusks. Squid somewhat resemble the latter, but their bodies are elongated instead of rounded, and the edible varieties are less than a foot long. Baby squid (called *calamaretti* in Italy) have a tender flesh and an especially sweet flavor and are highly prized by gourmets.

Squid must be skinned (by rubbing off the skin) before cooking. They have a long internal quill, or bone (which looks like stiff cellophane), which must be removed, as must the yellowish deposit and the ink sac under the head. This is usually done by the fish dealer, but in some cases the ink sac or the yellowish deposit must be retained for use in the sauce. After cleaning, squid must be thoroughly washed and dried.

922. SQUID WITH ANCHOVIES
Calamari alla teglia

3 pounds small squid, cleaned and cut into small pieces
$\frac{1}{2}$ cup oil
1 onion, chopped
18 anchovy fillets, washed free of salt [*see* No. 220], and cut in half
2 tablespoons chopped parsley
Salt (if necessary) and freshly ground pepper
Juice of 1 lemon

Heat the oil in a frying pan over medium heat, add the onion, and cook until limp but not brown. Add the squid pieces, reduce heat slightly, cook for 1 minute, season with pepper, mix in the anchovy pieces, cover the pan, and cook for 30 minutes, or until the squid are tender. About 5 minutes before the squid are done, correct seasoning, and add the parsley and the lemon juice. Turn them onto a hot serving platter. *Serves* 6.

923. SQUID WITH ARTICHOKES
Calamari coi carciofi

3 pounds small squid, cleaned and cut into bite-size pieces
6 artichokes, washed, trimmed, cut into quarters, and the chokes removed [*see* **introduction to** No. 1578]
$\frac{1}{4}$ cup oil
$\frac{1}{4}$ cup water
2 cloves garlic, crushed in the garlic-press
Salt and freshly ground pepper

Toss the artichoke quarters in 2 tablespoons of the oil in a frying pan over medium heat for a few minutes, season them with salt and pepper, add $\frac{1}{4}$ cup of water to the pan, cover tightly, reduce the heat to moderate, and cook for about 30 minutes. Heat the remaining oil in a heavy pot over medium heat, add the garlic, cook until golden, add the squid, and cook for 1 minute, stirring constantly. Add sufficient water barely to cover the squid, season with $\frac{1}{2}$ teaspoon salt and a little freshly ground pepper, bring to a boil, reduce the heat, cover the pot tightly, and cook for about 35 minutes. When both the squid and artichokes are tender, add the artichokes to the pot containing the squid, cook together for 2 minutes, and turn out onto serving platter. *Serves* 6.

Squid

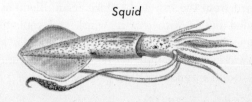

924. BAKED STUFFED SQUID
Calamaretti ripieni al forno

3 pounds small squid, cleaned
1 clove garlic, crushed in the garlic-press
2 tablespoons chopped parsley
1 cup fresh breadcrumbs
½ cup oil
1 teaspoon salt
Freshly ground pepper
½ cup dry white wine

Cut off the heads and the tentacles from the squid and put them through the meat grinder, using a very fine blade. Put the ground squid in bowl and add the garlic, parsley, breadcrumbs, and ¼ cup of the oil; season with salt and pepper and mix thoroughly. Stuff the squid bodies with this mixture and sew the opening with string or secure it with toothpicks. Oil a baking dish that is large enough to accommodate all of the fish, place the squid in it, pour the remaining oil over them, and add the wine. Bake the fish for 45 minutes in a medium (375°) oven. Remove and place them on a hot serving platter. *Serves 6.*

925. SQUID AND BEET GREENS
Calamaretti in zimino

3 pounds small squid, cleaned and cut into strips
2 pounds beet greens, trimmed and washed
½ cup oil
½ cup dry white wine
2 tablespoons tomato paste
2 tablespoons chopped parsley
Juice of 1 lemon
Salt and freshly ground pepper

Cook the beet greens in a covered saucepan over medium heat for 8 minutes in just the water that clings to the leaves after washing. Drain, cool slightly, press out excess water with the hands, and reserve. Heat the oil in a large, heavy saucepan over medium heat, add the squid, season lightly with salt and pepper, and allow the squid to brown slightly. Add the wine and the tomato paste. Reduce heat to the lowest possible flame, cover tightly, and cook for 40 minutes, stirring occasionally. About 10 minutes before the squid is done, add the beet greens and parsley. Remove the squid to a hot serving platter, reduce the sauce slightly over high heat, pour it over the squid, and squeeze the lemon juice over it. *Serves 6.*

The preparation of
Baked Stuffed Squid (No. 924)

926. FRIED SQUID
Calamaretti fritti

2 pounds baby squid, cleaned
Flour
Fat for deep frying
Salt
3 lemons, quartered

Dry the squid and dust them with flour. Place them in a wire frying basket, shake the basket to remove excess flour, and then fry in deep hot (375°) fat until the pieces are golden. This should take about 5 minutes. Drain on absorbent paper for a mixture, sprinkle with salt, and turn the pieces out onto a serving platter. Garnish with the lemon quarters. *Serves 6.*

927. GRILLED SQUID
Calamari gratellati

3 pounds small squid, cleaned, and cut into 2-inch
  pieces
1 cup oil
Salt and freshly ground pepper
3 lemons, quartered

Place the pieces of squid in a bowl, add the oil, and season them generously with salt and pepper. Marinate the pieces for 2 hours, stirring occasionally. Broil the pieces 5 inches below a medium broiler flame for about 15 minutes on each side, basting occasionally with the oil marinade. Remove them to a hot serving platter and garnish with the lemon quarters. *Serves 6.*

311

928. STEWED SQUID
Calamari in umido

3 pounds squid, cleaned and cut into strips
Yellow deposit from the squid
¼ cup oil
½ cup dry white wine
½ cup red wine
5 anchovy fillets, washed free of salt [see No. 220] and chopped
1 clove garlic, crushed in the garlic-press
1 pound tomatoes, peeled, seeded, drained, and chopped
1 cup water
Salt and freshly ground pepper
2 tablespoons chopped parsley

Bring the oil and both wines to a boil in a large, heavy saucepan over high heat; cook until the wine has almost completely evaporated. Add the tomatoes, garlic, and anchovies and cook for 5 minutes. Season lightly with salt and pepper, add the squid and 1 cup of water, reduce the heat to the lowest possible flame, cover the pan, and cook for 1 hour. About 10 minutes before the squid is cooked, add the yellow deposit and stir it in well. When the squid is tender, remove the pieces to a heated serving platter and keep hot. Raise the flame under the sauce in the pan and reduce it for 5 minutes, or until it has slightly thickened. Taste, and add salt and pepper, if necessary. Pour the sauce over the fish and sprinkle the parsley over the top. *Serves* 6.

STURGEON

Storione

Sturgeon are large, migratory fish that live alternately in fresh and salt water. They are highly prized for their roe, or caviar, and for their strongly flavored flesh, which is very firm and rather dry. Sturgeon is usually marketed in transverse slices, although occasionally small, whole sturgeon may be found.

929. STURGEON BORGHESE
Storione alla borghese

1 3-pound piece of sturgeon
½ cup butter, softened
1 onion, chopped
1 carrot, chopped

1 stalk celery, finely sliced
1 tablespoon chopped parsley
1 cup dry white wine
1 cup Fish Fumet [No. 2]
1½ tablespoons Kneaded Butter [No. 107]
½ cup heavy cream
Salt and freshly ground pepper

Grease an earthenware pot with ½ the butter, spread the vegetables and parsley in the bottom, place the fish on top, spread the remaining butter over the fish, add wine and Fumet, season lightly with salt and pepper, and bake in a moderate (350°) oven for about 40 minutes, basting frequently with the liquid in the pot. Transfer the fish to a hot serving platter, remove any skin, and keep warm. Strain the cooking liquid through a sieve into a saucepan and reduce over high heat to 1½ cups. Blend in the kneaded butter with a whisk, cook for 5 minutes, add the cream, reduce the heat, simmer 5 minutes longer, and correct the seasoning. Just before serving, slice the fish on the platter and pass the sauce separately. *Serves* 6.

930. STURGEON FRENCH STYLE
Storione alla francese

6 ⅓-pound slices of sturgeon
6 tablespoons butter, softened
1½ cups dry white wine
1 pound clams, washed and scrubbed
1 pound mussels, scrubbed and "beards" removed
1 pound shrimp, shelled and de-veined
2 tablespoons Kneaded Butter [No. 107]
1 truffle, sliced [or No. 1819a]
Salt and freshly ground pepper

Grease an earthenware (or enamel) pan with ½ of the butter, arrange the sturgeon slices in it, season very lightly with salt and pepper, spread the slices with the remaining butter, add 1 cup of the wine, cover tightly, and place in a moderate (350°) oven for 15 to 18 minutes, basting frequently with the cooking liquid. While the sturgeon is cooking, quickly steam the clams and the mussels, separately, in 2 covered saucepans over high heat with ¼ cup of wine in each; as soon as their shells open, pour them into a colander placed over a bowl; and remove them from their shells, allowing any liquid to drain into the bowl. Place the shellfish in another bowl, cover, and keep warm. Strain the liquid through several thicknesses of cheesecloth into a saucepan, add the shrimp, bring to a boil over high heat, reduce the heat, and simmer for 5 to 6 minutes. Remove the shrimp with a slotted spoon to the bowl with the shellfish. When the sturgeon is cooked, transfer the slices to a hot serving platter and keep warm. Add the cooking liquid to the shellfish liquid and reduce over high heat to 1½ cups. Blend in the kneaded butter with a whisk, correct the seasoning, and cook for 5 minutes longer. Pour the sauce over the sturgeon, surround with a border of the shellfish, and garnish the sauced fish with the slices of truffle. *Serves* 6.

TROUT
Trota

BROOK AND LAKE TROUT
Trotella di riviera

Brook or lake trout are as popular in Italy as in the United States. There are a great many varieties of this small fresh-water fish, and the coloring of even the same types may vary depending on the waters they inhabit. The average market size of brook trout is from ½ to 2 pounds, and they are nearly always cooked whole.

931. TROUT AU BLEU
Trotelle al blu

6 ¾-pound live brook trout
1 cup white wine vinegar
6 sprigs parsley
3 lemons, quartered
1 cup butter, melted
Salt

Strike the heads of the trout on a hard surface to kill them and then very quickly clean them (*see* page 258).

Dip them for a moment in vinegar and then drop them into a large pot of lightly salted boiling water. As soon as the water returns to a boil, reduce the heat and simmer for about 6 minutes. Place a fresh napkin on a hot serving platter, arrange the trout on top, and season lightly with salt. Garnish with the lemons and parsley and serve the melted butter on the side. *Serves* 6.

NOTE: This may *only* be accomplished with live trout.

932. COLD TROUT AU BLEU
Trotelle al blu fredde

Cook the trout in the manner described in the preceding recipe and allow them to cool in the cooking liquid. Garnish and serve them in the same manner and serve Sauce Ravigote [No. 96] in place of the melted butter. *Serves* 6.

933. TROUT IN CREAM
Trotelle alla crema

6 ¾-pound brook trout, cleaned
Flour
½ cup butter
½ cup heavy cream
Juice of 1 lemon
Salt

Season the trout with salt and dust them with flour. Heat the butter in a frying pan over high heat until golden and sauté the trout for about 4 minutes on each side, adjusting the heat so that the butter does not burn. Transfer the trout to a hot serving platter and keep warm. Add the cream and a little salt to the butter in the pan and simmer for 2 minutes. Add the lemon juice and pour over the fish. *Serves* 6.

934. TROUT ITALIANA
Trotelle all'italiana

6 ¾-pound brook trout, cleaned
6 tablespoons butter, softened
3 fennel hearts, sliced, parboiled for 15 minutes in
    1 cup water, and well drained (reserving the water)
1 cup dry white wine
Pinch paprika
Salt and freshly ground pepper

Butter a large baking dish with 3 tablespoons of the butter, spread the parboiled fennel in the bottom, arrange the fish on top, season lightly with salt and pepper, add the wine, cover the dish tightly, and place it in a moderate (350°) oven for 10 to 12 minutes, basting occasionally with the liquid in the dish. Transfer the fish to a hot serving platter and keep warm. Pour the fish cooking liquid and the fennel into a saucepan, add the fennel liquid, bring to a boil over high heat, and reduce to 1 cup. Correct the seasoning, remove from the heat, swirl in the remaining butter, bit by bit, add the paprika, and pour over the fish. *Serves* 6.

935. TROUT WITH LEMON
Trotelle fritte al limone

6 ³/₄-pound brook trout, cleaned
Milk
Flour, seasoned with salt and freshly ground pepper
¹/₂ cup oil
6 sprigs parsley, fried in deep fat [*see* No. 276]
3 lemons, quartered

Dip the fish in milk and dust with the seasoned flour. Heat the oil in a large frying pan over high heat until smoking hot and sauté the fish about 4 minutes on each side. Transfer them to a hot serving platter and garnish with the fried parsley and lemon quarters. *Serves* 6.

936. GRILLED TROUT MAÎTRE D'HÔTEL
Trotelle alla griglia maître d'hôtel

6 ³/₄-pound brook trout, cleaned
A marinade:
  1 cup oil
  ¹/₃ cup lemon juice
  1 teaspoon salt
  ¹/₄ teaspoon freshly ground pepper
1¹/₂ cups Maître d'Hôtel Butter [No. 111]

Marinate the trout in the marinade for 2 hours, turning the fish occasionally. Broil the fish under a hot broiler flame for about 4 minutes on each side, basting frequently with the marinade. Transfer them to a hot serving platter and serve the Maître d'Hôtel butter on the side. *Serves* 6.

937. TROUT MEUNIÈRE WITH SHRIMP AND MUSHROOMS
Trotelle alla mugnaia con code di gamberetti e funghi

6 ³/₄-pound brook trout, cleaned
Flour
³/₄ cup butter
¹/₄ pound mushrooms, sliced
1 pound shrimp, boiled for 8 minutes in salted water, shelled, and de-veined

2 tablespoons chopped parsley
Salt and freshly ground pepper

Season the trout lightly with salt and pepper and dust them with flour. Melt ¹/₂ cup of the butter in a large frying pan over high heat until it is golden and sauté the trout for about 4 minutes on each side. Transfer to a hot serving platter and keep warm. Sauté the mushrooms in the butter in the pan for about 6 minutes over moderate heat, add the remaining butter, raise the heat, cook until the butter is a light brown, and pour over the fish. Garnish the platter with the shrimp and sprinkle with the chopped parsley. *Serves* 6.

938. TROUT WITH TARTAR SAUCE
Trotelle lessate con salsa tartara

6 ³/₄-pound brook trout, cleaned
2 quarts Court Bouillon [No. 763]
3 lemons, quartered
6 sprigs parsley
1¹/₂ cups Tartar Sauce [No. 98]

Place the fish on a rack in a fish boiler, add the Court Bouillon, cover the pan tightly, bring to a boil over high heat, reduce the heat, and simmer for 3 minutes. Transfer the fish to a hot serving platter which has been covered with a fresh napkin, garnish with the parsley and lemon quarters, and serve the tartar sauce on the side. *Serves* 6.

939. TROUT IN RED WINE
Trotelle al vino rosso

6 ³/₄-pound brook trout, cleaned
6 tablespoons butter
2 carrots, sliced
1 onion, sliced
Bouquet Garni:
  2 sprigs thyme (or ¹/₄ teaspoon dried)
  1 bay leaf
  2 sprigs parsley
2 cups dry red wine
1 tablespoon Meat Essence [No. 10]
1¹/₂ tablespoons Kneaded Butter [No. 107]
Salt and freshly ground pepper

Melt 3 tablespoons of the butter in a frying pan over moderate heat, add the sliced carrots and onion, and cook for about 10 minutes, or until they are soft but not brown. Spread the cooked vegetables in the bottom of a large baking dish, place the trout on top, season lightly with salt and pepper, add the Bouquet Garni and the wine blended with the meat essence, cover the dish, place in a moderate (350°) oven for about 15 minutes, basting occasionally with the liquid in the dish. Transfer the fish to a hot serving platter and keep warm. Strain the cooking liquid into a saucepan and reduce over high heat to 1½ cups. Blend in the kneaded butter with a wire whisk, cook for 5 minutes, correct the seasoning, remove from the heat, swirl in the remaining butter, and pour over the fish. *Serves* 6.

SALMON TROUT

Trota salmonata

Salmon trout is often known as rainbow trout in various parts of the United States. It is a beautifully colored fish that can grow to a very large size, although it is usually caught in sizes from 2 to 8 pounds. The texture (and color) of its flesh is similar to salmon, but less oily, and it often has many of the same preparations as salmon, except that it is usually served whole. Salmon trout sometimes take to the sea and are then known as steelheads.

940. SALMON TROUT BELLA VISTA
Trota salmonata in bella vista

1 4-pound salmon trout, cleaned
2 quarts Court Bouillon [No. 763]
6 small tomatoes
3 hard-boiled eggs
18 tiny shrimp, cooked in boiling water for 5 minutes, shelled, and de-veined
1 quart Fish Aspic [No. 119]
 or Substitute Fish Aspic [No. 119a]

2 cups Russian Salad [No. 1879]
1 gherkin, sliced
6 sprigs parsley
2 cups Mayonnaise [No. 77]

Place the fish on the rack in a fish boiler, cover with the Court Bouillon, bring to a boil over high heat, reduce the heat, and simmer for about 20 minutes (the exact time will depend on the thickness of the fish). Remove from the heat, add a little cold water to the cooking liquid, and allow the fish to cool in the liquid. Carefully transfer the fish to a serving platter, remove a wide diagonal strip of the skin from the center of the fish, and chill fish thoroughly in the refrigerator. Slice off the top ⅓ of the tomatoes, squeeze them slightly to remove seeds and juice, and scoop out most of the pulp. Chill the tomatoes, eggs, shrimp, and Russian salad in the refrigerator. When all ingredients are very cold, arrange the shrimp decoratively on the exposed flesh of the fish where the skin has been removed. Place a bowl with the liquid aspic in another bowl filled with ice and stir until it becomes thick and syrupy. Spoon a generous cup over the fish until the entire surface is well glazed. If the aspic becomes too thick during this process, place it over a bowl of warm water and stir until it returns to the proper consistency. Fill the tomatoes with the Russian salad and arrange these alternately with halves of the hard-boiled eggs around the fish. Place a slice of pickle on each egg half and glaze the surface of the eggs and stuffed tomatoes with more aspic. Return the fish to the refrigerator to chill thoroughly. Pour the remaining aspic into a shallow dish, chill until firm in the refrigerator, turn this sheet of aspic out onto a board, cut it into large triangles, and decorate the edge of the platter with these. Stuff the fish's mouth with parsley just before serving and serve the mayonnaise on the side. *Serves* 6.

Salmon Trout Bella Vista (No. 940)

315

941. SALMON TROUT GOURMET
Trota salmonata farcita del "gourmet"

1 4-pound salmon trout, cleaned
2 cups Simple Fish Stuffing [No. 135]
6 tablespoons butter, softened
1 cup Fish Fumet [No. 2]
1 cup dry white wine
6 artichoke hearts, boiled, drained, and then cooked
    in butter [*see* **introduction to No. 1578**]
1 cup Sauce Béarnaise [No. 67]
Salt and freshly ground pepper

Remove the bone of the fish without separating the halves, as described in No. 862. Season the cavity lightly with salt and pepper, place the 2 cups of stuffing in it, and sew the opening with string. Spread a baking dish with 2 tablespoons of the butter, place the fish in it, spread another 2 tablespoons of the butter on the fish, season lightly with salt and pepper, add the wine and Fumet, cover the dish with a lid or aluminum foil, and place in a moderate (350°) oven for about 35 minutes, basting frequently with the liquid in the dish. Carefully transfer the fish to a hot serving platter, remove the string, and keep warm. Strain the cooking liquid into a saucepan and reduce over high heat to $\frac{1}{2}$ its quantity. Remove from the heat and swirl in the remaining butter, bit by bit. Pour the sauce into a sauceboat and garnish the fish with the artichoke hearts, each coated generously with the Béarnaise. *Serves* 6.

942. SALMON TROUT WITH HOLLANDAISE SAUCE
Trota salmonata lessata con salsa olandese

1 4-pound salmon trout, cleaned
2 quarts Court Bouillon [No. 763]
1 tablespoon butter, melted
6 sprigs parsley
3 lemons, quartered
2 cups Sauce Hollandaise [No. 72]

Place the fish on a rack in a fish boiler, cover with the Court Bouillon, bring to a boil over high heat, cover the pan tightly, reduce the heat, and simmer for 10 minutes. Turn the heat off under the pan and leave the fish in the hot cooking liquid for another 15 minutes. Carefully transfer the fish to a hot serving platter, brush it with the butter, garnish with the lemons and parsley, and serve the Hollandaise on the side. *Serves* 6.

943. SALMON TROUT NORWEGIAN
Trota salmonata alla "moda di Norvegia"

1 4-pound salmon trout, cleaned
2 quarts Court Bouillon [No. 763]
1 quart Fish Aspic [No. 119] or Substitute Fish
    Aspic [No. 119a]
Garnish for the surface of the fish:
    12 chervil leaves, parboiled
    12 tarragon leaves, parboiled
    1 hard-boiled egg, chopped
    Optional: 2 truffles, sliced and cut into fancy shapes
    18 tiny shrimp, cooked in boiling water for
        5 minutes, shelled, and de-veined
6 small tomatoes
1½ cups Anchovy Butter [No. 108]
3 hard-boiled eggs
1 gherkin, sliced
6 sprigs parsley
2 cups Mayonnaise [No. 77]

Cook and garnish the trout in the same manner as Salmon Trout Bella Vista [No. 940], except that the whole top surface of the fish from the head to the tail is skinned after it has cooled in the Court Bouillon. The garnish for the surface of the fish is somewhat different, as listed above, and the tomatoes are stuffed with anchovy butter, instead of Russian salad. The small bits of truffle left after cutting the slices into fancy shapes may be chopped and sprinkled over the stuffed tomatoes. *Serves* 6.

944. SALMON TROUT IN RED WINE
Trota salmonata al vino rosso

1 4-pound salmon trout, cleaned
3 sweet red and yellow peppers, roasted, scraped,
    seeded, and cut into strips [*see* No. 145]
1 tablespoon oil
6 tablespoons butter, softened
1 onion, chopped
1 carrot, chopped
1 stalk celery, chopped
Bouquet Garni:
    2 sprigs thyme (or ¼ teaspoon dried)
    1 bay leaf
    3 sprigs parsley
1 tablespoon Meat Essence [No. 10]
2 cups red wine
2 tablespoons Kneaded Butter [No. 107]
2 cooked carrots, cut in julienne strips
Salt and freshly ground pepper

Sauté the pepper strips gently in the oil for 5 minutes and reserve. Butter a large baking dish with 2 tablespoons of the butter, spread the chopped vegetables in the bottom, arrange the fish on top, season lightly with salt and pepper, and add the Bouquet Garni. Blend the meat essence with the wine, pour it into the dish, cover tightly, and place the dish in a moderate (350°) oven for about 35 minutes, basting frequently with the liquid in the dish. Carefully transfer the fish to a hot serving platter and keep warm. Strain the cooking liquid into a saucepan, reduce it over high heat to about 1½ cups, blend in the kneaded butter with a whisk, cook for 5 minutes longer, and correct the seasoning. Remove from the heat, swirl in the remaining butter, and pour over the fish. Garnish the surface of the fish with the carrots and pepper strips cut into any desired fancy shapes. *Serves* 6.

945. SALMON TROUT IN SOUR CREAM
Trota salmonata con crema acida

1 4-pound salmon trout, cleaned
½ cup butter, softened
1 onion, finely chopped
1 teaspoon chopped thyme (or ¼ teaspoon dried)
1 bay leaf, crumbled
½ cup dry white wine
1½ cups heavy cream, blended with the juice of 1 lemon, and allowed to stand at room temperature for 2 hours
Salt and freshly ground pepper

Season the cavity of the fish with salt and pepper. Spread a large baking dish with 3 tablespoons of the butter, sprinkle the chopped onion in the bottom, place the fish on top, and dot with 2 more tablespoons of butter. Place the dish in a moderate (350°) oven for about 35 minutes, basting frequently with the juices in the pan. Transfer the fish to a hot serving platter and keep warm. Add the thyme, bay leaf, and wine to the juices in the pan, bring to a boil over high heat, cook until the wine has nearly evaporated, add the cream, reduce the heat, and simmer for 10 minutes. Correct the seasoning, remove from the heat, swirl in the remaining butter, and pour over fish. *Serves* 6.

TUNA
Tonno

Tuna is a salt-water fish that can grow to an enormous size, well over 1000 pounds, although the size normally marketed is considerably smaller. Like sturgeon and other large fish, it is usually sold in transverse slices or steaks. Its flesh is firm and oily and lends itself easily to a number of different preparations. Fresh tuna is very popular in Italy and canned tuna in oil is very often part of a good antipasto.

946. BAKED TUNA
Tonno al forno

1 4-pound center slice of tuna
12 strips salt pork, cut ¼ inch square and 4 inches long, and parboiled for 15 minutes
A marinade:
  ½ cup oil
  2 tablespoons vinegar
  1 tablespoon chopped onion
  1 tablespoon chopped parsley
  1 teaspoon salt
  ¼ teaspoon freshly ground white pepper
1 cup butter, melted
3 lemons, quartered
Salt and freshly ground pepper

Lard the tuna with the strips of salt pork, using a larding needle. Marinate it in the marinade for 2 hours, turning it occasionally. Place the tuna in a baking dish, pour the marinade over it, and put it in a moderate (350°) oven for about 45 minutes, basting frequently with the juices in the dish. Transfer the fish to a hot serving platter, garnish with the lemon quarters, and serve the melted butter on the side. *Serves* 6.

Salmon Trout in Red Wine (No. 944): see page 316

947. TUNA BOLOGNESE
Tonno sott'olio alla bolognese

3 ½-pound pieces of tuna, canned in oil
3 tablespoons butter
A chopped mixture:
    1 onion
    1 clove garlic
    1 celery stalk
    2 sprigs parsley
    1 small carrot
½ cup dry white wine
¼ cup water
2 tablespoons butter, melted
Salt and freshly ground pepper

Melt the 3 tablespoons of butter in a frying pan over medium heat and, when it is golden, brown the pieces of tuna rather slowly on both sides. Transfer the pieces to a hot baking dish and keep warm. Add the chopped mixture to the butter in the pan and cook over medium heat until soft. Season lightly with salt and pepper, add the wine, and cook until ⁴/₅ has evaporated. Add ¼ cup of water and cook for 2 minutes longer. Slice the pieces of fish in the baking dish, spoon the chopped vegetables and their juices over the slices, sprinkle with the melted butter, and place in a hot (400°) oven for 3 minutes. Serve in the baking dish. *Serves* 6.

NOTE: Large pieces of canned tuna are available in certain Italian specialty shops. Fresh tuna may be used, cooking the pieces for 12 minutes in the butter, but the taste of the dish will not be the same.

948. BRAISED TUNA WITH SPINACH
Tonno brasato con spinaci

3 1-pound tuna steaks
½ cup butter, softened
1 carrot, chopped
1 onion, chopped
2 cups dry white wine
2 cups Fish Fumet [No. 2]
Bouquet Garni:
    2 sprigs thyme (or ¼ teaspoon dried)
    1 bay leaf
    3 sprigs parsley
2 pounds spinach, thoroughly washed
Salt and freshly ground white pepper

Grease a large baking dish or casserole with 1 tablespoon of the butter, spread the chopped onion and carrot in the bottom, place the slices of tuna over the vegetables, season lightly with salt and pepper, cover the dish very tightly, and place it in a moderate (350°) oven to "sweat" for 15 minutes. Heat the wine and Fumet to the boiling point in a saucepan, add them and the Bouquet Garni to the dish, and continue cooking, covered, for another 15 minutes. Cook the spinach in a covered saucepan over medium heat for about 8 minutes in just the water that clings to the leaves after washing. Drain thoroughly, press out excess water with the hands, chop it coarsely, place it in a saucepan with 2 tablespoons of the butter, season lightly with salt and pepper, and cook over a very gentle flame for 10 minutes. When the tuna is cooked, transfer the slices to a hot serving platter and keep warm. Strain the cooking liquid into a saucepan and reduce over high heat to 1 cup, correct the seasoning, remove from the heat, and swirl in the remaining butter, bit by bit. Pour over the fish and serve the spinach separately. *Serves* 6.

949. TUNA CONTADINA
Tonno alla contadina

3 1-pound tuna steaks
$\frac{1}{2}$ cup oil
1 onion, sliced
2 tablespoons flour
$1\frac{1}{2}$ cups dry white wine
$1\frac{1}{2}$ cups water
Bouquet Garni:
   2 sprigs thyme
   1 bay leaf
   2 sprigs parsley
3 tomatoes, peeled, seeded, drained, and chopped
Pinch sugar
$\frac{1}{4}$ cup white wine vinegar
3 tablespoons chopped pickles
1 tablespoon chopped parsley
Salt and freshly ground white pepper

Brown the tuna slices on both sides in smoking hot oil in a frying pan over high heat and then transfer them to a platter and keep warm. Cook the onion in the same oil until golden, add the flour, and stir for 1 minute. Add the wine, water, tomatoes, Bouquet Garni, sugar, and vinegar. Season with salt and pepper, bring to a boil, add the tuna slices, reduce the heat to a very low flame, and simmer for 20 minutes. About 5 minutes before removing from the heat, add the parsley and the chopped pickles. Transfer the slices to a hot serving platter, remove any skin attached to them, correct the seasoning of the sauce, and pour it over the fish. *Serves* 6.

950. TUNA ITALIANA
Tonno all'italiana

1 4-pound center slice of tuna
A marinade:
   $\frac{1}{2}$ cup oil
   Juice of 1 lemon
   1 tablespoon chopped parsley
   1 teaspoon salt
   $\frac{1}{4}$ teaspoon freshly ground white pepper
$\frac{1}{2}$ cup oil
2 onions, finely sliced
$\frac{1}{2}$ pound mushrooms, chopped
$1\frac{1}{2}$ cups dry white wine
1 cup Fish Fumet [No. 2]
2 tablespoons Kneaded Butter [No. 107]
Salt and freshly ground pepper

Marinate the fish in the marinade for 1 hour, turning it occasionally. Heat the oil until it is smoking hot in a heavy pot over high heat and brown the fish in it very quickly on all sides. Remove the fish temporarily to a dish. Add the onions to the oil in the pan, cook until golden, add the mushrooms, stir for 1 minute, return the fish to the pot, season with salt and pepper, add the wine and Fumet, cover the pot, bring to a boil, reduce the heat, and simmer for about 30 minutes. Transfer the fish to a hot serving platter, skin it, and keep it warm. Strain the cooking liquid into a saucepan and reduce to $1\frac{1}{2}$ cups over high heat. Blend in the kneaded butter with a whisk, cook for 5 minutes, correct the seasoning, and pour over the fish. *Serves* 6.

Tuna with Peas
(No. 952): see page 320

951. TUNA LUIGI VERONELLI
Tonno alla Luigi Veronelli

1 3-pound center slice of tuna
3 cloves garlic, cut in half
4 tablespoons oil
6 tablespoons butter
½ cup Marsala wine
1 pound tomatoes, peeled, seeded, drained, and chopped
1 onion, chopped
4 tablespoons heavy cream
Salt and freshly ground pepper

Skin the piece of tuna, make small incisions in it with a very sharp knife, and insert the pieces of garlic. Heat the oil until it is smoking in a frying pan over high heat and brown the tuna very quickly on all sides. Butter a casserole with 3 tablespoons of the butter, place the tuna in it, season lightly with salt and pepper, and add the Marsala, tomatoes, and onion. Dot with the remaining butter, cover the casserole tightly, and place in a moderate (350°) oven for 45 minutes. Transfer the fish to a hot serving platter and keep warm. Bring the cooking liquid to a boil over high heat, add the cream, cook for 2 minutes, correct the seasoning, and pour over the fish. *Serves* 6.

952. TUNA WITH PEAS
Tonno sott'olio con piselli

6 ½-pound pieces of tuna, canned in oil
    [*see* Note to No. 947]
1 onion, chopped
3 tablespoons oil (drained from the canned tuna)
½ cup Tomato Sauce [No. 19]
1 tablespoon chopped parsley
1 pound shelled peas
Salt and freshly ground pepper

Brown the onion in the oil in a large saucepan over medium heat. Add the tomato sauce, parsley, peas, and sufficient water barely to cover the peas. Season with salt and pepper, cover the pan, and cook for 5 minutes. Add the pieces of tuna and cook for 8 minutes longer. Transfer the pieces of tuna to the center of a hot serving platter and pour the peas and sauce around them. *Serves* 6.

953. TUNA WITH TARTAR SAUCE
Tonno alla graticola con salsa tartara

6 ½-pound tuna steaks
A marinade:
    1 cup oil
    ⅓ cup dry white wine
    ½ onion, chopped
    1 tablespoon chopped parsley
    1 teaspoon chopped thyme (or ¼ teaspoon dried)
    1 bay leaf, crumbled
    1 teaspoon salt
    ¼ teaspoon freshly ground white pepper
1 cup fresh breadcrumbs
3 lemons, quartered
1½ cups Tartar Sauce [No. 98]

Marinate the tuna steaks in the marinade for 1 hour, turning them occasionally. Arrange the slices on the rack of the broiler and broil under a hot flame for about 6 minutes on each side, basting occasionally with the marinade. About 1 minute before they are cooked, sprinkle with the breadcrumbs and marinade. Remove steaks when they are golden, transfer to a hot serving platter, garnish with the lemon quarters, and serve the sauce on the side. *Serves* 6.

954. TUNA VERDE
Tonno al verde

6 ½-pound tuna steaks
1 onion, chopped
1 clove garlic, crushed in the garlic-press
½ cup oil
¼ pound spinach, thoroughly washed and coarsely
    chopped
2 tablespoons chopped parsley
½ cup dry white wine
Flour
Juice of 1 lemon
Salt and freshly ground pepper

Lightly brown the onion and garlic in 2 tablespoons of hot oil in a frying pan over medium heat. Add the spinach and parsley, season lightly with salt and pepper, stir for 1 minute, add the wine, and cook until ⅘ has evaporated. Remove from the heat and keep warm. Season the tuna slices with salt and pepper, dust them with flour, and brown them quickly on both sides in the remaining oil in a frying pan over high heat. Transfer them to a baking dish, spoon the vegetables and their liquid over them, and place them in a moderate (350°) oven for 15 minutes. Squeeze the lemon juice over them and serve in the baking dish. *Serves* 6.

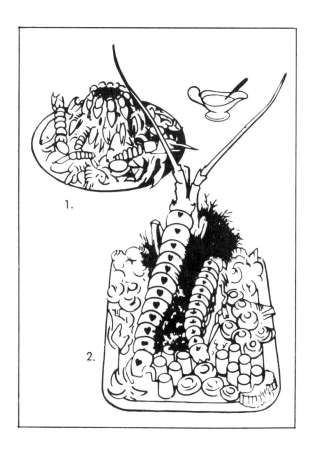

1. A platter of cooked crayfish (*see* Nos. 974 and 975) piled in a mound and surrounded by cooked scampi (*see* Nos. 998–1001). The latter demonstrate the difference between shrimp and true scampi.

2. Lobster Bella Vista (No. 977). In this presentation a rock lobster was used.

TURBOT

Rombo

Turbot has the most distinctively delicate flavor of all salt-water fish. It is, unfortunately, native only to European waters, but it is imported by fish dealers in the larger cities of the United States. Turbot is one of the so-called flat fish and it grows to considerable size, 25 pounds or even larger; thus it is usually sold in fillets or thick slices. Occasionally, small, whole turbot are available and these are especially delicious. Turbot is brownish in color and its flesh is very white, firm, flaky, and moist.

Halibut, while never attaining the distinction in flavor or texture of the best turbot, is the closest substitute native to American waters and it may replace turbot in any of the following recipes, although small, whole halibut are rarely found marketed.

955. CREAMED TURBOT AU GRATIN
Rombo con crema al gratino

3 1-pound turbot (or halibut) slices
2½ cups Duchesse Potatoes [No. 1771]
2 cups Velouté Sauce for Fish [No. 17a]
3 cups Court Bouillon [No. 762]
2 tablespoons butter, softened
1 egg, beaten
4 tablespoons grated Parmesan cheese

The Duchesse potatoes and the Velouté sauce should be prepared in advance. Place the turbot slices on a rack in a fish boiler, add the Court Bouillon, cover, bring to a boil over high heat, reduce the heat, and simmer for 10 minutes. Drain the fish and flake or break it into bite-size pieces, discarding any bones. Butter the bottom of a shallow oven-proof dish, spread ½ cup of the Velouté sauce in the bottom, and arrange the pieces of fish over the sauce. Pipe a thick border of the Duchesse potatoes around the edge, using a large star tip; brush the potatoes with beaten egg; pour the remaining sauce over the fish; and sprinkle all with the grated cheese. Place the dish in a hot (400°) oven for 5 or 6 minutes, or until the top is golden. *Serves* 6.

956. TURBOT GOURMET
Fricassea di rombetto del buongustaio

1 2-pound turbot (or substitute a single slice of the same weight)

24 Braised White Onions [No. 1721]
24 Fried Mussels [No. 1021]
2 ½-pound sole fillets
½ pound mushrooms, sliced
½ cup butter
1 onion, chopped
2½ cups heavy cream
2 egg yolks
Juice of 1 lemon
1½ cups Croûtons [No. 332], cut into heart shapes
Salt and freshly ground white pepper

The braised onions should be prepared in advance and kept warm. Make the preliminary preparation of the mussels so that they may be fried at the last moment before serving (shuck them and dip them in beaten egg and breadcrumbs, as described in No. 1021). Sauté the mushrooms in 3 tablespoons of the butter over low heat in a covered saucepan for 8 minutes; remove from the heat and keep warm. Slice the turbot and sole fillets into 2-inch slices. Melt the remaining butter in a large earthenware (or enamel) pot over moderate heat, add the chopped onion, and cook until transparent. Add the sliced fish, season very lightly with salt and pepper, and cook for 2 minutes, stirring gently. Add 2 cups of the cream, bring to a boil, reduce the heat, and simmer for 10 minutes. Remove the fish slices with a slotted spoon to a hot serving platter and keep warm. Raise the heat under the cooking liquid and reduce to 1½ cups. While it is reducing, quickly fry the mussels as described in No. 1021 and arrange them and the braised onions around the fish slices. Remove the cream from the heat, slowly pour in the egg yolks which have been beaten with the remaining ½ cup of cream, stir vigorously with a whisk until well blended, return to low heat, and cook until slightly thickened, stirring constantly; do not boil. Add the cooking liquid from the mushrooms and the onions and add any liquid which has drained from the fish. Add the lemon juice, correct the seasoning, spoon the mushrooms over the fish, pour the sauce over, and garnish with the croûtons. *Serves* 6.

957. TURBOT HOLLANDAISE
Rombo lessato con salsa olandese

1 3-pound turbot (or substitute 3 1-pound slices of halibut)
3 cups Court Bouillon [No. 762]
3 lemons, quartered
6 sprigs parsley
3 cups Sauce Hollandaise [No. 72]
Salt and freshly ground pepper

Bone the turbot (if a whole fish is available) by making a deep slit down the back the whole length of the fish, cut off the backbone with poultry shears close to the head and near the tail, separate the bone from the flesh with a very sharp knife, and remove the bone, taking as little of the flesh as possible. Season the cavity lightly with salt and pepper. Place the fish on a rack in a fish boiler, cover with the Court Bouillon (adding a little water, if necessary), cover, bring to a boil over high heat, reduce the heat, and simmer for 25 minutes. Drain the fish and transfer it to a hot serving platter. Garnish with the parsley and the lemon quarters and serve the Hollandaise sauce on the side. (If only slices of larger turbot—or halibut—are available, mask the slices on the serving platter with a little of the Hollandaise.) *Serves* 6.

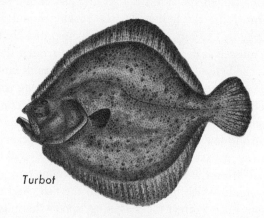

Turbot

958. STUFFED TURBOT ITALIANA
Rombetto farcito all'italiana

1 3-pound turbot, cleaned
1½ cups Simple Fish Stuffing [No. 135]
4 tablespoons butter, softened
1 cup dry white wine
1 cup Fish Fumet [No. 2]
2 cups American Sauce [No. 63]
2 teaspoons chopped tarragon
Salt and freshly ground pepper

Remove the backbone of the fish without separating

the 2 halves, as described in the preceding recipe. Season the cavity lightly with salt and pepper and stuff it. Sew up the opening with string, spread the softened butter over the fish, and place it in a baking dish. Add the wine and Fumet and place the dish in a moderate (350°) oven for about 30 minutes, basting often with the liquid in the pan. Transfer the fish to a hot serving platter and keep warm. Reduce the cooking liquid to ½ cup in a saucepan over high heat, add any liquid which drains from the fish, reduce again, and mix with the American sauce. Cook only long enough to heat thoroughly, correct the seasoning, pour over the fish, and sprinkle with the chopped tarragon. *Serves* 6.

959. TURBOT MAÎTRE D'HÔTEL
Rombo "maître d'hôtel"

3 1-pound slices turbot
A marinade of:
    ⅓ cup lemon juice
    ⅔ cup oil
    1 teaspoon salt
    ¼ teaspoon freshly ground white pepper
2 tablespoons butter, softened
8 tablespoons butter, melted
1 cup fresh breadcrumbs
2 tablespoons chopped parsley
1½ cups Maître d'Hôtel Butter [No. 111]

Marinate the turbot slices for 2 hours in the marinade. Butter a large baking dish with the softened butter, drain the fish slices thoroughly, arrange them in the baking dish, sprinkle them with 4 tablespoons of the melted butter and the breadcrumbs, and place them in a hot (375°) oven for 18 minutes, basting occasionally with the remaining melted butter. Remove from the oven, transfer to a hot serving platter, sprinkle with the chopped parsley, and serve the Maître d'Hôtel butter on the side. *Serves* 6.

WHITEBAIT
Bianchetti

Whitebait are tiny fish, less than an inch long, and are especially delicious when very fresh. They may be boiled or fried and are served either hot or cold. Italians frequently serve whitebait as an accompaniment to omelets or frittatas.

960. FRIED WHITEBAIT
Frittura di bianchetti

2 pounds whitebait
Flour
Fat for deep frying
Salt
6 sprigs parsley, fried in deep fat [see No. 276]

Dust the whitebait lightly with flour, place them in a frying basket, shake the basket to remove excess flour, and fry in deep, hot (375°) fat for about 1 minute, or until they are golden and crisp. Drain them on absorbent paper, season lightly with salt, heap them up on a serving dish, and garnish with the fried parsley. *Serves* 6.

961. WHITEBAIT SALAD
Insalata di bianchetti

2 pounds whitebait
1 teaspoon salt
1 cup Sauce Vinaigrette [No. 99]
2 tablespoons chopped parsley

Place the whitebait in a saucepan, cover with cold water, add the salt, bring to a boil over high heat, reduce heat, and cook for 2 minutes. Drain them, allow them to cool, dry them on a towel, place them on a serving dish, pour the Vinaigrette sauce over them, sprinkle the parsley over the top, and mix very lightly. *Serves* 6.

WHITING
Nasello o merlano

Whiting are salt-water fish, related to the cod. They are native to the North Atlantic and a great deal of whiting is caught off the coasts of New England, Long Island, and New Jersey. Usually, the sizes found in American fish markets are from 1 to 4 pounds. Their backs are gray-green running to silver on their undersides. The flesh of whiting is very white and has a delicate flavor. They are scaled and cleaned as described in the introduction (page 258).

Whiting Fines Herbes (No. 967): see page 324

962. WHITING WITH ANDALUSIAN SAUCE
Nasello fritto con salsa andalusa

6 small whiting (less than 1 pound each), cleaned
Flour
1 cup oil, or more as needed
3 lemons, quartered
Parsley sprigs
1½ cups Andalusian Sauce [No. 47]
Salt

Secure the tail of each fish in its mouth with a skewer. Dust each fish with flour and fry in hot oil in a frying pan over high heat for 8 to 10 minutes; the oil should come halfway up the sides of the fish, so that they cook evenly when turned over. Drain them when they are crisp and golden, arrange them on a hot serving platter, and garnish with the lemon quarters and the parsley. The parsley may be fried in deep fat, if desired [see No. 276]. Serve the sauce on the side. *Serves* 6.

963. BOILED WHITING WITH MELTED BUTTER
Nasello lessato con burro fuso

1 4-pound whiting, cleaned
1 tablespoon vinegar
2 pounds small "new" potatoes
Parsley sprigs
1 cup butter, melted
Salt

Place the fish on a rack in a fish boiler, cover with cold water, add the vinegar and a little salt, bring to a boil over high heat, reduce the heat, and simmer for 25 to 30 minutes. Boil the potatoes at the same time in lightly salted water until just tender, about 20 minutes. Transfer the fish to a serving platter, surround with the boiled potatoes, and garnish with the parsley. Serve the butter on the side. *Serves* 6.

964. WHITING CECILIA
Filetti di nasello Cecilia

3 2-pound whiting, filleted
1 pound asparagus, cleaned, peeled, and cooked until
    tender [see introduction to No. 1597]
1 egg, beaten
Flour, liberally seasoned with salt and freshly ground
    pepper
1/2 cup butter
1 tablespoon chopped parsley
2 lemons, quartered

Time the cooking of the asparagus so that it is done just as the fish is done. Cut each fillet in half, dip them in beaten egg, and dredge them with the seasoned flour. Melt the butter in a large frying pan over medium high heat until golden, add the pieces of fish, and cook for 3 minutes on each side, or until golden. Arrange the fish on a hot serving platter, sprinkle the parsley over it, and garnish with the cooked asparagus and the lemon quarters. *Serves 6.*

965. WHITING COLBERT
Nasello Colbert

6 small whiting (less than 1 pound each), cleaned
1 cup milk
Flour, liberally seasoned with salt and freshly ground
    pepper
2 eggs, beaten
Fresh breadcrumbs
1/2 cup oil
1/2 cup Maître d'Hôtel Butter [No. 111]
2 lemons, scalloped and sliced

Slit the fish down the back with a very sharp knife and remove the backbones, breaking them off at the head and close to the tail. Dip the fish in milk, dust with the seasoned flour, dip in the beaten egg, and dredge in the breadcrumbs. Heat the oil in a large frying pan over high heat until smoking and brown the fish for 3 to 4 minutes on each side. Arrange the fish on a hot serving platter, put a generous tablespoon of the Maître d'Hôtel butter inside each, and garnish with the lemon slices. *Serves 6.*

966. WHITING DIPLOMATICA
Nasello alla diplomatica

6 small whiting (less than 1 pound each), cleaned
A stuffing composed of:
    1/4 pound mushrooms, coarsely chopped
    2 shallots, chopped
    1 tablespoon chopped parsley
    1 tablespoon chopped tarragon (or 1 teaspoon dried)
    2 tomatoes, peeled, seeded, drained, and chopped
    1/2 teaspoon salt
    1 cup Sauce Mornay [No. 56], chilled
2 quarts Fish Fumet [No. 2] or substitute Court
    Bouillon [No. 763]
2 cups hot Sauce Mornay [No. 56]
3 tablespoons butter, melted
1/4 cup grated Parmesan cheese

Slit the fish down the back with a very sharp knife and remove the backbones, breaking them off at the head and close to the tail. Stuff each fish with about 1/2 cup of the stuffing and sew up the openings (or secure with skewers). Place the fish on a rack in a fish boiler and cover with the Fumet. Bring to a boil over high heat, reduce the heat, and simmer for 10 to 12 minutes. Drain them and transfer to an oven-proof serving platter; allow them to sit for 2 minutes; and remove any liquid they release with a bulb baster. Cover each fish with hot Mornay sauce, sprinkle with the grated cheese and the melted butter, and place them in the broiler under a high flame for 1 minute, or until lightly browned. *Serves 6.*

967. WHITING FINES HERBES
Nasello con erbe fini

6 small whiting (less than 1 pound each), cleaned
1/2 cup butter, softened
1 1/2 cups dry white wine
2 1/2 tablespoons flour
2 1/2 cups hot Fish Fumet [No. 2]
1 tablespoon chopped parsley
2 teaspoons chopped chervil
2 teaspoon chopped tarragon
2 egg yolks
1/2 cup heavy cream
Salt and freshly ground pepper

The preparation of Whiting Diplomatica (No. 966). Here, the stuffing is placed into a pastry bag and piped into the fish.

Season the cavities of the fish with salt and pepper, butter them very lightly with 3 tablespoons of the butter, place them on a rack in a fish boiler, pour in the wine, cover tightly, bring to a boil over high heat, and place the boiler in a moderate (350°) oven for 10 minutes. Transfer the cooked fish to an oven-proof serving platter and keep barely warm. While the fish are cooking, melt the remaining butter in a heavy saucepan over medium heat, add the flour, stir for 1 minute, add the boiling Fumet, and bring to a boil, stirring constantly. Reduce heat to the simmering point and cook for 10 minutes. Put the wine in which the fish cooked in another saucepan over high heat and reduce to about 4 tablespoons; add it to the other sauce along with the 3 herbs. Beat the egg yolks with the cream and, off the heat, slowly pour it into the sauce, stirring constantly. Return it to a very low flame and cook for about 3 minutes, stirring constantly, until slightly thickened. Correct the seasoning. Remove any liquid that the fish have released with a bulb baster and pour the sauce over them. Place the platter in a moderate (350°) oven just long enough to heat thoroughly. *Serves* 6.

968. WHITING AND MUSHROOMS AU GRATIN
Nasello farcito e gratinato

3 2-pound whiting, filleted
A stuffing composed of:
   1 1/2 cups Simple Fish Stuffing [No. 135]
   1/4 cup Duxelles [No. 138]
   2 tablespoons chopped parsley
4 tablespoons butter, softened
1/2 pound mushrooms, sliced
1 1/2 cups Duxelles Sauce [No. 31]
3/4 cup fresh breadcrumbs
4 tablespoons butter, melted
Juice of 1 lemon
Salt and freshly ground pepper

Season the 6 fillets lightly with salt and pepper and spread each with a generous 1/4 cup of the stuffing. Roll each fillet up and place in a baking dish that has been spread with the softened butter. Arrange the sliced mushrooms in a circle around the dish and season lightly with salt and pepper. Spread the Duxelles sauce over the fillets and sprinkle with the breadcrumbs and the melted butter. Place the dish in a medium (375°) oven for 20 minutes. Remove and squeeze the lemon juice over all. *Serves* 6.

MISCELLANEOUS FISH DISHES
Preparazioni diverse

969. FISHERMAN'S FISH FRY
Frittura di pesci misti del pescatore

This is one variation of the famous Italian Fritto Misto. *This recipe is for small whole fish, but any combination of fillets or small pieces of larger fish, as well as shellfish, may be used.*

A combination of very small fish weighing from 1/2 to
   3/4 pound, such as: fresh-water bass, butterfish,
   brook trout, fluke, mullet, perch, or pike
Flour
Oil as needed
Optional: 2 cloves of garlic, finely chopped (*see* Note
   below)
Lemon quarters
Chopped parsley
Salt and freshly ground pepper

Allow 2 to 3 fish for each person to be served. Clean the fish; liberally season the flour with salt and pepper and dredge the fish in this. Heat a generous amount of oil in several frying pans over high heat until smoking hot. Add the fish and cook them quickly for 2 or 3 minutes on each side. Heap them up on a very large serving platter, garnish with the lemon quarters and chopped parsley, and serve at once.

NOTE: One may omit the flour and merely season the fish with salt and pepper. If this method is followed, add 2 finely chopped cloves of garlic to the frying fish about 1 minute before they are done. Whichever method is followed, a good mixture of frying oil would be half olive oil, half lard.

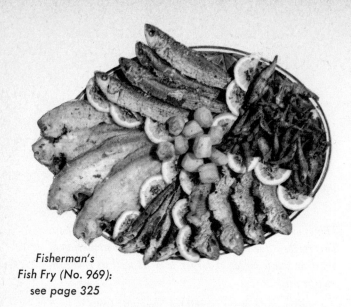

*Fisherman's
Fish Fry (No. 969):
see page 325*

970. FISH SOUFFLÉ CASALINGA
Pesce alla casalinga

1 pound cooked fish, boned, skinned, and flaked
2 cups Mashed Potatoes [No. 1780], well seasoned
    with salt, pepper, and nutmeg
8 tablespoons butter, softened
5 egg yolks
6 egg whites beaten into stiff peaks
¼ cup fresh breadcrumbs
6 slices bread, cut into triangles and sautéed in oil
    until golden

Place the fish flakes and the mashed potatoes in a heavy saucepan and stir constantly over medium heat until very hot, being careful not to scorch the mixture. Remove from the stove and add 4 tablespoons of the butter and the egg yolks, stirring vigorously. Add ¼ of the beaten egg whites and then carefully fold in the remaining whites. Grease a baking dish with 2 tablespoons of the butter, pour in the potato/fish mixture, sprinkle with the breadcrumbs, and dot with the remaining butter. Place in a medium (375°) oven for 30 to 40 minutes, or until well puffed. Remove and garnish with the sautéed triangles of bread. *Serves 6.*

971. CREAMED FISH AU GRATIN
Pesce con crema al gratino

1 pound cooked fish, boned, skinned, and flaked
3 cups Sauce Mornay [No. 56]
2 cups Duchesse Potatoes [No. 1771]
2 egg yolks, beaten
4 tablespoons Gruyère cheese, grated

Heat the Mornay sauce in a heavy saucepan over medium heat until thoroughly hot. Remove from the

326

heat, gently fold in the flaked fish, and pour the mixture into an oval, lightly greased baking dish. Place the Duchesse potatoes in a pastry bag fitted with a large star tip and pipe a border around the edge of the dish. Brush the potatoes with beaten egg yolks and sprinkle the sauced fish with the cheese. Place the dish in a hot (400°) oven for 10 to 15 minutes, or until the potatoes and the fish are lightly browned. *Serves 6.*

CRUSTACEANS
Crostacei

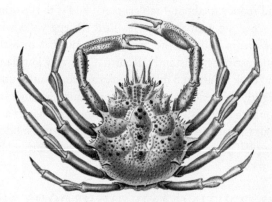

CRAB
Granzevola

In the United States the so-called blue crab is found in great abundance along the Atlantic coast and is particularly plentiful in the Chesapeake Bay area. A slightly different species is found along the Pacific coast, and this type provides much of the commercially available canned crab meat. It is somewhat time consuming to shell and extract the meat from crabs, particularly the eastern-seaboard variety, but their highly distinctive, delicate flavor makes it well worth the effort.

Crabs should be cooked live in boiling water, acidulated with vinegar and seasoned with salt, for about 10 minutes. The claws and legs are broken off and the meat removed from them. The flap that folds under the crab is cut off and a knife is inserted in the opening to force the two shell halves apart; the upper shell is then pulled off and the head and stomach are discarded; the hard covering around the edge should be cut with a knife, and the meat removed with a very fine knife or with a nut pick.

Crabs shed their shells annually and in this soft-shell condition they are delicious sautéed or fried in deep fat.

972. CRAB RICCA
Granzevola alla ricca

1½ pounds fresh crab meat (the meat extracted from approximately 10 cooked crabs, as described in the introduction), chilled
½ cup oil
¼ cup lemon juice
1 teaspoon salt
¼ teaspoon freshly ground pepper
6 crab shells, scrubbed and dried
6 leaves Boston lettuce
3 cups Macedoine of Vegetables [No. 198], substituting Mayonnaise [No. 77] for the Vinaigrette sauce

Mix the oil, lemon juice, salt, and pepper until well blended and pour over the crab flakes in a bowl. Toss lightly and then stuff the crab shells with the mixture. Arrange these on a serving platter garnished with the 6 lettuce leaves topped with a mound of the vegetables mixed with mayonnaise. *Serves 6.*

973. COLD BRANDIED CRABS
Granzevola alla semplice

These are prepared exactly as Crab Ricca [No. 972], adding ¼ cup brandy and a dash of Worcestershire sauce to the crab-meat dressing before stuffing the shells.

CRAYFISH
Gambero d'acqua dolce

Crayfish are a fresh-water crustacean which look very like tiny New England lobster; their average size is about 6 inches in length. Large numbers of crayfish are taken from Lake Michigan and, generally, they are more plentiful in the West and South than on the east coast.

Crayfish are often very simply cooked for about 10 minutes in boiling Court Bouillon [No. 764]. They may be attractively served by folding a napkin in the form of a cone in the center of a serving platter, the crayfish heaped around it, and the platter generously garnished with sprigs of parsley and scalloped lemon halves.

Traditionally, crayfish are always served in their shells; messy perhaps, but delicious.

974. CRAYFISH ALLEGRO
Gamberi allegri

36 live crayfish, their tails split on the underside
4 tablespoons butter
2 carrots, diced
2 onions, diced
1 stalk celery, diced
1 cup dry Marsala wine
1 cup heavy cream
Pinch Cayenne pepper
½ cup Béchamel Sauce [No. 18]
Salt and freshly ground pepper

Sauté the crayfish in the butter in a large frying pan over moderate heat for 3 minutes. Stir in the 3 vegetables, cook for 1 minute, and add the Marsala, cream, and Cayenne. Season with salt and pepper, bring to a boil, reduce the heat, and simmer for 5 minutes. Heap the crayfish on a hot serving platter and keep warm. Add the Béchamel to the sauce, raise the heat, and reduce to 1½ cups. Correct the seasoning. The sauce may be strained at this point, if desired, and then served separately. *Serves 6.*

975. CRAYFISH MONSIEUR LE PRIEUR
Gamberi à la mode de Monsieur Le Prieur

36 live crayfish, their tails split on the underside
1 cup dry white wine
1 cup white wine vinegar
½ cup Brown Stock [No. 4]
¼ cup Cognac
3 ounces pork fat, diced and parboiled 10 minutes
2 small carrots, sliced
4 medium onions, chopped
2 shallots, chopped
2 cloves of garlic, bruised
Bouquet Garni:
   2 sprigs thyme (or ¼ teaspoon dried)
   2 sprigs parsley
   2 sprigs chervil (or ¼ teaspoon dried)
   1 bay leaf
Rind of ½ orange (all white part removed)
½ teaspoon salt
4 peppercorns
3 pinches freshly ground white pepper
2 pinches Cayenne pepper

Simmer all of the ingredients, except the crayfish, in a saucepan over medium heat for 15 minutes. Add the crayfish, cover the pan, bring to a boil, and simmer for 6 minutes. Transfer the crayfish to a hot serving bowl and keep warm. Strain the cooking liquid and ingredients through a fine sieve, pressing through as much of the solids as possible. Return it to the fire just long enough to get thoroughly hot and serve separately. *Serves 6.*

LOBSTER

Astaco o aragosta

Much of the lobster in European waters is of the species known in the United States as rock lobster. In this country, this variety is found chiefly off the Florida reef, though a closely related type is taken in great numbers off the Pacific coast. Rock lobster is mottled with yellow, red, and blue and generally is more brilliantly colored than the blackish-green New England lobsters. Rock lobsters, sometimes called spiny lobsters, do not have large front claws like the New England variety. Both, however, turn bright red when subjected to heat, and the flavor of the flesh of both, while not entirely similar, is equally delicious.

Unless precooked, lobsters should always be bought live and cooked as soon thereafter as possible. It is not recommended they be kept even so long as overnight. Their flesh deteriorates very quickly if they have been dead any length of time before being cooked.

976. LOBSTER AMERICANA
Astaco all'americana

3 2-pound live lobsters
1 cup oil
1 shallot, chopped
1 clove garlic, crushed in the garlic-press
1 cup brandy
1 cup dry white wine
1 cup Fish Fumet [No. 2]
4 plump tomatoes, peeled, seeded, drained, and
     chopped
1 tablespoon Meat Essence [No. 10]
1 tablespoon chopped parsley
1 teaspoon chopped chervil
1 teaspoon chopped tarragon
Pinch Cayenne pepper
6 tablespoons butter, softened
Salt and freshly ground black pepper

Cut off the claws of the lobsters with a sharp knife or with poultry shears. Cut the tail off from the body

of each and slice it into 5 or 6 even slices at the joints. Cut the body of each in half lengthwise, discarding the small sac behind the head and the intestinal tract, but reserving the liver and coral. If you are using New England lobsters, crack the claws in such a way that the meat may be easily extracted from them after they are cooked.

Heat the oil in a very large frying pan over high heat until it is smoking, add the pieces of lobster, stir them in the oil for 5 or 6 minutes, and then drain off most of the oil with a bulb baster. Add the shallot and garlic, cook for 1 minute, add the brandy, allow it to get very hot, and ignite. Shake the pan over medium heat until the flames subside. Turn the contents of the pan into a large earthenware pot and add the wine, Fumet, and tomatoes. Season lightly with salt and pepper, bring to a boil over high heat, reduce the heat, cover the pot, and simmer for 15 minutes. Transfer the lobster pieces to a large, hot serving dish (the shells may be removed, if you wish) and keep warm. Reduce the cooking liquid over high heat to 1½ cups. Mash the coral and liver with a fork and stir them into the sauce. Blend in the meat essence with a wire whisk and add the chervil, tarragon, and Cayenne. Correct the seasoning, remove from the heat, and swirl in the butter, bit by bit. Pour the sauce over the lobster and sprinkle the top with parsley. *Serves 6.*

977. LOBSTER BELLA VISTA
Astaco freddo in "bella vista"

1 5-pound live lobster, or 3 2-pound lobsters
5 quarts Court Bouillon [No. 764]
2 heads Boston lettuce, washed and shredded
3 quarts Fish Aspic [No. 119], or Substitute Fish
     Aspic [No. 119a]
3 truffles, sliced and cut into fancy shapes
6 cooked artichoke hearts, chilled [*see* introduction to
     No. 1578]
3 cups Macedoine of Vegetables [No. 198]
3 cups Mayonnaise [No. 77]
6 hard-boiled eggs
Red vegetable coloring
6 small hearts of Boston lettuce
12 sprigs very fresh tarragon

A very large, whole lobster makes the most attractive and imposing presentation of this dish, although the meat of smaller lobsters is usually more tender. If smaller lobsters are chosen, the preparation is identical, except the cooking time should be reduced to about 25 minutes.

Tie the lobster to a small board, so that it will remain flat during the cooking. Place it and the Court Bouillon in a large pot, cover tightly, bring to a boil over high heat, reduce the heat, and simmer for about 40 minutes. Add a little cold water to the Court Bouillon, allow the lobster to cool in the liquid, and drain. Carefully cut out the underside of the tail shell with a sharp knife or poultry shears and remove the meat in 1 piece. If you are using New England lobster, twist off the large claws. Spread the rounded shell of the body slightly apart and from the underside pull out all of the insides and the small claws in 1 piece; remove all of the meat from the body, discarding the carcass; coarsely chop the meat from the claws and reserve. Slice the meat from the tail into $\frac{1}{2}$-inch slices. Wash out the whole shell and pat the inside dry. Stuff the shell loosely with the shredded lettuce and arrange the slices from the tail slightly overlapping in graduated sizes from the head to the tail. Place a fancily cut slice of truffle on the exposed part of each slice. Place the lobster on a very large serving platter and, if necessary, prop it firmly in place with large cubes of bread. Place the platter in the refrigerator until very cold.

Slice the hard-boiled eggs in half, mash the yolks with 1 cup of the mayonnaise, tint a pale pink with a drop of red vegetable coloring, place the mixture in a pastry bag fitted with a small star tip, and pipe the mixture back into the white halves. Pour $\frac{1}{2}$ cup of the liquid aspic into a small, shallow baking dish, tint it a deep red with the vegetable coloring, place it in the coldest part of the refrigerator for a few minutes to become very firm, turn out onto a board, and cut out 12 small rounds. Place 1 round on top of each stuffed egg, sprinkle each with small bits of chopped truffle (left from cutting them into fancy shapes), and chill them in the refrigerator. Chill 6 cup molds, whose diameter is slightly smaller than the artichoke hearts, in the refrigerator until very cold. Line the bottom and sides of these with a thin layer of aspic which has been stirred over ice until thick and syrupy; this may require 2 or more coatings, chilling the cups between each coating. Fill these almost to the brim with the macedoine of vegetables which has been mixed witht he chopped lobster meat from the claws, fill the cups with liquid aspic, and chill until firmly jellied.

When the lobster is very cold, stir more aspic over ice until it is thick and syrupy, and glaze the exposed pieces of lobster with a thin coating. Return the lobster to the refrigerator. Pour $\frac{1}{2}$ cup of the liquid aspic into a small, shallow dish, chill until firm, turn it out onto a board, and chop it finely. Sprinkle a little of this chopped aspic between each slice of the lobster. Fill 8 or 10 small, fluted crescent molds with liquid aspic and chill until firm. Finally, unmold the cups of vegetables in aspic on top of the artichoke hearts. Garnish the platter with these, the stuffed egg halves, the crescents of aspic, hearts of lettuce, and stuff the sprigs of tarragon around the lobster head. *Serves* 6.

NOTE: In the illustration, a rock lobster was used. This type may be employed in the preparation of the dish with equal success.

978. LOBSTER BORDELAISE
Astaco alla bordolese

3 2-pound live lobsters
6 tablespoons Clarified Butter [No. 102]
$\frac{1}{2}$ cup brandy
1 shallot, chopped
1 clove garlic, crushed in the garlic-press
$\frac{1}{2}$ cup dry white wine
Bouquet Garni:
    2 sprigs thyme (or $\frac{1}{2}$ teaspoon dried)
    2 sprigs parsley
    1 bay leaf
Pinch Cayenne pepper
$2\frac{1}{2}$ cups Fish Fumet [No. 2]
$1\frac{1}{2}$ cups Spanish Sauce [No. 16]
$1\frac{1}{2}$ cups Tomato Sauce [No. 19]
1 tablespoon chopped chervil
1 tablespoon chopped tarragon
2 tablespoons chopped parsley
Juice of 1 lemon
4 tablespoons butter, softened
Salt and freshly ground white pepper

Cut the lobsters into pieces, reserving the liver and coral, as described in Lobster Americana [No. 976]. Sauté the pieces in the clarified butter over fairly high heat in a frying pan for about 5 minutes, or until the shells turn a bright red. Add the brandy, allow it to become very hot, ignite, and shake the pan until the flames subside. Add the shallots, garlic, and wine. Continue cooking over high heat until the liquid is reduced by $\frac{1}{2}$. Add the Bouquet Garni, Cayenne, Fumet, and the Spanish and tomato sauces. Bring to a boil, reduce the heat, cover the pan tightly, and simmer for 15 minutes. Transfer the lobster pieces to a hot serving platter, remove the pieces from their shells, if desired, and keep warm. Pound the liver and coral in a mortar until it is very smooth, blend it into the sauce with a whisk, add the chopped herbs, and reduce

329

over high heat to 2 cups. Discard the Bouquet Garni, add the lemon juice, correct the seasoning, remove from the heat, and swirl in the softened butter bit by bit. Pour the sauce over the lobster and serve at once. *Serves* 6.

979. BROILED LOBSTER FLAMBÉ
Astaco al brandy

3 2-pound live lobsters
½ cup butter, melted
½ cup brandy
Salt and freshly ground white pepper
3 lemons, quartered

Split the lobsters in half lengthwise and discard the sac behind the head and the intestinal tract. Season the exposed meat lightly with salt and pepper and brush it with melted butter. Arrange the lobsters, cut side up, on the rack under a medium broiler flame and broil for about 15 minutes, basting occasionally with more butter. Transfer them to a large oven-proof platter, heat the brandy in a small saucepan until it is very hot, ignite, pour over the lobsters, and shake the platter until the flames subside; the brandy may be heated over a spirit lamp and the lobsters flambéed at the table, if desired. Pass the lemon quarters separately. *Serves* 6.

980. LOBSTER CASA DORATA
Medaglioni di astaco "Casa Dorata"

3 2-pound live lobsters
5 quarts Court Bouillon [No. 764]
½ pound mushrooms, sliced
¾ cup butter
½ cup brandy
3 cups Sauce Nantua [No. 57]
3 truffles, chopped
3 ½-pound sole fillets
1½ cups Sauce Villeroy [No. 59]
Fresh breadcrumbs
6 Potato Baskets [No. 1752], fried in deep fat
6 sprigs parsley
Salt and freshly ground pepper

Tie the lobsters to small boards so that they will remain flat during their cooking. Place them and the Court Bouillon in a large pot, cover, bring to a boil over high heat, reduce the heat, and simmer for 10 minutes. Allow them to cool in the cooking liquid for 10 minutes, drain, split them in half lengthwise, and discard the intestinal tract and the sac behind the head.

Remove the meat from the claws and discard the claw shells; remove the tail meat, leaving the shells of the bodies whole. Slice all of the meat and keep warm. Sauté the mushrooms in 3 tablespoons of the butter in a covered frying pan over moderate heat for 8 minutes and reserve. Melt 3 tablespoons of the butter in a frying pan over fairly high heat, add the pieces of lobster, stir for 1 minute, add the brandy, allow it to become very hot, ignite, and shake the pan until the flames are extinguished. Continue cooking for 3 minutes until the brandy is slightly reduced, then add the Nantua sauce and the mushrooms with their liquid. Reduce the heat and simmer for a few minutes, or until the sauce is slightly thickened. Portion out the sauce and the lobster pieces in the shell halves, sprinkle the tops with the chopped truffles, arrange the halves in a roasting pan, and place the pan in a moderate (350°) oven for 10 minutes. While the lobster is heating, quickly cut the sole fillets into ¾-inch cubes, dip the cubes in Villeroy sauce, roll them in breadcrumbs, and sauté them in the remaining butter in a frying pan over high heat until golden brown. Transfer the lobster halves to a serving platter and garnish with the parsley and the potato baskets filled with the cubes of sole. *Serves* 6.

981. COLD LOBSTER ITALIANA
Astaco freddo all'italiana

3 2-pound live lobsters
5 quarts boiling water, seasoned with 4 tablespoons
   salt and ¾ cup white wine vinegar
Bouquet Garni:
   3 sprigs parsley
   2 sprigs thyme (or ½ teaspoon dried)
   1 bay leaf
6 hearts of Boston lettuce
6 hard-boiled eggs, halved
3 tablespoons capers
3 ripe tomatoes, sliced
1 tablespoon chopped basil
2 cups Mayonnaise [No. 77]

Place the lobsters and the Bouquet Garni in a large pot, add the boiling water, bring back to a boil over high heat, reduce the heat, cover the pot, and simmer for 20 minutes. Remove from the heat, add 3 cups cold water, and allow the lobsters to cool in the liquid. Drain and chill them in the refrigerator until cold. Split them in half lengthwise, discard the sac behind the head and the intestinal tract, and arrange the halves on a serving platter. Garnish with the hearts of lettuce, the egg halves topped with capers, and the tomato slices seasoned with salt and pepper and sprinkled with chopped basil. Serve the mayonnaise on the side. *Serves 6.*

982. BROILED LOBSTER LUIGI VERONELLI
Astaco alla Luigi Veronelli

3 2-pound live lobsters
½ cup oil
3 cups Sauce Béarnaise [No. 67]
Salt and freshly ground pepper

Split the lobsters in half lengthwise, crack the claws, and discard the sac behind the head and the intestinal tract. Scoop out the liver and coral with a spoon and reserve. Season the exposed meat lightly with salt and pepper and brush it with oil. Arrange the lobsters, cut side up, on the rack under a medium broiler flame and broil for about 15 minutes, basting occasionally with a little more oil. Pound the liver and coral in a mortar until very smooth, blend it into the Béarnaise sauce with a whisk, and keep the sauce warm. When the lobsters are cooked, remove the tail meat from each half, cut it into slices, dip the slices into the Béarnaise, and put them back into their shells. Arrange them on an oven-proof platter and place them in a hot (450°) oven for 5 minutes to become glazed and thoroughly hot. Serve the remaining Béarnaise on the side. *Serves 6.*

983. LOBSTER IN CREAM
Astaco alla crema

3 2-pound live lobsters
¾ cup butter
½ cup brandy
3 cups heavy cream
Salt and freshly ground white pepper
Pinch Cayenne pepper
Juice of 1 lemon
2 tablespoons chopped parsley
1 recipe Pilaf [No. 595]

Cut the lobsters into pieces, as described in Lobster Americana [No. 976]. Heat ½ cup of the butter in a very large frying pan over high heat until it is golden. Add the pieces of lobster, season lightly with salt and pepper, and stir them in the butter for 5 minutes. Drain off most of the butter with a bulb baster, add the brandy, allow it to become very hot, ignite, and reduce it to ⅓ its quantity. Add the cream and season with the

Cayenne and a little more salt and white pepper. Bring the cream to a boil, reduce the heat, and simmer for about 15 minutes. Remove the pieces of lobster tail to a hot serving dish and keep warm. Remove the bodies and the claws from the sauce, extract their meat, and add it to the tail sections on the platter. Mash the liver and coral with a fork and blend it into the sauce with a whisk. Reduce the sauce over high heat to 2½ cups, remove from the heat, and swirl in the remaining butter, bit by bit. Pour the sauce through a fine sieve over the lobster pieces and sprinkle with the parsley. Serve the pilaf separately. *Serves 6.*

984. LOBSTER CROQUETTES
Crocchette di astaco Facchinetti

This recipe is an adaptation of a specialty of Saverio Facchinetti, head chef at the Hotel Cavalieri in Milan.

4 2-pound lobsters
½ cup oil
1 onion, chopped
1 small carrot, sliced
1 clove garlic, crushed in the garlic-press
1 cup dry white wine
½ cup Cognac
2 pounds tomatoes, peeled, seeded, chopped,
    and puréed through a food mill
2 bay leaves, crumbled
2 sprigs thyme (or ¼ teaspoon dried)
Pinch Cayenne pepper
2 eggs, beaten
1½ cups heavy cream
½ cup white Port wine
Fat for deep frying
Salt and freshly ground pepper
Croquette batter:
  4 cups milk
  2½ cups sifted flour
  ¾ cup butter
  6 egg yolks
  ½ teaspoon salt

Cut up the lobsters as described in Lobster Americana [No. 976], reserving the liver and coral, and sauté the pieces in smoking hot oil in a large frying pan over high heat for about 5 minutes, or until the shells turn bright red. Remove most of the oil with a bulb baster and add the onion, carrot, garlic, wine, ¼ cup of the Cognac, tomatoes, bay leaves, thyme. Season lightly with salt, pepper, and Cayenne. Bring to a boil, reduce the heat, cover the pan, and simmer for about 15 minutes.

Remove from the heat, drain the lobster pieces, reserving the liquid, and extract all of the meat from the shells. Chop the meat coarsely and reserve. Mash the liver and coral in a mortar, blend them into the cooking liquid in a saucepan with a whisk, bring to a boil over medium heat, add the carcasses of the lobster bodies, and cook for about 5 minutes. Pour the mixture through a fine sieve into a bowl, pressing through as much of the vegetables and lobster pulp as possible. There should be about 2½ cups; reserve this sauce until needed.

Prepare the croquette batter: bring the milk to a boil with the salt and the butter in a saucepan over medium heat; add the flour in a steady stream, stirring constantly until well blended; remove from the heat; cool slightly; and beat in the egg yolks. Mix in 1 cup of the lobster cooking liquid and all of the chopped lobster meat. Allow the mixture to cool completely.

Pour the remaining lobster cooking liquid into a saucepan and add the remaining ¼ cup Cognac, the cream, and the Port. Bring to a boil over medium heat, reduce the heat to the lowest possible flame, and simmer for about 15 minutes.

Drop the croquette batter by spoonful, a few at a time, in deep hot (375°) fat, fry until golden, drain briefly on absorbent paper, and arrange them on a serving platter. Correct the seasoning of the sauce and serve it separately in a sauceboat. *Serves 6.*

985. LOBSTER DIAVOLA
Astaco alla diavola

3 2-pound live lobsters
4 tablespoons butter, softened
½ cup brandy
3 tablespoons prepared mustard (Dijon-type preferred)
1 tablespoon oil
1½ cups breadcrumbs
6 sprigs parsley
3 lemons, quartered
Salt and freshly ground pepper

Split the lobsters in half lengthwise and discard the intestinal tract and the sac under the head. Mash the liver and the coral with the butter in a saucepan, place the pan over medium heat, add the brandy, heat for ½ minute, and ignite. When the flame subsides, add the mustard, and season lightly with salt and pepper. Stir the mixture until it is smooth and creamy, and remove from the fire. Grease a large baking dish with oil, arrange the lobsters, cut side up, in it, brush

them with ⅓ of the sauce, and place them in a medium (375°) oven for 15 minutes, basting occasionally with another ⅓ of the sauce. Remove the lobsters from the oven, spread them with the remaining sauce mixed with the breadcrumbs, and return them to the oven for another 5 minutes. Transfer them to a serving platter, crack the claws, and garnish with the parsley and lemon quarters. *Serves 6.*

986. LOBSTER HUNGARIAN
Aragosta all'ungherese

Prepare the lobster exactly as described in Lobster in Cream [No. 983], but season the sauce with 1 tablespoon paprika and add 1 chopped large onion, cooked until soft in 2 tablespoons of butter and puréed in a food mill or in the blender. *Serves 6.*

987. LOBSTER MARIA JOSÉ OF SAVOY
Astaco "Marie José di Savoia"

3 2-pound live lobsters
½ cup butter, melted
2 tablespoons chopped carrot
2 tablespoons chopped celery
2 tablespoons chopped onion
1 cup butter
4 egg yolks
¼ cup heavy cream
2 tablespoons chopped basil
½ cup brandy
Salt and freshly ground white pepper

Split the lobsters in half lengthwise, crack the claws, and discard the sac behind the head and the intestinal tract. Scoop out the liver and coral and reserve. Season the exposed meat lightly with salt and pepper and brush with melted butter. Arrange the halves, cut side up, on the rack under a medium broiler flame and broil for about 15 minutes, basting occasionally with more melted butter. While the lobsters are broiling, sauté the chopped vegetables in the butter very gently in a frying pan over moderate heat for 5 minutes. Do *not* allow the vegetables or the butter to brown. Beat the egg yolks with the cream in the top half of a double boiler over hot (not boiling) water. Very slowly pour the butter and chopped vegetables into the cream and egg yolks, beating constantly with a whisk. Remove from stove, and then pound the liver and coral in a mortar until smooth and blend them into the sauce. Place the pan over barely simmering water and stir constantly with a whisk until the sauce is quite thick.

332

Season with salt and pepper, press it through a fine strainer, add the chopped basil, and keep warm. When the lobsters are cooked, arrange the halves on a hot oven-proof platter. Serve at once with the sauce on the side. Heat the brandy in a small saucepan over a spirit lamp at the table, ignite, and pour over the lobster halves. *Serves 6.*

NOTE: Maria José of Savoy was the queen of Italy.

988. LOBSTER MOUSSE WITH CURRY SAUCE
Mousse di astaco con salsa al curry

3 2-pound live lobsters
5 quarts Court Bouillon [No. 764]
Pinch mace
Pinch nutmeg
5 egg whites
4 cups very cold heavy cream
2 tablespoons butter, softened
2 1/2 cups hot Curry Sauce [No. 70]
Salt and freshly ground white pepper

Split the lobsters in half and remove all of the meat from the tails, claws, and bodies. Be careful that the meat is free of any bits of shell or cartilage. Put all of this raw lobster meat through the meat grinder, using the finest blade, and then pound it to a paste in the mortar (or blend for a few seconds in the electric blender, but be careful that it does not liquefy). Season the paste generously with salt, pepper, mace, and nutmeg and place it in the refrigerator to chill for 1 hour. When it is cold, put it in a chilled bowl and beat in the unbeaten egg whites, a little at a time, with a wooden spoon. Place the bowl over ice and work in the chilled cream very slowly, beating well after each addition. Pour the mixture into a generously buttered mold, set the mold in a shallow roasting pan half filled with hot water, and bake in a moderate (350°) oven for 35 to 40 minutes, or until the mousse is firm and a knife inserted in the center comes out clean. Remove from oven, let stand for 10 minutes, and unmold the mousse onto a hot serving platter and pour the sauce over it. *Serves 6.*

989. LOBSTER NEWBURG
Astaco à la Newbourg

3 2-pound live lobsters
1/2 cup butter
1 cup dry Madeira wine
1 cup dry sherry wine
2 1/2 cups Fish Fumet [No. 2]
2 cups heavy cream
6 egg yolks, beaten
Pinch paprika
Salt and freshly ground pepper

Cut the lobsters into pieces as described in Lobster Americana [No. 976], reserving the liver and coral. Melt the butter in a large frying pan over high heat, add the lobster pieces, and sauté for about 5 minutes, or until the pieces turn a bright red. Remove lobster with a slotted spoon, add the Madeira and sherry, cook until wine is reduced by 1/2, add the Fumet, bring to a boil, add lobster, cover the pan, reduce the heat, and simmer for 15 minutes. Remove the lobster pieces with a slotted spoon, extract all of the meat from the shells, cut it into bite-size pieces, put them in a hot serving dish, and keep warm. Reduce the cooking liquid over high heat to 1 1/2 cups, remove from the heat, and slowly add the cream which has been beaten with the egg yolks, stirring constantly with a whisk. Return the pan to very low heat and stir constantly until the sauce has thickened. Add the paprika, correct the seasoning, and pour over the lobster pieces. *Serves 6.*

990. LOBSTER PILAF WITH SAUCE CARDINAL
Pilaff di astaco con salsa cardinale

3 2-pound live lobsters
4 quarts Court Bouillon [No. 764]
Sauce Cardinal:
  2 cups Velouté Sauce for Fish [No. 17a]
  1 cup Fish Fumet, reduced to 2 tablespoons
  1 tablespoon chopped truffle [or No. 1819a]
  1 tablespoon truffle juice [or *see* No. 1819a]
  4 tablespoons lobster butter, softened
    (*see* Note below)
3 tablespoons butter, softened
5 cups cooked rice Pilaf [No. 595]

Place the lobsters and the Court Bouillon in a large pot over high heat, cover, bring to a boil, reduce the heat, and simmer for 20 minutes. Drain the lobsters, and extract all of the meat from the shells; cut it into bite-size pieces, and keep warm. Prepare a Cardinal sauce by combining the Velouté, reduced Fumet, truffle, and truffle juice in a saucepan over medium heat. Simmer for 5 minutes, remove from the heat, and swirl in the lobster butter, bit by bit. Add the lobster pieces to the sauce and keep warm. Butter a large round mold with the softened butter, press ⅔ of the rice around the bottom and up the sides of the mold, pour the sauced lobster into the center, and cover with the remaining rice. Place the mold in a hot (400°) oven for 8 to 10 minutes to become thoroughly hot and then unmold on a hot serving platter. *Serves 6.*

NOTE: Classically, lobster butter is made by pounding lobster shells and butter in a mortar with a pestle. This is a somewhat arduous procedure and it may be simplified by using an electric blender. Break up approximately 1 pound of lobster shells and place them in the container of the blender with 1 cup water, 8 tablespoons of butter, and the coral from 1 lobster; blend on high speed for about 30 seconds, or until it has a smooth but grainy texture. Turn the mixture out into a saucepan and simmer for 5 minutes very slowly over the lowest possible heat. Pour the mixture into a bowl and chill in refrigerator until butter has formed a solidified layer. Any bits of shell will sink to the bottom of the bowl and the pinkish butter may be spooned off the top after it has solidified.

991. LOBSTER PILAF PIEMONTESE
Risotto di astaco alla piemontese

3 2-pound live lobsters
4 quarts Court Bouillon [No. 764]
3 tablespoons butter
2 truffles, sliced [or No. 1819a]
1 recipe Risotto with Butter and Parmesan Cheese
    [No. 572]
1½ cups grated Parmesan cheese
Salt

Place the lobsters and the Court Bouillon in a large pot over high heat, cover, bring to a boil, reduce the heat, and simmer for 20 minutes. Drain the lobsters, extract all of the meat from the shells, cut it into bite-size pieces, and sauté them in the butter in a frying pan over medium heat just until very hot. Season them lightly with salt, toss them lightly with the hot risotto, and turn the mixture out onto a hot serving platter. Garnish the top with the truffles and pass the grated cheese on the side. *Serves 6.*

334

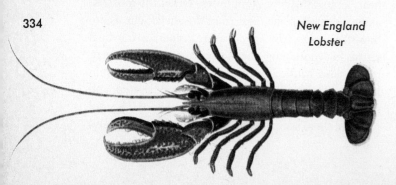

New England Lobster

992. LOBSTER PIQUANT UMBERTO OF SAVOY
Astaco piccante "Umberto di Savoia"

3 2-pound live lobsters
A basting mixture:
    ¾ cup oil
    ¾ cup butter, melted
    1 tablespoon chopped parsley
    1 teaspoon chopped oregano (or ½ teaspoon dried)
    1½ teaspoons dry mustard
    ¼ teaspoon freshly ground white pepper
    1 teaspoon salt
1 cup breadcrumbs
2 lemons, quartered

Split the lobsters in half lengthwise, crack the claws, and discard the intestinal tract and the sac behind the head. Brush the exposed meat of the lobsters generously with the basting mixture, place them, cut side up, on the rack under a medium broiler flame, and broil for about 13 minutes, basting occasionally with more of the basting mixture. Reserve about ⅓ of this mixture and blend with the breadcrumbs. Brush the lobsters with the breadcrumbs and broil for about 2 minutes longer under a high flame. Transfer the halves to a serving platter and garnish with the lemon quarters. *Serves 6.*

NOTE: Umberto of Savoy was the king of Italy, and the husband of Maria José of Savoy (*see* Note to No. 987).

993. LOBSTER RUSSE
Astaco freddo alla russa

1 5-pound live lobster
4 cups Mayonnaise [No. 77]
2 quarts Fish Aspic [No. 119] or Substitute Fish
    Aspic [No. 119a]
3 truffles, sliced
24 tiny sprigs parsley
1 cup caviar
4 cups Russian Salad [No. 1879], chilled

Cook the lobster as described in Lobster Bella Vista [No. 977], slicing the meat from the tail and chopping the meat from the body and claws. Discard the shells. Stir 2 cups of the aspic mixed with 2 cups of the mayonnaise in a bowl over ice until it becomes very thick. Dip each of the tail slices of the lobster in the mixture and place them, well separated, on a platter. Place a slice of truffle on the top of each and top with a small sprig of parsley. Chill in the refrigerator until very cold. Stir 2 more cups of the aspic over ice until thick and syrupy and glaze the tops of the lobster slices with a thin layer. Place them in the refrigerator again to chill. Chill a round, 1½-quart fluted mold in the freezer. Stir 2 more cups of the aspic over ice until thick and syrupy. Line the sides and bottom of the mold with a thick layer of aspic; this will require 2 or more coatings, chilling the mold between coatings. Put the Russian salad in the lined mold, pour in aspic to the top of the mold, and chill until firmly jellied. Pour the remaining aspic into a flat, shallow dish, chill until jelled, turn it out onto a board, and chop it finely. Unmold the jellied vegetables onto the center of a large, round serving platter, surround with the glazed lobster medallions, arrange small heaps of the caviar on the platter, and circle with a border of the chopped aspic. *Serves* 6.

994. LOBSTER THERMIDOR
Astaco alla Thermidor

3 2-pound live lobsters
⅓ cup oil
4 tablespoons butter
1 tablespoon chopped shallots
1 cup dry white wine
1½ cups Fish Fumet [No. 2]
1 teaspoon chopped tarragon (or ½ teaspoon dried)
1 teaspoon chopped chervil (or ½ teaspoon dried)
3 cups thick Sauce Mornay [No. 56]
1 teaspoon dry mustard
2 tablespoons Meat Essence [No. 10]
½ cup grated Parmesan cheese
Salt and freshly ground pepper

Split the lobsters in half lengthwise, crack the claws, discard the intestinal tract and the sac behind the head, and reserve the liver and the coral. Place the halves, cut side up, in a roasting pan, brush them liberally with oil, and put them in a hot (400°) oven for 20 minutes, basting occasionally with more oil. Extract all of the meat from the claws and discard the claw shells; remove the meat from the tails, leaving the shells whole; slice all of the meat and keep it warm. Melt the butter in a saucepan over medium heat, add the shallots, cook until transparent, and add the wine, Fumet, tarragon, and chervil. Cook over high heat until reduced to ½ cup and add the Mornay sauce, mustard, meat essence, and the reserved liver and coral which have been pounded smooth in a mortar. Bring to a boil, reduce the heat, and simmer for 5 minutes, correct the seasoning, and then strain the sauce through

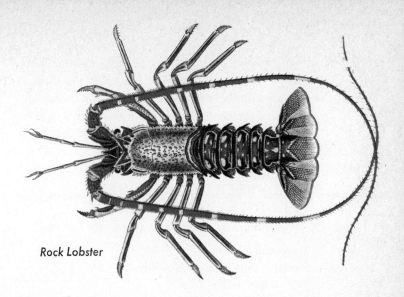

Rock Lobster

a fine sieve. Spoon a little of the sauce into each shell half, arrange the pieces of lobster on top, cover with the remaining sauce, and sprinkle with the grated cheese. Arrange the lobster halves in a large roasting pan and place in a hot (400°) oven for 6 to 8 minutes, or until the tops are golden brown. *Serves* 6.

995. LOBSTER TIRLI IN BIRLI
Conchiglie di astaco "tirli in birli"

3 2-pound live lobsters
4 quarts Court Bouillon [No. 764]
½ cup butter
3 tablespoons chopped onion
½ pound mushrooms, finely sliced
1 cup dry sherry wine
5 egg yolks, beaten
1 cup heavy cream
6 thin slices of truffle [or No. 1819a]
6 large scallop shells

Place the lobsters and the Court Bouillon in a large pot over high heat, bring to a boil, cover the pot, reduce the heat, and simmer for 25 minutes. Remove the lobsters from the liquid, extract all of the meat from the shells, cut it into bite-size pieces, and keep warm. Reduce 2 quarts of the Court Bouillon in a saucepan over high heat to 1 cup and reserve. Melt 3 tablespoons of the butter in another saucepan over medium heat, add the onion, cook until golden, add the mushrooms, stir for 1 minute, add the sherry, and cook until reduced by ½. Add the reduced Court Bouillon, bring to a boil, and remove from the heat. Slowly add the egg yolks which have been beaten with the cream, stirring constantly with a whisk. Return the pan to very low heat, stir constantly until the sauce has thickened, correct the seasoning, remove from the heat, and swirl in the remaining butter, bit by bit. Spoon a little of the sauce into each scallop shell, portion out the pieces of lobster in the shells, and cover with the remaining sauce. Garnish the top of each with a slice of truffle and place the shells in a hot (400°) oven for 6 minutes to become thoroughly hot. *Serves* 6.

996. LOBSTER TOURNEDOS LUIGI VERONELLI
Medaglioni di aragosta alla Luigi Veronelli

3 2-pound lobsters
5 quarts Court Bouillon [No. 764]
1 cup butter, softened
A marinade:
   3 tablespoons oil
   1 tablespoon chopped parsley
   1/2 teaspoon salt
   1/8 teaspoon freshly ground pepper
   Pinch nutmeg
Flour
3 eggs, beaten
Fresh breadcrumbs
6 slices bread, crusts removed, and sautéed
   in oil until golden
6 sprigs parsley
3 lemons, quartered

Place the lobsters and the Court Bouillon in a large heavy pot over high heat, cover tightly, bring to a boil, **reduce** the heat, and simmer for 15 minutes. Allow them to remain in the cooking liquid for 10 minutes, drain, cool somewhat, and extract all of the meat from the shells. Slice the meat from the tail into 1/2-inch slices. Chop the rest of the meat and then pound it in a mortar with 1/2 cup of the butter or blend both for a few seconds in the blender. Marinate the slices from the tail in the marinade for 1 hour, dip the pieces first in flour, then in beaten egg, and dust with breadcrumbs. Melt the remaining butter in a large frying pan over high heat until it is golden, add the lobster slices, and sauté quickly on both sides until golden. Spread the bread slices with the lobster/butter mixture, arrange the slices on a hot serving platter, place a few lobster slices on each, and garnish with the parsley and lemon quarters. *Serves* 6.

997. LOBSTER VILLA SASSI
Astaco "Villa Sassi"

3 2-pound live lobsters
1 cup butter, softened

2 tablespoons finely chopped onion
1 cup dry white vermouth
1/2 cup dry Marsala wine
1 1/2 cups heavy cream
4 egg yolks
Pinch Cayenne pepper
1/4 cup oil
3 lemons, quartered
6 sprigs parsley
Salt and freshly ground pepper

Melt 2 tablespoons of the butter in a frying pan over low heat, add the onion, cook until transparent, add the vermouth and Marsala, and cook until the liquid has almost entirely evaporated. Simmer the cream in another saucepan over moderate heat until reduced to 1/3 its original quantity. Combine reduced wine and cream in the top half of a double boiler, allow to cool slightly, beat in the egg yolks with a whisk, place the pan over barely simmering water, and stir constantly with a whisk while adding the remaining butter, bit by bit. When the sauce has thickened like Hollandaise, remove from the fire, add the Cayenne, correct the seasoning, press it through a very fine sieve, and keep warm.

Split the lobsters in half lengthwise, discard the intestinal tract and the sac behind the head, crack the claws, season the exposed meat with salt and pepper, and brush it with oil. Place the halves on the rack under a medium broiler flame and broil for about 15 minutes, basting occasionally with more oil. Remove from the broiler, transfer the halves to a serving platter, garnish with the parsley and lemon quarters, and serve the sauce on the side. *Serves* 6.

SCAMPI
Scampo

Scampi are medium-sized salt-water crustaceans which, unfortunately, are native only to Adriatic waters. Usually about 6 or 7 inches long, the tail meat is the only edible part. Scampi are occasionally imported by fish dealers in the larger cities of the eastern United States and, in spite of their high price, are well worth trying. They are rather a cross between a crayfish and a shrimp.

Jumbo shrimp or frozen baby rock-lobster tails are the closest equivalent to genuine scampi and may be substituted for them in the succeeding recipes.

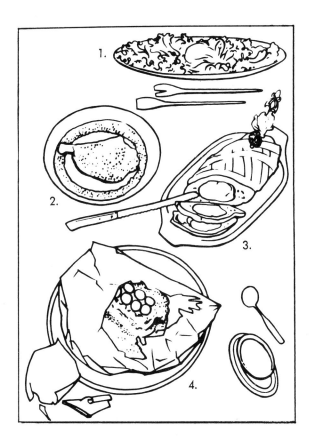

1. An excellent condiment to accompany beef is fresh, finely shredded horseradish. Here, it is presented garnished with leaves of escarole and Boston lettuce.

2. Individual serving of Roast Beef Pizzaiola (No. 1110)

3. Fillet of Beef en Croûte (No. 1097)

4. Roast Sirloin Château en Papillote (No. 1112)

998. SCAMPI BRUSSELS EXPOSITION 1958
Spiedini di scampi Esposizione di Bruxelles 1958

24 large scampi, shelled
6 skewers
24 large mushroom caps
24 slices prosciutto, 1½ inches square and ⅛ inch thick
24 slices mozzarella
½ teaspoon dried thyme
1 bay leaf, crumbled
2 teaspoons salt
¼ teaspoon freshly ground pepper
½ cup butter, melted
1 bunch watercress, washed and dried

Run the scampi on 6 skewers, alternating them with the mushroom caps, slices of prosciutto, and slices of mozzarella. Pound the salt, pepper, and dried herbs in a mortar, season the skewered ingredients with this mixture, arrange the skewers in a shallow roasting pan, pour the melted butter over them, and place the pan under a medium broiler flame for about 8 minutes, turning the skewers often and basting with the butter in the pan. Transfer the skewers to a bed of watercress on a hot serving platter and serve at once. *Serves 6.*

999. SCAMPI CAPRICCIO DI DIANA
Code di scampi "Capriccio di Diana"

24 large scampi, shelled
3 tablespoons butter
1 cup dry sherry
2 cups Sauce Mornay [No. 56]
3 truffles, sliced [or No. 1819a]
¼ cup grated Parmesan cheese
6 sprigs parsley
Salt

Cut out the underside of the tail shell of the scampi, remove the tail meat, and reserve the shells. Slice the meat into fairly thick slices, season them lightly with salt, and sauté them quickly in the butter in a frying pan over fairly high heat until they are faintly golden. Remove the slices with a slotted spoon and keep warm. Add the sherry to the juices in the pan and reduce over high heat to a few tablespoonsful. Add the Mornay sauce and cook only until thoroughly hot. Spoon a little of the sauce into each shell, arrange a few scampi slices in each, top with a few slices of truffle, and cover with the remaining sauce. Sprinkle a very

small amount of cheese over each, arrange the shells in a roasting pan, and place in a hot (400°) oven for 6 to 8 minutes, or until the tops are golden. Arrange the shells on a serving platter and garnish with the parsley. *Serves 6.*

NOTE: If jumbo shrimp are used, substitute 6 small ramekins or scallop shells for the scampi shells.

1000. SCAMPI CASINO DI VENEZIA
Code di scampi "Casino di Venezia"

24 scampi, shelled
Flour
½ cup butter (or more as needed)
1 clove garlic, crushed in the garlic-press
¾ pound mushrooms, thinly sliced
1 tablespoon chopped parsley
6 slices bread, crusts removed, large enough to hold 4 scampi each
3 cups Sauce Mornay [No. 56], to which 1 tablespoon curry powder has been added
3 tablespoons melted butter
¼ cup grated Parmesan cheese
24 thin slices of truffle [or No. 1819a]
½ cup brandy
Salt and freshly ground pepper

Season the scampi tails lightly with salt and pepper and dust them with the flour. Melt 4 tablespoons of the butter in a large frying pan over fairly high heat until golden, add the scampi, and cook for 5 minutes, or until they are a light gold on all sides. Transfer them to a bowl and keep warm. Add 1 more tablespoon of butter to the frying pan, add the garlic, cook for 1 minute, add the mushrooms and parsley, cover the pan, and cook over moderate heat for about 8 minutes. Remove from the heat and reserve. Sauté the slices of bread in another frying pan in 3 tablespoons of butter until golden brown on both sides, adding more butter as necessary. Arrange these slices in a circle around a large oven-proof platter, place 4 scampi on each slice, cover with Mornay sauce, sprinkle with a little cheese and melted butter, and place in a hot (400°) oven for 10 minutes. Remove from the oven, spoon the mushrooms into the center of the platter, and garnish each scampi with a slice of truffle. Add the brandy to the mushroom juices in the frying pan, reduce over high heat to ½ its quantity, and pour over the mushrooms. *Serves 6.*

1001. CURRIED SCAMPI
Code di scampi al curry

24 large scampi, shelled
2 tablespoons oil
2 tablespoons chopped onion
2 tablespoons chopped carrot
2 tablespoons chopped celery
1 clove garlic, crushed in the garlic-press
1 bay leaf, crumbled
½ cup brandy
2½ cups Cream Sauce [No. 55]
2 tablespoons curry powder
¼ cup heavy cream
2 egg yolks
Salt and freshly ground white pepper

Heat the oil in a large frying pan over medium heat; add the chopped vegetables, garlic, and bay leaf; and cook until the vegetables are soft. Add the scampi, season lightly with salt and pepper, raise the heat slightly, and cook until they are golden on all sides. Transfer the scampi to a hot serving platter and keep warm. Add the brandy to the pan and reduce over high heat to ½ its quantity. Add the cream sauce, simmer for 2 minutes, strain through a fine sieve, add the curry powder and the egg yolks which have been beaten with the cream, pour the sauce back into the pan, and return to very low heat. Stir the sauce constantly until it has thickened slightly, correct the seasoning, and pour over the scampi. *Serves 6.*

1002. FRIED SCAMPI ITALIANA
Code di scampi fritte all'italiana

24 large scampi, shelled
Flour
1¼ cups oil
2 pounds young, tender zucchini, sliced
3 lemons, quartered
Salt and freshly ground white pepper

Season the scampi lightly with salt and pepper, dust them with flour, and sauté them in 1 cup of very hot oil in a very large frying pan over high heat for about 5 minutes, or until they are golden on all sides. Heat the remaining oil in another frying pan over medium heat, add the zucchini, and cook for about 5 minutes, stirring often and seasoning lightly with salt and pepper. Place the scampi in the center of a hot serving platter, arrange a circle of the zucchini around them, and garnish with the lemon quarters. *Serves 6.*

Scampi New York's Fair 1939 (No. 1003)

1003. SCAMPI NEW YORK WORLD'S FAIR 1939
Spiedini di scampi Esposizione di New York 1939

24 large scampi, shelled
6 large tomatoes
1 tablespoon finely chopped oregano (or ½ teaspoon dried)
2 tablespoons chopped parsley
2 cloves garlic, crushed in the garlic-press
½ cup fresh breadcrumbs
½ cup oil (or more as needed)
2 pounds tender zucchini
Flour
24 thin slices salt pork, parboiled for 15 minutes
24 medium mushroom caps
Salt and freshly ground pepper

Slice off the tops of the tomatoes, squeeze them slightly to remove some of the seeds and juice, season them with salt and pepper, and sprinkle the tops with chopped oregano, parsley, garlic, breadcrumbs, and a few drops of oil. Arrange the tomatoes in a baking dish and bake them in a medium (375°) oven for 15 minutes. Season the zucchini with salt and pepper, dust it lightly with flour, and sauté it in very hot oil in a large frying pan over high heat for about 5 minutes, or until the slices are golden. Remove from the heat and keep warm. Wrap each of the scampi in a slice of salt pork and run them onto skewers, alternating them with the mushroom caps. Brush them lightly with oil and broil them under a medium flame for about 8

338

minutes, turning them often and basting with a little more oil. Arrange the tomatoes on a hot serving platter, place 2 or 3 of the scampi and a few mushrooms on top of each tomato. Arrange the remaining scampi and mushrooms around the platter, and garnish with small heaps of the zucchini. *Serves* 6.

1004. SCAMPI PARIS EXPOSITION 1937
Code di scampi Esposizione di Parigi 1937

24 large scampi, shelled
2 small globe eggplant, peeled and each cut into
    4 slices
Flour
2 eggs, beaten
6 tablespoons oil
$\frac{3}{4}$ cup butter
1 cup diced smoked tongue
$\frac{1}{2}$ pound mushrooms, thinly sliced
3 truffles, chopped [or No. 1819a]
2 tablespoons chopped onion
4 tomatoes, peeled, seeded, drained, and chopped
1 yellow pepper, roasted, peeled, seeded, and cut
    into strips [*see* No. 145]
1 cup dry sherry
Salt and freshly ground pepper

Liberally salt the eggplant slices and let them stand on paper towels for 2 hours to drain; then wash them off thoroughly and pat dry. Season the eggplant slices with pepper, dust them lightly with flour, dip them in the beaten eggs, and sauté in hot oil in a large frying pan over fairly high heat until golden on both sides. Transfer the slices to a hot platter and keep warm. Melt 3 tablespoons of the butter in another frying pan over moderate heat, add the diced tongue, cook for 1 minute, add the mushrooms and truffles, cover the pan, reduce the heat, and simmer for 8 minutes, shaking the pan occasionally. Remove from the heat and keep warm. Melt 3 tablespoons of the butter in a saucepan over medium heat, add the chopped onion, cook until golden, add the tomatoes and the pepper strips, season with salt and pepper, and simmer for 10 minutes. Melt another 4 tablespoons of the butter in a frying pan over fairly high heat, add the scampi tails, and sauté for 5 or 6 minutes, or until the scampi are golden on all sides. Arrange the scampi alternately with the eggplant slices around the edge of a large serving platter, place the mushroom/tongue mixture in the center, and garnish with small heaps of the tomatoes. Pour the sherry into the pan in which the scampi were cooked, reduce over high heat to $\frac{1}{2}$ its

quantity, remove from the heat, swirl in the remaining butter, and pour over all. *Serves* 6.

1005. SCAMPI SPUMANTE
Code di scampi allo spumante

24 large scampi, shelled
$\frac{1}{2}$ cup butter
2 tablespoons chopped onion
$\frac{1}{2}$ pound mushrooms, sliced
$\frac{1}{2}$ bottle dry spumante wine (or Champagne)
$1\frac{1}{2}$ cups heavy cream
3 egg yolks
Salt and freshly ground white pepper

Melt 4 tablespoons of the butter in a large, heavy saucepan over fairly high heat, add the chopped onion, cook until it is golden, add the scampi and the mushrooms, season lightly with salt and pepper, stir for 1 minute, add the wine, bring to a boil, reduce the heat, and simmer for 10 minutes. Remove the scampi and mushrooms with a slotted spoon to a hot oven-proof dish and keep warm. Reduce the wine over high heat to $\frac{1}{5}$ its quantity, add $1\frac{1}{4}$ cups of the cream, bring just to a boil, and remove from the heat. Beat the egg yolks with the remaining cream, blend them into the sauce with a whisk, return the pan to very low heat, and cook, stirring constantly, for about 5 minutes, or until the sauce has thickened slightly. Do not boil. Correct the seasoning, remove the pan from the heat, and swirl in the remaining butter, bit by bit. Strain the sauce through a fine sieve, if desired, and pour over the scampi. Place the dish in a hot (400°) oven for 5 minutes, or until the top is glazed. *Serves* 6.

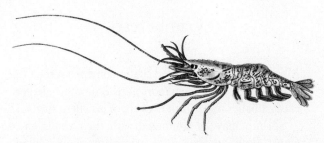

Above: *Shrimp*   **Left:** *Scampo*

These two drawings (not to scale) show the difference between these crustaceans. A scampo is about the size of a jumbo shrimp.

1006. SCAMPI VILLA SASSI
Spiedini di scampi "Villa Sassi"

24 large scampi
¼ cup oil
6 skewers
2 tablespoons butter
2 cloves garlic, crushed in the garlic-press
½ cup brandy
Dash Worcestershire sauce
1 tablespoon prepared mustard (Dijon-type preferred)
¼ cup Anchovy Butter [No. 108]
Juice of ½ lemon
6 sprigs parsley
Salt and freshly ground pepper

Separate the scampi tails from the bodies and discard the bodies. Cut out the underside of the tail shells with a very sharp knife or with poultry shears, season the meat lightly with salt and pepper, and brush the tails generously with oil. Run the scampi onto 6 skewers and broil under a medium broiler flame for about 8 minutes, turning them often and basting with more oil as they cook. Melt the butter in a saucepan, add the garlic, cook until golden, add the brandy and Worcestershire sauce, and reduce to ½ its quantity. Remove from the fire and beat in the mustard, anchovy butter, and lemon juice. Transfer the scampi to a hot serving platter, garnish with the parsley, and serve the sauce on the side. *Serves* 6.

SHRIMP

Gamberetti

Most shrimp in the United States come from the Gulf Coast. The shrimp from more northern waters are generally smaller in size, but they are of excellent flavor.

Shrimp may be simmered with their shells on in Court Bouillon [No. 765], cooled in their cooking liquid, shelled, and then de-veined by removing the black vein that runs just under the surface of their backs. Or they may be gently sautéed in butter or oil for about 5 minutes, either shelled and de-veined or in their shells and de-veined after cooking. Their skin under the translucent shell will turn a bright pink shortly after contact with heat.

1007. SHRIMP PILAF AMERICANA
Pilaff di gamberetti all'americana

2 pounds shrimp, cooked for 5 to 8 minutes in Court Bouillon [No. 765] to cover, shelled and de-veined
3 tablespoons butter, softened
5 cups rice Pilaf [No. 595]
2 cups American Sauce [No. 63]

Line the bottom and sides of a generously buttered mold with ⅔ of the rice, leaving a large hollow in the center. Combine the shrimp with 1½ cups of the American sauce and pour into the hollow. Cover with the remaining rice and bake in a moderate (350°) oven for about 15 minutes. Unmold onto a hot serving platter and circle with a ribbon of the remaining sauce. *Serves* 6.

1008. CREAMED SHRIMP PILAF
Pilaff di gamberetti alla crema

Prepare as described in the preceding recipe, substituting Cream Sauce [No. 55] for the American sauce. *Serves* 6.

1009. SHRIMP PILAF HUNGARIAN
Pilaff di gamberetti all'ungherese

Prepare as described in Shrimp Pilaf Americana [No. 1007], substituting White Wine Sauce [No. 76], which has been generously seasoned with 1 tablespoon paprika, for the American sauce. *Serves* 6.

340

1010. SHRIMP PILAF NANTUA
Pilaff di gamberetti alla Nantua

Prepare exactly as Shrimp Pilaf Americana [No. 1007], substituting Sauce Nantua [No. 57] for the American sauce. *Serves 6.*

FROGS AND MOLLUSKS

Rane e molluschi

FROGS

Rane

While frogs are not fish, custom has placed them in that category and they are sold by fish dealers. The white flesh of their legs, which is the edible part, is tender, delicate, and delicious. Usually dealers in the United States sell only the legs, skinned and ready for cooking. In Europe the bodies are often skinned, cleaned, and used as a flavoring agent for a sauce accompanying the legs.

1011. FROGS' LEGS BORDELAISE
Rane alla bordolese

36 pairs frogs' legs
Milk
Flour
1 cup Clarified Butter [No. 102]
2 shallots, chopped
2 tablespoons chopped parsley
½ cup fresh breadcrumbs
Juice of 1 lemon
Salt and freshly ground pepper

Wash the frogs' legs and soak them in milk for 1 hour. Drain them and pat dry on paper towels. Season them lightly with salt and pepper, dust with flour, and sauté them in hot clarified butter in a large frying pan over

medium heat for about 12 minutes. Adjust the heat during the cooking so that the frogs' legs will brown nicely but the butter does not burn. Transfer them to a hot serving platter and keep warm. Add the shallots, parsley, and breadcrumbs to the butter in the pan, cook for 2 minutes, pour over the frogs' legs, and sprinkle with the lemon juice. *Serves 6.*

1012. BRANDIED FROGS' LEGS
Rane al brandy

36 pairs frogs' legs
Milk
½ cup brandy
Flour
4 egg whites, beaten stiff
½ cup butter
6 sprigs parsley, fried in deep fat [*see* No. 276]
3 lemons, quartered
Salt and freshly ground pepper

Soak the frogs' legs in milk for 1 hour. Drain, pat dry on paper towels, place them in a bowl with the brandy, season lightly with salt and pepper, and marinate them for 2 hours, stirring occasionally. Drain and dry them again, dip them in flour, then in the beaten egg whites, and sauté them in foaming hot butter in a large frying pan over medium heat for about 12 minutes. Arrange them on a hot serving platter and garnish with the fried parsley and lemon quarters. *Serves 6.*

1013. FROGS' LEGS FINES HERBES
Rane con erbe fini

Prepare exactly as Frogs' Legs Bordelaise [No. 1011], omitting the breadcrumbs and adding to the butter in the pan 1 tablespoon each of 3 or 4 fresh herbs such as thyme, tarragon, oregano, basil, or savory.

1014. FROGS' LEGS FIORENTINA
Cosce di rane alla fiorentina

36 pairs frogs' legs
Milk
Flour
½ cup oil
12 eggs
2 tablespoons finely chopped parsley
Salt and freshly ground white pepper

Soak the frogs' legs in milk for 1 hour. Drain and dry them thoroughly. Season them lightly with salt and pepper, dust them with flour, and brown them quickly on both sides in hot oil in a very large frying pan over high heat. Reduce the heat and sauté them gently for 10 minutes longer. Break the eggs into a bowl, add the parsley, season lightly with salt and pepper, and beat very lightly with a fork. Pour them into the frying pan with the frogs' legs, raise the heat slightly, allow the eggs to set on the bottom of the pan for a few seconds, begin raising the edge of the eggs to allow uncooked egg to run underneath, continue only until the eggs are barely cooked but still soft, and then run a broad spatula under them to make certain they are not sticking to the bottom. Invert the contents of the pan onto a hot serving platter and sprinkle with the parsley. *Serves* 6.

1015. FROGS' LEGS ITALIANA
Cosce di rane all'italiana

36 pairs frogs' legs
Milk
3 eggs
2 tablespoons heavy cream
Pinch nutmeg
Fresh breadcrumbs
½ cup butter
6 sprigs parsley, fried in deep fat [*see* No. 276]
3 cups Tomato Sauce [No. 19]
Salt and freshly ground pepper

Soak the frogs' legs in milk for 1 hour. Drain and dry them thoroughly. Beat the eggs in a bowl with the cream and season with salt, pepper, and nutmeg. Dip the frogs' legs in this mixture and then roll in breadcrumbs. Heat the butter in a large frying pan over medium heat until golden, add the frogs' legs, and sauté them for about 12 minutes, or until they are golden on both sides. Transfer them to a hot serving platter, garnish with the fried parsley, and serve the tomato sauce on the side. *Serves* 6.

1016. FROGS' LEGS MILANESE
Costolettine di rane alla milanese

The trattorias "outside the gate" in Milan are famous for this dish.

48 pairs frogs' legs
Milk
3 eggs, beaten
Fresh breadcrumbs
½ cup butter
6 sprigs parsley, fried in deep fat [*see* No. 276]
3 lemons, quartered
Salt and freshly ground pepper

Soak the frogs' legs in milk for 1 hour. Drain, dry thoroughly, and remove all of the meat from the bones. Reserve 24 of the thigh bones which should be picked very clean. Place all of the meat on a board, season it lightly with salt and pepper, and pound it with the flat side of a cleaver. Wrap a generous amount of the flattened meat around each of the reserved bones, dip them in beaten egg, and roll them in breadcrumbs. Heat the butter in a large frying pan over medium heat until golden, add the reconstituted legs and sauté for 12 minutes, or until they are golden on all sides. Transfer them to a hot serving platter and garnish with the fried parsley and the lemon quarters. *Serves* 6.

NOTE: This dish may be simplified by merely shaping the chopped meat into small fingers instead of reconstituting it on the bones.

Garlic

1017. FROGS' LEGS WITH PEPPERS AND MUSHROOMS
Rane con peperoni e funghi

36 pairs frogs' legs
Milk
½ cup brandy
½ cup oil
½ pound mushrooms, sliced
3 medium green peppers, roasted, scraped, seeded, and cut into strips [*see* No. 145]
1 clove garlic, crushed in the garlic-press
Juice of 1 lemon
2 tablespoons chopped parsley
Salt and freshly ground pepper

Soak the frogs' legs in milk for 1 hour. Drain and pat dry on paper towels. Place them in a bowl with the brandy, season them lightly with salt and pepper, and allow them to steep for 2 hours, turning them occasionally. Drain and dry them again. Sauté them in ½ cup of very hot oil in a large frying pan over medium heat for about 12 minutes. Transfer them to a hot serving dish and keep warm. Add the pepper strips and the garlic to the hot oil, cook for 2 minutes, add the mushrooms, and continue cooking for about 8 minutes longer, stirring often. Spoon the peppers and mushrooms over the frogs' legs, squeeze the lemon juice over them, and sprinkle with the chopped parsley. *Serves* 6.

1018. FROGS' LEGS PROVENÇALE
Rane alla provenzale

36 pairs frogs' legs
Milk
Flour
6 tablespoons oil
2 cloves garlic, crushed in the garlic-press
2 tablespoons chopped parsley
Juice of 1 lemon
Salt and freshly ground pepper

Soak the frogs' legs in milk for 1 hour. Drain and pat dry on paper towels. Season them lightly with salt and pepper, dust them with flour, and sauté them in very hot oil in a large frying pan over a medium flame for about 12 minutes, or until they are golden brown. Remove them to a hot serving platter and keep warm. Add the garlic and parsley to the oil in the pan, cook for 2 minutes, pour them over the frogs' legs, and squeeze the lemon juice over them. Serve at once. *Serves 6.*

MUSSELS
Cozze o muscoli

Mussels are particularly abundant along the Atlantic coast and are often gathered in the harbors of its seaports. Particular care should be taken that mussels be live before cooking. They should first be thoroughly scrubbed under running water and the black "beard" pulled off (or, more easily, the "beard" may be removed after the shells have been steamed open). Discard any mussels whose shells do not close tightly when given a slight tap. Soak them for 1 hour in a large quantity of water and discard any which float to the top. Mussels may be shelled raw, or cooked in the shell by steaming the mussels for a few minutes with a small amount of liquid in a tightly covered pot over high heat. The pot is shaken during the cooking to facilitate their opening. The liquid in the shells is delicious, and normally forms the base of any accompanying sauce.

1019. MUSSELS AMMIRAGLIA
Cozze all'ammiraglia

48 large raw mussels, scrubbed, soaked, and shelled
6 skewers
12 very thin slices bacon
1/2 cup butter, melted
1 1/2 cups Tomato Sauce [No. 19], or substitute
    Marinara Sauce with Red Wine [No. 42]

Run a skewer through one end of 2 slices of bacon, allowing the bacon to dangle free; run the skewer through 8 mussels; stretch the bacon slices over the mussels so that they are almost entirely encased; and spear the other ends of the bacon securely on the skewer. Repeat until 6 skewers are filled. Brush them with melted butter and broil under a high broiler flame, turning the skewers occasionally, until the bacon is fully cooked and beginning to crisp. Transfer the skewers to a hot serving platter and serve the tomato or Marinara sauce separately. *Serves 6.*

Mussels Ammiraglia (No. 1019)

343

1020. CREAMED MUSSELS
Cozze alla crema

48 large mussels, scrubbed and soaked
½ cup dry red wine
4 tablespoons chopped parsley
2 stalks of celery, finely sliced
1 bay leaf
2 tablespoons chopped onion
2 cups heavy cream
3 tablespoons Kneaded Butter [No. 107]
Freshly ground pepper

Place the wine, 2 tablespoons parsley, the celery, bay leaf, and onion in a large heavy pot. Add the mussels, cover the pot tightly, bring to a boil over high heat, and shake the pot for a few minutes until the mussel shells open. Pour the contents of the pot into a colander placed over a bowl, drain all of the liquid from the mussels into the bowl, and place the mussels in another bowl in a warm place. Strain the liquid through several thicknesses of cheesecloth, return it to the pot, bring to a boil over high heat, and reduce to ½ its quantity. There should be about ¾ cup. Add the cream, bring just to a boil, blend in the kneaded butter with a whisk, reduce the heat, and simmer for 5 minutes. Grate a generous amount of pepper into the sauce, correct the seasoning, add the mussels in their shells, and heat for 2 minutes. Pour the mussels and the sauce into a shallow serving bowl and sprinkle with the remaining chopped parsley. *Serves 6.*

1021. FRIED MUSSELS
Cozze fritte

48 raw mussels, scrubbed, soaked, and shelled
3 eggs beaten
Fresh breadcrumbs, seasoned with salt and pepper
Fat for deep frying
12 sprigs parsley, fried in deep fat [*see* No. 276]
3 lemons, quartered
2 cups Tomato Sauce [No. 19], or substitute
    Tartar Sauce [No. 98]

Dip the mussels in beaten egg and then in breadcrumbs. Fry them in deep hot (375°) fat until golden brown, drain them on absorbent paper, and heap them on a hot serving platter. Garnish with the fried parsley and the lemon quarters and serve the tomato or tartar sauce on the side. *Serves 6.*

1022. MUSSELS MARINARA
Cozze "à la marinière"

48 mussels, scrubbed and soaked
½ cup butter, softened
4 tablespoons chopped parsley
1 tablespoon chopped shallots
Bouquet Garni:
    2 sprigs thyme (or ¼ teaspoon dried)
    1 bay leaf
1 cup dry white wine
Freshly ground pepper

Melt 3 tablespoons of the butter in a large heavy pot and add the parsley, shallots, Bouquet Garni, wine, and the mussels. Cover the pot, bring to a boil over high heat, and shake the pan for a few minutes until the mussel shells open. Remove the pot from the heat, discard the top shell of each mussel, and place the bottom shells with their mussels in a hot, shallow serving bowl. Bring the cooking liquid to a boil, season lightly with pepper, discard the Bouquet Garni, remove from the heat, and swirl in the remaining butter, bit by bit. Allow the sauce to sit for a moment so that any bits of grit will sink to the bottom and pour almost all of it over the mussels. *Serves 6.*

NOTE: The cooking liquid may be strained through several thicknesses of cheesecloth prior to bringing it to a boil again. In this case, return the Bouquet Garni to the liquid until it is time to remove it as indicated.

1023. NYMPHET'S MUSSELS
Cozze ninfetta

48 mussels, scrubbed, soaked, and opened on
    the half shell
½ cup butter
A chopped mixture:
    2 cloves garlic
    3 sprigs oregano (or ½ teaspoon dried)
    3 sprigs parsley
1½ cups fresh breadcrumbs
Dash Worcestershire sauce
Juice of 1 lemon
Salt and freshly ground pepper

Melt the butter in a frying pan over medium heat and add the chopped mixture, breadcrumbs, and Worcestershire sauce. Add the mussels and stir them gently for a few minutes until they become a good orange color. Turn them out into a hot serving dish, season lightly with salt and pepper, and sprinkle with the lemon juice. *Serves 6.*

1024. PARISIAN MUSSELS
Cozze alla parigina

48 large mussels, scrubbed and soaked
2 cups dry white wine
2 tablespoons finely chopped shallots
1 teaspoon chopped thyme (or ½ teaspoon dried)
1 bay leaf
3 tablespoons Kneaded Butter [No. 107]
1 tablespoon chopped parsley
Juice of ½ lemon
Freshly ground pepper
6 sprigs parsley

Place 1 cup of the wine, 1 tablespoon of the shallots, the thyme, bay leaf, and the mussels in a large heavy pot. Cover the pot, bring to a boil over high heat, and shake the pot for a few minutes until the shells open. Pour the contents of the pot into a colander placed over a bowl and extract the mussels from their shells, allowing any liquid to drain into the bowl. Keep the mussels warm in another bowl. Strain the liquid through several thicknesses of cheesecloth into a saucepan, add the remaining wine and shallots, bring to a boil over high heat, and reduce to about 2½ cups. Blend in the kneaded butter with a whisk, add the chopped parsley, and simmer for 5 minutes. Season with the pepper and lemon juice. Place the mussels on a hot serving dish, cover with the sauce, and garnish with the parsley sprigs. *Serves 6.*

1025. MUSSELS PROVENÇALE
Cozze alla provenzale

48 large raw mussels, scrubbed, soaked, and opened
    on the half shell
1 cup cooked snails (*see* page 349)
1 cup butter, softened
1½ cups fresh breadcrumbs

Pound the snail meat in a mortar until it is a paste and then blend in the softened butter, a little at a time (or whirl ingredients in the blender for 10 seconds). Spread a generous spoonful over each mussel on the halfshell, sprinkle each with breadcrumbs, arrange them in a large roasting pan, and place the pan in a very hot (450°) oven for about 8 minutes, or until the tops are golden brown. *Serves 6.*

OYSTERS
Ostriche

The oyster season starts the first of September and ends at the close of April, and thus a popular saying has evolved about consuming oysters during "R" months, especially January, when oysters are really at their best.

There are many different kinds of oysters. In England, the best are the Colchester and Whitstable Natives. In France, among the best oysters are the Marennes, the Belons, and the flat ones called Armoricaines. Also French are the so-called Portugaises, which were originally taken from the mouth of the Tagus, near Lisbon. In Marennes they have succeeded in growing the so-called *Portugaises claires*, which have an especially delicious flavor. The main Italian center for oyster breeding is the Mare Piccolo at Taranto. From there, the young oysters are taken to Lake Fusaro for their final growth.

In America, the native Indians enjoyed enormous wild oysters, some over a foot long, but after civilization developed, the natural beds were gradually exhausted. Today, cultivated oyster beds extend offshore from Massachusetts to Texas, as well as off the Pacific coast states. Until recently, half of the oysters consumed in this country came from Long Island Sound and Chesapeake Bay, but production there, especially in the Chesapeake, has fallen off. At this writing, the south Jersey coast is supplying most of the oysters, with some from Virginia waters and from Gardiner's Bay off Long Island, and a smaller quantity from the Eastern Shore of Maryland, while Cape Cod supplies the balance.

Formerly, their names indicated the source of the oyster, but now they more frequently refer to the size. "Blue Points" were oysters originating off Blue Point, Long Island, in Great South Bay, but now the name means a small, four-year old oyster served on the half shell. "Cape Cods" now mean medium or large (also known as "Box" or "Primes"). "Lynnhaven" is a long-tongued Virginia oyster, also sometimes called a "Box." Another big Virginia oyster is the "Chincoteague," from the bay of the same name. Oyster fanciers who favor shellfish raised in cold waters have spurred the importation of "Malpeques" from Prince Edward Island of Canada.

New York oyster lovers insist that the oysters raised in the Gulf of Mexico cannot compare with northern bivalves because the water is too warm and not salty enough, but New Orleans shellfish fanciers enjoy Louisiana oysters, including those bred near Pascagoula, near the mouth of the Mississippi, and "Bayou" oysters. Texans around Corpus Christi are proud of their "Texas Blue Points." In California, there are beds of "California Eastern" oysters, transplanted from Long Island. Off the Oregon coast large but not particularly tasty "Willapoints" are grown, having been relaid from Japan. The tiny "Olympics" of Washington State are considered the best of the Pacific oysters.

Shucking oysters can be a time-consuming chore, unless one is experienced at it. A small shucking knife is forced between the 2 shells at the thin edge of the oyster, the strong muscle attached to the shell is cut, and the 2 shell halves forced apart with a twisting motion of the knife. A fish dealer will always shuck oysters for you, but they are at their best if opened and served immediately, arranged on a bed of chopped ice, in the deeper of their shell halves. They may be served with slices of buttered rye bread, lemon quarters, and freshly ground or crushed pepper. They are also delicious when served with a sauce of scallions which have been finely chopped and mixed with white wine vinegar, salt, and freshly ground pepper.

1026. CURRIED OYSTERS ON THE HALF SHELL
Conchiglie di ostriche al curry

36 oysters, shucked (reserving the bottom shells)
1 cup heavy cream
1 tablespoon curry powder
1 cup fresh breadcrumbs
Salt and freshly ground pepper

Place the oysters and their liquid in a saucepan, bring just to a boil over medium heat, and remove immediately from the fire. Drain them in a sieve placed over a bowl and keep them warm. Strain the liquid through several thicknesses of cheesecloth into the saucepan, add the cream and curry powder, and simmer for 5 minutes. Correct the seasoning. Return the oysters to their warmed shells, spoon a little of the sauce over each, sprinkle with breadcrumbs, and place them in a moderate (350°) oven for about 5 minutes, or until the tops are golden. *Serves 6.*

Chervil

1027. OYSTER FRITTERS
Bignè di ostriche all'italiana

36 oysters, shucked
Fritter Batter [No. 275]
3 lemons, quartered
2 cups Tomato Sauce [No. 19]
Fat for deep frying

Put the oysters and their liquid into a saucepan, bring just to a boil over medium heat, and remove from the fire immediately. Allow them to cool in the cooking liquid, drain them, dry on absorbent paper, dip them in fritter batter, and fry in deep hot (375°) fat until golden brown. Heap them on a serving platter, garnish with the lemon quarters, and serve the tomato sauce separately. *Serves 6.*

SCALLOPS
Conchiglie Saint-Jacques

The scallop is a salt-water mollusk with a fluted shell. It is particularly abundant along the northern and middle Atlantic coast of the United States. Larger scallops are usually known as sea scallops, and the smaller ones, greatly prized by many for their tender, sweet flesh, are known as bay scallops. They are normally sold already shelled and cleaned by fish dealers. However, if the occasion arises when you must shell them, place them on the lowest rack of a very slow oven for a few minutes until the shells open; remove the scallop from the shell and trim off the beard and any black parts, leaving only the white flesh, which is the edible part. The shells, larger ones particularly, should be scrubbed and boiled and retained permanently as attractive serving containers.

Throughout the succeeding recipes the cooking times specified are for sea scallops. If bay scallops are used, the cooking time should be reduced by approximately one half.

1028. SCALLOPS ARMORICAINE
Conchiglie Saint-Jacques à l'armoricaine

2 pounds scallops
6 tablespoons butter
1 carrot, thinly sliced
1 onion, chopped
2 shallots, chopped
2 cups dry white wine

Bouquet Garni:
   1 bay leaf
   2 sprigs parsley
   2 sprigs thyme (or ½ teaspoon dried)
3 tomatoes, peeled, seeded, drained, and sliced
½ cup heavy cream
1 tablespoon chopped chervil (or 1 teaspoon dried)
1 tablespoon chopped tarragon (or 1 teaspoon dried)
Salt and freshly ground white pepper

Melt 3 tablespoons of the butter in a heavy saucepan over medium heat; add the carrot, onion, and shallots; and cook until very soft but not browned. Add the scallops, stir for 1 minute, season lightly with salt and pepper, and then add the wine, Bouquet Garni, and tomatoes. Season lightly again, cover the pan, bring to a boil, reduce the heat, and simmer for 10 minutes. Remove the scallops to a hot serving dish, cut them in half, if desired, and keep them warm. Reduce the cooking liquid over high heat to ½ its quantity, discard the Bouquet Garni, and strain the sauce through a very fine sieve, pressing through as much of the vegetables as possible (or blend for a few seconds in the electric blender). Return the sauce to the saucepan, add the cream, simmer for 5 minutes, correct the seasoning, and add the chopped herbs. Remove from the heat, swirl in the remaining butter, bit by bit, and pour over the scallops. *Serves* 6.

NOTE: If dried herbs are used, add them with the cream.

1029. SCALLOPS BÉARNAISE
Conchiglie Saint-Jacques béarnaise

2 pounds scallops, cut into ½-inch slices
2 eggs, beaten
Breadcrumbs
½ cup Clarified Butter [No. 102]
6 sprigs parsley, fried in deep fat [*see* No. 276]
6 scallop shells
2 cups Sauce Béarnaise [No. 67]
Salt and freshly ground white pepper

Season the scallop slices lightly with salt and pepper, dip them in egg, roll them in breadcrumbs, and sauté them until golden brown in the clarified butter in a frying pan over fairly high heat. Arrange the slices in 6 hot scallop shells, garnish the top of each with a sprig of fried parsley, and serve at once with the Béarnaise passed separately. *Serves* 6.

Tarragon

1030. SCALLOPS BRETONNE
Conchiglie Saint-Jacques alla brettone

2 pounds scallops, cut into ½-inch slices
4 tablespoons butter
1½ cups dry white wine
2 tablespoons chopped parsley
1 cup Croûtons [No. 332]
4 tablespoons butter, melted
1 cup breadcrumbs
Salt and freshly ground white pepper
6 large scallop shells

Melt 4 tablespoons of butter in a heavy saucepan over medium heat, add the scallops, season lightly with salt and pepper, stir for 1 minute, and then add the wine, parsley, and croûtons. Cover the pan tightly, bring to a boil, reduce the heat, and simmer for 8 minutes. Portion the mixture out into 6 hot scallop shells, sprinkle with breadcrumbs and melted butter, and brown for 1 minute under a high broiler flame. *Serves* 6.

1031. SCALLOPS EN BROCHETTE
Spiedini di conchiglie Saint-Jacques

24 large scallops
6 skewers
18 large mushroom caps
12 slices bacon, parboiled for 5 minutes
¼ cup butter, melted
1 cup Maître d'Hôtel Butter [No. 111]
Salt and freshly ground pepper

Sauté the mushroom caps in 2 tablespoons of the butter in a frying pan over medium heat for 2 minutes. Wrap each scallop in a half slice of bacon. Arrange 3 mushroom caps and 4 scallops, alternately, on each of 6 skewers, season them with salt and pepper, and brush generously with butter. Place the skewers under a medium broiler flame, and broil for about 10 minutes, turning them often and basting with more butter. Arrange the skewers on a hot serving platter and serve the Maître d'Hôtel butter separately. *Serves* 6.

1032. CURRIED SCALLOPS
Conchiglie Saint-Jacques al curry

2 pounds scallops
½ cup butter
1 tablespoon chopped shallots
2 cups dry white wine
Bouquet Garni:
   1 bay leaf
   2 sprigs parsley
   2 sprigs thyme (or ½ teaspoon dried)
1 tablespoon curry powder
½ cup heavy cream
Salt and freshly ground pepper

Melt 4 tablespoons of the butter in a heavy saucepan over medium heat, add the shallots, cook until golden, add the scallops, and stir for 1 minute. Add the wine, Bouquet Garni, and curry powder. Cover the pan, bring to a boil, reduce the heat, and simmer for 10 minutes. Transfer the scallops to a hot serving dish, slice them in half, if desired, and keep warm. Reduce the cooking liquid to ½ its quantity, discard the Bouquet Garni, add the cream, simmer 3 minutes longer, correct the seasoning, and pour over the scallops. *Serves* 6.

1033. SCALLOP FRITTERS
Bignè di conchiglie Saint-Jacques

2 pounds scallops, cut into ½-inch slices
A marinade:
   ¾ cup oil
   ¼ cup lemon juice
   1 tablespoon chopped parsley
   1 teaspoon salt
   ¼ teaspoon pepper
Fritter Batter [No. 275]
Fat for deep frying
6 sprigs parsley, fried in deep fat [*see* No. 276]
3 lemons, quartered

Marinate the scallop slices in the marinade for 1 hour, drain, and dry the slices on absorbent paper. Dip them in fritter batter and fry in deep hot (375°) fat until golden brown. Arrange them on a hot serving platter and garnish with the fried parsley and lemon quarters. *Serves* 6.

1034. SCALLOPS GRAN SUCCESSO
Conchiglie Saint-Jacques gran successo

2 pounds scallops, coarsely chopped
¼ pound mushrooms, thinly sliced

2 tablespoons butter
4 egg yolks
½ cup cream
Pinch nutmeg
¼ cup brandy
1 cup fresh breadcrumbs
4 tablespoons butter, melted
6 scallop shells
Salt and freshly ground white pepper

Sauté the mushrooms in 2 tablespoons of the butter in a covered frying pan over very gentle heat for 8 minutes, stirring occasionally, and reserve. Mix the scallops with the egg yolks and cream in a bowl and season lightly with salt, pepper, and nutmeg. Heat the brandy, ignite it, and pour it into the mixture. Place a layer of the mushrooms in the scallop shells, sprinkle lightly with breadcrumbs, cover with the scallop mixture, sprinkle with breadcrumbs and melted butter, and place the filled shells in a hot (400°) oven for about 8 minutes, or until bubbling and the tops are golden. *Serves* 6.

1035. SCALLOPS MORNAY
Conchiglie Saint-Jacques Mornay

2 pounds scallops, sliced ½-inch thick
4 tablespoons butter
2 cups hot Duchesse Potatoes [No. 1771]
1 egg, beaten
2 cups Sauce Mornay [No. 56]
½ cup grated Parmesan cheese
6 scallop shells
Salt and freshly ground white pepper

Melt the butter in a frying pan over medium heat, add the scallop slices, season lightly with salt and pepper, and sauté for about 3 minutes on each side. Using a pastry bag fitted with a star tip, pipe a border of the potatoes around the edge of the scallop shells and brush with beaten egg. Combine the scallop slices with the Mornay sauce, fill each shell with the mixture, sprinkle with grated cheese, and place in a hot (400°) oven for about 10 minutes, or until the mixture bubbles and the tops are brown. *Serves* 6.

1036. PARISIAN SCALLOPS
Conchiglie Saint-Jacques alla parigina

Prepare as described in the preceding recipe, substituting Duxelles Sauce [No. 31] for the Mornay.

348

1037. SCALLOPS SACHA GUITRY
Conchiglie Saint-Jacques "Sacha Guitry"

2 pounds scallops
6 tablespoons butter
½ pound mushrooms, sliced
1 clove garlic, crushed in the garlic-press
1 tablespoon chopped parsley
¾ cup dry sherry wine
Salt and freshly ground pepper

Melt 3 tablespoons of the butter in a frying pan over fairly high heat, add the scallops, season with salt and pepper, and brown them for about 3 minutes. Add the mushrooms, garlic, and parsley. Cover the pan, reduce the heat, and simmer for 5 minutes longer, shaking the pan occasionally. Transfer the scallops and mushrooms with a slotted spoon to a hot serving dish and keep warm. Add the sherry to the liquid in the pan and quickly reduce over high heat to about ½ its quantity. Remove from the heat, swirl in the remaining butter, bit by bit, and pour over the scallops. *Serves 6.*

SNAILS

Lumache o chiocciole

Snails have for centuries been considered a gastronomic delicacy in Europe and are just now becoming popular in the United States. They are commercially raised and fattened on various greens and they take approximately 3 years to reach an edible size of about 1 inch in diameter. Live snails must be purged (frequently this has already been done before purchasing) and very thoroughly cleaned, as described below, before cooking. Snails are also commercially available in cans, and cleaned snail shells are sold in packages.

Purging and basic preparation of live snails:
   Place several dozen live snails in a wicker basket with the loose leaves of 2 heads of lettuce and several slices of bread which have been soaked in water and wrung dry. Cover the basket and allow it to stand for 3 days. Remove snails from the basket, wash them under running water, and then soak them for 2 hours in a large enamel pot of cold water acidulated with 1 cup of vinegar and a handful of coarse salt. Drain them and put them through several changes of cold water until the water is absolutely clear. Drain again and discard any snails whose heads are not out of the shell. Place them in a pot, cover with cold water, and bring slowly to a boil over moderate heat. Simmer for 5 minutes and then drain them in a colander. Remove the snails from the shells and reserve the shells. Cut off the tips of the heads and the black part on their tail ends. Return them to the pot and cover with a generous amount of Court Bouillon [No. 764]. Season very lightly with salt, add 2 sliced cloves of garlic, bring very slowly to a boil, and simmer for 3 to 4 hours. Drain and dry them on a cloth.

   Do not, under any circumstances, prepare live snails that have not been purged and cleaned in this manner, as this process rids them of all poisonous vegetation (harmless to snails) that they may have ingested.

1038. SNAILS BOURGUIGNONNE
Lumache alla bourguignonne

6 dozen large live snails, cleaned and cooked as
    described in the introduction (or substitute
    canned snails)
2 cups butter, softened
4 shallots, finely chopped
2 tablespoons chopped parsley
3 cloves garlic, crushed in the garlic-press
1 teaspoon salt
¼ teaspoon freshly ground pepper
½ cup butter, melted
½ cup fresh breadcrumbs

Cream the softened butter with the shallots, parsley, garlic, salt, and pepper. Put a small amount of this butter in each snail shell, insert the snails, and cover the opening with a generous amount of the butter. Sprinkle with breadcrumbs and melted butter and arrange the snails on individual snail plates or on a baking sheet. Place them in a hot (400°) oven for about 10 minutes, or until the tops are golden. Serve them at once. *Serves 6.*

1039. SNAILS WITH CHEESE ITALIANA
Lumache al formaggio all'italiana

Prepare as the preceding recipe, adding ½ cup grated Parmesan cheese to the creamed butter mixture.

1040. SNAILS GENOVESE
Lumache alla genovese

6 dozen large live snails, cleaned and cooked as
   described in the introduction (or substitute
   canned snails)
Salt
Flour
1 cup oil
3 lemons, quartered

Dry the cooked snails on a cloth, season them lightly
with salt, dust them with flour, and sauté them in hot
oil in a large frying pan over high heat until they are
golden brown. Heap them on a hot serving platter and
garnish with the lemon quarters. *Serves* 6.

1041. SNAILS ROMANA
Lumache alla romana

6 dozen large live snails, cleaned and cooked as
   described in the introduction (or substitute
   canned snails)
4 tablespoons olive oil
4 cloves garlic, crushed in the garlic-press
3 tablespoons chopped parsley
12 anchovy fillets, washed free of salt [*see* No. 220]
   and chopped
6 tomatoes, peeled, seeded, drained, and chopped
1 yellow pepper, roasted, scraped, seeded, and cut
   into strips [*see* No. 145]
Optional: 1 teaspoon chopped mint
Salt and freshly ground pepper

Heat the oil in a large casserole over medium heat,
add the garlic, cook until golden, and add the parsley,
anchovies, tomatoes, yellow pepper, and optional mint.
Season with salt and pepper and simmer for 30 minutes.
Add the snails, cook for 3 minutes longer, and serve
in the casserole. *Serves* 6.

1042. SNAIL FRITTERS WITH TOMATO SAUCE
Bignè di lumache con salsa di pomodoro

6 dozen large live snails, cleaned and cooked as
   described in the introduction (or substitute
   canned snails)
A marinade:
   1 cup oil
   ¼ cup lemon juice
   2 tablespoons chopped parsley
   1 teaspoon salt
   ¼ teaspoon freshly ground pepper
Fritter Batter [No. 275]
Fat for deep frying
12 sprigs parsley, fried in deep fat [*see* No. 276]
3 lemons, quartered
3 cups Tomato Sauce [No. 19]

Marinate the snails in the marinade for 1 hour. Drain
them, pat dry on paper towels, dip them in the fritter
batter, and fry in deep hot (375°) fat until golden
brown. Arrange them on a hot serving platter, garnish
with the lemon quarters and fried parsley, and serve
the tomato sauce on the side. *Serves* 6.

FISH SOUPS OR STEWS
Zuppe di pesce

1043. ADRIATIC FISH SOUP
Brodetto delle coste adriatiche

3 pounds several kinds of fish, such as are used in
   Bouillabaisse [No. 1044]
½ cup oil
1 tablespoon chopped onion
2 cloves garlic, crushed in the garlic-press
2 sprigs thyme (or ¼ teaspoon dried)
2 sprigs sage (or ¼ teaspoon dried)
1 bay leaf, crumbled
¼ small red pepper
½ cup dry white wine

*Snails Bourguignonne (No. 1038),
shown before they are placed in the oven:
see page 349*

1 pound tomatoes, peeled, seeded, drained, and chopped
2 cups water
⅛ cup white wine vinegar
18 slices of dried bread, crusts removed, sautéed
    in oil until golden
Salt and freshly ground pepper

Cut the fish into thick 2-inch slices. Heat the oil in a large, heavy pot over medium heat and add the onion, garlic, thyme, sage, bay leaf, and red pepper. Cook until the onion is transparent, add the wine, and cook until almost evaporated. Add the tomatoes, season with salt and pepper, add the water and vinegar, and boil for 10 minutes. Press the mixture through a fine strainer into a bowl, extracting as much of the tomatoes as possible. Return it to the pot, add the more firmly fleshed fish [*see* No. 1044], cover the pot tightly, bring to a boil, reduce the heat, and cook for 8 minutes. Add any tender fish and cook for 8 minutes longer. Transfer the pieces of fish to a hot serving bowl, correct the seasoning of the soup, and pour over the fish. Serve the sautéed slices of bread on the side. *Serves 6.*

1044. BOUILLABAISSE
Bouillabaisse

This is the famous fish soup of Marseilles. It is a splendidly hearty dish and may be made as elaborate and with as many different kinds of fish as the cook desires, but classically it is a simple fishermen's soup originally made with the unsalable leftovers from the day's catch. The varieties of fish should include very firmly fleshed fish, as well as tender, flaky types, and shellfish. Since the special flavor of a good Bouillabaisse comes from using different types of fish in one dish, it is best saved for occasions when a large number of persons are to be served.

Firmly fleshed fish:
    1 pound Spanish mackerel
    1 pound red snapper
    1 pound sea bass
    1 pound halibut (or winter flounder)
    1 pound eel
Tender fish:
    1 pound mullet (or perch)
    1 pound fresh cod, from the tail end
Shellfish:
    12 mussels, scrubbed
    12 soft-shell clams
    2 2-pound lobsters
Boiling water, lightly salted
1 cup oil
2 onions, chopped

2 leeks (white part only), chopped
4 cloves garlic, crushed in the garlic-press
1 tablespoon powdered saffron
1 teaspoon fennel seeds, crushed in the mortar
2 tablespoons chopped parsley
5 ripe tomatoes, peeled, seeded, drained, and chopped
Salt and freshly ground pepper
18 slices oven-dried French or Italian bread

Cut all of the fish, except the mussels and the clams, into 2-inch slices. Heat the oil in a very large (10-quart or larger) earthenware (or enamel) pot; add the onions, leeks, and garlic; and cook until transparent. Add the saffron, fennel, parsley, and tomatoes. Stir for 1 minute, spread the pieces of lobster on top of the mixture, arrange the firmly fleshed fish on top of these, and cover them generously with boiling water. Bring back to a boil, reduce the heat, and simmer for 8 minutes. Add the mullet, cod, clams, and mussels, bring back to a boil, and simmer for 8 minutes longer. As quickly as possible transfer all of the fish to a large, hot serving dish. Correct the seasoning of the soup, arrange the sliced bread in a tureen, and pour the soup over them. The fish should not be allowed to remain in the hot soup, as it will overcook. Serve each guest a selection of the fish in a deep soup bowl and ladle a generous amount of the soup into it. *Serves 12.*

Some popular fish used in
Italian fish stews (many are exclusively Mediterranean)

1045. BRETON COTRIADE
Cotriade

Cotriade is the famous fish soup of Brittany. Like Bouillabaisse, the more different kinds of fish used in it, the more its flavor is enhanced.

1 pound sardines
1 pound mackerel
1 pound conger eel, skinned
1 pound mullet
1 pound halibut
1 pound fresh cod, cut from the tail end
$\frac{1}{2}$ cup lard
3 cloves garlic, crushed in the garlic-press
2 onions, sliced
Bouquet Garni:
   2 sprigs thyme (or $\frac{1}{4}$ teaspoon dried)
   2 sprigs parsley
   1 bay leaf
Boiling water, lightly salted
6 potatoes, peeled and quartered
Salt and freshly ground pepper
$\frac{1}{2}$ cup oil
Juice of 2 lemons

Cut all of the fish, except the sardines, into 2-inch slices. Melt the lard in a large earthenware (or enamel) pot over medium heat, add the garlic and onions, and cook until golden. Add the Bouquet Garni, potatoes, mackerel, eel, mullet, halibut, and sufficient boiling water to generously cover the potatoes and fish. Bring to a boil, reduce the heat, and simmer for 8 minutes. Add the sardines and cod, bring to a boil again, and simmer for another 8 minutes. Test the potatoes for doneness and cook a little longer if necessary. Carefully transfer the pieces of fish and the potatoes to a shallow serving bowl, season them lightly with salt and pepper, squeeze the lemon juice over them, and pour over the oil. Discard the Bouquet Garni, correct the seasoning of the broth, and serve it separately in a warm tureen. *Serves* 10.

1046. FISH SOUP CASALINGA
Zuppa di pesce per famiglia

1 pound squid
1 pound eels, skinned
1 pound skate
1 pound sea bass
$\frac{1}{2}$ cup oil
1 tablespoon chopped onion
3 cloves garlic, crushed in the garlic-press

4 anchovy fillets, washed free of salt [*see* No. 220]
   and pounded to a paste in the mortar
2 quarts Fish Fumet [No. 2]
Bouquet Garni:
   1 carrot, sliced
   1 stalk celery, sliced
   $\frac{1}{2}$ bay leaf
2 tablespoons chopped parsley
4 tomatoes, peeled, seeded, drained, and chopped
Salt and freshly ground pepper
12 slices bread, browned in the oven

Cut the squid into strips and the other fish into 2-inch slices. Heat the oil in a large earthenware (or enamel) pot over medium heat, add the onion and garlic, and cook until golden. Add the anchovy paste and stir for a few seconds. Add the Fumet, parsley, Bouquet Garni, and tomatoes. Season lightly with salt and pepper, bring to a boil, add the squid and skate, reduce the heat, cover the pot, and cook for 15 minutes. Add the eels and sea bass and cook for 10 minutes longer. Check each of the fish for doneness and cook a little longer, if necessary. Arrange the toast in a large tureen, place the pieces of fish over it, correct the seasoning of the broth, and pour over the fish. *Serves* 6.

1047. FISH SOUP CATTOLICA
Brodetto alla maniera di Cattolica

Cattolica is a very popular seaside resort on the Adriatic coast of Italy.

1 pound cuttlefish, cleaned and cut in large slices
1 pound rockfish (or rosefish, if available)
1 pound red snapper
1 pound sea bass
1 pound mullet
1 pound cod, cut from the tail end
$\frac{1}{2}$ pound shrimp, shelled and de-veined
1 cup oil
1 onion, chopped
4 cloves garlic, crushed in the garlic-press
4 tomatoes, peeled, seeded, drained, and chopped
2 tablespoons chopped parsley
2 cups water (or white wine)
Salt and freshly ground pepper
20 slices stale French bread, crusts removed, and
   sautéed in oil until golden

Cut all of the fish, except the shrimp, into 2-inch slices. Heat the oil in a very large earthenware (or enamel) pot over medium heat, add the onion and garlic,

SEE
VERSE
OR
TION

Bolliti Misti Italiana (No. 1078) served with all the appropriate condiments. At lower right is a bowl of *mostarda di frutta* (a mixture of fruits candied in a heavy syrup heavily spiced with hot oil of mustard—this is available in jars imported from Italy) and at lower left is a bowl of coarse (Kosher) salt.

and cook until golden. Add the tomatoes and parsley, season with salt and pepper, bring to a boil, and cook for 5 minutes. Add 2 cups of water and the cuttlefish, bring to a boil, reduce the heat, and simmer for 15 minutes. Add the rockfish and the red snapper, season again lightly with salt and pepper, cover the pot, and simmer for 5 minutes. Add the mullet, cod, sea bass, and shrimp, bring back to a boil, and simmer for 10 minutes longer. Place all of the fish in a hot serving bowl, correct the seasoning, allow the soup to cool slightly, and pour over the fish. Serve the sautéed slices of bread separately. *Serves* 10.

1048. CLAM SOUP NAPOLETANA
Zuppa di vongole alla napoletana

48 clams (steamers, if desired)
$\frac{1}{2}$ cup oil
2 cloves garlic, crushed in the garlic-press
1 cup dry white wine
6 cups Fish Fumet [No. 2]
4 peppercorns, crushed in the mortar
6 slices dried bread, crusts removed, sautéed in
    olive oil

Scrub the clams thoroughly under running water. Heat the oil in a heavy pot over high heat, add the garlic, cook until golden, add the wine, and cook until $\frac{1}{2}$ has evaporated. Add the clams and Fumet, cover the pot tightly, and shake the pot until the shells open. Put a slice of sautéed bread in each of 6 hot soup bowls, arrange 8 clams on each slice, strain the liquid in the pot through several thicknesses of cheesecloth, season it with the pepper, and pour a little of the liquid in each bowl. *Serves* 6.

1049. DRIED CODFISH SOUP ITALIANA
Zuppa di baccalà all'italiana

2 pounds dried cod, soaked for 12 hours in
    several changes of water (*see* page 268)
$\frac{1}{2}$ cup oil
2 onions, finely sliced
$\frac{1}{2}$ cup dry white wine
3 tomatoes, peeled, seeded, drained, and chopped
2 cloves garlic, bruised
Bouquet Garni:
  1 tablespoon celery leaves
  2 sprigs thyme (or $\frac{1}{4}$ teaspoon dried)
  1 bay leaf
  3 sprigs parsley

4 potatoes, peeled and thickly sliced
1 tablespoon chopped parsley
Salt and freshly ground pepper
24 slices bread, crusts removed, browned in the
    oven, and lightly rubbed with garlic

Remove all skin and bones from the pre-soaked cod and cut it into 2-inch slices. Heat the oil in a large earthenware (or enamel) pot over medium heat, add the onions, and cook until golden. Add the wine, tomatoes, garlic, and Bouquet Garni and cook until the wine has almost evaporated. Add the potatoes and sufficient water to cover them generously, season with salt and pepper, bring to boil, and cook for 15 minutes. Add the cod slices and the chopped parsley, bring back to a boil, reduce the heat, cover the pot, and cook for 8 to 10 minutes longer. Transfer the fish and potatoes to a large, deep serving dish, discard the garlic and Bouquet Garni, correct the seasoning of the soup, and pour over the fish. The slices of bread should be browned and rubbed with garlic just before serving. *Serves* 6.

1050. FROG SOUP
Zuppa di ranocchi alla campagnola

48 small whole frogs, skinned and cleaned
$\frac{1}{2}$ cup oil
A chopped mixture:
  2 sprigs thyme
  2 cloves garlic
  2 sprigs rosemary
  1 stalk celery
  1 sprig parsley
  1 bay leaf, crumbled
Pinch nutmeg
$\frac{1}{2}$ cup dry white wine
2 quarts cold water
Salt and freshly ground pepper
12 slices stale bread, sautéed in butter until golden
1 cup grated Parmesan cheese

Separate the frogs' legs from the bodies and set them aside until needed. Wash the bodies carefully, discard the innards, and chop them coarsely. Heat the oil in an earthenware (or enamel) pot over medium heat, add the chopped mixture, stir for 1 minute, add the frogs' bodies, and season lightly with salt, pepper, and nutmeg. Add the wine and cook until the wine has almost evaporated. Add 2 quarts of water, bring to a boil, reduce the heat, and cook for 1 hour. Strain through a fine sieve into a bowl, pressing as much of the frog meat through the sieve as possible. Return this liquid to the pot, add the frogs' legs, bring to a boil, and then simmer over moderate heat for about 15 minutes. Remove the legs with a slotted spoon, bone them, and return the meat from the legs to the pot. Cook over moderate heat only until very hot and correct the seasoning. Serve the soup in a tureen and pass the sautéed slices of bread and the cheese on the side. *Serves* 6.

NOTE: If whole frogs prove unavailable, the same amount of frogs' legs may be employed with equal success.

1051. FISH SOUP GENOVESE
Zuppa di pesce alla genovese

¾ pound each: conger eels, gray sole, mullet,
    cuttlefish, and squid
½ cup oil
1 onion, chopped
2 cloves garlic, crushed in the garlic-press
2 leeks, white part only, chopped
2 hearts of Boston lettuce, sliced
Bouquet Garni:
    2 sprigs thyme (or ¼ teaspoon dried)
    2 sprigs parsley
    1 bay leaf
½ cup dry white wine
4 anchovy fillets, washed free of salt [*see* No. 220],
    and pounded to a paste in the mortar

Fish Soup Cattolica (No. 1047): see page 352

354

1 quart boiling Fish Fumet [No. 2]
12 slices bread, crusts removed, browned in the oven
1 tablespoon chopped parsley
Salt and freshly ground pepper

Cut the cuttlefish and the squid into strips and cut the other fish into 2-inch slices. Heat the oil in a large earthenware (or enamel) pot over medium heat; add the onions, garlic, and leeks; and cook until transparent. Add the cuttlefish, squid, eels, sliced lettuce, and the Bouquet Garni; reduce the heat and cook very gently for 15 minutes, stirring occasionally. Add the wine and the anchovy paste and cook until the wine is reduced by ½. Add the sole, mullet, and Fumet; bring to a boil; and cook for about 10 minutes longer. Taste, and correct seasoning. Arrange the toast in the bottom of a large serving bowl, place the fish on top, correct the seasoning of the cooking liquid, pour it over the fish, and sprinkle with the parsley. *Serves* 6.

1052. FISH SOUP GOURMET
Zuppa di pesce del ghiottone

¾ pound each porgy, mullet, cod, and halibut
    (or any other desired fish in season)
2 pounds crayfish, lobster, or shrimp
2 pounds mussels, scrubbed, and "beards" removed
6 tablespoons butter
1 clove garlic, crushed in the garlic-press
1 onion, chopped
4 leeks (white part only), chopped
½ cup dry white wine
Bouquet Garni:
    2 sprigs thyme (or ¼ teaspoon dried)
    1 bay leaf
    2 sprigs parsley
    3 sprigs basil (or ½ teaspoon dried)
    1 sprig savory (or ½ teaspoon dried)
4 hearts Boston lettuce, sliced
2 quarts Fish Fumet [No. 2]
¼ cup oil
4 peppercorns, crushed
1 tablespoon chopped parsley
16 slices bread, crusts removed, browned in the oven
Salt and freshly ground pepper

Cut the porgy, mullet, cod, and halibut into 2-inch slices; peel and de-vein the shrimp or cut the lobster into 2-inch slices and remove its center vein. Melt the butter in a large earthenware (or enamel) pot over medium heat; add the garlic, onions, and leeks; and cook until golden. Add the wine, Bouquet Garni,

Fish Soup Napoletana (No. 1056): see page 356

lettuce, and all of the fish except the mussels. Season with salt and pepper and cook until the wine has almost evaporated. Add the Fumet, bring to a boil, reduce the heat, and simmer for another 10 minutes. While the fish are cooking, place the oil, peppercorns, and mussels in a tightly covered pot over high heat and shake the pot until the shells open. Pour the mussels and their liquid into a colander placed over a bowl, extract the mussels from their shells, and allow their liquid to drain into the bowl. Strain this liquid through several thicknesses of cheesecloth and add to the soup. Just before removing the soup from the fire, add the mussels. Arrange the toast in a large, shallow serving bowl, place the fish on top, discard the Bouquet Garni, correct the seasoning of the broth, pour over the fish, and sprinkle with parsley. *Serves* 8.

1053. MEDITERRANEAN FISH STEW
Caciucco delle coste mediterranee

3 pounds several kinds of fish (including shellfish)
½ cup oil
A paste pounded in the mortar:
   3 cloves garlic, peeled
   ¼ small red hot pepper
½ cup dry wine (either white or red)
1 pound tomatoes, peeled, seeded, drained, and puréed through a food mill
½ cup cold Fish Fumet [No. 2]
12 slices French or Italian bread, dried in the oven
Salt and freshly ground pepper

Cut the fish into 2-inch slices. Heat the oil in a large earthenware (or enamel) pot over medium heat, add the garlic/pepper paste, cook for 1 minute, add the wine, and cook until it has almost evaporated. Add the tomatoes, season with salt and pepper, cover the pot, reduce the heat, and simmer for 10 minutes. Add the more firmly fleshed fish, bring to a boil, and simmer for 8 minutes. Add any tender fish, season again lightly with salt and pepper, stir the fish gently into the tomatoes, bring to a boil, and simmer for another 8 minutes, covered. Remove the pot from the heat, add the cold Fumet to stop the cooking process, correct the seasoning, serve directly from the pot, and pass the plain, dried bread separately. *Serves* 6.

1054. FISHERMAN'S MUSSEL SOUP
Zuppa di cozze marinaia

48 mussels, scrubbed, and "beards" removed
¼ cup oil
2 cups dry white wine
2 cloves garlic, crushed in the garlic-press
2½ pounds tomatoes, peeled, seeded, drained, and chopped
1 tablespoon chopped oregano (or ½ teaspoon dried)
Salt and freshly ground pepper

Place the mussels and the oil in a tightly covered pot over high heat and shake the pot for a few minutes

355

until the shells open. Pour the mussels and the liquid in the pot into a colander placed over a bowl. Transfer the mussels in their shells to another bowl after first allowing any liquid in the shells to drain through the colander. Keep the mussels warm and strain the liquid through several thicknesses of cheesecloth. Put the mussel liquid, the wine, garlic, tomatoes, and oregano in an earthenware (or enamel) pot over fairly high heat, season with salt and pepper, and cook for 10 minutes, or until slightly thickened. Portion the soup out into 6 hot soup bowls and place 8 mussels in their shells in each bowl. Serve at once. *Serves 6.*

1055. MUSSEL SOUP MARINARA
Zuppa di cozze alla marinara

4 pounds fresh mussels, scrubbed
½ cup oil
1 tablespoon chopped onion
2 cloves garlic, crushed in the garlic-press
½ cup white wine
1 tablespoon chopped parsley
1 whole peppercorn, crushed in the mortar
12 slices bread, crusts removed, toasted

Heat the oil in a large, heavy pot over high heat, add the onions and garlic, and cook until they are a pale gold. Add the wine and parsley and season with the pepper. Cook until the wine has reduced by ½. Add the mussels, cover the pot tightly, and cook for a few minutes, just until the mussels open their shells; shake the pot fairly constantly to facilitate their opening. Arrange the slices of toast in 6 large, hot soup bowls. Portion out the mussels into the bowls and pour a little of the liquid in the pot into each, being careful not to pour it all, since the bottom may contain sand. *Serves 6.*

NOTE: The cooking liquid may be strained through a triple thickness of cheesecloth before pouring over the mussels. Also, if more "soup" is desired, a cup of Fish Fumet [No. 2] may be added with the mussels.

1056. FISH SOUP NAPOLETANA
Zuppa di pesce alla napoletana

¾ pound each gray sole fillets, sea bass, squid, and halibut
1 pound shrimp, shelled and de-veined
2 pounds mussels, scrubbed, and "beards" removed
1 pound clams
1 cup oil
1 onion, chopped
1 pound tomatoes, peeled, seeded, drained, and chopped
2 cloves garlic, finely sliced
2 quarts Fish Fumet [No. 2]
1 tablespoon chopped parsley
Salt and freshly ground pepper
12 slices bread, crusts removed, sautéed in oil until golden

Cut the squid into strips and cut the sole, bass, and halibut into 2-inch slices. Put ¼ cup of the oil with the mussels and clams in a tightly covered pot and shake the pot over high heat until the shells open. Pour the shellfish and their liquid into a colander placed over a bowl, remove the clams and mussels from their shells, and allow their liquid to drain into the bowl. Strain the liquid through several thicknesses of cheesecloth. Keep the mussels and clams warm in a covered bowl. Heat the remaining oil in a large earthenware (or enamel) pot over medium heat, add the onion, and cook until golden. Add the squid and the shellfish liquid, cover the pot, and cook for 10 minutes. Add the tomatoes and garlic, season with salt and pepper, and cook for another 5 minutes. Add the bass, halibut, sole, shrimp, and Fumet. Bring to a boil, reduce the heat, and simmer for about 10 minutes. Just before removing from the fire, add the parsley, mussels, and clams. Arrange the sautéed slices of bread in individual soup bowls, spoon a selection of the fish into each, correct the seasoning of the broth, and ladle a little broth into each bowl. Serve the remaining broth in a tureen. *Serves 6 to 8.*

MEATS

MEATS
Carni

European methods of grading and cutting meats vary considerably from American practices. In general, the European method is to cut meats according to the natural muscle separations; American butchers cut meats across the grain. Throughout this section we have recommended American cuts that are the closest equivalent to the European, or, more specifically, to the Italian.

In the United States, meats are graded and clearly marked into the following categories: Prime, Choice, Good, Standard, Commercial, and Utility. This system of grading is an indication not only of flavor and tenderness, but of the fat content in the meat. A Prime cut of beef, for instance, will be bright red and well marbled with fat, as well as having a thick layer of white fat around it. The same cut from the other grades will contain a decreasing proportion of fat and will be proportionately less tender and flavorful. It is always wise to use a better grade of meat for the simpler methods of cooking, such as roasting, broiling, or sautéeing, since the meat is cooked and eaten virtually in its natural state. Braising or stewing, however, will tenderize the lower grades of meats and, when simmered with vegetables and other seasonings, their flavor can be improved. In this same sense, it is important to choose the right cut of meat, as well as the right grade, for the right dish. The more tender cuts and those with less connective tissues from the loin or rib section are at their best when simply roasted, broiled, or sautéed. The tougher cuts from the shoulder, neck, or breast are better for braising or stewing, not only because they need slow tenderizing in liquid, but also because their flavor is usually stronger and can withstand slow simmering.

All meats are aged for varying lengths of time before being marketed. This aging process relaxes the fabric of the flesh and thus makes it more tender. Hence, when one speaks of a "ripe" steak, it is from a cut that has been properly aged for the maximum length of time before spoilage has set in. It is not recommended that this aging process be extended in the home refrigerator, chiefly because of the lack of proper ventilation. One's best guarantee of well-aged meat lies in a reliable butcher. If meat is to be stored for any length of time in the refrigerator, always leave it loosely wrapped to allow air to circulate around it.

The various methods of cooking meats—such as roasting, boiling, broiling, sautéeing, braising, and stewing—are discussed in the author's introduction, at the beginning of this book. Except for some dishes of boiled or stewed meats, Italian culinary practice nearly always requires meats to be first seared by high heat to seal in the juices before proceeding with the full cooking. Thus, a roast is always browned in a hot oven for about 15 minutes, the heat is then reduced, and the cooking completed in a moderate oven. Meats to be braised are always first browned in very hot fat and then are slowly simmered with liquid in a tightly covered pot. When meats are browned in fat, it is important that the fat be just hot enough for the meat to brown quickly, but the heat should be adjusted during the browning process to avoid burning the fat; if the fat does burn, it should be discarded at the end of the browning process and fresh butter or oil added to the cooking utensil before proceeding. Equally important in this browning process is that pieces of meat should not be crowded in a pan so that they steam or stew, rather than being quickly seared. If a large number of pieces of meat are to be browned, do only a few at a time, remove them with a slotted spoon as they become brown, and then add fresh pieces to the pan; or, alternatively, use 2 pans with slightly more fat, in order to brown them all at once.

Personal preference must, to some extent, dictate the cooking times for meat. In general, Italians prefer meat slightly less well done than most Americans. Thus the cooking times given in some of the following recipes may seem slightly short to some tastes. The times given in many of the beef recipes, for instance, are for medium rare. These cooking times should be increased slightly if your preference is for well-done meat. It must be remembered, however, that none of the specified cooking times can be absolutely exact, since the timing will depend far more on the thickness of a cut of meat than on the actual poundage. Instinct, which can become one of the joys of cooking, must partly guide you in cooking meats to the desired degree of doneness. A meat thermometer can be a useful tool, if absolute accuracy is the goal.

Carving can seem a chore, especially to the cook, who often feels that once the roast is on the table labor might well be shared at this point and someone else should face up to the task of carving. Whoever the carver may be, the one essential is a razor-sharp knife. Carving with a dull knife can never be anything but hacking. It is also helpful if a roast is allowed to rest after cooking for at least 15 minutes before it is carved. This resting allows the juices to retreat into the tissues, and the meat will have a firmer texture. Large roasts can sit for as long as 30 minutes out of the oven and still retain their heat.

Meat should nearly always be cut across the grain. If you are cutting down to a bone, such as in a leg of lamb, it is simpler to cut the desired number of uniform slices down to the bone without detaching them and then cut from the underside to free them all at once from the bone. Carving is actually not nearly the mystery it seems to the uninitiated and even the briefest acquaintance with animal anatomy can make it not only simple, but a pleasure, when one learns to do it with precision and, above all, dispatch.

Specific cuts of meats are called by a variety of names in different parts of the United States. Throughout this section, we have called the various cuts by what are, hopefully, their most commonly used and, hence, their most easily recognizable names.

1057. WHITE FOUNDATION FOR MEATS
Bianco speciale per carni

3 tablespoons flour
1 quart cold water
1 medium carrot, sliced
1 medium onion, stuck with 1 clove
Bouquet Garni:
   3 sprigs parsley
   2 sprigs thyme (or ¼ teaspoon dried)
   1 bay leaf
2 teaspoons salt

Mix the flour and an equal amount of water to a smooth paste in saucepan. Gradually add the remaining water, stirring constantly to prevent lumps. Add the remaining ingredients and simmer the mixture over medium heat for 15 minutes. It is now ready for cooking variety meats such as calf's head, kidneys, etc. *Makes* 1 *quart.*

BEEF
Bue

The best beef comes from young steers from 4 to 5 years old. After slaughter, the beef is aged from 2 to 6 weeks. This aging process is, if anything, more important for beef than for other meats. All of the previous remarks about meat in general apply specifically to beef.

Choosing the correct cut of beef for a particular dish can be a problem for an inexperienced cook. While it is wise to be guided by a helpful butcher, it is even wiser to begin to familiarize oneself with the various cuts and the cooking methods best applied to them. As experience grows and one's taste for the various cuts becomes educated, much waste of effort and money can be saved. It is foolish, for instance, to use an expensive cut of high-grade beef to simmer for hours in a stew; the results will not only prove to be a waste of money, but the beef will be disappointingly dry and lacking in flavor. In all of the recipes that follow, we are recommending specific cuts that are well adapted to, and most enhanced by, the flavorings and techniques involved.

359

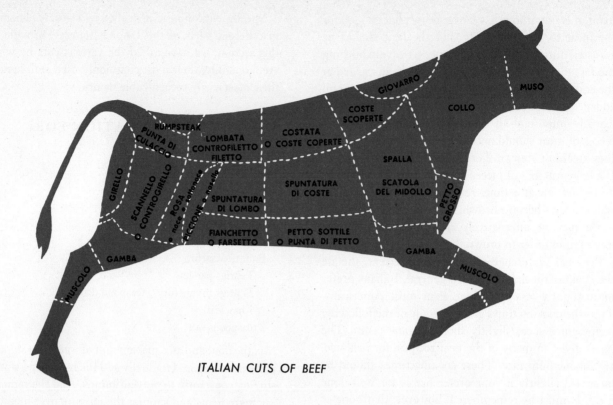

ITALIAN CUTS OF BEEF

1058. BEEF "BIRDS"
Uccelli scappati

12 thin slices sirloin, about ¼ inch thick
12 thin slices prosciutto (fat and lean)
24 sage leaves
24 small rectangles of stale bread, the same size
    as the beef "birds"
24 small thin rectangles of very lean salt pork,
    parboiled for 15 minutes
½ cup melted butter
6 sprigs parsley
Salt and freshly ground pepper

Flatten the slices of beef with the flat side of a meat
cleaver as thinly as possible, being careful not to break
through them. Cut these slices in half, season them
lightly with salt and pepper, and on each put a half
slice of prosciutto and a sage leaf. Roll each up and tie
securely with a string. The rolls should be about 2½
inches long, about the size of a small sausage. Arrange
4 of the rolls on each of 6 skewers, alternating each roll
with a piece of bread and a slice of salt pork. Brush
very generously with butter and broil them under a
medium broiler flame for about 5 minutes on each side,
or slightly longer if the rolls are very thick. Arrange
them on a hot serving platter and garnish with the
parsley. *Serves 6.*

1059. BEEF BRACIOLA
Braciola di manzo farcita

1 pound rump of beef, cut in one flat slice
½ pound lean veal, ground
¼ cup ground prosciutto (fat and lean)
¼ cup ground Italian salami (or substitute calt's liver)
½ cup grated Parmesan cheese
2 tablespoons butter, softened
1 cup fresh breadcrumbs, soaked in milk
    and squeezed almost dry
1 egg
A chopped mixture:
    ¼ pound fresh ham fat
    1 small onion
    1 carrot
    3 sprigs parsley
    1 clove garlic
1 bay leaf
1 clove
½ cup white wine
2 tablespoons flour
1 pound tomatoes, peeled, seeded, drained, and
    puréed through a food mill
Salt and freshly ground pepper

Flatten the piece of beef with the flat side of a meat
cleaver until it is as thin as possible, but be very

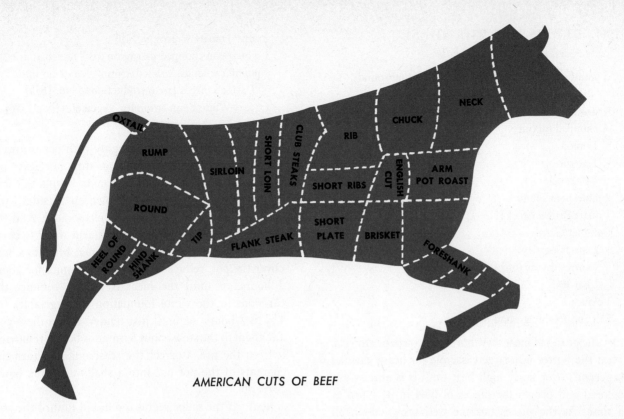

AMERICAN CUTS OF BEEF

careful not to break through it. Season it lightly with salt and pepper and reserve. Put the veal, prosciutto, and salami through the meat grinder, using the finest blade. Mix the ground meats thoroughly with the cheese, butter, breadcrumbs, and egg and season with salt and pepper. Spread this mixture evenly over the flattened beef, roll it up tightly, and tie very securely so that none of the stuffing can escape during the cooking. Put chopped mixture, clove, and bay leaf in a heavy pot large enough to contain the beef and sauté over medium heat until the mixture begins to color. Add the beef, raise the heat slightly, and brown the meat on all sides. Add the wine and cook until it has completely evaporated. Sprinkle the flour over the beef and turn the beef in the pot until the flour is brown. Add the tomatoes and sufficient water to barely cover the beef, season with salt and pepper, bring to a boil, reduce the heat, and simmer for about 2 hours, or until the beef is tender; turn the beef several times during the cooking. Transfer the beef to a serving platter and keep warm. Strain the sauce through a fine sieve, return it to the pot, and cook over high heat until slightly thickened. Slice the beef on the platter and pour the sauce over it. *Serves* 4.

NOTE: If more than 4 persons are to be served, prepare 2 beef rolls as described above, or prepare small individual rolls for each person.

1060. BEEF BRACIOLA NAPOLETANA
Braciola di manzo farcita alla napoletana

Prepare in the same way as the preceding recipe, except substitute the following stuffing:

⅓ cup pine nuts
½ cup raisins
2 cloves garlic, crushed in the garlic-press
2 tablespoons chopped marjoram
3 tablespoons chopped parsley
1 cup fresh breadcrumbs, soaked in milk and
    squeezed almost dry
1 egg

Serves 4.

361

1061. BEEF STEW BORGHESE
Ragù di bue alla borghese

3 pounds rump of beef (or chuck or bottom round),
    cut into 1½-inch cubes
4 tablespoons butter
A chopped mixture:
    1 onion
    1 carrot
    1 stalk celery
2 tablespoons flour
1 quart Brown Stock [No. 4]
Bouquet Garni:
    2 sprigs parsley
    2 sprigs thyme (or ½ teaspoon dried)
    1 bay leaf
1 clove
Salt and freshly ground pepper

Dry the pieces of meat very thoroughly on paper towels. Heat the butter in a large casserole (or heavy enamel saucepan) over fairly high heat until it is almost nut colored and brown the pieces of beef in it, a few at a time. As the pieces become well browned on all sides, remove them with a slotted spoon to a bowl. When all are browned, add the chopped vegetables to the fat in the casserole and cook until the onion becomes a light gold. Return the meat to the casserole, stir for 1 minute, sprinkle in the flour, and stir for 1 minute more, or until the flour begins to brown. Add the brown stock, Bouquet Garni, and clove; and season lightly with salt and pepper. Bring quickly to a boil over high heat, cover the casserole, reduce the heat, and simmer for 2 hours. Transfer the pieces of meat with a slotted spoon to a bowl, strain the sauce through a fine sieve, remove any excess fat from the surface, and then return the meat and the sauce to the casserole. Continue cooking over low heat for about 1 hour longer, or until the meat is tender. Serve in the casserole. *Serves* 6.

1062. BEEF STEW WITH CARDOONS ROMANA
Stufatino di bue coi cardi alla romana

3 pounds rump of beef (or chuck or bottom round),
    cut into 1½-inch cubes
1 tablespoon lard
A chopped mixture:
    2 ounces ham fat
    1 onion
    1 clove garlic
½ cup dry white wine
2 cups Tomato Sauce [No. 19]
1 tablespoon chopped marjoram (or 1 teaspoon dried)
1 pound cardoons, washed, trimmed, and cut into
    3-inch pieces [*see* introduction to No. 1636]
1 quart White Foundation for Vegetables [No. 1576]
Salt and freshly ground pepper

Dry the pieces of beef thoroughly with paper towels. Heat the lard with the chopped mixture in a heavy pot over fairly high heat until the onion begins to color, add the pieces of beef, and brown on all sides. Add the wine and cook until almost evaporated. Add the tomato sauce, marjoram, and sufficient water to cover the meat. Season with salt and pepper, bring to a boil, cover the pot, reduce the heat, and simmer for about 3 hours, or until the meat is tender. Simmer the cardoons in the white foundation for vegetables for 1½ to 2 hours, or until just tender. Drain them and add them to the stew about 5 minutes before removing it from the fire. Correct the seasoning and turn the contents of the pot out into a shallow serving bowl. *Serves* 6.

NOTE: If the sauce seems too liquid toward the end of the cooking, it may be thickened with a little Kneaded Butter [No. 107] about 15 minutes before removing it from the fire.

1063. BEEF STEW WITH FENNEL
Stufatino di bue al finocchio

3 pounds rump of beef (or substitute chuck or bottom
    round), cut into 1½-inch cubes
A chopped mixture:
    2 ounces ham fat
    2 ounces lean salt pork, parboiled for 10 minutes
    1 onion
    1 stalk celery
    1 clove garlic
1 tablespoon lard
½ cup dry white wine
2 cups Tomato Sauce [No. 19]
1 tablespoon marjoram (or 1 teaspoon dried)
1 tablespoon fennel seeds
Salt and freshly ground pepper

Prepare in the manner described in the previous recipe, omitting the cardoons and adding the fennel seeds with the tomato sauce. *Serves* 6.

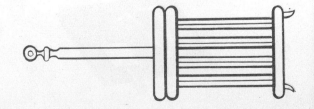

1064. BITOCHKI
Bitokes alla russa

1 pound ground beef (top or bottom round)
2 onions, chopped
$\frac{1}{2}$ cup butter
Pinch nutmeg
Flour
$\frac{1}{2}$ cup heavy cream
1 tablespoon Demi-Glaze Sauce [No. 20]
Juice of $\frac{1}{2}$ lemon
Salt and freshly ground pepper

Sauté the onions in a frying pan in 2 tablespoons of the butter over moderate heat for about 5 minutes, or until they are golden; remove from the heat and keep warm. Season ground meat with salt, pepper, and nutmeg; shape into 8 patties and dust them with flour. Melt the remaining butter in a frying pan over high heat and quickly brown the patties on both sides. Reduce the heat and continue cooking for 2 or 3 minutes on each side, or longer to taste. Transfer the patties to a hot serving platter and keep warm. Add the cream, Demi-Glaze, and lemon juice to the juices in the pan and boil for 2 minutes over high heat. Pour the sauce over the patties and top each with a generous spoonful of the onions. *Serves* 4.

1065. BEEF À LA MODE
Boeuf à la mode

4 pounds rump of beef in one piece
    (or substitute top or bottom round)
$\frac{1}{4}$ pound pork fat belly (or substitute salt
   pork, parboiled), cut into strips 4 inches long and
    $\frac{1}{4}$ inch square
3 tablespoons brandy
1 tablespoon chopped parsley
$1\frac{1}{2}$ cups red wine
4 tablespoons butter
2 carrots, sliced
2 onions, sliced
Bouquet Garni:
   2 sprigs thyme (or $\frac{1}{2}$ teaspoon dried)
   1 bay leaf
2 small calf's feet, parboiled for 10 minutes
2 quarts Brown Stock [No. 4]
$\frac{1}{8}$ pound fresh pork rind
2 veal bones (from the leg, if possible)
Salt and freshly ground pepper

Garnish:
   $1\frac{1}{2}$ pounds large carrots, cut into balls and
     cooked in butter [*see* No. 1644]
   18 Brown-Braised Onions [No. 1722]

Place the pork fat strips in a bowl with the brandy, season with salt (unless parboiled salt pork is substituted) and pepper, and marinate for 1 hour. Sprinkle the strips with the parsley and then insert them into the beef, regularly spaced, with a larding needle. Season the beef generously with salt and pepper, put it into a bowl, add the wine and pork strips marinade, and marinate it for 4 to 6 hours in a cool place, turning it occasionally. Dry the meat very thoroughly and then brown it on all sides in 4 tablespoons extremely hot butter in a frying pan over high heat. Transfer the beef to a large heavy pot and add the marinade, sliced carrots and onions, Bouquet Garni, calf's feet, veal bones, pork rind, and sufficient brown stock to bring the liquid to $\frac{2}{3}$ the depth of the meat. Cover the pot tightly, bring slowly to a boil over medium heat, reduce the heat to a very low flame, and simmer for 4 hours. Remove the beef and the calf's feet, cut off any meat from the calf's feet, and discard the bones. Strain the liquid in the pot through a fine sieve into a bowl, allow it to stand for a few minutes, skim off the fat from the surface, and return liquid to the pot. Return the beef and calf's foot meat to the pot, add the cooked carrots and onions, and simmer over moderate heat only until very hot. Transfer the meat to a hot serving platter, surround with the vegetables, and pour the sauce over both. *Serves* 6.

NOTE: The sauce may be thickened with an appropriate amount (1 tablespoon per cup of sauce) of Kneaded Butter [No. 107], if desired. It should be blended into the sauce after the latter has been strained and de-greased; then simmered for 10 minutes.

1066. BOILED BEEF CASALINGA
Bollito di famiglia

4 pounds hind shank (or heel of round) of beef
Aromatic vegetables:
  1 onion, stuck with 1 clove
  1 carrot, sliced
  1 clove garlic, bruised
  1 stalk celery, sliced
  2 tomatoes, peeled, seeded, drained, and chopped
3 peppercorns
Salt
Bouquet Garni:
  2 sprigs thyme (or ½ teaspoon dried)
  2 sprigs parsley
  1 bay leaf
1 cup Italian rice (or substitute ¼ pound pastina)
1 pound each of 4 seasonal vegetables, such as
    cabbage, peas, green beans, Brussels sprouts,
    carrots, etc.
1½ quarts White Stock [No. 1]
2 cups Green Sauce [No. 88]

Cook the beef with the aromatic vegetables, seasonings, and Bouquet Garni in about 4 quarts of water in the manner described for Bolliti Misti [No. 1077]; the beef should be tender in slightly less than 4 hours. Transfer the meat to a bowl with 3 cups of the broth and keep warm. Strain remaining broth, correct seasoning, return it to the pot, bring to a boil over high heat, add the rice, and cook until just *al dente*. Serve the rice and the broth as a first course and serve the meat with the seasonal vegetables, cooked separately until just tender in the white stock, as a second course. The green sauce should be served separately. *Serves 6.*

1067. BOILED BEEF CAMPAGNOLA
Manzo lesso alla campagnola

18 thin slices boiled beef [*see* No. 1066]
2 tablespoons oil
3 onions, sliced, parboiled for 5 minutes,
    and well drained
½ cup dry white wine
4 ripe tomatoes, peeled, seeded, drained, and chopped
½ cup Brown Stock [No. 4]
2 tablespoons chopped basil (or substitute parsley)
Salt and freshly ground pepper

Heat the oil in a casserole over medium heat, add the onions, cook until golden, add the wine, and continue cooking until the wine has almost evaporated. Add the tomatoes and brown stock, season with salt and pepper,

and cook for 10 minutes, stirring frequently. Add the slices of beef and chopped basil (or parsley), cook just long enough for the beef to become thoroughly hot, and serve in the casserole. *Serves 6.*

1068. BOILED BEEF AND CELERY
Manzo lesso in intingolo con cuori di sedano

18 thin slices boiled beef [*see* No. 1066]
1 tablespoon oil
¼ cup chopped ham fat
1 onion, chopped
2 hearts of celery, parboiled in lightly salted
    water for 20 minutes, drained, and thinly sliced
3 tomatoes, peeled, seeded, drained, and chopped
½ cup Brown Stock [No. 4]
Salt and freshly ground pepper

Heat the oil in a heavy saucepan over medium heat, add the ham fat and onion, cook until the onion begins to color, and add the celery, stock, and tomatoes. Season with salt and pepper and simmer for 15 minutes. Add the slices of beef, continue cooking only until the beef is thoroughly hot, and serve in the casserole. *Serves 6.*

1069. BOILED BEEF FLAMANDE
Manzo lesso alla fiamminga

18 slices boiled beef [*see* No. 1066]
3 tablespoons butter
2 onions, chopped
1½ tablespoons flour
3 cups red wine
Salt and freshly ground pepper

Heat the butter in a casserole over medium heat, add the onions, and cook until golden. Blend in the flour, cook for 1 minute, and slowly pour in the wine, stirring continuously with a wooden spoon. Continue cooking until the wine is reduced by ½. Season to taste with salt and pepper, add the slices of beef, cook only until the beef is thoroughly hot, and serve in the casserole. *Serves 6.*

1070. BOILED BEEF WITH TART SAUCE
Manzo lesso con salsa piccante

18 thin slices boiled beef [*see* No. 1066], chilled
3 hard-boiled eggs, sliced and chilled
3 tomatoes, sliced and chilled
2 pickles, sliced

1 recipe Pesto Genovese [No. 93], to which is added:
1 teaspoon dry mustard
1 tablespoon vinegar
3 additional tablespoons oil
2 hearts of Boston lettuce, quartered

Arrange the slices of cold beef on a chilled serving platter and garnish the platter with the slices of hard-boiled eggs, tomatoes, and pickles. Pour the Pesto sauce over the meat slices and garnish with the lettuce quarters. *Serves* 6.

1071. BOILED BEEF EN MIROTON
Manzo lesso "en miroton"

18 thin slices boiled beef [*see* No. 1066]
3 tablespoons butter
2 onions, thinly sliced
1 cup Spanish Sauce [No. 16], or substitute
    leftover meat gravy
1 cup Tomato Sauce [No. 19]
1 tablespoon vinegar
Salt and freshly ground pepper

Heat the butter in a casserole over medium heat, add the onions, and cook until golden. Add the Spanish and tomato sauces and season only if necessary with salt and pepper. Add the vinegar and simmer for 15 minutes. Add the slices of beef and cook only until the beef is thoroughly hot. Serve in the casserole. *Serves* 6.

NOTE: This dish is a means of dressing up leftover beef, and, thus, canned or fresh tomatoes may be substituted for the tomato sauce and any good stock thickened with Kneaded Butter [No. 107] for the Spanish sauce.

1072. BOILED BEEF NAPOLETANA
Manzo lesso alla napoletana

18 thin slices boiled beef [*see* No. 1066]
1½ pounds tomatoes, peeled, seeded, drained, and
    puréed through a food mill
3 cloves garlic, crushed in the garlic-press
2 tablespoons chopped oregano (or 1 teaspoon dried)
2 tablespoons chopped parsly
½ cup oil
Salt and freshly ground pepper

Mix together the tomato purée, garlic, oregano, and parsley. Season the mixture with salt and pepper. Brush a casserole generously with oil and arrange in it alternating layers of the tomato mixture and slices of beef, sprinkling each layer with some of the oil and ending with a layer of the tomato mixture. Place the casserole in a moderate (350°) oven for about 25 minutes and serve in the casserole. *Serves* 6.

1073. BOILED BEEF AND ONIONS AU GRATIN
Manzo lesso gratinato con cipolle

18 slices boiled beef [*see* No. 1066]
4 onions, sliced, parboiled 5 minutes, and well drained
3 tablespoons butter
¾ cup fresh breadcrumbs
3 tablespoons butter, melted
Juice of ½ lemon
3 tablespoons chopped parsley
Salt and freshly ground pepper

Gently sauté the onions in 3 tablespoons of butter in a frying pan over moderate heat until transparent, but not brown. Arrange alternating layers of the beef and onions in a casserole, seasoning each layer lightly with salt and pepper. Sprinkle the top with breadcrumbs and then with melted butter and place the casserole in a hot (400°) oven for 10 minutes, or just until the beef is thoroughly hot. Sprinkle the top with lemon juice and parsley and serve in the casserole. *Serves* 6.

1074. BOILED BEEF WITH PEPPERS
Manzo lesso con peperoni

This dish is prepared in the same way and with the same ingredients as Boiled Beef and Celery [No. 1068], except that 4 sweet red or yellow peppers are substituted for the celery. The peppers should be roasted, scraped, seeded, and cut into strips [*see* No. 145] before being added. *Serves* 6.

1075. BOILED BEEF SALAD
Manzo lesso in insalata

12 slices boiled beef [*see* No. 1066], cut into thin strips
    and chilled
2 onions, thinly sliced
12 mint leaves, crushed
2 tablespoons chopped parsley
1 tablespoon capers
2 pickles, sliced
¾ cup Sauce Vinaigrette [No. 99], mixed with
    1 tablespoon prepared mustard

Mix all of the ingredients except the Vinaigrette sauce in a salad bowl. Add the Vinaigrette just before serving and toss very lightly. *Serves* 6.

Boiled Beef Salad (No. 1075): see page 365

1076. BOILED BEEF MEATBALLS ROMANA
Manzo lesso in polpette alla romana

1 pound boiled beef [*see* No. 1066]
3 ounces prosciutto (fat and lean)
6 slices bread, soaked in milk and squeezed almost dry
3 sprigs parsley
1 clove garlic
2 tablespoons grated Parmesan cheese
Pinch nutmeg
3 eggs
1 cup fresh breadcrumbs
·Flour
A chopped mixture:
  2 ounces ham fat
  1 small onion
  1 small carrot
  1 small stalk celery
¼ cup oil
1 bay leaf
1 clove
1 pound tomatoes, peeled, seeded, drained, and puréed
    through a food mill
Salt and freshly ground pepper

Cut the beef into small pieces and put it through the meat grinder, using the fine blade, with the prosciutto, bread, parsley, and garlic. Add the grated cheese to the mixture; season with salt, pepper, and nutmeg; and blend in 2 eggs, slightly beaten. Stir the mixture

lightly with a two-pronged fork, form it into 18 small balls, dust these with flour, dip them in the remaining egg, beaten, and then into breadcrumbs. Gently sauté the chopped mixture in 1 teaspoon of the oil in a saucepan over moderate heat until it begins to color and then add the tomatoes, bay leaf, and clove. Season with salt, pepper, and nutmeg; and simmer for 15 minutes. Shortly before this sauce is fully cooked, heat the oil in a frying pan over fairly high heat and brown the meatballs quickly on all sides. Remove them with a slotted spoon to a hot serving platter and spoon the sauce over them. *Serves 6.*

1077. BOLLITI MISTI
Bolliti misti

An Italian bolliti misti *is somewhat reminiscent of a New England boiled dinner, but it is more elaborate, containing a variety of boiled meats and seasonal vegetables. Although popular throughout Italy,* bolliti misti *is a specialty of Piedmont. An annual scene in Bergamo, an hour's ride from Milan, is the hundreds of summer visitors sitting outside under the trees making a difficult choice from a large cart of* bolliti misti.

2 pounds lean short ribs of beef
4 pounds rump or bottom round of beef
1 pound beef hocks
1½ pounds shoulder of lamb
1 pound breast of veal
1 calf's foot, parboiled for 15 minutes
½ pound lean pork fat belly (or substitute lean salt
    pork, parboiled)
Aromatic vegetables:
  1 onion, stuck with 1 clove
  1 clove garlic
  2 carrots, sliced
  2 turnips, sliced
  2 tomatoes, peeled, seeded, drained, and sliced
Bouquet Garni:
  2 sprigs thyme (or ¼ teaspoon dried)
  2 sprigs parsley
  1 bay leaf
Vegetable garnish:
  1 pound each of 6 different vegetables in season,
    such as cabbage, peas, green beans, zucchini,
    carrots, Brussels sprouts, etc.
1 pound "new" potatoes
12 white onions
2 quarts White Stock [No. 1]
3 cups Green Sauce [No. 88]
Salt and freshly ground pepper

Place all of the meat and bones in a large, heavy pot, cover generously with cold water, bring very slowly to a boil over low heat, skim off any scum that rises to the surface, and then add the garlic, aromatic vegetables, and the Bouquet Garni. Season lightly with salt and pepper. Simmer for several hours removing each cut of meat as it becomes tender; the veal and lamb will be ready first, after cooking between 1½ and 2 hours; the beef will take up to 3 hours. As each cut of meat is removed from the pot, keep it warm in a covered bowl with a little of the broth. Shortly before the beef cuts are fully cooked, cook each of the garnishing vegetables separately until just tender in a little stock (the potatoes and onions may be cooked in water); time the cooking of each so that they all finish cooking at approximately the same time (if a shortage of burners necessitates their being cooked in advance, drain them, keep them barely warm in separate bowls, and then reheat them just before serving). Arrange the meats on a large serving platter, spoon a little of the strained broth over them, arrange the vegetables on another serving platter, and serve the green sauce on the side. *Serves 8 to 10.*

1078. BOLLITI MISTI ITALIANA
Bolliti misti all'italiana

1 5-pound capon, boned (*see* page 436)
2 pounds short ribs of beef
1 veal knuckle
1 pound spiced Italian sausage *(cotechino)*, or
    substitute Polish sausage, parboiled
½ pound lean salt pork, parboiled for 15 minutes
Stuffing for the capon:
  1 onion, chopped
  1 clove garlic, crushed in the garlic-press
  2 tablespoons butter
  ¼ pound prosciutto, finely chopped
  Gizzard, heart, and liver of the capon, sautéed
      5 minutes in 1 tablespoon butter and chopped
  3 cups fresh bread cubes, soaked in milk and
      squeezed almost dry
  2 tablespoons chopped parsley
  2 eggs
  Salt and freshly ground pepper
Bouquet Garni:
  2 sprigs thyme (or ½ teaspoon dried)
  2 sprigs parsley
  1 bay leaf

Aromatic vegetables:
  2 stalks celery, sliced
  1 onion, stuck with 2 cloves
  1 carrot, sliced
Vegetable garnish:
  1 pound each 6 fresh vegetables in season, such
      as cabbage, peas, green beans, zucchini,
      Brussels sprouts, etc.
  12 white onions
  2 quarts White Stock [No. 1]
3 cups Green Sauce [No. 88]
Salt and freshly ground pepper

For the capon stuffing, sauté the chopped onion and garlic in 2 tablespoons of butter in a frying pan over moderate heat until transparent, add the chopped prosciutto, and cook for 1 minute longer. Remove from the heat and mix thoroughly with the other stuffing ingredients in a bowl. Season with salt and pepper and then stuff capon loosely with the mixture, recreating as nearly as possible the original shape of the bird. Sew the openings very securely with string, so that none of the stuffing can escape, and truss the bird so that it will retain its shape during the cooking. Place the capon and all of the other meats in a large heavy pot, cover with cold water, and proceed with the cooking and serving as described in the previous recipe; the capon will require approximately 2 hours of simmering. Prepare and serve the vegetables as described in the previous recipe. *Serves 8 to 10.*

1079. BRAISED BEEF WITH GNOCCHI
Bue brasato con gnocchi

4 pounds rump of beef
¼ pound salt pork, cut into strips 4 inches long
    and ¼ inch square
2 cups red wine
3 tablespoons brandy
1 tablespoon chopped parsley
Pinch nutmeg
4 tablespoons oil
¼ cup flour
3 cups Brown Stock [No. 4]
Bouquet Garni:
  2 sprigs thyme (or ½ teaspoon dried)
  1 bay leaf
  2 sprigs parsley
Salt and freshly ground pepper
1 recipe Potato Gnocchi Romana [No. 620]

Mix the wine, brandy, chopped parsley, nutmeg, and

2 generous pinches pepper in a bowl; marinate the salt pork strips in this mixture for ½ hour. Lard the beef with the salt pork strips, using a larding needle. Heat the oil over high heat until it is smoking hot in a pot large enough to easily contain the beef, brown the beef on all sides, and then remove it from the pot. Add the flour, stir until it is golden, and then slowly add the marinade, stirring constantly with a whisk. Stir in the stock, season lightly with salt and pepper, bring to a boil, add the beef and the Bouquet Garni, cover the pot tightly, and place it in a moderate (350°) oven for 3 hours. Remove the pot from the oven, transfer the beef to a bowl for a few minutes, and strain the cooking liquid. Return the beef and the liquid to the pot and place the pot back in the oven for about 1 hour, or until the beef is tender. Slice the beef on a hot serving platter and pour the sauce over the slices. Serve the gnocchi on the side. *Serves* 6.

1080. BRAISED BEEF RICCA
Bue brasato alla ricca

Prepare in the same manner as the preceding recipe and add the following to the pot for the last 5 minutes of cooking:

¼ pound lean salt pork dice, parboiled
    for 5 minutes, drained, and sautéed over medium
    heat until golden brown
½ pound button mushrooms, gently sautéed for
    8 minutes in 2 tablespoons of butter
12 Brown-Braised Onions [No. 1722]

Omit gnocchi garnish and serve as described above. *Serves* 6.

1081. BROILED STEAK FIORENTINA
Bistecca fiorentina

1 sirloin or porterhouse steak, 2 inches thick
½ cup oil
1 teaspoon salt
½ teaspoon freshly ground pepper
Juice of ½ lemon
1 recipe Black-Eyed Beans Uccelletto [No. 1610]

Marinate the steak for ½ hour in the oil, salt, and pepper. Place it on a preheated rack about 5 inches beneath a very high broiler flame and broil for 6 minutes on each side, or longer to taste. Transfer the steak to a hot serving platter, squeeze the lemon juice over the top, and serve the black-eyed beans separately. *Serves* 6.

1082. CARBONNADES OF BEEF FLAMANDE
Carbonades di bue alla fiamminga

2 pounds lean beef (rump or chuck), cut in slices 4 by
    4 inches square and ½ inch thick
4 tablespoons oil
2 onions, sliced, parboiled for 6 minutes, drained,
    and thoroughly dried
3 cups beer
1 cup Brown Stock [No. 4]
3 tablespoons Kneaded Butter [No. 107]
1 tablespoon brown sugar
Bouquet Garni:
    2 sprigs thyme (or ½ teaspoon dried)
    1 bay leaf
    2 sprigs parsley
Salt and freshly ground pepper

Heat the oil in a frying pan over high heat and quickly brown the slices of meat, a few at a time, on both sides. Season the slices with salt and pepper as they cook and remove them with a slotted spoon when they are nicely browned. When all the slices are cooked, add the onions to the oil in the pan and cook until golden. Spoon a few of the onions in the bottom of a casserole, place a few slices of beef on top, and continue alternating layers until all of the onions and beef have been used. Add the beer and stock to the pan in which the beef and onions were cooked, and reduce to ¾ its quantity, scraping the bottom and sides of the pan to incorporate any drippings from the beef. Blend in the kneaded butter and the brown sugar, season with a little salt and pepper, and then pour into the casserole. Add the Bouquet Garni, pushing down so that it is submerged, cover tightly, bring to a boil over high heat, and then place the casserole in a moderate (350°) oven for 2½ hours. Serve in the casserole. *Serves* 6.

SEE
VERSE
OR
TION

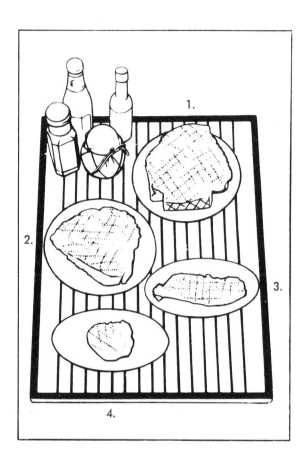

Various grilled steaks cut in the Italian manner
1. Chateaubriand (see No. 1083)
2. Broiled Steak Fiorentina (No. 1081)
3. Entrecôte (No. 1087)
4. Fillet of Beef à la Minute (No. 1103)

1083. CHATEAUBRIAND BÉARNAISE
Chateaubriand alla griglia

The Chateaubriand is the whole center cut of a fillet of beef. It is not as flavorful as many other cuts, but it is highly prized for its extreme tenderness. A Chateaubriand may be roasted whole or, more frequently, cut into slices about 1½ inches thick and broiled. Sauce Béarnaise makes the perfect accompaniment for Chateaubriand.

    3 pounds fillet of beef (center cut), at room
        temperature and cut into 3 equal-sized slices
    3 slices bacon
    4 tablespoons melted butter
    Salt
    1 bunch watercress, washed and dried
    2 cups Sauce Béarnaise [No. 67]

Tie a slice of bacon around the circumference of each slice of fillet, or secure the bacon with toothpicks. Brush the fillets with melted butter, place them on a hot rack of a preheated broiler about 4 inches beneath a very high flame, and brown them for 2 to 3 minutes on each side, basting occasionally with more butter (the exact cooking time will depend on personal preference and the thickness of the meat, but a Chateaubriand is nearly always served rare; when the center of each slice begins to offer slight resistance to the pressure of the finger, it will be sufficiently cooked). Spread the watercress out on a hot serving platter, and, when the fillets are cooked, arrange them on top. Sprinkle a little salt over them and serve the Béarnaise sauce on the side. *Serves 6.*

1084. CHOPPED BEEF ALLA CREMA
Bistecche alla crema

    1½ pounds ground beef (top or bottom round)
    ¼ cup finely chopped prosciutto (fat and lean)
    Pinch nutmeg
    Flour
    ¼ cup butter
    ½ cup heavy cream
    Juice of ½ lemon
    Salt and freshly ground pepper

Mix the ground beef with the prosciutto in a bowl; season with salt, pepper, and nutmeg; mix thoroughly with a two-pronged fork (to avoid packing the meat down); and shape into 4 round, flat patties. Dust these with flour. Heat the butter in a frying pan over high heat and sauté the patties until they are golden on each side. Lower the flame and continue cooking for 2 minutes on each side, or longer to taste. Arrange these

on a heated serving platter. Add the cream and the lemon juice to the butter in the pan, cook it over a brisk flame until it is somewhat reduced, and pour over the patties. *Serves 4.*

1085. CHOPPED BEEF NIÇOISE
Bistecche alla nizzarda

    1½ pounds ground beef (top or bottom round)
    3 large onions, finely chopped
    6 cloves garlic, crushed in the garlic-press
    1 egg white
    Pinch nutmeg
    Flour
    ½ cup butter
    Salt and freshly ground pepper

Put the chopped onion, garlic, ground meat, and egg white in a bowl; season with salt, pepper, and nutmeg; and mix thoroughly with a two-pronged fork (to avoid packing the meat down). Shape into 4 patties and dust lightly with flour. Heat the butter in a frying pan over high heat until it is nut colored and sauté the patties quickly on both sides; reduce the heat and cook for 2 minutes on each side, or longer to taste. Arrange the patties on a hot serving platter and pour the butter in the pan over them. *Serves 4.*

1086. GRANDMOTHER'S CHOPPED BEEF
Bistecche della nonna

    1½ pounds ground beef (top or bottom round)
    ½ cup thick Béchamel Sauce [No. 18]
    3 eggs
    ¼ cup grated Parmesan cheese
    ½ cup fresh breadcrumbs, soaked in milk
        and squeezed almost dry
    Flour
    ½ cup butter
    Salt and freshly ground pepper

Put the ground meat, Béchamel sauce, 2 of the eggs, grated Parmesan cheese, and breadcrumbs in a bowl; season with salt and pepper; and mix thoroughly with a two-pronged fork (to avoid packing the meat down). Shape the mixture into 6 patties, dip in the remaining egg, beaten, and dust with flour. Heat the butter in the frying pan over high heat and brown the patties quickly on both sides. Reduce the heat and continue cooking for 2 to 3 minutes on each side, or longer to taste. Transfer them to a hot serving platter and pour the butter in the pan over them. *Serves 6.*

1087. ENTRECÔTE

Lombatine—entrecôtes—alla griglia

6 club steaks, cut from the rib end of the short loin
½ cup Clarified Butter [No. 102]
Salt and freshly ground pepper
1 recipe Sautéed Potatoes [No. 1788]

Place 4 tablespoons of butter in each of 2 large frying pans over high heat until almost brown, put 3 steaks in each pan, and brown quickly on both sides. Reduce the heat slightly and cook for about 1 more minute on each side, or longer to taste. Arrange the steaks on a hot serving platter, season them lightly with salt and pepper, and pour the butter in the pans over them. Serve the sautéed potatoes separately. *Serves 6.*

1088. ENTRECÔTE WITH ANCHOVIES AND OLIVES

Lombatine—entrecôtes—con acciughe e olive

6 club steaks, cut from the rib end of the short loin
½ cup butter
½ cup chilled Anchovy Butter [No. 108]
12 anchovy fillets, washed free of salt
    [*see* No. 220] and rolled
1 cup pitted green olives, parboiled for 8 minutes
Salt and freshly ground pepper

Heat 4 tablespoons of butter in each of 2 frying pans over high heat until brown, add 3 steaks to each pan, and brown quickly on both sides. Reduce the heat slightly and cook for about 1 more minute on each side, or longer to taste. Arrange the steaks on a hot serving platter, season them with salt and pepper, place a few curls of anchovy butter and 2 rolled anchovy fillets on the top of each, and garnish the platter with the parboiled olives. *Serves 6.*

1089. ENTRECÔTE BÉARNAISE

Lombatine—entrecôtes—alla béarnaise

6 club steaks, cut from the rib end of the short loin
½ cup butter
2 tablespoons Meat Essence [No. 10]
1 bunch watercress
2 cups Sauce Béarnaise [No. 67]
Salt and freshly ground pepper

Pan-fry the steaks in the manner described in Entrecôte [No. 1087]. Arrange the steaks on a hot serving platter, season them lightly with salt and pepper, spread 1 teaspoon of meat essence on each, and garnish the platter with water cress. Serve the Béarnaise sauce separately. *Serves 6.*

1090. ENTRECÔTE BORDELAISE

Lombatine—entrecôtes—alla bordolese

6 club steaks, cut from the rib end of the short loin
½ cup butter
12 thin slices beef marrow, parboiled for 5 minutes
2 cups Sauce Bordelaise [No. 27]
Salt and freshly ground pepper

Pan-fry the steaks in the manner described in Entrecôte [No. 1087]. Arrange the steaks on a hot serving platter, season them lightly with salt and pepper, put 2 slices of beef marrow on each, and serve the Bordelaise sauce separately. *Serves 6.*

1091. ENTRECÔTE FORESTIERA

Lombatine—entrecôtes—alla forestiera

6 club steaks, cut from the rib end of the short loin
¼ pound lean salt pork, diced, parboiled for
    10 minutes, and drained
½ pound mushrooms
10 tablespoons butter
½ cup dry white wine
2 cups Spanish Sauce [No. 16]
2 tablespoons chopped parsley
Salt and freshly ground pepper

Place the parboiled salt pork dice in a frying pan and shake the pan over fairly high heat until pork is golden on all sides; remove the dice with a slotted spoon and drain them on absorbent paper. Gently sauté the mushrooms in 2 tablespoons of butter in a covered frying pan over moderate heat for about 8 minutes; remove from the heat and reserve. Pan-fry the steaks in the remaining butter in the manner described in Entrecôte [No. 1087]. Arrange the steaks on a hot serving platter, season them lightly with salt and pepper, and keep warm. Add the wine to the butter in the pan, reduce over high heat until almost evaporated, add the Spanish sauce, and bring just to a boil. Garnish the platter with heaps of the mushrooms, sprinkle the steaks with the parsley and salt pork dice, and serve the sauce separately. *Serves 6.*

1092. ENTRECÔTE PAPRIKA

Lombatine—entrecôtes—alla paprika

6 club steaks, cut from the rib end of the short loin
¼ pound lean salt pork, diced, parboiled for
    10 minutes, and drained
½ cup butter
2 cups Paprika Sauce [No. 53]
Salt and freshly ground pepper

Place the salt pork dice in a frying pan and shake the pan over fairly high heat until pork is golden on all sides; remove the dice with a slotted spoon and drain on absorbent paper. Pan-fry the steaks in the manner described in Entrecôte [No. 1087]. Arrange the steaks on a hot serving platter, season them lightly with salt and pepper, sprinkle the salt pork dice over them, and serve the sauce separately. *Serves* 6.

1093. ENTRECÔTE TIROLESE
Lombatine—entrecôtes—alla tirolese

6 club steaks, cut from the rib end of the short loin
1/2 cup butter
2 Bermuda onions, thinly sliced
1/2 cup Pepper Sauce [No. 25]
1/2 cup thick Tomato Sauce [No. 19]
Salt and freshly ground pepper

Pan-fry the steaks in the manner described in Entrecôte [No. 1087]. Arrange the steaks on a hot serving platter, season them lightly with salt and pepper, and keep warm. Add the onion rings to the butter in the pan, cook over fairly high heat until golden, add the pepper sauce, and simmer for 2 minutes. Spoon a little of the onions and sauce over each steak and circle the platter with a ribbon of tomato sauce. *Serves* 6.

1094. FILLET OF BEEF CAPRICCIOSO
Filetti di bue capricciosi

6 slices fillet of beef, cut 3/4 to 1 inch thick
A marinade:
    1/2 cup oil
    1 tablespoon chopped sage (or 1 teaspoon dried)
    1 tablespoon chopped rosemary (or 1 teaspoon dried)
    1 teaspoon salt
    1/4 teaspoon freshly ground pepper
1 cup fresh breadcrumbs
4 tablespoons butter
6 tablespoons Anchovy Butter [No. 108]
6 slices bread, crusts removed, lightly browned
    in butter

Marinate the slices of fillet in the marinade for 1 hour, turning the meat occasionally. Remove them from the marinade and roll immediately in breadcrumbs. Melt the butter in a large frying pan over fairly high heat until golden, add the slices of fillet, and cook for about 3 minutes on each side. Spread each of the browned slices of bread with a tablespoon of anchovy butter, arrange them on a hot serving platter, and place a slice of fillet on top of each piece of bread. *Serves* 6.

1095. FILLET OF BEEF CAVALLO
Bistecche a cavallo

6 slices fillet of beef, cut 3/4 to 1 inch thick
1/2 cup butter
6 eggs
Salt and freshly ground pepper

Heat 1/2 of the butter in a frying pan over fairly high heat, add the slices of fillet, and cook for 3 minutes on each side, or to taste. They will be medium rare when the center of each offers a little resistance to the finger and is no longer soft. Season the slices with salt and pepper and transfer them to a hot serving platter. Melt the remaining butter in another frying pan and quickly fry the eggs over medium high heat, basting them occasionally with the butter in the pan. Carefully cut away the egg whites from the yolks and place a cooked yolk on each slice of fillet. Combine the butters in both pans and pour over the fillets. *Serves* 6.

1096. FILLET OF BEEF CASINO
Filetti di bue "Casino"

6 slices fillet of beef, cut 3/4 to 1 inch thick
6 tablespoons butter
A chopped mixture:
    1/8 pound mushrooms
    1/8 pound prosciutto
    3 sprigs parsley
1/2 cup Brown Stock [No. 4]
1/2 cup dry white wine
Juice of 1/2 lemon
Salt and freshly ground pepper

Melt 3 tablespoons of the butter in a frying pan over high heat until golden, add the slices of fillet, and cook for about 3 minutes on each side. Season the slices with salt and pepper, transfer them to a hot serving platter, and keep warm. Add the chopped mixture to the pan, cook for 3 minutes, add the stock and wine, and cook until the liquid is reduced to 1/2 its quantity. Remove from the heat, swirl in the remaining butter, bit by bit, add the lemon juice, and spoon a little of the sauce over each slice of fillet. *Serves* 6.

371

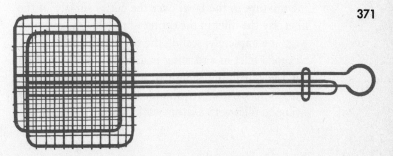

1097. FILLET OF BEEF EN CROÛTE
Filetto di bue in crosta alla francese

3 pounds fillet of beef, in 1 piece
6 strips salt pork, cut slightly longer than the beef
    and ¼ inch square, parboiled 5 minutes
6 tablespoons butter
2 carrots, chopped
2 onions, chopped
2 tablespoons chopped parsley
¼ teaspoon powdered bay leaf
¼ teaspoon powdered sage
¼ teaspoon powdered thyme
¼ pound chicken livers, chopped
2 ounces pork fat belly
2 ounces prosciutto
¾ cup Duxelles [No. 138]
1 egg
1 recipe Rich Pastry [No. 1955], made without sugar
1 egg yolk, beaten with 2 tablespoons milk
Salt and freshly ground pepper
Pinch nutmeg
¼ cup dry Madeira wine

Using a larding needle, lard the beef lengthwise with the strips of salt pork; the strips should protrude about ¼ inch from either end of the fillet. Melt 3 tablespoons of the butter in a frying pan over high heat until golden, add the fillet, and brown quickly on all sides, being careful that the ends of the larding strips become well browned and crisp. Remove the fillet from the pan and allow to cool to room temperature. Melt the remaining 3 tablespoons of butter in a saucepan over moderate heat and add the carrots, onions, parsley, bay leaf, sage, and thyme. Sauté gently for about 5 minutes, or until the onions are soft. Add the chicken livers, raise the heat slightly, and cook for 2 minutes longer. Remove from the heat and turn the contents of the pan into a bowl. Put the pork fat and prosciutto through the meat grinder, using the finest blade, and add them to the vegetable/chicken liver mixture. Add the Duxelles and egg; season with salt, pepper, and nutmeg; and stir the mixture vigorously to form a smooth paste. Roll out ¾ of the dough in a sheet large enough to encase the fillet, spread an even coating of the mixture in the bowl over the entire surface of the fillet, lay the fillet in the center of the dough, and then wrap it completely, sealing the edges tightly. Place the wrapped fillet in a roasting pan, seam side down. Roll out the remaining dough to a thickness of ¼ inch, cut it into narrow strips, and decorate the top of the wrapped fillet with a latticework of these strips. Brush

the surface with the egg yolk mixed with milk and insert a pastry tube (or small metal funnel) with a medium round opening in the center of the top to allow steam to escape during the cooking. Place the pan in a medium (375°) oven for about 50 minutes, or slightly longer if the fillet is very thick. About 10 minutes before the end of the cooking, pour the Madeira into the pastry-tube funnel. Remove the pan from the oven, carefully transfer the fillet to a hot serving platter, and allow it to rest for 10 minutes in a warm place before serving. *Serves* 6.

1098. FILLET OF BEEF DAUPHINE
Filetto di bue brasato alla Dauphine

3 pounds fillet of beef, in 1 piece
6 strips of salt pork, slightly longer than the beef
    and ¼ inch square, parboiled for 10 minutes
¼ pound pork rind, parboiled for 2 hours
4 tablespoons butter
1 onion, chopped
1 carrot, chopped
Bouquet Garni:
    2 sprigs thyme (or ½ teaspoon dried)
    1 bay leaf
    3 sprigs parsley
2 cups Brown Stock [No. 4]
1 cup dry Madeira wine
1 tablespoon arrowroot blended with
    2 tablespoons Madeira
12 small croquettes prepared from Potatoes
    Dauphine [No. 1768]
Salt and freshly ground pepper

Using a larding needle, lard the fillet lengthwise with the strips of salt pork; the strips should protrude about ¼ inch from either end of the fillet. Melt the butter over high heat in a heavy pot or casserole until it is golden and quickly brown the fillet on all sides, being careful that the ends of the larding strips get well browned and crisp. Remove the fillet from the pot for a few minutes, drain off most of the butter, and deglaze the pot with a small amount of the stock. Line the bottom of the pot with the pork rind, sprinkle the chopped carrot and onion over the rind, lay the fillet on top, and then add the Bouquet Garni, brown stock, and Madeira; the liquid should come about halfway up the sides of the fillet. Cover the pot, bring to a boil over high heat, and place the pot in a moderate (350°) oven for about 40 minutes (the exact time will depend on the thickness of the fillet; the Chateaubriand section of a fillet will require about 50 minutes). Baste the meat once or twice during the cooking with the liquid in the pot. Transfer the fillet to a hot serving platter and keep warm; it should rest for at least 10 minutes before serving. Reduce the cooking liquid in the pot to about 2 cups over high heat, strain through a fine sieve, return it to the pot, blend in the arrowroot, correct the seasoning, and simmer over medium heat for 3 minutes. Slice the fillet neatly, arrange the slices overlapping each other on the platter, spoon the sauce over the slices, and garnish the platter with the potato croquettes. *Serves* 6.

1099. FILLET OF BEEF FRASCATI
Filetto di bue brasato alla Frascati

Prepare in the same manner and with the same ingredients as Fillet of Beef Dauphine [No. 1098], except omit the potato croquettes and garnish the platter with the following:

6 round slices of pâté de foie gras, about
    ¼ inch thick
18 asparagus tips, cooked in lightly salted water
    until just tender and dressed with 3
    tablespoons butter
12 thin slices truffle
½ pound mushrooms, cooked in 3 tablespoons
    butter in a covered saucepan over moderate
    heat for 8 minutes

Serves 6.

1100. FILLET OF BEEF GOURMET
Filetti di bue del buongustaio

6 slices fillet of beef, cut ¾ to 1 inch thick
½ pound mushrooms, quartered
½ cup butter
6 round slices pâté de foie gras, ¼ inch thick and
    2 inches in diameter
6 slices truffle
¼ cup butter, melted
1 cup fresh breadcrumbs
6 slices bread, crusts removed, lightly browned
    in butter
¾ cup dry Marsala wine
½ cup Tomato Sauce [No. 19], reduced to ¼ cup
Salt and freshly ground pepper

Gently sauté the mushrooms in 2 tablespoons of butter in a frying pan over moderate heat for 8 minutes and reserve. Make a deep incision in the side of each slice of beef with a very sharp knife and insert a slice of foie gras and a slice of truffle into each. Season the slices with salt and pepper, dip them in melted butter,

and then cover with breadcrumbs. Melt 4 tablespoons of the butter in a large frying pan over fairly high heat until it is golden, add the slices of beef, and cook for about 3 minutes on each side. Arrange the browned slices of bread on a hot serving platter and place one slice of beef on top of each piece of bread. Add the Marsala to the pan and reduce it over high heat to ½ its quantity. Add the tomato sauce and the mushrooms, bring to a boil, remove from the heat, swirl in the remaining butter, bit by bit, and spoon a little of this sauce over each slice of fillet. *Serves* 6.

Bay

1101. FILLET OF BEEF GRAND HÔTEL
Filetti di bue "Grand Hôtel"

6 slices fillet of beef, cut ¾ to 1 inch thick
¾ cup butter
1 pound tomatoes, peeled, seeded, drained,
    and chopped
1 pound zucchini, sliced
1 cup pitted green olives
24 Noisette Potatoes [No. 1783]
¾ cup Italian Meat Sauce [No. 41]
Salt and freshly ground pepper

Melt 2 tablespoons of the butter in a saucepan over medium heat, add the tomatoes, season with salt and pepper, and simmer for 10 minutes. Sauté the zucchini in 3 tablespoons of butter in a large, covered frying pan over moderate heat for about 5 minutes, shaking the pan occasionally, remove from the heat, and season with a little salt and pepper. Parboil the olives for 10 minutes in water, drain them, and gently sauté them in a tablespoon of butter for about 5 minutes in a saucepan over moderate heat. Reserve each of these vegetables when they are cooked and keep warm. Melt 3 tablespoons of the butter in a large frying pan over fairly high heat until golden, add the slices of fillet, and cook for about 3 minutes on each side. Season the slices with salt and pepper and transfer them to a hot serving platter. Add the Italian meat sauce to the pan, bring to a boil, remove from the heat, and swirl in the remaining butter, bit by bit. Garnish the platter with small heaps of the vegetables and the potatoes and spoon a little of the sauce over each slice of fillet. *Serves* 6.

1102. FILLET OF BEEF ITALIANA
Filetti di bue all'italiana

6 slices fillet of beef, cut ¾ to 1 inch thick
6 thin slices mozzarella cheese, slightly smaller
    in diameter than the fillets
6 thin slices prosciutto, slightly smaller in diameter
    than the fillets
6 slices truffle
¼ cup butter, melted
1 cup fresh breadcrumbs
⅓ cup butter
6 slices bread, crusts removed, lightly browned
    in butter
½ cup Tomato Sauce [No. 19], reduced to ¼ cup
¾ cup dry Marsala wine
Salt and freshly ground pepper

Prepare in the same manner as described in Fillet of Beef Gourmet [No. 1100], except omit mushrooms and insert slices of the mozzarella and prosciutto into the meat instead of foie gras. *Serves 6.*

1103. FILLET OF BEEF À LA MINUTE
Filetti di bue "à la minute"

6 slices fillet of beef, cut ¾ to 1 inch thick
¼ cup oil
Salt and freshly ground pepper
12 curls of cold sweet butter
2 tablespoons chopped parsley
Juice of ½ lemon
6 Tomatoes Au Gratin [No. 1812]

Brush the slices of beef with oil and put them on a preheated rack about 4 inches beneath a high broiler flame. Broil them for 3 minutes on each side, season them with salt and pepper, and transfer them to a hot serving platter. Top each slice with 2 curls of icy cold sweet butter, a teaspoon of chopped parsley, and a few drops of lemon juice. Garnish the platter with the tomatoes. *Serves 6.*

1104. HAMBURGER
Bistecche all'amburghese

1½ pounds ground beef (top or bottom round)
2 onions, sliced, parboiled for 5 minutes,
    and dried
6 tablespoons butter
2 egg yolks
Pinch nutmeg

Flour
Salt and freshly ground pepper

Sauté the onions in 2 tablespoons of the butter in a frying pan over moderate heat for about 5 minutes, or until they are soft, but not brown. In a bowl, mix the ground beef with about ¼ of the onions and the egg yolks. Season lightly with salt, pepper, and nutmeg. Stir the mixture with a large two-pronged fork to avoid packing the meat down. Form the mixture into 4 patties and dust them with flour. Melt the remaining butter in a frying pan over fairly high heat until golden, add the beef patties, and cook for 2 to 4 minutes on each side, according to taste. Adjust the heat during the cooking so that the butter does not burn. Transfer the patties to a hot serving platter and keep warm. Add the remaining onions to the butter in the pan, sauté over high heat for 1 minute, and then pour the onions and the butter over the patties. *Serves 4.*

NOTE: Any additional desired seasonings, such as dry mustard or fresh herbs, may be added to the beef before mixing.

1105. HUNGARIAN GOULASH
Goulash all'ungherese

3 pounds lean beef (arm pot roast or shoulder),
    cut into 1½-inch cubes
4 tablespoons lard
½ pound onions, coarsely chopped
1½ tablespoons paprika
1 pound tomatoes, peeled, seeded, drained,
    and chopped
1½ cups water (or bouillon)
1 pound potatoes, quartered
Salt and freshly ground pepper

Melt the lard in a heavy casserole (or enamel pot) over high heat until smoking, add the cubes of beef, and brown on all sides (do not crowd the cubes; cook only a few at a time if necessary). Add the onions, reduce the heat slightly, and stir until the onions are golden. Add the paprika, stir it in well, add the tomatoes and ½ cup of water, season with salt and pepper, and cover the casserole. Bring to a boil over high heat and then place the casserole in a moderate oven for 1½ hours. Add the quartered potatoes and about 1 cup of water, or sufficient to barely submerge the potatoes, and continue cooking for 45 minutes, or until the meat is tender enough to cut with a fork. Serve in the casserole. *Serves 6.*

1106. MINUTE STEAK PAILLARD
Paillard

In Italy, a veal steak, pounded very thin and broiled, is commonly called Paillard. The true Paillard, however, as conceived by the famous French restaurateur of that name, is simply a very tender and well-aged beefsteak cut very thin (about ¼ inch), broiled quickly, and served with a sprig of watercress and potato chips [No. 1762].

1107. PEPPERED STEAK
Steak al pepe

3 sirloin or porterhouse steaks, cut 1 inch thick
2 tablespoons white peppercorns, coarsely
      pounded in the mortar
½ cup butter
½ cup Cognac
½ cup Brown Stock [No. 4]
Salt

Rub the pepper into both sides of the steaks and allow them to stand for 3 hours at room temperature to absorb the flavor of the pepper. Heat ¼ cup of the butter in a large frying pan over fairly high heat until it is almost nut colored and quickly brown the steaks in it, 1 or 2 at a time (or use 2 frying pans), for about 2 minutes on each side, or longer to taste. Transfer the steaks to a hot platter and keep warm. Pour off all the fat in the pan, add the Cognac and stock, reduce over high heat to ½ their quantity, remove from the heat, and swirl in the remaining butter, bit by bit. Season the steaks lightly with salt and pour the sauce over them. *Serves* 6.

1108. ROAST BEEF
Roast beef

In England, the traditional cut for roast beef is a section from the ribs cooked as a standing roast. This is an equally popular cut in the United States, either with the ribs, or boned and rolled. However, tenderloin, sirloin, or even rump can make excellent roasts.

Remove the beef from the refrigerator at least 3 hours before cooking. Dry it thoroughly with paper towels, rub it with a generous amount of salt, and brush it with butter or rendered beef fat. Place it on a rack in a shallow roasting pan in a very hot (500°) oven for 10 minutes to sear the meat and seal in its juices. Reduce the heat to moderate (325°) and cook for a total of 17 minutes to the pound for rare, or longer to taste. For a rolled, boned roast, add about 5 minutes per pound.

Baste 2 or 3 times during the cooking with the juices in the pan. When fully cooked, allow it to rest for a minimum of 10 minutes before carving to allow the juices to retreat back into the tissues. It may be served simply with the juices it renders when it is carved or the roasting pan may be de-glazed with 1 or 2 cups of Brown Stock [No. 4]. Pour off most of the fat in the pan before de-glazing.

If there are meat juices in the pan mixed with the fat, place the pan over high heat for a few minutes until the juices congeal and stick to the bottom of the pan, being very careful that they do not burn; pour off the fat; and then de-glaze with the stock.

1109. ROAST BEEF LUIGI VERONELLI
Costata di bue alla Luigi Veronelli

3 pounds boned rib roast of beef
1 carrot, thinly sliced
1 onion, thinly sliced
1 stalk celery, thinly sliced
2 cloves garlic, crushed in the garlic-press
2 cloves, bruised
3 peppercorns, crushed
1 bottle dry red wine
¼ cup chopped ham fat
1 tablespoon oil
1 pound mushroom caps
6 tablespoons butter
Salt and freshly ground pepper

Rub the beef with a generous amount of salt and put it into a bowl with the sliced vegetables, garlic, cloves, and peppercorns. Add the wine and marinate the meat in this mixture for 3 hours, turning it occasionally. Remove it from the marinade and dry thoroughly on paper towels. Reduce the marinade in a saucepan over high heat to ½ its quantity and strain through a fine sieve. Heat the oil and ham fat in a heavy pot until smoking hot and quickly brown the beef on all sides. Add the reduced marinade, bring to a boil, and place the pot in a moderate (350°) oven for 1¼ hours. Turn the beef twice during the cooking and baste frequently with the liquid in the pot. Shortly before the beef is fully cooked, sauté the mushrooms in 3 tablespoons of butter in a covered frying pan over moderate heat for about 8 minutes. Transfer the beef to a hot serving platter, and garnish with the mushrooms. Spoon off excess fat from the surface of the sauce, swirl in the remaining butter, bit by bit, and serve separately in a sauceboat. *Serves* 6.

1110. ROAST BEEF PIZZAIOLA
Costata di bue alla pizzaiola

6 ½-pound slices of beef, cut from a rib roast
3 tablespoons oil
3 cloves garlic, crushed in the garlic-press
6 very ripe tomatoes, peeled, seeded, drained, and
    chopped
1 tablespoon chopped oregano (or 1 teaspoon dried)
Salt and freshly ground pepper

Heat the oil in a heavy frying pan over high heat until smoking hot and quickly brown the slices of beef on both sides (do not crowd the slices; cook only 2 at a time, if necessary). Transfer the slices to a hot serving platter and keep warm. Add the garlic to the oil remaining in the pan, cook until golden, add the tomatoes and oregano, season with salt and pepper, and cook over medium high heat for 8 minutes. Return the slices of beef to the pan for 1 minute or just long enough to become thoroughly hot and then arrange them and the sauce on the platter. *Serves 6.*

1111. ROAST BEEF PRIMAVERILE
Costata di bue con primizie

4 pounds rib roast of beef
1 pound carrots, cut into ovals the size of olives
1 pound string beans
6 artichoke hearts
1 pound small young peas
¾ cup butter
2 cups dry Marsala wine
Salt

Roast the beef in the manner described in No. 1108. Cook each of the vegetables in lightly salted water until just tender (for the exact cooking times, see the section on vegetables beginning at page 539) and then dress each with 2 tablespoons of butter; time their cooking so that they are finished when the roast is ready to be served. When the beef is cooked, transfer it to a hot platter. Pour off excess fat in the roasting pan, add the Marsala, and de-glaze the drippings in the pan over high heat, scraping the bottom with a wooden spoon. Garnish the platter with small mounds of the vegetables and serve the sauce separately. *Serves 6.*

1112. ROAST SIRLOIN CHÂTEAU EN PAPILLOTE
Lombata di manzo château al cartoccio

3 pounds boneless sirloin, or boned rib roast
6 slices beef marrow, ¼ inch thick
12 large mushroom caps
½ cup butter
1 medium onion, finely chopped
½ teaspoon powdered bay leaf
1 tablespoon chopped thyme (or ½ teaspoon dried)
½ cup dry red wine
2 cups Consommé [No. 360], reduced to 1 cup
Parchment paper
4 tablespoons oil
½ cup Duxelles [No. 138]
Salt and freshly ground pepper

Poach the beef marrow in simmering water for 3 minutes, remove from the heat, and let it stay in the hot water until needed. Gently sauté the mushrooms in 2 tablespoons of butter in a covered frying pan over moderate heat for 8 minutes; remove from the heat and reserve. Put the onion, powdered bay leaf, thyme, and wine in a saucepan, bring to a boil over high heat, and reduce until only 2 or 3 tablespoons of liquid remain. Add the consommé, simmer for 3 minutes, strain through a fine sieve, return to the saucepan, and reserve. Heat 3 tablespoons of butter in a heavy pot over high heat until golden and quickly brown the beef on all sides; place the pot in a medium (375°) oven for about 25 minutes, or slightly longer if the beef is very thick. Remove the beef from the oven and sprinkle it with salt and pepper. Brush a large sheet of parchment paper with oil, place the beef in the center, and arrange the mushroom caps and slices of beef marrow on top. Combine the Duxelles with the reserved consommé sauce, bring it quickly to a boil, remove from the heat, and swirl in the remaining butter, bit by bit. Spoon a little of this sauce over the beef and wrap it securely in the paper, crimping the edges well to make a tight seal. Place the wrapped roast in an oiled roasting pan in a hot (450°) oven for about 25 minutes, or until the paper has swelled and turned brown. Carefully transfer the wrapped roast to a hot serving platter, tear open the paper at the table, slice the roast thinly, and spoon the remaining sauce over the slices. *Serves 6.*

376

1113. ROLLED RIB ROAST IN CASSEROLE
Costata di bue in casseruola

3 pounds boned rib roast of beef
Thin sheets of beef suet
6 tablespoons butter
1½ cups Brown Stock [No. 4]
Salt and freshly ground pepper

Wipe the roast completely dry with paper towels, wrap its circumference with the sheets of suet, and tie securely with string. Melt 3 tablespoons of butter in a heavy pot over high heat and quickly brown the meat on all sides. Reduce the heat and continue cooking for about 35 minutes (or longer, to taste), turning the meat frequently for even cooking. Remove the meat from the pot and keep warm. Add the brown stock to the pot, reduce over high heat to about 1 cup, remove from the heat, and swirl in the remaining butter, bit by bit. Slice the meat neatly on a hot serving platter, season lightly with salt and pepper, and spoon the sauce over the slices. *Serves* 6.

1114. SAUTÉ OF BEEF
Sauté di bue

Beef sautés differ from ordinary beef stews in that they employ pieces of a much finer cut of beef, usually fillet. Since the meat is more tender than the coarser cuts used in stews, it is quickly browned in butter, leaving the center of the pieces rare; removed from the pan; and then returned later to simmer for a very short time in a prepared sauce. A sauté is thus both somewhat more elegant and simpler to prepare than a stew.

2½ pounds fillet of beef (or substitute sirloin), cut
    into strips ½ inch thick and about 2 inches long
6 tablespoons butter
¼ cup dry red wine (or dry Madeira)
1 cup Brown Stock [No. 4]
½ cup heavy cream
2 teaspoons arrowroot
2 tablespoons chopped parsley
Salt and freshly ground pepper

Dry the strips of beef very thoroughly on paper towels. Heat 4 tablespoons of the butter in a heavy frying pan over fairly high heat until it is golden and quickly sauté the pieces of beef in it, a few pieces at a time, until they are nicely browned but still rare on the inside. As soon as the pieces are browned, transfer them to a bowl with a slotted spoon. Pour off all the fat in the pan, add the wine and brown stock, and de-glaze the pan over high heat by scraping the bottom and sides with a wooden spoon. Reduce over high heat to about ⅔ their quantity. Gently sauté the mushrooms in another frying pan over moderate heat in the remaining 2 tablespoons of butter for about 8 minutes. Blend the arrowroot with the cream, add it to the reduced wine and stock, and stir over moderate heat until the sauce has slightly thickened. Add the mushrooms and the pieces of beef, correct the seasoning, reduce the heat to a very low flame, cover the pan, and simmer for about 2 minutes. Be very careful not to overcook so that the beef becomes well done. Transfer the meat and sauce to a hot serving platter and sprinkle with the chopped parsley. *Serves* 6.

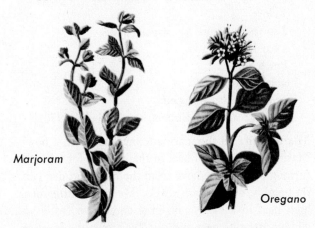

Marjoram

Oregano

1115. SAUTÉ OF BEEF TOLSTOY
Sauté di bue alla Tolstoi

2½ pounds fillet of beef (or substitute sirloin), cut into
    strips ½ inch thick and about 2 inches long
4 tablespoons butter
1 tablespoon chopped onion
5 tomatoes, peeled, seeded, drained, and puréed
    through a food mill
½ cup Tomato Sauce [No. 19]
2 cups White Stock [No. 1]
2 teaspoons paprika
½ cup sliced pickles
Salt and freshly ground pepper

Brown the pieces of beef in the butter in the manner described in the preceding recipe and then transfer them to a bowl. Add the onion to the butter in the pan, cook until transparent, and then add the tomatoes, tomato sauce, stock, paprika, and pickles. Season lightly with salt and pepper and simmer over medium heat until somewhat thickened. Add the pieces of beef, cover the pan, reduce the heat to a very low flame, and simmer for 2 minutes. Turn the beef and sauce out onto a hot serving platter. *Serves* 6.

1116. SIRLOIN MAESTRO
Controfiletto di bue alla maniera del maestro

3 pounds boned sirloin, in 1 piece
A marinade:
  1 cup dry white wine
  ½ cup oil
  1 tablespoon wine vinegar
  1 carrot, sliced
  1 onion, sliced
  1 stalk celery, sliced
  3 sprigs parsley, crushed
  3 peppercorns
  1 teaspoon salt
  1 clove garlic, crushed in the garlic-press
  1 clove
  2 sprigs thyme (or ½ teaspoon dried)
  1 bay leaf
  Pinch nutmeg
3 tablespoons butter
4 medium onions, chopped
1 recipe Creamed Mushrooms Au Gratin [No. 1707]

Mix together all the marinade ingredients in a bowl. Marinate the piece of beef in the mixture for 6 hours, turning it often. Remove from the bowl and dry very thoroughly with paper towels. Melt the butter over high heat in a heavy pot large enough to easily accommodate the meat and quickly brown the meat on all sides. Reduce the heat to moderate and continue cooking for about 30 minutes, turning the meat frequently (the exact cooking time will depend on personal preference and the thickness of the meat). Transfer the meat to a hot oven-proof serving platter and keep it warm in a 170° oven. While the beef is cooking, reduce the marinade in a saucepan over high heat to ⅓ its quantity, strain through a fine sieve, and reserve. When the beef is cooked, add the onions to the butter in the pan and cook over medium heat until golden. Add the reduced marinade and bring to a boil. Remove the beef from the oven, slice it neatly on the platter, and spoon the onions and sauce over the slices. Serve the creamed mushrooms on the side. *Serves 6.*

1117. SIRLOIN PRIMAVERILE
Controfiletto di bue primaverile

3 pounds boned sirloin, cut in 1 slice
8 strips of prosciutto (lean and fat), 3 inches long and ¼ inch square
8 strips of salt pork, 3 inches long and ¼ inch square, parboiled for 15 minutes

A marinade:
  1 cup dry Marsala wine
  ¼ cup brandy
  1 carrot, chopped
  1 stalk celery, chopped
  1 bay leaf
  Salt and freshly ground pepper
½ cup butter
A chopped mixture:
  1 onion
  1 carrot
  1 stalk celery
  3 sprigs parsley
½ cup Brown Stock [No. 4]
1½ pounds string beans, cooked until just tender in lightly salted water, drained, and dressed with 2 tablespoons butter
1½ pounds "new" potatoes, cooked until just tender in lightly salted water, drained, and dressed with 3 tablespoons butter

Using a larding needle, lard the beef with the strips of prosciutto and salt pork. Mix the marinade ingredients in a bowl and marinate the beef in the mixture for 6 hours, turning it occasionally. Remove from the marinade and dry thoroughly on paper towels. Melt 4 tablespoons of the butter over high heat in a pot large enough to easily contain the meat, add the chopped mixture, cook until golden, add the beef, and brown on all sides. Reduce the heat to moderate and continue cooking for about 30 minutes, turning the beef frequently (the exact cooking time will depend on the thickness of the beef and on personal preference). Remove the beef and keep warm in a very low (170°) oven. Add the marinade and the brown stock to the pot and reduce over high heat to about 1 cup. Strain through a fine sieve, return it to the pot, bring to a boil, remove from the heat, and swirl in the remaining butter, bit by bit. Slice the beef neatly on the platter, spoon the sauce over the slices, and garnish with the beans and potatoes. *Serves 6.*

1118. STEAK TARTARE
Bistecche alla tartara

Since the beef in this dish is eaten raw, it should be of excellent quality. Fillet of beef is the first choice, although sirloin or a comparable cut may be substituted. All fat should be trimmed off before grinding.

1 pound fillet of beef, finely ground
Parsley sprigs
1 cup Tartar Sauce [No. 98]

Brandy
Worcestershire sauce
Freshly ground pepper
Salt

Shape the beef into four round patties and arrange them on a serving platter garnished with parsley. Serve the tartar sauce, brandy, and condiments at the table to permit each guest to season his steak according to his preference. *Serves* 4.

1119. STEAK TARTARE AMERICANA
Bistecche all'americana

1 pound fillet of beef, finely ground
4 egg yolks
2 onions, chopped
½ cup chopped parsley
½ cup pickled capers
Worcestershire sauce
Brandy
Freshly ground pepper
Salt

Shape the beef into four round patties and arrange them on a serving platter. Make a depression in the center of each and place 1 raw egg yolk in it. Serve each guest with 1 patty on a cold plate and serve the remaining ingredients separately so that each guest may season his steak to taste. *Serves* 4.

1120. STUFFED BEEF ROLLS
Involtini di bue

12 thin slices of top or bottom round of beef
12 slices prosciutto (fat and lean)
1 stalk celery, finely chopped
1 carrot, finely chopped
Flour
2 tablespoons oil
A chopped mixture:
  2 ounces ham fat
  1 stalk celery
  1 clove garlic
  1 medium onion
½ cup dry white wine
1 pound tomatoes, peeled, seeded, drained, and
  chopped
1 bay leaf
1 clove
Salt and freshly ground pepper
2 tablespoons chopped parsley

Flatten the slices of beef as thinly as possible with the

flat side of a meat cleaver. Season the slices lightly with salt and pepper and on each place a slice of prosciutto and a little chopped celery and carrot. Roll the slices up and tie securely with string. Dust the rolls lightly with flour. Heat the oil over high heat in a pot large enough to contain the beef rolls in 1 layer, add the chopped mixture, cook for 1 minute, add the beef rolls, and brown quickly on all sides. Add the wine and stir until the wine is almost completely evaporated. Add the tomatoes, bay leaf, and clove; and season with salt and pepper. Cover the pot, bring to a boil, reduce the heat to a very low flame, and simmer for about 2 hours. Stir occasionally during the cooking to make certain the rolls do not stick to the bottom of the pot. Transfer the rolls to a hot serving platter and remove the string. Pour the sauce over them through a fine sieve and sprinkle with the chopped parsley. *Serves* 6.

1121. TOURNEDOS ANDALUSIA
Tournedos all'andalusa

Tournedos are slices cut from a fillet of beef near the tail end.

6 slices fillet of beef, cut 1½ inches thick and about
  2½ inches in diameter
6 sweet red peppers
1 clove garlic, crushed in the garlic press
1 cup Duxelles [No. 138]
1 cup dry white wine
½ cup Italian Meat Sauce [No. 41]
1 cup Tomato Sauce [No. 19]
1 tablespoon chopped parsley
1 cup fresh breadcrumbs
6 slices eggplant, ½ inch thick and 3 inches in diameter,
  sprinkled with salt and allowed to drain for 1 hour,
  then washed and patted dry
Flour
¾ cup butter
6 sweet Italian sausages
6 slices bread, crusts removed, cut the same diameter
  as the fillets
Salt and freshly ground pepper

Cut off and discard the top third of the peppers and remove the seeds. Parboil peppers in boiling water for 5 minutes, drain, and reserve. Cook the garlic, Duxelles, and ½ cup of the wine in a saucepan over fairly high heat until the wine has nearly evaporated. Add the meat and tomato sauces, season with salt and pepper, and simmer for 5 minutes. Stir in the parsley and the breadcrumbs, remove from the heat, and allow to cool

Tournedos Andalusia (No. 1121): see page 379

slightly. Fill the peppers loosely with the mixture, top each with a teaspoon of butter, place them in a buttered baking dish, and bake in a moderate (350°) oven for 15 minutes.

Season the slices of eggplant with a little pepper, dust them lightly with flour, and sauté them in 3 tablespoons of butter in a frying pan over high heat for 3 minutes on each side. Remove from the heat and keep warm.

Sauté sausages in another frying pan over medium heat for about 10 minutes. Remove them from the pan and keep warm.

Sauté the slices of bread in 3 tablespoons of butter in a frying pan over medium heat until golden on both sides. Remove from the pan and arrange them on a hot serving platter. Add 4 more tablespoons of butter to the pan, raise the heat, add the tournedos (slices of fillet), and cook for 3 to 4 minutes on each side. Place a tournedos on each slice of bread, season lightly with salt and pepper, top with a slice of eggplant, and arrange the sausages and stuffed peppers on the platter. Add the remaining wine to the pan in which the tournedos cooked, reduce over high heat to $\frac{1}{2}$ its quantity, and pour over the tournedos. *Serves* 6.

1122. TOURNEDOS BELLA ELENA
Tournedos Bella Elena

6 slices fillet of beef, cut 1½ inches thick and about
   2½ inches in diameter

4 tablespoons butter
6 Artichoke Croquettes [No. 250]
6 slices truffle
Salt and freshly ground pepper
Juice of 1 lemon

Heat the butter in a frying pan over fairly high heat until almost nut colored, add the tournedos, and cook for 3 to 4 minutes on each side. Arrange the tournedos and artichoke croquettes on a hot serving platter and season the tournedos with salt and pepper and top each with a truffle slice. Add the lemon juice to the butter in the frying pan, cook for 1 minute, and pour over the tournedos. *Serves* 6.

1123. TOURNEDOS BORDELAISE
Tournedos con midollo di bue

6 slices fillet of beef, cut 1½ inches thick and
   2½ inches in diameter
4 tablespoons butter
6 slices beef marrow, cut ¾ inch thick and parboiled
   5 minutes
1½ cups Sauce Bordelaise [No. 27]
Salt and freshly ground pepper

Sauté the tournedos as described in the previous recipe and arrange them on a serving platter. Season them lightly with salt and pepper, top each with a slice of beef marrow, and serve the sauce separately. *Serves* 6.

380

1124. TOURNEDOS CLAMART

Tournedos Clamart

6 slices fillet of beef, cut 1½ inches thick and
    2½ inches in diameter
4 tablespoons butter
6 small Potatoes Macaire [No. 1778]
Salt and freshly ground pepper

Sauté the tournedos as described in Tournedos Bella Elena [No. 1122]. Arrange them on a hot serving platter, season them lightly with salt and pepper, and garnish the platter with the small potato cakes. *Serves* 6.

1125. TOURNEDOS FAVORITA

Tournedos Favorita

6 slices fillet of beef, cut 1½ inches thick and
    2½ inches in diameter
4 tablespoons butter
6 rounds of bread, crusts removed, cut to the size of
    the tournedos, and lightly browned on both sides
    in butter
6 slices pâté de foie gras
6 slices truffle
18 asparagus tips, cooked until barely tender in lightly
    salted water and dressed with 2 tablespoons butter
1 tablespoon Meat Essence [No. 10]
½ cup Brown Stock [No. 4]
18 Noisette Potatoes [No. 1783]
1 tablespoon chopped parsley
Salt and freshly ground pepper

Sauté the tournedos as described in Tournedos Bella Elena [No. 1122]. Place a tournedos on each of the rounds of bread on a hot serving platter, season them lightly with salt and pepper, top each with a slice of foie gras and truffle, and garnish the platter with the asparagus tips. Add the meat essence and brown stock to the pan in which the tournedos cooked, bring to a fast boil, and pour over the tournedos. Sprinkle the potatoes with parsley and serve them separately. *Serves* 6.

1126. TOURNEDOS CONNOISSEUR

Tournedos del "connaisseur"

6 slices fillet of beef, cut 1½ inches thick and
    2½ inches in diameter
4 tablespoons butter, melted
½ cup Mustard Butter [No. 112], chilled
2 tablespoons chopped parsley
Juice of 1 lemon
Salt and freshly ground white pepper

Brush the slices of fillet with melted butter, place them on a heated rack about 5 inches beneath a high broiler flame, and broil for about 3 minutes on each side, basting occasionally with more butter. Arrange them on a hot serving platter, season them with salt and white pepper, and top each with several curls of mustard butter, a little parsley, and a few drops of lemon juice. *Serves* 6.

1127. TOURNEDOS MARQUIS DE SADE

Tournedos "Marquis de Sade"

6 slices fillet of beef, cut 1½ inches thick
    and 2½ inches in diameter
6 tablespoons butter
6 slices stale bread, crusts removed, cut to the size of
    the tournedos, and toasted
6 slices truffle
½ cup Brown Stock [No. 4]
¼ cup dry sherry wine
½ cup Tomato Sauce [No. 19]
½ cup heavy cream
1 tablespoon chopped truffle
Salt and freshly ground pepper

Sauté the tournedos as described in Tournedos Bella Elena [No. 1122] and season them lightly with salt and pepper. Arrange the toasted rounds of bread on a hot serving platter, place a tournedos on each, and top each with a slice of truffle. Add the sherry, stock, and tomato sauce to the pan in which the tournedos cooked and reduce over high heat to ½ their quantity. Add the cream and chopped truffle, bring just to a boil, remove from the heat, correct the seasoning, swirl in the remaining butter, bit by bit, and pour over the tournedos. *Serves* 6.

1128. TOURNEDOS MEXICO

Tournedos alla messicana

6 slices fillet of beef, cut 1½ inches thick and
    2½ inches in diameter
½ cup butter
3 sweet peppers, roasted, peeled, seeded, and cut into
    strips [*see* No. 145]
6 large mushroom caps
2 tablespoons oil
1 cup Tomato Sauce [No. 19]
¾ cup Brown Stock [No. 4]
Salt and freshly ground pepper

Sauté the tournedos as described in Tournedos Bella Elena [No. 1122] and season them lightly with salt and pepper. Sauté the strips of pepper in 2 tablespoons of butter in a frying pan over moderate heat for about 10 minutes. Brush the mushroom caps with oil and broil them under a medium broiler flame for about 3 minutes on each side. Fill each of the caps with tomato sauce (reserving a few tablespoons) and sprinkle with a little parsley. Arrange them and the tournedos on a hot serving platter and top each of the tournedos with a few strips of the peppers. Add the remaining tomato sauce and stock to the pan in which the tournedos cooked and reduce over high heat to ½ their quantity. Remove from the heat, swirl in the remaining butter, bit by bit, and pour over the tournedos. *Serves* 6.

1129. TOURNEDOS OPERA
Tournedos opera

6 slices fillet of beef, cut 1½ inches thick and
    2½ inches in diameter
6 tablespoons butter
½ pound chicken livers, coarsely chopped
2 tablespoons dry Madeira wine
18 asparagus tips, cooked until just tender in
    lightly salted water and dressed with 2
    tablespoons butter
12 baked tartlet shells [*see* No. 1959]
Salt and freshly ground pepper

Melt 2 tablespoons of the butter in a frying pan over medium heat, add the chicken livers, season lightly with salt and pepper, and sauté for 3 minutes. Add the Madeira and cook for 1 minute longer. Remove from the heat and reserve. Time the cooking of the asparagus tips so that they are ready at the same time as the tournedos. Sauté the tournedos in the manner described in Tournedos Bella Elena [No. 1122] and season them with salt and pepper. Arrange them on a hot serving platter and garnish the platter with the tartlet shells, half of them filled with asparagus tips and half with the chicken livers. *Serves* 6.

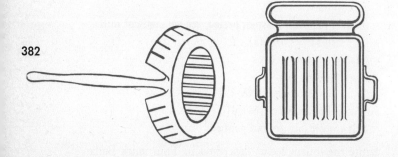

VEAL
Vitello

The best veal is very tender and has a very finely textured flesh of a pale pink color which becomes white on contact with heat. It comes from milk-fed calves between 6 and 12 months old that have been kept very quiet during their short life. This type of veal is, unfortunately, rarely found in American markets, although some suppliers experiment from time to time with techniques to produce meat of this quality. When it is to be found, it is naturally expensive, but well worth the cost. In any event, when buying veal, avoid meat of a dark or bright red color, as it will have come from a calf that has been at least partially fed on grain or grass. As a general rule, the paler the flesh, the more tender and flavorful the veal will be.

In America, we are more likely to associate veal with Italian cooking than any other meat, if for no other reason than the fact that veal *scaloppine* turns up so frequently on American menus. A beautifully prepared *scaloppine* in a Marsala sauce, or with mushrooms and prosciutto, can indeed be delicious and deserves its popularity. Equally rewarding are the many other veal dishes which are so distinctively Italian, such as a veal *piccata*, stuffed veal chops, or *ossobuco*, to name but a few. While many of these dishes contain a variety of ingredients, none of them is actually very difficult to prepare. Because it is so young, veal is lacking in a great deal of fat. For this reason it can toughen easily, and some care must be taken in its preparation so that it retains its natural juices, unless it is tenderized by slow braising or stewing. Thin slices of veal, such as for *scaloppine*, for instance, are always cooked very quickly in butter or oil and then removed from the pan while a sauce is prepared, so that they will not toughen from contact with boiling liquid. Veal can be delicious when roasted in an open pan, but it is wise to choose only a good grade of pale veal for such a simple treatment. If only darker veal is available, it will be more tender and juicier if roasted or braised in a covered pot. The best cuts for a roast are top round or rump, although shoulder or breast meat may be used. The loin is an expensive cut and, while it may be boned and roasted, it is more often reserved for chops. The neck, shoulder, or breast meat is best for stews. As with beef, it is important to choose the right cut of veal for the right dish.

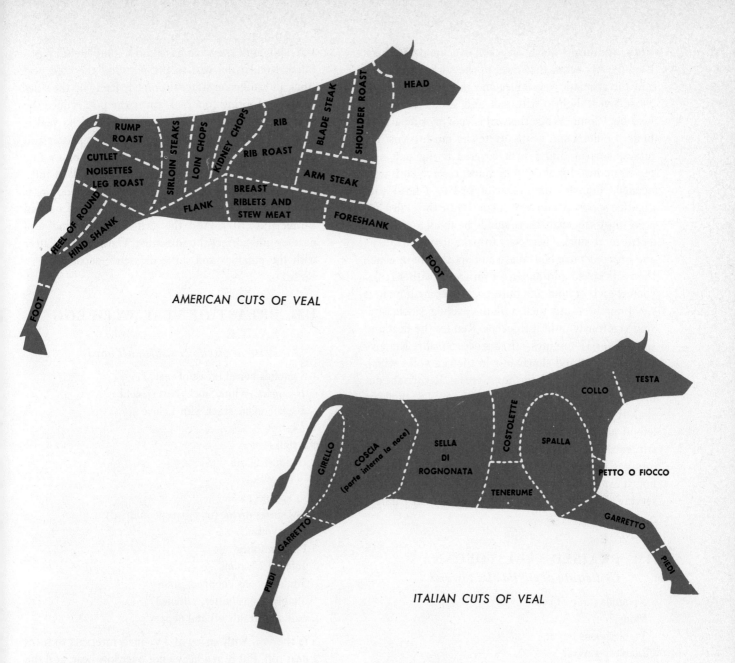

AMERICAN CUTS OF VEAL

ITALIAN CUTS OF VEAL

1130. BLANQUETTE DE VEAU À L'ANCIENNE
Blanquette di vitello all'antica

3 pounds veal (breast, shoulder, or neck), cut into 1½-inch cubes
1½ quarts White Stock [No. 1]
Aromatic vegetables:
   1 carrot, quartered
   1 onion, stuck with 1 clove
   1 stalk celery
Bouquet Garni:
   1 leek, chopped
   3 sprigs parsley
   2 sprigs thyme (or ½ teaspoon dried)
   1 bay leaf

18 Braised White Onions [No. 1721]
18 mushroom caps
6 tablespoons butter
3 tablespoons flour
5 egg yolks
½ cup heavy cream
1 lemon
Pinch nutmeg
2 tablespoons chopped parsley
Salt and freshly ground white pepper

Cover the pieces of veal with cold water in a large heavy pot, bring slowly to a boil over medium heat, simmer 2 minutes, pour the veal into a colander, and wash the pieces under cold running water. Clean the pot thoroughly, return the veal to it, add the white

383

stock, and bring slowly to a boil over moderate heat. Remove any scum that rises to the surface and then add the aromatic vegetables and the Bouquet Garni. Season very lightly with salt and simmer over low heat for 1 hour. While the veal is cooking prepare the braised onions and gently sauté the mushrooms in 2 tablespoons of butter in a covered frying pan over moderate heat for about 8 minutes; reserve both until needed. Transfer the pieces of veal to a bowl with a slotted spoon. Strain the cooking liquid through a fine sieve into a saucepan (there should be about 5 cups; add a little more stock if necessary to make up this quantity), and bring just to a boil. Wash and dry the pot in which the veal cooked and prepare a roux in it with 4 tablespoons each of flour and butter, stir over medium heat for 1 minute, and then add the boiling stock, stirring vigorously until it thickens. Reduce the heat and simmer for 15 minutes, stirring occasionally. Remove from the heat and slowly stir in the egg yolks which have been beaten with the heavy cream. Return the pot to very low heat and stir constantly until it thickens slightly. Do not boil. Add the veal, onions, mushrooms, lemon juice, and nutmeg. Correct the seasoning and stir constantly over a very low flame for about 5 minutes, or just long enough to get all ingredients very hot. Turn the contents of the pot out into a shallow serving dish and sprinkle with the chopped parsley. *Serves 6.*

1131. BRAISED VEAL TOSCANA
Grillettato di vitello alla toscana

3 pounds rump of veal
Flour
3 tablespoons butter
2 tablespoons oil
¼ cup chopped onion
1 clove garlic, crushed in the garlic-press
½ cup dry white wine
¼ pound prosciutto, cut in strips
1 quart Brown Veal Stock [No. 5], cold
½ teaspoon grated lemon rind (no white part)
Pinch nutmeg
1½ pounds "new" potatoes, cooked until just
        tender in lightly salted water
Salt and freshly ground pepper

Season the veal with salt and pepper and dust it with flour. Heat the butter and oil in a heavy pot over fairly high heat and brown the veal on all sides. Remove it temporarily from the pot, add the onion and garlic, cook until they are golden, add the prosciutto and wine,

and cook until the wine has almost completely evaporated. Return the veal to the pot, add the cold veal stock and sufficient water to come halfway up the sides of the veal, bring to a boil, cover the pot, reduce the heat, and simmer for 1½ hours, or until the veal is tender. Transfer the veal to a hot serving platter and keep warm. Strain the cooking liquid through a fine sieve into a saucepan and reduce over high heat until it is strongly flavored and slightly thickened; or, if desired, it may be thickened with a little Kneaded Butter [No. 107]. Add the grated lemon rind and nutmeg and correct the seasoning. Garnish the platter with the potatoes and serve the sauce separately. *Serves 6.*

1132. BREAST OF VEAL WITH EGG SAUCE
Petto di vitello con salsa all'uovo

3 pounds boned breast of veal
1½ quarts White Stock [No. 1], cold
1 small onion, stuck with 1 clove
2 carrots
2 stalks celery
Bouquet Garni:
    1 bay leaf
    3 sprigs parsley
    2 sprigs thyme (or ½ teaspoon dried)
5 egg yolks
Pinch nutmeg
Juice of 2 lemons
3 tablespoons chopped parsley
3 tablespoons butter, softened
Salt and freshly ground pepper

Tie the veal with string at 1½-inch intervals to form a neat roll. Put it in a heavy pot over low heat, add the cold white stock and sufficient cold water to barely cover it, and bring very slowly to a boil. Simmer for 5 minutes, skimming frequently to remove the scum that rises to the surface. Add the vegetables and Bouquet Garni and simmer for about 2 hours, or until the veal is tender. Transfer the veal to a hot serving platter and keep warm. Reduce the cooking liquid over high heat to slightly less than 3 cups. Strain it through a cheesecloth-lined colander into a bowl. Wash out the pot, and then return the strained cooking liquid to it. Beat the egg yolks with 1 cup of the liquid and gradually pour into the pot, stirring constantly. Place the pot over very low heat and stir constantly until slightly thickened. Do not boil. Add the nutmeg, lemon juice, and parsley, and season with salt and pepper.

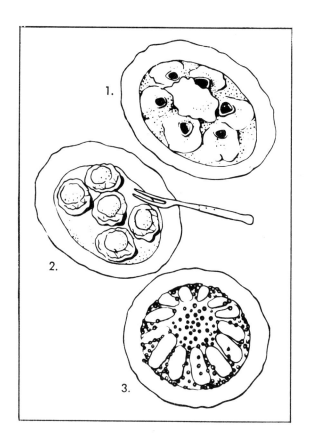

1. Ossobuco Milanese (No. 1159)
2. Veal Cutlets Partenopea (No. 1152)
3. Veal Rolls with Peas (No. 1175)

Swirl in the softened butter, bit by bit. Slice the veal neatly on the platter, spoon a little of the sauce over the slices, and serve the remainder separately. *Serves* 6.

1133. SKEWERED VEAL ROMANA
Spiedini di vitello alla romana

18 scallops of veal, cut from the upper
    leg, 1/4 inch thick
18 thin slices of prosciutto
18 very thin slices of salt pork, parboiled for
    15 minutes
6 skewers
18 cubes of stale bread, 1 1/2 inches square
    and 1/2 inch thick
18 sage leaves
1/2 cup butter, melted
1/2 cup dry white wine
Salt and freshly ground pepper

Place the slices of veal between sheets of wax paper and pound them with the flat side of a meat cleaver to make them as thin as possible without breaking through them. Season with salt and pepper, place a slice of prosciutto and salt pork on each, and roll the slices up (the rolls should have the appearance of small, fat sausages). Secure the ends with toothpicks. Place 3 of the rolls on each of 6 skewers, alternating them with cubes of bread and sage leaves. Brush them very generously with butter, place them in a buttered baking dish, add the wine, and bake in a moderate (350°) oven for 1/2 hour, basting frequently with more butter and the juices in the dish. Transfer them to a hot serving platter and serve at once. *Serves* 6.

1134. BROILED VEAL CHOPS
Costolette di vitello alla griglia

6 loin or rib veal chops, cut 1 inch thick
1/2 cup butter, melted
36 Noisette Potatoes [No. 1783]
Watercress
3 lemons, quartered
Salt and freshly ground pepper

Dry the chops thoroughly with paper towels, brush them with melted butter, and brown them quickly on both sides beneath a high broiler flame. Reduce the flame slightly and cook them for a total of about 8 minutes on each side, basting occasionally with a little more melted butter. Arrange them on a hot serving platter and garnish with the potatoes, watercress, and lemon quarters. *Serves* 6.

1135. VEAL CHOPS WITH BASIL
Costolette di vitello al basilico

6 loin or rib veal chops, cut 1 inch thick
6 tablespoons butter
1 cup dry white wine
1 clove garlic, crushed in the garlic-press
3 tablespoons chopped basil
2 tablespoons Demi-Glaze Sauce [No. 20]
Juice of 1/2 lemon
Salt and freshly ground pepper

Dry the chops thoroughly on paper towels. Heat 4 tablespoons of the butter in a large, heavy skillet over fairly high heat until golden, add 2 or 3 of the chops, and brown on each side for 3 minutes. Remove them from the pan and season with salt and pepper. Cook the remaining chops in the same manner, remove them from the pan, and season them. Add the wine to the pan and reduce over high heat to 1/2 its quantity. Return the chops to the pan, overlapping one another, and sprinkle with the garlic and basil. Cover the pan tightly and simmer over very low heat for about 20 minutes. Turn the chops over once during the cooking period and baste with the juices in the pan. They are fully cooked when their juices run clear yellow and they are easily pierced with a fork. Transfer the chops to a hot serving platter and keep warm. Add the Demi-Glaze to the juices in the pan and reduce over high heat to about 1/2 cup. Remove from the heat, add the lemon juice, and swirl in the remaining butter, bit by bit. Spoon a little of the sauce over each chop. *Serves* 6.

1136. VEAL CHOPS GOURMET
Costolette di vitello del "gourmet" con tagliatelle e tartufi

6 loin or rib veal chops, cut 1 inch thick
6 round slices pâté de foie gras, 1/4 inch thick
    and 1 1/2 inches in diameter
Flour
1 egg, beaten
1 cup fresh breadcrumbs
6 tablespoons butter
1 cup Port wine
1/2 pound tagliatelle, cooked [*see* No. 514]
4 tablespoons butter, softened
1 large truffle, sliced [or No. 1819a]
Salt and freshly ground white pepper

Dry the chops thoroughly with paper towels. Cut a horizontal slit in the side of each to make a pocket and insert a slice of foie gras. Season the chops with salt and pepper, dust with flour, dip in beaten egg, and cover them generously with breadcrumbs. Heat 4 tablespoons of butter in a large frying pan over fairly high heat, and brown the chops, 3 at a time, for about 3 minutes on each side. When they are all nicely browned, transfer them to a shallow baking dish, pour the melted butter in the pan over them, and bake in a moderate (350°) oven for about 20 minutes, basting occasionally with the butter in the dish. They are fully cooked when easily pierced with a fork. While the chops are cooking, add the Port to the frying pan, reduce over high heat to ⅔ its quantity, lower the heat, and keep hot until needed. Cook the tagliatelle in a large quantity of boiling salted water until just *al dente,* drain them, pour them into the center of a large hot serving platter, toss them with 4 tablespoons of softened butter, and sprinkle the sliced truffle on the top. Arrange the chops around the tagliatelle, remove the reduced Port from the heat, swirl in the remaining 2 tablespoons of butter, bit by bit, and pour over the chops. *Serves 6.*

1137. VEAL CHOPS LADY VIOLET GRAHAM
Costolette di vitello "Lady Violet Graham"

6 loin or rib veal chops, cut 1 inch thick
18 1-inch strips of prosciutto
9 anchovy fillets, washed free of salt [*see* No. 220]
12 thin slices dill pickle
12 very thin slices lean salt pork, cut approximately the same size as the chops, and parboiled for 20 minutes
4 tablespoons butter
1 onion, sliced
1 small stalk celery, sliced
1 tablespoon chopped parsley
1 tablespoon chopped basil (or ½ teaspoon dried)
½ cup dry white wine
½ cup White Stock [No. 1]
3 egg yolks
1 cup heavy cream
12 small rounds of bread, browned in butter
Salt and freshly ground white pepper

Cut small slits in each of the chops with a very sharply pointed knife and insert in these slits a few strips of prosciutto, halves of anchovy fillets, and slices of pickle. Season the chops with pepper. Cover both sides of each with slices of salt pork and tie very securely

with string. Melt the butter in a large frying pan and quickly brown the chops over fairly high heat, 3 at a time, for about 3 minutes on each side. Remove the chops from the pan for a few minutes. Add the onion, celery, parsley, and basil. Reduce the heat slightly and stir until the onion begins to color. Add the wine and stock, bring to a boil, return the chops to the pan, cover tightly, reduce the heat to a very low flame, and simmer for about 20 minutes. The chops are fully cooked when easily pierced with a fork. Transfer the chops to a hot serving platter and keep warm. Reduce the cooking liquid over high heat to ½ its quantity, strain through a fine sieve, and return to the pan. Add the egg yolks which have been beaten with the heavy cream, return the pan to a very low flame, and stir constantly for about 3 minutes, or until the sauce thickens slightly. Do not boil. Correct the seasoning, pour over the chops, and garnish with the rounds of bread. *Serves 6.*

1138. VEAL CHOPS VERONELLI
Costolette di vitello alla Veronelli

6 loin or rib veal chops, cut 1 inch thick
A marinade:
    3 tablespoons white wine
    ½ cup oil
    1 onion, chopped
    Juice of ½ lemon
    1 tablespoon chopped parsley
    1 tablespoon chopped thyme (or ½ teaspoon dried)
    1 bay leaf, crumbled
    1 teaspoon salt
Flour
2 eggs, slightly beaten
1½ cups breadcrumbs
4 tablespoons oil
½ cup butter
1 medium onion, chopped
½ cup chopped prosciutto
1 cup dry Marsala wine
1½ cups Brown Veal Stock [No. 5]
2 tablespoons Kneaded Butter [No. 107]
1 tablespoon chopped basil
1 tablespoon chopped marjoram
1 clove garlic, crushed in the mortar with 3 peppercorns
Salt and freshly ground white pepper

Marinate the chops in the marinade for 3 hours. Drain them, being careful to wipe off all the marinade ingredients, dust with flour, dip in beaten egg, and cover them

386

thoroughly with breadcrumbs. Heat 4 tablespoons of the butter and 4 tablespoons of oil in a large frying pan over high heat and brown the chops, a few at a time, for about 3 minutes on each side. When they are nicely browned, arrange them all in the pan, overlapping one another, reduce the heat, cover the pan, and simmer for about 20 minutes. Turn the chops once during the cooking and baste with the juices in the pan. While the chops are cooking, sauté the chopped onion in 2 tablespoons of butter in a heavy saucepan over medium heat until it is golden, add the prosciutto, cook for 1 minute longer, add the Marsala and stock, and reduce to $\frac{1}{2}$ their quantity. Blend in the kneaded butter with a whisk, simmer for 5 minutes, and then add the garlic, peppercorns, and chopped herbs. Arrange the chops on a hot serving platter and serve the sauce separately. *Serves* 6.

1139. VEAL CHOPS MARÉCHALE
Costolette di vitello à la maréchale

6 loin or rib veal chops, cut 1 inch thick
Flour
2 eggs, beaten
1 cup fresh breadcrumbs
$\frac{1}{2}$ cup grated Parmesan cheese
$\frac{1}{2}$ cup butter
2 truffles, sliced [or No. 1819a]
2 lemons quartered
24 asparagus tips, cooked until just tender in lightly
    salted water, drained, and dressed with
    3 tablespoons melted butter
$\frac{1}{2}$ cup Brown Veal Stock [No. 5]
Salt and freshly ground white pepper

Season the chops with salt and pepper, dust them with flour, dip in beaten egg, and then cover thoroughly with the breadcrumbs mixed with cheese. Heat 6 tablespoons of the butter in a large frying pan over fairly high heat until golden and quickly brown the chops, 3 at a time, for about 3 minutes on each side. When they are nicely browned, arrange them all in the pan, overlapping one another, cover the pan tightly, reduce the heat to a low flame, and simmer for about 20 minutes, turning them once during the cooking period and basting with the juices in the pan. They are fully cooked when their juices run clear yellow and they are easily pierced with a fork. Transfer them to a hot serving platter, put a few slices of truffle on each chop, and garnish the platter with the lemon quarters and asparagus tips. Add the veal stock to the frying pan, bring to a boil over high heat, remove from the heat, swirl in the remaining butter, bit by bit, and spoon a little of this sauce over each chop. *Serves* 6.

1140. VEAL CHOPS MARIA THERESA
Costolette di vitello "Maria Teresa"

6 loin or rib veal chops, cut 1 inch thick
6 thin slices prosciutto (fat and lean)
6 thin slices Swiss (or Gruyère) cheese
Flour
2 eggs, slightly beaten
2 cups fresh breadcrumbs
6 ripe tomatoes
6 tablespoons butter
$\frac{1}{4}$ cup oil
12 anchovy fillets, soaked free of salt [*see* No. 220]
Salt and freshly ground pepper

Cut a horizontal slit in the side of each chop to make a pocket and insert into each a slice of prosciutto and cheese. Season the chops with salt and pepper, dust with flour, dip in beaten egg, and cover thoroughly with breadcrumbs. Heat the butter in large frying pan over fairly high heat until golden and brown the chops, 3 at a time, for about 3 minutes on each side. When they are nicely browned, arrange them all in the pan, overlapping one another, reduce the heat, cover the pan tightly, and simmer for about 20 minutes, turning them once during the cooking and basting with the juices in the pan. They are fully cooked when their juices run yellow and they are easily pierced with a fork. While the chops are cooking, cut off the tops of the tomatoes, season them generously with salt and pepper, sprinkle with breadcrumbs and a little oil, and place them in an oiled dish in a moderate (350°) oven for 15 minutes. Remove them from the oven and place them under a high broiler flame for 1 or 2 minutes to brown the tops. Arrange the chops on a hot serving platter, place 2 anchovy fillets on each chop, and garnish with the tomatoes. *Serves* 6.

Veal Chops Maréchale (No. 1139):
see page 387

1141. VEAL CHOPS WITH MARSALA SAUCE

Costolette di vitello alla moda con salsa al marsala

6 loin or rib veal chops, cut 1 inch thick
Flour
2 eggs, slightly beaten
1½ cups fresh breadcrumbs
½ cup butter
1 pound mushrooms, sliced
1 clove garlic, crushed in the garlic-press
Salt and freshly ground pepper
2 cups Marsala Sauce [No. 43]

Season the chops with salt and pepper, dust with flour, dip in beaten egg, and cover thoroughly with bread-crumbs. Heat 5 tablespoons of the butter in a large frying pan over fairly high heat until golden and brown the chops, 3 at a time, for about 3 minutes on each side. When they are nicely browned, arrange them all in the pan, overlapping one another, lower the heat, cover the pan, and simmer for about 20 minutes, turning them once during the cooking and basting with the juices in the pan. While the chops are cooking, gently sauté the mushrooms and garlic in the remaining butter in a covered frying pan over moderate heat for about 8 minutes. Arrange the chops on a hot serving platter, spoon a little of the mushrooms over each, and serve the Marsala sauce separately. *Serves 6.*

1142. VEAL CHOPS MILANESE

Costolette di vitello alla milanese

6 loin or rib veal chops, cut 1 inch thick
Flour
2 eggs, slightly beaten
1½ cups fresh breadcrumbs mixed with ½ cup grated Parmesan cheese
½ cup butter
Salt and freshly ground pepper
3 lemons, quartered

Season the chops with salt and pepper, dust with flour, dip in beaten egg, and cover them thoroughly with breadcrumbs mixed with cheese. Heat the butter in a large frying pan over high heat until golden and brown the chops, 3 at a time, for about 3 minutes on each side, being careful to adjust the heat so that the butter does not burn. When they are nicely browned, arrange the chops overlapping one another in the pan, reduce the heat, cover the pan, and simmer for about 20 minutes. When they are fully cooked, remove the lid, raise the heat, and cook for 1 minute longer on each side to re-crisp them. Arrange them on a hot serving platter, pour the butter in the pan over them, garnish with the lemon quarters, and serve immediately. *Serves 6.*

1143. VEAL CHOPS MILANESE WITH SPAGHETTI

Costolette di vitello alla milanese con spaghetti

6 Veal Chops Milanese [No. 1142]
¼ pound mushrooms, sliced
½ cup butter
½ cup chopped prosciutto
2 truffles, chopped [or No. 1819a]
½ cup Italian Meat Sauce [No. 41]
1 pound spaghetti
½ cup grated Parmesan cheese
Salt and freshly ground pepper

Prepare the veal chops as described in the preceding recipe. Gently sauté the mushrooms in 2 tablespoons of the butter in a covered frying pan for about 8 minutes, remove the lid, add the prosciutto and truffles, simmer for 1 minute, add the Italian meat sauce, bring to a boil, remove from the heat, and keep hot. Cook the spaghetti in a large pot of vigorously boiling salted water until just *al dente*, drain, and turn the spaghetti out into the center of a large hot serving platter. Toss the spaghetti lightly with the Parmesan cheese and the remaining butter, season it with pepper, and then pour the reserved sauce over it. Arrange the chops in a circle around the spaghetti and serve immediately. *Serves 6.*

1144. VEAL CHOPS PAESANA
Costolette di vitello alla paesana

6 loin or rib veal chops, cut 1 inch thick
¼ pound salt pork, diced and parboiled for 10 minutes
1 carrot, sliced
1 leek (white part only), sliced
1 onion, sliced
1 stalk celery, sliced
Pinch sugar
½ cup butter
½ cup Brown Veal Stock [No. 5]
24 Noisette Potatoes [No. 1783]
Salt and freshly ground pepper

Sauté the salt pork dice in a frying pan over medium heat until golden on all sides, remove the dice with a slotted spoon, and drain on absorbent paper. Gently sauté the sliced vegetables with a pinch of sugar in 2 tablespoons of the butter in another frying pan over medium heat until the onion becomes lightly browned, add the brown stock, and continue cooking until the stock has evaporated; remove from the heat and reserve. Dry the costops thoroughly on paper towels. Heat the remaining butter in a shallow, heavy casserole over high heat and brown the chops, a few at a time, for about 3 minutes on each side. When they are nicely browned, arrange them all in the casserole overlapping one another, season them with salt and pepper, cover tightly, reduce the heat, and simmer for about 20 minutes, turning them once during the cooking and basting with the juices in the pan. About 5 minutes before they are fully cooked, add the salt pork dice, potatoes, and sliced vegetables. Complete the cooking and serve in the casserole. *Serves 6.*

1145. VEAL CHOPS PHILIP OF EDINBURGH
Costolette di vitello "Filippo di Edimburgo"

6 loin or rib veal chops, cut 1 inch thick
2 tablespoons chopped white truffle [or No. 1819a]
¼ cup chopped tongue
¼ cup chopped ham
2 cups thick cold Sauce Mornay [No. 56]
Flour
2 eggs, beaten

1 cup fresh breadcrumbs mixed with ½ cup grated Gruyère (or Parmesan) cheese
2 tablespoons butter
3 tablespoons oil
4 tablespoons butter, melted
Salt and freshly ground pepper
2 cups Marsala Sauce [No. 43]

Dry the chops thoroughly on paper towels. Cut a horizontal slit in the side of each chop to make a little pocket and stuff each with a little of the chopped truffle, tongue, and ham. Season them with salt and pepper, cover each with a thin layer of Mornay sauce, dust them with flour, dip in beaten egg, and then cover them with a generous layer of the breadcrumbs mixed with cheese. Put the chops in the refrigerator for ½ hour. Heat the 2 tablespoons of butter and the 3 tablespoons of oil in a large frying pan over high heat until almost smoking and brown the chops for about 3 minutes on each side. Do not crowd them during the browning; cook only 2 or 3 at a time, if necessary. Transfer them to a shallow baking dish, pour the melted butter over them, and bake in a moderate (350°) oven for about 25 minutes, basting occasionally with the butter in the dish. They are fully cooked when easily pricked with a fork. Transfer to a hot serving platter and serve the Marsala sauce on the side. *Serves 6.*

1146. VEAL CHOPS PORTUGUESE
Costolette di vitello alla portoghese

6 loin or rib veal chops, cut 1 inch thick
½ cup oil
½ cup Tomato Sauce [No. 19]
1 cup dry white wine
1 clove garlic, crushed in the garlic-press
Salt and freshly ground pepper
2 tablespoons chopped parsley

Dry the chops thoroughly on paper towels and season lightly with salt and pepper. Heat the oil in a large heavy frying pan over high heat until smoking, and brown the chops, a few at a time, for about 3 minutes on each side. When all are nicely browned, drain off most of the oil in the pan, arrange all of the chops in it, overlapping one another, reduce the heat, cover the pan, and simmer for about 20 minutes. Turn the chops once during the cooking and baste with the juices in the pan. Transfer the chops to a hot serving platter and keep warm. Add the tomato sauce, wine, and garlic to the pan, reduce over high heat until slightly thickened, correct seasoning, pour over the chops, and sprinkle with the chopped parsley. *Serves 6.*

389

1147. VEAL CHOPS SASSI
Nodini alla Sassi

Prepare in the manner described for Veal Chops with Basil [No. 1135], substituting 2 tablespoons of sage leaves (or 1 teaspoon dried sage) for the basil and adding to the pan, about 10 minutes before the chops are fully cooked, 12 "new" potatoes which have been parboiled for 10 minutes in lightly salted water, drained, and browned in 3 tablespoons of butter in a frying pan over medium heat. *Serves* 6.

1148. VEAL CHOPS IN WHITE WINE
Arrostini annegati al vino bianco

6 loin or rib veal chops, cut 1 inch thick
6 tablespoons butter
1 cup dry white wine
1 clove garlic, crushed in the garlic-press
1 teaspoon chopped rosemary (or ½ teaspoon dried)
2 tablespoons Demi-Glaze Sauce [No. 20]
Juice of ½ lemon
Salt and freshly ground pepper

Dry the chops thoroughly on paper towels. Heat 4 tablespoons of the butter in a large heavy skillet until golden, add 2 or 3 of the chops, and brown on each side for 3 minutes. Remove them from the pan and season with salt and pepper. Cook the remaining chops in the same manner, season them, and remove from the pan. Add the wine to the pan and reduce over high heat to ½ its quantity. Return the chops to the pan, overlapping one another, and sprinkle a little garlic and rosemary over each. Cover the pan tightly and simmer over very low heat for about 20 minutes. Turn the chops over and baste with the juices in the pan once during the cooking period. The chops are fully cooked when their juices run clear yellow and they are easily pierced with a fork. Transfer them to a hot serving platter and keep warm. Add the Demi-Glaze to the juices in the pan and reduce over high heat to about ½ cup. Remove from the heat, add the lemon juice, and swirl in the remaining butter, bit by bit. Spoon a little of the sauce over each chop. *Serves* 6.

1149. VEAL CUTLETS BOLOGNESE
Medaglioni di vitello alla bolognese con tartufi

6 oval ½-inch slices of veal, cut from the upper leg
Juice of 2 lemons
2 eggs, beaten

1 cup fresh breadcrumbs, mixed with ½ cup grated Parmesan cheese
6 tablespoons butter
6 slices prosciutto
6 slices Gruyère cheese
6 slices white truffle [or No. 1819a]
Salt and freshly ground pepper

Place the lemon juice in a bowl with 2 teaspoons of salt and ½ teaspoon of freshly ground pepper, mix thoroughly until the salt is dissolved. Brush a little of this mixture on each of the veal slices and let them rest in the bowl for 2 hours, turning them occasionally. Dry them on paper towels, dip in beaten egg, and cover thoroughly with the breadcrumbs mixed with cheese. Heat the butter over fairly high heat in a frying pan large enough to accommodate the veal slices without crowding (or use 2 pans with slightly more butter) and quickly brown the slices for about 3 minutes on each side. On top of each slice place a slice of prosciutto, a slice of cheese, and a slice of truffle. Cover the pan, reduce the heat slightly, and cook for about 4 minutes, or until the cheese melts. Transfer them to a hot serving platter and spoon a little of the butter in the pan over each. *Serves* 6.

1150. VEAL CUTLETS NINFETTA
Medaglioni di vitello alla ninfetta

6 oval ½-inch slices of veal, cut from the upper leg
Flour
6 tablespoons butter
½ pound mushrooms, sliced
½ cup Port wine
1 cup heavy cream
Salt and freshly ground pepper
24 asparagus tips, cooked until just tender in lightly salted water and dressed with 2 tablespoons butter

Season the slices of veal with salt and pepper and dust them with flour. Heat the butter in a large frying pan over fairly high heat until golden and quickly brown the veal slices for about 3 minutes on each side. Reduce the heat, cook for about 5 minutes longer, transfer the slices to a hot serving platter, and keep warm. Add the mushrooms to the butter in the pan, stir for 1 minute, add the Port, and cook until it is almost evaporated. Add the cream, boil for 2 minutes, season lightly with salt and pepper, spoon this sauce over the veal slices, and garnish the platter with the asparagus tips. *Serves* 6.

1151. VEAL CUTLETS EN PAPILLOTES
Medaglioni di vitello al cartoccio

6 oval ½-inch slices of veal, cut from the upper leg
6 tablespoons butter
12 thin slices prosciutto
6 sheets of parchment paper, cut in the shape of
    large hearts and oiled on both sides
¾ cup Duxelles Sauce [No. 31]
Salt and freshly ground pepper

Dry the slices of veal thoroughly with paper towels. Heat the butter in a large frying pan over fairly high heat and quickly brown the slices for about 3 minutes on each side. Brown only 2 or 3 of them at a time if necessary to avoid crowding. When they are browned, season with salt and pepper. Place a slice of prosciutto on one half of each of the paper hearts, spread a tablespoon of the Duxelles over the prosciutto, place a slice of veal on top, spread with another tablespoon of Duxelles, and top with a slice of prosciutto. Fold over the other half of the paper hearts and crimp the edges well to effect a tight seal. Place them in an oiled baking dish in a hot (400°) oven for about 10 minutes, or until the paper is puffed and browned. Serve on individual heated plates and allow each guest to open his own. *Serves* 6.

1152. VEAL CUTLETS PARTENOPEA
Medaglioni di vitello con prosciutto alla Partenopea

6 oval ½-inch slices of veal, cut from the upper leg
½ cup butter
4 tomatoes, peeled, seeded, drained, and sliced
1 tablespoon chopped basil (or 1 teaspoon dried)
6 slices prosciutto, cut slightly smaller than the
    veal and ¼ inch thick
6 slices bread, crusts removed, cut the size
    of the veal slices
Salt and freshly ground pepper

Heat 2 tablespoons of the butter in a saucepan over medium heat, add the tomatoes and basil, season with salt and pepper, and simmer for about 10 minutes. Heat the remaining butter in a large frying pan over fairly high heat until golden, add the veal slices—a few at a time if necessary to avoid crowding—and brown for about 3 minutes on each side. Reduce the heat slightly and cook for about 5 minutes longer, or until the slices are tender. Season them with salt and pepper, transfer them temporarily to a bowl, and keep warm. Add the slices of prosciutto to the butter in the pan and sauté them for about 1 minute on each side. Remove them with a slotted spoon, add the slices of bread, and sauté until golden on both sides. Arrange the bread on a hot serving platter, place a slice of veal on each, top with a slice of prosciutto, and spoon a little of the tomatoes over each. *Serves* 6.

1153. VEAL CUTLETS WITH PIQUANT BUTTER
Medaglioni di vitello con burro piccante

6 oval ½-inch slices of veal, cut from the upper leg
½ cup Anchovy Butter [No. 108]
1 clove garlic, crushed in the garlic-press
2 tablespoons chopped parsley
1 tablespoon lemon juice
½ cup butter, melted
Salt and freshly ground pepper
24 Noisette Potatoes [No. 1783]

Mix thoroughly the anchovy butter with the garlic, parsley, and lemon juice in a bowl and then chill until very firm in the refrigerator. Season the cutlets with salt and pepper, brush them with butter, and then broil them about 4 inches beneath a medium high broiler flame for about 4 minutes on each side, basting occasionally with a little more melted butter. Arrange the cutlets around a hot serving platter, place several curls of the piquant butter on top of each, and garnish the center of the platter with the noisette potatoes. *Serves* 6.

1154. VEAL CUTLETS PIEMONTESE
Medaglioni di vitello alla piemontese

6 oval ½-inch slices of veal, cut from the upper leg
A marinade:
    ½ cup oil
    2 tablespoons lemon juice
    2 teaspoons salt
    ½ teaspoon freshly ground pepper
    3 sprigs crushed basil (or 1 teaspoon dried)
6 thin slices fontina cheese (or substitute Munster)
6 slices white truffle [or No. 1819a]
Flour
2 eggs, beaten
1½ cups fresh breadcrumbs
6 tablespoons butter
1 recipe Risotto with Butter and Parmesan
    Cheese [No. 572]

Marinate the slices of veal in the marinade for 3 hours. Drain and dry them thoroughly on paper towels. Using a very sharp knife, carefully cut a horizontal slit in the side of each slice to form a pocket and insert a slice of cheese and a slice of truffle into each. Dust them with flour, dip in beaten egg, and then cover thoroughly with breadcrumbs. Heat the butter in a very large frying pan over fairly high heat until golden, add the slices of veal, and brown for about 3 minutes on each side. Reduce the heat slightly, and cook for about 5 minutes longer, or until the slices are tender. Turn the risotto out into the center of a hot serving platter, arrange the veal around it, and pour a little of the butter in the pan over each slice. *Serves 6.*

1155. VEAL CUTLETS RAMON NOVARRO
Medaglioni di vitello Ramon Novarro

6 oval ½-inch slices of veal, cut from the upper leg
½ cup butter
1 large onion, finely chopped
3 tablespoons dried mushrooms, soaked ½ hour
    in warm water, squeezed dry, chopped, and
    gently sautéed for 10 minutes in 2 tablespoons
    of butter
½ cup dry sherry wine
1 recipe Rich Pastry [No. 1955], made without sugar
6 thin slices prosciutto, cut the size of the veal slices
1 egg, beaten with 2 tablespoons milk
Salt and freshly ground pepper

Dry the slices of veal thoroughly on paper towels. Heat 6 tablespoons of the butter in a large frying pan over fairly high heat, add the slices of veal—a few at a time if necessary to avoid crowding—and brown for about 4 minutes on each side. Season them with salt and pepper, transfer them to a cold platter, and allow them to cool completely. Heat the remaining butter in another frying pan over moderate heat, add the onion, cook until transparent, add the mushrooms, and gently sauté for about 5 minutes. Add the sherry, reduce over high heat to about 3 tablespoons, remove from the heat, and allow to cool completely. Divide the pastry dough into 6 portions and roll each out to a thickness of ⅛ inch and into a shape slightly more than twice as large as the slices of veal. Place a slice of prosciutto in the center of each, spread a generous spoonful of mushrooms and sauce over the prosciutto, and top with a slice of veal. Encase completely in the dough, pressing the edges tightly together to effect a tight seal. Reverse the cases onto a slightly dampened baking sheet, seam side downward, brush them with the egg beaten with milk, and bake in a hot (400°) oven for 15 to 20 minutes, or until the pastry is nicely browned. Serve each on an individual heated plate. *Serves 6.*

1156. FRICADELLES OF VEAL
Polpette di vitello alla francese—fricadelles de veau

2 pounds ground lean veal (breast or heel of the round)
¼ pound very lean salt pork, parboiled for
    15 minutes

Veal Cutlets Ramon Novarro (No. 1155)

6 slices dry bread, crusts removed, soaked in
    White Stock [No. 1], and squeezed almost dry
1 onion, chopped, and cooked in 1 tablespoon of
    butter for 5 minutes
2 tablespoons chopped parsley
2 eggs, beaten
Pinch nutmeg
Flour
6 tablespoons butter
3 cups Brown Veal Stock [No. 5]
Salt and freshly ground pepper

Put the veal, salt pork, and bread through the meat grinder, using the finest blade. Mix this ground mixture thoroughly with the onion, parsley, and beaten eggs; and season with salt, pepper, and nutmeg. Form 18 meatballs from the mixture and roll them lightly in flour. Heat the butter in a large frying pan over high heat until golden and quickly brown the meatballs on all sides. Add the stock, bring to a boil, reduce the heat, cover the pan, and simmer for $\frac{1}{2}$ hour. Remove them with a slotted spoon to a hot serving platter, reduce the stock in the pan to $\frac{1}{2}$ its quantity, correct the seasoning, and pour over the veal balls. *Serves* 6.

1157. VEAL FRICASSEE
Fricassea di vitello

3 pounds veal (breast, shoulder, or neck), cut
    into $1\frac{1}{2}$-inch cubes
$\frac{1}{2}$ cup butter
4 tablespoons flour
6 cups hot White Stock [No. 1]
Bouquet Garni:
    2 sprigs thyme (or $\frac{1}{2}$ teaspoon dried)
    3 sprigs parsley
    1 bay leaf
Pinch nutmeg
$\frac{1}{2}$ pound mushroom caps
5 egg yolks
1 cup heavy cream
18 Braised White Onions [No. 1721]
Juice of 1 lemon
Salt and freshly ground white pepper

Dry the pieces of veal thoroughly with paper towels. Heat 4 tablespoons of the butter in a large, heavy pot over medium heat until the foam begins to subside, add the pieces of veal, a few at a time, and stir for 1 or 2 minutes in the hot butter to seal the juices in the meat, but do not allow them to brown. After this preliminary cooking, place all of the pieces in the pot, sprinkle with the flour, stir for 1 minute, and add the boiling hot stock and Bouquet Garni. Season with salt, white pepper, and nutmeg; bring to a boil; reduce the heat; and simmer for about $1\frac{1}{2}$ hours, or until the veal is tender. While the veal is cooking, gently sauté the mushrooms in 2 tablespoons of the butter in a covered frying pan for about 8 minutes; reserve until needed. When the veal is tender, transfer the pieces temporarily with a slotted spoon to a bowl and keep warm. Discard the Bouquet Garni, remove the pot from the heat, add the egg yolks which have been beaten with the cream, return the pot to very low heat, and stir constantly for about 5 minutes, or until slightly thickened. Add the pieces of veal, onions, and mushrooms; correct the seasoning; and cook only long enough to get thoroughly hot. Do not boil. Off the heat, blend in the lemon juice and the remaining butter, bit by bit, and turn contents of the pot out into a shallow hot serving dish. *Serves* 6.

1158. VEAL GRENADINS WITH MIXED VEGETABLES
Grenadine di vitello con macedonia di legumi

6 oval slices of veal, cut from the upper leg,
    about $\frac{1}{2}$ inch thick
24 1-inch strips of salt pork, parboiled for
    10 minutes
4 tablespoons butter
$\frac{1}{2}$ pound pork rind, parboiled for 2 hours
1 onion, sliced
1 carrot, sliced
Bouquet Garni:
    3 sprigs parsley
    2 sprigs thyme (or $\frac{1}{2}$ teaspoon dried)
    1 bay leaf
$\frac{1}{2}$ cup dry white wine
$1\frac{1}{4}$ cups Brown Veal Stock [No. 5]
A macedoine of several vegetables, such as string
    beans, plum tomatoes, zucchini, tiny artichokes,
    etc., each cooked separately until just tender
    in lightly salted water, drained, mixed together,
    and dressed with a little butter

Make 4 slits in each of the slices of veal with a sharply pointed knife and insert the salt pork strips into the veal. Heat the butter in a large frying pan over high heat until almost nut colored and very quickly brown the pieces of veal, a few at a time. Line the bottom of a casserole with the pork rind, sprinkle the sliced carrot and onion over the rind, and arrange the pieces of veal, overlapping one another, on top of the vegetables. Season lightly with salt and pepper, add the Bouquet Garni and the wine, and boil over high heat until the wine has almost evaporated. Add the veal stock, bring to a boil, reduce the heat, cover the casserole, and simmer for about 45 minutes, or until the veal is tender. Transfer the slices to a hot serving platter, garnish with a few of the cooked vegetables, and keep warm. Strain the liquid in the casserole through a fine sieve into a saucepan and reduce over high heat to about 3/4 cup. Serve the sauce and the macedoine of vegetables separately. *Serves* 6.

1159. OSSOBUCO MILANESE
Ossobuco con gremolata alla milanese

6 veal shin bones, 4 inches long and well covered with meat
1/2 cup butter
Flour
A chopped mixture:
　1 onion
　1 carrot
　1 stalk celery
　1 clove garlic
　3 sprigs marjoram (or 1 teaspoon dried)
　1 small piece lemon rind (no white part)
1/2 cup dry white wine
4 ripe tomatoes, peeled, seeded, drained, and chopped
1 1/2 cups Brown Veal Stock [No. 5]
1 clove garlic, crushed in the garlic-press
1 teaspoon grated orange rind (no white part)
1 teaspoon grated lemon rind (no white part)
Salt and freshly ground pepper

Heat 4 tablespoons of the butter in a heavy pot over fairly high heat until golden, dust the shin bones with flour, and brown them on all sides in the butter. Add the chopped mixture, season with salt and pepper, stir for 2 minutes, add the wine, and cook until it has evaporated. Place the veal bones upright so that their marrow will not fall out. Add the tomatoes and stock, season with a little more salt, bring to a boil, cover the pot, reduce the heat, and simmer for about 1 hour. About 10 minutes before the meat on the bones is fully cooked and tender, remove the lid, raise the heat, and reduce the sauce slightly. About 3 minutes before removing from the heat, add the garlic, grated lemon, and orange peel. Arrange the ossibuchi on a hot serving platter and cover with the sauce. *Serves* 6.

NOTE: This is traditionally served with Risotto Milanese [No. 578].

1160. VEAL PICCATA
Piccata al prezzemolo o frittura piccata

18 round veal scallops, cut 1/4 inch thick
Flour
1/2 cup butter
Juice of 2 lemons
2 tablespoons chopped parsley
Salt and freshly ground pepper

Place the veal scallops between sheets of wax paper and pound them with the flat side of a meat cleaver to make them as thin as possible without breaking through them. Season them with salt and pepper and dust with flour. Heat 5 tablespoons of the butter in a large frying pan over fairly high heat until it is golden and quickly brown the veal slices, a few at a time, for about 2 minutes on each side. Transfer them to a hot serving platter and keep warm. Add the lemon juice and parsley to the pan, remove from the heat, swirl in the remaining butter, bit by bit, and pour over the scallops. *Serves* 6.

1161. VEAL PICCATA BRUSSELS EXPOSITION 1958
Piccata di vitello "Esposizione di Bruxelles 1958"

18 round veal scallops, cut 1/4 inch thick
Flour
1/2 cup butter
1/2 cup dry white wine
1/2 cup Brown Veal Stock [No. 5]
1 tablespoon chopped shallots
4 ripe tomatoes, peeled, seeded, drained, and chopped
Pinch sugar
1 cup heavy cream
Juice of 1 lemon
Salt and freshly ground pepper
1 recipe Brussels Sprouts in Butter [No. 1628]

Place the slices of veal between sheets of wax paper and pound them with the flat side of a meat cleaver until they are as thin as possible. Season them with salt and pepper and dust with flour. Heat 6 tablespoons of the butter in a large frying pan over fairly high heat until golden and brown the veal, a few slices at a time, for about 2 minutes on each side. Transfer the slices to a hot serving platter and keep warm. Add the wine and stock to the pan and reduce to $\frac{1}{2}$ their quantity. Add the shallots and tomatoes, season with sugar, salt, and pepper, cook for about 5 minutes, add the cream, reduce the heat slightly, and simmer for 5 minutes longer. Remove from the heat, add the lemon juice, and swirl in the remaining butter, bit by bit. Pour this sauce over the slices of veal and garnish the center of the platter with the Brussels sprouts. *Serves 6.*

1162. VEAL PICCATA NEW YORK WORLD'S FAIR 1939

Piccata di vitello "Esposizione di New York 1939"

18 round veal scallops, cut $\frac{1}{4}$ inch thick
3 baked potatoes [No. 1748], halved
1 cup butter
2 white truffles, chopped [or No. 1819a]
6 cooked artichoke hearts [*see* introduction to No. 1578]
Flour
2 eggs, beaten
$\frac{1}{2}$ pound mushrooms, sliced
1 clove garlic, crushed in the garlic-press
1 tablespoon sage leaves (or 1 teaspoon dried)
$\frac{1}{3}$ cup brandy
Salt and freshly ground pepper

Carefully scoop the potato pulp out of the skins into a bowl, season with 1 teaspoon salt and a little freshly ground pepper, add 4 tablespoons butter and the chopped truffles, and mix thoroughly. Form into small cakes the size of the veal scallops and brown them on both sides in 3 tablespoons of the butter in a frying pan over fairly high heat. Remove from the heat and keep warm. Quarter the artichoke hearts, dust them with flour, dip them in beaten egg, drop them immediately in 5 tablespoons of the butter in a frying pan over fairly high heat, and shake them in the pan just until they are nicely browned on all sides. Remove from the heat and keep warm. Place the slices of veal between sheets of wax paper and pound them with the flat side of a meat cleaver to make them as thin as possible without breaking through them. Season them with salt and pepper and dust them with flour. Heat the remaining butter in a large frying pan over fairly high heat until golden and quickly brown the slices of veal, a few at a time, for about 2 minutes on each side. Transfer them to the center of a hot serving platter and keep warm. Add the mushrooms, garlic, and sage leaves to the pan, adding a little more butter if necessary, and sauté over moderate heat for

5 minutes. Add the brandy, reduce it slightly over high heat, and pour over the slices of veal. Arrange the potato cakes in a circle around the veal and top each with a few pieces of artichoke. *Serves 6.*

1163. VEAL PICCATA PARIS EXPOSITION 1937

Piccata di vitello "Esposizione di Parigi 1937"

18 round veal scallops, cut $\frac{1}{4}$ inch thick
$\frac{1}{2}$ pound mushrooms, sliced
1 cup butter
1 cup diced prosciutto
2 truffles, chopped [or No. 1819a]
1 onion, chopped
1 clove garlic, crushed in the garlic-press
1 pound tomatoes, peeled, seeded, drained, and chopped
4 zucchini, sliced
Flour
2 eggs, beaten
1 cup dry Marsala wine
Salt and freshly ground pepper

Gently sauté the mushrooms in 3 tablespoons of the butter in a covered frying pan over moderate heat for 5 minutes. Remove the cover, add the prosciutto and truffles, and cook for 3 minutes longer. Remove from the heat and keep warm. Heat 2 tablespoons of butter in a saucepan over medium heat, add the onions and garlic, cook until golden, add the tomatoes, season with salt and pepper, and simmer for 10 minutes. Dust the zucchini slices with flour, sprinkle with a little salt, dip in beaten egg, and drop them immediately in 4 tablespoons of the butter in a frying pan over medium heat. Cook for about 5 minutes or until they are nicely browned. Remove from the heat and keep warm. Place the slices of veal between sheets of wax paper and pound them with the flat side of a meat cleaver to make them as thin as possible without breaking through them. Season them with salt and pepper and dust them with flour. Heat the remaining butter in a large frying pan over fairly high heat until golden and quickly brown the slices of veal, a few at a time, for about 2 minutes on each side. Transfer the slices to the center of a hot serving platter and keep warm. Add the Marsala to the pan and reduce over high heat by $\frac{1}{4}$. Add the reserved mushroom/prosciutto/truffle mixture, cook for 1 minute, and then pour this sauce over the slices of veal. Garnish the platter with small heaps of the tomatoes and the zucchini. *Serves 6.*

1164. VEAL PICCATA CASINO DI VENEZIA
Piccata di vitello "Casino di Venezia"

18 round veal scallops, cut ¼ inch thick
1 recipe Duchesse Potatoes [No. 1771]
1 cup chopped prosciutto (or smoked ham)
¼ pound calf's brains, soaked in acidulated water
    and blanched for 20 minutes (*see* page 481)
¼ pound veal sweetbreads, soaked in acidulated water
    and blanched for 15 minutes (*see* page 496)
½ cup butter
½ cup brandy
6 tablespoons Tomato Sauce [No. 19]
18 thin slices salt pork, parboiled for 10 minutes
2 tablespoons chopped basil (or 1 teaspoon dried)
Flour
1 cup dry white wine
Salt and freshly ground pepper

Place the slices of veal between sheets of wax paper and pound them with the flat side of a meat cleaver to make them as thin as possible without breaking through them. Prepare the Duchesse potatoes, mix with the chopped prosciutto, and keep warm. Slice the parboiled brains and sweetbreads and sauté them gently in 2 tablespoons of the butter in a frying pan over medium heat for about 3 minutes on each side. Season them with salt and pepper, remove them with a slotted spoon, and keep warm. Add the brandy to the pan, reduce over high heat to ½ its quantity, add the tomato sauce, return the sweetbreads and brains to the pan, remove from the heat, and keep warm. Season the slices of veal with salt and pepper, place a slice of salt pork on each, and sprinkle with a little chopped basil. Roll the slices up, secure the ends with toothpicks (or tie with string), and dust with flour. Heat the remaining 6 tablespoons of butter in a large frying pan over fairly high heat until golden, add the veal rolls, brown quickly on all sides, reduce the heat, and cook for about 6 minutes longer, turning them occasionally. Pipe a thick border of the Duchesse potatoes around the edge of a hot serving platter, arrange the veal rolls in a circle next to the potatoes, and pour the sweetbreads and brains with their sauce in the center. Quickly de-glaze the pan in which the veal cooked with the wine, reduce to about ½ its quantity, and spoon a little of this sauce over each of the veal rolls. *Serves 6.*

Veal Grenadins with Mixed Vegetables (No. 1158): see page 393

1165. VEAL RIBLETS À L'ANCIENNE
Teneroni di vitello all'antica

6 veal riblets (cut from the ends of the ribs and
    extending to the full width of the breast), 1 inch
    thick
½ cup butter
½ cup dry white wine
1 bay leaf
1 cup Brown Veal Stock [No. 5]
¼ pound lean salt pork, diced and parboiled for
    10 minutes
1 recipe Braised White Onions [No. 1721]
1 recipe Glazed Carrots [No. 1647]
Salt and freshly ground pepper

Dry the riblets thoroughly with paper towels. Heat 4 tablespoons of the butter in a large heavy casserole over fairly high heat and brown the riblets for about 3 minutes on each side. Season them with salt and pepper, add the wine and bay leaf, and cook until the wine has almost evaporated. Add the veal stock, bring to a boil, reduce the heat, cover the casserole, and simmer for about 1 hour, or until the riblets are tender. Turn them once during the cooking. Sauté the salt pork dice in a frying pan over medium heat until the dice are golden on all sides and then drain on absorbent paper. When the riblets are fully cooked, transfer them to a hot serving platter, reduce the cooking liquid slightly over high heat, pour over the veal, and garnish the platter with the salt pork, carrots, and onions. *Serves 6.*

1166. VEAL RIBLETS WITH CELERY
Teneroni di vitello con sedani

6 veal riblets (cut from the ends of the ribs and
  extending to the full width of the breast), 1 inch
  thick
A chopped mixture:
  2 ounces ham fat
  1 onion
  1 clove garlic
1 tablespoon oil
1 bay leaf
½ cup dry Marsala wine
1 cup Brown Veal Stock [No. 5]
6 white celery hearts, parboiled 15 minutes in lightly
  salted water
Salt and freshly ground pepper

Dry the riblets very thoroughly with paper towels.
Place the chopped mixture and the oil in a heavy
casserole over medium high heat, cook until the onion
begins to color, add the riblets, and brown them on
both sides. Season with salt and pepper, add the bay
leaf and Marsala, and cook until the Marsala has
nearly evaporated. Add the stock, bring to a boil,
reduce the heat, cover the casserole, and simmer for
1 hour, or until the riblets are tender. About 15 minutes
before the riblets are fully cooked, slice the celery
hearts in half lengthwise, add them to the casserole,
and complete the cooking. Transfer the riblets to a hot
serving platter, surround them with the celery, reduce
the cooking liquid slightly over high heat, correct the
seasoning, and pour over the veal. *Serves 6.*

1167. VEAL RIBLETS WITH MUSHROOMS
Teneroni di vitello con funghi

This dish has the same ingredients and is prepared in
the same way as Veal Riblets à l'Ancienne [No. 1165]
except that 1 pound of mushrooms, sliced and gently
sautéed in 4 tablespoons of butter for about 10 minutes,
is substituted for the salt pork, onions, and carrots.
Serves 6.

1168. VEAL RIBLETS WITH RICE
Teneroni di vitello con risotto

This dish has the same ingredients and is prepared
in the same way as Veal Riblets à l'Ancienne [No.
1165], except the salt pork, onions, and carrots are
omitted and the riblets are served with a side dish of
Risotto with Butter and Parmesan Cheese [No. 572].
Serves 6.

1169. ROAST BREAST OF VEAL BORGHESE
Petto di vitello al forno alla borghese

3 pounds boned breast of veal
¼ pound prosciutto (fat and lean), cut into strips
6 tablespoons butter, softened
1½ pounds "new" potatoes, parboiled for 10 minutes
1½ cups Brown Veal Stock [No. 5]
Salt and freshly ground pepper

Lard the veal with the strips of prosciutto by using a
larding needle or make small slits with a sharply

*Veal
Piccata Casino
di Venezia
(No. 1164)*

397

pointed knife and insert the strips. Dry the roast thoroughly on paper towels, tie it into a neat roll with string, rub it with salt and pepper, place it in a shallow open roasting pan, and spread it with the softened butter. Place it in a hot (450°) oven for 10 minutes, reduce the heat to moderate (350°), and roast for a total of 1½ hours, or until its juices run a clear yellow when it is pierced with a fork. Baste every 10 or 15 minutes with the juices in the pan. About 30 minutes before it is fully cooked, arrange the potatoes around the roast, baste them with the fat in the pan, and complete the cooking. Transfer the veal and the potatoes to a hot serving platter and keep warm. Place the pan over fairly high heat until all the meat juices evaporate and stick to the bottom, being careful not to let them burn, and pour off all of the fat. Add the stock, and de-glaze the pan by scraping the bottom and sides with a wooden spoon. Continue cooking over high heat until slightly reduced and thickened. Carve the roast into neat slices and serve the sauce separately. *Serves* 6.

1170. ROAST SHOULDER OF VEAL
Spalla di vitello alla fornaia

Prepare in the same manner and with the same ingredients as Roast Breast of Veal Borghese [No. 1169], substituting a good cut from the shoulder for the breast of veal. *Serves* 6.

1171. ROAST VEAL MARIA
Noce di vitello arrostita tartufata "Maria"

3 pounds round or rump of veal
12 strips ham fat (or substitute salt pork)
2 truffles, sliced [or No. 1819a]
Several thin sheets of veal fat (or substitute suet)
3 tablespoons oil
¼ cup brandy
2 onions, sliced
2 carrots, sliced
4 tablespoons butter
Salt and freshly ground pepper
1 recipe Potato Croquettes [No. 1767]

Make slits in the veal with a sharply pointed knife and insert strips of the ham fat (or salt pork) and slices of truffle. Wrap the sides of the roast in the sheets of veal fat and tie with string at 1½-inch intervals to make a neat roll. Heat the oil in a frying pan over fairly high heat until smoking hot and brown the veal on all sides. Season it with salt and pepper, transfer it to a casserole

or heavy roasting pan, and add the brandy, onions, carrots, and butter. Bring liquid to a boil over high heat, cover the casserole, and place it in a moderate (350°) oven for 1½ hours, or until its juices run yellow when pierced with a fork. Baste several times during the cooking with the juices in the casserole. Transfer it to a hot serving platter, allow it to rest for 10 minutes before carving, cut it into neat slices, strain the juices in the casserole (or, if desired, mash the vegetables into the juices), and spoon over the slices. Serve the potato croquettes on the side. *Serves* 6.

1172. ROAST VEAL WITH SOUR CREAM
Noce di vitello alla crema acida

Roast the veal in the manner described in the preceding recipe, omitting the truffles. When it is fully cooked, transfer it to a hot serving platter and allow it to rest for 10 minutes before carving. Add 1½ cups heavy cream and the juice of 1 lemon to the juices in the casserole and reduce over medium heat by ⅓. Cut the veal into neat slices, correct the seasoning of the sauce, strain it, if desired, and spoon it over the slices. *Serves* 6.

NOTE: Commercial sour cream may be substituted for the heavy cream and lemon juice. Reduce the juices in the casserole by ½, add 1 cup of room-temperature sour cream, correct the seasoning, heat only long enough to get the sour cream very hot, and then spoon over the slices.

1173. VEAL ROLLS GOURMET
Involtini di vitello del ghiottone

12 veal scallops, cut ¼ inch thick and about 4 inches square
12 slices prosciutto (fat and lean)
Flour
2 eggs, slightly beaten
2 cups fresh breadcrumbs
6 ripe tomatoes
2 cloves garlic, crushed in the garlic-press
2 tablespoons chopped basil (or 2 teaspoons dried)
3 tablespoons oil
6 tablespoons butter
Salt and freshly ground pepper

Place the scallops between sheets of wax paper and pound with the flat side of a meat cleaver to make them as thin as possible without breaking through them. Season them lightly with salt and pepper, place a slice of prosciutto on each, roll them up, and secure the ends with toothpicks or tie with string. Dust them with flour, dip in beaten egg, and then cover thoroughly with breadcrumbs. Cut off the top third of each tomato, season generously with salt and pepper, and sprinkle with garlic, basil, breadcrumbs, and then with a few drops of oil. Place them in an oiled oven-proof dish and bake in a moderate (350°) oven for 15 minutes. Heat the butter in a large frying pan over medium heat until golden, add the veal rolls, and cook fairly slowly for about 15 minutes, or until they are nicely browned on all sides; do not cover the pan and use 2 frying pans if necessary to avoid crowding. Place the tomatoes under a high broiler flame for 1 minute to brown the tops. Arrange the veal rolls on a hot serving platter and garnish with the tomatoes. *Serves* 6.

1174. VEAL ROLLS MILANESE
Messicani alla milanese

12 veal scallops, cut about 4 inches square and ¼ inch thick
¼ pound lean pork
2 ounces ham fat
2 cloves garlic
3 slices bread, soaked in milk and squeezed almost dry
½ cup grated Parmesan cheese
1 teaspoon grated lemon rind (no white part)
2 eggs, slightly beaten
Pinch nutmeg
12 thin slices of lean pork fat (or substitute sheets of suet)
6 tablespoons butter
½ cup dry white wine
1 cup Brown Veal Stock [No. 5]
Salt and freshly ground pepper
1 recipe Risotto Milanese [No. 578]

Place the slices of veal between sheets of wax paper and pound them with the flat side of a meat cleaver until

they are as thin as possible, but be careful not to break through them. Put the pork, ham fat, garlic, and bread through a meat grinder, using the finest blade. To this ground mixture add the cheese, grated lemon rind, and eggs; season with salt, pepper, and nutmeg. Mix thoroughly and then spread a little of the mixture on each of the slices of veal. Roll them up, wrap each in a slice of lean pork fat, and secure with toothpicks. Heat the butter in a large frying pan over fairly high heat and quickly brown the rolls on all sides. Reduce the heat slightly and cook the rolls for a total of about 20 minutes. Turn the risotto out onto a hot serving platter, surround with the veal rolls, and keep hot. Add the wine and stock to the frying pan, reduce over high heat to ½ their quantity, and spoon a little of this sauce over each of the rolls. *Serves* 6.

1175. VEAL ROLLS WITH PEAS
Messicani con piselli

Prepare in the same manner as Veal Rolls Milanese [No. 1174], except substitute Peas with Prosciutto [No. 1739] for the risotto. *Serves* 6.

1176. SALTIMBOCCA ROMANA
Saltimbocca alla romana

Although generally considered to be a Roman specialty, this dish originated in Brescia.

12 slices of veal from the upper leg, cut ½ inch thick
12 thin slices prosciutto (fat and lean)
24 fresh sage leaves
Flour
6 tablespoons butter
1½ cups dry white wine
Salt and freshly ground pepper

Put the veal slices between sheets of wax paper and

Filling and rolling up the veal slices for
Veal Rolls Milanese (No. 1174)

Saltimbocca Romana (No. 1176): see page 399

pound them with the flat side of a meat cleaver to make them slightly thinner than they were cut. Season them with salt and pepper, place 2 sage leaves (dried sage is a poor substitute for this dish, but it may be used if necessary) and a slice of prosciutto on each slice, fold the slices in half, secure with toothpicks, and dust with flour. Melt the butter in a large frying pan (or use 2 frying pans with slightly more butter so that all of the veal may be cooked at the same time) over fairly high heat, add the slices of veal, brown quickly for about 2 minutes on each side, reduce the heat, and continue cooking for about 5 minutes, or until the veal is just tender. Do not overcook. Transfer the veal to a hot serving platter, remove the toothpicks, and keep warm. De-glaze the pan with the wine, scraping the sides and bottom with a wooden spoon, reduce by $\frac{1}{4}$, and pour over the veal. *Serves* 6.

400

Sage

1177. VEAL SAUTÉ WITH ARTICHOKES
Vitello all'uccelletto con carciofi

3 pounds veal, cut in $\frac{1}{2}$-inch slices from the round
3 very young artichokes
$\frac{1}{2}$ cup butter
$\frac{1}{2}$ cup dry white wine
12 sage leaves (or 1 teaspoon dried)
Juice of 1 lemon
Salt and freshly ground pepper

Cut the veal into bite-sized pieces and dry on paper towels. Remove all of the tough outer leaves from the artichokes, cut off the tips of the remaining leaves, cut the artichokes in half, discard the chokes, and then cut them in $\frac{1}{2}$-inch slices. Sauté them gently in 3 table-spoons of the butter in a frying pan over moderate heat for 15 minutes. Remove from the heat and reserve. Heat the remaining butter in another large frying pan over fairly high heat until it is golden and brown the pieces of veal very quickly, a few at a time. Season them with salt and pepper, transfer them temporarily to a bowl, and keep warm. Add the wine, sage leaves, and artichokes to the pan and cook until the wine has almost evaporated. Season the artichokes lightly with salt and pepper, return the pieces of veal to the pan, stir for 1 minute, add the lemon juice, and then turn the veal and artichokes out onto a hot serving platter. *Serves* 6.

1. Carrot Purée (No. 1648). In this presentation the purée has been placed in a casserole, its surface sprinkled with ½ cup fine breadcrumbs, and dotted with 3 tablespoons butter. It was then baked in a 375° oven until the crumbs were well browned.

2. Braised Leg of Lamb Abruzzi (No. 1195) served on a bed of Fettuccine with Triple Butter (No. 490). In this presentation legs of baby spring lamb were used. If these are available, cut cooking time of No. 1195 to 1 hour.

3. Lamb Chops à la Minute (No. 1207) served with Potato Chips (No. 1762)

4. Broiled Tomatoes (No. 1809)

1178. SCALOPPINE MARSALA
Scaloppine di vitello al marsala

18 veal scallops, ¼ inch thick, cut from the upper leg
Flour
½ cup butter
1 cup dry Marsala wine
½ cup Brown Veal Stock [No. 5]
Salt and freshly ground pepper

Place the slices of veal between sheets of wax paper and pound them with the flat side of a meat cleaver to make them as thin as possible without breaking through them. Season them with salt and pepper and dust lightly with flour. Heat 6 tablespoons of the butter in a large frying pan over fairly high heat until it is golden and quickly brown the slices of veal, a few at a time, for about 2 minutes on each side. Transfer the slices to a hot serving platter and keep warm. Add the stock and Marsala to the pan and reduce over high heat to ½ their quantity. Remove from the heat, swirl in the remaining butter, bit by bit, and pour this sauce over the veal. *Serves* 6.

1179. SCALOPPINE VIENNESE
Scaloppine di vitello alla viennese

12 oval veal scallops, cut from the leg ½ inch thick
Flour
2 eggs, beaten
1½ cups fresh breadcrumbs
5 tablespoons butter
3 tablespoons oil
12 anchovy fillets, washed free of salt [*see* No. 220]
12 slices lemon
12 olives, pitted
1 hard-boiled egg, finely chopped
2 tablespoons chopped parsley
Salt and freshly ground pepper

Place the slices of veal between sheets of wax paper and pound with the flat side of a meat cleaver to make the slices slightly thinner than their natural state. Season them with salt and pepper, dust with flour, dip them in beaten egg, and cover thoroughly with breadcrumbs. Heat 3 tablespoons of the butter and all of the oil in a large frying pan over fairly high heat and brown the slices, a few at a time, for about 3 minutes on each side. Adjust the heat while they are browning so that the butter does not burn. Transfer them to a hot serving platter and garnish the top of each with an anchovy fillet, a pitted olive, and a slice of lemon covered with chopped hard-boiled egg. Add the remaining butter

to the pan, heat until golden, pour over the veal, and sprinkle with the chopped parsley. *Serves* 6.

1180. SPEZZATINO OF VEAL CACCIATORA
Sauté o spezzatino di vitello alla cacciatora

3 pounds veal (breast, shoulder, or neck), cut into
    1-inch cubes
2 tablespoons butter
3 tablespoons oil
6 tomatoes, peeled, seeded, drained, and chopped
1 cup dry white wine
Bouquet Garni:
    3 sprigs parsley
    2 sprigs thyme (or ½ teaspoon dried)
    1 bay leaf
2 cups Cacciatora Sauce [No. 28]
Salt and freshly ground pepper
2 tablespoons chopped parsley

Dry the pieces of veal thoroughly on paper towels. Heat the butter and oil in a heavy pot over fairly high heat until it is very hot and brown the pieces of veal, a few at a time, on all sides. When they are all nicely browned, cover them with the tomatoes and wine, add the Bouquet Garni, season very lightly with salt and pepper, and add a little water if necessary to cover the meat. Bring to a boil, reduce the heat, and simmer for 1½ hours, or until the veal is tender. Remove the veal from the pot with a slotted spoon and keep warm. Reduce the remaining liquid over medium high heat until it is very thick, add the Cacciatora sauce, return the pieces of veal to the pot, and simmer for 5 minutes. Discard the Bouquet Garni, turn the veal and the sauce out onto a hot serving platter, and sprinkle with the chopped parsley. *Serves* 6.

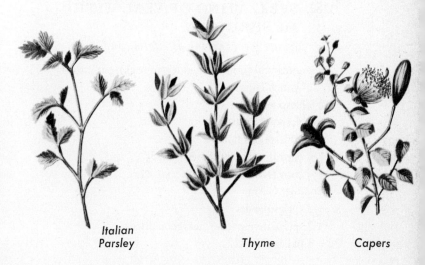

Italian
Parsley   Thyme   Capers

1181. SPEZZATINO OF VEAL CASALINGA

Sauté o spezzatino di vitello alla casalinga

3 pounds veal (breast, shoulder, or neck), cut into
    1-inch cubes
4 tablespoons butter
4 tablespoons oil
2 onions, sliced
1 clove garlic, crushed in the garlic-press
3 yellow sweet peppers, roasted, scraped, seeded,
    and cut into strips [*see* No. 145]
2 cups dry white wine
2 cups Brown Veal Stock [No. 5]
6 ripe tomatoes, peeled, seeded, drained, and chopped
Pinch sugar
3 tablespoons Kneaded Butter [No. 107]
2 tablespoons chopped parsley
Salt and freshly ground pepper

Dry the pieces of veal thoroughly on paper towels. Heat the butter and oil in a heavy pot over fairly high heat until the foam subsides and quickly brown the pieces of veal, a few at a time, on all sides. When they are all nicely browned, remove them temporarily from the pot with a slotted spoon. Add the onion and garlic, cook until the onion is transparent, add the strips of pepper, stir for 2 minutes, and then add the wine, stock, and tomatoes. Return the pieces of veal to the pot, season with sugar, salt, and pepper, bring to a boil, reduce the heat, and simmer for $1\frac{1}{2}$ hours, or until the veal is tender. Blend in the kneaded butter, simmer for 10 minutes longer, turn the pieces of veal and the sauce out onto a hot serving dish, and sprinkle with the parsley. *Serves* 6.

1182. SPEZZATINO OF VEAL WITH MUSHROOMS

Sauté o spezzatino di vitello con funghi

3 pounds veal (breast, shoulder, or neck), cut into
    1-inch cubes
2 tablespoons oil
6 tablespoons butter
$1\frac{1}{2}$ tablespoons flour
$1\frac{1}{2}$ cups Brown Veal Stock [No. 5]
$1\frac{1}{2}$ cups Demi-Glaze Sauce [No. 20]
Bouquet Garni:
    3 sprigs parsley
    2 sprigs thyme (or $\frac{1}{2}$ teaspoon dried)
    1 bay leaf

1 pound mushrooms, quartered
Salt and freshly ground pepper

Dry the pieces of veal thoroughly on paper towels. Heat the oil and 3 tablespoons of the butter in a heavy pot over fairly high heat until the butter foam subsides and quickly brown the pieces of veal, a few at a time, on all sides. Sprinkle with the flour, stir for 1 minute, and add the stock, Demi-Glaze sauce, and Bouquet Garni. Bring to a boil, reduce the heat, and simmer for $1\frac{1}{2}$ hours, or until the veal is tender. Shortly before the veal is fully cooked, gently sauté the mushrooms in the remaining butter in a frying pan over moderate heat for about 8 minutes. Add the mushrooms to the pot, discard the Bouquet Garni, simmer for a few minutes, and turn the veal and the sauce out onto a hot serving dish. *Serves* 6.

1183. SPEZZATINO OF VEAL WITH PEAS

Sauté o spezzatino di vitello con piselli

3 pounds veal (breast, shoulder, or neck), cut into
    1-inch cubes
$\frac{1}{2}$ cup chopped ham fat
2 tablespoons oil
$\frac{1}{2}$ cup dry white wine
3 tablespoons flour
Bouquet Garni:
    3 sprigs parsley
    2 sprigs thyme (or $\frac{1}{2}$ teaspoon dried)
    1 bay leaf
1 pound tiny peas, shelled
Salt and freshly ground pepper

Dry the pieces of veal thoroughly on paper towels. Put the ham fat and oil in a heavy pot over fairly high heat, stir until the oil is smoking hot, and quickly brown the pieces of veal, a few at a time, on all sides. Add the wine and cook until it is completely evaporated. Sprinkle with the flour and stir until the flour is lightly browned. Add sufficient water to barely cover the veal, season with salt and pepper, add the Bouquet Garni, bring to a boil, reduce the heat, and simmer for $1\frac{1}{2}$ hours, or until the veal is tender. Add a little more water from time to time during the cooking if necessary to keep the veal barely covered. About 15 minutes before the veal is fully cooked, add the peas. Complete the cooking, correct the seasoning, remove the Bouquet Garni, and turn the veal and the sauce out into a hot serving dish. *Serves* 6.

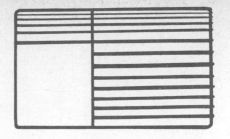

1184. SPEZZATINO OF VEAL WITH TAGLIATELLE

Sauté o spezzatino di vitello con tagliatelle fresche

Prepare in the same manner as Spezzatino of Veal with Mushrooms [No. 1182], except omit the mushrooms and serve with a side dish of tagliatelle [*see* No. 514], dressed with a generous amount of butter and Parmesan cheese. *Serves* 6.

1185. SPEZZATINO OF VEAL WITH TOMATOES

Sauté o spezzatino di vitello al pomodoro

3 pounds veal (breast, shoulder, or neck), cut into
    1-inch cubes
3 tablespoons oil
2 tablespoons butter
$\frac{1}{2}$ cup dry white wine
2 cloves garlic, crushed in the garlic-press
2 pounds tomatoes, peeled, seeded, drained, and
    chopped
1 bay leaf
2 tablespoons chopped marjoram (or 1 teaspoon dried)
2 tablespoons chopped parsley
Salt and freshly ground pepper

Dry the pieces of veal thoroughly with paper towels. Heat the butter and oil in a heavy pot over fairly high heat until the butter foam subsides and quickly brown the pieces of veal, a few at a time, on all sides. Add the wine and cook until it is completely evaporated. Add the garlic, tomatoes, bay leaf, and sufficient water to barely cover the veal (if only dried marjoram is available, it should be added at this point). Season with salt and pepper, bring to a boil, reduce the heat, and simmer for $1\frac{1}{2}$ hours, or until the veal is tender. Add a little more water from time to time during the cooking if neecssary to keep the veal barely covered. Add the chopped marjoram and parsley, correct the seasoning, and turn the veal and sauce out into a hot serving dish. *Serves* 6.

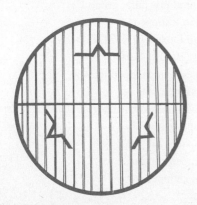

1186. VEAL STEW WITH MUSHROOMS

Muscoletti di vitello con funghi

3 pounds veal (shank or breast), cut into
    $1\frac{1}{2}$-inch cubes
2 tablespoons oil
6 tablespoons butter
A chopped mixture:
    4 tablespoons ham fat
    1 onion
    1 carrot
    1 clove garlic
$\frac{1}{2}$ cup dry white wine
3 tablespoons flour
1 clove
$\frac{1}{2}$ teaspoon powdered bay leaf
1 pound tomatoes, peeled, seeded, drained, and
    chopped
1 quart Brown Veal Stock [No. 5]
2 pounds mushrooms, sliced
Salt and freshly ground pepper

Dry the pieces of veal thoroughly on paper towels. Heat the oil and 3 tablespoons of the butter over high heat in a large heavy pot, add the chopped mixture, stir until the onion begins to color, add the pieces of veal, and brown them lightly on all sides. Cook only several pieces at a time if necessary to avoid crowding and adjust the heat so that the vegetables do not burn. When all the pieces are lightly browned add the wine, and cook until evaporated. Sprinkle with the flour and stir until it becomes golden. Add the clove, powdered bay leaf, tomatoes, and sufficient stock to completely cover the meat. Season lightly with salt and pepper, bring to a boil, reduce the heat, and simmer for about 2 hours, or until the veal is tender. Shortly before the veal is fully cooked, gently sauté the mushrooms in the remaining butter in a covered frying pan over moderate heat for about 8 minutes; remove from the heat and reserve. Transfer the pieces of veal to a bowl with a slotted spoon and keep warm. Strain the sauce through a fine sieve, return it to the pot, reduce it slightly over high heat if it is too thin, correct the seasoning, and then add the pieces of veal and the mushrooms. Simmer for 5 minutes and then turn out onto a hot serving dish. *Serves* 6.

Stuffed Breast of Veal Casalinga (No. 1187)

1187. STUFFED BREAST OF VEAL CASALINGA

Petto di vitello ripieno alla casalinga

3 pounds boned breast of veal
A finely ground stuffing:
   $\frac{1}{2}$ pound lean raw pork
   2 ounces ham (fat and lean)
   2 ounces sausage meat
   1 clove garlic
   3 sprigs parsley
2 eggs, slightly beaten
12 strips prosciutto, 3 inches long and $\frac{1}{4}$ inch square
3 sweet Italian sausages, quartered lengthwise
6 tablespoons butter
$\frac{1}{2}$ cup dry white wine
2 cups Brown Veal Stock [No. 5]
Salt and freshly ground pepper

Have the butcher prepare the veal for stuffing by cutting a lengthwise pocket in it. Mix the eggs with the stuffing ingredients, season with pepper, spread a layer in the pocket, press the strips of the prosciutto and sausage into the stuffing, and cover with the remaining stuffing. Sew the opening with string and then tie the veal into a neat roll so that it will retain its shape during the cooking. Heat the butter in a heavy casserole or roasting pan over fairly high heat until it is golden and brown the veal on all sides, taking care not to burn the butter. Add the wine and cook until it is almost evaporated. Season the veal with salt and pepper, add the stock, bring to a boil, cover the casserole, and place it in a moderate (350°) oven for about $1\frac{1}{2}$ hours, or until the juices run yellow when the veal is pierced with a fork. Transfer the veal to a hot serving platter and allow it to rest for 10 minutes before carving. Reduce the liquid in the casserole over high heat by $\frac{1}{3}$, cut the veal into neat slices, and spoon the sauce over the slices. *Serves 6.*

1188. STUFFED BREAST OF VEAL WITH GLAZED CARROTS

Petto di vitello farcito e brasato con carote glassate

3 pounds boned breast of veal
Stuffing:
   $\frac{1}{2}$ pound raw pork, ground
   1 onion, chopped
   $\frac{1}{4}$ cup Duxelles [No. 138]
   2 eggs, slightly beaten
   1 tablespoon chopped parsley
   $\frac{1}{2}$ teaspoon salt
   $\frac{1}{4}$ teaspoon black pepper, crushed in the mortar
   $\frac{1}{4}$ cup brandy
4 tablespoons oil
4 tablespoons butter
1 onion, chopped

1 carrot, chopped
½ cup dry white wine
¾ pound fresh pork rind, cut in wide strips and
    parboiled for 1 hour
2 veal knuckles, split and parboiled for 45 minutes
Bouquet Garni:
    3 sprigs parsley
    2 sprigs thyme (or ½ teaspoon dried)
    1 bay leaf
1 quart Brown Veal Stock [No. 5]
1 recipe Glazed Carrots [No. 1647]
Salt and freshly ground pepper

Have the butcher prepare the veal for stuffing by cutting a lengthwise pocket in it. Mix the stuffing ingredients thoroughly, stuff the veal, sew the opening with string, and then tie it at 1½-inch intervals to form a neat roll. Heat the oil in a frying pan over high heat until very hot and quickly brown the veal on all sides. Season it with salt and pepper, remove it from the pan, pour off the oil, lower heat, add the butter, heat until the foam subsides, add the carrot and onion, and stir over medium heat until the onion begins to color. Add the wine and cook until it has almost evaporated. Line a heavy casserole with the pork rind, pour the vegetables over it, lay the veal on top, and add the veal knuckles, Bouquet Garni, and stock. Bring to a boil, cover the casserole, and place it in a moderate (350°) oven for about 1½ hours. The veal is fully cooked when it is easily pierced with a fork and its juices run yellow. About 15 minutes before removing it from the oven, remove the lid, raise the heat slightly to allow the cooking liquid to reduce, and baste frequently. Transfer the veal to a hot serving platter and allow it to rest for about 10 minutes before carving. Reduce the cooking liquid still further, if necessary, to give it a good strong flavor, and strain it through a fine sieve into a sauceboat. Serve it and the glazed carrots separately. *Serves* 6.

NOTE: The flesh may be removed from the knuckles, cubed, and added to the sauce. Or it may be reserved for another purpose.

1189. STUFFED BREAST OF VEAL WITH BRAISED LETTUCE
Petto di vitello farcito e brasato con lattughe brasate

This has the same ingredients and is prepared in the same way as Stuffed Breast of Veal with Glazed Carrots [No. 1188], substituting Braised Lettuce [No. 1697] for the glazed carrots. *Serves* 6.

1190. STUFFED BREAST OF VEAL WITH TAGLIATELLE
Petto di vitello farcito e brasato con tagliatelle

This has the same ingredients and is prepared in the same way as Stuffed Breast of Veal with Glazed Carrots [No. 1188], substituting for the carrots a dish of tagliatelle or fettuccine [*see* No. 514] cooked *al dente* in a large quantity of lightly salted boiling water, drained, and generously dressed with butter and grated Parmesan cheese. *Serves* 6.

1191. STUFFED SHOULDER OF VEAL CASALINGA
Spalla di vitello farcita alla casalinga

Prepare in the same manner and with the same ingredients as Stuffed Breast of Veal Casalinga [No. 1187], substituting a good cut from the shoulder for the breast of veal. *Serves* 6.

LAMB
Agnello

Lamb comes from sheep between 3 months and 1 year old. After 1 year it becomes mutton which, perhaps because of its strong flavor, is not very popular with Americans. Very young lamb, from 3 to 5 months old, was formerly known as spring lamb, but now, since modern shipping and raising methods make very young lamb available the year round, it is more generally known as baby or milk-finished lamb. Baby lamb is naturally more tender and delicately flavored than a more mature animal.

The most popular cut of lamb for a roast is the leg, although a less expensive shoulder cut may be substituted. The leg adapts itself splendidly to the simple roasting process, and a nicely roasted leg, seasoned with garlic and rosemary in the Italian manner, can be an unforgettable delight. As with veal, the loin is more generally reserved for chops, for which Italian cooks have devised a variety of delicious preparations. Breast or shoulder is best for stews.

Generally, Italians prefer roasted, sautéed, or broiled lamb cooked medium rare; the meat is still pink, but no longer bloody. If your taste is for well-done lamb, the cooking times for many of the following recipes should be increased slightly, but lamb should never be cooked until it is very well done (a thermometer reading of over 170°), or it will become dry and tasteless and can only be partially redeemed by a well-flavored sauce.

1192. BOILED LEG OF LAMB INGLESE
Cosciotto d'agnello all'inglese

1 6-pound leg of lamb, boned and tied very
    securely to hold its shape
Cold water
2 carrots, quartered
2 onions
Bouquet Garni:
   3 sprigs parsley
   2 sprigs thyme (or 1/2 teaspoon dried)
   1 bay leaf
1 clove garlic
1 1/2 pounds turnips, washed and peeled
3 tablespoons butter
1 1/2 cups Bastard Sauce [No. 66], mixed with
   1 tablespoon capers
Salt and freshly ground pepper

Place the lamb in a large pot with the carrots, onions, Bouquet Garni, garlic, and turnips. Add sufficient water to cover the lamb and add 1 1/2 teaspoons salt for each quart of water. Bring to a boil over high heat, reduce the heat to moderate, and simmer for 1 3/4 hours. Transfer the lamb to a hot serving platter and allow it to rest for 15 minutes before carving. Remove the turnips with a slotted spoon, mash them with the butter, and season with salt and pepper. Cut the lamb into neat slices on the platter and serve the turnips and Bastard sauce separately. *Serves 6 to 8.*

1193. BRACIOLINE OF LAMB WITH ARTICHOKES
Bracioline d'agnello con carciofi

18 slices lamb, cut 1/4 inch thick from the leg
6 very young artichokes
1/2 cup chopped ham fat
1 tablespoon oil
1 onion, chopped
1 cup dry white wine
1 cup Tomato Sauce [No. 19]
1 clove garlic, crushed in the garlic-press
1 tablespoon chopped marjoram (or 1/2 teaspoon dried)
Juice of 1 lemon
Salt and freshly ground pepper

Break off the tough outer leaves of the artichokes, cut off the tips of the remaining leaves, quarter the artichokes, remove the chokes, and cut into slices. Parboil the slices in lightly salted acidulated water for 25 minutes, drain, and reserve until needed. Place the slices of lamb between sheets of wax paper and pound them with the flat side of a meat cleaver so that they are somewhat thinner than they were cut. Season the slices with salt and pepper on both sides. Heat the oil and ham fat in a large frying pan over fairly high heat and quickly brown the lamb, a few slices at a time, for about 2 minutes on each side. As the slices are browned, transfer them to a hot serving platter and keep warm. When all have been browned, add the chopped onion to the pan, cook until golden, add the wine, and reduce to 1/2 its quantity. Add the tomato sauce, garlic, marjoram, and reserved artichokes. Simmer for 10 minutes, add the lemon juice, and then spoon over the lamb slices. *Serves 6.*

1194. BRACIOLINE OF LAMB WITH POTATO CROQUETTES
Bracioline d'agnello al marsala con crocchettine di patate

18 slices of lamb, cut 1/4 inch thick from the leg
Flour
1/2 cup butter
1/2 cup dry Marsala wine
1 cup Brown Stock [No. 4]
Salt and freshly ground pepper
6 Potato Croquettes [No. 1767]

Place the slices of lamb between sheets of wax paper and pound them with the flat side of a meat cleaver so that they are somewhat thinner than they were cut. Season the slices with salt and pepper and dust

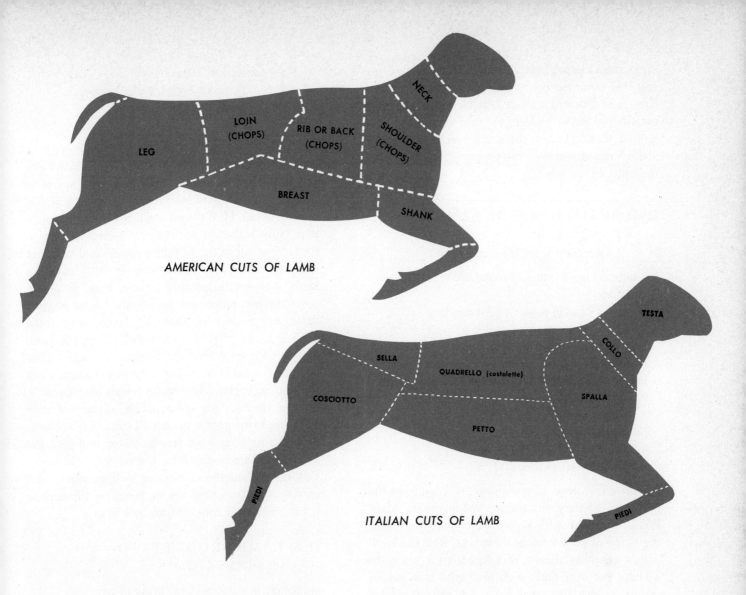

AMERICAN CUTS OF LAMB

ITALIAN CUTS OF LAMB

them with flour. Melt 6 tablespoons of the butter in a large frying pan over fairly high heat until it is golden and quickly brown the lamb, a few slices at a time, for about 2 minutes on each side. As the slices are browned transfer them to a hot platter and keep warm. When all are browned, add the Marsala and stock to the pan, reduce over high heat by $\frac{1}{3}$, remove from the heat, and swirl in the remaining butter, bit by bit. Spoon this sauce over the lamb and garnish the platter with the potato croquettes. *Serves 6.*

1195. BRAISED LEG OF LAMB ABRUZZI
Cosciotto d'agnello all'abruzzese

1 6-pound leg of lamb, boned and tied to hold its
   shape
$\frac{1}{4}$ pound lean salt pork, diced and parboiled for
   10 minutes

3 cloves garlic
6 sprigs rosemary
6 tablespoons oil
1 cup dry white wine
$1\frac{1}{2}$ pounds tomatoes, peeled, seeded, drained,
   and chopped
2 tablespoons chopped parsley
1 tablespoon chopped oregano (or 1 teaspoon dried)
Salt and freshly ground pepper

Put the salt pork dice in a frying pan over medium heat, shake the pan until the dice are golden on all sides, remove them with a slotted spoon, and drain on absorbent paper. Make small slits in the lamb with a very sharp knife and insert half cloves of garlic and small sprigs of rosemary in these slits. Rub the lamb with a generous amount of salt. Heat the oil in a large pot over fairly high heat and brown the lamb on all sides. Add the wine and cook until it is almost evaporated. Add the tomatoes, salt pork dice, parsley, oregano, and sufficient water to come about $\frac{1}{3}$ up the sides of the lamb. Season lightly with salt and pepper, bring to a boil, cover the pot, reduce the heat to a very low flame, and simmer for about 2 hours, or until the lamb is easily pierced with a fork. Transfer the lamb to a hot serving platter, reduce the sauce over high heat for about 5 minutes, correct the seasoning, and pour over the lamb. *Serves 6 to 8.*

1196. BRAISED LEG OF LAMB PASQUALE

Cosciotto d'agnello pasquale

1 6-pound leg of lamb, boned and tied to hold its shape
12 narrow strips of prosciutto, 3 inches long
$\frac{1}{2}$ cup red wine
1 clove garlic, crushed in the garlic-press
1 tablespoon chopped parsley
1 tablespoon chopped marjoram (or 1 teaspoon dried)
6 tablespoons butter
1 cup dry white wine
1 quart Brown Stock [No. 4]
4 tablespoons Kneaded Butter [No. 107]
36 Noisette Potatoes [No. 1783]

Marinate the strips of prosciutto for 2 hours in the red wine with the garlic, parsley, and marjoram. Make slits in the lamb with a very sharp knife and insert the strips of prosciutto in these slits. Rub the lamb with a generous amount of salt. Melt the butter in a heavy pot over fairly high heat until it is golden and brown the lamb on all sides. Add the white wine and marinade and cook until they have almost completely evaporated. Add the stock and sufficient water to come about $\frac{1}{3}$ up the sides of the lamb, bring to a boil, cover the pot, reduce the heat to a very low flame, and simmer for about 2 hours, or until the lamb is easily pierced with a fork. Transfer the lamb to a hot serving platter and keep warm. Blend the kneaded butter into the cooking liquid with a whisk and simmer for about 15 minutes. Cut the lamb into neat slices on the platter, pour the sauce over the slices, and serve the potatoes on the side. *Serves 6.*

1197. BRAISED LEG OF LAMB TOSCANA

Agnello con piselli alla toscana

1 6-pound leg of lamb, boned and tied to hold its shape
3 cloves garlic
6 sprigs rosemary

6 tablespoons oil
$1\frac{1}{2}$ pounds tomatoes, peeled, seeded, drained, and chopped
2 pounds shelled peas
Salt and freshly ground pepper

Make small slits in the lamb with a very sharp knife and insert half cloves of garlic and small sprigs of rosemary in these slits. Rub the lamb with a generous amount of salt. Heat the oil in a heavy pot or casserole over fairly high heat until it is smoking and brown the lamb on all sides. Add the tomatoes and sufficient water to come about $\frac{1}{3}$ the way up the sides of the lamb, season with salt and pepper, bring to a boil, cover the pot, reduce the heat to the lowest possible flame, and simmer for about $2\frac{1}{2}$ hours, or until the lamb is easily pierced with a fork. Turn the lamb every half hour during the cooking and add a little additional water if the liquid reduces too much. Cook the peas in lightly salted water for about 5 minutes, or until they are not quite tender, drain, and then add them to the pot for the last 10 minutes of cooking. Place the lamb on a hot serving platter and pour the sauce and the peas around it. *Serves 6.*

NOTE: Although it facilitates both browning and carving, the lamb need not be boned; if the bone is left in, reduce the cooking time by 1 hour.

1198. LAMB BRODETTATO

Agnello brodettato

3 pounds boned shoulder or breast of lamb, cut in $1\frac{1}{2}$-inch cubes
4 tablespoons oil
$\frac{1}{2}$ cup chopped prosciutto (fat and lean)
1 onion, chopped
$\frac{1}{2}$ cup dry white wine
3 tablespoons flour
1 quart White Stock [No. 1]
1 clove garlic, crushed in the garlic-press
2 tablespoons chopped parsley
3 egg yolks
2 tablespoons grated Parmesan cheese
Juice of 1 lemon
Pinch nutmeg
Salt and freshly ground pepper

Dry the pieces of lamb thoroughly on paper towels. Heat the oil in a large heavy pot over fairly high heat until smoking and quickly brown the lamb, a few pieces at a time, on all sides. When all the pieces are browned, drain off the oil with a bulb baster, sprinkle the chopped prosciutto and onion over the lamb, and stir over medium heat until the onion begins to color. Season lightly with salt and pepper, add the wine, and cook until the wine has completely evaporated. Sprinkle the flour over the meat and stir until the flour is lightly browned. Add the stock and sufficient water to barely cover the meat, bring to a boil, reduce the heat, cover the pot, and simmer for about 2 hours, or until the lamb is tender. About 10 minutes before the lamb is fully cooked, add the garlic and parsley. Beat the egg yolks in a bowl with about $\frac{1}{2}$ cup of the cooking liquid, the grated cheese, and the lemon juice. Remove the pot from the fire, add the egg yolk mixture, stirring constantly; return the pot to very low heat; and stir until the liquid is slightly thickened. Add the nutmeg, correct the seasoning, and turn the contents of the pot into a hot serving dish. *Serves 6.*

1199. LAMB BRODETTATO RICCA
Agnello brodettato alla ricca

Prepare in the same manner as described in the preceding recipe and serve a side dish of celery which has been boiled until tender in lightly salted water (*see* page 558), drained, and then braised for 10 minutes in a baking dish in a moderate (350°) oven with a generous cup of the lamb cooking liquid. *Serves 6.*

1200. LAMB CACCIATORA
Agnello alla cacciatora con aceto

3 pounds lamb, cut from the leg into 1-inch cubes
3 cloves garlic
4 anchovy fillets, soaked free of salt [*see* No. 220]
1 cup wine vinegar
3 tablespoons oil
4 sprigs rosemary, tied together with string
    (or substitute 1 tablespoon dried)
Salt and freshly ground pepper

Pound the garlic and the anchovy fillets in a mortar until they are a paste and then blend thoroughly with the vinegar. Dry the pieces of lamb on paper towels. Heat the oil and rosemary in a large frying pan over moderate heat for about 5 minutes until the oil becomes thoroughly impregnated with the rosemary and then discard the rosemary (if only dried rosemary is available, strain the oil after heating through a sieve into a bowl and then return it to the pan). Raise the heat until the oil is almost smoking and quickly brown the lamb, a few pieces at a time, on all sides. When all are browned, reduce the heat slightly and continue cooking

for about 5 minutes longer, or until the lamb is tender but still slightly pink on the inside. The pieces must not be crowded in the pan so that they steam and release their juices; use 2 pans if necessary. Transfer the pieces to a hot serving platter, season with salt and pepper, and keep warm. Add the vinegar mixed with the garlic and anchovies to the pan, reduce over high heat to $\frac{1}{3}$ its quantity, and pour it over the lamb. *Serves 6.*

1201. LAMB CHOPS WITH ARTICHOKES
Costolettine d'agnello con carciofi

12 loin lamb chops, cut 1 inch thick
6 very young artichokes
4 tablespoons oil
3 tablespoons butter
1 clove garlic, crushed in the garlic-press
$\frac{1}{2}$ cup chopped prosciutto (fat and lean)
$\frac{1}{2}$ cup dry white wine
2 tablespoons chopped marjoram
    (or substitute parsley)
Salt and freshly ground pepper

Break off the tough outer leaves of the artichokes and cut off the tips of the remaining leaves. Cut the artichokes into quarters, remove the chokes, parboil the quarters for 30 minutes in lightly salted acidulated water, drain, and reserve until needed. Heat the oil in a large frying pan over fairly high heat and brown the chops, a few at a time, for about 4 minutes on each side. Do not crowd them in the pan; if desired, use 2 pans with slightly more oil. When all are browned, transfer them to a hot serving platter, season them with salt and pepper, and keep warm. Pour off the fat in the pan and add the butter, garlic, and prosciutto. Cook until the garlic is golden, add the wine, de-glaze the pan by scraping the sides and bottom with a wooden spoon, add the artichokes and marjoram (or parsley), reduce the heat, and simmer for 5 minutes, stirring gently to make sure the artichokes get thoroughly hot. Garnish the platter with the artichokes and pour the liquids in the pan over the chops. *Serves 6.*

1202. BROILED LAMB CHOPS
Lamb chops o chops d'agnello alla griglia

12 loin lamb chops, cut 1 inch thick
$\frac{1}{2}$ cup oil
Salt and freshly ground pepper

Brush the chops with oil and place them on a rack

about 4 inches beneath a high broiler flame. Broil them for 4 to 5 minutes on each side, basting them with a little more oil when they are turned. Transfer them to a hot serving platter and serve at once. *Serves* 6.

1203. LAMB CHOPS CAPRICCIOSE
Costolettine d'agnello capricciose

12 loin lamb chops, cut 1 inch thick
12 thin slices salt pork, parboiled for 10 minutes
6 ripe tomatoes
3 tablespoons basil (or 1 tablespoon dried)
1/2 cup fresh breadcrumbs
1/2 cup oil
3 tablespoons butter
12 large mushroom caps
2 cloves garlic, crushed in the garlic-press
2 tablespoons chopped parsley
Salt and freshly ground pepper

Sauté the slices of salt pork in a frying pan over medium heat until they are crisp and golden on both sides; drain on absorbent paper until needed. Cut off the top third of the tomatoes, season with a generous amount of salt and pepper, and then sprinkle with basil, breadcrumbs, and a little oil. Place them in a baking dish in a moderate (350°) oven for 15 minutes. Melt the butter in a frying pan over moderate heat, add the mushrooms and garlic, cover the pan, and cook for about 8 minutes, shaking the pan occasionally. Heat 6 tablespoons of oil in a large frying pan over fairly high heat until smoking and brown the chops, a few at a time, for about 4 minutes on each side. Do not crowd the chops; if desired, use 2 pans with slightly more oil. When all the chops are browned, transfer them to a hot serving platter, season them with salt and pepper, top each with a slice of salt pork and mushroom cap, garnish the platter with the tomatoes, and sprinkle the whole with parsley. *Serves* 6.

1204. LAMB CHOPS FINANCIÈRE
Costolettine d'agnello alla finanziera

12 loin lamb chops, cut 1 inch thick
6 tablespoons butter
1 cup dry Madeira wine
1/4 cup Demi-Glaze Sauce [No. 20]
12 slices stale bread, crusts removed, cut in the shape of small hearts
3 tablespoons oil
2 cups Sauce Financière [No. 32]
Salt and freshly ground pepper

Heat the butter in a large frying pan over fairly high

heat until golden and brown the chops, a few at a time, for about 4 minutes on each side. Do not crowd the chops; if desired, use 2 pans with slightly more butter. When all are browned, transfer them to a hot serving platter, season them with salt and pepper, and keep warm. Pour off most of the fat in the pan, add the Madeira, de-glaze the pan by scraping the sides and bottom with a wooden spoon, cook until the wine is reduced to 2 or 3 tablespoons, and blend in the Demi-Glaze. Quickly sauté the pieces of bread in hot oil in another frying pan over medium heat until they are golden on both sides. Alternate the slices of bread with the chops in a circle around the platter, pour the Madeira/Demi-Glaze sauce over the chops, and pour the Sauce Financière in the center. *Serves* 6.

1205. LAMB CHOPS GOURMET
Costolettine d'agnello ghiotte

12 loin lamb chops, cut 1 inch thick
6 tablespoons butter
2 cups Sauce Soubise [No. 74]
1 1/2 cups fresh breadcrumbs
2 pounds zucchini, sliced, cooked until just tender in lightly salted boiling water, well drained, and dressed with 4 tablespoons butter
2 cups Tomato Sauce [No. 19]
Salt and freshly ground pepper

Heat the butter in a large frying pan over high heat until it is golden and very quickly brown the chops, a few at a time, for 2 minutes on each side. Do not crowd the chops; if desired, use 2 pans with slightly more butter. As the chops become browned, remove them with a slotted spoon and allow them to cool slightly on absorbent paper. When they are cool enough to handle, season them lightly with salt and pepper, spread a little Soubise sauce all over them, and cover them with a generous amount of breadcrumbs. Reheat the fat in the pan over medium heat, and cook the chops for about 3 minutes on each side, or until they are golden brown. Arrange them in a circle around a hot serving platter, heap the zucchini up in the center, and serve the tomato sauce on the side. *Serves* 6.

1206. LAMB CHOPS INGLESE
Costolettine d'agnello all'inglese

12 loin lamb chops, cut 1 inch thick
1/2 cup butter, melted
1 cup breadcrumbs
6 slices bacon

Watercress
Salt and freshly ground pepper

Season the chops with salt and pepper, brush them with butter, cover them generously with breadcrumbs, and sprinkle them again with butter. Place them on a rack about 5 inches beneath a fairly high broiler flame, broil for about 5 minutes, turn the chops, broil for 2 minutes, put a half slice of bacon on each chop, and broil for about 3 minutes longer, or until the bacon is crisp and golden. Transfer them to a hot serving platter and garnish the platter with sprigs of watercress. *Serves* 6.

NOTE: Watch chops carefully so that the breadcrumbs do not burn.

1207. LAMB CHOPS À LA MINUTE
Costolettine d'agnello à la minute

12 loin lamb chops, cut 1 inch thick
6 tablespoons butter
Juice of 2 lemons
2 tablespoons chopped parsley
Salt and freshly ground pepper

Heat the butter in a large frying pan over fairly high heat until golden and brown the chops, a few at a time, for about 4 minutes on each side, adjusting the heat during the cooking so that the butter does not burn. Do not crowd the chops; if desired, use 2 pans with slightly more butter. Transfer the chops to a hot serving platter, season them with salt and pepper, and keep warm. Add the lemon juice to the pan, stir for a few seconds, add the parsley, and pour over the chops. *Serves* 6.

1208. LAMB CHOPS EN PAPILLOTES
Costolettine d'agnello al cartoccio

6 large loin lamb chops, cut 1 inch thick
12 thin slices prosciutto (or smoked ham)
6 tablespoons butter
¼ cup oil
6 large sheets of parchment paper, cut in the shape of large hearts
6 tablespoons Duxelles Sauce [No. 31]
1½ cups Marsala Sauce [No. 43]
Salt and freshly ground pepper

Sauté the slices of prosciutto in 2 tablespoons of butter in a frying pan over medium heat for 2 or 3 minutes, then remove from the heat and keep warm. Heat the remaining butter in a large frying pan over fairly high heat and brown the chops for about 4 minutes on each side. Season them with salt and pepper and remove from the heat. Brush the paper hearts on both sides with oil, place a slice of ham on one side of each of the hearts, top with a chop, put a tablespoon of the Duxelles sauce on each chop, and cover with a slice of prosciutto. Fold the other half of the hearts over the chops and crimp the edges well to make a tight seal. Place them in an oiled baking dish in a very hot (550°) oven for about 10 minutes, or until they are puffed and golden brown. Transfer them to individual hot serving plates and allow each guest to open his own. Serve the Marsala sauce separately. *Serves* 6.

1209. LAMB CHOPS PARISIAN
Costolettine d'agnello alla parigina

12 loin lamb chops, cut 1 inch thick
Flour
2 eggs, beaten
2 cups fresh breadcrumbs
6 tablespoons butter
1 recipe Creamed Mushrooms Au Gratin [No. 1707]
18 asparagus tips, cooked until just tender in lightly salted water, drained, and dressed with 3 tablespoons butter
Salt and freshly ground pepper

Season the chops with salt and pepper, dust them with flour, dip in beaten egg, and cover with a generous amount of breadcrumbs. Heat the butter in a large frying pan over fairly high heat until golden and brown the chops very quickly, a few at a time, for about 2 minutes on each side. Reduce the heat and continue cooking for about 3 minutes longer on each side. Do not crowd the chops in the pan; if desired, use 2 pans with slightly more butter. Arrange the chops in a circle around a hot serving platter, fill the center with the creamed mushrooms, and garnish the edge of the platter with the asparagus tips. *Serves* 6.

1210. LAMB CHOPS SCOTTADITO
Costolettine d'agnello a "scottadito"

12 loin lamb chops, cut 1 inch thick
½ cup oil
Salt and freshly ground pepper

Season the chops with salt and pepper and brush them with oil. Place them on a grill about 4 inches above red-hot charcoal embers and cook for about 4 minutes on each side. The chops should be slightly blackened on the outside but very tender and still pink on the inside. Serve at once. *Serves* 6.

1211. LAMB CHOPS VILLEROY
Costolettine d'agnello alla Villeroy

12 loin lamb chops, cut 1 inch thick
½ cup butter
2 cups cold Sauce Villeroy [No. 59]
2 eggs, beaten
2 cups fresh breadcrumbs
1½ cups Tomato Sauce [No. 19]
Salt and freshly ground pepper

Heat 6 tablespoons of the butter in a large frying pan over fairly high heat until golden and brown the chops, a few at a time, for about 4 minutes on each side. Do not crowd the chops; if desired, use 2 pans with slightly more butter. Remove them with a slotted spoon, season lightly with salt and pepper, and allow them to cool completely on absorbent paper. When cool, coat them with a thin layer of Villeroy sauce, dip them quickly in beaten egg, and then cover completely with breadcrumbs. Reheat the fat in the pan, adding a little more butter if necessary, and brown the chops over moderate heat for about 3 minutes on each side. Transfer them to a hot serving platter and serve the tomato sauce separately. *Serves* 6.

1212. LAMB NOISETTES CACCIATORA
Nocciole d'agnello alla cacciatora

12 loin lamb chops, cut 1 inch thick and boned
6 tablespoons butter
¼ cup chopped onion
½ pound mushrooms, sliced
½ cup dry white wine
½ cup Brown Veal Stock [No. 5]
½ cup Tomato Sauce [No. 19]
Salt and freshly ground pepper

Heat the butter in a large frying pan over fairly high heat until it is golden and brown the pieces of lamb for about 4 minutes on each side. Adjust the heat during the cooking so that the butter does not burn. Do not crowd the pieces of lamb; if desired, use 2 pans with slightly more butter. Transfer the lamb to a hot serving platter, season with salt and pepper, and keep warm. Add the chopped onion to the butter in the pan, cook until the onion is transparent, add the mushrooms, lower the heat, and cook for about 5 minutes. Add the wine, raise the heat, and cook until the wine has almost entirely evaporated. Add the veal stock and tomato sauce, simmer for 5 minutes, and then spoon the sauce and the mushrooms over the lamb. *Serves* 6.

1213. LAMB NOISETTES ITALIANA
Nocciole d'agnello all'italiana

12 loin lamb chops, cut 1 inch thick and boned
12 thin slices prosciutto (or smoked ham)
½ cup butter
1 cup dry white wine
12 rounds of stale bread, crusts removed, sautéed
    until golden in butter
Salt and freshly ground pepper

Sauté the slices of prosciutto in 2 tablespoons of the butter in a frying pan over medium heat for about 2 minutes; remove from the heat and keep warm. Sauté the pieces of lamb in the remaining butter in the manner described in the preceding recipe and season with salt and pepper. Arrange the rounds of bread on a hot serving platter, place a slice of prosciutto on each, and top with a noisette of lamb. De-glaze the pan in which the lamb cooked with the wine over fairly high heat, scraping the sides and bottom with a wooden spoon. Cook for a few minutes to reduce slightly and pour over the lamb. *Serves* 6.

1214. LAMB NOISETTES MELBA
Nocciole d'agnello Melba

12 loin lamb chops, cut 1 inch thick and boned
6 large ripe tomatoes
2 cups diced cooked chicken meat
¼ pound mushrooms, sliced and gently sautéed in
    3 tablespoons butter for about 8 minutes
1 truffle, chopped [or No. 1819a]
1½ cups Velouté Sauce [No. 17]
6 tablespoons butter
1 cup dry Madeira wine
½ cup Brown Veal Stock [No. 5]
6 hearts of Boston lettuce, braised [*see* No. 1697]
12 rounds of stale bread, crusts removed, sautéed
    in butter until golden
Salt and freshly ground pepper

Cut off and discard the top thirds of the tomatoes, scoop out most of the pulp with a spoon, and season the interiors with salt and pepper. Heat the diced chicken, mushrooms, and chopped truffle in the Velouté sauce in a saucepan over moderate heat, fill the tomatoes with this mixture, and place them in a baking dish in a moderate (350°) oven for 15 minutes. Sauté the pieces of lamb in the manner described in Lamb Noisettes Cacciatora [No. 1212] and season them with salt and pepper. Arrange the rounds of bread on a hot serving platter and place a noisette of lamb on each. Add the Madeira and veal stock to the pan in which the lamb was cooked, reduce over high heat to ½ its quantity, spoon a little of this sauce over the noisettes, and garnish the platter with the tomatoes and the braised lettuce. *Serves* 6.

1215. LAMB NOISETTES NIÇOISE
Nocciole d'agnello alla nizzarda

12 loin lamb chops, cut 1 inch thick and boned
6 tablespoons butter
1 cup Brown Veal Stock [No. 5]
½ cup Tomato Sauce [No. 19]
1½ pounds string beans, cooked in lightly salted
    water until just tender, drained, and dressed
    with 3 tablespoons butter
1½ pounds Noisette Potatoes [No. 1783]
Salt and freshly ground pepper

Sauté the pieces of lamb in the butter in the manner described in Lamb Noisettes Cacciatora [No. 1212], season them with salt and pepper, transfer them to a hot serving platter, and keep warm. Add the stock and tomato sauce to the pan and reduce over high heat to ½ their quantity. Pour this sauce over the noisettes and garnish the platter with the potatoes and the string beans. *Serves* 6.

1216. ROAST LEG OF LAMB
Cosciotto d'agnello arrosto

1 6-pound leg of lamb
3 cloves garlic, halved
¼ cup butter, melted
¼ cup oil
1 cup dry white wine
½ bunch watercress
Salt and freshly ground pepper
1½ cups Mint Sauce [No. 91]

Make small slits in the lamb with a very sharp knife and insert half cloves of garlic into these slits. Rub the lamb with a generous amount of salt and brush it with a mixture of melted butter and oil. Place the lamb in a roasting pan in a hot (450°) oven for 15 minutes, or until it becomes lightly browned. Baste with more butter and oil, reduce the heat to moderate (350°), and continue cooking for 1 hour. Transfer it to a hot serving platter and keep warm; the lamb should rest for 15 minutes before carving to allow the juices to retreat back into the tissues. Pour off the fat in the pan, add the

wine, and de-glaze the pan over fairly high heat, scraping the bottom and sides with a wooden spoon, until the wine is reduced by ½. When ready to serve, carve the lamb into neat slices, garnish the platter with watercress, spoon the few tablespoons of sauce over the slices, and serve the mint sauce on the side. *Serves* 6 *to* 8.

NOTE: The lamb may be boned before cooking, if desired. In this event, increase the total cooking time by 45 minutes.

1217. ROAST LEG OF LAMB AREZZO
Cosciotto d'agnello all'aretina

1 6-pound leg of lamb
3 cloves garlic, halved
A marinade:
    3 cups red wine
    1 cup oil
    ¼ cup wine vinegar
    6 sprigs rosemary
    2 teaspoons salt
    ½ teaspoon freshly ground pepper
6 tablespoons oil

Make small slits in the lamb with a very sharp knife and insert half cloves of garlic in these slits. Mix the marinade ingredients thoroughly in a large enameled or porcelain bowl and marinate the lamb for 24 hours, turning it frequently. Drain it on a rack for 30 minutes, dry it with paper towels, brush it with oil, and then roast it in the manner described in Roast Leg of Lamb [No. 1216], basting it every 20 minutes with the marinade. Allow it to rest on a hot serving platter for 15 minutes before carving and serve it with just its own juices. *Serves* 6 *to* 8.

1218. ROAST LEG OF LAMB CASALINGA
Cosciotto d'agnello alla casalinga

1 6-pound leg of lamb
6 tablespoons oil
2 pounds potatoes, quartered and parboiled
    10 minutes in lightly salted water
2 onions, sliced and parboiled 5 minutes
2 tablespoons chopped rosemary
Salt

Rub the lamb with a generous amount of salt, brush it with oil, and roast it in a shallow enameled baking pan in the manner described in Roast Leg of Lamb [No. 1216]. About 20 minutes before the lamb is fully

413

cooked, arrange the potatoes and sliced onions around the lamb, sprinkle them with rosemary, and baste them with the fat in the pan. Raise the heat slightly and complete the cooking, basting the potatoes and onions every 5 minutes. Remove the baking pan from the oven, allow the lamb to rest for 15 minutes before carving, and serve in the baking pan. *Serves 6.*

1219. ROAST LEG OF LAMB WITH PARSLEY
Quarto d'agnello arrosto al prezzemolo

1 6-pound leg of lamb
12 long, narrow strips salt pork, parboiled for 10
    minutes
¼ cup butter, melted
¼ cup oil
3 cups fresh breadcrumbs
1 cup finely chopped parsley
2 cups Piquant Sauce [No. 94]
Salt and freshly ground pepper

Lard the leg of lamb with the strips of salt pork, using a larding needle or inserting them into deep slits made with a very sharp knife. Rub the lamb with a generous amount of salt and then brush with a mixture of melted butter and oil. Roast the lamb in the manner described in Roast Leg of Lamb [No. 1216]. About 15 minutes before the lamb is fully cooked, baste it with the fat in the pan, remove it from the oven, and coat it with a generous amount of breadcrumbs mixed with parsley. Return it to the pan, baste it again, being careful not to dislodge the breadcrumbs, and complete the cooking. Raise the heat slightly so that the breadcrumbs will become golden brown. Transfer the lamb to a hot serving platter and allow it to stand for 15 minutes before carving. Serve the piquant sauce separately. *Serves 6 to 8.*

1220. SAUTÉ OF LAMB WITH ARTICHOKES
Sauté d'agnello con carciofi

3 pounds lamb, cut from the leg into strips ½ inch
    thick and 2 inches long
½ cup butter
6 artichoke hearts [*see* introduction to No. 1578]
    parboiled for 30 minutes and sliced
1 cup dry white wine
½ cup Brown Stock [No. 4]
2 tablespoons chopped parsley
Salt and freshly ground pepper

Heat 6 tablespoons of the butter in a large frying pan over fairly high heat until it is golden and quickly brown the pieces of lamb, a few at a time, for about 2 minutes on each side. Do not crowd the pieces in the pan; if desired, use 2 frying pans with slightly more butter. The pieces should be nicely browned on the outside but still pink on the inside. Transfer them to a hot serving platter, season with salt and pepper, and keep warm. Gently sauté the sliced artichoke hearts in the remaining butter in another frying pan over moderate heat for 3 or 4 minutes and then arrange them on the platter with the lamb. Add the wine and stock to the pan in which the lamb cooked and reduce over high heat to ½ their quantity. Pour this sauce over the lamb and sprinkle with the parsley. *Serves 6.*

1221. SAUTÉ OF LAMB CACCIATORA
Sauté d'agnello alla cacciatora

3 pounds lamb, cut from the leg into strips ½ inch
    thick and 2 inches long
6 tablespoons butter
1 cup dry white wine
1 cup Cacciatora Sauce [No. 28]
2 tablespoons chopped parsley
Salt and freshly ground pepper

Heat the butter in a large frying pan over fairly high heat until it is golden and brown the pieces of lamb, a few at a time, on both sides. Do not crowd the pieces; if desired, use 2 frying pans with slightly more butter. The lamb should be nicely browned on the outside, but still pink on the inside. Transfer the pieces to a hot serving platter, season with salt and pepper, and keep warm. Add the wine and Cacciatora sauce to the pan and reduce over high heat by ⅓. Spoon this sauce over the lamb and sprinkle with the chopped parsley. *Serves 6.*

1222. SAUTÉ OF LAMB IN CREAM
Sauté d'agnello alla crema

3 pounds lamb, cut from the leg into strips ½ inch
    thick and 2 inches long
¾ cup butter
1½ cups heavy cream
Salt and freshly ground pepper

Sauté the pieces of lamb in 6 tablespoons of the butter as prescribed in the preceding recipe, transfer them to a hot serving platter, season with salt and pepper, and keep warm. Pour off most of the butter in the pan, add the cream, and reduce over fairly high heat by ⅓.

Remove from the heat, swirl in the remaining butter, bit by bit, correct the seasoning, and pour over the lamb. *Serves 6.*

1223. SAUTÉ OF LAMB WITH EGGPLANT
Sauté d'agnello con melanzane

3 pounds lamb, cut from the leg into strips ½ inch thick and 2 inches long
6 tablespoons butter
2 eggplants, peeled, cut into 1-inch cubes, salted, allowed to drain for 1 hour; then washed and thoroughly dried
Flour
½ cup oil
1 cup dry white wine
½ cup Thickened Brown Veal Stock [No. 6]
½ cup Tomato Sauce [No. 19]
2 tablespoons chopped parsley
Salt and freshly ground pepper

Sauté the pieces of lamb in the butter in the manner described in Sauté of Lamb with Artichokes [No. 1220], transfer them to a hot serving platter, season them with salt and pepper, and keep warm. Season the eggplant cubes lightly with pepper, dust them with flour, and sauté them in smoking hot oil in a frying pan over fairly high heat until they are golden brown. Arrange them on the platter with the lamb. Add the wine, stock, and tomato sauce to the pan in which the lamb cooked and reduce over high heat by ⅓. Pour this sauce over the lamb and sprinkle with the chopped parsley. *Serves 6.*

1224. SAUTÉ OF LAMB WITH MUSHROOMS
Sauté d'agnello con funghi

This is prepared with the same ingredients and in the same manner as Sauté of Lamb with Eggplant [No. 1223], substituting ½ pound of mushroom caps for the eggplant. The mushrooms should be gently sautéed in 3 tablespoons of butter in a covered frying pan over moderate heat for about 8 minutes. *Serves 6.*

1225. SAUTÉ OF LAMB WITH POTATOES
Sauté d'agnello con patate

This has the same ingredients and is prepared in the same manner as Sauté of Lamb with Eggplant [No. 1223], substituting 1½ pounds Noisette Potatoes [No. 1783] for the eggplant. *Serves 6.*

1226. SAUTÉ OF LAMB WITH TOMATOES
Sauté d'agnello al pomodoro

This has the same ingredients and is prepared in the same manner as Sauté of Lamb with Artichokes [No. 1220], except the artichokes are omitted, and the platter is garnished with 1 recipe Tomatoes Au Gratin [No. 1812]. *Serves 6.*

1227. LAMB STEW
Ragú d'agnello a bianco

3 pounds boned breast or shoulder of lamb, cut in 1½-inch pieces
2 onions, sliced
2 quarts White Stock [No. 1]
Bouquet Garni:
   3 sprigs parsley
   2 sprigs thyme (or ½ teaspoon dried)
   1 bay leaf
1½ pounds potatoes, sliced
2 tablespoons chopped parsley
Salt and freshly ground pepper

Place the lamb, onions, stock, and Bouquet Garni in a large, heavy pot, bring to a boil over high heat, reduce the heat, and simmer for 1½ hours. Correct the seasoning, add the potatoes, and cook for 30 minutes longer. Discard the Bouquet Garni, transfer the lamb and potatoes to a shallow hot serving bowl, sprinkle with the parsley, and spoon over a generous amount of the cooking liquid. *Serves 6.*

1228. LAMB STEW BUONA DONNA
Ragú d'agnello buona donna

3 pounds boned breast or shoulder of lamb, cut in 1½-inch cubes
4 tablespoons butter
1 teaspoon brown sugar
3 tablespoons flour
1 quart Brown Stock [No. 4]
1 clove garlic, crushed in the garlic-press
Bouquet Garni:
   3 sprigs parsley
   2 sprigs thyme (or ½ teaspoon dried)
   1 bay leaf
12 "new" potatoes
12 white onions
Salt and freshly ground pepper

Heat the butter in a large frying pan over fairly high heat and quickly brown the lamb, a few pieces at a time, on all sides. As the pieces become browned, transfer them to a large, heavy pot. Season the pieces in the pot with salt and pepper and sprinkle them with the sugar, place the pot over medium heat, and stir for 2 or 3 minutes. Sprinkle with the flour and continue stirring until the flour is lightly browned. Drain off the fat (if any) from the frying pan, add the stock, bring to a boil over high heat, de-glaze the pan by scraping the bottom and sides with a wooden spoon, and then pour the stock over the lamb. Add a little water if necessary to barely cover the lamb. Add the garlic and Bouquet Garni, bring to a boil, reduce the heat, cover the pot, and simmer for 1 hour. Add the potatoes and onions and continue cooking for 30 minutes longer, or until the lamb and vegetables are tender. Correct the seasoning and turn the contents of the pot out into a shallow serving dish. *Serves 6.*

1229. LAMB ROMANA
Agnello alla romana

2½ pounds lamb, cut from the leg into 1½-inch cubes
1½ cups breadcrumbs
½ cup chopped parsley
3 cloves garlic, crushed in the garlic-press
2 teaspoons salt
¼ teaspoon freshly ground pepper
¼ cup oil

Mix thoroughly together the breadcrumbs, parsley, garlic, salt, and pepper. Brush the lamb pieces with oil, roll them in the breadcrumb mixture, place them on a baking dish, sprinkle with oil, and bake in a moderate (350°) oven for 30 minutes, or until they are golden. *Serves 6.*

KID

Capretto

Kid is relatively unknown in American meat markets. It is, however, a delicious, tender meat, somewhat similar to lamb in texture and flavor. It can usually be obtained in Italian or Arab communities in the larger American cities.

Kid may be seasoned with garlic and rosemary and roasted in the manner described in Roast Leg of Lamb [No. 1216], or it may, in fact, be successfully substituted in any of the foregoing recipes for lamb.

1230. KID CACCIATORA
Capretto alla cacciatora

3 pounds kid, cut from the leg in 1½-inch cubes
½ cup oil
½ cup chopped onion
3 tablespoons flour
3 cups White Stock [No. 1]
1 cup Tomato Sauce [No. 19]
Bouquet Garni:
   3 sprigs parsley
   2 sprigs thyme (or ½ teaspoon dried)
   1 bay leaf
3 tablespoons brandy
½ pound mushrooms, sliced
3 tablespoons butter
2 tablespoons chopped parsley
Salt and freshly ground pepper

Dry the pieces of kid thoroughly on paper towels. Heat the oil until smoking hot in a large frying pan over fairly high heat and quickly brown the kid, a few pieces at a time, on all sides. Do not crowd the pieces in the pan; if desired, use 2 frying pans with slightly more oil. As the pieces become brown, transfer them to a heavy pot. Sprinkle the onion over the pieces of kid in the pot and stir over medium heat until the onion becomes golden. Sprinkle the flour over the meat and stir until it is lightly browned. Add the stock, tomato sauce, and Bouquet Garni. Season with a little salt and pepper and bring to a boil. Heat the brandy in a ladle over a medium flame, ignite, and add to the pot. Reduce the heat and simmer very gently for 1½ to 2 hours, or until the pieces of kid are tender. Shortly before the meat is fully cooked, gently sauté the mushrooms in the butter in a frying pan over moderate heat for about 8 minutes and then add them to the pot. Discard the Bouquet Garni, correct the seasoning, turn the contents of the pot out into a shallow serving dish, and sprinkle with the chopped parsley. *Serves 6.*

1. Ham Mousse (No. 1564), served with Paprika Sauce (No. 53)
2. Macedoine of Vegetables (No. 198)
3. Mashed Potatoes (No. 1780)
4. Fresh Ham Braised in Marsala (No. 1233)
5. Applesauce (see No. 1549)
6. Roast Pork (No. 1250)
7. French Fried Potatoes (No. 1773)

1231. KID ITALIANA
Capretto all'italiana

3 pounds boned shoulder of kid, wrapped with thin
    strips of salt pork (or beef suet) and tied into a roll
4 tablespoons butter, softened
4 tablespoons oil
1 cup fresh breadcrumbs
2 cloves garlic, crushed in the garlic-press
2 tablespoons chopped rosemary (or 2 teaspoons dried)
2 tablespoons chopped parsley
1 cup dry Marsala wine
Salt and freshly ground pepper

Season the kid with salt and pepper, place it in a roasting pan with the butter and oil in a hot (450°) oven for 15 minutes, basting it once or twice with the butter and oil. Reduce the heat to moderate (350°) and continue cooking for 55 minutes, basting occasionally with the fat in the pan. Mix the breadcrumbs thoroughly with the garlic, rosemary, and parsley. Remove the kid from the pan and roll it in the breadcrumb mixture. Return it to the pan, sprinkle it lightly with the fat in the pan, and continue cooking for another 15 minutes. Raise the heat slightly during the last 5 minutes of cooking, so that the breadcrumbs will brown. Transfer the roast to a hot serving platter and allow it to rest for 15 minutes before carving. Pour off most of the fat in the pan, add the Marsala, de-glaze the pan over high heat by scraping the sides and the bottom with a wooden spoon, and cook until the Marsala is reduced to about ½ cup. Cut the meat into neat slices on the platter and spoon the reduced Marsala over the slices. *Serves* 6.

PORK
Maiale

The best pork has very finely textured and firm flesh. Very young pork will have almost white flesh, and as a pig grows older, its flesh becomes progressively pinker. The meat is very fat, and because of this almost all cuts of pork—shoulder, loin, or leg—may be roasted.

Pork must be cooked until it is well done. Pigs are subject to a parasitic worm called trichina (the microscopic larvae of which are lodged in the muscles) which is killed at an internal meat temperature of 137°. Thus, to avoid any possibility of transmission of infection to the eater, pork should be cooked to an internal temperature of 185°. At this temperature the meat is no longer even pink and its juices will run clear yellow when pricked deeply with a fork. While caution on this point is certainly advisable, it is equally unnecessary to overcook pork until it is dry and tasteless. The thickness of the meat will determine the cooking time more than the actual poundage. Thus, a 5-pound loin of pork will be fully roasted in a 325° oven in about 3 hours, or slightly less; a fresh ham, which is much thicker, will require up to an hour longer cooked at the same temperature.

1232. BAKED HAM ITALIANA
Prosciutto all'italiana

1 8-pound smoked ham, soaked in water for 24 hours
2 cups Marsala wine (1 cup dry and 1 cup sweet, if
    desired)
2 cups light brown sugar
1 tablespoon dry mustard
1 double recipe Risotto with Butter and Parmesan
    Cheese [No. 572]
1 double recipe Asparagus Italiana [No. 1602]

Scrub the ham thoroughly under running water. Place it in a large kettle or ham boiler, cover with cold water, bring to a boil, reduce the heat, and simmer for 2 hours and 40 minutes (20 minutes to the pound). Remove it from the cooking liquid, and, when cool enough to handle, cut off the rind, leaving about ½ inch of fat on its top side. Place the ham in a roasting pan, add the Marsala, cover the pan tightly, and bake in a moderate (350°) oven for 30 minutes. Remove the cover, score the fat lightly with a knife, and sprinkle the top surface with the brown sugar which has been mixed with dry mustard. Raise the heat to 450° and continue baking uncovered, basting frequently, for about 15 minutes, or until the surface is well glazed. Transfer the ham to a serving platter and allow it to rest for 1 hour before

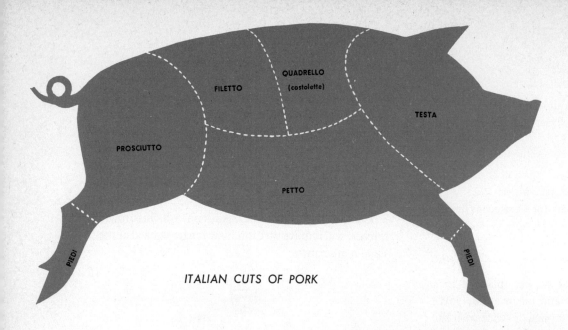

ITALIAN CUTS OF PORK

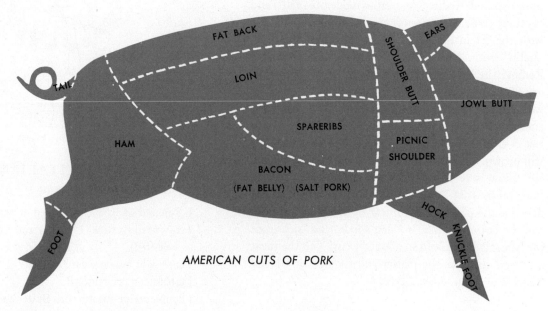

AMERICAN CUTS OF PORK

carving, or cool completely and serve at room temperature the following day. The simple risotto, dressed with butter and Parmesan cheese, and asparagus make ideal accompaniments. *Serves* 12 *to* 15.

1233. FRESH HAM BRAISED IN MARSALA
Prosciutto fresco di maiale al marsala

1 5-pound fresh ham
3½ cups Marsala wine (sweet or dry)
3 tablespoons oil
3 tablespoons butter
1 onion, sliced
2 carrots, sliced
2 stalks celery, sliced

Bouquet Garni:
   3 sprigs parsley
   2 sprigs thyme (or ½ teaspoon dried)
   1 bay leaf
1 cup Brown Stock [No. 4]
3 tablespoons Kneaded Butter [No. 107]
Salt and freshly ground pepper

Marinate the ham in the Marsala for 24 hours, turning it occasionally. Remove it from the marinade and dry thoroughly on paper towels. Heat the oil and butter in a large heavy pot or casserole and brown the meat on all sides. Remove the meat temporarily; drain off all but 2 tablespoons of the fat in the pan; add the onion, carrots, and celery; and sauté over moderate heat until the onion begins to color. Return the meat to the pot, season it with salt and pepper, add ½ cup

418

of the Marsala marinade and the Bouquet Garni, cover the pot, and place it in a moderate (325°) oven for about 2½ hours, or until the ham is tender and its juices run clear yellow when pierced with a fork. Transfer the ham to a hot serving platter and allow it to rest for 20 minutes before carving. Add the stock and another cup of the Marsala marinade to the juices in the pan (the ham should have rendered a generous cup of liquid as it cooked), bring to a boil, blend in the kneaded butter, and simmer for 15 minutes. Cut the ham into neat slices on the platter and spoon a generous amount of the sauce over the slices. *Serves* 8.

1234. HAM AND ASPARAGUS SURPRISE
Soufflé di prosciutto con punte di asparagi

2 cups finely ground or chopped cooked ham
3 tablespoons butter, softened
¾ cup grated Parmesan cheese
1 cup very thick Béchamel Sauce [No. 18]
5 egg yolks
7 egg whites
Pinch salt
Freshly ground pepper
18 asparagus tips, boiled in lightly salted boiling
    water until barely tender, and drained

Grease a 6-cup soufflé dish generously with butter and dust the inside with ¼ cup of the grated cheese. Mix together very thoroughly the chopped ham, Béchamel sauce, the remaining cheese, and the egg yolks. Season the mixture with a little pepper. Beat the egg whites with a pinch of salt until stiff peaks form, fold ¼ of the whites into the other mixture until well combined, and then very gently fold in the remainder. Do not overmix. Arrange 6 of the asparagus tips fanwise in the bottom of the soufflé dish, pour in ⅓ of the soufflé mixture, and continue with 2 more layers each of the asparagus and mixture. Place the dish in a medium (375°) oven, turn the heat down to moderate (350°), and bake for about 40 minutes, or until the top is golden brown and a knife inserted in the center comes out clean. Serve immediately. *Serves* 6.

1235. HAM AND TRUFFLE SOUFFLÉ
Soufflé di prosciutto con tartufi

Prepare with the same ingredients and in the same manner as the preceding recipe, omitting the asparagus tips. Garnish the surface of the soufflé just before baking with thick slices of white truffle and sprinkle with a little chopped truffle. *Serves* 6.

1236. HAM ROLLS RICCA
Involtini di prosciutto alla ricca

12 large thin slices prosciutto (or smoked ham)
4 cooked artichoke hearts [*see* introduction to No. 1578]
    cooled and thinly sliced
2 cups finely diced cooked white meat of chicken
1 truffle, chopped [or No. 1819a]
1½ cups thick Béchamel Sauce [No. 18]
4 tablespoons butter
2 cups Marsala Sauce [No. 43]
1 recipe Asparagus Italiana [No. 1602]

Blend lightly but thoroughly together the sliced artichoke hearts, chicken, chopped truffle, and Béchamel sauce. Spread a little of this mixture on each slice of prosciutto, roll the slices up, and tie with string so that the filling will not escape. Heat the butter in a large frying pan over medium heat and very gently sauté the rolls for 8 to 10 minutes, or just long enough to heat through. Arrange the rolls on a hot serving platter, spoon the Marsala sauce over them, and garnish the platter with the asparagus. *Serves* 6.

1237. BRAISED PIG'S EARS WITH LENTILS
Orecchie di maiale brasate con lenticchie

6 pig's ears, singed, scraped, cut in half lengthwise,
    and parboiled 15 minutes
½ pound fresh pork rind, parboiled for 1 hour
    and cut into wide strips
2 carrots, sliced
2 onions, sliced
Bouquet Garni:
    3 sprigs parsley
    2 sprigs thyme (or ½ teaspoon dried)
    1 bay leaf
1 cup white wine
2 cups White Stock [No. 1]
1 recipe Boiled Lentils [No. 1695]
Salt and freshly ground pepper

Line the bottom of a large heavy pot with the pork rind and then place on top the sliced carrots and onions, the Bouquet Garni, and the pig's ears. Add the wine and cook over high heat until the wine is reduced by ½. Add the stock, bring to a boil, cover the pot, and place it in a moderate (350°) oven for about 1 hour, or until the pig's ears are tender. Heap the lentils in the center of a large hot serving platter and arrange the pig's ears around them. Reduce the cooking liquid over high heat by ⅓, strain through a fine sieve, correct the seasoning, and pour over the pig's ears. *Serves* 6.

1238. PIG'S EARS VINAIGRETTE
Orecchie di maiale lessate con salsa vinaigrette

6 pig's ears, singed, scraped, cut in half lengthwise,
    and parboiled 5 minutes
1 carrot, sliced
1 onion, stuck with 1 clove
Bouquet Garni:
    3 sprigs parsley
    2 sprigs thyme (or ½ teaspoon dried)
    1 bay leaf
1 cup Sauce Vinaigrette [No. 99]
Salt and freshly ground pepper

Place the pig's ears in a heavy pot with the carrot,
onion, and Bouquet Garni. Cover with cold water,
season with salt and pepper, bring to a boil, reduce
the heat, and simmer for about 1 hour, or until the
ears are tender. Drain and serve the ears either hot or
cold marinated in the Vinaigrette sauce. *Serves 6.*

1239. BROILED PIG'S FEET
Piedini di maiale alla griglia

6 pig's feet, scrubbed in several changes of water
1 onion, sliced
1 carrot, sliced
2 stalks celery, sliced
Bouquet Garni:
    3 sprigs parsley
    2 sprigs thyme (or ½ teaspoon dried)
    1 bay leaf
1 lemon, sliced
3 cloves garlic
½ cup butter, melted
2 cups fresh breadcrumbs
Salt and freshly ground pepper

Place the pig's feet in a large heavy pot with the onion,
carrot, celery, Bouquet Garni, lemon slices, and garlic.
Cover with cold water, season with salt and pepper,
bring to a boil, reduce the heat, and simmer for about
4 hours, or slightly less if the feet are small. Remove
the feet from the cooking liquid, split them in half
lengthwise, brush them with melted butter, cover them
with a liberal coating of breadcrumbs, sprinkle with
more butter, and then broil them for about 5 minutes
on each side under a medium broiler flame. Arrange
them on a hot serving platter and, if desired, serve
a side dish of mashed potatoes. *Serves 6.*

*The preparation of
Pig's Feet Croquettes (No. 1240).
The photographs gives one
a good idea of what the caul,
or reticulum, looks like*

1240. PIG'S FEET CROQUETTES
Piedini di maiale farciti alla griglia

3 pig's feet (5 if they are small), simmered 4 hours
    in the aromatic vegetables, herbs, and
    seasonings described in the previous recipe
½ pound mushrooms, sliced
1 tablespoon butter
½ cup dry white wine
2 cups Forcemeat [No. 129], made with chicken
½ pound pig's caul (*see* Note below), or 6 thin
    sheets of fat belly
1½ cups fresh breadcrumbs
½ cup butter, melted
2 cups Tomato Sauce [No. 19]
Salt and freshly ground pepper

Remove the pig's feet from the cooking liquid when
they are tender, cool, remove all the meat from the
bones, and cut it into small dice. Cook the mushrooms
with the 1 tablespoon of butter and the wine in a
saucepan over medium heat for about 10 minutes, or
until the wine has evaporated, and cool. Mix the forcemeat with the meat from the pig's feet and the mushrooms in a bowl. Cut the caul into 6 pieces (or use
sheets of fat belly), spread these pieces out on a board,
portion out the stuffing mixture on each of the pieces,
and then fold the pieces up so that the stuffing will not
escape. Brush with melted butter, coat with breadcrumbs, and sprinkle with more melted butter. Broil
for about 10 minutes on each side under a medium
broiler flame, transfer to a hot serving platter, and serve
the tomato sauce on the side. *Serves 6.*

NOTE: Pig's caul, or *reticulum*, is a fatty membrane
surrounding the innards. It is available in butcher
shops in Italian neighborhoods, or pork stores in
German neighborhoods.

420

1241. PORK CHOPS GOURMET
Costolette di maiale alla ghiottona

6 loin or rib pork chops, cut 1 inch thick
3 cloves garlic, cut in slivers
A marinade:
 $\frac{1}{3}$ cup vinegar
 $\frac{1}{2}$ cup oil
 1 teaspoon salt
 $\frac{1}{4}$ teaspoon freshly ground pepper
 $\frac{1}{2}$ teaspoon powdered bay leaf
 $\frac{1}{2}$ teaspoon powdered rosemary
6 tablespoons oil
$\frac{3}{4}$ pound mushrooms, sliced
3 tablespoons butter
1 clove garlic, crushed in the garlic-press
1 tablespoon chopped rosemary (or $\frac{1}{2}$ teaspoon dried)
1 recipe Noisette Potatoes [No. 1783]
2 tablespoons chopped parsley

Make small slits in the chops with a sharply pointed knife and insert the slivers of garlic in these slits. Mix the marinade ingredients together thoroughly and marinate the pork chops in the mixture for at least 3 hours, turning them occasionally. Dry them on paper towels. Heat the oil in a shallow casserole or deep skillet over fairly high heat until smoking hot and quickly brown the chops for 2 minutes on each side. Reduce the heat to a very low flame, cover the pot, and cook the chops for 25 minutes longer, turning them over once during the cooking. While the chops are cooking, melt the butter in a frying pan over moderate heat, and gently sauté the mushrooms with the garlic and rosemary for about 10 minutes. When the chops are tender, arrange them on a hot serving platter, garnish with the potatoes on one end of the platter and the mushrooms on the other, and sprinkle with the chopped parsley. *Serves 6.*

1242. PORK CHOPS MODENESE
Costolette di maiale alla modenese

6 loin or rib pork chops, cut 1 inch thick
$\frac{1}{2}$ cup butter
$\frac{1}{2}$ cup dry white wine
1 tablespoon chopped rosemary (or 1 teaspoon dried)
1 tablespoon chopped sage (or 1 teaspoon dried)
2 cloves garlic, crushed in the garlic-press
Juice of 1 lemon
Salt and freshly ground pepper

Heat 6 tablespoons of the butter in a large shallow casserole or pot over medium high heat until golden

and quickly brown the chops for about 2 minutes on each side. Add the wine and cook until it has entirely evaporated. Season the chops with salt and pepper and sprinkle each with a little sage, rosemary, and garlic. Reduce the heat to a very low flame, cover the pot, and cook for about 25 minutes longer, turning the chops over once during the cooking. Transfer them to a hot serving platter, add the lemon juice to the liquid in the pan, cook for 1 minute over high heat, remove from the heat, swirl in the remaining butter, bit by bit, and pour over the chops. *Serves 6.*

1243. PORK CHOPS NAPOLETANA
Costolette di maiale alla napoletana

6 loin or rib pork chops, cut 1 inch thick
6 tablespoons oil
2 cloves garlic, crushed in the garlic-press
3 yellow peppers, roasted, scraped, seeded, and
 cut into strips [*see* No. 145]
$\frac{1}{2}$ pound ripe tomatoes, peeled, seeded, drained, and
 chopped
$\frac{1}{2}$ pound mushrooms, sliced
Salt and freshly ground pepper

Heat the oil in a large shallow casserole or pot over fairly high heat until smoking and quickly brown the chops for 2 minutes on each side. Remove them temporarily from the pan, add the garlic and peppers, reduce the heat, cook until the garlic begins to color, add the tomatoes, season with a little salt and pepper, and cook for 5 minutes. Return the chops to the pan overlapping one another, season them with salt and pepper, reduce the heat to a very low flame, cover the pan, and cook for 15 minutes longer. Turn the chops over, add the mushrooms, re-cover the pan, and cook for another 10 minutes. Transfer the chops to a hot serving platter and spoon the sauce over them. *Serves 6.*

421

Pork Cutlets in Wine (No. 1247): see page 422

1244. PIQUANT PORK CHOPS
Costolette di maiale piccanti

6 loin or rib pork chops, cut 1 inch thick
½ cup butter
1 tablespoon chopped onion
1 clove garlic, crushed in the garlic-press
½ cup dry white wine
½ cup Brown Stock [No. 4]
2 tablespoons chopped dill pickles
Dash Worcestershire sauce
Salt and freshly ground pepper

Heat 6 tablespoons of the butter in a large, shallow casserole or deep skillet over fairly high heat until foaming and quickly brown the chops for 2 minutes on each side. Reduce the heat to a very low flame, season the chops with salt and pepper, sprinkle with the chopped onion and garlic, cover the skillet, and cook for 25 minutes longer, turning the chops over once during the cooking. Transfer them to a hot serving platter and keep warm. Add the wine and stock to the pot, reduce over high heat by ¼, add the pickles and Worcestershire sauce, remove from the heat, swirl in the remaining butter, bit by bit, and pour over the chops. *Serves* 6.

1245. PORK CHOPS WITH RADISH SAUCE
Costolette di maiale con rafano

6 loin or rib pork chops, cut 1 inch thick
Flour
2 eggs, lightly beaten
1½ cups fresh breadcrumbs
6 tablespoons butter
1 cup Béchamel Sauce [No. 18]
¾ cup grated radishes
Salt and freshly ground pepper

Season the chops with salt and pepper, dust with flour, dip in beaten egg, and then cover with a generous coating of breadcrumbs. Heat the butter in a large, shallow casserole or deep skillet over fairly high heat until foaming and quickly brown the chops for 2 minutes on each side. Drain off most of the butter in the pan with a bulb baster, reduce the heat to a very low flame, cover, and cook for 25 minutes longer, turning the chops over once during the cooking. Remove the lid, raise the heat, and quickly re-crisp the covering on the chops. Transfer them to a hot serving platter and keep warm. Blend in the Béchamel sauce and the grated rad-

ishes with the juices in the pot, simmer for 5 minutes, and serve separately in a sauceboat. *Serves* 6.

1246. PORK CUTLETS IN CAPER SAUCE
Fettine di prosciutto di maiale fresco in salsa di capperi

12 slices pork from the leg, cut ½ inch thick
Flour
2 eggs, slightly beaten
2 cups fresh breadcrumbs
½ cup butter
1 medium onion, chopped
8 anchovy fillets, washed free of salt [*see* No. 220]
   and pounded to a paste in the mortar
3 tablespoons white wine vinegar
1 cup Brown Stock [No. 4]
2 tablespoons of very tiny capers
1 tablespoon parsley, chopped
Salt and freshly ground pepper

Place the slices of pork between sheets of wax paper and then pound them slightly flatter with the flat side of a meat cleaver. Season them with salt and pepper, dust them with flour, dip in beaten egg, and cover liberally with breadcrumbs. Heat 6 tablespoons of the butter in a large frying pan over fairly high heat until foaming and quickly brown the pork, a few slices at a time, for about 2 minutes on each side. Do not crowd the pieces in the pan; if desired, use 2 pans with slightly more butter. Reduce the heat and continue cooking for about 5 minutes longer on each side. Transfer the slices to a hot serving platter and keep warm. Add the onion to the remaining butter in the pan, cook until it begins to color, blend in the anchovy paste with a wire whisk, and then add the vinegar, stock, and capers. Reduce over high heat by ¼, remove from the heat, swirl in the remaining butter, bit by bit, pour this sauce over the pork, and sprinkle with the parsley. *Serves* 6.

1247. PORK CUTLETS IN WINE
Fettine di prosciutto di maiale fresco al vino

12 slices pork from the leg, cut ½ inch thick
Flour
½ cup butter
12 large leaves of Boston lettuce or romaine
1 cup dry white wine
Juice of 1 lemon
Salt and freshly ground pepper

Place the slices of pork between sheets of wax paper and then pound them slightly flatter with the flat side of a meat cleaver. Season them with salt and pepper and dust them with flour. Heat 6 tablespoons of the butter in a large frying pan over fairly high heat until golden and quickly brown the pork, a few slices at a time, for about 2 minutes on each side. Do not crowd the pieces in the pan; if desired, use 2 pans with slightly more butter. Reduce the heat and continue cooking for about 5 minutes longer on each side. Line a hot platter with the lettuce leaves, arrange the pork slices on top, and keep warm. Add the wine to the pan, reduce over high heat by $1/2$, add the lemon juice, remove from the heat, swirl in the remaining butter, bit by bit, and pour over the pork. The center of the platter may be garnished with mashed potatoes, if desired. *Serves 6.*

1248. PORK PIE INGLESE

Pasticcio di maiale all'inglese—Hot Pork Pie

$1/2$ pound boiled ham, sliced very thin
2 pounds lean leg or shoulder of pork, sliced
    $1/2$ inch thick
$1/2$ teaspoon powdered sage
$1/2$ teaspoon powdered thyme
$1/4$ teaspoon powdered bay leaf
1 cup Duxelles [No. 138]
1 pound potatoes, sliced
2 onions, chopped
2 tablespoons chopped parsley
2 cups Brown Stock [No. 4]
1 egg, slightly beaten
$1/2$ recipe Flaky Pastry [No. 1954]
Salt and freshly ground pepper

Line the bottom and sides of a baking dish or casserole with slices of boiled ham. Season the slices of pork with salt and pepper, sprinkle them with the powdered herbs, lay them on top of the boiled ham. Sprinkle the Duxelles over the pork and cover with layers of the potatoes and onions seasoned with a little salt and pepper. Sprinkle the top with parsley and add the stock. Roll out the dough in a sheet about $1/4$ inch thick, place the dough over the baking dish, and fasten it firmly to the outside edge of the dish by moistening the underside of the dough. Brush the dough with beaten egg, make a small hole in the center, and insert a pastry tube (or small metal funnel) in this hole to allow steam to escape during the cooking. Place in a moderate (350°) oven for $2\frac{1}{4}$ hours, and serve in the baking dish. *Serves 6.*

NOTE: If the crust browns too quickly, cover it lightly with aluminum foil.

1249. PORK RIND WITH BEANS

Cotenne di maiale con fagioli

1 pound fresh pork rind, parboiled for 1 hour
$1\frac{1}{2}$ pounds dried white beans, soaked in water
    overnight
4 sprigs rosemary, tied with string
3 cloves garlic, unpeeled
$1/4$ cup chopped ham fat
1 tablespoon oil
1 onion, chopped
1 clove garlic, crushed in the garlic-press
2 pounds tomatoes, peeled, seeded, drained, and
    chopped
3 tablespoons chopped parsley
2 tablespoons chopped basil
Salt and freshly ground pepper

Put the beans in a large earthenware pot with the pork rind, rosemary, and whole cloves of garlic. Season with salt and pepper, add sufficient water to barely cover the beans, bring to a boil over high heat, reduce the heat, cover pot, and simmer for $1\frac{1}{2}$ to 2 hours. About 30 minutes before the beans are tender, heat the oil with the ham fat in a large pot over medium heat, add the onion and garlic, cook until the onion begins to color, add the tomatoes, season with salt and pepper, and simmer for 20 minutes. When the beans are cooked, drain them in a colander, cut the pork rind in small strips, discard the rosemary and garlic, and then add the beans and pork rind to the tomato mixture. Add the parsley and basil, stir gently, and cook for 5 minutes longer. Serve in the pot. *Serves 6.*

1250. ROAST PORK

Carré di maiale arrostito

1 5-pound rib or loin roast of pork
1 teaspoon powdered sage
1 teaspoon dried rosemary
1 cup dry white wine
1 cup Brown Stock [No. 4]
Salt and freshly ground pepper

Rub the roast with salt, pepper, sage, and rosemary. Place it, fat side up, in a shallow open roasting pan in a hot (450°) oven, reduce the heat to moderate (325°), and cook it for about 30 minutes to the pound, or until its juices run clear yellow with no trace of pink when pierced with a fork. After the first hour of cooking, add the wine to the juices in the pan, and then baste every

10 minutes. The steam from the liquid will help render out much of the fat in the pork. Transfer the pork to a hot serving platter and keep warm. Place the pan over high heat and boil away all liquid in the pan, leaving only fat, but being careful not to burn the congealed "drippings" in the bottom. Pour off the fat, add the stock, de-glaze the pan over fairly high heat by scraping the bottom and sides with a wooden spoon, and reduce the stock by $1/4$. Cut the pork into neat slices on the platter and spoon the sauce over the slices. *Serves* 6.

NOTE: If desired, the roast may be boned, rolled, and tied before cooking; the cooking time should be increased to about 35 minutes per pound. A 3-pound boned roast will serve 6.

A side dish of applesauce or stewed apples is the traditional accompaniment for roast pork.

1251. ROAST PORK WITH CARDOONS
Arista di maiale con cardi

1 3-pound boneless rib or loin roast of pork, rolled and tied
1 teaspoon powdered sage
1 teaspoon dried rosemary
1 cup dry white wine
1 cup Brown Stock [No. 4]
2 pounds cardoons, trimmed and cut into 3-inch pieces
3 cups White Foundation for Vegetables [No. 1576]
3 tablespoons butter
1 clove garlic, crushed in the garlic-press
$1/4$ cup chopped onion
2 tablespoons chopped prosciutto (fat and lean)
1 pound tomatoes, peeled, seeded, drained, and chopped
Salt and freshly ground pepper

Roast the pork and prepare the sauce in the manner described in the preceding recipe. Since the roast is boned, it should be cooked about 35 minutes per pound. Parboil the cardoons in the white foundation for vegetables for $1\frac{1}{2}$ hours, drain, and reserve. About 30 minutes before removing the roast from the oven, melt the butter in a saucepan over medium heat and add the garlic, onion, and prosciutto. Cook until the onion begins to color, add the tomatoes and cardoons, season with salt and pepper, bring to a boil, and then simmer for about 20 minutes, or until the cardoons are tender. Cut the roast into neat slices on the platter, spoon the sauce over the slices, and serve the tomatoes and cardoons separately. *Serves* 6.

1252. ROAST PORK PAESANA
Carré di maiale alla paesana

1 3-pound boneless rib or loin roast of pork, rolled and tied
3 cloves garlic, halved
1 teaspoon powdered thyme
1 teaspoon dried rosemary
1 teaspoon powdered bay leaf
2 cups dry white wine
1 cup Brown Stock [No. 4]
Salt and freshly ground pepper

Cut small slits in the pork with a very sharply pointed knife and insert half cloves of garlic in these slits. Rub the roast with the powdered thyme, rosemary, bay leaf, and a generous amount of salt and pepper. Place the meat in a bowl, add the wine, and allow it to stand for 24 hours, turning it often. Dry it with paper towels and then roast it and prepare the sauce in the manner described in Roast Pork [No. 1250], using 1 cup of the wine marinade. Since the roast is boned, it should be cooked about 35 minutes to the pound. *Serves* 6.

1253. ROAST PORK TOSCANA
Arista di maiale alla toscana

1 5-pound rib or loin roast of pork
3 cloves garlic, halved
6 sprigs rosemary (or 1 tablespoon dried)
1 cup dry white wine
1 cup Brown Stock [No. 4]
Salt and freshly ground pepper
1 recipe Black-Eyed Beans Uccelletto [No. 1610]

Make small slits in the pork with a very sharply pointed knife and insert half cloves of garlic and sprigs of rosemary in these slits. Rub the roast with a generous amount of salt and pepper (and dried rosemary, if fresh rosemary is not available). Roast the pork and prepare the sauce in the manner described in Roast Pork [No. 1250]. Serve the black-eyed beans on the side. *Serves* 6.

1254. COTECHINO SAUSAGE
Cotechini fatti in casa

2 pounds lean shoulder of pork
1 pound fresh pork rind, parboiled for 2 hours
1 pound pork fat back
2 teaspoons salt
$1/2$ teaspoon freshly ground pepper
$1/4$ teaspoon powdered marjoram

¼ teaspoon powdered bay leaf
¼ teaspoon powdered thyme
¼ teaspoon powdered sage
¼ teaspoon vanilla
Commercial sausage casing

Using the finest blade, put the pork, pork rind, and fat back through the meat grinder twice. Season it with salt, pepper, the 4 herbs, and the vanilla. Place the mixture in a pastry bag fitted with a large round tip and fill the sausage casing, tying it off at 3-inch intervals. Store in the refrigerator until ready to cook. Cook by poaching in water for 1 hour. Makes about 4 pounds.

NOTE: If desired, a large pork intestine may be substituted for the commercial sausage casing, making 1 or more large sausages several inches in diameter. Before using, the intestine should be soaked in acidulated water for 2 hours. The intestine must not contain any holes through which the sausage meat may escape.

1255. COTECHINO SAUSAGE WITH BEANS CAMPAGNOLA
Cotechino con fagioli alla campagnola

1 2-pound cotechino sausage (*see* preceding recipe)
½ pound hog jowl
2 pig's tails
½ pound fresh pork rind
1½ pounds dried white beans, soaked in water overnight and drained
3 cloves garlic, unpeeled
Bouquet Garni:
   3 sprigs rosemary (or ½ teaspoon dried)
   1 bay leaf
1 onion stuck with 2 cloves

3 tablespoons oil
A chopped mixture:
   ¼ pound lean salt pork, parboiled for 10 minutes
   1 onion
   2 stalks celery
   3 sprigs parsley
2 pounds tomatoes, peeled, seeded, drained, and chopped
Salt and freshly ground pepper

Parboil the hog jowl, pig's tails, and pork rind in boiling water for 15 minutes. Drain, cut the tails into 2-inch lengths, and cut the hog jowl and pork rind into wide strips. Place all of these meats and the beans in a large earthenware pot, cover with cold water, and add the cloves of garlic, Bouquet Garni, and whole onion. Season lightly with salt and pepper, bring to a boil over high heat, reduce the heat, and simmer for 1½ to 2 hours, or until the beans are tender. While the beans are cooking, prick the sausage several times with a fork, place it in a saucepan, cover with cold water, bring to a boil over medium heat, and simmer for about 1½ to 2 hours. About 30 minutes before the beans and sausage are fully cooked, heat the oil in a large pot over medium heat, add the chopped mixture, cook until the onion begins to color, add the tomatoes, season with salt and pepper, and simmer for 20 minutes. Drain the beans, discard the Bouquet Garni and onion, and then add the beans and the pork meats to the tomatoes. Drain the sausage, slice it, and add to the pot with the beans. Mix very gently and simmer for 10 minutes longer. *Serves* 6.

1256. PORK SAUSAGE AND BEANS
Salsicce con fagioli stufati in umido

6 very large pork sausages
1 pound dry white beans, soaked in water overnight and drained
3 sprigs rosemary, tied with string (or 1 teaspoon dried, tied in a bag)
4 cloves garlic, unpeeled
1 onion, stuck with 1 clove
1 tablespoon lard
3 tablespoons oil
A chopped mixture:
   2 medium onions
   1 clove garlic
   1 stalk celery
2 pounds tomatoes, peeled, seeded, drained, and chopped
Salt and freshly ground pepper

425

Put the beans, rosemary, whole garlic cloves, and onion in a large, heavy pot, cover with cold water, season lightly with salt and pepper, bring to a boil, and then simmer over moderate heat for 1½ hours, or until the beans are tender. About ½ hour before the beans are cooked, heat the lard in a frying pan over medium heat and sauté the sausages for about 20 minutes, turning them frequently. Remove them from the pan and keep warm. Add the oil to the fat in the pan, heat for 1 minute, add the chopped mixture, and cook until the onion begins to color. Add the tomatoes, season with salt and pepper, and simmer for 10 minutes. Drain the beans and discard the rosemary, whole garlic cloves, and clove-stuck onion. Return the beans to the pot, add the sausage and tomatoes, mix lightly, cook over low heat for 5 minutes, and serve in the pot. *Serves 6.*

1257. PORK SAUSAGE IN WHITE WINE
Salsicce al vino bianco con purea di patate

6 very large pork sausages
1 tablespoon lard
1 cup dry white wine
1 tablespoon Kneaded Butter [No. 107]
1 cup Italian Meat Sauce [No. 41]

Heat the lard in a frying pan over medium heat and sauté the sausages for about 20 minutes, turning them frequently. Remove them to a hot serving platter and keep warm. Add the wine to the pan and reduce over high heat to ½ its quantity. Blend in the kneaded butter, add the meat sauce, simmer for 5 minutes, and pour over the sausages. A side dish of mashed potatoes is an excellent accompaniment for this dish. *Serves 6.*

1258. PORK STEW MILANESE
Cazzuola di maiale alla milanese

2½ pounds boneless shoulder of pork, cut into
    1½-inch cubes
1 pig's foot, split in half
¼ pound fresh pork rind
4 tablespoons oil
¼ cup chopped prosciutto (fat and lean)
1 onion, chopped
1 clove garlic, crushed in the garlic-press
2 small heads cabbage, quartered
6 sweet Italian sausages, pricked several times with
    a fork
Salt and freshly ground pepper

Place the pig's foot and pork rind in a saucepan, cover with 1 quart of cold water, bring to a boil over medium heat, cover the pan, and simmer for 2½ hours. Drain, reserving the cooking liquid; remove the meat from the pig's foot; and cut the pork rind into 2-inch strips. De-grease the cooking liquid. Dry the pieces of pork shoulder thoroughly on paper towels, heat the oil in a large, heavy pot, and quickly brown the pieces of pork on all sides. Add the prosciutto, onion, and garlic; cook until the onion begins to color; and then add the meat from the pig's foot, the pork rind, and the reserved cooking liquid. Season lightly with salt and pepper, bring to a boil, reduce the heat, cover the pot, and simmer for 1½ hours, or until the pieces of pork are not quite tender. Add the cabbage quarters and sausage (these need not be submerged in the cooking liquid, but may steam), re-cover the pot, and cook for about 25 minutes longer, or until the cabbage, sausage, and pieces of pork are all tender. Arrange the various ingredients on a hot serving platter, spoon a little of the cooking liquid over them, and grate a little freshly ground pepper over the cabbage. *Serves 6.*

1259. PORK AND GAMEBIRD STEW TOSCANA
Intingolo di maiale e uccelletti alla toscana

Traditionally, this Tuscan dish is garnished with very tiny roasted songbirds. Since these are never available in American markets, very small squabs may be successfully substituted.

2½ pounds boneless shoulder of pork, cut into
    1½-inch cubes
1 pig's foot
4 pig's tails
¼ pound fresh pork rind
½ cup oil
1 clove garlic, crushed in the garlic-press
1 pound tomatoes, peeled, seeded, drained, and
    chopped
12 sage leaves (or 1 teaspoon dried)
4 cloves garlic, unpeeled
½ cup red wine
6 1-pound squabs, cleaned
6 tablespoons butter, softened
12 slices bread, crusts removed, cut in half, and
    browned in butter
Salt and freshly ground pepper

Place the pig's foot, pig's tails, and pork rind in a large saucepan, cover with cold water, bring to a boil over high heat, reduce the heat, and simmer for 2 hours.

Drain, reserving the cooking liquid; remove all the meat from the tails and foot; cut it into pieces; and cut the rind into strips. De-grease the cooking liquid. Heat the oil in a large, heavy pot over fairly high heat and quickly brown the pieces of pork shoulder on all sides. Add the crushed garlic, stir until the garlic begins to color, and add the tomatoes, sage, unpeeled garlic, pig's tail and foot meat, pork rind, and enough of the reserved cooking liquid to barely cover the meat. Season with salt and pepper, bring to a boil, reduce the heat, and simmer for about 2 hours, or until the pork is tender. Add a little more of the cooking liquid from time to time as the liquid in the pot reduces. About 30 minutes before the pork is fully cooked, split the squabs down the backs, spread them out without separating the halves, flatten them slightly with the flat side of a meat cleaver, season them lightly with salt and pepper, spread them· with softened butter, and then broil them under a medium broiler flame for about 12 minutes on each side, basting occasionally with the butter in the broiler pan. Turn the contents of the pot out into a hot serving platter and garnish with the squabs and the browned slices of bread. *Serves* 6.

1260. PROSCIUTTO FANTASIA
Prosciutto crudo di montagna alla fiamma "fantasia"

6 slices raw smoked ham, cut ½ inch thick, soaked in
    milk overnight, washed under running water, and
    patted dry
3 tablespoons butter
3 tablespoons oil
½ cup brandy
2 cups Sauce Béarnaise [No. 67]

Heat the butter and oil in a very large frying pan over medium heat and sauté the slices of ham for about 15 minutes on each side. Transfer the slices to a very hot heat-proof serving platter. At table, place the platter over an alcohol burner, add the brandy, heat until the brandy is very hot, ignite, and shake the pan until the flames subside. Serve the Béarnaise sauce on the side. *Serves* 6.

1261. SAUERKRAUT ALSATIAN STYLE
Salcrauto guarnito all'alsaziana

Sauerkraut, generously flavored with juniper berries and fresh pepper, is a typical and popular dish of Northern Italy. The traditional garnishes may include sausages, cooked ham, smoked bacon or very lean salt pork, frankfurters, salami, and smoked goose.

2 pounds sauerkraut, thoroughly washed and
    squeezed dry
¼ pound fresh pork rind, parboiled for 10 minutes
1 green apple, peeled and sliced
1 onion stuck with 1 clove
1 carrot, quartered
12 juniper berries, tied in a muslin bag
Bouquet Garni:
   3 sprigs thyme (or ½ teaspoon dried)
   1 bay leaf
1 cup dry white wine
3 cups White Stock [No. 1]
½ cup lard, melted
½ pound bacon or very lean salt pork, cut in ¼-inch
    slices and parboiled 10 minutes
1 1-pound garlic salami
½ pound smoked goose
½ pound boiled ham
3 sweet Italian sausages
6 pork frankfurters (or substitute Polish sausage,
    knockwurst, etc.)
Salt and freshly ground pepper

Line the bottom of a large pot with the pork rind and place the sauerkraut on top. Add the apple, onion, carrot, juniper berries, Bouquet Garni, wine, and sufficient stock to cover the sauerkraut generously. Season lightly with salt and pepper, add the melted lard, cover the pot, bring to a boil, and simmer for 1 hour. Add the bacon and salami, mixing them into the sauerkraut, and cook for 20 minutes longer. Add the smoked goose and cook for 10 minutes longer. Add the ham, sausages, and frankfurters and cook for 20 minutes longer. Discard the carrot, onion, juniper berries, and Bouquet Garni. Spread the sauerkraut out on a hot serving platter, arrange the various meats neatly on top, and spoon over a little of the cooking liquid. Plain boiled potatoes and beer are the traditional accompaniment for this dish. *Serves* 8.

427

Sauerkraut
Alsatian Style
(No. 1261):
see page 427

1262. ZAMPONE MODENESE WITH LENTILS
Zampone di Modena con lenticchie in umido

Zampone *are very large cured pig's legs, stuffed with spiced chopped meat. They are available in Italian markets in larger American cities.*

2 2-pound zampone
1 onion, sliced
1 carrot, sliced
2 stalks celery, sliced
1 recipe Boiled Lentils [No. 1695]
1½ cups Marsala Sauce [No. 43]

Soak the zampone in several changes of water for 6 hours. Drain and tie each very securely in cheesecloth. Place them in a large, heavy pot with the sliced onion, carrot, and celery. Cover with cold water, bring to a boil, reduce the heat to a very low flame, and simmer for 3 hours. When they are tender, remove them from the cooking liquid, discard the cheesecloth covering, cut them into thick slices, and arrange them on a hot serving platter. Garnish the platter with the boiled lentils; serve the Marsala sauce separately. *Serves 6.*

SUCKLING PIG

Porcellino

Suckling pig is a very young milk-fed pig from 6 to 8 weeks old, normally weighing from 8 to 12 pounds.

Its flesh is extremely tender and of an almost sweet flavor. A whole suckling pig is at its best roasted and is particularly delicious roasted on a spit over charcoal. It makes a very festive dish, as testified by its traditionally fanciful garnish of cranberry necklace and earrings and an apple stuffed in its mouth.

1263. BRAISED HAUNCH OF SUCKLING PIG
Cosciotto di porcellino di latte con cipolline

1 4-pound haunch of suckling pig
A marinade:
  1½ cups dry white wine
  ½ cup wine vinegar
  3 onions, sliced
  1 carrot, sliced
  1 stalk celery, sliced
  ½ teaspoon powdered thyme
  ¼ teaspoon powdered bay leaf
  10 peppercorns, bruised
  2 cloves
  2 teaspoons salt
6 tablespoons oil
3 tablespoons butter
3 tablespoons flour
1½ pounds tomatoes, peeled, seeded, drained, and chopped
1 cup heavy cream
Juice of 1 lemon
18 Braised White Onions [No. 1721]

428

Mix all of the marinade ingredients very thoroughly together in a bowl and marinate the meat in the mixture for 24 hours, turning it frequently. Dry it well on paper towels. Heat the oil in a large, heavy pot over fairly high heat until smoking and brown the meat on all sides. Remove it temporarily from the pot and pour off the oil. Make a roux in the pot with the butter and flour, cook over medium heat until the flour begins to color, add the tomatoes, stir until they thicken, add the strained marinade liquid, and bring to a boil. Return the meat to the pot, cover tightly, and place the pot in a moderate (350°) oven for about 1 hour and 45 minutes, turning the meat over once during the cooking. Transfer the meat to a hot serving platter and keep warm. Reduce the cooking liquid over high heat to about 2 cups. Add the cream and lemon juice, correct the seasoning, and simmer for 5 minutes. Cut the meat into neat slices on the platter, garnish with the braised onions, spoon a little of the sauce over the slices of meat, and serve the remainder in a sauceboat. *Serves* 6.

1264. ROAST SUCKLING PIG
Porcellino di latte ripieno arrostito

1 10-pound suckling pig, cleaned, reserving
    the liver
A chopped mixture:
    ¼ pound salt pork
    ¼ pound dried mushrooms, soaked ½ hour in
        warm water and squeezed dry
3 tablespoons chopped basil
3 tablespoons chopped sage (or 2 tablespoons dried)
3 cups fresh bread cubes, soaked in milk and
    squeezed almost dry
2 eggs, lightly beaten
½ cup brandy
4 peppercorns crushed in the mortar

½ cup oil
6 tablespoons Kneaded Butter [No. 107]
3 cloves garlic, crushed in the garlic-press
2 tablespoons chopped rosemary
    (or 2 teaspoons dried)
4 tablespoons butter, melted
1 cup White Stock [No. 1]
1½ cups dry white wine
Salt
1 small red apple
Cranberries or cherries

Put the pig liver through the meat grinder, using the finest blade. Add it to the chopped mixture together with the basil, sage, bread, eggs, brandy, peppercorns, and oil; mix all of these thoroughly together. Mix the kneaded butter with the crushed garlic and rosemary and spread it throughout the inside of the pig. Stuff the pig loosely with the stuffing mixture and sew the opening securely with string. Truss the forelegs and hindlegs so that the pig will lie flat on its belly during the cooking. Place a block of wood in its mouth to hold it open and cover the ears and tail with aluminum foil to prevent their burning. Make small gashes with a very sharp knife over the pig's back to allow fat to escape. Brush it with melted butter and place it in a large shallow roasting pan in a moderate (325°) oven for 4 hours (25 minutes to the pound). Add a little stock to the pan from time to time and baste every 20 minutes. A few minutes before the pig is fully cooked remove the foil from the ears and tail. Transfer the pig to a large hot serving platter and keep warm. Remove the block of wood from the mouth and replace it with a small red apple. Put cherries or cranberries in the eye sockets and, if desired, make a necklace and earrings of cranberries. De-grease the juices in the pan, add the wine, and reduce over high heat to about 2 cups. Correct the seasoning of this sauce and serve separately in a sauceboat. *Serves* 12 *to* 15.

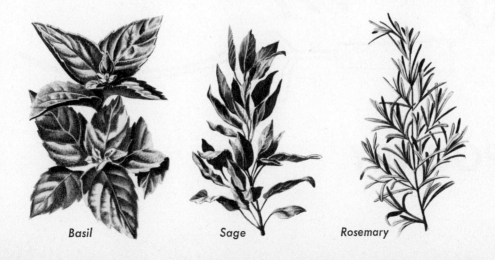

Basil   *Sage*   *Rosemary*

POULTRY

POULTRY

Pollame

In addition to the various types and sizes of chickens, we will deal in this section with turkey, duck, guinea hen, goose, and squab. Since most wild fowl require considerably different techniques of cooking, they will be dealt with in a subsequent chapter.

Some of the greatest glories in the whole repertoire of Italian cooking are reserved for poultry. While many of the recipes in this section are regional specialties, using ingredients or techniques native to a given locality, all of them can easily be adapted to the American kitchen.

Poultry is at its best if cooked between 8 and 24 hours after it is killed. In large American cities, especially, birds marketed so soon after slaughter are not so easily come by, and naturally the best guarantee of freshness of poultry, as well as of flavor, will lie in a reliable butcher or market. Modern techniques of freezing foods are unquestionably a blessing, but with poultry they are a mixed blessing. A frozen bird is better than no bird at all, but the freezing, or more correctly the defrosting process, necessitates a bird's losing a great deal of its natural juices and renders it much dryer and less flavorsome than an unfrozen one. If only frozen poultry is available, which is certainly often the case, the best method of defrosting is to do it as slowly as possible in the refrigerator over a period of 24 to 36 hours. Much less of the juices will be lost by this method than if a bird is allowed to thaw at room temperature.

While storing poultry for any length of time in a home refrigerator is not recommended, occasionally it becomes a necessity. Freshness will be better preserved if the wrappings around a bird are loosened, the giblets removed from the cavity, and the bird thoroughly washed inside and out, every 24 hours.

CHICKEN

Pollo

Italian classification of chickens into types and weights differs only slightly from the American. The chicken is, in fact, a thoroughly international bird. Italians rarely cook chickens of less than 1 pound, the type known in American markets as squab chickens. They also make a somewhat greater distinction or category of hens from 7 to 8 months old weighing about 3 pounds, dressed. These latter are called *pollastra* (pullets) and will be dealt with separately in this section. American cooks generally make less distinction than European cooks between roosters and hens, and with some reason, since the difference in flavor between the sexes of commercially raised chickens in the United States is slight indeed.

Briefly, chickens may be divided into the following categories:

Broilers (2 to 3 months old), weighing $1\frac{1}{2}$ to $2\frac{1}{2}$ pounds

Fryers (3 to 5 months old), weighing 2 to 3 pounds

Roasters (5 to 9 months old), weighing 3 to 5 pounds

Capons (7 to 10 months old), weighing over 4 pounds

Fowl (10 to 12 months old), weighing over $3\frac{1}{2}$ pounds

Old Hens or Roosters (over 12 months old), weighing over $3\frac{1}{2}$ pounds.

While roasters may be fried and fryers may be roasted, generally these categories are designed to give the maximum flavor and tenderness from the methods of cooking for each category. Roasters and capons may be poached or fricaseed, as well as roasted. Fowl are best used only for stews or fricassee, and old hens or roosters are best reserved for the stock or soup pot.

A chicken should always be brought to room temperature before cooking to ensure its cooking evenly. Italian cooks prefer chicken slightly less well done than American cooks. While a chicken that is still bloody on the inside is certainly inedible, a chicken that has been allowed to cook until it is dry and tough is equally so. A roasted chicken is fully cooked when its juices run clear yellow when pierced with a fork, or when, if the bird is raised slightly by the legs, all of the juices that drain from the vent run clear yellow. A poached or stewed chicken is cooked when it is easily pierced with a fork through its fleshiest part.

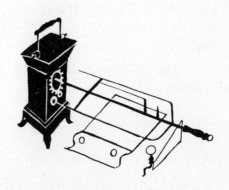

1265. BROILED CHICKEN AMERICANA WITH SAUCE REMOULADE
Pollo alla griglia all'americana con salsa remoulade

3 2-pound broiling chickens, split in half
¾ cup butter, melted
½ cup prepared mustard (Dijon-type preferred)
1½ cups breadcrumbs
12 slices bacon, broiled
3 lemons, quartered
Salt and freshly ground pepper
2 cups Sauce Remoulade [No. 97]

Brush the chicken halves with a generous amount of butter and place them on a rack about 6 inches beneath a medium broiler flame. Broil for about 8 minutes on each side, basting occasionally with more butter. Remove them from the rack, brush both sides of each half with prepared mustard, and cover liberally with breadcrumbs. Sprinkle with a little melted butter, return them to the broiler rack, reduce the flame slightly, and broil for about 5 minutes longer on each side. Transfer them to a hot serving platter, season them with salt and pepper, place 2 slices of bacon on each half, garnish the platter with the lemon quarters, and serve the Remoulade sauce on the side. *Serves* 6.

1266. BROILED CHICKEN DIAVOLA
Pollo alla diavola

3 1½-pound broiling chickens, split in half
½ cup butter, melted
Salt and freshly ground pepper
2 cups Diavola Sauce [No. 30]

Brush the chicken halves with a generous amount of butter and place them on the rack of a broiler about 5 inches beneath a medium flame. Broil for about 10 minutes on each side, basting occasionally with more butter. Arrange them on a hot serving platter and serve the Diavola sauce on the side. *Serves* 6.

1267. CHICKEN IN CASSEROLE BUONA DONNA
Pollo in cocotte "buona donna"

1 3-pound frying or roasting chicken, cleaned
6 sprigs parsley
½ cup butter
12 small "new" potatoes, parboiled 2 minutes in lightly salted water
12 white onions, parboiled 5 minutes

1 cup diced lean salt pork, parboiled 10 minutes, drained, and fried until golden brown
½ cup Chicken Stock [No. 3]
Salt and freshly ground pepper

Season the cavity of the chicken with salt and pepper and stuff it with the parsley. Truss it in the manner described in the introduction. Heat 6 tablespoons of the butter in a frying pan over fairly high heat until golden and brown the chicken on all sides. Remove it from the pan. Melt the remaining butter in a large, heavy casserole over medium heat, add the parboiled potatoes, and roll them in the butter for 2 minutes. Push them aside and place the chicken in the bottom of the casserole, breast side up. Add the onions, browned salt pork, and stock. Season lightly with salt and pepper, cover the casserole tightly, bring to a boil over high heat, and then place the casserole in a moderate (350°) oven for 1 hour and 15 minutes, basting frequently with the butter and juices in the casserole. Serve in the casserole. *Serves* 4.

NOTE: If more than 4 persons are to be served, it is recommended that 2 3-pound chickens in a larger casserole with appropriately more vegetables be cooked, rather than choosing a larger-sized chicken.

1268. CHICKEN IN CASSEROLE WITH MUSHROOMS AND POTATOES
Pollo in casseruola con funghi porcini e patate

Prepare in the same manner and with the same ingredients as the preceding recipe, omitting the onions and the "new" potatoes and substituting ¾ pound of sliced large mushrooms which have been gently sautéed in 4 tablespoons of butter for 8 minutes, and ½ recipe French Fried Potatoes [No. 1773]. The mushrooms and potatoes should not be added to the casserole until 5 minutes before removing it from the oven. *Serves* 4.

SEE
VERSE
FOR
PTION

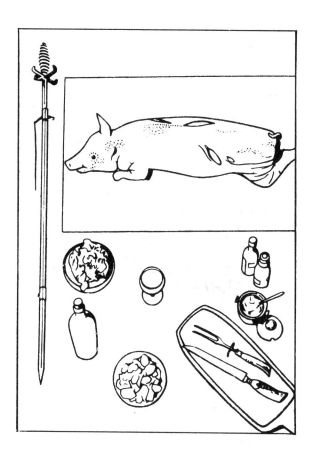

Roast Suckling Pig (No. 1264). This is the simplest—
and an extremely effective—presentation of this dish
and, as may be seen, the more festive and elaborate
preparation suggested in the recipe can be omitted
successfully, if so desired.

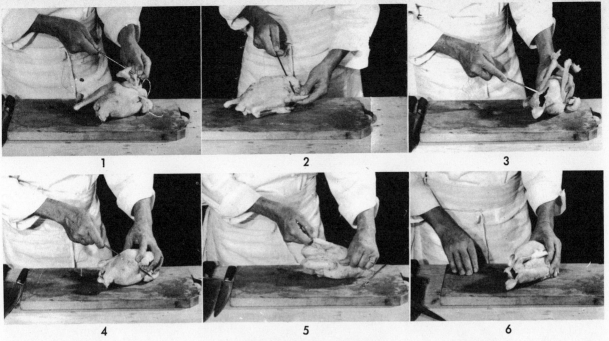

HOW TO TRUSS POULTRY

1. Push a large needle threaded with white twine through the carcass of the bird close to the joint of the drumsticks and the thighs. Fold each of the wing tips back under the wings. Push the needle through one wing.

2. Overlap the loose skin around the neck onto the backbone and sew it securely in place. Push the needle through the other wing, pull twine taut, and tie it off.

3. Pass the needle through the carcass slightly above the tail end

4. Pass the twine around the tip end of one drumstick and then push the needle back through the carcass

5. Pass the thread around the other drumstick, pull the twine taut, and tie off

6. The bird is now ready for roasting or poaching

1269. CHICKEN IN CASSEROLE PASTORELLA

Pollo farcito in casseruola pastorella con patatine nocciole

1 3-pound frying or roasting chicken, cleaned
2 onions, chopped
1 clove garlic, crushed in the garlic-press
¾ cup butter
¼ pound chicken livers, chopped
¼ pound mushrooms, chopped
4 sprigs parsley
1 cup diced lean salt pork, parboiled 10 minutes, drained, and fried until golden brown
½ cup Chicken Stock [No. 3]
18 Noisette Potatoes [No. 1783]
½ pound mushroom caps
Salt and freshly ground pepper

Sauté the onions and garlic in 3 tablespoons of the butter in a frying pan over medium heat until the onion becomes transparent, add the chopped livers, cook for 1 minute longer, add the chopped mushrooms, and cook for 3 minutes longer. Season the mixture lightly with salt and pepper, add the parsley, and remove from the heat. Season the cavity of the chicken with salt and pepper and then spoon the mixture into the cavity. Sew the opening and truss the chicken in the manner described in the introduction. Heat 6 tablespoons of the butter in a frying pan over fairly high heat and brown the chicken on all sides. Transfer it to a large heavy casserole, add the browned salt pork dice and the stock, season the chicken lightly with pepper, bring to a boil over high heat, cover the casserole, and then place it in a moderate (350°) oven for 1 hour and 15 minutes, basting frequently with the butter and juices in the casserole. While the chicken is cooking, prepare the noisette potatoes and gently sauté the mushroom caps in the remaining butter in a covered frying pan for about 8 minutes. When the chicken is fully cooked, cut it in half with poultry shears, and arrange the 2 halves on a round hot serving platter. Garnish the platter with small heaps of the stuffing, the Noisette potatoes, and the mushrooms; and spoon the juices in the casserole over the chicken. *Serves 4.*

433

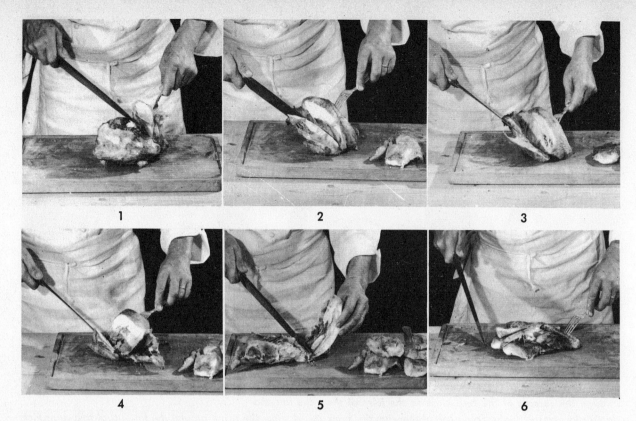

HOW TO CARVE ROAST CHICKEN

1. *Holding the chicken securely with a fork, pull the leg and thigh away from the carcass of the chicken with the flat side of the knife. Sever the thigh from the carcass.*

 2. *Cut off the wings and slice the white meat of the breast on one side*

3. *Cut off the breast meat*

4. *Slice and remove the breast meat on the other side*

5. *Cut off the white meat left along front end of the breast around the wishbone*

6. *Remove carcass and reassemble chicken neatly*

1270. SPRING CHICKENS IN CASSEROLE WITH MUSHROOMS
Polli farciti in casseruola con funghi

Prepare in the same manner and with the same ingredients as the preceding recipe, except using 2 young 1½-pound chickens and adding a ¼ cup chopped prosciutto to the stuffing. The cooking time for the chickens should be reduced to 45 minutes. *Serves* 4.

1271. CHICKEN FRICASSEE À L'ANCIENNE
Pollo in fricassea all'antica

1 4-pound roasting chicken, cut up for frying
5 tablespoons butter
3 tablespoons flour
3 cups boiling Chicken Stock [No. 3]
1 cup dry white wine
Bouquet Garni:
 2 sprigs thyme (or ½ teaspoon dried)
 2 sprigs parsley
 1 bay leaf

2 egg yolks
½ cup heavy cream
24 Braised White Onions [No. 1721]
24 mushroom caps, gently sautéed in 3 tablespoons of butter until just tender
Juice of 1 lemon
Pinch nutmeg
Salt and freshly ground pepper

Dry the pieces of chicken very thoroughly on paper towels. Heat the butter in a large, shallow pan over medium heat until the foam subsides. Add the pieces of chicken, a few at a time, and cook for about 2 minutes on each side, or until they stiffen slightly and turn a deep yellow. Do not allow them to brown. As the pieces turn yellow, remove them from the pan and add fresh pieces. When all have had this preliminary cooking, return them all to the pan, overlapping one another, cover, reduce the heat, and cook for 10 minutes. They should not cook long enough to render any juices. Remove the cover, season the pieces with salt and pepper, sprinkle them with flour, and turn the pieces in the butter until the flour begins

434

to color. Add the boiling stock and stir until the stock thickens. Add the wine and Bouquet Garni, season with salt and pepper only if necessary, bring to a boil, reduce the heat to a low flame, cover, and simmer for about 30 minutes. The chicken is fully cooked when the drumstick or thigh is easily pierced with a fork. Remove the pieces of chicken with a slotted spoon to a hot shallow serving dish and keep warm. If the sauce has become too thin, reduce it slightly over high heat. Discard the Bouquet Garni. Beat the egg yolks with the cream and any juice which the sautéed mushrooms have rendered, and then pour this mixture, off the heat, into the cooking liquid, stirring constantly with a whisk. Return it to a very low flame and stir until the sauce thickens slightly. Do not boil. Add the mushrooms and the white onions and cook only long enough to get thoroughly hot. Add the lemon juice and nutmeg, correct the seasoning, and pour over the chicken. *Serves* 6.

1272. FRIED CHICKEN FIORENTINA
Pollo fritto alla fiorentina

1 3-pound chicken, cut up for frying
A marinade:
   3 tablespoons oil
   4 tablespoons lemon juice
   1 teaspoon salt
   1/4 teaspoon freshly ground white pepper
   1 tablespoon chopped parsley
   1 clove garlic, crushed in the garlic-press
   1 tablespoon chopped rosemary (or 1 teaspoon dried)
2 cups Fritter Batter [No. 275]
Fat for deep frying
6 sprigs parsley, fried in deep fat [*see* No. 276]
3 lemons, quartered
2 cups Tomato Sauce [No. 19]

Mix the marinade ingredients thoroughly together and marinate the pieces of chicken for 3 hours, turning them occasionally. Wipe the pieces dry with paper towels and dip them in fritter batter. Drop the pieces in deep medium-hot fat (350°) for about 20 minutes. Adjust the heat as they cook so that they do not brown too quickly. Drain the pieces on paper towels for a few minutes, arrange them on a hot serving platter, garnish the platter with the fried parsley and lemon quarters, and serve the tomato sauce in a sauceboat. *Serves* 4.

1273. GOLDEN FRIED CHICKEN FIORIO
Pollo dorato alla fiorio

2 2 1/2-pound chickens, cut up for frying
1 quart milk
Flour
3 eggs, beaten
3 cups fresh breadcrumbs
3/4 cup Clarified Butter [No. 102]
3 lemons, quartered
6 pickles, sliced
Salt and freshly ground pepper

Marinate the pieces of chicken for 3 hours in the milk, turning the pieces occasionally. Drain them and dry thoroughly on paper towels. Season the pieces with salt and pepper, dust lightly with flour, dip in beaten egg, and then cover generously with breadcrumbs. Heat the butter in a very large frying pan over fairly high heat and brown the chicken, a few pieces at a time, on all sides. As the pieces become brown, remove them from the pan and add fresh ones. Adjust the heat during the browning so that the butter does not burn. When all are browned, return the drumsticks and thighs to the pan, reduce the heat to a low flame, cover the pan, and cook for 10 minutes. Add the wings and breasts (and the backs, if they are being used) and cook for 15 minutes longer. Remove the lid, raise the heat, and re-crisp the breadcrumb covering on the pieces. Transfer them to a hot serving platter and garnish with the lemon quarters and the pickles. *Serves* 6.

Chicken in Casserole with Mushrooms and Potatoes (No. 1268): see page 432

HOW TO BONE POULTRY

1. Using a very sharp knife, cut through the skin and flesh of the back from the neck to the tail
2. Using the fingers and the point of the knife, pull the flesh from the bones of the wings
3. Working from the inside, remove the flesh from the bones of the legs, thighs, back, and breast
4. Cut through the bone where the legs join the thighs
5. Remove the bones from legs, thighs, back, and breast
6. Remove the bones from the wings
7. The poultry is boned

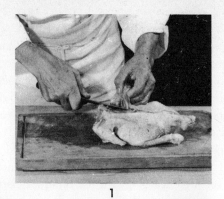

1

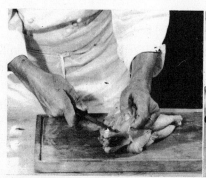

2

3

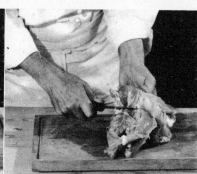

4

5

6

7

1274. CHICKEN MEUNIÈRE
Pollo farcito "bella mugnaia"

1 3-pound roasting chicken, cleaned
6 slices of truffle
6 chicken livers
2 cups fresh bread cubes, soaked in milk and
    squeezed almost dry
¼ pound mushrooms, chopped and twisted dry in
    a cloth
1 cup finely diced salt pork, parboiled for
    10 minutes
1 tablespoon brandy
1 onion, chopped
2 tablespoons chopped parsley
½ teaspoon powdered thyme
½ cup butter

¼ pound diced lean salt pork, parboiled for
    10 minutes, drained, and fried until golden brown
¼ pound mushrooms, sliced
Salt and freshly ground pepper

Insert the slices of truffle between the skin and the flesh of the breast of the chicken by pushing them in with the forefinger, being careful not to pierce the skin. Chop the chicken livers very finely and then mix them in a bowl with the bread cubes, chopped mushrooms, finely diced salt pork, brandy, chopped onion, parsley, and thyme. Season this stuffing lightly with salt and pepper. Season the cavity of the chicken with salt and then stuff it loosely. Sew the opening with string and truss the chicken in the manner described in the introduction. Heat 6 tablespoons of the butter in a large frying pan over fairly high heat until golden

436

and quickly brown the chicken on all sides. Transfer it to a large, heavy casserole which has been spread with the remaining butter. Season it lightly with salt, add the browned salt pork dice and sliced mushrooms, cover the casserole, heat over a high flame until it sizzles, and then place it in a moderate (350°) oven for 1½ hours, basting occasionally with the juices in the casserole. Transfer it to a hot serving platter, carve it, arrange heaps of the stuffing on the platter, and spoon the juices, mushrooms, and salt pork over the carved pieces. *Serves* 4.

1275. ROAST CHICKEN
Pollo arrosto

1 4-pound roasting chicken, cleaned
½ lemon
4 sprigs parsley
3 tablespoons butter, softened
3 tablespoons oil
2 cups Chicken Stock [No. 3]
Salt

Rub the cavity of the chicken with the lemon, season the cavity with a generous amount of salt, and stuff it with the sprigs of parsley (the parsley and lemon will prevent the cooked chicken from having any disagreeable poultry odor). Truss the chicken in the manner described in the introduction and spread it with the softened butter. Pour the oil in a shallow roasting pan, add a little stock, and lay the chicken on its side in the pan. Place the pan in a hot (425°) oven for 15 minutes, turning it on its other side and basting with the fat in the pan after 5 minutes and then turning it upright and basting again after another 5 minutes. Reduce the heat to moderate (350°) and continue cooking for a total cooking time of 1 hour and 15 to 30 minutes. Baste and turn the chicken every 15 minutes, adding a few tablespoons of stock. It will be fully cooked when the chicken is lifted by the legs and the juices from the vent run clear yellow without any trace of rosiness. Transfer it to a hot serving platter and keep warm. Place the roasting pan over fairly high heat until all of the juices have evaporated and only fat remains, being careful not to burn the "drippings" which adhere to the bottom. Pour off the fat, add the stock, and de-glaze the pan over medium heat by scraping the bottom and sides with a wooden spoon. Reduce this sauce slightly, correct the seasoning, and serve it separately in a sauceboat. *Serves* 6.

1276. ROAST CHICKEN FANTASIA
Pollo arrosto fantasia

2 3-pound roasting chickens, cleaned
6 thin slices lean salt pork, parboiled for
    10 minutes
12 sage leaves (or 1 teaspoon dried)
6 sprigs rosemary (or 1 teaspoon dried)
½ cup butter
1 cup oil
12 thin slices prosciutto (or smoked ham)
2 brown paper bags, each large enough to contain
    one of the chickens
Salt

Season the cavities of the chickens with salt and then place inside each cavity 3 slices of salt pork, 6 sage leaves, and 3 sprigs of rosemary. Truss the chickens in the manner described in the introduction. Heat 4 tablespoons each of butter and oil in each of 2 frying pans over fairly high heat until almost smoking and quickly brown the chickens on all sides. Remove them from the pans, allow to cool slightly, and then wrap them in the slices of prosciutto. Brush the paper bags, inside and out, with oil, place a chicken in each bag, and tie securely with string. Place the bags in an oiled pan in a moderate (350°) oven for 15 minutes. Pierce each bag in a couple of places with a sharply pointed knife and continue cooking for 1 hour longer. Remove from the oven and discard the bags, allowing any juices in the bags to drain onto a hot platter. Line the platter with the slices of prosciutto, and arrange the chickens on top. *Serves* 6.

1277. CHICKEN ON THE SPIT FANTASIA
Pollo allo spiedo "fantasia"
con salsa tartara

This dish is particularly delicious if the chicken is roasted on a spit over a medium hot charcoal fire. It may, however, be successfully roasted in the oven in the usual manner.

1 3-pound roasting chicken, cleaned
6 anchovy fillets, washed free of salt [*see* No. 220]
1 cup diced salt pork, parboiled for 10 minutes
½ pound sausage meat sautéed in a frying pan
    over medium heat for 5 minutes and well
    crumbled
2 cups soft bread cubes, soaked in milk and squeezed
    almost dry
½ teaspoon powdered thyme
½ cup butter, melted
Salt and freshly ground pepper
2 cups Tartar Sauce [No. 98]

Insert the anchovy fillets between the skin and the flesh of the chicken breast by pushing them in with the forefinger, being careful not to pierce the skin. Mix together in a bowl the salt pork dice, sausage meat, bread cubes, and thyme. Stuff the chicken loosely, sew the openings with string, and then truss the chicken in the manner described in the introduction. Skewer the chicken on a spit, brush it with melted butter, and roast it about 6 inches above a medium hot charcoal fire for about 1 hour and 30 minutes, basting frequently with more melted butter. (Or, alternatively, roast it in the oven in the manner described in Roast Chicken —No. 1275—cooking it for a total time of 1 hour and 30 minutes.) Transfer it to a hot serving platter and serve the tartar sauce separately. *Serves* 4.

1278. CHICKEN ON THE SPIT, VILLA SASSI
Asticciole di pollo "Villa Sassi"

3 2-pound chickens, cleaned
6 skewers
12 slices prosciutto, or smoked ham (fat and lean),
    cut ⅛ inch thick
24 sage leaves
3 tablespoons butter
1 onion, chopped
1 stalk celery, chopped
½ cup butter, melted
Flour
½ cup dry white wine
¼ pound mushrooms, sliced
6 ripe tomatoes, peeled, seeded, drained, and chopped
½ pound home-made tagliarini [*see* No. 511] or thin
    egg noodles, cooked until just *al dente* in lightly
    salted boiling water and dressed generously with
    butter and grated Parmesan cheese
2 white truffles, sliced [or No. 1819a]
Salt and freshly ground pepper

Bone the chickens in the manner described in the introduction and remove the skin. Cut the meat of each chicken into 8 pieces about 2 inches square. Season the pieces lightly with salt and pepper and then spear 4 pieces on each of 6 skewers, alternating them with half slices of prosciutto and sage leaves (if fresh sage leaves are not available, the chicken pieces may be rubbed with a very little powdered sage). Heat the 3 tablespoons of butter in a large oven-proof dish over medium heat, add the chopped onion and celery, and cook until the onion is soft. Brush the skewered chicken with the melted butter, dust it lightly with flour, and arrange the skewers in the baking dish. Place the dish on a rack about 5 inches below a medium broiler flame and broil for about 15 minutes, turning the skewers often and brushing occasionally with more melted butter. When the chicken is nicely browned and tender, transfer the skewers to a hot platter and keep warm. Add the wine and mushrooms to the baking dish and cook over high heat for 5 minutes. Add the tomatoes, season with salt and pepper, and cook for 10 minutes longer. Time the cooking of the pasta so that it is ready and dressed at just this point. Spread the pasta out on a shallow serving dish, spoon the tomato/mushroom sauce over it, arrange the skewered chicken and prosciutto on top, and sprinkle with the sliced white truffles. *Serves* 6.

Chicken on the Spit Villa Sassi (No. 1278)

CHICKEN SAUTÉS
Polli sautés

Chicken sautés are similar to other meat sautés in that the chicken is browned and cooked until just tender in butter or oil, removed from the pan, and then added only at the last minute to a prepared sauce. Thus it is a true sauté, although the finished dish may somewhat resemble a stew. Young frying chickens from 2 to 3 pounds are always used for sautés.

A frying chicken is disjointed into 2 drumsticks, 2 thighs, 2 wings, and 2 breast halves. The back may be cut in half and included, if desired, but since it has little meat on it, it is better reserved for the stock pot.

1279. CHICKEN SAUTÉ CACCIATORA
Pollo sauté alla cacciatora

3 pounds cut-up frying chicken
4 tablespoons butter
3 tablespoons oil
½ pound mushrooms, sliced
¼ cup chopped onion
½ cup dry white wine
1 tablespoon flour
1 cup boiling Chicken Stock [No. 3]
2 tablespoons brandy
4 ripe tomatoes, peeled, seeded, drained, and chopped
1 tablespoon chopped parsley
1 tablespoon chopped tarragon (or substitute
   1 teaspoon dried)
Salt and freshly ground pepper

Dry the chicken pieces thoroughly on paper towels. Heat the oil and 2 tablespoons of the butter in a very large frying pan over fairly high heat and brown the chicken, a few pieces at a time, for about 2 minutes on each side. As the pieces brown, remove them from the pan and add fresh pieces. When all are browned, return only the thighs and drumsticks to the pan, cover tightly, reduce the heat to a low flame, and simmer for 10 minutes. Add the breasts and wings and simmer for 15 minutes longer, or until all of the pieces are tender. Remove them from the pan to a hot platter, season them with salt and pepper, and keep warm. Sauté the mushrooms in the remaining butter in a covered

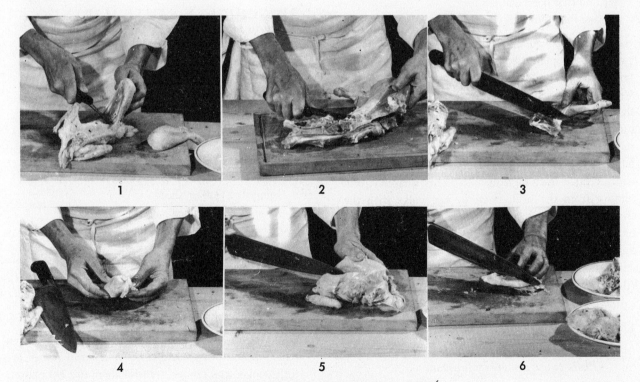

1   2   3

4   5   6

HOW TO PREPARE CHICKEN FOR A SAUTÉ

1. Begin the disjointing of the chicken by pulling the thighs and drumsticks away from the carcass. and cutting the two off in one piece

2. Sever the thighs from the carcass

3. Cut off the drumsticks from the thighs

4. If desired, the thighs may be boned and rolled

5. Remove breast from carcass and cut off wings

6. Cut the breast in half

frying pan for about 8 minutes; remove from the heat and reserve. Drain off most of the fat from the pan in which the chicken cooked, add the onion, cook over medium heat until the onion is golden, add the wine, raise the heat, and cook until it has evaporated. Stir in the flour, cook for 1 minute, add the boiling stock, and cook until thickened. Heat the brandy in a ladle over medium heat, ignite, and add to the pan. Add the tomatoes and herbs, season with salt and pepper, and simmer for 10 minutes. Return the pieces of chicken to the pan, add the mushrooms, simmer for 3 minutes, and turn the chicken and sauce out onto a hot serving platter. *Serves* 6.

1280. CHICKEN SAUTÉ IN CREAM WITH RICE PILAF
Pollo sauté alla crema con riso pilaff

3 pounds cut-up frying chicken
5 tablespoons butter
3 tablespoons oil
1/2 pound mushrooms, sliced
1/2 cup dry white wine
1 1/2 cups heavy cream
3 egg yolks
Salt and freshly ground pepper
1 recipe Pilaf [No. 595]

Sauté the chicken in the manner described in the preceding recipe. When the pieces are fully cooked and tender, transfer them to a hot serving platter, season with salt and pepper, and keep warm. Gently sauté the mushrooms in the remaining 3 tablespoons of the butter in a covered frying pan for about 8 minutes; remove from the heat and reserve. Drain off most of the fat from the pan in which the chicken cooked, add the wine, reduce over high heat to 1/2 its quantity, and remove from the heat. Beat the egg yolks with the cream, add them to the pan, stirring constantly, and return the pan to very low heat. Stir this sauce until it thickens slightly, add the mushrooms, season with salt and pepper, and pour over the chicken. Serve the Pilaf on the side. *Serves* 6.

1281. CURRIED CHICKEN SAUTÉ FANTASIA
Pollo sauté con curry fantasia

3 pounds cut-up frying chicken
2 tablespoons butter
3 tablespoons oil
2 tablespoons curry powder

3/4 cup dry white wine
1/4 cup brandy
6 ripe tomatoes, peeled, seeded, drained, and chopped
2 apples, peeled and sliced
1/2 cup pitted green olives, sliced and parboiled for 3 minutes
Bouquet Garni:
   3 sprigs parsley
   2 sprigs thyme (or 1/2 teaspoon dried)
Salt and freshly ground pepper

Sauté the chicken in the manner described in Chicken Sauté Cacciatora [No. 1279]. When the pieces are fully cooked and tender, transfer them to a hot platter, season them with salt and pepper, and keep warm. Drain off all but 2 tablespoons of the fat from the pan, add the curry powder, stir for 1 minute over medium heat, add the wine, and cook until reduced by 1/2. Heat the brandy in a ladle over medium heat, ignite, and add to the pan. Add the tomatoes, apples, olives, and Bouquet Garni. Season with salt and pepper, simmer for 10 minutes, return the chicken to the pan, simmer 5 minutes longer, remove the Bouquet Garni, and then turn the chicken and sauce out onto a hot serving dish. *Serves* 6.

1282. CHICKEN SAUTÉ MARENGO
Pollo sauté alla Marengo

3 pounds cut-up frying chicken
5 tablespoons butter
3 tablespoons oil
1/2 pound mushroom caps
2 cloves garlic, crushed in the garlic-press
1/2 cup sherry wine
1/2 cup Demi-Glaze Sauce [No. 20]
6 ripe tomatoes, peeled, seeded, drained, and chopped
Optional: 2 truffles, sliced
3 tablespoons chopped parsley
6 slices bread, crusts removed, browned in oil
6 fried eggs, fried in oil
6 jumbo shrimp, boiled for 6 minutes in Court Bouillon for Shrimp [No. 765], drained, peeled, and de-veined
Salt and freshly ground pepper

Sauté the chicken in the manner described in Chicken Sauté Cacciatora [No. 1279]. When the pieces are fully cooked and tender, transfer them to a hot platter, season them with salt and pepper, and keep warm. Gently sauté the mushrooms in the remaining tablespoon of butter in a covered frying pan over moderate heat for about 8 minutes; remove from the heat and reserve. Drain off most of the fat in the pan in which the chicken cooked, add the garlic, stir over medium heat for 1 minute, add the sherry, and cook until reduced by ½. Add the Demi-Glaze, tomatoes, optional sliced truffles, and parsley. Season with salt and pepper and simmer for 15 minutes. Return the pieces of chicken to the pan, add the mushrooms, and simmer for 5 minutes. Transfer the pieces of chicken to a hot serving platter, pour the sauce over the pieces, arrange the browned slices of bread around the platter, and garnish the top with the fried eggs and shrimp. *Serves* 6.

1283. CHICKEN SAUTÉ MARYLAND
Pollo sauté Maryland

3 pounds cut-up frying chicken
2 eggs, beaten with 1 tablespoon oil
3 cups fresh breadcrumbs
2 tablespoons butter
3 tablespoons oil
6 corn fritters (*see* Note below)
6 banana halves, fried until golden in 3 tablespoons butter
6 thick slices bacon, broiled

1½ cups Horseradish Sauce [No. 89]
Salt and freshly ground pepper

Season the pieces of chicken with salt and pepper, dip them in the beaten egg, and cover them generously with breadcrumbs. Sauté the pieces in the manner described in Chicken Sauté Cacciatora [No. 1279]. Arrange the pieces on a hot serving platter and garnish with the corn fritters, fried bananas, and bacon. Serve the horseradish sauce on the side. *Serves* 6.

NOTE: To prepare the corn fritters, mix 1 cup of fresh or canned corn kernels with ½ recipe Cream Puff Dough [No. 1990]. Drop 6 very large spoonsful of this batter into 5 tablespoons very hot butter in a frying pan over high heat and cook on both sides until puffed and golden.

BREAST OF CHICKEN
Filetti o costolette di pollo

Breast of chicken, skinned and boned, is exquisitely delicate and delicious, when properly prepared. Because the flesh of the breast is so delicate, extreme care must be taken not to overcook it. It is always quickly poached or sautéed in butter until just tender.

441

HOW TO BONE A POULTRY BREAST

The simplest method of removing and boning a poultry breast is to remove it all in a single piece with poultry shears, disjointing the wings where they join the carcass and severing the bases of the wishbone. Using a very sharp knife, cut along top ridge of breastbone and continue down each side to separate the flesh from the bone in one piece. Pull off skin, remove white tendons from underside of flesh, and flatten each of the breast fillets with the flat side of a meat cleaver.

1. Loosen the skin from one end of the breast
2. Pull off the skin in one piece
3. Cut off the wings from the breast
4. The whole breast attached to the breast bone
5. Loosen the flesh from the bone
6. Cut and pull off the bone

Chicken breasts are never cooked in liquid, as this will toughen them. A perfectly cooked chicken breast should be white with the barest tinge of rosiness and it should be very juicy, never dry.

The two breast halves are skinned and completely boned before cooking, or, if desired, the upper wing may be left attached (Italians call the latter *costolette di pollo,* or cutlets, as opposed to the boned breasts alone which are *filetti*).

The two methods of cooking breast of chicken are *a bianco,* or white-cooked, and *a bruno,* or brown-cooked. The first requires the chicken to be poached in butter in a covered casserole for about 5 minutes; the chicken should remain absolutely white. The second requires the chicken to be sautéed for about the same time in Clarified Butter [No. 102] which burns less quickly than ordinary butter and thus can be much hotter.

To test breast of chicken for doneness, press it lightly with the forefinger. If the flesh is still soft, it is underdone; if the flesh feels slightly spongy or springy, it is fully cooked. Even a minute of overcooking can toughen the breast, and thus, while it is very simple to cook, constant attention is required.

1284. BREAST OF CHICKEN WITH ARTICHOKES
Filetti di pollo con carciofi

6 boned breasts of chicken
6 small young artichokes, trimmed, cooked until just tender in White Foundation for Vegetables [No. 1576], drained, and sautéed 3 minutes in butter
24 Noisette Potatoes [No. 1783]
Flour
6 tablespoons Clarified Butter [No. 102]
1 cup dry white wine
2 tablespoons butter, softened
Salt and freshly ground pepper

Prepare the artichokes and potatoes in advance and keep warm. Season the chicken breasts very lightly with salt and pepper and dust them with flour. Heat the clarified butter in a large frying pan over medium high heat until its color deepens slightly. Add the chicken breasts, cook for 3 minutes on one side, turn and cook for 2 minutes on the other. Adjust the heat during the cooking so that the butter does not burn. Test for doneness by pressing with the finger. If the flesh is still soft, cook a little longer; if the flesh springs back to the touch, remove the breasts at once to a hot

serving platter. Add the wine to the pan and reduce over high heat to ½ its quantity. Remove from the heat and swirl in the 2 tablespoons of the softened butter, bit by bit. Pour over the chicken breasts and garnish the platter with the artichokes and the potatoes. *Serves 6.*

1285. BREAST OF CHICKEN GAUDENTE
Filetti di pollo alla gaudente

6 boned breasts of chicken
¼ pound chicken kidneys (or hearts), chopped
6 tablespoons butter
¼ pound chicken livers, chopped
½ cup pitted green olives, parboiled for 5 minutes and sliced
1 cup Marsala Sauce [No. 43]
1 clove garlic, crushed in the garlic-press
½ pound mushrooms, sliced
Flour
6 tablespoons Clarified Butter [No. 102]
6 slices bread, crusts removed, cut to the size of the chicken breasts, and browned in butter
Salt and freshly ground pepper

Sauté the chicken kidneys (or hearts) for 3 minutes in 3 tablespoons of butter in a frying pan over medium heat, add the chicken livers, and sauté for 3 minutes longer. Add the olives and Marsala sauce, simmer 2 minutes longer, and reserve. Heat the remaining 3 tablespoons of butter in another frying pan over medium heat, add the garlic, cook for 1 minute, add the mushrooms, and sauté gently for about 8 minutes. Combine the mushrooms with the kidneys (or hearts) and livers and keep warm. Season the chicken breasts with a little salt and pepper and dust them with flour.

Chicken Sauté Maryland
(No. 1283): see page 441

442

Heat the clarified butter in a large frying pan and sauté the chicken breasts in the manner described in the preceding recipe. When they are fully cooked, arrange them in a circle on the browned slices of bread on a hot serving platter and heap the livers, kidneys (or hearts), and mushrooms in the center. *Serves 6.*

1286. BREAST OF CHICKEN UNDER GLASS
Filetti di pollo sotto la campana

6 boned breasts of chicken
¼ pound mushrooms, sliced
6 tablespoons butter
Juice of 1 lemon
1 cup heavy cream
½ cup Brown Veal Stock [No. 5]
Salt and freshly ground pepper
6 glass bells

Gently sauté the mushrooms in 2 tablespoons of butter in a covered frying pan over medium heat for 8 minutes; remove from the heat and reserve. Rub the chicken breasts with a few drops of lemon juice and season them lightly with salt and pepper. Heat the remaining butter in a large, shallow casserole until it foams, very quickly roll the chicken breasts in the butter, cover the casserole, and put it in a hot (400°) oven for 6 minutes. Remove from the oven and test the breasts for doneness by pressing with the finger. If they are still soft, return the casserole to the oven for another minute. When the flesh feels slightly springy to the touch, the breasts are fully cooked. Transfer them quickly to individual hot serving plates and keep warm. Add the stock to the pan and reduce over high heat to a few tablespoons. Add the cream and continue cooking over high heat until it thickens slightly. Add the mushrooms, correct the seasoning, pour a little of the sauce over each breast, and cover each with a heated glass bell. *Serves 6.*

NOTE: Small Pyrex bowls may be substituted for the glass bells, or they may be omitted.

1287. BREAST OF CHICKEN LUIGI VERONELLI
Filetti di pollo alla Luigi Veronelli

6 boned breasts of chicken
1 recipe Pilaf [No. 595]
6 tablespoons butter
Juice of 1 lemon
6 slices boiled smoked tongue, cut ½ inch thick

Salt and freshly ground pepper
2 cups Sauce Suprême [No. 22]

Prepare the rice pilaf and keep hot. Cook the chicken breasts in the manner described in the preceding recipe and, when they are fully cooked, arrange them in a circle around the edge of a hot serving platter and keep warm. Pack the rice in a buttered ring mold and then unmold in the center of the platter. Sauté the slices of tongue for 1 minute in the butter remaining in the pan in which the chicken breasts were cooked and then arrange them around the rice alternately with the breasts. Spoon a little of the Suprême sauce over the chicken and tongue and serve the remainder in a sauceboat. *Serves 6.*

1288. BREAST OF CHICKEN MARÉCHALE
Filetti di pollo à la maréchale

6 boned breasts of chicken
Flour
2 eggs, beaten
2 cups fresh breadcrumbs
½ cup Clarified Butter [No. 102]
6 thick slices white truffle [or No. 1819a]
18 asparagus tips, boiled in lightly salted water until just tender, drained, and dressed with 2 tablespoons of butter
Juice of 1 lemon
Salt and freshly ground pepper

Season the chicken breasts with salt and pepper, dust them with flour, dip in beaten egg, and then cover them

Breast of Chicken Ricca
(No. 1293): see page 445

443

generously with breadcrumbs. Heat 5 tablespoons of the clarified butter in a large frying pan and sauté the breasts in the manner described in Breast of Chicken with Artichokes [No. 1284]. When they are fully cooked, arrange them on hot platter, top each with a slice of truffle, and garnish the platter with the asparagus tips. Add the remaining clarified butter to the pan, heat until golden, remove from the heat, add the lemon juice, and then pour over the chicken breasts. *Serves* 6.

1289. BREAST OF CHICKEN A BIANCO WITH MUSHROOMS
Filetti di pollo con funghi a bianco

6 boned breasts of chicken
18 mushroom caps, fluted [*see* Note to No. 866]
Juice of ½ lemon
10 tablespoons butter
2 cups Sauce Parisienne [No. 21]
Salt and freshly ground white pepper

Gently sauté the fluted mushrooms in 4 tablespoons of the butter and lemon juice in a covered frying pan over moderate heat for 8 minutes; season lightly, remove from the heat and reserve. Poach the chicken breasts in the remaining butter and salt and pepper in a covered casserole in the manner described in Breast of Chicken Under Glass [No. 1286]. When they are fully cooked, transfer them to a hot serving platter, cover each with a little of the Parisienne sauce, and garnish with the mushrooms. Serve the remaining sauce in a sauceboat. *Serves* 6.

1290. BREAST OF CHICKEN BRUNO WITH MUSHROOMS
Filetti di pollo con funghi a bruno

6 boned breasts of chicken
18 mushroom caps, fluted [*see* Note to No. 866]
4 tablespoons butter
Juice of ½ lemon
Flour
6 tablespoons Clarified Butter [No. 102]
2 cups Mushroom Sauce No. 2 [No. 58]
Salt and freshly ground pepper

Gently sauté the mushroom caps, lightly seasoned with salt and pepper and sprinkled with lemon juice, in the 4 tablespoons butter. Cover the pan and let cook over low heat for 8 minutes, remove from heat and keep warm. Lightly season the chicken breasts with salt and pepper and dust with flour. Heat the clarified butter in

a large pan over medium high heat until its color has deepened slightly. Add the chicken breasts, cook for 3 minutes on one side, turn and cook for 2 minutes on the other. Make sure they become browned. Adjust the heat during cooking so that the butter does not burn. Test for doneness by pressing with the finger. If the flesh is still soft, cook a little longer; if the flesh springs back to the touch, remove the breasts at once to a hot serving platter. Arrange them in a circle, top with the fluted mushroom caps, pour a thin ribbon of the mushroom sauce over them, and serve the rest of the sauce in a sauceboat. *Serves* 6.

1291. BREAST OF CHICKEN ORLY
Filetti di pollo à l'Orly

6 boned breasts of chicken
A marinade:
 ½ cup oil
 Juice of 1 lemon
 1 small onion, sliced
 1 tablespoon chopped parsley
 ½ teaspoon salt
 ¼ teaspoon freshly ground pepper
1 cup oil
1½ cups Fritter Batter [No. 275], into which is folded 1 stiffly beaten egg white
6 sprigs of parsley, fried in deep fat [*see* No. 276]
3 lemons, quartered
2 cups Tomato Sauce [No. 19]

Marinate the chicken breasts in the marinade for 2 hours. Drain and dry thoroughly on paper towels. Heat the oil in a large frying pan over medium high heat until it is very hot but not smoking. Dip the chicken breasts in the fritter batter and cook them in the oil on one side for 3 minutes. Turn and cook on the other side for 3 minutes longer. Test for doneness by pressing with the finger. If the flesh feels soft, cook a little longer. As soon as it feels springy to the touch, transfer the breasts to a hot serving platter, garnish with the fried parsley and lemon quarters, and serve the tomato sauce on the side. *Serves* 6.

1292. BREAST OF CHICKEN EN PAPILOTTE
Filetti di pollo al cartoccio

6 boned breasts of chicken
Flour
5 tablespoons Clarified Butter [No. 102]
12 thin slices prosciutto

444

1 cup Italian Meat Sauce [No. 41]
6 sheets of parchment paper, cut in the shape of large
    hearts and brushed with oil on both sides
Salt and freshly ground pepper

Season the chicken breasts with salt and pepper and dust lightly with flour. Heat the butter in a large frying pan over high heat and quickly sauté the chicken breasts for 2 minutes on each side. The butter should be hot enough so that the breasts will be browned in a total of 4 minutes. Place a slice of prosciutto on one half of each of the paper hearts, place a chicken breast on top, spoon a generous amount of Italian meat sauce over the chicken breasts, top with a slice of prosciutto, fold over the other half of the paper hearts, and seal the edges well by crimping. Place them on an oiled oven-proof platter in a hot (450°) oven for about 5 minutes, or until the paper is puffed and browned. Serve on the platter. *Serves* 6.

1293. BREAST OF CHICKEN RICCA
Filetti di pollo alla ricca

6 boned breasts of chicken
6 ½-inch slices of cold Polenta [No. 623]
Flour
10 tablespoons butter
6 ¼-inch slices very lean salt pork, parboiled for
    10 minutes
2 eggs, lightly beaten
1 cup grated Parmesan cheese
Salt and freshly ground pepper

Dust the slices of polenta with flour and brown them lightly on both sides in 4 tablespoons of butter in a frying pan over medium high heat. Transfer them to a hot serving platter and keep warm. Sauté the slices of salt pork in 4 tablespoon of the butter in another frying pan over medium heat until crisp and golden. Remove them with a slotted spoon and reserve. Season the chicken breasts with salt and pepper, dust them with flour, dip in beaten egg, and then roll in the grated cheese. Heat the fat in the pan in which the salt pork was cooked until it is very hot and sauté the chicken breasts for 3 minutes on one side and then for 2 minutes on the other. Test for doneness by pressing with the finger; as soon as the flesh feels springy to the touch, they are fully cooked. Arrange them over the slices of polenta, and top each with a slice of salt pork. Add the remaining butter to the pan, heat for a few seconds, and pour over the chicken. *Serves* 6.

1294. BREAST OF CHICKEN ROSSINI
Filetti di pollo Rossini

6 boned breasts of chicken
Flour
6 tablespoons butter
6 ¼-inch slices pâté de foie gras
6 slices truffle
1½ cups Demi-Glaze Sauce [No. 20]
Salt and freshly ground pepper

Cook the chicken breasts in the butter in the manner described in Chicken Breasts with Artichokes [No. 1284]. When they are fully cooked, arrange them on a hot serving platter and keep warm. Very quickly sauté the slices of pâté de foie gras in the butter remaining in the pan and then place them on top of the chicken breasts. Top each with a slice of truffle and spoon a little Demi-Glaze sauce over each. *Serves* 6.

1295. BREAST OF CHICKEN VILLEROY
Filetti di pollo alla Villeroy

6 boned breasts of chicken
Juice of 1 lemon
6 tablespoons butter
1½ cups cold Sauce Villeroy [No. 59]
2 cups fresh breadcrumbs
1 cup oil
6 sprigs parsley, fried in deep fat [*see* No. 276]
1½ cups Tomato Sauce [No. 19]
Salt and freshly ground pepper

Poach the lemon-rubbed chicken breasts in the butter in a covered casserole in the manner described in Breast of Chicken Under Glass [No. 1286]. When they are fully cooked, transfer them to a shallow bowl, cover tightly, and chill. When they are cold, coat them with a generous amount of Villeroy sauce and then roll in breadcrumbs. Heat the oil in a large frying pan over medium high heat and brown the chicken breasts for about 2 minutes on each side. Arrange them on a hot serving platter, garnish with the fried parsley, and serve the tomato sauce on the side. *Serves* 6.

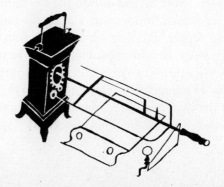

SPEZZATINI OF CHICKEN

Spezzatini di pollo

Spezzatini are similar to sautés in that the chicken is first browned, cooked until tender, and set aside while a sauce is prepared. The breasts are then usually only simmered in the sauce for a few minutes before serving. Frying chickens weighing about 2½ pounds are always used in *spezzatini*. They are thus young and tender enough to cook in about 30 minutes.

1296. SPEZZATINO OF CHICKEN ITALIANA

Spezzatino di pollo all'italiana

3 pounds cut-up frying chicken
Flour
⅔ cup oil
6 ripe tomatoes
2 cloves garlic, crushed in the garlic-press
3 tablespoons chopped parsley
1 cup fresh breadcrumbs
2 tablespoons butter
½ pound sweet Italian sausage, cut into 1-inch
    pieces, and poached 10 minutes
1 sweet yellow pepper, roasted, scraped, seeded,
    and cut into strips [*see* No. 145]
2 cups shelled young peas, simmered 10 minutes in
    lightly salted water
Salt and freshly ground pepper

Season the pieces of chicken with salt and pepper and dust with flour. Heat ½ cup of the oil in a large frying pan and brown the chicken, a few pieces at a time, on both sides. As the pieces become brown, remove them from the pan, and add fresh ones. When all are browned, return only the legs and thighs to the pan, cover tightly, reduce the heat, and simmer for 10 minutes. Add the breasts and wings and simmer for another 15 minutes. The pieces are fully cooked when the breast feels springy to the touch and the thigh can be easily pierced with a fork. Transfer them to a hot serving platter and keep warm. Slice off and discard the top third of the tomatoes, season the tops with a generous amount of salt and pepper, and then sprinkle each with a little garlic, parsley, breadcrumbs, and, finally, the remaining oil. Place them in a baking dish in a moderate (350°) oven for 15 minutes. Drain off the fat from the pan in which the chicken cooked, add the butter, and sauté the sausage over medium heat for about 5 minutes.

Add the peppers, cook 5 minutes longer, add the peas, season with salt and pepper, and cook only until the peas are very hot. Spoon this mixture over the chicken, and garnish the platter with the tomatoes. *Serves* 6.

1297. SPEZZATINO OF CHICKEN ITALIANA WITH RICE

Spezzatino di pollo all'italiana con riso

3 pounds cut-up frying chicken
6 tablespoons butter
1 onion, finely chopped
6 tomatoes, peeled, seeded, drained, and chopped
½ cup Tomato Sauce [No. 19]
Bouquet Garni:
    3 sprigs parsley
    2 sprigs thyme (or ½ teaspoon dried)
    1 bay leaf
3 cups Chicken Stock [No. 3]
2 cups Italian (short-grain) rice, well washed
Salt and freshly ground pepper

Dry the chicken thoroughly on paper towels. Heat the butter in a large casserole or enamel pot over fairly high heat and brown the chicken, a few pieces at a time, for about 2 minutes on each side. Adjust the heat so that the butter does not burn. As the pieces become brown, remove them from the pot and add fresh ones. When all are browned, return them all to the pot, add the onion, stir for 1 minute over medium heat, and then add the tomatoes, tomato sauce, Bouquet Garni, stock, and rice. Season with salt and pepper, bring to a boil, and then place in a moderate (350°) oven for 30 minutes. Discard the Bouquet Garni and serve in the casserole. *Serves* 6.

1298. SPEZZATINO OF CHICKEN WITH PEPPERS

Spezzatino di pollo con peperoni

3 pounds cut-up frying chicken
2 cloves garlic, crushed in the garlic-press
1 cup dry white wine
¼ cup brandy
3 sweet yellow peppers, roasted, scraped, seeded,
    and cut into strips [*see* No. 145]
¾ cup oil
½ cup chopped onion
Flour
6 tomatoes, peeled, seeded, drained, and chopped
1 tablespoon chopped basil (or 1 teaspoon dried)
Salt and freshly ground pepper

Put the garlic in a bowl with the wine and brandy and allow to stand for 1 hour. Gently sauté the peppers in 4 tablespoons of the oil in a frying pan over medium heat for about 10 minutes; remove from heat and set aside. Cook chicken in remaining oil as described in Spezzatino of Chicken Italiana [No. 1296]. When the pieces are fully cooked, transfer them to a hot serving platter and keep warm. Pour off all but 2 tablespoons of the oil in the pan, add the chopped onion, cook until golden, add the garlic/wine/brandy mixture, and reduce over high heat to ¹⁄₂ its quantity. Add the tomatoes and basil, season with salt and pepper, and simmer for 15 minutes. Return the pieces of chicken to the pan, simmer for 5 minutes, rearrange the chicken on the platter, pour the sauce over, and top with the strips of pepper. *Serves* 6.

1299. SPEZZATINO OF CHICKEN PIEMONTESE

Spezzatino di pollo alla piemontese

3 pounds cut-up frying chicken
Flour
¹⁄₂ cup oil
4 tablespoons butter
¹⁄₂ cup dry white wine
6 tomatoes, peeled, seeded, drained, and chopped
1 recipe Risotto with Butter and Parmesan Cheese [No. 572]
1 white truffle, sliced [or No. 1819a]
Salt and freshly ground pepper

Cook the chicken in the oil in the manner described in Spezzatino of Chicken Italiana [No. 1296]. When it is fully cooked, transfer it to a hot serving platter and keep warm. Drain off all of the oil in the pan, add the butter and wine, reduce over high heat until the wine has almost evaporated, add the tomatoes, season with salt and pepper, and simmer for 15 minutes. Return the pieces of chicken to the pan and simmer for 5 minutes. Time the cooking of the risotto so that it is cooked and dressed at this point. Press the rice into a large buttered ring mold. Unmold it onto a large serving platter, arrange the chicken and sauce in the center, and sprinkle the slices of truffle over the top. *Serves* 6.

1300. SPEZZATINO OF CHICKEN ROMAGNOLA

Spezzatino di pollo alla romagnola

3 pounds cut-up frying chicken

A marinade:
  1¹⁄₂ cups red wine
  1 clove garlic, crushed in the garlic-press
  1 teaspoon salt
  ¹⁄₄ teaspoon freshly ground pepper
  ¹⁄₂ teaspoon powdered thyme
  1 tablespoons chopped marjoram (or 1 teaspoon dried)
Flour
¹⁄₂ cup oil
6 tablespoons butter
1 clove garlic, crushed in the garlic-press
1 onion, chopped
¹⁄₂ cup Brown Veal Stock [No. 5]
3 egg yolks

Marinate the pieces of chicken in the marinade for 3 hours. Remove the pieces, dry thoroughly on paper towels, and dust with flour. Cook the chicken in the oil in the manner described in Spezzatino of Chicken Italiana [No. 1296]. When the pieces are fully cooked, transfer them to a hot serving platter and keep warm. Drain off the oil from the pan, add 3 tablespoons of the butter, heat for 1 minute, add the garlic and onion, cook until golden, and then add the stock and the strained marinade. Bring to a boil and reduce over high heat to ¹⁄₂ its quantity. Remove from the heat, beat a few tablespoons of the liquid with the egg yolks, pour the egg-yolk mixture into the pan, return it to a very low flame, and stir constantly until slightly thickened. Correct the seasoning and spoon this sauce over the chicken. *Serves* 6.

1301. SPEZZATINO OF CHICKEN AL SANGUE
Spezzatino di pollo al sangue

3 2-pound live chickens (*see* Note below)
2 cups red wine
Flour
$\frac{1}{2}$ cup butter
$\frac{1}{2}$ pound diced salt pork, parboiled for 15 minutes
$\frac{1}{2}$ pound mushrooms, sliced
2 tablespoons chopped shallots
2 tablespoons flour
1 cup boiling Brown Veal Stock [No. 5]
Bouquet Garni:
   3 sprigs parsley
   2 sprigs thyme (or $\frac{1}{2}$ teaspoon dried)
   6 celery leaves
   1 bay leaf
$\frac{1}{4}$ cup brandy
Salt and freshly ground pepper
12 Brown-Braised Onions [No. 1722]
6 slices of bread, crusts removed, cut in the shape
   of hearts, and browned in butter

Sever the heads of the chickens and allow their blood to drain into a bowl. Add 2 tablespoons of wine to the blood to prevent its coagulation. Pluck and clean the chickens. Cut them into pieces for frying, season them with salt and pepper, dust them with flour, and cook them in the butter in the manner described in Spezzatino of Chicken Italiana [No. 1296]. When they are fully cooked, transfer them to a hot serving platter and keep warm. Add the salt pork dice to the butter in the pan and sauté over medium heat until the dice are golden brown. Remove with a slotted spoon and reserve. Add the mushrooms to the pan, reduce the heat slightly, and sauté for about 10 minutes. Remove them with a slotted spoon and keep warm. Drain off all but 3 tablespoons of fat from the pan, add the shallots, cook over medium heat until they begin to color, add the flour, stir for 1 minute, add the boiling stock, stir until very thick, and then stir in the red wine. Add the Bouquet Garni, bring to a boil, and reduce over medium heat until slightly thickened. Add the chicken blood, return the pieces of chicken to the pan, and simmer for 5 minutes, stirring constantly. Heat the brandy in a ladle over medium heat, ignite, and pour over the chicken. Shake the pan until the flames subside. Arrange the chicken on a large serving platter, spoon the sauce over the pieces, and garnish the platter with the salt pork dice, mushrooms, braised onions, and the browned slices of bread. *Serves* 6.

NOTE: This dish may be made with killed, cleaned chickens. However, because it will be impossible to employ their blood in the sauce, the dish will not have the same taste and unctuousness.

1302. SPEZZATINO OF CHICKEN TRASTEVERINA
Spezzatino di pollo alla trasteverina

3 pounds cut-up frying chicken
Flour
$\frac{1}{2}$ cup oil
$\frac{1}{4}$ pound diced salt pork, parboiled for 10 minutes
2 cloves garlic, crushed in the garlic-press
$\frac{1}{2}$ cup dry white wine
3 ounces dried mushrooms, soaked $\frac{1}{2}$ hour in warm
   water, squeezed dry, and sliced
2 yellow peppers, roasted, scraped, seeded, and
   cut into strips [*see* No. 145]
$\frac{1}{2}$ pound zucchini, sliced
6 tomatoes, peeled, seeded, drained, and chopped
1 tablespoon chopped rosemary (or $\frac{1}{2}$ teaspoon dried)
1 tablespoon chopped marjoram (or 1 teaspoon dried)
1 tablespoon chopped parsley
Salt and freshly ground pepper

Cook the chicken in the manner described in Spezzatino of Chicken Italiana [No. 1296]. When the pieces are fully cooked, transfer them to a hot platter and keep warm. Add the salt pork dice to the fat in the pan and sauté over medium heat until golden brown. Remove the dice with a slotted spoon and reserve. Drain off all but 2 tablespoons of the fat in the pan, add the garlic, cook for 1 minute, add the wine, and cook until it has completely evaporated. Add the mushrooms, peppers, zucchini, tomatoes, and herbs. Season with salt and pepper and simmer for 10 minutes. Return the chicken pieces and the salt pork dice to the pan, mix lightly, and continue cooking for 5 minutes longer. Arrange the chicken on a hot serving platter and spoon the sauce over the pieces. *Serves* 6.

1303. SPEZZATINO OF CHICKEN IN VINEGAR
Spezzatino di pollo all'aceto

3 pounds cut-up frying chicken
4 anchovy fillets, washed free of salt [*see* No. 220]
2 cloves garlic
$\frac{1}{2}$ cup white wine vinegar
Flour
$\frac{1}{2}$ cup oil

1. Broiled Chicken Diavolo (No. 1266). Here the chicken has been broiled on a portable charcoal grill.

2. Guinea Hen in Clay (No. 1340)

3. Pullet in Casserole with Spring Vegetables (No. 1306). In this presentation additional amounts of the vegetables called for in the recipe are served in a separate casserole.

3 sprigs rosemary (or 1 teaspoon dried)
Salt and freshly ground pepper

Pound the anchovy fillets and the garlic to a paste in a mortar. Add the vinegar and blend until smooth. Season the chicken with salt and pepper and dust with flour. Heat the oil with the rosemary until smoking in a large frying pan over fairly high heat and cook the chicken in the manner described in Spezzatino of Chicken Italiana [No. 1296]. When the chicken is fully cooked, transfer it to a hot platter and keep warm. Drain off all but 2 tablespoons of the fat in the pan, add the vinegar mixture, and reduce over high heat to ½ its quantity. Return the pieces of chicken to the pan, cover tightly, and simmer over very low heat for 5 minutes. Transfer the chicken to a hot serving platter and spoon the sauce over. *Serves* 6.

PULLETS
Pollastra

As mentioned in the introduction to this section, Italians particularly prize young hens from 7 to 8 months old for their tenderness and their delicate flavor. Roasting chickens weighing about 3 pounds may be successfully used in any of the following recipes.

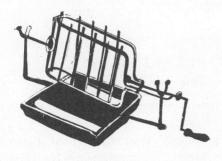

1304. BONED PULLET ITALIANA
Pollastra farcita lessata all'italiana

1 4-pound roasting chicken, cleaned and boned
Stuffing ingredients:
   ¼ pound chicken livers, chopped and sautéed
      3 minutes in 2 tablespoons of butter
   ½ cup diced lean salt pork, parboiled 10 minutes
   ½ cup chopped prosciutto (or smoked ham)
   1 tablespoon chopped parsley
   1 clove garlic, crushed in the garlic-press

1 onion, chopped
2 cups fresh bread cubes, soaked in milk and
      squeezed almost dry
1 teaspoon salt
¼ teaspoon freshly ground pepper
Pinch nutmeg
2 egg yolks
3 quarts Chicken Stock [No. 3]
Aromatic vegetables:
   2 carrots, sliced
   2 leeks (white part only), sliced
   3 stalks celery, sliced
   3 stalks beet greens
   1 onion, stuck with 1 clove
Sauce:
   2 hard-boiled eggs
   ¼ cup prepared mustard (Dijon-type preferred)
   3 tablespoons vinegar
   ¾ cup oil
   2 tablespoons finely chopped onion
   1 teaspoon salt
   ¼ teaspoon freshly ground white pepper

Bone the chicken whole as described on page 436, without breaking through the skin (a good butcher will do this for you). If desired, the drumstick and wing bones may be left intact to help give the chicken its original appearance after it is stuffed. Mix all of the stuffing ingredients in a bowl, season the cavity of the chicken with salt, and then stuff it loosely. Sew the openings with string and wrap the chicken in cheese-cloth, tying it securely, so that it will hold its shape during the cooking. Place it in a large, heavy pot with the stock and aromatic vegetables, bring to a boil, reduce the heat, and simmer for 1 hour and 30 minutes. Prepare the sauce while the chicken is cooking. Mash the hard-boiled egg yolks and mix them with the mustard and vinegar in a bowl. Beat in the oil in a slow stream so that the mixture maintains the smoothness and consistency of mayonnaise. Chop the egg whites and add them to the sauce with the onion, salt, and pepper. Unwrap the chicken on a hot serving platter. Carve it at the table in crosswise slices, spoon a little of the strained cooking liquid over each serving, and serve the sauce separately. *Serves* 6.

1305. BONED PULLET ROSA DI MAGGIO
Pollastra farcita "rosa di maggio"

1 4-pound roasting chicken, cleaned and boned
3 cups Forcemeat [No. 129], made with chicken
$\frac{1}{2}$ cup butter
$\frac{1}{4}$ pound pork rind, parboiled for 1 hour
1 carrot, sliced
1 onion, sliced
2 cups Chicken Stock [No. 3]
Bouquet Garni:
  3 sprigs parsley
  2 sprigs thyme (or $\frac{1}{2}$ teaspoon dried)
  1 bay leaf
1 pound veal sweetbreads, soaked, parboiled for
  15 minutes, trimmed, and sliced
Juice of 1 lemon
Salt and freshly ground pepper

Bone the chicken whole as described on page 436, without breaking through the skin, but leave the leg and wing bones intact so that the chicken will better hold its original shape. Stuff it loosely with the forcemeat, sew the openings, and truss it very securely. Dry it thoroughly with paper towels. Heat 4 tablespoons of the butter in a frying pan over fairly high heat until it is golden, and brown the chicken on all sides. Line a large, heavy casserole with the pork rind, add the carrot and onion, and lay the chicken on top, breast side up. Season it lightly with salt, add 1 cup of the stock and the Bouquet Garni, bring to a boil, cover the casserole, and place it in a moderate (350°) oven for 1 hour and 30 minutes. While the chicken is cooking, heat the remaining butter in a saucepan over moderate heat, add the sliced sweetbreads, and sauté very gently for 6 minutes. Add the remaining stock, bring slowly to a boil, cover the pan, and simmer for 25 minutes, or until the sweetbreads are tender. When the chicken is fully cooked, transfer it to a hot serving platter and spoon the sweetbreads around it. Strain the chicken cooking liquid, add it to the saucepan with the sweetbread cooking liquid, reduce over high heat to a generous cup, add the lemon juice, and spoon this sauce over the sweetbreads. *Serves* 6.

450

1306. PULLET IN CASSEROLE WITH SPRING VEGETABLES
Pollastra in casseruola con primizie

1 3-pound roasting chicken, cleaned
6 sprigs parsley

6 tablespoons Clarified Butter [No. 102]
$\frac{1}{4}$ cup brandy
1 pound carrots, cut into the shape of olives
12 white onions, parboiled 5 minutes
$\frac{1}{4}$ pound salt pork, diced, parboiled for 10 minutes,
  then drained and sautéed until golden brown
1 pound small "new" potatoes, parboiled 2 minutes
$\frac{1}{2}$ cup dry white wine
$\frac{1}{2}$ cup Chicken Stock [No. 3]
1 pound string beans, parboiled 3 minutes in salted
  water
Salt and freshly ground white pepper

Season the cavity of the chicken with salt and pepper, stuff it with the sprigs of parsley, and then truss in the manner described in the introduction. Heat the butter in a large, heavy pot over medium high heat until it is golden and brown the chicken on all sides, being careful to adjust the heat so that the butter does not burn. Heat the brandy in a ladle over medium heat, ignite, and pour over the chicken. Shake the pot until the flames subside. Add the carrots, onions, salt pork dice, and potatoes. Baste all of the vegetables with the butter and juices in the pot. Add the wine and stock, season with salt and pepper, cover the pot, bring to a boil, and then place the pot in a moderate (350°) oven for 1 hour and 15 minutes, basting occasionally with the juices in the pot. About 15 minutes before the chicken is fully cooked, add the string beans. Remove from the oven when the chicken is tender and, if desired, serve in the pot. *Serves* 4.

1307. PULLET FEDORA
Pollastra "Fedora"

1 3-pound roasting chicken, cleaned and cut up for
  frying
$\frac{1}{2}$ pound calf's sweetbreads, soaked, trimmed, and
  blanched [*see* introduction to No. 1434]
Optional: $\frac{1}{4}$ pound cocks' combs, parboiled 10 minutes
  and then skinned by rubbing with a coarse cloth
A marinade:
  1 cup Port wine
  1 truffle, sliced
  $\frac{1}{2}$ teaspoon salt
  $\frac{1}{8}$ teaspoon freshly ground pepper
$\frac{1}{2}$ pound mushrooms, sliced
$\frac{1}{2}$ cup Clarified Butter [No. 102]
18 Braised White Onions [No. 1721]
$\frac{1}{4}$ pound diced lean salt pork, parboiled for 10 minutes,
  drained, and sautéed until golden brown

Pullet Fedora (No. 1307)

½ recipe Flaky Pastry [No. 1954]
1 pound shelled peas, cooked until tender in lightly
    salted water, and dressed with 3 tablespoons butter
1½ pounds small carrots, quartered, cooked until
    tender in lightly salted water, and dressed with
    4 tablespoons butter
Salt and freshly ground pepper

Slice the calf's sweetbreads and marinate them with the optional cocks' combs in the marinade for 2 hours. Gently sauté the mushrooms in 2 tablespoons of the butter in a covered frying pan over moderate heat for about 8 minutes; remove from the heat and reserve. Dry the pieces of chicken thoroughly on paper towels. Heat the remaining butter in a large frying pan over fairly high heat until golden and brown the chicken, a few pieces at a time, for 3 minutes on each side. As they become brown, remove them from the pan and add fresh pieces. Adjust the heat so that the butter does not burn. When all are browned, remove from the pan. Drain the sweetbreads and optional cocks' combs, reserving the marinade, and dry them on paper towels. Add them to the pan in which the chicken cooked and sauté them over moderate heat for 5 minutes. Return the drumsticks and thighs to the pan, reduce the heat to a very low flame, cover the pan, and simmer for 10 minutes. Add the wings and breasts and cook for 15 minutes longer. Prepare the braised onions so that they will be ready at this point. Transfer all of the meats to a large, shallow casserole and add 6 of the braised onions, the salt pork dice, and the reserved mushrooms. De-glaze the pan in which the chicken cooked with the marinade liquid over high heat, scraping the bottom and sides of the pan with a wooden spoon, and then pour this over the meats in the casserole. Season them lightly with salt and pepper. Roll out the pastry in a sheet about ¼ inch thick, lay this sheet over the casserole, and trim the edges. If desired, cut out rosettes or other fancy shapes from any remaining bits of dough and decorate the top. Cut slits in the top to allow steam to escape. Place the casserole in a hot (450°) oven for about 20 minutes, or until the top is golden brown. Time the cooking of the carrots and peas so that they will be ready at the point when the casserole is removed from the oven, and serve these and the remaining onions in side dishes. *Serves* 6.

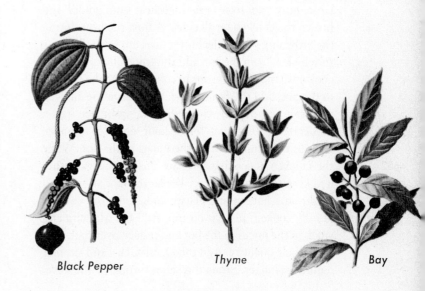

Black Pepper   Thyme   Bay

1308. PULLET FINANCIÈRE
Pollastra stufata alla finanziera

1 3-pound roasting chicken, cleaned
6 sprigs parsley
6 tablespoons Clarified Butter [No. 102]
1 onion, sliced
1 carrot, sliced
Bouquet Garni:
   3 sprigs parsley
   2 sprigs thyme (or $1/2$ teaspoon dried)
   1 bay leaf
Garnishes:
   $1/2$ pound mushrooms, gently sautéed in 3 tablespoons
      butter for 10 minutes
   12 medium-sized Quenelles [No. 339], made with
      Chicken Forcemeat [No. 129]
   $1/4$ pound chicken kidneys (or hearts), sliced, and
      gently sautéed in 3 tablespoons butter for
      10 minutes
   Optional: $1/4$ pound cocks' combs, simmered in lightly
      salted water for 10 minutes, drained, skinned by
      rubbing with a coarse cloth, and gently sautéed
      in 3 tablespoons butter for 3 minutes
1 large rectangle of bread, cut $1/2$-inch thick from an
   unsliced loaf and sautéed in butter until golden
   brown
$1/2$ cup dry Madeira wine
$1/2$ cup Brown Veal Stock [No. 5]
2 cups Demi-Glaze Sauce [No. 20]
2 truffles, sliced [or No. 1819a]
Salt and freshly ground pepper

Season the cavity of the chicken with salt and pepper, stuff it with the parsley, and truss in the manner described in the introduction. Heat the butter in a large, heavy pot over fairly high heat until golden and brown the chicken on all sides. Adjust the heat during the browning so that the butter does not burn. Remove the chicken from the pot, add the onion and carrot, and cook until the onion begins to color. Return the chicken to the pot, add the Bouquet Garni, season the chicken with salt and pepper, cover the pot, and place it in a moderate (350°) oven for 1 hour and 15 minutes, basting occasionally with the juices in the pot. While the chicken is cooking, prepare the various garnishes and keep them warm. Place the large piece of browned bread on a hot serving platter and, when the chicken is fully cooked, place it on top. Add the Madeira and stock to the juices in the pot and reduce over high heat to $1/2$ their quantity. Add the Demi-Glaze and simmer 5 minutes longer. Strain this sauce through a fine sieve,

return it to the pot, add the truffles, and simmer for 2 minutes. Arrange the various garnishes around the chicken and spoon the sauce over them. *Serves* 6.

1309. PULLET LEONE FILIPPI
Pollastra ripiena "Leone Filippi"

1 3-pound roasting chicken, cleaned
$1/4$ pound mushrooms, sliced
6 tablespoons butter
$1/2$ cup chopped prosciutto (or smoked ham)
3 cups Risotto with Butter and Parmesan Cheese
   [No. 572], cooled
$1/4$ cup brandy
1 cup Chicken Stock [No. 3]
1 cup heavy cream
Salt and freshly ground pepper

Gently sauté the mushrooms in 2 tablespoons of the butter in a frying pan over moderate heat for about 8 minutes, or until they are soft and tender. Mix them and the prosciutto with the cooled risotto. Season the cavity of the chicken with a little salt and pepper, stuff it loosely with the rice mixture, sew the openings with string, and truss in the manner described in the introduction. Heat the remaining butter in a heavy pot over fairly high heat until golden and brown the chicken on all sides. Adjust the heat so that the butter does not burn. Heat the brandy in a ladle over medium heat, ignite, pour over the chicken, and shake the pot until the flames subside. Season the chicken lightly with salt and pepper, cover the pot, and place it in a moderate (350°) oven for 1 hour and 30 minutes, or until the juices of the chicken run clear yellow when it is pierced with a fork. Baste it occasionally during the cooking with the juices in the pot. Transfer it to a hot serving platter and keep warm. Add the stock to the juices in the pot and reduce over high heat to $1/2$ their quantity. Add the cream, continue cooking until slightly thickened, correct the seasoning, and serve separately in a sauceboat. *Serves* 4.

1310. PULLET PHOENICIA DI MALTA
Pollastra "Phoenicia di Malta"

1 3-pound roasting chicken, cleaned
6 sprigs parsley
6 thin slices of truffle
6 tablespoons butter
1 onion, sliced
1 carrot, sliced
4 tablespoons dry Marsala wine

½ cup Velouté Sauce for Chicken [No. 17b]
1 cup heavy cream
Salt and freshly ground pepper

Season the cavity of the chicken with salt and stuff it with parsley. Put the slices of truffle between the skin and the flesh of the breast by pushing them in with the forefinger. Truss the chicken in the manner described in the introduction. Heat the butter in a large, heavy casserole over fairly high heat until golden and brown the chicken on all sides. Adjust the heat so the butter does not burn. Remove it from the casserole, add the carrot and onion, and sauté them until the onion begins to color. Return the chicken to the casserole, season it lightly with salt and pepper, cover the casserole, and place it in a moderate (350°) oven for 1 hour and 15 minutes, or until the juices of the chicken run clear yellow when pierced with a fork. Transfer to a hot serving platter and keep warm. Add the Marsala, Velouté, and cream to the juices in the pot, reduce over high heat for 5 minutes, correct the seasoning, strain through a fine sieve, and serve this sauce separately in a sauceboat. *Serves* 4.

CAPONS
Cappone

Capons are roosters that have been castrated while very young, and fattened on a special diet. Their weight is usually in excess of 4 pounds. "Caponettes" are available in the United States; these are hens which have been de-sexed. Many so-called "capons" available in supermarkets nowadays are "caponettes."

1311. BOILED CAPON WITH CAPER SAUCE
Cappone farcito lessato con salsa di capperi

1 5-pound capon, cleaned
Stuffing ingredients:
  4 cups soft bread cubes, soaked in milk and squeezed almost dry
  The capon liver, chopped and sautéed 3 minutes in 1 tablespoon butter
  ¼ pound mushrooms, sliced and gently sautéed in 2 tablespoons butter for 8 minutes
  ½ cup chopped prosciutto—or smoked ham—(fat and lean)

  2 tablespoons chopped parsley
  ½ teaspoon powdered thyme
  1 teaspoon salt
  ¼ teaspoon freshly ground pepper
  Pinch nutmeg
  2 eggs, beaten
Aromatic vegetables:
  1 onion stuck with 1 clove
  1 stalk celery
  1 carrot
Bouquet Garni:
  3 sprigs parsley
  2 sprigs thyme (or ½ teaspoon dried)
  1 bay leaf
2 cups Caper and Anchovy Sauce [No. 69]
Salt and freshly ground white pepper

Mix all of the stuffing ingredients thoroughly together in a bowl. A 5-pound bird will require about 4 cups of stuffing; use a little more bread, if necessary. Season the cavity of the capon lightly with salt, fill it loosely with the stuffing, sew the openings, and truss in the manner described in the introduction. Place the capon, aromatic vegetables, and Bouquet Garni in a large, heavy pot. Cover with cold water, season with a little salt and pepper, bring slowly to a boil, and simmer for 2 hours. Test for doneness by removing the capon from the pot and piercing the fleshy part of the thigh with a fork; if the juices run clear yellow, it is fully cooked. Transfer it to a hot serving platter and keep warm. Reduce the cooking liquid over high heat to ½. Serve a little of this liquid, strained, and the caper and anchovy sauce separately. *Serves* 6.

1312. BOILED CAPON WITH GREEN SAUCE
Cappone lessato al "sale grosso" con salsa verde

This is prepared in the same manner and with the same ingredients as the preceding recipe, except that Green Sauce [No. 88] is substituted for the caper and anchovy sauce. Serve with an accompaniment of coarse salt, and allow each guest to season his own portion. *Serves* 6.

453

1313. BRAISED CAPON ANGELA THERESA
Cappone in casseruola Angiola Teresa

1 5-pound capon, cleaned
6 sprigs parsley
6 tablespoons butter
1 cup chopped prosciutto (or smoked ham)
2 cups dry white wine
1 large oblong of bread, cut ½ inch thick from an
    unsliced loaf and browned in butter
1½ cups heavy cream
¼ cup pâté de foie gras
3 egg yolks
Juice of 1 lemon
Salt and freshly ground pepper

Season the cavity of the capon with salt, stuff it with the parsley, and truss in the manner described in the introduction. Heat the butter in a large, heavy pot over fairly high heat until golden and brown the capon on all sides. Adjust the heat during the browning so that the butter does not burn. Season lightly with salt and pepper, add the prosciutto and 1 cup of the wine, cover the pot, and place it in a moderate (350°) oven for about 2 hours, basting occasionally with the butter and rendered juices in the pot. Place the capon on the browned piece of bread on a hot serving platter and keep warm. Add the remaining wine to the pot and reduce the liquid over high heat to ½ its quantity. Add 1 cup of the cream, bring to a boil, and reduce until slightly thickened. Mash the foie gras with the egg yolks and then blend with the remaining cream. Off the heat, pour this mixture into the sauce, stirring constantly. Return the pot to very low heat and stir until slightly thickened. Add the lemon juice, correct the seasoning, and spoon this sauce over the capon. If desired, the platter may be garnished with Braised White Onions [No. 1721], sliced mushrooms which have been sautéed in butter, and sliced zucchini which has been boiled until tender and then dressed with butter. *Serves* 6.

1314. BRAISED CAPON PAESANA
Cappone in casseruola alla paesana

1 5-pound capon, cleaned
6 tablespoons butter
2 onions, sliced
2 cloves garlic, crushed in the garlic-press
3 yellow peppers, roasted, scraped, seeded, and cut
    into strips [*see* No. 145]

Bouquet Garni:
  3 sprigs parsley
  2 sprigs thyme (or ½ teaspoon dried)
  1 bay leaf
½ cup dry Marsala wine
6 ripe tomatoes, peeled, seeded, drained, and chopped
½ cup chopped prosciutto
2 medium zucchini, sliced
¼ cup chopped parsley
Salt and freshly ground pepper

Season the cavity of the capon with salt and pepper and truss in the manner described in the introduction. Heat the butter in a large, heavy pot over fairly high heat until golden and brown the capon on all sides. Adjust the heat during the browning so that the butter does not burn. Remove the capon from the pot, add the onions and garlic, cook until the onion begins to color, add the pepper strips, cook for 3 minutes longer, and then add the Bouquet Garni, Marsala, tomatoes, and prosciutto. Season with salt and pepper, bring to a simmering boil, and return the capon to the pot. Place it in a moderate (350°) oven for 2 hours. About 15 minutes before the capon is fully cooked, add the zucchini and the parsley, and complete the cooking. Transfer the capon to a hot serving platter. If the sauce is too liquid, reduce it slightly over high heat, and then spoon it around the capon. *Serves* 6.

1315. BREAST OF CAPON WITH ASPARAGUS TIPS
Filetti di cappone con punte d'asparagi violetti

6 capon breasts, boned
6 tablespoons butter
½ cup Brown Veal Stock [No. 5]
1 lemon
¼ pound mushrooms, sliced
1 cup heavy cream
Salt and freshly ground pepper
24 asparagus tips, cooked in salted water until tender,
    drained, and dressed with 4 tablespoons butter

Cook the capon breasts and prepare a sauce in the manner described in Breast of Chicken Under Glass [No. 1286]. If the breasts are very large, they will probably require 1 or 2 extra minutes of cooking. Be very careful not to overcook. Arrange them on a hot serving platter, spoon the sauce over them, and garnish the platter with the asparagus tips. *Serves* 6.

454

1316. CAPON "HAMS" IN CREAM
Giambonetti di cappone alla crema

6 legs and thighs (attached) of capon, boned and skinned
Stuffing ingredients:
    1/2 pound lean pork, ground
    1 truffle, chopped [or No. 1819a]
    1 teaspoon salt
    2 egg yolks
    1/4 teaspoon freshly ground pepper
    Pinch nutmeg
Flour
1/2 cup Clarified Butter [No. 102]
2 tablespoons brandy
1 cup dry white wine
1/4 cup Port wine
1 cup heavy cream.
Salt and freshly ground pepper

Place the 6 pieces of capon between sheets of wax paper and pound them slightly with the flat side of a meat cleaver. Mix the stuffing ingredients in a bowl to a smooth paste or blend in the blender on high speed for a few seconds. Spread a little of this mixture on each piece of capon, roll them up to resemble little hams, and tie securely with string. Season them with salt and pepper and dust with flour. Heat the butter in a large frying pan over fairly high heat and quickly brown the capon rolls on all sides. Adjust the heat so that the butter does not burn. Add the brandy to the pan, ignite, and shake the pan until the flames subside. Reduce the heat, cover the pan, and continue cooking for about 25 minutes. The rolls will be fully cooked when they are easily pierced with a fork and their juices run a clear yellow. Transfer them to a hot serving platter and keep warm. Add the 2 wines to the pan and reduce over high heat until they are slightly syrupy. Add the cream, reduce until slightly thickened, correct seasoning, and pour over the capon. *Serves* 6.

TURKEY
Tacchino

While very large turkeys of 16 to 20 pounds can be wonderfully impressive looking birds, smaller ones weighing 10 to 12 pounds, or even less, are usually considerably more tender and provide better eating. There exists a running controversy as to whether hens are to be preferred to tom turkeys for tenderness and flavor. Italian cooks, generally, prize hens as being more delicately flavored. In any event, tenderness will depend to a large extent on a turkey's age and flavor and the practices of the turkey grower.

Regrettably, turkeys are, more often than not, marketed frozen. This is especially true at Christmas and Thanksgiving when the enormous demand makes distribution a serious problem. If you live in an area where freshly killed turkeys are available, you are fortunate indeed. Like all frozen poultry, turkeys should be defrosted as slowly as possible under refrigeration to avoid an excess loss of juices and flavor. A 12-pound frozen turkey will require 2 to 3 days to defrost in the refrigerator.

Always bring a turkey to room temperature before cooking.

1317. BRAISED TURKEY FRANCESE
Tacchino in casseruola alla francese

1 8-pound turkey, cleaned
1 large bunch parsley
1/2 cup Clarified Butter [No. 102]
3 carrots, sliced
3 onions, sliced
Bouquet Garni:
    3 sprigs thyme (or 1/2 teaspoon dried)
    3 sprigs parsley
    1 bay leaf
1/2 pound diced salt pork, parboiled 15 minutes,
    drained, and sautéed until golden brown
10 small sausages
2 tablespoons butter
1 cup Thickened Brown Veal Stock [No. 6]
Salt and freshly ground pepper

Season the cavity of the turkey with salt and pepper, stuff it with parsley, and truss securely. Heat the butter in a very large casserole or enameled Dutch oven or roasting pan and brown the turkey on all sides, being careful to adjust the heat so the butter does not burn. Remove the turkey, add the carrots and onions, and cook until the onions begin to color. Return the turkey to the casserole, season it lightly with salt and pepper, add the Bouquet Garni and salt pork dice, cover the pot, and place it in a moderate (350°) oven for about 3 hours, basting frequently with the juices in the casserole. Begin testing the turkey for doneness after 2 1/2 hours. It is fully cooked if the juices from the fleshiest part of the thigh run clear yellow when pricked with a fork. Shortly before the turkey is done, gently sauté the sausages in the butter in a frying pan for about 10 minutes; remove them from the heat and reserve. Transfer the turkey to a hot serving platter, garnish with the sausages, and keep warm. Discard the Bouquet Garni and mash the vegetables slightly with the juices in the casserole. Add the veal stock, simmer over medium heat for 5 minutes, and serve this sauce separately in a sauceboat. *Serves* 10.

1318. ROAST TURKEY
Tacchino arrosto

1 10- to 12-pound turkey, cleaned
1 large bunch parsley
2 large sheets of fresh pork fat belly, cut ¼ inch thick
¾ cup butter, softened
4 cups Chicken Stock [No. 3], simmered for 1 hour
    with the turkey giblets
Salt and freshly ground pepper

Season the cavity of the turkey with salt, stuff it with the parsley, season the surface with salt and pepper, and then truss very securely in the manner described before (page 433). Tie the sheets of pork fat over the breast (they should be large enough so that the entire breast is covered). Spread the softened butter over the rest of the bird and place it on its side on a rack in a large, shallow roasting pan with ½ cup of the stock. Place the pan in a hot (450°) oven for 10 minutes. Turn the turkey on its other side, baste, and cook for another 10 minutes. Place it breast-side up, baste, and reduce the heat to moderate (325°). Roast for a total cooking time of 20 minutes to the pound. Turn the turkey and baste every 20 minutes. For the last 40 minutes of roasting, place it breast-side up, remove the pork fat, and allow the breast to brown, basting it frequently. It is fully cooked if, when raised by the legs, the juices from the vent run absolutely clear yellow without any trace of rosiness. Transfer it to a hot serving platter and keep warm. Place the pan over high heat until all of the juices in the pan have evaporated, leaving only fat, but be careful not to burn the coagulated "drippings" in the bottom. Pour off all of the fat and de-glaze the pan with the strained stock over high heat by scraping the bottom and sides with a wooden spoon. If the rack is crusted with drippings, de-glaze it also. (If desired, the gravy may be thickened slightly by sprinkling 2 tablespoons of flour in the pan and browning it for a few seconds before adding the stock.) Simmer for 5 minutes, correct the seasoning, and serve separately in a sauceboat. *Serves* 12.

NOTE: The above method of roasting will ensure an evenly cooked and beautifully crisped bird. There are,

however, a variety of other methods, each of which has its devotees. Most of these other methods are designed to save the cook labor. The best of these, we believe, is to cook the turkey breast-side up in a moderate (325°) oven with several thicknesses of cheesecloth, which have been dipped in melted butter, draped over the breast; this method requires only occasional basting and the cheesecloth is removed for the last ½ hour of cooking to allow the breast to brown. Another method is to encase the bird entirely in a large brown paper bag which has been brushed with oil or melted butter and then to roast in a moderate oven for the specified time; the paper bag is removed for the last 45 minutes of cooking to allow the bird to brown. Roasting a turkey wrapped in foil is not recommended, as the foil has no porosity and the turkey will steam, rather than roast, giving the meat a somewhat disagreeable wet quality.

1319. ROAST TURKEY À L'ANCIENNE
Tacchino arrosto all'antica moda

Roast a 10- to 12-pound turkey and prepare the gravy in the manner described in the preceding recipe. Chop the turkey liver, simmer it in ¾ cup of the gravy over medium heat for 3 minutes, and then pour this sauce over 12 small hearts of Boston or Bibb lettuce. Toss lightly and serve these separately. *Serves* 12.

1320. ROAST TURKEY WITH SAUSAGE AND CHESTNUT STUFFING
Tacchino ripieno con salsicce e castagne

1 10- to 12-pound turkey, cleaned
Stuffing ingredients:
    1½ pounds chestnuts
    3 cups Brown Stock [No. 4]
    3 stalks celery, chopped
    2 onions, chopped
    2 tablespoons butter
    1 pound sausage meat
    3 truffles, chopped [or No. 1819a]
    3 tablespoons brandy
    3 cups bread cubes, soaked in milk and squeezed dry
    2 tablespoons chopped parsley
    1 tablespoon chopped thyme (or 1 teaspoon dried)
    Salt and freshly ground pepper
2 large sheets fresh pork fat back, cut ¼ inch thick
¾ cup butter, softened
4 cups Chicken Stock [No. 3], simmered 1 hour with the
    turkey giblets and strained
Salt and freshly ground pepper

Cut a cross on the shell of each chestnut. Place them in a saucepan, cover with cold water, bring to a boil over high heat, and boil 2 minutes. Allow them to cool in the water and then, using a sharp knife, remove the shells and inner skin. Place the peeled chestnuts in a saucepan with the brown stock and simmer over medium heat for 45 minutes. Drain, mash $\frac{1}{3}$ of the chestnuts to a purée, and chop the remaining $\frac{2}{3}$ coarsely. Gently sauté the onions and celery in the 2 tablespoons of butter over moderate heat until the onions are soft. Sauté the sausage meat in a frying pan over medium heat for about 5 minutes, crumbling it well; remove from the heat; and drain off the fat. Combine all of these cooked ingredients with the truffles, brandy, bread cubes, and herbs in a bowl. Season to taste with salt and pepper and mix thoroughly. The mixture should be moist, but not wet. If it is too dry, add a little of the water in which the chestnuts cooked.

Stuff the cavity and the crop of the turkey loosely. Sew the openings with string and truss the turkey securely. Tie the sheets of pork fat over the breast and crop and spread the softened butter over the rest of the bird. Roast the turkey and prepare the sauce in the same manner as Roast Turkey [No. 1318]. *Serves* 12.

NOTE: Never stuff a turkey more than an hour or two in advance of cooking. The stuffing, even under refrigeration, will hasten deterioration.

1321. ROAST TURKEY UNCLE TOM
Tacchino come piace allo zio Tom

1 8-pound turkey, cleaned
2 large sheets fresh pork fat back, cut $\frac{1}{4}$ inch thick
$\frac{1}{2}$ cup Clarified Butter [No. 102]
$1\frac{1}{2}$ cups Chicken Stock [No. 3]
30 Braised White Onions [No. 1721]
30 Brussels Sprouts in Butter [No. 1628]
The turkey liver, chopped
The turkey gizzard, chopped
3 tablespoons butter
$\frac{1}{2}$ cup dry white wine
Salt and freshly ground pepper

Season the cavity of the turkey with salt and pepper, truss securely, and tie the sheets of pork fat over the breast. Heat the butter in a very large casserole or roasting pan over fairly high heat until golden, and brown the turkey on all sides except the fat-covered breast. Adjust the heat during the browning so that the butter does not burn. Turn the turkey breast-side up, add $\frac{1}{2}$ cup of the stock, bring it to a boil,

and place the casserole or pan in a moderate (350°) oven for about $2\frac{1}{2}$ hours. Baste every 15 minutes with the butter and stock in the casserole, adding a little more stock whenever necessary. About 30 minutes before it is fully cooked, remove the pork fat from the breast to allow it to brown. Transfer the turkey to a hot serving platter, garnish with the onions and Brussels sprouts, and keep warm. Sauté the liver and gizzard in butter for 3 minutes in a frying pan over high heat, remove them with a slotted spoon, and de-glaze the pan with the wine. Add the liver, gizzard, and the wine in the frying pan, plus any remaining stock, to the casserole. Correct the seasoning, simmer 2 minutes over medium heat, and serve this sauce separately in a sauceboat. *Serves* 10.

BREAST OF TURKEY
Filetti di Tacchino

Breasts are removed from a turkey in the same manner as chicken breasts and they receive much the same treatment (*see* page 441). They may be poached in butter *a bianco* or sautéed *a bruno* (*see* page 444). Small turkey breasts from a 4- to 5-pound bird are to be preferred to larger ones, as they are more tender and each half breast makes a convenient serving for 1 person.

1322. BREAST OF TURKEY BOLOGNESE
Filetti di tacchino alla bolognese

6 small breasts of turkey, skinned, boned, and flattened slightly
Flour
2 eggs, beaten
2 cups fresh breadcrumbs
6 tablespoons butter
6 thin slices Fontina (or Gruyère) cheese, cut the size of the turkey breasts
6 thin slices prosciutto (or smoked ham)
$\frac{1}{2}$ cup Italian Meat Sauce [No. 41]
Salt and freshly ground pepper

Season the breasts lightly with salt and pepper; dust with flour, dip in beaten egg, and then cover generously with breadcrumbs. Heat the butter in a large frying pan over fairly high heat until golden and brown the breasts for 4 minutes on one side. Turn them, brown for 3 minutes, and test for doneness by pressing with the finger. If the flesh is still soft, cook a little longer; if it feels slightly springy to the touch, it is fully cooked. Transfer them immediately to the rack of a broiler, cover each with a slice of cheese and prosciutto, and broil under a very hot flame for 1 minute to melt the cheese. Arrange them on a hot serving platter and top each with a spoonful of the meat sauce. *Serves 6.*

1323. BREAST OF TURKEY WITH LEMON
Filetti di tacchino fritti al limone

6 small breasts of turkey, skinned, boned, and flattened slightly
Flour
2 eggs, beaten
2 cups fresh breadcrumbs
6 tablespoons butter
Juice of 2 lemons
6 sprigs of parsley, fried in deep fat [*see* No. 276]
3 lemons, quartered
Salt and freshly ground pepper

Season, bread, and cook the turkey breasts in the manner described in the preceding recipe. Adjust the heat during the browning so that the butter does not burn. When they are fully cooked, transfer them to a hot serving platter, pour the butter in the pan over them, and squeeze a very generous amount of lemon juice over each. Garnish the platter with the fried parsley and the lemon quarters. *Serves 6.*

1324. BREAST OF TURKEY LUIGI VERONELLI
Filetti di tacchino alla Luigi Veronelli

6 small breasts of turkey, skinned, boned, and flattened slightly
Juice of 1 lemon
6 tablespoons butter
6 sage leaves (or ½ teaspoon dried)
6 Crêpes Célestine [No. 330], each large enough to wrap 1 breast
¾ cup Sauce Soubise [No. 74]
6 thin slices mozzarella cheese

1 cup butter, melted
2 cups fresh breadcrumbs
18 asparagus tips, cooked until just tender in salted water, drained, and dressed with 3 tablespoons butter
1½ cups Marsala Sauce [No. 43]
Salt and freshly ground pepper

Rub the turkey breasts with a little lemon juice and season them lightly with salt and pepper. Heat the 6 tablespoons of butter with the sage in a large frying pan until foaming and quickly roll the breasts in it. Cover the pan tightly and place it in a medium (400°) oven for 7 minutes. Test the breasts for doneness by pressing with the finger. If they are still soft, cook a little longer; if the flesh feels slightly springy to the touch, they are fully cooked. Remove them immediately from the pan, allow to cool, and then chill. Spread the crêpes out flat, spread each with a little Soubise, place a cooled breast in the center, top each with a slice of mozzarella, and then roll up. The crêpes must be large enough so that they will remain closed. Brush each with melted butter, and cover generously with breadcrumbs. Pour the remaining melted butter in a fying pan and sauté the wrapped breasts rather slowly over medium heat so that their covering will become golden and the breasts will just heat through but will not overcook. Arrange them on a hot serving platter, cover each with a little Marsala sauce, and garnish with the asparagus tips. *Serves 6.*

1325. BREAST OF TURKEY MEUNIÈRE
Filetti di tacchino al burro spumante

6 small breasts of turkey, skinned, boned, and slightly flattened
Flour
½ cup Clarified Butter [No. 102]
Juice of 2 lemons
Salt and freshly ground pepper

Season the turkey breasts with salt and pepper and dust them with flour. Heat 6 tablespoons of the butter in a large frying pan over fairly high heat and cook the breasts in the manner described in Breast of Turkey Bolognese [No. 1322]. Adjust the heat during the browning so that the butter does not burn. Transfer them to a hot serving platter when they are fully cooked. Add the remaining 2 tablespoons of butter and the lemon juice to the pan, heat for a few seconds, and pour over the breasts. *Serves 6.*

458

1326. BREAST OF TURKEY NERO
Filetti di tacchino alla Nerone

6 small breasts of turkey, skinned, boned,
    and slightly flattened
Flour
2 eggs, beaten
2 cups fresh breadcrumbs
6 tablespoons Clarified Butter [No. 102]
1/2 cup brandy
Salt and freshly ground pepper

Season, bread, and cook the turkey breasts in the manner described for Breast of Turkey Bolognese [No. 1322]. Adjust the heat during the cooking so that the butter does not burn. When they are fully cooked, transfer them to a hot serving platter. Quickly add the brandy to the pan, heat for 1 minute, ignite, and pour flaming over the breasts. *Serves 6.*

1327. BREAST OF TURKEY NEW YORK WORLD'S FAIR 1939
Filetti di tacchino "Fiera di New York 1939"

6 small breasts of turkey, skinned, boned,
    and slightly flattened
Juice of 1 lemon
Flour
6 tablespoons butter
12 sage leaves (or 1/2 teaspoon dried)
1/2 cup brandy
1 1/2 cups Sauce Mornay [No. 56]
6 thick slices veal sweetbreads, soaked, trimmed,
    and sautéed in butter [see No. 1333]
1 pound fettuccine [see No. 489], cooked until *al dente*
    in lightly salted water, drained, and dressed with
    a generous amount of butter and Parmesan cheese
2 white truffles, sliced
Salt and freshly ground pepper

Rub the turkey breasts with lemon juice, season with salt and pepper, dust them with flour, and then poach them in the butter and sage in the manner described in Breast of Turkey Luigi Veronelli [No. 1324]. When they are fully cooked, transfer them to a hot dish and keep warm. Add the brandy to the butter in the pan, and reduce by 1/2. Add the Mornay and simmer for 3 minutes. Time the cooking of the sweetbreads and the fettuccine so they are both ready at this point. Spread the fettuccine out on a hot oven-proof platter, arrange the turkey breasts on top, place a slice of sweetbread and a few truffle slices over each, and cover with the sauce. Place the platter under a high broiler flame for 1 minute to brown the top. *Serves 6.*

1328. BREAST OF TURKEY PIEMONTESE
Filetti di tacchino alla piemontese

6 small breasts of turkey, skinned, boned, and slightly
    flattened
Flour
6 tablespoons Clarified Butter [No. 102]
1/2 cup Marsala wine
1 cup Brown Veal Stock [No. 5]
3/4 cup grated Parmesan cheese
3 white truffles, sliced
2 tablespoons butter, softened
Salt and freshly ground pepper

Season the turkey breasts with salt and pepper, dust with flour, and cook them in the 6 tablespoons of clarified butter in the manner described for Breast of Turkey Bolognese [No. 1322]. When they are fully cooked, transfer them to a hot oven-proof platter and keep warm. Add the Marsala and stock to the pan and reduce over high heat to 1/2 their quantity. Sprinkle the grated cheese over the turkey breasts, place the platter under a high broiler flame for a few seconds to slightly melt the cheese, remove from the broiler, and sprinkle the truffles on top. Remove the sauce from the heat, swirl in the softened butter, bit by bit, and pour over the breasts. *Serves 6.*

1329. BREAST OF TURKEY VILLA SASSI
Filetti di tacchino "Villa Sassi"

6 small breasts of turkey, skinned, boned, and slightly
    flattened
Juice of 1 lemon
3/4 cup butter
1 onion, chopped
6 sage leaves (or 1/2 teaspoon dried)
1/4 pound mushrooms, sliced
2 truffles, chopped [or No. 1819a]
2 egg yolks, beaten
12 large thin slices prosciutto (or smoked ham)
6 slices bread, crusts removed, sautéed in
    butter until golden brown
1 1/2 cups Marsala Sauce [No. 43]
Salt and freshly ground pepper

Rub the turkey breasts with lemon juice, season them lightly with salt and pepper, and cook them in 6 tablespoons of the butter in the manner described in Breast of Turkey Luigi Veronelli [No. 1324]. Remove them from the pan 2 minutes before they are fully cooked, allow them to cool slightly, and then chop them rather coarsely. Add the onion and sage to the butter in the pan, cook over medium heat until the onion begins to color, add the mushrooms, and simmer for 8 minutes. Remove from the heat, allow to cool, and then add the truffles, chopped turkey, and egg yolks. Mix thoroughly, spread a little of the mixture on each of the slices of prosciutto, roll up, and secure with toothpicks. Arrange these rolls in a buttered baking dish and brush with the remaining butter, melted. Place the dish in a moderate (350°) oven for about 10 minutes, or until they are heated through and slightly sizzling. Arrange 2 of the rolls on each of the browned slices of bread on a hot serving platter, and spoon a little of the Marsala sauce over each. *Serves* 6.

DUCK

Anitra

Several varieties of duck are commercially raised in Europe, but in the United States the white Peking duck is usually the only type marketed. Their average weight is from 4 to 6 pounds. Heavier ducks are too old and tough to be suitable for roasting, although they may be tenderized by slow braising.

Ducks are often marketed frozen and, like all poultry, should be defrosted as slowly as possible in the refrigerator.

There is surprisingly little meat on duck and thus it is wise to allow 1½ pounds for each person to be served. They have, however, an enormous fat content, and should be lightly scored with a sharp knife and

pricked with a fork on their lower thighs, near the vent, and breast to allow the fat to escape during the cooking. Most of the meat on a duck is in a thin layer over the whole breast. It is simpler to carve it in long lengthwise strips, rather than to attempt to slice it as one would a chicken breast. The thigh and drumstick are removed in the same manner as from a chicken.

Wild duck may be substituted in any of the succeeding recipes for commercially raised birds. However, they have a much smaller fat content and thus, when roasted, should be spread with softened butter before cooking and basted frequently during the roasting. As a rule, wild ducks are fairly small; a 3-pound bird will serve 2 persons. Their cooking time is about 18 to 20 minutes to the pound (if you prefer wild fowl rare, as many Italians do, the cooking time should be reduced to 15 minutes per pound).

1330. BRAISED DUCK WITH LENTILS
Anitra brasata con lenticchie

1 5-pound duck, cleaned
3 tablespoons oil
A chopped mixture:
  3 tablespoons ham fat
  1 small onion
  1 small carrot
  1 stalk celery
1 cup dry white wine
Bouquet Garni:
  3 sprigs parsley
  2 sprigs thyme (or ½ teaspoon dried)
  1 bay leaf
½ cup Chicken Stock [No. 3]
1½ cups lentils, soaked in water overnight
Salt and freshly ground pepper

Remove as much fat from the duck as possible. Season the cavity of the duck with salt and pepper and truss it securely. Prick the skin around the vent, thighs, and lower part of the breast with a fork, and score lightly with a sharp knife. Heat the oil in a large pot or enameled Dutch oven over fairly high heat and brown the duck on all sides. Remove it from the pot and add the chopped mixture. Sauté it over medium heat and cook until the onion begins to turn gold. Add ½ cup of the wine and cook until it has almost evaporated. Add the duck and the Bouquet Garni, cover, and place it in a moderate (350°) oven for 2 hours. While the duck is cooking, put the lentils in a saucepan, cover with

cold water, season with 1 teaspoon of salt, bring to a boil, simmer for about 50 minutes (or until you estimate they are ¾ cooked), and then drain. Remove the duck from the oven and drain off all the fat with a bulb baster. Add the lentils, the stock, and remaining wine; re-cover the pot, and place it back in the oven for about 45 minutes. The duck will be fully cooked if, when pricked with a fork in the fleshy part of the thigh, its juices run clear yellow. Transfer it to a large hot serving platter and surround with the lentils. *Serves* 4.

1331. BRAISED DUCK WITH OLIVES
Anitra brasata con olive verdi

1 5-pound duck, cleaned
3 tablespoons oil
5 tablespoons butter
½ cup brandy
Bouquet Garni:
  3 sprigs parsley
  2 sprigs thyme
  1 bay leaf
2 tablespoons flour
½ cup dry white wine
2 cups boiling Chicken Stock [No. 3]
24 pitted green olives, parboiled 5 minutes
Salt and freshly ground pepper

Season the cavity of the duck with salt and pepper, truss it securely, and prick the vent, lower thigh, and lower breast several times with a fork and score with a sharp knife. Heat the oil in a large frying pan over high heat, brown the duck on all sides, and remove from the heat. Melt 3 tablespoons of the butter in a large casserole or enamel pot over medium heat, add the duck, and turn it for 1 minute in the hot butter. Heat the brandy in a ladle over medium heat, ignite, pour over the duck, and shake the casserole until the

flames subside. Add the Bouquet Garni, cover the casserole tightly, and place it in a moderate (350°) oven for 2 hours. Remove it from the oven, transfer the duck temporarily to a hot dish, discard the Bouquet Garni, and boil away any juices in the casserole over high heat, leaving only fat, but being careful not to burn the congealed "drippings" in the bottom. Pour off all of the fat and add the remaining butter. Stir in the flour, cook for 1 minute, add the boiling stock, stir until thickened, and then stir in the wine. Return the duck to the casserole, re-cover, and place it back in the oven for 30 minutes. About 5 minutes before it is fully cooked add the olives. Transfer the duck to a hot serving platter, carve it into neat slices, discard the carcass, and spoon the sauce over the slices. *Serves* 4.

1332. BRAISED DUCK WITH PEAS
Anitra brasata con piselli e lardoncini

1 5-pound duck, cleaned
3 tablespoons oil
A chopped mixture:
  3 tablespoons ham fat
  1 onion
  1 carrot
  1 stalk celery
½ cup dry white wine
Bouquet Garni:
  3 sprigs parsley
  2 sprigs thyme (or ½ teaspoon dried)
  1 bay leaf
1 tablespoon butter
1 tablespoon flour
1½ cups boiling Chicken Stock [No. 3]
½ pound diced lean salt pork, parboiled 10 minutes,
    drained, and sautéed until golden brown
1 pound shelled petits pois (or 2 boxes frozen),
    cooked until just tender in lightly salted water
Salt and freshly ground pepper

Season the cavity of the duck with salt and pepper and truss it securely. Prick the skin around the vent, thighs, and lower part of the breast with a fork and score with a sharp knife. Heat the oil in a large casserole or enamel pot over fairly high heat and brown the duck on all sides. Remove it from the pot. Add the chopped mixture, lower heat to medium, and cook until the onion has begun to color. Add the wine and cook until it has almost evaporated. Add the duck and the Bouquet Garni, cover the casserole, and place it in a moderate (350°) oven for 2 hours. Remove the casserole from the oven and transfer the duck temporarily to a hot dish. Place the casserole over high heat and boil away any juices, leaving only fat, but being careful not to burn the vegetables or the coagulated "drippings" in the bottom. Lower heat, pour off all the fat, and add the butter. Stir in the flour, cook for 1 minute, add the boiling stock, and stir until thickened. Return the duck to the casserole, add the salt pork dice, re-cover, and place the casserole back in the oven for 30 minutes. About 5 minutes before the duck is fully cooked, add the peas. Transfer the duck to a hot serving platter, carve it into neat slices, discard the carcass, and garnish the platter with small heaps of the sauced peas. *Serves 4.*

1333. BRAISED DUCK WITH TURNIPS
Anitra brasata con rape

This has the same ingredients and is prepared in the same way as Braised Duck with Lentils [No. 1330], except that 2 pounds of turnips are substituted for the lentils. The turnips should be peeled, cubed, and parboiled for 5 minutes before being added to the casserole for the last 30 minutes of cooking. *Serves 4.*

1334. ROAST DUCK
Anitra arrostita

1 5½-pound duck, cleaned
3 sprigs sage (or ½ teaspoon dried)
6 sprigs parsley
1 onion, sliced
2 cups Chicken Stock [No. 3]
2 tablespoons butter
Salt and freshly ground pepper

Season the cavity of the duck with salt and pepper and rub it with sage. Stuff it with the parsley and onion, truss it securely, and prick the vent, lower thighs, and lower breast several times with a fork and score with a sharp knife. Place it breast-side up on a rack in a shallow roasting pan in hot (450°) oven for 15 minutes. Add ½ cup of the stock, and reduce the heat to moderate (350°) and continue roasting for an additional 2 hours and 15 to 30 minutes, pricking the duck from time to time to permit more fat to run off. Test for doneness by lifting by the legs; if the juices that drain

from the vent run clear yellow, the duck is fully cooked. Transfer it to a hot serving platter and keep warm. Pour off all of the fat in the pan, add the stock, and de-glaze the pan over high heat by scraping the bottom and sides with a wooden spoon. Add the remaining stock and reduce to 1 cup over high heat. Correct the seasoning, remove from the heat, and swirl in the butter, bit by bit. Serve this sauce separately in a sauceboat. *Serves 4.*

NOTE: Alternative seasonings for the cavity of the duck may be sliced apples or dried soaked prunes.

1335. ROAST DUCK WITH ONIONS AND CARROTS
Anitra arrostita con cipolline e carotine

Prepare with the same ingredients and in the same manner as the preceding recipe and serve side dishes of Glazed Carrots [No. 1647] and Brown-Braised Onions [No. 1722].

1336. ROAST DUCK WITH ORANGE SAUCE
Anitra all' arancia

1 5½-pound duck, cleaned
3 sprigs parsley
1 onion, sliced
3 sprigs sage (or ½ teaspoon dried)
Rind of 2 oranges (no white part), cut in small julienne strips and parboiled 5 minutes
3 tablespoons sugar
¼ cup white wine vinegar
3 cups Chicken Stock [No. 3], simmered with the duck giblets and neck until reduced to 1 cup
3 tablespoons butter
1½ tablespoons potato flour mixed with ¼ cup Madeira or Port wine
1 cup orange juice
2 tablespoons Curaçao or Grand Marnier
4 oranges, peeled and divided into neat sections
Salt and freshly ground pepper

Season the cavity of the duck with the parsley, onion, and sage, truss it, and roast it in the manner described in Roast Duck [No. 1334]. Remove it when it is fully cooked and keep warm. Boil the orange peel, sugar, and vinegar in an enamel saucepan over medium heat until it is thick and syrupy and immediately add the stock, boiling hot, and blend well. Pour off all of the fat from the roasting pan, add the butter, stir in the potato flour over medium heat, cook until the flour mixture is smooth, and add the boiling stock mixture. Stir with a wooden spoon, scraping the sides and bottom of the pan, until the sauce is very thick. Add the orange juice and Curaçao. Correct the seasoning; if the sauce seems too sweet, correct by adding a little lemon juice. Simmer for 5 minutes while you carve the duck into neat slices on the platter. Garnish the edge of the platter with the orange sections and spoon the sauce over the carved duck. *Serves* 4.

1337. ROAST STUFFED DUCK
Anitra farcita ed arrostita

1 5½-pound duck, cleaned
Stuffing ingredients:
   ½ pound chicken livers, chopped
   The duck liver, chopped
   4 tablespoons butter
   5 green apples, cored, peeled, and thickly sliced
   1 tablespoon sugar
   ½ teaspoon cinnamon
   ½ teaspoon salt
   1 tablespoon chopped sage (or ½ teaspoon dried)
2 cups Chicken Stock [No. 3]
2 tablespoons butter
Salt and freshly ground pepper

Sauté the chopped livers in the 4 tablespoons of butter in a frying pan over medium heat for 3 minutes and then remove with a slotted spoon to a bowl. Add the sliced apples to the pan and turn lightly until they are barely soft but still hold their shape. Add them and any juices in the pan to the bowl with the livers. Add the remaining stuffing seasonings and mix gently. Stuff the duck loosely with the mixture, sew the openings, truss, and prick the vent, lower thighs, and lower breast with a fork and score with a sharp knife. Roast the duck and prepare a sauce in the manner described in Roast Duck [No. 1334]. Because of the stuffing, the total cooking time should be increased by ½ hour. *Serves* 4.

1338. DUCK STEW ITALIANA
Intingolo di anitra all'italiana

1 5-pound duck, cut up for frying
3 cups Chicken Stock [No. 3]
¼ cup oil
1 onion, stuck with 2 cloves
2 carrots, sliced
2 stalks celery, sliced

Bouquet Garni:
   3 sprigs rosemary (or ½ teaspoon dried)
   3 sprigs parsley
   1 bay leaf
¼ cup vinegar
Water (or red wine)
3 tablespoons Kneaded Butter [No. 107]
Salt and freshly ground pepper
6 slices bread, crusts removed, cut in half, and
   sautéed golden brown in oil

Cut the duck up for frying in advance and season lightly. It should be cut in the same manner as chicken, except each breast half should be cut in 2 pieces. Remove as much fat as possible. Put the back, wings, and giblets in a saucepan with the chicken stock over medium heat and simmer for 1 hour. Strain this stock and de-grease it. Heat the oil in a large, heavy pot over fairly high heat and quickly brown the remaining duck pieces on all sides. Drain off the fat in the pot and add onion, carrot, celery, Bouquet Garni, stock, vinegar, and sufficient water (or, if desired, red wine) to barely cover the duck pieces. Bring to a boil, reduce the heat, and simmer for about 1 hour, or until the duck pieces are tender. Remove them from the pot, strain and de-grease the cooking liquid, and return it to the pot. Bring to a boil, blend in the kneaded butter, and simmer for 5 minutes. Return the duck pieces to the pot, correct the seasoning, and simmer for 5 minutes longer. Arrange the duck pieces on a hot serving platter, pour the sauce over the pieces, and garnish with the slices of browned bread. *Serves* 4.

GUINEA HEN
Faraona

Guinea fowl were originally imported from Africa, but they are now commercially raised in the United States, as well as in most European countries. The flesh has a slightly gamy flavor and it is fairly dry, much less fat than chicken. The hens are generally more prized than roosters and they are usually marketed in sizes of about 2 pounds, although occasionally larger birds may be found.

1339. GUINEA HEN CACCIATORA
Faraona come piace al cacciatore

2 2-pound guinea hens, cleaned
6 large sprigs parsley
2 large, thin sheets of fresh pork fat back
6 tablespoons butter, softened
1 clove garlic, crushed in the garlic-press
1 pound mushrooms, sliced
1½ cups Game Stock [No. 7], or Chicken Stock [No. 3]
½ pound diced lean salt pork, parboiled 15 minutes, drained, and sautéed golden brown on all sides
Juice of 1 lemon
Salt and freshly ground pepper

Season the cavities of the guinea with salt and pepper and stuff 3 sprigs of parsley into each. Tie a sheet of fat over each breast, truss securely, and spread each with 3 tablespoons of the butter. Place the fowl on their sides in a shallow roasting pan in a hot (450°) oven. Turn them on the other side after 5 minutes and baste. Turn them upright after another 5 minutes. Cook 5 minutes longer, reduce the heat to moderate (350°), and roast them for a total cooking time of about 1 hour, turning them every 15 minutes and basting with the juices in the pan. About 15 minutes before they are fully cooked, remove the pork fat from the breasts to allow them to brown. Test them for doneness after 50 minutes by lifting by the legs; if the juices that drain from the vent have only a faint trace of rosiness, they are fully cooked. Transfer them to a hot serving platter and keep warm. Pour off all but 2 tablespoons of the fat in the pan, add the garlic and mushrooms, and stir over moderate heat for 5 minutes. Add the game (or chicken) stock, bring to a boil, and de-glaze the pan by scraping the sides and bottom with a wooden spoon. Add the salt pork dice and reduce the stock over high heat by ⅓. Add the lemon juice and correct the seasoning. Remove from the heat and swirl in the remaining 3 tablespoons of butter, bit by bit. Cut the guinea hens in half with poultry shears, lay them cut side down on the platter, and spoon the sauce over them. *Serves* 4.

1340. GUINEA HEN IN CLAY
Faraona alla creta

2 2-pound guinea hens, cleaned
3 pounds soft potter's clay
Cheesecloth or thin straw matting
2 large sheets parchment paper
8 thin slices smoked ham
2 tablespoons chopped sage

2 tablespoons juniper berries
2 tablespoons chopped thyme
2 tablespoons chopped rosemary
6 tablespoons butter, softened
Salt and freshly ground pepper

Season the cavities of the guineas with salt and pepper and truss the birds securely. Divide the clay in half and press or roll each half out into a sheet about ½ inch thick. Cover each of these sheets with several thicknesses of cheesecloth or thin straw matting (in ancient Roman times a layer of straw was used), lay the parchment paper on top, and then cover the paper entirely with the slices of ham. Pound the herbs in a mortar until they form a paste and blend with the softened butter. Spread a thin layer of this mixture over the ham and place a guinea hen in the center. Completely encase the birds in each of the coverings: first the buttered ham, then the parchment paper, crimping the edges well to effect a tight seal, then the cheesecloth or straw, and finally the clay. Make absolutely certain that there are no holes or thin places in the clay which might burst during the cooking. Place the wrapped fowl on an oiled baking sheet in a moderate (325°) oven for 2½ hours. Arrange them on a serving platter and break open the clay shells at the table. *Serves* 4.

1341. BRAISED GUINEA HENS IN CREAM
Faraona in casseruola alla crema

Prepare in the same way and with the same ingredients as Braised Pheasant in Cream [No. 1486]. *Serves* 6.

GOOSE
Oca

European geese are considered by many gourmets to be superior to the American-grown variety. The practice of overfeeding geese in some European countries, however, is unacceptably cruel to most American minds. In any event, American geese have a delicious flavor and are far less popular fare than they might be. Geese are marketed in the United States when they are less than 6 months old and weigh from 8 to 12 pounds. They are similar to duck in flavor and in fat content and they receive much the same cooking treatment. Like duck also, the proportion of meat on a goose is

SEE
VERSE
FOR
PTION

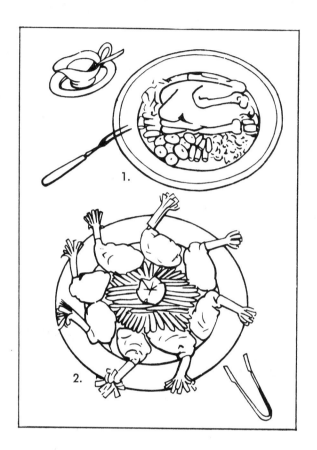

1. Braised Capon Angela Theresa (No. 1313)

2. Breast of Chicken Maréchale (No. 1288). In this presentation the wingbones of the chicken have been left in the breasts and the truffle garnish has been omitted.

1. Roast Turkey with Sausage and Chestnut Stuffing (No. 1320). In this presentation the garnish consists of additional whole boiled chestnuts on orange slices, strips of additional lean fatback, lightly broiled, and roast potatoes.

2. Squab with Black Olives (No. 1350)

relatively small, and thus it is wise to allow 1½ pounds of goose for each person to be served.

Goose liver is particularly delicious and generally considered superior to that of other poultry. Goose fat may be rendered and used as a sautéeing fat, or, although it is an acquired taste, cold rendered goose fat can be delicious simply spread on bread.

1342. BRAISED STUFFED GOOSE INGLESE
Oca farcita all'inglese

1 9-pound goose, cleaned
6 onions
4 cups bread cubes, soaked in milk and squeezed almost dry
2 tablespoons chopped sage (or 1 tablespoon dried)
Pinch nutmeg
6 tablespoons butter
1 cup dry white wine
1 cup Chicken Stock [No. 3]
Bouquet Garni:
　3 sprigs parsley
　2 sprigs thyme (or ½ teaspoon dried)
　1 bay leaf
3 tablespoons Kneaded Butter [No. 107]
Salt and pinch freshly ground pepper

Put the onions, unpeeled, on a baking sheet in a moderate (350°) oven for 20 minutes. Remove them from the oven, cool, peel, and then chop them coarsely. Mix them in a bowl with the bread, sage, nutmeg, and salt and pepper to taste. Remove as much fat as possible from the goose, and stuff it loosely with this mixture, sew the openings, truss securely, and prick the vent, lower thighs, and lower breast several times with a fork, and score the bird all over with a sharp knife. Heat the butter in a very large pot or Dutch oven over fairly high heat until golden and brown the goose on all sides. Add the wine and reduce to ½ its quantity. Add the stock and Bouquet Garni, bring to a boil, cover tightly, and then place the pot in a moderate (350°) oven for 4 hours. Baste several times during the cooking. The goose will be fully cooked when, if pricked with a fork in the fleshy part of the thigh, the juices run clear yellow. Transfer the goose to a hot serving platter and keep warm. Discard the Bouquet Garni, de-grease the liquid in the pot (there should be about 3 cups; if necessary, add a little more chicken stock to make up this quantity), bring to a boil, blend in the kneaded butter with a whisk, correct the seasoning, and simmer for 10 minutes. Serve this sauce

Roast Goose (No. 1343)

separately in a sauceboat and, if desired, serve a side dish of applesauce. *Serves* 6.

1343. ROAST GOOSE
Oca arrostita

1 9-pound goose, cleaned
1 onion, sliced
1 stalk celery, sliced
4 sprigs parsley
Boiling water
3 cups Chicken Stock [No. 3]
Giblets from the goose
3 tablespoons butter
Salt and freshly ground pepper

Remove as much fat from the goose as possible, and season the cavity with salt and pepper and stuff it with the onion, celery, and parsley. Truss it securely and prick it with a fork on the vent, lower thighs, and lower breast, and score it all over with a sharp knife. Place it breast-side up on a rack in a shallow roasting pan in a hot (450°) oven for 15 minutes. Baste it with 4 tablespoons of boiling water, reduce the heat to moderate (350°), and continue roasting for a total cooking time of about 4 hours, adding 2 tablespoons of boiling water to the pan every 15 minutes. After this time begin testing for doneness by pricking the fleshy part of the thigh with a fork; when the juices run clear yellow, it is fully cooked. Do not overcook so that the breast meat is dry. Remove the goose to a hot serving platter and keep warm. While the goose is roasting, simmer the giblets in the stock for 2 hours in a covered saucepan over low heat and then de-

465

grease. Place the roasting pan over high heat and evaporate all the juices, leaving only fat, but being careful not to burn the congealed "drippings" in the bottom. Drain off all the fat and de-glaze the pan with the stock over high heat by scraping the sides and bottom with a wooden spoon. Simmer until slightly reduced and of a good strong flavor. Correct the seasoning, remove from the heat, and swirl in the butter, bit by bit. Serve this sauce separately in a sauceboat. *Serves* 6.

1344. ROAST STUFFED GOOSE BORGHESE
Oca farcita alla borghese

1 9-pound goose, cleaned
Stuffing ingredients:
  2 onions, chopped
  2 tablespoons butter
  1 pound lean fresh pork, finely ground with
      ¼ pound salt pork
  6 green apples, cored and thickly sliced
  The goose liver, chopped and sautéed 2 minutes in
      1 tablespoon butter
  2 eggs, beaten
  3 tablespoons brandy
  3 tablespoons rendered goose fat
  1½ pounds chestnuts, peeled, cooked, and coarsely
      chopped [*see* No. 1320]
  ½ teaspoon allspice
  2 tablespoons pine nuts, coarsely chopped
  1 teaspoon salt
Boiling water
3 cups Chicken Stock [No. 3]
Giblets from the goose
3 tablespoons butter
Salt and freshly ground pepper

Gently sauté the chopped onion in 2 tablespoons of butter until it is soft and then mix it in a bowl with all of the other stuffing ingredients. The mixture should be moist; if it seems dry, add a little of the stock in which the chestnuts cooked. Stuff the goose loosely with the mixture, sew the openings, truss it securely, and prick it several times in the vent, lower thigh, and the lower breast, and score it all over with a sharp knife. Roast the goose and prepare the sauce in the manner described in Roast Goose [No. 1343]. Because of the stuffing, increase the total cooking time by 45 minutes. If desired, the goose may be garnished with sautéed Italian sausages and a dish of tart applesauce may be served on the side. *Serves* 6.

1345. ROAST GOOSE PAESANA
Oca alla paesana con salsa al rafano

1 9-pound goose, cleaned
Stuffing ingredients:
  The goose liver, chopped and sautéed 3 minutes in
      2 tablespoons butter
  ¼ pound chicken livers, chopped and sautéed
      3 minutes in 2 tablespoons butter
  4 cups fresh bread cubes, soaked in milk and
      squeezed almost dry
  1 cup diced lean salt pork, parboiled 5 minutes
  3 onions, chopped and sautéed in 3 tablespoons butter
      until soft
  1 tablespoon chopped parsley
  1 tablespoon chopped sage
  1 egg
  4 apples, peeled, cored, and sliced
  1 teaspoon salt
  ¼ teaspoon freshly ground pepper
Boiling water
3 cups Chicken Stock [No. 3]
Giblets from the goose
3 tablespoons butter
Salt and freshly ground pepper

Mix all of the stuffing ingredients thoroughly together in a bowl. Stuff the goose loosely, sew the openings, truss securely, and prick the vent, lower thighs, and lower breast several times with a fork, and score it all over with a sharp knife. Roast the goose and prepare the sauce in the manner described in Roast Goose [No. 1343]. Because of the stuffing, increase the total cooking time by 45 minutes. *Serves* 6.

1346. GOOSE STEW WITH SAUSAGE AND CHESTNUTS
Ragù d'oca con luganega e castagne

1 8-pound goose, cleaned, cut up for frying, and with
    as much fat as possible removed from the pieces
6 tablespoons fat from the above
1 clove garlic, crushed in the garlic-press
1 onion, sliced
1 carrot, sliced
1 dry cup white wine
½ teaspoon brown sugar
3 cups Chicken Stock [No. 3]
1 cup Tomato Sauce [No. 19]
Bouquet Garni:
  3 sprigs parsley
  2 sprigs thyme (or ½ teaspoon dried)
  1 bay leaf

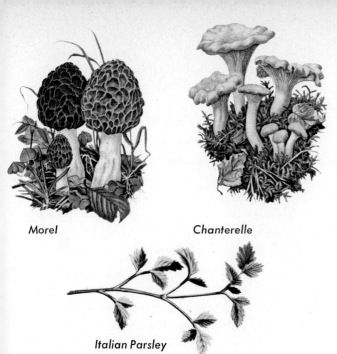

Morel

Chanterelle

Italian Parsley

1352. SQUAB WITH ONIONS AND MUSHROOMS
Piccioncelli in composta

4 1-pound squabs, cleaned
6 tablespoons Clarified Butter [No. 102]
½ cup dry white wine
2 tablespoons flour
2 cups hot Chicken Stock [No. 3]
Bouquet Garni:
   3 sprigs parsley
   2 sprigs thyme (or ½ teaspoon dried)
   1 bay leaf
1 cup diced lean salt pork, parboiled 10 minutes,
   drained, and sautéed until golden brown
12 Braised White Onions [No. 1721]
½ pound mushrooms, sliced and gently sautéed in
   3 tablespoons butter for 8 minutes
Salt and freshly ground pepper

Season the cavities of the squabs with salt and pepper and truss the birds securely. Heat the butter in a large casserole over fairly high heat and brown the squabs on all sides. Remove them temporarily from the casserole and drain off all but 2 tablespoons of the butter. Add the wine and cook until entirely evaporated. Add the flour, stir until it begins to color, add the hot stock, and stir until slightly thickened. Add the Bouquet Garni and the salt pork dice and return the squabs to the casserole. Cover tightly and cook for about 30 minutes, or until the squabs are tender. Turn them frequently during the cooking. Correct the seasoning, arrange the squabs on a hot serving platter, spoon the sauce over them, and garnish with the onions and small heaps of the mushrooms. *Serves* 4.

1353. SQUAB WITH FRESH PEAS
Piccioncelli con piselli freschi

Prepare with the same ingredients and in the same manner as described in the preceding recipe, omitting the onions and mushrooms and adding to the casserole 5 minutes before the squabs are fully cooked ½ cup of chopped prosciutto (or ham) and 1 pound shelled peas which have been cooked in lightly salted water until just tender.

1354. SQUAB RICHELIEU
Piccioncelli alla Richelieu

4 1-pound squabs, cleaned
2 eggs, beaten
2 cups fresh breadcrumbs
6 tablespoons Clarified Butter [No. 102]
2 white truffles, sliced [or No. 1819a]
1 cup Maître d'Hôtel Butter [No. 111], softened
Salt and freshly ground pepper

Split the squabs in half down their backs, spread them out without separating the halves, and flatten them slightly with the flat side of a meat cleaver. Season them with salt and pepper, dip in beaten egg, and cover with a generous amount of breadcrumbs. Heat the butter in a very large frying pan (or use 2 frying pans with slightly more butter if necessary to avoid crowding) and brown the squabs on both sides. Reduce the heat and sauté gently for about 25 minutes, turning them frequently. Arrange them on a hot serving platter, sprinkle with the sliced truffles, and top each with a generous spoonful of the maître d'hôtel butter. Serve the rest of the butter on the side. *Serves* 4.

Tarragon

Savory

469

1355. ROAST SQUAB
Piccioncelli arrostiti

4 1-pound squabs, cleaned
4 thin sheets pork fat belly
6 tablespoons butter, softened
1½ cups Chicken Stock [No. 3]
Juice of 1 lemon
3 tablespoons butter, softened
Salt and freshly ground pepper

Season the cavities of the squabs with salt and pepper, tie the sheets of pork fat over the breasts, and truss the birds securely. Spread them with the softened butter and place them on their sides in a roasting pan in a hot (450°) oven for 5 minutes. Turn them breast-side up and roast for another 5 minutes. Turn them on their other side and roast for another 5 minutes. Reduce the heat to moderate (350°) and roast for a total cooking time of about 45 minutes, turning them and basting frequently. About 15 minutes before they are fully cooked, remove the pork fat from the breasts and allow them to brown. Transfer the birds to a hot serving platter and keep warm. Pour off most of the fat in the pan, add the stock, and reduce over high heat by ⅓. Correct the seasoning, add the lemon juice, remove from the heat, swirl in the 3 tablespoons of butter, bit by bit, and spoon this sauce over the squabs. *Serves* 4.

1356. SQUAB ST. GERMAIN
Piccioncelli Saint-Germain

4 1-pound squabs, cleaned
1 cup butter, melted
2 cups fresh breadcrumbs
2 cups Sauce Béarnaise [No. 67]
3 tablespoons hot Brown Veal Stock [No. 5]
Salt and freshly ground pepper

Split the squabs in half down their backs, spread them out without separating the halves, and flatten them slightly with the flat side of a meat cleaver. Season them with salt and pepper, brush them with melted butter, cover generously with breadcrumbs, and sprinkle with more butter. Place them on a rack about 6 inches beneath a medium broiler flame for 15 minutes, basting them once with more butter and adjusting the heat so that they do not brown too quickly. Turn them over, baste with more butter, and cook for about 10 minutes longer. Arrange them on a hot serving platter and serve the Béarnaise, into which the veal stock has been beaten, separately in a sauceboat. *Serves* 4.

FRIED SPECIALTIES
AND VARIETY MEATS

CROQUETTES, FRITTI, STECCHI, AND SUPPLÌ

Crocchette, fritti, stecchi, e supplì

In this section we will deal with a number of special entrée dishes, most of which are fried in deep fat. Some of these, like croquettes, will be familiar to any American cook, but many are peculiarly and very specially Italian.

Basil

CROQUETTES

Crocchette

In addition to serving as an appetizer with cocktails or as a hot hors d'oeuvre, croquettes can be a delicious and delicate entrée dish. For general information on the preparation of croquettes, *see* page 84

1357. CROQUETTES
Preparazione di base

3 cups cooked chopped meat, chicken, fish, etc.
1 cup cooked chopped mushrooms (about ½ pound, sautéed in 3 tablespoons butter)
1 tablespoon chopped truffle [or No. 1819a]
½ cup dry white wine
3 egg yolks, beaten
2½ cups Velouté Sauce [No. 17] reduced to 1½ cups and cooled (*see* Note below)
2 tablespoons butter
3 eggs, beaten
2 cups breadcrumbs
Salt and freshly ground pepper
Fat for deep frying

Put the cooked meat, mushrooms, chopped truffle, and wine in a saucepan over medium heat, season with salt and pepper, and cook until the wine has almost evaporated. Mix the egg yolks with the cooled Velouté sauce and then stir the mixture into the saucepan. Place over low heat, stirring constantly until very thick, but do not boil. Remove from the heat, stir in the butter, and allow to cool completely. When cool, shape the mixture with moistened hands into 6 croquette shapes—cones, balls, cylinders, etc.—or form it into 12 smaller shapes. Dip in beaten egg, roll in breadcrumbs, and allow to rest for 10 minutes. Fry the croquettes in deep hot (375°) fat until golden brown. The croquettes must not touch one another during the cooking, or they will burst; it is advisable to use a wire basket for their easy submersion in the fat and their removal. When they are all cooked, sprinkle with a little salt and serve at once. *Serves* 6.

NOTE: Any thickened sauce appropriate to the other ingredients may be substituted for the Velouté, such as Sauce Mornay [No. 56], Italian Meat Sauce [No. 41], Demi-Glaze Sauce [No. 20], etc.

1358. CHICKEN CROQUETTES ACCADEMIA ITALIANA DELLA CUCINA
Crocchette di pollo "Accademia Italiana della Cucina"

3 cups cooked chopped chicken meat
1 cup cooked chopped mushrooms (about ½ pound, gently sautéed in 3 tablespoons butter)
¼ cup chopped prosciutto
2½ cups Sauce Mornay [No. 56], reduced to 1½ cups
½ cup Italian Meat Sauce [No. 41], reduced to ¼ cup
2 tablespoons butter, softened
2 eggs, beaten
2 cups breadcrumbs
6 sprigs parsley, fried in deep fat [*see* No. 276]
2 lemons, quartered
Salt and freshly ground pepper
Fat for deep frying

Proceed generally in the manner described in the preceding recipe. Combine the chicken, mushrooms, and the prosciutto in a saucepan with the Mornay and Italian meat sauce. Season, if necessary, with salt and pepper. Simmer the mixture over low heat until very hot, cool, beat in the butter, form into any desired croquette shapes, dip in beaten egg, roll in breadcrumbs, and allow to rest for 10 minutes. Fry the croquettes in deep hot (375°) fat until golden brown, drain, arrange them on a hot serving platter, and garnish with the fried parsley and lemon quarters. *Serves* 6.

472

1359. CODFISH CROQUETTES WITH TOMATO SAUCE
Crocchette di baccalà con salsa al pomodoro

3 cups salt codfish, soaked and cooked [*see* No. 790]
1½ cups Duchesse Potato Base [No. 1770]
2 cups hot Béchamel Sauce [No. 18], reduced to 1 cup
2 eggs, beaten
2 cups breadcrumbs
2 cups hot Tomato Sauce [No. 19]
Salt and freshly ground pepper
Fat for deep frying

Chop the cooked fish coarsely and then pound it to a paste in the mortar (or press through a fine sieve). Mix it thoroughly with the potato mixture and the Béchamel sauce and season only if necessary with salt and pepper. Allow the mixture to cool. Shape into croquettes and fry in deep fat in the manner described in Croquettes [No. 1357]. Drain them when they are golden brown, arrange them on a hot serving platter, and pour the tomato sauce over them. *Serves* 6.

1360. FONTINA CHEESE CROQUETTES
Crocchette di fontina

½ pound Fontina cheese, cubed
5 tablespoons butter
5 tablespoons flour
1 cup scalded milk
Pinch Cayenne pepper
Pinch nutmeg
Flour
2 eggs, beaten
2 cups breadcrumbs
Salt and freshly ground pepper
Fat for deep frying

Melt the butter in a saucepan over medium heat, stir in the flour, cook for 1 minute, add the hot milk, and stir constantly until very thick. Add the cheese and continue stirring until the cheese is melted. Season to taste with salt, pepper, Cayenne, and nutmeg. Pour the mixture into a shallow buttered dish and allow to cool completely. When cool, cut it into any desired shapes, dust the shapes with flour, dip in beaten egg, and coat completely with breadcrumbs. Allow the croquettes to rest for 10 minutes and then fry in deep hot (375°) fat in the manner described in Croquettes [No. 1357]. When they are golden brown, arrange them on a hot serving platter and season very lightly with salt. *Serves* 6.

1361. GRUYÈRE CHEESE CROQUETTES
Crocchette di groviera

Prepare in the same manner as the preceding recipe, substituting Gruyère cheese for the Fontina and adding, off the heat, 3 beaten egg yolks to the cheese mixture before it is allowed to cool. *Serves* 6.

1362. LAMB CROQUETTES WITH TOMATO SAUCE
Crocchette d'agnello con salsa al pomodoro

3 cups chopped cooked lamb
1 cup chopped cooked mushrooms (about ½ pound, gently sautéed in 3 tablespoons butter)
¼ cup chopped prosciutto
½ cup dry white wine
2½ cups Béchamel Sauce [No. 18], reduced to 1½ cups
3 egg yolks, beaten
2 tablespoons butter
3 eggs, beaten
2 cups breadcrumbs
Salt and freshly ground pepper
Fat for deep frying
2 cups hot Tomato Sauce [No. 19]

Prepare in the manner described in Croquettes [No. 1357], substituting the chopped prosciutto for the truffles. When all of the croquettes are fried golden brown, arrange them on a hot serving platter and pour the tomato sauce over them. *Serves* 6.

1363. MUSSEL CROQUETTES
Crocchette di cozze

24 mussels, scrubbed and soaked (*see* page 343)
1 onion, chopped
1 cup dry white wine
½ teaspoon dried thyme
1 bay leaf
2½ cups Béchamel Sauce [No. 18], reduced to 1½ cups
1 cup chopped cooked mushrooms (about ½ pound, gently sautéed in 3 tablespoons butter)
Flour
2 eggs, beaten
2 cups breadcrumbs
6 sprigs parsley, fried in deep fat [*see* No. 276]
2 lemons, quartered
Salt and freshly ground pepper
Fat for deep frying

Put the onion, wine, thyme, and bay leaf in a heavy pot, bring to a boil over medium heat, and simmer for 5 minutes. Add the mussels, cover the pot tightly, raise the heat, and cook for about 5 minutes, or until all of the mussels open. Shake the pan every few seconds to facilitate their opening. Pour the contents of the pot into a sieve placed over a bowl. Extract the mussels from their shells, allowing any liquid to drain into the bowl. Chop the mussels coarsely and reserve. Strain the mussel liquid through several thicknesses of damp cheesecloth into a saucepan and then reduce over high heat to a few tablespoons. Add the Béchamel sauce and, when well blended, add the mussels and mushrooms. Correct the seasoning and stir over medium heat until the mixture is heated through. Pour it into a shallow dish and allow to cool. When cool, form it into any desired croquette shapes, dust with flour, dip in beaten egg, coat completely with breadcrumbs, and then allow the croquettes to rest for 10 minutes. Fry the croquettes in the manner described in Croquettes [No. 1357], arrange them on a hot serving platter when they are golden brown, and garnish with the lemon quarters and the fried parsley. *Serves* 6.

Preparation of Polenta Croquettes Italiana (No. 1364)

1364. POLENTA CROQUETTES ITALIANA
Crocchette di polenta all'italiana

½ recipe hot Polenta [No. 623]
¾ cup grated Parmesan cheese
12 cubes of Gruyère cheese, about ¾ inch square
Flour
2 eggs, beaten
2 cups breadcrumbs
Fat for deep frying
2 cups hot Tomato Sauce [No. 19]

Blend the Parmesan cheese with the polenta in a saucepan over medium heat and stir until the cheese is melted. Drop the mixture by very large spoonsful (each spoonful should be about the size of an egg; gauge the size of each so that there will be 12 spoonsful in all) onto an enameled surface (or large platter) moistened with water. As quickly as each little clump of the polenta is cool enough to handle, press a cube of Gruyère cheese into the center and then close the polenta over the cheese so that it is entirely encased. Roll each in flour, dip in beaten egg, coat with breadcrumbs, and allow to rest for 10 minutes. Fry in deep hot (375°) fat in the manner described in Croquettes [No. 1357]. When they are golden brown, arrange the croquettes on a hot serving platter and spoon the sauce over them.

1365. POLENTA CROQUETTES ITALIANA WITH BACON
Crocchette di polenta all'italiana con "bacon"

Prepare in the same manner as the preceding recipe, alternating the croquettes on the platter with thick slices of broiled bacon. *Serves* 6.

1366. POTATO CROQUETTES STUFFED WITH CHEESE AND HAM
Crocchette di patate con mozzarella e prosciutto

1½ pounds "old" potatoes, peeled and quartered
6 tablespoons butter, melted
¼ cup grated Parmesan cheese
3 egg yolks
1 cup mozzarella cheese, cut into tiny cubes
½ cup chopped prosciutto
2 tablespoons chopped parsley
Flour
2 eggs, beaten
2 cups breadcrumbs
Salt and freshly ground pepper
Fat for deep frying

Cook the potatoes in lightly salted water in a saucepan over medium heat for about 20 minutes, or until they are barely tender. Drain, purée through a ricer or food mill, return them to the saucepan, and stir them over low heat for a few minutes to dry them, being careful not to scorch the bottom. Remove from the heat, stir in the butter and Parmesan cheese, season with salt

Preparation of Potato Croquettes Stuffed with Ham and Cheese (No. 1366)

and pepper, and then blend in the egg yolks. Pour the mixture into a shallow platter and allow to cool completely. When cool, turn it out onto a floured board, form it into a long roll about 3 inches in diameter, and then divide it into 12 equal slices. Mix the mozzarella, prosciutto, and parsley together, place a generous spoonful of this mixture in the center of each slice of the potato mixture, and then close the potatoes over the chopped mixture so that it is completely encased. Roll each into a ball, dust with flour, dip in beaten egg, roll in breadcrumbs, and then allow them to rest for 10 minutes. Fry in deep hot (375°) fat in the manner described in Croquettes [No. 1357] and, when golden brown, arrange them on a hot serving platter. *Serves 6.*

1367. SPAGHETTI CROQUETTES ITALIANA
Crocchette di spaghetti all'italiana

½ pound spaghetti
4 tablespoons butter
1 cup chopped cooked chicken
1 cup chopped boiled tongue
½ cup grated Parmesan cheese
2 cups Béchamel Sauce [No. 18], reduced to 1 cup
1 cup Tomato Sauce [No. 19]
Flour
2 eggs, beaten
2 cups breadcrumbs
Salt and freshly ground pepper
Fat for deep frying
2 cups hot Italian Meat Sauce [No. 41]

Break the spaghetti into very short pieces and cook it in lightly salted boiling water until just *al dente*. Drain

it well, turn it into a bowl, mix in the butter, and then add the chicken, tongue, grated cheese, and the Béchamel and tomato sauces. Season to taste with salt and pepper and allow the mixture to cool completely. When cool, form it into any desired croquette shapes, dust them with flour, dip in beaten egg, roll in breadcrumbs, and then allow them to rest for 10 minutes. Fry in deep hot (375°) fat in the manner described in Croquettes [No. 1357], arrange them on a hot serving platter when they are golden brown, and spoon the meat sauce over them. *Serves 6.*

FRITTI
Fritti

Fritti (fried foods) are an Italian specialty that can be very simple, or, like the famous *Fritto Misto,* can be a very impressive array of meats, fish, and vegetables. The contents of the more complicated *Fritti* naturally vary from region to region in Italy, each containing local specialties and whatever very fresh ingredients are seasonably available.

1368. FRITTO BOLOGNESE
Fritto composto alla bolognese

½ pound cooked lean veal
¾ pound lamb's or calf's brains, soaked and parboiled (*see* page 481)
½ cup chopped prosciutto (fat and lean)
3 tablespoons butter
1½ cups Béchamel Sauce [No. 18], reduced to 1 cup
1 whole egg and 1 egg yolk
2 tablespoons chopped truffle [or No. 1819a]
½ cup grated Parmesan cheese
Pinch nutmeg
Flour
2 eggs, beaten
2 cups fresh breadcrumbs
2 lemons, quartered
Salt and freshly ground pepper
Fat for deep frying

Put the veal, lamb's brains, and prosciutto through the meat grinder, using the finest blade. Heat the butter in a frying pan over medium heat; add the ground meats, Béchamel sauce, egg, and egg yolk; and stir just until very hot and slightly thickened. Remove from

475

the heat, stir in the chopped truffle and grated cheese, and season with salt, pepper, and nutmeg. Turn the mixture out into a shallow dish and allow to cool completely. When cool, form the mixture into small balls with moistened hands, dust them with flour, dip in beaten egg, and roll in breadcrumbs. Allow the balls to rest for 10 minutes and then fry in deep hot (375°) fat until golden brown, being careful that the balls do not touch each other as they cook. Drain, arrange them on a hot serving platter, and garnish with the lemon quarters. *Serves* 4.

1369. FRITTO MISTO BOLOGNESE
Fritto misto alla bolognese

6 very small Stecchi Bolognese [No. 1380]
6 small Chicken Croquettes Accademia Italiana
 della Cucina [No. 1358]
½ pound calf's brains, soaked and parboiled
 (*see* page 481)
6 small loin lamb chops, cut ½ inch thick and boned
6 slices calf's liver, cut ¼ inch thick
1 pound zucchini, quartered lengthwise
6 very small artichokes, cut in half, trimmed,
 and parboiled until just tender (*see* page 539)
6 flowerets of cauliflower, parboiled in lightly salted
 water for 10 minutes
Flour
1 cup Fritter Batter [No. 275]
3 eggs, beaten
1 cup breadcrumbs
¾ cup butter
Salt and freshly ground pepper
3 lemons, quartered
Fat for deep frying

Make all of the preliminary preparations, preparatory to frying, for the Stecchi and chicken croquettes. Drain thoroughly and dry the brains, slice them, season with salt and pepper, and dust them with flour. Season the lamb chops and calf's liver with salt and pepper and dust them with flour. Drain thoroughly and dry the artichokes and the cauliflower and then dust them and the zucchini with flour. In order to speed up the frying of the various ingredients, use, if possible, 2 or more pans of deep fat and 2 frying pans, all at the same time. The Stecchi and croquettes are fried in deep hot (375°) fat as described in Nos. 1380 and 1358, respectively. Dip the sliced calf's brains in beaten egg, and sauté immediately in 4 tablespoons of very hot butter in a frying pan until golden on both sides. Dip the lamb chops in beaten egg, cover with breadcrumbs, and sauté in 4 tablespoons of very hot butter for about 3 minutes on each side, or until they are golden brown. Sauté the calf's liver in another 4 tablespoons of very hot butter for about 2 minutes on each side. Fry the artichokes in deep hot (375°) fat until golden brown. Dip the cauliflower in fritter batter and then fry in deep fat until golden brown. Dip the zucchini in beaten egg, drop immediately into deep hot fat, and fry until golden brown. As each of these ingredients is fully cooked and brown, arrange on a hot serving platter and keep warm. When all are done, garnish the platter with lemon quarters and serve immediately. *Serves* 6 to 8.

*Fritto
Misto
Milanese
(No. 1370)*

1370. FRITTO MISTO MILANESE
Fritto misto alla milanese

Prepare in the same manner and with the same ingredients as the preceding recipe, omitting the Stecchi Bolognese and lamb chops. Substitute in their place 6 thin slices of veal cut from the upper leg (cooked in the same manner as the lamb chops) and ½ pound veal sweetbreads which have been soaked, parboiled (*see* page 496), and then sautéed in the same manner as the brains. An optional addition is 12 cocks' combs, parboiled until just tender in lightly salted boiling water, drained, dusted with flour, and then sautéed in 3 tablespoons of butter. The butter in which the various ingredients were cooked may be sprinkled over all of the ingredients just before serving and then the whole platter sprinkled with chopped parsley. *Serves* 6.

1371. GNOCCHI FRITTO PIEMONTESE
Fritto di gnocchetti alla piemontese

2 cups milk
6 tablespoons butter
½ cup sifted flour
¼ cup semolina
½ cup grated Parmesan cheese
½ cup Gruyère cheese, cubed
2 egg yolks
2 tablespoons chopped truffle [or No. 1819a]
Pinch sugar
Pinch nutmeg
Salt and freshly ground white pepper
Flour
2 eggs, beaten
2 cups breadcrumbs
Fat for deep frying

Put the milk and butter in a saucepan over medium heat, bring slowly to a boil, and then add the flour mixed with the semolina in a slow steady stream, stirring constantly to avoid any lumps. Add the Parmesan and Gruyère cheese and cook until they are melted and well blended. Remove from the heat, stir in the egg yolks and chopped truffle, and season with salt, pepper, nutmeg, and sugar. Pour the mixture out onto an enameled surface, spread it out to a thickness of ¾ inch, and allow it to cool completely. When cold, cut it into small rectangles, or any other desired shapes, dust them with flour, dip in beaten egg, and cover generously with breadcrumbs. Allow them to rest for 10 minutes and then fry in deep hot (375°) fat until

golden brown. Drain, heap them up on a hot serving platter, and serve at once. *Serves* 6.

1372. MOZZARELLA IN CARROZZA WITH ANCHOVY BUTTER
Mozzarella in carrozza con burro d'alici

6 slices bread, crusts removed, cut in half
(or use 12 thin slices of French or Italian bread)
12 slices mozzarella cheese, cut ½ inch thick and
about the same size as the half slices of bread
½ cup milk, slightly warmed
2 eggs, beaten
Fat for deep frying
1 cup Anchovy Butter [No. 108]

Place the mozzarella on the slices of bread, pressing it down firmly around the edges so that it will adhere. Sprinkle the undersides of the bread with a little milk, dust the bread and the cheese topping with flour, dip in beaten egg and then in flour again, and then drop immediately in deep hot (375°) fat until golden brown. Drain, arrange them on a hot serving platter, and serve the anchovy butter on the side. *Serves* 6.

1373. MOZZARELLA MILANESE
Mozzarella alla milanese

12 slices mozzarella cheese, ½ inch thick
Flour
2 eggs, beaten
6 tablespoons butter
Salt and freshly ground pepper

Heat the butter in a frying pan over medium heat until almost golden, dust the slices of cheese with flour, dip them in beaten egg, and drop immediately into the hot butter. Cook them on both sides until they are golden brown, drain on absorbent paper, arrange them on a hot serving platter, and sprinkle with a little salt and pepper. *Serves* 6.

477

1374. PROVOLA CHEESE FRITTO
Fritto di provola

Prepare in the same manner as the preceding recipe, substituting provola cheese for the mozzarella.

1375. RICOTTA CHEESE FRITTO
Fritto di ricotta

1/2 pound ricotta cheese
1/2 cup sifted flour
3 eggs
1/2 teaspoon salt
1 tablespoon sugar
Grated peel of 1 lemon
Flour
Fat for deep frying

Mix thoroughly together in a bowl the ricotta, 1/2 cup of flour, eggs, salt, sugar, and lemon peel. Chill for 2 hours. Roll the mixture, a generous spoonful at a time, in flour and then fry these balls in deep hot (375°) fat until they are golden brown. Drain and serve immediately. *Serves* 6.

1376. FRITTO ROMANA
Fritto composto alla romana

3 cups chopped cooked chicken meat
1 cup chopped boiled tongue
3 tablespoons butter
1 onion, chopped
2 1/2 cups Sauce Mornay [No. 56], reduced to 1 1/2 cups
Salt and freshly ground pepper
Flour
2 eggs, beaten
2 cups breadcrumbs
Fat for deep frying
2 lemons, quartered

Heat the butter in a frying pan over medium heat, add the onion, and cook until transparent. Add the chopped tongue, chopped chicken, and Mornay sauce. Season to taste with salt and pepper and heat just until thoroughly hot. Turn the mixture out into a shallow dish and allow to cool completely. When cool, shape the mixture into small ovals with moistened hands, dust with flour, dip in beaten egg, coat generously with breadcrumbs, and allow to rest for 10 minutes. Fry the ovals in deep hot (375°) fat until golden brown, drain, arrange them on a hot serving platter, and garnish with the lemon quarters. *Serves* 6.

1377. FRITTO MISTO ROMANA
Fritto misto alla romana

Prepare generally in the same manner and with the same ingredients as Fritto Misto Bolognese [No. 1369], but using 1 pound of calf's (or lamb's) brains, 1 pound veal sweetbreads, and 1 pound veal (or lamb's) kidneys in place of the meats specified in No. 1369. The sweetbreads should be soaked, parboiled (*see* page 496), sliced, and cooked in the same manner as the brains. The kidneys should be trimmed and cooked in the manner described in Veal Kidneys Trifolato with Lemon [No. 1428]. If desired, the platter may be additionally garnished with 6 rectangles of bread which have been dipped in 1 cup of milk beaten with 2 eggs and then fried until golden brown in deep hot (375°) fat. *Serves* 6.

1378. FROGS' LEGS FRITTO
Fritto di ranocchi

36 pairs frogs' legs
A marinade:
    1 onion, sliced
    2 tablespoons chopped parsley
    1 teaspoon salt
    1/4 teaspoon freshly ground pepper
    Pinch nutmeg
    1 1/2 cups dry Marsala wine
Flour
2 eggs, beaten
3 lemons, quartered
Fat for deep frying

Mix all of the marinade ingredients in a bowl and marinate the frogs' legs in the mixture for 3 hours, turning them occasionally. Drain them, dry very thoroughly on paper towels, dust with flour, dip in beaten egg, and then drop them immediately into deep hot (375°) fat until they are golden brown. Do not crowd the frogs' legs in the fat; cook only about 6 or 8 at a time, or, if desired, use 2 pans of deep fat. Arrange them on a hot serving platter and garnish with the lemon quarters. *Serves* 6.

1379. PANDORATO WITH MOZZARELLA AND ANCHOVIES
Pandorato con mozzarella e alici

1 loaf unsliced slightly stale bread, crusts removed, and cut into 6 slices about 1 inch thick
12 slices mozzarella cheese
12 anchovy fillets, washed free of salt [*see* No. 220]

478

1 cup milk, slightly warmed
Flour
3 eggs, beaten with $\frac{1}{2}$ teaspoon salt
$\frac{1}{2}$ cup butter
Salt

Halve the 6 slices of bread to form rectangles. Scoop out the center of each of these rectangles to form a long hollow about $\frac{1}{2}$ inch deep. Trim the slices of mozzarella so that they will fit neatly into the hollows and then top each with an anchovy fillet. Sprinkle the bread cases lightly with milk and dust them with flour. Put the beaten eggs in a shallow dish large enough to contain all of the rectangles of bread and let them sit in the eggs for about 20 minutes to absorb as much as possible, occasionally spooning a little of the egg over the tops of the cases. Heat 4 tablespoons of the butter in a large frying pan over medium heat and sauté the cases cheese side up, a few at a time, adding more butter as necessary (or use 2 frying pans with the remaining butter). When the undersides are golden brown and the cheese slightly melted, turn the cases quickly and brown the top side. When both sides are golden, transfer them to a hot serving platter and keep warm while the remaining cases are browned. Sprinkle the cases lightly with salt before serving. *Serves 6.*

STECCHI
Stecchi

Stecchi are prepared by spearing a variety of savory ingredients on thin wooden skewers and then frying them in deep fat.

1380. STECCHI BOLOGNESE
Stecchi alla bolognese

6 large slices veal, cut $\frac{1}{2}$ inch thick from the upper
    part of the leg
6 tablespoons butter
9 sweet Italian sausages
18 slices Gruyère cheese, cut $1\frac{1}{2}$ inches square
    and $\frac{1}{2}$ inch thick
18 cubes crustless bread, cut $1\frac{1}{2}$ inches square
    and 1 inch thick
6 thin wooden skewers
$1\frac{1}{2}$ cups milk, slightly warmed
Flour
4 eggs, beaten with 1 teaspoon salt

3 cups fresh breadcrumbs
Salt and freshly ground pepper
Fat for deep frying

Heat the butter in a large frying pan over fairly high heat until golden and sauté the slices of veal for about 3 minutes on each side. Remove them from the pan, season lightly with salt and pepper, cool, and cut each slice into 3 pieces; each piece should be about $1\frac{1}{2}$ inches square. Add the sausages to the frying pan and sauté over medium heat for about 15 minutes, turning them frequently. Remove them from the pan and cut them in half. Alternate the slices of veal, sausages, cheese, and bread cubes on the skewers, spearing 3 of each ingredient on each of the 6 skewers. Dip them quickly in milk, roll in flour, dip in beaten egg, and then coat with a generous amount of breadcrumbs. Allow them to rest for a few minutes and then fry them, a few at a time, in deep hot (375°) fat until golden brown on all sides. The pan of fat must be large enough so that the filled skewers are not crowded. If desired, use 2 pans of fat in order to fry all of them at once. Transfer them to a hot serving platter as soon as they are browned and season lightly with salt before serving. *Serves 6.*

1381. STECCHI GENOVESE
Stecchi alla genovese

9 large chicken livers, rapidly sautéed in 3 tablespoons
    of butter for 3 minutes and cut in half
$\frac{3}{4}$ pound veal sweetbreads, soaked, parboiled
    (*see* page 496), and cut into 18 slices about $\frac{1}{2}$ inch
    thick
9 slices boiled tongue, $\frac{1}{4}$ inch thick and cut in half
18 slices Gruyère cheese, cut $1\frac{1}{2}$ inches square
    and $\frac{1}{2}$ inch thick
6 thin wooden skewers
2 cups thick, cold Sauce Mornay [No. 56]
3 eggs, beaten
3 cups fresh breadcrumbs
Salt and freshly ground pepper
Fat for deep frying

Alternate the slices of sweetbreads, chicken livers, tongue, and cheese on the skewers, using 3 of each ingredient on each of the 6 skewers. Season them lightly with salt and pepper, spread the Mornay sauce over them so that they are completely covered, roll them in beaten egg, and then cover generously with breadcrumbs. Place the filled skewers in the refrigerator for 1 hour. When cold, fry them in deep hot (375°) fat until golden brown. Fry only 2 or 3 at a time so that they do not touch each other in the fat, or use 2 pans of fat in order to fry them all at once. Arrange them on a hot serving platter, season them lightly with salt, and serve immediately. *Serves 6.*

1382. STECCHI NAPOLETANA
Stecchi alla napoletana

18 slices eggplant, cut ½ inch thick and 1½ inches
    square
6 tablespoons oil
6 slightly green tomatoes, peeled, seeded, and cut into
    thirds
18 slices mozzarella cheese, cut ½ inch thick and
    1½ inches square
18 slices bread, cut ½ inch thick and 1½ inches square
6 wooden skewers
1½ cups milk, slightly warmed
Flour
3 eggs, beaten
Salt and freshly ground pepper
Fat for deep frying

Dust the squares of eggplant with flour and then sauté them, a few at a time, in hot oil in a very large frying pan for 1 to 2 minutes on each side, or until golden brown. When they are browned, remove them from the pan and allow them to cool on absorbent paper. Alternate the eggplant, tomatoes, mozzarella, and slices of bread on the skewers, using 3 of each ingredient on each of the 6 skewers, and sprinkle lightly with salt and pepper. Dip the filled skewers very quickly in milk, then in flour, dip in beaten egg, and then fry them immediately in deep hot (375°) fat until golden brown. Fry only 3 at a time to avoid crowding, or use 2 pans of deep fat in order to fry them all at once. Drain them when they are golden and serve immediately. *Serves 6.*

SUPPLÌ
Supplì

Supplì are a Roman specialty, resembling croquettes. They are most often made of large balls of rice, completely encasing a center of ham, cheese, or other savory ingredients, and are fried in deep fat. Italian rice, which is very glutinous, should be used. Long-grain rice is too "dry."

1383. RICE SUPPLÌ WITH HAM AND CHEESE
Supplì di riso con prosciutto e mozzarella

1 recipe Risotto with Butter and Parmesan Cheese
    [No. 572]
½ cup diced mozzarella cheese
½ cup grated Parmesan cheese
1 tablespoon chopped parsley
2 eggs
½ cup diced lean prosciutto
Pinch nutmeg
Salt and freshly ground pepper
Flour
2 eggs, beaten with ½ teaspoon salt
3 cups breadcrumbs
Fat for deep frying

Prepare the risotto and spread it out in a shallow dish to cool. The risotto should be slightly moist, but not wet. Mix the mozzarella in a bowl with the Parmesan, parsley, 2 eggs, and prosciutto. Season the mixture with salt, pepper, and nutmeg. When the rice is cold, form it with moistened hands into balls the size of small limes. Punch a fairly deep hole in the center

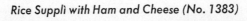
Rice Supplì with Ham and Cheese (No. 1383)

SEE
VERSE
FOR
PTION

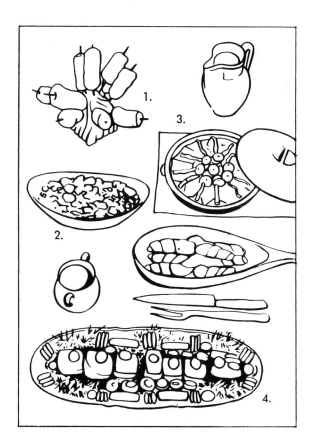

1. Stecchi Bolognese (No. 1380)

2. Rattatuia of Chicken Livers and Veal Kidneys (No. 1416)

3. Chicken Fricassee à l'Ancienne (No. 1271)

4. Oxtail Italiana (No. 1430). In this presentation the recipe has been additionally garnished with boiled chestnuts browned under the broiler, strips of sautéed lean fatback (or pre-parboiled and sautéed bacon), and Glazed Carrots (see No. 1647). For the preparation of boiled chestnuts see No. 1320 .

of each with the forefinger and place a generous spoonful of the ham and cheese mixture and a cube of mozzarella into each of the holes. Close the rice around the fillings so that they are completely encased. Coat the balls with flour, dip in beaten egg, and roll them in breadcrumbs. Allow the balls to rest for 10 minutes and then fry in deep medium-hot (350°) fat until golden brown. Do not crowd the balls in the fat; if desired, use 2 pans of fat so that they may all be browned at one time. Adjust the heat during the frying so that they do not brown too quickly and the heat may penetrate to the center of the balls. As they become brown, drain on absorbent paper and keep warm until all have been cooked. *Serves* 6.

1384. RICE SUPPLÌ WITH MUSHROOMS, CHICKEN LIVERS, AND SWEETBREADS
Supplì di riso con ragù e rigaglie

1 recipe Risotto with Butter and Parmesan Cheese [No. 572]
3 tablespoons butter
1 onion, chopped
½ cup dry white wine
½ cup chopped mushrooms
½ cup chopped prosciutto
1 small veal sweetbread, soaked and parboiled (*see* page 496)
6 small chicken livers, chopped and sautéed 3 minutes in 2 tablespoons butter
Flour
2 eggs, beaten with ½ teaspoon salt
3 cups breadcrumbs
Salt and freshly ground pepper
Fat for deep frying

Prepare the risotto and spread it out in a shallow dish to cool. The risotto should be slightly moist, but not wet. Melt the butter in a frying pan over medium heat, add the onion, cook until golden, add the wine, and cook until it has completely evaporated. Add the mushrooms, reduce the heat, and simmer until the mushrooms are almost soft. Add the prosciutto, sweetbread, and chicken livers; season lightly with salt and pepper; simmer for 3 minutes; and remove from the heat. When the rice is cold, form it into balls, place a very generous spoonful of the filling in the center of each, and proceed as described in the preceding recipe to coat with breadcrumbs and fry in deep fat. *Serves* 6.

VARIETY MEATS
Interiora

Careful preparation and cooking of internal organ meats has been a specialty of Italian (and European) cooks for centuries. All internal meats have their own special characteristics and require fairly special attention. Properly prepared, they can make superb dishes, with the added virtue of being high in nutritive value and many of them quite inexpensive. Some, like brains or sweetbreads, are extremely delicate; others, like tripe, require very long, slow cooking to tenderize them. Because internal organ meats are highly susceptible to deterioration, it is wise to make certain they are as fresh as possible.

In addition to internal organs, we include in this section calf's head, oxtail, and poultry wings.

BRAINS
Cervello di vitello

Although beef, lamb, and pork brains are all edible, calf's brains are generally preferred for their finer texture and greater delicacy of flavor.

Brains must be soaked for several hours before cooking. Soak them first for 2 hours in several changes of water and then remove as much of their covering membranes as possible without tearing their very delicate flesh. Soak them again in water lightly acidulated with lemon juice or vinegar for 2 hours, again pull off as much of the membrane as possible, and cut off the small white pieces at the base. If they are to be sautéed or fried, which is the more popular method of cooking them, they should now be blanched for 20 minutes in lightly acidulated water; the water must not be allowed to boil and should be kept just below the simmering point. Allow them to cool for 10 minutes in the water, drain them, plunge in cold water, and they are then ready to be sliced and sautéed. If they are to be braised, this blanching process is unnecessary.

1385. BRAINS IN BLACK BUTTER
Cervella di vitello al burro nero

1½ pounds calf's brains, soaked, blanched, and
 sliced ½ inch thick
Flour
3 tablespoons butter
1 tablespoon capers
1 tablespoon lemon juice
½ cup Black Butter [No. 100]
2 tablespoons chopped parsley
Salt and freshly ground pepper

Season the sliced brains with salt and pepper and dust them with flour. Heat the butter in a very large frying pan over fairly high heat until golden, add the brains, and sauté for about 3 minutes on each side, or until they are golden brown. Remove them with a slotted spoon to a hot serving platter, add the capers and lemon juice to the hot black butter, pour over the brains, and sprinkle with the parsley. *Serves* 6.

1386. BRAINS WITH CURRY SAUCE
Cervella di vitello all'indiana

1½ pounds calf's brains, soaked, blanched, and cut
 into ½ inch slices
Flour
3 tablespoons butter
1 recipe Indian Rice [No. 594]
2 cups Curry Sauce [No. 70]
Salt and freshly ground pepper

Sauté the brains in the manner described in the preceding recipe and arrange them in a circle around the edge of a large hot serving platter. Heap the rice in the center of the platter and pour the curry sauce over the brains. *Serves* 6.

1387. BRAINS FIORENTINA
Cervella fritta alla fiorentina

This has the same ingredients and preparation as Brains Inglese [No. 1389], except that the platter is garnished with 1 recipe Spinach in Butter [No. 1791] and ½ cup of Black Butter [No. 100] is poured over the brains. If desired, 12 anchovy fillets, which have been washed free of salt [*see* No. 220], may be arranged on top of the brains. *Serves* 6.

1388. BRAINS AU GRATIN
Cervella di vitello al gratino

1½ pounds calf's brains, soaked, blanched, and cut
 into ½-inch slices
2 cups Duxelles Sauce [No. 31]
½ cup fresh breadcrumbs
6 tablespoons butter, melted
2 tablespoons chopped parsley
Juice of 1 lemon
Salt and freshly ground pepper

Spread half of the Duxelles sauce in the bottom of a large shallow baking dish, arrange the sliced brains on top, season with salt and pepper, spread the remaining Duxelles sauce over the brains, sprinkle with breadcrumbs, and then sprinkle the melted butter over the top. Place the dish in a medium (375°) oven for about 15 minutes, or until the breadcrumbs are golden. Remove from the oven, sprinkle with the lemon juice and parsley, and serve in the baking dish. *Serves* 6.

1389. BRAINS INGLESE
Cervella di vitello all'inglese

1½ pounds calf's brains, soaked, blanched, and cut
 into ½-inch slices
A marinade:
 2 tablespoons oil
 Juice of 1 lemon
 2 tablespoons chopped parsley
 ½ teaspoon salt
 ¼ teaspoon freshly ground pepper
2 eggs, beaten
2 cups fresh breadcrumbs
Fat for deep frying

Mix the marinade ingredients thoroughly together in a bowl until the salt is dissolved. Add the brains to the bowl and marinate for 2 hours. Drain them well, dip in beaten egg, and then coat with a generous amount of breadcrumbs. Fry them in deep hot (375°) fat until they are golden brown, drain, and serve immediately on a hot platter. *Serves* 6.

1390. BRAINS PARTENOPEA
Cervella di vitello alla partenopea

1½ pounds calf's brains, soaked, blanched, and cut into ½-inch slices
½ cup oil
Salt and freshly ground pepper
1 cup pitted black olives, sliced
2 tablespoons capers
1 cup breadcrumbs

Brush a large shallow baking dish with oil, arrange the sliced brains in the dish, season lightly with salt and pepper, spread the olives and capers over the brains, cover with breadcrumbs, and sprinkle a generous amount of oil over the top. Place the dish in a medium (375°) oven for about 15 minutes, or until the breadcrumbs are golden brown, remove from the oven, and serve in the baking dish. *Serves* 6.

1391. BRAINS RICCA
Cervella di vitello alla ricca

1½ pounds calf's brains, soaked, blanched, and chopped
½ cup chopped prosciutto
2 tablespoons chopped truffles
½ cup cooked chopped mushrooms (about ¼ pound, gently sautéed in 3 tablespoons butter)
2½ cups Béchamel Sauce [No. 18], reduced to 1½ cups
Flour
2 eggs, beaten
2 cups fresh breadcrumbs
6 tablespoons butter
2½ cups Marsala Sauce [No. 43]
Salt and freshly ground pepper

Mix the chopped brains in a bowl with the prosciutto, truffles, mushrooms, and Béchamel. Season lightly with salt and pepper and allow the mixture to become completely cold. Shape the mixture into 6 large or 12 small patties, dust them with flour, dip in beaten egg, and cover with a generous amount of breadcrumbs. Heat the butter in a very large frying pan (or use 2 frying pans with slightly more butter) until golden and sauté the patties for about 3 minutes on each side, or until they are golden brown. Arrange them on a hot serving platter and pour the Marsala sauce over them. *Serves* 6.

1392. BRAINS TEDESCA
Cervella di vitello alla tedesca

1½ pounds calf's brains, soaked, blanched, and cut into ½-inch slices
Flour
3 tablespoons butter
6 slices bread, crusts removed, sautéed golden brown in butter
2 cups Sauce Parisienne [No. 21]
Salt and freshly ground pepper

Sauté the brains in the manner described in Brains in Black Butter [No. 1385], arrange them on top of the slices of browned bread on a hot serving platter, and spoon the Parisienne sauce over them. *Serves* 6.

CALF'S HEAD
Testa di vitello

Calf's head always receives the following preliminary preparation. Have the butcher clean and bone a calf's head, leaving the tongue and brain separate. Soak the head for 3 hours in several changes of water and then cook it slowly in a large enamel or earthenware pot generously covered with White Foundation for Meats [No. 1057] to which is added 1 tablespoon of vinegar per quart of foundation liquid and 1 cup of chopped beef suet or veal fat. It should simmer for about 2 hours, or until the meat is tender. If desired, the tongue and brain (after being soaked) may be cooked with the head; the tongue should simmer for the last hour of cooking and the brain for the last 20 minutes.

483

1393. CALF'S HEAD GOURMET
Testa di vitello alla buongustaia

1 calf's head, soaked, parboiled for 2 hours, and cut
    into pieces about 2 by 4 inches
A chopped mixture:
    1/8 pound dried mushrooms, soaked in warm water
        for 1 hour and squeezed almost dry
    1/4 pound lean prosciutto
    2 ounces pork fat back
    1 tablespoon butter
1 very large piece of pig's caul (*reticulum*), soaked
    in warm water until soft
2 cups breadcrumbs
6 tablespoons oil
2 cups Tomato Sauce [No. 19]
Salt and freshly ground pepper

Sauté the chopped mixture in the tablespoon of butter
for about 10 minutes in a frying pan over medium heat.
Season lightly with salt and pepper, remove from the
heat, and cool. Spread each of the pieces of calf's head
with a little of the chopped mixture, wrap each in a
small piece of pig's caul, roll in breadcrumbs, and
then sauté them in very hot oil in a large frying pan over
fairly high heat until golden brown. Transfer them to
a hot serving platter and serve the tomato sauce separately. *Serves 6.*

NOTE: If pig's caul is not available, paper-thin slices
of fresh pork fat back may be substituted. After wrapping the filling in the fat, dip in beaten egg so that the
breadcrumbs will adhere.

1394. CALF'S HEAD WITH TOMATO SAUCE
Testa di vitello fritta con salsa al pomodoro

1 calf's head, soaked, parboiled for 2 hours, and
    cut into bite-sized pieces
A marinade:
    1 cup oil
    1/4 cup lemon juice
    2 tablespoons chopped parsley
    1 teaspoon salt
    1/4 teaspoon freshly ground pepper
2 cups Fritter Batter [No. 275]
Fat for deep frying
3 lemons, quartered
6 sprigs parsley
2 cups Tomato Sauce [No. 19]

Place the pieces of calf's head in the marinade while
they are still hot and allow them to cool completely in

the marinade, stirring them occasionally. Drain them,
pat dry, dip in fritter batter, and drop immediately in
deep hot (375°) fat, frying them until golden brown.
Remove them from the fat, drain briefly on absorbent
paper, and arrange them on a hot serving platter.
Garnish the platter with the lemon quarters and parsley
and serve the tomato sauce separately. *Serves 6.*

CALF'S HEART
Cuore di vitello

1395. CALF'S HEART IN CASSEROLE
Cuore di vitello in casseruola

6 small calf's hearts, trimmed of fat and arteries
Salt and freshly ground pepper
6 tablespoons butter
2 cups Thickened Brown Veal Stock [No. 6]

Season the hearts lightly with salt and pepper. Heat
the butter in a large casserole over medium heat until
the foam subsides, add the hearts, and roll them in the
butter. Place the casserole in a medium (350°) oven for
about 1 1/2 hours (the exact time will depend on the size
of the hearts), turning them and basting frequently
with the butter in the casserole. When they are tender,
add the thickened veal stock and simmer over medium
heat just until the stock is hot. Serve in the casserole.
Serves 6.

1396. CALF'S HEART CIOCIARA
Cuore di vitello alla ciociara

6 small calf's hearts, trimmed of fat and arteries
    and cut in half
A marinade:
    1/2 cup oil
    1 clove garlic, crushed in the garlic-press
    2 tablespoons chopped parsley
    1 teaspoon salt
    1/4 teaspoon freshly ground pepper

Marinate the hearts in the marinade for 2 hours. Remove them and strain the marinade through a fine sieve into a large frying pan, heat until very hot over fairly high heat, add the hearts, brown for 1 minute on each side, reduce the heat, and simmer the hearts very slowly for about 30 minutes, or until they are tender, turning them frequently. Transfer the hearts to a hot serving platter and pour some of the pan juices over the hearts. *Serves* 6.

NOTE: An ideal accompaniment for these sautéed calf's hearts is a tart salad of dandelion leaves or any similar wild green.

1397. ROAST CALF'S HEARTS
Cuore di vitello arrosto

6 calf's hearts, trimmed of fat and arteries
A marinade:
  1/2 cup oil
  2 tablespoons lemon juice
  1 teaspoon salt
  1/4 teaspoon freshly ground pepper
18 "new" potatoes, cooked until just tender in lightly
      salted water

Marinate the hearts in the marinade for 1 hour. Arrange them in a shallow open roasting pan, pour the marinade over them, and roast in a moderate (350°) oven for about 1 1/2 hours, or until the hearts are tender. Baste them with the pan juices every 10 minutes. Transfer them to a hot serving platter and garnish with the boiled potatoes. De-glaze the roasting pan with 2 tablespoons water and pour over the hearts. *Serves* 6.

CALF'S LIVER AND PORK LIVER
Fegato di vitello e di maiale

Calf's liver is somewhat more tender than beef, lamb's, or pork liver, and, while it is expensive, is generally preferred. Pork liver, however, is prized by many for its rather special flavor and its rich fattiness.

Before cooking, whether liver is sliced or left whole, the membrane surrounding it and the tough tubular veins should be removed.

1398. CALF'S LIVER BORGHESE
Fegato di vitello alla borghese

1 3-pound piece calf's liver
12 4-inch strips pork fat back
A marinade:
  1/2 cup oil
  2 tablespoons lemon juice
  1 tablespoon brandy
  1 tablespoon chopped parsley
  1 teaspoon salt
  1/4 teaspoon freshly ground pepper
4 tablespoons butter
1 carrot, sliced
1 onion, sliced
Bouquet Garni:
  3 sprigs parsley
  2 sprigs thyme (or 1/2 teaspoon dried)
  1 bay leaf
1 1/2 cups diced lean salt pork, parboiled for
      15 minutes, drained, and sautéed until golden
      brown
12 Brown-Braised Onions [No. 1722]
18 small Glazed Carrots [No. 1647]
1 cup Brown Veal Stock [No. 5]
3/4 cup dry white wine
Salt and freshly ground pepper

Using a larding needle, lard the piece of liver with the strips of fat back. Place it in the marinade for 2 hours, drain, and dry thoroughly on paper towels. Heat the butter in a heavy casserole over fairly high heat until golden and quickly brown the liver on all sides. Adjust the heat during the browning so that the butter does not burn. Arrange the sliced carrot, onion, and the Bouquet Garni around the liver, season lightly with salt and pepper, cover the casserole, and place it in a moderate (350°) oven for about 1 hour and 15 minutes (the exact time will depend on the thickness of the piece of liver), basting frequently with the butter and juices in the casserole. Be very careful not to overcook, or the liver will toughen. Test after 1 hour by pricking with a fork; if the juices run pink instead of blood red, it will be fully cooked. When it is tender, transfer it to a hot serving platter, sprinkle with the browned salt pork dice, and arrange the glazed carrots and onions around it. Discard the Bouquet Garni, add the wine and veal stock to the casserole, and reduce over high heat to 1/2 their quantity. Correct the seasoning, and pour the sauce through a fine sieve over the liver. *Serves* 6.

1399. BREADED CALF'S LIVER
Fegato di vitello fritto

6 large slices calf's liver, cut ½ inch thick
Flour
2 eggs, beaten
2 cups fresh breadcrumbs
¼ cup oil
3 lemons, quartered
6 sprigs parsley, fried in deep fat [see No. 276]
Salt and freshly ground pepper

Season the slices of liver with salt and pepper, dust them with flour, dip in beaten egg, and coat with a generous amount of breadcrumbs. Heat 4 tablespoons of oil in each of 2 large frying pans over fairly high heat and quickly brown 3 slices of liver in each pan. Cook for 3 minutes on 1 side and then 2 minutes on the other. If the juices run pale pink when the slices are pricked with a fork, they will be sufficiently cooked. Do not overcook, or the liver will toughen. Transfer the slices to a hot serving platter and garnish with the fried parsley and lemon quarters. *Serves* 6.

1400. CALF'S LIVER CASALINGA
Fegato di vitello alla casalinga

6 slices calf's liver, cut ½ inch thick
Salt and freshly ground pepper
Flour
¼ cup oil
4 tablespoons chopped onion
1 cup dry white wine
4 tablespoons butter
2 tablespoons chopped parsley

Season the slices of liver with salt and pepper and dust them with flour. Heat 4 tablespoons of oil in each of 2 frying pans over fairly high heat, add 2 tablespoons of the chopped onion to each of the pans, and cook until golden. Add 3 slices of liver to each of the pans, and cook for 3 minutes on 1 side, and 2 minutes on the other. Test for doneness by pricking with a fork; if the juices run pale pink, the slices are fully cooked. Transfer them to a hot serving platter and keep warm. Add ½ cup of the wine to each of the pans and de-glaze over high heat. Combine the 2 liquids in 1 of the pans, reduce slightly, remove from the heat, and swirl in the butter, bit by bit. Pour this sauce over the liver and sprinkle with the parsley. *Serves* 6.

1401. CALF'S LIVER CONTADINA
Fegato di vitello alla contadina

6 slices calf's liver, cut ½ inch thick
Salt and freshly ground pepper
Flour
¼ cup oil
3 onions, thinly sliced
2 cloves garlic, crushed in the garlic-press
⅓ cup white wine vinegar
1 tablespoon chopped parsley

Season the slices of liver with salt and pepper and dust with flour. Heat 4 tablespoons of oil in each of 2 frying pans over fairly high heat until smoking, add 3 slices of liver to each pan, cook for 3 minutes on 1 side, and then 2 minutes on the other. Test for doneness by pricking with a fork; if the juices run pale pink, they are fully done. Transfer them to a hot serving platter and keep warm. Combine all of the oil in which the liver was cooked in one of the pans, add the onions, and sauté over medium heat until the onions are golden. At the same time, add the vinegar to the other pan and de-glaze over high heat until the vinegar is reduced to a few tablespoons. Spoon the onions over the liver, pour over the reduced vinegar, and sprinkle with the parsley. *Serves* 6.

1402. CALF'S LIVER INGLESE
Fegato di vitello all'inglese

6 slices calf's liver, cut ½ inch thick
Salt and freshly ground pepper
Flour
½ cup butter
6 thick slices lean bacon, broiled crisp
2 lemons, quartered

Season the slices of liver with salt and pepper and dust with flour. Heat 4 tablespoons of butter in each of 2 frying pans over fairly high heat until golden, add 3 slices of liver to each of the pans, cook for 3 minutes on 1 side, and then 2 minutes on the other. Test for doneness by pricking with a fork; if the juices run pale pink, the liver is fully cooked. Transfer them to a hot serving platter, pour the butter in which they cooked over them, and garnish the platter with the bacon and lemon quarters. *Serves* 6.

1403. CALF'S LIVER WITH LEMON
Fegato di vitello al limone

6 slices calf's liver, cut ½ inch thick
Salt and freshly ground pepper
Flour
½ cup butter
Juice of 2 lemons
2 lemons, very thinly sliced
2 tablespoons chopped parsley

Sauté the slices of liver in the manner described in the preceding recipe, arrange them on a hot serving platter, and squeeze the juice of 2 lemons over them. Add the very thinly sliced lemons to 1 of the pans in which the liver cooked, sauté for a few seconds over high heat, top each piece of liver with a few of the lemon slices, pour the butter from both pans over the liver, and sprinkle with the chopped parsley. *Serves* 6.

1404. CALF'S LIVER MILANESE
Fegato di vitello alla milanese

6 slices calf's liver, cut ½ inch thick
A marinade:
　½ cup oil
　3 tablespoons lemon juice
　1 teaspoon salt
　¼ teaspoon freshly ground pepper
Flour
2 eggs, beaten
2 cups fresh breadcrumbs
½ cup butter
6 sprigs parsley
2 lemons, quartered

Place the slices of liver in the marinade for 1 hour, turning them occasionally. Drain the slices and dry them on absorbent paper. Dust them with flour, dip in beaten egg, and cover generously with breadcrumbs. Heat 4 tablespoons of butter in each of 2 frying pans over fairly high heat until golden, add 3 pieces of liver to each pan, sauté for 3 minutes on 1 side, and then 2 minutes on the other. Test for doneness by pricking with a fork; if the juices run pale pink, the liver is fully cooked. Transfer them to a hot serving platter, pour the butter in which they cooked over them, and garnish with the parsley and lemon quarters. *Serves* 6.

1405. CALF'S LIVER WITH SAGE
Fegato di vitello con erba salvia

6 slices calf's liver, cut ½ inch thick
12 fresh sage leaves (or 1 tablespoon dried)
Salt and freshly ground pepper
Flour
½ cup butter
2 lemons, quartered

If only dried sage is available, rub a little on each side of the slices of liver. Season them with salt and pepper and dust with flour. If fresh sage is available, put half of the butter and half of the sage leaves in each of 2 frying pans over fairly high heat, cook until the butter is golden, add 3 slices of liver to each of the pans, cook for 3 minutes on 1 side, and then 2 minutes on the other. Test for doneness by pricking with a fork; if the juices run pale pink, the liver is fully cooked. Transfer them to a hot serving platter and garnish with the lemon quarters. *Serves* 6.

1406. CALF'S LIVER VENEZIANA
Fegato di vitello alla veneziana

1½ pounds calf's liver, sliced ¼ inch thick
　and then cut into narrow strips 2 inches long
Salt and freshly ground pepper
Flour
½ cup oil
4 onions, sliced
Optional: ½ cup white wine vinegar
2 lemons, quartered

Season the strips of liver with salt and pepper and dust them with flour. Heat 4 tablespoons of oil in each of 2 frying pans over fairly high heat until smoking, add half of the liver strips to each pan, and sauté very quickly, about 3 minutes in all, until the strips are browned on both sides. Remove them to a hot serving platter and keep warm. Add the onions to 1 pan and the optional vinegar to the other. Cook the onions until they begin to color and reduce the vinegar to a few tablespoons. Pour the reduced vinegar over the liver, spoon the onions on top, and garnish the platter with the lemon quarters. *Serves* 6.

1407. PORK LIVER BOLOGNESE
Fegatelli di maiale alla bolognese

18 1-inch cubes of pork liver
A marinade:
    $\frac{3}{4}$ cup oil
    2 tablespoons lemon juice
    1 tablespoon dried rosemary
    1 tablespoon dried sage leaves
    1 teaspoon salt
    $\frac{1}{4}$ teaspoon freshly ground pepper
Optional:
    18 fresh sage leaves
    1 large sheet of pig's caul, cut in 6 squares
18 cubes stale bread, cut $\frac{1}{2}$ inch thick and
    1 inch square
6 wooden skewers
6 large wedges bread, cut $\frac{1}{2}$ inch thick and
    sautéed in oil until golden brown

Place the cubes of liver in the marinade for 1 hour. Drain and then alternate the pieces of liver with the bread cubes and the optional sage leaves on 6 skewers, using 3 of each ingredient on each skewer. (Wrap each with a square of optional caul.) Brush each with a little of the marinade and then broil under a medium broiler flame for about 15 minutes, turning the skewers frequently and basting when necessary with more of the marinade or, if necessary, with a little more oil. Adjust the flame so that the liver and bread cubes do not brown too quickly. Arrange the skewers on a hot serving platter and garnish with the browned wedges of bread. *Serves* 6.

1408. PORK LIVER WITH FENNEL
Fegatelli di maiale al finocchio

24 1-inch cubes of pork liver
3 tablespoons fennel seeds, pounded in the mortar
Salt and freshly ground pepper
Flour
2 eggs, beaten
2 cups fresh breadcrumbs
12 bay leaves, cut in half
6 wooden skewers
1 cup oil
2 lemons, quartered
6 large wedges of cold Polenta [*see* No. 623], cut
    $\frac{1}{2}$ inch thick and sautéed in oil until golden
    brown

Rub each of the cubes of liver with a little of the crushed fennel seeds, season them with salt and pepper, dust with flour, dip in beaten egg, and cover with a generous amount of breadcrumbs. Alternate the cubes with the bay leaves on 6 skewers and then sprinkle with oil. Place the skewers under a medium broiler flame for about 15 minutes, turning them frequently and sprinkling with more oil whenever necessary. Adjust the broiler flame so that the breadcrumbs do not brown too quickly. Arrange the skewers on a hot serving platter and garnish with the lemon quarters and the fried wedges of polenta. *Serves* 6.

1409. PORK LIVER FIORENTINA
Fegatelli di maiale alla fiorentina

24 1-inch cubes of pork liver
2 cloves garlic, crushed in the garlic-press
3 tablespoons fennel seeds
Salt and freshly ground pepper
Flour
2 eggs, beaten
2 cups fresh breadcrumbs
24 cubes of stale bread, cut $\frac{1}{2}$ inch thick and
    1 inch square
12 bay leaves, cut in half
6 wooden skewers
$\frac{3}{4}$ cup oil
2 lemons, quartered

Pound the fennel seeds and the crushed garlic in the mortar and rub each of the cubes of liver with the mixture, season them with salt and pepper, dust with flour, dip in beaten egg, and cover generously with breadcrumbs. Alternate the cubes with the bay leaves on 6 skewers and sprinkle with oil. Broil in the manner described in the preceding recipe, arrange the skewers on a hot serving platter, and garnish with the lemon quarters. *Serves* 6.

1410. PORK LIVER WITH LENTILS
Involtini di fegato di maiale con purea di lenticchie

24 1-inch cubes of pork liver
Salt and freshly ground pepper
Pinch nutmeg
24 thin strips salt pork, 4 inches long and 1 inch wide,
    parboiled for 15 minutes
12 bay leaves, cut in half
6 wooden skewers
$\frac{1}{4}$ cup oil
1 recipe Lentil Purée [No. 1696]

Season the cubes of liver with salt, pepper, and nutmeg. Wrap each in a strip of salt pork and then alternate them with the bay leaves on 6 skewers. Brush with the oil and place the skewers under a medium broiler flame for about 15 minutes, turning them frequently. Adjust the flame as they cook so that they do not brown too quickly. Transfer them to a hot serving platter and serve the lentil purée on the side. *Serves* 6.

1411. SAUTÉED PORK LIVER
Fegato di maiale in padella

6 slices pork liver, cut ⅜ inch thick
Salt and freshly ground pepper
Flour
½ cup oil
¼ cup chopped onion
Juice of 1 lemon
2 tablespoons chopped parsley

Season the slices of liver with salt and pepper and dust with flour. Heat 4 tablespoons of oil in each of 2 frying pans over fairly high heat, add 2 tablespoons of chopped onion to each pan, and cook until the onion is golden. Add 3 slices of liver to each pan and brown for 2 minutes on each side. Reduce the heat and continue cooking for about 2 minutes longer on each side. Test for doneness by pricking with a fork; as soon as the juices run clear without any trace of rosiness, the liver is sufficiently cooked. Transfer the slices to a hot serving platter, squeeze the lemon juice over them, and sprinkle with the chopped parsley. *Serves* 6.

1412. SAUTÉED PORK LIVER WITH BAY LEAF
Fegato di maiale con foglia di lauro

6 slices pork liver, cut ⅜ inch thick
1 tablespoon powdered bay leaf
Salt and freshly ground pepper
Pinch nutmeg
Flour
3 bay leaves, crumbled
½ cup oil
2 lemons, quartered

Rub a little powdered bay leaf into each of the slices of liver; season them with salt, pepper, and nutmeg; and dust with flour. Heat 4 tablespoons of oil and a little crumbled bay leaf in each of 2 frying pans over fairly high heat until the oil is smoking, add 3 slices of liver to each pan, sauté for 2 minutes on each side, reduce the heat, and continue cooking for about 2 minutes longer on each side. Test for doneness by pricking with a fork; as soon as the juices run clear without any trace of rosiness, the liver is sufficiently

cooked. Transfer the slices to a hot serving platter and garnish with the lemon quarters. *Serves* 6.

1413. SAUTÉED PORK LIVER WITH TOMATO
Fegato di maiale al pomodoro

6 slices pork liver, cut ⅜ inch thick
Flour
½ cup oil
¼ cup chopped onion
1 pound ripe tomatoes, peeled, seeded, drained, and chopped
½ cup dry white wine
2 tablespoons chopped parsley
Salt and freshly ground pepper

Season and cook the pork liver in the manner described in Sautéed Pork Liver [No. 1411]. When it is fully cooked, transfer it to a hot serving platter and keep warm. Add the tomatoes to one of the pans and the white wine to the other. Season the tomatoes with salt and pepper and cook over fairly high heat for about 10 minutes, or until they are thick and soft; at the same time de-glaze the other pan with the wine, reduce over high heat to a generous tablespoon, and then add to the pan with the tomatoes. Spoon the tomatoes over the liver and sprinkle with the parsley. *Serves* 6.

CHICKEN LIVERS
Fegatini di pollo

Chicken livers are one of the most tender of all types of liver. Because of their small size, they cook very quickly and care should be taken not to overcook them so that they become dry. Do not crowd them when sautéeing, and cook them at high heat, otherwise the juice will run out of them and they will dry out.

1414. CHICKEN LIVERS WITH ARTICHOKES
Fegatini di pollo con carciofi

1½ pounds chicken livers, cut in half and patted dry
½ cup butter
6 small artichokes, trimmed, parboiled until barely tender (*see* page 539), drained, and sliced
1 cup chopped prosciutto (fat and lean)
2 tablespoons chopped parsley
Juice of 1 lemon
6 slices bread, crusts removed, browned in butter
Salt and freshly ground pepper

Heat 3 tablespoons of the butter in a saucepan over low heat, add the artichokes, and stir gently for 3 or 4 minutes to get them hot; remove from the heat and keep warm. Heat the remaining butter in a very large frying pan over medium high heat until the foam subsides, add the chicken livers, raise heat, and sauté for about 3 minutes, turning them frequently. Season them with salt and pepper, reduce the heat, add the prosciutto and artichokes, and stir gently for about 1 minute longer. Turn the contents of the pan out onto a hot serving platter, squeeze the lemon juice over all, sprinkle with the chopped parsley, and garnish the platter with the browned bread slices. *Serves* 6.

1415. CHICKEN LIVER PIE
Pasticcio di fegatini di pollo

1 recipe Flaky Pastry [No. 1954]
1 pound chicken livers, coarsely chopped
1½ cups finely diced cooked loin of pork
    (broiled chops or leftover roast)
2 tablespoons chopped truffle [or No. 1819a]
¾ cup heavy cream
2 tablespoons butter, melted
3 eggs, lightly beaten
Pinch nutmeg
Salt and freshly ground pepper
1 egg yolk, beaten with 2 tablespoons milk

Mix the chicken livers in a bowl with the pork, truffle, heavy cream, melted butter, and eggs; and season the mixture with the nutmeg and salt and pepper to taste. Roll out the pastry dough to a thickness of ⅛ inch and then line a 9-inch flan ring placed on a baking sheet (or use a 9-inch pie tin) with it, reserving a generous ⅓ of the dough to be used as a cover. Fill the pie with the chicken liver/pork mixture, cover with the remaining pastry, crimp the edges together decoratively, brush with the egg yolk beaten with milk, and make several slits in the top to allow steam to escape. Place the pie on the lowest rack in a moderate (375°) oven for 30 minutes and then transfer it to a higher rack for about 10 minutes to brown the crust. Slide the pie off the baking sheet onto a serving platter, remove the flan ring, and serve immediately; or allow to cool and serve warm. *Serves* 6.

NOTE: If baked in a pie tin, serve in tin and do not attempt to remove it.

490

1416. RATTATUIA OF CHICKEN LIVERS AND VEAL KIDNEYS
"Rattatuia" di fegatini di pollo e rognoni di vitello

1 pound chicken livers, cut in half and patted dry
1 pound veal kidneys, trimmed of fat and membrane, and split
6 tablespoons butter
½ pound mushrooms, sliced and gently sautéed for 8 minutes in 3 tablespoons butter
2 onions, parboiled for 10 minutes and thinly sliced
2 cloves garlic, crushed in the garlic-press
1 cup Marsala wine
2 tablespoons chopped parsley
Salt and freshly ground pepper

Heat 4 tablespoons of the butter in a large frying pan over medium heat until the foam subsides, add the kidneys, and sauté for about 10 minutes, turning them frequently and adjusting the heat so that the butter does not burn. Remove them from the pan and keep warm. Add the mushrooms, onions, and garlic to the pan; season lightly with salt and pepper; and stir gently. Add the chicken livers to the pan and sauté for 3 minutes, turning them frequently. Slice the kidneys about ¼ inch thick and add them to the pan. Reduce the heat and simmer gently for 2 minutes. Turn the contents of the pan out into a hot serving dish and keep warm. Add the Marsala to the pan, reduce over high heat by ⅓, remove from the heat, and swirl in the remaining butter, bit by bit. Pour this sauce over the kidneys and livers and sprinkle with the chopped parsley. *Serves* 6.

1417. RISOTTO AND CHICKEN LIVERS PIEMONTESE
Turbante di fegatini di pollo alla piemontese

1 recipe Risotto with Butter and Parmesan Cheese [No. 572]
2 truffles, sliced
4 tablespoons butter
1½ pounds chicken livers, patted dry
Salt and freshly ground pepper
1½ cups Demi-Glaze Sauce [No. 20]
2 tablespoons chopped parsley

Prepare the risotto, mix in the truffles, and then press the risotto into a large, lightly buttered ring mold. Heat the butter in a very large frying pan over medium heat until it is golden, add chicken livers, raise heat, and sauté for about 4 minutes, stirring frequently.

Season lightly with salt and pepper, add the Demi-Glaze sauce, and cook only long enough for the sauce to become hot. Unmold the risotto onto a hot serving platter, fill the center of the ring with the chicken livers, and sprinkle with the parsley. *Serves* 6.

1418. CHICKEN LIVERS WITH SAGE
Fegatini di pollo con erba salvia

2 pounds chicken livers
½ cup butter
2 tablespoons fresh sage leaves (or substitute dried)
1 cup chopped prosciutto
1 cup dry white wine
Salt and freshly ground pepper

Heat 4 tablespoon of the butter and the sage leaves in a very large frying pan over medium heat until the butter foam subsides, add the chicken livers, raise heat, and sauté for about 4 minutes, turning them frequently (do not crowd them in the pan; sauté only half at one time, if necessary). Add the prosciutto and simmer for 1 minute longer. Transfer the livers and prosciutto to a hot serving dish, and keep warm. Add the wine to the pan, reduce over high heat to ½ its quantity, remove from the heat, and swirl in the remaining butter, bit by bit. Correct seasoning, and pour this sauce over the livers and serve immediately. *Serves* 6.

1419. CHICKEN LIVER SPIEDINI LUIGI VERONELLI
Spiedini di fegatini di pollo alla Luigi Veronelli

24 chicken livers
12 wide strips salt pork, cut thinly, and parboiled for 10 minutes
18 large mushroom caps
Optional: 24 fresh sage leaves
6 skewers
1 cup butter, melted
1½ cups cold Duxelles [No. 138]
3 cups fresh breadcrumbs
Salt and freshly ground pepper

Broil the parboiled salt pork for a few minutes under a medium broiler flame until only partially cooked and not quite crisp. Cut the strips in half and wrap a half strip around each of the chicken livers. Alternate 4 wrapped livers, 3 mushroom caps, and 4 sage leaves on each of 6 skewers. Brush the skewered ingredients with melted butter; spread with the Duxelles, pressing

it on so that as much adheres as possible; and then coat generously with breadcrumbs. Sprinkle with melted butter and place the skewers under a medium high broiler flame for 6 to 8 minutes, turning them frequently and sprinkling with more butter as necessary. Transfer them to a hot serving platter and sprinkle lightly with salt and pepper. *Serves* 6.

1420. CHICKEN LIVERS ON TOAST POINTS GOURMET
Toasts di fegatini di pollo dei viveurs

2 pounds chicken livers
6 tablespoons butter
¼ cup brandy
2 tablespoons flour
2 cups Chicken Consommé [No. 361]
12 anchovy fillets, washed free of salt [*see* No. 220]
1 tablespoon capers
Salt and freshly ground pepper
6 slices bread, crusts removed, cut diagonally in half, and sautéed golden brown in butter
Juice of 1 lemon
2 tablespoons chopped parsley

Heat the butter in a very large frying pan over fairly high heat until golden, add the chicken livers, raise heat, and sauté for 3 minutes, turning them frequently. Add the brandy, heat for a few seconds, ignite, and shake the pan until the flames subside. Cook until the brandy has evaporated, sprinkle the flour over the livers, stir for a few seconds, add the chicken consommé, reduce the heat to a very low flame, and simmer for about 10 minutes. Pound the anchovy fillets and the capers in a mortar until they are a paste, spread a little of this mixture on each of the browned slices of bread, and arrange the slices on a hot serving platter. Correct the seasoning of the sauce, add the lemon juice, spoon the livers and sauce over the bread, and sprinkle with the chopped parsley. *Serves* 6.

KIDNEYS
Rognone

Veal kidneys are tender and delicately flavored and are generally to be preferred over beef, lamb, or pork kidneys. Before cooking, kidneys should be trimmed free of fat and the membrane that covers them should be peeled off. If not veal, they should then be split, washed, and patted dry. Kidneys should not be boiled in liquid, as this toughens them. Since kidneys tend to release a great deal of juice on contact with heat, it is wiser to cook them over a high flame. They are usually sautéed or broiled fairly quickly and, if served in a sauce, they are sliced after cooking and simmered in the sauce for only a minute to heat them through and to blend the flavors. If they are sautéed sliced, their released juices tend to make them boil and thus toughen them. Kidneys will be at their tenderest if cooked just long enough to leave their centers pink.

1421. VEAL KIDNEYS WITH ASPARAGUS PARMIGIANA
Rognone di vitello con asparagi alla parmigiana

5 veal kidneys, trimmed of fat and membrane
10 tablespoons butter
18 asparagus tips, parboiled in lightly salted water
    for 15 minutes, or until almost tender, and drained
½ cup grated Parmesan cheese
1 cup dry Marsala wine
1 cup Italian Meat Sauce [No. 41]
Salt and freshly ground pepper
2 tablespoons chopped parsley

Heat 4 tablespoons of the butter in a frying pan over medium heat until the foam subsides, add the whole kidneys, and sauté for about 10 minutes, turning them frequently and adjusting the heat so that the butter does not burn. Remove them from the pan and keep warm. Arrange the asparagus in a shallow baking dish, dot with 4 tablespoons of the butter, sprinkle with the Parmesan, and place the dish in a moderate (350°) oven for about 8 minutes. Add the Marsala to the pan in which the kidneys cooked, reduce over high heat to ½ its quantity, add the Italian meat sauce, and simmer for 3 minutes. Slice the kidneys about ¼ inch thick, add them to the sauce, simmer for 1 minute, correct the seasoning, remove from the heat, and swirl in the remaining butter, bit by bit. Correct seasoning, and turn the kidneys and the sauce out onto a hot serving platter, sprinkle with the parsley, and garnish with the gratinéed asparagus. *Serves* 6.

1422. BROILED VEAL KIDNEYS
Rognone di vitello alla griglia

6 large veal kidneys, trimmed of fat and membrane

A marinade:
    ¾ cup oil
    3 tablespoons lemon juice
    1 teaspoon salt
    ¼ teaspoon freshly ground pepper
6 thin skewers
2 lemons, quartered

Marinate the kidneys for 2 hours in the marinade, turning them frequently. Remove them, press them out as flat as possible with the palm of the hand, and run them through with a short skewer so that they will retain their flat shape during the cooking. Brush them with a little of the marinade and place them under a medium broiler flame for 12 to 15 minutes, turning them frequently and brushing with more of the marinade as necessary. Unskewer them onto a hot serving platter and garnish with the lemon quarters. *Serves* 6.

1423. VEAL KIDNEYS IN CASSEROLE
Rognone di vitello in casseruola

6 large veal kidneys, trimmed of fat and membrane
4 tablespoons butter
Salt and freshly ground pepper
2 cups Thickened Brown Veal Stock [No. 6]

Heat the butter in a heavy casserole over medium heat until the foam subsides, add the kidneys, raise heat, and sauté for 10 minutes, turning them frequently and adjusting the heat so that the butter does not burn. Remove them from the casserole, add the veal stock, and simmer for 5 minutes. Slice the kidneys about ¼ inch thick, add them to the sauce, simmer for 1 minute, correct the seasoning, and serve in the casserole. *Serves* 6.

1424. VEAL KIDNEYS GERMANA
Rognone di vitello "Germana"

6 large veal kidneys, trimmed of fat and membrane
2 onions, thinly sliced
4 tablespoons butter
½ pound mushrooms, sliced
4 tablespoons prepared mustard (Dijon-type preferred)
¼ cup brandy
2 tablespoons chopped parsley
Salt and freshly ground pepper

Sauté the kidneys, with the onions, as described in Veal Kidneys with Asparagus Parmigiana [No. 1421], remove them from the pan, add the mushrooms, reduce the heat, and simmer for 5 minutes. Slice the kidneys about ¼ inch thick; add them, the mustard, and brandy to the pan; season lightly with salt and pepper; and stir over medium heat for 2 minutes to get very hot and blend the flavors. Turn the contents of the pan out onto a hot serving platter and sprinkle with the parsley. *Serves 6.*

1425. VEAL KIDNEYS MAÎTRE D'HÔTEL
Rognone di vitello alla "Maître d'Hôtel"

6 large veal kidneys, trimmed of fat and membrane
6 skewers
Salt and freshly ground pepper
⅓ cup melted butter
1 cup breadcrumbs
1 cup Maître d'Hôtel Butter [No. 111]

Press the kidneys flat with the palm of the hand and pierce each with a short skewer so that they will not curl while they are cooked. Season them with salt and pepper, brush with some melted butter, and broil them under a medium flame for 12 to 15 minutes, turning and basting them frequently with more melted butter. Spread the Maître d'Hôtel butter out on a warm serving platter, unskewer the kidneys on the platter, slice them, toss them in the butter, and serve immediately. *Serves 6.*

1426. VEAL KIDNEYS MARSALA
Rognone di vitello al marsala

6 large veal kidneys, trimmed of fat and membrane
6 tablespoons butter
1½ cups dry Marsala wine
Juice of 1 lemon
2 tablespoons chopped parsley
Salt and freshly ground pepper

Heat 4 tablespoons of the butter in a frying pan over medium high heat until the foam subsides, add the whole kidneys, and sauté for about 15 minutes, turning them frequently and adjusting the heat as they cook to keep the butter from burning. Remove them from the pan and keep warm. Add the Marsala to the pan and reduce over high heat to ½ its quantity. Slice the kidneys, add them to the pan, season with salt and pepper, add the lemon juice, and heat for 1 minute. Remove the pan from the heat, and swirl in the remaining butter, bit by bit. Turn the kidneys and sauce out onto a hot serving platter and sprinkle with the parsley. *Serves 6.*

1427. VEAL KIDNEYS PAESANA
Rognone di vitello alla paesana

6 large veal kidneys, trimmed of fat and membrane
½ cup butter
2 cloves garlic, crushed in the garlic-press
1 pound ripe tomatoes, peeled, seeded, drained, and chopped
½ pound mushrooms, sliced
2 sweet Italian sausages, sautéed for 10 minutes and thinly sliced
2 tablespoons chopped parsley
Salt and freshly ground pepper

Melt 2 tablespoons of butter in a heavy pot over medium heat, add the garlic, cook for 2 minutes, add the tomatoes, season with salt and pepper, and cook for about 10 minutes, or until the tomatoes are soft. In a separate pan gently sauté the mushrooms in another 2 tablespoons of butter for about 8 minutes, remove from the heat, and reserve. Sauté the kidneys in the remaining 4 tablespoons of butter in the manner described in the preceding recipe, remove them from the pan, and slice them. Add the kidneys, mushrooms, and sausage to the pot with the tomatoes, season lightly with salt and pepper, and cook for 1 minute. Turn the contents of the pot out onto a hot serving platter and sprinkle with the parsley. *Serves 6.*

1428. VEAL KIDNEYS TRIFOLATO WITH LEMON
Rognone di vitello trifolato al limone

6 large veal kidneys, trimmed of fat and membrane
4 tablespoons butter
2 lemons, very thinly sliced
2 cups Croûtons [No. 332]
2 tablespoons chopped parsley
Salt and freshly ground pepper

Sauté the kidneys in the manner described in Veal Kidneys Marsala [No. 1426], remove them from the pan, and slice them. Add the paper-thin slices of lemon to the butter remaining in the pan and toss for a few seconds over high heat. Add the kidneys and croûtons, season lightly with salt and pepper, and stir for 1 minute. Turn the contents of the pan out onto a hot serving platter and sprinkle with the parsley. *Serves 6.*

493

OXTAIL
Coda di bue

When purchased from a butcher, oxtails have usually been skinned and cut at the joints into 1- to 2-inch pieces. They should be thoroughly washed and well dried before using.

1429. OXTAIL GOURMET
Coda di bue del buongustaio

4 pounds cut-up oxtail
3 large slices of fresh pork rind
2 onions, sliced
2 carrots, sliced
Bouquet Garni:
   3 sprigs parsley
   2 sprigs thyme (or ½ teaspoon dried)
   1 bay leaf
1 clove garlic, peeled
1 clove
Salt and freshly ground pepper
1 cup butter, melted
3 cups breadcrumbs
3 lemons, quartered

Line a large, heavy pot with the pork rind, and then place on top the sliced vegetables, Bouquet Garni, garlic, clove, and pieces of oxtail. Cover with cold water, season lightly with salt, bring to a boil, cover the pot, and simmer over very low heat for 3 to 4 hours, or until the meat of the oxtail is very tender and will separate easily from the bones. Remove the pieces of oxtail (the broth should be reserved for another use), drain, and dry them thoroughly. Season them lightly with salt and pepper, brush them with butter, roll in breadcrumbs, place them in a shallow baking dish, and

494

sprinkle with more melted butter. Place the dish in a hot (400°) oven for about 10 minutes, or until the pieces of oxtail are golden brown. Transfer them to a hot serving platter and garnish with the lemon quarters. *Serves 6.*

1430. OXTAIL ITALIANA
Coda di bue all'italiana

4 pounds cut-up oxtail
2 carrots, sliced
2 onions, sliced
1 stalk celery, sliced
Bouquet Garni:
   3 sprigs parsley
   2 sprigs thyme (or ½ teaspoon dried)
   1 bay leaf
3 cups Brown Stock [No. 4]
3 cups dry white wine
Salt and freshly ground pepper
3 tablespoons butter
1 clove garlic, crushed in the garlic-press
½ pound mushrooms, sliced
4 tablespoons Kneaded Butter [No. 107]
1 cup Tomato Sauce [No. 19]
3 sweet Italian sausages, sautéed for about 15 minutes
   and sliced
1 recipe Celery Au Gratin [No. 1659]

Place the pieces of oxtail in a large, heavy pot with the sliced vegetables and the Bouquet Garni. Add the stock and wine and sufficient water to barely cover the pieces of oxtail. Season lightly with salt and pepper, bring to a boil, cover the pot, and simmer over very low heat for 3 to 4 hours, or until the oxtail meat is very tender and will separate easily from the bones. While the oxtail is simmering, melt the butter in a frying pan over medium heat, add the garlic, cook for 1 minute, add the mushrooms, and sauté gently for about 8 minutes; remove from the heat and reserve. When the oxtail is fully cooked, remove the pieces from the pot. Strain the cooking liquid through a fine sieve, return it to the pot (there should be about 4 cups; reduce over high heat to this quantity, if necessary), bring to a boil, blend in the kneaded butter with a whisk, add the tomato sauce, and simmer for 10 minutes. Correct the seasoning and then add the oxtail pieces, mushrooms, and sausage. Simmer for 5 minutes and then turn the contents of the pot out into a deep hot serving dish. Serve the gratinéed celery on the side. *Serves 6.*

1431. OXTAIL VACCINARA
Coda di bue alla vaccinara

4 pounds cut-up oxtail
1 onion, sliced
1 leek (white part only), sliced
1 carrot, sliced
1 quart Brown Stock [No. 4]
Bouquet Garni:
  3 sprigs parsley
  2 sprigs thyme (or ½ teaspoon dried)
  1 bay leaf
2 tablespoons oil
A chopped mixture:
  ¼ pound prosciutto (fat and lean)
  1 onion
  3 sprigs marjoram (or 1 teaspoon dried)
1 cup dry white wine
2 pounds tomatoes, peeled, seeded, drained, and
    chopped
1 bunch celery, cut into 2-inch pieces and parboiled
    in lightly salted water for 10 minutes
1 tablespoon pine nuts
2 tablespoons seeded raisins
Pinch cinnamon
Pinch nutmeg
Salt and freshly ground pepper

Place the pieces of oxtail in a large, heavy pot with the sliced vegetables, stock, and Bouquet Garni. Add sufficient water to barely cover the oxtail and season lightly with salt. Bring to a boil, cover the pot, and simmer over very low heat for 2½ hours, or until the pieces of oxtail are not quite tender. Remove them from the pot and dry them thoroughly. Put the oil and the chopped mixture in a heavy casserole over medium heat and stir until the onion begins to color. Add the pieces of oxtail and turn them until they begin to brown. Add the wine and cook until it has completely evaporated. Add the tomatoes and 1 cup of the oxtail cooking liquid, season with salt and pepper, cover the pot very tightly, and simmer over low heat for about 1 hour, or until the meat is very tender and separates easily from the bones. About 15 minutes before the oxtail is fully cooked, add the parboiled celery, pine nuts, and raisins and then complete the cooking. Taste for salt and pepper and season with a little cinnamon and nutmeg. Serve in the casserole. *Serves* 6.

NOTE: The remaining oxtail cooking liquid can serve as the basis for soup or a sauce.

POULTRY WINGS
Alette di pollame

Although the wings of most poultry may be cooked separately, turkey wings lend themselves best to this separate treatment, since they are larger and have more meat on them.

1432. FRIED TURKEY WINGS
Alette di tacchino dorate

6 large or 12 small turkey wings
1 onion, sliced
1 carrot, sliced
1 stalk celery, sliced
Salt and freshly ground pepper
2 eggs, beaten
2 cups fresh breadcrumbs
4 tablespoons butter
2 cups Tomato Sauce [No. 19]

Put the turkey wings in a pot with the sliced vegetables and cover with cold water. Season lightly with salt and pepper, bring to a boil, and simmer over low heat for about 1 hour, or until the wings are very tender. Drain them, cool, and remove all of the bones but try to retain the original shape of the wings. Season them with salt and pepper, dip in beaten egg, and coat generously with breadcrumbs. Melt the butter in a large frying pan over fairly high heat and sauté the wings until they are golden brown on both sides. Transfer them to a hot serving platter and serve the tomato sauce separately. *Serves* 6.

1433. TURKEY WINGS NIÇOISE
Alette di tacchino alla nizzarda

6 large or 12 small turkey wings
3 tablespoons butter
3 tablespoons oil
1 cup chopped onion
2 cloves garlic, crushed in the garlic-press
1 cup dry white wine
1 cup Chicken Stock [No. 3]
1 pound ripe tomatoes, peeled, seeded, drained, and
    chopped
Bouquet Garni:
   3 sprigs parsley
   2 sprigs thyme (or $\frac{1}{2}$ teaspoon dried)
$1\frac{1}{2}$ cups pitted black olives
$\frac{1}{2}$ pound mushroom caps
2 tablespoons chopped parsley
Salt and freshly ground pepper

Heat the butter and oil until very hot in a large frying pan over fairly high heat, add the turkey wings, and brown on all sides. Remove them from the pan, add the onion and garlic, and cook until they begin to color. Add the wine and cook until it has completely evaporated. Add the tomatoes and stock and Bouquet Garni, season with salt and pepper, and bring to a boil. Return the wings to the pan, cover tightly, and cook for 20 minutes over low heat. Add the mushrooms and olives and simmer for 15 minutes longer. Turn the wings and sauce out onto a hot, shallow serving platter and sprinkle with the parsley. *Serves* 6.

SWEETBREADS
Animella di vitello

Veal sweetbreads are more tender and flavorful than any other variety and are the type most commonly found in American markets. Sweetbreads are very similar to brains in texture and flavor. However, they are somewhat less delicate, and they receive the same preliminary preparation and generally the same cooking treatment. A whole sweetbread is the thymus gland of the animal and consists of 2 nodules, or lobes, of which the more rounded is the tenderest and best part. This choicer lobe is sometimes available separately, although it is more expensive.

If sweetbreads are to be sautéed or broiled, first soak them in several changes of cold water for 2 hours.

Drain and carefully remove as much as possible of the membrane that covers them, being careful not to dig into the tender flesh. Soak them again in cold water acidulated with lemon juice or vinegar and again remove as much of the membrane as possible. Cut off the connective tubes and then blanch the sweetbreads over low heat for 15 minutes in lightly salted water acidulated with lemon juice (about 1 tablespoon of lemon juice to 1 quart of water). The water should be maintained at a point just below a simmer; do not boil. Drain and plunge them in cold water for 5 to 10 minutes. They are now ready to be sliced and sautéed.

Sautéeing is the more popular method of cooking sweetbreads. If, however, they are to be braised, blanching them is not necessary.

1434. SWEETBREADS WITH ARTICHOKES
Animella di vitello con carciofi

2 pounds sweetbreads, soaked, trimmed, and blanched
2 tablespoons oil
6 very small artichokes, cut in half, trimmed, and
    parboiled until just tender (*see* page 539)
Flour
$\frac{1}{2}$ cup butter
$1\frac{1}{2}$ cups dry white wine
1 cup chopped smoked ham (fat and lean)
6 slices bread, crusts removed, sautéed golden brown
    in butter
Salt and freshly ground pepper

Heat the oil in a frying pan over low heat, add the artichoke halves, and sauté very gently for about 5 minutes to get them very hot. Remove them from the heat and keep warm. Slice the sweetbreads about $\frac{1}{2}$ inch thick, season with salt and pepper, and dust with flour. Heat 5 tablespoons of the butter in a large frying pan over medium heat until the foam subsides, add the sweetbreads, and brown them for about 3 minutes on each side. Remove them with a slotted spoon to a hot serving platter and keep warm. Add the wine to the pan and reduce over high heat by $\frac{1}{2}$. Add the ham, cook for 1 minute, remove from the heat, and swirl in the remaining butter, bit by bit. Pour this sauce over the sweetbreads and garnish the platter with the browned slices of bread and the artichokes. *Serves* 6.

SEE
VERSE
FOR
PTION

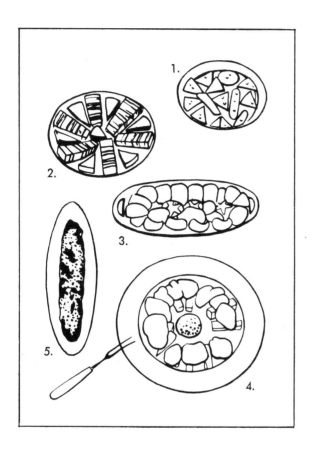

1. Chicken Livers on Toast Points (No. 1420)
2. Pork Liver Bolognese (No. 1407)
3. Gruyère Cheese Croquettes (No. 1361)
4. Broiled sweetbreads (see Nos. 1437–39) served on toast strips. This type of presentation may be accompanied with any of the sauces called for or described in the above-listed recipes.
5. Broiled Tomatoes (No. 1809)

1435. BRAISED SWEETBREADS BONNE MAMAN
Animella di vitello bonne maman

2 pounds sweetbreads, soaked and trimmed
6 tablespoons butter
2 stalks celery, sliced
2 carrots, sliced
2 onions, sliced
Bouquet Garni:
   3 sprigs parsley
   2 sprigs thyme (or ½ teaspoon dried)
   1 bay leaf
2 cups White Stock [No. 1]
1 cup dry white wine
Salt and freshly ground pepper

Heat 3 tablespoons of the butter in a casserole over medium heat, add the sliced vegetables and the Bouquet Garni, and sauté gently for 10 minutes. Add the sweetbreads and cook for 10 minutes, turning them frequently. Add the stock and wine, bring to a boil, cover the casserole tightly, and place it in a moderate (325°) oven for 40 minutes. Transfer the sweetbreads to a hot serving platter and keep warm. Discard the Bouquet Garni, reduce the cooking liquid to ½ its quantity, correct the seasoning, remove from the heat, and swirl in the remaining butter, bit by bit. Slice the sweetbreads on the platter and pour the sauce over them. *Serves* 6.

1436. BRAISED SWEETBREADS WITH CELERY AU GRATIN
Animella di vitello con sedani gratinati

Prepare in the same manner and with the same ingredients as the preceding recipe and serve with a side dish of Celery Au Gratin [No. 1659]. *Serves* 6.

1437. BROILED SWEETBREADS DIAVOLO
Animella di vitello alla diavolo

2 pounds sweetbreads, soaked, trimmed, and blanched
½ cup butter, melted
Salt and freshly ground white pepper
6 Tomatoes Au Gratin [No. 1812]
2 cups Diavolo Sauce [No. 30]

Cut the sweetbreads in half lengthwise, season them with salt and pepper, and brush with melted butter. Place them under a medium broiler flame for about 10 minutes, turning and basting frequently with more melted butter. Arrange them on a hot serving platter, garnish with the tomatoes, and serve the Diavolo sauce on the side. *Serves* 6.

1438. BROILED SWEETBREADS MAÎTRE D'HÔTEL
Animella di vitello alla "Maître d'Hôtel"

Prepare in the same manner and with the same ingredients as the preceding recipe, omitting the Diavolo sauce and spreading sweetbreads with a generous cup of softened Maître d'Hôtel Butter [No. 111] when they are arranged on the platter. *Serves* 6.

1439. BROILED SWEETBREADS PIQUANT
Animella di vitello con salsa piccante

Prepare in the same manner and with the same ingredients as Broiled Sweetbreads Diavolo [No. 1437], substituting Piquant Sauce [No. 94] for the Diavolo sauce. *Serves* 6.

1440. SWEETBREADS GOURMET
Animella di vitello dei gourmets

1 recipe Braised Sweetbreads Bonne Maman [No. 1435]
2 truffles, sliced
½ recipe Flaky Pastry [No. 1954]
1 egg yolk, beaten with 2 tablespoons milk

Prepare the braised sweetbreads. When they are fully cooked, slice them, arrange them in a shallow baking dish, sprinkle with the sliced truffles, and pour the braising sauce over them. Roll the pastry dough out ¼ inch thick, cover the baking dish with it, crimp the edges decoratively, and brush with the egg yolk mixed with milk. Place the dish in the upper level of a hot (450°) oven for 20 minutes, or until the crust is nicely browned. *Serves* 6.

1441. SWEETBREADS WITH HAM AND MASHED POTATOES
Animella di vitello al prosciutto con purea di patate

Prepare in the same manner and with the same ingredients as Sweetbreads with Artichokes [No. 1434], omitting the artichokes and the browned slices of bread and serving with a separate dish of Mashed Potatoes [No. 1780]. *Serves* 6.

1442. SWEETBREADS WITH LEMON
Animella di vitello fritta al limone

2 pounds sweetbreads, soaked, trimmed, blanched, and
    sliced
A marinade:
    $\frac{1}{2}$ cup oil
    $\frac{1}{2}$ cup lemon juice
    1 tablespoon chopped thyme (or 1 teaspoon dried)
    1 bay leaf, crumbled
    10 basil leaves
    1 clove garlic, crushed in the garlic-press
    1 teaspoon salt
    $\frac{1}{4}$ teaspoon freshly ground pepper
Flour
6 tablespoons butter
2 lemons, quartered

Place the sliced sweetbreads in the marinade for 2 hours. Drain thoroughly, and dust with flour. Heat the butter in a very large frying pan over fairly high heat and brown the sweetbreads for about 3 minutes on each side. Transfer them to a hot serving platter, pour the butter in the pan over them, and garnish with the lemon quarters. *Serves* 6.

1443. SCALOPPINE OF SWEETBREADS CAPRICCIOSE
Scaloppine di animella di vitello capricciose

2 pounds sweetbreads, soaked, trimmed, and blanched
Flour
2 eggs, beaten
2 cups fresh breadcrumbs
6 tablespoons butter
$\frac{1}{4}$ cup chopped onion
$1\frac{1}{2}$ cups dry Marsala wine
1 cup Consommé [No. 360]
2 tablespoons Kneaded Butter [No. 107]
Pinch paprika
2 tablespoons chopped parsley
Salt and freshly ground pepper

Slice the sweetbreads about $\frac{1}{2}$ inch thick, season the slices with salt and pepper, dust them with flour, dip in beaten egg, and coat generously with breadcrumbs. Heat 4 tablespoons of the butter in a large frying pan over medium high heat and brown the slices for about 3 minutes on each side. Transfer them to a hot serving platter and keep warm. Add the onion to the butter in the pan (adding another 2 tablespoons, if necessary), cook until the onion is transparent, add the Marsala,

and reduce over high heat to $\frac{1}{2}$ its quantity. Add the consommé, bring to a boil, blend in the kneaded butter with a whisk, and simmer for about 8 minutes. Taste for salt and pepper and season with a pinch of paprika. Pour this sauce over the sweetbreads and sprinkle with the parsley. *Serves* 6.

1444. SCALOPPINE OF SWEETBREADS IN CREAM
Scaloppine di animella di vitello alla crema

2 pounds sweetbreads, soaked, trimmed, and blanched
Flour
4 tablespoons butter
1 tablespoon chopped shallot
1 cup dry sherry wine
1 cup heavy cream
Salt and freshly ground white pepper
6 slices of bread, crusts removed, sautéed golden
    brown in butter

Cut the sweetbreads into $\frac{1}{2}$-inch slices, season them with salt and pepper, and dust lightly with flour. Heat the butter in a large frying pan over fairly high heat until the foam subsides and brown the sweetbreads for about 3 minutes on each side. Transfer them to a hot serving platter and keep warm. Add the shallot to the butter in the pan, cook until it begins to color, add the sherry, and reduce to $\frac{1}{2}$ its quantity. Add the cream and continue cooking until slightly reduced and thickened. Taste, and correct seasoning. Arrange a few pieces of the sweetbreads on each of the slices of toast and spoon a little of the sauce over each. *Serves* 6.

1445. SCALOPPINE OF SWEETBREADS WITH FETTUCINE
Scaloppine di animella di vitello con fettuccine al burro

2 pounds sweetbreads, soaked, trimmed, and blanched
Flour
2 eggs, beaten
2 cups fresh breadcrumbs mixed with $\frac{1}{2}$ cup grated
    Parmesan cheese
6 tablespoons butter
1 recipe Fettuccine with Triple Butter [No. 490]
2 lemons, quartered
Salt and freshly ground pepper

Cut the sweetbreads into $\frac{1}{2}$-inch slices, season them with salt and pepper, dust with flour, dip in beaten egg, and cover generously with breadcrumbs mixed with Parmesan cheese. Heat the butter in a large frying pan over medium high heat until the foam subsides and brown the sweetbreads for about 3 minutes on each side. Heap the hot fettuccine up in the center of a hot serving platter, surround with the sweetbreads generously covered with the butter in which they cooked, and garnish with the lemon quarters. *Serves* 6.

1446. SCALOPPINE OF SWEETBREADS WITH LEMON
Scaloppine di animella di vitello al burro e limone

2 pounds sweetbreads, soaked, trimmed, and blanched
Flour
Salt and freshly ground pepper
4 tablespoons butter
2 lemons, very thinly sliced

Cut the sweetbreads into slices ½ inch thick, season them with salt and pepper, and dust with flour. Heat the butter in a large frying pan over fairly high heat and brown the sweetbreads for about 3 minutes on each side. Transfer them to a hot serving platter and keep warm. Add the paper-thin slices of lemon to the butter remaining in the pan, toss over high heat for a few seconds, and then spoon them over the sweetbreads. *Serves* 6.

1447. SCALOPPINE OF SWEETBREADS MILANESE
Scaloppine di animella di vitello alla milanese

Prepare in the same manner and with the same ingredients as Scaloppine of Sweetbreads with Fettuccine [No. 1445], substituting 1 recipe Noisette Potatoes [No. 1783] for the fettuccine. *Serves* 6.

1448. SCALOPPINE OF SWEETBREADS WITH RISOTTO
Scaloppine di animella con risotto

Prepare in the same manner and with the same ingredients as Scaloppine of Sweetbreads with Fettuccine [No. 1445], substituting 1 recipe of Risotto with Butter and Parmesan Cheese [No. 572] for the fettuccine. *Serves* 6.

TONGUE
Lingua di bue

Beef tongue is generally superior in flavor and texture to that of veal, pork, or lamb. A 2- to 3-pound beef tongue is the best size, having a firm but tender texture; over 3 pounds, tongue tends to be somewhat tough.

Both fresh and smoked tongue receive generally the same cooking treatment. Some smoked tongue requires soaking for 24 hours in several changes of water; the packer's instructions should be followed with regard to soaking. Before boiling a tongue, scrub it thoroughly under cold running water; then place it in a pot with aromatic vegetables (sliced carrot, celery, and onion), 1 bay leaf, 5 peppercorns, 1 tablespoon salt (omit for smoked tongue), and cold water to cover; bring it to a boil, and simmer for 3 to 4 hours, or until the tongue can be easily pierced with a fork. Remove it from the cooking liquid, put it under cold running water to make it easy to handle, cut off the small bones and gristle from the root end, and carefully pull off all of the skin (the skin will come off much more easily while the tongue is hot). Return the tongue to the cooking liquid to cool. Unless pickled, tongue nearly always receives this same preliminary treatment.

1449. BOILED TONGUE WITH PIQUANT SAUCE
Lingua di bue in salsa piccante

1 3-pound boiled fresh tongue, sliced ¼ inch thick
3 tablespoons butter
1 cup chopped onion
1 clove garlic, crushed in the garlic-press
3 cups Italian Meat Sauce [No. 41]
2 tablespoons prepared mustard (Dijon-type preferred)
¼ cup wine vinegar
2 tablespoons small pickled capers
4 anchovy fillets, soaked free of salt [*see* No. 220] and chopped
½ cup chopped gherkins
2 tablespoons chopped parsley
Salt and freshly ground pepper

Boil the tongue as described in the introduction above. Heat the butter in a very large frying pan over medium heat, add the onion and garlic, and cook until the onion

499

begins to color. Add the meat sauce, mustard, and vinegar; and stir thoroughly to blend. Add the capers, anchovy fillets, and gherkins; and simmer 3 minutes. Add the slices of tongue and simmer just long enough to get very hot. Correct the seasoning of the sauce, turn the contents of the pan out onto a hot serving platter, and sprinkle with the parsley. *Serves* 6.

1450. BOILED TONGUE WITH SWEET AND SOUR SAUCE
Lingua di bue in agro-dolce

1 3-pound boiled smoked (or fresh) tongue, sliced
     ¼ inch thick
3 tablespoons butter
1 small carrot, chopped
1 small onion, chopped
1 bay leaf
1 tablespoon brown sugar
1 square grated bitter (unsweetened) chocolate
1 cup wine vinegar
1 tablespoon arrowroot
1 cup Brown Stock [No. 4]
½ cup pine nuts
1 cup pitted sour cherries
½ cup seeded raisins
½ cup pitted prunes, soaked for 10 minutes in very
     hot water
2 tablespoons mixed diced candied fruit
Salt

Boil the tongue as described in the introduction above. Heat the butter in a very large frying pan over medium heat, add the chopped carrot and onion and bay leaf, and cook fairly slowly until the vegetables are soft. Add the sugar and chocolate, stir until the chocolate is melted, and blend in the vinegar. Mix the arrowroot with the stock and then add it to the pan. Simmer for about 10 minutes. Add the pine nuts, cherries, raisins, prunes, and candied fruit. Season to taste with salt and add a little more sugar if the sauce seems too sour. Simmer 5 minutes, add the slices of tongue, continue cooking only long enough to get the tongue very hot, and then turn the contents of the pan out onto a hot serving platter. *Serves* 6.

1451. BRAISED TONGUE
Lingua di bue brasata

1 3-pound fresh tongue, scrubbed and boiled with
     aromatic vegetables as described in the
     introduction to this section, but removed from the
     cooking liquid after 2 hours

4 tablespoons oil
4 tablespoons flour
3 cups boiling Brown Stock [No. 4]
2 cups dry red wine
3 tablespoons brandy
Bouquet Garni:
   3 sprigs parsley
   2 sprigs thyme (or ½ teaspoon dried)
   1 bay leaf
Salt and freshly ground pepper

Remove the tongue from its cooking liquid before it is fully cooked, but tender enough to skin; if the skin does not come off easily, cook a little longer. After skinning, dry it thoroughly on paper towels. Heat the oil in a large, heavy pot, brown the tongue on all sides, and remove it from the pot. Add the flour, stir until it begins to color, add the boiling stock, and stir until it comes to a boil. Add the wine, brandy, and Bouquet Garni and bring to a boil. Reduce the heat, return the tongue to the pot, cover, and simmer for 1½ hours, or until the tongue is very tender. Remove it from the braising liquid, trim off the root end, and slice it on a hot serving platter. Discard the Bouquet Garni, correct the seasoning of the sauce, and pour over the tongue. *Serves* 6.

1452. BRAISED TONGUE BORGHESE
Lingua di bue alla borghese

Prepare in the same manner and with the same ingredients as the preceding recipe, except add to the pot for the last 15 minutes of cooking 2 cups of diced salt pork which has been parboiled for 15 minutes and then sautéed in a frying pan until golden brown. If desired, the platter may be garnished with a generous amount of Glazed Carrots [No. 1647]. *Serves* 6.

1453. BRAISED TONGUE AU GRATIN
Lingua di bue brasata e gratinata

1 3-pound Braised Tongue [No. 1451]
4 tablespoons butter
4 onions, sliced
½ pound mushrooms, sliced
3 tablespoons melted butter
1 cup fresh breadcrumbs
Salt and freshly ground pepper

Heat 4 tablespoons of butter in a large frying pan over medium heat, add the onions, and cook until they are soft. Add the mushrooms, mix them with the onions, season lightly with salt and pepper, and cook for about

8 minutes, or until the mushrooms are tender. Slice the tongue, put the slices in a baking dish, toss them with 1 cup of the braising sauce (reserving the remainder of the sauce for another use), and then arrange the slices overlapping one another in the dish. Spread the onion/mushroom mixture over the slices, sprinkle with breadcrumbs, and then with melted butter. Place the dish in a hot (400°) oven for 10 minutes, or until the crumbs are browned. Serve in the dish. *Serves* 6.

1454. BRAISED TONGUE WITH TAGLIATELLE
Lingua di bue brasata con tagliatelle

Prepare the tongue in the same manner and with the same ingredients as Braised Tongue [No. 1451]. Prepare 1 recipe of Fettuccine with Triple Butter [No. 490], heap it up in the center of a large serving platter, surround it with slices of the braised tongue, and spoon the sauce over the slices. *Serves* 6.

1455. PICKLED TONGUE
Lingua di bue salmistrata

Scrub a 3-pound fresh tongue thoroughly under running cold water and then submerge the tongue in a generous quantity of Pickling Brine for Tongue [No. 127] for about 8 to 10 days in a cool place. When the tongue feels hard to the touch, it is sufficiently pickled; if it still feels soft, it should remain longer in the brine. A pickled tongue should be boiled with aromatic vegetables in the manner described in the introduction to this section. *Serves* 6.

TRIPE
Trippe

Tripe is the lining of beef stomach. There are 4 types: the lining of the so-called second stomach—the end of the belly—provides 3 kinds of honeycomb tripe: dark, light, and partially honeycombed. The fat part of the belly provides the fourth type. Although light honeycomb tripe is the type most commonly found in American markets, all 4 types are used in some classic dishes, such as the famous *Tripes à la mode de Caen*. Nowadays tripe is frequently sold partially cooked and one should always inquire from a butcher whether it is or not. If not partially cooked, tripe requires extremely long—from 12 to 24 hours—slow cooking.

Uncooked tripe must be well scrubbed under cold running water and then soaked for a minimum of 12 hours in cold water. It is then blanched by simmering very slowly in lightly salted water for $\frac{1}{2}$ hour. Drain, cut it into pieces $1\frac{1}{2}$ inches square or any other desired small shapes, and it is then ready for cooking.

1456. TRIPE BOLOGNESE
Trippa alla bolognese

3 pounds pre-cooked light honeycomb tripe, cut into
    $1\frac{1}{2}$-inch squares
2 tablespoons oil
A chopped mixture:
    $\frac{1}{4}$ pound lean salt pork, parboiled 5 minutes
    1 onion
    1 clove garlic
    3 sprigs parsley
3 cups Brown Stock [No. 4]
2 tablespoons Kneaded Butter [No. 107]
$\frac{1}{2}$ cup Italian Meat Sauce [No. 41]
1 cup grated Parmesan cheese
Salt and freshly ground pepper

Put the oil in a large, heavy pot over medium heat, add the chopped mixture, and cook until the onion begins to color. Add the pieces of tripe, season with salt and pepper, and brown on both sides. Add the stock, bring to a boil, reduce the heat to a very low flame, cover the pot, and simmer for 3 hours, or until the tripe is very tender. Remove the pieces with a slotted spoon and keep warm. Reduce the cooking liquid over high heat to a scant 2 cups. Blend in the kneaded butter with a whisk, add the meat sauce, and simmer for 10 minutes. Correct the seasoning, return the tripe to the pot, heat for 1 minute, taste, and correct seasoning and then turn the contents of the pot out onto a hot serving platter. Serve the grated cheese on the side. *Serves* 6.

1457. TRIPE BORGHESE
Trippa alla borghese

3 pounds pre-cooked light honeycomb tripe, cut into
    $1\frac{1}{2}$-inch squares
$\frac{1}{2}$ cup butter
1 onion, sliced
1 carrot, sliced
4 tablespoons flour
1 quart boiling Brown Stock [No. 4]
Bouquet Garni:
    3 sprigs parsley
    2 sprigs thyme (or $\frac{1}{2}$ teaspoon dried)
    1 bay leaf
$\frac{1}{2}$ pound mushrooms, sliced
1 clove garlic, crushed in the garlic-press
Salt and freshly ground pepper
2 tablespoons chopped parsley

Heat 5 tablespoons of the butter in a large, heavy pot over medium heat, add the sliced onion and carrot, and cook until the onion begins to color. Sprinkle with the flour, stir for 1 minute, add the boiling stock, and stir until it comes back to a boil. Add the pieces of tripe and the Bouquet Garni and season if necessary with salt and pepper. Cover the pot and simmer very slowly for 3 hours, or until the tripe is tender. While the tripe is cooking, gently sauté the mushrooms and garlic in the remaining butter in a frying pan over medium heat for about 8 minutes; remove from the heat and reserve. About 5 minutes before removing the tripe from the heat, add the mushrooms and garlic. When tripe is fully cooked, discard the Bouquet Garni, turn the contents of the pot out onto a hot serving platter, and sprinkle with the parsley. *Serves* 6.

1458. BREADED TRIPE WITH PIQUANT SAUCE
Trippa fritta panata con salsa piccante

3 pounds pre-cooked light honeycomb tripe, cut into
    $1\frac{1}{2}$-inch squares
1 quart Brown Stock [No. 4]
Salt and freshly ground pepper
Flour
3 eggs, beaten
3 cups breadcrumbs
Fat for deep frying
2 cups Piquant Sauce [No. 94]

Put the pieces of tripe and the stock in a large, heavy pot over medium heat, bring to a boil, reduce the heat, and simmer for about 3 hours, or until the tripe is tender. Drain thoroughly, season the pieces with salt and pepper, dust them with flour, dip in beaten egg, and coat generously with breadcrumbs. Fry the pieces in deep hot (375°) fat until golden brown, drain, and arrange them on a hot serving platter. Serve the Piquant sauce on the side. *Serves* 6.

1459. TRIPE WITH BUTTER AND LEMON
Trippa al burro e limone

3 pounds pre-cooked light honeycomb tripe, cut into
    $1\frac{1}{2}$-inch squares
1 quart Brown Stock [No. 4]
Salt and freshly ground pepper
Flour
$\frac{1}{2}$ cup butter
2 tablespoons chopped parsley
Juice of 2 lemons

Simmer the tripe in the stock in the manner described in the preceding recipe, drain thoroughly, season the pieces with salt and pepper, and dust with flour. Heat 4 tablespoons of butter in each of 2 frying pans over fairly high heat, add half of the tripe to each pan, and brown on both sides. Transfer the pieces to a hot serving platter, squeeze the lemon juice over them, and sprinkle with the parsley. *Serves* 6.

1460. TRIPE WITH COGNAC
Trippa maritata al cognac

3 pounds uncooked tripe, soaked, blanched, and
    cut into $1\frac{1}{2}$-inch squares
1 carrot, sliced
2 onions, sliced
1 calf's foot, split
Bouquet Garni:
    3 sprigs thyme (or $\frac{1}{2}$ teaspoon dried)
    1 bay leaf
3 cloves garlic, crushed in the garlic-press
8 peppercorns
2 cups dry white wine
2 cups Brown Stock [No. 4]
$1\frac{1}{2}$ cups very thick flour and water paste
$\frac{1}{2}$ cup Cognac
Salt and freshly ground pepper

Line the bottom of a large earthenware casserole with the carrot and onions and then add the tripe, calf's foot, Bouquet Garni, garlic, peppercorns, wine, and stock. Season lightly with salt and pepper, bring to a boil, and then seal on the lid of the casserole with the flour and water paste. Place the pot in a slow (225°) oven for 18 hours. Break the seal and remove the lid. Discard the Bouquet Garni. Remove the calf's foot, pick off the meat from the bones, and return the meat to the casserole. Heat the Cognac in a ladle for a few seconds, ignite, and pour over the tripe. Shake the casserole for a few seconds until the flames die out and then serve the casserole. *Serves* 6.

1461. TRIPE WITH EGG SAUCE
Trippa legata all'uovo

Prepare in the same manner and with the same ingredients as Tripe Bolognese [No. 1456], except the sauce for the tripe is thickened with 3 egg yolks instead of the kneaded butter. The egg yolks should be mixed with the cold Italian meat sauce before being blended into the tripe sauce, and the sauce is then stirred constantly over low heat until slightly thickened. Do not boil. Stir in the juice of 1 lemon just before serving. *Serves* 6.

1462. TRIPE GENOVESE
Trippa alla genovese

3 pounds pre-cooked light honeycomb tripe, cut into
    1½-inch squares
3 tablespoons oil
½ cup chopped ham fat
1 onion, chopped
1 clove garlic, crushed in the garlic-press
1 cup dry white wine
2 tablespoons chopped parsley
1 tablespoon chopped rosemary (or 1 teaspoon dried)
1 pound ripe tomatoes, peeled, seeded, drained,
    and chopped
1 quart Brown Stock [No. 4]
Salt and freshly ground pepper
1 cup grated Parmesan cheese

Heat the oil and the ham fat in a large, heavy pot over medium heat and then add the onion and garlic. Cook until the onion begins to color, add the pieces of tripe, and sauté for about 3 minutes on each side. Add the wine and cook until it has completely evaporated. Add the parsley, rosemary, tomatoes, and sufficient stock to barely cover the tripe. Season with salt and pepper and cook uncovered over fairly low heat for about 3 hours. Add a little more stock from time to time, as necessary. During the last hour of cooking allow the liquid in the pot to reduce to a slightly thickened consistency, being careful to stir the pieces of tripe frequently so that they will cook evenly. When fully cooked and

tender, transfer the tripe and the sauce to a hot serving platter and serve the grated cheese on the side. *Serves* 6.

1463. TRIPE LUCCHESE
Trippa alla lucchese

Prepare in the same manner and with the same ingredients as Tripe with Butter and Lemon [No. 1459], except omit the lemon juice and just before removing the pieces from the pan, sprinkle with a little cinnamon and a very generous amount of grated Parmesan cheese. *Serves* 6.

1464. TRIPE MADRILÈNE
Trippa alla madrilena

3 pounds uncooked honeycomb tripe, soaked,
    blanched, and cut into 1½-inch squares
3 onions, sliced
2 carrots, sliced
1 calf's foot, cracked and split
Bouquet Garni:
    3 sprigs parsley
    2 sprigs thyme (or ½ teaspoon dried)
    1 bay leaf
6 peppercorns
1 quart Brown Stock [No. 4]
1½ cups very thick flour and water paste
3 tablespoons Kneaded Butter [No. 107]
½ cup tomato paste
6 small sweet Italian sausages
1 cup chopped smoked ham
5 sweet red or yellow peppers, roasted, scraped,
    seeded, and cut into strips [*see* No. 145]
3 tablespoons chopped parsley
Salt and freshly ground pepper

Line the bottom of a large, heavy pot with the sliced

Tripe Madrilène (No. 1464)

503

onions and carrots and lay on top the tripe, calf's foot, Bouquet Garni, and peppercorns. Add the stock and sufficient water to cover the tripe. Season lightly with salt and bring to a boil over medium heat. Spread the flour and water paste around the rim of the pot, put on the cover, and press down slightly so that it is hermetically sealed with the paste. Place the pot in a slow (225°) oven for 18 hours. Carefully prize off the lid and remove the pieces of tripe and the calf's foot with a slotted spoon. Strain the cooking liquid through a fine sieve, de-grease it, and return it to the pot. Reduce it over high heat to about 3 cups, blend in the kneaded butter and the tomato paste with a whisk, reduce the heat, and simmer for 10 minutes. Pick off the meat from the calf's foot and return it and the pieces of tripe to the pot. Add the sausages, ham, and pepper strips and simmer for 15 minutes longer. Correct the seasoning, turn the contents of the pot out into a shallow serving dish, and sprinkle with the parsley. *Serves* 6.

1465. TRIPE MILANESE
Trippa alla milanese

Prepare in the same manner and with the same ingredients as Tripe Bolognese [No. 1456], omitting the kneaded butter. Reduce the stock in which the tripe cooked to 1 cup and increase the Italian Meat Sauce [No. 41] to 1½ cups. Since the stock in which the tripe is cooked is reduced to ¼ its quantity, be careful that it is only very lightly salted at the beginning. *Serves* 6.

1466. TRIPES À LA MODE DE CAEN
Trippa alla moda di Caen

1 pound each of all 4 types of tripe (*see* introduction),
    uncooked, soaked, blanched, and cut into
    1½-inch squares
2 calf's feet, cracked and split
¼ pound chopped salt pork (or pork rind)
3 onions, each stuck with 1 clove
2 carrots, sliced
2 stalks celery, sliced
5 onions, sliced
3 cloves garlic, crushed in the garlic-press
3 small Bouquets Garnis, each made of:
    3 sprigs parsley
    2 sprigs thyme (or ½ teaspoon dried)
    1 bay leaf
2 quarts hard cider
3 teaspoons salt

½ teaspoon mace
2 teaspoons freshly ground pepper
Pinch nutmeg
1½ cups very thick flour and water paste
1 cup Calvados or applejack

Place the salt pork and the cracked calf's feet in the bottom of a very large earthenware pot. Arrange all of the following on top, more or less in layers, and season each layer with a little salt and pepper, mace, and nutmeg: the tripe, whole and sliced onions, carrots, celery, garlic, and Bouquets Garnis. The ingredients should nearly fill the pot. Add sufficient cider to barely cover the tripe. Bring to a boil over medium heat, remove from the heat, spread the flour and water paste around the rim of the pot, put on the cover, and press it down slightly so that the pot is hermetically sealed. Place the pot in a very slow (225°) oven for 24 hours. Carefully prize off the cover, remove the calf's feet, pick off the meat from the bones, and return it to the pot. Add the apple brandy, taste for salt and pepper, and serve in the pot. *Serves* 8.

NOTE: Cider has a tendency to darken the tripe and, if desired, Brown Stock [No. 4] may be substituted. Also, brandy may be substituted for the Calvados.

1467. TRIPES À LA MODE DE LYON
Trippa alla moda di Lione

Prepare in the same manner and with the same ingredients as Tripe with Butter and Lemon [No. 1459], substituting 1 cup of white wine vinegar for the lemon juice. Reduce the vinegar to ½ its quantity before pouring over the tripe. *Serves* 6.

1468. TRIPE ROMANA
Trippa alla romana

Prepare in the same manner and with the same ingredients as Tripe Bolognese [No. 1456], substituting White Stock [No. 1] for the brown stock, grated Pecorino cheese for the Parmesan, and sprinkling the tripe with 3 tablespoons chopped mint when served. *Serves* 6.

1469. TRIPE TOSCANA
Trippa alla toscana

Prepare in the same manner and with the same ingredients as Tripe Genovese [No. 1462], but substituting chopped or dried marjoram for rosemary to cook with the tripe and, if available, sprinkling the tripe with a generous amount of chopped fresh marjoram when served. *Serves* 6.

GAME

GAME
Cacciagione e selvaggina

GAME BIRDS

Pheasant

Mallard Duck

Woodcock

Partridge

Quail

Snipe

Wild fowl and game meats make glorious and unusual table fare and, sadly, they are all too seldom found in ordinary American markets. Unless there is a hunter in the family, game usually has to be sought out from special butchers. In Italian communities of the larger American cities, one can nearly always find a shop that carries a variety of fresh game that has been properly hung or aged. If possible, avoid frozen game meats, as most game is dryer and leaner than commercially raised animals and the freezing and defrosting process reduces the natural juices even further. If only frozen game meat is available, defrost as slowly as possible over a long period of time in the refrigerator.

PARTRIDGE

Pernice

Most of the wild partridge found in American markets is actually either a type of quail or grouse, but since the difference in flavor among them is slight, it takes a true wildfowl connoisseur to distinguish partridge from quail, once cooked. There is a controversy as to whether partridge should be ripened by hanging or not. Italians generally prefer it cooked within 24 hours after killing and American taste is inclined to ripen it for 4 days, or even longer, before cooking. Personal taste for or against ripe game meat must, to a large extent, be one's guide in the length of time to ripen all game meats.

1470. PARTRIDGE ACCADEMIA ITALIANA DELLA CUCINA
Pernici "Accademia Italiana della Cucina"

6 1-pound partridges, cleaned
1 lemon
6 thin sheets fresh pork fat back
6 tablespoons butter
6 large thin slices truffled pâté de foie gras
Salt and freshly ground pepper
1 recipe Dried White Beans with Ham [No. 1614]

Rub the cavities of the birds with lemon juice and season with salt and pepper. Truss and tie a thin sheet of fresh pork fat over the breast of each. Heat the butter in a large, shallow casserole over fairly high heat until the foam subsides and brown the partridges on all sides. Reduce the heat, cover the casserole, and cook for 40 minutes, turning and basting the birds frequently. Remove the pork fat and brown the breasts, uncovered, for the last 10 minutes of cooking. Transfer them to a hot serving platter, remove the trussing strings, and place a slice of foie gras over each breast. Serve the ham and beans on the side. *Serves 6.*

1471. PARTRIDGE BONNE MAMAN
Pernici bonne maman

6 1-pound partridges, cleaned
6 partridge livers
1½ pounds goose liver (or susbtitute chicken livers)
½ cup butter
½ cup pâté de foie gras
1 tablespoon chopped truffles

2 tablespoons chopped parsley
1½ cups fresh white breadcrumbs
¼ cup brandy
6 large thin slices fresh pork fat back
1 cup Armagnac (or brandy)
6 cloves garlic, peeled and parboiled for 10 minutes
Salt and freshly ground pepper

Coarsely chop the goose liver and the partridge livers and sauté gently in a frying pan over medium heat in 2 tablespoons of the butter for 4 minutes. Remove from the heat, mash, and mix with the pâté de foie gras. Turn this liver mixture into a bowl and mix thoroughly with the chopped truffles, parsley, breadcrumbs, and brandy; if the mixture seems too dry, add a little dry white wine. Season the mixture with salt and pepper and stuff each of the partridges. Sew the openings, truss, and tie a thin sheet of fresh pork fat over each of the breasts. Heat the remaining butter in a large, shallow casserole over medium high heat until almost golden and brown the partridges on all sides. Heat the Armagnac in a small saucepan, ignite, and pour over the partridges. Shake the casserole until the flames subside, add the garlic, cover the casserole, reduce the heat, and cook for 50 minutes, turning and basting the birds often. Remove the pork fat in order to brown the breasts, uncovered, about 10 minutes before the partridges are fully done. Serve in the casserole. *Serves 6.*

1472. BROILED PARTRIDGE DIAVOLO
Pernici arrostite alla diavolo

6 1-pound partridges, cleaned
Salt and freshly ground pepper
1 cup butter, melted
2 cups fresh breadcrumbs
1 bunch watercress
12 thin lemon slices, scalloped
2 cups Diavolo Sauce [No. 30]

Split the partridges down their backs, spread them out flat without separating the halves, and pound slightly with the flat side of a meat cleaver so that they will retain their flattened shape. Season them with salt and pepper and brush with butter. Place them on a rack under high broiler flame and brown them for 4 minutes on each side. Remove from the broiler, brush with more butter, cover generously with breadcrumbs, and sprinkle with more melted butter. Return them to the broiler, reduce the flame, and cook for 10 minutes on each side, sprinkling with more butter as necessary. Adjust the heat so that they will not brown too quickly. Transfer them to a hot serving platter, garnish with the water-cress and lemon slices, and serve the Diavolo sauce on the side. *Serves 6.*

1473. PARTRIDGE WITH BRUSSELS SPROUTS
Pernici con cavolini di Bruxelles

6 1-pound partridges, cleaned
1 lemon
6 large thin sheets fresh pork fat back
6 tablespoons butter
1 recipe Brussels Sprouts in Butter [No. 1628]
2 cups diced lean salt pork, parboiled 15 minutes, drained, and sautéed until golden brown
6 slices bread, crusts removed, sautéed golden brown in butter
Salt and freshly ground pepper

Rub the cavities of the partridges with lemon juice and season with salt and pepper. Truss the birds and tie a thin sheet of fresh pork fat over the breasts. Heat the butter in a large, shallow casserole over fairly high heat until almost golden and brown the birds on all sides. Reduce the heat, cover the casserole, and cook for 40 minutes, turning the birds frequently and basting with the butter and juices in the casserole. Remove the pork fat, and brown the breasts, uncovered, about 10 minutes before they are fully cooked. Arrange the partridges on the browned slices of bread on hot serving dish and keep warm. Add the Brussels sprouts and the browned salt pork dice to the casserole, stir for 1 minute, arrange them on the platter, and spoon the juices in the casserole over the partridges. *Serves 6.*

1474. PARTRIDGE IN CASSEROLE
Pernici in casseruola

6 1-pound partridges, cleaned
1 lemon
6 tablespoons butter
6 large thin sheets fresh pork fat back
1 cup Game Stock [No. 7] or Substitute Brown Stock [No. 4a]
½ cup brandy
Salt and freshly ground pepper

Rub the cavities of the partridges with lemon juice and season with salt and pepper. Truss the birds and tie the thin sheets of fresh pork fat over the breasts. Heat the butter in a large, shallow casserole over medium high heat until almost golden and brown the partridges on all sides. Add the game stock, bring to a boil, and place

the casserole, uncovered, in a moderate (350°) oven for 40 minutes, turning the birds frequently and basting with the juices in the casserole. If the stock in the casserole evaporates too quickly as the birds roast, add a very small amount of boiling water. Remove the pork fat and brown the breasts about 15 minutes before the partridges are fully cooked. Remove the casserole from the oven and discard the trussing strings. At the table, heat the brandy over a spirit lamp, ignite, and pour over the partridges. *Serves 6.*

1475. PARTRIDGE IN CREAM
Pernici alla crema

6 1-pound partridges, cleaned
2 lemons
6 tablespoons butter
6 large thin sheets fresh pork fat
½ cup Game Stock [No. 7] or Substitute Brown Stock [No. 4a]
1½ cups hot heavy cream
Salt and freshly ground pepper

Season, truss, and roast the partridges in the manner described in the preceding recipe. After they have been in the oven for 20 minutes, add the hot cream, and continue roasting for another 20 minutes, turning them often and basting frequently with the cream. When they are fully cooked, remove the casserole from the oven, correct the seasoning of the sauce, add the juice of 1 lemon, and serve in the casserole. *Serves 6.*

NOTE: If the cream in the casserole becomes curdled, it may be rectified by adding a few additional tablespoons of chilled cream off the heat just before serving.

1476. PARTRIDGE LUIGI VERONELLI
Pernici alla Luigi Veronelli

6 1-pound partridges, cleaned
1 lemon
6 tablespoons butter
6 medium Italian sausages
6 small carrots, sliced
1 head green (or Savoy) cabbage, cored and cut into 6 wedges
6 large thin slices salt pork, parboiled for 15 minutes
Bouquet Garni:
   3 sprigs parsley
   2 sprigs thyme (or ½ teaspoon dried)
   1 bay leaf
2 cups dry white wine

508

2 cups Game Stock [No. 7] or Substitute Brown
    Stock [No. 4a]
Salt and freshly ground pepper

Rub the cavities of the partridges with lemon, season them with salt and pepper, and truss them securely. Heat the butter in a large casserole over medium high heat until it is almost golden and brown the partridges on all sides. Remove them from the casserole, add the sausages, sauté for 8 minutes, remove from the casserole, and cut them into ½-inch pieces. Add the sliced carrots to the casserole, stir for 1 minute in the hot fat, lay half of the cabbage on top, season with a little salt and pepper, lay the partridges on top of the cabbage, arrange the pieces of sausage around and between them, cover each partridge with a slice of the salt pork, cover with the remaining cabbage, season with a little salt and pepper, and push the Bouquet Garni well down into the casserole. Add the wine and stock, bring to a boil, cover the pot, and place in a moderate (325°) oven for 1½ hours. Serve in the casserole or, if desired, arrange the birds and other ingredients on a hot serving platter. *Serves* 6.

1477. PARTRIDGE NORCIA
Pernici alla moda di Norcia

6 1-pound partridges, cleaned
1 pound lean sausage meat
2 truffles, chopped [or No. 1819a]
2 cups fresh white breadcrumbs
3 tablespoons chopped parsley
6 tablespoons butter
6 large thin slices fresh pork fat back
2 cups dry Marsala wine
2 lemons, sliced
Salt and freshly ground pepper

Sauté the sausage meat in a frying pan over medium heat for about 5 minutes, crumbling it well with a fork as it cooks. Mix it in a bowl with the truffles, breadcrumbs, and parsley. Stuff each of the partridges with a little of the mixture, sew the openings, truss securely, and tie a thin sheet of fresh pork fat over each of the breasts. Heat the butter in a large, shallow casserole over fairly high heat and brown the partridges on all sides. Reduce the heat, cover the casserole, and cook for 50 minutes, turning the birds often and basting frequently with the butter and juices in the casserole. Remove the pork fat and brown the breasts, uncovered, about 10 minutes before they are fully cooked. Transfer them to a hot serving platter and keep warm. Add the Marsala to the casserole, reduce over high heat to

½ its quantity, pour over the partridges, and garnish with the lemon slices. *Serves* 6.

1478. PARTRIDGE WITH GREEN OLIVES
Pernici con olive nere o verdi

Season and truss the partridges in the manner described in No. 1474. Prepare with same ingredients and in the same manner as Squab with Green Olives [No. 1351], substituting 6 1-pound partridges for the squabs. Black olives may also be used. *Serves* 6.

1479. ROAST PARTRIDGE ON TOAST
Pernici arrostite sul crostone

6 1-pound partridges, cleaned
1 lemon
6 large thin slices fresh pork fat
10 tablespoons butter
6 partridge livers, sliced
3 chicken livers, sliced
2 tablespoons brandy
6 slices bread, crusts removed, sautéed golden
    brown in butter
2 cups Game Stock [No. 7] or Substitute Brown
    Stock [No. 4a]
Salt and freshly ground pepper

Season, truss, and roast the partridges in the manner described in Partridge with Brussels Sprouts [No. 1473]. While they are roasting, gently sauté the chicken and partridge livers in 2 tablespoons of butter in a frying pan over medium heat for 4 minutes, remove from the heat, mash them to a paste, and blend in the brandy. Spread this paste on the browned slices of bread, arrange the slices on a hot serving platter, and put a roasted partridge on each slice. Add the game stock to the casserole in which the partridges cooked, reduce over high heat to ½ its quantity, remove from the heat, and swirl in the remaining butter, bit by bit. Serve this sauce on the side. *Serves* 6.

509

Partridge with Brussels Sprouts
(No. 1473): see page 508

1480. SALMIS OF PARTRIDGE
Pernici in salmì

6 1-pound partridges, cleaned
½ pound mushroom caps
¾ cup butter
6 partridge livers
2 chicken livers
½ cup brandy
1 onion, chopped
2 cloves garlic, crushed in the garlic-press
1 carrot, chopped
3 cups Italian Meat Sauce [No. 41]
1 tablespoon chopped thyme
1 bay leaf, crumbled
1 cup dry white wine
2 truffles, sliced
6 slices bread, crusts removed, sautéed golden
    brown in butter
Salt and freshly ground pepper

Gently sauté the mushroom caps in 3 tablespoons of butter in a frying pan over moderate heat for 8 minutes and reserve. Chop the partridge and chicken livers, gently sauté them in 3 tablespoons of butter in a frying pan over medium heat for 4 minutes, remove from the heat, mash them to a paste, and reserve. Season the partridges with salt and pepper and truss securely. Heat 6 tablespoons of butter in a large, shallow casserole over medium high heat and brown the partridges on all sides. Cover the casserole and place it in a moderate (350°) oven for 20 minutes, turning the partridges and basting twice during this time. Remove them from the oven, skin them, and cut each with

poultry shears into 5 pieces: 2 breast halves with wings attached, 2 thighs with drumsticks attached, and the back. Put the backs and the skin in a mortar. Put the remaining pieces in a shallow, hot dish, heat the brandy in a saucepan, ignite, pour over the pieces, shake the dish until the flames subside, and then cover the dish so that the exposed flesh of the partridges will not dry out. Pound the backs and skin as finely as possible with a pestle and reserve. Put the chopped onion, garlic, and carrot in the casserole in which the partridges were cooked, sauté over medium heat until the onion is transparent, add the wine, and cook until completely evaporated. Add the meat sauce, the pounded partridge bones, thyme, bay leaf, and salt and pepper to taste. Simmer for 20 minutes and then strain through a very fine sieve. Put this sauce in a large casserole or dish placed over barely simmering water and add the reserved partridge pieces, their juices, the reserved mushrooms, and the sliced truffles. Cover the pan and heat for 30 minutes, being careful that the water does not boil. Just before removing from this gentle heat, brown the slices of bread in butter and spread the slices with the reserved liver paste. Arrange them on a hot serving platter and spoon the pieces of partridge and the sauce over them. *Serves* 6.

NOTE: If desired, the backs and skin may be placed in the meat grinder, using the finest blade, and ground up instead of pounded in the mortar.

1481. PARTRIDGE ON THE SPIT
Pernici allo schidione

6 1-pound partridges, cleaned
1 lemon
6 large grape leaves
1 cup butter, melted
6 large thin slices fresh pork fat back
6 slices bread, crusts removed, sautéed golden brown
    in butter, and spread with Forcemeat Au Gratin
    [No. 130]
Salt and freshly ground pepper

Rub the cavities of the partridges with lemon and season them with salt and pepper. Truss securely and tie a buttered grape leaf covered with a slice of fresh pork fat over the breast of each. Brush with melted butter and grill the birds about 5 inches above a hot charcoal fire (if possible, on a rotating spit; if not, turning them often) for about 40 minutes, basting with more butter as necessary. Be careful to adjust the height of the birds from the fire so that they do not brown too quickly. Serve them on a hot serving platter, each bird placed on a slice of the browned bread spread with forcemeat. *Serves 6.*

PHEASANT

Fagiano

Pheasant holds a place of honor among wildfowl, not only for its rich distinctive flavor but for the beauty of its plumage with which many pheasant dishes may be garnished. Pheasant should be ripened by hanging for 4 days in a cool, dry place. Occasionally very small pheasants, weighing about 1 pound, are available, but the size recommended for roasting is a 2½- to 3-pound bird which will serve 3 persons generously (or 4, if additional courses are served).

1482. PHEASANT AMERICANA
Fagiano all'americana

6 1- to 1½-pound pheasants, cleaned
1 cup butter, melted
3 cups fresh breadcrumbs
½ cup Maître d'Hôtel Butter [No. 111]
12 slices bacon, broiled crisp
6 large mushroom caps, gently sautéed for 10 minutes in butter
1 recipe Tomatoes Au Gratin [No. 1812]
Salt and freshly ground pepper

Split the pheasants down the back, spread them out flat, and pound them slightly with the flat side of a meat cleaver so that they will retain their flattened shape as they cook. Season them with salt and pepper and brush them with melted butter. Place them on a rack about 5 inches from a high broiler flame and broil for about 5 minutes, or until golden on each side. Remove them from the broiler, cover them with a generous amount of breadcrumbs, sprinkle with melted butter, and return them to the rack of the broiler. Reduce the flame and broil for about 6 minutes longer on each side, basting with more butter as necessary. Arrange them on a hot serving platter, put a generous tablespoon of Maître d'Hôtel butter and 2 slices of bacon on each, and garnish the platter with the tomatoes and mushroom caps. *Serves 6.*

NOTE: If very small pheasants are not available, use 3 2-pound birds and broil for an additional 10 minutes.

1483. PHEASANT BELGIAN STYLE
Fagiano alla belga

1 2½- to 3-pound pheasant, cleaned
1 large thin sheet of fresh pork fat back
½ cup butter
1 onion, chopped
1 carrot, chopped
4 Belgian endives, trimmed, leaves separated, and broken in half
1 lemon
1 cup dry white wine
Salt and freshly ground pepper

Season cavity of the pheasant with salt and pepper, truss the bird securely, and tie the thin sheet of fresh pork fat over the breast. Heat 5 tablespoons of the butter in a large, heavy casserole over medium high heat, add the chopped onion and carrot, cook until the onion is golden, add the pheasant, and brown on all sides. Reduce the heat, cover the casserole, and cook for about 50 minutes, turning the pheasant often and basting with the butter and juices in the casserole. Remove the pork fat and brown the breasts uncovered for the last 10 minutes. While the pheasant is cooking, melt 3 tablespoons of butter in a saucepan over very low heat, add the pieces of endive, toss in the butter, season with salt and pepper, add the juice of 1 lemon and 3 tablespoons of water, and cook covered for 20 minutes. When the pheasant is cooked, remove it from the casserole and carve into serving pieces. Add the wine to the casserole in which the pheasant cooked and reduce over high heat to ½ its quantity, reduce the heat, add the pieces of endive, and arrange the cup-up pheasant on top. Baste with the juices in the casserole, cover tightly, and simmer over very low heat for 10 minutes. Serve in the casserole. *Serves 4.*

1484. BROILED PHEASANT
Fagiano alla griglia

Broil 6 small 1- to 1½-pound, or 3 2-pound pheasants in the manner described in Pheasant Americana [No. 1482], omitting the garnishes of bacon, tomatoes, and mushrooms. *Serves 6.*

Juniper Berries

1485. PHEASANT CONTE DI SAVOIA
Fagiano in casseruola "Conte di Savoia"

1 2½- to 3-pound pheasant, cleaned
1 large thin sheet fresh pork fat back
½ cup truffled pâté de foie gras
¾ cup butter
1 large rectangle of bread, 5 inches wide, 8 inches
    long, and ½ inch thick
1 cup dry Madeira wine
1 cup Game Stock [No. 7] or Substitute Brown
    Stock [No. 4a]
Pinch paprika
Juice of 1 lemon
Salt and freshly ground pepper
1 bunch watercress

Push the forefinger between the skin and the flesh of the breast of the pheasant, work on both sides of the breast until the skin is free, and insert the foie gras between the skin and the flesh. Then season, truss, and roast the pheasant in the manner described in Pheasant Belgian Style [No. 1483]. Sauté the rectangle of bread in 4 tablespoons of the butter until golden brown on both sides, arrange it on a hot serving platter, place the cooked pheasant on top, and keep warm. Add the Madeira and stock to the casserole in which the pheasant cooked, reduce over high heat by ⅓, correct the seasoning, add the lemon juice and paprika, remove from the heat, and swirl in 3 tablespoons of butter, bit by bit. Garnish the platter with the watercress and serve the sauce on the side. *Serves* 4.

1486. PHEASANT IN CREAM
Fagiano in casseruola alla crema

Prepare 6 small 1½-pound young pheasants in the same manner and with the same ingredients as Partridge in Cream [No. 1475]. If only larger pheasant is available, increase the total cooking time after browning to about 1 hour for a 3-pound bird. *Serves* 6.

1487. PHEASANT NORMANDA
Fagiano alla normanda

1 2½- to 3-pound pheasant, cleaned
1 large thin slice fresh pork fat back
6 tablespoons butter
½ cup Calvados (or applejack)
6 tart green apples, cored, peeled, and thickly sliced
1½ cups hot heavy cream
Salt and freshly ground pepper

Season the cavity of the pheasant with salt and pepper,

truss, and tie the sheet of fresh pork fat over the breast. Heat the butter in a large, heavy casserole over fairly high heat until almost golden and brown the pheasant on all sides. Heat the Calvados in a small saucepan, ignite, pour over the pheasant, and shake the casserole until the flames subside. Place the casserole in a moderate (350°) oven, uncovered, for 20 minutes, basting twice during this time. Arrange the apples around the pheasant, add the hot cream, and continue roasting for about 30 minutes longer, basting frequently with the juices in the casserole. Remove the pork fat and brown the breast for the last 10 minutes of cooking. Serve in the casserole. *Serves* 4.

    NOTE: If the cream in the casserole becomes curdled, it may be rectified by stirring in a few additional tablespoons of chilled cream off the heat just before serving.

1488. ROAST PHEASANT ON TOAST
Fagiano arrosto sul crostone

Prepare in the same manner and with the same ingredients as Pheasant Conte di Savoia [No. 1485], omitting the foie gras and paprika. *Serves* 6.

1489. SALMIS OF PHEASANT
Fagiano in salmì

Prepare in the same manner and with the same ingredients as Salmis of Partridge [No. 1480], substituting 3 2-pound pheasants for the partridges. The roasting time for the pheasants should be increased to 35 minutes. If only larger birds are available, increase the roasting time accordingly. *Serves* 6.

1490. SALMIS OF PHEASANT IN RED WINE
Fagiano in salmì al vino rosso

Prepare in the same manner and with the same ingredients as Salmis of Partridge [No. 1480] with the changes noted in the preceding recipe and substituting red wine for the white. *Serves* 6.

1491. PHEASANT WITH SOUR CREAM ENRICA
Fagiano con crema acida "Enrica"

1 2½- to 3-pound pheasant, cleaned
1 large thin sheet fresh pork fat back
½ cup butter
Juice of 2 lemons
1 cup hot Italian Meat Sauce [No. 41]

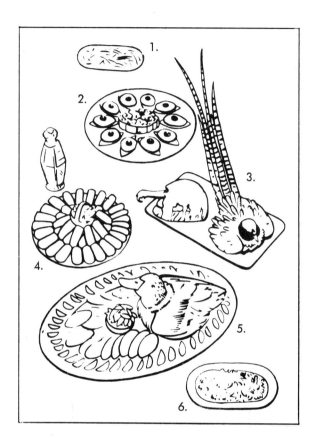

1. French Fried Potato Straws (No. 1776)
2. Fillet of Hare Lucullus (No. 1520)
3. Pheasant with Sour Cream Enrica (No. 1491)
4. Potato Croquettes (No. 1767)
5. Roast Duck with Orange Sauce (No. 1336). In this presentation the dish has been garnished with a wild duck's plumage.
6. Mushrooms with Garlic and Oregano (No. 1709)

1½ cups hot cream
½ pound mushrooms, sliced
Salt and freshly ground pepper

Season the cavity of the pheasant with salt and pepper, truss the bird, and tie the sheet of fresh pork fat over the breast. Heat 6 tablespoons of the butter in a large, heavy casserole over fairly high heat until almost golden and brown the pheasant on all sides. Place the casserole, uncovered, in a moderate (350°) oven for 20 minutes, basting and turning the bird twice during this period. Add the cream, lemon juice, and meat sauce to the casserole, and roast for another 30 minutes, basting frequently with the juices in the casserole. Remove the pork fat and brown the breast during the last 10 minutes of roasting. While the bird is roasting, gently sauté the mushrooms in the remaining butter in a covered frying pan over moderate heat for 8 minutes; add them to the casserole about 5 minutes before the pheasant is fully cooked. If the cream in the casserole curdles, it may be rectified by stirring in a few tablespoons of chilled cream off the heat just before serving. Serve in the casserole. *Serves 6.*

NOTE: In photograph facing page 528, the pheasant is placed on a thick rectangle of white bread (cut from an unsliced loaf, crust removed) treated in the same manner as in Pheasant Conte di Savoia [No. 1485]. The pheasant and bread are then placed on a large platter, the sauce poured over, and the platter garnished with the head and plumage of the bird.

QUAIL
Quaglia

As previously noted, quail is similar to partridge and even sometimes sold as partridge in American markets. It has a delicious white flesh with a strong gamy flavor. Unlike most game birds, quail should not be ripened and is best if eaten within 24 hours after being killed.

1492. QUAIL BORGHESE
Quaglie alla borghese

6 1-pound quails, cleaned
6 large thin slices fresh pork fat
6 large vine leaves
6 tablespoons butter
1 recipe Peas with Lettuce [No. 1736]
1 cup chopped smoked ham

½ cup heavy cream
Salt and freshly ground pepper

Season the cavities of the quails with salt and pepper, truss the birds securely, and tie a vine leaf covered with a sheet of fresh pork fat over the breasts. Heat the butter in a large, heavy casserole until almost golden and brown the quails on all sides. Place the casserole in a hot (450°) oven and roast for 25 minutes, basting 3 times during this period. While they are roasting, purée the peas and lettuce through a food mill or in the electric blender, turn the mixture into a bowl, add the ham and heavy cream, and correct the seasoning. Pour this mixture into a shallow casserole, arrange the cooked quails on top, after removing the trussing strings and pork fat, and place the casserole in a moderate (350°) oven for 10 minutes. *Serves 6.*

1493. BROILED QUAIL WITH ASPARAGUS
Quaglie grigliate con punte di asparagi

6 1-pound quails, cleaned
1 cup butter, melted
2 cups fresh white breadcrumbs
3 cups Duchesse Potato Base [No. 1770]
2 cups Demi-Glaze Sauce [No. 20]
½ cup Game Fumet [No. 9]
18 asparagus tips, cooked until just tender in boiling
    salted water, drained, and dressed with
    3 tablespoons butter
Salt and freshly ground pepper

Split the quails down the back, spread them out flat, and pound them slightly with the flat side of a meat cleaver so that they will retain their flattened shape during the cooking. Season them with salt and pepper, brush with melted butter, and broil under a high broiler flame for 4 minutes on each side. Remove from the rack, coat generously with breadcrumbs, and sprinkle with more butter. Return them to the broiler, reduce the heat slightly, and broil for about 4 minutes longer on each side, or until golden brown, basting with more butter as necessary. Arrange them on a hot serving platter, surround with a thick circle of Duchesse potatoes piped from a pastry bag through a large star tip, garnish with the asparagus tips, and serve the Demi-Glaze sauce mixed with the fumet on the side. *Serves 6.*

513

1494. QUAIL IN CASSEROLE
Quaglie in casseruola

6 1-pound quails, cleaned
6 large thin sheets fresh pork fat back
$\frac{1}{2}$ cup butter
$\frac{1}{2}$ cup brandy
1 cup Consommé [No. 360]
6 slices bread, crusts removed, sautéed golden
     brown in butter, and spread with Forcemeat au
     Gratin [No. 130]
Salt and freshly ground pepper

Season the cavities of the quails with salt and pepper, truss the birds securely, and tie sheets of fresh pork fat over the breasts. Heat 6 tablespoons of the butter in a large, heavy casserole over fairly high heat until almost golden and brown the quails on all sides. Place the casserole in a hot (450°) oven for 25 minutes, basting and turning the birds 3 times during this period. Remove the pork fat and brown the breasts for the last 10 minutes. Remove from the oven, heat the brandy in a saucepan, ignite, pour over the quails, and shake the casserole until the flames subside. Remove the quails from the casserole and keep warm. Add the consommé to the casserole, reduce slightly over high heat, remove from the heat, and swirl in the remaining butter, bit by bit. Return the quails to the casserole, spoon the sauce over them, and serve in the casserole. Serve the browned slices of bread spread with the forcemeat on the side. *Serves 6.*

1495. QUAIL IN CASSEROLE BUONA DONNA
Quaglie in casseruola "Buona donna"

Prepare in the same manner and with the same ingredients as the preceding recipe, adding to the casserole just before serving 18 Noisette Potatoes [No. 1783] and 1 cup of diced salt pork which has been parboiled for 15 minutes, drained, and then sautéed until golden brown and crisp. *Serves 6.*

1496. QUAIL IN CASSEROLE WITH CURRANT JELLY
Quaglie in casseruola con gelatina di ribes

Prepare in the same manner and with the same ingredients as Quail in Casserole [No. 1494], omitting the brandy and adding at the same time as the consommé: $\frac{1}{2}$ cup currant jelly, the juice of 1 lemon, and 1 cup Port wine in which has been soaked for 2 hours the rind from 2 oranges. *Serves 6.*

1497. QUAIL IN CASSEROLE WITH GRAPES
Quaglie in casseruola con acini d'uva moscata

Prepare in the same manner and with the same ingredients as Quail in Casserole [No. 1494], adding 2 cups of pitted Muscat or seedless white grapes to the sauce in the casserole about 3 minutes before removing it from the heat. *Serves 6.*

1498. QUAIL IN CASSEROLE WITH PÂTÉ DE FOIE GRAS
Quaglie in casseruola con fegato d'oca

6 1-pound quails, cleaned
2 cups pâté de foie gras
6 tablespoons butter
2 truffles, chopped
1 cup dry Madeira wine
$\frac{1}{2}$ cups Italian Meat Sauce [No. 41]
$1\frac{1}{2}$ cups very thick flour and water paste
Salt and freshly ground pepper

Season the cavities of the quails very lightly with salt and pepper, stuff each with $\frac{1}{3}$ cup of foie gras, sew up the opening, and truss the birds securely. Heat the butter in a large, heavy casserole over fairly high heat until almost golden and brown the quails on all sides. Add the truffles, Madeira, and meat sauce. Bring to a boil, remove from the heat, spread the flour and water paste around the rim of the casserole, and press on the lid to seal hermetically. Place the casserole in a moderate (350°) oven for 35 minutes. Open the casserole at the table so that the guests may inhale the aroma that escapes when the lid is first taken off. *Serves 6.*

1499. QUAIL DIAVOLO
Quaglie alla diavolo

6 1-pound quails, cleaned
1 cup butter, melted
3 cups fresh breadcrumbs
Salt and freshly ground pepper
2 cups Diavolo Sauce [No. 30]

Broil the quails in the manner described in Broiled Quail with Asparagus [No. 1493] and serve them with the Diavolo sauce on the side. *Serves 6.*

Rosemary

1500. QUAIL WITH NEW PEAS ROMANA
Quaglie con pisellini dolci alla romana

Prepare in the same manner and with the same ingredients as Quail in Casserole [No. 1494], omitting the browned slices of bread. Prepare 1 recipe of Peas with Prosciutto [No. 1739], heap them up in the center of a large hot serving platter, surround with the quails, and spoon their sauce over them. *Serves* 6.

1501. QUAIL RICHELIEU
Quaglie alla Richelieu

6 1-pound quails, cleaned
6 large thin slices fresh pork fat back
6 tablespoons butter
2 onions, chopped
2 carrots, sliced
2 stalks celery, sliced
½ cup brandy
2 cups thickened Brown Veal Stock [No. 6]
3 truffles, sliced
Salt and freshly ground pepper
1 recipe Pilaf [No. 595]

Season the cavities of the quails with salt and pepper, truss the birds securely, and tie a sheet of fresh pork fat over each of the breasts. Heat the butter in a large heavy casserole over fairly high heat until almost golden and brown the quails on all sides. Remove them temporarily from the casserole. Add the sliced vegetables, cook over medium heat until the onion begins to color, return the quails to the casserole, heat the brandy, ignite, pour over the quails, and shake the casserole until the flames subside. Add the veal stock and truffles, bring to a boil, cover the casserole, and place it in a moderate (350°) oven for 35 minutes, turning the quails occasionally. For the last 10 minutes of cooking remove the pork fat from the breasts and cook uncovered to allow the breasts to brown nicely. Heap the rice up in the center of a hot serving platter, surround with the quails, and spoon the cooking liquids over them. *Serves* 6.

1502. SAUTÉED QUAIL WITH CHERRIES
Quaglie arrosto con ciliege

12 very small ½- to ¾-pound quails, cleaned
12 thin slices of fresh pork fat back
6 tablespoons butter
3 cups pitted sour cherries, simmered 10 minutes in 2 cups Simple Syrup [No. 2294], and drained
6 Potato Baskets [No. 1752], each large enough to contain 2 quails
Juice of 1 lemon
Salt and freshly ground pepper

Season the cavities of the quails with salt and pepper, truss the birds securely, and tie a sheet of fresh pork fat over each of the breasts. Heat the butter in a very large frying pan over fairly high heat until golden and brown the quails on all sides. Reduce the heat and continue cooking for about 15 minutes, turning the birds often. Remove the pork fat from the breasts, raise the heat slightly, and cook for about 5 minutes longer, or until the breasts are brown. Arrange 2 of the quails in each of the potato baskets, spoon a few drained cherries into each basket, and squeeze a little lemon juice over each. *Serves* 6.

1503. QUAILS ON THE SPIT
Quaglie allo spiedo

6 1-pound quails, cleaned
6 large thin slices fresh pork fat back
1 cup butter, melted
1 bunch watercress
Salt and freshly ground pepper

Season the cavities of the quails with salt and pepper, truss the birds securely, and tie a sheet of fresh pork fat over each of the breasts. Impale the birds on a rotating spit about 5 inches above a hot charcoal fire, brush with melted butter, and roast for about 15 minutes, basting occasionally with more butter. Remove the pork fat from the breasts, roast for another 5 minutes, or until the breasts are nicely browned, and then arrange the birds on a bed of watercress on a hot serving platter. *Serves* 6.

RABBIT AND HARE
Coniglio e lepre

Both rabbit and hare are bred commercially in the United States, and it is largely a matter of taste whether one prefers their lighter and more delicately flavored flesh to wild rabbit or wild hare, which have a stronger gamy flavor. The wild variety may be cooked and eaten immediately after shooting while they are still warm, but if allowed to grow cold, their texture and flavor are improved by hanging for 3 or 4 days in a cool place.

When rabbit or hare is to be cut up for frying, sever the legs at the joints and cut the backs into pieces about 2 inches wide.

1504. RABBIT IN CASSEROLE GERMANA
Coniglio in casseruola "Germana"

2 3-pound rabbits, cleaned and cut up for frying
6 tablespoons butter
2 cloves garlic, crushed in the garlic-press
2 onions, chopped
6 shallots, chopped
$\frac{1}{2}$ cup brandy
$1\frac{1}{2}$ cups dry white wine
2 cups diced lean salt pork, parboiled 15 minutes, drained, and sautéed golden brown
$\frac{1}{2}$ pound small mushrooms
2 tablespoons Kneaded Butter [No. 107]
3 tablespoons chopped parsley
Salt and freshly ground white pepper

Dry the pieces of rabbit thoroughly on paper towels. Heat the butter in a large pot over fairly high heat until golden and brown the pieces of rabbit on all sides. Remove the pieces from the pot; add the garlic, onions, and shallots; and cook until the onions begin to color. Return the pieces of rabbit to the pot, heat the brandy, ignite, pour over the rabbit, and shake the pot until the flames subside. Add the wine, salt pork dice, and salt and pepper to taste. Bring just to a boil, reduce the heat to a very low flame, cover the pot, and simmer for about 1 hour (wild rabbit will require slightly longer cooking). About 15 minutes before the rabbit is fully cooked, add the mushrooms and stir in the kneaded butter. Complete the cooking uncovered, correct the seasoning, turn the contents of the pot out onto a hot serving platter, and sprinkle with the chopped parsley. *Serves* 6.

1505. FRIED RABBIT
Coniglio fritto dorato

2 3-pound rabbits, cleaned and cut up for frying
3 cups Cooked Marinade for Meat or Game [No. 123]
Flour
2 eggs, beaten with a pinch of salt
Fat for deep frying

6 sprigs fried parsley, fried in deep fat [*see* No. 276]
2 lemons, quartered

The more tender flesh of commercially bred rabbits is preferable for this dish. Marinate the pieces of rabbit in the marinade for 12 hours, drain thoroughly, dust with flour, dip in beaten egg, and drop immediately in deep hot (375°) fat, reduce the heat slightly, and fry for about 20 minutes, adjusting the heat so that they will brown in this time. Arrange the pieces on a hot serving platter and garnish with the fried parsley and lemon quarters. *Serves* 6.

1506. FILLET OF WILD RABBIT
Lombata di coniglio selvatico arrostita

2 $1\frac{1}{2}$-pound fillets from the backs of wild rabbit
24 narrow strips fresh pork fat back
Salt and freshly ground pepper
$\frac{1}{2}$ cup butter, softened
2 cups Game Stock [No. 7], prepared with the bones and trimmings of the rabbits
1 bunch watercress
2 lemons, quartered

Using a larding needle, lard the fillets with the strips of pork fat. Season with salt and pepper, spread with 6 tablespoons of the softened butter, and place them in a shallow roasting pan in a hot (400°) oven for about 25 minutes, basting occasionally with the butter in the pan. Transfer them to a hot serving platter and keep warm. Add the stock to the pan and reduce over high heat to $\frac{1}{2}$ its quantity. Correct the seasoning, remove from the heat, and swirl in the remaining butter, bit by bit. Pour this sauce over the fillets and garnish with the watercress and the lemon quarters. *Serves* 6.

1507. FILLET OF WILD RABBIT IN CREAM
Lombata di coniglio selvatico alla crema

2 $1\frac{1}{2}$-pound fillets from the backs of wild rabbit
24 narrow strips fresh pork fat back
3 cups Cooked Marinade for Meat or Game [No. 123]
$\frac{3}{4}$ cup prepared mustard (Dijon-type preferred), blended with 3 tablespoons oil
5 tablespoons butter
1 cup heavy cream
Salt and freshly ground pepper

Using a larding needle, lard the fillets with the strips of pork fat and then marinate them in the marinade for 12 hours. Drain, dry thoroughly, spread with the mustard, and place them and the butter in a shallow roasting pan in a hot (400°) oven for about 25 minutes (the exact time will depend on the thickness of the fillets), basting occasionally with the butter in the pan. Transfer the fillets to a hot serving platter and keep warm. Add 2 cups of the marinade liquid, strained, to the pan and reduce over high heat to $\frac{1}{2}$ its quantity. Add the cream and continue cooking until slightly thickened and of good consistency. Correct the seasoning and pour over the fillets. *Serves 6.*

1508. FILLET OF WILD RABBIT GOURMET

Lombata di coniglio selvatico alla gastronoma

2 1$\frac{1}{2}$-pound fillets from the backs of wild rabbit
24 narrow strips fresh pork fat back
Salt and freshly ground pepper
5 tablespoons butter
Flour
2 eggs, beaten with a pinch of salt
2 cups fresh white breadcrumbs
6 slices smoked ham, cut $\frac{1}{8}$ inch thick and gently
    sautéed for 3 minutes in 3 tablespoons butter
1 recipe French Fried Potato Straws [No. 1776]

Using a larding needle, lard the fillets with the strips of pork fat and season them with salt and pepper. Heat the butter in a large, shallow casserole over fairly high heat until almost golden and brown the fillets on all sides. Place the casserole in a hot (400°) oven for 15 minutes, basting twice with the butter in the casserole. Remove the fillets, dust them lightly with flour, dip in beaten egg, cover generously with breadcrumbs, and sprinkle with the butter with which they were roasted. Place them on a rack beneath a high broiler flame and broil for about 5 minutes on each side, or until their covering is golden brown. Baste occasionally with more butter as necessary. Line a hot serving platter with the slices of ham, lay the fillets on top, and garnish with the potato straws. *Serves 6.*

1509. FILLET OF WILD RABBIT WITH TARTAR SAUCE

Lombata di coniglio selvatico alla tartara

2 1$\frac{1}{2}$-pound fillets from the backs of wild rabbit
A marinade:
    1 cup olive oil
    2 tablespoons chopped parsley
    1 teaspoon salt
    $\frac{1}{4}$ teaspoon freshly ground pepper
Flour
2 eggs, beaten with a pinch of salt
2 cups breadcrumbs
$\frac{1}{2}$ cup butter, melted
2 cups Tartar Sauce [No. 98]

Place the fillets in the marinade for 2 hours. Drain, dry thoroughly, dust with flour, dip in beaten egg, and cover generously with breadcrumbs. Place the fillets in a shallow roasting pan, sprinkle with melted butter, and place in a hot (400°) oven for about 25 minutes, basting frequently with more butter. Spread the tartar sauce out on a hot serving platter and lay the fillets on top. *Serves 6.*

1510. WILD RABBIT FRANCESE

Coniglio selvatico alla francese

2 3-pound rabbits, cleaned and cut up for frying
$\frac{1}{2}$ cup butter
1 cup diced salt pork, parboiled for 15 minutes and
    drained
1 onion, chopped
2 shallots, chopped
$\frac{1}{2}$ cup brandy
2 cups dry white wine
1 tablespoon chopped thyme (or 1 teaspoon dried)
$\frac{1}{2}$ pound mushrooms, sliced
2 tablespoons chopped parsley
Salt and freshly ground pepper

Dry the pieces of rabbit thoroughly and season them with salt and pepper. Heat 5 tablespoons of the butter and the salt pork dice in a large heavy casserole over fairly high heat until the dice are almost golden, and brown the pieces of rabbit on all sides. Reduce the heat slightly, add the onion and shallots, and cook until the onions begin to color. Heat the brandy, ignite, pour over the rabbit, and shake the casserole until the flames subside. Cook until the brandy is evaporated, add the wine and thyme, bring to a boil, cover the casserole, and place it in a moderate (350°) oven for about 1$\frac{1}{2}$ hours. Add the mushrooms to the casserole for the last 10 minutes of cooking. Transfer the pieces to a hot serving platter, swirl the remaining 3 tablespoons of butter into the juices in the pan, correct the seasoning, pour this sauce over the rabbit, and sprinkle with the parsley. *Serves 6.*

1511. RABBIT STEW CIOCIARA
Spezzatino di coniglio alla ciociara

2 3-pound rabbits, cleaned and cut up for frying
6 tablespoons oil
2 cloves garlic, crushed in the garlic-press
1 cup chopped smoked ham
1 cup dry white wine
2 pounds tomatoes, peeled, seeded, drained, and chopped
3 tablespoons chopped parsley
Salt and freshly ground pepper

Dry the pieces of rabbit thoroughly and season them with salt and pepper. Heat the oil in a large, heavy casserole over fairly high heat and brown the pieces on all sides. Add the garlic and ham, cook until the garlic begins to color, add the wine, and cook until it has evaporated. Add the tomatoes, adjust seasoning, cover the casserole, and cook over low heat for about 1 hour. Sprinkle with the parsley and serve in the casserole. *Serves 6.*

1512. RABBIT STEW IN CREAM BORGHESE
Spezzatino di coniglio con crema alla borghese

2 3-pound rabbits, cleaned and cut up for frying
6 tablespoons butter
3 cups Game Stock [No. 7] or Substitute Brown Stock [No. 4a]
1 onion, stuck with 1 clove
1 stalk celery, sliced
1 carrot, sliced
Bouquet Garni:
   3 sprigs parsley
   2 sprigs thyme (or ½ teaspoon dried)
   1 bay leaf
Juice of 1 lemon
3 egg yolks
1 cup heavy cream
Pinch nutmeg
2 tablespoons chopped parsley
1 recipe Glazed Carrots [No. 1647]
1 recipe Brown-Braised Onions [No. 1722]
Salt and freshly ground pepper

Dry the pieces of rabbit thoroughly and season them with salt and pepper. Heat the butter in a large, heavy casserole over fairly high heat until almost golden and brown the pieces on all sides. Add the stock, onion, celery, carrot, Bouquet Garni, and a pinch of salt and pepper. Bring to a boil, cover the casserole, reduce the heat, and simmer for about 1 hour, or until the pieces of rabbit are tender. Remove them with a slotted spoon to a hot serving platter and keep warm. Strain the cooking liquid through a fine sieve, return it to the pot, and reduce over high heat to about 1½ cups. Mix the lemon juice, egg yolks, and cream and then pour this mixture into the reduced cooking liquid off the heat, stirring constantly with a whisk. Return to very low heat and simmer, stirring constantly, until slightly thickened. Do not boil. Correct the seasoning, add the nutmeg, pour over the rabbit, sprinkle with the parsley, and garnish with the glazed carrots and braised onions. *Serves 6.*

1513. RABBIT STEW ROMANA
Spezzatino di coniglio alla romana

Prepare in the same manner and with the same ingredients as Rabbit Stew Ciociara [No. 1511], omitting the ham and substituting dry Marsala for the white wine. If desired, garnish with 6 slices of crustless bread that have been sautéed golden brown in butter. *Serves 6.*

1514. RABBIT STEW IN WHITE WINE
Spezzatino di coniglio al vino bianco

Prepare in the same manner and with the same ingredients as Rabbit Stew in Cream Borghese [No. 1512], substituting dry white wine for the stock and instead of thickening the reduced cooking liquid with cream and egg yolks, reduce the liquid to 2 cups only and thicken with 2 tablespoons Kneaded Butter [No. 107]. Simmer the thickened sauce for about 10 minutes before pouring over the pieces of rabbit. *Serves 6.*

1515. CIVET OF HARE FIAMMINGA
Civet di lepre alla fiamminga

1 5-pound hare, cleaned and cut up for frying
6 tablespoons butter
4 onions, finely sliced
2 tablespoons flour
1 quart red wine, heated
⅓ cup wine vinegar
3 tablespoons brown sugar

Bouquet Garni:

   3 sprigs parsley

   2 sprigs thyme (or ½ teaspoon dried)

   1 bay leaf

Optional: the blood from the hare mixed with

   3 tablespoons red wine

The liver from the hare, chopped

Salt and freshly ground pepper

2 cups currant jelly

Dry the pieces of hare thoroughly and season them with salt and pepper. Heat the butter in a large, heavy pot over fairly high heat until almost golden and brown the pieces of hare on all sides. Add the onions, stir until they begin to color, sprinkle in the flour, cook for 1 minute, and add the wine, boiling hot. Stir until the liquid thickens slightly and add the vinegar, brown sugar, and the Bouquet Garni. Season with salt and pepper, reduce the heat, and simmer for 1 hour and 15 to 30 minutes, or until the pieces of hare are tender. Remove them to a hot serving platter and keep warm. Discard the Bouquet Garni, reduce the cooking liquid to about 3 cups, add the chopped liver, simmer 3 minutes, and slowly add the blood mixed with wine. Swirl the sauce over very low heat until it thickens slightly. Do not stir or boil. Correct the seasoning, pour over the pieces of hare, and serve the currant jelly on the side. *Serves* 6.

NOTE: If the hare's blood is not used, increase the quantity of flour to 3 tablespoons.

1516. CIVET OF HARE FRANCESE
Civet di lepre alla francese

1 5-pound hare, cleaned and cut up for frying

A marinade:

   2 cups red wine

   ¼ cup brandy

   2 tablespoons oil

   1 onion, sliced

   3 shallots, sliced

   1 bay leaf

   6 sprigs chopped parsley

   1 teaspoon salt

   ½ teaspoon freshly ground pepper

   Pinch powdered thyme

4 tablespoons butter

2 cups diced salt pork, parboiled for 15 minutes
      and drained

12 small white onions

2 cloves garlic, peeled

3 tablespoons flour

3 cups hot Game Stock [No. 7] or Substitute Brown
      Stock [No. 4a]

½ pound mushrooms, sliced

Optional: the blood from the hare mixed with

   3 tablespoons red wine

The hare liver, chopped

Place the pieces of hare in the marinade for 6 hours. Drain them and dry thoroughly. Heat the butter in a large, heavy pot over medium heat, add the salt pork dice, sauté until golden, and remove them with a slotted spoon. Add the onions, sauté until golden brown on all sides, and remove. Reserve the onions and salt pork dice until needed. Add the garlic and pieces of hare to the fat in the pan and brown them over high heat on both sides. Sprinkle the pieces with the flour, stir for 1 minute, and add the boiling stock. Stir until it boils, and add the strained marinade. Bring to a boil, reduce the heat, cover the pot, and place it in a moderate (350°) oven for 45 minutes. Remove the pieces of hare with a slotted spoon to a large heavy casserole, strain the cooking liquid into the casserole, and add the reserved salt pork dice and the onions. Bring to a boil over moderate heat and simmer for 15 minutes. Add the mushrooms and simmer for 15 to 30 minutes longer, or until the pieces of hare are tender. Add the chopped hare liver for the last 5 minutes of cooking. Correct the seasoning, mix a little of the sauce with the reserved blood, slowly add it to the casserole, and then swirl over very low heat until the sauce thickens slightly. Do not boil. Serve in the casserole. *Serves* 6.

1517. CIVET OF HARE WITH POLENTA
Civet di lepre con la polenta

Prepare in the same manner and with the same ingredients as Civet of Hare Fiamminga [No. 1515] and serve with a dish of hot Polenta [No. 623]. *Serves* 6.

1518. CIVET OF HARE LYONNAISE
Civet di lepre à la lyonnaise

Prepare in the same manner and with the same ingredients as Civet of Hare Francese [No. 1516], substituting ½ pound of chestnuts for the mushrooms. The chestnuts should be peeled and cooked until tender in any desired stock as described in No. 1320, browned in butter, and then added to the sauce for the last 15 minutes of cooking. *Serves* 6.

519

Italian Parsley

1519. FILLET OF HARE IN CREAM
Filetti di lepre alla crema

6 1-inch-thick slices fillet of hare
A marinade:
    ¼ cup brandy
    ½ cup oil
    2 tablespoons chopped rosemary (or 1 teaspoon dried)
    ½ teaspoon salt
    Pinch freshly ground pepper
6 tablespoons butter
2 cups heavy cream
½ cup Demi-Glaze Sauce [No. 20]
Salt and freshly ground pepper

Pound the slices of fillet slightly with the flat side of a meat cleaver and then place them in the marinade for 3 hours. Drain and dry them thoroughly. Heat the butter in a large frying pan over fairly high heat until almost golden and brown the slices for about 4 minutes on each side. Transfer them to a hot serving platter and keep warm. Add the cream and Demi-Glaze sauce to the frying pan and cook over high heat until slightly reduced and of a good consistency. Correct the seasoning and pour over the fillets. *Serves* 6.

1520. FILLET OF HARE LUCULLUS
Filetti di lepre "Lucullus"

12 1-inch-thick slices fillet of hare
24 small strips of smoked tongue
24 small strips of truffles
6 tablespoons butter
Salt and freshly ground pepper
12 2-inch rounds, made from very thin Puff Paste
    [No. 1960] and baked in a hot oven until golden
½ cup brandy
1 cup pâté de foie gras, diced
6 truffles, diced
1 cup Demi-Glaze Sauce [No. 20]

Pound the slices of fillet slightly with the flat side of a meat cleaver and, using a larding needle, lard them with the strips of tongue and truffle. Roll each of the slices into the shape of tight cones, secure with toothpicks, and season them with salt and pepper. Heat the butter in a large frying pan over fairly high heat until golden and brown the pieces of fillet on all sides. Reduce the heat and sauté gently for about 10 minutes longer (they should be slightly rare; the exact timing will depend on the thickness of the slices). Arrange them in a circle around the edge of a large hot serving platter, each cone placed on top of a round of baked puff paste.

Add the brandy to the frying pan and de-glaze over high heat. Spoon a little of this sauce over each of the cones. Quickly heat the diced foie gras and truffles in the Demi-Glaze sauce and pour into the center of the platter. *Serves* 6.

1521. FILLET OF HARE ON TOAST
Filetti di lepre sul crostone

6 1-inch-thick slices fillet of hare
24 strips of fresh pork fat back
Salt and freshly ground pepper
6 tablespoons butter
½ cup brandy
6 slices bread, crusts removed, sautéed golden
    brown in butter
2 cups Pepper Sauce [No. 25]

Flatten the slices of fillet slightly with the flat side of a meat cleaver, and, using a larding needle, lard the slices with the strips of fresh pork fat. Heat the butter in a large frying pan over fairly high heat until golden and brown the slices for about 4 minutes on each side. Season them with salt and pepper, heat the brandy, ignite, pour over the fillets, and shake the pan until the flames subside. Arrange each of the slices on a browned slice of bread on a hot serving platter, spoon a little of the pan juices over each, and serve the pepper sauce on the side. *Serves* 6.

1522. ROAST FILLET OF HARE WITH BRANDY AND MUSTARD
Dorso di lepre arrostito con brandy e mostarda

1 3-pound fillet of hare
12 strips fresh pork fat back
½ cup prepared mustard (Dijon-type preferred),
    mixed with 2 tablespoons oil
6 tablespoons melted butter
Salt and freshly ground pepper
¼ cup brandy

Using a larding needle, lard the fillet with the strips of fresh pork fat, season it with salt and pepper, and spread the mustard all over it. Place it in a shallow casserole with the butter in a hot (400°) oven for about 40 minutes, basting frequently with the butter in the casserole. Remove from the oven, heat the brandy, ignite, pour over the fillet, and shake the casserole until the flames subside (it may be flambéed at the table, if desired). Serve in the casserole. *Serves* 6.

1523. ROAST FILLET OF HARE IN CREAM
Dorso e coscetti di lepre alla crema

Prepare in the same manner and with the same ingredients as Fillet of Wild Rabbit in Cream [No. 1507], substituting 1 whole 3-pound fillet of hare for the rabbit and increasing the roasting time to 40 minutes. *Serves* 6.

1524. ROAST FILLET OF HARE TEDESCA
Dorso di lepre arrostito alla tedesca

Prepare in the same manner and with the same ingredients as Roast Fillet of Hare with Brandy and Mustard [No. 1522], larding the fillet with 12 narrow strips of prosciutto (fat and lean) and serving stewed prunes as a side dish. *Serves* 6.

1525. HARE SCALOPPINE WITH TRUFFLES
Scaloppine di lepre con tartufi

12 ½-inch-thick slices fillet of hare
Salt and freshly ground pepper
6 tablespoons butter
2 cups dry Marsala wine
½ cup Demi-Glaze Sauce [No. 20]
4 truffles, sliced

Flatten the slices of fillet with the flat side of a meat cleaver and season them with salt and pepper. Heat the butter in a large frying pan over fairly high heat until golden and brown the slices of fillet for about 4 minutes on each side. Transfer them to a hot serving platter and keep warm. Add the Marsala to the frying pan and reduce over high heat to ½ its quantity. Add the Demi-Glaze sauce and the truffles, heat for 1 minute, and pour over the slices of fillet. *Serves* 6.

SNIPE
Beccaccino

Snipe are very small wildfowl, similar to woodcock. They are improved by hanging for 3 or 4 days in a cool place. Snipe may be drawn, if desired, but the approved method of eating them is whole, entrails and all.

1526. SNIPE IN BRANDY
Beccaccini al brandy

12 snipe
6 tablespoons butter
2 tablespoons chopped shallot
½ cup brandy
¼ cup Meat Essence [No. 10]
Salt and freshly ground pepper

Heat the butter in a very large frying pan over fairly high heat until almost golden, add the shallots, stir for 1 minute, add the snipe, and brown on all sides. Reduce the heat slightly and turn the birds in the hot butter for about 10 minutes. Heat the brandy, ignite, pour over the snipe, and shake the pan until the flames subside. Transfer them to a hot serving platter and season them with salt and pepper. Blend the meat essence with the juices in the pan and pour over the snipe. *Serves* 6.

1527. SNIPE ON A SPIT
Beccaccini allo spiedo

12 snipe
1 cup butter, melted
6 thick slices toast, crusts removed
Salt and freshly ground pepper

Impale the snipe on a rotating spit about 5 inches above a hot charcoal fire, brush generously with butter, and grill them for about 10 minutes. Remove them from the spit, slit them open, scoop out their entrails with a spoon, and mash with a little of the melted butter. Spread a little of this mixture on each slice of toast, arrange 2 snipe on each slice, pour over remaining butter, and season them lightly with salt and pepper. *Serves* 6.

VENISON
Capriola

Venison refers loosely to any antlered game—moose, elk, deer, etc.—but the variety most prized by gourmets is the roe deer. It should be aged for 2 to 4 weeks to tenderize its flesh.

1528. ROAST HAUNCH OF VENISON FRANCESE
Cosciotto di capriolo arrosto alla francese

1 5-pound leg of venison
12 narrow strips of salt pork (or pork fat back)
1/2 cup butter, softened
Salt and freshly ground pepper
1 1/2 cups dry white wine
2 cups Pepper Sauce [No. 25]
1 recipe Lentil Purée [No. 1696]

Using a larding needle, lard the leg of venison with the strips of salt pork, rub it with salt and pepper, and spread with the softened butter. Place it in a shallow roasting pan in a hot (450°) oven for 15 minutes, reduce the heat to moderate (350°), and roast for about 1 hour and 15 minutes longer for medium rare, basting occasionally with the juices in the pan. Transfer the leg to a hot serving platter and keep warm. De-glaze the roasting pan with the wine over high heat and reduce to 1/3 its quantity. Pour this sauce over the venison and serve the pepper sauce and the lentils on the side. *Serves* 6.

1529. VENISON STEAKS WITH CHERRIES
Costolette di capriolo con ciliege

6 venison steaks, cut 3/4 inch thick from the loin
6 tablespoons oil
6 slices stale bread, cut into the shape of hearts and sautéed golden brown in butter
1/2 cup vinegar
3 cups pitted sour cherries, simmered 10 minutes in 1 cup Simple Syrup [No. 2294]
2 cups Pepper Sauce [No. 25]
Salt and freshly ground pepper

Season the steaks with salt and pepper and sauté them in smoking hot oil in a frying pan over high heat for about 4 minutes on each side. Alternate them with the browned hearts of bread, overlapping one another, on a hot serving platter, and place the cherries in the center. Pour off the oil from the pan, de-glaze the pan with vinegar, add the pepper sauce, and heat for 1 minute. Serve this sauce on the side. *Serves* 6.

1530. VENISON STEAKS CONTI
Costolette di capriolo Conti

Prepare in the same manner and with the same ingredients as the preceding recipe, substituting 1 recipe Lentil Purée [No. 1696] for the cherries. *Serves* 6.

1531. VENISON STEAKS IN CREAM
Costolette di capriolo alla crema

6 venison steaks, cut 3/4 inch thick from the loin
6 tablespoons butter
6 slices stale bread, cut in the shape of hearts and sautéed golden brown in butter
1 cup dry Madeira wine
1 1/2 cups heavy cream
2 cups Duxelles [No. 138]
Salt and freshly ground pepper

Season the steaks with salt and pepper. Heat the butter in a very large frying pan over fairly high heat until almost golden and brown the steaks for about 4 minutes on each side. Arrange them alternately with browned hearts of bread, overlapping each other, around a hot serving platter and heap the Duxelles in the center. De-glaze the frying pan with the Madeira and reduce over high heat to 1/2 its quantity. Add the cream, cook until slightly reduced and thickened, correct the seasoning, and spoon this sauce over the steaks. *Serves* 6.

1532. VENISON STEAKS WITH JUNIPER BERRIES
Costolette di capriolo al ginepro

6 venison steaks, cut 3/4 inch thick from the loin
6 tablespoons butter
6 slices stale bread, cut into the shape of hearts and sautéed golden brown in butter
12 juniper berries, crushed in the mortar
1/2 cup brandy
1 cup cream
1/2 cup Pepper Sauce [No. 25]
Juice of 1 lemon
Salt and freshly ground pepper
3 cups hot applesauce

Season and pan fry the steaks in the manner described in the preceding recipe. Alternate them with the browned hearts of bread on a hot serving platter and keep warm. Add the juniper berries and the brandy to the pan and reduce the brandy over high heat to 1/2 its quantity. Add the cream, continue cooking until the cream is slightly reduced and thickened, add the pepper sauce and lemon juice, and correct the seasoning. Spoon this sauce over the steaks and serve the applesauce on the side. *Serves 6.*

1533. VENISON STEAKS À LA MINUTE
Costolette di capriolo à la minute

6 venison steaks, cut ¾ inch thick from the loin
A marinade:
  ½ cup oil
  ½ cup brandy
  1 teaspoon salt
  ¼ teaspoon freshly ground pepper
  6 crushed juniper berries
6 tablespoons butter
6 slices stale bread, crusts removed, sautéed
  golden brown in butter
¼ cup wine vinegar
1½ cups Brown Stock [No. 4]
¼ cup Meat Essence [No. 10]
Salt and freshly ground pepper

Place the steaks in the marinade for 6 hours, turning them occasionally. Drain and dry them thoroughly on paper towels. Heat the butter in a very large frying pan over fairly high heat until almost golden and brown the steaks for about 4 minutes on each side. Arrange them alternately with the browned slices of bread, overlapping one another, on a hot serving platter, and keep warm. De-glaze the pan with the vinegar, reduce over high heat to 1 tablespoon, add the stock, reduce to ½ its quantity, blend in the meat essence, and spoon a generous tablespoon of this sauce over each of the steaks. *Serves 6.*

1534. VENISON STEAKS WITH MUSHROOMS
Costolette di capriolo con testine di funghi

Prepare in the same manner and with the same ingredients as Venison Steaks with Cherries [No. 1529], omitting the cherries and heaping in the center of the platter 1 pound of mushroom caps that have been gently sautéed in 3 tablespoons of butter for about 8 minutes and seasoned with salt, pepper, and a little lemon juice. *Serves 6.*

WOODCOCK
Beccaccia

Woodcock is prized by gourmets above all other wildfowl for its delicious, slightly piquant flavor. Like snipe, it is frequently eaten whole, entrails and all, or the cooked entrails may be used as a paste spread on toast on which the woodcock is served. Woodcock should be ripened by hanging in a cool, dry place for 3 to 4 days.

1535. WOODCOCK IN BRANDY
Beccaccia al fine champagne

6 woodcock, trussed
½ cup butter
½ cup Fine Champagne brandy (or Cognac)
1 cup Game Stock [No. 7]
Juice of 1 lemon
Pinch Cayenne pepper
6 slices bread, crusts removed, sautéed golden
  brown in butter
2 tablespoons pâté de foie gras
Salt and freshly ground pepper

Heat 5 tablespoons of the butter in a large frying pan over fairly high heat until almost golden and brown the woodcock on all sides. Reduce the heat slightly and turn the birds in the hot butter for about 12 minutes. Remove them from the pan and, with poultry shears, cut off the 2 breast halves and the 2 legs with thighs attached. Place these pieces on a hot serving platter and keep warm. Remove the entrails from each carcass and reserve. Crush the remaining carcasses of the birds in a duck press and extract all their juices (this may be done by grinding in meat grinder and then pressing in a fine sieve into a bowl, but it is not as effective). Pour off most of the fat from the frying pan, de-glaze over high heat with the brandy, add the game stock, and reduce by ⅓. Season to taste with salt and pepper and add the lemon juice and Cayenne. Add the reserved juice from the carcasses and stir constantly over very low heat for 1 minute. Do not boil. Remove from the heat and swirl in the remaining butter bit by bit. Spread the browned slices of bread with the reserved entrails blended with the foie gras, arrange the pieces of woodcock on the toast, and spoon a little of the sauce over each. *Serves 6.*

1536. WOODCOCK IN CASSEROLE WITH CREAM
Beccaccia in casseruola alla crema

6 woodcock, trussed
6 tablespoons butter
½ cup Cognac
1 cup heavy cream
Salt and freshly ground pepper

Heat the butter in a large, heavy casserole over fairly high heat and brown the woodcock on all sides. Reduce the heat slightly and turn the birds in the hot butter for about 12 minutes. Heat the Congac, ignite, pour over the birds, and shake the casserole until the flames subside. Remove the woodcocks to a hot serving platter and keep warm. Add the cream to the casserole, reduce for 3 or 4 minutes, correct the seasoning, and spoon a little of this sauce over the birds. *Serves* 6.

1537. SALMIS OF WOODCOCK
Beccaccia in salmì

Prepare in the same manner and with the same ingredients as Salmis of Partridge [No. 1480], substituting 6 woodcock for the partridges. The woodcock should not be drawn until after cooking, their entrails then mixed with a little pâté de foie gras, instead of chicken livers, and spread on the toast on which the carved woodcock is served. *Serves* 6.

1538. SALMIS OF WOODCOCK FERNANDA
Beccaccia in salmì Fernanda

Prepare in the same manner and with the same ingredients as Salmis of Partridge [No. 1480], except for the changes noted in the preceding recipe and substituting red wine for the white, and Demi-Glaze Sauce [No. 20] for the Italian meat sauce. *Serves* 6.

1539. WOODCOCK ON TOAST
Beccaccia sul crostone

Prepare in the same manner and with the same ingredients as Woodcock in Brandy [No. 1535], except the birds are served whole on toast, instead of being carved. After they are fully cooked, slit them open and remove the entrails with a spoon. Mix the entrails with the foie gras, spread on toast, arrange the birds on the toast on a hot platter, and keep warm while the sauce is being prepared. *Serves* 6.

1540. SAUTÉ OF WOODCOCK IN SPUMANTE
Beccaccia sautée allo spumante

6 woodcock, cut up for frying
6 tablespoons butter
2 cups Game Fumet [No. 9], prepared with the backs and heads of the woodcock
1 cup of dry Spumante wine (or Champagne)
¾ cup Demi-Glaze Sauce [No. 20]
Juice of 1 lemon
Pinch Cayenne pepper
Salt and freshly ground pepper

Cut up the woodcock into the following pieces: 2 breast halves with wings attached and 2 legs with thighs attached (prepare the game Fumet with remainder). Heat 4 tablespoons of the butter in a large frying pan over fairly high heat and brown the pieces on all sides. Reduce the heat slightly and turn the pieces in the hot butter for about 10 minutes. Transfer them to a hot serving platter, season them with salt and pepper, and keep warm. Add the Fumet to the pan and reduce over high heat to ½ cup. Add the wine and the Demi-Glaze sauce and reduce to about 1½ cups. Season with salt and pepper to taste and add the lemon juice and Cayenne. Remove from the heat, swirl in the remaining butter, bit by bit, and pour this sauce over the woodcock pieces. *Serves* 6.

COLD MEAT DISHES
AND PÂTÉS

COLD DISHES
Piatti freddi

COLD MEATS
Carni fredde

1541. BEEF IN ASPIC
Bue alla moda in gelatina

1 4-pound rump of beef, cooked in the manner described in Beef à la Mode [No. 1065] and cooled
4 carrots, sliced and cooked until just tender in lightly salted water
12 tiny white onions, cooked until just tender in lightly salted water
2 quarts Regular Aspic [No. 118]
2 cups tiny pickles or gherkins

Line a large mold with a thick layer of aspic (*see* page 49) and then press the onions and carrots decoratively in the bottom and around the sides. Spoon a little aspic over, chill until set, lay the beef on top, and fill the mold with liquid aspic. Chill until firm, unmold on a cold serving platter, and surround with the pickles. *Serves 6.*

1542. FILLET OF BEEF IN ASPIC
Filetto di bue in gelatina

1 4-pound fillet of beef
12 strips pork fat back
2 tablespoons butter, softened

6 truffles, cut in half
Salt and freshly ground pepper

Using a larding needle, lard the fillet lengthwise with the pork fat and truffles. Spread the fillet with the butter, season with salt and pepper, and roast in a hot (375°) oven for 40 minutes. Remove from oven, let cool to room temperature, then chill in the refrigerator for 2 hours. Continue to prepare, with same ingredients, as described in the preceding recipe. *Serves 6.*

1543. COLD FILLET OF BEEF
Cuore di filetto di bue picchettato

4 pounds fillet of beef, cut from the center of the loin
6 narrow strips salt pork, cut slightly longer than the fillet and parboiled for 15 minutes
6 tablespoons butter
1 onion, chopped
1 carrot, chopped
1 cup chopped smoked ham
1 tablespoon chopped parsley
Pinch dried thyme
1 bay leaf
1 cup dry white wine
1 large sheet of parchment paper, buttered on both sides
1 cup Brown Stock [No. 4]
1 bunch watercress
Salt and freshly ground pepper

Using a larding needle, lard the fillet lengthwise with the strips of salt pork and season it with salt and pepper. Heat the butter in a large frying pan over fairly high heat until golden and brown the fillet quickly on all sides. Remove it from the pan, add the chopped onion and carrot, cook until the onion is transparent, and then add the ham, parsley, thyme, bay leaf, and wine. Cook until the wine is reduced by $1/2$, remove from the heat, and cool. Lay the fillet of beef in the center of the parchment paper, pour the cooked vegetables and their cooking liquid over the top, and crimp the edges of the paper tightly together so that the fillet is completely encased. Lay it in a shallow roasting pan, add the stock to the pan, and place it in a moderate (350°) oven for 40 minutes. Remove the beef from the wrapping, chill, and serve cold on a platter garnished with watercress. *Serves 6.*

1544. GALANTINE OF CHICKEN
Galantina di gallinella

1 5-pound capon, split down the back, skinned, and
   boned (*see* page 436)
½ pound lean pork, diced
¼ pound cooked tongue, diced
¼ pound cooked ham, diced
1 pound lean veal, diced
1 pound fresh pork fat, diced
¾ cup dry Marsala wine
¼ cup brandy
½ teaspoon powdered thyme
Pinch powdered bay leaf
4 truffles, diced
2 tablespoons shelled pistachio nuts
2 eggs, beaten
1 calf's foot, split
2 onions, sliced
1 carrot, sliced
1 stalk celery, sliced
1 bay leaf
2 cloves
2 quarts Chicken Stock [No. 3]
Juice of 1 lemon
3 egg whites, lightly beaten
12 thin slices of cooked carrot
1 cooked egg white
6 tarragon leaves
Salt and freshly ground pepper

The skin must be removed from the chicken in 1 piece
without any holes or tears in it and all of the flesh
removed from the bones, reserving the meat from the
breasts and thighs separately. While this is not a difficult operation, it is time-consuming, and an ac-
comodating butcher will do it for you. Cut the flesh
from the breasts and the thighs into dice, place them
in a bowl with the diced pork, tongue, ham, half of the
diced veal, and half of the fresh pork fat. Add ¼ cup
Marsala, the brandy, thyme, bay leaf, and ½ teaspoon
salt. Mix thoroughly and marinate for 6 hours. Put
the remaining chicken flesh, and the remaining diced
veal, and the pork fat through the meat grinder,
using the finest blade. Mix this ground mixture in
a bowl with the diced meats, the marinade, truffles,
pistachio nuts, and the eggs. Season with a little salt
and pepper. Spread the chicken skin out flat, with
moistened hands form the mixture in the bowl into
a cylindrical roll, lay it on the skin, and fold the skin
over the mixture so that it is completely enclosed.
Wrap it tightly in a towel, tie the ends securely, and tie
the center of the roll in 2 or 3 places so that it will retain
its cylindrical shape during the cooking. Place the roll
in a large pot with the calf's foot, onions, carrot, celery,
bay leaf, cloves, and chicken stock. Add a little water
if necessary to cover the roll completely. Bring to a boil
and simmer for 1½ hours. Remove it from the pot,
cool slightly, and remove from the towel. Place it on
a platter and weight it with a board or heavy plate for
2 hours. Chill in the refrigerator overnight. Strain
the stock in which it cooked, de-grease it, return it to
the pot with ½ cup Marsala, the lemon juice, salt and
pepper to taste, and the beaten egg whites. Bring slowly
to a boil, simmer 10 minutes, remove from the heat,

Galantine of Chicken (No. 1544)

527

allow to stand for another 10 minutes, and then strain through several thicknesses of damp cheesecloth. When ready to garnish the galantine, cut the carrot and egg white into any desired fancy shapes and press them and the tarragon leaves onto the top of the galantine. Stir the liquid in which the galantine cooked in a bowl over ice until it becomes thick and syrupy, and completely coat the galantine with it. Pour a generous amount of the aspic on the platter around the galantine and then chill in the refrigerator until firm. *Serves 6 to 8.*

1545. CIMA GENOVESE
Cima alla genovese

4 pounds breast of veal
Stuffing ingredients:
   $\frac{3}{4}$ pound finely ground lean pork
   $\frac{1}{4}$ pound finely ground fresh pork fat
   3 cups fresh bread cubes, soaked in milk, and
      squeezed almost dry
   $\frac{1}{3}$ cup grated Parmesan cheese
   Optional: 1 pound turnip greens, cooked and chopped
   $\frac{1}{2}$ pound shelled peas, cooked
   $\frac{1}{4}$ pound diced cooked veal sweetbreads
      (*see* page 496)
   2 tablespoons chopped marjoram (or 1 teaspoon dried)
   2 tablespoons shelled pistachio nuts
   4 eggs
   1 teaspoon salt
   $\frac{1}{4}$ teaspoon freshly ground pepper
   Pinch nutmeg
1 onion, sliced
1 carrot, sliced
1 stalk celery, sliced
1 bay leaf
6 peppercorns
Salt

Have the butcher prepare the breast of veal for stuffing by cutting a deep lengthwise slit in it. Mix all of the stuffing ingredients thoroughly together and stuff the veal. Sew the opening securely with string and then tie the meat at 2-inch intervals so that it will hold its shape during the cooking. Place it in a large pot with the onion, carrot, celery, bay leaf, peppercorns, and a generous teaspoon of salt. Cover with cold water, bring slowly to a boil, and simmer for about 2 hours. Remove it from the cooking liquid, weight it for 2 hours with a board or heavy plate, and chill before serving. *Serves 6 to 8.*

1546. HARE IN ASPIC CASALINGA
Coniglio in gelatina alla casalinga

1 4-pound hare, cut up for frying
2 calf's feet, split lengthwise and parboiled for
   15 minutes
1$\frac{1}{2}$ cups wine vinegar
$\frac{1}{2}$ cup dry white wine
2 quarts Game Stock [No. 7] or Brown Stock [No. 4]
1 onion, stuck with 2 cloves
Bouquet Garni:
   3 sprigs parsley
   2 sprigs thyme (or $\frac{1}{2}$ teaspoon dried)
   1 bay leaf
1 carrot, sliced
1 onion, sliced
1 stalk celery, sliced
1 teaspoon salt
$\frac{1}{4}$ teaspoon freshly ground pepper
3 egg whites, beaten
1 bunch watercress

Place all ingredients except the egg whites and watercress in a large, heavy pot. Add a little water if necessary to completely cover the pieces of hare and calf's feet. Bring very slowly to a boil and simmer for about 2 hours, or until the pieces of hare are tender. Remove them from the pot to a serving platter. Remove the calf's feet, pick all of the meat from the bones, and arrange them on the platter. Cover the platter with a damp cloth and place it in the refrigerator to chill. Reduce the cooking liquid over high heat to a good strong flavor, strain through a very fine sieve, degrease it, and return it to the pot with the egg whites. Bring to a boil, simmer for 10 minutes, remove from the heat, allow it to rest for 10 minutes, and strain into a bowl through several thicknesses of damp cheesecloth. Cool and then stir over cracked ice until syrupy. Spoon some of this aspic over the cold pieces of hare and calf's foot meat. Chill the remainder in a shallow dish until it is firm, turn it out onto a board, chop it, and arrange small heaps of it around the platter alternating with sprigs of watercress *Serves 6.*

1547. COLD LAMB WITH MINT SAUCE
Schiena di agnello con salsa di menta

Roast a leg of lamb in the manner described in No. 1216 and allow it to remain overnight at room temperature. When ready to serve, slice it, and serve 2 cups of Mint Sauce [No. 91] on the side. *Serves 6.*

SEE
VERSE
FOR
TION

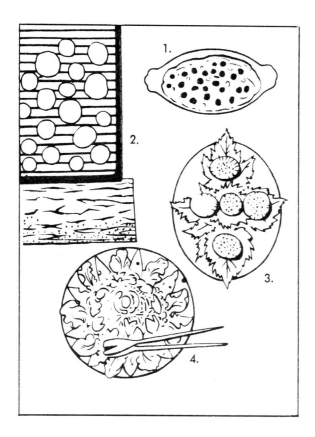

1. Broiled Mushrooms (No. 1703)
2. Creamed Mushrooms with Truffles (No. 1708)
3. Mushrooms on Vine Leaves (No. 1715)
4. Festival Salad (No. 1859)

Note: The mushrooms employed in this photograph are mainly the wild varieties, commonly procurable in markets in Italy. For a full discussion on mushrooms, see page 567

1548. COLD PARTRIDGE ARGENTINA
Pernici in escabecio all' Argentina

6 1-pound partridges, cleaned and trussed
6 tablespoons butter
4 tablespoons oil
2 onions, chopped
1 clove garlic, crushed in the garlic-press
1 cup red wine vinegar
2 cups dry white wine
2 tablespoons chopped tarragon (or 1 tablespoon dried)
2 tablespoons chopped rosemary (or 1 tablespoon dried)
2 tablespoons chopped sage (or 1 tablespoon dried)
6 juniper berries, crushed
Salt and freshly ground pepper
1 bunch watercress

Season the cavities of the partridges with salt and pepper. Heat the butter in a large casserole over moderate heat until the foam subsides, add the partridges, and sauté them very gently for about 25 minutes. They should turn a golden color, but not brown. Transfer them to a bowl. Heat the oil in a frying pan over medium heat, add the onion and garlic, and cook until the onion is transparent. At the same time, put the vinegar and wine in a saucepan with the herbs and simmer for 10 minutes; remove from the heat and cool slightly. Add the onions and garlic to the bowl with the partridges, pour in the wine and herbs, and season with a generous amount of salt and pepper. Marinate the birds in this mixture for 3 days in a cool place, turning them frequently. Drain them, arrange them on a cold serving platter, and garnish with the watercress. *Serves* 6.

1549. COLD PORK WITH RED CABBAGE AND SPICED APPLESAUCE
Maiale arrostito freddo con cavolo marinato e salsa di mele

1 recipe Roast Pork [No. 1250], cooled and thinly sliced
1 red cabbage, trimmed and finely shredded
2 teaspoons salt
3 cloves garlic, crushed in the garlic-press
6 peppercorns
1 bay leaf, crumbled
2 cups wine vinegar, boiled and cooled
6 large green apples, peeled, cored, and thinly sliced
6 tablespoons sugar
1 cup dry white wine
2 tablespoons prepared mustard (Dijon-type preferred)
¼ cup chopped pickle
Juice of 1 lemon
2 cups tiny pickles or gherkins
Salt and freshly ground pepper

Spread the shredded cabbage out on a platter and season it with the salt. Leave it in a cool place for 12 hours. Put it in a bowl with the garlic, peppercorns, bay leaf, and vinegar. Mix thoroughly and marinate in this mixture in a cool place for 1 week before serving. Prepare a tart applesauce by simmering the apples in a saucepan with the sugar and wine for about 15 minutes, or until they are very soft. Purée them through a food mill and then season them with the mustard, chopped pickles, lemon juice, and a tiny pinch of salt and pepper. Cool in the refrigerator before serving. Arrange the slices of pork on a cold serving platter, garnish with the pickles and small heaps of the marinated cabbage, and serve the applesauce on the side. *Serves* 6.

1550. VEAL ROLLS IN ASPIC
Messicani in gelatina

6 large slices veal, cut ¼ inch thick from the upper leg
¾ cup ground lean pork
¼ cup chopped prosciutto (fat and lean)
½ cup fresh breadcrumbs soaked in milk and
   squeezed almost dry
¼ cup grated Parmesan cheese
1 clove garlic, crushed in the garlic-press
2 egg yolks, beaten
Salt and freshly ground pepper
Pinch of nutmeg
Flour
6 tablespoons butter
1 pound each of 3 seasonable green vegetables, cooked
   until just tender in lightly salted water, drained,
   and chilled
1 quart Regular Aspic [No. 118]

Put the ground pork, prosciutto, and breadcrumbs through the meat grinder twice, using the finest blade. Mix them in a bowl with the cheese, garlic, egg yolks, a little salt and pepper, and the nutmeg. Flatten the slices of veal with the flat side of a meat cleaver until they are as thin as possible, but be very careful not to break through them. Season them with salt and pepper and spread each with a little of the ground mixture. Roll them up, secure with toothpicks (or tie with string), and dust them with flour. Heat the butter in a very large frying pan over fairly high heat until golden and brown the rolls on all sides. Reduce the heat slightly and sauté gently for about 6 minutes, turning them often in the pan. Remove them from the pan to a platter, cool, and then chill thoroughly. When cold, garnish the platter attractively with the 3 cold vegetables. Stir the liquid aspic in a bowl over cracked ice until it becomes syrupy and cover the veal and vegetables with a generous coat. Chill the remaining aspic in a shallow dish until jellied, turn it out on a board, chop it, and garnish the platter with small heaps. *Serves* 6.

1551. COLD PORK TOSCANA
Arista di maiale alla toscana

1 4-pound roast loin of pork [*see* No. 1250], cooled
   to room temperature
1 recipe Black-Eyed Beans Uccelletto [No. 1610],
   cooled to room temperature
½ cup oil
Juice of 1 lemon

Slice the cold roast pork attractively on a platter and serve the black-eyed beans, mixed with the oil and lemon juice, on the side. *Serves* 6.

1552. COLD TONGUE WITH PIQUANT SAUCE
Lingua di vitello fredda in salsa piccante

1 3-pound boiled fresh tongue (*see* page 499),
   skinned, cooled, and sliced
1 carrot, chopped
3 stalks celery, chopped
1 cup oil
6 anchovy fillets, soaked free of salt [*see* No. 220]
¼ cup capers
2 tablespoons chopped parsley
1 clove garlic, crushed in the garlic-press
½ cup fresh breadcrumbs, moistened with vinegar
   and squeezed almost dry
Juice of 2 lemons
Salt and freshly ground pepper

Sauté the chopped carrot and celery gently in 2 tablespoons of the oil over moderate heat in a frying pan until they are soft, but not brown. Remove from the heat and cool. Pound the anchovy fillets in a mortar with the capers, parsley, garlic, and breadcrumbs until they form a paste. Add the lemon juice and beat in the remaining oil in a slow steady stream. Add the cooked carrot and celery, season with salt and pepper, and mix thoroughly. Arrange the slices of tongue on a cold

serving platter and spoon the sauce over the slices. *Serves* 6.

1553. COLD VEAL
Noce di vitello arrostita fredda

Tie 4 pounds shoulder or breast of veal into a roll and braise it in the manner described in Braised Veal Toscana [No. 1131], omitting garnishes and thickened gravy. Remove it from the pot and cool it. Strain the juices in the pot, de-grease them, and chill in a bowl in the refrigerator until they are jellied. Slice the veal attractively on a cold serving platter and garnish with small heaps of the jellied sauce. *Serves* 6.

1554. COLD VEAL CUTLETS BELLA VISTA
Costolette di vitello in bella vista

6 slices of veal, cut ½ inch thick from the upper leg
Salt and freshly ground pepper
Flour
6 tablespoons butter
1 pound each of any 4 seasonal vegetables
   (such as carrots, green beans, peas, asparagus tips,
   etc.), each cooked separately until just tender
   in lightly salted water, drained, and chilled
1 quart Regular Aspic [No. 118]

Flatten the slices of veal slightly with the flat side of a meat cleaver, season them with salt and pepper, and dust lightly with flour. Heat the butter in a very large frying pan over fairly high heat and brown the slices on both sides. Reduce the heat slightly and cook for about 2 minutes longer on each side. Remove them from the pan, cool, and then chill in the refrigerator. When cold, arrange them on a cold serving platter and garnish with heaps of the chilled vegetables. Stir the liquid aspic in a bowl over cracked ice until it becomes syrupy, coat the veal and vegetables generously, chill the remaining aspic until firm, chop it, and arrange it in a ring around the platter. *Serves* 6.

GOOSE LIVER
Fegato d'oca

In Europe it is a fairly common practice to force-feed geese so that their livers become enormously fattened. In France, particularly, geese are bred whose livers can reach up to 4 pounds in weight. This practice is forbidden by law in the United States and thus these large livers are unknown here. In the succeeding recipes we are suggesting a quantity of small goose livers to replace a single large one, or, when goose livers are not available, chicken livers may be substituted.

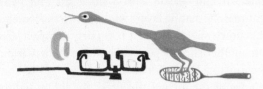

1555. GOOSE LIVER MOUSSE IN ASPIC
Mousse di fegato d'oca in gelatina

1½ pounds raw goose livers
1½ cups dry Madeira wine
1 cup thick Velouté Sauce [No. 17]
3 cups Chicken Aspic [No. 120]
1½ cups whipped cream
Salt

Simmer the goose livers with the Madeira in a saucepan over very gentle heat for about 6 minutes. Drain them, push them through a sieve into a bowl, add the Velouté sauce, season with a little salt, and mix thoroughly (if desired, the livers and Velouté may be mixed in the blender). Place in the refrigerator and chill until very cold. Chill a large decorative mold in the freezer and then line the bottom and sides with a thick coat of aspic (*see* page 49); this should take about 1½ cups. Stir the remaining liquid aspic in a bowl over cracked ice until it is thick and syrupy. Blend 1 cup of the aspic with the goose liver mixture and stir in the very cold whipped cream. Mix lightly and then pour into the mold. Cover the top with the remaining aspic and chill in the refrigerator for 3 hours. *Serves* 6.

1556. TRUFFLED GOOSE LIVER EN BRIOCHE STRASBOURG
Fegato d'oca in brioscia alla moda di Strasburgo

1½ pounds raw goose livers
3 truffles, cut in fine strips
¼ cup brandy
1 bay leaf, crumbled
Salt and freshly ground pepper
4 tablespoons butter
1 cup finely chopped pork fat
1 recipe Plain Brioche Dough [No. 1890], which has been allowed to rise once in a warm place
1 egg yolk, beaten

Put the truffle strips in a bowl and add the brandy, bay leaf, and a little salt and pepper; marinate the truffle for 1 hour, stirring several times. Make small slits in the livers with a sharply pointed knife and insert the pieces of truffle. Heat the butter in a very large frying pan over low heat and gently sauté the livers for about 6 minutes. Cool, season lightly with salt and pepper, and mix them in a bowl with the pork fat. Butter a round, scalloped cake tin (or any appropriately deep baking pan) and line it with ⅔ of the brioche dough. Place the liver mixture in the center, pressing it well together, cover with the remaining brioche dough, and press the edges of the top together with the edges of the dough lining the pan. Make a hole in the center and insert a tiny funnel to allow the steam to escape while the brioche is baking. Set the pan in a warm place until the dough has doubled in bulk. Brush the top with beaten egg yolk and bake it in a moderate oven (350°) for about 50 minutes. It is fully cooked when a long skewer, inserted into the center, comes out clean. The brioche may be eaten hot, or kept in a cool place and served cold. *Serves* 6.

1557. TRUFFLED GOOSE LIVER EN CROŪTE
Pâté di fegato d'oca tartufato

1½ pounds raw goose livers
6 truffles, cut in fine strips and marinated for 2 hours in 4 tablespoons of brandy
1 recipe Pastry for Pâtés [No. 1566]
6 large thin slices fresh pork fat (from the back, if possible)
4 cups Chicken Forcemeat for Pâtés [No. 131]
1 bay leaf, crumbled
3 sprigs thyme (or 1 teaspoon dried)
1 egg, beaten
½ cup rendered pork fat
Salt

Make small slits in the goose livers with a sharply pointed knife and stud them with the pieces of well-marinated truffles. Roll out ⅔ of the pastry and line the bottom and sides of a deep, round timbale mold, leaving ½ inch of pastry overlapping the edges. Line the mold with thin sheets of pork fat. Cover the bottom with half of the forcemeat and then add the goose livers, pressing them as close together as possible. Season with salt and cover them with the rest of the forcemeat. Fold the slices of pork fat over the top and lay the bay leaf and thyme on the fat. Roll out most of the rest of the pastry (reserving a little for decorating

531

Truffled Goose Liver en Croûte (No. 1557): see page 531

the top) to fit over the top, moisten the edges and press firmly together with the edges of the pastry lining the mold. Decorate the top by making a crimped roll of the remaining pastry and distributing it (*see* photograph this page) or by shaping it into leaves, flowers, triangles, or any desired shapes. Make a hole in the center of the top and insert a pastry tube with a round hole to allow the steam to escape during the baking. Brush the surface with beaten egg, set the mold in a pan partially filled with hot water, and put it into a moderate (350°) oven for 1½ hours. The liver is cooked when a skewer plunged into it comes out clean. Remove the pâté (which should be a rich golden color) from the oven and let it cool in the mold. While it is still warm pour through the hole in the top the rendered pork fat and chill for 12 hours before serving. *Serves* 8.

1558. TERRINE OF TRUFFLED GOOSE LIVER

Fegato d'oca con tartufi in terrina

1½ pounds raw goose livers
2 truffles, cut into narrow strips and soaked 1 hour in ¼ cup brandy
6 large thin slices fresh pork fat (from the back, if possible)
3 cups Chicken Forcemeat for Pâtés [No. 131], substituting lean pork for the raw chicken meat
1 bay leaf, crumbled
2 sprigs thyme (or 1 teaspoon dried)
1 cup thick flour and water paste
1 cup lard, melted
Salt and freshly ground pepper

Make small slits in the livers with a sharply pointed knife and insert the strips of truffle. Line an oblong terrine (or any oblong casserole with a cover) with 5 slices of pork fat and in the bottom spread a layer of ¼ of the forcemeat. Lay ⅓ of the livers over the forcemeat and season with a little salt and pepper. Continue alternating layers, ending with the forcemeat. Press down slightly so that it is fairly compact. Cover with another slice of pork fat and lay the bay leaf and thyme on top. Spread the flour and water paste around the edge of the terrine and press the lid on tightly to form a hermetic seal. Place the terrine in a pan of hot water reaching halfway up the sides of the terrine in a moderate (350°) oven for 1 hour. Remove the terrine from the oven, break and discard seal, remove the cover, and place a small weight on top of the pâté for 12 hours. Immerse the terrine in a bowl of hot water for a few seconds and then unmold it. Carefully remove the pork fat. Pour the lard into the terrine and mix with the fats and other substances left in the terrine during the baking. Carefully return the baked pâté to the terrine and spoon a few tablespoons of the hot fat over the top. Cool in the refrigerator for at least 10 hours. *Serves* 6.

1559. TRUFFLED GOOSE LIVER IN WINE ASPIC

Fegato d'oca in gelatina al chianti bianco

1½ pounds raw goose livers
3 truffles, cut into narrow strips and soaked 1 hour in ¼ cup brandy
3 cups Chicken Forcemeat for Pâtés [No. 131], substituting raw pork for the chicken
1 egg, beaten
4 large thin slices fresh pork fat (from the back, in possible)
Salt and freshly ground pepper
1 quart Regular Aspic [No. 118]
1 cup white Chianti wine

Make small slits in the livers with a sharply pointed knife and insert the strips of truffles. Mix the forcemeat with the egg in a bowl. Rinse out with cold water and wring dry several long thicknesses of cheesecloth. Spread these out on a table, cover with slightly overlapping sheets of fresh pork fat, spread the forcemeat on top, and place the livers in the center. Season the livers lightly with salt and pepper and then fold over the slices of pork fat so that the livers are completely encased, first in the forcemeat, then with the pork fat, and finally with the cheesecloth. It may be formed into a roll or ball, whichever is desired. Tie the cheese-cloth securely so that none of the ingredients can escape during the cooking. Place it in a saucepan large enough to hold it comfortably and cover with the liquid aspic mixed with the Chianti. Bring slowly to a boil and simmer for 40 minutes. Remove it from the cooking liquid, cool slightly, weight it on a platter with a heavy plate for 1 hour, and then chill in the refrigerator. De-grease the aspic and reserve (if it has become cloudy as the liver cooked, clarify it with 2 lightly beaten egg whites —*see* page 49). Line an appropriately sized mold with a thick coating of aspic (*see* page 49), and chill. Very carefully remove the cheesecloth and pork fat from the forcemeat covering the livers, and place the ball or roll in the mold. Cover with the remaining liquid aspic and chill in the refrigerator for 3 hours. *Serves* 6.

1560. PÂTÉ DE FOIE GRAS BELLA VISTA
Fegato d'oca in "bella vista"

1 pound canned pâté de foie gras
1 quart Chicken Aspic [No. 120]
2 truffles, sliced
2 whites of hard-boiled eggs

Line an appropriately sized mold with a thick layer of aspic (*see* page 49), chill, and then press into the sides and bottom of the mold slices of truffles and slices of hard-boiled egg white which have been cut into fancy shapes. Chill in the refrigerator and cover with a second layer of aspic. Lay the foie gras on top and fill the mold with aspic. Chill in the refrigerator for 3 hours and then unmold. *Serves* 6.

1561. DICED PÂTÉ DE FOIE GRAS IN ASPIC
Fegato d'oca in gelatina

Prepare in the same manner as the preceding recipe, except cut the foie gras into large dice and put only a little of the foie gras and aspic into the mold at a time, chilling between additions, so that it is well distributed in the mold. *Serves* 6.

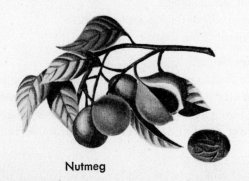

Nutmeg

MOUSSES, PÂTÉS, AND TERRINES
Mousses, pâtés, e terrine

1562. CHICKEN MOUSSE
Mousse di pollo

3 cups chopped cooked chicken meat
3 cups Velouté Sauce [No. 17], reduced to 2 cups
3 cups Chicken Aspic [No. 120]
1 cup heavy cream, whipped
Salt and freshly ground pepper

Pound the chicken in a mortar and then mix it thoroughly with the Velouté sauce (or whirl both together in the electric blender, 2 cups at a time, until smooth). Season with salt and pepper and chill in the refrigerator until very cold. Line a large mold with a thick layer (about 1½ cups) of aspic (*see* page 49), and chill. Stir the remaining aspic in a bowl over cracked ice until very thick and syrupy, stir in the chicken and Velouté mixture, and then blend in the whipped cream. Pour this mixture into the mold and chill for 6 hours. Dip the mold briefly into hot water and unmold on a cold serving platter. *Serves* 6.

1563. CHICKEN LIVER MOUSSE
Mousse di fegato di pollo

Prepare in the same manner and with the same ingredients as the preceding recipe, substituting 2 cups of chopped cooked chicken liver for the chopped chicken. *Serves* 6.

1564. HAM MOUSSE
Mousse di prosciutto

Prepare in the same manner and with the same ingredients as Chicken Mousse [No. 1562], substituting 3 cups chopped cooked ham for the chicken. *Serves* 6.

1565. TOMATO MOUSSE
Mousse di pomodoro

Prepare in the same manner and with the same ingredients as Chicken Mousse [No. 1562], substituting 2 cups of a very thick, freshly made Tomato Paste [No. 144] for the chopped chicken. Omit pounding in the mortar and simply mix thoroughly with the Velouté sauce before chilling. *Serves* 6.

LINING AND FILLING A MOLD FOR PÂTÉS

1. Roll out the pastry in a sheet about ⅛ inch thick. Line the bottom and sides of a deep timbale mold with the pastry, pressing it firmly in the mold and leaving a generous amount hanging over the sides. Then line the mold

with thin slices of fresh pork fat.

2. & 3. Alternate layers of the forcemeat and meat in the mold, ending with a top layer of forcemeat. Cover with a thin slice of pork fat and lay the bay leaf and thyme on top.

4. Bring the strips of pastry up from the sides and cover the top. Make a hole in the center and insert a pastry tube with a round hole or a tiny funnel through which the steam may escape during the cooking.

Brush the top of the pastry with beaten egg and place the mold in a pan half filled with hot water in a moderate (350°) oven for 1¾ hours. If the top browns too quickly, cover with foil. It may be unmolded and served hot or allowed to cool in the mold and served cold. If it is to be served cold, pour the liquid aspic through the hole in the top and chill.

534

1566. PASTRY FOR PÂTÉS
Pâté classico

5 cups sifted flour
¾ cup butter, well chilled
2 eggs, chilled
⅔ cup ice water (more or less, as needed)
1 teaspoon salt

Sift the flour into a mound, form a hollow in the center, and in it place the butter, salt, and eggs. Working with the fingers, blend the ingredients into a smooth dough, adding water little by little as it is needed. Press it into a firm ball and allow it to rest in a cool place for several hours before rolling it out. *Serves 6.*

1567. CLASSIC PÂTÉ EN CROUTE
Pâté crostato classico

4 cups of any desired seasoned meat and forcemeat
1 recipe Pastry for Pâtés [No. 1566]
6 large thin sheets fresh pork fat (from the back, if possible)
1 egg, beaten
1 bay leaf, crumbled
2 sprigs thyme (or ½ teaspoon dried)
Optional: 1 cup Regular Aspic [No. 118]

Baking the pâté:
Brush the top of the pastry with beaten egg and place the mold in a pan half filled with hot water in a moderate (350°) oven for 1¾ hours. If the top browns too quickly, cover with foil. It may be unmolded and served hot

HOW TO PREPARE A PÂTÉ WITHOUT A MOLD

1. Roll the pastry into a solid ball, flattening it out at the bottom so that it stands firmly. Hollow out the center with the fingers (reserving enough dough to make a cover), shaping it so that you have a thick, even wall of pastry.

2. Line the pastry mold with thin slices of the pork fat and fill it just as you would a metal mold.

3. Cover with a thin slice of pork fat, lay the bay leaf and thyme on top, and seal with a cover rolled out from the remaining pastry. Insert a funnel in the center to allow the steam to escape and also for filling with aspic if the dish is to be served cold.

or allowed to cool in the mold and served cold. If it is to be served cold, pour the liquid aspic through the hole in the top and chill. *Serves 8 to 10.*

1568. DUCK PÂTÉ
Pâté di anitroccolo

1 3½-pound duck, split down the back, skinned, and boned
½ cup dry Madeira wine
1 recipe Pastry for Pâtés [No. 1566]
6 large thin slices fresh pork fat
2 cups Chicken Forcemeat for Pâtés [No. 131]
2 truffles, chopped
1 sheet fresh pork fat back
1 bay leaf, crumbled
3 sprigs thyme (or ½ teaspoon dried)
1 egg, beaten
Optional: 1 cup Chicken Aspic [No. 120]
Salt and freshly ground pepper

The skin must be removed from the duck in 1 piece, being very careful not to tear it. Cut off all tendons or tough parts from the boned meat, cut it into strips, season the strips with a little salt and pepper, and marinate in the Madeira for 1 hour. Line a deep timbale mold with the pastry and with the slices of fresh pork fat in the manner described in the preceding recipe. Spread the duck skin out flat on a table, spread the forcemeat over it, sprinkle with the truffles, and lay the strips of duck meat on the forcemeat. Raise the whole by lifting the edges of the skin and then slide it down into the mold, pressing it down well so that

there are no air spaces. The mold may be banged once or twice on the table to make certain the filling is well settled. Pull the skin up over the top, cover with a sheet of fresh pork fat, and lay the bay leaf and thyme on top. Cover with a top made from the remaining pastry and bake the pâté in the manner described in the preceding recipe. *Serves 6.*

NOTE: The optional aspic may be poured into the pâté when it is cold, and then refrigerated until set.

1569. HARE PÂTÉ
Pâté di lepre

Remove the fillet from the back and bone the thigh meat from a 5-pound hare. Cut this meat into strips, season it with a little salt and pepper, and marinate it in ½ cup of brandy for 2 hours. Prepare 2 cups of Chicken Forcemeat for Pâtés [No. 131], substituting half boneless hare meat and half fresh lean pork for the raw chicken, and mix with the marinated strips of hare meat. Proceed to line a deep pâté mold, fill, and bake in the manner and with the ingredients in Classic Pâté en Croûte [No. 1567]. *Serves 6.*

1570. VEAL AND HAM PÂTÉ
Pâté di vitello e prosciutto

½ pound veal, cut from the upper leg into strips
½ cup brandy
½ pound boiled ham, cut into strips
6 large slices fresh pork fat (from the back, if possible)

2 cups Chicken Forcemeat for Pâtés [No. 131],
   substituting half raw veal and half raw lean pork
   for the chicken
1 recipe Pastry for Pâtés [No. 1566]
1 bay leaf, crumbled
2 sprigs thyme (or ½ teaspoon dried)
1 egg, beaten
Optional: 1 cup Regular Aspic [No. 118]
Salt and freshly ground pepper

Marinate the strips of veal in the brandy, seasoned
with a little salt and pepper, for 1 hour and then
prepare the pâté in the manner described in Classic
Pâté en Croûte [No. 1567]. *Serves* 6.

1571. WOODCOCK PÂTÉ
Pâté di beccaccia

Prepare in the same manner and with the same ingredients as Duck Pâté [No. 1568], substituting 2 or 3
woodcock, depending on their size, for the duck. After
lining the mold with pastry and pork fat, line it with
the skins of the woodcock and then fill the mold
with forcemeat and woodcock meat in alternate layers.
Serves 6.

TERRINES
Terrine

Terrines are pâtés baked in oval earthenware dishes
from which they take their name. A terrine is not
lined with pastry, the way a pâté mold is, but is simply
covered with its own lid before baking.

1572. TERRINE OF HARE
CACCIATORE
Terrina di lepre del cacciatore

1½ pounds fillet of hare, cut from the back into strips
A marinade:
   1 cup brandy
   6 peppercorns
   1 teaspoon salt
   1 bay leaf
   6 juniper berries, crushed

8 large thin slices fresh pork fat (from the back, if
   possible)
3 cups Chicken Forcemeat for Pâtés [No. 131],
   substituting raw veal for the chicken
6 large slices lean boiled ham, cut ⅛ inch thick

Marinate the strips of hare meat (there should be about
3 cups) in the marinade for 3 hours. Line a 2-quart
terrine with 7 slices of fresh pork fat, spread a layer
of forcemeat in the bottom, lay a few strips of hare
meat on the forcemeat, and cover with a slice of ham.
Continue to make layers in the terrine, ending with a
layer of forcemeat. Cover with a slice of fresh pork fat,
cover the terrine with its lid, and place it in a shallow
roasting pan half filled with boiling water in a moderate
(350°) oven for 1½ hours. Remove from the oven,
remove the lid, and weight the pâté until it is cooled
with a board or heavy casserole that will fit just inside
the terrine. It may then be chilled or not, as desired,
and either served in the terrine or unmolded on a
platter. *Serves* 6.

1573. TERRINE INGLESE
Terrina all'inglese

1 pound veal, cut from the upper leg and sliced ⅛ inch
   thick
1 pound fresh pork fat, sliced ⅛ inch thick
4 large onions, chopped
3 tablespoons chopped parsley
1½ cups dry white wine
3 sprigs thyme (or ½ teaspoon dried)
1 bay leaf
Salt and freshly ground pepper

Pound the slices of veal slightly with the flat side of a
meat cleaver and season them with salt and pepper.
Line the bottom of a 2-quart terrine with a slice (or
slices) of fresh pork fat, cover with a slice (or slices)
of veal, and sprinkle with a little chopped onion and
parsley. Continue to make layers in this manner until
the terrine is filled, ending with a slice of pork fat.
Add the wine, lay the thyme and bay leaf on top, and
cover the terrine with its lid. Place it in a roasting pan
half filled with boiling water in a moderate (350°)
oven for 1½ hours. Remove from the oven, remove the
lid, and weight the pâté in the terrine for several hours
with a board or heavy casserole that will fit just inside
the terrine. Chill and serve in the terrine, if desired,
or unmold on a platter. *Serves* 6.

1574. TERRINE OF RABBIT LUIGI VERONELLI
Terrina di coniglio alla Luigi Veronelli

1 4-pound rabbit, boned
A marinade:
  1 onion, sliced
  1 carrot, sliced
  1 clove garlic, sliced
  2 tablespoons chopped parsley
  1 bay leaf
  1 teaspoon salt
  $\frac{1}{4}$ teaspoon freshly ground pepper
  1 bottle dry white wine
Forcemeat:
  The rabbit liver, ground
  $\frac{1}{4}$ pound ground cooked ham
  $\frac{1}{4}$ pound ground lean pork
  $\frac{1}{4}$ pound ground fresh pork fat
  $\frac{1}{2}$ cup brandy
  1 teaspoon salt
  $\frac{1}{4}$ teaspoon freshly ground pepper
  1 egg, beaten
6 tablespoons rendered pork fat
2 envelopes unflavored gelatin softened in $\frac{1}{3}$ cup water

Marinate the boned rabbit in the marinade for 24 hours. Mix all of the forcemeat ingredients thoroughly together in a bowl. Remove the rabbit from the marinade, dry it, and spread it out flat. Lay the forcemeat in the center, pull the flesh of the rabbit around the forcemeat so that it is completely encased, and then sew and tie the rabbit with string so that none of the forcemeat can escape during the cooking. Place it in a large, heavy pot with the marinade, bring very slowly to a boil, and then simmer, covered, over very low heat for 2 hours. Remove the rabbit from the cooking liquid and place it in a terrine. Strain the cooking liquid, de-grease it, blend in the gelatin, stir over low heat until dissolved, and pour over the rabbit in the terrine. Cool and then chill for several hours before unmolding on a platter. *Serves 6.*

NOTE: This may also be made with a boned, de-fatted duck or large chicken.

1575. VEAL WITH TUNA
Vitello tonnato

$2\frac{1}{2}$ pounds veal, cut from the upper leg in a single piece
12 anchovy fillets, washed free of salt [*see* No. 220]
Aromatic vegetables:
  1 carrot, sliced

Veal with Tuna (No. 1575)

  1 onion, sliced
  2 stalks of celery, sliced
1 bottle dry white wine
1 lemon
$\frac{1}{4}$ cup oil
1 7-ounce can Italian-style tuna in olive oil
3 cups Mayonnaise [No. 77]
1 cup capers
1 cup gherkins
2 lemons, sliced
Salt and freshly ground pepper

Make tiny slits in the veal with a very sharp knife and insert half of the anchovy fillets. Put the veal in a large, heavy enamel pot, add the sliced aromatic vegetables, the white wine, the juice of 1 lemon, oil, and the peel (no white part) from the lemon. Cover the pot, bring slowly to a boil, and simmer for $1\frac{3}{4}$ to 2 hours, or until the veal is tender. Remove it from the pot, strain the cooking liquid, return it to the pot, and then return the veal to the liquid to cool completely. When it is cool, drain it and transfer to a serving platter. Reduce the cooking liquid over high heat to $\frac{1}{4}$ its quantity. Pound the tuna and remaining anchovy fillets in a mortar until they form a paste, dilute with a few tablespoons of the cooking liquid, stir this mixture into the mayonnaise, a little at a time. The mayonnaise should be still thick, but fairly runny. Slice the veal on the platter, spread a thick layer of the mayonnaise over the slices, garnish with a few of the capers and gherkins, and serve the remainder with the sliced lemons on the side. *Serves 6.*

537

VEGETABLES
AND SALADS

VEGETABLES
Legumi

In Italy, vegetables appear in the markets when they are in season. As yet, frozen vegetables have not become popular or widely available except in the larger cities. It is advised that the following recipes be made with only the freshest seasonal vegetables for the best results. Let crispness and color be your guide when purchasing. Remember that the smaller the vegetable, the tastier it is. Also remember that locally grown produce has a far superior taste and texture than that which has been shipped cross-country in refrigerated trucks or railway cars.

Most vegetables should be cooked in enamel pots and pans. Metal (especially aluminum) will discolor them, and act chemically with their acids and salts thereby changing their taste and texture. Earthenware vessels may also be used. If the worse comes to the worst, stainless steel pans may be employed, but *never* aluminum or copper.

1576. WHITE FOUNDATION FOR VEGETABLES
Bianco speciale per legumi

2 tablespoons flour
1 quart cold water
1 teaspoon salt
Juice of ½ lemon
2 tablespoons butter

Certain vegetables, such as artichokes, cardoons, etc., are blanched or parboiled in this foundation to keep them from darkening.

1577. MARINADE FOR VEGETABLES
Marinata per legumi

½ cup oil
3½ cups cold water
Juice of 2 lemons
Bouquet Garni:
   3 sprigs parsley
   1 stalk celery
   1 stalk fennel
   1 bay leaf
   2 sprigs thyme (or ½ teaspoon dried)
6 peppercorns
1 teaspoon salt

Put all the ingredients in an enamel saucepan, bring to a boil, and simmer for 20 minutes. Pour the hot mixture over the chosen vegetable and marinate for several hours or as long as 2 days.

ARTICHOKES
Carciofi

Artichokes are one of the most popular vegetables in Italy, and Italian cooks have made a fine art of their preparation. Small baby artichokes are very common in Italy and these are particularly prized since, after being trimmed, the whole leaf is edible. These may occasionally be found in American markets, although the usual size is fairly large, about the size of an orange. Of this larger type, only the hearts and the tender bases of the leaves are edible. In the recipes for baby artichokes to follow, do not attempt to substitute large artichokes, as no amount of cooking will tenderize the fibrous quality of the whole leaf.

The heart, or bottom, of the artichoke can darken to a very unattractive color unless specially treated. Whenever cutting into and exposing any part of the heart, always rub it immediately with lemon juice. Whole artichokes or the hearts alone should always be boiled in White Foundation for Vegetables [No. 1576].

Artichokes must be trimmed before cooking. First break off any tough outer leaves and cut off the stem. Rub the bottom immediately with lemon juice. Cut off the tips of all the leaves with scissors. (The artichokes may now be soaked in acidulated water for 1 hour if they are to be braised, but this is a useless step when they are to be boiled in acidulated water.) Drop them in a large quantity of boiling White Foundation for Vegetables [No. 1576], place a dish towel or several thicknesses of cheesecloth over their tips to keep them moist and prevent discoloration, cover the pan, and boil over moderate heat until the outer leaves can easily be pulled off and the bottoms are easily pierced with a knife. The exact time will depend on the size; a baby artichoke will be tender in 15 to 20 minutes, while large ones will require up to 50 minutes. Drain them upside down in a colander.

Occasionally they are only half-cooked, or parboiled in the foundation liquid, drained, and their cooking completed by braising.

Frequently the choke, or hairy growth at the bottom of the leaves and above the heart, is removed before cooking. If the artichokes are to be served halved or quartered, this is very simple: cut the artichoke in half or into quarters, rub the exposed parts with lemon juice, cut out the choke with a very sharp knife, and rub again with lemon juice. If the artichokes are to be served whole, spread the leaves apart with the fingers, turn the artichoke upside down, and press with the palm of the hand to force the leaves even further apart, being careful not to snap any of them off. Pull out the inner core of whitish leaves with the fingers and then cut out the choke with a sharp-edged spoon, a grapefruit knife, or melon-ball cutter. Rub the exposed heart with lemon juice and tie a string around the outer leaves so that the artichoke will hold its shape during the cooking.

If the hearts are to be cooked alone, break off all of the leaves, one by one, by bending them outward until they snap off. Rub frequently with lemon juice while breaking off the leaves to prevent discoloration. When only the whitish inner core of leaves remains, cut them off with a sharp knife and remove the choke with a sharp-edged spoon, or, if desired, the choke may be left attached to the heart and removed more easily after cooking.

Always cook artichokes in an enamel saucepan. Never cook them in aluminum, as it will discolor them.

1578. ARTICHOKES BARIGOULE
Carciofi Barigoule

6 medium artichokes, trimmed, parboiled for
    10 minutes in White Foundation for Vegetables
    [No. 1576], and drained
2 cups Duxelles [No. 138]
1 cup finely chopped fresh pork fat
2 tablespoons chopped parsley
6 long thin slices salt pork, parboiled for 15 minutes

5 slices fresh pork rind, parboiled in 2 cups of the white
    foundation for 1 hour
1 onion, sliced
1 carrot, sliced
1 cup dry white wine
Bouquet Garni:
    3 sprigs parsley
    2 sprigs thyme (or ½ teaspoon dried)
    1 bay leaf
1 quart White Stock [No. 1]
Salt and freshly ground pepper

Spread the leaves of the parboiled artichokes apart and remove the chokes. Combine the Duxelles, chopped pork fat, and parsley in a bowl and season with salt and pepper. Spoon a generous ½ cup of this mixture into the center of each of the artichokes, wrap each in a slice of salt pork, and tie with string. Line the bottom of an enamel casserole with the pork rind, scatter the sliced onion and carrot over the rind, and place the tied artichokes on top. Add the wine and Bouquet Garni and cook over medium heat until the wine has almost evaporated. Add the stock, which should come about halfway up the height of the artichokes. Bring to a boil, cover the casserole, reduce the heat, and simmer for about 30 minutes, or until the outer leaves may be easily pulled off. Remove the artichokes with a slotted spoon, untie them, arrange them on an oven-proof platter, and put them into a slow (250°) oven to dry for 10 minutes. Strain the liquid in the casserole through a very fine sieve, de-grease, and return to the casserole. Reduce over high heat to 1 cup, spoon a little of this sauce over each artichoke, and cover each with a small piece of the salt pork with which they were wrapped. *Serves 6.*

1579. ARTICHOKES WITH BASIL
Carciofi in spicchi al tegame con basilico

12 baby artichokes, trimmed, chokes removed, sliced
    ¼ inch thick (lengthwise), soaked in acidulated
    water for 1 hour, and well drained

THE PREPARATION OF ARTICHOKE HEARTS

Left: *Remove the leaves all around the base of the artichoke; trim the bottom into a rounded shape and remove the rest of the leaves attached to the base*
Right: *Rub each of the artichoke hearts with the cut side of a half lemon to prevent their darkening*

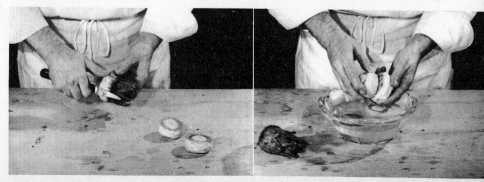

Artichokes
Barigoule
(No. 1578)

6 tablespoons oil
Salt and freshly ground pepper
¼ cup chopped basil
1 clove garlic, crushed in the garlic-press
1 cup dry white wine
6 slices bread, crusts removed, sautéed golden
    brown in oil

Heat the oil in an enamel frying pan over moderate heat, add the artichoke slices, season with salt and pepper, add the basil and garlic, stir for 1 minute, and add the wine. Cover tightly and simmer for 30 minutes. Remove the lid and allow the cooking liquid to reduce by ½. Transfer the slices to a hot serving platter and surround with browned slices of bread. *Serves* 6.

1580. ARTICHOKES WITH BASTARD SAUCE

Carciofi lessati con salsa al burro

6 medium artichokes, trimmed
2 quarts White Foundation for Vegetables [No. 1576]
2 cups Bastard Sauce [No. 66]

Cook the artichokes in the white foundation until tender as directed in the introduction to this section. Serve them hot with the sauce on the side. *Serves* 6.

1581. BRAISED ARTICHOKES ROMANA

Carciofi al tegame alla romana

6 medium artichokes, trimmed, parboiled for
    15 minutes in White Foundation for Vegetables
    [No. 1576], drained, and chokes removed
¼ cup chopped mint
4 cloves garlic, crushed in the garlic-press
1½ cups fresh breadcrumbs
½ cup oil

4 cups White Stock [No. 1]
Salt and freshly ground pepper

Mix together the mint, garlic, breadcrumbs, and 2 tablespoons oil in a bowl. Press a little of this mixture in the center and among the leaves of each of the artichokes. Season with salt and pepper and sprinkle each with a generous spoonful of oil. Tie a string around each of the artichokes, place them in an enamel casserole, add the white stock, bring to a boil over medium heat, cover the casserole, reduce the heat, and simmer for about 30 minutes, or until the outer leaves may easily be pulled off. Transfer them to a hot serving platter and keep warm while the liquid in the casserole is reduced over high heat to 1 scant cup. Spoon a little of this sauce over each and serve immediately or allow to cool to room temperature. *Serves* 6.

1582. ARTICHOKES CAVOUR

Carciofi alla Cavour

6 medium artichokes, trimmed, boiled until tender in
    White Foundation for Vegetables [No. 1576],
    drained, and chokes removed
¾ cup butter, melted
1 cup grated Parmesan cheese
4 tablespoons butter
4 hard-boiled eggs, chopped
2 tablespoons chopped parsley
6 anchovy fillets, washed free of salt [*see* No. 220]
    and finely chopped

Spread the leaves of each of the artichokes apart slightly and sprinkle with melted butter, Parmesan cheese, and then with more butter. Tie a string around each and place them on an oven-proof platter in a medium (375°) oven for 10 minutes. Melt the 4 tablespoons of butter in a frying pan over moderate heat

541

and add the chopped eggs, parsley, and anchovy fillets. Heat just until very hot, spoon a little of this mixture over each of the artichokes, and serve immediately. *Serves* 6.

1583. FRICASSEE OF ARTICHOKES
Carciofi in fricassea

12 baby artichokes, trimmed, chokes removed, sliced
  $\frac{1}{4}$ inch thick, and boiled until tender in White
  Foundation for Vegetables [No. 1576]
5 eggs
$\frac{1}{2}$ cup heavy cream
Juice of 1 lemon
2 tablespoons chopped parsley
Salt and freshly ground pepper
6 tablespoons butter

Drain the artichokes thoroughly and dry them on absorbent paper. Beat the eggs lightly with the cream, lemon juice, parsley, and salt and pepper to taste. Heat the butter in a frying pan over medium heat, add the artichoke slices, sauté gently for 3 minutes, pour in the egg mixture, and stir until the eggs are scrambled but still very moist. Turn out onto a hot serving platter and serve at once. *Serves* 6.

1584. ARTICHOKES WITH HOLLANDAISE SAUCE
Carciofi lessati con salsa olandese

6 medium artichokes, trimmed
2 quarts White Foundation for Vegetables [No. 1576]
2 cups Sauce Hollandaise [No. 72]

Cook the artichokes in the white foundation until tender, as described in the introduction to this section. Serve them hot with the Hollandaise sauce on the side. *Serves* 6.

1585. ARTICHOKES PAESANA
Carciofi in spicchi alla paesana

12 baby artichokes, trimmed, chokes removed, sliced
  $\frac{1}{4}$ inch thick (lengthwise), and soaked in acidulated
  water for 1 hour
1 cup chopped lean salt pork, parboiled for 15 minutes
2 onions, sliced
2 potatoes, sliced
1 head Boston lettuce, leaves separated
6 tablespoons butter
1 quart White Stock [No. 1]
Salt and freshly ground pepper

Place all the ingredients, except the salt and pepper,

in an enamel casserole over moderate heat and mix lightly. There should be sufficient stock to completely cover the other ingredients. Cook uncovered for about 30 minutes, or until all ingredients are tender and the stock is reduced to about 1 cup. Stir frequently to ensure even cooking. Season with salt and pepper and serve in the casserole. *Serves* 6.

1586. ARTICHOKES WITH PEAS AND LETTUCE CASALINGA
Carciofi con pisellini e lattughe alla casalinga

12 baby artichokes, trimmed, chokes removed, sliced
  $\frac{1}{4}$ inch thick, parboiled 10 minutes in White
  Foundation for Vegetables [No. 1576], and drained
3 tablespoons butter
$\frac{1}{4}$ cup chopped onion
2 heads Boston lettuce, leaves separated
1 pound shelled peas (petits pois, if available)
1 tablespoon lemon juice
Salt and freshly ground pepper

Heat the butter in an enamel casserole over medium heat, add the artichokes and onion, and sauté gently for 5 minutes. Season very lightly with salt and pepper, arrange the lettuce leaves over the artichoke slices, and place the peas on top of the leaves. Add the lemon juice and season the peas lightly with salt and pepper. Add 2 tablespoons of water, or, if the lettuce is wet from washing, no water is necessary. Cover tightly and simmer over low heat for 25 minutes. After 15 minutes, stir once or twice. Serve in the casserole. *Serves* 6.

1587. ARTICHOKES VINAIGRETTE
Carciofi lessati con salsa all'agro

6 medium artichokes, trimmed
2 quarts White Foundation for Vegetables [No. 1576]
1$\frac{1}{2}$ cups Sauce Vinaigrette [No. 99]

Cook the artichokes in the white foundation until tender, as directed in the introduction to this section. Serve them at room temperature with the Vinaigrette sauce on the side. *Serves* 6.

1588. ARTICHOKE HEARTS WITH ASPARAGUS TIPS RICCA
Fondi di carciofo con punte d'asparagi alla ricca

6 artichoke hearts, cooked until tender in White
  Foundation for Vegetables [No. 1576], drained,
  and cut into quarters

¼ cup Duxelles [No. 138]
2 cups Sauce Mornay [No. 56]
18 asparagus tips, cooked until just tender in lightly
    salted water
½ cup grated Gruyère cheese
¼ cup butter, melted

Combine the Mornay sauce with the Duxelles in a shallow, oven-proof dish, arrange the asparagus attractively in the center of the dish, and place the quartered artichoke hearts around the edge. Sprinkle with the cheese and melted butter. Place the dish in a very hot (500°) oven for 8 minutes, or until the cheese is light gold. Serve in the dish. *Serves* 6.

1589. ARTICHOKE HEARTS CAPRICCIO DEL MAESTRO
Fondi di carciofo "Capriccio del Maestro"

6 artichoke hearts, cooked until tender in White
    Foundation for Vegetables [No. 1576], as
    described in the introduction to this section, and
    cooled
6 tablespoons truffled pâté de foie gras
1½ cups Sauce Villeroy [No. 59]
2 cups fresh white breadcrumbs
6 tablespoons butter
6 sprigs parsley, fried in deep fat [*see* No. 276]
2 cups Marsala Sauce [No. 43]

Spread the hollow of each of the artichoke hearts with 1 tablespoon of foie gras, dip each into the Villeroy sauce, and cover with breadcrumbs. Heat the butter in a frying pan over medium heat until almost golden, and brown the artichokes on both sides. Heap them in a pyramid on a small serving platter, garnish with the sprigs of fried parsley, and serve the Marsala sauce on the side. *Serves* 6.

1590. ARTICHOKE HEARTS DIANA
Fondi di carciofo alla Diana

6 artichoke hearts, cooked until tender in White
    Foundation for Vegetables [No. 1576] as described
    in the introduction to this section, and cooled
1 pair sweetbreads, soaked, parboiled, and coarsely
    chopped (*see* page 496)
4 tablespoons butter
¼ cup dry Marsala wine
¾ cup Béchamel Sauce [No. 18]
2 egg yolks
2 tablespoons grated Parmesan cheese
¼ cup chopped smoked tongue

Salt and freshly ground pepper
2 cups fresh white breadcrumbs
½ cup butter, melted

Heat the 4 tablespoons of butter in a frying pan over medium heat until golden and lightly brown the sweetbreads. Transfer them to a bowl, de-glaze the frying pan with the Marsala, and reduce over high heat to 1 tablespoon. Pour it into the bowl with the sweetbreads and add the Béchamel, egg yolks, grated Parmesan, tongue, and salt and pepper to taste. Mix thoroughly and heap a generous amount of the mixture in the hollow of each of the artichoke hearts. Cover with breadcrumbs and sprinkle with melted butter. Arrange them on an oven-proof platter, place them in a hot (400°) oven for about 10 minutes, or until the tops are lightly browned, and serve on the platter. *Serves* 6.

1591. ARTICHOKE HEARTS FIORENTINA
Fondi di carciofo alla fiorentina

6 artichoke hearts, cooked until tender in White
    Foundation for Vegetables [No. 1576] as described
    in the introduction to this section, and cooled
1 cup Spinach in Butter [No. 1791]
1 cup Sauce Mornay [No. 56]
¾ cup grated Parmesan cheese
½ cup butter, melted

Heap a little of the spinach on top of each of the artichoke hearts, cover with the Mornay sauce, and sprinkle with the grated Parmesan cheese and melted butter. Place them on an oven-proof platter in a very hot (500°) oven until they are golden and serve on the platter. *Serves* 6.

1592. ARTICHOKE HEARTS GOURMET
Fondi di carciofo del ghiottone

6 artichoke hearts, cooked until tender in White
    Foundation for Vegetables [No. 1576] as described
    in the introduction to this section, and cooled
¾ cup finely ground cooked chicken
1 cup Béchamel Sauce [No. 18], reduced to ¾ cup
¾ cup grated Gruyère cheese
½ cup butter, melted

Combine the chicken with the Béchamel sauce and heap a little of the mixture on the top of each of the artichoke hearts. Sprinkle with the cheese, then with melted butter, and place them on an oven-proof

543

platter. Brown them in a very hot (500°) oven and serve on the platter. *Serves 6.*

1593. ARTICHOKE HEARTS LUCULLUS
Fondi di carciofo "Lucullus"

6 artichoke hearts, cooked until tender in White
    Foundation for Vegetables [No. 1576], and drained
1½ cups Marsala Sauce [No. 43]
2 truffles, chopped

Arrange the artichoke hearts on an oven-proof platter, spoon the Marsala sauce over them, and sprinkle each with the chopped truffles. Place the platter in a hot (400°) oven for 10 minutes and serve on the platter. *Serves 6.*

1594. ARTICHOKE HEARTS LUIGI VERONELLI
Fondi di carciofo alla Luigi Veronelli

12 baby artichoke hearts, cooked until tender in
    White Foundation for Vegetables [No. 1576],
    and drained
½ pound button mushroom caps
3 tablespoons butter
2 cups Béchamel Sauce [No. 18], made with heavy
    cream instead of milk
Salt and freshly ground white pepper
Pinch nutmeg
Juice of ½ lemon
2 truffles, chopped

Gently sauté the mushroom caps in the butter in a frying pan over moderate heat for about 8 minutes, or until they are tender. Add the Béchamel sauce, bring to the simmering point, and season with salt, pepper, nutmeg, and lemon juice. If the sauce is too thick, add a little heavy cream. Add the artichoke hearts, heat for 1 minute, turn the contents of the pan out onto a hot serving platter, and sprinkle with the truffles. *Serves 6.*

1595. ARTICHOKE VELOUTÉ WITH PUFF PASTE ROSETTES
Vellutata di carciofi con fioroni

6 artichoke hearts, cooked until tender in White
    Foundation for Vegetables [No. 1576], and drained
¼ pound mushrooms, chopped
3 tablespoons butter
2 cups Velouté Sauce [No. 17]
½ cup heavy cream

Salt and freshly ground pepper
18 tiny baked rosettes, made of Puff Paste [No. 1960]

Quickly sauté the mushrooms in a saucepan with the butter for 10 minutes, or until very soft. Add the Velouté, artichokes, and heavy cream. Simmer over moderate heat until the sauce is very thick. Rub the mixture through a fine strainer into another saucepan (or blend in the blender for a few seconds), heat very gently for 2 minutes, correct the seasoning, pour into a vegetable dish, and garnish with the pastry rosettes. *Serves 6.*

1596. SAUTÉED ARTICHOKE HEARTS
Fondi di carciofo trifolati

6 artichoke hearts, sliced and rubbed immediately
    with lemon juice
4 tablespoons butter
2 cloves garlic, crushed in the garlic-press
Salt and freshly ground pepper
2 tablespoons chopped parsley

Heat the butter in a frying pan over moderate heat, add the garlic and sliced artichoke hearts, and sauté very gently for about 15 minutes, or until the hearts are tender, turning them frequently in the pan. Raise the heat and lightly brown them, season with salt and pepper, turn them out onto a hot serving platter, and sprinkle with the parsley. *Serves 6.*

ASPARAGUS
Asparagi

Italians usually serve asparagus as a separate course, and only rarely as an accompaniment to the main entrée. White asparagus is quite common in Italy, but only occasionally can it be found in American markets. It is cooked in the same way as green asparagus.

SEE
VERSE
OR
TION

1. Bagna Cauda (No. 65)

2. Stuffed Onions (No. 1719). Also shown are zucchini prepared with the same stuffing. To prepare the zucchini, take 4 medium zucchini and cut them into 4-inch lengths. Peel the sections vertically with a rotary peeler, leaving a thin strip of skin between each peeled strip. Hollow out the sections with a grapefruit knife, making sure to leave a solid bottom in each section. Then proceed as for Stuffed Onions.

3. Cold Asparagus with Cream Mayonnaise (No. 1599)

4. Stuffed Peppers alla Turca (No. 1745)

5. Tomatoes Siciliana (No. 1817)

6. Artichoke Hearts Diana (No. 1590)

7. Eggplant Souflées (No. 1675)

It is not generally an American habit to peel asparagus, which is something of a loss, since nearly the whole of a spear of asparagus may be eaten if it is peeled. A rotary vegetable peeler may be used, but a sharp paring knife is somewhat better, since more of the tough outer skin should be removed from the lower portion of the spear than from the tender part near the tip and a vegetable peeler does not cut quite deep enough. Peel off just enough of the skin so that the tender flesh is exposed. When this is done, the whole spear will be about the same size and a pale green color. Only the very bottom of the butt end need be discarded.

Asparagus should always be cooked until just *al dente,* that is, when tender but still retaining texture. They should never be overcooked until soft and limp. Peeled asparagus may be cooked with the spears lying flat in a generous quantity of lightly salted water. Removal from the hot water will be facilitated if asparagus are tied in bundles, 6 or 7 spears to a bundle. The exact time will depend on the thickness of the spears; they are fully cooked when a knife easily pierces the bottom end of the spears. Begin testing for doneness after it has boiled for 12 minutes. Very thick spears will require as much as 17 minutes. Drain very briefly on a cloth before transferring to a hot serving platter.

If a variety of courses is being served, 2 pounds of asparagus is sufficient to serve 6; with fewer courses, prepare 3 pounds.

Always cook asparagus in an enamel pan. Special cookers for asparagus with removable racks are available.

1597. ASPARAGUS WITH ANCHOVY BUTTER
Asparagi di campo al burro e alici

2 pounds asparagus, peeled
4 tablespoons butter
1/4 cup Anchovy Butter [No. 108]
2 tablespoons chopped parsley
Juice of 1/2 lemon
1 cup Croûtons [No. 332]

Cook the asparagus as described in the introductory remarks above, but drain while still slightly under-done. Heat 4 tablespoons of butter in a large frying pan over moderate heat and sauté the asparagus very gently until tender, about 5 minutes. Remove from the heat, swirl in the anchovy butter, sprinkle with the parsley, and add the lemon juice. Arrange on a hot serving platter and garnish with the croûtons. *Serves* 6.

1598. ASPARAGUS IN CREAM
Punte di asparagi alla crema

2 pounds asparagus, peeled
6 tablespoons butter
3/4 cup heavy cream
Salt

Cook the asparagus as described in the introductory remarks above, but drain while still slightly under-done. Melt 3 tablespoons of the butter in a large frying pan, add the asparagus and the cream, and simmer over very low heat until the asparagus are tender. Remove it from the heat, swirl in the remaining butter, bit by bit, correct the seasoning, and then turn out onto a hot serving platter. *Serves* 6.

1599. COLD ASPARAGUS WITH CREAM MAYONNAISE
Asparagi con maionese e panna montata

2 pounds asparagus, peeled
2 cups Mayonnaise [No. 77], with 1 cup whipped
    cream folded in just before serving

Cook and drain the asparagus as directed in the introductory remarks above. Chill thoroughly and serve cold with the mayonnaise on the side. *Serves* 6.

1600. ASPARAGUS FLAMANDE
Asparagi alla fiamminga

2 pounds asparagus, peeled
3 hard-boiled eggs, finely chopped and seasoned with
    salt and pepper
1/2 cup butter, melted

Cook and drain the asparagus as described in the introductory remarks above. Arrange them on a hot serving platter, sprinkle with the chopped eggs, and pour the butter over. *Serves* 6.

1601. ASPARAGUS AU GRATIN FRANCESE
Punte di asparagi gratinate alla francese

2 pounds asparagus, peeled
2 cups Sauce Mornay [No. 56]
1/2 cup grated Parmesan cheese

Cook and drain the asparagus as directed in the introductory remarks above. Arrange them in an oven-proof shallow dish, cover with the Mornay sauce, sprinkle with the grated Parmesan cheese, and put into a very hot (450°) oven until the top is golden. *Serves* 6.

1602. ASPARAGUS ITALIANA
Asparagi all'italiana

2 pounds asparagus, peeled
½ cup grated Parmesan cheese
½ cup Hazelnut Butter [No. 103]

Cook and drain the asparagus as described in the introductory remarks above. Arrange them on a hot serving platter, sprinkle with the grated Parmesan cheese, and pour the butter over. *Serves* 6.

1603. ASPARAGUS WITH LEMON
Asparagi all'agro di limone

2 pounds asparagus, peeled
½ cup olive oil
2 tablespoons lemon juice
1 tablespoon chopped parsley
½ teaspoon salt
¼ teaspoon freshly ground pepper

Cook and drain the asparagus as described in the introductory remarks above. Mix the oil, lemon juice, parsley, salt, and pepper thoroughly. Arrange the asparagus on a hot serving platter and pour the sauce over them. *Serves* 6.

1604. ASPARAGUS MALTESE
Asparagi alla maltese

2 pounds asparagus, peeled
2 cups Sauce Hollandaise [No. 72], to which is added the juice of ½ orange and 1 tablespoon slivered orange peel (no white part) which has been parboiled for 5 minutes and drained

Cook and drain the asparagus as described in the introductory remarks above. Arrange them on a hot serving platter and pour the Hollandaise sauce over them. *Serves* 6.

1605. ASPARAGUS MILANESE
Asparagi alla milanese

2 pounds asparagus, peeled
½ cup grated Parmesan cheese
½ cup Hazlenut Butter [No. 103]
6 fried eggs

Cook and drain the asparagus as described in the introductory remarks above. Arrange them on a hot serving platter, sprinkle with the grated Parmesan cheese and with the hazlenut butter, and lay the fried eggs on top. *Serves* 6.

1606. ASPARAGUS POLONAISE
Asparagi alla polonese

2 pounds asparagus, peeled
4 hard-boiled egg yolks, chopped
2 tablespoons chopped parsley
½ cup butter
¼ cup white breadcrumbs

Cook and drain the asparagus as directed in the introductory remarks above. Arrange them on a hot serving platter and sprinkle with the chopped egg yolks and parsley. Melt the butter in a frying pan over medium heat, add the breadcrumbs, cook until foaming, and pour over the asparagus. *Serves* 6.

1607. ASPARAGUS WRAPPED IN PROSCIUTTO AU GRATIN
Punte di asparagi al prosciutto e parmigiano

18 very large asparagus stalks, peeled
18 thin slices prosciutto
½ cup butter, melted
½ cup grated Parmesan cheese
6 slices bread, crusts removed, sautéed golden in butter

Cook the asparagus as described in the introductory remarks above and drain when barely tender. Cool slightly, wrap each stalk in a slice of prosciutto, and arrange them in a lightly buttered baking dish. Sprinkle with melted butter, then with grated cheese, and then with the remaining butter. Place the dish in a hot (450°) oven until the top is golden, and serve in the baking dish, garnished with the browned slices of bread. *Serves* 6.

1608. SAUTÉED ASPARAGUS TIPS WRAPPED IN PROSCIUTTO
Punte di asparagi giganti al prosciutto

18 very large, fat asparagus stalks, peeled
18 thin slices prosciutto
Flour
2 eggs, beaten
6 tablespoons butter

Cook the asparagus as described in the introductory remarks above and drain when they are barely tender. Cool slightly, wrap each stalk tightly in a slice of prosciutto, dust with flour, and dip in beaten egg. Heat the butter in a very large frying pan over medium heat (or use 2 pans) and sauté the stalks until golden brown on all sides. Arrange them on a hot serving platter and serve at once. *Serves* 6.

1609. ASPARAGUS WITH ZABAGLIONE
Asparagi allo zabaione

2 pounds asparagus, peeled
1 recipe Zabaglione [No. 2116] omitting sugar, substituting dry white wine for the Marsala, and beating in 4 tablespoons softened sweet butter just before serving

Cook and drain the asparagus as directed in the introductory remarks above. Arrange them on a hot serving platter and pour the Zabaglione over. *Serves* 6.

DRIED BEANS
Fagioli

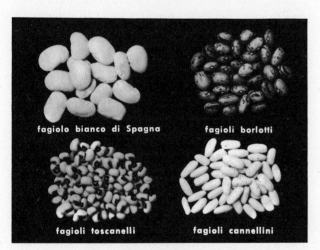

The English-language names
of these dried beans are:
dried lima beans (upper left);
cranberry beans (upper right);
black-eyed beans (bottom left);
white navy beans (bottom right).

Dried white beans and closely related types, such as black-eyed beans or cranberry beans, are a staple of the Italian diet and are served almost as frequently as potatoes or rice. While these are occasionally available freshly picked, more often they are dried and commercially packaged.

Dried beans must be soaked for 12 hours in a generous quantity of water, unless they are pre-processed and the packager's instructions clearly state that soaking is unnecessary. After soaking, discard any beans which float on the surface of the water. They should be brought to a boil in about twice the quantity of water as beans. The water should be lightly salted and may be flavored with onion, a Bouquet Garni, salt pork, a ham bone, or any other desired flavoring agent. After reaching a boil, they should simmer slowly until they are tender. The exact time will depend on the particular variety of bean: white beans will usually be tender in $1\frac{1}{2}$ hours, some types of navy beans require as much as $2\frac{1}{2}$ hours, and some dried lima beans will be fully cooked in $\frac{1}{2}$ hour. To test for doneness, remove a spoonful of beans from the cooking pot, blow on them, and if their outer skins immediately peel back, they are fully cooked.

Freshly picked beans need not be soaked, but they should be thoroughly washed. They are cooked in the same manner as dried beans, except that they will be tender in about $\frac{1}{3}$ the time.

1610. BLACK-EYED BEANS UCCELLETTO
Fagioli toscanelli all'uccelletto

1 pound black-eyed beans, soaked for 12 hours, simmered with 1 onion in lightly salted water until tender, and drained
$\frac{1}{2}$ cup oil
12 fresh sage leaves (or 2 teaspoons dried)
3 ripe tomatoes, peeled, seeded, drained, and chopped
Salt and freshly ground pepper

Heat the oil with the sage leaves in a large, heavy pot over medium heat until almost smoking, add the beans, and stir for 3 minutes, being careful not to scorch the beans. Add the tomatoes, season with salt and pepper, stir lightly until the moisture from the tomatoes has almost evaporated, and turn out into a hot vegetable dish. *Serves* 6.

1611. DRIED CRANBERRY BEANS IN RED WINE
Fagioli borlotti al vino rosso

1 pound dried cranberry beans, soaked for 12 hours and drained
2 cups dry red wine
$1\frac{1}{2}$ quarts cold water
1 onion, stuck with 1 clove
$\frac{1}{2}$ pound lean salt pork, parboiled for 20 minutes
1 teaspoon salt
2 tablespoons butter
1 tablespoon flour

Put the beans into a large, heavy pot with the wine, water, onion, salt pork, and salt. Bring slowly to a boil and then simmer for about 1½ hours, or until the beans are tender. Drain them into a colander, reserving the cooking liquid. Discard the onion and cut the salt pork into coarse dice. Heat the butter in the pot over medium heat, add the salt pork dice, and stir until golden on all sides. Stir in the flour, cook for 1 minute, and then stir in 1 cup of the hot cooking liquid. Simmer for 5 minutes, add the beans, toss lightly, cook just long enough to get the beans very hot, and then turn them out into a hot vegetable dish. *Serves 6.*

1612. DRIED WHITE BEANS AMERICANA
Fagioli all'americana

1 pound dried white beans, soaked for 12 hours, simmered until tender in lightly salted water, and drained
½ cup oil
½ pound salt pork, diced, parboiled for 15 minutes, and drained
1 onion, chopped
1 stalk celery, chopped
6 large ripe tomatoes, peeled, seeded, drained, and puréed through a food mill
2 tablespoons chopped parsley
Salt and freshly ground pepper

Heat the oil in a large, heavy casserole over medium heat until almost smoking, add the salt pork dice, and stir until they are golden. Add the onion and celery and cook until the onion is soft. Add the tomatoes and parsley, season with salt and pepper, and simmer for 30 minutes. Add the beans, mix lightly, correct the seasoning, and heat only long enough to get the beans very hot. Serve in the casserole, or, if desired, turn the beans out into a hot vegetable dish. *Serves 6.*

1613. DRIED WHITE BEANS PARISIAN STYLE
Fagioli alla parigina

The French, particularly Parisians, are especially fond of white beans as an accompaniment for roast lamb. Thus this recipe presupposes that there is on hand a generous cup of the juices which drain from a Roast Leg of Lamb [No. 1216] as it is being carved, or 1 cup of lamb gravy made by de-glazing the pan in which the lamb was roasted with Brown Stock [No.4].

1 pound dried white beans, soaked 12 hours, simmered in lightly salted water with 1 onion until tender, and drained
1 cup lamb juices or pan-gravy
1 cup fresh breadcrumbs
4 tablespoons butter, melted

Put the cooked beans in a shallow baking dish, add the lamb juices or gravy, mix lightly, cover with breadcrumbs, and sprinkle with melted butter. Place the dish in a very hot (500°) oven for about 10 minutes, or until the top is nicely browned, and serve in the baking dish. *Serves 6.*

1614. DRIED WHITE BEANS WITH HAM
Fagioli stufati con cotenne di prosciutto

1 pound dried white beans, soaked for 12 hours
1 ham bone (with some meat clinging to it)
3 sprigs rosemary (or 1 teaspoon dried, tied in a cloth bag)
2 large pieces fresh pork rind, parboiled for 1 hour and cut into ½-inch squares
1 tablespoon oil
A chopped mixture:
  ¼ cup ham fat
  1 onion
  1 clove garlic
  3 sprigs basil (or 1 teaspoon dried)
  3 sprigs parsley
1 pound ripe tomatoes, peeled, seeded, drained, and chopped
Salt and freshly ground pepper

Put the beans in a large pot with the ham bone, rosemary, pork rind, and a generous amount of water, also using the water in which the rind cooked. Season with a little salt, bring slowly to a boil, and simmer for about 1½ hours, or until the beans are tender. While the beans are cooking, heat the oil in another large

pot over medium heat, add the chopped mixture, cook until the onion begins to color, add the tomatoes, season with salt and pepper, and simmer 20 minutes. Drain the beans when they are tender, discard the ham bone and rosemary, add the beans to the tomato mixture, stir for 1 minute, and then turn them out into a hot vegetable dish. *Serves* 6.

1615. FRESH WHITE BEANS IN BUTTER
Fagioli al burro

2 pounds freshly picked white beans
1 onion
Salt
$\frac{1}{2}$ cup butter, softened

Put the beans in a large earthenware pot, cover with a generous amount of cold water, add the onion, and season with salt. Bring to a boil, reduce the heat, and simmer for about 30 minutes, or until the beans are tender. Drain them in a colander, discard the onion, return them to the pot over low heat, and shake the pot for a few minutes to eliminate any moisture. Add the butter, stir lightly until the butter is melted, and turn the beans out into a hot serving dish. *Serves* 6.

1616. PURÉE OF DRIED WHITE BEANS
Fagioli in purea

1 pound dried white beans, soaked, simmered in lightly salted water with 1 onion until tender, and drained
1 cup heavy cream
6 tablespoons butter

Discard the onion and purée the beans by passing them through a food mill. Return them to their pot over a low fire, stir with a wooden spoon, add the cream and butter, and stir until the butter is melted and the mixture is very smooth. If desired, they may be puréed in the blender, a little at a time, adding as much cream as necessary to each batch to keep the blender from clogging; when all are blended, return them to their pot, add the butter, and stir until the butter is melted. *Serves* 6.

BEETS
Barbabietole

The green tops of beets should be removed before they are cooked (the greens—which are delicious—

may be thoroughly washed and cooked like spinach) and the beets scrubbed, but not peeled. The American method of cooking beets is usually to boil them, but Italians generally prefer to simply put them on a baking sheet or pan and bake them until tender in a moderate (350°) oven. The exact time will depend on the age and size of the beets. Large, old beets will require as long as $1\frac{1}{2}$ hours, but medium-sized young beets will usually be tender in about 40 minutes. Test for doneness by pressing with the finger; if they yield slightly to this pressure, they are fully cooked. The skins will slip off easily after they are cooked.

1617. BEETS WITH BÉCHAMEL SAUCE
Barbabietole alla besciamella

2 pounds beets, trimmed, baked until tender as described in the introductory remarks above, skinned, and sliced
4 tablespoons butter, melted
Salt
2 cups hot Béchamel Sauce [No. 18]

Heat the butter in a saucepan over medium heat until melted, add the sliced beets, and stir lightly until they are very hot. Season them lightly with salt, turn them out into a hot vegetable dish, and cover with the hot Béchamel sauce. *Serves* 6.

1618. BEETS IN CREAM
Barbabietole alla crema

3 pounds beets, trimmed, baked until tender as described in the introductory remarks above, skinned, and cut into balls with a melon ball cutter
4 tablespoons butter
2 cups heavy cream
Salt

After cutting the beets into balls, reserve the trimmings as a garnish for cold dishes or for use in a salad. Heat the butter in a saucepan over medium heat, add the beets, and stir until they are very hot. Turn them out into a hot vegetable dish and keep warm. Add the cream to the saucepan, reserving 3 tablespoons, and boil over high heat until reduced by $\frac{1}{2}$. Remove from the fire, add the reserved cream, season with a little salt, and pour over the beets. *Serves* 6.

1619. BEETS WITH FRESH HERBS
Barbabietole con erbe fini

2 pounds beets, trimmed, baked until tender as
   described in the introductory remarks above,
   skinned, and sliced
4 tablespoons butter
1 onion, chopped
¼ cup Meat Essence [No. 10]
½ cup mixed chopped fresh herbs, such as parsley,
   marjoram, basil, chervil, mint, etc.
Salt

Heat the butter in a saucepan over medium heat until
melted, add the onion, and cook until it is soft. Add
the beets, season with a little salt, stir until very hot,
and then add the meat essence and chopped herbs.
Stir lightly for 1 minute and then turn out into a hot
vegetable dish. *Serves* 6.

1620. BEETS INGLESE
Barbabietole all'inglese

2 pounds beets, trimmed
6 tablespoons butter, softened
Salt

Drop the beets into a generous quantity of boiling
salted water. Reduce the heat and simmer for about
30 minutes, or until they are tender. Drain them, peel,
cut into thick slices, and put them in a hot vegetable
dish. Dot with the softened butter and season with a
little salt. *Serves* 6.

1621. BEETS PARMIGIANA
Barbabietole alla parmigiana

2 pounds beets, trimmed, baked until tender as
   described in the introductory remarks above,
   skinned, and sliced
2 cups Italian Meat Sauce [No. 41]
1 cup grated Parmesan cheese
¼ cup butter, melted

Butter a shallow baking dish and arrange the beets
in it in layers, covering each layer with a generous
amount of the Italian meat sauce. Sprinkle the top with
grated Parmesan cheese and melted butter and put the
dish in a hot (400°) oven until top is lightly browned.
Serve in the baking dish. *Serves* 6.

550

BROCCOLI
Broccoli

Italians frequently braise broccoli in wine, which will
be described in the following recipe, but the simplest
method of cooking is to boil it in water. Before cooking,
the tough outer leaves should be discarded, the tough
bottom ends of the stalks cut off, the stalks peeled, and
the thicker stalks split lengthwise from the base up to
2 inches of the floweret heads (this will allow the stalks
to cook more quickly). Tie the stalks into a bunch, set
them upright in a large enamel (never metal) saucepan,
add sufficient water to come halfway up the stalks,
season with a little salt, and cover the pan (if the broccoli is too tall for the saucepan, invert another pan on
top to serve as a lid). Bring to a boil, reduce the heat,
and simmer for about 15 minutes. When the base of
the thicker stalks is easily pierced with a fork, the
broccoli is fully cooked.

1622. BRAISED BROCCOLI ROMANA
Broccoli romani

2 pounds broccoli
4 tablespoons oil
2 cloves garlic, crushed in the garlic-press
1½ cups dry white wine
Salt and freshly ground pepper

Cut off the tough outer leaves of the broccoli and then
cut off the stalks about 2 inches below the heads.
Peel stalks, cut any thick stalks in half lengthwise, or,
if they are very thick, quarter them. Heat the oil in a
large skillet over medium heat, add the garlic, and cook
until the garlic begins to color. Add 1 cup of the wine
and the broccoli stalks, season with a little salt and
pepper, cover the pan, and simmer for 5 minutes.
Lay the heads of the broccoli on top of the stalks,

season again with a little salt and pepper, and cook uncovered for about 10 minutes longer, or until the stalks and the heads are tender. If too much wine evaporates, add a little more as it cooks, but 5 minutes before the broccoli is tender, raise the heat slightly and allow the wine to reduce to about $\frac{1}{2}$ cup. Arrange the broccoli on a hot serving dish and pour the liquids in the pan over it. *Serves* 6.

1623. BROCCOLI WITH PROSCIUTTO
Broccoli romani al prosciutto

2 pounds broccoli, boiled until tender in the manner described in the introductory remarks above
6 tablespoons oil
2 cloves garlic, crushed in the garlic-press
1 cup chopped prosciutto
Salt and freshly ground pepper
1 cup Croûtons [No. 332]

While the broccoli is cooking, heat the oil in a frying pan over medium heat, add the garlic, cook until golden, add the prosciutto, and cook long enough to heat it through. When the broccoli is tender, drain it thoroughly, arrange it on a hot serving platter, season with a little salt and pepper, pour the sauce over, and garnish with the croûtons. *Serves* 6.

1624. BROCCOLI SICILIANA
Broccoli alla siciliana

2 pounds broccoli
$\frac{1}{2}$ cup oil
1 cup sliced pitted black olives
1 onion, sliced
18 anchovy fillets washed free of salt [*see* No. 220] and chopped
1 cup finely diced Cacciocavallo cheese (or substitute provolone)
2 cups dry red wine
1 cup Croûtons [No. 332]
Salt and freshly ground pepper

Cut off the stalks of the broccoli about 1 inch below heads. Peel stalks, cut any thick stalks in half lengthwise, and if there are any very thick ones, quarter them lengthwise. All of the stalks should be roughly the same thickness. Oil a heavy casserole, arrange a layer of $\frac{1}{3}$ of the broccoli stalks in the bottom, season with a little salt and pepper, and sprinkle with a little more oil. Lay $\frac{1}{3}$ of the onion, olives, anchovies, and cheese on top of the broccoli. Continue making layers

in this fashion and then lay the broccoli heads on the top. Add the wine, place the casserole over medium heat, bring to a boil, and cook for about 20 minutes, or until the stalks of the broccoli are tender. Do not stir during the cooking. Serve in the casserole topped with the croûtons. *Serves* 6.

BROCCOLI-RAVE
Broccoletti di rape

Broccoli-rave is not too commonly seen in American markets. It has long, slender stalks sprouting tiny flowerets.

1625. BROCCOLI-RAVE VINAIGRETTE
Broccoletti di rape all'agro

2 pounds broccoli-rave, cut into 4-inch lengths
$\frac{3}{4}$ cup Sauce Vinaigrette [No. 99]

Cook the broccoli-rave in a generous quantity of lightly salted boiling water for about 15 minutes, or until tender. Drain it thoroughly, place it in a hot vegetable dish, and pour the Vinaigrette sauce over it (or, if desired, it may be chilled before being mixed with the Vinaigrette sauce). *Serves* 6.

1626. BROCCOLI-RAVE WITH GARLIC AND OIL NO. 1
Broccoletti di rape lessati e insaporiti con aglio e olio

2 pounds broccoli-rave, cut into 4-inch lengths
6 tablespoons oil
2 cloves garlic, crushed in the garlic-press
Salt and freshly ground pepper

Cook the broccoli-rave in a generous quantity of lightly salted boiling water for about 15 minutes, or until tender. Drain thoroughly, arrange on a hot serving platter, and season lightly with salt and pepper. Heat the oil and garlic in a saucepan until the garlic begins to color and pour over the broccoli. *Serves* 6.

1627. BROCCOLI-RAVE WITH GARLIC AND OIL NO. 2
Broccoli di rape stufati a crudo con aglio e olio

Instead of first boiling the broccoli-rave and then dressing it with garlic and oil as in the preceding recipe, heat the garlic and oil in a large, heavy saucepan for 1 minute over medium heat, add the broccoli-rave, season with salt and pepper, and mix lightly. Add ¼ cup of water, cover the saucepan, and cook for 10 minutes. Remove the cover, raise the heat slightly, and cook for about 10 minutes longer, or until the broccoli-rave is tender and the cooking liquid almost evaporated.

BRUSSELS SPROUTS
Cavolini di Bruxelles

Before cooking, any yellowish leaves on Brussels sprouts should be pulled off, the root end cut off, and a small cross cut in the base of each sprout to make it cook more quickly. It was formerly necessary to soak Brussels sprouts in acidulated water for 15 minutes to rid them of any insects buried in their leaves, but present-day growing methods seem to have eliminated these pests and soaking is unnecessary. They should, however, be briefly washed under running water.

1628. BRUSSELS SPROUTS IN BUTTER
Cavolini di Bruxelles al burro

1½ pounds Brussels sprouts
6 tablespoons butter
Salt and freshly ground pepper
Juice of 1 lemon

Cook the Brussels sprouts in a generous quantity of lightly salted boiling water for about 8 to 10 minutes, or until they are barely tender, and drain immediately. Heat the butter in a frying pan over medium heat, add the drained sprouts, season with a little salt and pepper, and roll them in the butter for 1 minute. Squeeze the lemon juice over them and turn them out into a hot vegetable dish. *Serves* 6.

1629. BRUSSELS SPROUTS IN CREAM
Cavolini di Bruxelles alla crema

1½ pounds Brussels sprouts
6 tablespoons butter
1 cup heavy cream
Salt and freshly ground pepper

Cook the sprouts as described in the preceding recipe, except drain them after 6 to 8 minutes, or when they are still slightly underdone. Heat the butter in a frying pan over medium heat, add the drained sprouts, roll them for a few seconds in the butter, add all but 2 tablespoons of the cream, and boil for about 4 minutes; the cream should reduce and thicken slightly. Remove from the fire, swirl in the remaining cream, and turn the sprouts and cream out into a hot vegetable dish. *Serves* 6.

1630. BRUSSELS SPROUTS WITH CURRY
Cavolini di Bruxelles all'indiana

1½ pounds Brussels sprouts
6 tablespoons butter
1½ cups Curry Sauce [No. 70]
3 cups Indian Rice [No. 594]

Cook, drain, and roll the Brussels sprouts in butter as described in Brussels Sprouts in Butter [No. 1628]. Add the curry sauce, heat for 1 minute, pour the sprouts and sauce into the center of a hot serving platter, and surround with a border of the rice. *Serves* 6.

1631. BRUSSELS SPROUTS INGLESE
Cavolini di Bruxelles all'inglese

1½ pounds Brussels sprouts
½ cup butter, softened
Salt and freshly ground pepper

Cook the Brussels sprouts as described in Brussels Sprouts in Butter [No. 1628], drain them, put them into a hot vegetable dish, season lightly with salt and pepper, and serve the butter on the side. *Serves* 6.

1632. BRUSSELS SPROUTS ITALIANA
Cavolini di Bruxelles all'italiana

Prepare in the same manner and with the same ingredients as Brussels Sprouts in Butter [No. 1628], except sprinkle the sprouts with ½ cup of grated Parmesan cheese just before serving.

CABBAGE
Cavolo

Green Cabbage   Savoy Cabbage

The familiar variety of red and green cabbage, as well as Savoy, are all available in Italy, although in contrast to the present-day American method of boiling cabbage very quickly, Italians generally prefer to braise it very slowly for a long period of time.

1633. BRAISED CABBAGE
Cavolo cappuccio brasato

1 head green cabbage, core removed, parboiled
   3 minutes, and the leaves separated
8 thin slices of lean salt pork, parboiled for 15 minutes
2 carrots, sliced
1 onion stuck with 1 clove
Bouquet Garni:
   3 sprigs parsley
   2 sprigs thyme (or ½ teaspoon dried)
   1 bay leaf
2 cups Brown Stock [No. 4]
Salt and freshly ground pepper

Line the bottom of a heavy casserole with 4 slices of the salt pork, sprinkle the carrots over the pork, add the loose cabbage leaves, season with a little salt and pepper, lay the onion and Bouquet Garni over the cabbage, cover with the remaining slices of salt pork, and pour in the stock. Bring to a boil over medium heat, cover the casserole, and place it in a moderate (350°) oven for 1½ hours. Discard the onion and Bouquet Garni and serve in the casserole. *Serves* 6.

1634. RED CABBAGE FIAMMINGA
Cavolo rosso alla fiamminga

1 large head red cabbage, core removed, shredded
6 tablespoons butter
1 tablespoon wine vinegar
2 cups Brown Stock [No. 4]
3 tart apples, peeled, cored, and quartered
1 tablespoon brown sugar
Salt and freshly ground pepper

Heat the butter in a heavy casserole over low heat, add the shredded cabbage, season with a little salt and pepper, cover the casserole, and simmer for 10 minutes, stirring occasionally. Add the vinegar, stock, apples, and brown sugar; turn the heat down to the lowest possible flame; and simmer for 3 hours. Check occasionally to make certain the stock has not evaporated and add a little more if necessary. Serve in the casserole or in a vegetable dish. *Serves* 6.

1635. STUFFED CABBAGE ITALIANA
Cavolo ripieno all'italiana

1 large head green cabbage
6 tablespoons butter
4 ½-inch-thick slices of veal, cut from the upper leg
1 pair sweetbreads, soaked, blanched (*see* page 496),
   and sliced
½ cup chicken livers
2 cups fresh breadcrumbs
¼ cup grated Parmesan cheese
1 egg, lightly beaten
Pinch nutmeg
Salt and freshly ground pepper
3 cups Brown Stock [No. 4]

Discard the core from the cabbage and parboil the cabbage for 5 minutes in lightly salted water. Drain it, cool slightly, and gently pull the leaves apart without separating them from the base. If the leaves do not come apart easily, pour a little boiling water over them. Cut out the very center leaves of the head, leaving a hole about the size of a large lemon. Turn the head upside

553

down to drain. Heat 4 tablespoons of the butter in a frying pan over medium high heat and brown the slices of veal for about 3 minutes on each side. Remove them from the pan with a slotted spoon and brown the slices of sweetbreads for about 2 minutes on each side, adding more butter if necessary. Remove them with a slotted spoon, and quickly sauté the chicken livers for about 3 minutes. Grind all 3 meats in the meat grinder, using the finest blade. Mix them in a bowl with the breadcrumbs, cheese, and beaten egg. Season the mixture with salt, pepper, and a little nutmeg. Fill the center of the head of cabbage with a little of this stuffing and then scatter generous spoonsful throughout the leaves, pushing it well down between them. Press the head together with both hands so that it resembles its original shape as closely as possible and tie with string. Place the cabbage in a deep casserole, pour in the stock, bring to a boil, cover tightly, and place it in a moderate (350°) oven for 2 hours. Check occasionally to see that the stock has not evaporated and add more if necessary. Carefully transfer the head of cabbage to a hot serving platter, remove string, and pour the reduced juices in the casserole over the cabbage. *Serves* 6.

CARDOONS
Cardi

Cardoons are a member of the thistle family and, like artichokes, when trimming any cut parts should be immediately rubbed with lemon juice to prevent their darkening. Discard the tough outer stalks, scrape off any strings on the remaining stalks as one would for celery (which they somewhat resemble), and cut the stalks into 3-inch pieces, rubbing the cut ends with lemon juice. If they are to be kept for any length of time before cooking, soak them in a bowl of acidulated water. Place in an enamel saucepan, and boil them in a generous quantity of White Foundation for Vegetables [No. 1276] for $1\frac{1}{2}$ to 2 hours, or until they are tender, and drain.

1636. CARDOONS IN BUTTER
Cardi al burro

Prepare and cook 2 bunches of cardoons as described in the preceding introduction. Drain them thoroughly and sauté them very gently in $\frac{1}{2}$ cup butter in a frying pan over low heat for 10 minutes. Season them lightly with salt and pepper and serve them in a hot vegetable dish. *Serves* 6.

1637. CARDOON FRITTERS
Cardi fritti

2 bunches cardoons, trimmed, cooked as described
    in the introductory remarks above, and drained
A marinade:
  1 cup olive oil
  $\frac{1}{3}$ cup lemon juice
  2 tablespoons chopped parsley
  1 teaspoon salt
3 cups Fritter Batter [No. 275]
Fat for deep frying
3 lemons, quartered

Marinate the still-hot cardoons for 1 hour in the marinade, drain thoroughly, pat dry, dip them in the fritter batter, and drop them into deep hot (375°) fat until they are crisp and golden. Heap them on a hot platter and garnish with the lemon quarters. *Serves* 6.

1638. CARDOONS AU GRATIN
Cardi al gratino

2 bunches cardoons, trimmed, cooked as described in
    the introductory remarks above, and well drained
3 cups Sauce Mornay [No. 56], mixed with $\frac{1}{2}$ cup
    Duxelles [No. 138]
$1\frac{1}{2}$ cups fresh white breadcrumbs, mixed with $\frac{1}{2}$ cup
    grated Parmesan cheese
$\frac{1}{4}$ cup butter, melted

Spread a shallow baking dish with a little of the Mornay sauce, arrange the pieces of cardoon in the dish, and cover them with the rest of the sauce. Sprinkle the top with breadcrumbs mixed with cheese and then with the melted butter. Put the dish in a very hot (500°) oven for 5 minutes, or until the surface is golden. *Serves* 6.

1639. CARDOONS WITH MEAT SAUCE AND MARROW
Cardi con salsa di carne e midollo

2 bunches cardoons, trimmed, cooked as described
    in the introductory remarks above, and well
    drained
$1/2$ pound beef marrow
3 tablespoons butter
2 cups Italian Meat Sauce [No. 41]

Cut the marrow into $1/4$-inch slices, drop into a saucepan of simmering water, and cook over very low heat for 5 minutes. Remove from the heat and reserve in the hot water. Melt the butter in a saucepan, add the cooked cardoons and the meat sauce, and simmer over low heat for 10 minutes. Turn the cardoons and sauce out into a hot serving dish and cover with the slices of poached marrow. *Serves* 6.

1640. CARDOONS MILANESE
Cardi alla milanese

2 bunches cardoons, trimmed, cooked as described
    in the introductory remarks above, and well
    drained
$1 1/2$ cups grated Parmesan cheese
$1/2$ cup butter, melted
$1/4$ cup Hazlenut Butter [No. 103]

Arrange layers of the cardoons in a shallow baking dish, sprinkling each layer with a little cheese and melted butter. Put the dish in a hot (450°) oven until the surface is brown. Pour the hazlenut butter over the top and serve in the baking dish. *Serves* 6.

1641. CARDOONS POLONAISE
Cardi alla polacca

2 bunches cardoons, trimmed, cooked as described
    in the introductory remarks above, and well
    drained
3 hard-boiled eggs, chopped
3 tablespoons chopped parsley
$1/2$ cup butter
$1/2$ cup breadcrumbs

Arrange the hot cardoons on a hot serving platter and sprinkle with the chopped hard-boiled eggs and parsley. Melt the butter in a frying pan over medium heat, add the breadcrumbs, and, when foaming, pour over the cardoons. *Serves* 6.

1642. RAW CARDOONS WITH BAGNA CAUDA
Cardi con bagna cauda

2 bunches raw cardoons, trimmed as described in the
    introductory remarks above and soaked in
    acidulated water
3 cups Bagna Cauda [No. 65]

The Piedmontese, whose specialty this dish is, traditionally serve raw cardoons in a bowl of acidulated water at the table and each guest serves himself by drying a piece of cardoon on a napkin, dipping it in the very hot Bagna Cauda sauce, and eating immediately. The sauce should be kept hot over a spirit lamp or in a chafing dish. *Serves* 6.

CARROTS
Carote

The tops and tails of carrots should be trimmed off before cooking and very young carrots may be simply scrubbed, but larger older ones should be peeled or scraped. They may be cut into any desired shape: sliced, cut into strips, quartered, etc. Whichever shape is chosen, they should be of uniform thickness in order to cook evenly.

Carrots are more often than not marketed packaged in plastic and have been kept for some time under refrigeration. Whenever very fresh carrots that are only a few hours out of the ground are available, take advantage of them. They have an unforgettable flavor.

1643. CARROTS WITH BRANDY
Carote al brandy

2 pounds young carrots, scrubbed and sliced
6 tablespoons butter
Salt and freshly ground pepper
1 teaspoon sugar
$1/3$ cup brandy
2 tablespoons chopped parsley

Heat the butter in a heavy frying pan over moderate heat and add the sliced carrots. Season them with salt, pepper, and the sugar. Cover the pan and cook them slowly for about 30 minutes, or until they are tender, stirring them frequently. Remove the cover, add the brandy, heat for a few seconds, ignite, and shake the pan until flames subside. Turn carrots out into a hot vegetable dish and sprinkle with the parsley. *Serves* 6.

1644. CARROTS IN BUTTER
Carote al burro

3 pounds large carrots, peeled and cut into the shape
of large olives with sharp knife (reserve the
trimmings for use in a stock or soup)
6 tablespoons butter
3 cups Brown Stock [No. 4]
1 teaspoon sugar
2 tablespoons chopped parsley
Salt and freshly ground pepper

Place the carrots, butter, stock, sugar, $\frac{1}{2}$ teaspoon salt,
and a pinch of pepper in a saucepan over medium
heat, bring to a boil, and simmer for 30 to 40 minutes,
or until the carrots are tender and the stock is very
reduced and thickened. Stir them frequently to ensure
even cooking and adjust the heat during the cooking so
that the stock does not evaporate too quickly. Turn
them out into a hot vegetable dish and sprinkle with the
parsley. *Serves* 6.

1645. CARROTS IN CREAM
Carote alla crema

Prepare in the same manner and with the same ingredients as Carrots with Brandy [No. 1643], omitting the
brandy. After the carrots have cooked for 15 minutes,
add $1\frac{1}{2}$ cups of heavy cream, and complete the cooking
uncovered, allowing the cream to reduce slightly.
Remove from the heat, swirl in $\frac{1}{4}$ cup more heavy
cream, correct the seasoning, turn out into a hot vegetable dish, and sprinkle with the parsley. *Serves* 6.

1646. FRICASSEE OF CARROTS
Carote in fricassea

Prepare in the same manner and with the same ingredients as Carrots with Brandy [No. 1643], omitting the
brandy. When the carrots are tender, remove the pan
from the heat and add 1 cup of heavy cream mixed
with 2 lightly beaten egg yolks. Return the pan to very
low heat and stir constantly until the cream is slightly
thickened. *Serves* 6.

1647. GLAZED CARROTS
Carote glassate al burro

Prepare in the same manner and with the same ingredients as Carrots in Butter [No. 1644], except when the
carrots are barely tender, add 3 tablespoons more of
butter and stir constantly until the stock has completely evaporated. *Serves* 6.

1648. CARROT PURÉE
Carote in purea

2 pounds carrots, peeled and sliced
$\frac{1}{2}$ cup butter
Salt and freshly ground pepper
Pinch sugar
$\frac{1}{2}$ cup heavy cream

Boil the carrots for 30 to 40 minutes, or until they are
tender, in a generous quantity of water lightly seasoned
with salt and sugar. Drain them, press them through
a ricer, return them to the saucepan, and add the butter
and cream. Stir them over low heat until the mixture
is very smooth, correct the seasoning, and turn them
out into a hot vegetable dish. *Serves* 6.

1649. CARROTS WITH MUSHROOMS MAJOR DOMO
Carote con funghi maggiordomo

2 pounds young carrots, scrubbed and cut into thin
strips
1 teaspoon sugar
$\frac{1}{2}$ pound mushrooms, sliced
6 tablespoons butter
3 tablespoons Meat Essence [No. 10]
Juice of $\frac{1}{2}$ lemon
Salt and freshly ground pepper
2 tablespoons chopped parsley

Boil the carrots in a generous quantity of water
seasoned with salt and sugar for 25 to 30 minutes, or
until they are barely tender. While the carrots are
cooking, heat the butter in a large frying pan over
moderate heat, and gently sauté the mushrooms for
about 10 minutes, or until they are tender. Drain the
carrots and add them to the frying pan, stir in the meat
essence and lemon juice, and season with salt and
pepper if necessary. Turn the carrots and mushrooms
out into a hot vegetable dish and sprinkle with the
parsley. *Serves* 6.

CAULIFLOWER
Cavolfiore

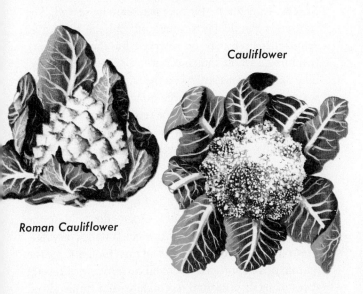

Cauliflower

Roman Cauliflower

The best cauliflower has very white closely packed flowerets and the surrounding leaves should be still fresh and green. Before cooking, all of the outside leaves should be broken off, and it will cook more evenly if it is then broken up into flowerets with no more than about 1½ inches of stem. Some recipes require it to be cooked whole, however, so that it makes a very attractive presentation. Before cooking it whole, cut off all of the thick central stem and make deep incisions with a sharp knife into all the remaining smaller stems so that the heat will penetrate them more easily.

1650. BOILED WHOLE CAULIFLOWER
Cavolfiore lessato

1 large cauliflower, trimmed but left whole as described in the introductory remarks above
½ cup butter, melted
Salt

Boil the head of cauliflower, stem down, in a large pot of lightly salted water for about 18 minutes. When the stems can be easily pierced with a fork, it is fully cooked. Drain it carefully without breaking off any of the flowerets, place it on a hot serving platter, and pour the melted butter over it. *Serves* 6.

NOTE: About 2 to 3 cups of any desired sauce, such as Hollandaise [No. 72], Mornay [No. 56], or Béchamel [No. 18], may be substituted for the butter.

1651. BOILED WHOLE CAULIFLOWER WITH MOUSSELINE SAUCE
Cavolfiore lessato con salsa mousseline

Prepare in the manner described in the preceding recipe, substituting for the butter 2 cups of Hollandaise sauce [No. 72] mixed just before serving with 1 cup whipped cream.

1652. CAULIFLOWER IN BUTTER
Cavolfiore al burro

1 large cauliflower, trimmed into flowerets as described in the introductory remarks above
½ cup butter, melted
Salt and freshly ground pepper
3 tablespoons chopped parsley

Drop the flowerets into a generous quantity of lightly salted boiling water for about 12 minutes. When the thickest stems of the flowerets can easily be pierced with a fork, they are fully cooked. Drain carefully in a colander, arrange on a hot serving platter, season with salt and pepper, pour the melted butter over, and sprinkle with the parsley. *Serves* 6.

1653. CAULIFLOWER FRITTERS
Bignè di cavolfiore

1 large cauliflower, trimmed into flowerets as described in the introductory remarks above
2 cups Fritter Batter [No. 275]
Fat for deep frying
Salt

Cook the cauliflower in the manner described in the preceding recipe (omitting butter and parsley), drain carefully, and cool slightly. Dip the flowerets in fritter batter and drop them in deep hot (375°) fat until they are crisp and golden brown. Arrange them on a hot serving platter and sprinkle lightly with salt. *Serves* 6.

1654. CAULIFLOWER AU GRATIN
Cavolfiore al gratino

1 large cauliflower, trimmed into flowerets as described in the introductory remarks above
3 cups Sauce Mornay [No. 56]
½ cup grated Parmesan cheese
¼ cup butter, melted

Cook the flowerets in a large quantity of boiling salted water for about 12 minutes, or until they are tender, and drain in a colander. Arrange them stem side down in a baking dish, cover with the Mornay sauce, sprinkle with Parmesan cheese, and then with melted butter. Bake in a hot (500°) oven for 5 or 6 minutes, or until the surface is golden. *Serves* 6.

1655. CAULIFLOWER PARMIGIANA
Cavolfiore alla parmigiana

1 large cauliflower, trimmed into flowerets as described in the introductory remarks above
$\frac{1}{2}$ cup grated Parmesan cheese
2 cups fresh breadcrumbs, fried in 6 tablespoons butter for a few seconds, cooled, and mixed with an additional $\frac{1}{2}$ cup grated Parmesan cheese
$\frac{1}{2}$ cup Hazlenut Butter [No. 103]

Boil the flowerets in a large quantity of lightly salted boiling water for about 12 minutes, or until they are tender, and drain them carefully in a colander. Butter a shallow baking dish, sprinkle it with the grated Parmesan cheese, arrange the flowerets in the dish, and sprinkle them with the breadcrumbs mixed with Parmesan cheese. Put the dish in a hot (500°) oven for about 8 minutes, or until the top is golden. Remove from the oven and pour the hazlenut butter over the flowerets. *Serves* 6.

CELERY

Sedano

558

Celery was very popular with the ancient Romans and its cultivation was resumed in Italy in the sixteenth century. In addition to its serving as a standard ingredient of an antipasto, Italians are fond of it as a cooked vegetable, usually as an accompaniment for roast meat or poultry.

Celery always has the same preliminary preparation before it is sauced. Allow 1 bunch of celery about 2 inches in diameter for each person to be served. The root ends should be trimmed off and the top leaves removed (these may be reserved for the stock pot), trimming a whole bunch down to about 7 inches long. The tough fibrous strings on the outer stalks should be scraped off, or, if using large bunches of green Pascal celery, the outer stalks may be removed (again, reserving these for the stock pot) and only the more tender inner stalks used. Wash the bunch very thoroughly under running water, pulling the stalks apart gently to wash out the grit at the base of the stalks. Drop the celery in a generous quantity of lightly salted boiling water and boil for 10 minutes. Drain and, holding the celery in a cloth, squeeze out as much water as possible. Tie several loops of string around each bunch. Line the bottom of an appropriately sized casserole with several slices of fresh pork rind, sprinkle with a thinly sliced carrot and onion, lay the celery on top in 1 layer, add a few sprigs of parsley and thyme tied together with a bay leaf, and cover the celery with Brown Stock [No. 4], about 3 to 4 cups. Season lightly with salt, bring to a boil, cover the casserole, and place it in a moderate (350°) oven for 1 to 2 hours. White celery will be tender in about 1 hour; Pascal celery will require from $1\frac{1}{2}$ to 2 hours. Drain it carefully in a colander and it is now ready to be sauced.

1656. CELERY WITH BÉCHAMEL SAUCE
Sedani alla besciamella

6 bunches celery, trimmed, cooked, and drained as described in the introductory remarks above
4 tablespoons butter
3 cups Béchamel Sauce [No. 18]

Melt the butter in a very large frying pan over moderate heat, add the celery, and turn it in the butter for 2 minutes. Transfer it to a hot serving dish and cover with the Béchamel sauce. *Serves* 6.

1657. CELERY IN BUTTER
Sedani al burro

6 bunches celery, trimmed, cooked, and drained as described in the introductory remarks above
6 tablespoons butter
Salt and freshly ground pepper

Heat the butter in a very large frying pan over moderate

heat, add the celery, and sauté gently for about 5 minutes, or until it is lightly browned. Season it with a little salt and pepper, arrange it on a hot serving dish, and pour the butter in the pan over it. *Serves* 6.

1658. CELERY GOURMET
Sedani del ghiottone

6 bunches celery, trimmed, cooked, and drained as
    described in the introductory remarks above
2 tablespoons butter, softened
2 cups Italian Meat Sauce [No. 41]
1 cup slivered prosciutto (or smoked ham)
¾ cup grated Parmesan cheese
¼ cup butter, melted

Spread a baking dish with the softened butter, arrange the celery on it, cover with the Italian meat sauce, and then sprinkle first with the slivers of prosciutto, then the grated cheese, and finally with the melted butter. Place the dish in a very hot (500°) oven for about 5 minutes, or until the top is lightly browned. Serve in the baking dish. *Serves* 6.

1659. CELERY AU GRATIN
Sedani gratinati al parmigiano

6 bunches celery, trimmed, cooked, and drained as
    described in the introductory remarks above
1 cup grated Parmesan cheese
½ cup butter, melted

Arrange the celery in a buttered baking dish, sprinkle with the grated Parmesan cheese, and then with melted butter. Put it into a very hot (500°) oven for about 5 minutes, or until the top is golden. *Serves* 6.

1660. CELERY WITH HOLLANDAISE SAUCE
Sedani lessati con salsa olandese

6 bunches celery, trimmed, cooked, and drained as
    described in the introductory remarks above
3 cups Sauce Hollandaise [No. 72]

Arrange the hot drained celery on a serving dish and pour the Hollandaise sauce over it. *Serves* 6.

1661. CELERY WITH MEAT SAUCE AND MARROW
Sedani alla midolla e sugo di carne

6 bunches celery, trimmed, cooked, and drained as
    described in the introductory remarks above

3 tablespoons butter, softened
¼ pound beef marrow
2 cups Italian Meat Sauce [No. 41]

Melt the butter in an enameled baking dish over moderate heat, arrange the celery in it, turn the bunches for 1 minute in the butter, place the marrow slices on top of the celery, pour the meat sauce over, and serve in the baking dish. *Serves* 6.

1662. CELERY MORNAY
Sedani Mornay

6 bunches celery, trimmed, cooked, and drained as
    described in the introductory remarks above
3 cups Sauce Mornay [No. 56]
2 cups fresh breadcrumbs, mixed with ½ cup grated
    Parmesan cheese
½ cup butter, melted

Spread ½ cup of the Mornay sauce in the bottom of a baking dish; arrange the celery bunches over it, cover with the remaining sauce, sprinkle with the breadcrumbs mixed with grated cheese, and then with melted butter. Put the dish in a very hot (550°) oven for 8 minutes, or until the surface is golden. *Serves* 6.

EGGPLANT
Melanzane

Eggplant was originally imported from India and was being cultivated in Italy by the seventeenth century. Although there are several varieties and sizes of eggplant, the best known and most generally used is the reddish-purple oval variety.

The flesh of eggplant is extremely watery and to eliminate as much water as possible before cooking, it should always be sprinkled with a liberal amount of salt and allowed to drain on absorbent paper or a rack. If it is being cooked sliced, salt both sides of the slices, lay the slices on absorbent paper, and weight with a pastry board or any convenient similar weight for 1 hour. The salt is thoroughly washed off and the slices dried on absorbent paper towels. If the eggplant is to be cooked cut in half, make deep incisions in the flesh of each half, going to within ¼ inch of the skin, sprinkle a generous amount of salt in the incisions, and place the halves cut side down on a rack for 1 hour. Squeeze the halves gently but firmly between the hands to press out as much of the remaining water as possible,

559

wash, and pat dry. Much of the salt will be washed out
of the incisions as the eggplant drains.

1663. BAKED EGGPLANT WITH GARLIC
Melanzane arrostite profumate all'aglio

3 small eggplant, cut in half, salted, and drained of
   water as described in the introductory remarks
   above
6 cloves garlic, crushed in the garlic-press
1 cup oil
Freshly ground pepper

After squeezing the eggplant to remove as much
water as possible, insert a little garlic, oil, and pepper
in the incisions in each half. Grease a large baking dish
with oil, place the eggplant, cut side up, in the dish,
and sprinkle the tops with more oil. Place the dish in a
moderate (350°) oven for 30 to 40 minutes, or until the
flesh is very tender and may be pierced easily with a
fork. Serve in the baking dish, or, if desired, transfer
them to a serving platter. *Serves 6.*

1664. BROILED EGGPLANT MAÎTRE D'HÔTEL
Melanzane alla griglia maître d'hôtel

2 large eggplant, peeled, sliced ½ inch thick, salted,
   and drained of water as described in the
   introductory remarks above
½ cup oil
1 cup Maître d'Hôtel Butter [No. 111]

Brush the eggplant slices liberally with oil and broil
them under a medium broiler flame for about 4 minutes
on each side, or until they are golden brown. Transfer
them to a hot serving platter and dot with the Maître
d'Hôtel butter. *Serves 6.*

The preparation
of Eggplant Catanese (No. 1665).
Note the small size
of the eggplant

1665. EGGPLANT CATANESE
Melanzane a ventaglio alla catanese

6 very small oval eggplant
1 cup oil
Flour
Salt

Peel the eggplant, but leave about 1 inch surrounding
the blossom end unpeeled. Hold them upright on their
blossom ends and cut them into strips about ¼ inch
square, leaving the strips attached to the blossom-end
base (*see* photograph). Sprinkle with a generous
amount of salt, spreading the strips apart so that the
salt will penetrate to the point where the strips are
attached to the blossom end. Place them on a rack and
allow them to drain for ½ hour. Squeeze them gently
to remove as much water as possible, wash thoroughly,
dry completely, and dust them lightly with flour, and
then shake them to remove excess flour. Heat the oil
in a very large frying pan over medium heat and sauté
the eggplant for about 10 minutes, turning them
frequently and adjusting the heat so that they will not
brown too quickly before the interior is tender. Arrange
them on a hot serving platter and sprinkle lightly with
salt. *Serves 6.*

1666. EGGPLANT FRITTERS
Bignè di melanzane

2 eggplant, peeled, sliced ½ inch thick, salted, and
   drained of water as described in the introductory
   remarks above
2 cups Fritter Batter [No. 275]
Fat for deep frying

Dip the eggplant slices in the fritter batter and drop
them in deep hot (375°) fat until they are crisp and
golden brown. Heap them up on a hot serving platter
and serve immediately. *Serves 6.*

1667. EGGPLANT AND MOZZARELLA FRITTERS
Melanzane filanti con mozzarella

2 large eggplant, peeled, sliced ¼ inch thick, salted, and drained of water as described in the introductory remarks above
1 cup flour
½ cup oil
1½ cups finely diced mozzarella cheese
½ cup Anchovy Butter [No. 108], softened
½ cup grated Parmesan cheese
2 tablespoons chopped basil
2 egg yolks
Salt and freshly ground pepper
2 cups Fritter Batter [No. 275]
Fat for deep frying

Dust the eggplant slices with flour. Heat the oil in a very large frying pan over high heat and very quickly brown the slices on both sides. Mix the mozzarella in a bowl with the anchovy butter, Parmesan cheese, basil, egg yolks, and salt and pepper to taste. Spread half of the eggplant slices with a little of this mixture and cover each of these with a slice of matching size. Press slices together and dip them in fritter batter and fry in deep hot (375°) fat until crisp and golden brown. Heap them up on a hot serving platter and serve immediately. *Serves 6.*

1668. EGGPLANT NAPOLETANA
Parmigiana di melanzane alla napoletana

2 eggplant, peeled, sliced ½ inch thick, salted, and drained of water as described in the introductory remarks above
Flour
½ cup oil
3 cups Tomato Sauce [No. 19]
1 cup grated Parmesan cheese
3 tablespoons chopped basil
½ pound mozzarella cheese, very thinly sliced

Dust the eggplant slices with flour. Heat the oil in a very large frying pan over high heat and brown the slices as quickly as possible on both sides. Arrange the slices in a lightly oiled, shallow baking dish in 3 layers, covering each layer with some of the tomato sauce, Parmesan cheese, chopped basil, and lastly the slices of mozzarella. Place the dish in a hot (450°) oven for about 8 minutes, or until the contents of the dish are bubbly and the mozzarella on top is very lightly browned. *Serves 6.*

1669. EGGPLANT PROVENÇALE
Melanzane alla provenzale

3 small eggplant, cut in half and drained of water as described in the introductory remarks above
½ cup oil
1 onion, chopped and gently sautéed in 1 tablespoon butter until soft
½ cup Duxelles [No. 138]
1 cup Tomato Sauce [No. 19], slowly reduced to ½ cup
⅓ cup ricotta cheese
⅓ cup cream cheese, softened
¾ cup Italian Meat Sauce [No. 41]
4 tablespoons chopped parsley
2 cloves garlic, crushed in the garlic-press
2 cups fresh breadcrumbs
½ cup butter, melted
Salt and freshly ground pepper

Heat the oil in a very large frying pan over medium heat and gently sauté the eggplant halves, flesh side down, for about 10 minutes. Remove them from the pan and scoop out all of their flesh, going to within ¼ inch of the skin. If all of the flesh does not come out easily, brush whatever remains in the halves with a little oil, place them in a roasting pan half filled with boiling water, and place the pan in a moderate (350°) oven for 5 to 10 minutes. The flesh should now be soft enough to scoop out easily. Coarsely chop all of the flesh and mix it in a bowl with the cooked onion, Duxelles, tomato sauce, ricotta, cream cheese, meat sauce, parsley, garlic, and salt and pepper. Fill each of the eggplant halves with this stuffing, cover each generously with breadcrumbs, and sprinkle with melted butter. Place them in a roasting pan in a medium (375°) oven for about 30 minutes, or until the tops are golden. Arrange them on hot serving platter. *Serves 6.*

1670. SAUTÉED EGGPLANT
Melanzane fritte

2 large eggplant, peeled, sliced ½ inch thick, salted, and drained of water as described in the introductory remarks above
Flour
1 cup oil

Cut the eggplant slices into strips about 3 inches long and ½ inch square. Dust them with flour and then sauté them in a large frying pan in smoking hot oil until they are golden brown on all sides. Drain them for a moment on absorbent paper and then heap them up on a hot serving platter. *Serves 6.*

1671. SAUTÉED BREADED EGGPLANT
Melanzane panate

Prepare in the same manner as in the preceding recipe, except after dusting the strips of eggplant with flour, dip them in beaten egg and then cover with fresh breadcrumbs before frying. About 2 cups of breadcrumbs and 2 beaten eggs will be sufficient for 2 eggplant. *Serves 6.*

1672. SAUTÉED DICED EGGPLANT
Melanzane al funghetto

Prepare in the same manner as Sautéed Eggplant [No. 1670], except cutting the eggplant into ½-inch dice instead of strips. *Serves 6.*

1673. SAUTÉED EGGPLANT MILANESE
Melanzane dorate alla milanese

Prepare in the same manner as Sautéed Eggplant [No. 1670], except after dusting eggplant with flour, dip it quickly in beaten egg before frying. *Serves 6.*

1674. EGGPLANT SICILIANA
Melanzane alla siciliana

2 large eggplant, peeled, sliced ½ inch thick, salted, and drained of water as described in the introductory remarks above
Flour
½ cup oil
½ pound mozzarella cheese, sliced
4 hard-boiled eggs, sliced
3 tablespoons chopped basil
2½ cups Tomato Sauce [No. 19]
1 cup grated Parmesan cheese
Salt and freshly ground pepper

Dust the eggplant slices with flour. Heat the oil in a very large frying pan over high heat and brown the slices very quickly on both sides. Arrange half of the slices in a shallow baking dish and cover with the slices of mozzarella, hard-boiled eggs, and chopped basil. Season lightly with salt and pepper, cover with the remaining slices of eggplant, spread the tomato sauce over the eggplant, and sprinkle with the grated cheese. Place the dish in a medium (375°) oven for about 20 minutes, or until the top is golden. *Serves 6.*

1675. EGGPLANT SOUFFLÉS
Melanzane soufflées all'emmenthal

3 small eggplant, cut in half and drained of salt as described in the introductory remarks above
½ cup oil
4 egg yolks, slightly beaten
2 cups Béchamel Sauce [No. 18], reduced over low heat to 1 cup
1 cup grated Swiss cheese
5 egg whites, beaten into stiff peaks
Salt and freshly ground pepper

Remove all of the pulp from the eggplant halves in the manner described in Eggplant Provençale [No. 1669]. Chop the pulp very finely and mix it in a bowl with the egg yolks, Béchamel sauce, Swiss cheese, and salt and pepper to taste. Fold in ¼ of the stiffly beaten egg whites until the mixture is smooth and then very gently fold in the remainder. Fill each of the eggplant halves with this mixture, place them in a roasting pan in a medium (375°) oven for about 20 minutes (the exact time will depend on the size of the eggplant), or until they are puffed and browned on the top. *Serves 6.*

1676. STUFFED EGGPLANT ITALIANA
Melanzane farcite all'italiana

3 small eggplant, cut in half and drained of water as described in the introductory remarks above
½ cup oil
1 onion, chopped and gently sautéed in 1 tablespoon butter until soft
4 ripe tomatoes, peeled, seeded, drained, and chopped
2 cups fresh bread cubes, soaked in Brown Stock [No. 4] and squeezed almost dry
2 cloves garlic, crushed in the garlic-press
3 tablespoons chopped parsley
1 cup fresh white breadcrumbs
½ cup butter, melted
Salt and freshly ground pepper

Remove all of the pulp from the eggplant halves in the manner described in Eggplant Provençale [No. 1669]. Coarsely chop the pulp and mix it in a bowl with the onion, tomatoes, bread cubes, garlic, parsley, and salt and pepper to taste. Fill the eggplant halves with this mixture, cover generously with breadcrumbs, and sprinkle with melted butter. Place them in a lightly oiled baking dish in a medium (375°) oven for 30 minutes, or until the tops are golden brown. *Serves 6.*

1677. STUFFED EGGPLANT SICILIANA
Melanzane riempite alla siciliana

Prepare in the same manner and with the same ingredients as the preceding recipe, adding to the stuffing ingredients 8 chopped anchovy fillets which have been washed free of salt [see No. 220], ¼ cup capers, and ½ cup pitted black olives, chopped. *Serves 6.*

ENDIVE
Indivia

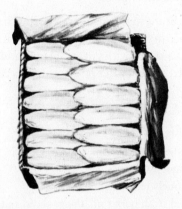

White or Belgian endive is mainly eaten raw in a salad, but it is delicious braised and makes a particularly fine accompaniment for roast or braised veal. The bases of endives should be slightly trimmed before cooking.

1678. BRAISED ENDIVE
Indivie alla mugnaia

12 endives
6 tablespoons butter, softened
Juice of 1 lemon
1 sheet of heavy, unglazed paper
Salt and freshly ground pepper

Spread the bottom of a casserole with 2 tablespoons of the softened butter, arrange the endives in it (if necessary in 2 layers), season them with a little salt and pepper, sprinkle with lemon juice, and dot with the remaining butter. Add 2 tablespoons of water, butter both sides of the heavy paper which has been trimmed to fit inside the casserole, lay it over the endives, cover the casserole, bring to a boil over medium heat, and then place the casserole in a very moderate (325°) oven for 1 hour. Remove the lid, but leave the paper over the endives, and continue braising for about 30 minutes longer, or until the endives are very tender and golden. Serve in the casserole. *Serves 6.*

1679. ENDIVE IN CREAM
Indivie alla crema

12 endives
6 tablespoons butter, softened
Juice of 1 lemon
1 sheet of heavy paper
Salt and freshly ground white pepper
2 cups Béchamel Sauce [No. 18]
½ cup heavy cream

Prepare in the same manner and with the same ingredients as the preceding recipe, and, when the endives are fully cooked, add to the casserole the Béchamel sauce which has been simmered with the heavy cream until slightly reduced and thickened. Stir the pieces of endive gently so that the sauce will become well blended with the butter and juices in the casserole. *Serves 6.*

1680. ENDIVE FIAMMINGA
Indivie alla fiamminga

Prepare in the same manner and with the same ingredients as Braised Endive [No. 1678], but add to the casserole after the first hour of braising 1 cup of finely diced smoked ham. When the endives are fully cooked, transfer them and the ham to a hot serving platter and keep warm. Add 1 cup Brown Stock [No. 4] to the casserole juices, reduce over high heat to ½ cup, and pour over the endives. *Serves 6.*

1681. ENDIVE AU GRATIN
Indivie alla parmigiana

Prepare in the same manner and with the same ingredients as Braised Endive [No. 1678], and, when the endives are fully cooked, sprinkle them with 1 cup of grated Parmesan cheese, spoon a little of the butter in the casserole over the cheese, and then quickly glaze the surface under a high broiler flame for about 2 minutes. *Serves 6.*

1682. ENDIVE IN MEAT SAUCE
Indivie al sugo di carne

Prepare in the same manner and with the same ingredients as Braised Endive [No. 1678], and, when the endives are fully cooked, add 2 cups of Italian Meat Sauce [No. 41] to the casserole. Lift the pieces of endive gently, so that the sauce will become well blended with the butter and juices in the casserole. *Serves 6.*

FAVE BEANS

Fave

These beans resemble very large Fordhook lima beans. When fresh, they have a rather starchy consistency and are not quite as sweet as limas. They come in large pods like the latter, but the pods are coarser and have a furry coating. If the beans are very large, each one should be slipped from its surrounding skin. This process becomes obligatory when the beans are purchased dried. They are then soaked in water to cover for 24 hours and after this time the skins are slipped off preparatory to cooking. Fresh fave beans take 30 to 35 minutes to cook, while the dried variety should cook for about 45 to 50 minutes after their preliminary soaking.

1683. FAVE BEANS IN BUTTER
Fave stufate con burro

4 cups shelled fresh fave beans
1 carrot
1 onion
1 stalk celery
4 tablespoons butter
Salt and freshly ground pepper

If beans are fresh and young they need not be skinned. Boil the onion, carrot, and celery in a large quantity of lightly salted water for 15 minutes. Add the beans and boil for about 30 minutes, or until they are tender. Drain them and discard the carrot, celery, and onion. Heat the butter in a saucepan over moderate heat, add the beans, stir for 3 minutes, season to taste with salt and pepper, and turn them out into a hot serving dish. *Serves* 6.

1684. FAVE BEANS IN CREAM
Fave alla crema

4 cups shelled fresh fave beans
4 tablespoons butter

2 cups heavy cream
Salt and freshly ground pepper

If beans are fresh and young they need not be skinned. Boil the beans in a generous quantity of lightly salted water for 15 minutes and drain. Heat the butter in a saucepan over medium heat, add the beans, stir for 3 minutes, add the cream, and cook for 15 minutes longer, or until the beans are tender and the cream is well reduced. Season to taste with salt and pepper and turn the beans out into a hot serving dish. *Serves* 6.

1685. FAVE BEANS INGLESE
Fave all'inglese

Cook the beans in the manner described in the preceding recipe, drain, and serve them in a hot vegetable dish well seasoned with salt and pepper and with 1/2 cup of softened sweet butter on the side. *Serves* 6.

1686. FAVE BEANS ROMANA
Fave con guanciale alla romana

4 cups shelled fave beans
5 tablespoons butter
1/4 cup finely chopped onion
1/4 pound fresh pork rind, thinly sliced and parboiled
    for 2 hours
Salt and freshly ground pepper

Melt the butter in a casserole over medium heat, add the onion, stir for a few minutes until soft, and then add the pork rind, beans, 1 cup of water (using water the pork rind has cooked in), and a pinch of salt. Cover the casserole and boil for about 20 minutes. Remove the lid and cook for about 10 minutes longer, or until the beans are tender and the water has almost evaporated. Correct the seasoning, and turn the beans out into a hot vegetable dish. *Serves* 6.

FENNEL

Finocchi

Fennel somewhat resembles celery but has the flavor of anise. It may be eaten raw in salads or as an ingre-

564

dient in an antipasto, but Italians frequently serve it as a cooked vegetable. Before cooking, all leaves and any very tough outer stalks should be discarded.

1687. FENNEL IN CASSEROLE CASALINGA
Finocchi al tegame alla casalinga

2 bunches fennel, trimmed
6 tablespoons oil
2 cloves garlic, crushed in the garlic-press
Salt and freshly ground pepper

Drop the fennel into a large pot of lightly salted boiling water and cook for 10 minutes. Drain and cut into 2-inch pieces. Heat the oil in a large, shallow casserole over medium heat, add the garlic, and cook until the garlic begins to color. Add the fennel, $\frac{1}{4}$ cup water, season with salt and pepper, cover, and braise gently for about 40 minutes, or until it is very lightly browned and tender. Serve in the casserole. *Serves* 6.

1688. FENNEL AU GRATIN
Finocchi al gratino

2 large bunches fennel, trimmed
3 cups Sauce Mornay [No. 56]
$\frac{1}{2}$ cup Duxelles [No. 138]
$\frac{1}{2}$ cup grated Parmesan cheese, mixed with 2 cups
    fresh breadcrumbs
$\frac{1}{2}$ cup butter, melted
Salt

Drop the fennel into a generous quantity of lightly salted boiling water and cook for about 35 minutes, or until it is barely tender. Drain and cut it into 2-inch lengths. Mix the Mornay sauce with the Duxelles and spread about $\frac{1}{2}$ cup in the bottom of a baking dish. Arrange the fennel in the dish, cover with the remaining sauce, sprinkle with the breadcrumbs and cheese, and then with melted butter. Place the dish in a moderate (350°) oven for about 30 minutes, or until the top is golden brown. *Serves* 6.

1689. FENNEL PARMIGIANA
Finocchi alla parmigiana

Prepare in the same manner as Fennel in Casserole Casalinga [No. 1687], except substitute butter for the oil and, when the fennel is fully cooked, sprinkle it with 1 cup grated Parmesan cheese. Run the casserole under a high broiler flame for 1 or 2 minutes to brown the surface. *Serves* 6.

1690. FENNEL WITH MEAT SAUCE
Finocchi al sugo di carne

Prepare in the same manner as Fennel in Casserole Casalinga [No. 1687], except turn the cooked fennel out into a hot serving dish and pour over it 3 cups hot Italian Meat Sauce [No. 41]. *Serves* 6.

LEEKS
Porri

Leeks are most often used to enhance the flavor of a good stock or soup, but they are also excellent as a cooked vegetable. Before cooking, the roots and all of the green tops must be trimmed off; only the white part of leeks is edible. Leeks usually have a great deal of dirt and grit between their leaves at the base of their stalks and they must be washed very thoroughly. If desired, they may be cut in half lengthwise, being careful to leave them attached at the base, and washed under running water while gently spreading their leaves apart. If they seem excessively dirty, they may be parboiled for 5 minutes in lightly salted water, drained, and washed again under running water.

1691. LEEKS WITH BÉCHAMEL SAUCE
Porri con besciamella

18 large leeks, trimmed and washed
6 tablespoons butter
1 teaspoon salt
3 cups Béchamel Sauce [No. 18]

Put the leeks in a saucepan with the butter, salt, and sufficient water to barely cover them. Partially cover the pan, bring to a boil over medium heat, and cook for about 20 minutes, or until they are tender. Toward the last 10 minutes of cooking remove the cover and allow the liquid to completely evaporate, raising the heat slightly if necessary, but being careful that they do not scorch on the bottom of the pan. When they are fully cooked and the liquid evaporated, transfer them to a shallow baking dish, add the Béchamel sauce, and stir the leeks gently so that the sauce is well combined with the butter and any small amount of remaining juices. Heat just until very hot and serve in the dish. *Serves* 6.

565

1692. LEEKS IN BUTTER
Porri con burro fuso

Prepare in the same manner as the preceding recipe, omitting the Béchamel sauce. When the leeks are tender, transfer them to a shallow baking dish, pour their cooking juices over them, cover loosely with foil, and place the dish in a hot (450°) oven for about 8 minutes, or until they are golden. *Serves* 6.

1693. BOILED LEEKS INGLESE
Porri all'inglese

18 leeks, trimmed and washed
2 tablespoons chopped parsley
½ cup butter, melted
Salt

Boil the leeks in a generous amount of lightly salted water for 15 to 20 minutes, or until they are tender. Drain them, transfer them to a hot serving dish, sprinkle with parsley, and serve the melted butter on the side. *Serves* 6.

1694. LEEKS PARMIGIANA
Porri alla parmigiana

Prepare in the same manner as Leeks with Béchamel Sauce [No. 1691], omitting the Béchamel. When they are tender, transfer them to a shallow baking dish, baste them with their cooking juices, sprinkle with 1 cup of grated Parmesan cheese, and place the dish under a high broiler flame for 1 to 2 minutes to lightly brown the surface. *Serves* 6.

LENTILS

Lenticchie

1695. BOILED LENTILS
Lenticchie in umido

1 pound lentils, soaked for 12 hours and drained
3 tablespoons oil
A chopped mixture:
   ¼ pound salt pork
   1 onion
   1 carrot
1 cup dry white wine
4 cups Brown Stock [No. 4]
2 cups Tomato Sauce [No. 19]
Salt and freshly ground pepper

Heat the oil in a large, heavy enamel pot over medium heat, add the chopped mixture, and cook until the onion begins to color. Add the wine and cook until it has completely evaporated. Add the lentils, stock, tomato sauce, and sufficient water to cover. Season very lightly with salt and pepper, bring to a boil, reduce the heat, and simmer for 1 hour. Raise the heat slightly so that the liquid in the pot will evaporate more quickly and stir frequently so that the lentils will not stick to the bottom of the pot. Cook for about 30 minutes longer, or until the lentils are tender and most of the cooking liquid has evaporated. Correct the seasoning and turn them out into a hot vegetable dish. *Serves* 6.

1696. LENTIL PURÉE
Purea di lenticchie

Prepare in the same manner and with the same ingredients as the preceding recipe, except cook the lentils slightly longer, or until they are very tender. Purée them with their juices through a food mill, return them to the pot over moderate heat, add 6 tablespoons of softened butter, stir until smooth, and serve in a hot vegetable dish. *Serves* 6.

LETTUCE

Lattuga

Lettuce, slowly braised with a variety of seasonings, is a delicate and refreshing accompaniment for roasted meats and poultry. Escarole, chicory, or Boston lettuce are excellent for braising, although any type of lettuce may be used. Iceberg lettuce, however, is slightly less flavorful than other types. Before braising, lettuce should be very thoroughly washed to remove all trace of dirt or grit, all outside wilted leaves discarded, the base trimmed, and very large heads may be cut in half.

It is then parboiled for 5 minutes in a large quantity of lightly salted water, drained, plunged for a moment in cold water, and squeezed with both hands to remove as much water as possible. Allow 1 medium head for each person to be served.

1697. BRAISED LETTUCE
Lattughe brasate

6 medium heads lettuce, trimmed, washed, parboiled,
    and squeezed to remove excess water
3 tablespoons butter, softened
Bouquet Garni:
   3 sprigs parsley
   2 sprigs thyme (or $\frac{1}{2}$ teaspoon dried)
   1 bay leaf
$\frac{1}{2}$ cup dry white wine
Pinch nutmeg
Pinch sugar
Salt and freshly ground pepper

After squeezing the lettuce to remove excess water, fold the tips of each head under so that they make fairly neat packets. Spread the butter in a large, shallow casserole, arrange the lettuce in it, add the Bouquet Garni and the wine, and season with salt, pepper, nutmeg, and sugar. Cover the casserole very tightly and simmer over very low heat for about 45 minutes. Remove the cover, raise the heat, and reduce the juices in the casserole very quickly. Serve in the casserole, or, if desired, transfer the lettuce and the reduced juices to a hot serving dish. *Serves 6.*

NOTE: If Boston lettuce is used, reduce braising time to 12 minutes.

1698. LETTUCE BRAISED IN CREAM
Lattughe alla crema

Prepare in the same manner and with the same ingredients as the preceding recipe, substituting $\frac{1}{2}$ cup heavy cream for the wine. After braising for 45 minutes, remove the cover of the casserole, reduce the juices over high heat to a few tablespoons, add 1 cup of boiling heavy cream, simmer for 2 minutes, correct the seasoning, and serve in the casserole. *Serves 6.*

1699. BRAISED LETTUCE GOURMET
Lattughe brasate alla ghiottona

6 medium heads lettuce, prepared for braising as
    described in the introductory remarks above
6 long, thin strips fresh pork fat back
3 tablespoons butter, softened

4 large, thin slices fresh pork rind, parboiled for
    1 hour
1 onion, sliced
1 carrot, sliced
1 cup Brown Stock [No. 4]
Bouquet Garni:
   3 sprigs parsley
   2 sprigs thyme (or $\frac{1}{2}$ teaspoon dried)
   1 bay leaf
Salt and freshly ground pepper

After squeezing the lettuce to remove excess water, fold the tips of the leaves under the heads to make each into a fairly compact packet. Wrap each head with a strip of fresh pork fat and tie with string. Spread the butter in the bottom of a large, shallow casserole, line the bottom with the pork rind, sprinkle the sliced vegetables over the rind, lay the lettuce on top, and add the stock and the Bouquet Garni. Season with salt and pepper, bring to a boil, cover the casserole tightly, and place it in a moderate (350°) oven for 55 minutes. Arrange the lettuce on a hot serving platter, discard the pork fat and string, and keep warm. Reduce the cooking liquid over high heat to about $\frac{1}{2}$ cup and spoon a generous tablespoon over each head of lettuce. *Serves 6.*

1700. BRAISED STUFFED LETTUCE
Lattughe farcite e brasate

Prepare in the same manner and with the same ingredients as the preceding recipe, except that after the lettuce has been parboiled and squeezed to remove excess water, spread the leaves of each head slightly apart and insert $\frac{1}{3}$ cup of Veal Forcemeat [No. 134] mixed with a generous tablespoon of Duxelles [No. 138]. Tie each head with pork fat and proceed with the braising as described. *Serves 6.*

MUSHROOMS
Funghi

Those who have traveled in Italy and other European countries have doubtless experienced the gastronomic joys of eating field mushrooms. Unfortunately, markets in the United States are supplied only with commercially grown mushrooms, namely, the *Agaricus bisporus*, which is the only variety of mushroom that (up until now) can be cultivated. Though delicate and subtle in flavor and texture, it runs a poor second to the rich

567

INEDIBLE

POISONOUS

Bitter Boletus or *Boletus felleus*

Edible Boletus or *Boletus edulis*

Boletus satanas

Boletus scaber

Imperial Agaric or *Amanita caesaria*

Boletus badlus

Armillaria mellea

Chanterelle or *Cantharellus cibarius*

Morel or *Morchella esculenta*

568

taste of such field mushrooms as the *Edible boletus* and Morel, which have so far resisted all attempts at cultivation.

The field mushrooms which are sold in European markets are harvested by country people with an unerring eye and instinct for distinguishing the edible from the poisonous varieties. During certain seasons of the year, however, some field mushrooms may be found in specialty food shops in the United States, where they command astronomical prices. Thus, in the spring one may find Morels, shipped from Michigan (usually), and in autumn some varieties of *Boletus* make their way into the shops (generally from the northeastern states).

Although field mushrooms are the most highly recommended, we do not advise gathering them unless you are absolutely certain of the distinctions (sometimes extremely subtle) between the poisonous and edible varieties. Since every edible mushroom has a poisonous look-alike, these are sometimes extremely difficult to ascertain and expert knowledge is required. This can be obtained by enrolling in a course on mycology (the study of fungi), going on field trips accompanied by an expert mycophile (mushroom-lover), or religiously consulting a reliable mushroom field guide (*see* Note below). To be on the safe side, we recommend all three steps. If none of these is practical for you, *do not resort to guesswork: poisonous mushrooms can be deadly* (the Destroying Angel, *Amanita phalloides,* can cause death within hours, and there is no antidote). However, if one possesses sufficient knowledge, the satisfactions of mushroom gathering can be very rewarding to the gourmet-naturalist.

Fortunately for the layman and city dweller, many types of European field mushrooms are available in dried form. Preserved in this manner they retain a surprisingly full flavor, and when properly reconstituted their texture is excellent. They have the added feature of lasting for quite a long time if kept in tightly covered jars on the pantry shelf. A couple of large dried mushrooms, soaked in 2 cups of very hot water and allowed to stand for $1/2$ hour, then drained, patted dry, and coarsely chopped, can be added to 1 pound of commercial fresh mushrooms before cooking. When cooked together, the penetrating flavor and aroma of the dried variety will infuse the fresh mushrooms, thereby lending the preparation an approximate flavor of field mushrooms.

The most frequently available (and desirable) dried mushrooms are the Morels and the *Edible boletus.* Most dried mushrooms are imported from Poland,

although an equally savory variety is imported from the Orient, chiefly Japan. Dried mushrooms are best when purchased strung on strings like a necklace (they seem fresher in taste, for some reason), but they are also available packed in plastic bags or containers. The stringed variety are usually found in shops in Italian, Jewish, or Slavic neighborhoods, while the packaged variety may be found in many supermarkets throughout the country.

Field mushrooms are also canned, France and Germany being the principal suppliers. The canned varieties are packed in either a light brine or broth. They are not quite as satisfactory as the dried variety as they tend to be somewhat pulpy in texture. However, if well drained, patted dry, and sautéed in melted butter only until hot (overcooking ruins them), they can provide a tasty dish.

If one wishes to use field mushrooms in any of the following recipes, the Italian name of the recipe will indicate the type of mushroom to be employed. "Funghi porcini" are *Edible boletus,* "funghi ovuli" are *Amanita caesarina,* "funghi freschi" would be any fresh field mushroom, and "funghi di serra" are cultivated mushrooms. If the latter are used in any of the recipes, their taste may be heightened by the method referred to above in the paragraph dealing with dried mushrooms.

A final word of warning for mycophiles who wish to pick their own. There is no sure method for detecting a poisonous mushroom other than recognizing its general appearance or subjecting it to a detailed chemical analysis. Dipping a silver spoon into the cooking mushrooms to see if it turns black will not work, nor will feeding a sample of the cooked mushrooms to the dog or cat. In the latter case, one's pampered house pet might even scorn an eminently edible (and delicious) Morel. Noting whether forest creatures such as squir-

rels or deer eat certain mushrooms is equally unreliable, as certain fungi harmful to man have no effect on certain rodents or ruminants. If you are not sure of a mushroom, do not pick it. Remember: even the contact of a very poisonous variety (such as the Destroying Angel) can contaminate a whole basket of edible mushrooms.

NOTE: For those who wish it, the following publications are considered reliable mushroom field guides.

GROVES, J. WALTON, *Edible and Poisonous Mushrooms of Canada*, 1962

HESLER, L. R., *Mushrooms of the Great Smokies*, 1960

KRIEGER, LOUIS C. C., *A Popular Guide to the Higher Fungi (Mushrooms) of New York State*, 1935

MCKENNEY, MARGARET, *The Savory Wild Mushroom*, 1962

POMERLEAU, RENÉ, *Mushrooms of Eastern Canada and the United States*, 1951

SMITH, ALEXANDER H., *The Mushroom Hunter's Field Guide*, 1963

ZAHL, PAUL A., "Bizarre World of Fungi," *National Geographic*, Vol. 128, No. 4 (October, 1965), pp. 502–27

1701. MUSHROOMS WITH ANCHOVY BUTTER
Funghi porcini trifolati

2 pounds large mushrooms, sliced
Optional: 3 tablespoons imported dried mushrooms, soaked ½ hour in hot water, drained, and chopped
5 tablespoons oil
3 cloves garlic, crushed in the garlic-press
Salt and freshly ground pepper
¾ cup Anchovy Butter [No. 108]
Juice of 1 lemon
3 tablespoons chopped parsley

Heat the oil in a large frying pan over moderate heat, add the garlic and mushrooms, and season with salt and pepper. Cover the pan and cook for 8 minutes, stirring occasionally. Remove the cover, raise the heat, cook for about 1 minute to reduce the juices in the pan, and turn the mushrooms out onto a hot serving platter. Heat the anchovy butter in a small saucepan until it foams, add the lemon juice, pour over the mushrooms, and sprinkle with the parsley. *Serves 6.*

1702. MUSHROOMS BORDELAISE
Funghi porcini alla bordolese

2 pounds large mushrooms, sliced
Optional: 3 tablespoons imported dried mushrooms, soaked in hot water for ½ hour, drained, and chopped
8 tablespoons butter
5 shallots, chopped (or ½ cup chopped scallions)
Juice of 1 lemon
Salt and freshly ground pepper
6 tablespoons chopped parsley

Heat the butter in a very large frying pan over medium heat until almost golden and sauté the mushrooms for about 4 minutes, or until they are lightly browned. Do not crowd them in the pan so that they steam, rather than sauté; cook only a few at a time, remove them with a slotted spoon when they are browned, and then add fresh ones to the pan; or, if desired, use 2 pans with slightly more butter. When they are all browned, return them all to the pan, add the shallots, and cook for 2 minutes longer, shaking the pan briskly to toss the mushrooms. Season them with salt and pepper, turn them out onto a hot serving dish, squeeze the lemon juice over them, and sprinkle with the chopped parsley. *Serves 6.*

1703. BROILED MUSHROOMS
Funghi di serra alla griglia

18 very large mushroom caps (reserving the stems for another use)
½ cup butter, melted
Salt and freshly ground pepper
6 slices bread, crusts removed, sautéed golden brown in butter

Brush both sides of the mushroom caps with melted butter and arrange them rounded side down in a large baking dish. Place them under a medium broiler flame for 4 minutes, turn them over, and broil for another 4 minutes. If necessary, raise the heat slightly so that they will brown. Season them with salt and pepper and place 3 mushrooms on each of the browned slices of bread on a hot serving platter. *Serves 6.*

1704. BROILED MUSHROOMS MAÎTRE D'HÔTEL
Cappelle di funghi porcini alla griglia con burro maître d'hôtel

Broil the mushrooms in the manner described in the

preceding recipe, arrange them hollow side up on the browned slices of bread, and fill each with a small spoonful of Maître d'Hôtel Butter [No. 111]. *Serves 6.*

1705. MUSHROOMS IN BUTTER
Funghi di serra al burro

Prepare in the same manner as Mushrooms Bordelaise [No. 1702], except omit the chopped shallots and add 4 tablespoons of fresh butter to the mushrooms just before removing them from the fire. *Serves 6.*

1706. MUSHROOMS CONTADINA
Funghi freschi alla contadina

Prepare in the same manner as Mushrooms Bordelaise [No. 1702], substituting 5 cloves of garlic, crushed in the garlic-press, for the shallots. *Serves 6.*

1707. CREAMED MUSHROOMS AU GRATIN
Funghi porcini alla crema gratinati

1½ pounds large mushrooms, sliced
Optional: ¼ cup imported dried mushrooms, soaked
    in hot water for ½ hour, drained, and chopped
6 tablespoons butter
⅓ cup chopped onion
2 cloves garlic, crushed in the garlic-press
Salt and freshly ground pepper
1½ cups dry Marsala wine
1½ cups heavy cream
1½ cups Béchamel Sauce [No. 18]
¾ cup grated Parmesan cheese

Heat the butter in a very large frying pan over moderate heat, add the onion and garlic, and cook until the onion begins to color. Add the mushrooms, cover the pan, and cook for 8 minutes, stirring occasionally. Remove the mushrooms with a slotted spoon and reserve. Add the Marsala to the pan and reduce over high heat to a few tablespoons. Add all but 2 tablespoons of the heavy cream and continue cooking until the cream is reduced and quite thick. Remove from the heat, stir in the remaining cream (this will smooth out the sauce), add the Béchamel sauce, and correct the seasoning. Mix the sauce with the mushrooms in a shallow baking dish, sprinkle with the grated cheese, and place the dish under a high broiler flame until the surface is golden brown. *Serves 6.*

1708. CREAMED MUSHROOMS WITH TRUFFLES
Funghi porcini alla crema e tartufi

1 pound mushrooms, sliced
4 tablespoons butter
2 white truffles, sliced
2 cups heavy cream
Salt and freshly ground pepper

Heat the butter in a large frying pan over fairly high heat and lightly brown the mushrooms, a few at a time, on both sides. As they brown, remove them with a slotted spoon, and then add fresh ones. When all are browned, return them all to the pan, add the truffles and all but ¼ cup of the cream, and cook until the cream is reduced to ½ its quantity. Remove from the heat, swirl in the remaining cream, season with salt and pepper, and serve in a hot vegetable dish. *Serves 4.*

1709. MUSHROOMS WITH GARLIC AND OREGANO
Funghi freschi al funghetto

1½ pounds mushrooms, sliced
6 tablespoons oil
3 tablespoons chopped oregano (or substitute any
    desired fresh herb)
3 cloves garlic, crushed in the garlic-press
Salt and freshly ground pepper
Pinch nutmeg

Heat the oil in a very large frying pan over fairly high heat and quickly brown the mushrooms, a few at a time. As they brown, remove them with a slotted spoon, and then add fresh ones to the pan. When all are browned, return them all to the pan, reduce the heat to a low flame, add the garlic and oregano, and season with salt, pepper, and a pinch of nutmeg. Cook slowly for about 3 minutes longer, stirring occasionally, and then turn them out onto a hot serving dish. *Serves 4.*

1710. MUSHROOMS GOURMET
Funghi di serra freddi alla ghiottona

18 large mushroom caps (reserving the stems for another use)
18 small cooked shrimp (*see* page 340)
18 cooked asparagus tips (*see* page 544)
3 braised hearts of white celery (*see* page 558), cut in half
6 cooked artichoke hearts (*see* page 540)
2 white truffles, sliced
3 cups Mayonnaise [No. 77]
¼ cup prepared mustard (Dijon-type preferred)
2 tablespoons brandy
Dash Worcestershire sauce
2 tablespoons tomato catsup
1 bunch watercress

Mix the mayonnaise with the mustard, brandy, Worcestershire sauce, and catsup. Drop the mushrooms in a pot of lightly salted boiling water and simmer over moderate heat for 15 minutes. Drain, cool, and then chill the mushrooms and all the other ingredients. When cold, arrange them attractively on a large platter, garnish with the watercress, and serve the seasoned mayonnaise on the side. *Serves* 6.

1711. MUSHROOMS WITH FRESH HERBS
Funghi di serra con erbe fini

Prepare in the same manner and with the same ingredients as Mushrooms Bordelaise [No. 1702], omitting the shallots and adding 1 generous tablespoon each of any available chopped fresh herbs, such as tarragon, basil, savory, marjoram, etc. The herbs should be mixed with the mushrooms just before removing them from the heat. *Serves* 6.

1712. MUSHROOMS LUIGI VERONELLI
Funghi di serra alla Luigi Veronelli

18 medium mushroom caps
6 tablespoons butter
½ cup chopped onion
2 cloves garlic, crushed in the garlic-press
¼ cup white wine vinegar
6 ripe tomatoes, peeled, seeded, drained, and chopped
Pinch sugar

Bouquet Garni:
  3 sprigs thyme (or ½ teaspoon dried)
  3 sprigs basil (or 1 teaspoon dried)
12 small Braised White Onions [No. 1721]
Salt and freshly ground pepper

Melt the butter in a large frying pan over fairly high heat until almost golden and quickly brown the mushroom caps on all sides. Reduce the heat and cook for about 5 minutes longer, or until the mushrooms are tender. Remove them with a slotted spoon and reserve. Add the chopped onion and garlic to the pan, raise the heat, cook until the onion begins to color, add the vinegar, and cook until it has evaporated. Add the tomatoes, sugar, and Bouquet Garni, season with salt and pepper, and cook for about 15 minutes, or until the tomatoes are reduced to a pulp. Add the mushrooms and braised onions, discard the Bouquet Garni, correct the seasoning, simmer for 2 minutes, and turn the mixture out into a hot serving dish. *Serves* 6.

1713. STUFFED MUSHROOMS
Cappelle di funghi porcini farcite

12 very large mushroom caps
¼ cup oil
2 tablespoons butter, softened
1½ cups Duxelles [No. 138]
½ cup Tomato Sauce [No. 19]
2 cups fresh breadcrumbs
Salt and freshly ground pepper
1 cup Demi-Glaze Sauce [No. 20]

Brush both sides of the mushroom caps with oil, season the hollows with a little salt and pepper, and arrange them hollow side up in a well-buttered roasting pan. Mix thoroughly together the Duxelles, tomato sauce, and breadcrumbs. Heap the hollows of the mushrooms generously with this mixture and sprinkle the tops with a few drops of oil. Place them in a hot (375°) oven for about 15 minutes, or until the caps are tender and the top is lightly browned. Arrange them on a hot serving platter and spoon a little of the Demi-Glaze sauce over each cap. *Serves* 6.

NOTE: The stems of the mushrooms may be chopped and used in the Duxelles.

1714. STUFFED MUSHROOMS AU GRATIN
Funghi porcini gratinati

Prepare in the same manner and with the same ingredients as the preceding recipe, except before baking the mushrooms, cover them with a generous amount of breadcrumbs and sprinkle with oil. The sauce may be served on the side, or, if desired, omitted.

1715. MUSHROOMS ON VINE LEAVES
Cappelle di funghi ovoli sulla foglia di vite

12 very large mushroom caps (reserving the stems for another use)
½ cup oil
12 grape leaves
2 cloves garlic, crushed in the garlic-press
1 tablespoon chopped oregano (or 1 teaspoon dried)
Salt and freshly ground pepper

Brush the grape leaves on both sides with oil and arrange them on an oven-proof platter. Heat the remaining oil in a small saucepan over moderate heat with the garlic and oregano for about 2 minutes. Brush the mushrooms on both sides with this seasoned oil, arrange them hollow side up on the grape leaves, and season the hollows with salt and pepper. Place the platter in a moderate (350°) oven for 10 minutes, turn the mushrooms over, bake for about 5 minutes longer, or until the mushrooms are tender, and serve on the platter. *Serves* 6.

ONIONS
Cipolle

1716. BAKED ONIONS
Cipolle al forno

18 medium white onions, parboiled in lightly salted water for 10 minutes
Salt and freshly ground pepper
½ cup oil
3 tablespoons chopped parsley

Cool the onions slightly and cut them in half. Grease a shallow baking pan with oil, arrange the half onions cut side up in the pan, season with salt and pepper, sprinkle with oil and the chopped parsley, and bake them in a moderate (350°) oven for 30 minutes. *Serves* 6.

1717. BOILED ONIONS NAPOLETANA
Cipolle lessate alla napoletana

18 medium white onions
1 cup oil
3 tablespoons chopped oregano (or 1 tablespoon dried)
3 tablespoons chopped parsley
Salt and freshly ground pepper

Mix the oil, oregano, parsley, 1 teaspoon salt, and a generous grating of pepper in a bowl and allow this mixture to stand for 1 hour. Boil the onions in a generous amount of lightly salted water for about 25 minutes, or until tender. Drain, cut them in half, arrange them cut side up on a hot serving platter, and spoon the seasoned oil over them. *Serves* 6.

1718. FRIED ONIONS
Cipolle fritte

6 medium onions
Flour
Salt
Fat for deep frying

Slice the onions, break them up into rings, season them with a little salt, and dust them with flour. Drop them in deep hot (375°) fat until they are crisp and golden brown, drain them briefly on absorbent paper, and then heap them up on a hot serving platter. *Serves* 6.

1719. STUFFED ONIONS
Cipolle farcite

18 medium white onions, parboiled in lightly salted water for 10 minutes
2 cups Forcemeat [No. 129], made with beef, veal, or chicken
3 tablespoons butter
½ cup Brown Stock [No. 4]
1 cup fresh breadcrumbs

Allow the parboiled onions to cool slightly and then with the sharp point of a knife press out the center of each while squeezing the sides slightly. About ⅓ of each of the onions should be removed in this manner. Chop these removed centers very finely and mix them with the forcemeat. Stuff the centers of the onions with this mixture, arrange them upright in a generously buttered shallow casserole, add the stock, bring to a

573

boil, cover the casserole, and place it in a moderate (350°) oven for about 25 minutes. Remove from the oven, sprinkle the stuffed centers of the onions with a little of the breadcrumbs, run them quickly under a high broiler flame to brown lightly, and serve in the casserole. *Serves 6.*

1720. ONIONS IN SWEET-AND-SOUR SAUCE
Cipolline in agro-dolce

18 medium white onions
3 tablespoons butter
½ cup chopped ham fat
1 clove garlic, crushed in the garlic-press
½ cup white wine vinegar
1 tablespoon sugar
2 tablespoons chopped parsley
Salt

Heat the butter and ham fat in a large, shallow casserole over medium heat until the ham fat is sizzling, add the garlic, and cook until the garlic begins to color. Add the onions and vinegar and season with a little salt. Cover the casserole tightly, lower the heat to a very low flame, and cook for about 25 minutes, or until the onions are barely tender, shaking the casserole occasionally to ensure even cooking. Remove the cover, raise the heat slightly, sprinkle the onions with the sugar, and shake the casserole constantly until the liquids are thickened and the onions are glazed. Transfer them to a hot serving dish and sprinkle with the parsley. *Serves 6.*

1721. BRAISED WHITE ONIONS
Cipolline glassate a bianco

18 medium white onions
½ cup White Stock [No. 1]
Bouquet Garni:
   3 sprigs parsley
   2 sprigs thyme (or ½ teaspoon dried)
   1 bay leaf
3 tablespoons butter
Salt and freshly ground pepper

Put the onions in a large, shallow casserole with the butter, stock, and Bouquet Garni. Season with a little salt and pepper, bring to a boil over medium heat, cover tightly, reduce the heat to a very low flame, and cook for about 30 minutes, or until the onions are tender, shaking the pan occasionally to ensure even cooking. Discard the Bouquet Garni and transfer

the onions to a hot serving dish, or use them as a garnish. *Serves 6.*

1722. BROWN-BRAISED ONIONS
Cipolline glassate a bruno

Prepare in the same manner and with the same ingredients as the preceding recipe, except before adding any of the other ingredients, brown the onions on all sides in the butter over fairly high heat and substitute Brown Stock [No. 4] for the white stock. *Serves 6.*

1723. GLAZED ONIONS FOR GARNISH
Cipolline glassate per guarnizioni

Prepare in the same manner and with the same ingredients as Braised White Onions [No. 1721], except that in addition to the changes indicated in the preceding recipe, remove the cover when the onions are fully cooked, sprinkle them with a teaspoon of sugar, raise the heat, and shake the casserole until the liquids have evaporated and the onions are golden and well glazed. *Serves 6.*

OYSTER PLANT

Scorzonera

Although oyster plant and salsify are not botanically related, they have the same flavor and may be prepared in the same way. In Italy, the black-skinned oyster plant, or *scorzonera,* is preferred for its better flavor to the white-skinned salsify. While the green tops of oyster plant may be cooked and eaten as a green vegetable, usually only the root part is considered edible. Before cooking, the root section should be peeled, cut into pieces about 3 inches long, and the pieces dropped at once into acidulated water to prevent them from darkening. When ready to cook, drop them in a generous quantity of boiling White Foundation for Vegetables [No. 1576] and simmer for 2 hours. If they are not to be used at once, they may be kept for several days in their cooking liquid in the refrigerator.

1724. OYSTER PLANT IN BROWN BUTTER
Scorzonera al burro nocciola

Prepare and cook 1½ pounds of oyster plant as described in the introductory remarks above. Drain and put it in a hot vegetable dish. Pour ½ cup of Hazlenut Butter [No. 103] over it and sprinkle with a tablespoon of parsley. *Serves 6.*

1725. OYSTER PLANT IN CREAM
Scorzonera alla crema

1½ pounds oyster plant, cleaned and cooked as
    described in the introductory remarks above
3 tablespoons butter
2 cups heavy cream
Salt and freshly ground pepper

Drain the oyster plant thoroughly. Heat the butter
in a large frying pan over medium heat, add the oyster
plant and the cream, reserving 3 tablespoons, and boil
until the cream is reduced by ½. Season with salt and
pepper, remove from the heat, swirl in the remaining
cream, and transfer the oyster plant and sauce to a hot
serving dish. *Serves 6.*

1726. OYSTER PLANT FRITTERS
Bignè di scorzonera

1½ pounds oyster plant, cleaned and cooked as
    described in the introductory remarks above
A marinade:
  1 cup oil
  ⅓ cup lemon juice
  2 tablespoons chopped parsley
2 cups Fritter Batter [No. 275]
Fat for deep frying
3 lemons, quartered
Salt and freshly ground pepper

Drain the cooked oyster plant, transfer it to a bowl,
season it with salt and pepper, pour the marinade over
it, and marinate for 1 hour, turning occasionally. Drain
the pieces, dip them in the fritter batter, and drop them
in deep hot (375°) fat until they are crisp and golden.
Drain them briefly on absorbent paper and then heap
them up on a hot serving platter and garnish with the
lemon quarters. *Serves 6.*

1727. OYSTER PLANT IN MEAT SAUCE
Scorzonera al sugo di carne

1½ pounds oyster plant, cleaned and cooked as
    described in the introductory remarks above
3 tablespoons butter
3 cups Italian Meat Sauce [No. 41]

Drain the pieces of oyster plant and then gently sauté
them in the butter in a frying pan over medium heat
for 3 or 4 minutes. Add the meat sauce, simmer for 5
minutes, and transfer them and the sauce to a hot
serving dish. *Serves 6.*

1728. OYSTER PLANT MORNAY
Scorzonera Mornay

1½ pounds oyster plant, cleaned and cooked as
    described in the introductory remarks above
3 tablespoons butter
3 cups Sauce Mornay [No. 56]
½ cup grated Parmesan cheese

Drain the pieces of oyster plant and then gently sauté
them in the butter in a frying pan over medium heat
for 3 minutes. Add the Mornay sauce, simmer for
3 minutes, pour the pieces and their sauce into a shallow baking dish, sprinkle with the Parmesan cheese,
and place the dish under a high broiler flame until the
top is golden brown. *Serves 6.*

1729. OYSTER PLANT POLONAISE
Scorzonera alla polacca

Prepare in the same manner and with the same ingredients as Asparagus Polonaise [No. 1606], substituting
1½ pounds of oyster plant, cleaned and cooked as
described in the introductory remarks above, for the
asparagus. *Serves 6.*

1730. OYSTER PLANT PROVENÇALE
Scorzonera alla provenzale

1½ pounds oyster plant, cleaned and cooked as
    described in the introductory remarks above
2 tablespoons oil
2 tablespoons butter
3 tablespoons chopped parsley
2 cloves garlic, crushed in the garlic-press
Salt and freshly ground pepper

Drain the pieces of oyster plant and sauté them in
the butter and oil in a frying pan over medium heat
until they are golden. Season with salt and pepper,
add the parsley and garlic, toss them lightly in the pan
for another 2 minutes, and then transfer to a hot serving
dish. *Serves 6.*

PEAS
Piselli

Peas are at their best when young, tiny, and very, very
fresh. Only rarely and only in special markets will this
type—known as petits pois—be found in American
markets. They are, however, widely available frozen,
and these can be surprisingly delicious and seem to

retain a fresh-tasting flavor, if carefully and very briefly cooked. Larger and more mature peas are not to be scoffed at, however, especially if they are still quite fresh. As a general rule in the succeeding recipes, if very young peas are used, cook them very briefly, for as little as 4 to 8 minutes; if only more mature peas are available, cook them very slowly from 12 to as long as 30 minutes, depending on their size. As they cook, taste them frequently for doneness. Allow about 2 pounds of peas, or 3 cups shelled, for 6 persons.

1731. PEAS IN BUTTER
Piselli al burro

2 pounds peas, shelled
4 tablespoons butter, softened
Pinch sugar
Salt and freshly ground pepper

Cook the peas in a generous quantity of lightly salted boiling water until they are just tender, from 5 to 30 minutes depending on their size. Taste frequently to test for doneness. Do not overcook. Drain them, put them in a frying pan over moderate heat, and shake the pan constantly for 1 minute to dry them, being very careful not to scorch them. Add the butter and season with salt, pepper, and sugar. Shake the pan until the butter is melted and then turn them out onto a hot serving dish. *Serves 6.*

1732. PEAS CASALINGA
Piselli alla casalinga

2 pounds peas, shelled
3 tablespoons butter
1 tablespoon flour
1 cup boiling White Stock [No. 1]
¼ pound diced lean salt pork, parboiled for 15
    minutes, drained, and sautéed golden brown
12 tiny white onions, parboiled 5 minutes in lightly
    salted water
Bouquet Garni:
    3 sprigs basil (or ½ teaspoon dried)
    2 sprigs rosemary (or ½ teaspoon dried)
    2 sprigs marjoram (or ½ teaspoon dried)
Salt and freshly ground pepper

Heat the butter in a casserole over medium heat, add the flour, stir for 1 minute, add the stock, and stir until boiling and thickened. Reduce the heat to a low flame, add the peas, salt pork dice, onions, Bouquet Garni, and a pinch of salt and pepper. Cover the casserole and simmer very gently for about 15 minutes,

or until the peas are tender. Discard the Bouquet Garni and serve in the casserole. *Serves 6.*

1733. PEAS FIAMMINGA
Piselli alla fiamminga

2 pounds peas, shelled
6 small young carrots, sliced
1½ cups White Stock [No. 1]
½ cup butter
Pinch sugar
Salt

Put the sliced carrots in a saucepan with the stock, 6 tablespoons of butter, and a pinch of sugar. Season very lightly with salt, bring to a boil over medium heat, and cook for 15 minutes, or until the carrots are about half cooked. Add the peas, mix them lightly with the carrots, cover the saucepan, and cook until they are not quite tender. Remove the cover, raise the heat, and cook until the peas and carrots are tender and the stock reduced to a few tablespoons. Remove from the heat, swirl in the remaining butter, and turn out into a hot serving dish. *Serves 6.*

Peas Francese (No. 1734)

1734. PEAS FRANCESE
Piselli alla francese

2 pounds large mature peas, shelled
4 tablespoons butter, softened
1 head Boston lettuce, washed and leaves separated
12 small white onions

576

Bouquet Garni:
    3 sprigs chervil (or 1 teaspoon dried)
    3 sprigs parsley
    1 bay leaf
Pinch sugar
Salt and freshly ground pepper

Spread the softened butter in the bottom of a casserole, arrange the lettuce leaves on top (they should be dripping wet from being washed), place the peas on top, and then push the onions and the Bouquet Garni down among the peas. Season with salt, pepper, and sugar. Place the casserole over low heat, cover it tightly, and simmer for 30 minutes without stirring. Remove Bouquet Garni and serve in casserole. *Serves* 6.

1735. PEAS INGLESE
Piselli all'inglese

Prepare as described in Peas in Butter [No. 1731], except serve the butter separately in a small bowl. *Serves* 6.

1736. PEAS WITH LETTUCE
Piselli con lattughe

2 pounds peas, shelled
3 hearts of Boston lettuce, shredded
6 tablespoons butter
Pinch sugar
Salt and freshly ground pepper

Cook the peas in a generous amount of lightly salted boiling water until they are just tender, from 5 to 30 minutes, depending on their size. Taste frequently for doneness. Do not overcook. While the peas are cooking, very gently sauté the lettuce in the butter in a saucepan over moderate heat until all the moisture in the lettuce has evaporated. Add the cooked peas, stir for 1 minute, and season with salt, pepper, and sugar. Turn the peas out into a pre-heated serving dish. *Serves* 6.

1737. PEAS WITH MINT
Piselli alla menta

Prepare in the same manner and with the same ingredients as Peas in Butter [No. 1731] and add to the peas, just before they are removed from the heat, ¼ cup of fresh mint leaves which have been dipped for 3 seconds in boiling water. *Serves* 6.

1738. PEAS AND ONIONS IN CREAM
Piselli e cipolline alla crema

2 pounds large mature peas, shelled
18 tiny white onions
6 tablespoons butter
Bouquet Garni:
    3 sprigs chervil (or 1 teaspoon dried)
    3 sprigs parsley
Pinch sugar
2 cups heavy cream
¼ teaspoon freshly ground pepper
1 teaspoon salt

Put all of the ingredients in a saucepan, reserving ¼ cup of the cream. Bring to a boil over medium heat and simmer for about 25 minutes, or until the peas and onions are tender and the cream reduced by ½. Correct the seasoning, remove from the heat, discard the Bouquet Garni, swirl in the reserved cream, and turn out into a hot serving dish. *Serves* 6.

1739. PEAS WITH PROSCIUTTO
Pisellini al prosciutto

Prepare in the same manner and with the same ingredients as Peas in Butter [No. 1731]. While the peas are cooking, gently sauté ½ cup of chopped onion in 2 tablespoons of butter in a saucepan over medium heat until the onion begins to color, add 1 cup of chopped prosciutto (or smoked ham), sauté for 2 minutes, and then add this mixture to the peas after they have been drained and dressed with butter. *Serves* 6.

Peppers Au Gratin Partenopea
(No. 1741): see page 578

PEPPERS
Peperoni

Peppers, which belong to the nightshade family, originated in tropical America. In Europe they are cultivated in central and southern Italy, in Spain, and in southern France. Peppers come in a wide range of sizes, colors, and tastes, ranging from sweet to hot. Before cooking, peppers should nearly always be skinned. The simplest method of doing this is to hold them by a long fork over an open flame until they are charred and blackened, rinse them under cold water, and scrape the charred skin off with a knife. The core end should then be cut out and the pith and seeds removed.

1740. FRIED PEPPERS ROMANA
Peperoni in padella alla romana

8 sweet peppers, roasted, scraped, seeded, and cut into strips
6 tablespoons oil
2 onions, chopped
6 ripe tomatoes, peeled, seeded, drained, and chopped
Salt and freshly ground pepper

Heat the oil in a large frying pan over medium heat, add the onion, and cook until the onion begins to color. Add the tomatoes, season with salt and pepper, and cook for 5 minutes. Add the peppers and simmer for about 15 minutes. Turn the mixture out into a hot serving dish and serve at once. *Serves 6.*

1741. PEPPERS AU GRATIN PARTENOPEA
Peperoni gratinati alla partenopea

8 red or yellow sweet peppers, roasted, scraped, seeded, and cut into strips
½ cup tiny capers

1 cup pitted black olives, cut in half
18 anchovy fillets, washed free of salt [*see* No. 220] and chopped
½ cup pine nuts
¾ cup oil
2 cups fresh breadcrumbs

Mix the pepper strips in a shallow baking dish with the capers, olives, anchovies, pine nuts, and ½ cup of oil. Sprinkle with breadcrumbs and then with the remaining oil. Place the dish in a medium (375°) oven for about 20 minutes, or until the top is lightly browned. *Serves 6.*

1742. PEPPERS AND PORK RIND
Peperoni con guanciale

8 sweet peppers, roasted, scraped, seeded, and cut into strips
½ pound fresh pork rind, parboiled for 2 hours, drained, and cut into strips
4 tablespoons oil
1 onion, chopped
6 ripe tomatoes, peeled, seeded, drained, and chopped

Heat the oil in a frying pan over medium heat, add the onion, and cook until the onion begins to color. Add the tomatoes, pepper strips, and the pork rind. Season with salt and pepper, simmer for about 15 minutes, and turn out onto a hot serving dish. *Serves 6.*

1743. STUFFED PEPPERS BARESE
Peperoni imbottiti alla barese

8 yellow peppers, roasted, tops cut off, scraped, and seeded
4 cups fresh white breadcrumbs
8 anchovy fillets, washed free of salt [*see* No. 220] and chopped
¼ cup tiny capers
1 cup pitted black olives, sliced
½ cup sultana raisins, softened in warm water and seeded
½ cup pine nuts
2 tablespoons chopped parsley
1 tablespoon chopped basil
¾ cup oil
Pinch nutmeg
Salt and freshly ground pepper
3 cups Tomato Sauce [No. 19]

Mix thoroughly together in a bowl the breadcrumbs, anchovies, capers, olives, raisins, pine nuts, parsley, basil, and ½ cup of the oil. Season with salt, pepper, and nutmeg and then stuff the peppers with the mixture. Arrange the peppers in a roasting pan and sprinkle the tops with the remaining oil. Pour the tomato sauce mixed with 1 cup of water into the pan and place it in a moderate (350°) oven for 1 hour. If the tomato sauce becomes too thick while the peppers are baking, add a little more water. Arrange the peppers on a serving dish, pour the tomato sauce around them, and serve hot or at room temperature. *Serves 6.*

1744. STUFFED PEPPERS FRANCESE
Peperoni farciti alla francese

6 sweet peppers, roasted, tops cut off, scraped, and
    seeded
4 tablespoons butter
½ pound chicken livers
4 cups Pilaf [No. 595]
Salt and freshly ground pepper
3 cups Italian Meat Sauce [No. 41]

Gently sauté the chicken livers in the butter in a frying pan over medium heat for 3 minutes, remove them from the pan, chop them, and mix them in a bowl with the rice. Season this mixture with salt and pepper to taste and then stuff the peppers with it. Bake and serve the peppers in the manner described in the preceding recipe, substituting the meat sauce for the tomato sauce. *Serves 6.*

1745. STUFFED PEPPERS ALLA TURCA
Peperoni farciti alla turca

6 sweet peppers, roasted, scraped, and seeded
½ cup oil
1 clove garlic, crushed in the garlic-press
3 onions, chopped
3 cups Pilaf [No. 595]
3 cups chopped cooked lamb
3 tablespoons chopped parsley
3 cups Tomato Sauce [No. 19]
Salt and freshly ground pepper

Heat 4 tablespoons of the oil in a frying pan over medium heat, add the garlic and onion, and cook until the onion begins to color. Remove from the heat, add the rice, lamb, parsley, and salt and pepper to taste. Stuff the peppers with this mixture, sprinkle the tops with the remaining oil, arrange them in a roasting pan, pour over 1 cup of the tomato sauce and 1 cup of water, and then bake and serve them in the manner described in Stuffed Peppers Barese [No. 1743]. *Serves 6.*

POTATOES
Patate

Potatoes are such a familiar staple of the American diet that they require no introduction. Throughout the succeeding recipes it is important to use "new" or Idaho potatoes when these are specified; when not so specified, "old" or "boiling" potatoes should be used. They should always be peeled before cooking unless otherwise directed, and if peeled in advance, may be kept in a bowl of cold water.

1746. POTATOES AMERICANA
Patate tritate all'americana

2 pounds "new" potatoes, unpeeled
6 tablespoons butter
1 onion, chopped
Salt and freshly ground pepper

Boil the unpeeled potatoes in a generous quantity of lightly salted water for 20 minutes, or until tender. Drain, cool, peel, and cut them into large dice. Heat the butter in a very large frying pan over medium heat, add the onion, cook until golden, add the potatoes, season with salt and pepper, and cook until they are golden brown. Shake the pan frequently to brown them evenly and then turn them out onto a hot serving dish. *Serves 6.*

1747. POTATOES ANNA
Patate Anna o galletta di patate al burro

6 Idaho potatoes
¾ cup butter, melted
Salt and freshly ground pepper

Slice the potatoes paper thin, soak them in cold water for 20 minutes, and dry them completely on an absorbent towel. Brush a baking dish with butter and arrange the potatoes in it in layers, seasoning each layer

579

with a little salt and pepper and sprinkling with a little melted butter. Put the dish in a hot (425°) oven for 30 minutes, remove from the oven, and allow the dish to stand for 3 minutes. Jerk the dish sharply once or twice to make sure the potatoes are not sticking to the bottom and then invert the dish onto a hot serving platter. *Serves* 6.

NOTE: If the potatoes are not bone-dry, they will stick to the pan.

1748. BAKED POTATOES
Patate al forno

6 Idaho potatoes, unpeeled
1 slice bacon
6 tablespoons butter
Paprika

Scrub the potatoes well, rub them with the bacon, and bake them in a hot (425°) oven for 50 minutes. Slash the tops twice in the shape of a cross, drop a pat of fresh butter into the center, sprinkle with a little paprika, and arrange them on a serving dish. *Serves* 6.

1749. BAKED POTATOES FANTASIA
Patate farcite "fantasia"

6 Idaho potatoes, unpeeled
½ cup grated Parmesan cheese
1 cup chopped smoked ham
½ cup chopped onion, cooked gently in 2 tablespoons
    butter until soft but not brown
2 tablespoons chopped parsley
¾ cup butter, melted
Salt and freshly ground pepper
1 cup fresh white breadcrumbs

Bake the potatoes in the manner described in the preceding recipe, cut them in half lengthwise, and scoop out almost all of their pulp, leaving just enough so that the halves are still firm. Put the pulp through a ricer into a bowl and add the cheese, ham, onion, parsley, ½ cup of the melted butter, and salt and pepper to taste. Mix thoroughly, stuff each of the potato halves with the mixture, cover with breadcrumbs, and sprinkle with the remaining melted butter. Arrange them in a roasting pan, bake them in a hot (450°) oven

Potatoes Anna (No. 1747)

Potato Brioches (No. 1760)

Potato Chips (No. 1762)

Potatoes Berny (No. 1753)

Duchesse Potatoes (No. 1771)

Baked Potatoes (No. 1748)

Baked Potatoes Fantasia (No. 1749)

French Fried Potatoes (No. 1773)

French Fried Potato Sticks (No. 1775)

for about 10 minutes, or until their tops are brown, and then arrange them on a hot platter. *Serves 6.*

1750. BAKED POTATOES GOURMET
Patate farcite "ghiotte"

Prepare in the same manner and with the same ingredients as the preceding recipe, except omit the Parmesan and ham and substitute ¼ pound of finely crumbled cooked sausage meat and ¼ pound chopped mushrooms that have been gently sautéed until soft in 2 tablespoons of butter. *Serves 6.*

1751. BAKED POTATOES GUSTOSE
Patate farcite "gustose"

Prepare in the same manner and with the same ingredients as Baked Potatoes Fantasia [No. 1749], except omit the Parmesan and the ham and substitute 1 cup of very finely diced mozzarella cheese and 12 chopped anchovy fillets which have been washed free of salt [*see* No. 220]. *Serves 6.*

1752. POTATO BASKETS
Cestini o nidi di patate

While it is possible to actually weave potato baskets, it is far simpler to use a wire mold especially made for this purpose. They are available in specialty kitchen equipment shops (*see* photograph below).

Cut 4 Idaho potatoes into very thin long strips, about ⅛ inch thick. Wash them in cold water and dry them thoroughly on some absorbent paper towels. Line a wire potato-basket mold with some of the strips, being careful that they do not stick through the wires of the mold, press on the cover, and fry in deep hot (375°) fat until crisp and golden brown. Drain on absorbent paper and proceed to make 6 baskets in this fashion. If desired, the baskets may be prepared in advance, then reheated and re-crisped for a few seconds in hot fat. Sprinkle with salt before serving. *Makes 6 baskets.*

Potato Croquettes (No. 1767)

Potatoes Dauphine (No. 1768)

French Fried Potatoes Copeaux (No. 1774)

Noisette Potatoes I (No. 1783)

Potato Baskets (No. 1752).
Above: The potatoes are placed in their special molds and are being lowered into hot fat. Below: The prepared baskets ready to serve.

French Fried Potato Straws (No. 1776)

Souffléed Potatoes (No. 1789). Here, slices have been square-cut.

1753. POTATOES BERNY
Patate Berny

3 cups Duchesse Potato Base [No. 1770]
3 truffles, chopped
2 eggs, beaten
1½ cups finely chopped almonds, toasted in a hot
(400°) oven for 5 minutes
Fat for deep frying

Mix the Duchesse potato base with the truffles, roll the mixture into 12 balls, dip in beaten egg, and cover generously with the chopped almonds. Drop the balls into deep hot (375°) fat until golden brown, drain briefly on absorbent paper, and transfer to a hot serving dish. *Serves* 6.

1754. BOILED POTATOES WITH BASIL
Patate al basilico

2 pounds "new" potatoes
6 tablespoons butter, melted
3 tablespoons coarsely chopped fresh basil
Salt

Boil the potatoes in a generous quantity of lightly salted water for about 20 minutes, or until they are just tender. Drain, put them in a hot serving dish, pour the melted butter over them, and sprinkle with the basil. *Serves* 6.

1755. BOILED POTATOES INGLESE
Patate all'inglese

2 pounds "new" potatoes
Salt

Put the potatoes in a colander placed over a saucepan of boiling water, cover the colander, and steam the potatoes for about 25 minutes, or until they are tender. Transfer them to a hot serving dish and sprinkle with a little salt. *Serves* 6.

1756. BOILED POTATOES IN THEIR JACKETS
Patate in camicia

2 pounds "new" potatoes, unpeeled
Salt
½ cup butter, softened

Boil the potatoes unpeeled in a generous quantity of lightly salted water for about 20 minutes, or until they are tender. Drain, transfer them to a serving dish, and serve the butter on the side. *Serves* 6.

1757. BOILED POTATOES WITH MINT
Patate alla menta

Prepare in the same manner as Boiled Potatoes with Basil [No. 1754], substituting fresh mint leaves for the basil. *Serves* 6.

1758. BOILED POTATOES WITH PARSLEY
Patate al prezzemolo

Prepare in the same manner as Boiled Potatoes with Basil [No. 1754], substituting parsley for the basil. *Serves* 6.

1759. POTATOES BERRICHONNE
Patate alla berrichonne

2 pounds potatoes, sliced
2 onions, sliced
¼ pound diced lean salt pork, parboiled for 15 minutes, drained, and sautéed golden brown
4 tablespoons butter, softened
Salt and freshly ground pepper
2 cups boiling Brown Stock [No. 4]
2 tablespoons chopped parsley

Put the potatoes, onions, and salt pork in a buttered baking dish, toss them lightly together, season with salt and pepper, and spread softened butter over the top. Add the boiling stock and place the dish in a hot (400°) oven for 30 to 40 minutes, or until the potatoes are soft and the liquid has evaporated. Sprinkle with the parsley and serve in the dish. *Serves* 6.

1760. POTATO BRIOCHES
Patate briosce

3 cups Duchesse Potato Base [No. 1770]
1 egg, beaten
2 tablespoons butter

Divide the Duchesse potato mixture into 6 equal portions and shape each in the traditional brioche form [*see* No. 1891]. Brush them with beaten egg, put them on a buttered baking dish, and bake them in a hot (450°) oven for 10 minutes, or until they are lightly golden. *Serves* 6.

1761. POTATOES CHÂTEAU
Patate château

2 pounds "new" potatoes
½ cup butter
Salt and freshly ground pepper

Cut the potatoes into smooth 1-inch balls or into the shape of large olives. Wash them in cold water and dry thoroughly. Heat the butter in a large frying pan over medium heat and sauté the potatoes for about 10 minutes, or until they are golden and tender. Adjust the heat as they sauté so that they do not brown too quickly and shake the pan frequently so that they brown evenly on all sides. Transfer them to a hot serving dish and season with salt and pepper. *Serves* 6.

1762. POTATO CHIPS
Patate chips—sfogliate

6 Idaho potatoes
Fat for deep frying
Salt

Slice the potatoes paper-thin with a vegetable slicer and soak them for 2 hours in several changes of ice water. Drain and dry them very thoroughly on paper towels. Drop them, a handful at a time, into deep hot (375°) fat until they are crisp and golden, being careful that they do not stick together. Drain on absorbent paper and proceed until all are deep fried. Arrange them on a paper doily on a serving platter and sprinkle with salt. *Serves* 6.

1763. POTATOES COLLERETTE
Patate collerette

Prepare in the same manner as the preceding recipe, except first cut the potatoes into equal-sized long cylinders, and then slice them paper thin. The result will be uniformly sized round chips. *Serves* 6.

1764. POTATOES COLOMBINA
Patate colombina

2 pounds potatoes, sliced
3 tablespoons oil
4 sweet peppers, roasted, scraped, seeded, and cut
    into strips [*see* No. 145]
6 tablespoons butter
Salt and freshly ground pepper

Heat the oil in a frying pan over medium heat, add the peppers, and sauté them gently for about 10 minutes, or until they are tender. Remove from the heat and reserve. Heat the butter in another large frying pan over medium heat until almost golden, add the potatoes, season with salt and pepper, cover the pan, and cook for about 15 minutes, or until they are tender. Toss them frequently with a spatula so that they will partially brown. Add the peppers to the potatoes, toss lightly, and transfer to a hot serving dish. *Serves* 6.

1765. POTATOES IN CREAM
Patate alla crema

2 pounds "new" potatoes, unpeeled
2 cups heavy cream
Salt and freshly ground pepper

Boil the unpeeled potatoes in a generous quantity of lightly salted water for about 20 minutes, or until they are just tender. Drain, cool, and cut them into slices. Place them in a large frying pan with 1¾ cups of the cream, bring to a boil over high heat, and cook until the cream is reduced by ½. Correct the seasoning, remove from the heat, swirl in the remaining cream, and turn out into a hot vegetable dish. *Serves* 6.

1766. POTATOES IN CREAM AU GRATIN
Patate alla crema gratinate

Prepare the potatoes as described in the preceding recipe, except turn them out into a baking dish, sprinkle with ½ cup of grated Parmesan cheese and ¼ cup melted butter, and brown very briefly under a high broiler flame. *Serves* 6.

1767. POTATO CROQUETTES
Patate crocchette

2 pounds potatoes, quartered
6 tablespoons butter
6 egg yolks
Pinch nutmeg
Flour
2 eggs, beaten
2 cups fresh breadcrumbs
Fat for deep frying
Salt and freshly ground pepper

Boil the potatoes in a generous quantity of lightly salted boiling water for about 20 minutes, or until they are tender. Put them through a ricer into a bowl and mix them thoroughly with the butter, egg yolks, nutmeg, and salt and pepper to taste. Form the mixture into 12 balls or any other desired shape, dust them with flour, dip in beaten egg, and cover with breadcrumbs. Drop them into deep hot (375°) fat until golden brown, drain briefly on absorbent paper, and arrange them on a hot serving platter. *Serves* 6.

583

1768. POTATOES DAUPHINE
Patate Dauphine

3 cups Duchesse Potato Base [No. 1770]
1 cup Plain Cream Puff Dough [No. 1991]
2 eggs, beaten
2 cups breadcrumbs
Fat for deep frying

Mix the Duchesse potato base thoroughly with the dough, form the mixture into rings about 3 inches in diameter, dip in beaten egg, cover generously with breadcrumbs, and carefully drop the rings into deep hot (375°) fat until they are golden brown. Drain briefly on absorbent paper and then heap them up on a hot serving dish. *Serves* 6.

1769. POTATOES DORATE
Patate dorate

4 Idaho potatoes, cut into the shape of large
    hazelnuts
6 tablespoons butter
Salt and freshly ground pepper

Soak the cut potatoes in ice water for 1 hour, drain, and dry them very thoroughly on an absorbent towel. Season them with salt and pepper. Heat the butter in a very large frying pan over medium heat until golden, place the potatoes in the pan without stirring them into the butter, cover the pan tightly, and cook for about 15 minutes shaking the pan every 5 minutes. Remove cover and cook 5 more minutes. They are fully cooked when they can be easily pierced with a fork; do not overcook until they are mushy. Remove from the heat and allow them to sit for 3 minutes, and then turn them onto a hot serving platter. *Serves* 6.

1770. DUCHESSE POTATO BASE
Composto per patate duchessa

2 pounds potatoes, quartered
6 tablespoons butter
4 egg yolks plus 1 whole egg, beaten together
Salt and freshly ground pepper
Pinch nutmeg

Boil the potatoes in a generous quantity of lightly salted water for about 20 minutes or until they are tender. Drain, purée them through a ricer into a saucepan, and heat them over a very low flame for 1 minute, stirring constantly, to rid them of all moisture. Add the butter and eggs and season them to taste with salt, pepper, and nutmeg. *Makes about* 4 *cups.*

1771. DUCHESSE POTATOES
Patate duchessa

4 cups Duchesse Potato Base [No. 1770]
2 eggs, beaten
2 tablespoons butter, softened

Put the Duchesse potato mixture into a pastry bag fitted with any desired large tip, squeeze out 6 large mounds onto a buttered oven-proof platter, brush with beaten egg, and bake in a hot (500°) oven for about 5 minutes, or until they are golden brown. *Serves* 6.

1772. POTATOES FONDANT
Patate fondanti

Prepare in the same manner as Potatoes Château [No. 1761], except cut the potatoes slightly larger, about the size of small eggs, and cook them about 5 minutes longer, being careful to adjust the heat so that they do not brown too quickly. *Serves* 6.

1773. FRENCH FRIED POTATOES
Patate fritte o Pont Neuf

6 Idaho potatoes, cut in long strips about ½ inch thick
Fat for deep frying
Salt

Soak the strips of potatoes in ice water for 30 minutes, drain, and dry them thoroughly on an absorbent towel. Drop them in a frying basket immersed in fat that has been pre-heated to 300° and cook for 15 minutes. Adjust the heat as they cook so that the temperature does not rise above 300°. Remove the basket from the fat, raise the heat, and immerse the potatoes again when the fat reaches 375°. Cook until the potatoes are crisp and golden, drain briefly on absorbent paper, transfer them to a serving dish, and sprinkle with salt. *Serves* 6.

1774. FRENCH FRIED POTATOES COPEAUX
Patate fritte en copeaux

Prepare in the same manner as the preceding recipe, except cut the potatoes into long irregular ribbons by cutting off slices spirally, about ⅛ inch thick. Cook them for only 5 minutes for their first immersion in the fat. *Serves* 6.

1775. FRENCH FRIED POTATO STICKS
Patate fritte a bastoncini

Prepare in the same manner as French Fried Potatoes

[No. 1773], except cut the potatoes into long strips ¼ inch thick and cook them for only 10 minutes for their first immersion in the fat. *Serves* 6.

1776. FRENCH FRIED POTATO STRAWS
Patate paglia

Prepare in the same manner as French Fried Potatoes [No. 1773], except cut them into long strips ⅛ inch thick and cook them for only 3 minutes for their first immersion in the fat. *Serves* 6.

1777. POTATOES LYONNAISE
Patate alla lyonnaise

2 pounds "new" potatoes, unpeeled
2 onions, sliced
½ cup butter
Salt and freshly ground pepper

Boil the unpeeled potatoes in a generous quantity of lightly salted water for about 20 minutes, or until they are tender. Drain, cool, peel, and slice them about ¼ inch thick. Heat half of the butter in a large frying pan over medium heat until golden, add as many of the potato slices as will conveniently fit the pan, and brown them on both sides. Remove them with a slotted spoon and proceed until all are browned, adding more butter as necessary. Add the onions to the pan, cook until golden, return the potatoes to the pan, heat thoroughly, season with salt and pepper, and turn them out into a hot serving dish. *Serves* 6.

1778. POTATOES MACAIRE
Patate Macaire

4 Idaho potatoes, unpeeled
½ cup butter, softened
6 tablespoons oil
Salt and freshly ground pepper

Bake the potatoes in the manner described in Baked Potatoes [No. 1748], scoop out all of the pulp into a bowl, add the butter, and season to taste with salt and pepper. Form into 6 patties, brown them on both sides in a frying pan in hot oil, and transfer them to a hot serving platter. *Serves* 6.

1779. POTATOES MAÎTRE D'HÔTEL
Patate maître d'hôtel

2 pounds "new" potatoes
6 tablespoons butter

3 cups boiling milk
Salt and freshly ground pepper
3 tablespoons chopped parsley

Boil the potatoes in a generous quantity of lightly salted water for about 15 minutes, or until they are not quite tender. Drain and slice them about ¼ inch thick while they are still hot. Melt the butter in a frying pan over medium heat, add the potatoes and the boiling milk, season with salt and pepper, and cook until the milk has cooked away, stirring them frequently (but gently) to keep from scorching. Transfer them to a hot serving dish and sprinkle with the parsley. *Serves* 6.

1780. MASHED POTATOES
Patate in purea

2 pounds potatoes, quartered
6 tablespoons butter
½ cup hot heavy cream (or rich milk)
Salt and freshly ground white pepper

Boil the potatoes in a generous quantity of lightly salted water for about 20 minutes, or until just tender. Do not overcook. Drain, purée them through a ricer into a saucepan, and place the pan over low heat for 1 minute, stirring constantly, to rid them of excess moisture. Add the butter, season to taste with salt and pepper, and beat them for about 5 minutes with a wooden spoon (or with an electric mixer), add the hot cream, bit by bit. Turn them into a hot vegetable dish and serve immediately. *Serves* 6.

1781. MASHED POTATOES AU GRATIN
Patate in purea gratinate

Prepare mashed potatoes as described in the preceding recipe, pour them into a shallow baking dish, cover them with ½ cup grated Parmesan cheese mixed with ½ cup fresh breadcrumbs, and sprinkle with ¼ cup melted butter. Place the dish under a high broiler flame for 3 minutes, or until the surface is golden. *Serves* 6.

1782. POTATOES MOUSSELINE
Patate mousseline

6 Idaho potatoes, unpeeled
½ cup butter, softened
1 cup heavy cream
4 egg yolks
Pinch nutmeg
Salt and freshly ground pepper
4 egg whites, beaten stiff
½ cup butter, melted

Bake the potatoes in the manner described in Baked Potatoes [No. 1748], remove all of the pulp, and mix with the softened butter, cream, egg yolks, nutmeg, and salt and pepper to taste. Mix well, fold in the beaten whites, and heap up the mixture in a mound on an oven-proof platter, brush with melted butter, place the platter in a hot (400°) oven for about 15 minutes, or until nicely browned and puffed, and serve on the platter. *Serves* 6.

1783. NOISETTE POTATOES I
Patate nocciole I

Prepare in the same manner as Potatoes Château [No. 1761], except cut the potatoes into smaller shapes, about the size of an olive. *Serves* 6.

1784. NOISETTE POTATOES II
Patate nocciole II

Prepare in the same manner as Potatoes Château [No. 1761], except use "old" potatoes and cut them into the shape of olives before cooking. *Serves* 6.

1785. POTATOES PARMENTIER
Patate Parmentier

2 pounds potatoes
6 tablespoons butter
3 tablespoons chopped parsley
Salt and freshly ground pepper

Cut the potatoes into ⅓-inch dice. Heat the butter in a very large frying pan over medium heat until almost golden, add the potatoes, and stir almost constantly until they are nicely browned on all sides. Season with salt and pepper, turn them out into a hot vegetable dish, and sprinkle with the parsley. *Serves* 6.

1786. POTATOES PIZZAIOLA
Patate alla pizzaiola

2 pounds "new" potatoes, unpeeled
3 tablespoons oil
2 cloves garlic, crushed in the garlic-press
2 tablespoons chopped oregano (or 1 teaspoon dried)
6 ripe tomatoes, peeled, seeded, drained, and chopped
6 tablespoons butter
Salt and freshly ground pepper

Boil the potatoes in a generous quantity of lightly salted water for about 20 minutes, or until they are tender. Drain, peel, and cut them into slices about ¼ inch thick. Heat the oil in a saucepan over medium heat, add the garlic, cook for 1 minute, add the tomatoes and oregano, season with salt and pepper, and simmer for 15 minutes. While the tomatoes are cooking, heat the butter in a large frying pan over medium heat until almost golden and brown the potato slices on both sides. Add the tomato mixture, toss lightly, correct the seasoning, and turn out onto a pre-heated serving dish. *Serves* 6.

1787. POTATOES WITH SALT PORK AND ONIONS
Patate con cipolline e lardo

2 pounds potatoes, sliced
4 tablespoons butter
3 onions, sliced and broken into rings
½ pound lean salt pork, cut into small thin slices and parboiled for 15 minutes and drained
2 tablespoons chopped parsley
Salt and freshly ground pepper

Melt the butter in a very large frying pan over medium heat, add the onions and sliced salt pork, and cook until the onions begin to color. Add the sliced potatoes, season with salt and pepper, mix lightly with the onions and salt pork, cover the pan, and cook for about 15 minutes, or until the potatoes are tender. Remove the cover briefly and turn the potatoes over with a spatula every 3 or 4 minutes so that they will all partially brown. Transfer them to a hot serving platter, sprinkle with parsley, and serve immediately. *Serves* 6.

1788. SAUTÉED POTATOES
Patate sautées

Prepare in the same manner as Potatoes Lyonnaise [No. 1777], omitting the onions. *Serves* 6.

1789. SOUFFLÉED POTATOES
Patate soufflées

Souffléed potatoes are not difficult to make, but they do require careful preparation. The first requirement is that only large, mature Idaho potatoes be used and these should be aged in a cool, dry place for at least a week. One test to see if they are properly aged is to scrape the potato with the fingernail and if the skin will no longer come off easily, it is old enough.

    6 mature, aged Idaho potatoes
    Fat for deep frying
    Salt

Trim each potato into a perfect oblong shape and then cut them into $\frac{1}{8}$-inch slices, lengthwise. The slices must be cut lengthwise with the grain. Each slice must be of absolutely uniform thickness over its whole length. This is difficult to do with a knife and is most easily accomplished with a mechanical slicer. The slices may now be trimmed into any desired shape, such as ovals, squares, diamonds, etc., but the traditional shape is a small rectangle with all 4 corners trimmed off. Soak the slices for 2 hours in several changes of ice water, drain them, and then dry very quickly but absolutely thoroughly on an absorbent towel. Drop the slices, a few at a time, into deep fat pre-heated to 275° and cook them for 7 minutes, taking great care that they are not crowded in the pan and that none of them stick together. Remove them and drain on absorbent paper. Repeat this process until all the slices have been cooked. They may now rest for several hours, if desired, before completing their cooking. A few minutes before serving, drop them, a few at a time, into deep hot (375°) fat. Agitate the pan slightly so that they will move in the fat. They should puff immediately. Cook until they are golden brown, and drain on absorbent paper. Proceed in this manner with the remaining slices until all have been cooked. Discard any that do not puff (usually about 10%) or eat them as ordinary French fries. Serve them in a wicker basket lined with a napkin and season them lightly with salt. *Serves* 6.

1790. POTATO TARTS WITH SPINACH
Cassolette di patate con spinaci

    4 cups Duchesse Potato Base [No. 1770]
    2 tablespoons butter, softened
    3 cups Spinach in Butter [No. 1791]
    2 eggs, beaten

Form the Duchesse potato mixture with the hands into 6 neatly shaped cups or tart shells, arrange them on a buttered baking dish, fill each with spinach, brush with beaten egg, and place them in a very hot (500°) oven for 5 or 6 minutes, or until the cups are golden brown. *Serves* 6.

SPINACH
Spinaci

Spinach has the virtue of being a very agreeable accompaniment to a wide variety of meat, poultry, and egg dishes. Before being cooked, it must be exceptionally well washed to rid it of all dirt that is buried in its tightly wrinkled leaves. If spinach is very young and fresh, nearly all of the stem is edible, as well as the leaves, and only the root end need be cut off; older, tougher spinach should have the stems trimmed off. *Never* cook it in aluminum, as it induces a chemical reaction that brings out a bitter flavor. Allow about 2 pounds of spinach for 6 persons.

Spinach may be cooked in two ways: if it is very young and fresh, it is delicious if simply put into a heavy enamel pot with just the water that clings to the leaves after washing, 1 tablespoon of butter, and a pinch of salt; cook it tightly covered over fairly high heat for about 5 minutes, turning it with a fork from the bottom of the pot once or twice to aid its cooking evenly. This method will allow the spinach to retain its maximum flavor. Older spinach, however, that is not as fresh as it might be, will react better to being boiled in a very large quantity of lightly salted water for about 5 minutes. This method will refresh the spinach somewhat and, while it will lose a little of its flavor in the water, it will also lose most of its bitterness. After cooking, it should be drained immediately in a colander and then squeezed to rid it of as much water as possible. It is now ready to be chopped or puréed if desired, and dressed with butter or any desired seasoning.

587

1791. SPINACH IN BUTTER
Spinaci al burro

2 pounds spinach, trimmed, washed, cooked, and
   drained as described in the introductory
   remarks above
6 tablespoons butter, softened
Salt and freshly ground pepper
Pinch nutmeg

After squeezing the spinach thoroughly to rid it of
as much water as possible, chop it coarsely and then
put it in an enamel saucepan with the softened butter.
Season with salt, pepper, and nutmeg. Stir over very
low heat for about 5 minutes, or until the butter has
been almost absorbed by the spinach, and turn it out
into a hot vegetable dish. *Serves* 6.

1792. CREAMED SPINACH
Spinaci alla crema

Prepare in the same manner as described in the preceding recipe and then sprinkle with 1 tablespoon of flour,
stir for 1 minute, add 1½ cups of boiling heavy cream,
simmer for 10 minutes, taste, and correct the seasoning.
Serves 6.

1793. SPINACH AU GRATIN
Spinaci stufati e gratinati

Prepare in the same manner as described in Spinach
in Butter [No. 1791], turn it out into a shallow baking
dish, sprinkle with ¾ cup of grated Parmesan cheese
and then with 3 tablespoons of melted butter, brown
the top under a high broiler flame for about 2 minutes,
and serve in the baking dish. *Serves* 6.

1794. SPINACH INGLESE
Spinaci all'inglese

2 pounds spinach, trimmed, washed, cooked, and
   drained in the manner described in the introductory remarks above
Salt and freshly ground pepper
½ cup butter, softened

After cooking the spinach, drain it in a colander,
but do not squeeze it dry. Turn it into a hot vegetable
dish, season to taste with salt and pepper, and serve
the softened butter on the side. *Serves* 6.

1795. SPINACH WITH MEAT SAUCE
Spinaci al sugo di carne

Prepare in the same manner as described in Spinach
in Butter [No. 1791], add 2 cups hot Italian Meat

Sauce [No. 41], and simmer for 5 minutes before
serving. *Serves* 6.

1796. SPINACH MILANESE
Spinaci alla milanese

Prepare 1 recipe of Spinach au Gratin [No. 1793] and
just before serving spoon a narrow border of 4 Scrambled Eggs [No. 688] around the outside edge of the
baking dish. *Serves* 6.

1797. SPINACH PARMIGIANO
Pane di spinaci al parmigiano

1 recipe puréed spinach [*see* No. 1798]
1 cup thick Béchamel Sauce [No. 18]
6 eggs, separated
3 tablespoons flour
2 cups freshly grated Parmesan cheese
Pinch salt
2 tablespoons butter, softened
3 tablespoons breadcrumbs
2 cups very thick Cream Sauce [No. 55]

Mix the puréed spinach with the Béchamel, the egg
yolks, and the flour. Beat until smooth, and then beat
in 1 cup of the Parmesan cheese. Beat the egg whites
with a pinch of salt, stir ¼ into the spinach mixture
until well blended, and then carefully fold in the remaining egg whites. Butter a 2-quart mold with the
softened butter, sprinkle with the breadcrumbs and
1 tablespoon of the remaining Parmesan, tilt mold in
all directions to coat insides completely, and knock
out excess. Pour in the soufflé mixture, place mold in a
pan containing very hot water, and bake in a moderate
(350°) oven for 1 hour, or until a knife blade inserted
in the center comes out clean. Remove mold from
oven, let it rest for a moment, unmold on a round,
pre-heated platter. Coat it, as though icing a cake, with
the cream sauce, which has been mixed with the remaining scant cup of Parmesan cheese. *Serves* 6.

1798. SPINACH PURÉE WITH CROÛTONS
Purea di spinaci con crostini

2 pounds spinach, trimmed, washed, cooked, and
   drained as described in the introductory
   remarks above
6 tablespoons butter, softened
Salt and freshly ground pepper
Pinch nutmeg
2 cups Croûtons [No. 332]

After draining, squeeze the spinach especially well
to rid it of as much water as possible. Purée it in a

food mill, place it in a saucepan, add the butter, and season to taste with salt, pepper, and nutmeg. Stir constantly over very low heat for about 5 minutes, turn it out into a hot vegetable dish, and sprinkle with the croûtons. *Serves* 6.

1799. SPINACH ROMANA
Spinaci alla romana

1 recipe Spinach in Butter [No. 1791]
2 cloves garlic, crushed in the garlic-press
1 cup chopped smoked ham
$\frac{1}{2}$ cup pine nuts
$\frac{1}{2}$ cup seeded raisins, softened for 5 minutes in
    hot water

Prepare the spinach as described in No. 1791 and then add the remaining ingredients. Cook over very low heat for about 5 minutes, stirring constantly, and then turn out into a hot vegetable dish. *Serves* 6.

1800. SPINACH SOUFFLÉ WITH MUSHROOMS
Soufflé di spinaci con funghi

Prepare in the same manner and with the same ingredients as Spinach and Ham Soufflé [No. 637], omitting the ham and substituting $\frac{3}{4}$ pound of chopped mushrooms which have been very gently sautéed in 3 tablespoons of butter with 2 crushed cloves of garlic in a frying pan for about 10 minutes. *Serves* 6.

STRING BEANS
Fagiolini verdi

There are a great variety of string or green beans on the market and most of these are now stringless which means only their ends have to be broken off before cooking. They should first be boiled in a generous quantity of lightly salted water from 8 to 15 minutes depending on their size, or until they are barely tender. Begin testing for doneness by tasting a bean after 8 minutes. It is important that they not be overcooked, as they will lose not only flavor but texture. Drain them in a colander, plunge them very briefly in cold water to halt the cooking process, and they may now wait for an hour or more before finishing them off. Just before dressing them and completing their cooking, place them in a large frying pan and shake the pan over moderate heat for about 2 minutes to heat them and rid them of excess moisture.

1801. STRING BEANS ARETINA
Fagiolini verdi all'aretina

2 pounds string beans, trimmed, cooked, drained,
    and dried as described in the introduction to
    this section
4 tablespoons oil
2 cloves garlic, crushed in the garlic-press
$\frac{1}{2}$ cup chopped onion
6 large ripe tomatoes, peeled, seeded, drained,
    and chopped
6 sage leaves (or $\frac{1}{2}$ teaspoon dried)
Salt and freshly ground pepper

Heat the oil in a large saucepan over medium heat, add the garlic and onion, and cook until the onion begins to color. Add the tomatoes and sage, season with salt and pepper, and simmer for about 15 minutes. Add the beans, toss them lightly with the tomatoes, correct the seasoning, simmer for 2 or 3 minutes, and then turn them out into a hot vegetable dish. *Serves* 6.

1802. STRING BEANS BONNE FEMME
Fagiolini verdi bonne femme

2 pounds string beans, trimmed, cooked, drained,
    and dried as described in the introduction to
    this section
$\frac{1}{2}$ pound lean salt pork, diced, parboiled for 15 minutes,
    drained, and sautéed golden brown
6 tablespoons butter
2 tablespoons chopped parsley
Salt and freshly ground pepper

Add the butter and the browned salt pork dice to the beans in the frying pan in which they were briefly dried. Shake the pan over medium heat until the butter is melted, correct the seasoning, turn them out into a hot serving dish, and sprinkle them with the parsley. *Serves* 6.

1803. STRING BEANS IN BUTTER
Fagiolini verdi al burro

2 pounds string beans, trimmed, cooked, drained,
    and dried as described in the introduction to
    this section
6 tablespoons butter
Juice of $\frac{1}{2}$ lemon
Salt and freshly ground pepper

Add the butter to the beans in the frying pan in which they were briefly dried and shake the pan over medium heat for 2 or 3 minutes until the butter is melted. Correct the seasoning, squeeze the lemon juice over them, and turn them out into a hot vegetable dish. *Serves* 6.

1804. STRING BEANS IN CREAM
Fagiolini verdi alla crema

2 pounds string beans, trimmed
2 cups heavy cream
Salt and freshly ground pepper

Boil the beans in a generous quantity of lightly salted water for about 5 minutes, or until they are about half cooked. Drain them in a colander, put them in a large frying pan over moderate heat, and shake the pan for a minute to rid them of excess moisture. Add 1¾ cups of the cream, bring to a boil, and simmer until the cream is reduced by ½ and the beans are fully tender. Season with salt and pepper, remove from the heat, swirl in the remaining cream, and turn them out into a hot vegetable dish. *Serves* 6.

1805. STRING BEANS INGLESE
Fagiolini verdi all'inglese

2 pounds string beans, trimmed and cooked as described in the introduction to this section
½ cup butter, softened
Salt and freshly ground pepper

Drain the beans when they are just tender, turn them out immediately into a hot vegetable dish, season them with a little salt and pepper, and serve the softened butter on the side. *Serves* 6.

1806. STRING BEANS WITH PROSCIUTTO
Fagiolini verdi al prosciutto

Prepare in the same manner as String Beans Bonne Femme [No. 1802], substituting 1 cup diced prosciutto (or smoked ham) for the salt pork and, if desired, garnish the beans with 1 cup Croûtons [No. 332] just before serving. *Serves* 6.

1807. STRING BEANS TOURANGELLE
Fagiolini verdi à la Tourangelle

Prepare in the same manner as String Beans in Butter [No. 1803] and blend in 2 cups of boiling Béchamel Sauce [No. 18] just before removing the beans from the heat. *Serves* 6.

TOMATOES
Pomodori

The tomatoes in American markets are all too often sad, hard little specimens wrapped in cellophane, lacking in flavor; and whatever tenderness they possess has been achieved by ripening them off the vine rather than on it. This is perhaps inevitable, especially in large cities, where the problems of distribution of such a highly perishable item as a ripe tomato are great. It is, however, a great loss, since nothing can quite equal the tangy flavor of a very fresh tomato that has been fully ripened on the vine. Whenever these are available, usually at the height of summer, take advantage of them and, if necessary, adapt your menu to include them.

Often tomatoes should be peeled, seeded, and drained of excess juice before cooking. This is most simply accomplished by first plunging them in boiling water for a few seconds. Then peel off the skin, cut off the top ¼ of the tomato at the stem end (this top section may be reserved for the stock pot), and, squeezing the tomato gently in the palm of the hand, shake out as many of the seeds and as much of the juice as possible. If the tomato is to be chopped, the juice and seeds may even more easily be drained off by cutting the tomato in half before squeezing and then only the core need be discarded.

1808. TOMATOES ANTICA
Pomodori all'antica

6 large ripe tomatoes
1 cup Duxelles [No. 138]
½ cup diced prosciutto (or smoked ham)
1 cup Italian Meat Sauce [No. 41]
1 tablespoon butter
Salt and freshly ground pepper

Cut off the top ¼ of the tomatoes, squeeze them gently to remove as much of the seeds and juice as possible, and then cut out a little of the center of each to make a slight hollow. Season the cut part generously with salt and lightly with pepper, spoon a little of the Duxelles and a spoonful of the meat sauce into each, arrange them on a lightly buttered baking dish, and bake them in a moderate (350°) oven for about 15 minutes, or slightly less if the tomatoes are quite ripe. Remove them from the oven, spoon another tablespoon of the meat sauce over each, and serve in the baking dish. *Serves* 6.

1809. BROILED TOMATOES
Pomodori alla griglia

6 large ripe tomatoes
4 shallots, chopped
2 tablespoons dried basil
1 cup fresh breadcrumbs
3 tablespoons butter
Salt and freshly ground pepper

Cut off the top ¼ of each of the tomatoes, season generously with salt and lightly with pepper, sprinkle each with a little of the shallots and basil, top with breadcrumbs, and put a generous dot of butter on the top of each. Arrange them in a buttered baking dish, and bake them in moderate (350°) oven for 10 minutes. Remove them from the oven and brown the tops under a medium broiler flame for about 3 minutes. Serve in the baking dish. *Serves* 6.

1810. TOMATO FRITTERS
Bignè di pomodori

6 tomatoes, not fully ripe
2 cups Fritter Batter [No. 275]
Fat for deep frying
6 sprigs parsley, fried in deep fat [*see* No. 276]
Salt and freshly ground pepper

Cut the tomatoes into slices about ½ inch thick, season them generously with salt and pepper, dip them in fritter batter, and drop them in deep hot (375°) fat, a few at a time, until they are golden brown. Drain and arrange them on a hot serving dish. Garnish with the fried parsley sprigs. *Serves* 6.

1811. TOMATOES GOURMET
Pomodori del ghiottone

6 large ripe tomatoes
1 tablespoon oil
4 Scrambled Eggs [No. 688]
¼ pound mushrooms, sliced and sautéed gently
    for 10 minutes in 2 tablespoons butter
½ cup chopped prosciutto (or smoked ham)
1 cup fresh breadcrumbs·
4 tablespoons butter
Salt and freshly ground pepper

Cut off the top ¼ of each of the tomatoes, squeeze them gently to remove as much of the seeds and juice as possible, and then cut out a small portion of their centers to form a slight hollow. Season them generously with salt and lightly with pepper, place them in an oiled baking dish, and bake in a moderate (350°) oven for about 15 minutes, or slightly less if the tomatoes are very ripe. Prepare the mushrooms and the scrambled eggs while the tomatoes are cooking and then mix them lightly together with the prosciutto. Heap a generous amount of this mixture on each tomato and then cover each with the breadcrumbs which have been fried for a few seconds in the butter. Serve in the baking dish. *Serves* 6.

1812. TOMATOES AU GRATIN
Pomodori gratinati

6 large ripe tomatoes
6 tablespoons oil
Salt and freshly ground pepper
2 cups fresh breadcrumbs

Cut the tomatoes into ½-inch slices and arrange them overlapping in a lightly oiled baking dish. Season them generously with salt and pepper, sprinkle with the breadcrumbs, and then with oil. Place the dish under a medium broiler flame for 5 or 6 minutes, or until the tomatoes are tender and the surface is lightly browned. Serve in the baking dish. *Serves* 6.

1813. TOMATOES AND EGGPLANT AU GRATIN
Pomodori e melanzane gratinati

Prepare in the same manner as the preceding recipe, except before broiling, intersperse the overlapping slices of tomatoes in the dish with 12 equal-sized slices of eggplant which have been treated as described on page 559, dusted with flour, and very quickly browned in oil in a frying pan over fairly high heat. *Serves* 6.

1814. TOMATOES WITH MIXED HERBS
Pomodori con erbe fini

6 large ripe tomatoes
½ cup butter
½ cup mixed chopped fresh herbs, such as parsley,
    marjoram, oregano, basil, tarragon, etc.
2 cups fresh breadcrumbs
Salt and freshly ground pepper

Cut the tomatoes into ½-inch slices. Heat 4 tablespoons of the butter in a large frying pan over fairly high heat and very quickly sauté the slices of tomato, a few at a time, for about 2 minutes on each side. Transfer them to a hot serving dish and keep warm until all of the tomatoes have been sautéed. Season them with salt and pepper, sprinkle with the chopped herbs, and then pour them over the fresh breadcrumbs which have been fried for a few seconds in the remaining butter. *Serves* 6.

1815. TOMATOES MASSAIA
Pomodori alla moda della massaia

Prepare in the same manner as Tomatoes Antica [No. 1808], omitting the Duxelles, prosciutto, and meat sauce. Substitute a filling made of $\frac{1}{4}$ pound of chopped mushrooms which have been gently sautéed for 10 minutes with 2 crushed cloves of garlic in 2 tablespoons of butter in a frying pan over moderate heat and then mixed with $\frac{1}{2}$ cup of Tomato Paste [No. 144]. *Serves* 6.

1816. TOMATOES WITH RICE ROMANA
Pomodori con riso alla romana

6 medium tomatoes, slightly underripe
$\frac{3}{4}$ cup uncooked rice
2 tablespoons oil
$1\frac{1}{2}$ cups hot Brown Stock [No. 4]
2 cloves garlic, crushed in the garlic-press
2 tablespoons chopped basil
3 cups Tomato Sauce [No. 19]
Salt and freshly ground pepper

Cut off the top $\frac{1}{4}$ of each of the tomatoes and then scoop out most of the pulp, leaving a shell about $\frac{1}{2}$ to $\frac{1}{4}$ inch thick. Season the insides with salt and pepper. Pound the rice in a mortar (or place in blender) until it is very finely grained and then mix it with the garlic and chopped basil. Put 2 very generous tablespoons of this mixture in each of the tomatoes and then pour a little of the hot stock and 1 teaspoon of the oil into each. The tomatoes should be no more than $\frac{3}{4}$ full. Cover each tomato with its top. Arrange them in a baking dish and pour the tomato sauce mixed with 1 cup of water around them. Bake in a moderate (300°) oven for 50 minutes and serve in the baking dish. *Serves* 6.

1817. TOMATOES SICILIANA
Pomodori alla siciliana

6 medium tomatoes, slightly underripe
6 tablespoons oil
2 onions, chopped
12 anchovy fillets, washed free of salt [*see* No. 220] and finely chopped
3 tablespoons chopped parsley
2 tablespoons capers
1 cup pitted black olives, sliced
$\frac{1}{2}$ cup fresh breadcrumbs
Salt and freshly ground pepper

Cut off the top $\frac{1}{4}$ of each of the tomatoes, squeeze each slightly to remove seeds and juice, and scoop out about half of the pulp from each. Season generously with salt and pepper. Heat 3 tablespoons of the oil in a frying pan over medium heat, add the onion, cook until soft, remove from the heat, and mix the onions with the anchovies, parsley, capers, black olives, breadcrumbs, and salt and pepper to taste. Stuff each of the tomatoes with this mixture, cover each with its top, and then arrange them in an oiled baking dish. Bake in a moderate (350°) oven for about 25 minutes, or slightly less if the tomatoes are fairly ripe, and serve in the baking dish. *Serves* 6.

1818. TOMATOES STUFFED WITH TUNA AND PEPPERS
Pomodori di magro

6 medium tomatoes, slightly underripe
4 tablespoons oil
$1\frac{1}{2}$ cups Italian-style tuna canned in oil, crumbled
3 sweet peppers, roasted, scraped, seeded, and cut into strips [*see* No. 145]
$\frac{1}{2}$ cup Anchovy Butter [No. 108], softened
1 cup fresh breadcrumbs
Salt and freshly ground pepper

Cut off the top $\frac{1}{4}$ of each of the tomatoes and scoop out most of the pulp from each. Season them generously with salt and pepper. Heat 2 tablespoons of the oil in a frying pan over moderate heat and gently sauté the strips of pepper for about 10 minutes, or until they are soft. Remove them from the heat and mix them with the tuna and the anchovy butter. Stuff each of the tomatoes lightly with this mixture, top with breadcrumbs, and sprinkle with a little oil. Arrange them in an oiled baking dish, bake in a moderate (350°) oven for about 25 minutes, or slightly less if the tomatoes are fairly ripe, and serve in baking dish. *Serves* 6.

Tomatoes with Rice Romana (No. 1816)

TRUFFLES
Tartufi

Truffles are a fungus growth that are found underground around the bases of oak trees. No method of cultivating them has ever been found and thus they are extremely expensive, even in the regions of France and Italy where they are most abundant. The French use pigs, which seem to have an instinct for finding them, to root them out with their snouts; the Italians use dogs to dig for them with their paws. Truffles are highly prized in cooking for their extraordinary pungency and flavor. Even a small fresh truffle can perfume a whole dish with its unmistakable aroma. Among gourmets, the most highly prized varieties are the black truffles from Périgord in France and the white truffles from Piedmont in Northern Italy (which aren't actually white at all, but range from pale beige to light brown). They are found, however, throughout Europe in a wide variety of colors and intensities of flavor. They have never been found in any abundance in the United States, perhaps for want of trying. Fresh truffles are incomparably superior to the imported canned ones that are generally available in the United States, but so strong is the truffle flavor that even the canned ones are worth their expense. White Piedmontese truffles seem to survive the canning process somewhat better than other types and are more pungent. Fresh truffles are occasionally imported airborne by a few specialty food shops in large American cities and their price is astronomical. In spite of this, we are including a few recipes for fresh truffles, if only because they can provide an unforgettable gastronomic delight. While canned truffles may be substituted in the succeeding recipes, we do not recommend it, as they will quite likely prove a very expensive disappointment.

Fresh truffles have very rough skins and must be washed and scraped or brushed before cooking.

1819. TRUFFLES IN BUTTER
Tartufi al burro

½ pound fresh truffles, washed and brushed
1 cup brandy
6 tablespoons butter
Salt and freshly ground pepper

Marinate the truffles in the brandy for 1 hour, turning them occasionally. Drain and dry them thoroughly. Melt the butter in a shallow casserole over low heat and very gently sauté the truffles for about 15 minutes, or until they are tender. Season them with salt and pepper and serve in the casserole. *Serves 6.*

NOTE: The brandy marinade will have gained a subtle truffle aroma, and may be employed with great effect in many dishes calling for brandy.

1819a. MOCK TRUFFLES

4 tablespoons imported dried mushrooms
1 pound large mushrooms
¼ cup olive oil
1 shallot, crushed in the garlic-press
¼ clove of garlic, crushed in the garlic-press
¼ teaspoon salt
¼ teaspoon freshly ground black pepper

Soak dried mushrooms in 1 cup very hot water for ½ hour. Do not wash fresh mushrooms unless they feel gritty. Discard their stems but do not peel the caps. Slice caps ¼ inch thick, put in a frying pan with olive oil, and fry over very high heat until brown, paper thin (through loss of practically all their moisture), and crisp—this should take about 15 to 20 minutes. When they are ¾ done, drain dried mushrooms, pat dry and chop finely, and add to frying fresh mushrooms. When the latter are cooked, pour the entire contents of frying pan into a small, deep bowl. Add shallot, garlic, salt and pepper, mix well, cover, and leave at room temperature for 6 to 12 hours. After this time has elapsed, store, covered, in refrigerator until needed. *Makes about 1 cup.*

1820. TRUFFLES IN CREAM
Tartufi alla crema

Prepare in the same manner described No. 1819, except add 1½ cups of heavy cream after the truffles have sautéed for 5 minutes, raise the heat slightly, cook until the cream is reduced by ½, remove from the heat, and swirl in ¼ cup more of fresh heavy cream. *Serves 6.*

1821. TRUFFLES ROASTED IN THE ASHES
Tartufi sotto la cenere

18 small fresh truffles
1 cup brandy [*see* Note to No. 1819]
18 small thin strips fresh pork fat back
6 sheets parchment paper
4 tablespoons oil

Marinate the truffles in the brandy for 1 hour, turning

them occasionally. Wrap each of the truffles with a strip of fresh pork fat and brush both sides of each sheet of the parchment paper with oil. Place 3 of the truffles on one side of each of the sheets of paper, fold the paper over them, and crimp the edges to make a very tight seal. Place these packets in a pan resting on the dying remains of a charcoal fire. The fire should be well past its prime, but still contain glowing embers. Place a few of the embers around the packets of truffles in the pan and sprinkle with a liberal amount of hot ashes. Allow the packets to remain for 1/2 hour. Carefully brush away the ashes and transfer the packets to individual serving plates. Allow each guest to open his own packet. The aroma that escapes as the packets are opened is unforgettable. *Serves* 6.

1822. TRUFFLES IN MARSALA
Tartufi al marsala

1/2 pound fresh truffles, washed and brushed
2 tablespoons butter
3 shallots, chopped
1 small carrot, chopped
1 tablespoon chopped parsley
1 teaspoon chopped thyme (or 1/2 teaspoon dried)
1 cup dry Marsala wine
1/2 cup Consommé [No. 360]
Salt and freshly ground pepper
1 cup thick flour and water paste

Heat the butter in a small earthenware casserole over moderate heat, add the shallots and carrot, and sauté very gently until the carrot is soft. Add the truffles, parsley, thyme, Marsala, consommé, and a pinch of salt and pepper. Bring to a boil, spread the rim of the casserole with the flour and water paste, press the cover on firmly to seal the casserole hermetically, and cook over low heat for about 20 minutes, or slightly longer if the truffles are very large. Remove from the heat and open the casserole at the table. *Serves* 6.

1823. TRUFFLES RICCA
Tartufi alla ricca

18 small truffles, washed and brushed
1 cup brandy [*see* Note to No. 1819]
18 very thin small slices fresh pork fat back
1/2 recipe Puff Paste [No. 1960], rolled out 1/4 inch thick and cut into 2 1/2-inch circles
1 egg yolk, beaten with 1 tablespoon water
2 cups Demi-Glaze Sauce [No. 20]
Salt

Marinate the truffles for 1 hour in the brandy, drain, and dry them well. Season them lightly with salt and wrap each in a very thin slice of pork fat. Place 1 truffle on each of the circles of dough, moisten the edges with water, fold the dough over the truffles to form half moons, press edges firmly together, and then brush the pastry cases with the egg yolk. Place them on a baking sheet in a fairly hot (400°) oven for about 20 minutes, or until they are puffed and golden brown. Heap them up on a serving platter and serve the Demi-Glaze sauce on the side. *Serves* 6.

TURNIPS
Rape

Turnips are a particularly fine accompaniment to game or more strongly flavored poultry, such as turkey or duck. Before cooking the tops should be cut off (these may be cooked separately in the same manner as spinach, if desired) and they should be peeled.

1824. TURNIPS IN BUTTER
Rape al burro

1 1/2 pounds turnips, peeled
1/2 cup butter
Salt and freshly ground pepper

Boil the turnips in a generous quantity of lightly salted water for about 25 minutes, or until they are tender. Drain, cool, and cut into thick slices. Heat 4 tablespoons of the butter in a large frying pan over medium heat and brown the slices, a few at a time. Season them with salt and pepper as they cook. Remove them from the pan to a hot serving dish, brown the remaining slices, adding more butter as necessary, and serve at once with the butter in the pan poured over them. *Serves* 6.

594

1825. CREAMED TURNIPS
Rape alla crema

1½ pounds turnips, peeled
4 tablespoons butter
2½ cups heavy cream
Salt and freshly ground pepper

Cut the turnips up into the shape of long olives. Drop olive-shaped pieces in a generous quantity of lightly salted boiling water, cook for about 10 minutes, or until they are not quite tender, and drain them. Melt the butter in a large frying pan over medium heat, add the turnips, roll them in the butter for 1 minute, add the cream, season with salt and pepper, cook until the cream is reduced by ½ and the turnips are tender, then turn them out into a hot vegetable dish. *Serves* 6.

1826. TURNIPS AU GRATIN
Rape gratinate

Prepare in the same manner as described in Turnips in Butter [No. 1824], except arrange the sautéed turnips in a shallow casserole, spread 2 cups of Béchamel Sauce [No. 18] over them, sprinkle with ½ cup grated Parmesan cheese, and brown the surface for about 2 minutes under a high broiler flame. *Serves* 6.

ZUCCHINI
Zucchine

Zucchini possesses a very delicate but pleasing flavor and is one of the most popular vegetables among Italians. Before cooking, it need only be washed, both ends cut off, and then usually sliced about ½ inch thick. It is frequently cooked in lightly salted boiling water and great care should be taken not to overcook it. Zucchini is deceptive in that it will soften considerably after it is drained, and 4 or 5 minutes is usually sufficient to tenderize it.

1827. ZUCCHINI CASALINGA
Zucchine alla casalinga

2 pounds zucchini, washed and sliced
4 tablespoons oil
4 tablespoons butter
½ cup grated Parmesan cheese
3 tablespoons chopped basil
Salt and freshly ground pepper

Heat the butter and oil in a very large frying pan over moderate heat, add the zucchini, season with salt and pepper, and shake the pan rather briskly for about 5 minutes so that the zucchini will be tossed in the pan and will cook evenly. Do not overcook. Sprinkle with the grated cheese and the basil, toss lightly, and then turn it out into a hot vegetable dish. *Serves* 6.

1828. ZUCCHINI FRITTERS CARNACINA
Zucchine fritte a modo mio

2 pounds zucchini, quartered lengthwise if small, or
    cut into eighths lengthwise if large
A marinade:
  1 cup oil
  ⅓ cup lemon juice
  2 tablespoons chopped parsley
  1 teaspoon salt
  ¼ teaspoon freshly ground pepper
2 cups Fritter Batter [No. 275]
Fat for deep frying
3 lemons, quartered

Marinate the zucchini in the marinade for 2 hours, drain and dry thoroughly, dip the pieces in fritter batter, and drop them in deep hot (375°) fat until golden brown. Heap them up on a hot serving platter and garnish with the lemon quarters. *Serves* 6.

1829. ZUCCHINI AU GRATIN ITALIANA
Zucchine gratinate all'italiana

2 pounds zucchini, sliced
6 tablespoons butter
½ cup heavy cream, or Brown Stock [No. 4]
½ cup grated Parmesan cheese
2 eggs, slightly beaten
Salt and freshly ground pepper

Boil the zucchini in lightly salted water for about 3 minutes, leaving it slightly underdone. Drain it in a colander for 5 minutes. Heat the butter in a very large frying pan over medium heat, add the zucchini, season with salt and pepper, and heat for 2 minutes, tossing it lightly. Add the cream and eggs and stir very lightly for another minute, or until the eggs are well distributed and appear somewhat curdled. Turn the zucchini out into a shallow casserole, sprinkle with the grated cheese, brown very briefly under a high broiler flame, and serve in the casserole. *Serves* 6.

1830. ZUCCHINI WITH MIXED HERBS
Zucchine con erbe fini

Prepare in the same manner as described in Zucchini Casalinga [No. 1827], omitting the cheese and adding, in addition to the basil, ½ cup of any desired mixed freshly chopped herbs, such as tarragon, oregano, marjoram, thyme, parsley, etc. *Serves* 6.

1831. ZUCCHINI INGLESE
Zucchine all'inglese

2 pounds zucchini, sliced
½ cup butter, softened
Salt and freshly ground pepper

Boil the zucchini in lightly salted water for about 5 minutes, or until it is just tender. Drain, put it in a hot vegetable dish, season with salt and pepper, and serve the butter on the side. *Serves* 6.

1832. ZUCCHINI WITH OREGANO
Zucchine all'origano

Prepare in the same manner as described in Zucchini Casalinga [No. 1827], adding 2 chopped cloves of garlic to the butter and oil before cooking the zucchini and substituting oregano for the basil. *Serves* 6.

1833. ZUCCHINI ROMANA
Zucchine al tegame alla romana

2 pounds zucchini, sliced
4 tablespoons oil
1 onion, chopped
6 ripe tomatoes, peeled, seeded, drained, and chopped
2 tablespoons chopped parsley
Salt and freshly ground pepper

Heat the oil in a casserole over medium heat, add the chopped onion, and cook until the onion begins to color. Add the tomatoes, season with salt and pepper, and simmer for 15 minutes. Add the zucchini, season again with salt and pepper, and stir frequently for about 5 minutes, or until the zucchini is just tender. Sprinkle with parsley and serve in the casserole. *Serves* 6.

1834. SAUTÉED ZUCCHINI
Zucchine fritte

2 pounds zucchini, sliced or, if small, quartered
    lengthwise
Flour

6 tablespoons oil
Salt and freshly ground pepper

Heat the oil until smoking hot in a very large frying pan over fairly high heat. Dust the pieces of zucchini with flour and brown them quickly in the oil. Brown only a few at a time so that they are not crowded in the pan, remove them to a hot serving dish with a slotted spoon, and continue until all are browned. Sprinkle lightly with salt and pepper and serve immediately. *Serves* 6.

1835. SCALLOPED ZUCCHINI AND TOMATOES
Zucchine e pomodori gratinati

2 pounds zucchini, sliced
6 ripe tomatoes, peeled and sliced
6 tablespoons oil
1½ cups fresh breadcrumbs
Salt and freshly ground pepper

Heat 3 tablespoons of the oil in a very large frying pan over fairly high heat until smoking hot and very quickly brown the tomatoes for a few seconds on each side. Arrange a layer of them in a shallow baking dish, season it with salt and pepper, cover with a layer of zucchini, season again with salt and pepper, and continue forming layers until all are used up, ending with a layer of the tomatoes. Sprinkle the top with breadcrumbs, sprinkle with the remaining oil, and bake in a moderate (350°) oven for about 40 minutes. If the top is not browned in this time, run the dish briefly under a high broiler flame. Serve in the baking dish. *Serves* 6.

1836. SCALLOPED ZUCCHINI WITH EGGPLANT, PEPPERS, AND TOMATOES
Legumi in fricassea

6 medium zucchini, sliced
1 eggplant, peeled, sliced, cut into 2-inch squares, and
    drained of moisture (*see* page 559)
½ cup oil
2 onions, chopped
2 cloves garlic, crushed in the garlic-press
3 sweet peppers, roasted, scraped, seeded, and
    cut into strips [*see* No. 145]
6 ripe tomatoes, peeled, seeded, drained, and chopped
1 tablespoon chopped rosemary (or 1 teaspoon dried)
Salt and freshly ground pepper
2 tablespoons chopped basil
2 tablespoons chopped parsley

Heat 3 tablespoons of the oil in a large heavy casserole over medium heat, add the onion and garlic, and cook until the onion begins to color. Add the peppers and sauté gently for 3 minutes. Add the tomatoes and rosemary, season with salt and pepper, and simmer for 15 minutes. Dust the slices of zucchini and eggplant with flour and brown them very quickly in smoking hot oil in a very large frying pan over high heat; cook only a few slices at a time so that they are not crowded in the pan, drain them on absorbent paper when they are browned, and season them with salt and pepper. When they are all browned, add them to the casserole with the tomatoes and peppers, mix lightly, simmer for 1 minute, sprinkle with the chopped basil and parsley, and serve in the casserole. *Serves* 6.

SALADS

Insalate

The simplest and most popular salad in Italy, as in America, is fresh greens dressed with oil and vinegar and seasoned with salt and pepper. We are including in this section, however, an array of salads, some simple, some very complicated, some known throughout the world, and some very specially Italian. Many of these are substantial enough to serve as a luncheon entrée or as the main dish of a cold buffet.

The standard dressing for a basic salad of greens is Sauce Vinaigrette [No. 99]. Its proportions of 3 parts oil to 1 part vinegar or lemon juice may be varied according to taste and, in addition to salt and pepper, it may be seasoned with fresh or dried herbs, mustard, garlic, shallots, etc. The possible variations of seasonings are almost infinite. Italians frequently place separate cruets of oil and vinegar with a variety of seasonings on the table and allow each guest to dress his own greens. Many Italian gourmets prefer this to a pre-mixed dressing and, indeed, have strong feelings as to whether the vinegar should be poured over the greens first so that they absorb it slightly or the greens coated first with oil so that they are somewhat insulated from the vinegar. Salads mixed at table in this fashion tend to have a fresher taste, but they are perhaps less subtle than when dressed with oil and vinegar and pre-mixed with herbs and other seasonings whose flavors have intermingled and blended. Another popular variation is to pre-season oil with whole cloves of garlic and/or shallots and allow it to stand for several hours before mixing it with vinegar and other desired seasonings just before serving.

Greens for a salad should always be thoroughly washed and totally dried well in advance of serving. Never pour a dressing over freshly washed greens, as the water that clings to the leaves will dissipate the flavors of the dressing. Greens may be partially dried by shaking or swinging them in a wire salad basket, but the simplest method of drying them is to spread them out on an absorbent towel, roll them up in the towel, and place them in the refrigerator for at least 1 hour before serving. Even slightly wilted greens will be crisped by this method.

Throughout this section we shall not specify a particular type of green to be used. Boston lettuce would be a first choice for many of the recipes in this section because of its sweetness and tenderness, but romaine, Bibb, or even iceberg lettuce may be successfully substituted. Chicory, watercress, dandelion leaves, and field lettuce all have a delicious but slightly bitterish taste and are perhaps better reserved for mixed green salads rather than for the more complicated salads that contain vegetables, meat, fish, or fruits.

Belgian Endives   Chicory or Curly Endive   Boston Lettuce

Romaine   Lamb's Tongues or Field Lettuce (Arugula)   Escarole

In any case, the choice of a green should be dictated largely by what is freshly available.

In all of the recipes in this section the ingredients should be well chilled before being used, unless otherwise specified. Any cooked ingredients should be prepared well in advance to allow them time to cool and then should be chilled in the refrigerator.

1837. SALAD ALBA
Insalata alla moda d'Alba

1 head lettuce, leaves separated, washed, and dried
18 cooked green asparagus tips (*see* page 544)
6 stalks celery, cut into 2-inch lengths and then into julienne strips
6 white Alba truffles, sliced
¾ cup Sauce Vinaigrette [No. 99]

Line salad bowl with the lettuce leaves and arrange the asparagus tips, julienne strips of celery, and white truffles over them. Pour the Vinaigrette over them and mix at the table. *Serves* 6.

1838. ALABAMA SALAD
Insalata Alabama

6 red apples
1 small cantaloupe (or any desired available melon)
2 bananas
½ cup nut meats, coarsely chopped
1 cup black raspberries, cleaned
1½ cups Sauce Vinaigrette [No. 99], made with lemon juice and seasoned with a pinch of sugar
1 cup cottage cheese
1 lemon
6 large lettuce leaves

Slice off the top ¼ of each of the apples and reserve these tops as lids. Throughout the following preparation, rub any exposed part of the apple with lemon juice to prevent its darkening. Using a very small melon ball cutter, cut out small balls from the apples and drop them into the prepared Vinaigrette sauce, discarding the central core and seeds as the balls are removed. When as many balls as possible have been

598

removed from each apple, trim it neatly so that it forms a shell about $\frac{1}{4}$ inch thick. Using a slightly larger cutter, cut out balls from the melon and bananas and drop them in the Vinaigrette. Add the nut meats, raspberries, and the cottage cheese dropped by small spoonsful. Mix very lightly and fill each of the apple shells with this mixture, and cover with their lids. Line a serving platter with chopped ice, arrange the lettuce leaves on the ice, and place 1 apple on each of the leaves. *Serves* 6.

1839. SALAD AMERICANA
Insalata americana

6 ripe tomatoes, sliced
6 "new" potatoes, boiled and sliced
4 stalks celery, cut into julienne strips
4 hard-boiled eggs, sliced
1 Bermuda onion, thinly sliced and broken into rings
1 cup Sauce Vinaigrette [No. 99]

Arrange the tomatoes, potatoes, and the celery attractively in a salad bowl. Cover with slices of hard-boiled egg and onion rings, pour the Vinaigrette sauce over, and mix at the table. *Serves* 6.

1840. APPETIZING SALAD
Insalata appetitosa

1 head lettuce, leaves separated, washed, and dried
6 cooked beets (*see* page 549), sliced
6 stalks celery, cut into short julienne strips
4 white Alba truffles, sliced
1 cup chopped smoked tongue
1 cup chopped cooked ham
2 cups Mayonnaise [No. 77], slightly thinned with $\frac{1}{4}$ cup heavy cream and 3 tablespoons tomato catsup

Mix all of the ingredients, except the lettuce leaves, lightly in a bowl. Line a salad bowl with the leaves, heap the mixed ingredients on them in a mound, and chill for 1 hour. *Serves* 6.

1841. ARGENTINE SALAD
Insalata argentina

1 celeriac (celery root), sliced and boiled in lightly salted water until tender
1 cucumber, peeled, sliced, soaked for $\frac{1}{2}$ hour in salted water, and well dried
6 cooked artichoke hearts (*see* page 539)
6 hard-boiled eggs, the whites sliced into rings and the yolks crumbled

6 stalks celery, cut in short julienne strips
4 cooked beets (*see* page 549), sliced
4 small Belgian endives, leaves separated
1$\frac{1}{2}$ cups Sauce Vinaigrette [No. 99], made with lemon juice
$\frac{1}{4}$ cup sliced pitted olives
$\frac{1}{4}$ cup chopped gherkins

Heap the celeriac in the center of a large shallow salad bowl and surround it with separate circles of cucumbers, artichoke hearts, egg whites, celery, beets, and endives in that order. Sprinkle with the crumbled egg yolks and chill until cold. Mix the Vinaigrette sauce with the olives and pickles, pour over the various ingredients in the bowl, and mix at the table. *Serves* 6.

1842. ARTICHOKE AND TRUFFLE SALAD
Insalata di carciofi crudi e tartufi

12 raw baby artichoke hearts (*see* page 539), sliced
6 white Alba truffles, sliced
1 cup Sauce Vinaigrette [No. 99], made with lemon juice

Arrange the two vegetables attractively in a glass salad bowl, pour the dressing over them, and mix at the table. *Serves* 6.

NOTE: The artichoke hearts may also be cooked, if desired.

1843. ASPARAGUS TIP SALAD
Insalata di punte d'asparagi

36 asparagus tips, cooked until just tender (*see* page 544)
1 cup Sauce Vinaigrette [No. 99]
2 tablespoons chopped parsley
2 hard-boiled eggs, chopped

Arrange the asparagus tips attractively on a platter, pour over the Vinaigrette sauce, and sprinkle with the parsley and chopped egg. *Serves* 6.

1844. AUSTRIAN SALAD FANTASIA
Insalata fantasia austriaca

6 "new" potatoes, boiled in lightly salted water, drained, and diced
2 cups cooked dried white beans (*see* page 547)
$\frac{1}{2}$ head Savoy cabbage, shredded, boiled about 15 minutes in lightly salted water, and drained
2 cups chopped cooked spinach (*see* page 587)
1 cup prosciutto, cut into strips
3 hard-boiled eggs, sliced
2 cups Sauce Vinaigrette [No. 99]

Marinate each of the 4 vegetables separately in ½ cup of the Vinaigrette sauce for about 1 hour in the refrigerator. Arrange them attractively in separate heaps on a cold serving platter and garnish with the hard-boiled eggs and the prosciutto strips. *Serves* 6.

1845. BAGRATION SALAD
Insalata Bagration

3 cups diced cooked white meat of chicken
4 stalks celery, thinly sliced
4 cooked artichoke hearts (*see* page 539), sliced
½ pound elbow macaroni, cooked until *al dente* in lightly salted boiling water
½ cup chopped lean cooked ham
2 cups Mayonnaise [No. 77], mixed with 1 cup cold Tomato Sauce [No. 19]
3 hard-boiled eggs, chopped
3 tablespoons chopped parsley

Gently mix the vegetables, meats, and pasta in a bowl with the tomato mayonnaise, chill for 1 hour, and sprinkle with the chopped eggs and parsley. *Serves* 6.

1846. BEET AND RADISH SALAD
Insalata di barbabietole e rafano

6 cooked beets (*see* page 549), sliced
1½ cups sliced radishes
3 hard-boiled eggs, chopped
2 tablespoons chopped parsley
¾ cup Sauce Vinaigrette [No. 99]

Heap the slices of beets in the center of a salad bowl, surround them with the radishes, sprinkle with the

hard-boiled eggs and parsley, and pour the Vinaigrette over all. *Serves* 6.

1847. BELGIAN SALAD FANTASIA
Insalata fantasia belga

6 large Belgian endives, leaves separated
½ pound diced salt pork, parboiled for 15 minutes, well drained, and sautéed golden brown
¾ cup Sauce Vinaigrette [No. 99], mixed with 2 finely chopped hard-boiled eggs, 2 tablespoons chopped parsley, and 1 tablespoon chopped chervil (or 1 teaspoon dried)

Toss the leaves of endive lightly in dressing in a salad bowl, sprinkle with the salt pork dice, add the Vinaigrette, toss again, and serve at once. *Serves* 6.

1848. BUTTERFLY SALAD
Insalata Butterfly

6 large leaves green lettuce
6 stalks celery, finely sliced
4 cups watermelon balls
3 hard-boiled eggs, sliced
½ cup nut meats, broken in pieces
¾ cup Sauce Vinaigrette [No. 99], mixed with ½ cup Mayonnaise [No. 77]

Mix the celery, watermelon, hard-boiled eggs, and nut meats in a bowl. Arrange the lettuce leaves on a serving platter, spoon a generous amount of the mixed ingredients on each leaf, and top with a little of the dressing. *Serves* 6.

600

Alabama Salad (No. 1838): see page 598

1849. CALIFORNIA SALAD
Insalata californiana

12 lettuce leaves
12 cooked prunes, pitted
1½ cups fresh pineapple, sliced
4 stalks celery, diced
½ cup blanched almonds [*see* No. 2280]
¾ cup Sauce Vinaigrette [No. 99], made with
 orange juice instead of vinegar and seasoned
 with a pinch of paprika, ½ teaspoon dry mustard,
 and 2 tablespoons chopped parsley

Arrange all the ingredients decoratively in a salad bowl (*see* photograph at the right) and cover with the dressing. *Serves* 6.

California Salad (No. 1849)

1850. CAULIFOWER SALAD NAPOLETANA
Insalata di rinforzo alla napoletana

1 head cauliflower, trimmed into flowerets and
 cooked in boiling salted water [*see* No.1560]
12 anchovy fillets, washed free of salt [*see* No. 220]
12 pitted black olives
¼ cup tiny capers
3 hard-boiled eggs, quartered
1 cup Sauce Vinaigrette [No. 99]

Arrange the cauliflower in a salad bowl and garnish with the anchovies, olives, capers, and hard-boiled eggs. Pour the Vinaigrette sauce over and mix at the table. *Serves* 6.

1851. CELERY SALAD
Insalata di sedani

2 bunches celery, cut into short julienne strips and
 parboiled 5 minutes in lightly salted water
1 cup Sauce Vinaigrette [No. 99], seasoned with 2
 tablespoons prepared mustard (Dijon-type
 preferred) and 2 tablespoons chopped parsley

Marinate the celery in the marinade for 2 hours in the refrigerator, turning it occasionally. Transfer it to a salad bowl when ready to serve. *Serves* 6.

1852. CHEF'S SALAD
Insalata del cuoco

The flowers only from 3 pounds cooked broccoli
 (*see* page 550)
12 small radishes, cleaned
4 cooked beets (*see* page 549), diced

1 cup Sauce Vinaigrette [No. 99]
6 scallions, chopped

Arrange the broccoli in a salad bowl, surround with the radishes and the diced beets in small heaps, pour the Vinaigrette over, and sprinkle with the scallions. *Serves* 6.

1853. CINEMA SALAD
Insalata "Diva del cinema"

3 grapefruit, divided into sections
4 seedless oranges, divided into sections
6 fresh figs, peeled and sliced
6 cooked artichoke hearts (*see* page 539), sliced
6 large lettuce leaves
A dressing:
 1 cup heavy cream
 ⅓ cup lemon juice
 ½ teaspoon sugar

Serve this salad in individual portions in 6 small salad bowls. Put a lettuce leaf in each, add a few of the grapefruit and orange sections, top with the figs and artichoke hearts, and pour a little of the dressing over each. *Serves* 6.

601

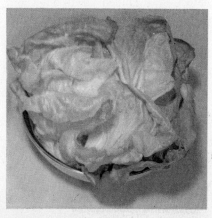
Boston lettuce, one of the best salad greens commonly available throughout the year

1854. SALAD CONTADINA
Insalata alla contadina

1 pound "new" potatoes, boiled and sliced
1 pound string beans, cooked in lightly salted boiling
    water
2 cups cooked black-eyed beans (*see* page 547)
3 tomatoes, peeled and sliced
1 cup Sauce Vinaigrette [No. 99]
1 Bermuda onion, sliced and broken into rings
2 tablespoons chopped basil

Toss the potatoes, beans, and black-eyed beans with
the Vinaigrette sauce in a salad bowl, surround with
a decorative ring of the tomatoes and onions, and
sprinkle with the basil. *Serves* 6.

1855. CURATE'S SALAD
Insalata del curato

1 head chicory, leaves separated, washed, and
    dried
6 radishes, sliced
1/2 cup thin strips of Swiss cheese
1/2 cup finely diced gorgonzola cheese
2 slices stale bread, rubbed with a cut clove of garlic
    and then broken into small pieces
3/4 cup Sauce Vinaigrette [No. 99]

Toss all of the ingredients lightly in a salad bowl.
Serves 6.

1856. SALAD ECCITANTE
Insalata eccitante

1 pound "new" potatoes, boiled and sliced
12 anchovy fillets, washed free of salt [*see* No. 220]
2 mackerel fillets steamed in 1/2 cup white wine,
    cooled, and flaked
3/4 cup Sauce Vinaigrette [No. 99], seasoned with
    1/2 teaspoon dry mustard
6 scallions, minced
2 tablespoons chopped basil
2 tablespoons chopped parsley

Arrange the potatoes in a chilled salad bowl and
decorate the top with the anchovy fillets and the
flaked mackerel. Pour the Vinaigrette sauce over,
sprinkle with the minced scallions and chopped herbs,
and mix at the table. *Serves* 6.

1857. EPICUREAN SALAD
Insalata "Epicuro"

2 pounds "new" potatoes, unpeeled, boiled until
    tender, drained, peeled, and sliced while still hot
1/4 cup Marsala wine, mixed with 2 tablespoons dry
    white wine
2 onions, chopped
2 stalks celery, very finely sliced
2 tablespoons chopped basil
1 tablespoon chopped truffle [or No. 1819a]
1 cup Sauce Vinaigrette [No. 99]

Sprinkle the hot potato slices in a salad bowl with the
Marsala and white wine and toss lightly until they
absorb the wines. Add the onion, celery, basil, truffle,
and Vinaigrette; mix lightly; and serve at room temperature. *Serves* 6.

1858. FARMER'S SALAD FANTASIA
Insalata fantasia del fattore

1 large head lettuce, leaves separated, washed, and
    dried
1/4 cup gorgonzola cheese
1/2 cup heavy cream
1/2 cup oil
2 tablespoons vinegar
1 tablespoon chopped tarragon (or 1 teaspoon dried)
1 tablespoon chopped chervil (or 1 teaspoon dried)
Salt and freshly ground pepper

Mash the cheese in a bowl with a fork and slowly blend
in the cream until the mixture is smooth. Beat in the
oil, drop by drop, add the vinegar and the chopped
herbs, and season to taste with salt and pepper. Pour
this dressing over the lettuce in a salad bowl and serve
at once. *Serves* 6.

1859. FESTIVAL SALAD
Insalata festival

1 pound button mushrooms, gently sautéed in
    3 tablespoons oil for 10 minutes and chilled
3 stalks celery, very thinly sliced
1/2 cup slivers of Gruyère cheese
3/4 cup Sauce Vinaigrette [No. 99]
    made with lemon juice
6 large lettuce leaves
2 truffles, chopped

Toss the mushrooms with the celery, cheese, and the
Vinaigrette sauce in a bowl. Arrange the lettuce leaves
on a serving platter, fill each with the mushroom mixture, and sprinkle with the truffles. *Serves* 6.

1860. SALAD FIAMMINGA
Insalata fiamminga

8 tiny heads of Bibb lettuce, washed and dried
12 anchovy fillets, washed free of salt [*see* No. 220]
18 small cooked shrimp, peeled and de-veined
    (*see* page 340)
3 hard-boiled eggs, sliced
3 hard-boiled egg yolks
3 tablespoons prepared mustard (Dijon-type preferred)
1 teaspoon salt
1/4 teaspoon freshly ground pepper
2 tablespoons brandy
2 tablespoons dry white wine
3/4 cup oil

Mash the hard-boiled egg yolks in a bowl with a fork and blend in the prepared mustard. Beat in the oil, drop by drop, alternating it with the brandy and wine, as the mixture becomes thick. Season with salt and pepper and chill in the refrigerator. Put the lettuce in a large salad bowl and arrange the hard-boiled eggs, shrimp, and anchovies decoratively on top (*see* photograph on page 604). Serve the chilled dressing on the side. *Serves* 6.

1861. SALAD GENOVESE
Cappon magro

1 1/2 cups cooked oyster plant (*see* page 574)
1 1/2 cups cooked beets (*see* page 549)
1 1/2 cups cooked string beans (*see* page 589)
1 1/2 cups cooked cauliflower flowerets [*see* No. 1560]
1 cup Sauce Vinaigrette [No. 99]
2 cloves garlic, halved
3 cups flaked cooked fish (halibut, salmon, or any
    desired kind)
18 cooked shrimp, shelled and de-veined (*see* page 340)
6 stalks celery, cut into short julienne strips
1 cup pitted ripe olives
12 anchovy fillets, soaked free of salt [*see* No. 220]
4 hard-boiled eggs, quartered
6 lettuce hearts
3 ripe tomatoes, sliced
3 cups Pesto Genovese [No. 93]

Put the oyster plant, beets, beans, and cauliflower in separate bowls and mix each with 1/4 cup of Vinaigrette. Rub a very large, deep platter with 2 cut cloves of garlic and arrange the 4 vegetables in the center. Surround them with a circle of the flaked fish and shrimp, and then garnish the platter decoratively with the celery, olives, anchovies, hard-boiled eggs, lettuce, and tomatoes. Serve the Pesto sauce on the side. *Serves* 8.

1862. SALAD GERMANA
Insalata Germana

1 small head lettuce, leaves separated, washed, and
    dried
18 cooked asparagus tips (*see* page 544)
2 cups cooked string beans (*see* page 589)
1 small head cauliflower, broken into flowerets and
    cooked [*see* No. 1560]
1 bunch watercress
1 cup red radishes, sliced
2 cups Mayonnaise [No. 77], thinned with 1/2 cup
    Sauce Vinaigrette [No. 99] and seasoned with
    1 tablespoon chopped taragon

Arrange the various cooked vegetables decoratively on a serving platter, garnish with the sliced radishes, and surround with lettuce leaves and watercress. Pour the dressing over and mix at the table. *Serves* 6.

1863. SALAD GOURMET
Insalata alla ghiottona

1 bunch chicory, leaves separated, washed, and dried
1/4 cup chopped scallions
1/2 pound diced salt pork, parboiled for 15 minutes,
    drained, and sautéed golden brown
1/2 cup Sauce Vinaigrette [No. 99]

Arrange the chicory in a salad bowl, sprinkle with the scallions and browned salt pork dice, and pour the Vinaigrette over. *Serves* 6.

1864. SALAD IN HALF-MOURNING
Insalata demi-deuil

Juice of 1 lemon
2 tablespoons prepared mustard (Dijon-type preferred)
1 1/2 cups cold Cream Sauce [No. 55]
1/2 cup heavy cream
1 1/2 pounds "new" potatoes, boiled and sliced
4 very large black truffles, sliced
1 truffle, chopped

Beat the lemon juice and the mustard into the cream sauce and then thin with sufficient heavy cream to make it of a pouring consistency. Toss the potatoes lightly with the sliced truffles in a salad bowl, cover with the cream sauce, and sprinkle with the chopped truffles. *Serves* 6.

603

Salad Musetta (No. 1873): see page 606　　　*Salad Fiamminga (No. 1860): see page 603*

1865. HEARTS OF LETTUCE SALAD WITH TOMATOES
Insalata di cuori di lattuga e pomodori

6 small hearts of lettuce, cut in half
6 ripe tomatoes, peeled and quartered
¾ cup Sauce Vinaigrette [No. 99], seasoned with
　　1 tablespoon each chopped basil and oregano
　　(or 1 teaspoon each dried)

Arrange the lettuce in a salad bowl, place the tomato quarters on top, pour the dressing over, and mix at the table. *Serves 6.*

1866. JAPANESE SALAD
Insalata giapponese

6 large lettuce leaves
6 slices fresh pineapple
Juice of ½ lemon
3 large ripe tomatoes, peeled and sliced
Pinch sugar
24 sections from seedless oranges
1 cup Sauce Vinaigrette [No. 99], blended with
　　¼ cup heavy cream

Arrange the lettuce leaves on a large serving platter, cover each with 3 tomato slices seasoned with sugar, place a slice of pineapple on each of the 3 tomato slices, squeeze a little lemon juice on the pineapple, and garnish each leaf with 4 orange sections (*see* photograph opposite).　Serve the vinaigrette sauce on the side. *Serves 6.*

1867. HOLLYWOOD SALAD
Insalata Hollywood

6 large lettuce leaves
1 carrot, grated
1½ cups fresh pineapple cubes
1 can hearts of palm, drained
2 avocado pears, peeled and sliced
½ cup freshly shelled almonds
1 cup Sauce Vinaigrette [No. 99], made with grape-
　　fruit juice instead of vinegar and seasoned with
　　½ teaspoon dry mustard and ½ teaspoon paprika

Arrange the lettuce leaves on a serving platter. Toss all the remaining ingredients lightly in a bowl and then place a generous amount in each of the leaves. *Serves 6.*

1868. HINDU SALAD
Insalata indiana

4 ripe tomatoes, sliced
6 stalks white celery, thinly sliced
6 cooked beets (*see* page 549), cut into strips
18 cooked asparagus tips (*see* page 544)
2 onions, broken into rings
2 green peppers, roasted, scraped, seeded
　　[*see* No. 145], and cut into strips
2 cups Mayonnaise [No. 77], mixed with ¼ cup
　　minced onion

Arrange the various ingredients decoratively in a salad bowl (*see* photograph opposite) and serve the mayonnaise on the side. *Serves 6.*

604

1869. SALAD LAKMÉ
Insalata Lakmé

1 head of cauliflower, broken into flowerets and
    cooked [*see* No. 1560]
12 tiny red radishes
1 bunch watercress
¾ cup Sauce Vinaigrette [No. 99], mixed with
    3 tablespoons heavy cream

Heap the cauliflower flowerets in the center of a salad
bowl, make a circle of small red radishes around it,
garnish with small bunches of watercress, and pour
the dressing over. *Serves 6.*

1870. SALAD LILY
Insalata Lily

6 white hearts of lettuce, cut in half
1 pound cooked shrimp (*see* page 340), shelled and
    de-veined (reserving the shells)
½ cup oil
2 tablespoons lemon juice
1 drop red vegetable coloring
4 tablespoons heavy cream
2 hard-boiled eggs, chopped
1 tablespoon chopped marjoram (or substitute
    parsley)
Salt and freshly ground pepper

Pound the (cooked) shrimp shells thoroughly in a
mortar and then continue pounding while adding the
oil, bit by bit (or blend the shells and oil for a few
seconds in an electric blender). Pour the oil through
several thicknesses of dampened cheesecloth into a
bowl, add the lemon juice and vegetable coloring,
season to taste with salt and pepper, and then slowly
beat in the cream. Arrange the lettuce in a salad bowl,
place the shrimp on top, pour the prepared dressing
over, and sprinkle with the chopped egg and marjoram.
Serves 6.

1871. SALAD MARIA THERESA
Insalata Maria Teresa

1 pound celeriac (celery root), sliced and cooked until
    tender in lightly salted boiling water
1½ cups Mayonnaise [No. 77]
3 hearts of lettuce, quartered
3 hard-boiled eggs, quartered
1½ cups julienne strips of cooked chicken meat
2 white truffles, sliced
2 black truffles, sliced
½ cup Sauce Vinaigrette [No. 99], made with
    lemon juice

Mix the celeriac with the mayonnaise and arrange it
in the center of a large serving platter. Toss half of
the Vinaigrette with the hearts of lettuce and the other
half separately with the strips of chicken meat. Arrange these and the hard-boiled eggs decoratively
around the celeriac and garnish the top of the celeriac
with the truffles. *Serves 6.*

1872. SALAD MELBA
Insalata "Melba"

6 large lettuce leaves
½ cup fresh pineapple cubes
3 cooked artichoke hearts (*see* page 539), sliced
1 cup pitted sour cherries, cut in half
1 cup raspberries
½ cup blanched almonds [*see* No. 2280], halved
½ cup Sauce Vinaigrette [No. 99], made with lemon
    juice and blended with ½ cup Mayonnaise
    [No. 77]

Arrange the lettuce leaves on a serving platter. Toss
all the remaining ingredients lightly in a bowl and
spoon a generous amount into each leaf. *Serves 6.*

605

Japanese Salad (No. 1866)   *Hindu Salad (No. 1868)*

1873. SALAD MUSETTA
Insalata fantasia di Musetta

6 endives, cut into 1-inch slices
6 cooked artichoke hearts (*see* page 539), sliced
4 "new" potatoes, boiled and sliced
1 cup pitted black olives
3 tomatoes, sliced
1 cup Sauce Vinaigrette [No. 99]

Arrange the various ingredients decoratively in a salad bowl (*see* photograph on page 604) and serve the Vinaigrette on the side. *Serves* 6.

1874. SALAD NIÇOISE
Insalata nizzarda

1 pound cooked string beans (*see* page 589), cut in
    pieces and chilled
1 pound "new" potatoes, boiled and diced
3 ripe tomatoes, quartered
1 tablespoon capers
1 cup pitted green olives
12 anchovy fillets, washed free of salt [*see* No. 220]
1 cup Sauce Vinaigrette [No. 99]

Mix the beans and potatoes lightly together with the Vinaigrette in a salad bowl, sprinkle with the capers, and garnish with the tomatoes, olives, and anchovy fillets. *Serves* 6.

1875. ORANGE SALAD
Insalata di arancie

6 navel oranges
1 medium Bermuda onion
½ cup dry sherry wine
Juice of 1 lemon, strained
⅓ cup neutral-tasting vegetable oil (or walnut oil)
3 tablespoons orange blossom honey
¼ teaspoon freshly ground white pepper
Optional: 3 tablespoons Pernod (or any anise liqueur)
1 bunch watercress, washed and trimmed

Carefully peel the oranges and remove all traces of the bitter white membrane. Slice the onion very thinly and separate the slices into rings. Place the rings in a sieve and run cold water over them for 5 minutes. Pat dry on paper towels, place in a small bowl, and pour over the sherry. Cover bowl and marinate the onions for 2 hours.

Meanwhile, place the lemon juice, oil, honey, pepper, and optional liqueur in a bowl. Add 2 tablespoons of

the sherry marinade from the onions, and beat with a wire whisk until blended. Let stand until the onions have completed their marination.

Before serving, arrange the watercress in a shallow glass bowl, slice the oranges very thinly and lay them over the watercress in overlapping circles. Drain the sherry from the onions (it can be reserved for use in a stew or sauce) and scatter the onion rings over the oranges. Beat the dressing and pour over all. Mix at table. *Serves* 6.

1876. RADISH AND GRUYÉRE CHEESE SALAD
Insalata di radicchio e groviera

1 slice stale bread
1 clove garlic
2 cups radishes, sliced
½ cup thin strips of Gruyère cheese
½ cup Sauce Vinaigrette [No. 99]

Rub the slice of bread with a cut side of the clove of garlic, break it into pieces, and put it in a salad bowl with the radishes and strips of cheese. Add the Vinaigrette and mix well. *Serves* 4.

1877. RADISH SALAD TREVISO
Insalata di radicchio di Treviso

¾ cup Sauce Vinaigrette [No. 99], seasoned with
    3 tablespoons prepared mustard (Dijon-type
    preferred), 1 tablespoon anchovy paste, and
    1 chopped clove of garlic
1 egg yolk
2 cups radishes, sliced

Beat the egg yolk in a bowl and slowly pour the seasoned Vinaigrette sauce over it, beating constantly. Mix this dressing thoroughly with the radishes in a salad bowl. *Serves* 4.

1878. RED CABBAGE SALAD
Insalata di cavoli rossi

1 small red cabbage, shredded
Salt
2 cups vinegar, boiled and cooled
1 bay leaf, crumbled
2 cloves garlic, crushed in the garlic-press

Sprinkle the cabbage very generously with salt and allow it to sit in a covered bowl for 48 hours. Wash it, drain it, and squeeze firmly to remove excess moisture. Pour the vinegar over it in a bowl, add the garlic and bay leaf, and marinate for 24 hours before serving. *Serves* 6.

1879. RUSSIAN SALAD
Insalata russa

1 cup diced cooked carrots [*see* No. 1644]
1 cup diced cooked turnips [*see* No. 1824]
1 cup cooked string beans (*see* page 589)
1 cup cooked peas (*see* page 575)
$\frac{1}{4}$ pound mushrooms, gently sautéed in 2 tablespoons butter for 8 minutes
4 "new" potatoes, boiled and diced
1 cup diced cooked lobster meat
$\frac{1}{2}$ cup diced pickled tongue
$\frac{1}{2}$ cup sliced gherkins
2 tablespoons very tiny capers
6 anchovy fillets, washed free of salt [*see* No. 220]
$\frac{1}{2}$ cup diced cooked beets (*see* page 549)
3 cups Mayonnaise [No. 77]

Mix the various ingredients, except the gherkins, capers, anchovies, and beets, in a bowl with $2\frac{1}{2}$ cups of the mayonnaise. They should be sufficiently well bound by the mayonnaise so that they will hold their shape. Heap them up in a mound on a large serving platter, cover with a thin coat of the remaining mayonnaise, and garnish the surface decoratively with the gherkins, capers, anchovies, and beets. *Serves* 8.

1880. SALAD SALLY LOU
Insalata "Sally Lou"

1 head lettuce, leaves separated, washed, and dried
4 stalks celery, thinly sliced
2 sweet peppers, roasted, peeled, seeded, and cut into strips [*see* No. 145]
3 hard-boiled eggs, quartered
1 cup finely diced Swiss or bland cheddar cheese

1 onion, sliced and broken into rings
1 cup Sauce Vinaigrette [No. 99]

Place the lettuce in a salad bowl, arrange the various ingredients decoratively on top, pour the Vinaigrette over, and mix at the table. *Serves* 6.

1881. SARATOGA SALAD
Insalata Saratoga

6 large lettuce leaves
2 stalks celery, thinly sliced
4 cooked beets (*see* page 549), diced
1 cup cooked string beans (*see* page 589)
3 fresh pears, peeled, cored, and sliced
$\frac{1}{2}$ cup chopped nut meats
1 cup Sauce Vinaigrette [No. 99], blended with 2 tablespoons heavy cream

Put each of the lettuce leaves on an individual salad plate. Mix the various ingredients gently with the Vinaigrette and spoon a generous amount over each of the leaves. *Serves* 6.

1882. SALAD SICILIANA
Insalata alla siciliana

6 large tomatoes
1 pound mushrooms, sliced, gently sautéed in 4 tablespoons oil for 10 minutes, and cooled
1 cup chopped pickles
4 stalks celery, finely sliced
1 pound cooked string beans (*see* page 589)
1 cup Sauce Vinaigrette [No. 99]
1 cup Mayonnaise [No. 77]
12 anchovy fillets, washed free of salt [*see* No. 220]
2 tablespoons tiny capers
12 thin slices of pickle
Salt and freshly ground pepper

Cut off the top $\frac{1}{4}$ of each of the tomatoes and reserve the tops as lids. Scoop out most of the pulp from the tomatoes, leaving a case about $\frac{1}{4}$ inch thick, and season the cases with salt and pepper. Toss the mushrooms, chopped pickles, celery, and string beans with the Vinaigrette in a bowl and stuff the tomatoes with part of this mixture. Put the lids on the tomatoes, arrange them around the edge of a large serving platter, heap the remaining vegetable mixture in a mound in the center of the platter, cover it with a thin coat of the mayonnaise, and decorate the surface of the mound with the anchovies, capers, and pickle slices. *Serves* 6.

1883. SUMMER SALAD
Insalata estiva

18 cooked asparagus tips (*see* page 544)
½ pound cooked string beans (*see* page 589)
6 cooked artichoke hearts (*see* page 539), sliced
3 ripe tomatoes, peeled, seeded, drained, and
    quartered
1 small cucumber, peeled and thinly sliced
1 cup Sauce Vinaigrette [No. 99], seasoned with
    2 tablespoons chopped basil or any desired fresh
    herb

Place the various ingredients in a salad bowl, pour the
Vinaigrette over, and toss lightly. *Serves* 6.

1884. TOMATO SALAD NAPOLETANA
Insalata di pomodori alla napoletana

6 large ripe tomatoes, peeled and sliced
1 cup Sauce Vinaigrette, seasoned with 2 cloves of
    chopped garlic and 2 tablespoons chopped basil

Arrange the tomatoes overlapping one another on a
large serving platter and pour the Vinaigrette over
them. *Serves* 6.

1885. TUTTI FRUTTI SALAD
Insalata "tutti frutti"

6 large lettuce leaves
1 cup pitted sweet red cherries
1 cup ripe strawberries
1½ cups cubed honeydew melon (or cantaloupe,
    Persian, etc.)
1 cup white seedless grapes
½ cup nut meats, coarsely chopped
1 cup Sauce Vinaigrette [No. 99], blended with ¼ cup
    heavy cream and 2 tablespoons maraschino liqueur

Arrange the lettuce leaves on a serving platter, toss the
various fruits and the nuts with the dressing in a bowl,
and spoon a generous amount onto each leaf. *Serves* 6.

1886. WALDORF SALAD
Insalata Waldorf

1½ cups diced apples
1½ cups finely sliced celery
1 cup coarsely chopped walnuts
1½ cups Mayonnaise [No. 77]

Mix all the ingredients in a salad bowl and chill until
very cold. *Serves* 6.

Chervil

Basil

Tarragon

SEE
VERSE
FOR
PTION

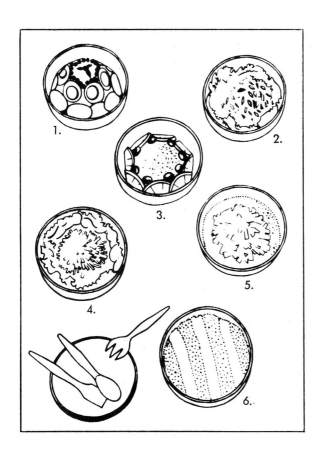

Suggested presentations for salads (see Nos. 1837–89). Many salads may be decorated or garnished along the general lines of those shown here. One must keep in mind, however, that the garnish should not be composed of ingredients inappropriate to the type of salad being served.

1. Sliced tomatoes, sliced hard boiled eggs, sliced pickles, peas, slices of black olives, and mayonnaise

2. Leaves of Boston lettuce and julienne strips of carrots, beets, green peppers, and celery

3. Sliced oranges and halved radishes

4. Boston lettuce, quartered tomatoes, and shredded scallions and Belgian endives

5. Chopped raw mushrooms, vertically sliced leaves of Belgian endive, and fresh tarragon leaves

6. Alternating bands of chopped hard-boiled egg yolks and whites

DESSERTS

DESSERTS
Dolci

Desserts play a smaller part in Italian homes than in American; the idea of building a whole meal around a culminating dessert, not unknown in the United States, is entirely alien to concepts of good eating and good cooking in Italy. Most meals at home there end with fruit or cheese, and this is also true of meals served in the majority of small restaurants and *trattorie*. Pastry making is so generally regarded as a specialized art that even in many larger restaurants an elaborate cake, tart, or *torta,* listed on the menu is often brought in from the local confectioner's, the *pasticceria*. The number of these shops and the frequency with which a steady stream of Italians visit them from early morning to late at night (sometimes to purchase a bite-sized pastry with or without espresso, sometimes to consume inordinate numbers even before a large meal) testify to the sweet tooth of the Italians, for all that it is not indulged at the end of regular meals. The range, delicacy, and richness of pastries in these shops have to be seen (and sampled) to be believed. Since *pasticceria* is more accurately translated as "sweet" or "confection," these shops often also sell chocolates, hard candies, and ice cream.

"Sweets" in Italian cooking include: hot sweets, usually prepared at home; cold sweets, which may be prepared either at home or at the pastry shop; "French" pastries and fine cookies (usually prepared at the confectioner's shop), mousses, bavarians, pies, cakes, tarts, and ices and ice creams.

This section will provide directions, in introductions to each subdivision, for the basic mixtures from which various specific recipes are derived. The opening section will provide the general directions for making a sweet raised dough, giving proportions for a more and a less rich, sweet product. Later subdivisions indicate the basic preparation for pastry dough, fritters, ice creams; for custard and bavarians; for gelatins; for almond preparations (a specialty of Italian as of French pastry making); meringues; sauces, etc. The full range of desserts—both those prepared in the home and the more professional productions of the confectioner—will be covered.

Except in pastry doughs, *all ingredients should be at room temperature*. If eggs are chilled, warm them by running hot tap water over them for 5 minutes. Butter or shortening will lose its chill faster if first cut into small pieces.

Freezing baked and unbaked cakes and pastries:

Since many homes are equipped with freezers, a time-saving device when a larger quantity than is immediately needed has been prepared, a word is included on various cakes and pastries that may be frozen before or after baking without impairing their flavor or delicacy.

Any of the pastry (non-yeast) doughs except cream-puff dough may be frozen without baking. Store these in amounts required (for 1 pie or for several tarts) or roll out and freeze in foil plates in the shape to be used eventually. Allow approximately 3 hours for frozen balls of dough to defrost; 20 minutes for the rolled and shaped dough.

Pies and tarts are best thawed and filled when ready to use. Eclairs and cream puffs may be filled and frozen, although they should not be kept more than 3 weeks if they have a custard or pastry cream filling. They may be frozen for twice this length of time if unfilled. Unfilled meringues may be kept frozen for months, but once filled with cream, 10 days should be the limit.

Cookies may be frozen baked or unbaked and will last in either form up to 6 months, the baked cookies even twice as long. They take less than $\frac{1}{2}$ hour to thaw.

Baked brioches, babas, and savarins may be kept frozen for months, up to a year; they should be frozen "dry," before they are steeped in liqueurs or syrups which are added after they are defrosted. Cakes, fully decorated, may be frozen for months, the freezing, however, depending upon the filling and icing. It is best to avoid freezing cakes with custard fillings. Butter icings and fillings keep frozen excellently for months at a time. Frostings made with confectioners' sugar or fondant are apt to become brittle and break. Uniced and unfilled layers may be frozen for periods as long as a year, thawed in 30 to 50 minutes (depending on size), then filled and decorated according to choice. This—with the exception of cakes with butter icings (which help to retain the cake's moisture)—is the safest method.

It goes without saying that all frozen cakes and pastries must be well sealed in airtight freezer bags or containers.

SWEET YEAST DOUGHS

Impasti

THE MATERIALS

Flour : Although Italian flour is available in both a more and a less white form, Italy has nothing comparable to the highly refined, bleached, powdery products available in the United States. Unbleached flour and the once common, but now rare, specifically marked "bread flour" is nearest the more natural Italian product which, containing more gluten, also requires more yeast and is slower in rising when used in yeast-raised cakes. The recipes given here have therefore been adapted to the American "all-purpose" flour, which should always be sifted at least once before measuring and, as in the baking of all cakes, sifted twice more when making delicate cakes. Unbleached flour is strongly recommended, as the bleached variety is too refined. Try not to use cake flour, as it is too powdery and its gluten content is too low.

Butter : In Italian baking as in all Italian cooking, this means unsalted butter, and the very best available.

Eggs : These are assumed to be the freshest possible; but where a particular point is made of the freshness, this quality is the determining factor in the result. As eggs vary greatly in size, it is assumed in these recipes that 1 extra-large egg is about $\frac{1}{4}$ cup.

Yeast : This may be either the fresh, compressed yeast (which is perishable and may not be kept too many days after purchase) or the dried yeast purchased in dated envelopes, which may be kept a considerable time if the envelopes are kept unopened in a cool place. The former provides 1 ounce, the latter about $\frac{1}{4}$ ounce, and both types will double the dough in approximately 3 hours if used with 1 to 2 cups of liquid and 3 to 4 cups of flour. Fresh yeast should be dissolved in warm water that is no higher than 85°, at which temperature the yeast should dissolve in about 5 minutes. This temperature is barely perceptible when a drop is touched to the inside of the wrist. Liquid for dissolving dry yeast should be distinctly warmer, from 105° to 115° (as directions on the package indicate) and takes 10 minutes before it foams, at which point it should be added to the recipe. Until familiar with the "feel" of the required liquid, use a thermometer.

Sugar : A teaspoon or more of sugar (if taken from the sugar in the recipe it may be up to 1 tablespoon) will speed the foaming of the yeast. Never rub the sugar into the yeast as it will bruise the fragile yeast cells. When the yeast has foamed, gently stir it through the liquid. Although a little sugar will hasten the foaming, too much sugar (with the yeast or in the recipe) will retard later rising, which explains why sweet doughs require more time to rise than plain doughs. Excessive amounts of butter in a recipe also inhibit rising.

Milk : When used in yeast-raised dough, milk should first be scalded (unless using evaporated milk—already canned at a high temperature—diluted with its equal quantity of water) or it may "sour" the mixture. Milk is scalded in a heavy-bottomed pan first rinsed in cold water and is ready when little bubbles appear around the edge or, if you are using a thermometer, at 150°.

BASIC PROCEDURES

Mixing : In most current American recipes, yeast is dissolved until it foams (see above), then added to the lukewarm liquid, just before the flour is added. The flour is added a cup at a time and very vigorously beaten in with the first 2 cups. The distribution and thorough incorporation of the yeast at this beginning stage influence its efficiency. In former times, and in occasional recipes today, the "sponge" method was used, by which the foaming yeast is added to $\frac{1}{2}$ to 1 cup of flour and set in a warm place until it bubbles, about 15 to 20 minutes. The classic Italian (and French) methods of preparing the basic sweet doughs—brioche, baba, savarin—are somewhat similar. By this method, 1 cake or envelope of yeast is softened in $\frac{1}{4}$ cup of warm water or milk, allowed to foam, and added to enough flour (up to 1 cup) to form a soft dough. This is rolled into a ball without over-handling, cut on the top with

2 shallow slashes forming a cross, set into a little bowl, covered, put in a warm place (80° to 90°) to double in volume (from 15 to 20 minutes). Occasionally—as in one recipe in this book—the ball of dough is dropped into a bowl of warm liquid (water or milk) and is ready for further use when it rises to the surface. In either case, the ball of dough or "leavening" is folded, beaten, or kneaded into the other ingredients which are mixed while the yeast is rising.

NOTE: Recently, a variety of dried yeast has come on the market that is "instantly" dissolved. It may be employed according to the directions printed on the envelope it is packed in.

Rising: The temperature at which leavened dough is set to rise is important: it should be even and free from sudden drafts. Rinse the bowl in which the dough is to be set with hot water and dry well. Rub the bowl lightly with shortening, putting a little more in the bottom than on the sides. Set the dough in the bowl with its top downward and coat it with the butter in the bottom of the bowl, then reverse the dough. The top is then buttered so as not to form a crust but keep elastic and permit the necessary rising and development of gluten. Cover the bowl lightly with a clean cloth, dry or dampened.

Leavened dough rises best in an 80° temperature, which is rarely found in the ordinary home. Setting the bowl of dough in the sunlight helps. Otherwise use the ancient method of setting the bowl into a deep pillow and surrounding it with a nest of pillows that rise above the bowl and may partially (but not wholly) cover it. These may be set next to a warm radiator, adjusting the pillows so that the mild warmth reaches the bowl. Never set dough to rise *on* a hot radiator or *in* a heated oven. One may place it in a cool oven with a pan of very hot water on the bottom, at least 1 foot away from the dough. Another aid in securing even heat is to use a heating pad, set at a low to moderate heat. If the internal or surrounding temperature at which the dough is raised is too hot, the dough may smell yeasty or turn sour; if the temperature is too low and the rising too long, texture may be sacrificed and the resultant product have large holes; it may even fall in the oven, giving a soggy result. Another, simpler, method is to set the bowl in a larger container of warm *(not hot!)* water.

Kneading: Leavened dough, unlike pastry which toughens with excessive handling, may be handled as much as you like. Indeed, if you are too busy to deal with the dough when it has risen properly the first time (it has so risen when two fingers pressed firmly into the top edge leave an impression that does not quickly disappear), you may punch it down and let it rise not only the second time that is usually required, but even a third. Two risings, however, and plenty of kneading (at least 8 minutes and, even better, 10 and up to 15) improve the texture and flavor of the product, so long as more flour than specified in the recipe is not added with the additional kneading. Such surplus flour may toughen the product or alter the flavor (since it may obscure the sugar and butter). As dough is kneaded it becomes more elastic and less sticky (so that additional flour is not needed) and is ready when it is shiny and slight bubbles appear under the surface.

Ovens should always be preheated at the desired temperature for at least 25 minutes before the cake or pastry is set into the oven.

BASIC RECIPES FOR SWEET YEAST-RAISED CAKES
Impasti di base

There is nothing difficult in the preparation of such classic yeast-raised sweet doughs as those for brioche, baba, and savarin. Brioche, however, requires a rest in the refrigerator overnight so that time must be allowed for its preparation. While all of these doughs may be kneaded in the usual fashion, they are best made in the Italian and French method, in which brioche dough is subjected to a slapping and paddling, and baba dough to a pulling that resembles the pulling of taffy.

1887. BABA DOUGH
Pasta per babà

2½ cups sifted all-purpose flour (remove 1 tablespoon for kneading with the butter, as noted below)
1 cake of fresh yeast or 1 envelope of dried yeast dissolved at temperatures indicated in introduction (page 611)
¼ cup milk, scalded and cooled to lukewarm
⅛ teaspoon salt
2 tablespoons sugar
4 eggs, lightly beaten
6 tablespoons butter, softened, kneaded with 1 tablespoon flour

Dissolve the yeast in a little water of the right temperature, add milk, and stir it into ½ cup of the flour to make a soft dough. Roll it into a ball, cut a

612

cross on the top, place it in a bowl, cover lightly, and set it in a warm place (80° to 90°) to rise: about 15 to 20 minutes. When it has risen, rinse a large bowl in very hot water, wipe dry, and put the rest of the flour into it. Make a well in the center and into it drop the sugar, salt, eggs, and the now-risen yeast ball. Using the fingers of the right hand slightly cupped (or use a wooden spoon if you prefer), mix the flour into the central liquids until all ingredients are thoroughly blended, pushing down any pieces of dough that stick to the side, and work in the butter. Then lift, pull, stretch, and slap the dough against the sides of the bowl; after about 15 minutes it will lose its stickiness and detach from the hands and become smooth and elastic. When it can be lifted in a single rope and pulled 12 inches apart without breaking, it has reached its proper elasticity (the gluten in the flour has been released). Form it into a ball, put it into a greased bowl, cover with greased wax paper and cover that with a clean cloth (see page 612), and set to rise in a warm place (see page 612) until it has doubled in bulk (it should be ready in about 1 hour).

The dough is now ready to be kneaded and put into baba molds (deep cylindrical pans) which it should fill ⅓ full, as described in Rum Babas [No. 1888]. *Makes 1 8-inch baba, or 15 small ones.*

NOTE: For baking instructions, see the following recipes.

1888. RUM BABAS
Babà al rhum

Double recipe of Baba Dough [No. 1887]
¾ cup currants (or seedless raisins), soaked for 1 hour
    in 3 tablespoons rum
1 tablespoon butter, softened

Sugar syrup:
  2 cups sugar
  2 cups water
  1 cup dark rum

Knead the currants or raisins into the dough after it has risen for the first time. Generously butter 2 8-inch baba molds (or 2 deep 8-inch fluted ring molds) and half-fill each with the dough. Cover lightly and set in a warm place to double in bulk (about 1 to 2 hours). When risen, bake in a moderate (350°) oven for 35 minutes (or bake for 10 minutes at 450°, reduce heat to 350°, and bake for another 15 to 20 minutes). The babas are done when a finger pressed to their surface leaves no impression, and when the sides of the cakes are slightly drawn away from the sides of the pans. Remove pans to a wire rack, and after the babas have cooled slightly (but are still a little warm), unmold them onto a large platter. Prick them all over with a skewer or knitting needle, and pour over the sugar syrup, made as follows: bring the water and sugar to a rolling boil over high heat in a small, heavy saucepan. Cook for 8 minutes, remove from fire, and add the dark rum. Slowly spoon the hot syrup over the babas gradually, so that it is absorbed and does not run down the sides. When all the syrup has been used up, put the babas back in their molds, prick their tops, and pour on the syrup left in the bottom of the platter. Let them stand for at least 1 hour to soak up this excess syrup. *Makes 2 8-inch babas.*

NOTE: Another syrup could be: 2 cups sugar boiled with 1½ cups water to 220° on the candy thermometer, removed from stove, and 1 cup dark rum poured into it. The babas may also be merely sprinkled with any preferred liquor or liqueur instead of the syrup (in which case they will not be as sweet or moist). If

Left to right: *Brioche with a "Head" (No. 1891):* see page 615. *Brioche Mousseline (No. 1895):* see page 616. *Rum Baba, baked in a large mold:* (see Nos. 1887 and 1888).

desired, they may also be iced (see picture) after they have soaked up the syrup. Mix 1 cup confectioners' sugar with 2 or 3 tablespoons heavy cream and dribble this over the tops of the cakes.

1889. DELICATE BRIOCHE DOUGH
Pasta per brioscia fine

This brioche should be reserved for special occasions since its preparation requires particular care. It is considered rather difficult to make, and requires 2 days. It must have 3 risings, the first taking up to 3 or 4 hours, the second in the refrigerator, and the third on the next day, before the brioche is to be baked. After the first rising it is placed in the refrigerator overnight (this may prove a convenience rather than a difficulty), closely covered. The peculiarity of this dough lies in its kneading [described in No. 1887], which is more like paddling, slapping, or beating than kneading in the usual sense of the term. This is accomplished with a flick of the wrist to bring the dough down hard on the board, or against the side of a large bowl. The dough is then grasped at its other end by the other hand, and brought down in the same way, the process continuing until it is properly smooth and elastic. The dough will be very loose at first, and it is best to work it in a large bowl rather than on a pastry board. Once the gluten in the flour has been released, however, it will become firmer and hold its shape, and may be transferred to a pastry board if desired. Nonetheless, it will be much looser than bread dough.

3 cups sifted all-purpose flour
2 cakes compressed yeast (or 2 envelopes dried yeast)
$\frac{1}{3}$ cup warm water
5 tablespoons sugar
4 eggs, lightly beaten
$\frac{1}{2}$ teaspoon salt
$\frac{3}{4}$ cup butter, softened
1 egg yolk, beaten with 1 tablespoon water

Dissolve the yeast and 1 tablespoon of the sugar in $\frac{1}{4}$ cup warm water of the proper temperature (*see* page 611). Let it stand until it foams, and then mix it with $\frac{1}{2}$ cup of the flour to make a soft dough. Mix only until smooth, form into a ball, place in a small bowl, slash a cross in its top, cover, and let rise until doubled in bulk (about 20 minutes). Meanwhile, rinse a very large mixing bowl with hot water, dry it thoroughly, and put the rest of the flour into it. Make a well in the center of the flour, and into this pour the beaten eggs, salt, and remaining sugar dissolved in the rest of the warm water. Mix this into a smooth dough with your hands (or a large wooden spoon), and then add the

butter, bit by bit, working it in until you have a quite soft, perfectly smooth dough. Work this vigorously, as described above, slapping and banging it against the bowl until it loses its stickiness and becomes elastic. Spread it out on a lightly floured pastry board in a large circle (or spread in the bowl); take the now-doubled yeast ball and spread it onto the dough. Knead together for at least 10 minutes until both are thoroughly blended, and form into a ball. Place this in a greased, warmed bowl as described in the introduction, dust the top very lightly with flour, cover, and set in a warm place to rise until doubled in bulk (*see* Note below). Punch it down to its original bulk and knead it for 2 or 3 minutes; then return it to the bowl, grease the top lightly, cover the bowl tightly with greased wax paper, and cover that with a towel. Place the bowl in the refrigerator for at least 7 hours, or overnight. After this time, knead the dough again and then put it in the traditionally shaped, fluted brioche pan, which has been lightly buttered (or put it in a round, high-sided baking tin). Brush the top lightly with a little butter, cover the pan with a cloth, and set it in a warm place until doubled in bulk. At this point, brush the surface of the dough with an egg yolk beaten in 1 tablespoon water, place the pan in a hot (450°) oven, and bake for 10 minutes, lower heat to 350°, and continue to bake for another 20 minutes, or until the brioche leaves the sides of the pan or a finger pressed into the top leaves no impression. Remove from the oven, place on a rack, and allow to cool. *Makes 1 large (8-inch) brioche.*

NOTE: Because of the richness of this dough, it will take a long time to rise, and, until removed from refrigerator, it will be a soft dough. Do *not* try to hurry the rising process or you will get a yeasty tasting result.

1890. PLAIN BRIOCHE DOUGH
Pasta per brioscia comune

$3\frac{1}{2}$ cups sifted all-purpose flour
2 cakes compressed yeast (or 2 envelopes dry yeast)
$\frac{1}{3}$ cup warm water of the proper temperature (*see* page 611)
4 teaspoons sugar
3 eggs, lightly beaten
$\frac{1}{2}$ teaspoon salt
$\frac{1}{2}$ cup butter
1 egg yolk, beaten with 1 tablespoon water

This is prepared in the same way as Delicate Brioche Dough [No. 1889]. If the dough seems too solid—it should be soft—add a little warm milk that has been first scalded and cooled (about ¼ cup). *Makes 1 large (8-inch) brioche.*

NOTE: For baking instructions, see the following recipes.

1891. BRIOCHE WITH A "HEAD"
Brioscia a testa

This is the traditional brioche with a small "head" set in its center. It is traditionally baked in a fluted mold. However, any deep, round pan may be used so long as the dough only half-fills the pan.

Use the Plain Brioche Dough [No. 1890], since it has less sugar and will therefore brown less quickly. (Indeed, if you do not mind a less sweet brioche, it would be better to reduce the sugar to 2 teaspoons.)

When the brioche dough is taken from the refrigerator, punch it down, knead for 1 or 2 minutes, and set ¼ of it aside. Shape the rest and put it into a buttered pan which should be only half-filled. Shape the remaining piece of dough like a pear, long and pointed at one end, wider at the rounded end. Poke a hole in the center of the dough in the pan and set the "head," slightly moistened at the tip, into the hole, narrow end in. Cover with a cloth and set in a warm place to rise until doubled in bulk. Brush top with an egg yolk beaten with 1 tablespoon water, and bake in a 400° oven for 25 minutes, or until a finger pressed on its surface leaves no impression. If the "head" browns too quickly before the rest is done, cover it with a buttered piece of brown paper. *Makes 1 large (8-inch) brioche.*

1892. INDIVIDUAL BRIOCHES
Briosce

1 recipe Plain Brioche Dough [No. 1890]
Butter as needed
Flour as needed
1 egg yolk, beaten with 1 tablespoon water

Reserve ¼ of the dough. Divide the rest into 12 pieces and roll each piece into a ball on a lightly floured pastry board. Set into well-buttered individual brioche molds: fluted cupcake-size molds (or substitute small custard cups or muffin tins). Make an indentation in the center of each with the finger and set 12 little "caps" made by rolling the remaining dough between the palms into 12 tiny pear shapes. Moisten their narrow ends and set into the holes. Cover tins and set in a warm place to rise until doubled in bulk. Brush the surfaces with the beaten egg yolk, but do not paint the place where the little "cap" is joined. Bake in a 425°

oven for 20 minutes, or until they are well browned. *Makes 12 brioches.*

1893. BRIOCHE RING
Brioscia a corona

This is one way of shaping any brioche dough (except Brioche Mousseline—No. 1895) after it has risen in the refrigerator overnight.

Remove the dough from the refrigerator, dust it very lightly with flour, and roll it into a smooth ball. Make a hole in the center with the index finger and then, using both hands, pull and flatten gently, enlarging the central hole until you have a ring of the desired size. It can then be placed either in a buttered ring mold (which it should only half-fill) or on a buttered cooky sheet or baking tin. Cover, let it rise in a warm place until it has doubled, brush it with beaten egg yolk, and decorate it by cutting the top surface in shallow slashes, so that when baked a risen edge outlines the pattern. One of the most attractive patterns (*see* drawing) is obtained by holding scissors at right angles to the top and snipping in a zigzag from the center toward the edge (without perforating either the center or the edge). When baked, the brioche ring will be broken in this pattern with a raised ridge. Bake at 425° for about 30 minutes. *Makes 1 ring.*

NOTE: A variant, rather like a rich coffee ring, may be made by rolling out the dough, after it has been removed from the refrigerator, into an oblong ½ inch thick, spreading the surface with ½ cup butter, softened, ½ cup finely chopped raisins soaked in 4 tablespoons of brandy, and 2 tablespoons brown sugar; then rolling up the dough as for jelly roll. Fasten ends firmly together in a ring, set on a buttered cooky sheet, and, using the scissors, cut from the edge toward the center (but not through the center) so that you have a circle of attached slices around the edge. Turn these gently so that one side of each slice is downward on the baking sheet. Cover lightly, and set in a warm place to rise until doubled in bulk. Just before baking (at 375° for 45 minutes) brush with beaten egg or melted butter (if with butter, sprinkle surface with granulated sugar).

1894. SQUARE BRIOCHES
Brioscia in stampi rettangolari

Prepare a brioche dough of your choice (except Brioche Mousseline—No. 1895). Take it from the refrigerator, knead it, divide it into 6 parts, and with lightly floured hands shape these into squares or oblongs. Arrange them, not touching, in 2 rows on a buttered, rectangular baking pan, cover with a cloth, and set them in a warm place to rise until doubled in bulk. Bake them at 425° for 30 minutes. (Brush them with beaten egg before baking if you prefer a darker brown, glazed surface.) *Makes 6 brioches.*

1895. BRIOCHE MOUSSELINE
Brioscia mussolina

Make the same dough as indicated in Delicate Brioche Dough [No. 1889], increasing the amount of butter to 1½ cups, and decreasing the flour to 2 cups. After kneading in the softened butter, this dough becomes almost as loose as cake batter, and an electric mixer would be advisable if one does not wish to use one's hands. Once the dough has been removed from its overnight stay in the refrigerator, however, the butter has stiffened sufficiently to allow the dough to be kneaded for a few minutes before placing in the pans for the third rising. When ready to bake, one should employ the traditionally shaped tin used for Brioche Mousseline: a tall, narrow, cylindrical mold. A large tin can may be substituted for this if a Mousseline pan is not readily available. Generously butter the pan. At the same time butter a large sheet of heavy brown or white paper. Fill the tin ⅔ full of the brioche dough. Make a collar of the greased paper to extend the height of the pan by 4 inches, and tie this on with string. Lightly butter the top of the dough, cover with a cloth, and set in a warm place to double in bulk (this may take up to 6 hours because of the richness of the dough). Brush the top of the brioche with beaten egg and bake in a 425° oven for 45 minutes, or until a cake tester or fine knitting needle comes out clean after being inserted in the center of the brioche.

NOTE: After brushing the top with beaten egg, a deep cross may be cut in the top of the dough before baking. Also, this dough may be baked in an ordinary high-sided, spring form, or angel-cake tin.

1896. BRIOCHE MOUSSELINE CASALINGA
Brioscia alla casalinga

This recipe resembles an even richer version of the popular Zuppa Inglese [No. 2093].

1 Brioche Mousseline [No. 1895], baked in a
    9-inch spring form pan
Syrup:
    ¾ cup sugar
    ½ cup water
    3 tablespoons butter
    2 strips orange rind (no white part)
    ½ teaspoon vanilla extract (or 1-inch piece of
        vanilla bean)
2 cups Pastry Cream [No. 2267]
¼ cup dark rum
¼ cup finely chopped candied orange peel
1 recipe Zabaglione Sauce [No. 2279]

Boil the sugar, water, butter, and orange rind in a small saucepan over high heat for 10 minutes (if using the vanilla bean, add it to the above ingredients). Slice a baked brioche mousseline horizontally into ¾-inch-thick layers. Set 1 layer in a mold slightly higher than that in which the brioche was baked. Remove syrup from stove after 10 minutes, discard orange rind (and the vanilla bean, if used), and add the vanilla extract (do not add if vanilla bean was used). Mix the pastry cream with the rum and candied orange peel. Spoon a little syrup over the brioche slice in the mold (not too much—the slice should be moist, not soggy), and spread a layer of pastry cream over this. Top with another slice of brioche, and repeat the process until all the ingredients have been used, ending with a top slice of brioche. Spoon any remaining syrup over this. Cover lightly with a piece of aluminum foil, and place in a cool place for at least 5 hours, or overnight. When ready to serve, unmold it carefully on a platter, and pour over ½ the Zabaglione sauce, and serve the rest of the sauce on the side. *Serves 6 to 8.*

Brioche Sévigné (No. 1897)

NOTE: If desired, the dessert may be assembled in the same pan in which it was baked, extending the height of the pan with heavy-duty aluminum foil if necessary.

1897. BRIOCHE SÉVIGNÉ
Brioscia alla Sévigné

1 recipe Brioche Mousseline [No. 1895], baked in
    an 8-inch spring form pan
Syrup:
    $^2/_3$ cup sugar
    $^2/_3$ cup strained strawberry preserves (or jelly)
    $^1/_2$ cup water
    1 cup mashed strawberries (if using frozen
        strawberries, decrease sugar to $^1/_2$ cup)
    2 tablespoons lemon juice
$^1/_4$ cup kirsch
$^1/_2$ cup blanched pistachio nuts, coarsely chopped

In a small, heavy enamel saucepan place the sugar, strawberry preserves, and water and bring to a boil over high heat. Lower heat, and simmer for 8 minutes; add the mashed strawberries and lemon juice; and cook for 8 minutes more. Meanwhile, slice the brioche into 4 or 5 horizontal layers, and place the first in the bottom of the spring form pan. When the syrup is cooked, remove it from the fire and add the kirsch. Spoon some of the hot syrup over the brioche layer, coating it evenly; top with the next brioche layer; and repeat the process. When the final layer has been added, spoon the rest of the syrup over it, and let the cake rest in a cool place (not the refrigerator) for 1 hour. Before serving, remove the sides of the spring form, and place the cake on a platter. Sprinkle the top and sides with the pistachio nuts. *Serves 6 to 8.*

NOTE: To blanch shelled pistachios, place them in a single layer on a baking sheet and place in a hot (375°) oven for 5 minutes. Dump them out on a towel while they are still blazing hot, and fold the towel over them several times. Firmly but gently, rub the nuts around in the towel, unwrap, and brush away the skins.

1898. BRIOCHE SURPRISE
Brioscia in sorpresa

1 recipe Delicate Brioche Dough [No. 1889], or
    Brioche Mousseline [No. 1895]
$1^1/_2$ cups fresh fruit (apricots, peaches, strawberries,
    cherries, blueberries, or seedless grapes; or any
    combination of these), cut into small pieces
$^3/_4$ cup apricot jam

3 tablespoons sugar (or more, if the fruit is tart)
$^1/_4$ cup kirsch

Peel, pit, or hull the fruit, and cut into bite-sized pieces (the blueberries may be left whole, but the grapes should be cut in half). Mix the apricot jam, sugar, and kirsch together, and pour over the fruit. Let this stand, covered, for 1 or 2 hours. Take the dough from the refrigerator and give it a final kneading. Butter an 8-inch spring form pan, and put half the brioche dough in it; make a depression in the top of this, about 1 inch in from the edge, deep enough to hold the fruit, and pour this in, reserving about $^2/_3$ cup of juice. Cover the fruit with the remaining dough, cover the pan lightly, and set in a warm place to rise until doubled in bulk. Bake in a hot (375°) oven for 45 minutes. After brioche has been removed from the oven, take the leftover juices from the fruit and reduce them in a small enamel saucepan over high heat to $^1/_2$ cup. Remove the sides of the spring form, and brush the cake with the reduced fruit juices. Serve while still warm. This cake is also excellent when served cold, accompanied by sweetened whipped cream flavored with kirsch. *Serves 6 to 8.*

NOTE: This may also be made by baking the brioche in an 8-inch spring form, cooling it, cutting off the top, scooping out some of the center, and filling it with a combination of fresh fruit, candied fruits and peels, apricot jam, and kirsch (in the proportions given above). Replace the top and serve. For a richer version, bind the fruits with 1 cup Pastry Cream [No. 2267].

Savarins (No. 1900): see page 618

617

1899. CROISSANTS
Croissants

4 cups sifted all-purpose flour

1 cake compressed yeast (or 1 envelope dry yeast)

1½ cups milk (or more as required), scalded and cooled to the proper temperature (*see* page 611)

½ cup butter, softened

4 tablespoons sugar

1 teaspoon salt

1 egg, beaten

Dissolve 3 tablespoons of the sugar in 1¼ cups of the lukewarm, pre-scalded milk. Place 3 cups of the flour in a large bowl, and, working the flour with the fingers of the right hand, gradually add enough of the sweetened milk to make a firm, moist dough (it may take less than 2 cups of milk, depending upon the type of flour employed). Knead this in the bowl for 10 minutes, or until it begins to become smooth and elastic, then transfer it to a lightly floured pastry board and knead for another 5 minutes. Cover this with a cloth and let it rest for 20 minutes. Meanwhile, dissolve the yeast and the remaining sugar in ¼ cup lukewarm milk. Let it stand until it foams (*see* page 611). Place the remaining flour in a small bowl, and pour in the foamed yeast, working it with the fingers until it is a smooth, moist dough. Cover the bowl, set in a warm place, and let this rise until doubled in bulk (about 20 minutes).

Take the flour/milk dough, and spread it out in a large circle on a lightly floured pastry board. Take the yeast dough and spread it onto the first dough and work and knead both together until they are smooth and thoroughly blended. Incorporate as much air into the dough as possible by folding it over on itself and sealing up the edges; do this for about 15 minutes. Roll out the dough into a square sheet about ½ inch thick. Dot this with pieces of butter, which should be firm but not hard, and fold the corners of the dough into the center of the square, making an envelope sealing in the butter. Seal the edges together by pinching them, so that the butter cannot break loose. Turn the dough upside down, and roll it out again, being careful not to let the butter escape. When it is the size of the original square, fold into an envelope again, turn upside down, and roll out again. Fold again, and place in the refrigerator for 20 minutes, loosely covered, then take it out and repeat the rolling and folding 2 more times. When it has been rolled out for the last time, wrap the square of dough loosely in wax paper (or roll it loosely in wax paper), wrap this loosely in a towel, and place in the least cold part of the refrigerator for at least 6 hours,

or overnight. Before baking, remove the dough from the refrigerator, fold it as before, and roll it out on a lightly floured pastry board into a ¼-inch-thick circle. Cut this into pie-shaped wedges, about 3½ inches at the wide end, and, starting with this end, roll them up loosely. Place on a baking sheet, and curve the ends to form crescents. Each crescent should be about 2 inches apart from its neighbor. When all the crescents have been made, cover them lightly with a cloth, set them in a warm place, and let them rise for about 1 hour, or until doubled in bulk. Brush lightly with the beaten egg, and bake in a 375° oven for about 35 minutes, or until well glazed and brown. *Makes about 18 croissants.*

1900. SAVARIN
Pasta per savarini

This yeast-raised dough is similar to that employed for babas and brioches, and often is used for them in both Italy and France. The difference is that savarins are baked in ring molds no less than 3 inches deep, 7 to 9 inches in diameter, and occasionally in smaller ring molds 2½ to 4 inches in diameter.

3 cups triple-sifted all-purpose flour

1 cake compressed yeast (or 1 envelope dry yeast)

⅓ cup sugar

¼ cup milk, scalded and cooled to the proper temperature (*see* page 611)

3 eggs, lightly beaten

¾ teaspoon salt

⅔ cup butter

3 tablespoons flour

1 egg yolk

6 tablespoons slivered almonds [*see* No. 2288]

Dissolve the yeast and 1 tablespoon of the sugar in the milk. Let it stand until it foams (*see* page 611). Take ½ cup of the flour, place it in a small bowl, and mix in the foamed yeast to make a smooth, soft dough. Cover, and set in a warm place until doubled in bulk (about 20 minutes). While it is rising, rinse out a large bowl in hot water and dry well, put the rest of the flour in this and make a well in the center. Beat the eggs and egg yolk with the rest of the sugar and the salt, and pour this into the center of the flour. Work the flour into the center with the fingertips of the right hand until you have a smooth but soft dough. Take this up and beat it and bang it against the sides of the bowl until it loses its stickiness and becomes elastic [*see* No. 1887]. Pat it out on a lightly floured pastry board into a ½-inch-thick circle; take the now-risen yeast dough and spread this out over it to within 1 inch of its edge. Knead the two together for about 5 to 8 minutes; roll into a ball and place in a large, lightly greased bowl; and set in a warm place. Knead the butter with 3 tablespoons flour, and divide it into 3 parts. When the dough has risen a little (before it has touched the sides of the bowl) divide it into 3 parts and knead each with the butter until you have 3 smooth, thoroughly blended balls of dough. Knead these 3 together for about 5 minutes, shape into a ball, put back in the greased bowl, cover, and set in a warm place to rise until doubled in bulk. When it has risen, punch it down and knead again for about 5 minutes. It is now ready for use, but may be kept tightly covered in the refrigerator overnight.

Baking the savarins:
Generously butter 2 9-inch ring molds, sprinkle the bottoms of each with 3 tablespoons thinly sliced almonds, and arrange the dough in the mold carefully so as not to disturb the almonds. Do not fill them more than ½ full, cover, and let rise until doubled in bulk. Bake in a 425° oven for 25 minutes, or until the sides of the savarins have shrunk away from the molds or until a finger pressed on the top leaves no indentation. *Makes 2 9-inch savarins.*

1901. BERRY-FILLED SAVARIN
Savarino con frutta di bosco

½ recipe Savarin [No. 1900], baked in a ring mold
    and cooled
¾ cup fresh strawberries (wild strawberries, if
    available)
¾ cup fresh raspberries
¾ cup fresh blackberries
1 cup superfine sugar (more, if berries are tart)
¼ cup maraschino liqueur
3 tablespoons slivered almonds [*see* No. 2288]

Hull the berries (if wild strawberries are used, leave them whole if cultivated are used, cut them in halves). Place the berries in a bowl, pour the sugar over them, and toss them carefully so as not to bruise them. Pour over the maraschino, cover the bowl, and place in the refrigerator for 2 hours. Just before serving put the savarin on a platter and pour the marinated fruits into the center. *Serves 6 to 8.*

NOTE: Sweetened whipped cream may be served with this and is especially delicious. The fruits may also be marinated in framboise or kirsch instead of maraschino.

1902. SAVARIN RICCA
Savarino alla ricca

½ recipe Savarin [No. 1900], baked in a ring mold
    and cooled
1 dead-ripe pineapple, peeled, cored, and thinly sliced
5 tablespoons superfine sugar
2 tablespoons maraschino liqueur
Sugar syrup:
    1 cup sugar
    ¾ cup water
    ¼ cup Aurum liqueur
1 cup heavy cream, whipped
3 tablespoons chocolate shot
1 recipe Strawberry Sauce [No. 2278]

Marinate the pineapple slices in 3 tablespoons of the superfine sugar and the maraschino for 2 or 3 hours in the refrigerator. When ready to serve, prepare the syrup by boiling the sugar and water in a small, heavy saucepan over high heat for 10 minutes; remove from stove, mix in the Aurum, and spoon the syrup slowly over the savarin which has been sliced in ¾-inch slices and arranged in a circle, slices slightly overlapping, on a large round platter. Drain the pineapple slices, reserving their juice. Arrange the pieces of pineapple on the savarin slices, taking care to accomplish this neatly, so that the fruit doesn't overlap the outer edges of the savarin slices. Whip the cream until stiff and sweeten it with the remaining superfine sugar, and heap the cream in the center of the platter and sprinkle it with the chocolate shot. Mix the pineapple juices with the strawberry sauce and serve in a sauce bowl on the side. *Serves 8 to 10.*

1903. SAVARIN WITH WHIPPED CREAM
Savarino con panna montata

½ recipe Savarin [No. 1900], baked in a ring mold
    and cooled
Sugar syrup:
    1 cup sugar
    ¾ cup water
    2 tablespoons butter
    1-inch piece vanilla bean (or 1 teaspoon vanilla
      extract)
¼ cup dark rum
1½ cups heavy cream, whipped
3 tablespoons superfine sugar

After you have removed the savarin from the oven place it on a rack to cool slightly while you prepare the sugar syrup. In a small, heavy saucepan put the sugar, water, butter, and vanilla bean. Place over high heat and bring to a boil, lower heat, and simmer for 15 minutes. Remove the vanilla bean and take off heat (if vanilla extract is being used add it at this point). Place the still-warm savarin on a platter, prick it all over with a skewer. Pour the rum into the hot sugar syrup and slowly spoon the syrup over the savarin a little at a time, so that it is absorbed and does not run off. Put the cake back in its mold and pour the excess syrup on the platter over it and let it stand in a cool place for 1 hour or until ready to serve (it should not stand over 2 hours or it will become soggy). Just before serving, whip the cream until stiff and fold in the superfine sugar. Unmold the savarin on a serving plate and pile the sweetened whipped cream in the center. *Serves 6 to 8.*

NOTE: An already cooled savarin may be used if first lightly wrapped in aluminum foil and heated for 10 minutes in a 375° oven, before pouring on the syrup.

1904. YEAST BUTTER CAKE
Pasta per torte

2 cups triple-sifted all-purpose flour
1 cake compressed yeast (or 1 envelope dry yeast)
½ cup milk, scalded and cooled to the proper temperature (*see* page 611)
¼ teaspoon salt
1⅓ cups butter, softened
1 cup plus 5 tablespoons sugar
9 egg yolks
1 teaspoon grated lemon rind (no white part included)
1 teaspoon vanilla extract (or 1 teaspoon orange extract)
Confectioners' sugar

Dissolve the yeast and 1 tablespoon of the sugar in the scalded milk and let it stand until it foams. While waiting, sift the flour once again with the salt. Cream the butter and the sugar together until pale and fluffy, using a wooden spoon or an electric mixer; add the egg yolks one at a time, beating well after each addition. Alternately beat in the flour and the foamed yeast, being careful to beat only enough to obtain a smooth batter. Fold in the flavorings, cover the bowl with a cloth, and let rise until doubled in bulk (about ½ to 1 hour). When risen, beat down again. Generously butter a large tube pan (an angel cake pan is fine), sprinkle it with flour, and tap out the excess. Pour the batter into the pan, cover it lightly and let stand in a warm place for about 25 minutes. Bake in a 375° oven for 40 to 50 minutes, or until a cake tester comes out clean. Cool on a cake rack, and serve sprinkled with confectioners' sugar. *Makes 1 9-inch cake.*

CAKES AND TORTES
Torte

Italian cakes are usually based upon a plain sponge or a sponge cake made with melted butter, called a Margherita. Baking powder cakes are not usually made—the only exceptions in this book are Nos. 1919 and 1921, the latter being a basically British recipe.

Unless otherwise specified, all the ingredients for cakes must be at room temperature.

1905. ALMOND CAKE
Gâteau mandorlato

1½ cups triple-sifted all-purpose flour
½ cup blanched almonds [*see* No. 2280]
4 bitter almonds, blanched (*see* Note, below)
1 cup plus 3 tablespoons sugar
6 eggs
½ teaspoon salt
⅔ cup plus 1 tablespoon butter, melted
½ cup apricot jam
½ cup Fondant Icing [No. 2255], barely lukewarm
1 tablespoon kirsch

Pound the almonds, bitter almonds, and sugar to a paste in the mortar (or whirl in the electric blender for 15 seconds). Put the eggs, almond paste, salt, and remaining sugar in a large, deep, very heavy enamel saucepan. Place the pan over very low fire and beat constantly with a wire whisk or rotary egg beater, until the mixture is thick and straw colored, and falls in a slowly dissolving ribbon on the surface when the beater is lifted from the pan. Remove from heat and alternately fold in the flour and melted butter. Lightly butter 2 8-inch cake pans and dust them with flour, tap out the excess, and divide the cake batter between the 2 pans. Bake in a 350° oven for 35 minutes. (The cake should be rather moist in the middle.) Remove from the oven and let cool on a cake rack. Spread one layer with the apricot jam, cover with the second layer, and ice the top with a thin coating of fondant icing mixed with 1 tablespoon kirsch. *Serves 8.*

·NOTE: Bitter almonds may be purchased in some specialty stores. They may also be extracted from peach pits by cracking the pit with a hammer. Too many bitter almonds can be poisonous (they contain amounts of prussic acid), so avoid using more than specified.

1906. ALSATIAN TORTE
Torta—crostata—all'alsaziana

2 cups triple-sifted all-purpose flour
1½ cups blanched almonds [see No. 2280]
½ teaspoon salt
1 cup butter, softened
1½ cups sugar
1 egg, beaten
⅓ cup strawberry preserves
⅓ cup raspberry preserves
⅓ cup cherry preserves
2 tablespoons confectioners' sugar

Pound the blanched almonds to a paste in the mortar (or whirl, ⅓ at a time, for 10 seconds in the blender). Cream the butter and the sugar in a large bowl until it is very fluffy; then beat in the egg. Alternately add the flour (to which the salt has been added) and almond paste to the creamed butter, working with a wooden spoon until you have a rather thick dough. Gather this into a ball, wrap it in foil or wax paper, and place in the refrigerator for at least 2 hours.

Lightly flour a pastry board and roll out ¾ of the dough into a rather thick circle large enough to fit a 9-inch shallow spring form pan. Lightly butter the pan and fit the circle of dough into it (or pat out the circle of dough in the bottom of the pan instead of previously rolling it out). Roll out the rest of dough into a ¼-inch-thick rectangle. Cut this into ¼-inch-wide strips. With a pastry brush lightly moisten the edge of the dough in the cake pan and press in a border, using 2 or 3 of the strips, making a little wall around the edge of the pan. Arrange the rest of the strips in a lattice formation across the dough. Into the inter-stices place alternating spoonsful of the various preserves. Bake in a 350° oven for 50 minutes. Place on a cake rack to cool. When ready to serve remove the sides of the spring form, transfer the cake to a platter, and lightly dust the top with a little confectioners' sugar. *Serves 8 to 10.*

NOTE: Any combination of 2 or more jams may be used. Also, instead of a spring form, this may be baked in a flan ring on a cooky sheet. Failing this, a 9-inch cake pan may be lined with aluminum foil, leaving about 1 inch extending above the edge, foil buttered, the dough placed in this. When the torte is baked it may be lifted out by grasping the protruding portion of the foil.

1907. APRICOT ROLL
Biscotto arrotolato

5 egg yolks
¾ cup sugar
1 cup triple-sifted all-purpose flour
4 egg whites
½ teaspoon salt
4 tablespoons butter, melted
Confectioners' sugar
2 cups apricot preserves, pressed through a fine sieve
3 tablespoons coarse white sugar crystals (if not
    available, use 2 tablespoons confectioners' sugar)

Beat the egg yolks and gradually add ½ cup of the sugar, beating until the mixture is lemon colored and fluffy. Still beating, add the sifted flour, a little at a time. In another bowl beat the egg whites with the salt until they form soft peaks and add the remaining ¼

cup of sugar to them. Continue beating until sugar is incorporated, and then gently fold the beaten egg whites into the sugar/egg/flour mixture. Finally, fold in the melted butter, mixing only until blended. Generously butter a 15- by 10-inch jelly roll pan, line with wax paper, butter the wax paper, sprinkle it with flour, and shake out the excess. Pour in the cake batter, and bake in a 375° oven for about 15 minutes. Remove from oven and immediately invert onto a sheet of wax paper which has been evenly dusted with confectioners' sugar. Carefully peel off the paper from the bottom of the cake, and if the cake has any hard edges, trim them off with a sharp knife. Dust a dish towel with confectioners' sugar and gently roll up the cake (from its wide end) in the towel; let it stand for about 30 minutes, or until completely cool. Carefully unroll the cooled cake, spread it with the apricot preserves, and roll up as gently as possible so as not to squeeze out the filling. Place on an oval platter or serving board and sprinkle lightly with the sugar. *Serves 6 to 8.*

NOTE: If desired, one may brush the surface of the roll with $\frac{1}{2}$ additional cup of strained apricot preserves before sprinkling the sugar over the cake.

1908. BASQUE CAKE
Gâteau alla basca

1 cup butter, softened
1 cup plus 2 teaspoons superfine sugar
2 whole eggs
3 eggs, separated (reserve 1 egg white)
1 tablespoon dark rum
$\frac{1}{2}$ teaspoon salt
4 cups sifted flour
3 teaspoon baking powder
3 cups Pastry Cream [No. 2267]

Cream the butter in a large bowl with a wooden spoon until light and fluffy. Gradually add 1 cup of the sugar, beating well until the mixture is smooth and light. Beat the 2 eggs and 3 yolks lightly with the salt and rum and add this alternately with the flour, mixing with a large fork until you have a smooth dough: do *not* overmix, however. Generously butter a 9-inch cake tin, dust it with flour, and shake out the excess. Pat out $\frac{2}{3}$ of the dough on a floured pastry cloth or board into a circle large enough to fit the tin and carefully place it in, pressing down the bottom and sides. Pour in the pastry cream. Pat out the remaining dough into a circle, and cover the top of the cake with it. Pinch the top and sides together to effect a tight seal, and cut a few decorative slashes in the top. Stir the reserved egg white

with the remaining sugar until the sugar is dissolved and paint the top of the cake with this mixture. Bake in a preheated 375° oven for 1 hour. Cool on a cake rack for 2 hours before carefully turning it out onto a round plate. Serve at room temperature. *Serves 8.*

NOTE: Do not refrigerate this cake, as cold will ruin its texture. To prevent it from spoiling serve at most 5 hours after baking (3 hours in summer).

1909. CHOCOLATE CAKE CAPRICCIO
Gâteau capriccio al cioccolato

$\frac{1}{2}$ recipe Italian Sponge Cake [No. 1913]
$\frac{1}{2}$ recipe Ganache Cream [No. 2265]
1 recipe Chocolate Icing [No. 2253]
1 cup sugar
$\frac{1}{2}$ cup water
4 tablespoons maraschino liqueur
11 small poached peach halves (prepared as in Peach Compote—No. 2188—or canned in heavy syrup), well drained
11 candied cherries
1 cup Fondant Icing [No. 2255]
3 tablespoons semi-sweet chocolate, melted
$\frac{1}{4}$ cup chocolate shot

Bake the cake in a 9-inch cake tin the day before. It should be somewhat dry to soak in the maraschino syrup. Boil the sugar and water in a small saucepan until it reaches the large thread stage (219° on the candy thermometer). Allow it to cool for 20 minutes and then stir in the maraschino. Split the cake in two, horizontally, and sprinkle the cut surfaces with the maraschino syrup. Spread the bottom layer with $\frac{1}{2}$ of the Ganache cream and cover with the top layer. Ice the entire cake with the chocolate frosting. Press the chocolate shot into the sides of the cake. Place a candied cherry in the cut half of each peach and arrange 10 of the halves around the top of the cake, convex side upward, and place the last one in the center. Melt the fondant in a small double boiler until it is syrupy (dilute with hot water if necessary), and carefully mask the peaches with this. Take care not to let the fondant dribble down the sides of the cake. Place the remaining Ganache in a pastry bag fitted with a large star tip and pipe a decorative border around the center peach and around the rim of the cake. Melt the semi-sweet chocolate in a small cup placed in a pan of hot water and pour the chocolate into a cornucopia made of parchment paper. Snip off the end of the cornucopia to make a very small hole and decorate the fondant-masked peach halves with delicate spiral lines of chocolate (*see* photograph on page 688). Place in refrigerator until ready to serve. *Serves* 10.

1910. FLORENTINE CASTAGNACCIO
Pizza di farina di castagne alla toscana—castagnaccio

This unusual "cake" is a Tuscan specialty. It is usually made in the autumn, and sold on street corners in Florence at that season. It has an unusual flavor, is very heavy in texture, and should be made and sampled at least once. Some people are addicted to it.

2¾ cups chestnut flour
½ cup sugar
½ teaspoon salt
1 cup water (more or less)
1 teaspoon fennel seeds
Optional: 1 sprig rosemary (or 1 teaspoon dried)
½ cup pine nuts
⅓ cup olive oil

Sift the chestnut flour, sugar, and salt into a bowl. Add the water, and beat well with a wooden spoon until you have a smooth, soft, batter-like dough with no lumps (more than 1 cup water may be needed, depending on the quality of the flour). Stir in the fennel seeds, optional rosemary, and pine nuts, reserving a few of each of these ingredients to sprinkle on the top before baking. Take 3 tablespoons of the oil and generously grease a large cake tin (traditionally a large round tin-lined copper pan), large enough so that the batter will be ½ inch deep. Pour in the batter, decorate the top with the reserved fennel seeds, rosemary, and pine nuts, pour the rest of the oil over the top, and bake in a 375° oven for ½ hour, or until the surface is dark brown and a cake tester emerges clean. Serve warm or at room temperature.

NOTE: Bacon grease may be substituted for the oil, and makes an even coarser, more peasanty preparation. Chestnut flour may be purchased in specialty food shops.

1911. GÂTEAU ST. HONORÉ
St. Honoré

This is the famous, spectacular French pastry named after Saint Honoratus, sixth-century bishop of Amiens, patron saint of bakers and confectioners.

⅓ recipe Flaky Pastry [No. 1954]
1 recipe Cream Puff Dough [No. 1990]
3 cups St. Honoré Cream [No. 2269]
2 cups heavy cream, whipped

4 tablespoons superfine sugar
1½ teaspoons vanilla extract
1 cup sugar
⅓ cup water
1 tablespoon white corn syrup

Roll out the pastry dough on a floured cloth or pastry board to a 10-inch circle (this may be easily accomplished by rolling out the dough and pressing the edge of a 10-inch cake tin in the dough). Place the circle of dough on a lightly moistened baking sheet. Fill a large pastry bag fitted with a large plain tube with the cream puff dough and carefully pipe a 1-inch border onto the rim of the pastry circle. Then pipe out the rest of the dough in small puffs about the size of a walnut on the unused portions of the baking sheet (at random, leaving at least 2 inches space between them). Place the sheet in a 375° oven for 30 minutes, or until the cream puff dough is well risen and golden brown. Carefully remove the puffs and the large dough circle and cool them on a pastry rack.

When cool, fill each of the puffs with a bit of whipped cream sweetened with the superfine sugar and vanilla. This may be best accomplished by piping the cream through a pastry bag fitted with a small plain tip.

Cook the sugar, water, and corn syrup in a small, heavy saucepan over medium heat until it caramelizes. Remove it at once from the heat when it turns honey colored. With a pair of tongs carefully dip each cream puff into the caramel and immediately affix it to the large cream puff dough border. Continue this until the entire circle is studded with cream puffs (*see* photograph, page 688). If caramel stiffens during this process, return it to the stove for a few seconds. Be careful not to let it burn, however. Fill the center of the circle with the St. Honoré cream. Decorate the surface with the whipped cream by dipping a tablespoon in lukewarm water, scooping out some cream, and making little mounds of it atop the St. Honoré cream. Dip spoon in water for each cream mound, and arrange the mounds in a neat pattern. Chill for 2 hours before serving. *Serves* 10.

NOTE: Employ great caution in dipping the puffs into the hot caramel, as you can burn your fingers badly. Do not chill the cake for more than 3 hours or it will become soggy.

623

1912. GERMAN ALMOND TORTE
Torta tedesca

1 cup blanched almonds [*see* No. 2280]
5 egg whites
7 tablespoons butter, softened
1 cup plus 2 teaspoons superfine sugar
8 egg yolks
1 cup sifted all-purpose flour
$\frac{1}{4}$ teaspoon salt
$1\frac{1}{4}$ teaspoons baking powder
For the icing:
   3 tablespoons instant coffee powder
   2 tablespoons heavy cream
   $\frac{3}{4}$ cup butter
   $\frac{1}{8}$ teaspoon salt
   $1\frac{1}{2}$ cups confectioners' sugar, sifted
   $\frac{1}{2}$ teaspoon vanilla extract

Pound the almonds in the mortar with one of the egg whites until they are a paste (or whirl in the blender, $\frac{1}{2}$ cup at a time, without the egg white, at high speed until pulverized). Cream the butter in a large warmed bowl with a wooden spoon until it is creamy and fluffy. Gradually add 1 cup of the sugar, beating rapidly. Beat in the egg yolks 1 at a time. The entire creaming process should take 30 minutes to ensure a maximum of lightness and delicacy. An electric beater will not give as light a result, although it may be used. Beat the egg whites with a pinch of the salt and the remaining sugar until they form soft peaks. Sift the flour again with the salt and baking powder. Alternately fold in small amounts of the sifted flour, beaten whites, and pulverized almonds. Grease a 10-inch cake tin and dust the inside with flour, tapping out the excess. Pour the cake batter into the tin, tilt slightly in all directions to coat the upper rim, and bake in a 350° oven for 35 to 45 minutes, or until a cake tester comes out clean. Cool on a cake rack.

Meanwhile, prepare the icing. Warm the cream slightly in a small cup over hot water. Stir the powdered instant coffee into it. Cream the butter with the salt in a large bowl (an electric mixer is fine for this) and gradually add alternating amounts of confectioners' sugar, coffee, and vanilla. When the cake is thoroughly cooled, spread it with the icing. *Serves 8 to 10.*

NOTE: If desired, the cake may be decorated with candied coffee beans and slivered toasted almonds [*see* No. 2288].

1913. ITALIAN SPONGE CAKE
Pasta per pan di Spagna

1 cup plus 2 teaspoons superfine sugar
8 eggs, separated
$\frac{1}{2}$ teaspoon grated lemon rind (no white part)
2 tablespoons vanilla sugar [*see* No. 2296], or substitute
   $1\frac{1}{2}$ teaspoons vanilla extract
$\frac{1}{2}$ teaspoon salt
$\frac{3}{4}$ cup triple-sifted all-purpose flour
5 tablespoons potato flour (or substitute $1\frac{1}{4}$ cups
   all-purpose flour for the above 2 flours)
5 tablespoons melted butter

Place 1 cup of sugar, yolks, lemon rind, vanilla sugar (if extract is used, add later on), and most of the salt in a large bowl. Place the bowl over a pan of hot (not boiling) water and beat (with a wire whisk, rotary or electric beater) until light and fluffy. When the batter falls in a dissolving ribbon from the beater, remove from stove and continue beating until cool. Beat the egg whites until fluffy with the remaining sugar and the remaining salt. Sift the 2 flours together. Alternately fold in small amounts of the flour and beaten egg whites (if vanilla extract is used, add now). Fold in the melted butter. Generously grease 1 10-inch cake tin or 2 8-inch tins. Dust with flour and tap out the excess. Pour in the batter and bake in a 350° oven for 40 minutes (less, if 8-inch pans are used) or until a cake tester comes out clean. Cool on cake racks. Ice the cake as desired. *Serves 8.*

1914. LINZERTORTE
Torta—crostata—all'austriaca: linzertorte

1 recipe Flaky Pastry [No. 1954]
$\frac{1}{2}$ cup blanched almonds [*see* No. 2280], finely ground
1 teaspoon cinnamon
$\frac{1}{3}$ cup sugar
2 cups raspberry jam
1 teaspoon lemon juice
1 egg yolk
1 tablespoon heavy cream

Make the pastry, adding the ground almonds, cinnamon, and all but 1 teaspoon of the sugar when you incorporate the flour. Let it rest, well wrapped, in the refrigerator for at least 3 hours. Roll out $\frac{2}{3}$ of the chilled dough on a floured cloth or pastry board. Fit it into a 9-inch flan ring or low-sided spring form pan, pressing down the bottom and sides, and crimping the edge decoratively. Prick bottom a few times with a fork. Fill with the jam which has been mixed with the

SEE
REVERSE
FOR
APTION

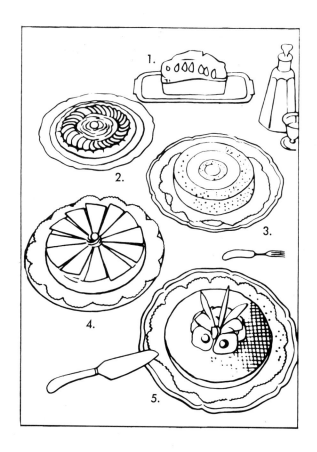

1. Plum Cake (No. 1921)
2. Apple Tart (No. 1962)
3. Paradiso Torte (No. 1919)
4. Sachertorte (No. 1924)
5. Pineapple Tart (No. 1980)

Croquembouche (No. 1997)

lemon juice. Roll out the rest of the pastry and cut it into ¼-inch-wide strips. Mix the yolk, remaining sugar, and cream, and paint the pastry strips with the mixture. Arrange the strips in a lattice over the pie. Trim neatly. Carefully brush the yolk mixture around the exposed rim of pastry (taking care not to touch the jam). Place in a 400° oven for about 35 minutes. If it browns too quickly, lightly cover top with a piece of aluminum foil. Cool on a cake rack. If the jam has sunk after cooling, fill in the spaces with additional jam, if desired. *Serves 8.*

1915. FANCY MARGHERITA CAKE
Pasta margherita fine

2 cups triple-sifted all-purpose flour (or, better, 1 cup all-purpose flour sifted 3 times with ⅔ cup potato flour)
1 cup plus 1 tablespoon superfine sugar
¼ teaspoon salt
8 eggs, separated
1 cup Clarified Butter [No. 102], cooled
1 teaspoon vanilla extract

Place 1 cup of the sugar and egg yolks in a bowl (an unlined copper bowl is excellent for this purpose) and place over a pan of hot (*not* boiling) water. Beat with a wire whisk, rotary or electric beater until it has increased by ⅓ and is barely warm. Remove bowl from hot water and continue beating until the mixture is cool and falls from the beater in a slowly dissolving ribbon onto the surface of the batter. Beat the egg whites with the remaining sugar and the salt until they form soft peaks. Slowly fold in ⅓ of the flour into the yolk mixture, then fold in ⅓ of the whites. Repeat process until all have been added, folding in each addition gently. Gently fold in the clarified butter and vanilla. Do *not* overmix at any time or the cake will be tough: fold and cut in all the additions with great gentleness. Grease a 10-inch cake tin or 2 8-inch tins. Line the bottom with a circle of wax paper, grease this, then dust lightly with flour and tap out the excess. Pour in the cake batter, and bake in a 350° oven for 35 to 40 minutes, or until a cake tester comes out clean. Let it remain in the pan for 10 minutes on a cake rack, then turn out on the rack, peel off the paper carefully, and cool on rack. Ice as desired. *Serves 8 to 10.*

1916. SIMPLE MARGHERITA CAKE
Pasta margherita comune

Same ingredients as in preceeding recipe, except that the butter is reduced to 5 tablespoons and all-purpose flour is used exclusively. Prepare and bake exactly as above recipe indicates.

1917. MOCHA CAKE WITH BUTTER CREAM
Gâteau al caffè

1 Italian Sponge Cake [No. 1913], baked in a 10-inch pan
½ cup sugar
¼ cup water
4 tablespoons maraschino (or coffee-flavored) liqueur
Butter cream icing:
 ½ cup plus 1 tablespoon butter, softened
 1¼ cups sifted confectioners' sugar
 5 tablespoons very strong coffee (or 3 tablespoons instant coffee powder mixed with 4 tablespoons hot water, and cooled)
 1 tablespoon powdered cocoa
 1 teaspoon vanilla extract
 Pinch salt
 ½ cup cold Pastry Cream [No. 2267]
½ cup slivered almonds [*see* No. 2288], toasted in the oven until golden brown

Bake the sponge cake the day before assembling this cake. It should dry out somewhat, the better to absorb the syrup. Boil the sugar and water in a small, heavy saucepan until it reaches the large thread stage (219° on the candy thermometer). Let it cool for 10 minutes, then add the liqueur. Split the cake horizontally and drizzle the syrup over the bottom piece. While the cake is soaking in the syrup, prepare the butter cream icing. Cream the butter and sugar in a warmed bowl. Beat (an electric beater is good for this) until light and fluffy. Mix the coffee, cocoa, vanilla, and salt together and gradually beat into the butter/sugar mixture. Beat in the pastry cream little by little. If the butter cream is too soft, place it in the refrigerator for 10 minutes, or until firm enough to spread. Carefully spread ½ cup of the cream on the syrup-soaked layer, cover with the upper piece of cake, and spread the rest of the cream over the top and sides. Decorate with the slivered almonds arranged in whatever pattern you desire. If the weather is warm, put the cake in a cool place (the least cold part of the refrigerator) until ready to serve. It is best if allowed to "ripen" for about 2 hours. *Serves 8 to 10.*

1918. ORANGE CAKE
Gâteau all'arancia

$^{1}/_{2}$ cup butter, softened
$^{2}/_{3}$ cup superfine sugar
$^{1}/_{4}$ teaspoon salt
$^{3}/_{4}$ cup triple-sifted all-purpose flour
$^{1}/_{3}$ cup sifted potato flour
$^{1}/_{2}$ scant cup finely diced candied orange peel
1 tablespoon grated orange rind (no white part)
$^{1}/_{4}$ cup dark rum
3 eggs, separated
Pinch salt

Have all ingredients at room temperature and heat the oven to 350° at least 35 minutes before placing the cake in it. Soak the candied peel, grated rind, and rum together for $^{1}/_{2}$ hour. Cream the butter, sugar (reserve 1 tablespoon), and salt in a large, warmed bowl. Beat with a wooden spoon or electric beater until light and fluffy. Beat in the egg yolks 1 at a time, beating well after each addition. Beat in the rum/candied peel/rind mixture. Beat the egg whites with 1 tablespoon of the sugar and a pinch of salt until they form soft peaks. Sift the 2 flours together. Alternately fold in the flours and the egg whites into the batter $^{1}/_{3}$ at a time, folding gently, being careful not to overmix. Butter an 8-inch cake tin that is $1^{1}/_{2}$ inches deep. Cover the bottom with a circle of wax paper, butter that, dust with flour, and tap out the excess. Pour the batter into the pan, tilt in all directions to bring batter up around the rim of the pan, and bake in a 350° oven for 35 to 45 minutes, or until a cake tester comes out clean. Place pan on cake rack for 10 minutes, then turn out, carefully peel off the paper, and let cool. *Serves 6 to 8.*

NOTE: This cake may be iced with 1 cup of Fondant Icing [No. 2255] flavored with 2 tablespoons orange juice (or any preferred orange liqueur).

1919. PARADISO TORTE
Torta—crostata—del paradiso

1 cup butter, softened
1 cup superfine sugar
2 tablespoons vanilla sugar [*see* No. 2296]
1 scant cup triple-sifted potato flour
1 teaspoon grated lemon rind (no white part)
5 egg yolks
3 eggs
1 cup sifted all-purpose flour
$^{1}/_{4}$ teaspoon salt
1 teaspoon baking powder

3 tablespoons vanilla confectioners' sugar
[*see* No. 2296]

Cream the butter in a large, warm bowl until light and fluffy. A wire whisk will accomplish this best. Gradually beat in the 2 sugars, and beat until very light in texture. Add 1 tablespoon of the potato flour and the lemon rind and beat until well blended. In another bowl (an unlined copper one if possible) beat the egg yolks until they are thick and lemon colored, using a wire whisk or an electric beater. Add the whole eggs, 1 at a time, beating for 2 minutes after each addition. When all have been added beat for another 20 minutes. Resift both flours together with the salt and baking powder. Beat $^{1}/_{4}$ of the eggs into the butter/sugar mixture until well blended, fold in $^{1}/_{4}$ of the sifted flour, and continue folding in alternate amounts of egg and flour, $^{1}/_{4}$ at a time. Take care to fold lightly; do *not* beat after the first addition of the eggs. Butter a 10-inch cake tin or 2 8-inch tins. Cover the bottom with a circle of wax paper and butter that. Dust with flour and tap out the excess. Pour in the cake batter and tilt the pan in all directions to bring it up to the rim. Place in a 350° oven for 35 to 40 minutes, or until a cake tester emerges clean. Remove to a cake rack and let sit in the pan for 10 minutes, then carefully turn out onto the rack and gently peel off the paper. Turn it right side up immediately, and allow to cool. When cool, sprinkle it heavily with the vanilla confectioners' sugar. *Serves 8 to 10.*

NOTE: This is a very delicate cake with an extraordinary texture. The lengthy beating of the eggs gives it its lightness, and time should not be skimped or the result will not be totally successful. Vanilla sugar is preferred to vanilla extract, as it lends a more subtle and pervasive aroma.

1920. PITHIVIERS CAKE
Gâteau Pithiviers

This is a famous French regional specialty, a cross between a pie and an almond cake. It originated in Pithiviers, a town in northeastern France not far from Orléans.

1 recipe Puff Paste [No. 1960]
Almond cream:
  $^{3}/_{4}$ cup blanched almonds [*see* No. 2280], ground to a powder, or whirled in the blender at high speed until pulverized
  $^{3}/_{4}$ cup superfine sugar
  $^{1}/_{4}$ cup butter, softened

1 egg

1 egg yolk

Pinch salt

1 tablespoon dark rum or orange flower water

2 tablespoons sifted confectioners' sugar

1 egg white

1 tablespoon water

Make the puff paste the day before and let it rest, covered, in the refrigerator overnight. Mix the powdered almonds with the sugar. Cream the butter until light and fluffy. Gradually beat in the almond/sugar mixture. Beat the egg and the yolk with the salt until light and fluffy, add the rum or orange flower water, and lightly mix into the almond/sugar/butter cream. Mix only until well blended. Roll out ⅔ of the puff paste into a circle large enough to fit the bottom and sides of an 8-inch flan ring. Place the ring on a baking sheet, fit in the pastry, press well into the sides and bottom, and prick with a fork a few times. Pour in the almond cream. Roll out the remaining dough into a smaller circle and cover the top of the flan ring. Seal both edges together, pressing well with your fingers. Do *not* allow the pastry to hang over the edge of the flan ring—it will be lifted off during the baking, and any overhanging pastry would make this impossible. Brush the surface with the egg white which has been lightly beaten until it is watery but not foamy. Place the cake in the refrigerator for 10 minutes. Heat the oven to 400°. Before placing the cake in the oven mark the top of the cake with fine parallel lines (not slits) with a sharp knife. The lines are traditionally in the shape of a rosette. Bake for 30 minutes, remove from the oven, carefully lift off the flan ring, and continue to bake for another 10 minutes. Remove it again, evenly sprinkle the confectioners' sugar over its surface, and put back in the oven for 2 minutes, or until the sugar has melted and formed a glaze (watch this carefully or it will burn). Remove from oven, let sit on baking sheet for 10 minutes, then carefully slide off onto a cake rack. Serve when cooled, but do not refrigerate. *Serves* 8.

1921. PLUM CAKE
Plum-cake

This is an adaptation of a famous English specialty. It is best if allowed to "ripen" for a few days.

1 cup butter, softened

1 cup superfine sugar

2 tablespoons vanilla sugar [*see* No. 2296]

4 eggs

1¾ cups triple-sifted all-purpose flour

½ teaspoon salt

1 teaspoon baking powder

3 tablespoons each of candied citron, candied lemon peel, and candied orange peel, finely chopped

1 scant cup seeded raisins, soaked in warm water for 30 minutes and well drained

1 scant cup currants, soaked in warm water for 30 minutes and well drained

1 tablespoon grated lemon rind (no white part)

¼ cup dark rum (*see* Note below)

Cream the butter in a large warm bowl with a wire whisk until it is almost white in color. Gradually beat in the sugars, beating briskly until the mixture is fluffy. Beat in the eggs, 1 at a time, beating for 2 minutes after each addition. Sift the flour with the salt and the baking powder, and beat in about ⅓ of it. When thoroughly blended add ½ the remaining ingredients, and mix well. Add the remaining flour by thirds, alternating with thirds of the remaining fruits and peels, beating to blend thoroughly. Generously grease a rectangular loaf pan (a bread pan is excellent) and line it with brown paper (a cut-up paper bag may be employed); grease the paper as well. Dust with flour and tap out the excess. Spoon the batter into the pan, tamping down well to avoid any air pockets, and bake in a preheated 350° oven for about 1 hour and 10 minutes, or until a cake tester comes out clean. Place on a cake rack and let it cool in the pan. *Makes 1 loaf serving* 12.

NOTE: The flavor may be further improved by sprinkling the cooled cake with ¼ cup (or more, if desired) of dark rum and wrapping it well in aluminum foil. Keep it for 1 week before using.

1922. QUEEN OF NUTS TORTE
Torta regina di noci

1 cup finely ground pecans, walnuts, or blanched almonds [*see* No. 2280], or a combination of all 3

1 cup superfine sugar

½ cup (generous) finely grated semi-sweet chocolate

¼ cup finely ground candied citron

4 eggs, separated

1 teaspoon vanilla extract

¼ teaspoon salt

4 tablespoons extra fine breadcrumbs

Mix the ground nuts (they may be ground in the meat grinder, using the finest blade, or whirled in the blender, ⅓ at a time, at high speed until pulverized) and the sugar together in a large bowl. Add the grated chocolate and the ground citron and mix well. Beat the egg yolks until thick and lemon colored and beat them into the mixture with the vanilla. Beat the egg whites with the salt until they form soft peaks, and carefully fold them into the mixture. Be careful not to overmix, or the egg whites will collapse. Generously butter an 8-inch cake pan. Pat in the breadcrumbs on the bottom and sides and tap out the excess. Pour the batter into the pan and bake in a 350° oven for 40 minutes, or until a cake tester comes out clean. Place on a cake rack and let cool in the pan for 10 minutes, then carefully turn it out onto the rack. Ice as desired, or sprinkle with vanilla confectioners' sugar [see No. 2296]. *Serves 6.*

1923. RUSSIAN CAKE
Gâteau alla russa

1¾ cups blanched almonds [see No. 2280], ground
1¼ cups superfine sugar
10 egg whites
½ teaspoon salt
3 tablespoons vanilla sugar [see No. 2296]
1 cup triple-sifted all-purpose flour
⅔ cup butter, heated until pale nut colored and cooled
Syrup:
   ½ cup sugar
   ¼ cup water
   3 tablespoons kirsch
1 cup apricot preserves, pressed through a fine sieve
½ recipe Almond Paste [No. 2282]
¼ cup finely cubed glacéed fruit or candied peel

Grind the almonds in the meat grinder, using the finest blade, or whirl them in the blender, ⅓ at a time, at high speed until pulverized. Make sure they are dry; if necessary, spread them out and dry them in a baking pan in a 250° oven. Do not let them brown. Mix the almonds, 1 cup of the sugar, and 2 of the egg whites. Beat until the mixture is smooth. Beat the remaining egg whites with the salt and the rest of the sugar and the vanilla sugar until they form soft peaks. Alternately add the whites, the flour, and the melted butter to the almond mixture, folding in each addition well but being careful not to overmix. Generously butter 2 8-inch cake tins, cover each of the bottoms with a circle of wax paper, butter this, then dust with flour, tapping out the excess. Divide the cake batter between the pans and bake in a 375° oven for 25 minutes, or until a cake tester comes out clean. Remove pans to a cake rack and let stand for 10 minutes, and carefully turn out onto the rack and gently peel off the paper.

While the cake is cooling, prepare the syrup. Boil the sugar and water in a small, heavy saucepan until it reaches the large thread stage (219° on the candy thermometer). Let it cool for 10 minutes, and then add the kirsch. When the cake is cool take a layer and place it on a cake plate. Sprinkle it with the syrup, making sure it soaks in well. Do not overload with syrup to make it soggy. If there is any syrup left over, sprinkle the second layer with it as well. Spread ⅓ of the apricot preserves mixed with ½ of the almond paste over the bottom layer and cover with the other layer. Spread the rest of the jam thinly over the top and sides of the assembled cake. Place the rest of the almond paste in a pastry bag fitted with a star tip, and pipe out a decorative pattern over the top of the cake and around its rim. Stud the top with the glacéed fruits in a decorative arrangement. *Serves 12.*

NOTE: This cake is better if covered with a cake cover (or placed in a large airtight tin) and left to "ripen" for a day or two.

1924. SACHERTORTE
Sachertorte

This famous cake was created at Vienna's celebrated Hotel Sacher. The original recipe is a closely guarded secret. This adaptation is especially delicious, though.

1½ cups superfine sugar
½ cup butter, softened
6 eggs, separated
1 cup dark cocoa (or 4 squares bitter chocolate, melted)
2 tablespoons vanilla sugar [see No. 2296]
½ teaspoon salt
1⅛ cups triple-sifted all-purpose flour
1 cup apricot preserves, pressed through a fine sieve
1 recipe Chocolate Icing [No. 2253], or 1½ cups chocolate Fondant Icing [see No. 2255]

Using a wire whisk and a warm bowl, cream the butter and ¾ cup of the sugar until light and fluffy. In another bowl beat the egg yolks with a wire whisk until thick and lemon colored. Gradually add the remaining sugar and beat briskly for 5 minutes. Combine the cocoa (or melted chocolate) with the creamed butter, and then beat the yolk mixture into the butter. Beat this for another 5 minutes. Beat the egg whites with the salt and the vanilla sugar until they form soft peaks. Gradually add the egg whites and flour to the first mixture, ⅓ at a time, folding each addition in gently. Do *not* overmix. Generously butter an 8-inch cake pan that is at least 1½ inches deep. Dust with flour and tap out the excess. Pour the batter into the pan and tip in all directions to coat the rim of the pan. Bake in a 325° oven for about 35 minutes, or until a cake tester plunged into the center of the cake comes out slightly oily (the cake should be a little underdone). Place the pan on a cake rack for 15 minutes, then turn out onto the rack. While still warm (but not hot) brush the entire surface with the strained apricot preserves. Let cool for at least 2 hours before icing with the chocolate icing. The cake shown in the photo facing page 624 was further decorated with triangular sheets of bittersweet chocolate. These are almost impossible to make at home, but thin sheets of chocolate may be purchased at certain candy shops which specialize in "homemade" confections. *Serves* 10.

1925. VACHERIN PRIMAVERA
Vacherin "sogno di primavera"

6 egg whites
$\frac{1}{2}$ teaspoon salt
$\frac{1}{2}$ teaspoon lemon juice
$1\frac{1}{4}$ cups superfine sugar
$\frac{1}{2}$ cup blanched almonds [*see* No. 2280], ground
2 tablespoons slivered almonds [*see* No. 2288]
2 cups heavy cream, whipped
$\frac{3}{4}$ cup Praline powder [*see* No. 2290]
1 teaspoon vanilla extract

Beat the egg whites with the salt and lemon juice in a large bowl. Use an unlined copper bowl if available, and beat with a large wire whisk for maximum lightness. When the eggs are foamy, gradually add the sugar, beating after each addition so that the meringue will not become grainy. When the eggs are beaten to soft peaks, gently fold in the ground almonds. Lightly butter a large baking sheet (or 2 baking sheets) and dust with flour, tapping off the excess. Draw 3 circles on the baking sheets, using a 7- or 8-inch cake tin as an outline. Fill a large pastry bag (without a tube, just use the aperture) with the meringue. Pipe a tight coil of meringue into each circle (filling it completely so it looks like a layer of cake), and sprinkle 1 circle with the slivered almonds. Bake in a 200° oven (or 175° if your oven can go that low) until the meringue circles are thoroughly dry. They must not become brown, or even golden, only the palest bisque in color. When they are baked, carefully remove them by sliding a spatula under each with a gently sawing motion. As the meringue layers are quite brittle, this is a tricky operation, and must be done patiently and with great gentleness. Let them cool on a cake rack. Whip the cream until stiff in a chilled bowl, fold in the crushed

praline and the vanilla extract. Place one of the layers on a round cake platter (or silver dish with a lace-paper doily) and spread it with $\frac{1}{3}$ of the cream, top with the second layer, and spread that with another $\frac{1}{3}$ of cream. Cover this with the almond-topped layer, and spread the rest of the cream carefully over the sides, leaving the top free. (The sides may be decorated with slivered toasted almonds, if desired.) Place the cake in the refrigerator for no more than 4 hours and no less than 2 hours. It should be slightly crisp, but not so crisp as to shatter under the knife. *Serves* 8.

1926. VACHERIN WITH CUSTARD CREAM
Vacherin con crema pasticcera

3 baked meringue layers [*see* No. 1925]
3 cups Pastry Cream [No. 2267], well chilled
$\frac{1}{2}$ cup butter, softened
$\frac{1}{2}$ cup superfine sugar
1 cup Chocolate Butter Cream [No. 2261]
$\frac{1}{2}$ cup heavy cream, whipped, sweetened with
    1 tablespoon superfine sugar
8 thin slices candied citron
1 candied cherry

Place 1 meringue layer on a round platter and carefully spread it evenly with 1 cup of pastry cream. Use light pressure since the meringue is very brittle. Top with the second meringue layer and spread this with another cup of the pastry cream. Top with the third meringue layer. Cream the butter with a wooden spoon in a warm bowl until pale in color, gradually beat in the sugar, beating until light and fluffy. Beat in the remaining pastry cream, 2 tablespoons at a time. When smooth, carefully ice the meringue layers with the mixture, smoothing it on with a spatula. Place the chocolate butter cream in a pastry bag fitted with a medium star tip. Pipe on swirls of cream on the sides of the vacherin and pipe on a star-like pattern on the top with a large rosette in the center (*see* photo facing page 720). Fill another pastry bag (or wash out the one used for the chocolate butter cream), fitted with the same star tip, with the whipped cream and pipe parallel lines of cream next to those of chocolate on the top surface of the cake. Arrange the slices of citron on the top, wedging them into the chocolate butter cream rosette in the center, and place the cherry in the middle. Place in refrigerator and let it "ripen" for 6 hours. *Serves* 8 *to* 10.

COOKIES AND SMALL CAKES

Pasticcini di tè

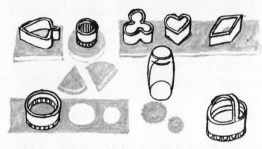

At one time cookies were considered a minor adjunct to the art of cake-making and fine pastries in general. However, during the past century, their variety, ingredients, and uses have become so extended in scope as to have become a specialty in their own right.

Many Italians, especially in the north, have become fond of afternoon tea *alla inglese,* and tea time in cities like Milan, Florence, and Rome brings out surprising numbers of smartly dressed women who sit at the tables of chic cafés and consume a no less surprising quantity of tiny cakes and cookies with their afternoon tea.

The best mixing bowl for these preparations is a large, unlined copper bowl. This must be kept scrupulously clean, and the batters must not remain in it longer than ½ hour or the copper will begin to oxidize, and this can cause serious poisoning. Despite the danger, however, a copper bowl is best, and if well taken care of will repay your labors with exquisite batters. It is also superb for beating egg whites, since it acts chemically with the albumen and makes them light and fluffy in a very short time. It also helps them hold their shape over short periods of waiting.

1927. ANISE BISCUITS
Biscotti all'anice

3 eggs
1 egg yolk
Pinch salt
½ cup plus 2 tablespoons superfine sugar
1 cup triple-sifted all-purpose flour
½ cup potato flour
3 tablespoons anise seeds

With a wire whisk beat the eggs, egg yolk, salt, and sugar in a large bowl (of unlined copper, if possible) placed over hot (not boiling) water until they double in volume and become lemon colored. Sift the 2 flours together, and gradually sift ½ the amount into the egg mixture, beating lightly with the whisk to incorporate as much air as possible into the batter. Remove from stove, sprinkle in the anise seeds, and cut in the rest of the flour. Lightly butter a large cooky sheet, sprinkle lightly with flour, and tap off the excess. Fill the pastry bag fitted with a large tube with the mixture, and pipe out on the sheet in 4-inch strips about 1½ inches wide. Bake until light gold (about 15 minutes) in a 350° oven. Remove from oven, slice each strip in half, slantwise, separate the pieces, return to oven, and bake until deep gold (about 15 minutes). Remove from oven and carefully place the biscuits on a cake rack to cool. *Makes about 4 dozen.*

NOTE: These may also be baked as follows. Butter a 9- by 12-inch baking pan, sprinkle lightly with flour, and tap out excess. Pour batter into pan and bake until pale gold and well puffed. Remove from oven, let cool for 15 minutes, cut into strips, remove from pan, and place on a baking sheet. Place sheet in a 300° oven until biscuits are deep gold (about 25 minutes). Whichever method is employed, however, the biscuits should be rather on the dry side.

1928. ALMOND MERINGUE COOKIES
Berrichons

¾ cup blanched almonds [*see* No. 2280], very finely ground
4 egg whites
Pinch salt
¾ cup vanilla sugar [*see* No. 2296], or 1 tablespoon vanilla extract and ¾ cup granulated sugar
¼ cup triple-sifted cake flour

Grind the almonds to a fine powder in the meat grinder (or whirl in the blender at high speed until pulverized). Beat the egg whites in a bowl (one of unlined copper, if possible) with the salt until they begin to form very soft peaks and gradually beat in the sugar until whites are stiff but not dry (if vanilla extract is used, add it now). Mix the flour with the powdered almonds and gently fold into the egg whites, making sure that they are well blended, but taking care not to overmix so that the egg whites lose volume. Butter a large baking sheet, dust with flour, and tap off excess. Put the mixture into a pastry bag with a medium plain tip and pipe out onto the baking sheet in 2-inch strips (or use a medium star tip and pipe out into little rosettes). Bake in a 250° oven until well puffed and pale bisque in color. Remove at once with spatula and place on a cake rack to cool. These cookies will keep a long time if placed in an airtight container. *Makes about 4 dozen.*

1929. BUTTER COOKIES
Pasta al burro per biscotti

4 eggs, separated
½ cup plus 2 tablespoons superfine sugar
¼ teaspoon salt
¾ cup triple-sifted all-purpose flour
1 teaspoon vanilla extract
6 tablespoons melted butter, still warm

Beat the egg yolks in a rather large bowl with a wire whisk, gradually adding ⅓ cup of the sugar. Beat until thick and lemon colored. Beat the whites in another bowl (preferably of unlined copper) with the salt until they form soft peaks. Gradually add the rest of the sugar to them, beating thoroughly after each addition. Sift the flour into the yolk mixture, folding and cutting it in gently, then fold and cut in the beaten whites, the vanilla, and, lastly, the melted butter. All these operations must be performed with speed and care; overmixing will make the batter fall. Butter a large baking sheet, sprinkle lightly with flour, and tap off excess. Drop batter by teaspoonful, 2 inches apart (or pipe into rosettes through a pastry bag fitted with a large star tip), and bake about 8 to 10 minutes in a 325° oven until golden (the edges should be browned). Remove from cooky sheet at once and cool on brown paper. *Makes about 4 dozen.*

1930. CAT'S TONGUES
Linguine di gatto mignonnes

These thin, dry cookies (whose long shape suggests a cat's tongue) are frequently served with iced desserts, sweet wines, or coffee. They sometimes serve as basis for more elaborate desserts [see No. 2122].

¾ cup butter, softened
¾ cup superfine sugar
2 egg whites
½ cup triple-sifted all-purpose flour
¼ teaspoon salt
1 teaspoon vanilla extract
½ teaspoon grated lemon rind (no white part)

Cream the butter with a wooden spoon in a warm bowl until pale and light. Gradually add the sugar and beat until fluffy. Beat in the egg whites, 1 at a time, beating thoroughly after each addition. Sift the flour with the salt and add gradually, beating well after each addition (an electric mixer may be used at this point). Finally, add the vanilla and the lemon rind. Lightly butter a large baking sheet, dust with flour, and tap off the excess. Place the batter in a pastry bag fitted with

a medium flat tip and pipe out into 2-inch strips, 1 inch apart. Bake in a 350° oven for 10 minutes, or until pale gold (the edges will be browned). Remove at once with spatula to a cake rack. When cool, store in an airtight container. *Makes about 4 dozen.*

1931. CHOCOLATE ALMOND SQUARES
Negretti

¾ cup blanched almonds [*see* No. 2280], ground
5 egg whites
1 cup superfine sugar
3 squares bitter chocolate
Pinch salt
½ recipe Ganache Cream [No. 2265]
1 recipe Chocolate Icing [No. 2253]

Grind the almonds to a powder in the meat grinder, using the finest blade (or whirl in the blender, ¼ cup at a time, at high speed until pulverized). Place in a bowl and work in 2 of the egg whites until the mixture becomes a smooth, rather granular paste. Work in ½ cup of the sugar. Melt the chocolate over hot water and add to the almond paste, mixing it in well. With a wire whisk beat the remaining egg whites and salt in a large bowl (of unlined copper, if possible) until they form soft peaks. Gradually add the remaining sugar, beating well after each addition. Fold the egg whites into the chocolate/almond mixture, mixing only until both are blended. Line a 10- by 14-inch baking pan with wax paper, butter well, sprinkle with flour, and tap out excess. Pour in the batter, spreading it out evenly with a moistened spatula. Bake for 10 minutes in a 350° oven. Remove at once and carefully reverse pan onto a dish towel which has been lightly dusted with confectioners' sugar (or powdered cocoa). Quickly peel off wax paper, and let the cake cool (it will be very thin). When cool, cut in half, making 2 sheets each 5 by 7 inches. Spread one of them with the Ganache, top with the other sheet, and spread it with the icing. Cut into 1-inch squares with a knife frequently dipped in hot water. *Makes 35 squares.*

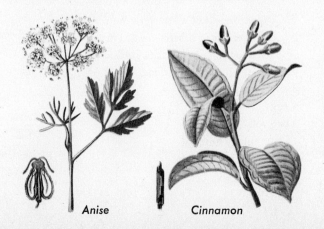

Anise   Cinnamon

1932. COOKIES CASALINGA
Pasticcini casalinghi

4 cups triple-sifted all-purpose flour
1¾ cups superfine sugar
Grated rind of 1 lemon (no white part)
1 cup butter, softened
½ teaspoon salt
4 egg yolks
½ teaspoon baking powder
3 tablespoons heavy cream
1 egg, lightly beaten
2 tablespoons Caramel Syrup [see No. 2293]
Decorations:
    Blanched almonds [see No. 2280]
    Diamond-shaped pieces of candied angelica
    Diamond-shaped pieces of candied orange or
        lemon peel
    Small candied cherries

Sift the flour into a large bowl, scoop out a hollow in the center, and into it put the sugar, lemon rind, butter, and salt. Mix thoroughly with the tips of the fingers (or a pastry blender) until it is like very fine cornmeal. Mix the yolks with the baking powder and cream, add to the flour mixture, and mix thoroughly to form a rather stiff dough. Gather it together with your hands, shape it into a flattened ball, wrap in wax paper, and place in the refrigerator for about 3 hours. After this time, roll it out on a lightly floured cloth or pastry board to a thickness of ¼ inch. Cut it into shapes using a knife or cooky cutter. Beat the egg with the caramel syrup and brush each cooky twice with this mixture. Decorate variously with any (or all) the ingredients listed above. Lightly butter a large baking sheet and place the cookies on it, ¾ inch apart. Bake in a 400° oven for 10 minutes, or until lightly brown. Remove from oven and cool cookies on a cake rack. *Makes about 4 dozen.*

1933. COOKY RINGS
Ciambelle di casa

3¼ cups triple-sifted all-purpose flour
½ cup hazelnuts or filberts, toasted in a 350°
    oven for 10 minutes, skins rubbed off with a towel,
    and the nuts finely ground
1 cup superfine sugar
1 egg
1 egg yolk
¼ cup butter, softened
½ teaspoon baking soda
¼ teaspoon salt

Sift flour into a large bowl, scoop out a hollow in the center and into it put the remaining ingredients. With a pastry blender mix together thoroughly and knead for several minutes with your hands until it forms a perfectly blended, very stiff dough. Wrap in wax paper and place dough in the refrigerator for 2 hours. After this time, roll dough out on a lightly floured cloth or pastry board to a thickness of ¼ inch, cut it into rings using a doughnut cutter (or cut into thin strips 6 inches long, and twist into rings, pinching edges together). Lightly butter a large baking sheet and place the rings on it ½ inch apart. Bake in a 425° oven for 10 minutes, or until deep gold. Remove and cool on a cake rack. *Makes about 4 dozen.*

1934. DAMES
Dame

½ cup butter, softened
½ cup superfine sugar
1 egg
1 cup triple-sifted all-purpose flour
¼ teaspoon salt
4 tablespoons yellow raisins, soaked in 2 tablespoons
    dark rum for 1 hour
Confectioners' sugar

Place the butter in a warmed bowl and cream it with a wooden spoon until light in color. Add the sugar, a tablespoonful at a time, beating well after each addition. When all the sugar has been added, beat vigorously for 5 minutes (if possible, do not use an electric beater as it will not make the mixture as light). Add the egg and beat well until thoroughly incorporated. Beat in the flour, the salt, and the raisins which have been well drained (the rum may be reserved for another use). Lightly butter a 9- by 12-inch baking pan, line it with wax paper, butter this, dust with flour, and tap out the excess. Put the batter in the pan, spreading it evenly with a moistened spatula. Bake in a 400° oven for 8 minutes, or until golden brown. Remove from oven, let rest for 2 minutes, turn it out onto a dish towel lightly dusted with confectioners' sugar, peel off paper quickly, and carefully cut into small rectangles about 1½ by 1 inches and place on a cake rack to cool. *Makes about 6 dozen.*

NOTE: The batter may also be placed in a pastry bag fitted with a large plain tip and piped into little mounds, 1½ inches apart, on a baking sheet.

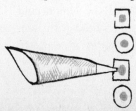

1935. FAMILY COOKIES
Biscotti di famiglia

These are excellent served with tea. They may be kept for quite a long time in an airtight container.

4 cups triple-sifted all-purpose flour
1 cup butter, softened
1 cup plus 3 tablespoons superfine sugar
3 eggs
2 tablespoons orange flower water
¼ teaspoon salt
1 egg yolk
2 tablespoons milk
Glaze:
    4 tablespoons confectioners' sugar
    1 tablespoon heavy cream

Sift the flour into a large bowl. Make a well in the center and in it place the butter and ½ of the sugar. Mix with a pastry blender until it resembles fine corn-meal. Beat the eggs with the rest of the sugar, the orange flower water, and the salt. Beat only until blended. Mix this into the flour mixture and form into a stiff dough, using a large fork or your hands to accomplish this. Gather the dough up into a flattish ball, wrap in wax paper, and place in refrigerator for 2 hours. After this time roll it out on a floured cloth or pastry board to a thickness of ¼ inch. Cut out cookies, using a cooky cutter (or a small glass), or simply cut in squares and diamonds with a sharp knife. Lightly butter a baking sheet, place the cookies on it, 1 inch apart, and bake in a 375° oven for 15 minutes, or until pale golden brown. Mix confectioners' sugar and cream to form a glaze, and brush each cooky with it. Cool on cake racks. *Makes about 4 dozen.*

1936. LEMON COOKIES
Biscotti al limone

6 eggs
1 cup plus 2 tablespoons superfine sugar
Pinch salt
Juice of 1 lemon, strained
Grated rind of 1 lemon (no white part)
1½ cups triple-sifted all-purpose flour
3 tablespoons coarse sugar crystals (or substitute
    colored cooky shot)

Place the eggs, sugar, salt, and lemon juice in a deep bowl (preferably of unlined copper) and place the bowl over a pan of hot (*not* boiling) water. With a wire whisk beat until greatly increased in volume and light in color. At this point remove from hot water, add lemon rind, and beat until somewhat cool. Sift in the flour, gradually, lightly incorporating it into the eggs with the whisk. Lightly butter a large baking sheet, dust it with flour, and tap off the excess. Drop the batter by teaspoonful 2 inches apart on the sheet and sprinkle each cooky with a few grains of the crystals. Bake in a 350° oven for 10 minutes, or until the edges are golden brown. Remove from oven and transfer cookies onto a cake rack at once. *Makes about 3 dozen.*

1937. LITTLE ALMOND TUBES
Tegoline alle mandorle

2 egg whites
Pinch salt
½ cup superfine sugar
½ cup triple-sifted all-purpose flour
3 tablespoons butter, melted
¼ cup thinly slivered almonds [*see* No. 2288]

Place the egg whites, salt, and sugar in a large, deep bowl (preferably of unlined copper) and place this over hot (not boiling) water. Beat with a wire whisk until the egg whites form soft peaks. Remove from hot water and beat for 5 minutes. Fold in the flour carefully, making sure you do not overmix. Fold in the melted butter and the almonds. Mix only until well blended. Lightly butter a large cooky sheet, dust with flour, and tap off the excess. Drop the batter by scant teaspoonful onto the sheet, spacing them 2 inches apart. Bake for 8 minutes in a 375° oven, remove, and while still hot, curl them around the handle of a wooden spoon. If any become brittle before they are so treated, place the sheet back in the oven for a few seconds to restore their pliability. *Makes about 2½ dozen.*

1938. MADELEINES
Maddalene

This is an Italian adaptation of those exquisite shell-shaped morsels which originated in Commercy in France. Readers of Marcel Proust will no doubt recall them as the memory-inducing catalyst that plays so large a part in his Remembrance of Things Past.

4 eggs
Pinch salt
½ cup superfine sugar
1 tablespoon orange flower water (or 1 teaspoon vanilla
    extract, or ½ teaspoon vanilla extract and
    1 teaspoon orange flower water)
¾ cup triple-sifted all-purpose flour
½ cup Clarified Butter [No. 102], cooled

Beat the eggs and salt in a large bowl (preferably one of unlined copper) with a wire whisk until they are very frothy and light in color. Gradually beat in the sugar and orange flower water. Fold in the flour, incorporating it well, but taking care not to overmix. Lastly, add the clarified butter, stirring it in until no trace remains (*stir*, do not beat or fold). Lightly butter 12 shell-shaped madeleine tins (these are traditional, although shallow muffin tins may be substituted), dust with flour, and tap out the excess. Divide the batter among the tins and bake in a 400° oven for 10 to 12 minutes, or until golden brown. Remove from tins and cool on a cake rack. *Makes 1 dozen.*

1939. NOVARA BISCUITS
Biscotti di Novara

Novara is a town in Lombardy, west of Milan, at the foot of the Italian Alps.

    4 eggs
    1 egg yolk
    1 heaping cup superfine sugar
    $\frac{1}{4}$ teaspoon salt
    1 teaspoon vanilla extract
    1$\frac{3}{4}$ cups triple-sifted all-purpose flour
    8 vanilla wafers, crushed (or whirled in the blender)
        until they are as fine as sugar

Place the eggs, egg yolk, sugar, and salt in a large bowl (preferably of unlined copper), place over hot (not boiling) water, and beat with a wire whisk until very light and greatly increased in bulk. Remove from heat and continue beating for 10 minutes (an electric beater may be used at this point, but not while the egg mixture is over hot water). When cool, add the vanilla and then gradually fold in the flour, mixing only until it is incorporated. Lightly butter a large baking sheet, dust it with flour, and tap off the excess. Place the batter in a pastry bag fitted with a medium plain tip, and pipe out 2-inch lengths of the batter, placed 2 inches apart. Lightly dust each biscuit with the crumbs and place the sheet in a 350° oven for 8 to 10 minutes, or until biscuits are deep gold. Cool on a cake rack. *Makes about 3 dozen.*

634

1940. ORANGE WAFERS
Gallettine all'arancia

    $\frac{3}{4}$ cup blanched almonds [*see* No. 2280], finely ground
    $\frac{2}{3}$ cup superfine sugar
    $\frac{1}{2}$ cup candied orange peel, very finely chopped
    $\frac{1}{4}$ scant cup triple-sifted all-purpose flour

    $\frac{1}{4}$ teaspoon salt
    $\frac{1}{2}$ teaspoon orange extract
    1 scant cup heavy cream

Grind the almonds in the meat grinder, using the finest blade (or whirl in the blender at high speed until pulverized). Place these and all the remaining ingredients in a large bowl and beat with a wire whisk until smooth (about 5 minutes). Lightly butter a large cooky sheet, dust it with flour, and tap off the excess. Drop batter onto sheet by scant teaspoonful, 2 inches apart. Bake in a 350° oven for no more than 10 minutes. Remove from sheet at once and cool on unglazed brown paper. *Makes about 3 dozen.*

1941. PALM LEAVES
Palmiers

These are a Parisian specialty. They are exquisite if cut half as thin as directed, and a generous amount of sweetened whipped cream sandwiched between 2 of them.

    1 recipe Puff Paste [No. 1960]
    Granulated sugar

Let the puff paste stay in the refrigerator overnight. When ready to make the palm leaves, liberally sprinkle a large pastry board with sugar. Roll out the pastry on this, sprinkling it with more sugar as you do so. When it is rolled out to a thickness of $\frac{1}{4}$ inch, sprinkle the entire surface with more sugar. Fold the left-hand side lengthwise until it meets the center, do the same for the right-hand side. Then fold each side again until they meet in the center (*see* illustration). With a very sharp knife cut off $\frac{1}{4}$-inch slices, sprinkle them with more sugar, and place them on a moistened baking sheet, 2 inches apart. Bake in a 425° oven for

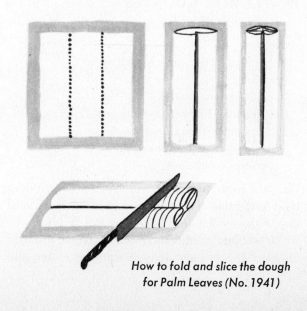

How to fold and slice the dough for Palm Leaves (No. 1941)

10 minutes, or until they are well puffed and the sugar on the bottom has begun to caramelize (the tops will be rather pale as opposed to the rich brown glaze on the bottoms). Remove them at once with a spatula and cool them, glazed side up, on a cake rack. *Makes about 3½ dozen.*

1942. PAVIA COOKIES
Biscotti tipo pavesini

Pavia is a city not far from Milan, famed for its university and magnificent Renaissance monastery, the Certosa. Although no longer housing a religious order, the Certosa still manufactures an exquisite liqueur called Gra-Car *(short for* Gratium Cartusia, *or "Gift of the Carthusians"). Pavia is well worth a visit, both for the Certosa and for this liqueur (which, so far as we know, is not exported).*

6 eggs
1 cup plus 3 tablespoons superfine sugar
¼ teaspoon salt
1 teaspoon vanilla extract
½ cup triple-sifted all-purpose flour
¼ cup coarsely chopped blanched almonds
　[*see* No. 2280], lightly toasted

Put the eggs, 1 cup of the sugar, and salt in a large, deep bowl (preferably of unlined copper). Place bowl over a pan of hot (not boiling) water and beat with a wire whisk until light in color and greatly increased in volume. Remove from over hot water and beat for 5 minutes, or until somewhat cooled (at this point an electric beater may be used). Beat in the vanilla extract and then gradually fold in the flour, a little at a time. Take care not to overmix, or the batter will be heavy. Lightly butter a large baking sheet, sprinkle it with flour, and tap off the excess. Drop batter by scant teaspoonsful onto the sheet, spacing them 2 inches apart. Sprinkle the surface of each with a little of the chopped, toasted almonds which have been mixed with the remaining sugar. Bake in a 350° oven for 10 minutes, or until they are a deep gold. *Makes about 4 dozen.*

1943. PINE NUT AND ALMOND PASTE COOKIES
Pinoccate

This is a very famous Italian cooky.

2 cups blanched almonds [*see* No. 2280], ground
2 cups plus 1 tablespoon superfine sugar

1 teaspoon vanilla extract
4 egg whites
Pinch salt
2 cups pine nuts

Place 1 cup of the sugar and the almonds in the mortar and pound them until they become a paste (or place them in the blender, ½ cup at a time, and whirl at high speed until reduced to a powder), and add the vanilla. Beat the egg whites with the salt until they form soft peaks, beat in the remaining sugar, and gradually fold into the almond paste. Place the pine nuts in a shallow bowl or dish and drop the almond mixture by spoonsful into them, rolling gently to cover the surface with nuts. Lightly butter a large cooky sheet, dust it with flour, and tap off the excess. Place the nut-coated dollops of cooky batter on it, 1 inch apart, flattening them lightly with a moistened spatula. Bake in a 400° oven for 10 minutes, or until golden. *Makes about 3 dozen.*

1944. PINE NUT COOKIES PERUGINA
Pinoccate alla perugina

This requires the use of paper-like wafers made from egg white and rice flour. It is the same sort of wafer used in torrone *or nougat candy. Impossible to make at home (it looks like sheets of paper), it can be bought at Italian confectioners in large cities.*

2 heaping cups superfine sugar
1½ cups cold water
½ teaspoon cream of tartar
¾ cup pine nuts
½ cup candied orange peel, finely chopped, soaked in
　2 tablespoons maraschino liqueur
Sheets of edible rice paper, as required

Place sugar, water, and cream of tartar in a heavy pan, and stir for 5 minutes off heat until the sugar has mostly dissolved and the mixture becomes translucent. Place it over medium heat and cover for a few minutes, so that the steam will wash down any sugar clinging to the sides of the pan. Uncover, and cook without stirring (stirring will make the sugar crystallize, something to be avoided at all costs) until it reaches the soft ball stage (230° on the candy thermometer). If any sugar crystals appear on the sides of the pan, wash them down with dampened cheesecloth wrapped on a fork. When sugar has reached its proper temperature remove pan from the stove and stir with a wooden spoon or small paddle. Keep stirring (not beating) in a

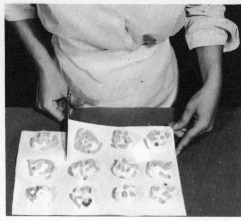

The preparation of Pine Nut Cookies Perugina (No. 1944). Left: Batter is being stirred, and pine nuts and orange peel are kept in readiness. Right: Mounds of batter are spaced out on the edible wafer paper, which is then cut into squares.

circular motion until the syrup becomes white, thick, and opaque. When it begins to whiten add the maraschino-soaked orange peel and its liquid and the pine nuts. Working very quickly (so the mixture does not harden), distribute generous spoonsful on a sheet of the rice-wafer paper (*see* photograph). Cut wafer paper with scissors as shown, and keep in a dry place. The part of the wafer protruding around the mounds may be crimped up around them. *Makes about 1½ dozen.*

1945. SABLÉS
Sablés

This delicate preparation is an Italian adaptation of a specialty of Normandy.

½ cup blanched almonds [*see* No. 2280], lightly toasted
¾ cup superfine sugar
⅔ cup butter, softened (or ⅓ cup butter, ⅓ cup lard)
4 egg yolks
1 teaspoon vanilla extract
⅓ teaspoon salt
2 cups triple-sifted all-purpose flour

Pound the almonds in the mortar with ¼ cup of the sugar (or whirl in blender on high speed until pulverized). Cream the butter and the rest of the sugar in a warm bowl with a wooden spoon. Beat in the egg yolks, 1 at a time, beating well after each addition. Add vanilla and salt, then beat in almonds. Gradually work in the flour, a little at a time, until you have a rather firm and stiff dough. Avoid overhandling (as in pie crust). Form into a ball, wrap well in wax paper or foil, and let it rest in the least cold part of the refrigerator for 2 hours. Lightly flour a cloth or pastry board and roll out chilled dough to the thickness of ¼ inch. Cut out with a scalloped round or oval cutter (*see* illustration) about 2 inches in diameter. Butter a

large cooky sheet and arrange the sablés on it, 1 inch apart. Bake in a 350° oven for 18 to 20 minutes, or until golden brown. *Makes about 3 dozen.*

NOTE: As in pie crust (*see* page 640), this dough must not be overhandled once the flour has been added. Work quickly and methodically.

1946. SAVOYARD LADYFINGERS
Savoiardi

8 eggs, separated
1¼ cups superfine sugar
½ cup plus 1 tablespoon twice-sifted arrowroot (or substitute potato flour)
1 tablespoon orange flower water
Pinch salt
4 tablespoons triple-sifted confectioners' sugar

Beat the egg yolks with 1 cup of the sugar in a large, deep bowl. If possible use a wicker whisk instead of a wire one. Beat until the mixture falls from the whisk in a slowly dissolving ribbon of batter. Sift in the arrowroot (arrowroot is a neutral starch and is very delicate; it does not alter the flavor of the preparation)

Cutting Sablés (No. 1945)

636

and fold it in very carefully, making sure you mix only until it is incorporated. Add the orange flower water next. Beat the egg whites and the salt with a wire whisk until they are foamy. Gradually add the remaining sugar and beat until they form soft peaks. Fold the whites into the yolk mixture, cutting the mixture in lightly. Mix only until they are blended. Lightly butter a large cooky sheet, dust it with flour, and tap off the excess. Fill a large pastry bag fitted with a large plain tip with the batter, and pipe it onto the sheet in 3-inch "fingers," leaving a 2-inch space between them. Sprinkle lightly with the confectioners' sugar and bake in a 350° oven for 15 minutes, or until pale gold. Remove with a spatula and cool on a cake rack. *Makes about 2½ dozen.*

NOTE: These are a superlative version of ladyfingers. Besides being delectable in their own right, they may be used in a number of other desserts.

1947. RAISED SWEET BISCUITS
Biscotti comuni

4 cups triple-sifted all-purpose flour
1 cake fresh compressed yeast, dissolved in ¼ cup lukewarm, scalded milk and left until foaming (about 5 minutes) in a warm (85°) place, (or 1 envelope dried yeast dissolved in hotter (110°) scalded milk, and left until foaming
7 tablespoons butter, softened
½ cup plus 2 tablespoons superfine sugar
2 eggs, lightly beaten
Grated rind of 1 lemon (no white part)
Pinch salt
¾ cup scalded milk, cooled to barely lukewarm

Take ½ of the flour and mix it with the dissolved yeast until it forms a smooth, rather loose dough (do not overmix). Roll it into a ball, cut a cross into the top with a sharp floured knife, and place in a warm bowl. Cover, and let rise until doubled (10 to 15 minutes). Place the remaining flour in a large bowl, make a well in the center, and into it put the remaining ingredients and the risen yeast ball. Knead the flour into the ingredients, working from the outer edge of the bowl toward the center, down and around. Mix and knead until the dough no longer sticks to the sides of the bowl and is smooth and satiny. Cover lightly, set in a warm place, and let rise until doubled in bulk (about 45 minutes). Punch down, and put dough on a lightly floured pastry cloth or board. Knead for a minute, and divide in 2 pieces. Form each piece into a smallish, rather long loaf and set them at least 7 inches

apart on a lightly buttered cooky sheet. Cover with a cloth and set in a warm place until doubled in bulk. Bake in a 350° oven for about 35 to 40 minutes, or until deep gold. Place on a cake rack to cool. When still slightly warm, slice with a bread knife into the thinnest possible slices. (Since the loaves are freshly baked this will be rather difficult: use a serrated bread knife and employ a gently sawing motion.) Arrange the slices on an unbuttered cooky sheet and return to the 350° oven to bake until dry and golden brown. Cool on a cake rack and when thoroughly cool store in an airtight container. *Make about 4 dozen.*

NOTE: For hints on yeast dough, *see page 611.*

1948. VANILLA ALMOND STICKS
Bastoncini alla vaniglia

1 cup blanched almonds [*see* No. 2280]
¼ teaspoon salt
½ cup superfine sugar
3 teaspoons warm water (more or less, as needed)
Triple-sifted confectioners' sugar
1 cup Royal Icing [No. 2257]

Pound the almonds, salt, and sugar to a paste in the mortar (or place in the blender and whirl at high speed until pulverized). Place in a bowl and work for a few minutes with a wooden spoon. Add the water, a teaspoon at a time, until you have a very firm, granular dough. Dust a pastry cloth or board with the sifted confectioners' sugar and roll the almond dough into a sheet about ½ inch thick. Spread a thin layer of icing over the sheet, and cut into strips 3 inches long and 1¼ inches wide. Lightly butter a large cooky sheet, place the strips on it, and bake in a 250° oven for 15 minutes. The strips should not darken, and the icing should melt and form a glaze. *Makes about 2½ dozen.*

SMALL CAKES AND PETITS FOURS
Pasticcini diversi

The name *petits fours* means literally "little ovens" in French. These should be made bite size, and are perfect served with afternoon tea, after-dinner coffee, or as accompaniments to ice cream, iced desserts, or fruit compotes. They may be elaborately decorated or not, but they must be very small, and whatever icing or decoration you choose should be neatly executed.

1949. INDIVIDUAL RUM BABAS
Piccoli babàs al rhum

1 recipe Baba Dough [No. 1887]
½ cup seedless raisins (or currants)
3 tablespoons dark rum
A syrup:
   1 cup sugar
   ¾ cup water
   ½ cup dark rum

Soak the raisins (or currants) in the rum while the dough is rising. Add them to the dough when the butter is added. Let dough rise as indicated. Generously butter individual tiny cylindrical molds (or very small muffin or jumble tins and fill them ½ full of dough. Cover with a cloth and set in a warm place until doubled in bulk. Bake in a 400° oven for 15 minutes, or until well puffed and golden brown. Remove from oven and let cool in their tins for 5 minutes, and then turn out onto a cake rack.

Bring the sugar and water to a boil in a small saucepan and let it cook for 5 minutes; remove from stove and add the rum. Prick each baba with a fork and dunk in the hot syrup, rolling it around to make sure it is well coated. Repeat until all babas have been treated in this manner, then dip them all once again. Continue until all the syrup has been used up. Place the babas on a plate and serve at room temperature or while still warm. They may also be served cold, accompanied by a bowl of sweetened whipped cream. *Makes about 2 dozen babas.*

1950. PETITS FOURS
Petits fours

.1 recipe of No. 1951, 1952, or 1953
1 recipe Fondant Icing [No. 2255], plain white or
   tinted with a few drops food coloring, or flavored
   with coffee, chocolate, orange or lemon extract, etc.
Optional: 1 recipe Butter Cream [No. 2260]
Decorations (any one, or in combination):
   Candied cherries
   Candied angelica
   Blanched almonds [*see* No. 2280], split and toasted
   Candied pineapple
   Candied orange or lemon peel
   Candied coffee beans

Butter a 9- by 12-inch baking tin (or, if you are making them in 2 layers, a 10- by 14-inch pan), line with wax paper, butter this, dust it lightly with flour, and tap out the excess. Pour in the cake batter of your choice and bake in a 350° oven for 25 minutes, or until a cake tester comes out clean. Turn out on a cake rack, carefully peel off the wax paper, and allow to cool thoroughly. Cut into small, bite-sized pieces: either diamond shapes, triangles, small rounds, or crescents (these last with a 1½-inch-round cooky cutter). Dust off any loose crumbs with a pastry brush, and place the little cakes on a cake rack, 1 inch apart. Prepare the icing as indicated, flavor and color as desired, and pour a little over each cake, making sure it is well coated. A piece of wax paper under the rack will catch the excess icing, which may then be gathered up, heated until soft, and reused. *Makes about 2 dozen.*

If desired, the cake may be baked in a wider pan, to produce a thinner cake. It is then cut into 2 equal halves, one placed over the other, cut into shapes as indicated above, and a little butter cream (flavored as desired) sandwiched between the layers. Ice as indicated above.

The cakes are now ready to be decorated. They must be festive in appearance, but the colors should be pale—use no more than 1 or 2 drops of food coloring in the icing. Here are some suggestions:

Chocolate Petits Fours: Ice with chocolate fondant, and decorate with split, toasted blanched almonds. Fill a small pastry bag fitted with the smallest tip (or use a paper cornucopia) with plain white fondant and pipe thin lines or swirls around the almonds and the edges of the cake. (If filled, use chocolate butter cream.)

White Petits Fours: Ice with plain white fondant (flavored with vanilla or almond extract) and decorate with a small piece of candied cherry or pineapple surrounded by tiny diamonds of candied angelica. Pink or green fondant may be piped on as indicated above. (If filled, fill with plain butter cream, or one flavored with the liqueur of your choice).

Pink Petits Fours: Color the fondant pale pink with a few drops red food coloring. Flavor with a little kirsch if desired. Decorate with pieces of candied cherry. White or chocolate fondant may be piped on as indicated above. (If filled, fill with plain butter cream flavored with kirsch or cherry brandy.)

Orange or Lemon Petits Fours: Color fondant pale orange or lemon yellow with a few drops food coloring and flavor with Grand Marnier (for orange) or lemon extract (for yellow). Decorate with tiny strips or diamonds of candied orange or lemon peel, and tiny diamonds of candied angelica. White (for orange) or pale green (for lemon) fondant may be piped on as indicated above. (If filled, use butter cream flavored

1 2 3

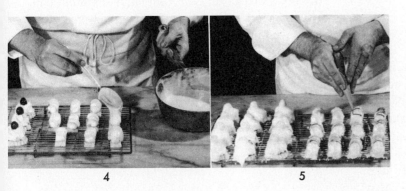

4 5

HOW TO ICE PETITS FOURS

1. Pipe on the butter cream (if used) with a pastry bag fitted with a medium plain tip

2. Garnish with cherries or candied fruit (this may also be done after the fondant has been poured over the cakes). To lessen danger of melting when fondant is applied, butter-cream-topped cakes may be chilled for 2 hours.

3. Soften the fondant in a pan over the lowest possible heat until it is syrupy, stirring constantly with a wooden spoon

4. Pour the fondant over each cake, making sure that it coats evenly

5. Pipe on lines of fondant, flavored and colored as desired. (At this point the cakes may be further decorated with the candied fruits and nuts listed in No. 1950.)

with Grand Marnier for the orange, and lemon-flavored butter cream for the lemon.)

Coffee Petits Fours: Flavor icing with 1 teaspoon instant coffee and a drop of vanilla extract. Decorate with candied coffee beans. White or chocolate fondant may be piped on as indicated above. (If filled, fill with coffee or chocolate butter cream.)

NOTE: The photographs above demonstrate the basic procedures for icing and decorating the cakes. You will notice that the butter cream has been piped on with a pastry bag and the warm fondant spooned over it. Your own ingenuity may create other combinations of flavors and decoration for the petits fours. However, since neatness is paramount, work calmly and methodically. If the decorations seem too elaborate or difficult, omit them and merely ice and/or fill the cakes.

1951. ALMOND CAKE BASE FOR PETITS FOURS

Pasta per petits fours in stampi

5 eggs
½ teaspoon salt
1 cup superfine sugar
5 egg yolks
1 cup Clarified Butter [No. 102], almost hot
1 cup blanched almonds [*see* No. 2280], ground to a powder

1¼ cups triple-sifted all-purpose flour
1 teaspoon almond extract

Beat the whole eggs and salt with a wire whisk in a large bowl (preferably of unlined copper) until they are foamy; gradually beat in the sugar. When it has all been added, add the yolks, 1 at a time, beating well after each addition. Beat until the batter falls in a slowly dissolving ribbon from the whisk. At this point, beat in the hot clarified butter in a thin stream. Grind the almonds in the meat grinder, using the finest blade (or whirl in blender at high speed, ½ cup at a time, until they are pulverized). Alternately add the flour and the almonds to the batter, mixing and folding them in. Take care not to overmix. Butter a baking pan of the size desired [*see* No. 1950], line it with wax paper, butter that, and dust with flour, tapping out the excess. Pour in the batter and bake in a 350° oven for 25 minutes, or until a cake tester comes out clean. Turn out onto a cake rack, carefully peel off paper, and proceed as indicated in No. 1950.

639

1952. BUTTER CAKE MIXTURE FOR PETITS FOURS
Biscotti al burro

½ cup butter, softened
1 cup superfine sugar
7 egg yolks
1½ cups triple-sifted all-purpose flour
2 eggs, lightly beaten
4 egg whites
¼ teaspoon salt
1 teaspoon vanilla (or almond, lemon, or orange) extract

Cream the butter with a wooden spoon in a large, warmed bowl until very pale. Gradually add ¾ cup of the sugar, beating until the mixture is light and fluffy. Add 3 of the yolks, all at once, and beat until thoroughly incorporated. Add a few tablespoons of the flour and then alternate with the beaten eggs, the remaining yolks, and the rest of the flour. Beat thoroughly after each addition. When all the ingredients have been added, beat the egg whites and the salt with a wire whisk in a large bowl (preferably of unlined copper) until foamy, and then add the remaining sugar. Beat until they form soft peaks and then fold and cut into the cake batter. Mix only until well blended, and add the flavoring. Butter and flour the size pan desired [see No. 1950], lining it with wax paper, and bake in a 350° oven for 25 minutes, or until a cake tester comes out clean. Turn out on a cake rack, carefully peel off the paper, and proceed as indicated in No. 1950.

1953. GÉNOISE MIXTURE FOR PETITS FOURS
Pasta genovese per biscotti e per petits fours

This is the classic base. It is very delicate, and the butter lends it added richness.

8 eggs
1 cup superfine sugar
Pinch salt
1½ cups triple-sifted cake flour
¾ cup lukewarm Clarified Butter [No. 102]
1 teaspoon vanilla (or other) extract

Put the eggs, sugar, and salt into a large, deep bowl (preferably of unlined copper), and place the bowl over hot (not boiling) water. Beat with a wire whisk until pale and lemon colored and greatly increased in volume. When the batter falls from the beater in a

slowly dissolving ribbon, remove from heat. Continue beating until the mixture is cool. Gradually stir in the flour (do not beat, but stir, blending it in well) and finally stir in the clarified butter gradually, a tablespoon at a time, mixing only until no trace remains. Flavor as desired. Butter a baking pan of the size most suitable [see No. 1950], line it with wax paper, butter that, and dust with flour, tapping out the excess. Pour in batter and bake in a 350° oven for 35 minutes, or until a cake tester comes out clean. Turn out onto a cake rack, carefully peel off paper, and proceed as indicated in No. 1950.

PASTRY, PIES, AND TARTS
Impasti

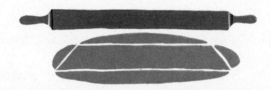

Unlike yeast-raised dough, the dough for pies and tarts must be handled as little as possible. "Quick and cold" should be the guiding words. Put your bowl and your implements for mixing the pastry (whether knives or pastry blender) in the refrigerator before you start. Where water is called for, use ice water. Only the butter, if too hard when it emerges from the refrigerator, may be allowed to warm up a slight bit. In certain recipes, this cook book follows the standard Italian practice of preparing pastry on a marble surface. An enamel or Formica table top will also serve, especially if wiped with a piece of ice and dried before mixing the pastry on it.

Many cooks prefer mixing the pastry by hand, because it is faster once you have the knack of it. The danger here, however, is of too much handling: the palms of the hands are treacherously warm. It is all-important that the bits of butter, however small or flaked, should stay firm and discrete, not be allowed to turn greasy.

Pastry dough should be very cold, and should be placed in a very hot oven (about 375° or 400°) to bake. This allows the dough to set rapidly and reduces the danger of a shortening-rich dough "melting," and

1. Crêpes Suzette (No. 2027)
2. Pastry Cream (No. 2267)
3. Rothschild Soufflé (No. 2046)
4. San Giuseppe Fritters (No. 2038)
5. Pears Cecilia (No. 2169)
6. Bananas Lucullus (No. 2148),
   with an accompanying bowl of
   Apricot Sauce (No. 2270) at right

thereby either dissolving or becoming too granular in texture to hold its shape when baked. If the unbaked dough is to be filled, the filling should not be hot, as this would cause the dough to melt before it has had time to set in the oven. If a hot filling must be added to an unbaked crust, then the dough should be baked "blind" for about 8 minutes before the filling is poured in.

Baking "blind":

This means that the dough is pre-baked (and usually cooled) before the filling is added. There are several methods that can be employed for pre-baking. The first is best for a pie shell that is to be kept in the pie pan; therefore one with sloping sides may be used.

1. Roll out the dough on a floured pastry cloth, board, or marble slab. Roll lightly in a single direction (not back and forth) using only enough flour to keep the dough from sticking. Too much flour will make the dough tough. Roll into as even a circle as possible, accomplishing this by rolling from the center outward in all directions. When rolled out, the dough should be no more than $\frac{1}{8}$ inch thick.

2. Gently position the pie tin in the center of the rolled-out circle of dough and run a sharp knife around the dough, about 2 inches beyond the outer rim of the pie tin.

3. Lift off the pie tin, carefully roll the trimmed circle of dough around the rolling pin, and unroll it onto the pie tin. (This is less tricky than trying to pick it up with your hands.)

4. Press the dough firmly into the bottom and sides of the tin. This is best accomplished by rolling the dough trimmings into a ball, and using this dough ball to press down the lining dough. Your fingers may be used, but because they are warm there is the danger that they may melt the shortening.

5. When the dough is pressed down and no air remains trapped between it and the tin, fold the overhanging dough around the rim over on itself and crimp decoratively, using floured fingers, a pastry crimper, or the well-floured tines of a fork.

6. Prick the bottom and the sides of the dough with a fork. (This prevents any air trapped between the dough and the tin from expanding with heat during baking, and thereby causing the crust to bubble up.)

7. Take a square of foil or wax paper, large enough to project about 2 inches beyond the upper rim of the tin, and place it over the tin. Pour in enough dried beans or peas so that the tin is filled.

8. Place the bean-filled tin in a 400° oven for 10

minutes, or until the crust is set, but not yet browned. After this time, remove from oven, carefully pour off the beans, lift out the foil or wax paper, return tin to oven, and bake until the crust is golden brown.

9. Remove from oven and cool on a cake rack before filling (or fill with a hot mixture and serve at once). The beans may be stored (when cool) in a large, tightly covered jar and used over and over for this purpose.

Baking "blind" in a straight-sided pan:

This method is best employed for tarts or pies that are to be served in a crust that has been removed from the tin. A straight-sided tin is used, as the slope-sided variety would make a crust lacking the tensile strength to support a filling. There are two ways of baking this type of crust. The first employs a flan ring or a low-sided spring form pan, and the second (and perhaps simpler method) calls for a regular straight-sided cake pan.

First method: Roll out the pastry and proceed up to step 4 as indicated above. Place a flan ring on a baking sheet and line it with the dough, or line a spring form with the dough. If the dough is not very rich, the spring form or flan ring may be lightly greased. The overhanging dough should not be folded so that it overlaps the rim of the pan; this would make it impossible to remove the baked crust. Merely trim it off flush with the rim of the pan and press it firmly against the inner sides with the point of a knife or the tines of a fork. Proceed as directed in steps 6 through 9. When cool, carefully lift off the flan ring, or loosen the sides of the spring form, and slide the baked shell onto a platter or serving dish.

Second method: This method is simpler and does not require the use of a special tin, or the bean lining. Proceed up to step 4. Grease the *outside* of a cake tin, dust it with flour, and tap off the excess. Place the tin (upside down so that its bottom surface faces upward) on a baking sheet. Press dough onto the tin, and, if desired, fold the excess dough over onto itself and crimp decoratively (or trim off flush with a sharp knife— however, it would be well to remember that the added thickness around the rim adds strength to the finished product). Prick the surface all over with a fork and proceed as directed in steps 6 through 9. When baked, leave on baking sheet to cool for a few minutes, then carefully lift off tin with the crust, and gently turn it over onto a platter or serving dish. Lift out the cake tin, and let the crust stand until absolutely cool.

NOTE: When following any of the above-listed instructions, one may place the unbaked crust-lined tin in the refrigerator for 1 hour if the day, or the kitchen, is warm. Also, the tin may be prepared well ahead of baking time and can rest in the refrigerator for a few hours until ready to bake. Baking directions for filled crusts will be found under the individual recipes for pies and tarts.

TWO CLASSIC FLAKY PASTRIES
Due pasti classici

This pair of recipes are based on the classic French *pâte brisée* and *pâte à foncer*. "Broken" and "to be kneaded" refer to the manner of preparing the dough which, like all pastry doughs, should rest in the refrigerator for at least 2 hours, or overnight, before being rolled out. Such rest removes any elasticity the dough may have acquired when being made. Tightly wrapped in wax paper, plastic food wrap, or foil, pastry dough may be kept in the refrigerator for 5 days. On freezing, see page 610.

The characteristic manner of preparing these doughs consists of breaking off small pieces of the mixed dough, and pushing them down with the heel of the hand (the palm is too warm) against the pastry board. When the entire mass of dough has been treated in this manner, gather the pieces and scattered flakes into a ball and repeat the breaking and pushing-down processes. Gather them into a ball again, wrap well, and place in the refrigerator.

1954. FLAKY PASTRY
Pasta brisée

2 cups sifted all-purpose flour
⅔ cup chilled butter (or ½ butter, ½ lard)
½ teaspoon salt
1 tablespoon sugar
Ice water as required (no more than 6 tablespoons)

Chill bowl and implements, also the flour, in refrigerator for 2 hours. Sift the flour, sugar, and salt into the bowl. With 2 knives, or a pastry blender, cut the butter quickly into the flour until the mixture resembles large peas. Using a big fork, or the tips of your fingers, dribble the ice water into the mixture, a very little at a time, working the butter/flour mixture into it from the center. Do not rework any part of the mixture if at all possible. When all the water has been in-

corporated, turn out the dough onto a floured pastry board, marble slab, or pastry cloth, and proceed to work the dough twice, as described in the introductory note above. When the pastry has rested in the refrigerator (for a minimum of 2 hours), take it out and let stand for 20 minutes or so to become workable. Divide it into 2 parts and roll out into 2 10- or 11-inch circles, or into a large sheet from which tart shells may be made. *Makes enough for 2 single-crust pies, 1 2-crust pie, or 12 tart shells.*

1955. RICH PASTRY
Pasta à foncer fine

2 cups sifted all-purpose flour
½ cup chilled butter (or ½ butter, ½ lard)
1 tablespoon sugar
1 teaspoon salt
1 egg yolk
Ice water as required (up to ⅓ cup)

Before beginning chill utensils and flour in refrigerator for 2 hours. Proceed exactly as in preceding recipe, except cut the butter into small slices when adding it to the flour/sugar/salt mixture, and, before adding the ice water, beat the egg yolk with 1 tablespoon of the water. Add the water/yolk mixture before the rest of the ice water. *Makes 2 single-crust pies, 1 2-crust pie, or 12 tart shells.*

1956. DELICATE SWEET PASTRY
Pasta zuccherata fine o pasta secca

2 cups sifted all-purpose flour
½ cup granulated sugar
Pinch salt
½ cup butter, softened
2 eggs (or 3, enough to bind the dough)

Put the flour, sugar, and salt in a large bowl. Make

a well in the center. Beat the eggs with a fork until they are blended but not foamy. Pour into the well. Add the butter in pieces, and proceed as directed in No. 1958. Another egg may be added if the dough will not bind properly. *Makes 2 single-crust pies, 1 2-crust pie, or 12 tart shells.*

NOTE: Whole eggs are used here, and a good deal of sugar, so this dough is less flaky than the preceding ones. If difficult to roll out, simply pat thin in the pie tin. If holes appear, patch with scraps of dough. Although less delicate than some pastry doughs, still it should not be overhandled.

1957. SWEET EGG PASTRY
Pasta frolla comune

2 cups sifted all-purpose flour
Pinch salt
½ cup granulated sugar
1 egg
Milk as required
5 tablespoons butter

Sift the flour, salt, and sugar together 3 times. Beat the egg with 3 tablespoons of milk, and proceed as directed in following recipe. More milk may be added if dough seems too dry. *Makes 2 single-crust pies, 1 2-crust pie, or 12 tart shells.*

NOTE: This mixture provides a rather heavy, cooky-like crust, and is used mainly as a base for tarts or for pies filled with sweetened rice or ricotta, also for desserts served at religious festivals in Italy.

1958. SWEET AND TENDER EGG PASTRY
Pasta frolla fine

For pies, tarts, and tartlets requiring a pre-baked crust.

2 cups sifted all-purpose flour
5 tablespoons superfine sugar
Pinch salt
3 egg yolks
½ teaspoon grated lemon rind (no white part)
½ cup butter, softened
Ice water (if needed)

The utensils do not need to be chilled for this recipe, but the dough should not be permitted to gather heat, as this will release the gluten in the flour and create a tough, elastic dough.

Sift the flour, sugar, and salt into a very large bowl. Make a well in the center of the mound. Beat the egg yolks slightly and add the lemon rind to them. Place the butter and the egg yolk/lemon rind mixture into the hollow in the flour. With a large fork or the tips of the fingers work the mixture into the flour, starting at the center and working in and down. Water should not be needed, but if after mixing the dough thoroughly you find it still too dry, 1 tablespoon of water may be added. However, this will not make as flaky a crust as one without water. When the dough is well mixed (it should be a little crumbly; do not overhandle it), pat it gently into a ball, wrap it well in foil or wax paper, and let it rest in the refrigerator for at least 3 hours. After this time proceed as directed on page 641. *Makes 2 10-inch crusts, or 12 tartlet shells.*

NOTE: Because of the egg yolks, this crust is not recommended for baking with a filling, as this might make it soggy. It is at its best when baked "blind" (*see* page 641).

1959. BARQUETTE AND TARTLET PASTRY
Pasta à foncer per barchette e tartelette

As the Italian name suggests, this pastry is very much like the recipe for kneaded pie pastry. Since these tart shells, however, are sometimes used for entrées or antipasto, the sugar has been omitted and the pastry is less rich. It is shaped either in the conventional round tart pan or the elongated, boat-shaped (barque) tin, and may be baked "blind" (unfilled) and filled afterward.

2 cups sifted all-purpose flour
½ cup sweet butter, softened
¾ teaspoon salt
½ cup ice water

Proceed as for Rich Pastry [No. 1897]. *Makes 12 tart shells.*

Shaping and baking:
In addition to the special barquette and tartlet pastry described in the preceding recipe, many other kinds of pastry may be employed, especially when pieces have been left over from other preparations, in the making of round or oval (barquette) tarts: Flaky Pastry [No. 1954], Rich Pastry [No. 1955], and Half Puff Paste [No. 1961]. Roll out the pastry until it is ⅛ inch thick and with a large cooky cutter cut out as many pieces of dough as there are to be tarts, making sure they are large enough to fit well into the bottom and cover the sides of the mold to be used. Butter the molds (round for tarts, oval for barquettes), line them with the pastry, prick the bottoms with a fork to prevent "bubbling," cover with a large circle of wax paper or

643

foil, and fill this with dried peas or beans. Set the molds on a cooky sheet or in a pan and bake 12 to 15 minutes at 450°, removing the paper and dried beans during the last 5 minutes of baking. Turn off the oven. Brush the insides of the tarts with an egg white beaten with $\frac{1}{2}$ teaspoon water and keep the tarts in the oven with the door open for minute or two to dry them thoroughly. Unmold them. They are now ready to be filled.

1960. PUFF PASTE
Pasta sfogliata

The Italian word sfogliata *means "leafy" or "leaf-like," and one characteristic of this pastry is the leafy layers into which it flakes apart. It also puffs up to 3 times its height when baked, which accounts for its English name.*

To be able to produce a good puff paste is something even an experienced cook may be proud of. The beginner should not despair if the first attempt does not succeed as well as hoped, for with more practice any terrors this pastry holds will surely be banished. Eventually, the results will be spectacular, and its preparation much less of a chore. Mastering puff paste is well worth the effort, for it has endless uses and its taste and texture are beyond compare.

The delicacy and lightness of puff paste are the result of 3 separate, relatively simple steps: the mixing of the flour and water, the incorporation of the butter in the "turns," and baking in a very hot oven.

As with most other pastries, the cook's byword should be "quick and cold." Old cookbooks used to warn that puff paste should be made only on cold, windy days, but if the kitchen is not overly hot, and if it has the added feature of being air-conditioned, puff paste can be made any day of the year.

A marble slab makes the best working surface, especially on warm days, since it may be pre-chilled by putting ice over it for 10 minutes, removing the ice, and wiping the slab dry. However, any broad, smooth working surface (such as a Formica counter-top or a large pastry board) can serve.

All the ingredients should be very cold, including the flour, which should be chilled 1 hour in the refrigerator. Although the butter must be cold, it must not be too hard, or it will be difficult to roll out. Many cooks soften the butter by kneading it under ice water, a process that also eliminates the milky sediment. The following recipe calls for the butter to be kneaded with a little flour: this helps to absorb the sediment, softens the butter to a workable consistency, and is much easier than kneading the butter under water.

> 4 cups sifted all-purpose flour, chilled
> 2 cups butter
> 1 teaspoon salt
> $\frac{1}{2}$ cup ice water (or more as needed)

Place the butter in a bowl. Sprinkle it with $\frac{1}{2}$ cup of the flour, and knead this in thoroughly. When the flour and butter have been thoroughly blended, shape the mixture into a brick 6 inches long and 4 inches wide. Wrap butter brick in wax paper or foil, and chill in the coldest part of the refrigerator for at least 15 minutes. Be careful, however, not to let it get as hard as ordinary chilled butter.

Place the remaining chilled flour in a large bowl, previously chilled (or on a pastry board—*see* photograph), make a well in the center, and pour in the salt and ice water. Mix this together thoroughly with the tips of the fingers, adding more ice water if necessary, to make a firm but pliable dough. This step is very important in determining the delicacy of the pastry, and care must be taken to mix rather than knead. However, one should work this mixture more thoroughly than ordinary pie-crust dough, to make it perfectly smooth. It should not, however, become elastic. The end product should be a tender, moist dough. Wrap it loosely in wax paper and place it in refrigerator until the butter is ready. It should rest a minimum of 10 minutes.

Combining the flour/water dough with the butter—the "turns":
The purpose of this operation is to distribute the butter so evenly (without handling or heat to make it melt or become "greasy") that when the pastry is baked, it will "flake" into many paper-thin, crisp layers. The secret of success is to have the flour/water dough and the butter of the same consistency. If one seems harder than the other on removing from the refrigerator, leave the harder one out for 5 minutes, and return the softer to a less cold part of the refrigerator.

Lightly flour your working surface (marble, wood, or Formica; *see* above), and roll out the flour/water dough into a rectangle that is approximately 15 by 18 inches and $\frac{1}{2}$ inch thick. Place the brick of kneaded butter in the center of this (*see* photograph). Fold $\frac{1}{3}$ of the dough rectangle over the butter, and then fold the remaining portion of dough over this, forming a sort of "envelope." Tamp down the open edges with a

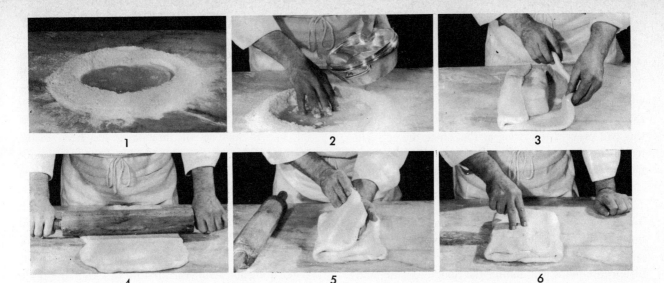

HOW TO PREPARE DOUGH FOR PUFF PASTE

1. Heap the flour on a cold marble (or other) surface, making a well in the center

2. Into the well, place the salt and some of the ice water. Work the flour into the center with the fingertips, adding more ice water as required

3. Pat or roll out the flour-and-water dough to make a square ½ inch thick, and set the brick of kneaded butter on it

4. Roll out the dough evenly into a rectangle, being careful to keep the butter from breaking through the surface

5. With the wide edge paralleling the edge of your working surface, fold the dough into thirds (giving it its first "turn")

6. So as not to forget how many "turns" you have given the pastry, make a mark on it with your index finger. Here, the pastry has had its fourth "turn."

rolling pin (this traps air inside) and lightly pinch the top edge together. Now, turn the folded rectangle so that the end (the smaller part of the rectangle) faces you. Keep it in this direction; turn rectangle upside down, so it presents a smooth surface, and roll it away from you to the size it was originally. *Never* return the rolling pin toward you. Now, fold the rolled-out strip as before: ⅓ to the center, and the other ⅓ over the folded part. Then turn it toward you again (this is a "turn"), tamp down the open ends, and mark it with 2 finger depressions (*see* photograph). These marks will allow you to keep track of the turn. Wrap loosely in wax paper and place the dough in the refrigerator for ½ hour.

Repeat this rolling, folding process until you have "turned" the pastry 6 times in all. Replace it in the refrigerator after each 2 turns (signaling the number of turns completed with finger marks). When all 6 turns have been made, let the pastry rest in the refrigerator for at least 2 hours.

During all the rolling, the butter should stay inside the dough. If it does break through, all is not lost: break off a piece of dough from one of the ends, moisten it slightly, and seal the patch. After a little practice this will not occur, and it will be very simple to keep the butter below the surface.

Always keep the end (i.e., the narrow part of the rectangle) toward you. Always roll the dough away from you, and, after folding the dough, tamp down the edges sharply with the rolling pin. This traps air that will ultimately expand when the dough is in the oven, and thereby help the puff paste to rise. After folding the dough, always turn it upside down before making the "turn," so that the smooth surface (the one without the fold showing) will face upward. After the 6 turns have been accomplished, let the dough rest as indicated. Before baking, it should be given 2 more turns. For best results, however, the dough should rest overnight. It may even be frozen at this stage. If this is done, let it thaw out for 2 hours at room temperature, or for 4 hours in the less cold part of the refrigerator.

Baking:

The main principle here is to have the oven blazing hot and the pastry very cold. This contrast helps the trapped air to expand rapidly and also seals the outer parts of the pastry, thereby preventing the trapped air from escaping. Preheat the oven to 400°. Roll out the folded pastry rectangle and make 2 more turns. For the final rolling out, roll it out about ¼ inch thick, cut into desired shapes, and place on a baking tin which has been lightly moistened with water. If desired, before placing on the baking tin, the pieces of pastry may be chilled for ½ hour. Place the tin in the oven and bake the pastry until it is well puffed and golden brown. If it is browning too fast, turn the oven down after 10 minutes to 350°.

Glazing puff paste:

To obtain a shiny top surface, brush the unbaked pastry with a beaten egg yolk. However, care must be taken that the egg yolk does not dribble over the sides: this will prevent the rising action, since the egg will harden in a few seconds, thereby forming an inhibiting factor—rather like a string holding down a balloon.

Uses for puff paste:

The dough may be used for practically any filling, but it is not recommended that it be used for a pie or tart whose filling must be baked in a crust. The moisture in the filling will inhibit the dough's rising, and although the top crust will be perfectly puffed and golden, the bottom will be soggy and heavy. However, a perfect top-crust pie can be prepared by covering the desired preparation with a layer of puff paste dough, baking as directed.

NOTE: Since the preparation of puff paste is time consuming and laborious, all scraps should be saved. They may be rolled out and cut into fancy shapes for use as garnishes, etc.

1961. HALF PUFF PASTE, OR ECONOMICAL FLAKY PASTRY
Pasta mezza sfogliata o pasta economica

2 cups sifted flour
1/2 cup cold margarine (if too hard, keep at room temperature 10 to 15 minutes)
1/2 teaspoon salt
1 egg white, beaten with 1/3 cup (about) ice water

Proceed as for the preceding classic Puff Paste [No. 1960], adding the egg white with the water, and giving the pastry only 5 turns, reserving the last 2 for the time when the pastry is to be shaped and baked.

1962. APPLE TART
Torta—crostata—di mele

1/2 recipe Sweet and Tender Egg Pastry [No. 1958] or Half Puff Paste [No. 1961]
1 1/2 pounds crisp, tart apples (greenings, if available), peeled, cored, quartered, and very thinly sliced
3/4 cup sugar
1 tablespoon lemon juice
Grated rind of 1/2 lemon (no white part)
1/2 cup apricot preserves, pressed through a fine sieve
2 tablespoons apple brandy (Calvados or applejack)

Line an 8-inch pie tin with the pastry, pricking the bottom in a few places. Crimp the edges decoratively. Arrange the thinly sliced apples in evenly spaced overlapping circles, starting from the outer edge and working in. As soon as the first layer has been made, sprinkle with 1/4 cup sugar and a bit of the lemon juice and grated rind. Repeat until all the apples have been used, ending with a layer of sugar. Bake in a 400° oven for 35 to 45 minutes, or until the apples are tender and the top has begun to glaze. Remove from oven and cool on a cake rack. While still warm, heat the sieved apricot preserves in a small saucepan over medium heat. When quite hot, remove from stove and stir in the apple brandy. Pour this over the apples in an even coating. *Serves* 6.

1963. APPLE DUMPLINGS
Mele in gabbia

1 recipe Sweet and Tender Egg Pastry [No. 1958], made the day before and allowed to rest in the refrigerator overnight
6 large, tart, firm apples (greenings, if available), peeled and cored
3/4 cup apricot preserves
1/2 cup sugar
1 egg, beaten lightly
Vanilla confectioners' sugar [*see* No. 2296]
1 recipe Apricot Sauce [No. 2270]

Roll out the pastry on a floured pastry cloth or board until it is about 1/8 inch thick. Cut into 6 equal squares. Roll the apples in the preserves until they are well coated, then sprinkle them all over with the sugar. Place a coated apple in the center of each pastry square. Mix the remaining sugar and preserves together and fill the hollow core with this mixture. Brush the edges of the squares with some cold water and bring the pastry up around the apples, pinching the pastry, sealing them in. If there is any pastry left over, gather up the scraps, roll them out again, and cut 6 3-inch circles from it with a floured glass or cooky cutter. Moisten the edges lightly and press into the top of each pastry-covered apple (this makes a perfect seal). Brush each dumpling with the beaten egg and place them in a lightly buttered baking dish. Place in a 375° oven and bake for 35 to 45 minutes (depending on the size of the apples). Remove when baked, place on a serving platter, dust with confectioners' sugar, and serve at once, accompanied by a bowl of apricot sauce. *Serves* 6.

NOTE: One may also use Half Puff Paste [No. 1961] for the dough.

1964. APRICOT TART
Torta—crostate—di albicocche

1/2 recipe Flaky Pastry [No. 1954], which has been
    allowed to rest overnight in the refrigerator
3 cups peeled apricot halves (canned or fresh;
    see Note below)
1 cup sugar (1/2 cup if canned apricots are used)
1 teaspoon lemon juice
1/4 cup halved blanched almonds [*see* No. 2280]
1 egg yolk, beaten with 1 tablespoon heavy cream
1/2 cup apricot preserves, pressed through a fine sieve
    (*see* Note below)

Roll out the pastry on a floured pastry cloth or board.
Make sure it is large enough to line an 8-inch flan ring.
Place the ring on a baking sheet and line it with the
pastry. Press it down well on the bottom and sides,
turn the excess pastry over on itself around the top
rim, and crimp it decoratively. Lightly prick the
bottom of the pastry with a fork to prevent it puffing
up while baking. Arrange the halved apricots in a
circular pattern over the crust (if using canned apricots,
make sure they have been well drained), cut side upward. Sprinkle them with the sugar and lemon juice
and place half a blanched almond in the center of each
half. Bake the tart in a 375° oven for 40 minutes. If any
apricots or almonds begin to brown too quickly,
cover the surface of the tart lightly with a piece of
aluminum foil. After 40 minutes, remove from oven,
carefully lift off the flan ring, and brush the surface of
the pastry with the egg yolk/cream mixture, and return
to oven for 5 minutes to allow the glaze to set. Remove
from oven, and allow to cool for 45 minutes before
sliding the tart off the baking sheet and onto a plate.
Brush the top with the apricot preserves and serve the
tart at room temperature. *Serves 6 to 8.*

NOTE: If canned apricots are used, drain them well
and reserve their syrup. Boil this down in a small
heavy saucepan until 1/4 cup remains and glaze the
tart with this reduced syrup instead of the apricot
preserves.

1965. BLUEBERRY TARTLETS
Tartelette di mirtillo

1/2 recipe Half Puff Paste [No. 1961]
2 cups blueberries
3/4 cup sugar
1 teaspoon lemon juice
1/2 recipe Almond Butter Cream [No. 2266], flavored
    with 1 tablespoon kirsch

Roll out the pastry less than 1/4 inch in thickness.
Line 12 tartlet molds with it, and prick the bottom of
the pastry with a fork a few times. Mix the blueberries,
sugar, and lemon juice lightly, coating all berries
evenly. Pile into the tartlet shells to within 1/4 inch of
the top. Pour over the almond cream to within 1/8 inch
of the top (any more will overflow during baking).
Put the tartlets on a baking sheet and bake in a 375°
oven for 25 to 30 minutes, or until the tops are well
glazed. Cool on a cake rack and serve cold. *Makes
12 tartlets.*

NOTE: This may be made into a tart by lining an
8-inch pie tin with the pastry, pricking the bottom,
crimping the edge, and proceeding as above. Increase
baking time by 10 to 15 minutes. *Serves 6.*

1966. CHERRY CUSTARD MERINGUE TART
Flan dolce di ciliege meringate

1/2 recipe Rich Pastry [No. 1955] or Flaky Pastry
    [No. 1954]
4 cups sour pie cherries, pitted
1/4 teaspoon almond extract
1 1/2 cups sugar (if Bing cherries are used, decrease
    sugar to 3/4 cup)
Optional: Juice of 1 lemon (only if Bing cherries are
    used)
Custard:
  2 eggs
  2 egg yolks
  6 tablespoons sugar
  1 cup milk, scalded
  Pinch salt
  1/2 teaspoon vanilla extract
3 egg whites
Pinch cream of tartar
6 tablespoons superfine sugar

Roll out the pastry until it is large enough to fit a
12-inch flan ring (or use a shallow 12-inch spring
form cake pan). Place the flan ring on a baking sheet
and fit the dough into it, being careful not to let the

crust overhang the rim (this will make it impossible to remove the ring or spring form when the tart has been baked). Mix the cherries with the almond extract and sugar (decrease sugar and add lemon juice if using Bing cherries) and put them into the tart. Beat the eggs and yolks with the sugar and salt, pour in the scalded milk and mix well, then add the vanilla. Pour this over the cherries. Place in a 350° oven for 45 to 55 minutes or until the top is puffed and golden. Remove from oven and cool to lukewarm. Carefully lift off the flan ring (or remove the sides of the spring form) and gently slide the tart onto an oven-proof platter. Beat the egg whites with the cream of tartar in a large bowl (preferably of unlined copper) until they are foamy. Add the superfine sugar and beat until they form soft peaks. Drop the meringue by tablespoonsful onto the surface of the tart, making sure the surface is completely covered by it. (It may also be smoothed on, with about 1/2 cup reserved and put into a pastry bag fitted with a large star tip, then piped on the smooth meringue in decorative swirls.) Sprinkle evenly with the remaining sugar and place in a 400° oven until the meringue is golden brown. This tart may be served warm, but is better if allowed to cool thoroughly. Do not, however, chill in the refrigerator as this will cause the meringue to turn rubbery. *Serves 8 to 10.*

1967. CHERRY CUSTARD PIE ROMANA
Crostata dolce alla romana

1 recipe Sweet and Tender Egg Pastry [No. 1958], using equal amounts of lard and butter for the shortening
2 cups sour cherry preserves
Custard:
   3 egg yolks
   2 eggs
   Pinch salt
   1/2 cup sugar
   1/3 cup flour
   2 cups milk, scalded
   1/2 teaspoon vanilla extract
1 egg, lightly beaten
1 tablespoon milk
1 teaspoon sugar

Roll out 2/3 of the pastry until large enough to fit a 9-inch pie tin. Fit it in, pricking the bottom lightly with a fork and leaving the pastry hanging over the rim. Fill the bottom with the cherry preserves and place in the refrigerator while preparing the custard. Beat the egg yolks, eggs, salt, and sugar until they are thick and lemon colored, then beat in the flour. Gradually add the scalding milk, beating all the time. Finally, add the vanilla. Pour the mixture into a heavy saucepan and place it over medium heat. Beat constantly with a wire whisk. When the mixture is thick and lumpy, remove from stove and beat until smooth. Return to stove and cook for 3 minutes more. Allow it to cool for 45 minutes in a small bowl, stirring from time to time to prevent a crust from forming. Roll out the remaining pastry to the thickness of 1/8 inch. Cut it in thin strips. Beat together the egg, milk, and sugar and paint the strips with this mixture. Remove pie from refrigerator and pour the custard over the preserves. Arrange the strips in a lattice pattern over the top, fold over the overhanging edges, and crimp decoratively. Place the pie on a 350° oven and bake for 1 hour. Remove and cool on a cake rack. Serve cold but not chilled. *Serves 8.*

1968. CHERRY TART
Torta—crostata—di ciliege

1/2 recipe Flaky Pastry [No. 1954], which has been allowed to rest overnight in the refrigerator
3 cups pie cherries, pitted (canned or fresh; *see* Note below)
1 1/2 cups sugar (1/2 cup if canned, sweetened cherries are used)
1 egg yolk, beaten with 1 tablespoon cream
1/2 cup currant jelly (*see* Note below)
2 tablespoons cherry brandy

Proceed exactly as in directions for Apricot Tart [No. 1964], omitting the almonds. After it has baked, melt the currant jelly in a small saucepan, add the cherry brandy, and paint the surface of the tart with this mixture. Serve at room temperature. *Serves 6 to 8.*

NOTE: If canned cherries packed in heavy syrup are used, drain them well and reserve the liquid. Boil this down in a small, heavy saucepan until 1/2 cup remains, add the cherry brandy, and use this as a glaze in place of the currant jelly. It is recommended, however, that water-pack pie cherries be used, in which case the liquid is discarded, and the currant jelly glaze is used.

1969. CHESTNUT TART
Flan dolce di castagne

1/2 recipe Sweet Egg Pastry [No. 1957]
1 1/2 pounds chestnuts
2 cups milk
2-inch strip of vanilla bean

¾ cup sugar
Pinch salt
½ cup heavy cream
3 egg whites
Vanilla sugar [see No. 2296]

Roll out the dough until it is large enough to fit a 9-inch flan ring. Place the ring on a lightly buttered baking sheet. Fit the dough into the ring, pressing it down well. Fold the crust over on itself at the top and crimp decoratively to form a little wall, higher than the rim of the ring. (Do not let it sit on the rim, however, as this will make it impossible to lift off the ring once the tart is baked.) Place in refrigerator to chill. Cut a cross in the flat part of the chestnuts and place in a pan. Bake in the bottom of a 400° oven until their skins split and peel back somewhat (about 12 minutes). Quickly remove the shells and skins while still hot. Place the peeled chestnuts, milk, vanilla bean, ½ cup of the sugar, and salt in an enamel saucepan. Bring to a boil over medium heat and cook until the chestnuts are very tender (about 30 to 40 minutes). Remove from fire, discard the piece of vanilla, and mash the chestnuts (with the cooking liquid) through a fine sieve or a potato ricer. Beat in the heavy cream and beat the mixture well for about 5 minutes. Beat the egg whites until stiff with a pinch of salt and the remaining sugar and fold them into the chestnut purée. Do this carefully to keep the mixture light. Remove the pie crust from the refrigerator, pour in the chestnut purée, and place in a 350° oven. Bake for 35 to 40 minutes, or until the top is well puffed and browned. Remove from oven and let it cool to lukewarm. Lift off the flan ring and slide carefully onto a plate. Sprinkle the top with vanilla sugar and let the pie cool in the least cool part of the refrigerator. *Serves* 8.

1970. CUSTARD TARTLETS
Tartelette con crema

1 recipe Half Puff Paste [No. 1961]
1 recipe Pastry Cream [No. 2267], chilled

Roll out the dough until it is ⅛ inch thick. Cut it into circles large enough to fit 12 tartlet tins. Press in well, and prick the bottom once or twice with a fork. Divide the pastry cream among them. Gather up the leftover dough and roll it out again. Cut into ¼-inch strips. Make a lattice of these strips over each tart. Press edges well into the sides of the tarts. Place tarts on a baking sheet and place in a 350° oven and bake for 30 minutes. Remove and cool on a cake rack. Chill slightly before serving. *Makes 12 tartlets.*

NOTE: This may be baked in an 8-inch pie tin. Increase baking time by 10 to 15 minutes. *Serves* 6.

1971. ENGLISH APPLE PIE
Torta—crostata—di mele all'inglese

½ recipe Flaky Pastry [No. 1954]
2 pounds firm, tart apples (greenings, if possible), peeled, cored, and cut into eighths
1¼ cups sugar
2 teaspoons cinnamon
Grated rind of ½ lemon (no white part)
1 tablespoon lemon juice
3 tablespoons butter, softened

Mix the apples, sugar, cinnamon, lemon rind and juice until the apples are well coated. Place them in a round, straight-sided baking dish about 8 or 9 inches in diameter, and dot with butter. Roll out the dough until it is slightly larger than the dish and cover the apples. Fold over the overlapping dough on itself and crimp. Cut a few slashes in the top of the crust and place in a 375° oven for 40 minutes, or until the apples are tender and the crust golden brown. This is equally good hot or cold. *Serves* 6.

NOTE: Puff Paste [No. 1960] would also provide a very good cover for this top-crust pie.

1972. ENGLISH RHUBARB PIE
Torta—crostata—di rabarbaro all'inglese

½ recipe Half Puff Paste [No. 1961] or Puff Paste [No. 1960]
1½ pounds strawberry rhubarb, cut in 2-inch pieces (if very thick, cut stalks in half)
¾ cup sugar
¾ cup (well packed) light brown sugar
2 teaspoons arrowroot (or potato flour)
2 tablespoons butter, softened
1 cup heavy cream, whipped, sweetened with 2 tablespoons sugar

Lightly butter a 10-inch straight-sided baking dish. Mix the two sugars together. Place alternate layers of sugar and rhubarb in the dish, ending with a layer of sugar. Sprinkle each layer with a little arrowroot (or potato flour). Dot the top with butter. Roll out the pastry to a thickness of ¼ inch. Place on dish and crimp overhanging edges, pressing them into inner sides of dish. Cut a slash in the top to permit the steam to escape. Place in a 375° oven and bake for 1 hour. Cool in a cake rack, and when cold place in refrigerator to chill thoroughly. Serve with the whipped cream on the side. *Serves* 8.

1973. FIG TART
Torta—crostata—di fichi

½ recipe Flaky Pastry [No. 1954]
3 cups peeled fresh figs (or canned figs in syrup)
1 cup sugar (omit if figs canned in syrup are used)
¼ cup water (omit if canned figs are used)
3 tablespoons dark rum
3 tablespoons Aurum liqueur
1 teaspoon lemon juice
½ cup apricot preserves, pressed through a fine sieve

Roll out the dough on a floured cloth or pastry board. Line an 8-inch tart tin with straight sides with the pastry. Press it well into the bottom and sides and prick it with a fork in several places. Fold the excess over on itself, and crimp decoratively. Line the crust with aluminum foil and fill the foil with dried peas or beans. Place in a 425° oven and bake for 10 minutes. Remove the tin, carefully pour out the dried peas (saving them for the same use another time), remove the foil, and return the crust to the oven to bake until golden brown. Cool on a baking rack, and when thoroughly cooled carefully lift the crust out onto a platter. While the crust is baking, boil the sugar and water together until they reach the large thread stage (219° on the candy thermometer). Cool for 20 minutes and then add the rum, Aurum, and lemon juice. Pour this over the figs, and let them steep for at least 3 hours in the refrigerator. Before serving, arrange the figs in the cooled crust, pour over a little of the syrup, and paint with the apricot preserves. *Serves 6 to 8.*

NOTE: If canned figs in heavy syrup are used, drain them well, place them in a bowl and pour over the Aurum and rum. Place the syrup in a small heavy saucepan, add the lemon juice, and cook until reduced to ¼ cup. Pour this over the figs and chill well. Proceed as above.

1974. ITALIAN RICOTTA TART
Crostata dolce di ricotta

Pastry as indicated for Ricotta Tart Romana [No. 1982], substituting lemon rind for the orange rind
Filling:
    1½ pounds ricotta cheese, as fresh as possible
    1½ cups superfine sugar
    5 egg yolks
    1 egg
    1 teaspoon grated orange rind (no white part)
    1 teaspoon grated lemon rind (no white part)
    ½ cup seedless raisins or currants

    ¼ cup candied fruits and peels, diced
    Pinch cinnamon
    Pinch salt
Glaze:
    1 egg yolk, slightly beaten
    1 tablespoon melted lard
    1 teaspoon sugar
Vanilla confectioners' sugar [*see* No. 2296]

Prepare the dough as indicated in No. 1982 and let it rest in the refrigerator for 2 hours. Press the ricotta through a fine sieve into a large bowl and beat until smooth. Add the remaining filling ingredients and blend well. Liberally grease a 9- or 10-inch pie tin with lard. Roll out ⅔ of the pastry into a circle large enough to fit it, and place it in the tin, pressing down lightly but firmly. Pour in the filling. Roll out the remaining dough to the thickness of ⅛ inch and cut in ¼-inch strips. Brush these thoroughly with the glaze which has been lightly beaten with a fork until well blended. Place the strips in a lattice formation on the pie. Take the overhang of the bottom crust and fold it over the strips, pinching together well. Crimp this edge decoratively. Brush the edge carefully with the remaining glaze, taking care that it does not dribble on the filling. Place in a 350° oven and bake for 1 hour, or until the top is golden brown and the filling seems firm. Remove from oven and cool on a cake rack. When cooled, carefully place a large plate over the pie and turn the pie and the plate over so that the bottom of the tin faces upward. Give it several sharp taps and remove the tin. Place another plate over the bottom crust and turn upside down again, so that the top of the pie faces upward. This takes finesse and calm, and the pie must be totally cool, otherwise it will crack. Sprinkle the top with the vanilla confectioners' sugar. Serve at room temperature. *Serves 8 to 10.*

1975. NEAPOLITAN CHEESE TART
Pastiera alla napoletana

Whole-grain wheat is a featured ingredient here. As it is all but unavailable in the United States, except in a few health food shops, barley may be substituted.

1 cup whole-grain, hulled wheat, soaked in 3 changes
    of water for 3 days (or substitute ¾ cup pearl
    barley, soaked in water for 12 hours)
1 recipe Rich Pastry [No. 1955], made with lard instead
    of butter
2 cups rich milk (or 1 cup milk and 1 cup cream)
2 slices lemon rind (no white part)
Pinch cinnamon

6 tablespoons light brown sugar
$\frac{1}{2}$ teaspoon salt
Filling:
   $1\frac{1}{2}$ cups superfine sugar
   6 egg yolks
   1 pound ricotta, pressed through a fine sieve
   $\frac{3}{4}$ cup candied citron, chopped
   1 tablespoon grated lemon rind (no white part)
   $\frac{1}{4}$ teaspoon cinnamon
   2 tablespoons orange flower water
   4 egg whites
Pinch salt
Glaze:
   1 tablespoon lard, melted
   1 tablespoon sugar
   1 egg yolk
Vanilla confectioners' sugar [see No. 2296]

Drain the pre-soaked wheat (or barley), place in a pot, and cover with plenty of cold water (at least 2 quarts). Bring to a boil and cook for 1 hour. Drain thoroughly and put into a large, heavy saucepan with the milk, slices of lemon rind, pinch of cinnamon, brown sugar, and salt. Bring to a boil over moderate heat, then lower heat as much as possible and cook until the milk has been entirely absorbed. Allow the mixture to cool, and remove the lemon rind. Beat the egg yolks with 1 cup of the superfine sugar until foamy, beat in the ricotta, and add the remaining filling ingredients, then fold this into the cooled cooked grain mixture and blend thoroughly. Beat the egg whites and pinch of salt in a large bowl (preferably of unlined copper) until foamy and then add the remaining $\frac{1}{2}$ cup of superfine sugar. Beat until they stand in soft peaks and then gently fold into the ricotta/grain mixture. Line a deep, large (about 10 to 12 inches in diameter, depending on its depth) pie tin with $\frac{2}{3}$ of the pastry which has been rolled out to the thickness of $\frac{1}{8}$ inch. Prick the bottom a few times with a fork. Fill with the ricotta/grain mixture. Roll out the remaining dough and cut it in $\frac{1}{4}$-inch strips. Beat the melted glaze ingredients together and lightly brush the strips with this mixture, making sure to coat them well. Arrange the strips lattice-fashion over the filling. Fold the overhanging dough around the edge over them and crimp decoratively. Brush the edge with the glaze mixture, taking care not to get any on the filling. Place the tart in a 350° oven and bake for 1 hour. If the top browns too quickly, lightly cover it with a sheet of aluminum foil. Remove from oven and cool on a cake rack. Let it chill slightly. When ready to serve sprinkle with a little vanilla confectioners' sugar. *Serves* 12.

1976. NUT TARTLETS
Tartelette con nocciole

1 recipe Flaky Pastry [No. 1954], made with the
   addition of 2 egg yolks
4 tablespoons maraschino liqueur
$1\frac{1}{4}$ cups Pastry Cream [No. 2267], chilled
$\frac{3}{4}$ cup currant jelly, melted
$\frac{3}{4}$ cup thinly sliced almonds [see No. 2288],
   unblanched

Make the pastry the day before and let it rest, covered, in the refrigerator overnight. Remove it 15 minutes before rolling it out. Mix the maraschino with the pastry cream. Place the currant jelly in a small, heavy saucepan over low heat until melted. Roll out the dough to the thickness of $\frac{1}{8}$ inch and cut it into 12 circles large enough to fit 12 tartlet tins. Line the tins with the dough, pressing down well, and prick once with a fork. Spoon some of the melted currant jelly into each of the tarts and then fill them $\frac{4}{5}$ full of the pastry cream. Sprinkle the tops with the almond slices. Place the tarts on a baking sheet and bake in a 375° oven for 20 minutes. Remove from oven and cool on a cake rack. Chill slightly before serving. *Makes 12 to 24 tartlets (depending on the size of the tins).*

NOTE: This may also be prepared in an 8-inch pie tin. In this case increase baking time by 15 minutes.

1977. ORANGE TARTLETS
Tartelette all'arancia

12 or 24 baked tartlet shells (depending on the size
   of the tins) made from Tartlet Pastry [No. 1959]
   or Flaky Pastry [No. 1954]
2 cups orange marmalade ("vintage" marmalade, if
   available)
$\frac{1}{3}$ cup candied orange peel, finely chopped
Optional: 2 tablespoons lemon juice
       1 cup Pastry Cream [No. 2267]
       Juice of 1 orange

Bake the tartlets "blind": that is, after lining the tins with the dough, line the dough with aluminum foil, pressing it down gently but firmly. Fill the foil-lined tartlets with dried beans, place on a baking sheet, and place in a 400° oven. After 12 minutes, remove from oven, pour out the beans (which may be kept in a covered jar and used again), and discard the foil. Return the tarts to the oven to brown. Remove from oven and cool on a cake rack.

Before serving, fill them with the marmalade which has been mixed with the chopped candied orange peel.

(Or, if desired, mix the marmalade, lemon juice, pastry cream, and orange juice together and fill the tarts with this mixture—which is less sweet and much creamier than the former filling.) *Makes 12 to 24 tartlets, depending on the size of the tins.*

1978. PEACH TARTLETS
Tartelette con pesche

1 recipe Rich Pastry [No. 1955], made with 2 additional
    tablespoons sugar
2 cups canned applesauce
3 tablespoons butter
1 cup Pastry Cream [No. 2267]
½ teaspoon vanilla extract
Syrup:
  1 cup sugar
  ½ cup water
6 medium freestone peaches
½ cup apple jelly, melted

Cook the applesauce in a small, heavy saucepan over medium heat until reduced to about 1 cup. Stir from time to time to prevent its scorching. Remove from heat, pour into a bowl, and let cool for 10 minutes. Beat in the butter, then the pastry cream and vanilla. Place the sugar and water for the syrup in a small, heavy saucepan and cook until it reaches the large thread stage (219° on the candy thermometer). Peel the peaches by plunging them into boiling water for 1 minute and then stripping off the loosened skins. Halve them carefully and poach for 5 minutes in the syrup. Remove from syrup and cool somewhat. Roll out the dough to the thickness of ⅛ inch and line 12 3-inch tart tins with it, pressing down well and pricking the bottoms with a fork once or twice. Pour some of the applesauce/pastry cream into each, place the tins on a baking sheet, and bake in a 375° oven for 20 minutes or until the filling is well puffed and firm. Remove from oven and cool on a baking rack. When cool, top each with a peach half, convex side upward, and brush a little of the melted apple jelly over each. *Makes 12 tartlets.*

NOTE: If desired, the syrup in which the peaches were cooked may be reduced until quite thick, 1 teaspoon lemon juice added to it, and the resulting glaze may be used in place of the melted jelly.

1979. PEAR TART
Torta—crostata—di pere

Same preparation and ingredients as indicated for Apple Tart [No. 1962], except that peeled, sliced pears are substituted for the apples. If they are somewhat underripe (which makes for a better-textured tart), bake at 400° for the first 10 minutes, then reduce heat to 350° and bake until the pears are tender. *Serves 6.*

1980. PINEAPPLE TART
Torta—crostata—all'ananasso

½ recipe Flaky Pastry [No. 1954], which has been
    allowed to rest overnight in the refrigerator
1 large fresh pineapple, peeled, cored, and cut into
    ½-inch slices
1 cup sugar (increase by ½ cup if pineapple is tart)
½ cup water
1 cup apricot jam, pressed through a fine sieve
¼ cup dark rum
Optional decorations:
  1 cup Fondant Icing [No. 2255]
  3 thin rounds candied pineapple
  3 candied cherries
  4 large, thin slices candied citron
  1 drop yellow food coloring

Boil the sugar and water in a medium, heavy saucepan until it reaches the large thread stage (219° on the candy thermometer). Add the pineapple and poach the slices until they are just tender. Remove them to a plate to cool, and reduce the remaining liquid until it is very thick. Remove from stove, place the pineapple back in the syrup, add the jam and rum, cover, and let cool in the refrigerator. Meanwhile prepare, line, and bake a flan ring with the pastry as described in Fig Tart [No. 1973]. When it has cooled fill it with the sliced pineapple, arranged in a decorative pattern. Spoon the syrup over the fruit. If desired, the tart may be decorated as shown in photograph facing page 624. Fill a pastry bag fitted with the smallest plain tip with the fondant icing and pipe it over the surface of the tart in a very fine lattice pattern. Twist the candied pineapple slices into cones, and place a cherry in each. Arrange around the center of the tart, open side facing outward. In the middle of this, arrange the slices of candied citron like the points of a crown. *Serves 8.*

1981. RASPBERRY TART
Torta—crostata—di lamponi

Same preparation and ingredients as indicated for Strawberry Tart [No. 1984], substituting the same amount of fresh raspberries. Frozen raspberries are unsuitable as they are too juicy. *Serves 6.*

NOTE: This may be served with 1 cup heavy cream, whipped until stiff, and sweetened with 1 tablespoon superfine sugar.

1982. RICOTTA TART ROMANA
Bocconotti di ricotta alla romana

Tart pastry:
 2¼ cups sifted all-purpose flour
 ½ cup superfine sugar
 ¼ teaspoon salt
 1 teaspoon grated orange rind (no white part)
 Pinch cinnamon
 ¼ cup plus 1 tablespoon cold butter
 ¼ cup plus 1 tablespoon cold lard
 3 eggs, lightly beaten
Filling:
 1 pound ricotta cheese, as fresh as possible
 ½ cup superfine sugar
 Pinch salt
 5 egg yolks, lightly beaten
 1 tablespoon cinnamon
 ½ cup candied fruits and peels, finely diced
Garnish:
 8 candied cherries
 8 strips candied orange peel
Glaze:
 2 tablespoons lard, melted
 1 egg yolk, slightly beaten
 1 tablespoon sugar

Prepare the pastry by mixing the flour, sugar, salt, orange rind, and cinnamon in a large bowl. With 2 knives or a pastry blender cut in the cold butter and lard until the mixture resembles coarse meal. Add the beaten eggs and mix lightly with a fork until the dough forms a loose ball (do not overwork). Gather up the dough with floured hands and press it very lightly together. Wrap it in wax paper and chill in refrigerator for 2 hours.

Prepare the filling. Press the ricotta through a fine sieve into a large bowl. Beat it with a rotary beater or wire whisk until smooth. Mix in the sugar, salt, egg yolks, cinnamon, and candied fruits and peels. Mix well to blend all ingredients.

After the dough has chilled for 2 hours roll ⅔ of it out on a floured pastry cloth or board into a circle large enough to fit an 8-inch pie tin. Fit it in, pressing down well, and prick the bottom a few times with a fork. Pour in the filling. Roll out the remaining dough until it is large enough to fit over the top, cover the filling with it, and gather up the edges of the dough and

Ricotta Tart Romana (No. 1982)

pinch them together and crimp decoratively. Garnish the border of the pie with the candied fruit, pressing it into the border. Brush with the glaze which has been beaten lightly with a fork. Prick top in a few places. Bake in a 350° oven for 1 hour or until the cheese filling seems firm and the top is golden brown. Remove from oven and place on a cake rack. When barely warm cut it into squares and remove them to a platter, reassembling the pie into its original shape. Serve at room temperature. *Serves* 8.

1983. PUFF-PASTE SQUARES WITH STRAWBERRIES
Gâteau millefoglie con fragoline e panna montata

1 recipe Puff Paste [No. 1960], prepared the day
 before and allowed to rest in the refrigerator
 overnight
3 cups small strawberries (wild strawberries, if possible), hulled (if berries are large, cut them in half)
1 cup superfine sugar (for tart berries; otherwise less)
2 tablespoons Aurum or kirsch
1½ cups heavy cream, whipped
3 tablespoons vanilla sugar [*see* No. 2296]
Vanilla confectioners' sugar [*see* No. 2296]

Divide the chilled puff paste in half and roll out into 2 equal-sized rectangles, ½ inch thick. Place on a slightly dampened baking sheet, prick all over with a fork, and bake in a 400° oven for 20 minutes or until well puffed and golden. They should not get too brown. Remove from oven and carefully transfer the baked sheets to a cake rack to cool. Sprinkle the berries with the sugar and liqueur and let them marinate in this in the refrigerator for 2 hours. Just before serving whip the cream in a chilled bowl and sweeten with the vanilla sugar. Mix with the strawberries. Place 1 of

653

the pastry sheets on a large platter, cover with the cream/strawberry mixture. Cover with the other pastry half and sprinkle the top with confectioners' sugar. Serve at once or it will become soggy. *Serves 6 to 8.*

1984. STRAWBERRY TART
Torta—crostata—di fragole

½ recipe Flaky Pastry [No. 1954], which has been
    allowed to rest overnight in the refrigerator
1 cup currant jelly
1 pint fresh strawberries, washed, hulled, and
    thoroughly dried

Prepare, line, and bake a flan ring with the pastry as described in Fig Tart [No. 1973]. Allow it to cool thoroughly. Melt the currant jelly over low heat in a small, heavy saucepan. When it is all melted and no lumps remain, brush a thin layer over the bottom of the crust. Arrange the strawberries in a circular pattern in the crust, and paint them completely with the melted currant jelly, pouring the excess into the spaces between the berries. Take care that no jelly runs down the outer side of crust. Serve no more than 1 hour after making, or crust will become soggy. *Serves 6.*

NOTE: This may be accompanied by a bowl of whipped cream made by whipping 1 cup of heavy cream until stiff, sweetened with 1 tablespoon of superfine sugar (and, if desired, flavored with ½ teaspoon of vanilla extract).

1985. STRAWBERRY TARTLETS
Tartelette con fragole

These should be made with wild strawberries, or at least the smallest available cultivated ones. Halved berries or big plump ones will not give the desired effect. The tart shells should also be small enough to consume in a few bites. If tins about 2 inches (or less) are not available, make the shells in small muffin or jumble tins.

½ recipe Sweet and Tender Egg Pastry [No. 1958]
    or Flaky Pastry [No. 1954]
1 pint wild strawberries (or the tiniest available
    cultivated variety), hulled
¼ to ½ cup superfine sugar (amount depends on
    sweetness of the berries)
3 tablespoons kirsch
½ cup currant jelly, melted

Place the berries in a bowl and sprinkle them with the sugar and kirsch. Place in refrigerator for 1 hour. Meanwhile, roll out the pastry dough to a thickness of ⅛ inch. Line the smallest tartlet tins (or small muffin

tins) with it and line them with foil, filling with dried beans. Bake them "blind" [*see* No. 1977], and let them cool on a cake rack. Just before serving, melt the currant jelly in a small, heavy saucepan over low heat. Fill the baked shells with the berries, mounding them high in the center. Brush the surface of the berries with the melted jelly. Do not let stand longer than 1 or 2 hours or they will get soggy. *Makes about 24 tartlets 2 inches (or less) in diameter.*

PASTRIES
Pasticceria

This section contains many "French" pastries, and others of German or Austrian origin. Since Northern Italy was under Austrian rule for many years (down to the middle of the nineteenth century), the latter influence is not surprising. Many of the recipes in this section are composed of pastry dough, custard, and whipped cream. In order to keep the pastry crisp, they should be assembled no more than 2 hours before serving and then placed in the refrigerator until serving time. Many of them are delectable when made bite size and served with afternoon tea.

1986. APPLE ROLL FANTASIA DI CLARA
Mele fantasia di Clara

1 recipe Half Puff Paste [No. 1961]
2 pounds firm, tart apples (greenings, if available),
    peeled, cored, and rather thickly sliced
½ cup butter
1 cup sugar (less, if apples are sweet)
⅓ cup currants
¼ cup pine nuts
1 teaspoon grated orange rind (no white part)
1 teaspoon lemon juice

¼ cup sweet Marsala wine
1 cup fine breadcrumbs
1 egg yolk, lightly beaten
1 tablespoon cream
1½ cups Apricot Sauce [No. 2270], flavored with
    2 tablespoons maraschino liqueur

Put the apple slices, sugar, and ¼ cup of the butter in a heavy enamel saucepan. Cook over medium heat, stirring occasionally to prevent scorching, until apples are tender but not reduced to a pulp. Remove from stove and allow to cool. Place in a bowl the currants, pine nuts, orange rind, lemon juice, and Marsala and let steep for 1 hour, stirring a few times with a wooden spoon. Melt the remaining butter in a skillet and brown the breadcrumbs in it over medium heat. Allow them to cool and stir into the stewed apples. Roll the dough out on a floured pastry cloth or board until it forms a rectangle 18 inches wide by 20 inches long. Mix the apples and the Marsala-soaked mixture together and spread this on the pastry to within 1 inch of 3 of its edges and 2½ inches on the remaining edge (which should be the long edge). Roll up as for a jelly roll. Pinch the edges together well and brush the surface of the roll with the egg yolk which has been beaten with the cream. Cover a large baking sheet with a sheet of aluminum foil and butter the foil lightly. Slide the apple roll onto the foil with its sealed edge downward, and raise the edges of the foil to form a little fence (this prevents any juice that oozes out during the baking from dripping onto the oven bottom). Place the roll in a 375° oven for 45 minutes, or until golden brown. Remove from oven, let it cool to lukewarm, and carefully slide it onto a serving platter. Serve the apricot sauce on the side. The roll should be served while still barely warm. *Serves 8 to 10.*

1987. APPLE STRUDEL
Strüdel

Homemade strudel dough is one of the greatest triumphs a cook can produce. It should be so thin you can read a book through it. Considerable practice is required to perfect the technique, so first efforts might best be approached in a "rehearsal" spirit. Learning from the mistakes made the first time, a second batch of dough can be prepared with more confidence. Fortunately, persons lacking the time or intrepidity (not to mention the table required) for its preparation can now find fully prepared leaves of strudel dough available commercially. Sealed in plastic film, they are marketed frozen and may be kept in the freezer a long time. They need little thawing,

and are practically as good as the homemade variety—but not quite comparable to the triumph of bringing off the whole production yourself.

Dough:
    2 cups sifted all-purpose flour
    1 egg, lightly beaten
    1 tablespoon superfine sugar
    Pinch salt
    1 teaspoon lemon juice
    ½ cup warm water
    2 tablespoons vegetable oil

Sift the flour into a large bowl. Make a well in the center and in it place the remaining ingredients, reserving 2 tablespoons of the water. Work the flour into the center of the well, and mix and knead until you have a fairly stiff dough. If it seems a little crumbly, add the remaining water; if it seems sticky add a little more flour. Gather the dough into a ball and place it on a lightly floured pastry cloth or board. Knead it well for 20 minutes or until perfectly smooth, then cover it with a warm bowl and let it rest for 45 minutes. When this time has elapsed cover a table at least 36 inches square with a clean tablecloth (a round table is ideal, and even a firm card table may be used: the main point is to be able to move all around it), dust the cloth with flour, and rub the flour in well, making sure the entire cloth is covered with it. Place the dough in the center of the cloth and roll it out with a rolling pin (preferably covered with a floured "stocking") until it has formed a large, thin circle. When it has become as thin as you can roll it, oil your hands lightly with vegetable oil, make fists of both your hands, place the knuckles under the dough, and stretch. Walk around the table, stretching and pulling all parts of the dough. It will become thinner and thinner. Continue this process until the dough hangs down at least 2 inches below the edge of the table. Trim off the thick edge with scissors and spread dough at once with the filling ingredients. If left for more than 5 minutes it will become brittle and harden.

Filling:
    2½ pounds firm, tart apples (greenings, if available),
        peeled, cored, and thinly sliced
    1½ cups melted butter
    2 cups sugar
    2 cups fine breadcrumbs
    ¾ cup seeded raisins or currants
    ¾ cup coarsely chopped walnuts or almonds
    Optional: 1 cup apricot preserves

Have all the filling ingredients ready, and placed in

bowls, before the dough is stretched out. The moment the dough has been prepared, brush its entire surface lightly with some of the melted butter and sprinkle it evenly with 1 cup of the sugar and breadcrumbs. Mix the rest of the ingredients together with all but 2 tablespoons of the melted butter (add the apricot preserves for a richer, more delicate filling) and place the filling along the edge of the dough, 3 inches in. It should form a 4-inch-wide strip. Flip the 3-inch bare strip of dough over the filling and then, taking the cloth in your hands, gently roll up the dough by lifting the cloth higher and higher. When it is all rolled up you will have a 3-foot-long roll. Lightly butter a large baking sheet and roll the dough onto it. It will probably be too large to fit lengthwise, so carefully curve it in to a horsehoe. (Or it may be halved and the 2 strips placed on the sheet lengthwise.) Brush the surface with the rest of the butter, place it in a 350° oven, and bake it for about 30 minutes or until it is golden brown. Remove it from the oven, allow it to cool for 30 minutes, and then slide it carefully onto a large platter. Serve while still warm. *Serves* 10.

NOTE: The strudel may be dusted with a little confectioners' sugar before serving.

1988. CANNOLI SICILIANA
Cannoli alla siciliana

The word cannoli *means "pipes," and these pastries take their name from the round metal tubes or pipes around which they are rolled before being fried in deep fat.*

Dough:
    1¼ cups sifted all-purpose flour
    5 tablespoons (more or less) Marsala wine (or use
        any other fortified wine)
    1 tablespoon superfine sugar
    Pinch salt
    12 metal tubes (*see* Note below)
Fat for deep frying
Filling:
    2 cups ricotta cheese, as fresh as possible
    ½ cup superfine sugar
    ¼ cup candied fruit (citron, orange peel, etc.),
        finely diced
    ¼ cup pistachio nuts, coarsely chopped
    Optional: ¼ cup semi-sweet chocolate, cut in fine
        dice
    Optional: 1 teaspoon vanilla extract (or 1 teaspoon
        orange flower water)

Sift the flour and salt into a bowl, make a well in the center, and add the wine and sugar. Work the flour into the center until you have a rather firm dough, something like noodle dough [*see* No. 482]. If the dough is too crumbly add more wine, but do not let it become sticky. Place dough on a lightly floured pastry cloth or board and knead it and pound it vigorously for about 15 minutes. It should be perfectly smooth by then. Form it into a ball, wrap in a clean, slightly dampened cloth, and let it rest for 2 hours. When it has rested roll it out on the pastry cloth or board until very thin (no more than 1/16 inch). Cut it into 5-inch squares and roll it around the metal tubes as follows: take a square and place it before you diamond fashion, one of the points toward you. Place the tube vertically across the middle of the diamond, each end at a point of the dough. Fold the sides over the tube, moistening the overlap with a little water and pressing together. When all the squares have been thus rolled, place them, a few at a time, into deep fat preheated to 375°. Remove them when they are golden brown (tongs are best for this, as the rolls are fragile) and let them drain on absorbent paper. When they are cool, slip off the tubes, and fill with the ricotta filling.

Press the ricotta through a fine sieve into a bowl. Beat it until it is creamy and smooth (an electric beater is fine), add the sugar, and beat until the mixture is no longer grainy in texture but velvet smooth. Beat in the rest of the ingredients with a large fork. Fill a pastry bag fitted with a large plain tube (or merely use the nozzle, without a tube) and pipe the filling into the cooled shells. *Makes* 12 *Cannoli.*

NOTE: The Cannoli may also have the ends showing the filling dipped in chopped pistachio nuts and the pastry then sprinkled with confectioners' sugar.

Cannoli forms may be made from 1-inch aluminum tubing (or 1-inch wooden doweling) cut in 5-inch lengths. They are rarely found commercially, it being the custom even in Italian-American families to cut their own.

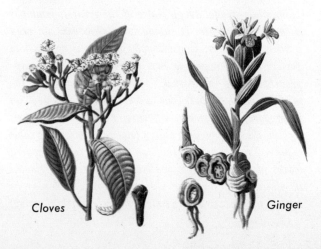

Cloves   *Ginger*

SEE

VERSE

FOR

PTION

1. Mont Blanc (No. 2081)
2. Holland Pudding with Currant Sauce (No. 2080).
   Additional sauce is in the bowl below.
3. Melon Surprise (No. 2154)
4. Charlotte Desiderio di Venus (No. 2068)

1989. CHERRY BARQUETTES

Barchette con ciliege

1 recipe Barquette Pastry [No. 1959]
3 cups sour pie cherries, pitted (or use 1 large can sour
    cherries packed in water, *not* syrup)
1¼ cups sugar
Optional: ½ teaspoon almond extract
¾ cup currant jelly, melted

Mix the cherries with the sugar (if canned cherries are used, drain thoroughly and pat dry on paper towels) and the optional almond extract. Let rest while you roll out the pastry dough. Roll out dough on a lightly floured pastry cloth or board to the thickness of ⅛ inch. Line 12 barquette (boat-shaped) molds with it. Fill with the cherries. Place molds on a baking sheet and bake in a 400° oven for 15 to 20 minutes. Remove from oven and cool on a cake rack. When cool, melt the currant jelly in a small, heavy saucepan over medium heat until it is syrupy and no lumps remain. Glaze each of the barquettes with the still liquid warm jelly. *Makes 12 barquettes.*

NOTE: These may also be baked in tart shells.

1990. CREAM PUFF DOUGH

Pasta per choux fine

1 cup cold water
½ cup butter
¼ teaspoon salt
Optional: 1 tablespoon sugar
1 cup sifted all-purpose flour
4 eggs

Place the water, butter, salt, and optional sugar in a heavy saucepan and bring to a rapid boil over high heat. When the butter has melted remove the pan from the fire and dump in the flour, all at once. Stir briskly with a wooden spoon until the flour has been thoroughly incorporated and return the pan to the stove, reducing the heat to very low, and continue stirring until the mixture forms a ball and leaves the sides and bottom of the pan. Remove from the stove, let cool for 5 minutes, and then add the eggs, 1 at a time, beating vigorously after each addition (an electric mixer is a help here). After the last egg has been added, beat the mixture until it becomes smooth and glossy. When this has been accomplished, the dough is now ready for a variety of uses: cream puffs, eclairs, etc.

Shaping and baking:

The dough may be placed in a large pastry bag fitted with a large plain tip, or dropped by spoonful onto a lightly greased baking sheet. The dough expands to twice its size when baked, so this should be your guide when spacing the puffs on the baking sheet. Place in a 425° oven for 15 minutes, then reduce the heat to 300° and bake for an additional 15 to 20 minutes. They should be well puffed by now and no traces of moisture should be left on the surfaces. One may make a test at this point by cutting one open and seeing if the inside is dryish. It will not be totally dry, however. Remove the puffs from the oven, cut a slit in the side of each, and allow them to cool thoroughly on a cake rack. Do not cover them while the least bit warm, as this will make them soggy. Also, do not fill until just before serving. *Makes 12 large puffs or 24 small ones.*

NOTE: Care should be taken that the oven is not too hot, for then the dough will rise too rapidly and subsequently collapse. If the puffs are large, split them open, scrape out any moist parts clinging to the insides, and dry them in a 350° oven for 10 minutes. Never fill a hot puff with a cold mixture or vice versa. Baked puffs may also be frozen, unfilled (*see* page 610).

THE PREPARATION OF CREAM PUFF DOUGH

1. Boil the water, salt, and butter in a saucepan; remove from the stove and stir in the flour
2. Stir the mixture continuously with a wooden spoon until it forms a ball, and no longer sticks to sides and bottom of the pan. Remove from fire and add the eggs, 1 at a time, beating vigorously until the dough is glossy before adding another egg.
3. Beat the dough until it is perfectly smooth and glossy

1   2   3

1991. PLAIN CREAM PUFF DOUGH
Pasta per choux comune

1 cup water
¼ teaspoon salt
4 tablespoons butter (lard may be substituted)
1 cup sifted all-purpose flour
5 small eggs

Proceed exactly as for Cream Puff Dough [No. 1990].

1992. CUSTARD CREAM PUFFS
Choux alla crema vanigliata

1 recipe Cream Puff Dough [No. 1990], flavored with
    1 tablespoon orange flower water
1 recipe Pastry Cream [No. 2267]
3 tablespoons unblanched almonds, sliced paper thin
    [see No. 2288]
3 tablespoons vanilla confectioners' sugar
    [see No. 2296]

Prepare the dough as indicated in No. 1990, adding the orange flower water just before the flour is dumped in. Lightly butter a large baking sheet, place the dough in a pastry bag fitted with a large plain tip (or just use the nozzle of the bag) and pipe on 12 medium balls of dough or 24 small ones. Bake as directed in No. 1990. Before cooling, pierce the bottoms with the tip of a small sharp knife. When cool, place the pastry cream in a pastry bag fitted with a medium plain tip, and fill each puff with the cream. Mix the almonds and sugar together and dust the surface of each puff with the mixture. *Makes 24 small puffs or 12 medium ones.*

1993. CHOCOLATE CREAM PUFFS
Choux alla crema al cioccolato

1 recipe Cream Puff Dough [No. 1990]
1 recipe Pastry Cream [No. 2267], flavored with
    2 squares melted bitter chocolate
½ cup Chocolate Fondant Icing [see No. 2255]

Prepare and bake as indicated in No. 1990. When filled, glaze the top of each puff with a little of the fondant icing. *Makes 24 small or 12 medium puffs.*

1994. MOCHA CREAM PUFFS
Choux alla crema al caffè

1 recipe Cream Puff Dough [No. 1990]
1 recipe Pastry Cream [No. 2267], flavored with
    2 tablespoons powdered instant coffee (or ¼ cup
    triple-strength brewed coffee), 1 tablespoon cocoa,
    and 2 teaspoons vanilla extract
½ cup Coffee Fondant Icing [see No. 2255]

Prepare and bake as indicated in No. 1990. When filled, glaze the top of each puff with a little of the fondant icing. *Makes 24 small or 12 medium puffs.*

1995. WHIPPED-CREAM-FILLED CREAM PUFFS
Choux alla panna montata

1 recipe Cream Puff Dough [No. 1990]
2 cups heavy cream
6 tablespoons vanilla superfine sugar [see No. 2296],
    or 6 tablespoons superfine sugar and 2 teaspoons
    vanilla extract
Confectioners' sugar, sifted

Prepare and bake as indicated in No. 1990. When cool fill with the following: whip the cream in well-chilled bowl until it is thick. Beat in the vanilla-flavored sugar (or sugar and vanilla extract). Fill as indicated in No. 1990, and dust the top of each puff with the confectioners' sugar. *Makes 24 small or 12 medium puffs.*

1996. ZABAGLIONE CREAM PUFFS
Choux allo zabaione

1 recipe Cream Puff Dough [No. 1990]
1 recipe Cold Zabaglione [No. 2117]
½ cup Fondant Icing [No. 2255]

Prepare and fill as indicated in No. 1990. When filled, glaze the top of each puff with the white fondant. *Makes 24 small or 12 medium puffs.*

1997. CROQUEMBOUCHE
Croquembouche

This magnificent dessert is extremely festive and impressive to look at, delightful to eat, and not terribly difficult to make. If one can make cream puffs and caramel, the effort expended on this confection is mainly patience. Although it is time consuming to prepare, one should not become panicky or hasty. Work calmly and all will be well.

1½ recipe Cream Puff Dough [No. 1990]
1 recipe Pastry Cream [No. 2267]
1 cup Fondant Icing [No. 2255]
1 cup Chocolate Icing [No. 2253]
½ recipe Génoise Base for Petits Fours [No. 1953]
Caramel:
  1 cup sugar
  ⅓ cup cold water
Garnishes:
  6 thin wedges candied citron
  9 small wedges candied pineapple
  15 Glacéed Strawberries [No. 2308], made with the tiniest berries available
  ¼ cup pistachio nuts, chopped
  ½ cup Fondant Icing [No. 2255]
  Optional: chocolate lattice crown (*see* Note below)

Place the cream puff dough in a pastry bag fitted with the large plain tip (or use the nozzle of the bag) and pipe out 40 small puffs about the size of a very small walnut onto a lightly buttered baking sheet. (When baked they should be 1½ inches in diameter.) Bake as indicated in No. 1990. Butter a 9-inch cake tin, line it with wax paper, butter that, dust with flour, and shake out the excess. Pour in the Génoise batter and bake as directed in No. 1953. When baked, remove from oven, turn out on a cake rack, carefully peel off the paper, and cool. It should be a *very* thin cake. Meanwhile prepare the pastry cream and allow it to chill, and prepare the fondant and icing. Have the garnishes all prepared and set out on plates. When the cake, puffs, and cream are properly cooked, begin your preparation.

Fill each of the puffs with the pastry cream as indicated in No. 1990. Spread the sides of 18 of the puffs with the fondant icing, leaving their tops and bottoms un-iced. Pour the rest of the icing over the cake, which has been placed on a large platter. While the icing is still warm, press in 18 of the puffs as follows: draw an 8-inch circle on top of the cake and arrange 11 of the fondant-iced puffs around it, with their sides touching. Fill the center space with 7 of the un-iced filled puffs. Ice the remaining puffs with chocolate icing (some of them may be merely decorated with thin lines and swirls of chocolate icing, squeezed from a stiff paper cornucopia with the end snipped off). Leave 1 puff un-iced and undecorated. Place all the puffs and the puff-topped iced cake in the refrigerator. Make sure the loose puffs do not touch.

Place the sugar and water for the caramel in a small, very heavy saucepan. Stir to dissolve the sugar for about 5 minutes and then cook until a caramel syrup is formed, deep golden in color (356° on the candy thermometer). Remove from fire at once and place the pan in a larger pan of boiling water. (This arrests the cooking of the caramel, which must not burn, yet keeps it hot.) Remove the puffs from the refrigerator. Take the chocolate-iced puffs and dip their bottoms in the caramel, 1 at a time. Use tongs for this as the caramel is very hot and can cause a serious burn. Arrange them over the un-iced puffs on top of the iced cake. This will give you a small circle of puffs, leaving the outer layer of fondant-iced puffs uncovered. This is to be the "second story" of the cake. It should take 8 or 9 puffs. When this has been done, fill the empty space in the center with 1 or 2 more puffs, dipping the bottom of each in the caramel. The third "story" should take 6 puffs, the fourth 4 puffs, each dipped in caramel and placed on the lower story at once, before the syrup has cooled. The caramel acts as a cement holding the layers together. Take the single un-iced puff and dip it totally in the caramel and place it on the peak (*see* photograph preceding page 625 for the way the assembled dessert is to look). Press the chopped pistachios around the side of the cake base. Place a glacéed strawberry between each puff of the first layer; place a wedge of candied pineapple between each puff of the second layer; place a wedge of candied citron between those of the third and fourth layers; and place a glacéed strawberry between each puff of the fifth layer. Place the ½ cup of fondant icing in a pastry bag fitted with a medium star tip and pipe on little dabs of icing as shown in the photograph. Crown it with the optional chocolate crown. Serve as soon as possible. *Serves* 12.

NOTE: The chocolate crown is almost impossible to make without a special type of chocolate used by candy makers, called "dipping" chocolate, which hardens after it has melted. Regular baking chocolate will not harden enough. If you can obtain dipping chocolate, make the lattice as follows. Lightly butter a large sheet of aluminum foil, drape it over rolling pin, leaving a wide "skirt" at the bottom. This will give you a curved surface. Heat the chocolate in a cup over warm water until it is just melted. Pour it into a cornucopia made of stiff paper. Snip off the end to create a tiny hole. Pipe the chocolate in strips on to the foil, to create 3 tear-shaped lattices as shown in the photograph. Let it cool, and then carefully peel off the foil. Tuck the bottom edges of each lattice under the top puff and fix it in place with a little cool fondant icing.

For additional effect, the example shown in the photograph has been made in 7 layers. If you wish to accomplish this, increase all ingredients by $\frac{1}{2}$ and make 60 puffs, etc. Also, the photographed example is further garnished with glacéed apple slices. These are made by slicing a red unpeeled apple into very thin wedges and treating them in the same manner as Glacéed Strawberries [No. 2308].

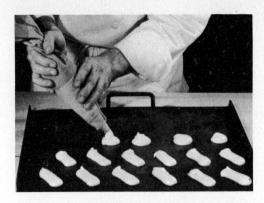

Piping out the dough
for Cream Puffs (No. 1990)
and Eclairs (No. 1998)

ECLAIRS

Eclairs

Eclairs are basically the same as cream puffs: they employ the same dough and take the same types of fillings and icings. However, they are finger shaped, and in some ways more decorative and festive in appearance. For serving with afternoon tea (or after-dinner coffee) they should be very tiny—about $1\frac{3}{4}$ inches long. The dough should be treated in approximately the same way indicated for Cream Puffs [No. 1990]. *See* photograph above right for the proper way to pipe the dough onto the sheet.

1998. CHOCOLATE ECLAIRS
Éclairs al cioccolato

1 recipe Cream Puff Dough [No. 1990]
1 recipe Pastry Cream [No. 2267]
$\frac{1}{2}$ cup Chocolate Fondant Icing [*see* No. 2255]

Fill a pastry bag fitted with a large plain tip (or use the nozzle of the bag) with the cream puff dough. Lightly butter a baking sheet and pipe on the dough in strips 4 inches long and $\frac{3}{4}$ inches wide (for tiny eclairs, pipe it on $1\frac{1}{2}$ inches long and $\frac{1}{4}$ inch wide, and use a medium plain tip). Place in a 425° oven for 20 minutes, then reduce heat to 300° and bake for another 10 minutes to dry them out. Remove to rack and cool. (For tiny eclairs bake at 400° for 10 minutes and at 300° for 7 minutes.) Before cooling slit the eclairs through the middle with a sharp knife (you may leave 1 side uncut and open them like a book, if you like) and fill with the pastry cream. Close them and ice the tops with the icing. *Makes* 12 *large eclairs or* 30 *small ones.*

1999. COFFEE ECLAIRS
Éclairs al caffè

1 recipe Cream Puff Dough [No. 1990]
1 recipe Pastry Cream [No. 2267], flavored with 2 tablespoons powdered instant coffee (or $\frac{1}{4}$ cup triple-strength brewed coffee) and 1 teaspoon vanilla extract
Optional: $\frac{1}{2}$ cup apricot preserves, pressed through a fine sieve
$\frac{1}{2}$ cup Coffee Fondant Icing [*see* No. 2255]

Proceed exactly as indicated in No. 1998. *Makes* 12 *large eclairs or* 30 *small ones.*

NOTE: Before icing them with the fondant icing, the eclairs may be brushed with the strained apricot preserves for extra richness.

2000. CUSTARD AND FRUIT ECLAIRS
Éclairs con crema pasticcera e frutta

1 recipe Cream Puff Dough [No. 1990]
1 recipe Pastry Cream [No. 2267]
$\frac{1}{3}$ cup candied fruit, diced (cherries, pineapple, orange or lemon peel, singly or in combination)
2 tablespoons dark rum
$\frac{1}{2}$ cup Fondant Icing [No. 2255]
Optional: 2 tablespoons candied angelica, cut into tiny diamonds
1 tablespoon candied cherries, cut into tiny dice

Prepare exactly as indicated in No. 1998, except: marinate the candied fruit in the rum for 2 hours and then mix into the cream before filling the eclairs. The eclairs may further be garnished by arranging the angelica and cherries in decorative patterns over the white fondant. *Makes* 12 *large eclairs or* 30 *small ones.*

2001. WHIPPED CREAM ECLAIRS
Éclairs con panna montata

1 recipe Cream Puff Dough [No. 1990]
2 cups heavy cream, whipped
6 tablespoons superfine sugar
1½ teaspoons vanilla extract
Fondant Icing [No. 2255]

Proceed as indicated in No. 1998. Fill the eclairs with the whipped cream which has been flavored with the sugar and vanilla. Coat tops with white fondant. *Makes 12 large eclairs or 30 small ones.*

NOTE: Chocolate or Coffee Fondant [*see* No. 2255] may be used in place of the white icing.

2002. ZABAGLIONE ECLAIRS
Éclairs al zabaione

1 recipe Cream Puff Dough [No. 1990]
1 recipe Cold Zabaglione [No. 2117]
½ cup Fondant Icing [No. 2255]

Proceed exactly as indicated in No. 1998. *Makes 12 large eclairs or 30 small ones.*

2003. DIPLOMATS
Diplomatici

½ recipe Italian Sponge Cake [No. 1913]
1 recipe Puff Paste [No. 1960], prepared the day before and left overnight in the refrigerator
1 recipe Pastry Cream [No. 2267]
4 tablespoons Alkermes liqueur (*see* Note below)
3 tablespoons sifted confectioners' sugar

Make sure that the puff paste dough has rested for at least 24 hours in the refrigerator. Butter a 9- by 9-inch baking tin, line it with wax paper, butter that, and dust with flour. Tap out the excess. Pour the cake batter into the pan and bake as indicated in Italian Sponge Cake [No. 1913]. Remove from oven when done (it will take about 10 minutes less to bake because it is thin), turn out on a cake rack, carefully peel off the paper, and cool. Roll out the puff paste on a lightly floured pastry cloth or board until it forms a rectangle 9 inches wide by 18 inches long, cut into 2 9- by 9-inch squares, place on a slightly dampened baking sheet, prick all over lightly with a fork, and bake in a 375° to 400° oven until well puffed and crisp. Do not let it get too brown. Remove from oven and cool on a cake rack. When the cake is cold, sprinkle it with the liqueur. Place one of the puff paste squares on a square serving dish and cover it with part of the pastry cream, top it with the liqueur-soaked cake square, top this with the remaining pastry cream, and finish it off with the second pastry square. Coat the top with the sifted confectioners' sugar and cut with a sharp knife into rectangles 3 inches long by 1½ inches wide. *Makes 18 pieces.*

NOTE: Alkermes is an Italian liqueur with a brandy base, flavored with an infusion of mace, nutmeg, cloves, and cinnamon, and colored a brilliant red. Benedictine or Chartreuse may be substituted for Alkermes.

2004. CREAM-FILLED PASTRY HORNS
Cornetti con panna montata

This recipe requires the use of little tin molds, slightly cone-shaped, about 5½ inches long. The cone shape makes it easier to remove the pastry when baked. The forms used in Cannoli [see No. 1988] might be made to serve, but the cylindrical shape will make the pastry harder to remove.

1 recipe Puff Paste [No. 1960], prepared the day before and left overnight in the refrigerator
6 cream horn tubes
2 cups heavy cream, whipped
6 tablespoons superfine sugar
1½ teaspoons vanilla extract
Optional: 2 tablespoons confectioners' sugar, sifted

Make sure that the puff paste dough has rested for at least 24 hours in the refrigerator. Roll out the dough on a lightly floured pastry cloth or board until it forms a rectangle 30 inches long. Cut lengthwise with a sharp knife into strips ½ inch wide. Lightly moisten the metal tubes (you need use only 6 tubes, baking the horns in relays of 6 at a time), and roll a strip of pastry around each, overlapping the edges slightly. Do not stretch the dough or it will not rise evenly. Place the horns on a lightly moistened baking sheet, 3 inches apart, and bake in a 400° oven for 15 minutes, or until well puffed and golden brown. Slip off the pastry horns the moment they leave the oven, and cool on a cake rack. Repeat until all have been made.

Whip the cream in a chilled bowl until stiff and flavor

with the vanilla and sugar. Place it in a pastry bag fitted with a large plain tip (or use the nozzle of the bag), and fill each horn with the cream. Dust the surface, if desired, with the confectioners' sugar. *Makes 24 horns.*

NOTE: These may be kept, unfilled, for a week or so if kept in an airtight container. Also the horns may be filled with Pastry Cream [No. 2267], if desired.

2005. NAPOLEONS
Gâteau millefoglie

1 recipe Puff Paste [No. 1960], prepared the day before and left overnight in the refrigerator
1 recipe Pastry Cream [No. 2267]
½ cup Fondant Icing [No. 2255], or 3 tablespoons vanilla confectioners' sugar [*see* No. 2296]
Optional: 1 square bitter chocolate, melted

Make sure that the puff paste dough has rested for at least 24 hours in the refrigerator. Roll out the dough on a lightly floured pastry cloth or board until it forms a rectangle 9 by 24 inches. Cut this into 4 equal 9- by 6-inch rectangles. Place them on a lightly dampened baking sheet and bake them in a 400° oven until they are well puffed, crisp, and golden brown. Remove from oven and let cool on a cake rack. When cool, scrape a few leaves off each rectangle, so that you have about ½ cup of crumbs. Put together as shown in photograph, and ice the top with the fondant (or sprinkle with confectioners' sugar). The cake may be served whole or cut into 12 rectangles. *Serves 10 to 12.*

NOTE: For the traditional patterned top, place the melted chocolate in a paper cornucopia. Cut off the tip to make a tiny hole and draw evenly spaced lines across the top. Immediately (before the chocolate and fondant harden) take a toothpick and lightly drag it across the lines.

2006. WAFERS FOR CORNUCOPIAS
Cialde per cornetti

These are waffles, actually, but should be baked in special utensils consisting of 2 hinged plates of cast iron (round, in this case) whose inner surfaces are stamped with a decorative pattern. The iron plates are attached to long metal handles. These wafer irons are available at certain shops specializing in European kitchenware: they are known as "Belgian" or "Swedish" waffle-irons. Do not attempt these wafers in the standard American waffle-iron.

2¾ cups triple-sifted all-purpose flour
1¾ cups superfine sugar
¼ teaspoon salt
1¾ tablespoons melted margarine (or butter)
2 egg yolks, lightly beaten
½ cup (more or less) cold water
¼ cup Clarified Butter [No. 102]

Sift the dry ingredients into a bowl. Make a well in the center and in it place the yolks, melted margarine, and ¼ cup of the water. Work the flour into the center and knead into a soft dough, adding more water as needed, 1 tablespoon at a time. Knead it for 5 minutes until smooth. Divide it into balls the size of a filbert or hazelnut. Lightly flour a pastry cloth or board and roll out the dough balls to the thickness of ⅛ inch. Heat the iron on the top of the stove over a high flame. It is sufficiently heated when a drop of water dances around the inner surface in a little ball. Brush both surfaces of the iron with the clarified butter and place a dough circle onto the iron. Close it and put it back on the fire. Turn it over after 30 seconds. When it has baked for 50 seconds open the iron a bit and if the waffle is golden brown turn it out onto a clean cloth. While it is still hot twist it into a cone, using a wooden mold or the handle of a wooden spoon. Let cool for a few

The preparation of Napoleons (No. 2005). Left: Spread a pastry rectangle with some of the pastry cream.
Center: When 3 of the pastry rectangles have been spread with the cream and piled on top
of each other, top with the fourth rectangle and spread the cream
oozing from between the layers evenly with a spatula to coat the sides lightly.
Right: Pat the reserved crumbs into the cream-spread sides.

minutes and then slip off the mold. Repeat this process until all the dough has been used up. The cones may then be filled with sweetened whipped cream, ice cream (in which case they are the authentic "ice-cream cones"), fruit, etc. *Makes about 40 cones.*

NOTE: The dough may be rolled out to the thickness of $1/16$ inch and cut into 5-inch circles, placed on a lightly buttered baking sheet, brushed with a little butter, and baked in a 400° oven for 10 minutes, or until golden, and then treated as indicated above. They will not, however, have as nutty a flavor.

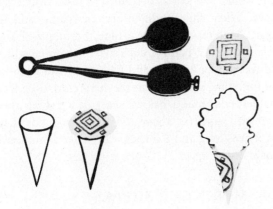

2007. ROLLED WAFFLES
Cialdoni—cialde arrotolate

2½ cups triple-sifted all-purpose flour
¾ cup superfine sugar
½ cup butter, softened
4 tablespoons heavy cream
3 egg whites, lightly beaten until liquid, not stiff
¼ cup warm water
Pinch salt
¼ cup Clarified Butter [No. 102]

Mix, form, roll, and bake as indicated in No. 2006. When baked, roll around the handle of a wooden spoon to form large tubes. When cool the tubes may be filled with sweetened whipped cream, or whipped cream flavored with any crushed, sweetened fruit or berries. *Makes about 30 tubes.*

2008. FLEMISH WAFERS OR WAFFLES
Cialde alla fiamminga—gaufres

This recipe also requires a special iron, this time square or rectangular, about the same dimensions as a slice of bread.

2 cups plus 2 tablespoons triple-sifted all-purpose flour

1 cake fresh compressed yeast dissolved in ¼ cup warm (85°) water for 5 minutes (or 1 envelope dry yeast dissolved in ¼ cup warmer—110°— water, and left until foaming, about 10 minutes, *see* page 611)
3 tablespoons butter, melted
½ teaspoon salt
2 cups milk, scalded and cooled
½ cup heavy cream, scalded and cooled
7 egg whites
Optional: ¼ cup superfine sugar
¼ cup Clarified Butter [No. 102]

Sift the flour into a large bowl. Make a well in the center and into it place the dissolved yeast, the 3 table-spoons melted butter, salt, and the scalded milk and cream. Mix with a wooden spoon until blended (do not beat too much) and then whip the egg whites in a large bowl (preferably of unlined copper) with a pinch of salt. When they are foamy add the optional sugar, if desired, and beat until they stand in soft peaks. Fold the whites into the batter and mix until thoroughly incorporated. Pour the mixture through a fine sieve into a large bowl, cover lightly with a towel, and leave in a warm place for 1 hour. Heat the waffle-iron as described in No. 2006. When hot, brush it with some of the clarified butter. Beat the batter down, and pour a large spoonful into the iron, holding the iron over the bowl to catch any overflow. Close the iron and bake the waffle as described in No. 2006. When baked, turn out onto a plate, keep in a warm place, and continue baking until batter is used up. Butter iron for each new waffle. The waffles may be sprinkled with confectioners' sugar, or else served with sweetened whipped cream and fresh strawberries or raspberries. *Makes about 24 waffles.*

NOTE: It is possible to prepare these waffles in an electric waffle iron, following the manufacturer's directions for baking. They will not, however, have the same flavor or texture as those baked in the special iron.

MERINGUES
Meringhe

Meringues are among the most delicate dessert preparations known. They should be crisp and light and melt on the tongue. When not baked properly, and are still even so slightly moist, they turn tough and chewy in your mouth. Ideally, the egg whites should be beaten in a large bowl of unlined copper. The chemical action of the copper, egg whites, and salt (or cream of tartar) gives the egg whites body and lets them incorporate more air. A big balloon wire whisk should be used, nearly as big as the bowl. Using these utensils (a stainless steel bowl is almost as good), you will discover that it is faster than with an electric mixer or rotary beater, and that the whites will rise at least $\frac{1}{8}$ higher.

Egg whites for meringues should be at room temperature; cold, they will not rise as high or as light. They should always be beaten with a pinch of salt, cream of tartar, or a few drops of lemon juice. The acid gives them staying power, and they will not collapse if left in the bowl for a few minutes.

The slightest trace of yolk in the whites will inhibit their rising, as yolks contain fat. The same holds true for bowl and beater: both must be totally free of fat or grease. It is best to wash bowl and beater with hot water and dry them with a clean, fresh towel before beating your whites.

The sugar should be added gradually when the whites become foamy. The meringue has been sufficiently whipped when the whites form soft peaks and cling to the beater in a mass. You have overbeaten if they look dry and stand in sharp, jagged peaks, and the mixture will probably fall when placed in the oven.

The oven temperature should be as low as possible. The point is to get the moisture out of the meringues, not to bake them. A temperature of 200° is as high as it should go, and if your oven will go as low as 175° that is the perfect temperature. Higher than this, the meringues brown too quickly, turn leathery, and collapse—are ruined. Properly baked, a meringue is crisp, feather-light, the palest bisque in color— almost white. Bake meringues for about 1 hour.

Once they have completely cooled, meringues keep a long time in airtight containers. Excess moisture in the air makes them soggy, so it is best not to bake meringues on a very damp or rainy day. It is wise not to have anything steaming on the stove when they are out of the oven and cooling on cake racks.

The baking sheets on which the meringues are put in the oven should either be lightly buttered, dusted with flour, and the excess flour tapped off, or they should be covered with unglazed paper (brown wrapping paper is fine). Baking sheets coated with the new non-stick plastics are excellent. When buttering the baking sheet, use a very light hand, for any greasiness will make the meringues leathery. If meringues are hard to remove from the baking sheet, use a gently

sawing motion with your knife or spatula. If they stick to paper, moisten it slightly on the reverse side.

2009. MERINGUES
Meringa ordinaria

8 egg whites
2 cups superfine sugar
$\frac{1}{2}$ teaspoon salt (or a big pinch of cream of tartar, or 1 teaspoon lemon juice)
$1\frac{1}{2}$ teaspoons vanilla or almond extract

Beat whites and salt as described in the introduction, above. When they begin to become foamy, add the sugar, 2 tablespoonsful at a time, beating well after each addition. When $1\frac{1}{2}$ cups sugar have been added, add the rest all at once, and fold it in. Add flavoring and fold it in well. To form the meringues, drop from a tablespoon onto a baking sheet or a baking sheet lined with paper (see above). Make oval mounds about $2\frac{1}{2}$ inches long and 2 inches wide. Bake as indicated above. *Makes about $2\frac{1}{2}$ dozen meringues.*

2010. MERINGUE SHELLS
Gusci di meringa

6 egg whites
$1\frac{1}{2}$ cups superfine sugar
$\frac{1}{4}$ teaspoon salt (or pinch cream of tartar, or $\frac{1}{2}$ teaspoon lemon juice)
1 teaspoon vanilla or almond extract

Beat as described in the introduction, above. Add sugar as described in No. 2009. When beaten place meringue in a pastry bag fitted with a large plain tip (or use the nozzle of the bag) and pipe out onto a baking sheet (see above) into little $3\frac{1}{2}$-inch round nests. Bake as described above. When cooled, these shells may be filled with ice cream, berries, custard, etc. *Makes about 16 meringue shells.*

2011. ALMOND CUSTARD MERINGUE ALLA RICCA
Meringa con mandorle alla ricca

This dessert is poached in the oven, rather than baked. Its texture is smooth and spongy rather than crisp.

5 egg whites
Pinch salt (or cream of tartar)
¾ cup plus 1 tablespoon superfine sugar
½ teaspoon almond extract
¾ cup almonds, sliced paper thin [*see* No. 2288], lightly toasted in the oven
2 tablespoons butter, softened
2 cups English Custard [No. 2111]
1 cup heavy cream, whipped, flavored with 2 tablespoons superfine sugar
Optional: paper-thin chocolate wafers (purchased at a candy shop)
1 candied cherry

Beat the egg whites with the salt as described in the introduction (*see* above). Fold in sugar as described in No. 2009. When meringue stands in soft peaks it is done. Liberally grease a 9-inch ring mold with the softened butter. Sprinkle the bottom and sides liberally with ½ cup of sliced almonds, making sure all surfaces are well coated. Carefully spoon in the meringue, taking care that the almonds are not dislodged. Place the mold in a shallow pan filled with hot water, and place in a 250° oven. Bake for 1½ hours or until the meringue is well puffed and springs back when lightly pressed with a finger. Remove from oven, let stand for 10 minutes, and then carefully reverse the mold onto a large round plate. Give the top of the mold several sharp taps with a large spoon, and carefully lift it off. Allow it to cool, then place in refrigerator for 2 hours. When chilled, fill the center of the ring with the custard. Fill a pastry bag fitted with a large star tip with the whipped cream and pipe swags around the sides of meringue (*see* photograph facing page 720) and over the center portion containing the custard. Sprinkle the remaining almonds over the top. The center may be further decorated (as shown) with chocolate wafers, slightly warmed, twisted into cornucopias, chilled, and arranged in a rosette around the center of the meringue. A swirl of whipped cream is then piped into the center, and the whole topped off with a candied cherry. The entire dish is then chilled for 1 or 2 hours before serving (it may rest in the refrigerator overnight). *Serves 8 to 10.*

2012. CUSTARD-FILLED MERINGUE SHELLS
Meringhe con crema inglese

8 Meringue Shells [No. 2010]
2 cups English Custard [No. 2111], made with 8 egg yolks, well chilled and flavored with 1 teaspoon vanilla extract or 1 tablespoon preferred liqueur

Fill the meringue shells with the custard. Serve as soon as possible, so that the meringues do not become soggy. *Serves 8.*

2013. MERINGUE SHELLS WITH CURRANT WHIPPED CREAM
Meringhe con panna montata e gelatina di ribes

8 Meringue Shells [No. 2010]
½ cup black currant jelly
4 tablespoons white wine
1½ cups heavy cream, whipped

Place the currant jelly in a small, heavy saucepan over low heat and beat with a small wire whisk until all lumps disappear and it becomes syrupy. Do not let it heat too much or come to a boil. Add wine and let jelly cool. Beat it into the whipped cream. Pile the currant-flavored cream into the shells and place in the refrigerator for no more than 1 hour before serving. *Serves 8.*

2014. MERINGUES WITH MOCHA BUTTER CREAM
Meringhe con crema al caffè

16 Meringues [No. 2009], 2½ inches long by 2 inches wide
2 cups Coffee Butter Cream [No. 2262]
2 tablespoons powdered cocoa
½ cup apricot preserves, pressed through a fine sieve
½ cup Coffee Fondant Icing [*see* No. 2255]

Hollow out the flat side of the meringues by pressing gently with your thumb. Mix the cocoa into the butter cream. Place a heaping tablespoon of the butter cream in each hollow, and press the meringues together in pairs. Place the rest of the butter cream in a pastry bag fitted with a plain tip and fill the empty space between the paired meringues. Brush this cream with a bit of the strained apricot preserves (being careful not to get it on the meringues), and coat the preserves with a thin coating of fondant. Let "ripen" in the least cold part of the refrigerator for 2 hours. *Serves 8.*

2015. MERINGUES WITH WHIPPED CREAM
Meringhe con panna montata

16 Meringues [No. 2009], 2½ inches long by 2 inches wide
2 cups heavy cream, whipped

Hollow out the flat side of the meringues by pressing gently with your thumb. Whip cream until stiff in a chilled bowl. Place a generous dollop of cream in each hollow and press the meringues together in pairs. Serve within the hour or they will become soggy.

NOTE: The cream should not be sweetened.

2016. MERINGUES WITH CREAM AND MARRONS GLACÉS
Meringhe con panna montata e marrons glacés

16 Meringues [No. 2009], 2½ inches long by 2 inches wide
1 cup marrons glacés, pushed through a fine sieve
   (or 1 cup canned purée of marrons glacés)
2 cups heavy cream, whipped
Pinch salt

Hollow out the flat side of the meringues by pressing gently with your thumb. Mix the mashed marrons with the cream, which has been whipped with the pinch of salt in a chilled bowl. Fold the cream into the marrons. Make a sandwich of the meringues using the whipped cream/marrons mixture as a filling. Additional unsweetened whipped cream may be placed in a pastry bag fitted with a medium star tip and the cream piped into decorative swirls over the exposed parts of the filling. *Serves 8.*

NOTE: Do not sweeten the cream as the marrons provide sufficient sweetness.

CRÊPES
Crespelle

Crêpes (or thin pancakes) are among the most versatile preparations in a cook's repertoire. They lend themselves to all sorts of fillings (both sweet and savory), and they have the added advantage of keeping for a while after they have been prepared. Once a batch of crêpes has been fried, one may store them for as long as 2 days in the refrigerator. They may be kept frozen for as long as 2 months. In this way one can make a large number of crêpes at one time, wrap them in plastic food wrap in batches of 18, and store them in the freezer for use as needed. They take about 1 hour to thaw because they are so thin, and because of this are invaluable to have on hand for unexpected emergencies.

To keep freshly made crêpes warm for periods up to 3 hours, one may pile them on a plate and place the plate over a pan of simmering water. Since many of the crêpe recipes that follow call for them to be baked and/or bathed in a heated sauce, it may not be necessary to have them piping hot. After they are prepared they may stand at room temperature for a few hours before they are given their final preparation.

The batter for crêpes *must* rest for at least 2 hours in the refrigerator. It can remain there as long as 24 hours—but not more, as it may ferment if left longer than that time. Before being fried the batter must be well mixed again, and if it has thickened after its stay (which is more than likely), a little water is added to thin it back to its required consistency.

The consistency of the batter should be that of heavy cream. Thinner batters will not hold together, and thicker ones will produce leathery crêpes. A fried crêpe should be thin enough that one can make out the pattern of the plate underneath it.

The pan in which you fry the crêpes must be no more than 7 inches in diameter. It must have gently sloping sides curving into the bottom of the pan (no sharp corner like a regular skillet). It should be as heavy as possible, in order to distribute the heat evenly. Heavy cast aluminum is the best; iron may lend a "taste" to the crêpes, and enamel will not conduct the heat as well. Ideally, the crêpe pan should never be washed with soap and water, since this destroys the thin coating of fat it absorbs over the years, and also mars the surface of the metal. For the same reason the pan should never be scoured with abrasives or steel wool. The best way to clean the pan is to wipe it out with paper toweling, wiping vigorously until a fresh towel, when applied, shows no stains. If there are scorched particles, put a little salt and a drop or two of vegetable oil in the pan and scrub well with the paper towels.

If the pan must be washed (or you do not wish to keep a pan just for crêpes), it must be greased lightly before frying crêpes by brushing it with a thin film of flavorless vegetable oil or clarified butter. Regular butter will burn and impart a scorched taste to the crêpes. The crêpes must never swim in oil, only the lightest coat should be given the pan after every 6 crêpes have been fried in it.

2017. CRÊPE BATTER
Pasta per crespelle

1½ cups sifted all-purpose flour
2 tablespoons superfine sugar
Pinch salt
3 eggs, lightly beaten
2 tablespoons melted butter
1½ cups milk (or ¾ cup milk and ¾ cup water)
1½ tablespoons orange flower water (or 1 table-
     spoon grated orange rind—no white part)
1½ tablespoons brandy (or rum, kirsch, or other
     preferred liqueur)

Sift the flour, sugar, and salt into a deep bowl. Add the lightly beaten eggs, beating them in with a wooden spoon until you have a smooth, thick paste with no lumps. Do not, however, beat after you have reached this stage. Gradually stir (do not beat) in the melted butter, milk (or milk and water), and orange flower water. The liquor is added just before the crêpes are to be fried. If the liquids are added gradually and gently stirred in, you will have a smooth batter. Place the bowl in the refrigerator and let it rest for at least 2 hours (*see* above).

If desired, this batter may be made in the blender. Place all ingredients except the brandy in the container and whirl on high speed for 1 minute. Scrape down the sides of the container if necessary and blend for another 1 or 2 seconds. Store as above before using.

Preparing the crêpes:

Read the preceding introduction on the type of pan to be used. Remove the batter from the refrigerator and stir it well. Add the brandy or liqueur. If still too thick (*see* page 666), dilute with a little water (not milk or cream). Heat the pan over moderate heat until a drop of water splashed onto its surface dances about in a little ball, without ever resting on the surface. (If your pan has not been seasoned, then you will now need to grease it slightly.) Place the bowl of batter on the stove next to the pan. Using a ladle pour a thin coating of batter in the pan (about a serving-spoon full), tilting the pan in all directions to coat it thoroughly and also bringing a coating up around the sides. If there are holes in the batter, leave them: more batter will make heavy lumps in the crêpe. Cook the crêpe until the edges look brown and the top is dry. Turn with a spatula and fry the other side until no more steam rises from the surface of the crêpe. If desired, lift an edge to make sure the crêpe is not browning too fast. Adjust heat during the cooking. Repeat until all batter is used up. It may get somewhat thick toward the last, so thin it out with a little water. As the crêpes are cooked, cool them on a large platter, piling them on top of one another as they become cool. You will notice that the side that was cooked first is the more attractive, so keep that side facing upward when you fold or roll them before giving them their final preparation. Store them as indicated on page 666. *Makes about 18 crêpes, or enough for 6 servings.*

2018. CRÊPES BUONGUSTAIO
Crespelle buongustaio

18 crêpes [*see* No. 2017]
4 tart, crisp apples (as large as possible), peeled,
     cored, and thinly sliced
4 tablespoons butter
3 tablespoons apricot preserves
5 tablespoons Praline powder [*see* No. 2290]
¼ cup heavy cream, whipped
4 tablespoons maraschino liqueur
4 dry almond macaroons (the imported Italian variety,
     if possible), crushed
2 tablespoons sugar

Cook the apples in 2 tablespoons of the butter in a small heavy saucepan until they are soft but not mushy. Remove from stove, place in a bowl, and allow to cool. When cooled add the apricot preserves, Praline powder, whipped cream, and liqueur. This should form a rather thick mixture. Spread each crêpe with some of the mixture, fold them in quarters, put them on a lightly buttered oven-proof platter, dot with the remaining butter, and sprinkle with the macaroon crumbs and sugar. Bake in a 375° oven for 10 minutes, and serve piping hot. *Serves* 6.

NOTE: The crêpes may be prepared and filled earlier in the day and baked before serving.

2019. CRÊPES CONVENTO WITH KIRSCH
Crespelle convento al kirsch

18 crêpes [*see* No. 2017]
3 firm, ripe pears, peeled, seeded, cored, and sliced
4 tablespoons butter
4 tablespoons sugar (more, if pears are tart)
1 cup Pastry Cream [No. 2267]
¼ cup kirsch

Cook the pear slices in 2 tablespoons of the butter and all the sugar in a small, heavy saucepan until they are soft but not mushy. Remove from stove and cool. (If they have produced too much liquid while cooking, remove the pears with a slotted spoon and reduce the pan liquids to 3 tablespoons over high heat and pour over pears.) When pears are cooled mix them with the pastry cream. Spread each of the crêpes with this mixture and roll them up loosely. Align them on an oven-proof platter and dot with the rest of the butter. Bake in a 375° oven for 10 minutes. Remove from oven. Heat kirsch in a ladle over a low flame, set alight, and pour it over the hot crêpes, and bring to the table flaming (or flame at the table). *Serves 6.*

NOTE: The crêpes may be prepared and filled earlier in the day and baked before serving.

2020. CRÊPES DELIZIOSE WITH FRESH RASPBERRIES
Crespelle deliziose con lamponi

18 crêpes [*see* No. 2017]
2 cups fresh raspberries
2 tablespoons Curaçao
1 tablespoon maraschino liqueur
Juice of 2 oranges
1/2 cup superfine sugar
4 tablespoons Praline powder [*see* No. 2290]
1 cup Pastry Cream [No. 2267]
3 tablespoons butter
1/4 cup brandy

Pick over the raspberries to make sure they are perfect. Place them in a glass bowl and sprinkle them with the Curaçao, maraschino, orange juice, and sugar. Turn them once or twice with a large wooden spoon, taking care you do not crush them, and place them in the refrigerator to chill for 1 hour. Mix the Praline powder with the pastry cream, and spread each of the crêpes with some of this mixture to within 1/2 inch of their edges. Roll the crêpes up. Just before serving, heat the butter in a large frying pan, place the crêpes in it, and heat them quickly, making sure, however, that the butter does not burn. Heat the brandy in a ladle over a low flame, set it aflame, pour it over the crêpes, and bring it to the table. flaming. Serve the chilled raspberries separately, and let each guest spoon some over the hot crêpes. *Serves 6.*

NOTE: Frozen raspberries may be used, if desired. Thaw 2 boxes and drain them. Proceed as directed above. Decrease sugar to taste. This dish may be prepared ahead of time (whether you use fresh or frozen berries) and heated just before serving.

2021. CRÊPES DIANA
Crespelle di ananasso Diana

18 crêpes [*see* No. 2017]
1 cup candied pineapple, cut in small pieces
1/4 cup superfine sugar
1/2 cup butter, softened
1/3 cup brandy or preferred liqueur

Spread each crêpe out flat and place a few pieces of pineapple on each. Roll up the crêpes and align them in an oven-proof serving dish. Cream the sugar and the butter together until light and fluffy and spread it over the crêpes. Place in a 375° oven for 10 minutes, or until the butter has melted and the crêpes are golden. Heat the brandy or liqueur in a ladle, set it aflame, pour it over the crêpes, and bring to the table flaming. *Serves 6.*

NOTE: The crêpes may be assembled ahead of time and placed in the oven 10 minutes before serving. If they have been chilled, take them out of the refrigerator 1 hour before placing them in the oven.

2022. CRÊPES GIL-BLAS
Crespelle Gil-Blas

18 crêpes [*see* No. 2017]
7 tablespoons butter, softened
1/2 cup superfine sugar
3 tablespoons Cognac or brandy
3 tablespoons butter, heated until nut colored and cooled
1/2 teaspoon lemon juice

Cream the softened butter and sugar in a small bowl until light and fluffy. Add the Cognac, a tablespoonful at a time, beating well to incorporate. Finally, beat in the cooled nut-colored butter and the lemon juice. Spread each of the crêpes with some of this mixture, roll up, and align them on an oven-proof serving dish. Place in a 400° oven for 7 minutes, and serve at once. *Serves 6.*

NOTE: The crêpes may be assembled ahead of time and placed in the oven just before serving. If chilled, remove them from the refrigerator 1 hour before serving time.

2023. CRÊPES GIORGETTA
Crespelle Giorgetta

18 crêpes [see No. 2017]
1 cup candied pineapple, cut in small pieces
¼ cup maraschino liqueur
1 cup Pastry Cream [No. 2267]
2 tablespoons butter, softened
2 tablespoons superfine sugar
3 tablespoons brandy

Marinate the pieces of candied pineapple in the maraschino for 3 hours. Drain, reserving the liqueur, spread each crêpe with some of the Pastry Cream to within ½ inch of the edge, sprinkle with a few pieces of pineapple, roll up, and align on an oven-proof serving dish. Cream the butter and sugar together, spread it over the crêpes, and pour over the reserved maraschino marinade. Place in a 375° oven for 10 minutes, or until the butter has melted and the pan liquids are bubbling. Heat the brandy in a ladle over a low flame, set it aflame, and pour it over the hot crêpes. Bring to the table flaming. *Serves* 6.

NOTE: The crêpes may be assembled and placed in the serving dish ahead of time. If chilled, remove from refrigerator 1 hour before placing in the oven.

2024. CRÊPES ITALIANA
Crespelle all'italiana

18 crêpes [see No. 2017]
1 cup heavy cream, whipped
½ teaspoon grated orange rind (no white part)
1 teaspoon vanilla extract
3 tablespoons superfine sugar
4 tablespoons vanilla sugar [see No. 2296]
1½ cups Apricot Sauce [No. 2270]
4 tablespoons Strega liqueur

Whip the cream in a chilled bowl and flavor it with the grated orange rind, vanilla, and sugar. Spread out the crêpes and place some of the whipped cream on each to within ½ inch of the edge. Fold each crêpe in half and align on a lightly buttered oven-proof serving dish. Sprinkle the surface of the crêpes with the vanilla sugar, and place in a 425° oven for 5 minutes. Flavor the sauce with the Strega and place it in a serving bowl. Remove the crêpes from the oven and serve at once. Allow each guest to help himself to the sauce. *Serves* 6.

NOTE: The crêpes should be at room temperature and the whipped cream should be well chilled. This dish should be assembled just before serving.

2025. CRÊPES WITH JAM
Crespelle alla confettura

18 crêpes [see No. 2017]
1½ cups preferred fruit preserves (strawberry, raspberry, apricot, etc.)
⅓ cup butter, softened
4 tablespoons superfine sugar

Spread each crêpe with some of the preserves, roll them up, and align on a lightly buttered oven-proof dish. Cream the butter and sugar together until fluffy and spread over the crêpes. Place in a 375° oven for 10 minutes, and serve at once. *Serves* 6.

NOTE: The crêpes may be assembled ahead of time and placed in the oven before serving. If chilled, remove them from the refrigerator 1 hour before placing them in the oven.

2026. CRÊPES WITH RUM-FLAVORED MARRONS GLACÉS
Crespelle con marrons glacés profumati al rhum

18 crêpes [see No. 2017]
1 cup marrons glacés, broken in small pieces
¼ cup dark rum
⅓ cup butter, softened
4 tablespoons superfine sugar

Place the crumbled marrons in a small bowl and pour over the rum. Let them marinate for 3 hours. Spread each of the crêpes with some of the marrons and fold them up so that their sides meet in the center—envelope fashion. Place them, folded side downward, on a lightly buttered oven-proof serving dish. Cream the butter and the sugar together until fluffy, add any of the remaining rum marinade from the marrons, and spread over the crêpes. Place in a 375° oven for 10 minutes, or until the crêpes are well glazed. Serve at once. *Serves* 6.

NOTE: The crêpes may be assembled ahead of time and placed in the oven just before serving. If chilled, remove from the refrigerator 1 hour before placing in the oven.

669

2027. CRÊPES SUZETTE
Crêpes Suzette

This is probably the most famous of crêpes recipes. When well made at home, they are usually much better than the restaurant variety, which are usually too sweet and too heavily laden with liquor.

> 18 crêpes [*see* No. 2017]
> 8 lumps sugar rubbed over the rind of 1 orange and 1 lemon until they have absorbed their essential oils
> ½ cup butter, softened
> Juice of 1 orange, strained
> ½ cup superfine sugar
> 2 strips orange rind (no white part)
> 2 strips lemon rind (no white part)
> ⅓ cup Grand Marnier
> 3 tablespoons maraschino liqueur
> ¼ cup brandy

Place the rubbed sugar lumps in a bowl and crush them. Mix in the butter and let stand 15 minutes (this allows the butter to absorb the orange and lemon zest, giving this recipe its particular fragrance). Cream in a tablespoon of the orange juice and ¼ cup of the superfine sugar. Then cream in the remaining orange juice and mix well. Place the mixture in a glass serving bowl. The rest of the ingredients are now ready to be prepared at the table (*see* photograph facing page 640).

In the frying pan of a chafing dish place the remaining sugar, the orange and lemon peel, the Grand Marnier, and the maraschino. Light the burner of the chafing dish, and dissolve the sugar, stirring gently with a silver spoon. Add the creamed butter/sugar/orange mixture, and let it melt, tipping the pan in all directions. Let this simmer for 2 minutes. Then add the crêpes, 1 at a time, coating each with the sauce, folding in half and then in quarters, and pushing to one side of the pan. Repeat until all have been treated in this manner. Remove the pan from the burner for a moment, and pour the brandy into a ladle. Heat this for a moment over the burner, set it aflame, and pour it over the sauced crêpes. Return the pan to the burner and shake it gently until the flames die out. Serve the crêpes on warmed plates, spooning some of the sauce over each portion. *Serves 6.*

670

NOTE: If a chafing dish is not available, prepare this in your most attractive frying pan in the kitchen. Follow the above directions up to the point where the warmed brandy is added. At this point, bring the pan into the dining room and set it on a heat-proof mat on the table. Pour over the warmed brandy, and flame. Continue as directed above.

FRIED CAKES AND FRITTERS
Bignè e frittelle

Many of the recipes are regional dishes served once a year, on a certain saint's day or holiday. In Italy, the fat for frying these cakes is usually lard, but any neutral vegetable oil may be used. Since these are sweet preparations, make sure that the fat or oil has not been used for any other fried preparation. However, since lard or olive oil break down when subjected to high heat, it is suggested that they be heated to 350° or 360°.

2028. BEIGNETS SOUFFLÉS
Pasta per bignè soufflés

> 1¼ cup sifted all-purpose flour
> ¼ cup butter
> 1 cup water
> ⅛ teaspoon salt
> 3 tablespoons sugar
> 4 eggs
> ¼ teaspoon vanilla extract (or 1 teaspoon orange flower water)
> Fat for deep frying

Place the butter, water, salt, and sugar in a small, heavy saucepan. Bring to a boil over high heat. When the butter has melted add the flour all at once. Stir until the flour and water forms a ball and leaves the sides of the pan. Stir for a minute or two to make a very dry mixture. Place in a large bowl and let cool for 5 minutes. Beat in the eggs, 1 at a time, beating well after each addition. After the last egg has been added, add the vanilla and beat the mixture for 5 minutes, or until it is smooth and very glossy. Drop by spoonsful into the fat, which has been preheated to 360°. Fry until the fritters are browned on all sides. Do not fry too many at a time, as they swell on contact in the hot fat. Drain on absorbent paper in a warm place. When all are fried, sprinkle with vanilla superfine sugar [see No. 2296] or serve with Apricot Sauce [No. 2270]. *Serves 6.*

NOTE: The fritters may also be split and filled with jam or preserves.

2029. CUSTARD FRITTERS
Bignè di crema rovesciata

1 recipe Baked Custard [No. 2103] (made with 3
    additional whole eggs)
1 recipe Fritter Batter for Fruit [No. 2031]
Fat for deep frying
Vanilla superfine sugar [see No. 2296]

Butter a 9- by 12-inch baking dish, line it with wax paper, and butter that. Pour in the custard and bake as directed in No. 2103. When done, chill for at least 6 hours (or, better, overnight). Before serving, turn the custard out onto a large platter or a wax-paper-covered board. Carefully peel off the wax paper adhering to the bottom of the custard, and cut the custard into 1½-inch squares (no larger, as it is very delicate and hard to handle). Dip them in the batter and then place them, a few at a time, in the fat, which has been preheated to 375°. When golden, remove with a slotted spoon and drain on absorbent paper in a warm place. When all have been fried, place them on an oven-proof serving dish, sprinkle with the sugar, and place in a 425° oven until they are well glazed (about 5 minutes). Serve at once. *Serves 8.*

NOTE: These are very delicate and hard to handle. It is best if they are dipped into the batter on a pair of tongs and placed directly into the fat. The latter should be about 2 inches deep. A large, deep skillet is the best utensil for frying.

2030. FRIED CREAM
Crema fritta

2 cups rich milk (or 1 cup milk and 1 cup cream),
    scalded
2-inch piece of vanilla bean, split
2 eggs
6 egg yolks
¾ cup sugar
1 cup sifted all-purpose flour
Pinch salt
3 dry almond macaroons (Italian macaroons, if
    possible), crushed
4 tablespoons butter, softened
2 eggs, lightly beaten
Fine breadcrumbs
Fat for deep frying
5 tablespoons vanilla confectioners' sugar [see No. 2296]

Scald the milk with the vanilla bean in a small, heavy saucepan. As soon as scalded, remove from fire, cover pan, and let steep for 15 minutes. Beat the 2 eggs, yolks, and sugar together until light and fluffy. Beat in the flour and salt, and gradually strain in the steeped milk. Beat until thoroughly blended (an electric beater works well here). Pour into a heavy saucepan, and stir with a wire whisk over a medium flame until very thick. Scrape the bottom constantly to prevent scorching. It will be a very thick and lumpy mixture. When thickened, remove from fire for a minute and beat with the whisk (*not* the electric beater) until smooth. Return to fire and let cook, stirring constantly, for 3 or 4 minutes. Remove, and beat in the macaroon crumbs and 2 tablespoons of the butter. Butter a 9- by 12-inch pan with 1 tablespoon of the butter and pour in the hot cream. Rub the remaining butter over the top to prevent a crust from forming, cover the pan lightly with wax paper, and chill the cream in the refrigerator for at least 6 hours (or, better, overnight).

When well chilled turn out carefully on a sheet of wax paper and cut into 1½-inch squares (no larger or it will be hard to handle). Dip into the beaten egg and then coat well with the breadcrumbs, making sure the squares have no bare spots. Place on a large platter and chill for at least 1 hour. Before serving heat the fat to 375° and fry the cream, a few squares at a time, until they are golden. Do not crowd them in the pan, or they will burst on contact with each other. Remove with a slotted spoon and drain on absorbent paper. When all are fried, pile them on a heated platter and dust them generously with the vanilla confectioners' sugar. *Serves 6 to 8.*

2031. FRITTER BATTER FOR FRUIT
Pasta—o pastella—per friggere bignè di frutta

1 cup sifted all-purpose flour
½ scant teaspoon salt
1 tablespoon melted butter
⅓ cup beer
¾ cup lukewarm water
1 egg white, beaten stiff
1 tablespoon brandy

Mix all ingredients, except the egg white and brandy, in a large bowl, beating thoroughly with a wooden spoon until smooth. Do not overbeat. Place in the refrigerator for at least 2 hours. Just before using, fold in the stiffly beaten egg white and brandy. *Makes about 2 cups.*

2032. APPLE FRITTERS WITH APRICOT SAUCE
Bignè di mele con salsa di albicocche

8 tart, firm apples (greenings, if available), peeled,
    cored, and cut into eighths
1 cup superfine sugar
3 tablespoons Calvados (or any preferred liqueur)
Fritter Batter for Fruit [No. 2031]
Fat for deep frying (vegetable oil preferred)
¼ cup superfine sugar
1 recipe Apricot Sauce [No. 2270]

Place the apple sections in a bowl and add the sugar
and liqueur. Mix well, and place in the refrigerator
for 5 hours, turning them with a spoon every hour or
so to blend the flavors. Remove them from the marinade
and pat dry on paper towels (so that the fritter batter
will adhere to them). Dip them in the batter and fry
them, a few at a time, in deep fat preheated to 375°.
Remove them when golden brown and well puffed and
drain on absorbent paper in a warm place. When all
are fried, sprinkle them with the superfine sugar, align
them on an oven-proof platter, and place in a 375° oven
for 5 or 10 minutes until well glazed. Serve at once
with the apricot sauce to which you have added the
marinade liquid from the apples. *Serves* 6.

2033. APRICOT FRITTERS
Bignè di albicocche

18 dead-ripe apricots, peeled, halved, and stoned
1 cup superfine sugar
¼ cup Aurum or maraschino liqueur
Fritter Batter for Fruit [No. 2031]
Fat for deep frying (vegetable oil preferred)
¼ cup superfine sugar

Place the apricot halves in a bowl and pour the sugar
and liqueur over them. Stir them gently and place the
bowl in a cool place for 5 or 6 hours, stirring every
hour or so to blend the flavors. Remove the apricots
from the marinade, dry them with paper towels (to
allow batter to adhere to them), and dip them in the
batter. Drop them, a few at a time, in deep fat, pre-
heated to 375°. Remove with a slotted spoon when
golden brown and well puffed, and drain on absorbent
paper in a warm place. When all have been fried,
sprinkle them with the sugar and place them on an
oven-proof serving plate and place in a 350° oven until
they are glazed (about 5 to 10 minutes). Serve at once.
Serves 6.

NOTE: If desired, the marinade may be cooked in a
small saucepan over high heat until it reaches the large
thread stage (219° on the candy thermometer), and
served as a sauce for the fritters.

2034. CENCI FIORENTINA
Cenci alla fiorentina o frappe alla romana

The word cenci *means "rags," referring to the rather
tattered and crumpled appearance of these paper-thin
strips of fried dough. They are known by various names
throughout Italy, but this version is traditionally
Florentine or Roman.*

1½ cups sifted all-purpose flour
3 tablespoons butter, softened and creamed with a
    wooden spoon until pale and fluffy
2 eggs, lightly beaten
⅛ teaspoon salt
1 tablespoon superfine sugar
Fat for deep frying (traditionally olive oil or lard)
Vanilla confectioners' sugar [*see* No. 2296]
Optional: 2 cups Custard Sauce [No. 2274]

Sift the flour into a large bowl. Make a well in the
center and into it drop the creamed butter, eggs, salt,
and sugar. Using the fingers of the right hand, slightly
curved or cupped, work the flour from the outer edge
into the center. As soon as the dough is blended (it
should be like noodle dough, *see* No. 482), knead it
with the palm of the hand until perfectly smooth and
no longer sticky. Form it into a ball, wrap it loosely in
a clean cloth, and let it rest in the least cold part of the
refrigerator for 1 hour. When ready to fry, divide the
dough into 4 pieces and roll them out to a thickness of
slightly less than 1/16 inch. Cut into 1-inch-wide strips
and cut the strips into 6-inch lengths. (A zig-zagged
pastry wheel is good for this.) Twist the strips into
loose knots, if desired, and fry them, a few at a time, in
deep fat preheated to 375°. When golden brown,
remove with a slotted spoon and drain on absorbent
paper in a warm place. When all are fried, pile them on a
large, warm platter and sprinkle generously with confectioners' sugar. Serve warm. If desired, they may be
accompanied by the custard sauce, served separately
in a small bowl. *Serves* 6.

2035. GRANDMOTHER'S RAISED RICE FRITTERS
Frittelle di riso della nonna

2 cups milk
½ scant cup short-grain rice (Italian rice, if available)
Pinch salt
¾ cup sifted all-purpose flour
1 cake fresh compressed yeast, dissolved in ¼ cup warm (85°) scalded milk for 5 minutes (or 1 envelope dry yeast dissolved in warmer—110°—scalded milk until foaming: about 10 minutes. *See section on yeast doughs, page 611*)
1 egg
2 egg yolks
½ cup currants, soaked for ½ hour in warm water and drained
Grated rind of ½ lemon (no white part)
¼ cup pine nuts, very coarsely chopped
Fat for deep frying (traditionally lard or olive oil)
Confectioners' sugar

Place the milk and rice with the salt in a small, heavy saucepan. Place over medium heat, and stir up occasionally until it comes to a boil. Lower heat, cover pan, and cook until milk has been totally absorbed and the rice is mushy (about 35 to 40 minutes). Pour into a large bowl, let cool, and when cooled beat in ¼ cup of the flour until well blended. Place the remaining flour in another bowl and mix it with the yeast mixture, stirring only until you have a small, smooth ball of moist dough. Cut a cross in the top of the ball, cover the bowl, and place in a warm place until doubled in bulk. Beat the whole egg and yolks together, and mix them into the rice/flour mixture together with the soaked currants, grated lemon rind, and pine nuts. When the yeast ball has doubled in bulk, knead or mix it into this mixture. You should have a very moist dough. If too stiff add a little warm milk, 1 teaspoonful at a time. Cover the bowl, and let the mixture rise in a warm place for 1 hour. When risen, stir down gently. Preheat the deep fat in a deep skillet to 360°. (The fat should be 3 inches deep.) Drop the dough into the hot fat by tablespoonsful, a few spoonsful at a time. Fry until the fritters are well puffed and brown on both sides. Remove with a slotted spoon and drain on absorbent paper. When all are fried, pile them on a warm platter, sprinkle them lavishly with confectioners' sugar, and serve while still warm. *Serves 8 to 10.*

2036. JAM- OR CREAM-FILLED FRITTERS
Bignè soufflés ripieni di confettura—o crema—calda

1 recipe San Giuseppe Fritters [No. 2038], or Beignets Soufflés [No. 2028]
Fat for deep frying
2 cups fruit preserves, pressed through a fine sieve and heated (or 2 cups hot Pastry Cream—No. 2267)
Optional: 2 tablespoons maraschino liqueur

Heat the fat to 360° and drop in the batter by scant tablespoonsful. Fry only 3 or 4 at a time. Remove them with a slotted spoon when they are well puffed and golden brown on both sides. Drain on absorbent paper in a warm place. When all have been fried, cut a deep slit in the side of each and fill with the hot, strained preserves (strawberry, apricot, plum, or whatever you prefer) or with the pastry cream. (The preserves or cream may be additonally flavored with maraschino, if desired.) Place in a 375° oven for a few minutes, and serve piping hot. *Makes about 30 fritters.*

2037. NEAPOLITAN ZEPPOLE
Zeppole alla napoletana

The name means "puffs," and these puffs are a Neapolitan specialty.

2 cups water
½ cup plus 1 tablespoon sugar
3 tablespoons olive oil
½ teaspoon salt
1 bay leaf
2 cups sifted all-purpose flour
2 tablespoons semolina (or substitute farina)
4 egg yolks
¼ scant cup sweet Marsala wine
Olive oil
Fat for deep frying (traditionally lard or olive oil)
Confectioners' sugar

Place the water, sugar, oil, salt, and bay leaf in a heavy saucepan and bring to a boil. Mix the flour with the semolina. When the water is boiling rapidly dump the flour/semolina mixture in all at once. Remove from stove and stir with a wooden spoon until the mixture forms a doughy mass and leaves the sides of the pan. Return to stove, lower heat, and cook for 7 minutes, stirring all the while (this dries out the dough mass). Remove from fire and discard the bay leaf. Let the dough cool for 5 minutes, and then beat in the egg yolks, 1 at a time, beating vigorously after each addition. Add the Marsala and beat until the dough is glossy (this will be hard work, as it is very stiff; a dough hook attached to an electric mixer is useful here). Liberally grease a marble slab (or enamel table top) with olive oil, and spread the dough on it to cool thoroughly. Brush the top with more oil. Pat the dough out, fold it over on itself 3 times, pat out again, and repeat the process 6 times. Then roll it between your hands until it forms a rope about as thick as your finger and cut it into 6-inch lengths. Form the lengths into rings, pressing the ends together firmly. Drop the rings a few at a time into the fat which has been pre-heated to 360°. When they are well puffed and brown on both sides, remove them with a slotted spoon and drain on absorbent paper in a warm place. While they are frying, prick the rings with the tines of a sharp fork. This makes particles of the uncooked dough emerge, a characteristic of this Neapolitan specialty. When all the rings have been thus fried, sprinkle them with confectioners' sugar and pile them on a heated platter. Serve warm. *Serves 6 to 8.*

2038. SAN GIUSEPPE FRITTERS
Bignè di San Giuseppe

These are traditionally served on Saint Joseph's day (March 19). In Naples they are known as Zeppole di San Giuseppe.

5 tablespoons butter
1¼ cups water
Pinch salt
Grated rind of 1 lemon (no white part)
2 tablespoons sugar
1¼ cups sifted all-purpose flour
4 egg yolks
2 eggs
Fat for deep frying (traditionally lard or olive oil)
Vanilla confectioners' sugar [*see* No. 2296]

Place the butter, water, salt, grated lemon rind, and sugar in a saucepan and bring to a boil. When boiling vigorously, dump in the flour all at once. Remove from stove and stir with a wooden spoon until the dough mixture forms a ball and leaves the sides of the pan. Return to stove, lower heat, and stir vigorously to dry out the dough somewhat. Remove from stove when the dough makes a slight hissing noise. Put into a large bowl and cool to lukewarm. Add the eggs and yolks, 1 at a time, and beat thoroughly after each has been added. When all the eggs have been added, beat vigorously until the dough begins to blister (this is the

secret of the dough's lightness; it takes 5 to 10 minutes of hard work: an electric mixer is useful here). Cover the bowl, and put in a cool place (not the refrigerator) for 1 hour. Heat the fat to 360° and drop in the dough by scant teaspoonsful. Fry a few at a time, and remove with a slotted spoon when they are well puffed and golden brown on both sides. The pan with fat should be swirled slightly so that the fritters will move about in it while they are frying. Drain on absorbent paper in a warm place. When all are fried serve warm, generously sprinkled with the confectioners' sugar. *Makes about 40 fritters.*

2039. VIENNESE RAISED FRITTERS
Bignè viennesi

This is a version of the famous Faschings Krapfen, *"Shrove-Tuesday Fritters," served in the Austrian capital at Carnival time. They are like our jelly doughnuts.*

½ cake (liberal) fresh compressed yeast, dissolved in 2 tablespoons warm (85°) water for 5 minutes (or ½—liberal—envelope dry yeast dissolved in warmer—110°—water until it foams, about 10 minutes)
2¼ cups sifted all-purpose flour
6½ tablespoons butter, softened
4 eggs, lightly beaten
¼ cup lukewarm water
Pinch salt
1 cup Frangipane Cream [No. 2268], or 1 cup apricot preserves
Fat for deep frying
Confectioners' sugar

Sift the flour into a large bowl. Make a well in the center and into it place the butter, eggs, water, and salt. Mix together, working the flour from the outer edge into the center. Knead with your hands until you have a smooth, rather moist dough. When it is no longer sticky (about 10 minutes), form it into a ball and cover the bowl. Set in a warm place to rise until doubled in bulk (about 40 minutes or less). Punch down and place on a lightly floured pastry cloth or board and roll out to the thickness of ¼ inch. Cut out rounds with a cooky cutter (or a glass, dipped in flour) about 3½ inches in diameter. Place a teaspoonful of the cream (or preserves) in the center of each circle, moisten the edges well, and fold over into half moons, pinching the edges firmly to prevent the filling from leaking out when the fritters are fried. Align them on a lightly floured board, cover with a lightly floured cloth, and set them in a warm place to rise until doubled in bulk. When risen, fry them a few at a time in deep fat preheated to 360°. When golden brown, remove with a slotted spoon and drain on absorbent paper in a warm place. When all have been fried, sprinkle liberally with the confectioners' sugar, pile on a warm platter, and serve while still quite hot. *Makes about 30 fritters.*

SOUFFLÉS

Soufflés

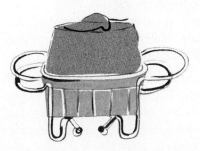

The same principles apply to dessert soufflés as to Entrée Soufflés (*see* page 221). Of course, there are certain differences. Sweet soufflés fall into two categories: those based on a cream-sauce mixture, and those based on puréed fruit. The former is the variety most frequently used, the basic cream being varied by different flavoring ingredients according to the recipe.

Instead of being sprinkled with breadcrumbs or cheese (as in entrée soufflés), the sides of the pan are buttered and generously coated with granulated sugar or with macaroon or cooky crumbs.

Sweet soufflés are subject to the same baking procedures as entrée soufflés, except that about 2 minutes before they are done, the top surface is evenly sprinkled with a thin layer of superfine sugar and the soufflé is placed in the hottest part of the oven so that the sugar will melt and form a glaze.

Individual soufflés may be made from these recipes. These are baked in small china soufflé dishes, glass or metal *cassoulettes,* or in pleated paper cases. Containers for individual soufflés should be filled to ¾ of their capacity. They should be baked in a 325° oven for about 10 to 12 minutes, or until well puffed. Large sweet soufflés are baked in straight-sided dishes or timbale molds and take a slightly shorter time than entrée soufflés; about 30 minutes. The oven temperature is also a bit lower: preheated to 375° and then lowered

to 350° when the soufflé is put in.

A sweet sauce may be served with a dessert soufflé: although it is not really necessary, it is sometimes a way of making it "go further," since an 8-inch baking dish is the largest size one should use. If many people have to be served, make 2 soufflés rather than a big one.

Full details on methods of mixing, shortcuts, hints, and pitfalls in soufflé preparation may be found on page 221.

2040. VANILLA SOUFFLÉ
Soufflé dolce alla vaniglia

This is the master recipe for cream-based soufflés.

6 tablespoons butter, softened
¾ cup sugar
1 cup milk
1 2-inch piece of vanilla bean, split (*see* Note below)
¼ cup sifted all-purpose flour
⅓ cup cold milk
4 egg yolks
5 egg whites
Pinch salt
2 tablespoons superfine sugar

Preheat oven to 375°. Generously coat the soufflé dish with 1 tablespoon of the butter. Sprinkle in the 2 tablespoons sugar and tilt the dish in all directions so that the interior is encrusted with sugar. Knock out any excess.

Place the 1 cup of milk in a heavy saucepan. Add the vanilla bean and bring to a simmer. Remove from stove, stir in ⅓ cup of the sugar, cover the pan, and let steep for 15 minutes. After this time remove the piece of vanilla bean. Mix the flour with the cold milk, stirring until you have a smooth paste. Beating with a wire whisk, add this to the milk/sugar mixture. Place the pan over a moderate flame, and beating constantly with the wire whisk, bring to a boil. Let it cook for 5 minutes, beating to prevent lumps and avoid scorching. Remove from stove, let it cool for 5 minutes, and then beat in the egg yolks, 1 at a time, beating well after each addition. Beat in the rest of the butter until it has melted into the mixture. Beat the egg whites with a wire whisk in a large bowl (preferably of unlined copper) with a pinch of salt until foamy. Gradually add the remaining sugar and beat until the whites form soft peaks. Stir ⅕ into the egg/milk base, mixing until well blended, then carefully fold and cut in the rest of the whites. Pour into the prepared soufflé dish and run the point of a sharp knife around the top, about

675

1 inch in from the inner side. This makes the top of the soufflé rise like a "hat." Place the dish in the preheated oven and lower heat to 350°. Bake for about 30 minutes, then open the oven and slide out the rack and quickly sprinkle the top of the soufflé with a little superfine sugar. Push the rack back in, and slide the soufflé to the back of the oven (usually the hottest place), raise the heat to 400°, and bake for another 2 or 3 minutes, or until the top is slightly glazed. Serve at once. *Serves 5 to 6.*

NOTE: The use of a piece of vanilla bean ensures a beautiful flavor of vanilla. However, if vanilla extract is to be used, proceed as follows: heat the milk to lukewarm, add the sugar and the flour pastes and proceed as above. Add 1 or 2 teaspoons vanilla extract just before the whites are folded in.

Any dessert sauce [Nos. 2270–2279] may be served with this soufflé.

2041. CHERRY SOUFFLÉ
Soufflé dolce con ciliege

1 recipe Vanilla Soufflé [No. 2040]
2 cups canned, pitted cherries packed in heavy syrup
1 cup raspberries (or 1 box frozen raspberries, drained)
3 tablespoons kirsch

Cook the canned cherries in their syrup until syrup is very thick (add the liquid from the drained frozen raspberries, if you are using them). Prepare the soufflé dish and the soufflé as indicated in No. 2040. Mix ¾ cup of the thickened cherries, slightly mashed, with the soufflé base just before the beaten whites are added. Bake as directed in No. 2040. While the soufflé is baking mix the rest of the cherries with the raspberries and add the kirsch. Keep warm, and serve this sauce with the soufflé. *Serves 6.*

2042. COFFEE SOUFFLÉ
Soufflé dolce al caffè

1 recipe Vanilla Soufflé [No. 2040]
5 tablespoons triple-strength freshly brewed coffee
(or 1½ tablespoons powdered instant coffee)

Prepare the soufflé as indicated in No. 2040, adding the coffee just before the whites are folded in. Bake as directed in No. 2040. Custard Sauce [No. 2274] may be served with the soufflé. *Serves 6.*

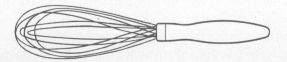

2043. CURAÇAO SOUFFLÉ
Soufflé dolce al curaçao

1 recipe Vanilla Soufflé [No. 2040]
1 teaspoon grated orange rind (no white part)
¼ cup Curaçao liqueur

Prepare the soufflé as indicated in No. 2040, adding the grated rind and the Curaçao just before the whites are folded in. Bake as directed in No. 2040. Orange Sauce [No. 2276] may be served with the soufflé. *Serves 6.*

2044. LEMON SOUFFLÉ
Soufflé dolce al limone

1 recipe Vanilla Soufflé [No. 2040]
1 teaspoon grated lemon rind (no white part)
Optional: 3 tablespoons lemon juice, strained
(or 1 teaspoon lemon extract)

Prepare the soufflé as indicated in No. 2040, omitting the vanilla. Fold in the lemon flavorings just before the whites are folded in. Bake as directed in No. 2040. Raspberry Sauce [No. 2277] may be served with the soufflé. *Serves 6.*

2045. ORANGE SOUFFLÉ
Soufflé dolce all'arancia

1 recipe Vanilla Soufflé [No. 2040]
1 tablespoon grated orange rind (no white part)
Optional: 1 tablespoon orange flower water

Prepare the soufflé as indicated in No. 2040 (omitting the vanilla, if desired). Fold in the orange flavorings just before the whites are folded in. Bake as directed in No. 2040. Orange Sauce [No. 2276] may be served with the soufflé. *Serves 6.*

2046. ROTHSCHILD SOUFFLÉ
Soufflé dolce Rothschild

A coarsely chopped mixture:
  2 tablespoons candied cherries
  2 tablespoons candied pineapple
  2 tablespoons candied citron
  2 tablespoons candied orange peel
4 tablespoons kirsch
1 recipe Vanilla Soufflé [No. 2040]

Soak the chopped candied fruits in the kirsch for 3 hours. Prepare the soufflé as indicated in No. 2040. Add the candied fruits and kirsch, reserving 2 tablespoons of the fruits, just before the whites are folded in. Sprinkle the remaining chopped mixture over the top of the soufflé. Bake as directed in No. 2040. Zabaglione Sauce [No. 2279] may be served with the soufflé. *Serves* 6.

2047. SOUFFLÉ AMBASCIATRICE
Soufflé dolce ambasciatrice

1 recipe Vanilla Soufflé [No. 2040]
4 tablespoons almonds cut in very fine slivers
    [*see* No. 2288]
2 tablespoons dark rum
6 dry almond macaroons (Italian almond macaroons,
    if available), crushed

Soak the almonds in the rum for 2 hours. Prepare the soufflé as directed in No. 2040. Fold in the macaroon crumbs and the rum and almonds just before the whites are folded in. Bake as directed in No. 2040. Custard Sauce Praliné [No. 2275] may be served with the soufflé. *Serves* 6.

NOTE: Instead of sugar, the soufflé mold may be coated with 2 additional tablespoons macaroon crumbs.

2048. TANGERINE SOUFFLÉ
Soufflé dolce di mandarino

1 recipe Vanilla Soufflé [No. 2040]
1 tablespoon grated tangerine rind (no white part)
Optional: 3 tablespoons tangerine juice (strained)

Prepare the soufflé as indicated in No. 2040, omitting the vanilla. Fold in the tangerine flavorings just before the whites are folded in. Bake as directed in No. 2040.

NOTE: A tangerine sauce, made by flavoring Custard Sauce [No. 2274] with 3 tablespoons tangerine juice and 1 teaspoon grated tangerine rind, may be served with the soufflé. *Serves* 6.

2049. TEA SOUFFLÉ
Soufflé dolce al tè

1 recipe Vanilla Soufflé [No. 2040]
3 tablespoons tea leaves

Prepare the soufflé as directed in No. 2040. Omit the vanilla bean and steep the tea leaves in the hot milk for 5 minutes. Strain, and proceed as directed. Bake as indicated in No. 2040. *Serves* 6.

NOTE: Orange Sauce [No. 2276] may be served with the soufflé.

2050. TORRONE (NOUGAT) SOUFFLÉ
Soufflé dolce al torrone

1 recipe Vanilla Soufflé [No. 2040]
½ cup (or 6 pieces) torrone (Italian nougat candy,
    commercially available), rather dry, and coarsely
    crushed

Prepare the soufflé as indicated in No. 2040. Fold in the torrone just before the whites are folded in. Bake as directed in No. 2040. *Serves* 6.

NOTE: Custard Sauce Praliné [No. 2275] may be served with the soufflé.

2051. CHOCOLATE SOUFFLÉ
Soufflé dolce al cioccolato

4 tablespoons butter, softened
2 tablespoons sugar
2½ squares bitter chocolate, grated or finely chopped
2 cups milk
⅔ cup superfine sugar
1 2-inch piece of vanilla bean (*see* Note below)
¼ scant cup potato flour (or cornstarch or rice flour)
4 egg yolks
Large pinch salt
5 egg whites
2 tablespoons sifted confectioners' sugar

Preheat the oven to 375°. Generously coat the soufflé dish with 1 tablespoon of the butter. Sprinkle in the 2 tablespoons sugar and tilt the dish in all directions so that the interior is encrusted with sugar. Knock out any excess.

Place the grated chocolate, ½ cup of the milk, ½ cup of the sugar, and the piece of vanilla bean in a small, heavy saucepan over a low flame. Stir until the chocolate has melted, and cover the pan and let steep for 15 minutes. After this time, remove the vanilla bean. Add 1 cup of the milk to the pan and put back on the stove over low heat. Dissolve the potato flour with the remaining milk, stirring until you have a smooth paste. Stir into the chocolate/milk mixture, beating with a wire whisk until it comes to a boil. Cook for 5 minutes, beating constantly to avoid lumps. Beat in the remaining 3 tablespoons of butter, and remove from stove. Let cool for 5 minutes and beat in the yolks, 1 at a time, beating well after each addition. Beat the egg whites and the salt with a wire whisk in a large bowl (preferably of unlined copper) until foamy. Gradually add the remaining sugar and beat until they stand in soft peaks. Mix ¼ of the beaten whites into the chocolate base, mixing and folding thoroughly.

Carefully fold in the rest of the whites, folding and cutting them in until both mixtures are blended. Pour into the prepared soufflé dish and run the point of a sharp knife around the top, about 1 inch in from the inner side. This makes the top of the soufflé rise like a "hat." Place the dish in the preheated oven and lower heat to 350°. Bake for about 30 minutes, then open the oven, slide out the rack, and quickly sprinkle the top of the soufflé with an even coating of the confectioners' sugar. Push the rack back in, and slide the soufflé to the back of the oven (usually the hottest part), raise heat to 400°, and bake for another 3 minutes, or until the top is slightly glazed. Serve at once. *Serves 6.*

NOTE: If vanilla extract is to be used instead of the vanilla bean, add 2 teaspoons extract just before the whites are folded in.

If desired, the soufflé may be accompanied by a bowl of sweetened whipped cream.

2052. FRUIT SOUFFLÉ
Soufflé dolce di frutta

This is a master recipe which may be adapted to whatever fresh fruit is in season. It differs from the cream-based soufflés in that it not only omits milk and flour, but contains no egg yolks. It is light, not very rich, and provides the perfect ending for a heavy meal. The egg yolks left from the whites may be used in a custard sauce [see No. 2274] to be served with the soufflé, adding a note of richness and suavity.

1 tablespoon butter
2 tablespoons sugar
1 cup water
1½ cups sugar
3 cups preferred fruit or berries (if fruit, it should be peeled and stoned, puréed
2 tablespoons lemon juice (unless fruit is very tart)
6 egg whites
Pinch cream of tartar

Generously coat the soufflé dish with the butter. Sprinkle with the 2 tablespoons of sugar and tilt dish in all directions so that the interior is encrusted with sugar. Knock out any excess. Preheat the oven to 375°.

Place the water and 1 cup of sugar in a heavy enamel saucepan and bring to a boil and cook to the hard crack stage (289° on the candy thermometer). Immediately add the puréed fruit, taking care that the sugar does not boil over. Lower heat and cook for 5 minutes. Remove from stove, add lemon juice, and

cool for 10 minutes. Beat the egg whites and the cream of tartar with a wire whisk in a large bowl (preferably of unlined copper) until they are foamy. Gradually add the remaining sugar until they stand in soft peaks. Fold ¼ of the whites into the fruit purée mixture, stirring well until thoroughly blended. Carefully fold and cut in the remaining whites, mixing only until incorporated. Pour into the prepared soufflé dish and place in the preheated oven. Lower heat to 350° and bake for 30 minutes, or until the top has risen well above the rim of the dish. Serve at once, with a custard sauce, if desired. *Serves 5 to 6.*

NOTE: The next best accompaniment for a fruit soufflé of this variety is a bowl of very slightly sweetened whipped cream.

DESSERT OMELETS
Omeletti dolci

The same rules apply to dessert omelets as those specified for regular omelets. Full discussion of this is supplied in the section on omelets, page 241. Dessert omelets are an excellent "emergency" dessert for unexpected company since they are relatively quick to prepare. The master recipe for preparing an omelet is No. 701.

2053. CHERRY OMELET
Omelette dolce con ciliege

This omelet is somewhat different: a sort of sandwich.

2 cups fresh cherries, pitted
¼ cup water
½ cup sugar (more, if cherries are very tart)
1 cup black currant jelly
9 eggs

678

½ teaspoon salt

4 tablespoons superfine sugar

8 tablespoons butter

¼ cup maraschino liqueur

Have ready 2 large frying pans, each about 12 inches in diameter. Poach the cherries in the sugar and water until they are tender but not mushy. Remove with a slotted spoon and add the currant jelly to the cherry liquid. Cook until very thick and syrupy, mix with the cherries, and keep hot. Beat the eggs in a large bowl with the salt and 2 tablespoons of the superfine sugar. Melt 4 tablespoons butter in each frying pan. When nut colored, pour in slightly more than ½ the egg mixture in 1 of the pans. Tilt in all directions, shake, and lift the edges to let the uncooked eggs slide underneath. Quickly spread the cherries and the currant jelly mixture over the top, lower the flame, and rapidly prepare the second omelet. Pour the rest of the eggs into the other pan and cook it as described in No. 701, without, however, attempting to fold. When the top is barely set, remove from stove. Slide the cherry-covered omelet out onto a large heated serving platter, cherry side up. Reverse the plain omelet over it, so that its cooked surface is upward. Sprinkle evenly with the rest of the superfine sugar. Heat the maraschino in a ladle, set aflame, pour over the omelet, and bring to the table flaming. *Serves* 6.

NOTE: Canned cherries in syrup may be substituted for the fresh variety. Drain them and cook the syrup with the jelly until thick. Do not cook the cherries, but add them to the mixture at the last minute to heat through.

2054. JAM OMELET
Omelette dolce alla confettura

This is excellent for a late breakfast or light lunch. For the former use the rum may be omitted.

8 eggs

½ teaspoon salt

6 tablespoons superfine sugar

8 tablespoons butter

1 cup jam or preserves (apricot, strawberry, plum, raspberry, etc.), heated in a small saucepan

Optional: 2 tablespoons dark rum or brandy

Break the eggs into a large bowl, add the salt and 2 tablespoons of the sugar, and beat with a fork. Prepare 4 omelets from this mixture as described in No. 701, using 2 tablespoons of butter and a generous ½ cup beaten eggs for each. Just before folding each

omelet, spread ¼ cup jam over its surface. Sprinkle each omelet with 1 tablespoon of the sugar in a lattice pattern and melt the sugar by passing a red-hot iron rod or poker across the surface (or place under a blazing hot broiler for a few seconds until glazed). If desired, heat the rum or brandy in a ladle, set aflame, pour over the omelets, and bring to the table flaming. *Serves* 4.

2055. KIRSCH OMELET
Omelette dolce al kirsch

12 eggs

½ cup superfine sugar

½ teaspoon salt

9 tablespoons butter

⅓ cup kirsch

Beat the eggs in a large bowl with 2 tablespoons sugar and the salt. Prepare 3 omelets as described in No. 701. As soon as each is done, place it on a large, warmed platter and set in a warm place. When all 3 are made, sprinkle them with the rest of the sugar, heat the kirsch in a ladle over a low flame, set it aflame, pour it over the omelets, and bring to the table flaming. *Serves* 6.

2056. OMELET WITH MARRONS GLACÉS
Omelette dolce con marrons glacés

This is a pair of frittate *with marrons and cream sandwiched between. For full instructions, see the master recipe for Plain Frittata* [No. 700].

The filling and topping:

1 cup marrons glacés, crumbled

1 cup heavy cream, whipped

⅓ cup Strega liqueur

3 tablespoons blanched almonds [*see* No. 2280], chopped

3 tablespoons superfine sugar

The frittata:

10 eggs

2 tablespoons superfine sugar

1 scant teaspoon salt

6 tablespoons butter

Prepare the filling by folding the crumbled marrons into the unsweetened whipped cream. Fold in 2 tablespoons of the Strega and keep in a cool place until needed. Mix the almonds with the sugar, and keep near at hand.

679

Have ready 2 large frying pans about 12 inches in diameter. Beat the eggs in a large bowl with the sugar and salt. Melt 3 tablespoons of butter in each pan and pour slightly more than ½ the egg mixture into one, the rest into the other. Cook as described in No. 700. When done, turn the thicker one out onto a heated platter, spread with the filling, and top with the other frittata, cooked side up. Sprinkle the top of this with the sugar/almond mixture. Heat the remaining Strega in a ladle over a low flame, set alight, and pour over the omelet, and bring to the table flaming. *Serves 6.*

2057. RUM OMELET
Omelette dolce al rhum

This is made with the same ingredients and in the same manner as Kirsch Omelet [No. 2055], substituting ⅓ cup dark rum for the kirsch. *Serves 6.*

2058. SOUFFLÉ OMELET FLAMBÉ
Omelette soufflée alla fiamma

This is a cross between an omelet and a soufflé. Though baked in the oven rather than cooked on top of the stove, it does not contain flour or milk, and is baked in a shallow baking dish rather than a soufflé dish. Fairly easy to make, it creates a spectacular effect and makes an excellent substitute for a soufflé.

6 egg yolks
1 cup superfine sugar
1 teaspoon vanilla extract (or 1 tablespoon any liqueur)
½ teaspoon grated orange or lemon rind (no white part)
10 egg whites
Pinch salt
2 tablespoons granulated sugar
1 tablespoon butter
2 tablespoons sifted confectioners' sugar
½ cup dark rum or brandy (or a preferred liqueur)

Beat the egg yolks with ¾ cup of the superfine sugar with a wire whisk in a large bowl. Beat until the mixture is light in color and falls in a slowly dissolving ribbon on the surface when the beater is lifted above the bowl. At this point beat in the vanilla and grated rind. In another large bowl (preferably of unlined copper) beat the whites and salt with a wire whisk (if the same used for the yolks, make sure it is thoroughly washed free of all traces of yolk) until foamy. Add the remaining ¼ cup of sugar and continue beating until it stands in soft peaks. Butter a large, oval baking dish about 2½ inches deep (a rectangular one will do, but is not

680

traditional) and sprinkle it with the granulated sugar, tilting in all directions so that it is completely coated, and knock out the excess. Fold ⅕ of the whites into the yolks, mixing lightly until totally incorporated. Mix in the rest of the whites, folding and cutting them in until blended. Pour the mixture into the prepared dish and mound it up in the center using a lightly moistened spatula. Cut a trench down the middle, lengthwise, about 1 inch deep (this allows the heat to penetrate into the interior). Place in a preheated 350° oven, and after 20 minutes sprinkle the entire surface with an even coating of the confectioners' sugar. Continue baking for another 10 minutes, or until the top is lightly glazed. Remove, and immediately heat the liquor in a ladle over a low flame, set it alight, and slowly pour it over the omelet. Bring to the table flaming. *Serves 6.*

PUDDINGS
Budini

Many of these puddings employ stale cake or ladyfingers as a base. Others are elaborations of rice pudding, and some are *croste,* a uniquely Italian concoction to be mentioned in due course. Many of these puddings are of British origin, reflecting the influence of many generations of British tourists who wished for a "touch of home" when dining in Italy. However, the damp British puddings have undergone a pleasant change when "translated" in Italian kitchens.

2059. ACCADEMIA PUDDING
Budino freddo all'accademia

½ cup fresh breadcrumbs (made by toasting slices of crustless bread in a 250° oven until dry and golden, and then crushed or grated into fine crumbs)
3½ cups rich milk
½ cup short-grain rice (Italian rice, if available)
1 cup plus 2 tablespoons sugar
Pinch salt
2 eggs
2 egg yolks
1½ cups strawberries, puréed (if frozen strawberries are used, decrease sugar to 1 scant cup)
1 teaspoon vanilla extract
2 tablespoons butter
Strawberry Sauce [No. 2278], flavored with 2 tablespoons kirsch and 1 teaspoon vanilla extract

Bring the milk to a boil in a heavy saucepan. Add the rice, sugar, and salt. Stir with a fork until it comes to a boil again, then lower heat, cover the pan, and cook for about 30 minutes, or until the rice has absorbed most of the milk (an asbestos pad placed between the pan and the flame will prevent scorching). Pour the rice into a large bowl. Beat the eggs and the yolks together. Add the strawberry purée to the rice, mixing well. Slowly add the eggs, stirring constantly. Finally, add the vanilla. Butter an appropriately sized (about 2-quart) scalloped mold. Coat with the breadcrumbs, tapping out any excess. Pour the rice mixture carefully into the mold, making sure the breadcrumbs are not dislodged. Cover the top loosely with a piece of aluminum foil, slashed in several places to allow steam to escape, and place in a 350° oven until the center of the pudding is firm (about 45 to 55 minutes). Remove from oven and let it stand until lukewarm. Carefully unmold it on a round platter, and place in the refrigerator for at least 4 hours. Serve accompanied by the strawberry sauce. *Serves 6 to 8.*

NOTE: It is advisable that the breadcrumbs be freshly made. The commercial variety lacks freshness and taste.

2060. APPLE CHARLOTTE CASALINGA
Crema alla casalinga

There are 2 types of charlotte: hot and cold. The former consists of cooked fruit (especially apples) poured into a deep mold lined with thin slices of stale bread or cake, and then baked. The other variety is a cream and cake preparation that is chilled [see Nos. 2068–70].

8 eggs
4 egg yolks
1 cup sugar
Pinch salt
3 cups rich milk, scalded
30 (or more) $\frac{1}{4}$-inch-thick slices stale sponge cake, brioche, or pound cake
$\frac{1}{4}$ cup kirsch
$\frac{1}{4}$ cup maraschino liqueur
2 tablespoons butter, softened
3 cups stewed apples (made by cooking 8 cups peeled apple sections in $\frac{1}{2}$ cup sugar and the juice of $\frac{1}{2}$ lemon until soft and transparent)

Beat the eggs, egg yolks, sugar, and salt in a large bowl until pale in color. Pour in the hot milk and mix well. Sprinkle the cake slices with the liqueurs. Butter a 3-quart mold and line with some of the cake, making sure no bare spots show through the cake. Place $\frac{1}{3}$ of the apples in the mold, top with a few slices of cake, and repeat the process, ending with the cake. Slowly pour in the egg/milk mixture. Set the mold in a pan of hot water deep enough to reach $\frac{1}{2}$ up its sides, and place in a 350° oven until the custard has set (about 1 hour). Remove from oven, lift out of the water bath, and let the mold stand for 45 minutes. Unmold on a serving platter and serve warm. *Serves 6.*

2061. APPLE CHARLOTTE WITH RUM
Charlotte di mele al rhum

2 pounds firm, tart apples (greenings, if possible), peeled, cored, and cut into sections
1 cup sugar
Pinch cinnamon
1 tablespoon lemon juice
1 cup butter
1 cup apricot preserves
1 teaspoon vanilla extract
4 tablespoons currants, plumped in warm water and drained
1 loaf slightly stale white bread, crust removed, sliced $\frac{1}{4}$ inch thick
$\frac{1}{4}$ cup dark rum
1 recipe Apricot Sauce [No. 2270], flavored with 4 tablespoons kirsch

Mix the apples, sugar, cinnamon, and lemon juice in a large bowl. Place apples in a baking pan, dot with 3 tablespoons of the butter, cover loosely with aluminum foil, and bake in a 350° oven until the apples are soft, but still keep their shape. Remove from oven, mix in the apricot preserves, vanilla, and currants, and leave in a warm place until needed. Butter a 2-quart charlotte or timbale mold (or any round, straight-sided metal mold) with some of the butter. Cut the bread into enough long triangles so that you are able to line the bottom of the mold. The triangles radiate outward, apexes meeting in the middle. They should overlap slightly. Cut an equal number of triangles for the top and set these aside. Cut the remaining bread into rectangles and trim them so that they fit upright in the mold without extending over the top. Melt the rest of the butter over low heat, taking care that it does not color. Brush some melted butter over the bread lining the bottom of the mold. Dip the rectangular slices of bread into the butter, and line the sides of the mold, overlapping the slices. Pour the apple mixture into the center, and top with the reserved bread triangles, laying them on in the same way that the bottom ones were positioned. Pour the rest of the butter over the top. Place the mold in a 350° oven and bake for 1 hour, or until the bread is golden brown. Remove from oven, let the mold stand for 25 or 35 minutes, and then unmold on a round serving platter. Spoon a little of the apricot sauce around it. Heat the rum in a ladle over a low flame, set it alight, and pour over the charlotte. Bring to the table flaming. Serve the remaining apricot sauce separately. *Serves 6 to 8.*

2062. APPLE MERINGUE PUDDING
Mele ranette meringate

10 firm, tart apples (greenings, if available), peeled
5 tablespoons butter
Grated rind of 1 small orange (no white part)
4 tablespoons sweet Marsala wine
3 tablespoons apricot preserves
Vanilla syrup:
   ⅔ cup sugar
   ⅓ cup water
   1-inch piece vanilla bean
3 egg whites
Pinch salt

Core 6 of the apples and cut them into pieces. Place them in a heavy saucepan with 3 tablespoons of the butter, the orange rind, and the Marsala. Cook over medium heat, stirring occasionally, until the apples are cooked to a pulp. Remove from stove and add the apricot preserves, and let cool. Prepare the vanilla syrup by cooking the sugar, water, and vanilla bean together until the mixture reaches the large thread stage (219° on the candy thermometer). Cut the remaining apples into neat segments (from 8 to 16 per apple, depending on their size) and poach them in the syrup until they are tender but not pulpy. Remove them with a slotted spoon. Grease a round, shallow baking dish with the remaining butter, and spread the apple purée over the bottom. Top with the slices of poached apple. Continue cooking the syrup until it reaches the soft ball stage (230° on the candy thermometer). Beat the egg whites and the salt with a wire whisk in a large bowl (preferably of unlined copper). When it forms very soft peaks, remove the vanilla bean from the hot syrup and pour the syrup into the meringue in a thin stream, beating all the time. Beat until the meringue is glossy and forms firm peaks. Spread the apple slices with the meringue (reserving ⅓ of it), mounding it up in the center of the dish and smoothing it with a dampened spatula. Place the remaining meringue in a pastry bag fitted with a large star tip, and pipe

decorative swirls and rosettes over the surface. Place the pudding in a 250° oven, and bake for 30 minutes, or until the meringue is pale golden brown. Serve hot. *Serves 6.*

NOTE: A pitcher of heavy cream (unsweetened) goes very well with this dessert.

2063. APRICOTS CONDÉ
Albicocche Condé

⅓ cup short-grain rice (Italian rice, if available)
2 cups milk
Pinch salt
2 scant cups sugar
3 tablespoons butter, softened
3 egg yolks
¼ cup heavy cream
1 teaspoon vanilla extract
12 plump, dead-ripe apricots, peeled, stoned, and
   halved
½ cup water
9 candied cherries, halved
18 small diamond-shaped pieces of candied angelica
4 tablespoons kirsch

Place the rice in a large pot of boiling water, and boil vigorously for 6 minutes. Drain into a strainer and rinse with cold water. Place the rice in a heavy saucepan with the milk, salt, ⅔ cup of the sugar, and 1 tablespoon of the butter. Bring to a boil over medium heat, fluff up a few times with a fork, cover pan, lower heat, and cook for 30 to 35 minutes, or until all the milk has been absorbed (an asbestos pad between the pan

Capricciosa Cream (No. 2067):
see page 684

682

and the flame will reduce the danger of scorching). Remove pan from stove and beat in another tablespoon of butter. Beat the egg yolks with the cream, beat the mixture into the rice, and add the vanilla extract. Butter a small, round-bottomed metal bowl with the remaining butter and pour in the rice, packing it down well with a spoon. Place the bowl in a deep pan filled with hot water, cover bowl loosely with aluminum foil, and bake in a 300° oven for 30 minutes. Remove from oven, lift bowl out of water, and let stand while you prepare the fruit.

Place remaining sugar and the water in a saucepan over medium heat and cook until it reaches the large thread stage (219° on the candy thermometer). Add the apricots and poach them until tender but not pulpy. Remove 18 of the halves with a slotted spoon and keep warm in a covered bowl. Raise the flame and cook the remaining apricots in the syrup until they become pulpy and the syrup and apricots attain the consistency of apricot preserves. Stir every so often to prevent scorching.

Unmold the rice in the center of a round shallow serving platter. Surround it with the reserved apricots, flat sides upward, and top each with one of the candied cherry halves. Top the cherry with a piece of angelica. Add the kirsch to the apricot pulp, and carefully pour it around the rice and decorated apricots. Serve warm. *Serves* 6.

2064. APPLES CONDÉ
Melė Condé

Same ingredients as for Apricots Condé [No. 2063], except that 10 tart apples, peeled, cored, and cut in segments, are substituted for the apricots
1-inch piece of vanilla bean

Prepare exactly as Apricots Condé, except the apples are poached with the vanilla bean. The piece of bean is removed before the puréed apples and syrup are poured on. *Serves* 6.

2065. BREAD AND BUTTER PUDDING
Bread and Butter Pudding

Every English cook is a master of this recipe, which is one of the most famous and delicious specialties of English cooking. Although simple and unassuming, it can be a magnificent dessert when made as indicated below.

4 eggs
¾ cup superfine sugar
Pinch salt

4 cups milk, scalded
1 teaspoon vanilla extract
½ cup butter, softened
7 thick slices stale bread, crusts removed, each cut into 4 pieces
1 cup currants, plumped for ½ hour in 2 cups warm water and well drained

Beat the eggs with 6 tablespoons sugar and the salt until well mixed. Pour in the hot milk and vanilla and beat until blended. Spread each slice of bread with some of the butter, reserving 1 tablespoon. Grease a 2-quart baking dish or glass casserole with the remaining butter. Arrange some of the bread slices, buttered side down, sprinkle with some of the remaining sugar and some of the currants. Repeat until all has been used, ending with a sprinkling of sugar and currants. Slowly pour in the egg/milk mixture, doing so by intervals and waiting until the bread has absorbed the milk before adding more. Place the baking dish in a 350° oven and bake for 45 minutes, or until well puffed and golden brown on the top. Serve either warm or chilled. *Serves* 6 *to* 8.

NOTE: If desired, Custard Sauce [No. 2274] may be served with the pudding. Whether the pudding is hot or cold, the sauce should be chilled.

2066. CABINET PUDDING WITH RUM ZABAGLIONE SAUCE
Budino cabinet con zabaione al rhum

2 dozen ladyfingers (or 1 recipe Savoyard Ladyfingers— No. 1946), split
1 tablespoon butter, softened
⅓ cup seedless raisins
¼ cup candied fruit (cherries, pineapple, orange peel, etc.), finely diced
4 egg yolks
1 egg
4 tablespoons superfine sugar
Pinch salt
2½ cups milk, scalded
1 teaspoon vanilla extract
1 recipe Zabaglione Sauce [No. 2279], made with ¼ cup dark rum instead of wine

Butter a 2-quart charlotte mold (or any deep, straight-sided casserole of 2-quart capacity) and line it with the ladyfingers (*see* Note below) so that the interior of the mold is covered completely and none of it is exposed. (Cut the ladyfingers neatly and arrange them symmetrically, since they are what will be seen when the dessert is unmolded.) Take the ladyfinger trimmings, raisins, and candied fruit and mix them together and place in the ladyfinger-lined mold. Beat the egg and yolks with the sugar and salt. Pour in the milk and beat until blended, then add the vanilla. Carefully pour this into the mold, taking care that the ladyfingers are not dislodged. If necessary, pour in a little at a time, and wait for a minute or so between pourings. Cover top with any leftover ladyfingers and let the pudding stand for 30 minutes. After this time, place it in a pan of hot water deep enough so that it reaches ⅔ up the sides of the mold. Cover the top of the mold with a piece of buttered paper (or aluminum foil), and bake in a 350° oven for 45 minutes, or until a knife inserted in the center emerges clean. Remove from the water bath and let the mold sit until it is warm to the touch. Carefully unmold on a round plate and chill until cool but not ice cold. When ready to serve, spoon a little sauce over the top and serve the rest separately. *Serves 6 to 8.*

NOTE: In this recipe (and others which call for ladyfingers) it is advised that the homemade variety be employed. They are not difficult to make, and their superlative texture and flavor cannot be matched by the purchased variety.

2067. CAPRICCIOSA CREAM
Crema capricciosa

3 cups heavy cream
2 teaspoons vanilla extract
15 Meringues [*see* No. 2009], crumbled in fairly big pieces
½ cup raspberries, puréed (if using frozen raspberries, drain them well before puréeing) and strained of seeds

Whip 2½ cups of the cream and the vanilla in a chilled bowl until very stiff. Fold in the crumbled bits of meringue. Lightly dampen a 2-quart round-bottomed bowl or mold, and pour in the cream/meringue mixture. Cover with wax paper and place in the refrigerator to chill for at least 6 hours. Unmold on a round platter (if it refuses to come out of the mold, dip it in hot water for 2 seconds, making sure the water does not spill over the edge of the bowl). Whip the rest of the cream until stiff, mix it with the raspberry purée, place it in a pastry bag fitted with a medium star tube, and pipe a decoration over the surface of the cream (*see* photograph on page 682). Chill until served. *Serves 6 to 8.*

NOTE: The cream may be additionally decorated with fresh, whole raspberries and served with Raspberry Sauce [No. 2277].

2068. CHARLOTTE DESIDERIO DI VENUS
Charlotte "desiderio di Venus"

1 recipe Italian Sponge Cake [No. 1913], baked in a 9- by 12-inch pan, cooled, and cut into ¼-inch-thick slices cut as long as the timbale is deep
2 dead-ripe pears, peeled, cored, and diced
3 large peaches, peeled, stoned, and halved, prepared as in Peach Compote [No. 2188], using ¾ cup sugar and ⅓ cup water
2 bananas, peeled, scraped free of filaments, and diced
¼ cup unblanched almonds, finely shredded
3 tablespoons kirsch
1 cup English Custard [*see* No. 2111], hot
1½ envelopes unflavored gelatin, softened in ¼ cup heavy cream
1¾ cups heavy cream, whipped
3 tablespoons superfine sugar
3 slices pineapple, about the same diameter as the bottoms of the timbale molds
3 candied cherries
1¾ cups marrons glacés, chopped

Cut the sponge cake and let it stand for a few hours to dry somewhat while the dessert is being prepared. Place the pears in a bowl. Cut the poached peaches into dice and while still hot pour them and their syrup over the pears. Add the bananas and almonds, mix well, let stand until cooled to room temperature, then place in refrigerator to chill. Prepare the custard and when cooked add the gelatin to the hot custard and stir until dissolved. Let stand until cooled to room temperature, then place in refrigerator until thick and almost set, but still liquid. Place the cream in a bowl in the freezing compartment of the refrigerator until mushy, then whip with a wire whisk until stiff. Leave in refrigerator until needed. Line 3 small timbale molds, about 3½ inches in diameter and 6 inches deep, with the slices of cake. Trim off any projecting ends and use these to line the bottoms of the molds. Remove chilled fruit, custard, and cream from the refrigerator. Fold the cream into the fruit, then blend in the custard, mix well, and divide among the 3 molds. Cover with remaining pieces of cake. Place in refrigerator for at least 5 hours. Unmold by running a sharp knife between the cake and the mold, dipping molds in hot water for 1 second, and then turn them out on a round serving platter. Top each charlotte with a pineapple slice, place a cherry in the center, and surround the bases with the chopped marrons. *Serves 8 to 10.*

2069. CHARLOTTE RUSSE
Charlotte alla russa

30 ladyfingers (more or less), left whole (or 1 recipe Savoyard Ladyfingers—No. 1946)

3 egg yolks

1 egg

Pinch salt

$\frac{1}{2}$ cup superfine sugar

1 cup milk, scalded

1 envelope unflavored gelatin, softened in $\frac{1}{4}$ cup cold milk

$1\frac{1}{2}$ cups heavy cream, whipped

2 teaspoons vanilla extract

15 candied cherries

Line a large, deep ring mold with the ladyfingers. Place a circle of ladyfingers on the bottom, touching one another but not overlapping, and then line the sides with a fence of ladyfingers, making sure that they stand very close together, leaving no space at all between them. Trim off any part of the ladyfingers projecting above the top of the mold. Cut up a few more ladyfingers into neat, small triangles, and use these pieces to fill in any spaces left between the bottom ones and those lining the inner and outer sides of the ring mold. Reserve any leftovers.

Beat the egg yolks with the egg, salt, and sugar until well blended. Pour in the scalded milk and stir until both are combined. Place in a small, heavy saucepan over very low heat and stir constantly until the mixture coats the spoon. Add the softened gelatin and stir until dissolved. Remove from stove and pour into a bowl. Whip the cream until stiff in a chilled bowl, and place to one side. Place the bowl with the custard in a larger bowl filled with ice, and beat the custard until it cools and becomes thick, but still fluid. Immediately remove the bowl from its bed of ice and fold in the whipped cream (reserving $\frac{1}{2}$ cup for decorating) and the vanilla. (Work quickly, for once gelatin begins to set, it does so with great speed. If it has gotten too stiff, place the bowl with the custard over warm water and stir until loose enough to fold in the whipped cream.) Pour the cream/custard mixture into the ladyfinger-lined mold, and top with the pieces of leftover ladyfingers. Place in the refrigerator for at least 4 hours. Unmold on a large platter and

decorate with the candied cherries, and the rest of the cream, placed in a pastry bag fitted with a medium star tip, and piped out in little spurts on the top of the ladyfingers. *Serves 6.*

NOTE: The best way to unmold this type of dessert is to place the platter over the mold and reverse both at the same time, bringing them down with a sharp jerk. If desired, the sides and bottom of the mold may be lined with white paper before adding the ladyfingers. The paper is carefully peeled off after the charlotte has been unmolded.

2070. CHARLOTTE SOGNO D'AUTUNNO
Charlotte sogno d'autunno

1 Italian Sponge Cake [No. 1913], baked in a loaf pan, cooled, and sliced into 20 pieces $\frac{1}{2}$ inch thick, $1\frac{1}{2}$ inches wide, and long enough to rise $\frac{1}{2}$ inch above the rim of the straight-sided mold employed

Custard:

  2 egg yolks

  1 egg

  3 tablespoons sugar

  Pinch salt

  $\frac{3}{4}$ cup rich milk, scalded

  $\frac{1}{2}$ envelope unflavored gelatin, softened in 2 tablespoons milk

  $\frac{1}{2}$ teaspoon vanilla extract

1 cup sugar

$\frac{1}{2}$ cup water

1 teaspoon lemon juice

2 pears, peeled, cored, and thinly sliced

3 peaches, peeled, stoned, and thinly sliced

2 bananas, peeled and sliced

3 tablespoons kirsch

1 slice candied pineapple, diced

$\frac{1}{2}$ cup marrons glacés, crumbled

$\frac{1}{4}$ cup candied fruit (cherries, orange peel, etc.), diced (the cherries halved)

2 tablespoons Drambuie liqueur

$1\frac{1}{2}$ cups heavy cream, whipped

Line a 3-quart charlotte mold (or straight-sided casserole of the same capacity) with the sponge cake slices. Line the bottom first, cutting the slices into wedges so that the cake will fit evenly, then line the sides, making sure there are no spaces between slices. Reserve any leftover pieces for the top.

Prepare the custard: Beat the egg and yolks with the sugar and salt, pour in the milk and stir until blended

685

Pour into a small, heavy saucepan and cook over a medium flame, stirring constantly until the mixture coats the spoon. Add the softened gelatin and stir until dissolved, add the vanilla, pour the custard into a bowl, and cool until slightly thickened but not solid.

Meanwhile, cook the sugar, water, and lemon juice in a small saucepan until it reaches the soft thread stage (219° on the candy thermometer). Add the sliced pears and peaches, and poach for 5 minutes. Remove fruit with a slotted spoon to a bowl, and let syrup cool in the refrigerator. Add the sliced bananas to the poached fruit, pour the kirsch over, add the candied pineapple and marron pieces, mix well, and let stand 1 hour. Soak the candied fruit pieces in the Drambuie and let stand until needed.

When the custard has become syrupy, whip the cream in a chilled bowl until thick. Sweeten it with 3 or 4 tablespoons of the cooled syrup in which the fruit has poached, and fold in the custard, mixing well. Add the fruits and marrons, and the kirsch in which they soaked, and mix well. Pour this into the cake-lined mold. Cover the top with the remaining pieces of cake, cover with wax paper, and chill for at least 6 hours (if the sides of exposed cake buckle when the filling is added, reinforce them with a strip of aluminum foil, twisting the ends together). When ready to serve, carefully unmold on a platter, bottom side of the charlotte upward, and garnish the surface with the Drambuie-soaked fruits. *Serves 8 to 10.*

NOTE: If desired, the unmolded charlotte may be decorated with whipped cream placed in a pastry bag fitted with a star tip and piped out in decorative swirls on the surface of the charlotte.

2071. CHESTNUT PUDDING
Budino freddo di marroni

1½ pounds very plump chestnuts
2 cups rich milk
Pinch salt
1½ cups superfine sugar
1½ teaspoons vanilla extract
1 cup blanched almonds [see No. 2280], toasted until golden brown in a 300° oven, and ground to a powder
1½ cups heavy cream, whipped
½ cup candied fruit (cherries, pineapple, citron, orange peel, etc.), cut in large dice
4 tablespoons kirsch

Cut a cross on the flat side of the chestnuts with a sharp knife. Place them in a skillet or large baking pan, and place them near the bottom of a 400° oven for 10 to 15 minutes, or until the skins peel back. Carefully peel off the skins while they are still hot. Place the peeled chestnuts in the milk, add the salt, and place over medium heat until boiling. Lower flame and simmer for 30 minutes. After this time, add the sugar and stir until dissolved. Pass the chestnuts and milk through a strainer, pressing them through to make a purée (or put them in the blender, ½ cup at a time, and whirl on low speed until puréed). Let the purée cool, and add the vanilla extract. Grind the almonds in the meat grinder, using the finest blade (or whirl them in the blender, ¼ cup at a time, until pulverized), and beat them into the purée. Beat the cream in a chilled bowl until stiff, and gently fold it into the chestnut/almond mixture. Dampen a 5-cup melon mold with cold water. Pour in ¼ of the mixture, and sprinkle with ¼ of the candied fruits, which have been soaked in the kirsch for 1 hour Repeat with layers of chestnut purée and fruit, ending with the purée. Place in the coldest part of the refrigerator for at least 6 hours. Unmold by dipping the mold in hot water for a few seconds and then turning out onto a platter. *Serves 6 to 8.*

NOTE: If desired, the pudding may be decorated with 1 cup whipped cream, piped in decorative swirls through a pastry bag fitted with a medium star tip, a few whole marrons glacés, and some additional candied fruit arranged in decorative patterns.

2072. CHOCOLATE PUDDING WITH CUSTARD SAUCE
Budino al cioccolato con crema all'inglese

¾ cup butter, softened
2 cups superfine sugar
8 egg yolks
1 cup plus 2 tablespoons fresh breadcrumbs (made by toasting slices of crustless bread in a 250° oven until dry and golden, and then crushing or grating them until reduced to fine crumbs)
Pinch cinnamon
4 squares bitter chocolate, finely grated
2 tablespoons vanilla extract
6 egg whites
¼ teaspoon salt
2 tablespoons butter, softened
1 recipe Custard Sauce [No. 2274]

Cream the butter with a wooden spoon in a warm bowl until it is pale in color, gradually beat in the sugar, and continue beating until the mixture is light and fluffy. Beat in 4 of the yolks, 1 at a time, beating well after each addition. Gradually beat in 1 cup of the breadcrumbs. When they are well blended, beat in the other 4 yolks, 1 at a time, beating well after each addition. Beat in the cinnamon, grated chocolate, and vanilla. Beat the egg whites and salt with a wire whisk in a large bowl (preferably of unlined copper) until they form soft peaks, and then fold carefully into the chocolate mixture, mixing only until blended. Liberally butter a 2½-quart charlotte mold (or any large, straight-sided casserole) and sprinkle it with the remaining crumbs, tilting in all directions, and shaking out the excess. Carefully pour in the chocolate pudding, place the mold in a pan of hot water that is deep enough to reach ⅔ up the sides of the mold, and place in a 350° oven for 55 minutes, or until a sharp knife inserted in the center of the pudding emerges clean. Remove from the oven, lift the mold out of the water bath, and let the pudding rest for 10 minutes. Unmold it on a large, round serving platter, surround it with a little of the custard sauce, and serve the rest of the sauce separately. *Serves* 8.

NOTE: This pudding is also delicious cold. Let it rest for 1 hour before unmolding, and then chill it in the refrigerator for 3 hours.

CROSTE

Croste

There is no equivalent word for this type of dessert in English. These preparations are familiar to Italian home kitchens, and the 3 recipes listed below are but a few of the many varieties that exist. Taking these as a starting point, the imaginative cook can create a number of delicious variations. These desserts are economical (if using stale baked goods), relatively simple to make, and provide a satisfying end to a light meal.

2073. CHERRY CROSTE
Croste con ciliege

2 cups cherries, pitted (or substitute 2 cups canned cherries in heavy syrup)
1 cup water
1 cup sugar
Juice of ½ lemon
1 day-old Brioche [No. 1890] or Savarin [No. 1900], baked in a loaf tin, or loaf of commercial egg bread (Challah), crust removed, sliced in ¼-inch-thick slices
¼ cup superfine sugar
¼ cup butter, softened
1 cup apricot preserves, pressed through a fine sieve
¼ cup blanched almonds [*see* No. 2280], halved
¼ cup candied fruits (pineapple, orange peel, citron, etc.), diced
¼ cup kirsch

Place the water, sugar, and lemon juice in a saucepan, bring to a boil, and cook until it reaches the large thread stage (219° on the candy thermometer). Add the cherries and cook until they are tender. Remove from stove and reserve. (If using canned cherries, omit the sugar/water syrup, drain the cherries, and cook the syrup they were packed in until reduced by ½, then add the cherries and heat through, removing them from the stove when they are hot.) Slice loaf and re-form by pressing the slices together carefully and neatly (a long, thin skewer pierced through the slices will hold the loaf together while it is baking). Cream the sugar and butter together until very creamy, and spread this over the surface of the re-formed, crustless loaf. Place this on a baking sheet and place in a 400° oven for 10 minutes, or until the exterior is well glazed. Remove from oven and carefully pull out the skewer. Spread each slice on 1 side only with some of the apricot preserves (reserving ¼ cup) and arrange the slices (spread side upward) in a tightly overlapping circle on a round, oven-proof serving platter. Pile the cherries with some of their syrup in the center of the circle, and decorate the slices with the almonds and candied fruit. Mix the remaining apricot preserves with the rest of the cherry syrup and the kirsch, and slowly pour ½ of it over the slices, making sure it soaks in, and does not run off. Do this at intervals, if necessary, to allow the first pouring sufficient time to absorb before pouring on more syrup. Place in a 350° oven for 10 to 15 minutes, or until bubbling. Remove from oven, pour over the rest of the syrup, and let cool for 15 to 20 minutes before serving. *Serves* 8.

2074. MARRON CROSTE
Croste con marroni

1 day-old Brioche [No. 1890] or Savarin [No. 1900], baked in a loaf tin, or loaf of commercial egg bread (Challah), crust removed, sliced in ¼-inch-thick slices
¼ cup superfine sugar
¼ cup butter, softened
1½ cups puréed marrons glacés (commercially available in cans)
1½ cups apricot preserves, pressed through a sieve
¼ cup slivered almonds [*see* No. 2288]
½ cup whole marrons glacés packed in syrup (commercially available)
½ cup raisins, plumped in warm water for ½ hour and drained
½ cup currants, plumped in warm water for ½ hour and drained
½ cup sweet Madeira wine

Slice loaf and re-form as indicated in No. 2073. Cream the sugar and butter together until creamy, and spread this over the re-formed, crustless loaf. Place this on a baking sheet and place in a 400° oven for 10 minutes, or until the exterior is well glazed. Remove from oven and carefully pull out the skewer. Spread each slice on 1 side only with the marron purée, coat with ¾ cup of the apricot preserves, and arrange the slices (spread side upward) in a tightly overlapping circle on a round, oven-proof serving platter. Sprinkle with the slivered almonds and pile the whole marrons, raisins, and currants in the center of the circle. Heat the remaining apricot preserves with the Madeira and spoon a ribbon of this around the slices, pouring the rest of it over the marrons, raisins, and currants in the center. Serve at once, or reheat for 5 minutes in a 250° oven. *Serves* 8.

2075. PINEAPPLE CROSTE
Croste all'ananasso

1 pineapple, peeled, cored, and sliced in ¼-inch rounds
2 cups sugar
1½ cups water

1 very fresh Brioche [No. 1890] or Savarin [No. 1900], baked in a loaf tin, or loaf of commercial egg bread (Challah), crust removed, sliced in ¼-inch-thick slices
¼ cup superfine sugar
¼ cup butter, softened
1 cup Apricot Sauce [No. 2270]
¼ cup sweet Madeira or sweet Marsala wine

Place the sugar and water in a large, deep skillet or shallow pot. Bring to a boil and cook to the large thread stage (219° on the candy thermometer). Add the pineapple slices and poach until the fruit is tender and somewhat translucent. Remove from stove and leave in syrup. Slice the loaf carefully, and when sliced, press it together into its original form (a long, thin skewer pierced through the slices will hold it together). Cream the butter and sugar together until very creamy, and spread this over the surface of the re-formed, crustless loaf. Place this on a baking sheet and place in a 400° oven for 10 minutes, or until the exterior is well glazed. Remove from oven and carefully pull out the skewer. Sandwich in a slice of pineapple (including a bit of syrup) between each slice of the loaf, carefully reassemble (the skewer may be reinserted for staying power). Put on a platter and let the loaf sit, lightly covered with a piece of wax paper, for 2 hours. Brush it with a bit of syrup if desired, but do not make it soggy. Before serving mix the wine with the sauce, and pour it over the loaf. *Serves* 8 *to* 10.

2076. DIPLOMAT PUDDING
Budino freddo alla diplomatica

1 recipe Vanilla Bavarian Cream [No. 2094]
16 dry ladyfingers (or 12 Savoyard Ladyfingers— No. 1946), split
½ cup kirsch
⅓ cup candied fruits (cherries, pineapple, orange peel, etc.), very finely diced

Chill a large, scalloped charlotte mold (or a straight-sided casserole). Soak the ladyfingers in the kirsch

SEE
REVERSE
FOR
CAPTION

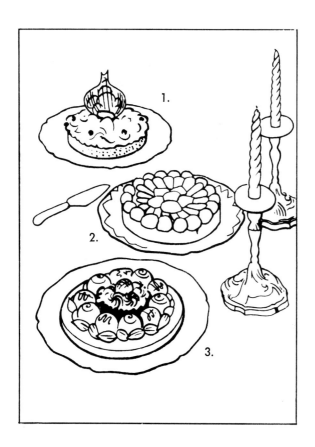

1. Chocolate Bavarian Cream (No. 2097)
2. Gâteau St. Honoré (No. 1911)
3. Chocolate Cake Capriccio (No. 1909)

Diplomat Pudding (No. 2076)

(it would be preferable to use the homemade Savoyards rather than purchased ladyfingers)—reserving 2 tablespoons, which is to be mixed with the candied fruits. Prepare the bavarian. Pour a shallow layer of the bavarian in the mold, top with 8 ladyfinger halves arranged like the spokes of a wheel, and sprinkle with some of the kirsch-soaked fruit. Cover with another layer of bavarian, add ladyfinger halves and fruit, and repeat until you end with a layer of cream. Place the mold in the coldest part of the refrigerator for 3 hours. Unmold by dipping the mold in very hot water for 2 seconds and then quickly turning the mold upside down on a round serving platter. *Serves* 8.

NOTE: This may be decorated as shown in the photograph above by arranging candied cherries and candied orange sections over and around the pudding.

2077. DIPLOMAT PUDDING WITH CUSTARD SAUCE

Budino diplomatico con salsa alla vaniglia

4 eggs
$\frac{1}{2}$ cup superfine sugar
Pinch salt
2 cups milk, scalded
1 teaspoon vanilla extract
1 tablespoon butter
2 tablespoons sugar
12 day-old ladyfingers (or 12 Savoyard Ladyfingers—No. 1946), split

$\frac{1}{2}$ cup seedless white raisins, plumped in hot water for $\frac{1}{2}$ hour and drained
$\frac{1}{2}$ cup candied fruits (cherries, pineapple, citron, orange peel, etc.), soaked for 3 hours in $\frac{1}{4}$ cup rum
1 recipe Custard Sauce [No. 2274]

Stir (do not beat) the eggs in a large bowl. When they are totally blended add the sugar and continue stirring until it is blended in. Add the salt and then stir in the scalded milk, a little at a time. If there is any foam on the mixture, skim it off. Add the vanilla. Butter a large ring mold and sprinkle it with the sugar, tilting in all directions to coat it well, and tapping out the excess. Place alternate layers of ladyfinger pieces (it would be preferable to use the homemade Savoyards rather than purchased ladyfingers), raisins, and rum-soaked fruit. Carefully pour in the egg/milk mixture, adding it by intervals so that the ladyfingers become well soaked and do not float. Place the mold in a pan of hot water deep enough to come $\frac{2}{3}$ up its sides, cover the mold loosely with a sheet of aluminum foil slashed in several places to allow steam to escape, and place in a 300° oven for 45 minutes, or until a knife inserted in the center of the pudding emerges clean. Remove from oven, lift out of the water bath, let it rest for 20 minutes, and unmold it onto a round serving platter. Pour over $\frac{1}{2}$ cup of the sauce, and serve the rest separately. *Serves 6 to 8.*

NOTE: This is also delicious cold. Leave it in the mold for 45 minutes, then unmold onto the platter, place in a refrigerator for 3 hours to chill, and serve as indicated above.

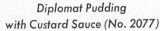

Diplomat Pudding
with Custard Sauce (No. 2077)

689

2078. EMPRESS RICE
Riso all'imperatrice

This is a version of the classic French Riz à l'impératrice, *a glorified and supremely delicious rice pudding.*

½ cup short-grain rice (Italian rice, if available)

2 cups rich milk

4 lumps sugar

2-inch piece of vanilla bean

Pinch salt

1 tablespoon butter

4 tablespoons apricot preserves, pressed through a fine sieve

¼ cup candied fruits (cherries, pineapple, orange peel, etc.), soaked for 2 hours in 4 tablespoons kirsch

Custard:

3 eggs

2 egg yolks

1 cup sugar

Pinch salt

2 cups rich milk, scalded

2 envelopes unflavored gelatin, softened in ⅓ cup cold milk

1 cup heavy cream, whipped

1 cup currant (or raspberry) jelly, melted over low heat and mixed with ¼ cup maraschino liqueur

12 candied cherries

12 thin strips candied orange peel

Place the milk in a small, heavy saucepan with the sugar lumps and vanilla bean. Bring to a boil over low heat, remove from stove, cover pan, and let steep for 15 minutes. Cook the rice for 6 minutes in about 1 quart boiling water, drain, and rinse well with cold water. When milk has steeped, add the rice and salt, place the pan over low heat, and bring to a simmer. Stir up rice once or twice with a fork. Cover pan and cook for ½ hour over very low heat. Remove from fire, discard vanilla bean, and pour rice into a bowl, fluffing rice with a fork. Fold in the butter, apricot preserves, and the kirsch-soaked fruits; mix well and allow to cool.

Meanwhile, make the custard. Beat the eggs and egg yolks with the sugar and salt until well blended. Slowly pour in the scalded milk and mix well. Place the custard in a small, heavy saucepan over low heat and stir constantly until the mixture coats the spoon. Add the softened gelatin, remove from heat, and stir until gelatin is dissolved. Allow the custard to cool to room temperature, stirring it every so often to prevent a crust from forming. When cooled, stir it into the rice mixture. Place the bowl containing the rice/custard mixture into a large bowl filled with cracked ice, and

stir constantly until the mixture gets thick but is still manageable. Immediately fold in the whipped cream and pour the mixture into a lightly oiled (or dampened) 3-quart mold. Place mold in refrigerator for at least 6 hours. Before serving melt the currant (or raspberry) jelly in a small saucepan over very low heat. When smooth, stir in the liqueur, pour into a small bowl, and allow to cool. Unmold the rice by dipping the mold in hot water for 1 or 2 seconds (taking care that the water does not spill over the top onto the pudding) and unmold on round serving platter. Decorate with the cherries and orange peel and serve at once. Serve the sauce separately. *Serves 8 to 10.*

2079. FRANKFURT PUDDING WITH STRAWBERRY SAUCE
Budino di Francoforte con salsa di fragole

1½ cups stale pumpernickel bread, crusts removed, cut in small cubes

⅔ cup good-quality red wine (sweet, if desired), warmed

1½ cups blanched almonds [*see* No. 2280], ground into powder

1 cup plus 2 tablespoons butter, softened

1½ cups superfine sugar

8 eggs, separated

2 tablespoons candied fruits (cherries, pineapple, orange peel, etc.), finely chopped

Pinch cinnamon

Pinch salt

2 tablespoons breadcrumbs (freshly made, if possible)

1 recipe Strawberry Sauce [No. 2278]

Warm the wine in a small, heavy enamel saucepan and pour it over the cubed pumpernickel. Mix well and let soak for ½ hour. Grind the almonds in the meat grinder using the finest blade (or place in blender, ½ cup at a time, and whirl at high speed until pulverized). When bread has soaked, press it through a fine sieve. Cream the butter in a warm bowl with a wooden spoon until pale in color. Add 1 cup of the sugar and cream until light and fluffy. Add the egg yolks, 1 at a time, alternating with small amounts of the pumpernickel, beating thoroughly after each addition. Then add the ground almonds, candied fruits, and cinnamon, mixing them in well. Beat the egg whites with the salt in a large bowl (preferably of unlined copper) with a wire whisk. When foamy add ½ cup of the sugar and beat until they stand in soft peaks. Fold ¼ of the beaten whites into the pudding mixture and stir in well. When incorporated, fold in the rest of the whites, cutting them in until both mixtures are blended. Butter a 2½-quart mold with the 2 tablespoons of butter and sprinkle it with the crumbs, tilting in all directions until well coated, and knocking out the excess. Carefully pour the pudding into the mold and place the mold into a pan of hot water deep enough to reach ⅔ up its sides. Place in a 325° oven and bake for 45 minutes to 1 hour, or until a knife blade inserted in its center emerges clean. Remove from oven, lift it out of its water bath, and let it stand for 15 minutes. Carefully unmold onto a serving platter and serve warm. Serve the strawberry sauce separately. *Serves 8 to 10.*

2080. HOLLAND PUDDING WITH CURRANT SAUCE
Budino all'olandese con salsa di ribes

2 cups rich milk
1 cup plus 2 tablespoons sugar
Pinch salt
Pinch nutmeg
½ cup butter
½ cup flour
10 egg yolks
4 egg whites
1 teaspoon vanilla (or almond) extract
Currant sauce (*see* Note below)

Place the milk, ½ cup of the sugar, salt, and nutmeg in a small, heavy saucepan. Stir over medium heat until sugar is dissolved, and bring to the scalding point. In another, larger saucepan melt all but 2 tablespoons of the butter over very low heat, taking care it does not brown. Add the flour, and mix until blended. Slowly pour in the hot milk, whipping with a wire whisk to prevent lumps. Cook over low heat for 5 minutes until very thick and smooth. Remove from stove and pour into a large bowl. Add the yolks, 1 at a time, beating well after each addition. Beat the egg whites with another pinch of salt with a wire whisk in a large bowl (preferably of unlined copper) until foamy. Gradually add ½ cup of the sugar and beat until they stand in soft peaks. Fold into the egg mixture, cutting in well, but not overmixing. Fold in the vanilla. Grease a 2½-quart mold with the rest of the butter, and sprinkle it with the remaining sugar, tilting in all directions to coat it well, and tapping out the excess. Pour in the batter. Place the mold in a pan of hot water deep enough to reach ⅔ up its sides, and place in a 400° oven to bake for 20 minutes. Lower the heat to 325° and continue baking until the pudding is well puffed and a knife inserted in its center emerges clean. Remove from oven, lift out of the water bath, and let the mold stand for 25 minutes. Unmold onto a deep serving dish and surround with 1 cup of the sauce. Serve the remaining sauce on the side. Serve warm or hot. *Serves 6 to 8.*

NOTE: The currant sauce is prepared as follows:
1 cup black currant jam
½ cup red currant jelly
½ cup raspberry jelly
2 tablespoons butter
1 tablespoon lemon juice

Place all ingredients in a small, heavy saucepan, and cook over low heat until the jellies are melted and all the ingredients are well blended. Stir from time to time to prevent scorching. Serve warm.

2081. MONT BLANC
Monte Bianco

This delectable and easily made dessert of chestnut purée and whipped cream takes its name from its resemblance to the snow-capped Alpine peak.

2 pounds chestnuts
3½ cups milk
2-inch piece of vanilla bean
1½ cups sugar
½ cup water
¼ teaspoon salt
3 tablespoons butter, softened
1½ cups heavy cream, whipped
1 teaspoon vanilla extract
3 tablespoons superfine sugar

Cut a cross in the flat side of the chestnuts with a sharp knife. Place them on a large baking pan or cooky sheet and place in a 400° oven for 15 minutes, or until the skins begin to curl back. Remove from oven and skin them while they are still hot. Place the milk in a heavy saucepan, add the peeled chestnuts and the vanilla bean, place over medium heat, and cook for about 30 minutes, or until tender. Drain the chestnuts in a colander and discard the vanilla bean. Cook the sugar and water in a small saucepan over rather high heat until they reach the soft ball stage (228° on the candy thermometer). Press the drained chestnuts through a fine sieve and mix the purée with the salt, butter, and sugar syrup. When well mixed, leave the purée until lukewarm. Place the purée in a potato ricer and press it out in the form of a broad cone onto a serving platter (or press it into a lightly oiled,

691

cone-shaped mold and turn it out onto the platter). Whip the cream in a chilled bowl until thickened. Add the superfine sugar and vanilla extract and whip until stiff. Cover the chestnut purée with the cream, smoothing it into a peak with a dampened spatula, and leaving the base partially free of cream. When finished the dessert should look like a snow-capped mountain peak (*see* photograph facing page 656). *Serves* 8 *to* 10.

NOTE: The purée may be passed through the holes of a fine colander if a potato ricer is not available. However, no matter what is used, the coils of purée should be loosely packed, not mashed down.

2082. MONT BLANC WITH STREGA
Monte Bianco al profumo di Strega

2 pounds chestnuts
1½ cups sugar
½ cup water
Pinch salt
⅓ cup Strega liqueur
1½ cups heavy cream, whipped
1 teaspoon vanilla extract

Skin the chestnuts as described in the preceding recipe. Cook the sugar and water in a saucepan over high heat until the syrup reaches the large thread stage (219° on the candy thermometer). Add the peeled chestnuts, and salt, and poach them in the syrup over medium heat for 30 minutes, or until tender. Remove with a slotted spoon, press them through a fine sieve, pour the syrup over them, mix well, and add the Strega. When well mixed, spoon the purée into a shallow glass serving bowl, heaping it into the form of a small mountain, and allow to cool at room temperature. Whip the cream until stiff and fold in the vanilla. Cover the purée with the cream as described in the preceding recipe. Place in refrigerator and chill for 2 hours. *Serves* 8 *to* 10.

NOTE: This is somewhat heavier than No. 2081, because the purée is not passed through a ricer. Since it is so sweet, the cream is flavored but unsweetened. One may also pile the purée on 9-inch layer of Italian Sponge Cake [No. 1913] which has been sprinkled with some Strega, and then icing it with the cream.

2083. NORMANDY APPLES WITH ALMOND CREAM AND CALVADOS
Mele alla normanda

2 cups sugar
2 cups water
1 lemon slice
2-inch piece of vanilla bean
5 firm, tart apples (greenings, if available), peeled, halved, and cored
¼ cup Calvados (or applejack)
Almond cream:
    1 cup blanched almonds [*see* No. 2280], ground to a powder
    1 cup butter, softened
    1 cup superfine sugar
    5 eggs, separated
    3 tablespoons Calvados (or applejack)
    Pinch salt
    2 tablespoons butter
    2 tablespoons granulated sugar

Place the sugar, water, lemon, and vanilla bean in a large enamel saucepan. Bring to a boil and add the apple halves. Poach over a low flame until the apples are tender but not mushy. Remove them to a bowl with a slotted spoon, and cook the syrup until it reaches the large thread stage (219° on the candy thermometer). Discard the vanilla and lemon, then add the Calvados to 1½ cups of the syrup, and chill the apples and the syrup separately.

Prepare the almond cream. Grind the almonds into powder in the meat grinder, using the finest blade (or whirl in the blender, ⅓ cup at a time, until pulverized). Cream the butter and the sugar until light and fluffy, beat in the egg yolks, 1 at a time, alternating with small amounts of the ground almonds, beating well after each addition. Cream in the Calvados. Beat the whites with the salt in a large bowl (preferably of unlined copper) with a wire whisk until they form soft peaks. Fold them into the egg/almond mixture. Generously butter a ring mold and sprinkle the inside with sugar, tilting in all directions to ensure an even coating and tapping out the excess. Pour the batter into the mold, place it in a pan of hot water reaching ½ the height of the mold, and bake in a 350° oven for 35 minutes. Remove from oven, take it out of its water bath, and cool until lukewarm. Carefully unmold on a round platter. Place in the refrigerator to chill. When chilled, pile the poached apples in the center of the ring and cover them and the almond cream with a generous amount of the apple syrup, and serve chilled. *Serves 6 to 8.*

NOTE: If desired, whipped cream flavored with almond (or vanilla) extract may be served on the side.

2084. ORANGE PUDDING MADRILENA
Arance alla madrilena

¾ cup short-grain rice (Italian rice, if available)
4 cups rich milk
Pinch salt
½ cup plus 2 tablespoons sugar
1-inch piece of vanilla bean (or 2 teaspoons vanilla extract)
2 teaspoons grated orange rind (no white part)
4 egg yolks
1 egg
Syrup:
  1 cup sugar
  ½ cup water
4 large strips orange rind (no white part), cut in fine julienne strips
2 navel oranges, peeled and separated into segments, with white membranes removed
1 recipe Zabaglione Sauce [No. 2279]

Put the rice into 3 quarts of vigorously boiling water and boil for 6 minutes. Drain into a sieve and wash the rice under cold running water. Place the milk, the salt, ½ cup of the sugar, and the vanilla bean in a heavy saucepan. Bring to a simmer over low heat and add the rice and 1 teaspoon grated orange rind. Fluff the rice a few times with a fork, cover pan, and cook over very low heat for 35 minutes, or until all the milk has been absorbed (an asbestos pad between the pan and the fire will reduce the danger of scorching). When the rice is cooked, remove from stove, pour it into a bowl, and remove the vanilla bean. Butter a 2-quart straight-sided mold (or a round-bottom oven-proof bowl) and sprinkle it with the remaining sugar, tilting in all directions to coat it well and shaking out the excess. Beat the egg yolks and egg together. Beat the eggs into the hot rice (and add vanilla extract, if using it), and pour into the mold. Cover with a sheet of aluminum foil, slashed with a knife to allow steam to escape, and place the mold in a pan of hot water deep enough to reach ⅔ up the sides of the mold. Place in a 350° oven and bake for 45 minutes. Remove from oven, lift out of water bath, and let stand for 20 minutes.

While the rice is baking, cook the sugar syrup in a small saucepan until it reaches the large thread stage (219° on the candy thermometer). Add the julienned orange rind and the orange sections, and poach until the sections are tender but still hold their shape. Remove them with a slotted spoon, and continue to poach the strips of rind. Make the Zabaglione, and add the rest of the grated rind to it. Unmold the pudding on a deep serving dish. Surround it with the orange sections, remove the strips of rind from the syrup and arrange them decoratively over the rice, and pour a little Zabaglione around the pudding (being careful not to drown the orange sections). Serve at once, accompanied by the remaining Zabaglione in a sauce bowl. *Serves 6.*

2085. PEACHES CONDÉ
Pesche Condé

Same ingredients as for Apricots Condé [No. 2063],
  except that 12 small freestone peaches, peeled,
  stoned, and halved, are substituted for the apricots
1-inch piece of vanilla bean

Prepare exactly as Apricots Condé, except that the peaches are poached in the syrup to which the vanilla bean has been added. The piece of bean is removed before the puréed peaches and syrup are poured on. *Serves 6.*

2086. PEARS CONDÉ
Pere Condé

Same ingredients as for Apricots Condé [No. 2063],
  except that 12 small russet pears, peeled, halved,
  and cored, are substituted for the apricots
1-inch piece of vanilla bean

Prepare exactly as Apricots Condè, except that the pears are poached in the syrup to which the vanilla bean has been added. The piece of bean is removed before the puréed pears and syrup are poured on. *Serves 6.*

2087. PINEAPPLE CHARLOTTE
Charlotte vanigliata con panna e ananasso

30 ladyfingers (more or less), left whole (or 1 recipe
    Savoyard Ladyfingers—No. 1946)
2 cups sugar
1 cup water
Juice of 1 lemon
1 fresh pineapple, peeled, cored, and cut into small
    cubes
⅓ cup Drambuie liqueur
2 cups cream, whipped
3 tablespoons candied fruits (cherries, orange peel,
    citron, etc.), cut in cubes

Line a ring mold with the ladyfingers (or, better still,
the homemade Savoyards) as described in Charlotte
Russe [No. 2069]. Cook the sugar and water in a small
saucepan over medium heat until it reaches the soft ball
stage (228° on the candy thermometer). Add the pineapple and lemon juice and poach for 5 minutes. Remove
from stove, add 4 tablespoons of the Drambuie, cover
and let steep until cool. Whip the cream until stiff in a
chilled bowl, and sweeten with 2 or 3 tablespoons of
the Drambuie-flavored syrup. Sprinkle the ladyfingers
lining the mold with about ¼ cup of the syrup. Remove
the pineapple from the remaining syrup with a slotted
spoon and fold the cubes into the whipped cream. Pour
this mixture into the ladyfinger-lined mold, cover the
top with any leftover ladyfingers or ladyfinger pieces,
and chill in the refrigerator for 5 hours. While the
dessert is chilling, soak the candied fruit in the remaining Drambuie. Unmold the charlotte on a serving
platter, decorate with the liqueur-soaked fruits, pour
the liqueur over the charlotte, and serve well chilled.
Serves 8 *to* 10.

2088. REGENZA CREAM
Crema reggenza

30 stale ladyfingers (or 1 recipe Savoyard
    Ladyfingers—No. 1946)
4 tablespoons kirsch
4 tablespoons maraschino liqueur
3 cups milk, scalded
3 tablespoons butter, softened
3 eggs
6 egg yolks
1 cup sugar
⅓ cup water
8 apricots, peeled and halved (*see* Note below)
16 candied cherries

Sprinkle the dry ladyfingers (or, better still, the homemade Savoyards) with 2 tablespoons each of the kirsch
and maraschino. Place them in a large bowl, and pour
the scalding milk over them, mix well until batter-
like, add 2 tablespoons of the butter, and pass through
a sieve. Beat the eggs and egg yolks with the sugar and
salt until foamy. Pour into the milk/ladyfinger mixture
and mix well. Butter a 2-quart mold with the remaining
butter (sprinkle it with a few tablespoons ladyfinger
crumbs, if desired, tipping the mold in all directions
to coat it well), pour in the pudding, set the mold in a
pan of hot water that reaches ⅔ up its sides, and place in
a 325° oven for 1 hour, or until a knife inserted in the
center comes out clean.

Meanwhile, cook the sugar and water in a saucepan
over medium heat until it reaches the large thread stage
(219° on the candy thermometer). Add the apricot
halves and poach them for 5 minutes. Remove them
with a slotted spoon, and reduce the liquid over a high
flame until very thick and syrupy. Return the apricots
to the syrup, add remaining kirsch and maraschino,
and let them marinate until the pudding is done. When
the pudding is cooked, remove it from the oven, lift it
out of its water bath, and let it sit for 25 minutes. After
that time, unmold it on a deep serving platter, arrange
the poached apricot halves around it, flat sides facing
upward, fill their hollows with the cherries, and pour
the syrup over both the pudding and the apricots.
Serve warm. *Serves* 8 *to* 10.

NOTE: If canned apricots in heavy syrup are used,
omit the sugar/water syrup and merely drain the
apricot syrup into a pan, add ½ cup sugar, cook until
thick, add liqueurs, place apricots in syrup, and let
marinate until cool. Then proceed as above.

The preparation of
Pineapple Charlotte (No. 2087)

2089. REGINA PUDDING
Budino regina

1 cup milk
$\frac{1}{2}$ cup butter
Pinch salt
$\frac{2}{3}$ cup sugar
$\frac{1}{2}$ cup plus 2 tablespoons sifted all-purpose flour
4 eggs, separated
Pinch cream of tartar
1 cup dry almond macaroons (Italian macaroons, if available), crushed into crumbs
$\frac{1}{4}$ cup pistachio nuts, finely chopped
1 recipe English Custard [No. 2111], hot
3 tablespoons Praline powder [*see* No. 2290]

Place the milk, butter, salt, and sugar in a heavy saucepan over medium heat and bring to a boil. When the butter has melted, remove from stove, stir in the flour, and stir until lumps disappear. Return to the stove and stir until it is very thick and smooth and starts to come away from the sides of the pan. Remove from stove and let cool for 5 minutes. Beat in the egg yolks, 1 at a time, beating well after each addition. Beat the egg whites and cream of tartar with a wire whisk in a large bowl (preferably of unlined copper) and fold them into the batter, mixing well to make a smooth, light mixture. Generously butter a 2-quart mold and sprinkle it with some of the macaroon crumbs and some of the chopped pistachios, tilting in all directions so that it is well coated. Allow the excess to settle in the bottom. Spoon a layer of pudding batter into the mold, top with a sprinkling of nuts and macaroons, and continue the layering process, ending with a layer of batter. Reserve 1 tablespoon of macaroon crumbs. Cover the mold with aluminum foil, making a slash in the foil to allow steam to escape, and place the covered mold in a pan of hot water deep enough to reach $\frac{2}{3}$ up the sides of the mold. Place in a 350° oven for 55 minutes, or until a knife inserted in the center emerges clean. Remove from oven, take the mold out of the water bath, and let it stand for 20 minutes. Mix the remaining macaroon crumbs and Praline powder into the warm custard, and pour into a small bowl, reserving about $\frac{1}{2}$ cup of custard. Unmold the pudding onto a shallow serving dish, pour over the reserved custard, and serve at once. Serve the custard sauce separately. *Serves* 6 *to* 8.

2090. RICE PUDDING WITH ALMONDS
Budino di riso con mandorle

1 cup short-grain rice (Italian rice, if available)
4 cups rich milk
2 pinches salt
5 tablespoons butter, softened
$\frac{3}{4}$ cup plus 2 tablespoons sugar
4 eggs, separated
$\frac{1}{4}$ cup heavy cream
$\frac{1}{3}$ cup blanched almonds [*see* No. 2280], lightly toasted in a 350° oven and finely chopped
2 tablespoons brandy
$1\frac{1}{2}$ teaspoons vanilla extract
1 recipe Apricot Sauce [No. 2270]
$\frac{1}{4}$ cup maraschino liqueur

Place the rice in 3 quarts of rapidly boiling water for 6 minutes. Drain through a strainer and rinse well under cold running water. Pour the milk into a heavy enamel saucepan and bring to a simmer over medium heat. Add the rice, salt, 4 tablespoons of the butter, and 4 tablespoons of the sugar. Fluff up with a fork a few times, lower heat, cover the pan, and cook for 30 minutes (an asbestos pad placed between the pan and the flame will reduce the danger of scorching), or until the rice is very tender and all the milk has been absorbed. Pour the rice into a bowl, fluff it up with a fork, and let cool for 15 minutes. Beat egg yolks with the cream until well mixed. Stir into the rice together with the chopped almonds and 4 tablespoons of the sugar. Beat the whites and another pinch of salt with a wire whisk in a large bowl (preferably of unlined copper) until foamy. Add the remaining sugar and beat until they stand in soft peaks. Beat in the vanilla and brandy, and carefully fold the whites into the rice mixture. Butter a $2\frac{1}{2}$-quart charlotte mold (or any deep-sided mold) with the remaining butter and pour in the rice pudding. Place the mold in a pan of hot water deep enough to reach $\frac{2}{3}$ up its sides and place in a 325° oven for 45 minutes, or until a knife inserted into the center emerges clean. Remove from oven, lift the mold out of the water bath, and let the pudding rest for 15 minutes. Mix the maraschino with the apricot sauce. Unmold the pudding on a serving platter, pour some of the apricot sauce over it, and serve warm. Serve the rest of the apricot sauce separately. *Serves* 6 *to* 8.

695

2091. RICE PUDDING WITH CANDIED FRUIT
Budino di riso con frutti canditi

1 recipe Rice Pudding with Almonds [No. 2090],
    omitting the almonds
¼ cup candied fruits (cherries, pineapple, orange peel,
    etc.), finely diced
¼ cup seedless raisins, soaked for 1 hour in
    4 tablespoons brandy
1 recipe Strawberry Sauce [No. 2278]
¼ cup Aurum liqueur

Prepare the pudding as indicated in No. 2090. Instead of adding the almonds, add the diced candied fruits and the brandy-soaked raisins. Bake as indicated in No. 2090. Mix the strawberry sauce with the Aurum, and proceed as in No. 2090. *Serves 6 to 8.*

2092. TOASTED ALMOND PUDDING
Budino di mandorle tostate

1 cup blanched almonds [*see* No. 2280], toasted in a
    350° oven until golden brown, and then ground
    to a powder
30 dry ladyfingers (or Savoyard Ladyfingers—No. 1946),
    crumbled
4 cups rich milk
6 eggs
¾ cup superfine sugar
Pinch salt
1 tablespoon butter, softened
1 cup Strawberry Sauce [No. 2278]

Grind the almonds in the meat grinder, using the finest blade (or put in the blender ⅓ cup at a time, and whirl at high speed until they are pulverized). Pour the milk into a heavy enamel saucepan, add the crumbled ladyfingers and ground almonds, and bring to a boil over low heat, stirring every so often to prevent scorching. When the mixture comes to a boil, remove from stove, and press through a very fine sieve (or place in blender ⅓ at a time and whirl at high speed for a few seconds) into a large bowl. Beat the eggs with all but 2 tablespoons of the sugar, add the salt, and add the eggs to the almond/ladyfinger mixture, beating well. Butter a straight-sided 3-quart mold and sprinkle it with the remaining sugar, tilting in all directions to coat it well, tapping out the excess, and pour the pudding into the mold. Place the mold in a pan of hot water deep enough to reach ⅔ up its sides and place in a 325° oven for 45 minutes, or until a knife inserted into the center comes out clean. Remove from oven, lift the mold out of the water bath, and let the pudding rest for 25 minutes. Unmold it on a shallow serving platter, surround it with the sauce, and serve warm. *Serves 6.*

2093. ZUPPA INGLESE
Zuppa inglese

Literally, "English soup." The reader may recall that in the section on soups it was stated that "A zuppa almost invariably includes bread." The origin of zuppa inglese probably goes back to the nineteenth century, when British tourists in some numbers began to visit Italy. No doubt they demanded trifle for dessert, and since it reminded the Italians of the way certain of their regional soups are put together, they called it "English soup." Other attempts have been made to account for the name, but this seems the most likely. The following is but one of an endless number of variations to be found throughout Italy.

1 recipe Italian Sponge Cake [No. 1913], baked in a
    single layer
1 recipe Pastry Cream [No. 2267], made with
    3 tablespoons flour, and chilled
3 tablespoons candied pineapple, finely diced
3 tablespoons candied cherries, finely diced
3 tablespoons candied orange peel, finely diced
½ cup rum
Optional: ¼ cup Alkermes liqueur (if using Alkermes,
    decrease rum to ¼ cup)
3 egg whites
Pinch salt
½ cup superfine sugar
4 thin strips candied peel

Split the sponge cake horizontally. Place the bottom layer, cut side up, on a round, oven-proof serving platter. Sprinkle it with ¼ cup of the rum (or the Alkermes liqueur). Mix the candied fruits with the pastry cream, and pile the cream onto the cake, mounding it up in the center. Cut the other layer of the cake into 2-inch fingers and sprinkle with the remaining rum. Pile the cake fingers over the cream, adding more in the center, so that the preparation is mounded. Whip the whites and salt with a wire whisk in a large bowl (preferably of unlined copper) until light and foamy, add all but 2 tablespoons of the sugar, and beat until it stands in soft peaks. Cover the entire surface of the dessert with the meringue, making sure there are no exposed or thin places. Smooth its sides with a moistened spatula until it resembles a squat cone. Decorate the top with the candied peel and sprinkle evenly with the remaining sugar. Place in a 350° oven until the meringue turns a pale ivory in color (it must not brown). Remove from oven, let cool to room temperature, and then chill in the refrigerator for at least 6 hours. *Serves 6 to 8.*

BAVARIANS, CUSTARDS, MOUSSES, AND GELATINS

Bavaresi, creme, moscovite, e gelatine

These are egg- and/or gelatin-based desserts. Bavarians are gelatin-strengthened custards enriched with whipped cream and flavored as indicated in the recipes listed, or according to one's own tastes. If crushed fruits, cake, or macaroon crumbs, etc. are used, make sure they are not so weighty that they will sink through the cream before it solidifies. Mousses are custardless bavarians, and are usually chilled in cracked ice (although the freezing compartment of the refrigerator works just as well). Many of the gelatins are wine- or liqueur-based preparations, and provide the perfect climax to a heavy meal. A light hand and a quick, steady approach is important in the making of all these preparations.

2094. VANILLA BAVARIAN CREAM
Bavarese alla vaniglia

This is the master recipe for the bavarians which follow.

1½ cups rich milk
2-inch piece of vanilla bean (or 2 teaspoons vanilla extract)

5 egg yolks
¾ cup superfine sugar
Pinch salt
1 envelope unflavored gelatin, softened in ¼ cup cold milk
1½ cups heavy cream, whipped

Place the milk and vanilla bean in a small, heavy saucepan over medium heat and bring to a simmer. Remove from stove, cover pan, and let steep for 15 minutes (if using extract, merely scald milk). Beat the yolks with the sugar and salt until lemon colored. Pour in the milk, discarding the vanilla bean, and mix well. Pour into a heavy saucepan, place over low heat, and stir constantly until the mixture coats the spoon. Add the softened gelatin, stir until dissolved, and remove from stove. Pour the custard through a very fine sieve into a bowl. (If vanilla extract is used, add it now.) Place the bowl in a larger bowl filled with cracked ice, and stir the custard until almost cold. Remove from over ice, and whip the cream in a chilled bowl until thick. Return the custard to the ice and stir until it is almost set. Immediately remove from over the ice, and fold in the whipped cream. Pour into a slightly moistened 1½-quart scalloped mold, place in refrigerator, and chill for at least 5 hours. Unmold by dipping the mold in hot water for 1 second (taking care that the water does not spill over onto the surface of the cream) and turn out onto a round serving platter. *Serves 6.*

2095. BAVARIAN CREAM MARCHESA REGINA
Marchesa regina

1 recipe Vanilla Bavarian Cream [No. 2094], using ½ envelope unflavored gelatin and 1 cup sugar
3 squares bitter chocolate
20 ladyfingers, split (or 20 Savoyard Ladyfingers—No. 1946)
¼ cup maraschino liqueur
1 cup heavy cream, whipped
2 tablespoons superfine sugar
1 teaspoon vanilla extract
3 tablespoons candied fruits (cherries, pineapple, citron, etc.), diced

Make the bavarian as indicated in No. 2094, using ½ envelope unflavored gelatin softened in 2 tablespoons cold milk. Melt the chocolate in a small bowl over hot water and add it to the custard while it is hot, and before adding the dissolved gelatin. Sprinkle the ladyfingers (or, better still, the homemade Savoyards) with the liqueur and line a deep straight-sided mold with them. Pour in the chocolate mixture, and top with any leftover ladyfingers. Place in refrigerator for at least 8 hours, or overnight. When ready to serve, unmold on a large, round platter. Whip the cream in a chilled bowl and flavor it with the vanilla and sugar. Place it in a pastry bag fitted with a large star tip, and pipe decorative swirls over the unmolded dessert. Sprinkle the top with a ring of the candied fruits. *Serves 6 to 8.*

2096. BLANCMANGE WITH MARASCHINO LIQUEUR
Blanc-manger al maraschino

This is the classic version, and is quite different from the quaking, glutinous cornstarch pudding remembered from childhood. Here is a superior, suave pudding to serve with pride.

1 cup blanched almonds [*see* No. 2280], ground to a
    powder
2 bitter almonds (*see* Note below), ground with the
    blanched almonds
2 cups rich milk
2-inch length of vanilla bean
3/4 cup superfine sugar
1 1/2 envelopes unflavored gelatin, softened in
    1/4 cup milk
1 cup heavy cream, whipped
2 tablespoons maraschino liqueur
3 tablespoons candied fruits (cherries, pineapple,
    orange peel, etc.), coarsely chopped and soaked in
    1 tablespoon maraschino liqueur

Grind all almonds to a powder in the meat grinder, using the finest blade (or whirl in the blender, 1/3 cup at a time, until pulverized). Place the ground almonds, milk, 1/2 cup of the sugar, and the vanilla bean in a heavy enamel saucepan and bring to a boil over low heat. Simmer for 10 minutes, remove from the stove, cover the pan, and let steep for 1 hour. After this time, dip a napkin or a clean linen cloth in cold water, line a sieve with it, and pour the almond milk through the cloth. Gather up the cloth and squeeze out every possible drop of liquid, and discard the now-flavorless ground almonds (if desired, an additional 1/4 cup of hot milk may be poured over the squeezed almonds in the cloth, and the liquid squeezed into the almond milk: this will ensure that every bit of almond essence has been extracted). Place the almond milk back on the stove, add 4 more tablespoons of the sugar, and heat until scalding hot. Add the softened gelatin and stir

until dissolved. Do not allow to boil. Remove from fire, pour into a bowl, and chill until thickened and syrupy. At this point, whip the cream in a chilled bowl until stiff, add the rest of the sugar, and fold it and the maraschino into the slightly thickened almond cream. Moisten a 1-quart melon mold with a little water, scatter the maraschino-soaked fruit over the inside, and carefully pour in the almond cream. Chill in the refrigerator for 5 hours. Unmold by running a sharp knife around the edge and then dipping the mold for 2 seconds in hot water. Turn out onto a platter and serve chilled. *Serves 6.*

NOTE: A bitter almond is the kernel of a peach stone. Crack 2 peach stones with a hammer or heavy nutcracker and extract the "almond" in the center. Peel it and proceed as directed above.

2097. CHOCOLATE BAVARIAN CREAM
Bavarese al cioccolato

1 recipe Vanilla Bavarian Cream [No. 2094], made
    with 1 cup sugar
3 squares bitter chocolate
2 tablespoons freshly brewed coffee
Garnishes:
    1 cup heavy cream, whipped
    2 tablespoons superfine sugar
    1 teaspoon vanilla extract
    6 paper-thin slices fresh pineapple
    12 candied cherries
    6 sections candied pineapple
    2 squares semi-sweet chocolate, melted
    2 tablespoons coffee
    Optional: 3-part chocolate lattice [*see* No. 1997]

Melt the chocolate in a small bowl placed in a pan of hot water. Add the coffee and mix well. Add this to the custard when it is placed on the stove, and continue as directed in No. 2094. When the cream has been made, pour it into a 9-inch straight-sided mold (or a deep cake tin) and chill as directed. Unmold on a round serving platter and decorate.

Whip the cream until stiff in a chilled bowl and flavor it with the sugar and vanilla. Spread 1/2 of it all over the bavarian, smoothing it with a moistened spatula. Place the rest in a pastry bag fitted with a large star tip and pipe a series of swirls in the center of the bavarian. Twist the slices of pineapple into shallow cones and place them at evenly spaced intervals around the center swirls of cream. Fill each pineapple cone with a cherry. Stick the candied pineapple sections into the sides of the center cream swirls in evenly spaced intervals. Pipe the rest of the cream around the cherry centers of the pineapple cones, and make a scalloped border around the top edge of the bavarian. Melt the chocolate in a small bowl over hot water, add the coffee, mix well, and pour into a small cornucopia made of stiff white paper. Snip off the end to make a tiny hole, and pipe random swirls of chocolate all over the sides of the bavarian. Heap the rest of the cherries into the center, and crown with the optional chocolate lattice. *Serves* 8.

NOTE: The photograph opposite page 672 gives an approximate idea of how the dessert should look. However, you may garnish it as desired, or merely pipe on swirls of whipped cream.

2098. COFFEE BAVARIAN CREAM
Bavarese al caffè

1 recipe Vanilla Bavarian Cream [No. 2094]
½ cup freshly ground coffee (all-purpose grind)

Place the coffee with the vanilla bean in the milk, place over medium heat, remove when simmering, cover pan, and steep for 15 minutes. Pour the coffee/vanilla milk through a sieve lined with a double layer of cheesecloth, and proceed exactly as indicated in No. 2094. *Serves* 6.

NOTE: If desired, the bavarian may be garnished as follows after it has been unmolded:

1 cup heavy cream, whipped
1 teaspoon powdered instant coffee
1 teaspoon vanilla extract
2 tablespoons superfine sugar
3 tablespoons candy coffee beans
12 thin strips candied orange peel

Whip the cream in a chilled bowl and flavor it with the coffee, vanilla, and sugar. Place it in a pastry bag fitted with a large star tip and pipe decorative swirls all over the cream. Decorate with the candy coffee beans and strips of orange peel.

2099. HAZELNUT BAVARIAN CREAM
Bavarese alle nocciole

1 recipe Vanilla Bavarian Cream [No. 2094]
¾ cup hazelnuts or filberts, ground to a powder
4 tablespoons maraschino liqueur

Grind the nuts in the meat grinder, using the finest blade (or place in blender, ¼ cup at a time, and whirl at high speed until pulverized). Mix the ground nuts with the maraschino liqueur. Make the bavarian as indicated in No. 2094. Add the ground nuts and maraschino mixture to the custard just before the whipped cream is folded in. Proceed exactly as directed in No. 2094. *Serves* 6.

NOTE: If desired, ¾ cup Italian macaroons (dry almond macaroons), crushed, may be substituted for the nuts. Whichever is used, the bavarian may be decorated as follows:

1 cup heavy cream, whipped
1 teaspoon vanilla extract (or 1 tablespoon maraschino)
2 tablespoons superfine sugar
10 candied cherries
4 tablespoons Praline powder [*see* No. 2290]

Whip the cream in a chilled bowl and flavor it with the vanilla (or maraschino) and sugar. Place in a pastry bag fitted with a large star tip, and pipe decorative swirls all over the cream. Decorate with candied cherries and dust the sides with the Praline powder.

2100. NESSELRODE PUDDING
Budino Nesselrode

This version does not contain the traditional rum-soaked fruits, and resembles a chestnut bavarian. It is, none-theless, delicious.

1 pound chestnuts
2 cups milk
Pinch salt
1-inch piece of vanilla bean
1 recipe Vanilla Bavarian Cream [No 2094]
½ cup heavy cream, whipped
1 tablespoon superfine sugar
4 marrons glacés, cut in sections
8 candied cherries

Skin the chestnuts as described in No. 2081. Cook them in the milk with the salt and vanilla bean for 30 minutes, or until tender. Drain them, discard the vanilla, and press the cooked chestnuts through a fine sieve. Let cool to room temperature. Prepare the bavarian, and fold in the chestnut purée just before the whipped cream is folded in. Pour into a lightly dampened mold and chill for 5 hours or more. Unmold by dipping the mold in hot water for 1 or 2 seconds, taking care that the water does not overflow over the sides of the mold, and turn out onto a serving platter. Whip the cream and superfine sugar in a chilled bowl until stiff, put it into a pastry bag fitted with a medium star tip, and pipe decorative swirls of cream over the surface of the pudding. Decorate further with the marrons and

699

cherries, and place in the refrigerator until serving time. *Serves 6 to 8.*

NOTE: If desired, rum-soaked fruit may be added. Soak ¼ cup chopped candied fruits (pineapple, citron, orange peel, etc.) in 3 tablespoons dark rum for 2 hours and fold into the chestnut purée before it is added to the bavarian mixture. Chill, and proceed as indicated above.

2101. ORANGE BAVARIAN CREAM
Bavarese all'arancia

1 recipe Vanilla Bavarian Cream [No. 2094], omitting the vanilla bean, and dissolving the unflavored gelatin in ⅓ cup strained orange juice
Grated rind of 1½ oranges (no white part)

Make the bavarian as indicated in No. 2094, but instead of steeping the vanilla bean in the hot milk, add ⅔ of the grated orange peel and steep for 15 minutes. Proceed exactly as indicated in No. 2094. Add the remaining orange peel to the whipped cream before it is folded into the custard, and continue as directed in No. 2094. *Serves 6.*

NOTE: If desired, the bavarian may be garnished as follows after it has been unmolded:

1 cup heavy cream, whipped
1 tablespoon orange flower water (or 1 teaspoon orange extract)
2 tablespoons superfine sugar
1 navel orange, separated into segments
1 cup sugar
⅓ cup water

Cook the sugar and water in a small, heavy saucepan until it reaches the large thread stage (219° on the candy thermometer). Add the orange segments and poach them for 2 minutes. Remove the segments with a slotted spoon and cook the syrup until it reaches the hard crack stage (289° on the candy thermometer). Remove the pan at once from the fire before the syrup begins to color, and place the pan in a large pan of boiling water. Working rapidly, dip each orange segment in the hot syrup until well coated, using tongs for this procedure as the syrup can cause a serious burn if it touches the skin. Place each segment on a sheet of lightly oiled aluminum foil (or wax paper) after it has been dipped, and allow to cool thoroughly. Whip the cream in a chilled bowl and flavor it with the orange flower water (or vanilla) and sugar. Place it in a pastry bag fitted with a large star tip and pipe decorative swirls all over the bavarian. Decorate with the glacéed orange segments.

2102. STRAWBERRY BAVARIAN CREAM
Bavarese alle fragole

1 recipe Vanilla Bavarian Cream [No. 2094], increasing unflavored gelatin to 1½ envelopes
1½ cups crushed strawberries
½ cup superfine sugar (if using frozen berries, omit sugar)
½ cup whole strawberries (the smallest obtainable), hulled

Make the Vanilla Bavarian Cream exactly as indicated in No. 2094. Mix the sugar with the crushed berries, and add them to the custard just before the whipped cream is folded in. Fold in the whole strawberries just before the mixture is poured into the mold. *Serves 6.*

NOTE: If desired, the bavarian may be garnished as follows after it has been unmolded:

1 cup heavy cream, whipped
1 teaspoon vanilla extract
4 tablespoons superfine sugar
15 perfect whole strawberries

Whip the cream in a chilled bowl and flavor it with the vanilla and 2 tablespoons of the sugar. Place it in a pastry bag fitted with a large star tip and pipe decorative swirls all over the bavarian. Dip the strawberries in the rest of the sugar, coating them well, and stud the cream-decorated bavarian with them.

CUSTARD
Crema

Custard is not difficult to make if it is not allowed to come to a boil. Once it does, the danger of curdling is almost unavoidable. A curdled custard can sometimes be saved by removing it at once from the heat and beating into it 1 very cold egg yolk beaten with 3 or 4

tablespoons of very cold heavy cream. However, to avoid this unhappy situation, the following steps must be followed. 1.) Use a very heavy cast-iron enamel saucepan. 2.) Keep the flame as low as possible. 3.) Stir constantly with a wooden spoon or wire whisk, scraping the bottom and sides of the pan at each stir. 4.) Remove from fire as soon as custard coats the spoon and becomes thick (in other words, when it reaches 165° on the candy thermometer). If these steps are followed, a successful custard will result.

Baked custards should be placed in a very slow oven, and the pan in which they are baked should be placed in a pan of hot water, deep enough to reach ²/₃ up the sides of the custard container. The custard should be baked only until the center is no longer liquid. It will still be a little shaky, but internal heat will finish the cooking once the custard has been removed from the oven. Inserting a knife in the center to see if it comes out clean is not advisable. If it is left in the oven until this stage is reached, there is danger of overcooking, and this results in the custard becoming watery or separating into curds. Chill a baked custard for at least 6 hours, and by that time it will be firm enough to unmold. Do not, however, place it in the refrigerator until it is completely cool.

2103. BAKED CUSTARD
Crema rovesciata alla vaniglia

This is a master recipe used as the basis for many variations and adaptations in other recipes.

- 1 quart rich milk
- 2-inch piece of vanilla bean (or 2 teaspoons vanilla extract)
- 4 eggs
- 8 egg yolks
- 1 cup sugar
- Pinch salt
- 1 tablespoon butter, softened

Place the vanilla bean (if used) in a heavy saucepan and bring to a simmer over a low flame. Remove from stove at once, cover pan, and let steep for 15 minutes (if not using vanilla bean, merely bring the milk to the scalding point). Beat the eggs, yolks, sugar, and salt together until very pale in color. Pour in the milk, stirring well (add the vanilla extract, if used, at this point), and when well mixed, pour through a fine strainer into a deep, round 2-quart baking dish, which has been greased with the butter. Place the dish in a pan of hot water deep enough to reach ²/₃ up the sides of the dish. Place the pan in a 300° oven and bake for

1 hour and 10 minutes, or until the center of the custard is only slightly shaky. Remove from oven, lift out of the water bath, and let the custard cool to room temperature. Place in refrigerator and chill for at least 8 hours. To unmold it, run a sharp knife around the edge to loosen it, place a serving platter over the baking dish, and reverse the dish and custard with a sharp motion. The custard should then drop onto the dish. Lift the baking dish off and serve. *Serves 6.*

NOTE: Do not let the water in the pan boil. If it begins to simmer add an ice cube to it. The custard may also be served in its baking dish, if you do not wish to unmold it.

2104. ALMOND CUSTARD CAPRICCIO DI DIANA
Crema rovesciata "Capriccio di Diana"

- 1 recipe Baked Custard [No. 2103]
- 1 tablespoon butter, softened
- ¹/₂ cup Praline powder [*see* No. 2290]
- 1 cup heavy cream, whipped
- 1 teaspon vanilla extract
- 2 tablespoons candied pineapple, finely diced

Prepare the custard as indicated in No. 2103. Grease the mold with butter, strain the custard into it, and bake as indicated in No. 2103. Chill for at least 8 hours, and unmold as indicated in No. 2103. Whip the cream in a chilled bowl and flavor it with ¹/₄ cup of the Praline powder and the vanilla. Place it in a pastry bag fitted with a large star tip, and pipe decorative swirls all over the custard. Sprinkle with the remaining Praline, and decorate with the candied pineapple. Chill until served. *Serves 6 to 8.*

2105. CARAMEL CUSTARD
Crema al caramello

- ¹/₂ cup sugar
- 3 tablespoons water
- 1 quart rich milk
- 2-inch piece of vanilla bean (or 2 teaspoons vanilla extract)
- ³/₄ cup sugar
- 4 eggs
- 8 egg yolks
- Pinch salt

Place the sugar and water in a small, heavy saucepan and stir for a few minutes until the sugar is somewhat dissolved. Place the pan over medium heat and cook without stirring until the sugar begins to turn straw colored (all the water has evaporated and the sugar is now caramelizing). Tilt the pan in all directions to ensure even cooking. Do not let the sugar burn, and remove the pan from the stove the moment the sugar has turned a deep ruddy gold (if it turns dark brown, it has burned and will be bitter). Immediately pour it into a 2-quart mold, and lift the mold (using asbestos potholders or gloves) and tilt in all directions until the caramel forms an even coating over the inside of the mold. This must be done quickly, as caramel hardens with great rapidity, and also with caution, as the sugar is very hot and can cause a bad burn. Place the mold aside to cool while you prepare the custard exactly as directed in Baked Custard [No. 2103]. Pour into the caramel-lined mold, and proceed exactly as in No. 2103, chilling for at least 8 hours. *Serves* 6.

NOTE: The custard will be very easy to turn out after it has chilled, because the caramel has melted and lubricates the mold.

2106. CARAMEL CUSTARD WITH WILD STRAWBERRY COMPOTE
Crema al caramello con composta di fragoline di bosco

1 recipe Caramel Custard [No. 2105], chilled and
    unmolded
1 pint wild strawberries, hulled (or 1 pint smallest
    available cultivated strawberries, washed, hulled,
    and cut in sections if large)
¾ cup sugar (less, if berries are sweet)
¼ cup water
Juice of ½ lemon
3 tablespoons kirsch

Keep the unmolded custard in the refrigerator until serving time. Pick over the strawberries and place them in a shallow glass serving bowl. Cook the sugar and water in a small, heavy saucepan until it reaches the large thread stage (219° on the candy thermometer). Remove from stove, let cool for 10 minutes, add the lemon juice, and then pour the hot syrup over the berries, mixing gently but thoroughly. Place in the refrigerator until well chilled and add the kirsch just before serving. Serve the compote separately with the caramel custard. *Serves 6 to 8.*

NOTE: For those who may grow their own "wild" strawberries (the tiny variety), or who may be using this cookbook in Italy and France, where wild strawberries may be purchased (in season) at any street corner, this recipe is given in its original form. Im-

ported wild strawberries are flown to the United States in season (late spring and early summer) and are available at specialty food shops. However, they are so expensive that nobody would dream of using them in this manner—they should just be served as is. Local strawberries make an excellent substitute, especially if one lives near a strawberry farm and can put in a special order for the smallest, reddest berries.

CUP CUSTARDS
Creme in tazzette

Individual cup custards do not have to be as firm as baked custards, and therefore may be made with fewer egg yolks. Custard cups usually hold from ½ cup to ¾ cup. The same principles applicable to the temperature of baked custards (*see* page 701) apply to cup custards. However, after placing the cups in the pan of hot water, they may be covered with aluminum foil and a slash cut in the foil to let the steam escape. This prevents the tops from becoming baked before the rest of the custard is done.

2107. VANILLA CUP CUSTARD
Crema alla vaniglia in tazzette

2¼ cups rich milk
1-inch piece of vanilla bean (or 1 teaspoon vanilla
    extract)
½ cup sugar
Pinch salt
1 egg
3 egg yolks

Prepare exactly as in Baked Custard [No. 2103]. Pour into custard cups and set them in a pan of hot water deep enough to reach ⅔ up their sides. Cover all loosely with a sheet of aluminum foil, slashed in several places to allow the steam to escape, and place in a 300° oven for 20 minutes. Remove from oven, lift out of the water bath, and let cool to room temperature before placing in the refrigerator. Chill for 2 hours before serving. *Makes about 6 cup custards.*

2108. COFFEE CUP CUSTARD
Crema al caffè in tazzette

2¼ cups milk
⅓ cup freshly ground coffee (all-purpose grind)

1-inch piece of vanilla bean (or 1 teaspoon vanilla
    extract)
1 egg
3 yolks
½ cup sugar
Pinch salt

Pour the milk into a small, heavy saucepan and add the
ground coffee and vanilla bean (if used). Place over
low heat, bring to a simmer, remove from stove, cover
pan, and let steep for 15 minutes. Beat egg, egg yolks,
salt, and sugar until well mixed, and gradually add
the coffee-infused milk, pouring it through a strainer
lined with a double thickness of cheesecloth (if using
vanilla extract, add it now). Pour into custard cups
and proceed as directed in Vanilla Cup Custard
[No. 2107]. *Makes about 6 cup custards.*

2109. CUSTARD DELIZIOSA WITH RASPBERRY SAUCE
Crema deliziosa con salsa di lamponi

3 cups rich milk
2-inch piece of vanilla bean (or 1 teaspoon vanilla
    extract)
6 eggs
⅔ scant cup sugar
Pinch salt
6 dry ladyfingers (or 6 Savoyard Ladyfingers—
    No. 1946), crumbled
6 large almond macaroons (Italian macaroons, if
    available), dry enough to grate
2 tablespoons butter, softened
1½ cups raspberry preserves (*see* Note below)
4 tablespoons kirsch

Place the milk and vanilla bean (if used) in a heavy
saucepan over low heat and bring to a simmer. Remove
from stove, cover pan, and let steep for 15 minutes
(if not using vanilla bean, merely bring milk to the
scalding point). Beat the eggs with the sugar and salt

until well mixed. Pour the milk into the eggs (discarding the vanilla bean) and mix well (if using vanilla
extract, add at this point). Pour the mixture through a
sieve lined with a double thickness of cheesecloth, to
eliminate any foam, into another bowl. Mix in the
crumbled ladyfingers and macaroons and stir the
mixture for a few minutes. Butter a 1½-quart casserole
or Pyrex baking dish with 1 tablespoon of the butter,
pour in the custard, dot the surface with the remaining
butter, and proceed as directed in Baked Custard
[No. 2103]. After the custard has chilled, run a sharp
knife all around the edge to loosen it, and unmold it
on a serving platter. Put back in the refrigerator while
the sauce is being made.

Heat the raspberry preserves in a small saucepan,
press through a fine sieve to eliminate the seeds, and
mix with the kirsch. Let cool for 15 minutes, then
remove the unmolded custard from the refrigerator,
pour the sauce over it, and serve. *Serves 6.*

NOTE: If desired, the sauce may be made with frozen
raspberries:

1 box frozen raspberries, thawed
½ cup raspberry jelly
4 tablespoons kirsch
Juice of ½ lemon, strained

Strain the raspberries carefully, leaving the berries
in the strainer (do not crush them) and keeping their
liquid in a small bowl. Heat the raspberry jelly in a
small saucepan over low heat until it has completely
melted. Stir in the juice strained from the raspberries,
and cook the mixture until it is somewhat thickened.
Remove from stove and cool for 15 minutes. Press the
raspberries through a fine sieve to eliminate the seeds
and mix the pulp with the sauce. Stir in the kirsch and
lemon juice, and pour the sauce over the custard.

2110. CUSTARD PUDDING
Custard Pudding

*This is a favorite English dessert (a somewhat less rich
version of Baked Custard—No. 2103) which may be
served either warm or cold. It is not unmolded, but
served in its baking dish. Because it is so simple, and not
at all rich, it is particularly suitable for small children
and invalids.*

1 quart milk, scalded
6 eggs
½ cup sugar
Pinch salt
1 teaspoon vanilla extract

Scald the milk in a heavy saucepan. Beat the eggs with the sugar and salt, and when well blended, slowly pour in the hot milk. Mix well, add the vanilla, and pour into a 1½-quart oven-proof casserole or round Pyrex baking dish. Place in a pan of hot water deep enough to reach ⅔ up the sides of the dish, and bake in a 300° oven for 1 hour, or until the center of the custard shakes only slightly. Remove from oven, lift out of the water bath, and let cool at room temperature. Serve warm, or chill for 3 or 4 hours in the refrigerator after the custard has cooled to room temperature. *Serves* 6.

2111. ENGLISH CUSTARD
Crema inglese

This is also known as "boiled custard." Of course, it should never be boiled. See page 700 for rules pertaining to custards cooked on top of the stove.

2½ cups rich milk (or ½ cup heavy cream and 2 cups milk)
2-inch piece of vanilla bean (or 1½ teaspoons vanilla extract)
8 egg yolks
Pinch salt
¾ cup sugar

Place the milk and vanilla bean (if used) in a small, heavy saucepan. Bring to a simmer over low heat, remove from the stove, cover pan, and let steep for 15 minutes. (If not using vanilla bean, merely bring milk to the scalding point.) Beat the yolks with the salt and sugar until well mixed. Discard the vanilla bean, and pour the milk slowly into the egg/sugar mixture. Stir until well blended. Pour the mixture into a heavy enamel saucepan (an enameled cast-iron pan is best) and place over very low heat. Stir constantly (*see* page 700 for detailed instructions) until the mixture thickens and coats the spoon. Do *not* ever let it boil. Remove from stove the moment it is thick; if let cook too long it will curdle (*see* page 700 for the remedy for curdled custard). Pour into a bowl (add the vanilla extract, if you are using it, at this point), and stir every so often until it has cooled to room temperature. (The stirring prevents a crust from forming.) Cover the bowl, and chill in the refrigerator. *Makes about 3¾ cups.*

2112. FLOATING ISLAND
Uova alla neve

In this version of an old favorite the meringue "islands" are poached, which makes them more delicate.

5 egg whites
Pinch cream of tartar
1½ cups sugar
2 teaspoons vanilla extract
1 quart rich milk
Pinch salt
2 tablespoons cornstarch
5 egg yolks

Place the egg whites and cream of tartar in a large bowl (preferably of unlined copper) and beat with a wire whisk until foamy. Add 1 cup of the sugar, a little at a time, beat until the whites stand in soft peaks, and then beat in 1 teaspoon of the vanilla. Heat the milk to simmering in a wide, shallow enamel pan (a deep enamel skillet may be used). When it simmers, lower heat and drop in the meringue by tablespoonsful. Poach for 1 minute, turn with a skimmer or slotted spoon and poach for 1 minute on the other side. Remove poached meringues with a slotted spoon and set them on a well-dampened cloth or dish towel. Mix the rest of the sugar with the salt, cornstarch, and yolks. Slowly add in the milk in which the meringues were poached, pouring it through a fine sieve. Place the custard in a heavy saucepan over medium heat, and stir with a wire whisk until it thickens. If it becomes lumpy, remove from stove and whip vigorously with the whisk until smooth. Return to stove and stir until it begins to simmer. Remove from stove at once, add the remaining vanilla, and pour through a fine sieve into a bowl. Cool to room temperature, stirring from time to time to prevent a crust from forming on the surface. Chill in the refrigerator for 2 hours, then pour the custard into a wide, shallow glass serving bowl. Top with the poached meringues, and chill for another 2 hours. *Serves* 6.

NOTE: If desired, this may be made with English Custard [No. 2111], and the milk used for poaching the meringues may be employed in some other pudding or even for cakes or brioches.

2113. FLOATING ISLAND IN A MOLD
Uova alla neve in stampo

This consists of a large center "island" surrounded by custard, rather than a lot of little floating meringues. It is actually more of a "floating iceberg," although it does not actually float, since it is too big.

4 egg whites
Pinch cream of tartar
¾ cup superfine sugar

704

1 teaspoon vanilla extract
1 tablespoon butter, softened
1 recipe English Custard [No. 2111], chilled
3 tablespoons kirsch

Beat the egg whites and the cream of tartar in a large bowl (preferably of unlined copper). When they are foamy add all but 2 tablespoons of the sugar, a little at a time, continue beating until they stand in soft peaks, and beat the vanilla into the meringue. Butter a 1-quart melon mold or round-bottomed oven-proof bowl, sprinkle in the remaining sugar, tilt in all directions to coat the inside well, and tap out the excess. Fill mold with the meringue by spoonsful, and when it is filled bring it down sharply on the table once or twice to expel any air pockets. Cover the mold tightly with a piece of aluminum foil, slashed in several places to permit steam to escape, and place the mold in a pan of hot water deep enough to reach ⅔ up the sides of the mold (since the meringue is light, and the mold may not be heavy if it is a tin one, the water level may have to be reduced to prevent the mold from floating in the water). Place in a 300° oven and bake for 45 minutes. Remove from oven, lift out of the water bath, remove the foil, and let stand for 5 minutes. Unmold in the center of a wide, shallow glass serving dish and let cool to room temperature. Flavor the custard with the kirsch and pour it around the meringue. Place the dish in the refrigerator and chill for 2 hours or more. *Serves* 6.

NOTE: If a lighter custard is desired, reserve a few spoonsful of meringue from the mold and fold them into the custard.

2114. MOLDED CUSTARD CREAM
Crema inglese con gelatina

1 recipe English Custard [No. 2111]
1½ envelopes unflavored gelatin, softened in ⅓ cup cold milk

Prepare the English custard as directed in No. 2111. Add the softened gelatin just as the custard begins to thicken. Continue stirring, and when properly thickened, pour into a moistened 1-quart mold. Chill in refrigerator for 5 hours, or until solid, and unmold by dipping the mold in hot water for 1 second (being careful the water does not spill over the top of the mold onto the custard) and turn out on a serving platter. Serve with stewed fruit or any sauce desired. *Serves* 6.

NOTE: This is the type of custard that frequently forms the base for bavarians [Nos. 2094–2102], etc.

2115. VIENNESE CUSTARD
Crema alla viennese

Because this has flour in it, the custard may be allowed to simmer for a while, since the flour lessens the chance of curdling.

2¼ cups rich milk
2-inch piece of vanilla bean (or 2 teaspoons vanilla extract)
3 tablespoons flour
½ cup sugar
Pinch salt
3 egg yolks
6 Meringues [No. 2009], crumbled
12 candied violets (or 12 small pieces candied fruit)

Place the milk in a small, heavy saucepan, add the vanilla bean (if used), place over low heat, and bring to a simmer. Remove from stove, cover pan, and let steep for 15 minutes (if not using vanilla bean, merely bring milk to the scalding point). Mix the flour, sugar, and salt in a bowl. Slowly pour on the 2 cups of hot milk (discarding the vanilla bean), stirring with a wire whisk to avoid lumps. Place the mixture in a heavy saucepan and place over medium heat, whisking and stirring until thick. It will probably be lumpy, so when it comes to a simmer, remove from stove for a minute and whisk vigorously to eliminate the lumps. Return to stove and stir for 5 minutes. Beat the yolks with the rest of the milk, and slowly pour the thickened flour/milk mixture into them, stirring all the time. Mix well, return to pan, and stir constantly over low heat until it begins to simmer. Remove from stove at once and pour through a fine sieve (to eliminate any remaining flour lumps) into a glass serving bowl. Stir in the crumbled meringues, cover bowl with plastic food wrap or aluminum foil, and place in the refrigerator for 4 hours. When ready to serve garnish with the candied violets. *Serves* 6.

2116. ZABAGLIONE
Zabaione al marsala

This is one of the most famous of Italian desserts. Quick to make, it is a fine "emergency" dessert. The "Italian" spelling currently used in the United States is no longer employed in Italy, as it is considered archaic. Zabaglione is very low in calories, since each helping contains but 1 egg yolk (about 70 calories), 1 tablespoon sugar (50 calories), and the Marsala has lost most of its alcohol by evaporation over the heat. Thus, the total calorie

705

count for a single portion of this rich-tasting dessert is only about 125–130 calories.

6 egg yolks
6 tablespoons superfine sugar
1 tablespoon warm water
²⁄₃ cup sweet Marsala wine

Place the first 3 ingredients in the top of a double boiler (it should be a round-bottomed container, but if none is available, use a heat-proof bowl that will fit into the top of a pot) and place over hot (not boiling) water. The bottom of the container holding the eggs should never touch the water. Beat with a wire whisk, scraping the sides and bottom, constantly until the mixture begins to foam up. Gradually add the Marsala in a steady trickle. Continue beating until the mixture forms very soft mounds. Immediately remove it from the heat and spoon it into 6 champagne glasses (with solid stems—do not use the hollow-stem variety) or shallow sherbet glasses. Serve at once, as it separates if left standing more than 5 minutes.

NOTE: If desired, a dusting of powdered cinnamon may be placed over each helping. Madeira or Port wine may be used, even sweet sherry, but Marsala is traditional.

2117. COLD ZABAGLIONE
Zabaione ghiacciato al Marsala

Since regular Zabaglione will not stand without separating, this is an excellent recipe for those who wish for the taste and texture of Zabaglione but desire a cold dessert. It makes an excellent filling for small cream puffs or eclairs, and might even be used to fill a cake.

7 egg yolks
¾ cup superfine sugar
1 cup sweet Marsala wine
½ teaspoon vanilla extract
Grated peel of ½ lemon (no white part)
Pinch cinnamon
1 cup heavy cream, whipped

Make the Zabaglione with the first 3 ingredients (no water here) as directed in No. 2116. As soon as it has reached the point where it forms soft mounds (as opposed to soft peaks in a meringue), remove it from the stove and continue beating until cool. Here, an electric beater may be used, although a whisk must be used in the basic preparation, since it is far more efficient in scraping the sides and bottom of the pan, and incorporates much more air into the preparation. When cooled to room temperature, add the vanilla,

lemon peel, and cinnamon. Place the bowl in a larger bowl filled with cracked ice, and continue beating until the mixture is chilled through. Beat the cream in a chilled bowl until stiff and fold it into the ice-cold Zabaglione. Pour into tall glasses (or into a glass serving bowl) and chill until ready to serve. *Serves 8.*

MOUSSES
Moscovite

Mousses are somewhat similar to bavarians, except that they are almost frozen. The traditional method is to pack the mold (preferably a tin mold) in cracked ice mixed with rock salt (like ice cream). Naturally, the mold must be tightly covered to prevent the salted ice from leaking in. However, with the modern convenience of freezers, the mold may be merely placed in the freezer for 2 or more hours, then unmolded (the same way as a bavarian: by dipping the mold for 1 or 2 seconds in hot water—taking care that the water does not spill over onto the top of the mousse—and unmolding on a serving platter).

2118. APRICOT MOUSSE
Moscovita di albicocche

4 cups apricot pulp (made from peeled, stoned, dead-ripe apricots passed through a food mill)
1½ cups superfine sugar (more, if fruit is tart)
2 envelopes unflavored gelatin softened in ¼ cup water and 1½ tablespoons lemon juice
¼ cup kirsch
2 cups heavy cream, whipped

Take 1 cup of the apricot pulp, the sugar, and softened gelatin, and place in a small saucepan over medium heat. Stir until the sugar and gelatin are completely dissolved. Remove from heat, mix with the rest of the pulp and the kirsch, and let cool to room temperature. Whip the cream until stiff in a chilled bowl, and fold it into the apricot mixture. Moisten a 2-quart tin mold and fill it with the mixture. Put the cover on the mold (or cover it tightly with aluminum foil) and place in the freezing compartment of the refrigerator (or in a bowl of cracked ice) for 5 hours (*see* above). Unmold, and serve at once. *Serves 6 to 8.*

NOTE: Canned, peeled apricots packed in syrup may be used. Increase the lemon juice to 4 tablespoons and taste the pulp before adding sugar to taste (about ½ cup should be sufficient, but remember that iced desserts taste less sweet once they are frozen.)

2119. CHERRY MOUSSE
Moscovita di ciliege

4 cups cherry purée (made from ripe sweet cherries, pitted and passed through a food mill)
1½ cups superfine sugar
¼ cup cherry brandy (or Cherry Heering)
2 envelopes unflavored gelatin softened in ¼ cup cold water and 2 tablespoons lemon juice
2 cups heavy cream, whipped

Prepare exactly as directed for Apricot Mousse [No. 2118]. *Serves 6 to 8.*

NOTE: Canned cherries packed in syrup may be used. Follow the same instructions given in the Note for Apricot Mousse [No. 2118].

2120. CUSTARD MOUSSE
Moscovita alla crema

1 recipe English Custard [No. 2111]
2 envelopes unflavored gelatin softened in ½ cup cold milk
2 cups heavy cream, whipped

Prepare the custard as directed in No. 2111. Just before you remove it from the stove, stir in the softened gelatin and stir until it is dissolved. Pour it through a fine sieve into a bowl and place it in a large bowl filled with cracked ice. Stir until the custard begins to thicken,

and remove it from the ice at once. Whip the cream until stiff and fold it into the custard. Pour into a 2-quart metal mold and chill in the freezer for 5 hours, or packed in ice. Unmold before serving. *Serves 6 to 8.*

NOTE: If desired, this may be served with any crushed, sweetened fruit or fruit sauce.

2121. PINEAPPLE MOUSSE
Moscovita di ananasso

4 cups pineapple pulp (made by grinding fresh, peeled, and cored pineapple in the meat grinder, using the coarse blade)
1¾ cups superfine sugar (or less if fruit is very sweet)
¼ cup Curaçao liqueur
2 cups heavy cream, whipped

Stir the pineapple pulp with the sugar until sugar is dissolved. Add the Curaçao. Whip the cream in a chilled bowl until stiff and fold into the pineapple mixture. Moisten a 2-quart mold, and pour the mixture in. Place in the freezing compartment of the refrigerator (or pack in salted cracked ice, making sure the mold is hermetically sealed) for 5 to 6 hours. Unmold on a serving platter just before serving. *Serves 6.*

NOTE: Since fresh pineapple contains an enzyme that prevents gelatin from setting, this dessert must be frozen to keep its shape. If you wish to use gelatin, then canned pineapple must be used. Follow the recipe for Apricot Mousse [No. 2118], reducing the sugar to ½ cup and substituting 4 cups well-drained canned pineapple pulp for the apricots.

2122. ST. AMBROEUS MOUSSE
St. Ambroeus

The Café St. Ambroeus in Milan is the most fashionable place to take afternoon tea. The pastries, tea sandwiches, and ice creams served there are superlative. This elaborate dessert epitomizes North Italian cuisine at its finest.

The base:

9 egg yolks

¾ cup plus 1 tablespoon superfine sugar

2 tablespoons ice water

1⅓ cups best quality sweet Marsala wine

2 envelopes unflavored gelatin, softened in ⅓ cup sweet Marsala wine

Grated rind of 1 lemon (no white part)

1½ teaspoons vanilla extract

Large pinch cinnamon

1½ cups heavy cream, whipped

The garnishes:

6 dozen (approximately) Cat's Tongues [No. 1930]

2 cups heavy cream, whipped

2 tablespoons superfine sugar

1 teaspoon vanilla extract

1 pint strawberries (the smallest available—wild ones, if possible)

4 thin wedges candied citron

Chocolate horns:

5 egg whites

1 cup superfine sugar

¼ teaspoon salt

1 cup blanched almonds [see No. 2280], ground to a powder

½ cup dark powdered cocoa

¾ cup triple-sifted cake flour

⅔ cup Clarified Butter [No. 102]

½ pound best-quality bittersweet chocolate

2 tablespoons brandy

2 tablespoons hot water

The base should be made first. Place the yolks, sugar, and ice water in the top of a very large double boiler (or into a large, round-bottomed bowl) and beat with a wire whisk until the mixture begins to become fluffy. Place the pan (or bowl) over hot (not boiling) water, and continue to beat until the mixture has increased considerably in volume, and forms a slowly dissolving ribbon when the beater is lifted above the pan. Begin to add the Marsala at this point, pouring it on in a fine stream. When all the wine has been added, beat in the softened gelatin, and beat for 2 minutes longer (or until the mixture is light, foamy, and begins to hold its shape—do not cook too long, or the egg yolks will begin to curdle). Remove the pan (or bowl) from the hot water and place it in a large bowl filled with cracked ice. Add the lemon rind, vanilla, and cinnamon, and beat over the ice until the mixture is room temperature. Remove from ice and whip the cream in a chilled bowl until stiff. Return the egg mixture to the ice, and beat until it becomes quite stiff but still loose enough to beat. Immediately remove from ice and fold in the whipped cream. Moisten 3 charlotte molds of decreasing size (or any similar straight-sided containers): 8 inches, 6 inches, and 4 inches (or use a 3-quart cone-shaped mold). Pour the mixture into the molds (or mold) and place in the refrigerator.

Make the Cat's Tongues (or purchase them at a reliable bakery) and set aside. Make the chocolate horns by beating the egg whites and salt in a large bowl (preferably of unlined copper) with a wire whisk until foamy, gradually beat in the sugar, and beat until they stand in soft peaks. Grind the almonds in meat grinder, using the finest blade (or place them in the blender, ½ cup at a time, and whirl at high speed until pulverized). Add the almonds, cocoa, and flour, alternately in small amounts, folding and cutting them into the whites. Finally, fold in the clarified butter, pouring it on in a thin stream. Mix only until the batter is blended. Butter 2 large baking sheets with ½-inch sides, line them with sheets of wax paper, butter that, and dust the surfaces with flour, making sure that they are well covered, and tap out the excess. Divide the batter among the 2 pans, smoothing it out with a moistened spatula. The batter must be very thin, no more than a coating. Place the pans in a 300° oven and bake until the batter is set but not yet browned. Remove the pans and immediately cut the sheets of dough into 3-inch squares with a sharp knife. Return pans to oven and bake until the dough begins to crisp. Take 1 of the pans from the oven and roll each square into a little cornucopia, using the handle of a wooden spoon to roll it around. This must be done while the dough is still warm; if it cools, return pan to the oven for a few seconds to become flexible again. When the first batch has been rolled, remove the other pan from the oven and roll those squares into cornucopias. Cool them on cake racks. When they are cool, melt the chocolate in a small, deep bowl placed over hot (not boiling) water. Add the brandy and water and stir until mixed. Keep the bowl in the hot water but remove it from stove. Take each cornucopia up in a pair of tongs and dip it into the chocolate, coating the outside thoroughly (if some gets into the inside, that will not matter). As each has been dipped, place it on a platter covered with wax paper. When all have been dipped, place the platter in the refrigerator.

After the cold base has remained in the refrigerator for 5 hours it may be unmolded and the dessert assembled. Dip the molds (or mold) into hot water for 1 second, taking care the water does not spill over onto the surface of the preparation. Unmold the first mold on a round serving platter, unmold the second on top of it, and the third on top of the second. You will now have a 3-tiered construction (if using the cone-shaped mold, you will, of course, have a single unit). Whip the cream until stiff in a chilled bowl, flavor it with the sugar and vanilla, and place it in a pastry bag fitted with a star tip. Fill each of the chocolate-covered cornucopias with the cream (or fill them with 1 cup of Cold Zabaglione—No. 2117). Lean some of them all around the base of the molded preparation, making sure they touch one another. Pipe a little of the cream in the spaces at the bottom. Place a pair of Cat's Tongues butterfly-fashion on top of the cornucopias, leaning them against the molded preparation, and pipe some cream between each pair (*see* photo facing page 736) top with another circle of cornucopias, then a ring of Cat's Tongues (this time place flat against the molded dessert). End with a final ring of cornucopias. Pipe some cream between and against each Cat's Tongue or cornucopia, to "cement" it against the mold. Crown the creation with a large dollop of cream, and set the slices of citron alternating with Cat's Tongues into the top to form its peak. Top each cornucopia with a strawberry (if the berries are big, cut them into sections) and place a few between the citron wedges. Serve at once, or no more than 2 hours after putting it together (if left for a longer time, the Cat's Tongues will become soggy). *Serves* 10 *to* 12.

NOTE: The photo facing page 736 will give you an approximate idea of the appearance of the assembled dessert. To serve, begin at the top and work down.

2123. STRAWBERRY MOUSSE
Moscovita di fragole

4 cups strawberry purée (made by passing fresh
    strawberries through the food mill)
1½ cups superfine sugar (more if berries are tart)
2 envelopes unflavored gelatin, softened in ⅓ cup cold
    water and 2 tablespoons lemon juice
¼ cup Strega liqueur
2 cups heavy cream, whipped

Make exactly as directed in Apricot Mousse [No. 2118]. *Serves* 6.

NOTE: Frozen strawberries may be used, if desired.

Use the kind that are not packed in syrup, if possible; otherwise decrease sugar to ½ cup and increase lemon juice to 4 tablespoonsful.

2124. VANILLA MOUSSE
Mousse dolce di vaniglia

7 egg yolks
1 egg
⅔ cup superfine sugar
Pinch salt
2 cups heavy cream, whipped
2 teaspoons vanilla extract

Beat the egg yolks, egg, sugar, and salt with a wire whisk in the top part of a double boiler (this should be round-bottomed; if such a utensil is not available, use a large heat-proof bowl that will fit over a pan of water). When thick and lemon colored, place over hot (not boiling) water and beat constantly (the water should never touch the container holding the eggs) until it begins to thicken. Remove from stove and continue beating until cooled to room temperature. Place the bowl in another bowl containing cracked ice, and beat until the eggs are well chilled. Beat the cream until stiff in a chilled bowl, add the vanilla, and fold into the eggs. Moisten a 2-quart metal mold and pour in the mousse. Chill as directed on page 706. Unmold just before serving. *Serves* 6.

2125. WHIPPED CREAM SORRISO DI MARIA
Panna montata "sorriso di Maria"

This is neither a mousse nor a bavarian, but it is delicate and very light, and should prove a great success as it is relatively quick and easy to assemble.

2 cups heavy cream, whipped
⅓ cup vanilla sugar [*see* No. 2296]
1 tablespoon grated orange peel (no white part)
8 marrons glacés, crumbled
4 tablespoons semi-sweet chocolate, shaved or grated

Whip the cream until stiff in a chilled bowl. Fold in the vanilla sugar, orange peel, and crumbled marrons. Spoon into 6 champagne glasses (not the hollow-stem variety) or sherbet glasses, and sprinkle with the chocolate. Chill before serving. *Serves* 6.

709

GELATINS
Gelatine

These gelatins are exquisite, crystal-clear preparations flavored with fruits or liqueurs. They are a far cry from the powdered fruit gelatins ubiquitously present on many American tables. The following desserts provide a perfect climax for a heavy meal, and are most suitable as a sweet for a midnight supper. Since they are light and delicate, they may be also served at luncheon. Unless otherwise noted, the instructions given in the master recipe for Orange Gelatin [No. 2127] apply to all the succeeding recipes in this category.

2126. CURRANT GELATIN
Gelatina al ribes

Made with fresh currants, this is a truly seasonal (early summer) dessert. It has an exquisite flavor and the color is beautiful. One may enjoy this during other parts of the year if the recipe below is made without gelatin and frozen. The juice is then heated to a simmer and the softened gelatin is stirred in until dissolved. The best results are achieved with this recipe when ⅔ of the currants are the red variety and ⅓ the white, although all red may be used if the white are unavailable.

1¾ pounds fresh currants (⅔ red, ⅓ white), washed
1 pint fresh strawberries, washed and hulled
2 cups fresh raspberries, washed
Optional: ½ cup water
2 envelopes unflavored gelatin, softened in ⅓ cup cold water and 3 tablespoons lemon juice

The juice may be extracted from the currants by either of 2 methods. 1.) Crush the currants and berries in a large bowl with a potato masher until they have yielded all their juice. Line a colander with a triple layer of cheesecloth and place it over a large pan. Pour in the crushed fruit, gather up the cheesecloth, and squeeze until all the juice has been extracted. 2.) Pull the currants off their stems and place them and the berries in a large enamel pan. Add ½ cup of water and place over medium heat until the mixture simmers. Simmer gently until the skins burst and the juice flows freely (no more than 15 minutes), crushing and turning the mixture with a slotted spoon. Pass through cheesecloth as above.

Place the strained currant/berry juice in a large enamel pan. Add the sugar, place over medium heat, and stir until the mixture comes to a boil. Skim off

the foam until it no longer rises and turn off the heat. Add the softened gelatin and stir until dissolved. Pour into a 1½-quart mold and chill and unmold as directed for Basic Orange Gelatin [No. 2127]. *Serves 6.*

NOTE: This is perfectly delicious served with a pitcher of very heavy unsweetened cream.

2127. BASIC ORANGE GELATIN
Gelatina all'arancia

This is the master recipe for most of those that follow. The addition of egg white and a crushed eggshell ensures the crystal clarity of the final result.

2 cups cold water
1 cup plus 2 tablespoons superfine sugar
1 egg white
1 eggshell, crushed
4 tablespoons white wine
Juice of 1 lemon
2 cups fresh orange juice
2 strips lemon rind (no white part)
2 strips orange rind (no white part)
2 envelopes unflavored gelatin, softened in ⅓ cup cold water

Place the water and sugar in a heavy saucepan over medium heat, and stir until the sugar is dissolved. Beat the egg white, crushed eggshell, wine, and lemon juice in a bowl with a large fork until frothy. Add the orange juice, and lemon and orange rind. Pour in the warm sugar syrup and beat for few seconds. Pour the mixture into an enamel pot and slowly bring to a simmer over low heat. Simmer for 5 minutes, add the softened gelatin, and stir until it is dissolved. Pour the mixture into a 1½-quart mold through a sieve lined with a triple layer of cheesecloth which has been dipped in cold water and well wrung out. Place in the refrigerator and chill for at least 5 hours. Unmold by dipping the mold in hot water for 1 or 2 seconds (taking care that the water does not spill over onto the top of the gelatin), and reverse the mold on a serving platter. *Serves 6.*

NOTE: If desired, fresh fruit sections may be added to the gelatin. To keep them from sinking to the bottom of the mold, pour the strained gelatin into a bowl and set this in another bowl filled with cracked ice. Stir until it becomes thick and syrupy, and add well-chilled fruit sections of your choice. Pour into an ice-cold mold and chill as above.

To use this (or any of the other gelatins listed here) as a glaze for fruit or fruit compotes, make sure that the ingredients to be coated are well chilled. Stir the gelatin over ice as above, and when very thick (but still runny), spoon a layer over the fruit. Chill the fruit for a few minutes (keep the gelatin out of the ice, or it will harden; if it does, then place it over hot water for a few minutes, and stir until it returns to the desired consistency), and repeat the glazing process to your satisfaction.

2128. LEMON GELATIN
Gelatina al limone

3 cups cold water
1½ cups superfine sugar
1 egg white
1 eggshell, crushed
4 tablespoons white wine
Juice of 1 orange
⅔ cup lemon juice
2 strips lemon peel (no white part)
2 strips orange peel (no white part)
2 envelopes unflavored gelatin, softened in ⅓ cup
    cold water

Proceed exactly as in Basic Orange Gelatin [No. 2127]. More sugar may be added to taste if a sweeter mixture is desired. *Serves* 6.

2129. AURUM GELATIN
Gelatina all' Aurum

Same ingredients listed for Basic Orange Gelatin
    [No. 2127]
½ cup Aurum liqueur

Prepare in the same way as in Basic Orange Gelatin [No. 2127], adding the Aurum after the orange mixture has simmered for 2 minutes. *Serves* 6.

2130. BRANDY GELATIN
Gelatina al brandy

Same ingredients listed for Basic Orange Gelatin
    [No. 2127]
½ cup good brandy (or Cognac)

Prepare in the same way as Basic Orange Gelatin [No. 2127], adding the brandy after the orange mixture has simmered for 2 minutes. *Serves* 6.

2131. KIRSCH GELATIN
Gelatina al kirsch

Same ingredients listed for Basic Orange Gelatin
    [No. 2127]
½ cup kirsch

Prepare in the same way as Basic Orange Gelatin [No. 2127], adding the kirsch after the orange mixture has simmered for 2 minutes. *Serves* 6.

NOTE: 1 cup pitted fresh cherries, cooked for 10 minutes with ½ cup sugar and then chilled, may be added to the gelatin before it is poured into the mold [*see* Note for No. 2127].

2132. MARASCHINO GELATIN
Gelatina al maraschino

Same ingredients listed for Basic Orange Gelatin
    [No. 2127]
½ cup maraschino liqueur

Prepare in the same way as Basic Orange Gelatin [No. 2127], adding the maraschino after the orange mixture has simmered for 2 minutes. *Serves* 6.

NOTE: 1 cup pitted fresh cherries, cooked for 10 minutes with ½ cup sugar and then chilled, may be added to the gelatin just before it is poured into the mold [*see* Note for No. 2127].

2133. MARSALA GELATIN
Gelatina al marsala

1½ cups sweet Marsala wine
1 egg white
1 eggshell, crushed
2½ cups cold water
⅔ cup sugar
2 envelopes unflavored gelatin, softened in ¼ cup
    cold water and 2 tablespoons lemon juice

Mix ¼ cup Marsala, the egg white, and eggshell in a large enamel pan. Beat with a whisk until frothy. Add the water and sugar and beat until the sugar is dissolved. Place the pan over moderate heat and bring to a simmer. Add the rest of the wine and simmer for 2 minutes. Add the softened gelatin and stir until dissolved. Proceed exactly as directed in Basic Orange Gelatin [No. 2127]. *Serves* 6.

NOTE: If desired this may be served with a bowl of well-chilled English Custard [No. 2111] as a sauce.

711

FRUIT DESSERTS AND COMPOTES

Entremets di frutta e composti

The climax of many an Italian meal is a big bowl of assorted fruits in season. However, the Italian cuisine includes an infinite number of ways of preparing fruits. This is not surprising, as Italy has been famous for its orchards for centuries. Fruit, in Italy, is prized not so much for its size, as for its perfume and flavor, which are exquisite. Since Italian fruit is usually only available during its proper season, it is always at the peak of perfection. Although canned or frozen fruits could be substituted in many of the following recipes, it is advised that only the freshest seasonal (local, if possible) fruit be employed for complete success. Fresh fruit that has been shipped from distant locales is apt to be tasteless (since it is shipped when only partially ripe).

2134. APPLES IN BAROLO WINE
Mele fredde al barolo

12 cooking apples (greenings, if available), peeled, cored, and cut into thick segments
3 cups Barolo wine (or any good-quality dry red Italian wine)
1½ cups sugar

Place the sugar and wine in an enamel saucepan, bring to a simmer, and cook over medium heat for 10 minutes. Add the apples, lower the heat, and poach until the apples are tender but still keep their shape. Remove the apples to a serving dish, and reduce the syrup by ½ over high heat. Pour over the apples, and chill the dish in the refrigerator. Serve ice cold. *Serves 6.*

2135. APRICOTS WITH CUSTARD SAUCE
Albicocche con crema inglese

18 dead-ripe apricots, peeled, but left whole and unstoned
Sugar syrup:
    ¾ cup water
    1½ cups sugar
Juice of 1 lemon

½ cup strawberry preserves
1 recipe Custard Sauce [No. 2274]
2 cups raspberries, passed through a fine sieve
2 tablespoons maraschino liqueur
18 small, ripe strawberries, hulled and washed

Cook the sugar and water in an enamel pan over low heat until the large thread stage is reached (219° on the candy thermometer). Add the apricots and lemon juice, and poach until fruit is tender but still holds its shape. Remove with a slotted spoon, and let fruit cool on a plate. Slit open on one side with a sharp knife and extract the pit, fill the space left by the pit with a little strawberry preserves, inserted with an after-dinner coffee spoon. Pour the custard sauce into a shallow serving bowl, and arrange the apricots in it, slit side down. Continue to cook the syrup in which the apricots poached until it reaches the hard ball stage (246° on the candy thermometer). Add the raspberry purée, and remove from stove at once. Place the apricot/custard preparation in the refrigerator to chill, and also the raspberry purée. When the latter is cool, add the maraschino and carefully pour it over the custard, spooning it out gently so that it floats on the custard, and does not coat the apricots. Top each apricot with a strawberry, and keep the dessert in the refrigerator until serving time. *Serves 6.*

2136. APRICOTS LILY
Albicocche deliziose "Lily"

12 large, dead-ripe apricots, peeled, stoned, and halved
⅓ cup superfine sugar
⅓ cup unblanched almonds, cut in fine slivers
⅓ cup sweet Madeira wine (or sweet Marsala)
Juice of 2 oranges, strained
1 cup heavy cream, whipped
2 tablespoons sugar
1 teaspoon vanilla extract
3 tablespoons candied violets
3 tablespoons bitter chocolate, shaved or grated

Arrange the apricots in a shallow glass serving bowl. Sprinkle with the sugar and the almonds. Mix the wine with the orange juice and pour over. Place the dish in the refrigerator until well chilled. Before serving, whip the cream until stiff in a chilled bowl, add the sugar and vanilla, mix well, and spread the cream over the fruit. Border the dish with a ring of candied violets, and sprinkle the shaved chocolate in the center. Serve at once. *Serves 6.*

2137. APRICOTS NINON
Albicocche Ninon

24 large, dead-ripe apricots, peeled, stoned, and halved
Sugar syrup:
  1 cup water
  1½ cups sugar
  1-inch piece of vanilla bean
1½ cups heavy cream, whipped
¼ cup unblanched almonds, cut in fine slivers
1 cup black currant jelly
4 tablespoons kirsch

Cook the sugar syrup in a shallow, wide pan until it reaches the large thread stage (219° on the candy thermometer). Add the halved apricots and poach them until tender but not mushy. Remove 18 of the halves with a slotted spoon. Place them on a plate and chill them in the refrigerator. Cook the rest of the syrup and remaining apricots down until they form a thick purée. Pour the purée into a bowl, remove the vanilla bean, and chill thoroughly in the refrigerator. Whip the cream until stiff in a chilled bowl, and then fold it into the very cold apricot purée. Arrange this in a shallow serving dish, and place the apricots, convex sides down, over the surface. Sprinkle over the almonds. Melt the currant jelly in a small saucepan over medium heat until it is completely smooth and free from lumps, stir the kirsch into it, and let it cool somewhat. Spoon a little of the currant sauce into each hollow of the apricots, and place the rest in a sauce bowl. Serve the apricots well chilled, accompanied by the still-warm sauce. *Serves 6.*

2138. APRICOTS REALE
Albicocche alla reale

4 very large dead-ripe apricots, peeled, halved, and
    stoned
½ cup water
1 cup sugar
1-inch piece of vanilla bean
1 recipe Kirsch Gelatin [No. 2131]
2 tablespoons anisette (or Strega) liqueur
Few drops red food coloring
2 cups fresh raspberries (or 2 boxes frozen raspberries)
1 9-inch layer Italian Sponge Cake [No. 1913]
½ cup pistachio nuts, coarsely chopped

Cook the sugar and water until they reach the large thread stage (219° on the candy thermometer). Add the vanilla and the apricots, and poach until they are tender. Remove with a slotted spoon, and let them cool.

Chill 8 small tartlet tins or individual fancy gelatin molds. Pour 2 tablespoons of the kirsch gelatin in each, and place in refrigerator until set. Place 1 apricot half in each gelatin-lined mold, convex side down, and fill the molds with the rest of the gelatin. Add the liqueur and food coloring (enough to tint it a deep rose-red) to the remaining gelatin, and pour it into a 9- by 12-inch baking tin. Place in refrigerator until set. Take the raspberries and add them to the syrup in which the apricots were cooked. Remove the vanilla bean, and cook the berries and syrup until thick. Strain through a fine sieve. Slit the sponge cake horizontally and spread the lower half with a little hot raspberry purée. Place the other half on top, and cover completely with the rest of the purée. Sprinkle with the chopped pistachios, and chill in the refrigerator. When all the component parts are well chilled and the gelatin set, unmold the small apricot-filled molds in a circle on top of the cake. Unmold the colored gelatin, chop it coarsely with a large knife, and pile it in the center. Place the dessert in the refrigerator until ready to serve. *Serves 8.*

NOTE: A bowl of Custard Sauce [No. 2274] may accompany this dessert.

2139. BAKED APPLE SLICES
GRATINATE
Mele ranette gratinate

12 baking apples (or greenings, if available), peeled,
    cored, and thickly sliced
½ cup butter, softened
¾ cup superfine sugar
¼ cup vanilla sugar [*see* No. 2296]
⅓ cup sweet Marsala wine
⅓ cup unblanched almonds, coarsely chopped
1 cup heavy cream, whipped

Apricots Reale (No. 2138)

Slice the apples rather thickly (at least ½ inch thick). Cream the butter, ¼ cup of the superfine sugar, and all the vanilla sugar together. Spread the bottom of a large, heavy enamel skillet with this mixture, lay the apples on top, and dot with the remaining butter. Place over medium heat, cover skillet, and cook for 5 minutes. Uncover, add the Marsala, raise heat to very high, and cook until the pan liquids have almost evaporated. Stir apples with a wooden spoon from time to time. When the apples are well glazed, but not pulpy, turn off the heat. Sprinkle the surface evenly with the almonds, and then the rest of the superfine sugar. Put under a medium broiler flame for 5 minutes, or until the top is nicely glazed. Serve warm, accompanied by a bowl of cream, whipped until stiff in a chilled bowl, but not sweetened. *Serves* 6.

NOTE: The cooking times will vary with the quality of apples used. However, the apple slices should never cook so long that they begin to disintegrate. If desired, a pinch of grated nutmeg may be mixed into the whipped cream.

2140. BAKED APPLES
Mele bonne femme

6 large baking apples, cored
¼ cup butter, softened
½ cup sugar
½ cup white wine (a sweet white wine such as a
    Sauternes may be used)

Peel the apples around their top thirds (this prevents them from bursting). Cream the butter and ⅓ cup of the sugar together and place some of this in the hollow space left by the core, and spread the surface of the apples with the rest. Place in a baking pan and pour in the wine. Bake in a 350° oven for ½ hour, or until their skins begin to wrinkle. Baste at least 3 times with the pan juices while they are baking. About 5 minutes before they are to be removed, sprinkle them with the remaining sugar, and raise the heat to 450°. Remove from oven, place on a warm serving dish, and pour the pan juices over them. This dish may be served either hot or cold. *Serves* 6.

NOTE: A pitcher of unwhipped heavy cream, sweetened with 2 tablespoons superfine sugar and a pinch nutmeg, goes very well with this dish.

2141. BAKED APPLES CASALINGA WITH WHIPPED CREAM
Mele alla casalinga con panna montata

6 large baking apples, cored and peeled
Juice of 1 lemon
6 slices crustless bread, cut in 3-inch rounds
⅓ cup butter, softened
½ cup sugar
½ teaspoon cinnamon
1 cup heavy cream, whipped
3 tablespoons superfine sugar

Slice the apples horizontally into slices ½ inch thick. Put each apple back in its original shape after it has been sliced. Butter the rounds of bread on both sides, and sprinkle with sugar. Cream the rest of the sugar and butter together, add the cinnamon, and spread each apple with the mixture. Place an apple on each bread round, put in a baking dish, and place in a 325° oven for 30 minutes, or until the apples are tender. Baste from time to time. Remove from oven, place on a serving dish, and serve warm accompanied by the cream which has been whipped until stiff in a chilled bowl and sweetened with the superfine sugar. *Serves* 6.

2142. BAKED APPLES CERTOSA
Mele alla certosa

6 large baking apples, unpeeled
Juice of 1 lemon
6 tablespoons seedless raisins, plumped for ½ hour in
    warm water, and drained
4 tablespoons pine nuts
¾ cup sweet Marsala wine
2 cups Pastry Cream [No. 2267], hot
12 pieces candied orange peel (or candied citron),
    large enough to plug the hollowed-out apples
¼ cup butter, softened
⅓ cup superfine sugar

Cut off a tiny portion of the stem end, and hollow out the apples with a melon ball cutter, taking care not to cut through the apples. The hollowed apples should have a wall about ¼ inch thick. Sprinkle the insides with lemon juice (to keep them from discoloring), and set aside. Soak the plumped raisins and the pine nuts in the Marsala for 2 hours. After that time remove them from the wine with a slotted spoon and mix them with the hot pastry cream. Fill each apple ⅔ full of this mixture (do not fill up to the top or they will burst in baking), and cover the top hole with a "plug" of candied peel. Cream the sugar and the butter

714

together and spread a teaspoonful over the top of each apple. Place the apples in a baking dish, pour in the Marsala, and add the rest of the creamed butter. Bake in a 375° oven for ½ hour or 45 minutes, or until the skins of the apples begin to wrinkle. Baste them with the pan juices at least 4 times during baking. Remove from oven when done, and arrange them on a serving platter. Pour the pan liquids into a small saucepan, and reduce until syrupy over high heat. Pour over the apples. This may be served either hot or cold. *Serves* 6.

2143. BAKED APPLES MELBA
Mele ranette al forno Melba

6 large baking apples (or greenings, if available),
    cored, and peeled only on their upper thirds
½ cup butter, softened
⅔ cup superfine sugar
Pinch salt
¼ cup sweet Marsala wine
6 ½-inch-thick slices stale cake, brioche, or bread,
    cut in 3-inch rounds
¼ cup brandy
1 cup raspberry preserves, passed through a fine sieve
Optional: 3 tablespoons Aurum liqueur
1 recipe Pastry Cream [No. 2267], well chilled

The apples should be peeled as indicated to prevent bursting while being baked. Cream the butter, sugar, and salt together. Fill the empty space left by the core with it and spread the apples thickly with the remaining butter/sugar mixture. Place in· a baking pan, sprinkle with the Marsala, and bake in a 350° oven for 25 minutes, or until the apples are tender and their skins begin to wrinkle. Baste them 3 or 4 times with the pan liquids during the baking. Toast the bread or cake rounds until they are golden, and arrange them in a circle on a platter (leaving an empty space in the middle). Pour a very little of the pan liquids on each round and top with an apple. Keep warm. Pour the brandy into the remaining liquid in the pan, place over medium heat, and ignite. Let the flames burn out, and stir in the raspberry preserves (strained, to eliminate the seeds). Stir until the preserves are well mixed with the rest of the ingredients and the mixture begins to bubble. Lower the heat and add the Aurum, mixing it in well. Pour this mixture over the apples, and fill the center of the platter with the well-chilled pastry cream, mounded up. Serve at once. *Serves* 6.

2144. BANANAS DESIDERIO DI EVA
Banane desiderio di Eva

6 ripe bananas, peeled and cut in half lengthwise
4 tablespoons butter, softened
½ cup superfine sugar
3 tablespoons Aurum liqueur
3 tablespoons maraschino liqueur
¼ cup dark rum
¾ cup very heavy cream, at room temperature
6 large dry almond macaroons (Italian macaroons, if
    possible), crushed

Butter an oven-proof baking dish (attractive enough to bring to the table) with 2 tablespoons of the butter. Lay the bananas in it in a single layer, flat sides downward. Sprinkle them with the sugar and the various liqueurs. Place in a 425° oven for 6 minutes, then pour in the cream, tilt the pan to mix it with the juices, and sprinkle the surface with the crushed macaroons. Dot with the remaining butter, and place in the oven for another 5 minutes, or until the tops are well browned and the pan juices are bubbling vigorously. Remove from oven, let stand 5 minutes (no more), and serve at once. *Serves* 6.

NOTE: Sour cream at room temperature may be used in place of heavy cream.

2145. BANANAS FLAMBÉ
Banane sciroppate al brandy

12 ripe bananas, peeled and sliced crosswise
4 tablespoons warm water
⅔ cup superfine sugar
Rind of 2 oranges (no white part), cut in fine julienne
    strips
Rind of 1 lemon (no white part), cut in fine julienne
    strips
Juice of 2 oranges, strained
Juice of ½ lemon, strained
½ cup best brandy

Do not peel and slice the bananas until the syrup is ready, otherwise they will turn brown. Place the water, sugar, and strips of rind in a small, heavy saucepan. Cook over medium heat until the sugar reaches the soft ball stage (220° on the candy thermometer). Add the orange and lemon juices and cook for another 2 minutes. Pour syrup into a bowl, and let cool. Slice the bananas into a heat-proof, shallow glass bowl, and pour the syrup over them, tossing lightly so that they are well coated. Cover the bowl, and chill in the refrigerator for at least 2 hours. Just before serving,

715

Baked Apples Certosa (No. 2142):
see page 714

warm the brandy in a ladle over a low flame, ignite, and pour over the bananas. Bring to the table flaming. *Serves 6.*

NOTE: A pleasant accompaniment to this dish would be Sablés [No. 1945].

2146. BANANAS FLAMBÉ IN ARMAGNAC
Banane infiammate all'armagnac

This dish is prepared in a chafing dish at the dinner table.

6 ripe bananas, peeled and sliced crossways in thinnish slices
4 tablespoons butter
1 large strip orange rind (no white part)
Juice of 1 large orange, strained
¼ cup maraschino liqueur
⅓ cup Armagnac brandy
1 cup heavy cream, poured into a serving pitcher
A small bowl filled with superfine sugar

Slice the bananas just before they are to be used, otherwise they will turn brown. Melt the butter in the frying pan of a chafing dish, using a high flame. When it sizzles, add the banana slices, and stir gently. Add the orange rind and some of the orange juice; stir until it evaporates and add the rest of the juice. Cook for a few more minutes. When the liquid has evaporated, spoon the banana slices onto dessert plates, leaving the butter in the pan. Add the liqueurs to the pan, ignite, let burn for a few seconds, pour in a

716

little cream and a spoonful of sugar, and stir well. Spoon over the bananas, and let each guest help himself to additional sugar and cream. *Serves 6.*

2147. BANANAS FLAMBÉ IN KIRSCH
Banane infiammate al kirsch

6 ripe bananas, peeled and left whole
⅓ cup butter
½ cup sugar
⅓ cup kirsch
1 cup heavy cream, whipped
2 tablespoons superfine sugar
1 teaspoon vanilla extract

Melt the butter in a baking dish attractive enough to bring to the table. Place the bananas in it, and roll them around until they are well coated with butter. Sprinkle them with sugar, and place the dish in a 350° oven for 15 minutes, or until the bananas are soft and are beginning to glaze. Remove from oven, heat the kirsch in a ladle over a low flame, ignite, pour over the bananas, and bring to the table flaming. Serve accompanied by the cream which has been whipped until stiff in a chilled bowl and flavored with the sugar and vanilla. *Serves 6.*

NOTE: This dish is also good served cold. Flame the bananas, let the flame go out, and chill them in the refrigerator until ice cold. The cream may then be piped over them through a pastry bag fitted with a large star tip.

2148. BANANAS LUCULLUS
Banane "Lucullo"

6 ripe bananas, unpeeled
4 tablespoons butter
2 tablespoons flour
½ cup superfine sugar
Pinch salt
¾ cup milk, scalded
3 egg yolks, lightly beaten
3 egg whites
Apricot Sauce [No. 2270], hot
3 tablespoons Curaçao liqueur

Melt the butter in a small saucepan over medium heat. Add the flour, stir well, and cook for 1 minute. Add ¼ cup of the sugar and the salt, and stir until the sugar is dissolved. Slowly pour in the hot milk, stirring vigorously to prevent lumps. Cook, stirring constantly, for 5 minutes, and remove from stove. Slice the side off the bananas lengthwise, leaving a good ¾ of the banana whole. Scoop out all the pulp and mash it thoroughly. Mix it into the flour/milk mixture, and beat in the yolks. Beat the whites with a wire whisk in a bowl (preferably of unlined copper) and when foamy add the remaining sugar. Beat until they form soft peaks and then fold into the banana mixture. Fill the scooped-out banana shells with this mixture, piling it in neatly. Place the bananas on a lightly greased baking dish (attractive enough to bring to the table) and place in a 400° oven for 10 minutes. Remove from oven, sprinkle with a little more superfine sugar, and return to oven until the tops are lightly glazed. Mix the Curaçao with the apricot sauce, and pour in a sauce bowl. Serve the bananas as soon as they are glazed, accompanied by the sauce. *Serves 6.*

NOTE: These bananas are rather like a soufflé, and must be brought from oven to table, otherwise they will fall.

2149. CHERRIES JUBILEE
Ciliege giubileo

6 cups large black cherries, pitted (if out of season use canned Bing cherries packed in syrup, and use the latter to supplement the syrup indicated below)
2 cups sugar
½ cup water
½ cup currant jelly
½ cup kirsch (or best brandy)

Place the sugar and water in a large saucepan and cook until it reaches the large thread stage (219° on the candy thermometer). Stir in the currant jelly and cook until it dissolves. Add the cherries and poach until they are tender. Do not overcook them until they become mushy. Pour the cherries and syrup into a heat-proof serving dish. Heat the kirsch (or brandy)

in a ladle over low heat, ignite, pour over the cherries, and bring to the table flaming. *Serves 6.*

NOTE: This is best served over vanilla ice cream, although it could also be served accompanied by a bowl of ice cold whipped cream.

2150. CHERRIES AND PINEAPPLE REALE
Ciliege e ananasso alla reale

2 pounds fresh, ripe cherries, pitted (save 20 of the pits)
1 large, dead-ripe pineapple, peeled, cored, and sliced ⅛ inch thick
2 cups superfine sugar
½ cup kirsch
2 cups good red wine (a sweetish wine may be used)
20 cherry pits crushed in the mortar (or placed in a heavy canvas bag and pounded with a hammer), tied in a cheesecloth bag

Place the sliced pineapple in a bowl, sprinkle 5 tablespoons sugar over the slices, and pour on the kirsch. Cover the bowl and chill in the refrigerator for 3 hours, turning the slices every so often to ensure their absorbing the kirsch flavor. Place the cherries, remaining sugar, and wine in an enamel saucepan. Add the bag of crushed cherry pits (which give an exquisitely subtle flavor to the mixture) and place over medium heat. Cook about 10 minutes, or until the cherries are tender. Remove the cherries with a slotted spoon and place them in a bowl. Cook down the syrup until reduced by ½ and pour it through a fine sieve over the cherries. Place in the refrigerator until well chilled. When ready to serve, arrange the kirsch-soaked pineapple slices in an overlapping circle around a shallow glass serving bowl. Add their marinating juice to the cherries, and pile the cherries and their syrup into the center of the dish. Place the dish into a larger bowl which has been filled with finely crushed ice, and serve ice cold. *Serves 6.*

2151. BRANDIED CHERRIES PRALINÉ
Ciliege al cherry brandy con croccante

2 pounds fresh, ripe cherries, pitted
2 cups sugar
¾ cup water
2-inch piece of vanilla bean
1 teaspoon cornstarch
⅓ cup Cherry Heering (or any good cherry brandy)
⅓ cup Praline powder [*see* No. 2290]

Cook the sugar and water in a heavy saucepan until it

reaches the large thread stage (219° on the candy thermometer). Add the cherries and cook for 5 minutes, or until not quite tender. Remove them with a slotted spoon and place in a bowl. Cook the syrup over high heat for 5 minutes. Remove a few tablespoons syrup from the pan, cool for a second or two, and mix with the cornstarch, stirring until smooth. Pour into the cooking syrup and let simmer for 3 minutes. Place the cherries back in the syrup, let cook for 2 minutes, and then pour into a glass serving bowl. Let cool at room temperature until the cherries are lukewarm, and stir in the cherry brandy. Place in the refrigerator until ice cold. Before serving, sprinkle the top with the Praline powder. *Serves* 6.

2152. CHERRIES IN WINE
Ciliege al vino barolo

2 pounds fresh, ripe cherries, pitted

1¾ cups sugar

1 stick cinnamon

4 strips orange rind (no white part)

3 cups Barolo wine (or any good-quality Italian red wine)

½ cup currant jelly

Place the cherries in an enamel saucepan and add the remaining ingredients. Cook over moderate heat until the mixture comes to a boil. Lower heat and cook for 10 minutes. Pour into a bowl, and place in the refrigerator until well chilled. *Serves* 6.

NOTE: Cat's Tongues [No. 1930] would provide a perfect accompaniment to this dish.

2153. FRESH FIGS BELVEDERE
Fichi freschi Belvedere

2 dozen plump, ripe, green (or purple) figs, peeled and halved

1½ cups Frangipane Cream [No. 2268]

1 cup heavy cream, whipped

2 cups ripe strawberries

½ cup ripe raspberries

⅔ cup superfine sugar

2 tablespoons Aurum liqueur

2 tablespoons maraschino liqueur

Chill the figs well. Mix the Frangipane cream with the heavy cream, which has been whipped until stiff in a chilled bowl. Spread this mixture in the bottom of a wide, shallow serving bowl. Press the strawberries and raspberries through a very fine sieve into a bowl. Add the sugar and stir until dissolved, then add the liqueurs. Chill all ingredients well. Before serving, place the figs over the cream, pour the berry purée into the center of the dish, and serve ice cold. *Serves* 6.

2154. MELON SURPRISE
Melone in sorpresa

1 good-size casaba or Cranshaw melon, perfectly ripe

4 to 6 cups assorted fruits in season (amount depends on the size of the melon), diced

Superfine sugar to taste

½ cup blanched almonds [*see* No. 2280], halved

⅓ cup Curaçao liqueur

¼ cup maraschino liqueur

Raspberry sauce:

   3 cups fresh raspberries

   1 cup superfine sugar

   Juice of ½ lemon

   ½ cup raspberry jelly

Cut the top off the melon, about 1 inch down from the stem end. This is its "lid" and is put aside until later. Scoop out the melon with a ball cutter, and discard the seeds. Mix the melon balls with the assorted fruits (apples, oranges, seedless grapes, plums, apricots, peaches, etc.—*no* canned fruits under *any* circumstances) and flavor to taste with sugar. Add the Curaçao and maraschino, toss well to incorporate the flavors, and place this mélange in the hollowed-out melon. Cover it with the "lid" and chill in the refrigerator for at least 6 hours. Make the raspberry sauce by passing the berries through a fine sieve (to eliminate all seeds) and mixing with the sugar, stirring until the sugar is dissolved. Heat the jelly in a small saucepan over medium heat until it has completely dissolved, and pour it into the raspberry purée. Mix well, add the lemon juice, pour into a sauceboat, and chill well. Serve the melon nested in a large bowl filled with ice cubes, and let each guest help himself to the sauce. *Serves 6 to 10 (depending on the size of the melon).*

2155. MELON WITH STRAWBERRIES
Melone con fragoline di bosco

1 casaba or Spanish melon, perfectly ripe

2 to 4 cups (depending on the size of the melon) strawberries (wild strawberries, if available), hulled

Superfine sugar (⅓ cup to each cup of berries)

¼ cup maraschino liqueur

2 tablespoons Aurum liqueur

Juice of ½ lemon, strained

Cut off the top of the melon, about 1 inch down from

the stem end. Place this "lid" aside for later use. Scoop out the melon with a ball cutter, discarding the seeds. Place melon balls in a bowl and sprinkle with a little of the sugar and the maraschino. Sprinkle the berries with remaining sugar, Aurum, and lemon juice in another bowl. Place both bowls, and the hollowed-out melon (if the melon is not sweet enough, sprinkle the inside with more sugar), in the refrigerator to chill thoroughly. Just before serving mix the melon balls with the berries, and place in the hollowed-out melon. Cover the melon with its "lid" and place the melon in a large bowl filled with cracked ice. Garnish ice with mint leaves and seasonal flowers, if desired. Serve ice cold. *Serves* 6.

NOTE: Although wild strawberries are called for in the original recipe, small cultivated ones may be employed with equal success.

2156. ICED MELON WITH WHIPPED CREAM
Melone ghiacciato con panna montata

1 Cranshaw, casaba, or Spanish melon, perfectly ripe
Superfine sugar to taste (amount depends upon the sweetness of the melon)
½ cup sweet Marsala wine
2 cups heavy cream, whipped
Optional: 2 or 3 tablespoons preferred liqueur

Cut off the top of the melon, about 1 inch down from the stem end. Place this "lid" aside for later use. Scoop out the melon with a ball cutter, discarding the seeds. Place melon balls in a large bowl, sprinkle with sugar to taste, and pour the Marsala over all. Mix lightly. Place balls back in melon, cover with the "lid," and place in refrigerator for at least 6 hours. When ready to serve, whip the cream until stiff in a chilled bowl, sweeten with 4 tablespoons of superfine sugar (and flavor, if desired, with preferred liqueur), and place in a glass serving bowl. Place the melon in a large bowl packed with crushed ice, and serve the whipped cream separately. *Serves 6 to 8 (depending on the size of the melon).*

2157. ORANGES CZARINA
Dessert alla zarina

6 large navel oranges
1 cup heavy cream, whipped
2 drops red food coloring
2 tablespoons superfine sugar
½ recipe Basic Orange Gelatin [No. 2127], made from the pulp from the above-listed oranges

Cut off the top eighth of the oranges. Scoop out all the pulp with a melon ball cutter, and press it through a fine sieve. Use the juice to make the orange gelatin. When gelatin is prepared, place it in a bowl over cracked ice, and stir until it becomes soupy. Remove bowl from ice at once, and mix ½ the gelatin with the food coloring and the cream, which has been whipped until stiff in a chilled bowl and sweetened with the sugar. Pour the rest of the gelatin into the orange containers, filling them halfway, and fill with the cream/gelatin mixture. Reserve some of the latter and place it in a pastry bag fitted with a large star tip. Pipe this onto the top of each orange, twisting it into a spiraled peak. Place oranges in the refrigerator for at least 4 hours. When ready to serve, set them into a large serving bowl packed with crushed ice. *Serves 6.*

2158. PEACHES WITH CANDIED VIOLETS
Pesche alla violetta

6 large, perfect, dead-ripe peaches, peeled, stoned, and sliced into 8 segments each
Juice of 2 oranges, strained
3 tablespoons Aurum liqueur
2 tablespoons brandy (or Cognac)
Superfine sugar to taste (depending on sweetness of the fruit)
1 cup heavy cream, whipped
Optional: 1 teaspoon almond extract
1 dozen candied violets

Place the peach sections in a wide, shallow glass serving bowl. Mix them lightly with the orange juice, Aurum, brandy, and sugar to taste. Place in refrigerator to chill for at least 2 hours. Before serving, whip the cream until stiff in a chilled bowl, flavor with 3 tablespoons of the sugar (and 1 teaspoon almond extract, if desired), place in a pastry bag fitted with a large star tip, and pipe over the peaches in decorative swirls and rosettes. Crown each rosette with a candied violet, and serve at once. *Serves 6.*

Peaches Flambé Brillat Savarin (No. 2159)

2159. PEACHES FLAMBÉ BRILLAT SAVARIN
Pesche alla fiamma Brillat Savarin

6 Savarins [*see* No. 1900], baked in small individual
    ring molds
3 very large, perfect peaches, peeled, halved, and stoned
Syrup:
  1 cup sugar
  ½ cup water
  1 thin slice lemon
½ cup apricot preserves, pressed through a fine sieve
2 tablespoons candied fruits (cherries, pineapple, orange
    rind, etc.), very finely chopped
5 tablespoons kirsch
5 tablespoons maraschino liqueur
1½ cups Pastry Cream [No. 2267]
4 tablespoons almond macaroon crumbs
2 tablespoons melted butter

Place the sugar, water, and lemon slice in an enamel saucepan and cook until it reaches the large thread stage (219° on the candy thermometer). Add the peaches and poach them until they are tender, but not mushy. Remove them with a slotted spoon and place them on a plate. Raise the flame and let the syrup cook down until it is very thick. Add the apricot preserves, mix well, pour into a sauceboat, and keep in a warm place.

Soak the candied fruits in 1 tablespoon each kirsch and maraschino and mix them into the pastry cream. Mix the liqueurs together and sprinkle about 6 tablespoons over the little savarins. Place them on a lightly buttered oven-proof serving platter, and fill their centers with the pastry cream. Top each with a peach half, round side up, and paint each with a little of the sauce. Sprinkle with macaroon crumbs, brush with melted butter, and place in a 350° oven for 10 minutes, or until crumbs are brown, and remove from oven. Heat the remaining liqueur in a ladle over low heat, set alight, and pour over the peaches. Bring to the table flaming. Serve sauce separately. *Serves* 6.

2160. PEACHES FLAMBÉ NAPOLEON
Pesche alla fiamma di Napoleone

6 large, perfect peaches, skinned and left whole
Syrup:
  1 cup sugar
  ½ cup water
  Rind of 1 orange (no white part), cut in large strips
1 teaspoon arrowroot mixed with 1 tablespoon orange
    juice
½ cup best brandy

Cook the sugar, water, and rind in an enamel saucepan until it reaches the large thread stage (219° on the candy thermometer). Add the peaches and let them poach until tender. Remove them with a slotted spoon and place them in a wide, shallow serving bowl. Cook the syrup until quite thick, stir in the arrowroot/orange juice mixture, and cook until the syrup is clear. Discard the orange rind, add 3 tablespoons brandy to the syrup, and pour over the peaches. Cool until lukewarm, and then heat the remaining brandy in a ladle over low heat, set alight, and pour over the peaches. Bring to the table flaming. *Serves* 6.

NOTE: Vanilla ice cream would be a perfect accompaniment to this dish.

SEE
REVERSE
FOR
CAPTION

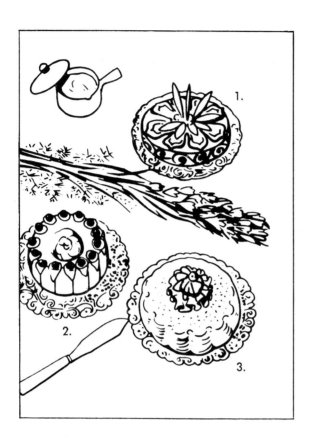

1. Vacherin with Custard Cream (No. 1926)
2. Charlotte Russe (No. 2069)
3. Almond Custard Meringue alla Ricca (No. 2011)

2161. PEACHES IMPERIAL
Pesche all'imperiale

6 large, perfect, dead-ripe freestone peaches, peeled
Juice of $\frac{1}{2}$ lemon
3 cups strawberries (wild strawberries, if available), hulled
2 tablespoons maraschino liqueur
$\frac{1}{2}$ cup superfine sugar
Juice of 1 orange, strained
6 glacéed walnuts [see No. 2302]
1 recipe Cold Zabaglione [No. 2117], made with Spumante wine (or Champagne) instead of Marsala

Peel the peaches and rub them with the lemon juice to keep them from turning dark, and place in refrigerator until chilled. Mix the berries with the liqueur, sugar, and orange juice and keep them in a bowl in the refrigerator until well chilled. Before serving, cut each peach in half, remove the stone, and replace it with a glacéed nut. Put the halves back together so that they look like a whole peach, and arrange them in a circle around a shallow glass serving dish. Place the berries in the center of the dish, coat each peach with the cold Zabaglione, and serve ice cold. Serve the remaining Zabaglione as a sauce. *Serves* 6.

2162. PEACHES AND RASPBERRIES
Pesche con lamponi

6 large, perfect peaches, peeled, halved, and stoned
Syrup:
   1 cup sugar
   $\frac{1}{2}$ cup water
   1 slice lemon
2 cups raspberries
2 tablespoons kirsch
2 tablespoons Aurum liqueur
$\frac{1}{2}$ teaspoon vanilla extract

Cook the sugar, water, and lemon slice in an enamel saucepan until it reaches the large thread stage (219° on the candy thermometer). Add the peaches, and poach until they are tender but not pulpy. Remove the peaches with a slotted spoon, and cook the syrup until it is very thick. Remove syrup from stove and pour $\frac{1}{2}$ of it over the peaches. Place the peaches in the refrigerator to chill. Press the raspberries through a fine sieve (to eliminate the seeds) and mix them with the remaining syrup, the liqueurs, and the vanilla. Chill them in another bowl in the refrigerator. Just before serving, pour the puréed raspberries over the peaches. Serve ice cold. *Serves* 6.

NOTE: A bowl of unsweetened whipped cream would be an excellent accompaniment to this dish.

2163. PEACHES REALE
Pesche alla reale

6 large, perfect freestone peaches, peeled
Syrup:
   Juice of 1 orange, strained
   1 cup sugar
   1 stick cinnamon
   1 whole clove
   Rind of $\frac{1}{2}$ orange (no white part), cut in fine julienne strips
   Rind of $\frac{1}{2}$ lemon (no white part), cut in fine julienne strips
1 cup Pastry Cream [No. 2267]
1 tablespoon candied fruit (pineapple and angelica), finely diced
3 tablespoons maraschino liqueur

Slit the peaches down the side and remove the pit (leaving the peach partly unslit, or "hinged together") and a bit of the center pulp (a ball cutter is useful here). Place the syrup ingredients in an enamel saucepan and cook until it reaches the large thread stage (219° on the candy thermometer). Place the peaches in the syrup and cook them for just 5 minutes, then remove pan from stove and allow the peaches to cool in the syrup. When cooled to room temperature, remove the peaches with a slotted spoon, and place the syrup back on the stove over medium heat and cook it until the syrup is very thick. Mix the candied fruit with the pastry cream and stuff the peaches with this mixture, wiping off any traces of cream that might smear onto the outside of the peaches. Close the peaches so that they look whole. Arrange them on a glass serving dish (slit side down) and chill in refrigerator. When syrup is thick, remove from stove, add the maraschino, cool somewhat, and pour through a sieve over peaches. Chill until ice cold. *Serves* 6.

Peaches Imperial (No. 2161)

2164. STUFFED BRANDIED PEACHES
Pesche farcite e profumate al liquore

6 large, perfect freestone peaches, peeled, halved, and
    stoned
Juice of ½ lemon, strained
Syrup:
    1 cup sugar
    ½ cup white wine
    2-inch piece of vanilla bean
1 cup heavy cream, whipped
½ cup coarsely chopped Praline [see No. 2290]
2 tablespoons Aurum liqueur
¼ cup best brandy

Rub the peaches with the lemon juice. Make the syrup
by cooking the sugar, wine, and vanilla in an enamel
saucepan over medium heat until it reaches the large
thread stage (219° on the candy thermometer). Add
the peaches and poach them for about 6 minutes,
remove with a slotted spoon, and arrange them on a
glass platter. Place in refrigerator until well chilled.
Cook down the syrup until it is very thick. Remove
the peaches from the refrigerator and scoop out some
of their centers with a melon ball cutter. Add the discarded pulp to the syrup. Chill the syrup well. Whip
the cream until stiff in a chilled bowl. Fold in the
Praline. Place some on each peach half, and join the
halves together so that the peaches look whole. Add
the liqueur and brandy to the syrup and pour it over
the peaches and leave in refrigerator until ready to
serve. *Serves* 6.

2165. STUFFED PEACHES FLAMBÉ
Pesche ripiene infiammate al liquore

6 large, dead-ripe freestone peaches, peeled
Syrup:
    2 cups white wine
    1¼ cups sugar
    1-inch piece of vanilla bean
1 cup heavy cream, whipped
½ cup dry almond macaroons (Italian macaroons,
    if possible), crushed
¼ cup brandy
3 tablespoons Aurum liqueur

Place the wine, sugar, and vanilla bean in an enamel
saucepan. Cook over high heat until it reaches the
large thread stage (219° on the candy thermometer).
Add the peaches and poach them over low heat until
they are tender but not mushy. Drain them with a
slotted spoon and place them on a plate until cool

enough to handle. Carefully split them, remove the
stones, and scoop out a little of the pulp from the
center. Keep the halves matched so that they will fit
when put together again. Whip the cream until stiff.
Sweeten with 1 or 2 tablespoons of the syrup, and
fold in the crushed macaroons. Mix well, and stuff
the peaches with this mixture. Put each peach back
together so that it looks whole, and place on a deep
serving platter. Heat the syrup until it simmers, and
pour a little over each peach (do not pour it all on).
Heat the brandy and Aurum in a ladle over low heat,
set alight, and pour over the peaches. Bring to the
table flaming. *Serves 6.*

NOTE: The remaining syrup may be poured into a
jar, tightly covered, and refrigerated for future use.

2166. STUFFED PEACHES GENOVESE
Pesche ripiene alla genovese

6 perfect, rather underripe peaches, peeled, halved,
    and stoned
3 medium, dead-ripe peaches, peeled, stoned,
    and mashed
⅔ cup sugar (more or less, depending on sweetness
    of the peaches)
½ cup dry almond macaroons (Italian macaroons,
    if available), crushed
1 egg yolk, lightly beaten
3 tablespoons preferred liqueur (kirsch, maraschino,
    peach) or brandy
½ cup vanilla wafers, crushed to fine crumbs
¼ cup butter, softened

Scoop out some of the center pulp of the halved
peaches so that their cavities will be large enough to
contain the stuffing. Keep the halves matched so that
they will fit when put together again. Mix the pulp
of the ripe peaches with ½ cup of the sugar, the
crushed macaroons, the egg yolk, and liqueur. Mix
together well, fill the peach halves with this mixture,
and place the halves back together so that the peaches
look whole. Mix the remaining sugar with the vanilla
wafer crumbs, and roll the peaches in the mixture.
Dot the peaches with the butter, place them in a
baking dish, and put into a 325° oven until very tender
(about 45 minutes). Baste at least 4 times during baking.
Serve warm. *Serves 6.*

NOTE: These peaches may be flamed with a little
brandy on serving, or they may be accompanied by a
bowl of sweetened whipped cream.

2167. PEARS ACCADEMICA
Pere all'accademica

6 large, rather underripe pears, peeled, halved, and
    stoned
Syrup:
  2 cups sugar
  1 cup water
  2-inch piece of vanilla bean
2 cups fresh raspberries
¼ cup Aurum liqueur
2 cups Cold Zabaglione [No. 2117]
6 marrons glacés, crumbled

Scoop out the centers and cores of the pears with a
melon ball cutter, leaving a shell about ¼ inch thick.
Cook the sugar, water, and vanilla bean in an enamel
pan until it reaches the large thread stage (219° on the
candy thermometer). Add the pears and poach them
until they are barely tender but still keep their shape.
Remove pears with a slotted spoon, place them on a
plate, and chill in the refrigerator. Let syrup cool to
room temperature. Mix the raspberries (taking care
not to crush them) with the Aurum, sweeten to taste
with some of the syrup, and place them in the refrigerator, covered, for at least 2 hours. When ready
to serve, place 2 pear halves in a sherbet (or champagne
glass), fill them with the raspberries, and cover them
with the cold Zabaglione. Repeat this until you have
filled 6 glasses. Sprinkle each with the crumbled marrons, and serve at once. *Serves* 6.

NOTE: Palm Leaves [No. 1941] provide a perfect
accompaniment to this dish.

2168. PEARS ALMONDINE BENEDETTA
Pere mandorlate "benedetta"

9 perfectly ripe pears, peeled, halved, and cored
⅔ cup vanilla sugar [*see* No. 2296]
¼ cup sweet Marsala wine
½ cup apricot preserves, pressed through a fine sieve
½ cup blanched almonds [*see* No. 2280], coarsely
    chopped and toasted
1 cup heavy cream, whipped

Place the pears in a baking dish, sprinkle them with
½ cup of the sugar and the Marsala, and place in a
400° oven for 8 minutes. Remove from oven, drain off
their cooking liquid with a bulb baster, and place
liquid in a small, heavy saucepan. Reduce this over
high heat until very thick. Mix this syrup with the
pears, and pile them in a pyramid on an oven-proof
serving platter. Spread with the strained preserves,

sprinkle with the almonds and 2 tablespoons of the
sugar, and place in the oven for another 5 minutes.
Whip the cream until stiff in a chilled bowl, and
sweeten it with the remaining sugar. Remove pears
from the oven and serve accompanied by a bowl of the
whipped cream. *Serves* 6.

NOTE: Palm Leaves [No. 1941] provide a perfect
accompaniment to this dish.

2169. PEARS CECILIA
Pere Cecilia

1 recipe Baked Custard [No. 2103]
6 pears, peeled, cored, and cut into segments
1 pear, peeled, halved, and cored
Syrup:
  1½ cups sugar
  ¾ cup water
  1-inch piece of vanilla bean
½ cup currant jelly
½ cup heavy cream
2 tablespoons kirsch

Pour the custard in a ring mold which has been generously buttered and sprinkled with sugar. Bake as
directed in No. 2103, and place in refrigerator until
chilled. Cook the sugar, water, and vanilla bean in an
enamel pan until it reaches the large thread stage
(219° on the candy thermometer). Add the pear segments and poach for 5 minutes, or until just tender.
Remove with a slotted spoon, and let them cool in a
bowl. Melt the currant jelly in a heavy saucepan. Add
½ cup of the syrup in which the pears cooked, and
place the halved pear in this mixture. Poach for 10
minutes, and remove pear with slotted spoon. Cool
this in another bowl (it will be pink from the syrup and
should not touch the segments or they will become
pink tinged also). Chill the pears and the currant syrup.
When all the ingredients are well chilled, unmold
the custard on a large, round serving platter. Surround
the rim with the segments. Mix the cream and kirsch
with the currant syrup and pour some in the center of
the custard; pour the rest around the outside, being
careful not to get any on the pear segments. Place the
currant-poached pear halves in the center of the custard
and serve well chilled. *Serves* 6.

Pears Almondine Benedetta
(No. 2168): see page 723

2170. PEARS IN RED WINE ITALIANA
Pere al vino rosso all'italiana

6 very large, underripe pears, left whole and unpeeled
1 cup sugar
1 stick cinnamon
1 or 2 whole cloves
2 strips orange rind (no white part)
2 strips lemon rind (no white part)
1 cup good-quality sweet red wine (or Port wine)

Wash the pears and remove their stems. Place them upright in a baking dish (which should be small enough so that they touch one another). Sprinkle them with the sugar, add the cinnamon and rinds, and pour over the wine. Place in a 375° oven and bake until the wine has almost cooked away. Baste 4 or 5 times during the baking. Serve either warm or thoroughly chilled. *Serves* 6.

NOTE: Whipped cream is an excellent accompaniment to the pears if they are to be served chilled. Vanilla ice cream would go well with them if they are warm.

2171. PEARS IN WHITE WINE WITH CUSTARD SAUCE
Pere al vino bianco con crema all'inglese

6 large pears, peeled and cored but left whole
$\frac{1}{2}$ cup sugar
1-inch piece of vanilla bean
$\frac{1}{2}$ stick cinnamon
1 whole clove

2 strips lemon rind (no white part)
2 strips orange rind (no white part)
1 cup white wine
2 cups English Custard [No. 2111]
3 tablespoons Aurum liqueur
3 tablespoons maraschino liqueur

Place the pears in an enamel saucepan small enough so that they stand upright. Add all the remaining ingredients except the custard and liqueurs and bring to a simmer over medium heat. Cover pan, lower heat, and cook until pears are tender, but still keep their shape. Remove them with a slotted spoon, place them in a shallow serving bowl, and keep warm. Reduce the cooking liquids in the pan over high heat until very thick and syrupy. Remove from fire, discard vanilla and strips of rind, and let cool for about 15 minutes. Stir into the custard, add the liqueurs, and pour over the pears. Serve while still warm. *Serves* 6.

2172. PEARS IN WHITE WINE ITALIANA
Pere al vino bianco all'italiana

6 large, ripe pears, peeled and cored but left whole
1 cup sugar
2 cups dry white wine
1 tablespoon grated orange rind (no white part)
1 tablespoon grated lemon rind (no white part)
1-inch piece of vanilla bean
$\frac{1}{2}$ cup coarsely crushed Praline [*see* No. 2290]
1 Italian sponge cake [No. 1913], sliced into
    3-inch fingers and lightly toasted

Place the pears in an enamel saucepan small enough so that they stand upright. Add all the remaining ingredients except the Praline and cake, and bring to a boil over high heat. Cover pan, lower heat, and poach until the pears are easily pierced with a fork. Remove them with a slotted spoon and place them in a glass serving bowl. Raise the heat and reduce the cooking liquid to a scant $\frac{3}{4}$ cup over high heat. Pour through a fine sieve over the pears, and place in the refrigerator until well chilled. Just before serving, sprinkle them with the crushed Praline, and serve the toasted sponge cake separately. *Serves* 6.

NOTE: A bowl of sweetened whipped cream may also accompany this dish.

2173. PINEAPPLE ACCADEMICA
Ananasso all'accademica

1 small, dead-ripe pineapple, peeled, cored, and
    thinly sliced

1 cup superfine sugar
¼ cup maraschino liqueur
Rind of ½ orange (no white part)
4 navel oranges, peeled, all white membranes discarded, and separated into segments (or cut in thin slices)
3 cups strawberries, hulled and washed
3 tablespoons Aurum liqueur
Juice of 2 tangerines, strained
1 cup heavy cream, whipped
¼ cup candied pineapple, cubed

Place the pineapple slices in a bowl and sprinkle with ½ cup of the sugar. Add the maraschino and rind, mix well until all the slices are coated, and place in the refrigerator for 2 hours. Chill the orange sections at the same time. Mix the berries with the remaining sugar, the Aurum, and tangerine juice, and place them in the refrigerator. When ready to serve, arrange the pineapple slices in an overlapping circle around a shallow glass serving bowl. Pile the berries in the center. Combine the juices from the 2 fruits and pour over through a fine sieve. Arrange the orange sections around the berries. Whip the cream until stiff in a chilled bowl, place in a pastry bag fitted with a large star tip, and pipe a border and rosettes around and over the fruit. Decorate with the candied pineapple, and serve well chilled. *Serves 6 to 8.*

2174. PINEAPPLE GLAZED IN LIQUEURS
Ananasso caramellato con liquori

12 thick slices of fresh pineapple
⅓ cup Aurum liqueur
⅓ cup best brandy
3 tablespoons kirsch
Juice of 1 orange, strained
3 tablespoons butter
¾ cup superfine sugar
¼ cup vanilla sugar [*see* No. 2296]

This is prepared in a chafing dish at the dining table. Place the liqueurs, orange juice, butter, and sugars in the pan of the chafing dish. Place over a lively flame, and simmer until the butter melts. Add the pineapple and cook until the liquid has evaporated and the sugar forms a glaze. Stir occasionally while the liquid cooks away. Serve as soon as the fruit slices are well glazed. *Serves 6.*

NOTE: If desired, a scoop of vanilla ice cream could be placed on each serving of fruit.

2175. STRAWBERRIES CASTA DIVA
Fragole di giardino casta diva

1 recipe Caramel Custard [No. 2105], baked in a ring mold
3 cups strawberries, washed, hulled, and patted dry
½ cup superfine sugar
3 tablespoons kümmel liqueur
1 cup heavy cream, whipped
¼ cup blanched almonds [*see* No. 2280], slivered

Prepare the custard as directed in No. 2105. When baked, chill in the refrigerator for at least 6 hours. Mix the berries with the sugar and liqueur, and let them steep in the refrigerator for 2 hours. Before serving, unmold the custard in the center of a serving dish. Pile the berries and their juices in the center. Whip the cream until stiff in a chilled bowl (do not sweeten), place it in a pastry bag fitted with a large star tip, and pipe a decorative border around the custard, and rosettes over the berries. Sprinkle with the almonds, and serve well chilled. *Serves 6.*

2176. STRAWBERRIES ROMANOFF
Fragole di bosco Romanoff

4 cups small, ripe strawberries (wild strawberries, if available), washed, hulled, and patted dry
½ cup superfine sugar
Juice of 1 large orange, strained
⅓ cup Curaçao (or Cointreau) liqueur
1 cup heavy cream, whipped
3 tablespoons vanilla superfine sugar [*see* No. 2296]

Place the berries in a crystal bowl. Mix the sugar with the orange juice, and stir until the sugar has dissolved (it may be whirled in the blender for a few seconds, to make the dissolving easier). Add the liqueur, pour over the berries, and toss lightly, being careful not to crush the berries. Cover the bowl, and chill in the refrigerator for 2 hours. Whip the cream until stiff in a chilled bowl, sweeten it with the vanilla sugar, place it in a pastry bag fitted with a large star tip, and pipe decorative rosettes and swirls around the berries. Place the bowl with the berries in a larger bowl filled with crushed ice. *Serves 6.*

Vanilla

2177. WILD STRAWBERRIES CAPRICCIO DI WANDA
Fragole di bosco "Capriccio di Wanda"

4 cups wild strawberries, hulled (or substitute the smallest, reddest cultivated berries available)

2 cups dry white wine

$\frac{2}{3}$ to 1 cup superfine sugar (depending upon the sweetness of the berries)

3 tablespoons maraschino liqueur

3 tablespoons Aurum liqueur

6 large navel oranges

3 small navel oranges

$\frac{1}{2}$ cup sugar

1 cup heavy cream, whipped

6 whole glacéed walnuts [*see* No. 2302]

Place the berries in a large bowl and pour over the wine. Stir them a few times to allow the wine to wash them, and then pour off the wine. Sprinkle them with the sugar and add the liqueurs. Cover the bowl and place the berries in the refrigerator to chill for 2 hours. Cut a small round (about the size of a quarter) in the top of each large navel orange, and scoop out the pulp with a melon ball cutter. Take care not to pierce the skin of the oranges. Press the pulp from the oranges through a fine sieve to extract the juice and pour the juice over the strawberries. Stir a few times, while the berries are chilling, taking great care not to crush them. Peel the small oranges, discarding all white membranes, and separate them into sections. Dip each section in sugar and place in refrigerator. Whip the cream until stiff in a chilled bowl. When ready to serve, drain most of the liquid from the berries and spoon them into the orange shells, alternating with spoonsful of cream. Cover the top of each orange with a glacéed nut, and place them in a shallow serving bowl. Surround with the orange sections. Place the serving bowl into a large bowl packed with crushed ice. *Serves* 6.

NOTE: The wine and juice from the marinating strawberries may be used in making a fruit gelatin. *See* the master recipe for Basic Orange Gelatin [No. 2127]. Any additional cream that might be left over in filling the oranges may be piped around them in decorative swirls.

726

2178. WILD STRAWBERRIES MARIA JOSÉ
Fragole di bosco alla Maria José

5 cups wild strawberries, hulled (or substitute the smallest, reddest cultivated berries available)

$1\frac{1}{4}$ cups superfine sugar (more, if berries are tart, less if very sweet)

$\frac{1}{2}$ tablespoon grated orange rind (no white part)

$\frac{1}{2}$ cup maraschino liqueur

1 cup heavy cream, whipped

3 tablespoons superfine vanilla sugar [*see* No. 2296]

6 candied violets

$\frac{1}{2}$ cup candied rose petals

Gently mix the berries with the sugar, orange peel, and maraschino. Take great care not to crush the berries. Place them in the refrigerator, covered, for at least 2 hours. Chill 6 large champagne glasses or sherbet cups. When ready to serve, spoon out the berries with a slotted spoon into the glasses. Pour their liquid through a fine sieve and pour some in each glass. Whip the cream until stiff in a chilled bowl, sweeten with the vanilla sugar, place it in a pastry bag fitted with a large star tip, and pipe a large rosette on each mound of berries. Top the rosette with a violet, and surround it with some candied petals. Serve at once. *Serves* 6.

NOTE: Candied violets, rose petals, and other such candied flowers, are imported from Europe and may be purchased in specialty food shops.

FRUIT COMPOTES
Composti di frutta

Compotes consist of fresh and/or dried fruit poached whole, in segments, or in slices, in a sugar syrup flavored with such aromatics as orange or lemon rind, vanilla, cloves, etc. Dried fruits must be soaked in warm water until plump before they are poached in the syrup. Some fresh fruit need not be poached, but merely allowed to marinate in the syrup.

Compotes are served ice cold, and before serving they are sometimes sprinkled with brandy or a fruit liqueur. The syrup may also be enriched by adding strained fruit preserves (strawberry, apricot, currant, or raspberry being the best for this use).

The secret of a good compote lies in the cooking of the fruit. Whether dried or fresh, it must be poached only until tender, and must never be allowed to go pulpy. Care must also be taken that certain fruits should not soak too long in the syrup (raspberries and strawberries, for instance), otherwise they will lose their color and flavor and become pulpy messes. Nothing is less appetizing than overcooked and/or oversoaked fruit lacking shape, texture, and native color and flavor. The fruits must be wisely "orchestrated" to provide a symphony of flavor.

All fruit should be poached in an enamel pan, as metal might give the fruit a "flavor" due to the latter's acid content.

2179. SYRUP FOR FRUIT COMPOTES

Most fruits benefit from the addition of lemon juice, which points up their flavor and makes bland fruits take on a little more character.

2 cups sugar
1 cup water
3 slices lemon

Cook the ingredients in an enamel pan over medium heat until the syrup reaches the large thread stage (219° on the candy thermometer). At this point either add the fruit to be poached, or cool the syrup until warm and pour over the fruit to be marinated. The lemon slices may be discarded at any point after the syrup has cooked. *Makes about 1½ cups.*

2180. APPLE COMPOTE
Composta di mele

8 large cooking apples (*see* Note below), peeled and cored
1 recipe Syrup for Fruit Compotes [No. 2179]
Optional: 1 or 2 teaspoons "red-hot" cinnamon drops, for their flavor and pink tint

Poach the apples in the simmering syrup until they are tender but still hold their shape (this is not applesauce or stewed apples, and they must be *al dente*: as it is impossible to determine the cooking time due to the various types of apples, it is suggested that you taste a piece after they have cooked for 6 minutes). Add the optional cinnamon drops and stir until dissolved, pour the apples into a glass compote dish, and place in refrigerator to chill well before serving. *Serves 6.*

NOTE: A pitcher of unwhipped heavy cream sweetened with 2 tablespoons superfine sugar and a grating of fresh nutmeg would be a perfect accompaniment to this dish.

The apples used vary according to the season. Mackintosh apples may be used whole (peeled and cored, of course), Rome Beauties halved, but Baldwins, greenings, or any hard winter apples should be quartered.

2181. APRICOT COMPOTE
Composta di albicocche

24 perfect apricots, peeled, pitted, and halved
Optional: 6 apricot pits, crushed with a hammer and tied in a cheesecloth bag
1 recipe Syrup for Fruit Compotes [No. 2179]

Place the fruit and the optional crushed pits (which will give the fruit a delicate bitter almond flavor) in an enamel pan with the hot syrup. Poach for 5 minutes or until the fruit is barely tender and then remove from stove to cool to room temperature (the fruit will cook while staying in the hot syrup). Discard optional bag of pits and pour into a compote dish and place in the refrigerator for 2 hours, or until well chilled. *Serves 6.*

NOTE: Custard Sauce [No. 2274] provides an excellent accompaniment for this compote.

2182. BANANA COMPOTE
Composta di banane

8 slightly underripe bananas, peeled, lightly scraped to remove surface filaments, and sliced crosswise in ½-inch slices
1 recipe Syrup for Fruit Compotes [No. 2179], substituting a 2-inch piece of vanilla bean for the lemon

Place sliced bananas in an enamel pan with the hot syrup. Poach for 5 minutes. Remove from stove and allow them to cool in the syrup to room temperature. Place fruit and syrup (discarding vanilla bean) in a compote dish and place in refrigerator for 2 hours, or until well chilled. *Serves 6.*

2183. CHERRY COMPOTE
Composta di ciliege

5 cups fresh cherries, pitted
12 cherry pits, crushed with a hammer and tied in a cheesecloth bag
1 recipe Syrup for Fruit Compotes [No. 2179]

Place cherries and pits in an enamel pan and cover with hot syrup. Poach for 5 minutes. Remove from stove and allow to cool in syrup to room temperature. Remove cheesecloth bag, pour mixture into a compote dish, and place in refrigerator for 2 hours, or until well chilled. *Serves 6.*

2184. COMPOTE ARMONIOSA
Coppa di frutta armoniosa

4 cups fresh cherries, pitted
1 recipe Syrup for Fruit Compotes [No. 2179]
4 ripe bananas, peeled, filament scraped off, and cut
    into ¼-inch slices
4 tablespoons maraschino liqueur
3 navel oranges, peeled, white membranes discarded,
    and separated into segments
1 cup heavy cream
2 tablespoons superfine sugar

Place cherries in an enamel saucepan and cover with the hot syrup. Poach for 5 minutes. Remove from stove and cool in syrup to room temperature. Pour into a compote dish and place in refrigerator for 2 hours, or until well chilled. Just before serving, slice the bananas into the cherry compote, add the maraschino, mix gently so as not to bruise the fruit, and surround the edge of the mixture with the orange sections, arranged in an overlapping circle. Mix the sugar with the cream until it has dissolved, and pour into a serving pitcher or sauceboat, and serve separately. *Serves 6.*

2185. COMPOTE GASTRONOME
Timballo di frutta alla ghiotta

4 large apples, peeled, cored, and cut into eighths
3 large pears, peeled, cored, and cut into eighths

1 recipe Syrup for Fruit Compotes [No. 2179]
½ cup kirsch
4 tablespoons marrons glacés, reduced to a purée
½ cup glacéed greengages (if available), diced
⅓ cup candied cherries, halved
1 cup heavy cream, whipped
½ teaspoon vanilla extract

Place the apples and pears in an enamel pan and cover with the hot syrup. Poach for 5 minutes. Remove from stove and allow to cool in syrup to room temperature. Remove fruit from syrup with a slotted spoon, place in a compote dish, and mix with ⅓ cup of the kirsch. Cover dish, and place in refrigerator. Place the remaining syrup back on the stove and reduce over high flame to about ¾ cup. Allow to cool for 10 minutes, then stir in the marron purée and the candied fruits. Cool to room temperature, then place in refrigerator. When well chilled, add the remaining kirsch and mix well. Whip the cream until stiff in a chilled bowl, fold in the vanilla, and place cream in a small serving bowl. Mix the chilled syrup with the candied fruits. Serve well chilled, with the whipped cream on the side. *Serves* 6.

2186. DRIED FIG COMPOTE
Composta di fichi secchi

24 best-quality sun-dried figs, soaked in cold water
    (or wine) to cover until they are plump

Although fresh fruit is to be preferred in most of the recipes in this section, the best substitutes are home-preserved fruits

1 recipe Syrup for Fruit Compotes [No. 2179], using
½ cup water and ½ cup dry red wine

Soak the figs until they are just plump, then drain
them immediately. Place them in an enamel pan and
cover with the hot syrup. Poach for 10 minutes, remove
from stove, and cool in syrup to room temperature.
Pour into a compote dish and place in refrigerator for
2 hours, or until well chilled. *Serves* 6.

2187. FRESH FIG COMPOTE
Composta di fichi freschi

24 fresh figs, peeled
1 recipe Syrup for Fruit Compotes [No. 2179],
    substituting a 2-inch piece of vanilla bean for the
    lemon

Place figs in an enamel saucepan and cover with the
hot syrup. Poach for 5 minutes. Remove from stove and
cool in syrup to room temperature. Remove vanilla
bean, pour into a compote dish, and place in refrigerator for 2 hours, or until well chilled. *Serves* 6.

2188. PEACH COMPOTE
Composta di pesche

24 small freestone peaches (or 12 medium), peeled,
    halved, and stoned
Optional: 3 peach stones, crushed with a hammer and
    tied in a cheesecloth bag
1 recipe Syrup for Fruit Compotes [No. 2179]

Place peaches and optional peach stones in an enamel
saucepan. Cover with hot syrup and poach 5 minutes
(8 minutes for larger peaches). Remove from stove and
cool in syrup to room temperature. Remove optional
peach stones and pour peaches and syrup into a compote dish. Place in refrigerator for 2 hours, or until well
chilled. *Serves* 6.

NOTE: Custard Sauce [No. 2274] would provide
an excellent accompaniment for this compote.

2189. PEAR COMPOTE
Composta di pere

8 perfect pears, peeled, cored, and halved
    (*see* Note below)
1 recipe Syrup for Fruit Compotes [No. 2179],
    substituting a 2-inch piece of vanilla bean for the
    lemon

Place the pears in an enamel saucepan and cover with
the hot syrup. Poach for 5 minutes. Remove from stove
and let cool in syrup to room temperature. Remove

vanilla bean and pour fruit and syrup into a compote
dish. Place in refrigerator for 2 hours, or until well
chilled. *Serves* 6.

NOTE: If the pears are hard, they may be cut into
quarters or eighths. Anjous, although green, are very
juicy and may be halved. If pears are quite hard, rub
them with a little lemon juice before poaching them.
This keeps them white.

2190. PINEAPPLE COMPOTE
Composta di ananasso

1 ripe pineapple, peeled, cored, and thinly sliced
1 recipe Syrup for Fruit Compotes [No. 2179], substi-
    tuting, if desired, a 2-inch piece of vanilla bean for
    the lemon

Place the pineapple slices in an enamel saucepan and
cover with the hot syrup. Poach for 5 minutes, remove
from stove, and allow to cool in syrup to room temperature. Arrange the slices in overlapping circles in a
shallow compote dish, pour over the syrup through
a fine sieve, and place in refrigerator for 2 hours, or
until well chilled. *Serves* 6.

2191. PRUNE COMPOTE
Composta di prugne secche

24 largest dried prunes available, soaked in cold water
    (or wine) to cover until plump (*see* Note below)
1 recipe Syrup for Fruit Compotes [No. 2179], made
    with ½ cup water and ½ cup red wine

Drain prunes the instant they are well plumped. (Pit,
if desired.) Pat dry, place in enamel saucepan, and
cover with the hot syrup. Poach for 5 minutes, remove
from stove, and allow to cool in syrup to room temperature. Pour into a compote dish and place in refrigerator for 2 hours, or until well chilled. *Serves* 6.

NOTE: Most American prunes require very little
soaking to plump them. Follow directions on box if
using domestic prunes. Imported prunes, of course,
require longer soaking—depending upon the variety
used.

2192. RASPBERRY COMPOTE
Composta di lamponi

6 cups perfect raspberries, picked over
½ recipe Syrup for Fruit Compotes [No. 2179]

Place raspberries in a compote dish and pour over
the hot syrup. Mix carefully so as not to bruise the

berries, and place in refrigerator for 2 hours, or until well chilled. *Serves* 6.

NOTE: If desired, a few tablespoons preferred liqueur may be added with the syrup, and the berries may be served with an accompanying bowl of whipped, unsweetened heavy cream.

2193. STRAWBERRY COMPOTE
Composta di fragole

6 cups perfect strawberries, hulled
½ recipe Syrup for Fruit Compotes [No. 2179]

Place berries in a compote dish and pour over the hot syrup. Mix carefully so as not to bruise the berries, and place in refrigerator for 2 hours, or until well chilled. *Serves* 6.

NOTE: If desired, a few tablespoons preferred liqueur may be added with the syrup, and the berries may be served with Custard Sauce [No. 2274].

ICE CREAM

Gelati

It is said that ice cream was invented in Italy and was introduced to France by Marie de' Medici when she went there to marry King Henry IV in 1600. Fruit ices, or sherbets, are known to have existed at the time of the Roman Empire, and it is recorded that Nero had special runners bring snow from the Alps in summertime to provide him with ices. These early sherbets were probably only snow or crushed ice flavored with fruit syrups and/or wine.

In Italy, ices and ice creams are great favorites, and Italian ice creams are among the best in the world.

Although American ice cream is available commercially in varying degrees of richness, it is rare nowadays to find "store-bought" ice cream made from fresh egg yolks, real cream, and pure flavorings. Nothing can compare to the homemade variety.

Fortunately, electrically powered ice-cream freezers are available to make the onerous task of churning a thing of the past. Ice cream may even be made in the ice trays of a refrigerator, but the end result is not as rich or as smooth as that churned in a special mixer.

The standard base for ice cream is a cream/milk/egg/sugar custard which is first cooked slightly and then mixed with the desired flavorings. The sugar and flavoring content must be slightly stronger than if the mixture were to be served unfrozen, as freezing tends to mask flavoring. If vanilla is to be used, it must be a crushed vanilla bean for maximum success, not vanilla extract. The same principle of freshness applies to other flavorings.

As soon as the custard/cream base has been prepared, it is cooled as quickly as possible before being poured into the freezing can of the freezer. The freezer can must not be filled more than ⅔ of capacity, to allow for expansion during freezing.

The following steps should be followed in making ice cream after the base has been prepared:

1. Pour custard/cream into can of freezer and place in freezer tub. Position dasher in can, cover tightly with lid, cover with gear case, and adjust until handle turns freely. Pack the tub with a mixture consisting of 8 parts coarsely crushed ice and 1 part rock salt. Turn the crank until mixture is half frozen: about 15 minutes of turning.

2. If crushed fruits or other solid ingredients are to be added, carefully scoop ice out of tub leaving the can well exposed. Lift off the gear case, wipe can and lid with a clean cloth (no salt ice must get into can), lift off lid, add ingredients desired, and replace lid and gear case as directed above. Pack with more ice and salt, and continue to crank until it impossible to turn. At this point the mixture is frozen. (If no other ingredient is to be added, omit this step, simply turning from the first until it is impossible to do so.)

3. Carefully scrape ice and salt away from can, remove gear case, wipe can free of salt and ice, remove lid, lift out dasher, scraping off cream with a rubber scraper, cover top of can with aluminum foil, and replace lid. Drain off all excess water from the tub and pack to the rim with 4 parts crushed ice to 1 part rock salt. Cover with several thicknesses of an old towel or piece of carpeting, and let the cream "ripen" for at

least 6 hours. (It *must* ripen, otherwise it lacks the proper flavor and texture.)

If you are using an electrically operated freezer, follow manufacturer's instructions.

Many households do not possess an ice cream freezer, and small city apartments may not have room to store one. Therefore, we will give a method for freezing in ice trays in the freezing compartment of the refrigerator. The result will not be as creamily smooth as is obtained with a freezer, but it will be head and shoulders above the purchased kind.

1. Set the control of the refrigerator to the coldest point $\frac{1}{2}$ hour before the cream is to be placed in the freezing compartment.

2. Chill the cream/custard base well. Wash out the ice trays thoroughly with water and soda to rid them of any stale food odors. (Do not use plastic ice trays, only the metal ones.) Pour cream/custard base in trays and place in coldest part of the freezing compartment. Leave it there until it has almost frozen solid, but is still mushy in the center.

3. Place the mushy cream/custard base in an ice-cold bowl and beat it vigorously with a wire whisk or electric beater until it is smooth and fluffy. It will be best if the bowl is set in a larger bowl containing crushed ice. Add fruit, if desired, making sure it is also well chilled, beat again, and return to ice trays. Cover trays with aluminum foil and freeze for at least 2 more hours. If a really smooth texture is desired, the mixture may be removed again after an hour and beaten as above, then returned to the trays and frozen for 2 additional hours.

2194. VANILLA ICE CREAM
Gelato alla vaniglia

2 cups milk
2 cups cream
1 cup sugar
1 4-inch length of vanilla bean, split and crushed
    in the mortar
6 egg yolks
Pinch salt

Place the milk, cream, sugar, and crushed vanilla bean in an enamel pan over low heat. Bring to the scalding point. Beat the yolks with the salt until foamy, then pour in the scalded cream mixture, mixing well. Pour back in enamel pan and place over lowest possible heat. Stir constantly until the mixture coats a metal spoon. Pour through a sieve into a bowl and chill thoroughly before freezing according to directions on page 730. *Makes about 7 cups (or 1 quart 1 $\frac{1}{2}$ pints).*

NOTE: The little specks of vanilla bean should not worry you: they are an indication that the best ingredients have been used.

2195. VANILLA ICE CREAM WITH WHIPPED CREAM
Gelato alla vaniglia con panna montata

1 recipe Vanilla Ice Cream [No. 2194], using only
    1 cup milk and 1 cup cream
1 $\frac{1}{2}$ cups heavy cream, whipped

Make cream/custard base as directed in No. 2194. Pour into can of freezer. Whip the cream in a chilled bowl till stiff and add $\frac{1}{3}$ of it to custard base in freezer. Proceed up to step 2 on page 730. Remove top of can and add the rest of the whipped cream and proceed as directed on page 730. *Makes about 1 $\frac{1}{2}$ quarts.*

2196. FRENCH VANILLA ICE CREAM
Gelato alla crema

1 cup milk
2 cups heavy cream
1 4-inch piece of vanilla bean, split and crushed
    in the mortar
1 $\frac{1}{4}$ cups sugar
10 egg yolks
Pinch salt

Proceed as directed in Vanilla Ice Cream [No. 2194]. Freeze as directed on page 730. *Make about 1 $\frac{1}{2}$ quarts.*

2197. ECONOMICAL VANILLA ICE CREAM
Gelato alla vaniglia economico

1 quart rich milk (or 2 cups milk and 2 cups light cream)
1 cup sugar
3 tablespoons light corn syrup
Pinch salt
4 eggs
1 $\frac{1}{2}$ tablespoons vanilla extract

Place milk, sugar, corn syrup, and salt in an enamel pan and bring to the scalding point over low heat. Beat eggs until very light and pour in hot milk, mix well, and pour back in pan. Place over lowest possible heat and stir constantly until mixture coats a metal spoon. Pour through a strainer into a bowl, beat in the vanilla, and chill thoroughly. Freeze as directed on page 730. *Makes about 1 $\frac{1}{2}$ quarts.*

2198. ALMOND ICE CREAM
Gelato di mandorla

1 recipe Vanilla Ice Cream [No. 2194], or French
    Vanilla Ice Cream [No. 2196]
1½ cups blanched almonds [see No. 2280], toasted
    in a 350° oven until golden brown
¼ cup superfine sugar
Pinch salt

Make ice cream/custard base as directed in No. 2194
or No. 2196. Chop the toasted almonds coarsely and
mix with the sugar and salt. When cream/custard base
is poured into freezer can, add the almond/sugar
mixture. Freeze as directed on page 730. *Makes about
1½ quarts.*

2199. CARAMEL ICE CREAM
Gelato alla vaniglia caramellata

1½ cups sugar
⅓ cup water
1 recipe Vanilla Ice Cream [No. 2194], or French
    Vanilla Ice Cream [No. 2196], reducing the sugar
    to ½ cup

Place sugar and water in a heavy saucepan and cook
over low heat until the sugar becomes straw colored.
At this point tip pan back and forth until sugar turns
a deep ruddy gold. Do not let it get dark brown or it
will be bitter. Remove from stove and pour in 1 cup
of the milk (or cream) to be used in the custard/cream
base. Take great care as it will bubble up and sputter
since the caramel is blazing hot. Let stand for ½ hour,
then place over low heat and stir until all caramel is
dissolved. Add the remaining milk and cream and
proceed as directed in No. 2194. Freeze as directed
on page 730. *Makes about 1½ quarts.*

2200. CHOCOLATE ICE CREAM
Gelato al cioccolato

1 recipe Vanilla Ice Cream [No. 2914]
3 squares unsweetened chocolate
½ cup superfine sugar
Optional: 4 tablespoons freshly brewed coffee

While scalding the milk/cream mixture, melt the
chocolate in a bowl over hot water. Add the sugar and
optional coffee (which adds richness to the chocolate
flavor). Pour the scalded milk/cream mixture slowly
into the melted chocolate, stirring vigorously to blend
well, and then pour into the eggs and proceed as directed in No. 2194. Freeze as directed on page 730. *Makes
about 1⅔ quarts.*

2201. COFFEE ICE CREAM
Gelato al caffé

1 recipe Vanilla Ice Cream [No. 2194]
1 cup all-purpose-grind coffee
Optional: 1 tablespoon dark cocoa

Pour the ground coffee into the milk/cream mixture
and add the optional cocoa (which adds richness to
the coffee). Bring to scalding, cover pan, and let
steep in a warm place for 15 minutes. Pour through
a very fine strainer (or a triple thickness of cheesecloth)
into another enamel pan, bring to scalding point
again, and proceed as directed in No. 2194. Freeze as
directed on page 730. *Makes about 1⅔ quarts.*

2202. FRESH COFFEE-BEAN ICE CREAM
Gelato al caffé a modo mio

1 recipe Coffee Ice Cream [No. 2201]
⅔ cup freshly roasted coffee beans (French-roast
    coffee, if available)
½ cup superfine sugar

Prepare the coffee infusion as directed in No. 2201.
While it is steeping, place the beans and sugar in a
baking pan and place in a 350° oven for 15 minutes.
Strain the coffee infusion as directed in No. 2201.
Place it back on the stove over low heat, and pour in
the heated beans and sugar the moment you take them
from the oven. Bring the milk to scalding once again,
and then pour, beans and all, into the eggs. Proceed
as directed in Vanilla Ice Cream [No. 2194], straining
the mixture into a bowl before chilling. A few coffee
beans may be frozen witn the cream for texture. *Makes
about 1⅔ quarts.*

2203. HAZELNUT ICE CREAM
Gelato alla nocciola

1 recipe Vanilla Ice Cream [No. 2194]
1½ cups hazelnuts or filberts, blanched and ground

If the nuts have not been blanched, spread them out
on a large baking tin and place them in a 350° oven
for 10 minutes. Dump them out on a large towel and
rub them in the towel until their skins come loose.
Put them in a colander and rinse under running water
until they are free from any adhering skin. Place them
in a 250° oven for 20 minutes to dry out. Grind them
to a powder in the meat grinder, using the finest blade
(or whirl them, ½ cup at a time, in the blender at high
speed until pulverized). Mix them with the custard/
cream base before it is cooked, and proceed as directed

in No. 2194. Freeze as directed on page 730. *Makes about 1²/₃ quarts.*

2204. MARASCHINO ICE CREAM
Gelato di maraschino

1 recipe Vanilla Ice Cream [No. 2194], or French
    Vanilla Ice Cream [No. 2196], omitting the vanilla
½ cup maraschino liqueur
Optional: 3 or 4 drops desired food coloring

Add the maraschino to the custard/cream base just before it is strained into the bowl. Add food coloring, if desired, and proceed as directed in No. 2194. Freeze as directed on page 730. *Makes about 1²/₃ quarts.*

2205. MARRON GLACÉ ICE CREAM
Gelato di marrons glacés

1 recipe Vanilla Ice Cream [No. 2194]
2 cups marrons glacés, crumbled

Proceed with the making of ice cream up to step 2 on page 730. Add the crumbled marrons to the partially frozen cream, and continue as directed on page 730. *Makes about 1²/₃ quarts.*

2206. NOUGAT ICE CREAM
Gelato al torrone

1 recipe Vanilla Ice Cream [No. 2194]
1½ cups *torrone* candy (Italian nougat, available
    commercially), cut into large dice

Proceed with the making of ice cream up to step 2 on page 730. Add the diced nougat to the partially frozen cream, and continue as directed on page 730. *Makes about 1²/₃ quarts.*

2207. PISTACHIO ICE CREAM
Gelato al pistacchio

1 recipe Vanilla Ice Cream [No. 2194]
1½ cups pistachio nuts, shelled and coarsely chopped
1 tablespoon almond extract
Few drops green food coloring

Make the custard/cream base as directed in No. 2194. Add the pistachios, almond extract, and enough coloring to tint it a pale green just before the custard/cream is placed in refrigerator to chill preparatory to freezing. Freeze as directed on page 730. *Makes about 1²/₃ quarts.*

2208. RUM ICE CREAM
Gelato al rhum

1 recipe French Vanilla Ice Cream [No. 2196], or
    Vanilla Ice Cream [No. 2194], omitting the vanilla,
    if desired
½ cup dark rum
Optional: few drops preferred food coloring

Make the custard/cream as described in No. 2194. Add the ½ cup dark rum just before the mixture is taken off the stove and strained through the sieve. Proceed as directed, and freeze as indicated on page 730. *Makes about 1²/₃ quarts.*

2209. PRESERVED OR FRESH FRUIT ICE CREAM
Gelato di frutta

1 recipe Vanilla Ice Cream [No. 2194], or French
    Vanilla Ice Cream [No. 2196]
2 cups fruit desired (peaches, apricots, strawberries,
    raspberries, cherries, currants, or firm melon),
    peeled, pitted, and cut into sections, according to
    nature of fruit
1 cup superfine sugar

Peel and cut the fruit into small dice. Strawberries may be halved, raspberries left whole, and currants pressed through a fine sieve after cooking. Mix with the sugar and let them stand for 2 hours until the sugar has dissolved. Then place in refrigerator until thoroughly chilled. Currants must be cooked for 5 minutes in an enamel pan over low heat until their skins burst. The fruit is added to the cream at step 2 on page 730. Continue as directed on page 730. *Makes about 2 quarts.*

NOTE: If desired, one may preserve one's own fruit for future use by freezing it. Merely prepare the desired amount of fresh fruit in season, using the proportions given above (1 cup sugar to every 2 cups fruit). After the sugar has dissolved pour the fruit into pint containers, cover tightly, and freeze until needed. This is a better way to enjoy fresh fruit out of season than to purchase commercially available frozen fruit.

ICES AND GRANITE
Gelati e granite

Freshly made water ices and *granite* are among the most delectable frozen desserts to be found in Italy. *Granite* are merely sweetened fruit purées frozen until granular or gritty in texture. They combine magnificently with a scoop of vanilla ice cream or with a dollop of whipped cream. It is impossible to obtain true *granite* commercially, but they are not hard to make. They do not require a special ice-cream freezer, and since the texture of a *granita* is supposed to be coarse, they are perfectly suited to making in the freezing compartment of your refrigerator.

1. Turn down the temperature control of the refrigerator to its coldest point ½ hour before placing the mixture in the freezing compartment. Wash out ice trays thoroughly with soda and hot water to eliminate any foreign odors they may have acquired. Prepare the mixture of your choice. Freeze mixture until it is almost frozen solid (the amount of sugar employed will usually prevent the mixture from turning into a block of ice).

2. Place frozen mixture in a chilled bowl and chop thoroughly. A mechanical ice crusher may be used, but care must be taken that the mixture is frozen to maximum hardness before crushing it in this manner.

3. Place the mushy mixture back in the freezer trays and freeze for another hour, or until solid again. Repeat step 2, and place in chilled sherbet glasses or parfait glasses, and keep them in the freezing compartment until ready to serve.

If a finer-grained water ice is desired, add an egg white to the mixture (as indicated in the following recipes), and freeze as ice cream (*see* pages 730–31).

2210. COFFEE GRANITA
Granita di caffè con panna

This glorified version of iced coffee will provide the perfect dessert after a rich, heavy meal. It is also superb served on hot summer nights, accompanied by cookies or petits fours.

2 cups triple-strength espresso coffee (or French-roast coffee prepared in a drip or filter coffee maker)
2 cups superfine sugar
1½ cups water

1¼ cups very cold water
1½ cups heavy cream

Prepare the coffee just before the mixture is to be assembled. Cook the sugar and the 1½ cups water in an enamel pan over medium heat until it reaches the large thread stage (219° on the candy thermometer). Remove from stove and allow to cool to lukewarm. Prepare the coffee while waiting for this. Mix the coffee and sugar syrup together, and add the 1¼ cups of very cold water. Pour the mixture into ice trays and freeze as directed at the left until stiff and mushy. Place coffee mush into a large, chilled bowl and chop until it resembles finely crushed ice. Place back in refrigerator and freeze for 1 hour more, chop, and repeat the process. Whip the cream until stiff in a chilled bowl. Do not sweeten it. Place a few spoonsful of the *granita* in the bottoms of 6 or 8 (depending on the size) chilled parfait glasses, top with a tablespoon or 2 of whipped cream. Continue layering, ending with a dollop of the cream. Place in freezing compartment until ready to serve.

NOTE: 1 tablespoon vanilla extract or 3 tablespoons brandy or rum may be added to the coffee while still hot.

2211. FRUIT ICE OR GRANITA
Gelato o granita di frutta

This is the master recipe, adapted to particular fruits in most of the recipes that follow.

5 cups fresh fruit, peeled, pitted, and puréed by passing through a food mill or pressing through a sieve
2½ cups superfine sugar
1½ cups water
Juice of 2 oranges, strained
Juice of 1 lemon, strained
Optional: 2 egg whites (if mixture is to be frozen in ice-cream freezer)

Place the puréed fruit in a large bowl. Place the sugar and water in a heavy saucepan over medium heat and cook until it reaches the large thread stage (219° on the candy thermometer). Pour it over the fruit, mix well, and let stand until cooled to room temperature. Add the orange and lemon juice, mix well, and place in the refrigerator until well chilled. Freeze as directed on the left. If a fine-grained water ice is desired, beat the egg white with 2 or 3 tablespoons of the juices from the fruit until well blended. Beat into the fruit purée and freeze as directed for ice cream on page 730. *Makes about 1⅔ quarts.*

2212. LEMON ICE OR GRANITA
Gelato o granita di limone

1 cup freshly squeezed lemon juice, strained
Juice of 1 orange, strained
Grated rind of 2 lemons (no white part)
1 cup water
2 cups superfine sugar
1 cup cold water
Optional: 2 egg whites (if mixture is to be frozen in
    ice-cream freezer)

Mix the lemon and orange juice with the grated rind. Cook the sugar and water in a small saucepan over medium heat until it reaches the large thread stage (219° on the candy thermometer). Remove from stove, cool to room temperature, and mix with fruit juices. Add cold water, mix well, and place in refrigerator until well chilled. Freeze as directed on page 734. If a fine-grained water ice is desired, beat the egg white with 2 or 3 tablespoons of the liquid until well blended. Beat into the rest of the liquid with a wire whisk, and freeze as directed for ice cream on page 730. *Makes about 1 scant quart.*

2213. ORANGE ICE OR GRANITA
Gelato o granita di arancia

2 cups freshly squeezed orange juice, strained
Grated rind of 1 orange (no white part)
1 cup water
1½ cups superfine sugar
Juice of 2 lemons, strained
Optional: 2 egg whites (if mixture is to be frozen in
    ice-cream freezer)

Mix the orange juice with the grated rind. Cook the sugar and water in a small saucepan over medium heat until it reaches the large thread stage (219° on the candy thermometer). Allow to cool to room temperature, then mix with orange juice. Add lemon juice and mix well. Place in refrigerator until well chilled. Freeze as directed on page 734. If a fine-grained water ice is desired, beat the egg white with 2 or 3 tablespoons of the liquid until well blended. Beat into the rest of the liquid with a wire whisk, and freeze as directed for ice cream on page 730. *Makes about 1 scant quart.*

2214. RASPBERRY ICE OR GRANITA
Gelato o granita di lamponi

5 cups fresh raspberries, puréed by pressing through a
    very fine sieve (all seeds should be eliminated)
Same ingredients as in Fruit Ice or Granita [No. 2211]

Prepare as directed in No. 2211. *Makes about 1⅔ quarts.*

NOTE: 2 cups heavy cream, whipped and unsweetened, make an excellent accompaniment to this preparation. Vanilla Ice Cream [No. 2194] or French Vanilla Ice Cream [No. 2196] also go very well with it.

2215. STRAWBERRY ICE OR GRANITA
Gelato o granita di fragole

5 cups fresh strawberries, hulled and puréed by passing
    through a food mill or pressing through a sieve
Same ingredients as in Fruit Ice or Granita [No. 2211]

Prepare as directed in No. 2211. *Makes about 1⅔ quarts.*

NOTE: 2 cups heavy cream, whipped and unsweetened, make an excellent accompaniment to this preparation. Vanilla Ice Cream [No. 2194] or French Vanilla Ice Cream [No. 2196] also go very well with it.

2216. TANGERINE ICE OR GRANITA
Gelato o granita di mandarino

2 cups freshly squeezed tangerine juice
Grated rind of 1 tangerine (no white part)
1 cup water
1¼ cups superfine sugar
Juice of 2 lemons, strained
Juice of 1 orange, strained
Optional: 2 egg whites (if mixture is to be frozen in
    ice-cream freezer)

Proceed exactly as directed in Orange Ice or Granita [No. 2213]. *Makes about 1 quart.*

COUPES
Coppe

Coupes are glorified sundaes made with ice cream, water-ices or *granite,* fruits, sauces, liqueurs, and other ingredients. The traditional containers for serving these preparations are champagne glasses (the solid-stem variety). Sherbet glasses, or even parfait glasses in some cases, would serve as well. Only a few of the better-known combinations are listed here, and as one grows more expert, others can be devised according to one's personal taste. The thing to remember is that the freshest and best ingredients should be employed, and, if time permits, homemade ice creams and ices should be used. Canned fruits are not recommended, nor commercially available syrups.

2217. COUPE DAMA BIANCA
Coppa "Dama bianca"

6 large scoops Almond Ice Cream [No. 2198]
6 pear halves, prepared as in Pear Compote [No. 2189], well chilled
6 teaspoons currant jelly
1½ cups Lemon Ice [No. 2212]

Place a scoop of ice cream in the bottom of 6 well-chilled champagne or sherbet glasses. Flatten out slightly with a spoon and place a pear half on each scoop, convex side down. Fill the hollow of each pear with 1 teaspoon of the jelly. Soften the lemon ice slightly and place it in a pastry bag fitted with a large plain tip (or the nozzle of the bag itself) and pipe a border of lemon ice around the ice cream. Place in freezer until ready to serve. *Serves* 6.

2218. COUPE DELIZIOSA
Coppa deliziosa

½ recipe Apricot Compote [No. 2181], well chilled
⅓ cup kirsch
6 very large scoops apricot ice cream, made according to Preserved or Fresh Fruit Ice Cream [No. 2209]
½ cup blanched almonds [*see* No. 2288], slivered, toasted in a 350° oven until golden brown, and cooled
3 tablespoons superfine sugar

Finely dice all but 6 of the apricots in the compote. Mix the fruit with 3 tablespoons of the kirsch. Place a large scoop of the ice cream in the bottoms of 6 well-chilled champagne or sherbet glasses. Cover with the diced apricots and their syrup, top each scoop with an apricot half, convex side upward, and sprinkle each with some of the slivered almonds. Mix the rest of the kirsch with the sugar until dissolved, and sprinkle some over each coupe. Place in freezer until ready to serve. *Serves* 6.

2219. COUPE GRAND HOTEL
Coppa Grand Hôtel

6 large scoops Maraschino Ice Cream [No. 2204]
½ recipe Cherry Compote [No. 2183], chilled until almost frozen
⅓ cup Curaçao liqueur
½ recipe Apricot Sauce [No. 2270], well chilled
4 tablespoons maraschino liqueur

Place the ice cream in a bowl and work with a wooden spoon until softened. Mix in the cherries and the Curaçao. Place in a metal ice tray, cover with foil,

and place in freezing compartment of the refrigerator until frozen back to its original consistency. Place a scoop of the ice cream in the bottoms of 6 champagne glasses or coupes. Mix the apricot sauce with the maraschino and pour some over each scoop. Keep in freezer until ready to serve. *Serves* 6.

2220. COUPE HAWAIIAN
Coppa hawaiana

6 large scoops Vanilla Ice Cream [No. 2194]
½ cup candied pineapple, diced
1 cup heavy cream, poured into a bowl and placed in freezing compartment until mushy
3 tablespoons superfine sugar
½ cup coarsely chopped Praline [*see* No. 2290]
½ cup heavy cream, whipped

Place the ice cream in a bowl, work with a spoon until softened, and work in the pineapple bits. Whip the almost-frozen cream until stiff and sweeten it with the sugar. Mix the whipped cream with the ice cream until perfectly blended. Place in clean metal ice trays, cover with foil, and place in freezing compartment until frozen back to its original consistency. Place a scoop of the cream in the bottoms of 6 well-chilled champagne or sherbet glasses. Sprinkle with the Praline and top each with a dollop of the whipped cream. Keep in freezer until ready to serve. *Serves* 6.

2221. COUPE JACQUES
Coppa Jacques

½ cup strawberries
½ cup raspberries
2 perfect peaches, peeled, stoned, and diced
2 large apples, peeled, cored, and diced
½ cup fresh black cherries, pitted and halved
1 cup superfine sugar
½ cup kirsch
6 small scoops Lemon Ice [No. 2212]
6 small scoops Strawberry Ice [No. 2215]
18 candied cherries
24 blanched almonds [*see* No. 2280], halved

Mix the fruits with the sugar and kirsch and let stand in the refrigerator for at least 6 hours or overnight. Place 1 scoop of lemon ice and 1 scoop of strawberry ice in the bottom of 6 well-chilled champagne or sherbet glasses. Fill the space between the scoops with the mixed fruits and their juice and place a candied cherry on each scoop and surround it with the blanched almonds like flower petals (*see* photograph on page 737). Keep in freezer until ready to serve. *Serves* 6.

SEE
EVERSE
FOR
APTION

Ambroeus Mousse (No. 2122)

2222. COUPE MARIA THERESA
Coppa Maria Teresa

1 recipe Peach Compote [No. 2188], made with halved
    peaches
⅓ cup Drambuie liqueur
6 large scoops peach ice cream made according to
    Preserved or Fresh Fruit Ice Cream [No. 2209]
12 blanched almonds [*see* No. 2280], halved

Reserve 6 of the most perfect peach halves. Dice the
rest coarsely. Drain off all but ¾ cup of the syrup.
Mix all the peaches and the syrup with the Drambuie,
and place in the refrigerator for at least 3 hours. Place
1 large scoop of ice cream in the bottom of 6 well-
chilled champagne or sherbet glasses. Surround with
the diced peaches and liqueur-flavored syrup, top
each scoop with a halved peach, and arrange 4 halved
almonds on top of that. Keep in freezer until ready
to serve. *Serves 6.*

SPECIAL DESSERTS WITH
ICE CREAM
Preparazioni diverse con gelati

These recipes employ ice cream in various manners.
Some are baked desserts, concealing ice cream beneath
a hot exterior, and others use various fruits and cakes.
The possible variations are endless, and one can soon
invent one's own combinations after trying those listed
here. Of course, commercial ice creams may be used,
but care should be taken to obtain the best available.
Naturally, homemade ice cream will provide a far
better result. However, only homemade fruit ices

should be used, as the commercial varieties are now
made from overcooked or reconstituted fruits, artificial
flavorings, and citric acid. The resulting mixture is
ersatz and not very palatable.

2223. BAKED ALASKA
Omelette en surprise

*Solidly frozen ice cream enclosed in a hot meringue crust
is always a mystery to the guests, besides providing a
delicious contrast of flavors, textures, and heat and cold.
Actually, the dish is based upon a sound scientific principle : insulation. The cake and meringue contain so many
tiny air holes, and provide such excellent insulation
against heat, that rock-hard ice cream will remain rock
hard, and defy cutting. It is best to use firm but man-
ageably frozen cream. A baked Alaska must be served
at once, so that the meringue is still hot.*

1 rectangle or round of sponge cake, at least 1 inch
    thick
3 tablespoons preferred liqueur, brandy, or rum
1 quart Vanilla Ice Cream [No. 2194], frozen in a brick
    or a round charlotte mold
½ recipe Italian Meringue [No. 2256]
Optional: ¼ cup candied fruits (cherries, pineapple,
    orange peel, citron, etc.) soaked for 2 hours in
    3 tablespoons dark rum

Trim the cake so that it is 1 inch larger all around
than the block of ice cream. This is important, as the
ice cream must not come to the edge of the cake.
Sprinkle it with the liqueur. If desired, a richer dessert
may be obtained by then sprinkling the cake with the

737

optional rum-soaked fruits. Place the cake on an oven-proof platter (*not* metal). Place the ice cream on top of the cake and quickly cover it and the cake with an even, thick coating of some of the meringue. Smooth the meringue evenly with a dampened spatula and make sure there are no gaps or thin spots. Place the remaining meringue in a pastry bag fitted with a large star tip and pipe decorative swirls and rosettes all over the smooth coating of meringue. (Once the ice cream has been placed on the cake, work quickly and calmly, and do not let the cream start to melt.) Place the meringue-covered cake/cream in a 400° oven and leave it there until the meringue turns golden brown (from 5 to 8 minutes). Remove from oven and serve at once. *Serves 8.*

NOTE: Although vanilla is the standard ice cream employed, one may make this with any flavor. Water ices, however, are not recommended as they have a lower melting point and disaster could result.

2224. BAKED CHERRY ALASKA
Ciliege gelate alla moda di Norvegia

1 rectangle or round of slightly stale sponge cake,
    at least 1 inch thick
½ recipe Cherry Compote [No. 2183], well chilled
¼ cup kirsch
1 quart Maraschino Ice Cream [No. 2204], frozen in a
    brick mold or a round charlotte mold
½ recipe Italian Meringue [No. 2256]

Trim the cake as directed in Baked Alaska [No. 2223]. Sprinkle it with the kirsch. Place on an oven-proof platter (*not* metal), and cover it with the compote and its syrup. Cover with the ice cream and meringue and bake exactly as directed in No. 2223. Serve at once. *Serves 6 to 8.*

2225. CHERRY ICE-CREAM TARTS ALLA DIVA
Tartelette di ciliege gelate alla diva

All ingredients must be at hand before assembling this dessert.

1 cup fresh cherries, pitted and halved
1 cup fresh raspberries
¼ cup Cherry Heering (or any good cherry brandy)
½ cup superfine sugar
6 large baked tartlet shells made with Flaky Pastry
    [No. 1954], or Sweet and Tender Egg Pastry
    [No. 1958]
½ recipe Italian Meringue [No. 2256]

6 scoops Vanilla Ice Cream [No. 2194]
¼ cup pistachio nuts, coarsely chopped

Place the cherries, raspberries, cherry brandy, and sugar in a bowl. Stir lightly to mix the ingredients, and place in the refrigerator for at least 3 hours. For the last hour place in freezing compartment so that they are almost frozen. When they have reached this stage, divide the mixture among the 6 tart shells. Top with the ice cream. Have the meringue ready and placed in a pastry bag fitted with a large star tip. Pipe a thick coating over the cream. Make sure that it covers the edges of the tart shells; leave no gaps. Sprinkle with the nuts. Place the tarts on a wooden board and place in a 400° oven until the meringue is golden brown. Remove from oven, transfer to a platter, and serve at once. *Serves 6.*

2226. CRÊPE-WRAPPED ICE CREAM CASINO POURVILLE SUR MER
Gelato fritto "Casino Pourville sur Mer"

This is one of the great classic desserts. It is assembled at the dining table, served with a flourish, and is perfectly delicious. If one works calmly with all the ingredients at hand, it is not difficult to assemble.

Have ready at the table:
1 recipe sauce for Crêpes Suzette [*see* No. 2027]
8 large, paper-thin crêpes, about 8 inches in diameter
    [*see* No. 2017]
1 cup candied fruits (cherries, pineapple, orange peel,
    citron, etc.) soaked for 2 hours in 5 tablespoons
    brandy and placed in a small serving bowl
1 cup coarsely chopped Praline [*see* No. 2290],
    placed in a small serving bowl
1 bottle Aurum liqueur
1 bottle maraschino liqueur
1 quart Caramel Ice Cream [No. 2199], colored pink,
    if desired, with a few drops of red food
    coloring, frozen in a brick-shaped mold,
    unmolded, and decorated with paper-thin squares
    of bittersweet chocolate

Before starting, make sure that the ice cream is really hard and well frozen. Place ⅛ of the crêpe sauce in the frying pan of the chafing dish. Light the flame of the chafing dish and, when the sauce is bubbling, dip a crêpe in it, and turn once, making sure it is well coated with the sauce and has heated through. Sprinkle with some of the brandy-soaked fruit, place a slice of ice cream in the center of the crêpe, sprinkle with a few drops of Aurum and maraschino, and fold the sides of the crêpe over the ice cream, envelope fashion. Place folded crêpe on a dessert plate and pour over the sauce remaining in the pan. Repeat this process for the rest of the crêpes. Each guest should eat his helping as soon as it is served him, otherwise the crêpe will get cold and the ice cream will melt. *Serves 8.*

2227. ICED APRICOTS IN KÜMMEL
Albicocche al kümmel

1 recipe Apricot Compote [No. 2181], well chilled
⅓ cup kümmel liqueur
8 dry almond macaroons (Italian macaroons, if available), crushed
1 quart Vanilla Ice Cream [No. 2194]
1 cup heavy cream, placed in a bowl in the freezing compartment of the refrigerator until mushy
3 tablespoons superfine sugar
¼ cup Glacéed Almonds [No. 2285], chopped

Pour all but 2 tablespoons of the kümmel over the apricots and place them in the coldest part of the refrigerator for at least 2 hours. When ready to serve, crumble the macaroons over the bottom of a well-chilled glass bowl. Spread the ice cream over the top and cover with the well-chilled apricot compote. Whip the cream until stiff and flavor with the sugar and the remaining kümmel. Spread this over the ice cream, and sprinkle the surface with the glacéed almonds. Serve at once. *Serves 6 to 8.*

2228. ICED MELON SURPRISE
Melone gelato in sorpresa

1 large, perfectly ripe casaba or Spanish melon
1 recipe Fruit Ice Cream [*see* No. 2209], made with the flesh of the melon and flavored with ½ cup kirsch

Cut off the top of the melon, about 1 inch down from the stem end. Place this "lid" aside for future use. Scoop out the melon with a ball cutter, discarding the seeds. Cut the melon balls in small pieces, flavor with kirsch, and use them in making the ice cream. Freeze ice cream according to the directions on page 730. Place the melon in the refrigerator to chill thoroughly (to ensure proper chilling, it may be filled with ice cubes after it has been in the refrigerator for 2 hours, and the ice cubes left in until just before it is to be filled with the ice cream). When the ice cream has "ripened" for the time specified on page 730 (or longer, if desired), dry the interior of the chilled melon, pack it with the ice cream, place the melon in a large bowl packed with cracked ice, and serve at once. If desired, the ice in the bowl may be decorated with seasonal flowers and foliage. *Serves 6 to 8.*

2229. ICED MELON SURPRISE WITH WHIPPED CREAM
Melone gelato in sorpresa con panna montata

Same ingredients listed in No. 2228
1 cup heavy cream, whipped

Proceed exactly as directed in the previous recipe. Add the whipped cream at step 2 on page 730. Continue as directed both on page 730 and in the preceding recipe. *Serves 6 to 8.*

2230. ICED PEACHES CARDINALE
Pesche alla cardinale

1 recipe Peach Compote [No. 2188], using halved peaches, well chilled
1 cup currant jelly
¼ cup kirsch
1 quart Strawberry Ice [*see* No. 2215]
1 cup fresh whole strawberries (wild strawberries, if available)

Prepare the compote and chill it in the coldest part of the refrigerator. Melt the currant jelly in a small, heavy saucepan over a low flame. When no lumps remain, dilute it with 6 tablespoons of the syrup from the compote. Pour into a small bowl, stir in the kirsch, and chill the now-liquid jelly in the refrigerator. When ready to serve, spoon the strawberry ice into a well-chilled glass bowl. Remove the peaches from the syrup with a slotted spoon and place them over the cream, and pour the currant jelly over the peaches. Garnish with the strawberries. Serve at once. If desired, the bowl may be placed in a larger bowl packed with crushed ice. *Serves 6.*

2231. ICED PEARS CHARLIE CHAPLIN
Pere gelate Charlie Chaplin

6 perfect pears, peeled, halved, and cored
Syrup:
  2 cups sugar
  $\frac{2}{3}$ cup water
  1-inch piece of vanilla bean
2 cups raspberries (preferably fresh but, if using frozen,
    drain well and add only enough syrup to taste)
$\frac{1}{4}$ cup Strega liqueur
12 small scoops French Vanilla Ice Cream [No. 2196]
$\frac{1}{2}$ recipe Cold Zabaglione [No. 2117], made with white
    wine instead of Marsala
3 marrons glacés, crumbled

Scoop out the interiors of the pear halves with a melon
ball cutter, leaving a shell no more than $\frac{1}{2}$ inch thick.
Cook the sugar, water, and vanilla bean in an enamel
saucepan until it reaches the large thread stage (219°
on the candy thermometer). Poach the pears in the
syrup for no more than 5 minutes, remove them with
a slotted spoon, and place in refrigerator to chill thoroughly. Raise the heat under the pan with the syrup,
and reduce it by $\frac{1}{2}$. Cool the syrup and pour $\frac{1}{2}$ of it
over the raspberries, add the Strega, and chill them
well. Prepare the cold Zabaglione and chill it well.
Before serving, place 2 pear halves in large, well-iced
champagne or sherbet glasses. Fill the hollows of the
pears with the raspberries, place a scoop of ice cream
in each pear half, coat with the cold Zabaglione, and
sprinkle some of the crumbled marrons on each serving.
Serve at once. *Serves* 6.

NOTE: A platter of Palm Leaves [No. 1941] provides
a perfect accompaniment to this dessert.

2232. ICED PEARS CONTE DI SAVOIA
Pere "Conte di Savoia"

3 large, perfect pears, peeled and halved
Syrup:
  2 cups sugar
  $\frac{1}{2}$ cup freshly squeezed orange juice, strained
  $\frac{1}{4}$ cup cold water
  1 stick cinnamon
  2 strips orange rind (no white part)
  2 strips lemon rind (no white part)
1 recipe Italian Sponge Cake [No. 1913], baked the day
    before in a 9- by 12-inch baking tin and cut into
    6 evenly sized rectangles
2 cups fresh raspberries
$\frac{1}{4}$ cup freshly squeezed orange juice, strained
3 tablespoons Aurum liqueur
$\frac{1}{2}$ cup superfine sugar
$\frac{1}{2}$ recipe Cold Zabaglione [No. 2117], made with
    white wine instead of Marsala
6 scoops Vanilla Ice Cream [No. 2194]
$\frac{1}{2}$ cup heavy cream
6 marrons glacés, finely crumbled

Scoop out the interiors of the pear halves with a melon
ball cutter, leaving a shell no more than $\frac{1}{2}$ inch thick.
Place the ingredients for the syrup in an enamel saucepan and cook over medium heat until it almost reaches
the soft ball stage (222° on the candy thermometer).
Place the pear cases in a large bowl and pour the boiling
syrup over them. Allow them to cool to room temperature and then place them in the refrigerator to chill
thoroughly. Hollow out the 6 rectangles of sponge cake
with a grapefruit knife, making little "boxes" of them.
Be careful not to break the cake. Soak the raspberries

Crêpe-wrapped Ice Cream Casino
Pourville-sur-Mer (No. 2226): see page 738

in the orange juice, Aurum, and sugar. Place them in the refrigerator for 2 hours or more to chill thoroughly. Prepare the cold Zabaglione, and allow that to chill thoroughly in the refrigerator. Just before serving, arrange cake boxes in a circle on a large platter, sprinkle each of them with a tablespoonful of the cold pear syrup. Place 1 pear half in each box and fill the pears with the raspberries and their juice. Place a scoop of ice cream in each pear and coat with the Zabaglione. Place the cream in a pastry bag fitted with a large star tip and pipe rosettes over each pear. Sprinkle with the crumbled marrons, and place in freezer until ready to serve (or serve at once). *Serves 6.*

NOTE: The unused pear syrup may be placed in a tightly covered jar and stored in the refrigerator for future use in fruit compotes or any other preparation desired.

2233. ICED PEARS DUCHESSA
Pere gelate duchessa

6 large, perfect pears, peeled and halved
Same syrup as in Iced Pears Conte di Savoia [No. 2232]
12 scoops French Vanilla Ice Cream [No. 2196]

Prepare the pears exactly as directed in No. 2232. When they are well chilled, fill their hollows with scoops of the ice cream, place them on a platter, drizzle over some of the syrup, and place in the freezer for 2 hours before serving. *Serves 6.*

2234. ICED PEARS NYMPHET
Pere gelate ninfetta

6 large, perfect pears, peeled
Same syrup as in Iced Pears Conte di Savoia [No. 2232]
1/4 cup Curaçao liqueur
1/2 recipe meringue mixture [*see* No. 2009]
1 quart Caramel Ice Cream [No. 2199]
1 cup currant jelly

Peel the pears, leaving them whole, and cut off their tops, about 1 inch below the stem. Hollow them out with a grapefruit knife or a melon ball cutter. Heat the syrup indicated in No. 2232 to the large thread stage (219° on the candy thermometer), and poach the pears (and their cut-off tops) for 2 minutes. Remove from stove, add the Curaçao, cool to room temperature, and then place in the coldest part of the refrigerator for at least 2 hours, or until thoroughly chilled. Lightly butter a baking sheet, dust with flour, tapping off the excess, and spread the meringue on it in an 8-inch circle. Bake in a 200° oven until the meringue is dry.

Remove it carefully and place it on a platter. When the pears are ice cold, melt the currant jelly until it liquifies in a small, deep saucepan over low heat. Dip each pear into it, coating it well, but taking care that the jelly does not run over into the hollowed-out interiors. Dip the pear tops in the jelly also. Place the pears in the freezing compartment for 10 minutes to chill well, and to set the jelly. Before serving, arrange the pears in a border on the meringue circle. Fill them with some of the ice cream, cover with their caps, and heap the rest of the cream in the center of the pear circle. Pour a little syrup over the ice cream and serve at once. *Serves 6.*

2235. ICED PINEAPPLE ITALIANA
Ananasso all'italiana

1 large, dead-ripe pineapple
1 1/2 cups superfine sugar (less if fruit is very sweet)
1/2 cup kirsch
3 or 4 cups (amount depends on size of pineapple)
    Strawberry Ice [No. 2215]

Prepare exactly as in Iced Pineapple Surprise [No. 2236]. *Serves 6 to 8 (depending on size of fruit).*

2236. ICED PINEAPPLE SURPRISE
Ananasso in sorpresa

1 large, dead-ripe pineapple
1 1/2 cups superfine sugar (less if fruit is very sweet)
1/2 cup dark rum
3 or 4 cups (amount depends on size of pineapple)
    Rum Ice Cream [No. 2208]

Cut off the top of the pineapple about 1 inch below the spiny leaf crown. Place this to one side and scoop out the inside of the fruit with a grapefruit knife and a melon ball cutter. Make sure you do not cut through the skin, and leave a shell about 1/2 inch thick. Discard the woody core of the fruit, cut up the rest, and sprinkle it with 1 cup of the sugar and all but 3 tablespoons of the rum. Place the fruit bits in the freezing compartment. Sprinkle the inside of the hollowed-out pineapple with the rest of the sugar and the rum and place it in the freezing compartment also. When the fruit and pineapple shell are ice cold, fill with alternating layers of the fruit pieces and the rum ice cream. Cover with the top of the pineapple, set the fruit in a bowl packed with crushed ice, and serve at once. *Serves 6 to 8 (depending on the size of the fruit).*

2237. ICED PINEAPPLE VILLA SASSI
Ananasso "Villa Sassi"

6 thick slices ripe pineapple
1 cup superfine sugar
¼ cup dark rum
3 tablespoons kirsch
3 tablespoons Aurum liqueur
6 scoops Vanilla Ice Cream [No. 2194]
¼ cup slivered almonds [see No. 2288]
1 cup Chocolate Sauce [No. 2272], hot

This dish is prepared at the dinner table in a chafing dish. Place the pineapple slices in the frying pan of the chafing dish. Light the flame and let it burn at maximum. Glaze the fruit by adding, little by little, the sugar, rum, and kirsch. Let the liquid cook away before adding more liquor. When all has been added, and the fruit is well glazed, portion it out onto 6 dessert plates, pour a little Aurum over each, top with a scoop of ice cream, pour the hot syrup over, sprinkle with the almonds, and pour a ribbon of chocolate sauce around each pineapple slice. *Serves 6.*

2238. LEMON ICE AND STRAWBERRIES DELIZIA DEL SUD
Fragoline di bosco gelate "Delizia del Sud"

½ cup dry Spumante wine (or Champagne)
3 tablespoons Aurum liqueur
3 tablespoons superfine sugar
Grated rind of ½ orange (no white part)
3 cups strawberries (wild strawberries, if available, otherwise use the smallest, reddest cultivated variety), hulled
1 quart Lemon Ice [No. 2212]
1½ cups heavy cream, placed in a bowl in the freezing compartment of the refrigerator until mushy
3 tablespoons superfine sugar
1 teaspoon vanilla extract
¼ cup candied orange peel, diced
6 marrons glacés, crumbled

Mix the wine, Aurum, sugar, and grated rind together and pour over the strawberries. Place in the coldest part of the refrigerator for at least 2 hours. When ready to serve, place the lemon ice in a well-chilled glass bowl. Cover it with the berries and their marinade. Whip the almost-frozen cream until stiff and flavor with the sugar and vanilla. Spread over the berries and garnish the surface of the cream with the diced candied peel and crumbled marrons. Place the bowl in a larger bowl filled with crushed ice and serve at once. *Serves 6 to 8.*

2239. MERINGUE GLACÉ CAPRICCIO DI DAMA
Meringaggio gelato capriccio di dama

1 recipe Italian Meringue [No. 2256]
1 pint Vanilla Ice Cream [No. 2194], slightly softened
1 pint Fruit Ice Cream [No. 2209], made with cherries, slightly softened
1 pint Chocolate Ice Cream [No. 2200]
1 cup heavy cream, placed in a bowl in the freezing compartment until mushy
2 cups currant jelly
5 tablespoons kirsch

Lightly butter 2 large baking sheets. Sprinkle with flour, tap off the excess, and trace 3 8-inch circles on the sheets (2 circles on 1 sheet, the third on the other; or bake 2 circles and then the other on the same sheet in relays). Spread a layer of meringue on each, carefully keeping within the traced outlines. Place the rest of the meringue in a pastry bag fitted with a large plain tip (or use the nozzle of the bag itself) and pipe a border (like a fence) around the outer edge of each layer. Bake in a 200° oven until dry and crisp. Carefully remove from baking sheets (by sawing them off with a serrated knife, if necessary). Allow to cool on cake racks. When quite cool, place the first layer on a cake platter and fill it with the vanilla ice cream, top with the next layer and fill it with the cherry ice cream. End with the final layer, topped by the chocolate ice cream. Place platter in freezing compartment. Take the mushy heavy cream and whip until stiff. Place it in a pastry bag fitted with a large star tip, remove meringue from freezer, and cover the sides showing ice cream layers with strips of cream. Pipe a lattice over the chocolate ice cream on the top. Return to freezer. Melt currant jelly in a small saucepan over low heat until completely liquefied. Add the kirsch, pour into a sauceboat, and let cool. Serve with the meringue cake. *Serves 8 to 10.*

2240. PEACH MELBA
Pesche Melba

This is one version of the famous dessert originally created in London by the renowned chef, Auguste Escoffier, in honor of the Australian diva, Nellie Melba.

1 recipe Peach Compote [No. 2188], made with very large, perfect peaches, peeled, halved, and stoned

2 cups fresh raspberries

¼ cup kirsch

6 large scoops Vanilla Ice Cream [No. 2194], or French Vanilla Ice Cream [No. 2196]

Chill the peaches in their syrup in the coldest part of the refrigerator until ice cold. Press the berries through a fine sieve to eliminate the seeds, and sweeten to taste with the syrup from the peaches. Add the kirsch, and place this purée in the coldest part of the refrigerator until ice cold. Before serving, place the ice cream in a chilled silver bowl. Cover with the peaches, removed with a slotted spoon from their syrup, and pour the raspberry purée over all. Serve at once. *Serves 6.*

2241. PEACHES REX
Pesche "Rex"

6 ripe peaches, peeled, halved, and stoned

Same syrup as in Iced Pears Conte di Savoia [No. 2232]

1 quart Caramel Ice Cream [No. 2199]

12 Glacéed Almonds [No. 2285]

3 tablespoons Aurum liqueur

1 recipe Cold Zabaglione [No. 2117], made with white wine instead of Marsala

½ cup heavy cream, whipped

1 square bitter chocolate, grated or shaved

Place the peaches in a bowl. Cook the syrup until it reaches the large thread stage (219° on the candy thermometer) and pour it over the peaches. Let cool at room temperature and then place in the coldest part of the refrigerator to chill for at least 2 hours. Before serving, place the ice cream in a mound in a shallow glass serving bowl. Remove peaches from syrup with a slotted spoon and arrange around the sides of the mound, convex sides against the cream, and place a nut in the hollows left by the peach stones. Sprinkle the fruit with the Aurum, cover all with the cold Zabaglione, place the cream in a pastry bag fitted with a large star tip, and pipe rosettes over each Zabaglione-covered peach. Sprinkle the chocolate over the top, and serve at once. *Serves 6 to 8.*

NOTE: The leftover peach syrup may be placed in a tightly covered jar and kept in the refrigerator for future use.

2242. PEAR ICE-CREAM CAKE ALMA
Pere gelate Alma

This delicate and delicious dessert may be assembled at the dining table. It should create a considerable effect if performed with both ease and a flourish. As in the case of all such desserts, the components must be ready at hand, and the person preparing the dessert must work quickly but calmly, and without apparent effort.

6 pears, peeled, halved, and cored

Same syrup as in Iced Pears Conte di Savoia [No. 2232]

6 sponge-cake boxes, prepared as directed in Iced Pears Conte di Savoia [No. 2232]

1½ cups heavy cream, placed in a bowl in the freezing compartment of the refrigerator until mushy

1 quart Vanilla Ice Cream [No. 2194], or French Vanilla Ice Cream [No. 2196]

⅓ cup Aurum liqueur

¼ cup maraschino liqueur

⅓ cup candied fruits (cherries, pineapple, orange peel, citron, etc.), diced and soaked in ¼ cup brandy for 3 hours

1 square bitter chocolate, grated or shaved

Place the pears in a bowl and pour the boiling syrup over them. Let them cool to room temperature and then place them in the coldest part of the refrigerator for 2 hours, or until well chilled. Let the sponge-cake boxes stand uncovered so that they become slightly dry. Before serving, place the sponge-cake boxes on a platter, and place the candied brandy-soaked fruits and the chocolate in individual bowls. Set a glass serving bowl into a larger bowl packed with crushed ice. Whip the cream until stiff. Mix the ice cream with the Aurum and maraschino and then mix in the whipped cream and place in the bowl packed in ice. Bring all components to the table: the pears in syrup, the platter with the sponge-cake boxes, the ice cream, and the bowls of candied fruit and grated chocolate. Place a cake case on each plate, and then top with the peach halves and a little syrup. Beat the brandy-soaked candied fruit into the ice cream and spoon a portion over the peaches and sprinkle each portion with chocolate.

NOTE: This may also be assembled in the kitchen before serving.

2243. STRAWBERRY ICE-CREAM CAKE CAPRICCIO DI EVA
Fragoline di bosco gelate capriccio di Eva

1 8-inch layer Italian Sponge Cake [No. 1913], made
    the day before
½ recipe sugar syrup for Iced Pears Conte di Savoia
    [No. 2232]
⅓ cup Aurum liqueur
½ cup maraschino liqueur
2 cups strawberries (wild strawberries, if available)
½ cup superfine sugar
1 quart Vanilla Ice Cream [No. 2194]
1 cup currant jelly

Allow the sponge cake to become slightly dry. Make the sugar syrup and cook it until it reaches the large thread stage (219° on the candy thermometer). Add 2 tablespoons each of the liqueurs, and pour all but 4 tablespoons of the hot syrup onto the cake, a little at a time, waiting until the cake has absorbed the poured-on syrup before adding more. Mix the berries with the sugar and the rest of the Aurum and 2 tablespoons of the maraschino. Chill both the syrup-soaked cake and the berries. Melt the currant jelly until liquified in a small saucepan over low heat. Mix in the remaining syrup and maraschino and pour it into a sauce bowl and place in refrigerator until well chilled. Before serving, place the cake on a large glass platter, cover it with the strawberries and their juice, and cover the berries with scoops of the ice cream. Serve at once, accompanied by the currant sauce. *Serves 6 to 8.*

2244. TANGERINE SURPRISE
Mandarini gelati in sorpresa

6 large, plump temple oranges, or tangelos
1 recipe Tangerine Ice [No. 2216], made with the
    pulp of the temple oranges

Cut the tops off the oranges and reserve. Scoop out the pulp, leaving a shell of rind. Take care not to pierce the rind when scooping out the pulp. Prepare the tangerine ice as directed in No. 2216. When "ripened" fill each of the orange shells with the ice and place them in the freezing compartment of the refrigerator. Before serving, pack a glass bowl with crushed ice. Arrange the oranges in the ice bed, and garnish with mountain laurel leaves (or orange leaves, if available). If desired, affix 1 or 2 leaves to the stem ends of the oranges with toothpicks, so that they look as though they had been freshly picked. *Serves 6.*

SPUMONIS AND CASSATAS
Spumoni e cassate

Spumoni and *Cassate* are special ice-cream mixtures frozen in a brick-shaped or cyclindrical mold. They usually comprise an outer coating of ice cream concealing a filling of whipped cream, brandied fruits or nuts, and other flavors of ice cream or fruit ices.

Typically Italian, these delicious preparations make a festive appearance at the table. Although it is recommended they be assembled with homemade ice creams, the best quality commercial ice creams may be employed. However, fruit ices should be homemade for the reasons given on page 730.

Assembling these preparations is not terribly hard, the only trick being to have the container ice cold. If one possesses a freezer, then packing in ice is not really necessary. The freezing compartment of the refrigerator is not recommended, however, as it never really gets as cold as a freezer. The method of assembling follows.

1. The first, outer layer of ice cream is softened a bit, and spooned into the bottom and sides of a prechilled metal mold (usually loaf shaped, or in the form of a half cylinder) and smoothed down as evenly as possible with the back of the spoon. The mold is then covered with its lid, and placed in a mixture of 4 parts crushed ice to 1 part rock salt, covered with the ice, and left for 1 hour for the coating to freeze firmly.

2. The mold is then removed, wiped with a damp cloth (to remove any traces of salt and ice), uncovered, and the filling is spooned in. The filling is topped with a layer of the same cream that was used in coating the mold, and the mold tightly covered again (a little softened butter spread over the join of the cover and the mold makes a tight seal), and buried in the ice, where it is left for at least 4 hours, or longer.

3. When ready to unmold, the mold is removed from its ice packing, dipped in a pan of very cold water (to wash off the salt and ice), uncovered, and reversed on a chilled platter. Several hard thumps will usually unmold it. However, if it proves hard to budge, a cloth dipped in hot water and well wrung out may be draped over the mold, and the cream will usually fall out of its own accord.

These preparations may be made in advance and kept for several months in a freezer until ready to use.

2245. SNOWSTORM CASSATA OR SPUMONE

Spumone—o cassata—albufera

3½ cups Vanilla Ice Cream [No. 2194]

2 cups heavy cream, placed in a bowl and kept in the freezing compartment of the refrigerator until mushy

¾ cup puréed marrons glacés, well chilled

¼ cup Pernod (or any anise liqueur), well chilled

Line the bottom and sides of a 2½-quart well-chilled melon mold with 2½ cups vanilla ice cream. Cover mold and freeze as directed in step 2 above. While it is freezing, whip the mushy cream until stiff. Mix the well-chilled marron purée and preferred anise liqueur until blended and then fold into the whipped cream, stirring and folding until blended. Place this mixture in the freezing compartment for 2 hours, stirring every ½ hour. Remove the mold from its ice pack, fill with the marron/whipped cream mixture, and cover with the remaining vanilla ice cream. Cover mold tightly again and freeze as directed in step 3 above. Unmold just before serving. *Serves 8 to 10.*

2246. SPUMONE AFRICANA

Spumone africana

3 cups Chocolate Ice Cream [No. 2200]

1 quart fruit ice cream made with apricots [*see* No. 2209]

¼ cup dark rum

Soften 2 cups of the chocolate ice cream in a bowl. Coat the bottom and sides of a long pre-chilled loaf mold with the cream. Cover mold tightly and freeze as directed in step 1 on page 744. When frozen, remove mold and fill as directed in step 2 with the apricot ice cream, which has been slightly softened in a bowl and the rum beaten into it. The top is then smoothed down and covered with the remaining chocolate ice cream, also softened in a bowl before spreading on. Cover mold again, and freeze as directed in step 3. Unmold just before serving. *Serves 8 to 10.*

NOTE: The example shown in the photograph was further decorated by strips of pistachio ice cream piped onto the sides of the mold before filling, and is garnished with marrons glacés.

2247. SPUMONE CARLTON

Spumone Carlton

3 cups Caramel Ice Cream [No. 2199]

3 cups Strawberry Ice [No. 2215]

1 cup heavy cream, placed in a bowl in the freezing compartment until mushy

1½ cups small Glacéed Strawberries [No. 2308]

Line the bottom and sides of a round, straight-sided metal ice-cream mold (of 2-quart capacity) with 2 cups of the caramel ice cream, smoothing it down with the back of the spoon. Cover mold tightly and freeze as directed in step 1 on page 744. When coating is frozen, whip the mushy heavy cream until stiff. Soften the

Left to right: *Tutti Frutti Spumone* (No. 2252); *Spumone Carlton* (No. 2247); *Spumone Africana* (No. 2246)

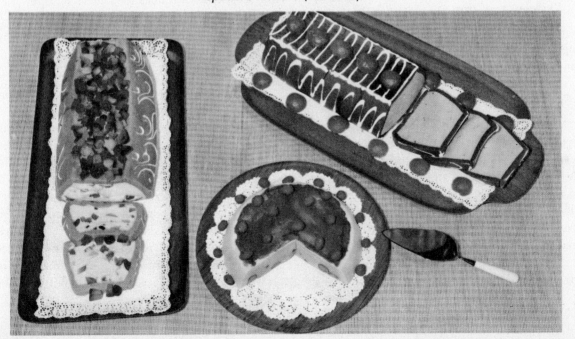

strawberry ice in a large bowl, and fold in the whipped cream and 1 cup of the glacéed berries. Pour into the center of the ice-cream-lined mold, smooth down the top carefully, and cover with the remaining caramel ice cream. Cover mold tightly and freeze as directed in step 3. Unmold just before serving and decorate the top with the remaining glacéed berries. *Serves 8 to 10.*

NOTE: The example shown in the photograph on page 745 was spread with a little softened chocolate ice cream after it was unmolded, and then decorated with the berries. This may be done, if desired.

2248. SPUMONE COPPELIA
Spumone Coppelia

3 cups Chocolate Ice Cream [No. 2200]
5 cups Hazelnut Ice Cream [No. 2203]
A few whole hazelnuts

Line the bottom and sides of a long, pre-chilled loaf mold with 2 cups of the chocolate ice cream. Cover mold and freeze as directed in step 2 on page 744. When frozen, remove mold and fill with the hazelnut ice cream and cover with the remaining chocolate ice cream. Cover mold tightly again, and freeze as directed in step 3 on page 744. Unmold just before serving, and decorate the top with the whole hazelnuts. *Serves 8 to 10.*

NOTE: If using commercial ice creams, use 5 cups vanilla ice cream, soften slightly in a large bowl, and mix in 1 cup ground hazelnuts, prepared as directed for No. 2203.

2249. SPUMONE FROU-FROU
Spumone frou-frou

3 cups Chocolate Ice Cream [No. 2200]
4 cups Rum Ice Cream [No. 2208]
¾ cup candied fruits (cherries, pineapple, citron, orange peel, etc.), diced
¼ cup dark rum

Line the bottom and sides of a long, pre-chilled loaf mold with 2 cups of the chocolate ice cream. Cover mold and freeze as directed in step 2 on page 744. When frozen, remove mold and fill with the rum ice cream, into which has been mixed the candied fruit and the additional rum. Cover with the remaining chocolate ice cream, cover mold tightly again, and freeze as directed in step 3 on page 744. Unmold just before serving. *Serves 8 to 10.*

NOTE: If using commercial ice creams, use 4 cups

rum-raisin ice cream, for the rum ice cream, soften slightly in a large bowl, and mix in the rum and candied fruits.

2250. SPUMONE MALTESE
Spumone maltese

4 cups Orange Ice [No. 2213], made with blood oranges
2½ cups heavy cream, placed in a bowl in the freezing compartment of the refrigerator until mushy
½ cup superfine sugar
1 tablespoon vanilla extract

Line the bottom and sides of a long, pre-chilled loaf mold with 2¾ cups of the orange ice. Cover mold and freeze as directed in step 2 on page 744. While it is freezing, whip mushy cream until stiff, add the sugar and vanilla, and place in freezing compartment for 2 hours, stirring every ½ hour. Remove mold from ice pack, uncover, and add the almost-frozen whipped cream. Cover with the remaining orange ice, cover mold tightly again, and freeze as directed in step 3 on page 744. Unmold just before serving. *Serves 8.*

NOTE: If blood oranges (oranges with deep red flesh) are not available, color regular orange juice with a few drops of red food coloring.

2251. SPUMONE MARIA LUISA
Spumone Maria-Luisa

3 cups raspberry ice cream, following recipe for Preserved or Fresh Fruit Ice Cream [No. 2209], using raspberries
1½ cups candied fruits (cherries, pineapple, citron, orange peel, etc.), finely diced
4 cups French Vanilla Ice Cream [No. 2196]

Line the bottom and sides of a long, pre-chilled loaf mold with 2 cups of the raspberry ice cream. Cover mold and freeze as directed in step 2 on page 744. When frozen, mix 1 cup of the candied fruits with the vanilla ice cream, and fill the mold with this mixture, covering it with the remaining raspberry ice cream. Tightly cover the mold again, and freeze as directed in step 3 on page 744. Unmold just before serving, and spread the remaining candied fruits over the top. *Serves 8 to 10.*

NOTE: If commercial ice cream is used, take 1 box frozen raspberries, partially defrost, and press through a fine sieve. Place the resulting purée in an ice tray and freeze in the freezing compartment of the refrigerator until mushy and almost frozen. Mix this with 2 cups vanilla ice cream, stir until well blended, then place in freezing compartment until firm and proceed as directed above.

In the photograph on page 745, the further decoration consists of swirls of vanilla ice cream piped on the mold through a pastry bag fitted with a small plain tip.

2252. TUTTI-FRUTTI SPUMONE
Spumone tutti frutti

3 cups strawberry ice cream, following recipe for Preserved or Fresh Fruit Ice Cream [No. 2209], using strawberries
4 cups French Vanilla Ice Cream [No. 2196]
1 cup candied fruits (cherries, pineapple, citron, orange peel, etc.), finely diced

Line the bottom and sides of a long, pre-chilled loaf mold with 2 cups of the strawberry ice cream. Cover mold and freeze as directed in step 2 on page 744. When frozen, mix the vanilla ice cream with the candied fruits and fill the mold with this mixture. Cover with the remaining strawberry ice cream. Cover mold tightly and freeze as directed in step 3 on page 744. Unmold just before serving. *Serves 8 to 10.*

ICINGS AND FILLINGS

Ghiacce di zucchero e creme di basi

Wherever a sugar syrup is called for in the following recipes, it would be safest to use a candy thermometer to gauge the proper temperature. This lessens the chance of overcooking or undercooking the syrup, which may result in either a granular or too-liquid icing.

2253. CHOCOLATE ICING
Ghiaccia al cioccolato

4 squares bitter chocolate, grated
1/3 cup heavy cream
4 cups (more or less) sifted confectioners' sugar
Pinch salt
1 1/2 teaspoons vanilla extract

Place the grated chocolate and cream in a small bowl. Place over boiling water until chocolate has melted. Mix well until blended. Place 3 cups of the sugar and the pinch salt in a large bowl and gradually add the melted chocolate. Beat until blended. If too thin to spread, add more sugar; if too thick, add warm cream by the teaspoonful until desired consistency is reached. Beat in vanilla. Spread at once with a spatula dipped from time to time in hot water. *Makes an amount sufficient to fill and ice 2 8-inch layers.*

2254. COFFEE ICING
Ghiaccia al caffè

1/3 cup triple-strength freshly brewed coffee
4 cups (more or less) sifted confectioners' sugar
2 teaspoons vanilla extract

Place 3 cups of the sugar in a large bowl. Beat in the still-warm coffee and the vanilla. Add additional sugar until mixture is creamy enough to spread. If too thick, dilute with driblets of coffee until mixture is of desired consistency. Spread at once, using a spatula dipped from time to time in hot water. *Makes an amount sufficient to fill and ice 2 8-inch layers.*

2255. FONDANT ICING
Ghiaccia al fondante

2 cups superfine sugar
2/3 cup warm water
Pinch cream of tartar (or 1 tablespoon white corn syrup)

Mix all ingredients together and stir for at least 10 minutes until the sugar dissolves (or place in blender and whirl at high speed for 2 minutes). This *must* be done previous to cooking, as the syrup must never be stirred once it is placed on the stove—if it is stirred at that point, the sugar will crystallize and the fondant will be impossible to make. When the sugar is dissolved, place it in a small, heavy saucepan and bring to a boil over moderate heat. When it comes to a boil, cover the pan to allow the steam to wash down any sugar crystals clinging to its sides. Remove cover after 2 minutes and continue cooking until syrup reaches the soft ball stage (238° on the candy thermometer). Pour it out immediately onto a lightly oiled marble slab or a large platter. Let it cool until it is cool to the touch and does not stick to the fingers. Then take a spatula and knead the paste over onto itself until it turns opaque white (this takes about 3 minutes). Gather the mass into your hands and knead it until it becomes white and creamy (it must be done in the hands as body heat is vital here). Shape it into a roll or ball and place it in a jar with a screw top. Cover tightly and allow it to ripen in the refrigerator for 2 days before using.

To use as icing, treat it as follows: take the amount needed and place it in a small, heavy enamel saucepan. Place the pan on an asbestos pad over medium heat and thin the fondant with a little boiling milk or water to the proportion of about 1 or 2 drops to $\frac{1}{2}$ cup fondant. Remove from stove and stir until lukewarm. If still too thick, add a few more drops of hot liquid. Flavor and color as follows:

Chocolate Fondant: 1 tablespoon grated bitter chocolate added to fondant while melting; add no liquid.
Coffee Fondant: Use strong coffee in place of milk or water in thinning fondant.
Green (Pistachio) Fondant: 2 drops green vegetable color and $\frac{1}{2}$ teaspoon almond extract.
Pink Fondant: 1 or 2 drops red vegetable color and $\frac{1}{2}$ teaspoon almond extract.
Lemon (Yellow) Fondant: 1 or 2 drops yellow food coloring and $\frac{1}{2}$ teaspoon lemon extract.
Orange Fondant: $\frac{1}{2}$ drop yellow food coloring and $\frac{1}{2}$ drop red food coloring, plus $\frac{1}{2}$ teaspoon orange extract or 1 teaspoon orange flower water.

The color choices are unlimited. Liqueurs of your choice may be used as flavoring. Do not, however, overflavor or overcolor. Deep blue might have a distressing effect, not because of its taste, but because of its psychological effects. The same applies to any color not pastel in shade. The amounts given above are for $\frac{1}{2}$ cup fondant and 1 teaspoonful (or more) hot liquid.
Warning: Do not overheat fondant or it will lose its gloss. Do not add cold liquid to the fondant or it might revert to clear sugar syrup.

2256. ITALIAN MERINGUE
Meringa italiana

This is probably the original version of "7-minute frosting." It is not cooked on the stove, however. The hot sugar syrup does give it body, and the heat of the syrup will cook it somewhat. The egg whites should be at room temperature, never cold.

    8 egg whites
    Pinch salt
    Pinch cream of tartar (or 1 tablespoon white corn syrup)
    3 cups sugar
    1 cup water

Place the egg whites, salt, and cream of tartar in a large, round-bottomed metal bowl. Let stand at room temperature while you prepare the sugar syrup. Place the sugar and water in an enamel pan and stir until the mixture is almost clear (or whirl in the blender at high speed for 10 to 15 seconds). Cover pan and bring sugar to a simmer over low heat. Remove cover (it allows the steam to wash down any sugar crystals clinging to the sides of the pan), and cook without stirring until it reaches the soft ball stage (238° on the candy thermometer). When sugar has reached 230° begin to beat the egg whites with a wire whisk or electric mixer (one hand must be used for beating, the other for pouring in the syrup: for this reason a rotary beater is impractical). When egg whites are beaten until they form soft peaks and sugar has reached 238° pour in the syrup in a slow, very fine, steady stream, beating whites vigorously all the time. When syrup has been used up, continue beating until cool. Use as desired: for meringue topping or for icing 3 8-inch layers.

NOTE: 2 teaspoons vanilla extract may be added after syrup has been incorporated.

Kneading Fondant (No. 2255).
Left to right: The cooled fondant
on the marble slab worked
with a spatula; the completely
opaque mass at the end
of the working process;
kneading fondant until it is smooth
and creamy

2257. ROYAL ICING
Ghiaccia reale

2 egg whites
½ teaspoon white vinegar
Pinch salt
4 cups sifted confectioners' sugar

Place the egg whites, vinegar, and salt in a round-bottomed metal bowl. Beat with a fork or a whisk until frothy (but not stiff and white) and slowly add sugar until the desired consistency is reached. If too stiff to spread with ease, dilute with a little hot water, 1 teaspoonful at a time. *Makes enough to ice 2 8-inch layers.*

NOTE: 1½ teaspoons vanilla or almond extract may be added after the sugar has been incorporated.

2258. ROYAL ICING PRALINÉ
Ghiaccia reale al croccante

1 recipe Royal Icing [No. 2257]
¾ cup Praline powder [*see* No. 2290]
1 teaspoon vanilla or almond extract

Prepare icing as directed in No. 2257. When ready, fold in the Praline powder and mix well. Add flavoring and mix in. If too stiff to spread easily, dilute with a little hot water, 1 teaspoonful at a time. *Makes enough to ice 2 8-inch layers.*

2259. UNCOOKED FONDANT ICING
Ghiaccia a freddo o ghiaccia all'acqua

If one desires a fondant-like icing and has no time to prepare fondant, this will prove an acceptable substitute. Once made, it may be flavored and colored just as true fondant.

¾ cup cold water
4 cups sifted confectioners' sugar
Flavoring and coloring desired [*see* No. 2255]

Place 3 cups of the sugar in a bowl. Slowly add the water. Mix with a wooden spoon until smooth. Add the remaining sugar until the mixture is very thick, but not thick enough to stand in peaks. It must "pour" slowly, like chilled molasses. *Makes about 2 cups.*

BASIC BUTTER CREAMS
Creme di base al burro

These basic creams are compounded of cornstarch-thickened custards, sugar, and butter. They must be kept chilled once they have been spread on cakes. If they are too loose to spread after being made, they may be kept in the refrigerator until they have thickened to the desired consistency.

2260. BUTTER CREAM
Crema al burro

½ cup sugar
6 egg yolks
Pinch salt
2 tablespoons cornstarch
1 cup milk
1 cup butter, softened
1½ cups superfine sugar
1½ teaspoons vanilla (or other preferred flavor) extract

Beat the sugar with the yolks and salt until pale and fluffy. Make a smooth paste of the cornstarch and ¼ cup of the milk, and beat into the yolk/sugar mixture. Place the rest of the milk in a small, heavy saucepan and bring to scalding over low heat. Pour into yolk mixture, mixing well. Pour into a heavy saucepan and cook over very low heat, stirring constantly, until it begins to bubble. Cook for 2 minutes longer, reducing heat to the lowest degree possible and stirring briskly. Remove from stove and let cool to room temperature, stirring every few minutes to prevent a crust from forming (to speed the process, the custard may be poured into a small bowl, placed in a larger bowl filled with ice, and stirred until cool but not chilled), and place in refrigerator until cool. Cream the butter until pale, slowly add the superfine sugar, and beat until very creamy and fluffy. Slowly beat in the well-chilled custard, 2 or 3 tablespoonsful at a time. When all the custard has been added and the mixture is smooth, add the flavoring extract and mix well. When cake has been iced, refrigerate until served. *Makes enough to ice 2 8-inch layers.*

749

2261. CHOCOLATE BUTTER CREAM
Crema al burro con cioccolato

Same ingredients as in Butter Cream [No. 2260], increasing the superfine sugar to 2 cups
2½ squares bitter chocolate, grated

Proceed as directed in No. 2260. Add the grated chocolate to the egg/sugar mixture before the hot milk is added. Continue as directed in No. 2260. When cake has been iced, refrigerate until served. *Makes enough to ice 2 8-inch layers.*

NOTE: A mocha butter cream may be created by adding the chocolate to the Coffee Butter Cream [No. 2262].

2262. COFFEE BUTTER CREAM
Crema al burro con caffè

Same ingredients as in Butter Cream [No. 2260]
$\frac{1}{2}$ cup ground coffee

Proceed as in No. 2260. When scalding the milk, add the ground coffee, mix in well, and bring to scalding. Cover pan, remove from stove, and let steep for 10 minutes. Strain coffee/milk through a triple layer of cheesecloth and beat into yolk/sugar mixture. Continue as directed in No. 2260. When cake has been iced, refrigerate until served. *Makes enough to ice 2 8-inch layers.*

2263. ENGLISH BUTTER CREAM
Crema al burro all'inglese

1 recipe English Custard [No. 2111], well chilled
$2\frac{1}{2}$ cups superfine sugar
$1\frac{1}{2}$ cups butter, softened

Place the custard in the refrigerator until chilled. Cream the butter until fluffy and gradually beat in the sugar. When all the sugar has been beaten in and the mixture is smooth and light, beat in the chilled custard, a few tablespoonfuls at a time. Beat for a few minutes after all the custard has been added. When cake has been iced, refrigerate until served. *Makes enough to ice 3 8-inch layers.*

NOTE: Chocolate or coffee may be added by either mixing 3 squares grated bitter chocolate with the hot custard before chilling, or making the custard from coffee-steeped milk, using $\frac{1}{2}$ cup ground coffee and straining the mixture before adding it to the eggs and sugar.

2264. ITALIAN MERINGUE BUTTER CREAM
Crema al burro alla meringa

$\frac{1}{2}$ recipe Italian Meringue [No. 2256]
1 cup butter, softened

Prepare meringue as directed in No. 2256. Beat until

cold. Place bowl in a larger bowl filled with ice. Beating constantly, add the softened butter, 1 tablespoonful at a time. When well blended, ice the cake with this mixture. When cake has been iced, refrigerate until served. *Makes enough to ice 2 8-inch layers.*

2265. GANACHE CREAM
Crema ganache

6 squares bitter chocolate, grated
$\frac{1}{2}$ teaspoon salt
1 cup heavy cream, warmed
1 cup butter, softened
$2\frac{1}{2}$ cups superfine sugar
1 tablespoon vanilla extract

Place the chocolate, salt, 3 tablespoons of the cream, 4 tablespoons of the butter, and $\frac{1}{2}$ cup of the sugar in a small, heavy saucepan. Place over low heat and stir constantly until melted and bubbling. Remove from fire and beat vigorously with a wooden spoon until cool. Gradually beat in the heavy cream. Place mixture in refrigerator until thick and cool. Cream the remaining butter in a warmed bowl until pale in color. Gradually beat in sugar. When all sugar has been added, beat until very fluffy. Add vanilla and then beat in the thickened chocolate mixture, beating until well blended. If too loose to spread, chill in refrigerator until desired consistency is reached. *Makes enough to ice 2 9-inch layers.*

NOTE: This is a very rich mixture, and is usually used in combination with other icings as a decorative (and flavorsome) accent. It may, however, be used with great effect in filling a plain cake which may then be iced with lightly sweetened whipped cream.

FILLINGS
Ripieni

Most of these recipes are based on pastry cream. Because they contain flour, these thick custards may be simmered for a few minutes without danger of curdling. They must be cooked longer than flourless custards so that they do not taste granular and "raw."

2266. ALMOND BUTTER CREAM
Crema di mandorle

$\frac{3}{4}$ cup blanched almonds [see No. 2280]

2 cups superfine sugar
1 cup butter, softened
Pinch salt
2 eggs
3 egg yolks

Grind the almonds in the meat grinder, using the finest blade (or whirl in the blender at high speed, ¼ cup at a time, until pulverized). Mix ground almonds with sugar. Cream the butter until pale in color and add the salt. Slowly beat in 1 cup of the almond/sugar mixture, beating well until fluffy. Beat the eggs and yolks together lightly, and add small amounts of this mixture alternating with the remaining almond/sugar. Beat until all is well blended and light. Place in refrigerator until firm enough to spread, and beat again to restore fluffiness. *Makes enough to fill 3 8-inch layers.*

NOTE: If desired, 1½ teaspoons almond extract may be added (with the eggs) for a more pronounced almond flavor.

2267. PASTRY CREAM
Crema pasticcera

¾ cup superfine sugar
6 or 7 egg yolks
⅓ cup sifted flour
Pinch salt
2-inch piece vanilla bean (or 1½ teaspoons vanilla extract)
2 cups milk, scalded

Beat the sugar with the yolks until pale and fluffy. Slowly add the flour and then the salt. Scald the milk with the vanilla bean, and stir into egg mixture. Pour into a heavy saucepan, place over low heat, and stir constantly with a wire whisk until thick and lumpy. Remove from stove, discard vanilla bean, and whip vigorously with whisk (do not use a rotary or electric beater, as it will "break down" the flour and thin the mixture) until smooth. Return to stove and stir constantly with whisk, scraping bottom often to prevent scorching, until it begins to bubble slowly. Turn down heat as low as possible, and continue beating and stirring for 3 more minutes. Remove from stove (beat in vanilla extract at this point, if vanilla bean was not used) and pour into a bowl. Cover with plastic self-adhesive food wrap, pressing it into the surface of the cream (this prevents a crust from forming). Chill in refrigerator until cold and stiff. *Makes about 3 cups.*

2268. FRANGIPANE CREAM
Crema frangipane

1 recipe Pastry Cream [No. 2267]
½ cup dry almond macaroons (Italian macaroons, if available), crushed to fine crumbs
4 tablespoons butter, softened

Prepare pastry cream as directed in No. 2267. When properly cooked, remove from stove, beat in macaroon crumbs, then beat in butter, 1 tablespoon at a time. Proceed as directed for pastry cream. *Makes about 3 cups.*

2269. ST. HONORÉ CREAM
Crema St. Honoré

1 recipe Pastry Cream [No. 2267], still warm
6 egg whites
Pinch salt
½ cup superfine sugar

Prepare the pastry cream and let it stand at room temperature until lukewarm. Beat the egg whites and salt with a wire whisk in a large bowl (preferably of unlined copper) until fluffy, beat in the sugar slowly and continue beating until the whites stand in soft peaks. Fold into the pastry cream until well blended. *Makes about 6 cups.*

NOTE: To make a stiffer, richer version, proceed as follows:

1 recipe Pastry Cream [No. 2267]
1½ envelopes unflavored gelatin, softened in ⅓ cup cream
3 egg whites
Pinch salt
⅓ cup superfine sugar
1 cup heavy cream, whipped

As soon as pastry cream is removed from stove, add gelatin and stir until dissolved. Let stand at room temperature until warm. Whip egg whites and salt with a wire whisk in a large bowl (preferably of unlined copper) until fluffy. Slowly add sugar and beat until the whites stand in soft peaks. Fold into the still-warm pastry cream. Place in refrigerator until cool but not set. Whip cream until stiff in a chilled bowl and fold into the egg white/pastry cream mixture. Make sure that the resulting mixture is used as a filling before the gelatin sets. *Makes about 6 cups.*

DESSERT SAUCES
Salse per i dolci

Although there are many dessert sauces, Italians prefer to rely on a repertoire limited to the classic few suited for almost any dessert needing a sauce. The fruit sauces may be made in large quantities, if desired, and then frozen in pint containers for future use. Do not, however, freeze any of the egg-based sauces, or they will separate when defrosted.

2270. APRICOT SAUCE
Salsa di albicocche

Enough ripe apricots, peeled and pitted, to make
    3 cups pulp
2 cups sugar
1 cup water
Optional: 2 slices lemon
Optional: 6 apricot pits, crushed with a hammer and
    tied in a cheesecloth bag

Pass the apricots through a sieve into a bowl. Place the sugar and water in an enamel pan over high heat and cook until it reaches the large thread stage (219° on the candy thermometer). Add the apricot pulp and the optional lemon slices and crushed apricot pits. Cook over low heat until very thick (about ½ hour), remove lemon slices and pits, and pour into a bowl. Let cool before chilling, or serve either warm or at room temperature. *Makes about 3 cups.*

NOTE: If desired, the sauce may be further flavored with 3 tablespoons apricot brandy when cool. Other suitable liqueurs are brandy, Grand Marnier, maraschino, kirsch, or Aurum.

2271. CHERRY SAUCE
Salsa di ciliege

3 cups fresh cherries, pitted
1 cup sugar (more, to taste, if cherries are very tart)
Optional: 2 slices lemon
Optional: 12 cherry pits, crushed with a hammer and
    tied in a cheesecloth bag
1 cup currant jelly

Place the cherries and sugar in an enamel pan, stir a few times, and let stand for 1 hour. Add the optional lemon slices and pits, and place over medium heat and cook for 15 minutes, stirring occasionally to prevent scorching. Lower heat, add the currant jelly, and cook for 15 more minutes, or until sauce is thick. Remove from stove, cool to room temperature, and remove lemon and cheesecloth bag. Serve at room temperature, chilled, or warm. *Makes about 2½ cups.*

NOTE: The cherries may also be passed through a fine sieve after cooking, if a smooth sauce is desired. A few tablespoons of any cherry-based liqueur may be added to flavor the sauce: kirsch, Cherry Heering, or maraschino.

2272. CHOCOLATE SAUCE
Salsa al cioccolato

4 squares bitter chocolate, diced
1 cup lukewarm milk or water
1 cup superfine vanilla sugar [*see* No. 2296]
¼ teaspoon salt
¼ cup heavy cream (or more)
3 tablespoons butter, softened

Place the chocolate, milk (or water), sugar, and salt in a heavy enamel saucepan over low heat. Cook for 10 minutes, stirring constantly. Place an asbestos pad between the pan and the flame, and cook, uncovered, until the mixture almost reaches the small ball stage (about 230° on the candy thermometer). Remove from stove and slowly beat in the cream and the butter (if not using vanilla sugar, add 1 teaspoon vanilla extract at this point). If too thick, add more cream until the mixture reaches the desired consistency (it will get thicker when cold: if too thick then, thin to desired consistency with some warm cream). Cool to room temperature before chilling. Serve warm, at room temperature, or well chilled. *Makes about 1½ cups.*

NOTE: If desired, the sauce may be further flavored with 2 tablespoons dark rum, added when sauce has cooled to room temperature.

2273. CURRANT SAUCE
Salsa di ribes

2 cups Currant Gelatin [No. 2126]
¼ cup kirsch

Melt currant gelatin over low heat in an enamel pan until liquefied. Add kirsch, remove from heat, and let cool to room temperature. Do not chill, or it may jell again. *Makes about 2 cups.*

NOTE: If desired, the following variation may be employed:

2 cups currant jelly
¼ cup boiling water
Juice of 1 lemon
¼ cup kirsch

Melt currant jelly in an enamel pan over low heat. When totally liquefied (no lumps remaining), add boiling water. Stir for a minute, remove from stove, add lemon juice, cool to room temperature, and add kirsch. Chill if desired (this will not jell again, because the kirsch and water have diluted it sufficiently). *Makes about 2¼ cups.*

2274. CUSTARD SAUCE
Salsa di crema alla vaniglia

2 cups rich milk, scalded
4 egg yolks
½ cup sugar
Pinch salt
Grated rind of ½ lemon (no white part)
1 teaspoon vanilla extract

Scald the milk in a heavy enamel saucepan. Beat the eggs, sugar, salt, and lemon rind with a wire whisk until light and lemon colored. Slowly beat in the hot milk. When well mixed, pour into a heavy enamel saucepan, place over very low heat, and stir constantly until the custard coats the spoon. Do not allow to boil or it will curdle. As soon as the custard has thickened sufficiently, remove from stove and pour into a bowl. Add the vanilla, stir well, and cool to room temperature, stirring from time to time to prevent a skin from forming on the custard. Chill in the refrigerator until very cold. *Makes 2¼ cups.*

2275. CUSTARD SAUCE PRALINÉ
Salsa di nocciole

1 recipe Custard Sauce [No. 2274], substituting
    ¾ cup Praline powder [*see* No. 2290] for the sugar
3 tablespoons sweet Marsala wine

Make the custard sauce as directed in No. 2274, using the Praline powder. After adding the vanilla, beat in the Marsala, and continue as directed in No. 2274. *Makes about 2¼ cups.*

2276. ORANGE SAUCE
Salsa di arance

1 cup Apricot Sauce [No. 2270]
2 cups orange marmalade (the bitter, "vintage" type,
    if available)
¼ cup Grand Marnier or Aurum liqueur

Mix the apricot sauce and marmalade together in a small enamel saucepan. Place over low heat, and stir constantly for 15 minutes. Remove from stove, let cool to room temperature, and stir in liqueur. Chill, or serve either warm or at room temperature. *Makes 3 cups.*

NOTE: If a less sweet sauce is desired, mix the marmalade with 1 cup unsweetened apricot purée, and proceed as directed above.

2277. RASPBERRY SAUCE
Salsa di lamponi

Same ingredients listed in Strawberry Sauce [No. 2278],
    substituting raspberries for the strawberries

Proceed as directed in No. 2278. Framboise (a raspberry liqueur) may be substituted for the kirsch. *Makes about 2½ cups.*

2278. STRAWBERRY SAUCE
Salsa di fragole

4 cups strawberries, hulled
1½ cups sugar
¾ cup water
Optional: 2 slices lemon
¼ cup kirsch

Cut the berries into small pieces. Cook the sugar and water in a small enamel saucepan over high heat until it reaches the soft ball stage (238° on the candy thermometer). Add the berries and the optional lemon slices, and cook until the berries are mushy. Remove from stove, discard the lemon slices, and pass the mixture through a fine sieve. Add the kirsch, mix well, and place in refrigerator until well chilled. *Makes about 2½ cups.*

NOTE: If frozen strawberries are used, defrost them, drain off their liquid, reduce sugar to ½ cup, cook syrup with berry liquid, and proceed as above.

2279. ZABAGLIONE SAUCE
Salsa allo zabaione

4 egg yolks
½ cup superfine sugar
1 tablespoon ice water
½ cup white wine (a sweet Sauternes may be used)
Optional: Pinch powdered cinnamon or ½ teaspoon
    vanilla extract

Place first 3 ingredients in the top part of a double boiler (top part should have a rounded bottom; otherwise use a heat-proof bowl which will fit over a pan of water without touching water). Place over hot (not boiling) water and beat with a wire whisk until very foamy and light. Slowly pour in the wine, beating vigorously. After all the wine has been added, continue beating for 3 more minutes. Remove from over hot water, and continue beating until the mixture is cool (the top part of the double boiler—or the bowl—may be placed in a large bowl filled with ice to speed the process). The cinnamon or vanilla (if used) should be added when the mixture is cool. Do not keep for longer than 24 hours, or it may separate. If, however, it does separate before serving, beat it with a wire whisk for a few minutes until it is blended again. *Makes about 1½ cups.*

MISCELLANEOUS BASIC DESSERT PREPARATIONS

Preparazione di base per i dolci—e diversi per pasticceria

ALMONDS
Mandorle

Almonds are the most frequently used nut in Italian dessert making. There are many ways to prepare them, none of which is very difficult. Almonds in many forms (blanched, shredded, thinly sliced, halved, roasted, chopped, and ground) may be purchased in packages in supermarkets throughout the United States. However, it is perhaps more convenient (and economical) to have on hand a few pounds of unblanched, shelled almonds, kept in a tightly covered jar in the refrigerator (to keep them from turning rancid).

An electric blender will prove handy for grinding almonds to a powder or reducing them to a paste. Because of its tremendous speed it lessens the chance of the almonds becoming oily. Of course, the time-honored mortar and pestle may be used, also the meat grinder.

2280. BLANCHED ALMONDS
Mandorle mondate

2 pounds shelled almonds
2 quarts boiling water

Place the almonds in a large bowl or pot. Pour the boiling water over them and let them stand until the water is warm enough to touch. Slip the skins off the almonds. When all are blanched, spread them out on a large baking pan in a single layer and place them in a 200° oven for ½ hour or until they are dried out. Do not let them brown. Remove from oven, let stand until thoroughly cooled, and store in a tightly covered jar in the refrigerator.

2281. ALMOND MILK
Latte di mandorle

½ pound blanched almonds [*see* No. 2280]
3 tablespoons superfine sugar
½ cup distilled water (or bottled spring water)

Pound the almonds to a paste in the mortar. Mix with the sugar and water and force through a hair sieve. (To simplify the process, place the almonds, ⅓ cup at a time, in the blender. Whirl at high speed until pulverized. When all are thus treated, place the almond powder back in the blender container, heat the water until simmering, pour over the almonds, add sugar, and turn the blender on at high speed and whirl for 20 seconds. Pour through a fine sieve.) Whichever method is used, the almond milk may be placed in a tightly stoppered bottle and stored in the refrigerator for 1 week. *Makes about 1½ cups.*

2282. ALMOND PASTE (MARZIPAN)
Pasta di mandorle

½ pound blanched almonds [*see* No. 2280]
1 cup plus 2 tablespoons superfine sugar
3 egg whites

Place the almonds and sugar, $\frac{1}{3}$ cup at a time, in the blender, and whirl at high speed until pulverized. When all are thus treated, place back in blender and add egg whites. Whirl on low speed, scraping down the sides with a rubber scraper, until well mixed. Turn on high speed and blend for 5 seconds. Turn out into a bowl, and work with a wooden spoon for 5 minutes. Gather paste up in your hands and knead into a smooth ball. Store in a tightly covered jar in the refrigerator. *Makes about 2 cups.*

2283. DRY ALMOND PASTE
Pasta di mandorle a secco

$\frac{1}{2}$ pound freshly blanched almonds [*see* No. 2280],
    still damp
1 cup superfine sugar

Pound the almonds in a mortar with the sugar until they become pasty. Knead with your hands for a few minutes until smooth, and store in a tightly covered jar in the refrigerator. *Makes about 2 cups.*

NOTE: The blender may be used here, but the mortar and pestle are the best utensils for this preparation.

2284. CHOPPED ALMONDS
Mandorle tritate

If one does not possess a chopping machine (either the modestly priced small graters made especially for nuts, or a meat grinder fitted with the finest blade), finely chop the blanched almonds on a board, using a razor-sharp knife. Spread them in a baking pan, dry them in a 200° oven for 20 minutes, let them cool to room temperature, and pass through a strainer. Keep the finer portions in a jar and take the coarser parts remaining in the strainer and keep them in another jar. Store in a cool place to keep them from turning rancid.

NOTE: It is not advisable to use a blender for chopping almonds, as they will be pulverized, not chopped.

2285. GLACÉED ALMONDS
Mandorle caramellate

2 cups sugar
2 tablespoons white corn syrup
2 cups unblanched almonds

Place the sugar and syrup in a heavy skillet over a low flame. Place the almonds in a 350° oven to heat while the sugar melts. As soon as sugar begins to turn a pale gold, tilt pan in all directions to distribute the heat evenly and to melt the sugar. As soon as it is a ruddy gold, remove the almonds from the oven and dump them in. Poke mixture with a wooden spoon for a moment, then tip out onto a lightly greased smooth surface and separate the nuts with 2 forks while they are still blazing hot. Let cool for at least 2 hours before storing in a tightly covered jar. Keep jar in a dry place.

NOTE: Blanched almonds [*see* No. 2280], or any nut, may be treated in this manner. The nuts, however, must be hot when added to the sugar or they will solidify it on contact. Work as quickly as possible when separating the nuts or they will all stick together.

2286. ROASTED ALMONDS
Mandorle grillées

1 pound blanched almonds [*see* No. 2280], left whole or
    halved
1 tablespoon neutral-tasting vegetable oil

If the almonds are to be split, do so right after they have been skinned. Dry them in the oven for 10 minutes [*see* No. 2280], and then place them in a bowl. When cool enough to handle pour on the oil and toss the almonds with your hands until they are all coated with a slight film of oil. Lay them out in a single layer in a large baking pan and place them in a 300° oven until they are golden brown. Remove from oven, let cool at room temperature for 2 hours, place in a tightly covered jar, and store in a cool place. *Makes 2 cups.*

2287. SALTED ALMONDS
Mandorle salate

2 pounds freshly blanched almonds [*see* No. 2280]
$\frac{1}{4}$ cup Clarified Butter [No. 102]
Pinch Cayenne pepper
Salt to taste
Optional: 3 tablespoons clear gum arabic solution
    (*see* Note below)

Place the almonds in a bowl. Pour over the clarified butter and Cayenne. Mix well with the hands until all almonds are coated. Spread out in a single layer in a large baking pan. Place in a 350° oven until golden brown, stirring them from time to time if they are not browning evenly. Remove from oven, sprinkle with salt, and, if desired, the solution of gum arabic (which makes them very glossy). Spread out on sheets of unglazed paper to cool. After 2 hours, place them in a tightly sealed jar. Use at most 2 weeks after making or they will turn rancid. Chilling will make them a bit soggy. *Makes about 3 cups.*

NOTE: The gum arabic solution may be obtained at a drug store.

2288. SHREDDED, SLIVERED, OR SLICED ALMONDS
Mandorle sfilettate

½ pound freshly blanched almonds [see No. 2280]
1 quart boiling lightly salted water

Place the freshly blanched almonds in the boiling water and cook them for 10 minutes. Remove pan from stove and leave the almonds in it until the water is cool. Take them out, a few at a time, and with a very sharp paring knife cut them in thin slices, lengthwise slivers, or thin shreds. Place these in a single layer in a baking pan and dry them out in a 200° oven for 1 hour, turning from time to time with a spatula. They should not brown. If they do, lower the oven to 150°. When dry, spread them out on paper towels to cool, and when totally cool store in tightly covered jars, which may be kept in the refrigerator if the weather is warm. *Makes about 2 cups.*

2289. TOASTED SUGARED ALMONDS
Mandorle dolci tostate

½ pound freshly blanched almonds [see No. 2280], left whole or shredded [see No. 2288]
3 tablespoons Clarified Butter [No. 102]
1 cup superfine sugar
Pinch salt

Dry the freshly blanched almonds in the oven for a few minutes. Place them in a bowl, and when cool enough to handle, pour on the butter and mix well with your hands. Mix the sugar and pinch of salt together and sprinkle over the almonds, mixing well with the hands so that they are all well coated. Place them in a single layer in a large baking pan and place them in a 325° oven until brown and well glazed. Turn them from time to time with a wooden spoon or spatula to let them brown evenly. Remove from oven when browned, turn out on unglazed paper, and let cool for 2 hours or more. When cool, store in a tightly sealed jar, which may be kept in the refrigerator if the weather is very warm. *Makes about 2 cups.*

2290. PRALINE
Croccante

This preparation is invaluable in dessert making. It lends itself to all sorts of uses, and can be kept for a long time, either crushed or whole, if stored in an airtight container. Dampness reaching crushed Praline will turn it into a solid mass. Chunks of Praline may also provide a pleasant candy. Crushed Praline is delicious sprinkled on ice cream.

1 pound unblanched, shelled almonds
2 cups sugar
2-inch piece vanilla bean
2 or 3 tablespoons warm water

Place all ingredients in a heavy enamel pan. Place over medium heat and stir until sugar is dissolved. Lower heat and cook until sugar turns granular. Remove piece of vanilla bean and continue cooking until sugar begins to caramelize. Tip pan in all directions to ensure even cooking and to avoid scorching. Continue cooking until all is reduced to caramel. Do not let it turn dark brown, merely a deep, ruddy gold. At this point pour it out onto a lightly oiled baking sheet and smooth it out with a hot spatula. Let stand until perfectly cold and then break into pieces. Listed below are two of the variations for praline:
Crushed Praline: Grind pieces of praline in a meat grinder, using the coarse blade, and store the resulting preparation in an airtight jar.
Praline Powder: Grind praline in the meat grinder, using the finest blade (or whirl in the blender, about ½ cup at a time, at high speed, until pulverized). Store in an airtight jar.

2291. CANDIED CITRON
Cedro candito

The citron is a large, lemon-like fruit that grows in warm climates. It has a very thick, wrinkled skin, and very little flesh. The skin is delicately perfumed, and in candied form is used in many desserts, including fruit cakes. Whole candied citrons are getting harder to find in specialty shops, so the following recipe will be useful. Also, freshly candied peel has a flavor far superior to the commercially available variety. Fresh citrons may be purchased at fancy fruit markets, or ordered from citrus growers by mail.

2 large citrons
6 cups sugar
3 cups water

Cut the citrons in half and scoop out the pulp. Soak the halves in cold water to cover for at least 8 hours, or overnight. Change the water 3 times during the soaking. Next day, place the soaked halves in a large enamel pan of boiling water, poach for 1 hour, drain, and pat dry. Place the sugar and water in a large enamel pan and cook until it reaches the large thread stage (219° on the candy thermometer). Add the citron halves and poach for 10 minutes. Remove pan from stove and leave citron in syrup overnight. The next day, remove citron from syrup with a slotted spoon, place pan on stove and cook syrup to the first part of the small ball stage (230° on the candy thermometer). Add the citron and poach for 15 minutes. Remove pan from fire and let citron cool in syrup overnight. Remove citron from syrup again, place pan back on stove and cook syrup to the hard ball stage (252° on the candy thermometer). Place citron back in syrup and poach for 20 minutes. Remove pan from stove and let citron cool in syrup overnight. The final preparation consists of removing citron halves from syrup (make sure they are well drained), placing on baking tin, and drying in a very slow (150°) oven for 1 or 2 hours. The citron may then be kept in airtight jars and used as needed. The jars may be stored in the refrigerator.

NOTE: If desired, once the citron has poached for the last time it may immediately be placed in sterilized jars, the jars filled to overflowing with the boiling syrup, and then sealed.

2292. CANDIED ORANGE OR LEMON PEEL
Scorzette di arancia o limone candite

    6 oranges or large lemons
    4 cups sugar
    1½ cups water

Cut oranges or lemons in half. Scoop out pulp (which may be used in other recipes), and wash peel in cold water. Place sugar and water in an enamel saucepan and cook over medium heat until it reaches the large thread stage (219° on the candy thermometer). Proceed exactly as directed for Candied Citron [No. 2291].

2293. CARAMEL SYRUP
Caramello

This is very useful for flavoring custards, cakes, icings, etc. Kept in a tightly stoppered bottle in the refrigerator it will last for several months.

    4 cups sugar
    1 cup water
    ½ cup boiling water

Place sugar and water in a heavy metal saucepan. Place over medium heat and stir until sugar is dissolved. Continue to cook over medium heat until the water cooks away and the sugar begins to turn straw

colored. Tip the pan in all directions to ensure even cooking. When caramel turns a deep, ruddy gold, remove pan from heat. Carefully pour on boiling water, taking great care not to get splattered by the blazing hot sugar, which foams up when the water is added. Leave pan for 5 minutes, then return to stove over low heat and cook until the remainder of the hardened caramel dissolves. Stir a few times to hasten the process. The moment the syrup is smooth, pour into a sterilized bottle and cork tightly. When cool, keep in refrigerator. *Makes slightly more than 1 pint.*

2294. SIMPLE SYRUP
Sciroppo di base

This may be used to sweeten iced drinks, fruit juices, and fruit compotes. Like the preceding caramel syrup, it keeps for a long time in the refrigerator.

    4 cups sugar
    2 cups cold water
    ½ egg white

Place all ingredients in a heavy saucepan and stir until blended. Place over moderate heat and cook until it reaches the large thread stage (219° on the candy thermometer). Pour through a cheesecloth-lined strainer into sterilized bottles, cork tightly, and store in refrigerator until needed. *Makes about 3 cups.*

2295. SPUN SUGAR
Zucchero filato

When successfully made, this resembles the "angels' hair" put under Christmas trees. It is not hard to make, though tricky. A candy thermometer must be used to gauge the proper temperature of the sugar. It must never be made on a damp day or in a steamy kitchen, or it will collapse. It will not keep for more than 3 hours; after this time it "melts." It must be spun with a special wire brush that looks rather like the brushes drummers use. One can be made by tying together 4-inch lengths of fine stainless steel or aluminum wire and spreading them out a bit, until the mass looks like a badly dried paint brush. This is then wired onto a small dowel. Old cookbooks used to specify that the sugar be spun between "2 oiled broom handles." However, 2 large dowels will serve just as well, and are more sanitary. The handles of 2 wooden spoons will also act as "spinners."

    2 cups sugar
    ¾ cup water
    1 teaspoon white corn syrup
    Pinch cream of tartar

Place all ingredients in a saucepan and stir until dissolved. Place over medium heat and cook until the syrup reaches the first part of the small ball stage (232° on the candy thermometer). Place 2 lightly oiled dowel sticks projecting about 2 feet from the edge of the kitchen counter. Hold them down with heavy weights to keep them from falling. Place a sheet of clean, unglazed paper on the floor. Take a special wire brush and dip it in the syrup. With a light, waving motion, spread the sugar filaments between the dowels. They will fall onto the paper below. When all the sugar has been spun, gather it up and surround the dessert with it. Serve at once. If dessert is moist the sugar will collapse within 20 minutes or so.

NOTE: Spun sugar is used with great effect to decorate ice-cream desserts such as coupes. It melts pleasantly on the tongue.

Vanilla

2296. VANILLA SUGAR
Zucchero vanigliato

Vanilla sugar provides a more concentrated and fresher vanilla flavor in desserts than vanilla extract. It keeps for a long time, in fact, the longer the better. The vanilla beans will have to be replaced after about 6 months.

2 pounds sugar
2 vanilla beans, split and cut in 1-inch lengths

Mix sugar and vanilla beans together. Pour into a jar with a tight-fitting cover and let stand for 3 days before using. As sugar is used, replace it with fresh sugar, mixing it with the sugar remaining in the jar. Store in a dry place.
Confectioners' Vanilla Sugar: Use sifted confectioners' sugar.
Superfine Vanilla Sugar: Use superfine sugar.

2297. WHIPPED CREAM
Panna montata

Although whipped cream is a common-enough prepara-tion, many people do not know that there is a proper way to go about it to obtain a superlative result. By following the hints below, your cream will be lighter and better than ever.

Cream should be whipped ice cold, in a cold bowl, and with a cold beater. The best method is to pour the cream into a deep, round-bottomed bowl and place it and the beater in the freezing compartment of the refrigerator for at least 20 minutes. (A wire whisk makes the best beater, a rotary beater next best; electric beaters should be avoided.) Then remove and whip lightly until the cream forms soft mounds. Overbeating will turn the cream to butter. The sugar should be added just when the cream begins to thicken.

Heavy cream, or "all-purpose" cream, will whip. All other varieties lack sufficient butterfat to increase in volume. When overwhipped, cream separates before it becomes butter. Should this happen, continue beating and make butter. It will be delicious.

Whipped cream will keep in the refrigerator for a day. However, there will be a layer of liquid at the bottom of the bowl. The cream should be spooned from the bowl, rather than poured out, to avoid using this watery drainage.

Only the freshest cream should be whipped. Old cream will taste "off" and will separate more readily.

CANDIES AND CONFECTIONERY
Confetteria

The following recipes list but a few of the many candies favored in Italian homes. They have been chosen be-cause they are relatively easy to make, yet typically Italian and very popular. A candy thermometer must be used in all recipes calling for a specific temperature of sugar.

2298. ALMOND BRITTLE
Croccantini di famiglia

2 cups sugar
Pinch salt
2 tablespoons butter
2 tablespoons water
½ teaspoon lemon juice
1 cup blanched almonds [*see* No. 2280], very coarsely chopped

Place the first 5 ingredients in a saucepan over medium

heat. Stir for a few minutes until sugar is dissolved. Place the almonds in a 300° oven so that they become heated through (if added cold to the caramel they will congeal it). As soon as water has cooked away and the syrup begins to turn straw colored, tip the pan in all directions to cook caramel evenly. When it is a ruddy gold, add the hot almonds, taking them right from the oven and pouring them into the caramel. Stir with a wooden spoon for a few seconds, turn off the heat, let stand for 1 or 2 minutes, and then pour out onto a lightly buttered cooky sheet. Let cool for 1 hour, then break up in small chunks and, if desired, place in little frilled paper candy cups.

NOTE: If desired, the chunks of brittle may be dipped in bitter chocolate (melted in a double boiler over hot water), then aligned on a buttered surface until cool.

2299. ALMOND LOZENGES
Pasticche alle mandorle

⅔ cup freshly blanched almonds [*see* No. 2280], still damp
1 cup superfine sugar
2 egg whites, unbeaten
1 teaspoon vanilla extract
Confectioners' sugar

Pound the almonds in a mortar with the sugar until reduced to a paste (or whirl with the sugar in the blender, ⅓ cup at a time, at high speed until pulverized). Place in a bowl and stir in the egg white a little at a time, adding more only when the previously added amount has been absorbed. Stir in the vanilla, and if mixture is too loose, bind with a few tablespoons of confectioners' sugar. When ready, the mixture should have the consistency of softish pie crust dough. Place in a pastry bag fitted with a large, flat, plain or serrated tip, and pipe little lozenges of the paste onto a buttered cooky sheet. Brush each with a little warm water and dust with confectioners' sugar. Bake in a 250° oven for 12 to 15 minutes (they should not become brown). Remove from oven and lift them onto unglazed paper immediately with a spatula. Allow to cool,

and then place in pleated paper candy cases, if desired. *Makes about 4 to 5 dozen.*

NOTE: The paste may be colored with a few drops of any vegetable coloring before being placed in the pastry bag.

2300. ANISE BALLS
Pallini all'anice

1 recipe Almond Paste or Marzipan [No. 2282]
1 teaspoon anise seeds, crushed in the mortar
3 tablespoons anisette liqueur or Pernod
2 egg whites, lightly beaten
Coarse sugar crystals
Confectioners' sugar

Knead the anise and liqueur into the marzipan. Roll bits of the mixture between the palms of your hands into little balls about the size of cherries. When all are made, roll them in the egg white and then in the coarse sugar. Butter a cooky sheet, sprinkle evenly with confectioners' sugar, tapping off the excess, and align the anise balls on the sheet. Place in a 200° oven for 30 minutes, remove from oven, and lift off balls with a spatula onto unglazed paper. When cool, place in pleated paper candy cases, if desired. *Makes about 4 dozen.*

NOTE: If desired, the almond paste or the coarse sugar (or both) may be colored with a few drops of vegetable coloring.

2301. CANDIED FIGS
Fichi caramellati

12 small figs, canned in heavy syrup
½ recipe Almond Paste or Marzipan [No. 2282], divided into 3 equal parts, each part colored with a drop of vegetable coloring: pink, green, and yellow
3 cups sugar
⅔ cup water
1 tablespoon white corn syrup

Cut the figs in half lengthwise. Let them drain on cheesecloth for at least 6 hours or until the syrup has drained away. Scoop out the inside of each with a small spoon. Make small balls of the colored marzipan, rolling between the palms of the hands to about the size of a small nut. Place 3 balls in each half fig, 1 of each color. Cook the sugar, water, and corn syrup as directed in No. 2302, and glaze each fig by dipping in the syrup with tongs. Be careful not to let the marzipan balls fall out. When all are dipped, they may be re-dipped, if desired. Place on an oiled cooky sheet until cool. *Makes 24.*

2302. CANDIED WALNUTS
Noci al caramello

2 cups unbroken walnut halves
1 cup Almond Paste or Marzipan [No. 2282], colored
    pale green with a few drops of food coloring
2 cups sugar
½ cup water
2 teaspoons white corn syrup

Roll the marzipan into small balls the size of a cherry and place between 2 walnut halves, pressing together firmly. Cook the sugar, water, and corn syrup in a small, heavy saucepan until it reaches the hard crack stage (280° on the candy thermometer). Do not allow it to turn to caramel. Remove pan from stove and dip in the walnuts 1 at a time (*see* photograph) using a spoon or tongs. Align on lightly buttered wax paper until cool, and then place in pleated paper candy cases. If kept in a dry place, these will keep quite a long time. *Makes about 2 or 3 dozen.*

Candied Walnuts (No. 2302)
in the course of preparation

2303. CHOCOLATE TRUFFLES
Tartufi al cioccolato

1 pound best-quality dark sweet chocolate, broken
    in small pieces
3 tablespoons heavy cream
Pinch salt
6 egg yolks
¾ cup butter, softened
Chocolate shot, powdered cocoa, or finely grated bitter
    chocolate

Melt the chocolate in an enamel saucepan placed in a larger pan filled with hot water. When melted, remove from hot water bath and stir in the cream and salt. Stir until slightly cooled, and beat in 2 of the egg yolks. Return to hot water bath and cook slowly, beating in an egg yolk every minute or so. When all the

yolks have been added, beat until quite thick. Remove from water bath and beat until cool. Beat in the butter, bit by bit. Stir until mixture is absolutely cool. Drop by teaspoonful onto a flat surface and roll into small balls. Roll balls in chocolate shot, cocoa, or grated chocolate (or roll ⅓ in each of these). Store in a cool place. These will keep for about 1 week. *Makes about 3 dozen truffles.*

2304. CHOCOLATE CARAMELS
Caramelle molli al cioccolato

2 cups sugar
1 cup heavy cream
Pinch salt
3 tablespoons corn syrup
3 squares bitter chocolate

Place all ingredients in a heavy saucepan over medium heat. Stir constantly until the mixture reaches the hard ball stage (246° on the candy thermometer). Remove from heat and pour into a lightly buttered square baking pan. When cool, cut into squares and keep in a cool place. *Makes about 30 pieces of caramel.*

2305. CHOCOLATE-COVERED HAZELNUTS
Nocciole mascherate

1½ cups best-quality dark semi-sweet chocolate
2 cups large hazelnuts or filberts, shelled

Melt the chocolate in a small bowl over hot water. Do not stir it. When melted, dip the nuts in it 1 tablespoonful at a time. When coated, remove from chocolate, separating them, and align on lightly buttered wax paper. *Makes about 1 pound.*

2306. COFFEE CARAMELS
Caramelle molli al caffè

Same ingredients listed in Chocolate Caramels
    [No. 2304], substituting 4 tablespoons triple-
    strength coffee for the bitter chocolate

Proceed exactly as directed in No. 2304. *Makes about 30 pieces of caramel.*

2307. GLACÉED ORANGE SECTIONS
Spicchi di arance canditi

These, and the glacéed strawberries that follow, should be served no more than 3 or 4 hours after they have been dipped in the syrup, or dampness will cause the coating to melt. For the same reason, do not store in the refrigerator.

> 4 navel oranges, tangerines, or temple oranges, peeled, separated into segments, and freed of white membrane
>
> 3 cups sugar
>
> 1 cup water
>
> 1 tablespoon white corn syrup

Have the orange sections aligned on a plate. Place the sugar, water, and corn syrup in a small, deep, heavy saucepan. Place over medium heat and stir until sugar is dissolved. Allow to cook until it almost reaches the caramel stage (290° on the candy thermometer), turn off the heat, and place the pan in a larger pan filled with boiling water. (This arrests the cooking process, yet keeps the syrup hot and liquid.) Using tongs, dip the orange sections in the blazing hot syrup 1 at a time, coating each well, and then aligning on a lightly oiled cooky sheet. Serve as soon as the sugar coating has hardened and cooled.

NOTE: These are perfect served with vanilla ice cream.

2308. GLACÉED STRAWBERRIES
Fragole caramellate

> 3 dozen extra-large, perfect strawberries (with long stems attached, if possible)
>
> 3 cups sugar
>
> 1 cup water
>
> 1 tablespoon white corn syrup

Prepare syrup as directed in Glacéed Orange Sections [No. 2307]. When syrup is ready, dip the berries, holding them by their stems. Serve as soon as coating is cool.

NOTE: Ordinary strawberries, hulled, may be dipped into the syrup with tongs.

2309. HOMEMADE NOUGAT
Torrone casalingo

> 1 pound (about 2 cups) strained orange-blossom honey
>
> ¼ teaspoon salt
>
> 2 cups sugar
>
> 1 tablespoon white corn syrup
>
> ½ cup water
>
> 3 egg whites
>
> 1½ cups unblanched almonds, whole (or an equal amount of pistachios or hazelnuts)
>
> 1 tablespoon vanilla extract

> Optional: 2 squares edible rice paper (available from certain Italian confectioners or Oriental food shops)

Place the honey, a pinch of the salt, 1½ cups of the sugar, the corn syrup, and water in a heavy saucepan. Stir over medium heat until the sugar is dissolved, and then cook until it reaches the large thread stage (219° on the candy thermometer). Remove from heat. Beat the egg whites with the rest of the salt in a bowl (preferably of unlined copper) until foamy. Beat in the rest of the sugar and beat the whites until they stand in soft peaks. Rapidly incorporate the beaten whites into the hot honey mixture, beating vigorously. Place pan back on fire and stir occasionally until the mixture reaches the hard ball stage (246° on the candy thermometer). Immediately stir in the nuts and vanilla, mix well, remove from stove, and pour into a square baking tin lined with the sheets of edible rice paper (or a buttered tin, lined with a sheet of buttered aluminum foil dusted with an even coating of sifted confectioners' sugar). Top with another sheet of rice paper (or buttered, sugared foil) and place a board with a weight on it over the paper. Leave until cool and then cut in rectangles about 1½ inches long by 1 inch wide (if foil has been used, peel off; keep the edible rice paper on the candy, however). Store in an airtight container when absolutely cool. *Makes about 35 pieces.*

2310. PRUSSIANS
Prussiani

> 1 cup hazelnuts or filberts, blanched [*see* No. 2203]
>
> 1 tablespoon Strega liqueur
>
> 1 tablespoon triple-strength coffee
>
> 2 cups sifted confectioners' sugar
>
> 4 squares bitter chocolate, grated
>
> 5 tablespoons hot milk
>
> Chocolate shot (or grated bitter chocolate)

Pound the nuts to a paste in the mortar, adding the liqueur and coffee by drops (or whirl in the blender ⅓ cup at a time, until pulverized, then place in a bowl and stir in the coffee and liqueur). Stir in ½ cup of the sugar, and mix to a rather stiff paste. Melt the chocolate in a small bowl placed over hot (not boiling) water. When melted, stir in the hot milk and then beat into the nut mixture. Gradually add the rest of the sugar, mixing until you have a very stiff mass. Roll by small teaspoonsful on a flat surface into balls the size of cherries and roll these in the chocolate shot, coating them well. Stored in a cool place, these will keep for a few weeks. *Makes about 4 dozen.*

2311. SNOWBALLS
Palle di neve

½ cup hazelnuts or filberts, blanched [see No. 2203]
½ cup blanched almonds [see No. 2280]
2 cups sifted vanilla confectioners' sugar [see No. 2296]
Pinch salt
2 egg whites
½ cup superfine sugar

Grind the almonds and hazelnuts to a powder in the meat grinder, using the finest blade (or whirl them, ⅓ cup at a time, in the blender at high speed until pulverized). Place in a bowl and stir in 1 cup of the confectioners' sugar and the salt. Beat 1 of the egg whites until barely foamy and stir about 2 teaspoonsful of it into the nut mixture. Knead with your hands into a smooth paste. Knead in the rest of the confectioners' sugar, and add the remaining egg white by drops until you obtain a smooth, stiff paste that does not crack or crumble (you may not need all the egg white to accomplish this). When smooth, break off small pieces of paste and roll them on a flat surface (or between your hands) into balls the size of a cherry. Beat the remaining egg white until it is barely foamy (it must lose its gelatinous quality, but must still remain a translucent liquid). Dip each ball into the white, then roll in the sugar, coating well. Place the sugar-coated balls in stiff pleated paper candy cases, align them on a board, and place in a 225° oven until they are well puffed but still white (from 20 to 30 minutes). Remove before they begin to color and let cool in paper cases. Store in an airtight container when absolutely cold. *Makes about 3 dozen.*

2312. STUFFED DATES
Datteri farciti

3 dozen plump, sun-ripened dates
2 cups Almond Paste or Marzipan [No. 2282]
1½ cups Fondant Icing [No. 2255]

Carefully pit the dates, taking care you do not tear them apart. Stuff them generously with the almond paste, smoothing down the exposed portion with a dampened spoon. Align the stuffed dates on a cake rack, leaving space between each, and carefully spoon the warmed and diluted fondant over them. When the upper coating has dried, turn them over and coat their undersides. Leave them on the rack until the icing is perfectly dry, and then place in pleated paper candy cases and store in a dry place. If kept cool (not in the refrigerator) these will keep for about a month. *Makes 3 dozen.*

2313. STUFFED PRUNES
Prugne farcite

3 dozen small sun-dried prunes
2 cups Almond Paste or Marzipan [No. 2282]
Syrup:
  2 cups sugar
  ½ cup water
  1 tablespoon white corn syrup

Make sure the prunes are plump and moist, but do not soak them. Slit the prunes down the side, remove the pits carefully, and fill them with a generous amount of the almond paste, smoothing down the exposed portion with a dampened spoon. Cook the sugar, water, and corn syrup in a heavy, deep saucepan until it reaches the hard crack stage (about 290° on the candy thermometer), making sure that it does not begin to color and turn into caramel. The moment it is ready, remove pan from fire and place it in a larger pan filled with boiling water. (This arrests cooking process, but keeps syrup hot.) Immediately dip each of the prunes in the clear syrup, using tongs or a pair of forks. Align them on a sheet of lightly buttered wax paper, making sure they do not touch. Let them cool for about 2 hours before placing them in pleated paper candy cases. If kept in a dry place they will keep for about 1 week. *Makes 3 dozen.*

NOTE: Make sure that this is made in a non-steamy kitchen, otherwise the hard sugar coating will begin to melt and turn soft.

2314. TOKENS
Gettoni

6 tablespoons butter, softened
¾ cup sifted confectioners' sugar
¾ cup Praline powder [see No. 2290]
1 egg
1 egg yolk
Pinch salt
½ teaspoon vanilla extract
Confectioners' sugar

Cream the butter until pale in a small deep bowl. Gradually add the sugar and praline powder, mixing until smooth and fluffy. Beat in the egg and then the yolk, beating vigorously after each addition. Finally, add the salt and the vanilla and beat for 5 minutes. Place the mixture in a pastry bag fitted with a medium plain tip. Squeeze out little mounds about the size of a large pea on a lightly greased baking sheet. Leave 1 inch of space between each mound. Press each portion down flat with a moistened knife blade. Place in a 400° oven for about 8 minutes. Remove from oven and lift off the "tokens" with a spatula, aligning them on unglazed paper. When cool, dust lightly with confectioners' sugar and keep in a cool place. Will keep for about 1 week. *Makes about 4 dozen.*

THE ELECTRIC BLENDER IN THE KITCHEN
Il frullatore in cucina

With the sole exception of an electric mixer, perhaps no other kitchen tool is as useful and time saving as an electric blender. It transforms the old-fashioned, laborious methods of making purées into the work of a few seconds; moreover, many sauces can be made in the blender in a quarter of the time they take to make by other means. Its use in making cold fruit and vegetable drinks is well known. Less well known is its ability to perform such simple but time-consuming tasks as making fresh breadcrumbs and grating nuts and hard cheeses.

Many modern labor-saving devices necessarily entail a loss of quality or flavor. This is not true of the blender. If for no other reason, we are including this separate section of blender recipes.

a. ANCHOVY SAUCE
Salsa alle acciughe

2 hard-boiled egg yolks
6 anchovy fillets, washed free of salt [*see* No. 220]
3 tablespoons oil
1 tablespoon vinegar
1 tablespoon lukewarm water
1 sprig thyme (or ¼ teaspoon dried)
2 sprigs parsley

½ teaspoon salt
⅛ teaspoon freshly ground pepper

Put all ingredients in blender container, mix for 20 seconds at low speed, and then for 10 seconds at high speed. *Makes more than ½ cup.*

b. BÉCHAMEL SAUCE
Salsa besciamella

4 tablespoons butter
2 tablespoons minced onion
3 tablespoons flour
2 cups scalded milk
1 teaspoon chopped thyme (or a pinch dried)
Pinch nutmeg
Salt and freshly ground pepper

Melt the butter in a saucepan over medium heat, add the onion, and cook until soft. Add the flour, blend well with the onion, and then slowly add the milk, stirring constantly. Add the thyme and nutmeg and season to taste with salt and pepper. Stir until the mixture reaches a boil, reduce the heat slightly, and simmer for 10 minutes, stirring occasionally. Pour into the blender container and mix for 30 seconds at low speed. *Makes 2 cups.*

c. BREAD SAUCE
Salsa di pane

2 cups milk
¾ cup fresh white bread, cubed (no crusts included)
Pinch salt
1 onion stuck with 1 clove
2 tablespoons butter
2 tablespoons heavy cream

Pour milk in saucepan, bring to boil, add bread cubes, salt, onion, and butter. Cook over moderate heat for 10 minutes, stirring occasionally. Cool, remove onion, and pour into blender container. Mix at low speed for a few seconds, at high speed for a few more seconds, and again at low speed, slowly adding the cream. Warm sauce over low flame a few minutes before serving. *Makes over 2 cups.*

763

Cayenne Pepper

d. SAUCE HOLLANDAISE
Salsa all'olandese

2 egg yolks
2 eggs (warmed by running hot tap water over them for
    2 minutes)
2 tablespoons lemon juice
Optional: 1 tablespoon minced onion
Optional: $\frac{1}{2}$ clove garlic, crushed in the garlic-press
Pinch white or Cayenne pepper (freshly ground, if
    possible)
2 pinches salt
$\frac{1}{2}$ cup butter, melted

Put egg yolks, eggs, lemon juice, optional onion and
garlic, pepper and salt in blender container and mix
at low speed 3 seconds. Remove cover and pour in hot
butter in steady stream (butter must be very hot, but
not brown). When all butter has been added, turn off
motor. If sauce has not thickened after standing for
3 minutes, put mixture in the top part of a double
boiler over barely simmering water and cook, stirring
continuously, until desired consistency is reached.
Makes $1\frac{1}{4}$ *cups.*

e. MAYONNAISE
Salsa maionese

2 egg yolks
1 tablespoon vinegar
1 tablespoon hot water
$\frac{1}{2}$ teaspoon salt
$\frac{1}{8}$ teaspoon freshly ground pepper
1 cup oil

Put egg yolks, water, vinegar, salt, and pepper in the
blender container. Add $\frac{1}{4}$ cup of the oil. Cover and
mix at low speed for 5 seconds. Raise speed to high,
uncover, and carefully pour in remaining oil in a steady
stream. As soon as all the oil has been added, shut off
motor. *Makes* $1\frac{1}{4}$ *cups.*

    NOTE: If the mayonnaise is too thick (depending on
the quality of the oil), add a little more oil. Lemon
juice may be substituted for the vinegar, but it will
whiten the mayonnaise slightly.

f. MINT SAUCE
Salsa alla menta—per agnello arrosto

For roast lamb
$\frac{1}{2}$ cup chopped fresh mint leaves
$\frac{1}{2}$ cup Consommé [No. 360]
$\frac{1}{2}$ cup white wine vinegar
2 tablespoons sugar
Pinch salt

Place all ingredients in the blender container and mix
for 30 seconds at high speed. *Makes* $1\frac{1}{4}$ *cups.*

g. SAUCE MORNAY
Salsa mornay

1 cup Béchamel Sauce [*see* recipe b.]
$\frac{1}{2}$ cup light cream
1 tablespoon butter
4 tablespoons grated Parmesan cheese

Add cream to Béchamel and bring to boil in a saucepan
over medium heat. Remove from stove and cool. Add
butter and cheese. Pour in blender container and mix
for 30 seconds at low speed. Taste and correct seasoning. Pour back into saucepan and heat through, stirring
occasionally. *Makes* $1\frac{1}{2}$ *cups.*

h. PESTO GENOVESE
Pesto alla genovese

1 cup fresh basil leaves (dried basil *cannot* be
    substituted)
2 cloves garlic, crushed in the garlic-press
4 tablespoons oil
1 tablespoon water
2 tablespoons pine nuts
1 tablespoon butter
2 tablespoons grated Sardinian pecorino (or Romano)
    cheese
2 tablespoons grated Parmesan cheese

Put the basil, garlic, 2 tablespoons of the oil, pine nuts,
and water in the blender container and mix at low
speed for 1 minute. Add the remaining ingredients,
mix for 30 seconds at low speed, and then for 30 seconds
at high speed. Serve at once or it will blacken. *Makes
about* $\frac{3}{4}$ *cup.*

i. RED WINE SAUCE
Salsa al vino rosso

3 tablespoons butter
5 carrots, sliced
5 scallions, chopped
1 clove garlic, crushed in the garlic-press
2 tablespoons flour
2 cups dry red wine
Pinch powdered thyme
Pinch powdered bay leaf
Salt and freshly ground pepper

Melt the butter in a saucepan over medium heat; add the carrots, scallions, and garlic; and cook until the carrots are lightly browned. Add the flour, mix it in well, slowly add the wine, stir until it comes to a boil, and season with thyme, bay leaf, and salt and pepper to taste. Reduce the heat slightly and simmer for 1 hour. Pour the mixture into the blender container and mix for 30 seconds at low speed. *Makes 1½ cups.*

j. TARTAR SAUCE
Salsa tartara

1 cup oil
2 hard-boiled egg yolks
1 teaspoon chopped chives (or scallion)
¼ teaspoon prepared mustard (Dijon-type preferred)
¼ teaspoon vinegar
½ teaspoon salt
⅛ teaspoon freshly ground pepper

Pour all ingredients in blender container and mix, alternating low and high speeds until an even blend results. *Makes 1 cup.*

NOTE: If desired, 1 teaspoon each finely chopped pickles and capers may be added to the sauce after it has been removed from the blender.

k. TOMATO SAUCE
Salsa al pomodoro

2 tablespoons oil
¼ cup chopped onion
1 clove garlic, crushed in the garlic-press
1 stalk celery with leaves, finely chopped
4 ripe tomatoes, peeled, seeded, drained, and chopped
4 sprigs fresh basil (or ½ teaspoon dried)
4 sprigs fresh parsley
Salt and freshly ground pepper
Pinch sugar

Heat the oil in a saucepan over medium heat; add the onion, garlic, and celery; and cook until the onion is soft. Add the tomatoes, basil, and parsley; and season to taste with salt, pepper, and sugar. Simmer for 45 minutes, stirring occasionally. Pour the mixture into the blender container and mix for 30 seconds at low speed. *Makes 3 cups.*

l. CREAM OF ASPARAGUS SOUP
Crema di asparagi

4 tablespoons butter
2 tablespoons flour
6 cups Chicken Consommé [No. 361]
1 pound asparagus tips, trimmed
½ cup light cream
2 egg yolks
Salt and freshly ground pepper
1 cup Croûtons [No. 332]

Melt the butter in a saucepan over medium heat, add the flour, and cook until golden, stirring constantly. Slowly stir in 2 cups of the consommé and then add the asparagus. Cook over a low flame for 30 minutes, stirring occasionally. Pour the mixture into the blender container and mix, alternating high and low speeds, until it is very smooth. Return the mixture to the saucepan and bring to the boiling point again. Beat egg yolks and cream together in blender container, add one cup of the unheated consommé, and, while motor is at medium speed, add 1 cup of the hot mixture. Blend for 3 seconds at medium speed. Pour the mixture in the container into remaining hot mixture in saucepan, and add the rest of the unheated consommé. Add salt and pepper to taste and place over low heat, stirring constantly, until it has slightly thickened. *Do not boil* or the soup will curdle. Serve at once accompanied by the croûtons. *Serves 6.*

m. CREAM SOUP PARMENTIER
Crema alla Parmentier

6 tablespoons butter
2 leeks, sliced (white part only)
10 cups Consommé [No. 360]
2 pounds potatoes, diced
½ cup heavy cream
4 egg yolks
Salt and freshly ground pepper

Melt 3 tablespoons of the butter in a large, heavy pot over medium heat, add the sliced leeks, and cook until golden but not brown. Add 4 cups of consommé, salt and pepper to taste, and the diced potatoes. Simmer for 1 hour. Pour the mixture into the blender container, about 3 cups at a time, mixing alternately at low and high speed until the mixture is velvet smooth. Return the mixture to the pot, reserving 1 cup in the blender container, with which blend the cream, remaining butter, and egg yolks for 5 seconds. Put to one side. Add the remaining consommé to the blended mixture in the pot and bring just to a boil. About 5 minutes before serving, remove from the heat and slowly stir the reserved mixture into the soup. Return the pot to low heat and stir until slightly thickened. Do not boil or the mixture will curdle. Correct the seasoning and serve at once. *Serves* 8.

n. CREAM OF PEA SOUP
Crema di piselli

2 pounds peas, shelled and cooked in lightly salted water until just tender (*see* page 575)
2 quarts White Bouillon [No. 323]
2 ounces smoked ham (fat and lean)
2 leeks, coarsely chopped
2 stalks celery, coarsely chopped
2 sprigs parsley
Salt and freshly ground pepper
Pinch nutmeg
3 egg yolks
4 tablespoons butter, softened
½ cup heavy cream, warmed

Reserve 3 tablespoons of the peas and put to one side. To remaining peas add the bouillon, ham, leeks, celery, and parsley. Put this mixture in blender container, about 3 cups at a time, mixing alternately at high and low speed until each batch is velvet smooth. Pour this mixture into a large saucepan or soup pot; season to taste with salt, pepper, and nutmeg; and simmer for 30 minutes over a low flame. Place the egg yolks, butter, and cream in the blender container and mix for 10 seconds at high speed. Pour this mixture into a tureen, slowly pour in the hot soup, stirring constantly to prevent curdling, garnish with reserved peas, and serve immediately. *Serves* 8.

o. CONSOMMÉ WITH SOUFFLÉ CROÛTONS
Zuppa alla de Pisis

5 tablespoons flour
1 teaspoon butter
3 eggs, separated
1 cup grated Parmesan cheese
1½ quarts hot Consommé [No. 360]

Place flour, butter, and egg yolks in the blender container. Mix for 3 seconds, add ⅓ cup of grated Parmesan, and blend for 3 more seconds at low speed. Beat the egg whites in a bowl until stiff but not dry and then gently fold in the blended mixture. Pour this into a jelly-roll pan or an edged baking sheet which has been buttered and floured. Bake in a moderate (325°) oven for 15 to 20 minutes. Turn out on a board, cool for a few minutes, and then cut into small squares. Put the squares in a warmed tureen, add the consommé, and serve immediately. Serve the remaining Parmesan on the side. *Serves* 4.

p. SWISS CHEESE SOUFFLÉ
Sformate di groviera

6 tablespoons butter
5 tablespoons flour
1½ cups milk, scalded
6 eggs, separated
1 teaspoon salt
¼ teaspoon freshly ground pepper
1 cup Swiss cheese, finely diced

Grease an 8-cup soufflé dish with 1 tablespoon of the butter and then dust with ½ tablespoon of the flour. Heat the remaining butter in a saucepan over medium heat, add the remaining flour, stir until well blended, add the hot milk all at once, and stir until the mixture is very smooth. Pour into the blender container, season with the salt and pepper, and then, mixing at low speed, add the egg yolks one at a time and the cheese. Beat the egg whites until stiff peaks form, stir ¼ of them into the blended mixture in a bowl, and then very gently fold in the remaining whites. Pour the mixture into the soufflé dish and bake in a hot (375°) oven for about 30 minutes, or until a knife inserted in the center comes out clean. Serve at once. *Serves* 4 *to* 6.

q. STEWED OCTOPUS
Polpi in umido

3 1-pound octopuses, cleaned and cut into bite-sized pieces
3 tablespoons oil
2 cloves garlic, crushed in the garlic-press
1 cup dry white wine
1 pound tomatoes, peeled, seeded, drained, and puréed in blender
2 tablespoons chopped parsley
1 teaspoon salt
⅛ teaspoon freshly ground pepper

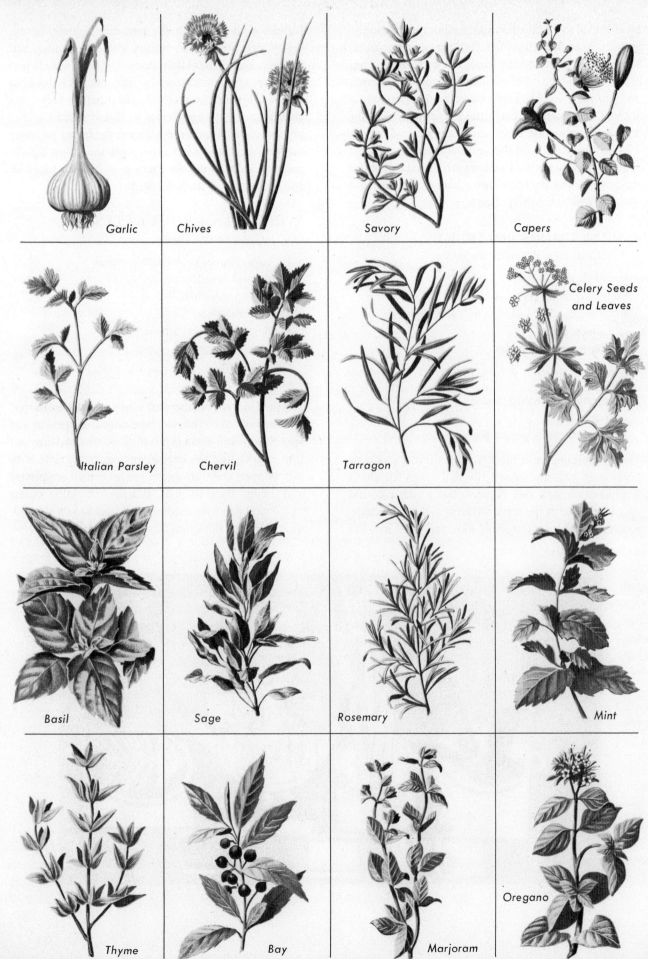

Garlic

Chives

Savory

Capers

Italian Parsley

Chervil

Tarragon

Celery Seeds and Leaves

Basil

Sage

Rosemary

Mint

Thyme

Bay

Marjoram

Oregano

Heat the oil in a heavy pot over medium heat, add the garlic, and cook until golden. Add the octopus pieces, stir for 1 minute, add the wine, and cook until it has almost evaporated. Add the blender-puréed tomatoes and sufficient water to barely cover the octopus, season with salt and pepper, cover the pot, and simmer for 1 hour. Remove the cover and continue cooking for 1 hour longer, or until the octopus is tender and the sauce is greatly reduced and slightly thickened. Pour the octopus and the sauce into a hot serving dish and sprinkle with the parsley. *Serves* 4.

r. VEAL CHOPS POJARSKY
Costolette di vitello Pojarsky

$\frac{1}{2}$ cup butter
6 loin veal chops, cut $\frac{3}{4}$ inch thick
1 cup bread cubes, soaked in milk and squeezed
    almost dry
2 tablespoons heavy cream
1 egg
Pinch nutmeg
$\frac{1}{2}$ cup grated Parmesan cheese
1 teaspoon salt
$\frac{1}{8}$ teaspoon freshly ground pepper

Heat 4 tablespoons of the butter in a frying pan over fairly high heat and brown the veal chops for about 3 minutes on each side. Remove them with a slotted spoon and reserve the butter in the pan. Bone the chops neatly, cut the meat into small dice, and put it into the blender container with the remaining butter, bread, cream, egg, and cheese. Season with salt, pepper, and nutmeg. Blend alternately at low and high speeds just until the ingredients are well mixed, but not reduced to a purée. Divide the mixture into 6 patties and press each against the chop bones so that it resembles the original chop. Reheat the butter in the frying pan over medium heat and carefully brown the chops lightly on both sides. Transfer them to a hot serving dish and serve immediately. *Serves* 6.

s. CHICKEN CROQUETTES
Crocchette di pollo

$1\frac{1}{2}$ cups chopped cooked chicken meat
$\frac{1}{2}$ cup fresh breadcrumbs
$\frac{1}{2}$ cup butter, melted
4 tablespoons milk
4 tablespoons grated Parmesan cheese
Salt and freshly ground pepper
Pinch nutmeg
Flour

Put the chicken, breadcrumbs, half the melted butter, and the milk in the blender container and blend at low speed until well homogenized. Turn the mixture out into a bowl, add the cheese, and season to taste with salt, pepper, and nutmeg. Shape into small croquettes and dredge them in flour. Put the remaining butter in a frying pan over medium heat and brown the croquettes rather slowly on all sides. *Serves* 4.

WINES, CHEESES, MENUS, AND INDEX

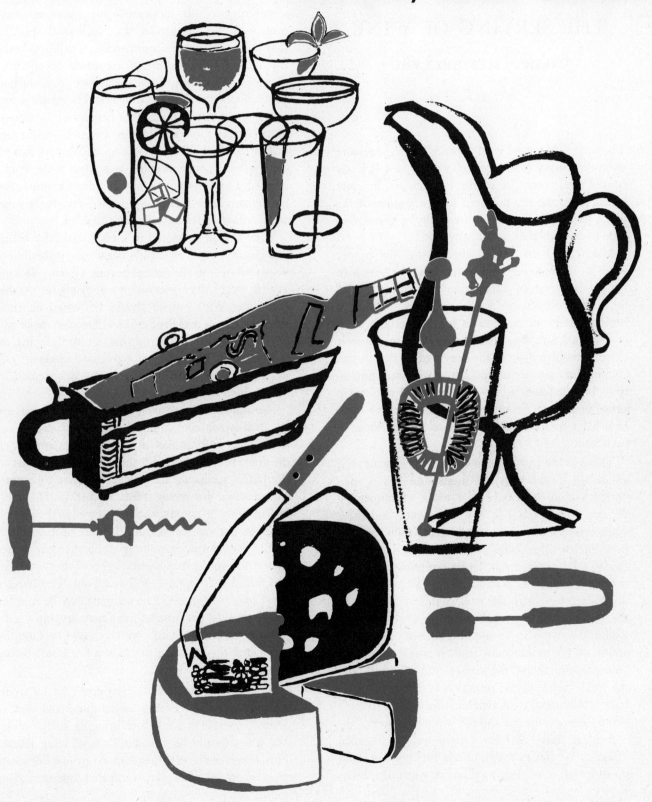

WINES
Vini

THE SERVING OF WINE
Come si servono i vini

The success of a good meal depends in great measure upon the quality of the accompanying wines. A badly cooked meal cannot, of course, be redeemed by great wines; but carefully prepared food will suffer if the wines served with it are poor in quality or unsuited in taste to the food they accompany.

Much has been written about wine: the proper ways in which to serve it; which foods go best with which wines; stern admonitions on vintages; and other types of advice. Much of this is sound, but (unfortunately) in many cases it is set forth in such over-refined language that the novice wine-lover is either intimidated or totally confused. Space in this volume does not permit an exhaustive dissertation on wine, but the following remarks, lists, and charts will (it is hoped) prove useful to anyone desiring a basic knowledge of wines in general, and Italian wines in particular.

There is one basic rule in the serving of wine: red wines are served with red meats and heavy, rich entrées; white wines are best when accompanying delicate white meats, fish, and light dishes; and sweet wines are served with dessert. (The list following this introduction names Italian wines best suited to various foods.) Of course the rule has its exceptions, the most notable of which is personal taste. If one wants to drink a red wine with sole or a white wine with steak, the heavens will not rumble in anger. However, it would be well to keep in mind the taste of your guests, and to try not to inflict any really personal oddities of your palate on theirs: the wines served at a meal (and the meal itself) are the reflection of the host's good taste and hospitality. A general Italian rule is to serve white wines in summer and red wines in winter.

A great deal has been written on the so-called "fragility" of Italian wines: of how they will not stand up to travel, or of their total failure when drunk but a few miles away from the zone in which they were produced. Much of this is a rather *chi-chi* mystique that has been built up through the years. It is, however, true that certain wines meant to be drunk young will not survive the motion inflicted on them in transporting them long distances. They are either too fresh (and therefore not fully fermented) to survive excessive motion or they are produced in such small quantity that it has not proved commercially feasible to bottle them (and for this reason they are served directly from the cask). In the former case the danger lies in the bottles exploding because the wine is still fermenting, and in the latter case exporting an entire cask of wine is not practical. However, any good wine bearing a reputable label is perfectly strong enough to survive export, but because motion does affect wine, it is a good idea to store bottles for a couple of months after having purchased them. This rest will restore the wine, and it will be all the better when you drink it.

Wine should be stored in a cool, dark, dry cellar, away from any vibration (in other words, it should not be placed next to the central heating system); lacking a cellar, a cool, dry closet makes a perfectly respectable substitute. Wine bottles should be stored on their sides (chiefly so that their corks will remain moist and not shrivel, thereby permitting air to leak in) on special racks. These may be purchased in almost any well-stocked department store in the larger cities, or may be built by those who are handy.

Because of Italy's equable climate, Italian wines are not usually sold as "vintage" wines. The vagaries of the weather in France is of paramount importance to the grape harvest, but since the climatic conditions on the Italian peninsula are usually the same each year, Italian wines are pretty steady in quality. However, Italian wines do not take to aging as well as the French varieties, and for this reason, the date on the bottles should be carefully noted. In general, white wines should be no older than 5 years, light reds the same age, and robust reds about 6 or 7 years old. The sweeter wines (with a high alcoholic content) may be kept for longer periods, but some of them may develop a sediment or "crust" with age, which should be carefully eliminated by decanting the wine a few hours before serving.

White wines should be served cool (not *ice* cold), with the sparkling varieties served quite cold, and, if desired, packed in ice before bringing to the table. Red wines should be served at "room" temperature. This, however, refers to the temperature of a European room: about 60–65°, *not* an overheated American room (usually about 70° or more). Naturally, if the day is warm the wine should not be served warm. On hot summer days it may be placed in the least cold part of the refrigerator for ½ hour (no more) if it has not been stored in a cool place. Red wine should be uncorked about 1 hour before serving. This allows it to "breathe," which improves its bouquet (the action of fresh air on the wine is the catalyst).

APPROPRIATE WINES
Accoppiamenti vini-vivande

ANTIPASTI: *Light, dry white wines*—Cortese, Lugana, Procanico, Soave, Torre Giulia, Verdicchio, Vermentino di Gallura

PICKLED APPETIZERS: *No wine*

OYSTERS, CLAMS, OTHER BIVALVES, AND SMOKED SALMON: *Robust, dry white wines*—Corvo, Cinqueterre, Morasca, Procanico

BOUILLON AND CONSOMMÉ: *Dry fortified wines*—the very dry Sherries, white Ports, and Marsalas

ROBUST SOUPS (CREAMS, MINESTRONES, AND ZUPPE): *Robust, dry white wines*—Cinqueterre, Lacrima Christi, Orvieto, Terlano, Vernaccia

PASTAS: *The sauce served on the pasta should be the guide to the proper wine*—Fish-based sauces: *dry white wine*. Meat-based sauces: *light, dry red wine*. Game-based sauces: *robust, dry red wine*

EGG DISHES: *Dry, or moderately dry, white wines*—Asprinio, Coronata, Polcevera, Termeno

FISH: *Dry, light white wines*—Asprinio, Cinqueterre, Coronata, Vernaccia. *Or moderately dry:* Lacrima Christi, Orvieto, Tocai

DELICATE FISH (SOLE, etc.): *Dry, light white wines*—Capri, Falerno Bianco, Montecarlo Bianco, Procanico, Soave, Termeno, Torre Giulia, Verdicchio

FISH SOUPS AND STEWS: *Moderately dry white wines with a full-bodied bouquet*—Albana, Castelli Romani, Est Est Est, Termeno, Vernaccia

WHITE- OR PINK-FLESHED MEATS: *moderately full-bodied, smooth, dry red wines*—Aglianico, Carmignano, Carema, Ghemme, Lago di Caldaro, Montecarlo Rosso, Sangiovese, Valpantena, Valpolicella

RED MEATS: *Austere, full-bodied red wines*—Barbaresco, Barolo, Brunello, Chianti, Falerno (red), Faro, Gattinara, Grumello, Inferno, Lessona, Montepulciano, Nipozzano, Santa Maddalena, Sassella

BOILED MEATS: *Full-bodied, rather young red wines*—Barbera, Bardolino, Dolcetto, Grignolino, Lambrusco di Sorbara, Nebbiolo, Sangiovese

POULTRY: *Light, dry red wines with a full bouquet*—Bardolino, Carema, Cesanese del Pilo, Freisa, Ghemme, Grignolino, Montepulciano, Teroldego

GOOSE LIVER AND PATÉS DE FOIE GRAS: *Champagne, or any of the truly great red wines (either French or Italian)*

GAME: *Robust, full-bodied red wines with a heavy bouquet*—Barolo, Brunello, well-aged Chianti, Gattinara, Lessona, Oliena, Recioto, Taurasi

SALADS: *No wine*

CHEESES: *Generally either sparkling dry wines or strong full-bodied varieties (however, each cheese ideally should have its own accompanying wine. A good rule to follow would be the more robust wines with the strong cheeses and lighter wines with the more delicate cheeses)*

DESSERTS: *Sparkling, semi-sweet white or red wines, sweet and rich*—Aleatico di Portoferraio, moderately dry Caluso, Malvasia di Lipari, Monica, Moscadello, Moscato dell'Elba, Moscato di Siracusa, sparkling Moscato, Nasco, Sanguinella, Zucco

FRUIT: *Sweet, heavy wines*—Aleatico di Portoferraio, sweet Caluso, Moscato dell'Elba, Moscato di Pantelleria

CITRUS FRUIT: *No wine*

CHART OF WELL-KNOWN
ITALIAN WINES
Vini d'Italia

The following list contains some of Italy's most famous wines, chiefly those which are widely available throughout the peninsula. The compilation reflects the author's personal taste, and therefore a number of various types of wines which might be favorites of the individual reader might not be mentioned. Also not mentioned are the very local wines which are never exported outside the region in which they are grown.

Many of the wines listed here will not be readily available in the United States. However, they have been included as a handy guide for those who will visit Italy, and who would like to have a brief survey of the local vintner's products. Those wines which are available in the United States are indicated by an asterisk (*). Not all these may be found in a single city at a single time. The best place to search out the more recondite varieties would be a well-stocked liquor store in an Italian neighborhood.

WHITE WINES

Wine	Region	Proper Age	Color and Bouquet	Taste	Alcoholic Content	Best Served With
ALBANA	*Forli:* the hills around Bertinoro, Castrocaro, and Cesena	Drinkable when 2 years old. Reaches perfection at 4 years	Golden yellow. A subtle and pervasive bouquet	Delicate, pleasant, harmonious, moderately dry	12–13%	Pastas (with light sauces: butter and cheese, fish, etc.). Seafood. Serve cold, about 50°
ASPRINIO	*Naples:* Aversa, Frattamaggiore, and the region around Caserta	Ready for drinking as soon as it has been made. Best drunk young	A greenish-yellow-white. Clear. A subtle, fleeting bouquet	Light, rather sharp, herbaceous, refreshing	6–12%	Devotees of this wine say it is best served in summer. Superb with dishes based on pike, eel, perch. Serve cold, about 50°
CALUSO	*Turin:* Caluso	Drinkable when 2 years old	Golden yellow. An exquisite and unique bouquet	Robust. Warm on the tongue. Comes in two varieties: sweet and moderately dry	12–16%	Chiefly a dessert wine. The moderately dry may accompany certain sharp cheeses. Serve iced at about 38°
*CAPRI	*Naples:* Islands in the Bay of Naples	Best drunk when 2–3 years old	Straw-colored. A pronounced bouquet which increases with the age of the wine	Rather dry. Has an aftertaste that is rather sharp. Robust, refreshing, unsubtle	About 12%	A classic wine for fish. Serve cold, about 45°
*CASTELLI ROMANI	*Latium:* especially the hills around Velletri	At least 5 or 6 years old, no sooner	Velletri wines: straw-colored. Frascati: clear gold. Colonna: deep gold. All have a strongly winey bouquet	The dry varieties are rather austere and smooth. The sweet varieties are mellow	10–13%	Dry varieties best served with fish. Serve cold, about 50°. All varieties are eminently suitable for dishes of the region, especially with any dishes made with peas

WHITE WINES

Wine	Region	Proper Age	Color and Bouquet	Taste	Alcoholic Content	Best Served With
*CINQUETERRE	*La Spezia:* Monterosso al Mare, Riomaggiore, and Vernazza	At least 4–5 years old	Golden yellow, which becomes deeper (almost brownish) with age. Clear and fresh	Moderately dry, smooth, full-flavored	12–14%	Superb with fish. Serve cold, about 45°
CORONATA	*Genoa:* Coronata and the vicinity around the hills near Cornigliano	Ready as soon as it has fermented	A clear, pale straw color. Rather limpid. Fresh	Dryish, subtle, refreshing	About 12%	Superb with fish. Serve cold, about 50°
CORTESE	*Alessandria:* Gavi, Sezzadio, Val Bormida	Ready in 2 years. Reaches perfection when 4 years old	Greenish white. A unique and delicate bouquet	Dry, light, pleasingly sharp, refreshing	10–11%	Excellent with antipasto and fish. Serve cold, about 50°
*CORVO	*Palermo:* Casteldaccia	Ready in 2 years. Reaches perfection when 4 years old	Golden yellow, limpid. A superb, "noble" bouquet. (Also available as a red wine)	Dry and velvety	About 13%	An aristocratic white wine that compares favorably with the best *crus* of Chablis. Unexcelled with antipasto and fish. Serve cold, about 45°
*EST EST EST	*Viterbo:* Bolsena and Montefiascone	Ready in 2 years. Reaches perfection when 4 years old	Moderately dry variety: golden yellow, with a full, winey bouquet. Sweeter variety: straw-colored, with the perfume of fresh grapes	The dryer is robust with a pleasantly bitter aftertaste. The sweeter has the characteristic flavor of Muscat grapes	10–11%	The dryer may be served with light pastas and fish. The sweeter is best with dessert. Serve cold, about 45°
*FALERNO	*Naples:* the Campi Flegrei (Phlegraean Fields)	Ready in 2 years. Reaches perfection when 4 years old	Pale straw-colored with amber lights. Uniquely pleasant bouquet	Moderately dry and delicate	12–13%	Excellent with fish. Unequaled when served with Mullet au Gratin [No. 821]. Serve cold, about 45°
*LACRIMA CHRISTI	*Naples:* Resina and Torre del Greco	Ready in 2 years. Reaches perfection when 4 years old	Golden amber, clear. A subtle and delicate bouquet	Full-bodied, with slightly aromatic taste. Very smooth and velvety	11–13%	Unexcelled with fish. Has a certain similarity to the Johannisberger Rhine wines. Serve cold, about 45°
*LUGANA	*Brescia:* Desenzano, Pozzolengo, and Sirmione	Ready when 4 years old	Pale greenish gold, clear. With a characteristic and pronounced bouquet	Dry, with a slight hint of tartness. Refreshing	11–13%	Very good with antipasto and fish. Serve well chilled, about 40°
*MALVASIA DI LIPARI	*Messina:* the islands of Stromboli and Salina	Best drunk when from 4–6 years old	Brilliant golden yellow. Delightfully suave bouquet	Sweet, ingratiating, subtle	15–16%	Magnificent dessert wine with a high alcoholic content. Serve very cold, about 35° (serve iced, if possible)
MONTECARLO	*Lucca:* Montecarlo	Ready when 3 years old, reaches perfection when 5 years old	Clear straw-colored with bright lights. Subtle bouquet	Brisk, full-bodied, very smooth and light	About 13%	A superior choice for antipasto and fish. Has a similarity to Chablis. Serve cold, about 45°
MORASCA CINQUETERRE	*Genoa:* around Chiavari	Ready when 4 years old, reaches perfection when 6 years old	Pale greenish yellow, clear and limpid. Very delicate bouquet	Dry, with a pleasantly tart accent. Brisk and refreshing	12–13%	Excellent with shellfish and antipasto. Serve cold, about 45°

WHITE WINES

Wine	Region	Proper Age	Color and Bouquet	Taste	Alcoholic Content	Best Served With
MOSCADELLO	*Siena:* Montalcino	Drink young; does not age well	Clear golden yellow. Delicate perfume	Sweet, smooth, lightly sparkling. A lively wine	7–8%	A pleasant wine to serve with small cakes or cookies. May be served before dinner. Serve cool, about 50°
MOSCATO DELL'ELBA	*Leghorn:* the island of Elba	Ready to drink in 4 years	Brilliant golden yellow. A "noble" bouquet	Sweet, smooth, rather heavy	12–15%	Delicious served with small cakes or cookies. May also be served before dinner. Serve very cold, about 35° (iced, if possible)
*MOSCATO DI PANTELLERIA	*Trapani:* the island of Pantelleria	Ready after 4–6 years	Brilliant golden amber. A unique and "noble" bouquet	Sweet, smooth, and with an ample taste	About 14%	A superior desser wine also suitable to serve before dinner. Serve very cold, about 35° (iced, if possible)
MOSCATO DI SIRACUSA	*Ragusa:* Noto, Pachino, Syracuse, and Vittoria	Gets better with age	Lively, clear, golden yellow. Has its own characteristic intense bouquet	Soft, smooth, delicate, very fragrant	13–15%	A dessert wine. Served at room temperature (an exception to the rule for white wines). Similar to the muscatels of Lunel in France
*MOSCATO (ASTI) SPUMANTE	*Asti:* the region surrounding Canelli	Ready to drink in 2 years, perfect when 4 years old	In its natural state: amber (color is toned down when wine is sold commercially). A delightfully musky bouquet	Sweet, delicate, and pure. Has lasting bubbles. The best varieties are not oversweet.	Varies: medium in content	Dessert wine. Serve very, very cold, iced, about 30°
NASCO	The areas around Cagliari and Oristano (Sardinia)	Ready to drink in 4 years, perfect when 6 years old	Brilliant golden amber. Has a subtle bouquet recalling the best Hungarian Tokay	Moderately sweet, with a vaguely bitterish undertone. Very smooth	15–16%	Magnificent wine suitable for serving with delicate pasta dishes and desserts. At its best served iced, about 32°
*ORVIETO	The hills around Orvieto	Ready to drink in 2 years, perfect when 4 years old	Pale straw-colored, with brilliant gold highlights. Has a delicate and characteristic bouquet	Dry to moderately dry. Full-bodied aroma and taste	11–13%	Excellent with light pastas and fish. Serve cold, about 40°
POLCEVERA	*Genoa:* Polcevera Valley	Ready to drink as soon as fermented	Clear, limpid, pale straw-colored. Refreshing and delicate	Dry, very light and fresh	About 12%	Best served with fish. Serve lightly chilled, about 45°
PROCANICO	*Leghorn:* the island of Elba	Ready to drink in 3 years, perfect when 5 years old	Very clear, pale straw-colored. Delicate and refreshing	Moderately dry, pure, very pleasant	11–13%	A superb wine for antipasto and fish (especially oysters and other bivalves and shellfish). Serve cold, about 38°. Similar to Chablis
*PROSECCO	*Treviso:* Conegliano and Valdobbiadene	Ready to drink in 3 years	Straw-colored. Fresh and lively, with a rather subtle aromatic bouquet	Mildly sweet with a slightly sharp edge	11–12%	(This wine is also available sparkling.) Best served with antipasto and cheeses. Serve chilled, about 40°

WHITE WINES

Wine	Region	Proper Age	Color and Bouquet	Taste	Alcoholic Content	Best Served With
SANGINELLA	*Salerno:* Giovi and Pastena	Ready to drink in 3 years, perfect when 5 years old	Golden yellow. Delicate aroma	Mild and subtle. Slightly sparkling (the sparkling increases as the wine ages in the bottle)	12–14%	A fine table wine. Serve cool, about 48°
*SOAVE	*Verona:* Montecchia di Crosara, Soave, Monteforte d'Alpone, and Vestena Nuova	Ready to drink in 3 years	Clear, limpid, straw-colored. Delicate and characteristic bouquet	Dry, smooth, refreshing	About 12%	A superior wine to serve with antipasto and fish. Serve chilled, about 40°. Somewhat similar to Chablis
*TERLANO	*Bolzano:* Andriano, Nalles, Terlano	Ready to drink in 3 years	Straw-colored. Lively bouquet	Moderately dry with a hint of aromatics. Soft and pleasant	11–13%	Serve with fish. Also good with soup. Serve chilled, about 40°
TERMENO	Mainly Termeno, but good varieties also produced in the Trento region and also in Friuli	Ready to drink in 3 years	Straw-colored. Fleeting bouquet	Aromatic, with a subtly bitter aftertaste. Full bodied and robust	13–14%	Serve with antipasto, delicately sauced pastas, and fish. Serve chilled, about 40°
TOCAI	*Udine:* the hills around Buttrio	Ages well: best drunk after 5 years	Greenish yellow. Lively bouquet	Moderately dry and rather aromatic, with a slightly bitter aftertaste	11–12%	Though similar in name to Tokay, it bears no resemblance to that Hungarian wine. Excellent with fish, it may also be served with white-fleshed roast meat. Serve chilled, about 40°
TORRE GIULIA	*Foggia:* Cerignola	Ages well: best drunk after 3 years	Clear, brilliant greenish gold. Subtle bouquet	Dry, neutral, harmonious	13–14%	Excellent wine for antipasto and fish. Serve well chilled, about 35°
*VERDICCHIO DEI CASTELLI DI JESI	*Ancona:* Castelbellino, Castelplanio, Cupramontana, Maiolati, Spontini, Montecaroto, Monte Roberto, Staffolo, and Rosora Mergo	Ready to drink in 1 year, reaches perfection when 3 years old	Clear, brilliant, pale amber. Delicate bouquet	Dry, lively, full-bodied, harmonious	14–15%	One of the best wines for antipasto and fish. Serve chilled, about 35°
VERMENTINO DI GALLURA	*Sassari:* Santa Teresa di Gallura	Ages well: best drunk after 3 years	Amber, clear and brilliant. Delicate, characteristic bouquet	Moderately dry with a pervasive bitterish aftertaste	15–16%	A superior wine for antipasto and fish. Serve very cold, about 35°
VERNACCIA	*Cagliari:* Cabras, Oristano, Riola Sardo, Sanvero, Milils, Solarussa, Zeddiani (all on Sardinia)	Ready after 3 years, it can age for as long as 30 years	Amber yellow, clear and brilliant. Delicate and delicious bouquet	Moderately dry with a mild bitter aftertaste and a pleasing tartness. Very fruity and fresh	15–16%	When young it may be served with fish. When well aged the alcoholic content increases to 18 or 20%: it is then an unparalleled wine to serve at the close of a meal. Serve chilled, about 40°
ZUCCO	*Palermo:* Carini, Giardinello, Torre San Cataldo	Ready to drink at 2 years, perfect when 8 years old	Two varieties: One is straw-colored, brilliant, and with a heavy bouquet. The other is amber, and delicately perfumed	The first is moderately dry and full-bodied. The other rich, smooth, and robust	13–16%	The dryer should be served with fish and the richer with dessert. Both should be served chilled, about 40°

RED WINES

Wine	Region	Proper Age	Color and Bouquet	Taste	Alcoholic Content	Best Served With
AGLIANICO	*Avellino:* the area around Tufo	Ready to drink at 2 years, perfect when 4 years old	Intense ruby red. Pervasive winey bouquet, which, when wine has aged, recalls certain Piemontese wines	Refreshing and tangy when 2 years old. At 5 years, moderately dry, smooth and pleasing	12–14%	Excellent wine with pastas, superb with main courses, and, when well aged, may also be served with roast veal or pork. Serve at room temperature
AGLIANICO DEL VULTURE	*Potenza:* the region around Rionero in Vulture	Ready to drink at 2 years, perfect when 4 years old	Ruby red. Delicate, lasting bouquet	Sparkling wine with smooth, full-bodied taste	12–14%	Excellent with pastas, and, even though a red wine, it may be served with practically any dish. Serve at room temperature
ALEATICO DI PORTOFERRAIO	*Leghorn:* the island of Elba	Ready to drink in 3–4 years	Deep ruby red. Delicate and penetrating bouquet	Mellow, sweet, smooth, and very warming	14–15%	A heavy wine; serve before dinner or with dessert
*BARBARESCO	*Cuneo:* Barbaresco	Ready to drink and perfect when 3 years old	Brilliant ruby red with the delicate aroma of violets	Moderately dry and a bit more severe than Barolo: smoother, more ample and tangy	12–14%	An exquisite accompaniment to roasts of beef or lamb, also capon, turkey, and goose liver. Serve rather warm, about 65°
*BARBERA	The valley of Tiglione, southeast of Asti	Ready to drink as soon as fermented. Lasts up to 2 years, but after 3 it loses its savor	Intense ruby red. Bouquet of both violets and marasca cherries	Flavorsome, full-bodied, robust, and warming	12–15%	Best served with highly spiced main courses. Serve at about 65°
*BARDOLINO	*Verona:* the municipalities of Bardolino and Garda	Drink young: does not age well	Clear, lively ruby red. Subtle and delicate bouquet	Dryish, vigorous, with a slightly tart edge	10–11%	A fine table wine: especially good with lean meats and poultry. Serve at room temperature
*BAROLO	*Cuneo:* Barolo, Castiglione Falletto, Grinzano, La Morra, Monforte d'Alba, Perno, Serralunga, Verduneo	Ready to drink at 4 years, perfect when 9 years old	Brilliant ruby red. After 6 or 7 years, if not disturbed, it will take on golden-orange glints. Subtle bouquet of violets, wood, and dried rose petals	Dry, severe, full-bodied, and rich	13–15%	An exquisite accompaniment to roast red meats, goose liver, and all game. Serve at about 68°
BRACHETTO	*Asti:* Montabone, Sesame	Ready to drink as soon as fermented	Clear ruby red. Characteristic aroma or perfume of roses	Rich, aromatic, and full-bodied with a hint of Muscat grapes. Rather sweet	13–15%	An excellent table or dessert wine. Serve at room temperature
BRUNELLO	*Siena:* Montalcino	Mature and ready to drink at 5 years. Magnificent when aged to 30 years	Garnet red, assumes orangey gleams when old. Full bouquet	Moderately dry, very smooth, full-bodied, and rich	About 13%	An aristocratic wine for roast meats, mixed grills, goose liver, and all game. Comparable to Burgundies of the highest *cru*
CAREMA	The vineyards on the left bank of the Dora Baltea River from Fort Bard to Ivrea	Ready to drink in 3 years	Clear ruby red. Subtle bouquet of raspberries	Dry and slightly, but delightfully, bitter	12–14%	A main-course wine, exceptionally fine with sweetbreads. Serve at room temperature

RED WINES

Wine	Region	Proper Age	Color and Bouquet	Taste	Alcoholic Content	Best Served With
CARMIGNANO	*Florence:* Carmignano	Ready to drink in 1 year, reaches perfection when 3–4 years old	Vivid and lively ruby red. Emits a strong fragrance of Parma violets	Dryish, very smooth, full-bodied, and straightforward	11–12%	An excellent table wine. When aged, it is perfect with roasts. Comparable to the Burgundies. Serve at room temperature
CESANESE DEL PIGLIO	*Frosinone:* Piglio	Ready to drink in 2 years	Ruby red. Two varieties: one with a subtle bouquet, the other with a uniquely special fragrance	The first is full-bodied and savory, the second smooth and very rich	9–12%	The first is excellent with poultry, especially if aged for more than 3 years. The second is excellent as a table wine with delicate dishes
*CHIANTI	*Siena:* Cajole, Radda, and various small estates in the Monti Chianti	Ready to drink in 3 years, reaching perfection when 6 years old	Lively ruby red. With age takes on orange-colored highlights. Has a unique bouquet of Parma violets and sweet iris, combined	Dry, with a delightfully bitterish aftertaste or tang. Straightforward, full-bodied, and fresh	12–14%	One of the great wines for red-meat roasts, all game, and light meals. Serve at about 65°
DOLCEACQUA	The hillsides around Imperia	Should be very well aged: at least 6 years (no less, preferably much more)	Clear, brilliant ruby red. Light bouquet of strawberries, and a delicate fragrance	Dry, with a pleasantly bitterish undertone, quite soft on the palate	12–13%	A superior table wine. Serve at room temperature
DOLCETTO	Produced in several parts of Piedmont; notably Alba, Cortemilia, Dogliani, Mango, Mondovi, and Ovada	Although ready to drink in 1 year, it is fully mature when 2 years old	Clear ruby red	Despite its name (which means "sweet") it is robustly dry with a pleasantly bitter aftertaste	10–12%	A superior table wine. Serve at room temperature
*FALERNO	*Naples:* the Campi Flegrei (Phlegraean Fields)	Ages well: should not be drunk before it is 2 years old	Intense ruby red. Subtle bouquet	Dry, rather austere, very warming. (Also comes in a white variety)	12–13%	When well aged, it is a very good wine to serve with red meat. Serve at room temperature
FARO	*Messina:* Faro Superiore, Ganzirri, and Santa Agata	Ready to drink in 2 years. Reaches perfection when 5 years old	Brilliant, lively ruby red. A steady, winey bouquet	Severe, smooth, dry, full-bodied, and rich	12–14%	One of the best wines for red meat and game. Serve at about 60°
*FREISA	*Turin:* the region around Chieri	Ready to drink when 3–4 years old	Garnet red. A delicate and pleasing aroma and bouquet	Severe, dry, with a delightful undertone. Rather rough when it is 2 to 3 years old	10–12%	A superior table wine. When well aged it is excellent with poultry, game, and red meat. Serve at room temperature
*GATTINARA	*Vercelli:* The hills around Gattinara	Reaches maturity in 5 years. Each additional year in the bottle brings it closer to perfection	Lively, brilliant ruby red. With each passing year it turns brick red, then clear garnet, and, finally, an orange red of crystalline clarity. First, the subtle fragrance of raspberries; then roses; finally, violets	Characterized by a fine, delicate savor, with a lively yet caressing richness: harmonious, velvet smooth—perfect	About 13%	An aristocratic wine to serve with red meat, dishes containing truffles, goose liver, game, and Risotto Milanese [No. 578]. Uncork 2 or 3 hours before pouring. Is comparable to Bordeaux of the finest *cru*. Serve at about 67°

RED WINES

Wine	Region	Proper Age	Color and Bouquet	Taste	Alcoholic Content	Best Served With
GHEMME	*Novara:* the slopes near Romagnano Sesia and Sizzano	Reaches maturity in 3 years. Attains perfection when 7 years old	Deep ruby red with highlights of an amber glow. A mildly resinous and violet-fragranced bouquet	Dry, smooth, with the delicate hint of raspberries	11–13%	Excellent with red meat and poultry. Superb with regional specialties. Serve at room temperature
GIOVI	*Salerno:* Giovi	Improves with age (4 or more years)	Deep ruby red. Unique and strongly heady bouquet	Dry, with a pleasant, bitter aftertaste	14–15%	When well aged it is best with game stews. Serve at room temperature
*GRIGNOLINO	*Asti:* Castell'Alfero, Castiglione, and Portocomaro	Reaches maturity in 2 years	Vivid ruby red. Ingratiating fragrance	Light and dry, with a pleasantly bitter undertone	11–12%	A fine table wine, especially good with main courses. Serve at room temperature
*GRUMELLO	*Valtellina:* the municipalities of Sondrio and Montagna	Reaches maturity in 2 years. Perfect when 5 years old	Lively, brilliant ruby red. A lasting (but light) fragrance of strawberries that intensifies with age	Dry, with a subtle tang. Smooth and warm	About 13%	A great wine with roast meat and game. Serve at room temperature
*INFERNO	Montagna, Poggiridenti (in Sondrio), and Treviso	Reaches maturity in 2 years. Perfect when 5 years old	Deep, brilliant ruby red. A delicate and lasting bouquet that increases with age	Dryish, with a light, nutty undertone. Smooth and warm	About 12%	A great wine with roast meat and game. Serve at room temperature
LAGO DI CALDARO	*Bolzano:* the north and west coast of Lake Caldaro	Reaches maturity in 2 years. Perfect when 5 years old	Garnet red, with orange gleams coming with age. Has a characteristic almond fragrance	Full-bodied, smooth, and harmonious	10–12%	A superior wine for red meat. Serve at room temperature
*LAMBRUSCO DI SORBARA	*Modena:* Villa di Sorbara	Should be drunk when no more than 3 or 4 years old	Lively, brilliant ruby red. Characteristic fragrance of violets	Smooth, light, and fresh	10–11%	A table wine. Serve at room temperature
LESSONA	*Vercelli:* Lessona	Reaches maturity in 3 years. Ages well, and is at its superb peak when 25 years old	A fine garnet red that turns orangey as the wine ages. A delicate and penetrating bouquet of roses and violets	Dry, with a brisk, straightforward taste overlaid by a velvety smoothness	12–14%	One of the great wines to serve with red meat and game. Unequaled when served with cold game dishes. Serve at room temperature
MONICA	*Cagliari:* the Campidano region (the island of Sardinia)	Keeps very well. Improves with great age	Ruby red with orange highlights. A subtle but penetrating fragrance	Sweet, heavy, and with a velvety smoothness	15–17%	A fine dessert wine that may also (according to personal taste) serve as a table wine. Serve at room temperature
MONTECARLO	*Lucca:* Montecarlo	Ready for drinking in 2–5 years	Brilliant garnet red. A full fragrance and bouquet. (A white variety is also produced)	Dry, velvet smooth, and harmonious	12–13%	When well aged, it is very fine with meat, especially roast veal or pork. Indispensable with small game birds (snipe or woodcock). Serve at room temperature
MONTEPULCIANO	*Siena:* the hills of Montepulciano	Reaches maturity in 4 years. Perfect when 6 years old	Deep, vivid garnet red. A lasting bouquet of Parma violets	Dry, austere, with a pleasantly bitterish aftertaste. Warm and full-bodied	12–13%	Serve with red meat, turkey, capon, duck, and goose. Serve at room temperature
*NEBBIOLO	*Cuneo:* the left bank of the Tanaro River	Reaches maturity in 3 years. Perfect when 4 years old	Clear ruby red. A heady fragrance	Dry and austere. Depending on the vineyard, it is similar to either Barolo or Bardolino, but a bit more tangy	11–13%	A superior table wine. Serve at room temperature

RED WINES

Wine	Region	Proper Age	Color and Bouquet	Taste	Alcoholic Content	Best Served With
*NIPOZZANO (CHIANTI)	*Florence:* Pelago	Ages well	Dark ruby red. A "noble" bouquet and fragrance	Dry and harmonious. Rich and full-bodied	11–13%	Superb with red meat, especially broiled steaks. Serve at room temperature
OLIENA	*Nuoro:* Oliena	Reaches maturity in 2 years. Perfect when 5 years old	Garnet red, becoming more delicate with age. Has a characteristic fragrance of strawberries	Dry, flavorsome, and with a slightly resinous aftertaste	12–15%	An excellent wine for red meat. Especially fine with roast boar. Serve at about 62°.
*RECIOTO AMARONE	*Verona:* Valpolicella and Valpantena	Reaches maturity in 4 years. Perfect when 8 years old	Garnet red. A heady and "noble" fragrance and bouquet	Two varieties: mellow and sweet, with a full-bodied smoothness and robustness. The dry type is rich, full-bodied, harmonious, and with a pleasantly bitter aftertaste	13%	The sweeter variety is best with desserts and the dry is one of the great wines for red meat. Serve at about 65°
SANGIOVESE	*Forlì:* the hillsides around Predappio, Civitella di Romagna, Cesena, Cevignano, and Rimini	Reaches maturity in 1 year. Perfect when 4 or 5 years old	Garnet red with a strong, heady fragrance	Dry, full-bodied, and harmonious with a pleasant hint of bitterness	11–13%	A good table wine. When well aged it is excellent with red meat. Serve at room temperature
SANTA MADDALENA	*Bolzano:* Santa Maddalena, Santa Giustina, and San Pietro	Reaches maturity in 2 years. Perfect when 6 years old	Ruby red, with increasingly orange tints as it ages. A subtle and heavenly fragrance and bouquet	Full-bodied, very smooth, and warm	12–13%	A good wine for red meat and game. Serve at about 62°
*SASSELLA	The region around Sondrio	Reaches maturity in 3 years	Vivid, brilliant ruby red. A delicate, lasting fragrance that increases with age	Dry, vigorous, tangy, harmonious, and warm	12–13%	A good wine for red meat and game. Serve at about 60°
TAURASI	*Avellino:* Taurasi	Reaches maturity in 1 year. Perfect when 4 years old	Heavy ruby red. A definite and unique fragrance	Dry, harmonious, and full-bodied	12–13%	Excellent with red meat, goose liver, and dishes containing truffles. Goes very well with highly seasoned and piquant dishes. Serve at about 60°
TEROLDEGO	*Trento:* Mezzolombardo, Mezzacorona, and San Michele all'Adige	Reaches maturity in 1 year. Perfect when 3 years old	Garnet red (or deep rose). A characteristic bouquet of violets, almonds, and raspberries	Dry and robust	11–13%	A fine table wine. Serve at room temperature
*VALPANTENA	*Verona:* Grescana, the Valley of Progno di Valpantena	Takes well to moderate aging	Beautiful ruby red. A fleeting and subtle bouquet and fragrance	Dry, smooth, and harmonious	11–12%	Excellent with red meat. Serve at around 60°
*VALPOLICELLA	*Verona:* the hillsides of Valpolicella	Two varieties: the first takes well to moderate ageing, the other is best drunk quite young	Two varieties. Brilliant ruby red. A delicate fragrance of bitter almonds that becomes more subtle with age	Both are rather flavorsome, dry, smooth, with a light, pleasant quality	12–13%	The first variety is excellent with red meat, the other is a fine table wine. Serve at room temperature

WINES OF ITALY

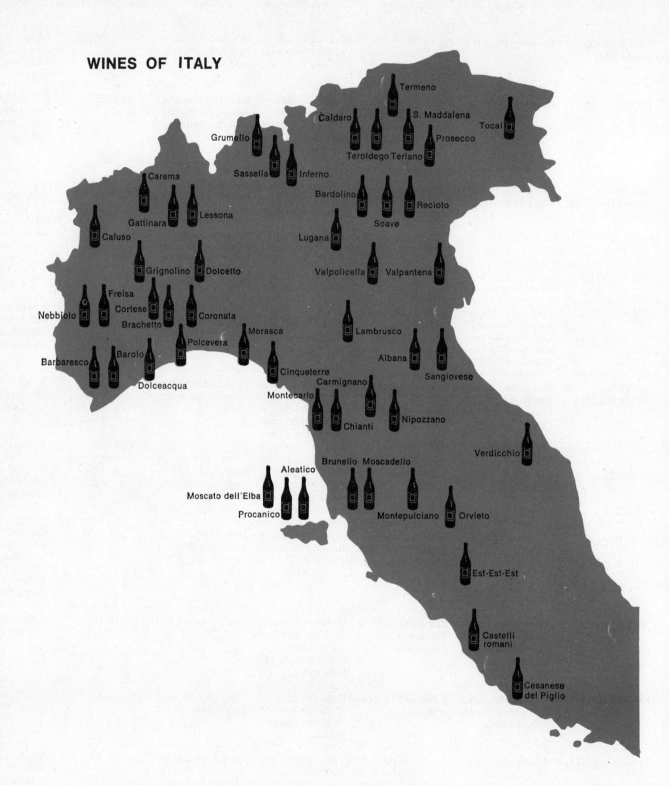

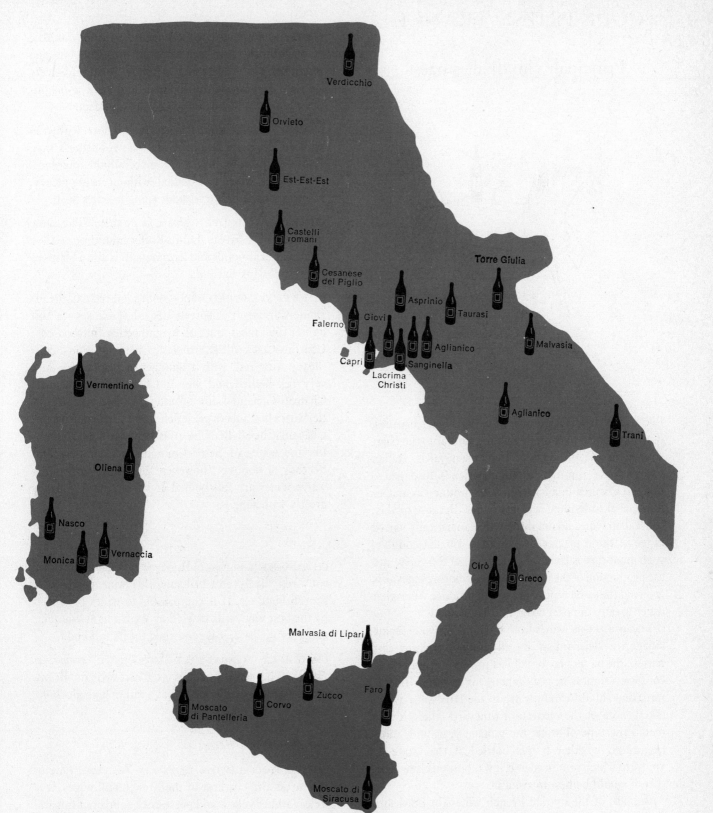

Verdicchio

Orvieto

Est-Est-Est

Castelli
romani

Cesanese
del Piglio

Torre Giulia

Asprinio
Taurasi

Giovi

Falerno

Malvasia

Aglianico

Capri

Sanginella

Lacrima
Christi

Aglianico

Vermentino

Trani

Oliena

Nasco

Monica
Vernaccia

Cirò
Greco

Malvasia di Lipari

Faro

Moscato
di Pantelleria
Corvo
Zucco

Moscato di
Siracusa

781

FAMOUS WINES OF OTHER COUNTRIES: FRANCE

Principali vini di altri paesi

Because of the great number of various French wines, it is impractical to compile a listing similar to the chart shown for the products of Italian vineyards. Italian vintners have, through years of experience, managed to unite the wines in each region to produce a smaller number of individual regional wines. Because of this, the Italian wines do not display the fantastically varied range of those produced in France. In that country, such great care is lavished on the care of the vines, and the production of the wines, that neighboring vineyards growing the same type of grape will produce wines that differ greatly in taste, color, and bouquet.

Because of this, wines from the same province, same village, or department are all unique, and for this reason, the buyer may be subject to a certain amount of confusion (unless he is a connoisseur of wine). Therefore, one should carefully study the label of a wine, taking note of the château or vineyard where it was made, the type of wine, the vintage year, and, most important, whether it was bottled at the estate or vineyard which produced it. If it was bottled elsewhere, then it would be best to avoid it.

Because of the myriad French wines (in Bordeaux alone there are over 3000 separate *crus,* or vineyards) the following is merely a selected list of the most famous and desirable wines.

BORDEAUX

Médoc

CHÂTEAU-LAFITE-ROTHSCHILD (red): *grown in Pauillac.* A magnificent ruby red with an exquisite bouquet reminiscent of violets and almonds. Austere, velvety smooth, generously full-bodied, and with a magnificently robust flavor: in other words, perfect.

CHÂTEAU-MARGAUX (red): *grown in Margaux.* Ruby red with an exquisite bouquet. Has less robustness than Lafite-Rothschild, but a far more subtle fragrance. A very fine wine, full-bodied without being heavy, it refreshes the palate without going to one's head.

CHÂTEAU-LATOUR (red): *grown in Pauillac.* The same qualities of Château-Lafite-Rothschild, but with a fragrance of almonds and hazelnuts. It is also a bit more fruity and winy in taste.

OTHER RECOMMENDED MÉDOC WINES (all red). Château-Brane-Cantenac; Château-Léoville-Lascases (a bit lighter than most, but still magnificently full-bodied); Château-Cos d'Estournal; Château-Calon-Ségur (heavy ruby red, with a bouquet of raspberries, and very full-bodied and winy); Château-Pontet-Canet; Château-Gruaud-Larose-Sarget (full-bodied and subtle, with a bouquet of great delicacy); Château Ausone; Château-Cheval-Blanche (the last mentioned pair—like the wines of Saint Emilion—lack subtlety and delicacy of bouquet; however, these heavy ruby-red, warm wines are full-bodied and fruity, and improve greatly with age).

Graves

CHÂTEAU-HAUT-BRION (red): *grown in Pessac.* A splendid ruby red, lively and brilliant, this wine possesses a superb bouquet. It is comparable to wines produced by the best vineyards in Médoc. With a light bouquet, and very delicate, it is renowned for its full body.

CHÂTEAU-LA MISSION-HAUT-BRION (red): *grown in Pessac.* The same qualities as Château-Haut-Brion, but not quite as superior. It has a rather high alcoholic content.

Sauternes and Barsac

CHÂTEAU-YQUEM (white): *grown in Sauternes.* One of the rarest and costliest of the French still wines, it is a clear amber yellow and possesses a subtle but full and rich bouquet. It is unique in character, being both rich and delicate, and is smooth and sweet. It is considered the best white dessert wine in the world.

CHÂTEAU-LA TOUR BLANCHE (white): *grown in Bommes*. White gold in color with the faintest fragrance of Muscat grapes. Softly smooth, subtle, very delicate, and winy, it ranks close to Château-Yquem as one of the great dessert wines.

CHÂTEAU-COUTET (white): *grown in Barsac*. Although similar to the above-mentioned pair it lacks their finesse. However, it is more full-bodied and it boasts a heady bouquet. The taste has overtones of Muscat grapes. Smoothly soft, delicate, and fragrant, it is one of the great dessert wines.

BURGUNDY

Côte d'Or

ROMANÉE CONTI (red): *grown in Vosne*. Rich ruby red with a subtle, soft velvety bouquet. It possesses a truly extraordinary finesse and is dry, austere, and full-bodied.

LA TÂCHE (red): *grown in Vosne*. At its best when moderately well aged, it is a rich ruby red, possesses a pronounced bouquet, and is dry, vigorous, full-bodied, and harmonious.

MUSIGNY (red): *grown in Chambolle*. A wine with a beautiful ruby-red color, it has a delicate bouquet and is full-bodied, very smooth, and superbly rich tasting.

CHAMBERTIN (red): *grown in Gevrey-Chambertin*. At its best when well aged, this wine is a limpid ruby red, has a suave bouquet, and is light and dry with a full-bodied taste.

CLOS-VOUGEOT (red): *grown in Vougeot*. Although fully mature after 4 years, it is best drunk when 6 years old or more. Beautifully ruby red in color, it has a pronounced and characteristic bouquet, is dry, and has a pleasantly bitter aftertaste.

SAINT-GEORGES (red): *grown in Nuits*. Possesses the characteristics of all the wines of the Côte d'Or, with a superb and pronounced bouquet. It is dry, full-bodied, satisfying, and robust.

Côte de Beaune

CORTON (red): *grown in Aloxe*. Hard and astringent when young, aging gives this wine a pronounced bouquet, magnificent body, and fullness. It is at its best when 20 years old.

VOLNAY (red): *grown in Volnay*. At its best when well aged, it has a seductive fragrance.

POMMARD (red): *grown in Pommard*. Very pronounced bouquet and fragrance. Full-bodied, with a robust character. Travels very well.

MONTRACHET (white): *grown in Chassagne and Puligny*. Takes well to extensive aging. This wine possesses all the distinctive characteristics of the great dry white wines of France. It is a lively amber yellow in color and has a delightful bouquet. Exceptionally full-bodied, very smooth, rich, and harmonious, it has a faintly nutlike savor. Since it is both robust and delicate, certain connoisseurs say that it combines the qualities of both Meursault and Chablis.

MEURSAULT (white): *grown in Meursault*. A beautiful amber yellow with a refined and delicate bouquet. In Burgundy it is referred to as an honest (*carré*, literally "square") wine. Meursault is produced by a number of vineyards in the locality, and each of these estates produces a wine with its own distinctive characteristics.

CHABLIS (white): *grown in Chablis*. Pale yellow when young, this wine becomes increasingly amber-colored with age. It has a delicious bouquet, is dry, delicate, fragrant, and lively, and possesses a pleasantly flinty taste. The most preferred variety is Chablis Moutonne. Chablis is unrivaled as an accompaniment to oysters.

POUILLY FUISSÉ (white): *grown in Pouilly*. The wine keeps very well. It is the whitest of all the white wines. Possessing a subtle bouquet, it has a delicate, refined, and light savor. The most preferred varieties are Château de Fuissé and Le Clos, both of which are of equal excellence.

Beaujolais

MOULIN-Â-VENT (red): *grown in Beaujolais*. All the best wines produced in this region bear its name. It reaches maturity in 3 years and perfection when 4 years old. It does not age well. A beautiful ruby red, it possesses the distinctive *gout de terroir*, or "earthy taste." A dry wine, it is full, delicate, and has excellent body.

Côte du Rhône

HERMITAGE (red): *grown in Tain-L'Hermitage*. A beautiful, clear ruby red with the delicate fragrance of raspberries, this wine is a trifle sharp when young, but with aging it assumes smoothness and full body, and may be considered a select wine of great harmoniousness.

CHÂTEAUNEUF-DU-PAPE (red): *grown north of Avignon.* A deep cardinal-red wine, vigorous and at the same time delicate, with a delightfully pungent aftertaste.

CÔTE ROTIE (red): *grown in Ampuis.* This wine reaches maturity in 4 to 5 years, and is at the peak of perfection when 13 years old. It is a deep purplish red, which gradually changes to a brilliant orange brown with age. It has a fragrant bouquet reminiscent of violets and raspberries. A trifle hard when young, it gains body and smoothness with age.

HERMITAGE (white): *grown in Tain-L'Hermitage.* A pale yellow in color, it has a characteristically heady fragrance and bouquet. It is fresh, dry, rich, and winy.

HERMITAGE PAILLE (white): *grown in Tain-L'Hermitage.* A straw-colored wine with a rich body, it is soft and sweetish with a pleasantly tart aftertaste. It is unctuous, refreshing, and winy.

CHAMPAGNE

WINES OF CHAMPAGNE (white): Without a doubt the most famous of all wines, this sparkling nectar is the apex of the vintner's art. It is produced only in the province of Champagne (any wine called "Champagne" produced in the United States—or elsewhere—may be acceptable as a sparkling wine, but can *never* approach the true Champagne in bouquet, quality, and delicacy); it is mainly produced in three separate zones or departments: (1) the slopes of the *Montagne de Reims;* (2) the northeast hillsides of Epernay facing the Marne; and (3) the *Côte Blanche* facing Epernay (which takes its name from the white grapes grown on the slopes). Space does not permit a discussion of the methods employed in producing this wine, its individual and unique characteristics, and its flavor. These are well known by lovers of fine wines. As far as the best wines of the region are concerned, this is a matter of individual taste. However, the following may be considered a representative selection of the most superb Champagnes. From the first district: Verzeay, Sillery, Mailly, Bouzy, and Ambonnay. From the second district: Avenay, Ay, Mareuil, Hautvillers, Cumières, Damery, Pierry, and Vinay. From the third: Avize, Cramant, Oger, and Le Mesnil.

JURA

ARBOIS ROUGE: *grown between Salins and Poligny.* At its best when very old, it reaches perfection at 50 years. Lightly herbaceous when young, it becomes dryer and smoother with age.

ARBOIS BLANC: *grown between Salins and Poligny.* Yellow in color with a strong, heady bouquet. Because of its characteristics, it is known as the "Madeira of the North." It was a favored wine of the high-born ladies of the eighteenth century.

OTHER PROVINCES AND REGIONS

POUILLY-FUMÉ (white): *grown in Pouilly-sur-Loire.* A unique watery green in color, it is very dry, slightly mineral in taste, exceptionally delicate, and rather smoky (the last-named quality disappears with age). It is best drunk young, as aging makes it gain in finesse but lose its character. The best wine is produced by Château du Nozet.

LAYON (white): *grown along the banks of the Layon in Anjou.* Amber-colored shading into topaz, it is best when well aged. It is sweet, fruity, winy, and warm. When old, it takes on the characteristics of Madeira.

MUSCADET (white): *grown between Nantes and Saint Nazaire in Brittany.* At its best when well aged. An extremely dry wine with a delightful aftertaste of Muscat grapes, and rather flinty in character. Rivals Chablis as a superb accompaniment to oysters. It is sold in bottles called *fillettes.*

MUSCAT DE LUNEL (white): *grown in Lunel in Languedoc.* An amber-yellow, sweet dessert wine with the flavor of Muscat grapes. It is high in alcoholic content, delicate, and heady.

MOUSSEUX DE SAUMUR (white): *grown in Saumur in Anjou.* Next to the Champagnes, this is considered the best dry sparkling wine in France. It has a smoky bouquet, is a clear amber yellow, and has a marvelously light quality that caresses the palate.

VOUVRAY (white): *grown in Vouvray in Touraine.* A lightly sparkling wine that becomes dryer as it ages. In its first year it is somewhat sweet, but after a few years it gathers austerity and a pleasant muskiness. It is then heady, bright, and delicate.

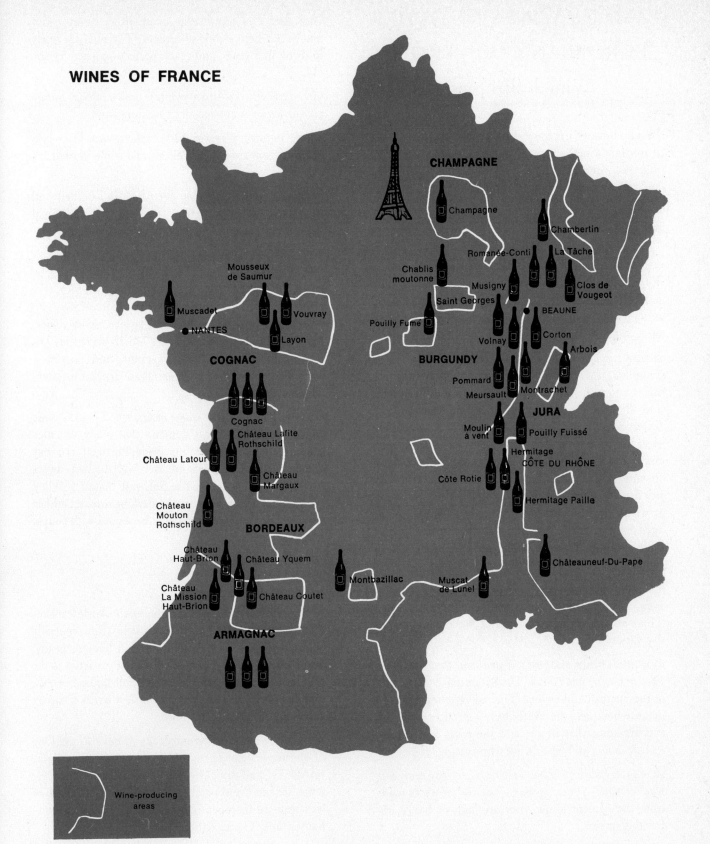

WINES OF FRANCE

CHAMPAGNE

Champagne

Chambertin

Romanée-Conti

La Tâche

Mousseux
de Saumur

Chablis
moutonne

Musigny

Clos de
Vougeot

Muscadet

Vouvray

Saint Georges

BEAUNE

NANTES

Layon

Pouilly Fumé

Volnay

Corton

Arbois

COGNAC

BURGUNDY

Pommard

Montrachet

Meursault

Cognac

JURA

Château Lafite
Rothschild

Moulin
à vent

Pouilly Fuissé

Château Latour

Hermitage

CÔTE DU RHÔNE

Château
Margaux

Côte Rotie

Château
Mouton
Rothschild

Hermitage Paille

BORDEAUX

Château
Haut-Brion

Château Yquem

Châteauneuf-Du-Pape

Château
La Mission
Haut-Brion

Château Coutet

Montbazillac

Muscat
de Lunel

ARMAGNAC

Wine-producing
areas

785

FAMOUS WINES OF OTHER EUROPEAN COUNTRIES
Vini di altri paesi

Besides those of France and Italy, there are many other European wines whose excellence deserves mention. The following listing presents a selection of the best and most widely acclaimed varieties.

SPAIN

ALICANTE (generally white): *grown around Alicante in Valencia.* A heavy, sweet dessert wine with a high alcoholic content. It has a heady, Muscat flavor and is robustly full-bodied. It is sometimes blended with other Spanish wines.

SHERRY: *grown in the region surrounding Jerez de la Frontiera, Andalusia.* Sherries range from the very sweet and rich (the Creams and Browns) to the light and dry (the Finos, Amontillados, and Manzanillas). Colors vary from the palest of amber yellows to rich, clear nut browns. Sherry is noted for its aromatic nuttiness and its rich smoothness. The dry varieties (and the intermediate) may be served as an aperitif (the very dry may be served with a soup course), while the sweeter wines are best served after dinner. Sherry can be aged for extremely long periods without losing any of its qualities (palatable 150-year-old sherries have been found).

MALAGA (red or white): *grown around Malaga in Andalusia.* A very rich, sweet, full-bodied dessert wine. There also exists an excellent and much sought-after dry variety.

RIOJA (red, white, and rosé): *grown along the banks of the Ebro in Castile and Alava.* The Riojas make up the best of the Spanish table wines. The red varieties possess a delicate bouquet; the whites have a stronger bouquet, and are somewhat dryer; and the rosés are fruitier, less alcoholic, and best drunk while young.

MUSCATEL (white): *grown in various regions near both Valencia and Sitges, in Barcelona.* Sweet wines made from the Muscat grape, they are light or heavy, refreshing or rich.

VAL DE PEÑAS (red or white): *grown on the rocky slopes of La Mancha.* The red varieties are preferred, and are rich in color, full-bodied, and have a subtle, bitter aftertaste. The white varieties are either sweet or dry and have a high alcoholic content. The reds are ready to drink in 3 years, and reach perfection when 5 years old.

SAN SATURNINO DE NOYA (white): *grown in San Saturnino de Noya.* A not-too-dry sparkling wine.

ALELLA (white): *grown in Allela in Barcelona.* The wines of this region are golden yellow, and come in both dry and sweet varieties.

PRIORATO (red): *grown in Priorato.* Full-bodied and winy, the sweet varieties (fortified by additional sugar syrup) resemble Port in flavor and bouquet.

PORTUGAL

DRY MADEIRAS (red and white): *grown in Madeira.* Rather acid when young, after 10 to 15 years they become full-bodied, smooth, fragrant, and possess a rich, winy savor. Sweet Madeiras are aperitif or after-dinner wines.

PORT (red and white): *grown in Oporto.* These famous wines are in such great demand that many varieties called "Port" and coming from Portugal are not genuine. The true Ports are rich, full-bodied, sweet (or semi-dry), possessing a rich full bouquet. They range in color from ruby red to dark brown and amber yellow. The dryer varieties may be served with soups.

GERMANY

AUSLESE (white): *grown in the Palatinate.* Auslese means "select," and these wines are made from specially selected grapes. The Auslese are full-bodied, heady, and fruity. One of the most celebrated varieties is the Diedesheimer, golden in color, full-bodied, fresh, and delicate. The great vintage Auslese wines compare favorably to certain Sauternes.

MOSELLE (white): *grown along the Moselle River.* One of the most delicate of the Rhine wines, it is light, refreshing, and dry. The best types in order of excellence are the Bernkastler (called "Doktor" because of its supposed therapeutic qualities), Piesporter, Grünhauser, and Theingartner.

NECKAR (white): *grown in the valley of the Neckar.* Generally very fragrant and rather high in alcoholic content, they should be drunk young.

WINES OF GERMANY

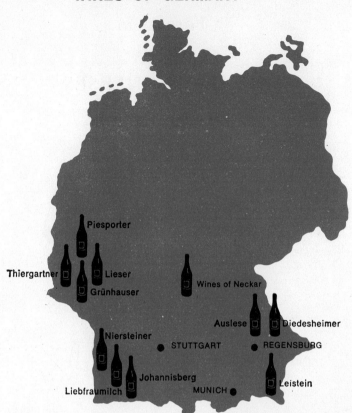

Piesporter

Thiergartner

Lieser

Grünhauser

Wines of Neckar

Auslese   Diedesheimer

Niersteiner

STUTTGART   REGENSBURG

Liebfraumilch   Johannisberg

Leistein

MUNICH

WINES OF HUNGARY

Tokay Essenz

BUDAPEST

Tokay Szamorodni

WINES OF SPAIN

Rioja

Muscatel

Rioja

Rioja

BARCELONA

Other Wines

San Sadurni
del Noya

Wines of Aletla

MADRID

Wines of Priorato   Rioja

Muscatel

Val de Peñas   ALICANTE

SEVILLE

MALAGA   Malaga

Sherry

Manzanilla

WINES OF PORTUGAL

OPORTO   Port

Sergial

Port

Wines of Madeira

787

RHINE WINES (white): *grown in the Rhine Valley*. The best of the Rhine wines is undoubtedly that produced by the Schloss Johannisberg. The Rhine wines are pale gold in color, fragrant with a delightful bouquet, dry, full-bodied, and with a mildly bitter aftertaste. They are ready to drink in 8 years and reach perfection when 12 years old. Certain Rhine wines (those made from the vine-dried grapes, picked with fanatical care, and labeled as *trockenbeere auslese*) can be kept as long as 100 years.

BAVARIAN WINES (white). The two great Bavarian wines are Stein and Leistein. The former is golden, with a delicate and lasting bouquet, and has an extraordinary vigor, both fiery and suave. It is said to be at its best when 100 years old. The Leistein has the same qualities, but is even more delicate and flavorsome.

HUNGARY

The most renowned Hungarian wines are the Tokays. These are produced in the region of Mount Tokaj in northeast Hungary. The best of these wines are listed below.

TOKAY ESSENZ (white). An unctuously sweet wine with a rich, heady fragrance and an unforgettable savor. This wine is made from specially selected grapes and is allowed to rest in great casks for 30 years before bottling. This is essential (therefore the appelation) to the production of this type of Tokay, which is unrivaled in its richness and bouquet.

TOKAY SZAMORODNI (white). Pale gold in color, this dry table wine has a distinctive, delicate bouquet. It is smooth, full-bodied, and has a unique and very pleasantly tart aftertaste.

CHEESE
Formaggio

ITALIAN CHEESES
Formaggi italiani

Cheeses are widely used in Italy as the climax of a meal, and some of the varieties described below serve primarily as dessert cheeses. However, as the reader of this cook book has by now discovered, cheese also plays an important role in Italian cooking as a necessary ingredient in many recipes. Most widely used for this purpose are Parmesan (known in Italy as *grana*, meaning "granular"), mozzarella, ricotta, and pecorino.

The cheeses listed below are those most widely used throughout Italy. Most of them are available in the United States in Italian foodshops, and some even in supermarkets. In Italy, cheeses of the same name may vary in flavor and sharpness, depending upon where they were made; in certain regions sheep, goat, or buffalo milk may be substituted for or combined with the cow's milk used exclusively in another region. And besides the varieties listed, there are innumerable local varieties which, like some purely local wines, rarely travel far from their place of origin. In this respect, the adventurous gourmet traveling through the Italian countryside might make some pleasant discoveries on his own by paying a visit to the markets of the smaller towns.

Unless otherwise noted, all cheeses should be served at room temperature.

BELPAESE

Although originating in Lombardy—with Melzo, Pavia, and Corteolona the major centers of production—this cheese is found throughout Italy. It has a soft, creamy, yellow, tender texture with a delicate, only slightly salty flavor, and because of its blandness is generally pleasing. In Italy it is produced all year and marketed in solid rounds weighing approximately 2 pounds. (Both imported and domestic varieties are widely available in the United States).

BITTO

A product of Valtellina in Lombardy, especially in the valley of that name above Morbegno and in the valleys of Masino and Tartano. This is a rather fat cheese prepared from whole cow's milk mixed with goat's milk. When it is fresh, it has a rather buttery texture, is soft and mild. When it has been aged 1 or 2 years, it becomes sharper and firmer with little spots of savory moisture.

BURRINI (also called BURRI and BUTIRRI)

This cheese is found throughout Southern Italy. It is especially good as made in Sorrento and elsewhere around the Naples area, in Calitri and Lacedonia, in Gioai del Colle, and in the province of Bari where it is called *manteche*. Burrini (or burri or butirri) takes its name from the Italian word for butter—*burro*—since the cheese is really a caciocavallo (*see* below) with a ball of fresh butter imbedded in the center, so that when it is sliced you get a thin slice of butter at the center of the cheese. It is usually prepared in small pieces weighing 5 or 6 ounces.

CACIOCAVALLO

This is another cheese made in Southern Italy (especially around Naples) and in Sicily, but widely available throughout Italy. The caciocavallo made at Capua, near Naples, is especially prized. It should be made entirely with cow's milk, but sometimes buffalo, goat, or sheep milk is combined with the former. It is always sold in the characteristic shape of a pair of coupled gourds. Aged, it becomes drier and a little sharp, and so is especially useful in cooking as a seasoning. In ancient Rome, it was smoked. Its name derives from the custom of hanging these cheeses in pairs (*a cavallo*—"on horseback") to ripen.

CASO FORTE (sometimes called SATICULANO)

This is a really great specialty, the recipe for the manufacture of which has been handed down over the generations at Statigliano in the Naples area. It is a rather strong-smelling cheese with a pleasantly sharp flavor.

It has one unique characteristic: eaten at the beginning of the meal, it acts exactly like an aperitif and stimulates the taste buds.

CASTELMAGNO

This is a Piedmont cheese made chiefly at Cuneo, about 50 miles south of Turin. It is a fatty, herb-flavored cheese, rather strong, salty, and sharp.

CRESCENZA

This Lombard cheese is especially prized when it comes from Melzo, near Milan. It is made with whole milk which must have been freshly milked from the cow. It has a soft texture, is creamy yellow, and has a buttery, delicate taste. It is usually prepared in a square form and only in winter.

FIOR D'ALPE

The most famous center of production of this Lombard cheese is Lodi. Made of whole cow's milk, the cheese is creamy, soft, and elastic, without holes. It has a pleasantly buttery flavor. Produced throughout the year, it comes in disks weighing about 4 pounds.

FIORE MOLLE

This cheese from the province of Lazio (of which Rome is the center) is especially prized when it comes from Leonessa, slightly northwest of Rome. It is a soft cheese, bright creamy yellow (the color is often heightened with saffron), with a slightly salty, aromatic taste. It somewhat resembles Belpaese.

FONTINA

This Piedmont cheese originating in the Val d'Aosta—and especially prized when it comes from Chatillon and Valtournanche—is like a rich, creamy Gruyère. Usually white or yellowish, it has few holes and a sweet, soft, delicate flavor. It is prepared in 20- to 60-pound forms. It is universally used in Piedmont for the characteristic *fonduta* or fondue. (Available in United States supermarkets.)

FORMAGGIO FIORE

This is the typical pecorino (*see* below) of Sardinia. It has a solid, rather close texture, with few holes; white in color, it has a pleasantly sharp taste. When just made, it is excellent for table use. After 3 months, however, it is better used as a condiment in other dishes. Its characteristic shape is like a round cake with sloping sides, and it may weigh from 2 to 10 pounds.

GORGONZOLA

This is a famous Lombard cheese prepared from whole milk until it forms a smooth, soft, buttery, translucent cheese with a strong fragrance and a very sharp

789

flavor. It is one of the so-called "herbed" cheeses, of a yellowish white color, streaked with greenish or bluish lines that result from a mold (a yellow penicillium mold) which develops during the ripening of the cheese (or can be induced later by the insertion of copper wires). Sometimes confused with Roquefort, it is more crumbly than the French cheese and, as noted above, is made from cow's milk, not the sheep's milk that goes into Roquefort. (Widely available in the United States.)

LODI GRANA

This is the Lombard equivalent of Parmesan and a close relative of the Emilian *grana,* or Parmesan. As its name suggests (*grana,* meaning "granular"), it is fine grained, but Parmans consider it coarser and stronger than Parmesan. In color it is somewhat yellower, though still light, and it is pitted with tiny holes. In general, however, it resembles Parmesan in smell and flavor, though commonly it is somewhat sharper. Gourmets praise its unique savoriness.

PARMESAN CHEESE (called GRANA PARMIGIANO E REGGIANO in Emilia)

Although Parma has given its name to this cheese, excellent *grana* (the common Italian name) is made in other cities of Emilia and the Romagna, the small area just north of Florence: notably in Modena, Reggio, Piacenza, and Bologna. Bibbiano (a town that originally belonged to Parma, and like it is in Emilia) is claimed as the first city where Parmesan cheese was made and as the place, in any case, where most of it is made. Local tradition has it that the best Parmesan comes from the Val d'Enza, between Bibbiano and Traversetolo, where the peculiarly fine pasturage imparts to the milk (and from it to the cheese) the fragrance and flavor that set Parmesan cheese apart from and (in the view of Italian cooks and gourmets) above all other cheeses, whether of Italy or other lands.

Parmesan cheese is of ancient origin, some claiming that it has been made in the region for 2000 years. Certainly it is referred to in one twelfth-century chronicle and figures by name in the third story (Eighth Day) of Boccaccio's fourteenth-century *Decameron,* in which one Calendrino is induced to set out on a journey to a "mountain made wholly of grated Parmesan cheese on which stand people who do nothing but make macaroni and ravioli" to go with it.

Grana takes its name from the fine and closely grained texture of the cheese which is interspersed with tiny pin-point holes. Good Parmesan is a rich golden

yellow. It should be compact and solid (soft spots, detected by periodic tapping with hammers during the lengthy ripening process, are surgically excised and cauterized). It has a characteristic fragrance and flavor and, though sharp, is never biting or acid. Parmesan is made from April to November in great wheels weighing from 50 to 60 pounds, colored greenish black on the outside. The age (from 2 to 4 or more years) is of primary importance and determines price, as well as markedly improving the texture. In Italy, where good Parmesan is by no means cheap, the old (*vecchio*) of 2 years is distinguished from that of 3 years (*vecchione*), and both from the very old, aged 4 or more years (*stravecchione*).

In good Italian cooking there is no substitute for Parmesan, where called for, as it is in an infinite number of dishes. Its especial virtue in cooking is that it does not become tough on contact with heat, does not melt rapidly, and does not produce—as the famous gourmet Edouard de Pomiane says in his *Bien manger pour bien vivre* ("Eat Well To Live Well")—those "intolerable strings" so ruinous in cooking. Nutritionists maintain that 4 ounces of grated Parmesan cheese provide as much energy as twice the quantity of lean beef.

If a good deal of space has been devoted here to Parmesan cheese, it is because as much time, energy, and specialized care go into its production as into fine vintage wines in other countries. Domestic "Parmesan" is a poor substitute, and Romano should *never* be used in place of Parmesan. (Widely available in the United States.)

MASCARPONE

This is a fresh, snow-white cream cheese made entirely with fresh, sweet cream, with a delicate, buttery flavor. It is produced during the autumn and winter and is wrapped in white muslin packets weighing from 4 to 8 ounces. It must be eaten immediately, since it rapidly "turns." Made in Lombardy, it is especially prized when it comes from Abbiategrasso and Lodi (near Milan), from Soresina (near Cremona), and from Mortare (near Pavia). The whipped cream cheese found in American supermarkets could serve as a substitute. However, it is not as rich, lacking the high butterfat content of mascarpone. Serve chilled.

MOZZARELLA

This cheese originating in Campania (the area south of Rome, around Naples) is made in many places there: Acerra, Aversa, Capua, Cardito, Castellamare di Stabia, and Mondragone; it is excellent, too, when it comes from the plain of Salerno farther to the south. It is the outstanding cheese originally (and best) made with buffalo milk, produced according to a method known as *pasta filata* which consists of shaping the thickened milk mixture into elastic ropes or strings. Since buffaloes are becoming rarer in Italy and increased demand has stimulated other industrial methods of production, it is now commercially produced with cow's milk but this, according to those who know the original product, is at the cost of both flavor and aroma. It should be of the whitest color, soft but solid, slightly moist on the surface, with a fresh, fragrant, mild, fine, delicate flavor. It usually contains a certain amount of creamy or milky whey which, after it is cut, begins to "leak" out. It is sold in round packets (originally called "buffalo eggs") and, generally, not above 1 pound in weight. It may be eaten a day after it has been made and should be eaten while as fresh as possible. (Widely available in the United States.) Serve chilled.

PECORINO

This hard, sharp cheese originally made with whole sheep's milk is made in many places in Italy and in a number of versions, but especially in the Roman countryside. The most famous source in Latium is Moliterno, which produces an especially strong, dry, sharp, solid but tender and smooth cheese. Siena, Sardinia, the Abruzzi have their own variants. The cheese is especially popular in cooking in and around Rome, but it is also widely used (as in Genoa) in country places as a substitute for the more expensive Parmesan. It is now produced commercially on a scale commensurate with the wide demand for it. White or grayish-white and oily, with a strong sheep's smell, it has a sharp, salty taste. When fresh, it makes an excellent table cheese; aged, it is much used as a condiment in cooking. It figures in a great many regional dishes, for its extremely sharp flavor. It is sold in cylinders usually wider than they are high, with a hard outside crust, weighing from 12 to 20 pounds. (Widely available in the United States.)

PROVATURA

This is another cheese of the Roman countryside, its most famous center of production being Roccagorga. It is made with buffalo milk (by the method known as *pasta filata*) and sold in the shape and size of a large egg. It should be eaten fresh. Like all buffalo-milk cheeses, it is becoming rarer and being replaced by provolone (*see* below). Serve chilled.

PROVOLA

Another cheese from the South, the provola of Sorrento and the Salerno plain being especially notable. It is made with buffalo milk by the method known as *pasta filata*. It is highly prized for its fragrance and flavor. It is usually sold in 2- to 4-pound packets. It should be eaten fresh. If it is to be aged, it must first be lightly smoked, in which case it is known as smoked provola. It, too, is becoming rare and increasingly replaced in cooking by provolone.

PROVOLONE

This, like the preceding provola from which it differs only in size and form (being larger than provola and spherical or slightly ovoid in form) was also originally a buffalo-milk cheese (although it may also be made with cow's milk). It is usually found in 8-pound long ovals. It has a soft, slightly fat texture and a characteristic flavor and aroma. It may be eaten fresh or aged. (Readily available in the United States.)

RICOTTA

This is an unsalted fresh cheese made in many ways, primarily in South-central Italy. Ricotta (meaning "twice-cooked") is the product obtained by cooking again the whey left when other cheese is made. There are also smoked and salted versions. A strong ricotta, made in Putignano and in Ruvo di Puglia in the province of Bari (down at the bottom of the "boot"), is subjected to a number of processes. March ricotta, produced in San Nicandro Garganico (in the province of Foggia) is salted and preserved between aromatic leaves and owes its name to the fact that it is eaten during the month of March. Roman ricotta, produced from sheep's milk, has a smooth, bland texture and is fragrant and delicate; it is much used in preparing various special Roman dishes. Hard ricotta, sometimes called "ricotta with rind," is salted and has a sharp taste; it is usually used as a condiment. (The fresh, unsalted ricotta, resembling the Roman variety most closely, is widely available in the United States, in supermarkets as well as at Italian grocers.) Serve cold.

ROBIOLA

This is a soft (in some cases, almost runny) cheese made in varying (milder and stronger) forms at many places in Lombardy and Piedmont. Its name derives from a red covering (*rubeus, rosso,* meaning red) in which it was formerly encased. Especially prized are the robiolas made in Albugnano, Cocconato, Casalborgone, and Montabone (province of Alessandria), Alba, Ceva, and Mondovi (province of Cuneo), and Melzo and Codogno (province of Milan). By far the most famous, however, are the robiolas from the Val-sassina (at Ballabio, Introbbio, and Maggianico). Of a soft, smooth, delicate texture, it is pressed down sometimes into a square, sometimes into a round shape. Its delicate fragrance remotely resembles that of truffles; it has a delicate, delicious flavor. Robiola may be eaten fresh or aged. It is usually put up in weights not exceeding ³⁄₄ pound.

ROBIOLINI

Although excellent robiolini is produced in Melle (in the province of Cuneo in Piedmont), the best robiolini comes from Lombardy. It may be made with whole cow's milk or with cow's milk mixed with milk of goats or sheep. It has a smooth texture and a flavor all its own.

SCAMORZA

This is another south Italian (Campanian) cheese most of which is made at Lioni in the province of Avellino. It is made of cow's milk by the *pasta filata* method already mentioned. It is eaten fresh and sold in a characteristic pear-shape, weighing about 6 ounces.

STRACCHINO (also called TALEGGIO)

This Lombard cheese is especially prized when made in Taleggio. Its name derives from a word in the local dialect *(stracco)* which in Italian would be *stanco* ("tired"), because it used to be believed that the best stracchino was made from the milk of cows "tired" after a long period of grazing in good pastures. The cheese must be made with cow's milk still warm from the milking. It is smooth, evenly textured, soft, and melts in your mouth, of a creamy yellow color, with a delicate but insistent flavor peculiar to it. It is produced only in cool or cold months and sold in a square form weighing about 2 pounds.

TOMINI

The best of this Piedmont cheese is produced in Chiaverano, Cumana, Cuorgné, and Pinerolo (province of Turin), also at Candelo (province of Vercelli). These are a special kind of small cheese made with goat's milk and preserved with pepper.

792

CHEESES OF OTHER NATIONS
Formaggi d'altri paesi

AUSTRIA

LIPTAUER

This is a strange cheese about which there has been a good deal of discussion. It has never been satisfactorily established whether its paternity is Hungarian or Austrian; it is assigned to Austria simply because Liptau is Austrian today. Originally Liptauer cheese was a soft white pecorino that was marketed in little white cartons. What is known today as Liptauer is a mixture of the original cheese with paprika, mustard, anchovy paste, and other spices. It has numberless variations.

ENGLAND

STILTON

Stilton is considered the king of English cheeses. It is prepared with whole milk to which cream is added. Its smooth texture is marbled with green, its flavor is both delicate and sharp. It takes a long time to ripen. English gourmets like to take a small Stilton cheese (about 10 pounds), make holes in it, and pour some Port wine into it. They then keep it about 2 months in a cool place, well covered with wax paper. It is then sliced and served. (Stilton and Stilton mixed with Port or other wines, or brandy, are available throughout the United States.)

FRANCE

BEAUFORT

This is a cheese made in shepherds' huts in the Alps,

especially in the Savoie. It is made of the very best milk produced by cows that are pastured within a specially enclosed area of about ½ mile square. It has a soft, smooth, almost oily texture, close without holes, translucent, in color a light yellow. It somewhat resembles fontina. It comes in large rounds of 60 to 120 pounds, unusual for being slightly concave around the edge.

BRIE

This cheese has been made at Brie in the Île de France for centuries. Round in shape and from 13 to 22 inches in diameter, it is pressed down rather like a pie. (It may be served under a rustic covering of rye straw.) It is soft and creamy (but should not be runny) and smooth; creamy yellow in color, its flavor is inimitable and indescribable. A truly noble cheese, it is extremely fragile. It is quickly aged to its proper point and then must be refrigerated to keep any length of time. It should be eaten quite soon after being removed from the refrigerator. (Generally available in the United States.)

CAMEMBERT

This Norman cheese, believed to have originated at Camembert, is of great and ancient fame. It is made from the whole milk of a famous breed of French cows, the richness of whose milk derives from the fertile soil and gentle climate of their Normandy pastures. Camembert has a unique, inimitable flavor with a slightly bitterish edge to it. It is a soft but solid cheese, without holes, pale yellow in color, with a taste that is strong yet suave. It is made in small disks, ranging from 8 to 12 ounces, packed in little wooden boxes. Its ritual preparation is legally controlled by the *Syndicat du Véritable Camembert*—"Company Producing True Camembert." (Generally available in the United States, in both domestic and imported form.)

MUNSTER

Made in the Münster valley (Upper Rhine) and in Alsace-Lorraine, this cheese is attributed to the patient art of monks who were developing agriculture in the seventh century along the lower slopes of both sides of the Vosges mountains. It is a soft to semi-hard cheese protected by a characteristic crust, the preservative action of which is due to a beneficent mold. It has a unique, subtly piquant flavor due to the milk from the particular breed of Vosges cows. (Readily available in the United States.)

REBLOCHON

This little-known cheese is the special product of the so-called Aravis Massif, high up in the mountains of the Savoie. It has a firm to solid texture, is soft in color, and has a delicate, slightly "country" fragrance; its taste is rich and full. It is usually prepared in perfect rounds weighing 2 to 4 pounds.

ROQUEFORT

This is one of the most famous of all cheeses. True Roquefort is made only of whole sheep's milk, produced by the hardy breed that makes its home in the arid Causses pastures of the Pyrenees. The process of making it, though very ancient, has remained a closely guarded secret. The cheeses are ripened in the cool, damp caves to be found in the Causses. It has a smooth, full texture, is of pale creamy color (but not white or gray, which means it is not fully ripened), streaked with green or blue. The French call it the "miracle cheese," and one must agree with them, for its rich, full-bodied, indefinable taste is inimitable. (Available in the United States in imported and domestic varieties.)

HOLLAND

EDAM

This is one of the classic cheeses, that comes in a round ball covered with a waxy red coating. When fresh its has a clear creamy color, is soft, and when subjected to heat melts rapidly and smoothly. This makes it extremely useful in cooking. Aged from 5 months to 1 year or more, the color darkens, the cheese becomes harder, and when heated melts less readily. It also becomes sharper in taste. The aged cheese is more commonly used as a condiment.

GOUDA

This cheese also comes in a characteristic round shape, with a bright red covering. It is rather like Edam.

SWITZERLAND

EMMENTHAL

This is a very famous cheese which is exported to the whole world. Produced originally in the Emme valley in the canton of Berne, it is today produced industrially on a vast scale. It is usually made from whole milk, but a semi-fat variety is also made. It has a firm, almost hard, compact texture, is yellowish in color, with fairly large holes. In taste it is rich, firm, and delicious. (Available throughout the United States as "Swiss Cheese," in both imported and domestic varieties.)

GRUYÈRE

Originally, Gruyère cheese was made in the canton of Fribourg, and the authentic product still comes only from French Switzerland. However, Gruyère is today manufactured throughout that country. It is very much like Emmenthal, except it lacks the holes. Ceding to the ignorance and preference of consumers, lately, producers have been making it with holes! Actually, it is a firmer, saltier, more pungent cheese than the ordinary Swiss. It is made in large rounds of about 100 pounds. (In the United States, small triangles of the processed variety wrapped in silver paper are also sold under the name of Gruyère.)

MENUS

HOW TO PREPARE A MENU
Come si compone un menu

For most occasions, the host or hostess has to deal with only two types of menu: the everyday, simple, informal one, which can be prepared in accordance with personal and family likes (always trying to avoid monotony), and those menus designed for formal luncheons and dinners, where one will be expected to show one's creative ability and culinary and decorative good taste. At the end of this section is a series of sample menus which, we hope, will be helpful for various occasions.

794

To be practical, menus must be divided according to the season of the year, so that full advantage can be taken of the different vegetables, fruits, and meats on the market, although today, because of swift freight transportation and frozen foods, seasons are no longer as important as they formerly were.

However, we have given menus for the four seasons, as well as those for formal, vegetarian, and meatless menus.

Here are some menu suggestions for rather informal luncheons and dinners with friends. The menus are divided according to the seasons.

SPRING LUNCHEONS AND DINNERS
Colazioni e pranzi di primavera

LUNCHEONS

Fried Eggs Napoletana [No. 666]
Braised Leg of Lamb Toscana [No. 1197]
Bananas Flambé in Armagnac [No. 2146]

Linguini with Garlic and Oil [No. 525]
Rabbit Stew in White Wine [No. 1514]
Mixed green salad (*see* page 597)
Mascarpone cheese with sugar and rum (*see* page 790)

Spaghetti and Shellfish Timbale [No. 570]
Veal Chops Sassi [No. 1147]
Mixed green salad (*see* page 597)
Cheese platter (*see* page 788)

Risotto with Sweetbreads [No. 589]
Veal Rolls Gourmet [No. 1173]
Tomatoes with oil, vinegar, and basil
Strawberries Casta Diva [No. 2175]

Fettuccine Guitar [No. 493]
Fritto Misto Milanese [No. 1370]
Bananas Flambé in Kirsch [No. 2147]

Penne or Maltagliati with Ricotta [No. 532]
Spezzatino of Chicken with Peppers [No. 1298]
A bowl of fresh fruit

Cheese and Ham Panzarotti [No. 562]
Squab Richelieu [No. 1354]
Mushrooms in Butter [No. 1705]
Strawberry Tart [No. 1984]

Risotto Verde [No. 540]
Scampi Casino di Venezia [No. 1000]
A bowl of fresh fruit

Potato Gnocchi Romana [No. 620]
Cold Pike Ricca [No. 855]
Crêpes Gil-Blas [No. 2022]

Spinach Soufflé with Mushrooms [No. 1800]
Sauté of Beef Tolstoy [No. 1115]
Boiled Potatoes Inglese [No. 1755]
Cheese platter (*see* page 788)

Risotto Milanese [No. 578]
Veal Rolls Milanese [No.1174]
Peas Casalinga [No. 1732]
A bowl of fresh fruit

Shrimp or Scampi Soufflé Italiana [No. 636]
Veal Riblets with Mushrooms [No. 1167]
Frankfurt Pudding with Strawberry Sauce [No. 2079]

DINNERS

Bouillon with Lettuce [No. 351]
Baked Ham Italiana [No. 1232]
Asparagus in Cream [No. 1598]
Meringues with Whipped Cream [No. 2015]

Roman Soup [No. 451]
Tuna Verde [No. 954]
Hollywood Salad [No. 1867]
Chocolate Soufflé [No. 2051]

Breton Cotriade [No. 1045]
Artichoke Hearts Lucullus [No. 1593]
Chocolate Cake Capriccio [No. 1909]

Asparagus Velouté Soup [No. 401]
Roast Beef Primaverile [No. 1111]
Iced Pears Duchessa [No. 2233]

Bouillon with Tortellini Bolognese [No. 357]
Mullets Marseillaise [No. 832]
Salad Germana [No. 1862]
Crêpes with Jam [No. 2025]

Consommé Celestine [No. 367]
Lamb Chops Gourmet [No. 1205]
Wild Strawberries Maria-José [No. 2178]

Cream of Artichoke Soup [No. 392]
Porgy Italiana [No. 863]
Apricots Condé [No. 2063]

Spinach Soup [No. 416]
Entrecôte Paprika [No. 1092]
Caramel Custard with Wild Strawberry Compote
[No. 2106]

Minestrone Genovese [No. 456]
Veal Cutlets en Papillotes [No. 1151]
Artichokes with Peas and Lettuce Casalinga
[No. 1586]
Crêpes Buongustaio [No. 2018]

Pea and Pasta Soup [No. 442]
Squabs with Black Olives [No. 1350]
Apple Charlotte Casalinga [No. 2060]

Rice Soup with Chicken Livers [No. 443]
Porgy Casalinga [No. 836]
Cherry Tart [No. 1968]

Purée of Tomato Soup [No. 391]
Veal Grenadins with Mixed Vegetables [No. 1158]
Wild Strawberries Capriccio di Wanda [No. 2177]

SUMMER LUNCHEONS AND DINNERS
Colazioni e pranzi d'estate

LUNCHEONS

Prosciutto and Melon [No. 213]
Veal Chops in White Wine [No. 1148]
Tomatoes with oil, vinegar, and basil
Cheese platter (*see* page 788)

Linguini with Garlic and Oil [No. 525]
Boiled Tongue with Piquant Sauce [No. 1449]
Celery Hearts [No. 190]
Banana Compote [No. 2182]

Prosciutto and Figs [No. 212]
Entrecôte [No. 1087]
Baked Potatoes [No. 1748]
A bowl of fresh fruit

Stuffed Calzone [No. 561]
Alabama Salad [No. 1838]
Baked Custard [No. 2103]

Neapolitan Pizza with Fresh Anchovies [No. 556]
Braised Duck with Olives [No. 1331]
Mixed green salad (*see* page 597)
A bowl of fresh fruit

795

Prosciutto and Melon [No. 213]
Chicken in Casserole Pastorella [No. 1269]
Noisette Potatoes [No. 1783 or 1784]
Peaches Reale [No. 2163]

Rice Cagnone [No. 592]
Roast Squab [No. 1355]
French Fried Potato Straws [No. 1776]
Mixed green salad (see page 597)
Apricots with Custard Sauce [No. 2135]

Molded Gruyère Cheese Soufflé [No. 644]
Eels Provençale [No. 811]
Butterfly Salad [No. 1848]
Fruit Soufflé [No. 2052]

Cold Summer Taglierini [No. 513]
Chopped Beef Niçoise [No. 1085]
Oysters on Horseback [No. 302]
Brandied Cherries Praliné [No. 2151]

Mosaic of Eggs in Aspic [No. 733]
Veal Chops with Basil [No. 1135]
Half-Mourning Salad [No. 1864]
A bowl of fresh fruit

Molded Eggplant Soufflé [No. 641]
Terrine Inglese [No. 1573]
Peppers Au Gratin Partenopea [No. 1741]
Peaches Reale [No. 2163]

Scalloped Zucchini with Eggplant, Peppers, and
    Tomatoes [No. 1836]
Veal with Tuna [No. 1575]
Apricot Tart [No. 1964]

DINNERS

Cold Minestrone Milanese [No. 459]
Veal Chops Luigi Veronelli [No. 1138]
Salad Sally Lou [No. 1880]
Coupe Dama Bianca [No. 2217]

Neapolitan Soup [No. 441]
Chicken Liver Pie [No. 1415]
Beets with Fresh Herbs [No. 1619]
Melon Surprise [No. 2154]

Minestrone Montefredine [No. 460]
Chicken Breasts en Papilottes [No. 1292]
Sautéed Eggplant Milanese [No. 1673]
Apricot Mousse [No. 2118]

Tomato Soup with Tarragon [No. 418]
Cold Trout Au Bleu [No. 932]
Boiled Potatoes with Parsley [No. 1758]
Frankfurt Pudding with Strawberry Sauce [No. 2079]

Bouillon with Passatelli Marchigiana [No. 352]
Filet of Sole Gran Successo No. 4 [No. 908]
Stuffed Brandied Peaches [No. 2164]

Consommé with Tomato Essence [No. 384]
Cima Genovese [No. 1545]
Baked Eggplant with Garlic [No. 1663]
Coffee Granita [No. 2210]

Consommé with Julienne Vegetables [No. 375]
Veal Rolls Gourmet [No. 1173]
Rum Ice Cream [No. 2208]

Zucchini Soup [No. 423]
Veal Rolls in Aspic [No. 1550]
Peppers Au Gratin Partenopea [No. 1741]
Peaches and Raspberries [No. 2162]

Minestrone Genovese [No. 456]
Cold Veal Cutlets Bella Vista [No. 1554]
A bowl of fresh fruit

Bean Soup with Pasta [No. 427]
Hare in Aspic Casalinga [No. 1546]
Custard Delizioza with Raspberry Sauce [No. 2109]

Tomato Mousse [No. 1565]
Steak Tartare [No. 1118]
Cold Zabaglione [No. 2117]

Rice and Parsley Soup Casalinga [No. 444]
Hamburger [No. 1104]
Coupe Maria Theresa [No. 2222]

AUTUMN LUNCHEONS AND DINNERS
Colazioni e pranzi di autunno

LUNCHEONS

Ravioli Timbale with Meat Sauce [No. 568]
Lamb Chops Villeroy [No. 1211]
Apples Condé [No. 2064]

Coddled Eggs Napoletana [No. 699]
Pork Chops Napoletana [No. 1243]
Pears in Red Wine Italiana [No. 2170]

Macaroni Au Gratin [No. 529]
Tournedos Marquis de Sade [No. 1127]
Broiled Mushrooms [No. 1703]
A bowl of fresh fruit

Risotto Milanese [No. 578]
Sauté of Beef [No. 1114]
Scalloped Zucchini with Eggplant, Peppers, and
    Tomatoes [No. 1836]
Chestnut Pudding [No. 2071]

Gnocchi Verde Italiana [No. 622]
Frogs' Legs Fines Herbes [No. 1013]
Mushrooms Contadina [No. 1706]
A bowl of fresh fruit

Fettuccine with Triple Butter [No. 490]
Roast Pork with Cardoons [No. 1251]
Cheese platter (*see* page 788)

Fried Mussels [No. 1021]
Beef Braciola [No. 1059]
Spinach in Butter [No. 1791]
Rum Babas [No. 1888]

Scampi Paris Exposition 1937 [No. 1004]
Saratoga Salad [No. 1881]
Coffee Soufflé [No. 2042]

Macaroni Timbale Italiana [No. 566]
Broiled Pig's Feet [No. 1239]
String Beans Aretina [No. 1801]
Platter of mild cheeses (*see* page 788)

Lasagna Italiana [No. 499]
Broiled Steak Fiorentina [No. 1081]
Black-Eyed Beans Uccelleto [No. 1610]
A bowl of fresh fruit

Risotto Campo Antico [No. 573]
Partridge with Brussels Sprouts [No. 1473]
Melon Surprise [No. 2154]

Shellfish Flan [No. 613]
Roast Sirloin Château en Papillote [No. 1112]
Souffléed Potatoes [No. 1789]
Peaches Reale [No. 2163]

DINNERS

Consommé with Mushroom Essence [No. 383]
Oxtail Italiana [No. 1430]
Fresh Figs Belvedere [No. 2153]

Consommé Chasseur [No. 368]
Salmis of Pheasant [No. 1489]
A bowl of fresh fruit

Zucchini Soup [No. 423]
Quail in Casserole with Grapes [No. 1497]
Savarin with Whipped Cream [No. 1903]

Bouillon with Pastina [No. 354]
Braised Beef with Gnocchi [No. 1079]
Nesselrode Pudding [No. 2100]

Chickpea Soup Toscana [No. 434]
Veal Fricassee [No. 1157]
Cabinet Pudding with Rum Zabaglione Sauce
    [No. 2066]

Cabbage Minestrone [No. 455]
Veal Cutlets Bolognese [No. 1149]
Chocolate Bavarian Cream [No. 2097]

Cream of Chestnut Soup Brunoise [No. 397]
Broiled Partridge Diavolo [No. 1472]
Charlotte Russe [No. 2069]

Bouillon Bolognese [No. 343]
Broiled Lamb Chops [No. 1202]
Stuffed Mushrooms [No. 1713]
A bowl of fresh fruit

Bouillon with Homemade Taglierini [No. 356]
Breast of Turkey New York World's Fair 1939
    [No. 1327]
Vanilla Mousse [No. 2124]

Minestrone Borghese [No. 454]
Quail Diavolo [No. 1499]
Apple Dumplings [No. 1963]

Chickpea Soup Contadina [No. 432]
Bolliti Misti Italiana [No. 1078]
Boiled Potatoes with Basil [No. 1754]
A bowl of fresh fruit

Mock-Turtle Soup [No. 469]
Roast Pheasant on Toast [No. 1488] with Diavolo Sauce
    [No. 30]
Chocolate Pudding with Custard Sauce [No. 2072]

WINTER LUNCHEONS AND DINNERS
Colazioni e pranzi d'inverno

LUNCHEONS

Risotto Campo Antico [No. 573]
Roast Duck [No. 1334]
Orange Salad [No. 1874]
Platter of assorted cheeses (*see* page 788)

Carrot Flan [No. 606]
Hungarian Goulash [No. 1105]
A bowl of fresh fruit

Mezze Zite with "Four" Cheeses [No. 552]
Breast of Turkey Nero [No. 1326]
Noisette Potatoes [No. 1783 or 1784]
Apple Compote [No. 2180]

Braised Sweetbreads with Celery Au Gratin [No. 1436]
Salad Musetta [No. 1873]
Pears with Red Wine Italiana [No. 2170]

Paella Valenciana [No. 481]
Iced Pineapple Surprise [No. 2236]

Cannelloni Italiana [No. 485]
Bass Gourmet [No. 772]
French Fried Potato Straws [No. 1776]
Platter of assorted cheeses (*see* page 788)

Fettuccine with Butter and Anchovies [No. 489]
Veal Chops Milanese [No. 1142]
French Fried Potatoes [No. 1773]
Apple Charlotte Casalinga [No. 2060]

Greek Pilaf [No. 598]
Pepper Steak [No. 1107]
Broccoli-Rave Vinaigrette [No. 1625]
Pears Cecilia [No. 2169]

Molded Artichoke Soufflé [No. 638]
Broiled Sweetbreads Piquant [No. 1439]
Peas in Butter [No. 1731]
Oranges Czarina [No. 2157]

Macaroncelli with Ham Au Gratin [No. 527]
Fillets of Perch with Sage [No. 850]
Boiled Potatoes in Their Jackets [No. 1756]
Platter of assorted cheeses (*see* page 788)

Piedmontese Fondue [No. 274]
Guinea Hen in Clay [No. 1340]
Braised Cabbage [No. 1633]
Banana Compote [No. 2182]

Creamed Eggs and Onions [No. 686]
Broiled Veal Kidneys [No. 1422]
Baked Potatoes [No. 1748]
Apples in Barolo Wine [No. 2134]

DINNERS

Cream of Barley Soup [No. 395]
Rattatuia of Chicken Livers and Veal Kidneys
    [No. 1416]
Radish Salad Treviso [No. 1877]
Brioche Surprise [No. 1898]

Stracciato [No. 342]
Goose Stew with Sausage and Chestnuts [No. 1346]
Orange Pudding Madrilena [No. 2084]

Bouillon with Homemade Taglierini [No. 356]
Fillets of Sole Indienne [No. 909]
Indian Rice [No. 594]
Charlotte Sogno d'Autunno [No. 2070]

Lettuce Velouté Soup [No. 403]
Breast of Turkey Villa Sassi [No. 1329]
Celery Salad [No. 1851]
Gâteau St. Honoré [No. 1911]

Cabbage Soup Milanese [No. 431]
Minute Steak Paillard [No. 1106]
Potato Chips [No. 1762]
Caramel Custard [No. 2105]

Rice and Potato Soup [No. 446]
Pork Sausages in White Wine [No. 1257]
Purée of Dried White Beans [No. 1616]
Dried Fig Compote [No. 2186]
Palm Leaves [No. 1941]

Bouillon with Breadcrumbs [No. 344]
Chateaubriand Béarnaise [No. 1083]
Nesselrode Pudding [No. 2100]

Bouillon with Semolina Gnocchi [No. 349]
Zampone Modenese [No. 1262]
Apple Fritters with Apricot Sauce [No. 2032]

Bouillon with Pastina [No. 354]
Boiled Capon with Green Sauce [No. 1312]
Crêpes with Rum-Flavored Marrons Glacés [No. 2026]

Cabbage Soup [No. 410]
Fried Chicken Fiorentina [No. 1272]
Celery Salad [No. 1851]
Regina Pudding [No. 2089]

Consommé Madrilène [No. 376]
Turkey Wing Niçoise [No. 1433]
Hazelnut Bavarian Cream [No. 2099]

Bouillon Bolognese [No. 343]
Braised Pig's Ears with Lentils [No. 1237]
Marron Croste [No. 2074]

FORMAL LUNCHEONS AND DINNERS
Colazioni e pranzi importanti

*Here are some suggested menus for formal meals, occasions
where one wishes to serve the finest foods to distinguished
guests. These dishes require more skill and experience than
the preceding suggestions. The luncheon menus can also
be used for dinners, if desired.*

LUNCHEONS

Oyster Fritters [No. 1027]
Tortellini Romagnola [No. 520]
Lamb Chops Cacciatora [No. 1212]
Potatoes in Cream Au Gratin [No. 1766]
Fricassee of Artichoke [No. 1583]
Bananas Lucullus [No. 2148]

Mushrooms Gourmet [No. 1710]
Easter Pie Genovese [No. 288]
Veal Rolls Milanese [No. 1174]
Boiled Potatoes with Basil [No. 1754]
Celery with Meat Sauce and Marrow [No. 1661]
Coffee Cup Custard [No. 2108]

Piedmontese Fondue [No. 274]
Spiedini Lucullus [No. 312]
Veal Chops in White Wine [No. 1148]
Potatoes Dorate [No. 1769]
Fennel Parmigiana [No. 1689]
Cherry Custard Meringue Tart [No. 1966]

Poached Eggs with Anchovies [No. 651]
Green Tagliatelle with Oil and Garlic [*see* Nos. 516
    and 525]
Veal Riblets à l'Ancienne [No. 1165]
Mashed Potatoes [No. 1780]
Eggplant Catanese [No. 1655]
Fresh Figs with Zabaglione Sauce [No. 2279]

Mussels Ravigote [No. 169]
Polenta Ciociara [No. 625]
Roast Pork Toscana [No. 1253]
Black-Eyed Beans Uccelleto [No. 1610]
Platter of assorted cheeses (*see* page 788)
Chestnut Tart [No. 1969]

Mullet with Saffron [No. 165]
Creamed Mushroom Pie [No. 289]
Spezzatino of Chicken in Vinegar [No. 1303]
Potatoes Macaire [No. 1778]
Sautéed Asparagus Tips Wrapped in Prosciutto
    [No. 1608]
Wild Strawberries Maria-José [No. 2178]

Cheese Tartlets [No. 316]
Carthusian Risotto [No. 574]
Fillet of Beef Gourmet [No. 1100]
Cauliflower Fritters [No. 1653]
Platter of assorted cheeses (*see* page 788)
Apricots Lily [No. 2136]

Gruyère Cheese Croquettes [No. 1361]
Vol-au-Vent Financière [No. 648]
Roast Beef Pizzaiola [No. 1110]
Potatoes Fondant [No. 1772]
Cardoons au Gratin [No. 1638]
Cheese plate: Provola, Mozzarella, Scamorza
    (see page 788)
Crêpes Suzette [No. 2027]

DINNERS

Fresh fruit compote with orange juice [see Nos. 2180–93]
Bouillon with Spinach Gnocchi [No. 350]
Golden Skate [No. 896] with Remoulade Sauce [No. 97]
Roast Sirloin Château en Papillote [No. 1112]
French Fried Potatoes [No. 1773]
Radish Salad Treviso [No. 1877]
Vacherin Primavera [No. 1925]

Shrimp Cocktail [No. 176]
Rice Soup with Chicken Livers [No. 443]
Fillet of Sole Bonne Femme [No. 899]
Sautéed Quail with Cherries [No. 1502]
Peas Francese [No. 1734]
Cold Zabaglione [No. 2117]
Cat's Tongues [No. 1930]

Norwegian or Scottish Smoked Salmon [No. 172]
Grandmother's Vegetable Soup [No. 421]
Bass Meunière with Peppers [No. 775]
Roast Duck with Orange Sauce [No. 1336]
Mixed green salad (see page 597)
Potato Croquettes [No. 1767]
Spumone Africana [No. 2246]

Pâté de foie gras and thin toast (see page 530)
Stracciatella [No. 359]
Whiting Fines Herbes [No. 967]
Entrecôte Bordelaise [No. 1090]
Hearts of lettuce salad (see page 597)
Orange Bavarian Cream [No. 2101]

800

Oysters with Lemon Wedges [see No. 171] and buttered
    slices of rye bread
Consommé à la Reine [No. 379]
Fillets of Sole Indienne [No. 909]
Roast Veal Maria [No. 1171]
Lettuce and tomato salad (see page 597)
Coupe Dama Bianca [No. 2217]

Caviar Canapés [No. 221]
Cream of Artichoke Soup [No. 392]
Coffered Mullet with Mushrooms [No. 824]
Roast Fillet of Hare with Brandy and Mustard
    [No. 1552]
Beet and Radish Salad [No. 1846]
Crêpe-Wrapped Ice Cream Casino Pourville Sur Mer
    [No. 2226]

Terrine of Truffled Goose Liver [No. 1558]
Minestrone Milanese [No. 458]
Fillets of Sole Colbert [No. 901]
Turkey with Sausage and Chestnut Stuffing [No. 1320]
Salad Musetta [No. 1873]
Curaçao Soufflé [No. 2043]

Fresh Tomato Juice Cocktail [No. 218]
Rice and Pea Soup [No. 445]
Fillets of Perch with Anchovy Butter [No. 845]
Breast of Chicken Rossini [No. 1294]
Noisette Potatoes [No. 1783 or 1784]
Chicory salad (see page 597)
Mont Blanc [No. 2081]

VEGETARIAN LUNCHEONS AND DINNERS
Colazioni e pranzi vegetariani

The following menus should clearly demonstrate that
vegetarian meals need not be dull or insipid. They provide
perfect Lenten meals, so delicious that meat will not be
missed.

LUNCHEONS

Fettuccine with Triple Butter [No. 490]
Artichoke Omelet [No. 716]
Japanese Salad [No. 1866]
Grandmother's Raised Rice Fritters [No. 2035]

Fried Eggs Romana [No. 670]
Potato Croquettes [No. 1767] with Tomato Sauce
    [No. 19]
Fig Tart [No. 1973]

Bucatini Gourmet [No. 522]
Shirred Eggs Diavola [No. 677]
Artichoke Hearts Lucullus [No. 1593]
A bowl of fresh fruit

Spaghetti with Broccoli [No. 537]
Mozzarella in Carrozza with Anchovy Butter [No. 1372]
Hindu Salad [No. 1868]
Baked Custard [No. 2103]

Vegetable Antipasto [No. 219]
Sliced tomatoes and onions marinated in Sauce
    Vinaigrette [see No. 99]
Parmesan Fritters [No. 279]
Artichoke Croquettes [No. 250]
Potatoes Pizzaiola [No. 1786]
Rice Pudding with Almonds [No. 2090]

Artichokes Vinaigrette [No. 1587]
Celery [No. 190]
Stuffed Olives Siciliana [No. 204]
Fettuccine with Butter and Anchovies [No. 489]
Piedmontese Fondue [No. 274]
Eggplant Catanese [No. 1665]
Apple Charlotte with Rum [No. 2061]

Macedoine of Vegetables [No. 198]
Artichoke Hearts, Greek Style [No. 182]
Neapolitan Black Olives [No. 206]
Gnocchi au Gratin [No. 614]
Spinach Frittata [No. 712]
Broccoli Siciliana [No. 1624]
Crêpes Gil-Blas [No. 2022]

Eggs Mayonnaise [No. 727]
Tomato sections with fresh basil
Russian Salad [No. 1879]

Spaghetti with Anchovies [No. 535]
Spinach Soufflé with Mushrooms [No. 1800]
String Beans Aretina [No. 1801]
Peaches Flambé Brillat-Savarin [No. 2159]

DINNERS

Purée of Vegetable Soup Italiana [No. 453]
Shirred Eggs Contadina [No. 676]
Cinema Salad [No. 1853]
Accademia Pudding [No. 2059]

Purée of Dried Pea Soup [No. 389]
Molded Harlequin Soufflé [No. 645]
Radish and Gruyère Cheese Salad [No. 1876]
Iced Melon Surprise [No. 2228]

Bean Soup Ciociara [No. 408]
Flan Italiana [No. 609]
Mushrooms Bordelaise [No. 1702]
Normandy Apples with Almond Cream and Calvados
    [No. 2083]

Zuppa Pavese [No. 425]
Polenta Croquettes Italiana [No. 1364]
Peas Fiamminga [No. 1733]
Compote Armoniosa [No. 2184]

Purée of Tomato Soup [No. 391]
Egg Canapés [No. 224]
Pilaf with Mushrooms [No. 600]
Braised Artichokes Romana [No. 1581]
Bagration Salad [No. 1845]
Rothschild Soufflé [No. 2046]

Chickpea Soup Contadina [No. 432]
Cannelloni Partenopea [No. 486], omitting the meat
Tomatoes Massaia [No. 1815]
Braised Lettuce [No. 1697]
Mixed green salad (see page 597)
Pineapple Tart [No. 1980]

Cream of Chicory Soup [No. 396]
Parmesan Fritters [No. 279]
Molded Mushroom Soufflé [No. 646]
Peas in Butter [No. 1731]
Hearts of Lettuce Salad with Tomatoes [No. 1865]
Bananas Flambé in Armagnac [No. 2146]

Celery Velouté Soup [No. 402]
Spinach in butter with hard-boiled eggs [see No. 1791]
Risotto with Butter and Parmesan Cheese [No. 572]
Creamed Mushroom Pie [No. 289]
Tomato Salad Napoletana [No. 1884]
Baked Apples Melba [No. 2143]

MEATLESS LUNCHEONS AND DINNERS
Colazioni e pranzi di magro

*For Lent and Fast days, here are some suggested menus
both simple and elaborate.*

LUNCHEONS

Tomatoes and Rice Romana [No. 1816]
Mediterranean Fish Stew [No. 1053]
A bowl of fresh fruit

Cheese Soufflé [No. 630]
Fillets of Sole Fantasia Marma [No. 903]
Rice Pudding with Candied Fruit [No. 2091]

Seafood Antipasto [*see* Nos. 147–79]
Shrimp Tart [No. 291]
Curate's Salad [No. 1855]
A bowl of fresh fruit

Risotto Paesana [No. 582]
Fillet of Mackerel in White Wine [No. 820]
Boiled potatoes [*see* No. 1755] with Sauce
　　Hollandaise [No. 72]
Platter of assorted cheeses (*see* page 788)

Mussels in Saffron Sauce [No. 170]
Easter Pie Genovese [No. 288]
Trout in Red Wine [No. 939]
Fennel in Casserole Casalinga [No. 1687]
Strawberries Romanoff [No. 2176]

Oysters [No. 171] with
　　buttered rye bread and lemon wedges
Tortelli Lombarda [No. 517]
Whiting Colbert [No. 965]
Peas with Lettuce [No. 1763]
Tangerine Soufflé [No. 2048]

Marinated Sardines [No. 173]
Ricotta Ravioli [No. 509]
Lobster Diavola [No. 985]
Celery Au Gratin [No. 1959]
Caramel Custard [No. 2105]
Petits Fours [No. 1950]

Anchovies Carbiniera [No. 147]
Cheese Frittata [No. 705]
Lobster in Cream [No. 983]
Baked Eggplant with Garlic [No. 1663]
Strawberry Tart [No. 1984]

DINNERS

Bouillon with Breadcrumbs [No. 344]
Frogs' Legs with Peppers and Mushrooms [No. 1017]
Crêpes Convento with Kirsch [No. 2019]

Mushroom Soup [No. 440]
Mullet Madrilène [No. 831]
Fried Peppers Romana [No. 1740]
Pear Compote [No. 2189]

Rice and Parsley Soup Casalinga [No. 444]
Baked Pike Luigi Veronelli [No. 853]
Broiled Mushrooms [No. 1703]
Florentine Castagnaccio [No. 1910]

Minestrone Toscana [No. 461]
Mozzarella in Carozza with Anchovy Butter [No. 1372]
Salad Americana [No. 1839]
Lemon Soufflé [No. 2044]

Fresh melon with brandy
Potage Parmentier [No. 388]
Mushrooms on Vine Leaves [No. 1715]
Fillets of Bass Au Gratin [No. 220]
Cauliflower Parmigiana [No. 1655]
Apple Strudel [No. 1987]

Caviar Toast [No. 295]
Lentil Soup [No. 413]
Tartlets Marion Delorme [No. 318]
Adriatic Fish Soup [No. 1043]
Bananas Lucullus [No. 2148]

Seafood Croquettes Dieppe [No. 255]
Squash Soup Casalinga [No. 415]
Fillets of Perch with Sage [No. 850]
Oyster Plant Provençale [No. 1730]
Soufflé Omelet Flambé [No. 2058]

Shrimp Cocktail [No. 176]
Cream of Green Asparagus Soup [No. 394]
Trout Italiana [No. 934]
Spinach in Butter [No. 1791]
Iced Pineapple Surprise [No. 2236]

COLD BUFFET
Buffet freddo

Today, the cold buffet is a popular feature of home entertaining which frequently takes the place of the elaborate formal dinners of the past. It is an excellent way to bring together many guests, especially when a large dining room is not available. There are almost countless variations of what can be offered at a cold buffet, but an excellent idea is to interrupt the meal in the

802

middle with a good hot consommé. Here is a list from which anyone can draw inspiration:

Various salads [*see* Nos. 1837–86]
Italian Antipasti [*see* Nos. 145–219]
Hot and Cold Canapés, Barquettes, Tartlets
    [*see* Nos. 221–322]
Easter Pie Genovese [No. 288]
Neapolitan Specialties [*see* Nos. 554–62]
Eggs in Aspic [*see* Nos. 728, 733, 743, etc.]
Salmon Trout Bella Vista [No. 940]
Cold Lobster Italiana [No. 981]
Ham Mousse [No. 1564]
Truffled Goose Liver in Wine Aspic [No. 1559]
Duck Pâté [No. 1568]
Galantine of Chicken [No. 1544]
Fillet of Beef in Aspic [No. 1542]
Cima Genovese [No. 1545]
Cold Veal Tongue with Piquant Sauce [No. 1552]
Vacherin with Custard Cream [No. 1926]
Gâteau St. Honoré [No. 1911]
Tangerine Surprise [No. 2244]

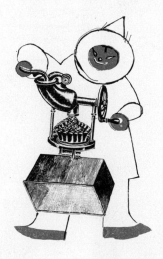

MIDNIGHT SUPPER
Cena di mezzanotte

A midnight supper can prolong a happy evening at the theater. It should be a rather smart occasion, and an array of light but stylish dishes is suggested. The menu should

be prepared according to the season, and should be accompanied by a good wine, preferably Champagne.

For light, refreshing midnight supper dishes in the summer, we suggest:

Melon Surprise [No. 2154]
Mussels in Aspic with Sardine Butter [No. 166]
Mullet with Saffron [No. 167]
Cold barquettes and tartlets [*see* Nos. 316–22]
Cold canapés [*see* Nos. 220–37]
Steak Tartare Americana [No. 1119]
Fillet of Beef in Aspic [No. 1542]
Cold Veal Cutlets Bella Vista [No. 1554]
Mussels Capricciose [No. 166]
Marinated Sardines [No. 173]
Lobster Bella Vista [No. 977]
Stuffed Eggs [*see* Nos. 739–51]
Cold Summer Taglierini [No. 513]
Celery Salad [No. 1851]
Ice Cream and/or Ices [*see* Nos. 2194–2252]
Hot antipasti served as entrées [*see* Nos. 250–324]
Mushroom Soup [No. 440]
Molded Mushroom Soufflé [No. 646]
Gruyère Cheese Soufflé [No. 631]
Hot egg dishes [*see* Nos. 650–99]
Broiled steaks [*see* Nos. 1083–1129]
Salad Americana [No. 1839]
Appetizing Salad [No. 1840]
Truffle dishes [*see* Nos. 1819–23]
Apricots Condé [No. 2063]

During the winter, hearty and spicy dishes are appreciated. Among the variety you can choose from are the celebrated English Savouries [see Nos. 292–305], as well as the most famous dishes of the international cuisine.

All oyster and shellfish dishes
Hot antipasti served as entrées (*see* pages 343–46)
Consommés, purées, veloutés [*see* Nos. 360–406]
Hot egg dishes [*see* Nos. 1083–1129]
Game (*see* pages 506–24)
Broiled meats (*see* pages 358–429)
Stecchi [*see* Nos. 1380–82]
Pork Liver with Fennel [No. 1408]
Broiled Pig's Feet [No. 1239]
Soufflés [*see* Nos. 2040–52]
Hot Puddings [*see* Nos. 2061, etc.)

On cold spring nights, serve winter dishes, and for warm spring nights, summer dishes will be appreciated. For every occasion, there is one "must"—interesting and inventive salads.

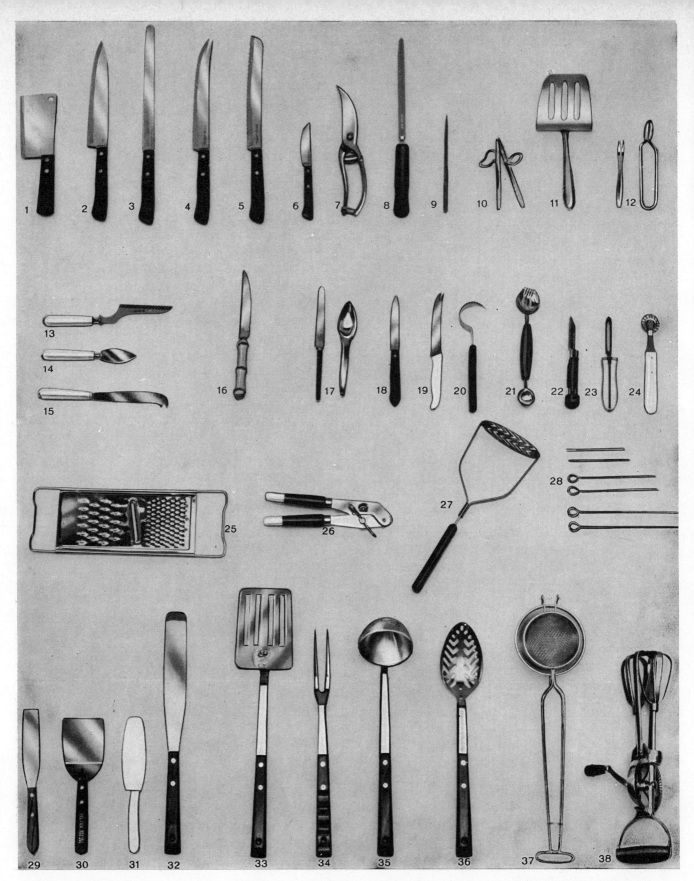

KITCHEN EQUIPMENT I—1. Cleaver; 2. Butcher's knife; 3 Slicer; 4. Carving knife; 5. Serrated knife; 6. Paring knife; 7. Poultry shears; 8. Knife sharpener; 9. Larding needle; 10. Asparagus tongs; 11. Asparagus server; 12. Fork and tongs for snails; 13. Knife for soft cheeses; 14. Knife for hard cheeses; 15. Cheese slicer/server; 16. Steak knife; 17. Grapefruit knife and spoon; 18. Grapefruit or citrus-fruit knife; 19. Fruit knife; 20. Butter curler; 21. Melon ball cutter; 22. Apple corer; 23. Rotary peeler; 24. Pastry wheel; 25. Grater; 26. Can opener; 27. Potato masher; 28. Skewers; 29–32. Various spatulas; 33. Pancake turner or spatula; 34. Kitchen fork; 35. Ladle; 36. Slotted spoon; 37. Wire utensil for making potato baskets; 38. Rotary beater

KITCHEN EQUIPMENT II—1. & 2. Large cooking pots; 3. Fish boiler or steamer; 4. Small saucepan; 5. Special covered frying pan (reversible) for making *frittate*; 6. Broth strainer; 7. Colander; 8. Vegetable steamer; 9. Pan for scalding milk; 10. Frying pan or skillet; 11. Shallow saucepan or baker; 12. Au gratin pan; 13. Snail baking pan; 14. Ramekin for shirred eggs; 15. Rubber scraper; 16. Oval oven-proof baking dish; 17. Individual soufflé dishes or custard cups; 18. Oven-proof ramekin or cocotte; 19. Soufflé dish

KITCHEN EQUIPMENT III—1. Heavy copper saucepan; 2. Electric blender; 3. Portable charcoal grill; 4. Baking sheet; 5. Deep fat fryer and removable frying basket; 6. Rolling pin; 7. Round baking pan; 8. Cheese grater; 9. Chopping board and half-moon chopper; 10. Ravioli mold and roller; 11. Mortar and pestle

KITCHEN EQUIPMENT IV—1. Metal pastry-decorating tube; 2. Cloth pastry bag and decorative tips; 3. Metal tubes for making cannoli; 4. Hand-turned ice cream freezer; 5. Loaf pans; 6. Wire whisk; 7. Shallow baking pan; 8. Roasting pans; 9. Covered ice cream or gelatin molds and various fancy molds for cakes, bavarians, and mousses

ITALIAN INDEX

For the convenience of those who wish to find a recipe under its
original Italian name, the following strictly alphabetical
listing is included. Unlike the English-language index, which follows,
it is not cross-referenced. All numbers refer to recipe numbers.

819

INDEX

Unless otherwise noted, all numbers refer to recipe numbers.
For the convenience of those who wish to find a recipe under its
original Italian name, we have included an Italian-language
index, which commences on page 808.

827

835